W9-BKM-752

Macmillan 180.00 set

Mystery and Suspense Writers

R
823.087
Mys
v.1

Mystery and Suspense Writers

The Literature of Crime, Detection, and Espionage

Robin W. Winks
Editor in Chief

Maureen Corrigan
Associate Editor

VOLUME 1

Margery Allingham
to
John D. MacDonald

FRANKLIN REGIONAL
SENIOR HIGH
LIBRARY

CHARLES SCRIBNER'S SONS
An Imprint of Macmillan Library Reference USA
NEW YORK

Copyright © 1998 Charles Scribner's Sons

All rights reserved. No part of this book may be reproduced or transmitted in any form or by any means, electronic or mechanical, including photocopying, recording, or by any information storage or retrieval system, without permission in writing from the Publisher.

Charles Scribner's Sons
An imprint of Macmillan Library Reference USA
1633 Broadway
New York, NY 10019

Library of Congress Cataloging-in-Publication Data

Mystery and suspense writers : the literature of crime, detection, and espionage / Robin W. Winks, editor in chief ; Maureen Corrigan, associate editor.
p. cm.
Includes bibliographical references and index.
ISBN 0-684-80492-1 (set : alk. paper). — ISBN 0-684-80519-7 (v. 1 : alk. paper)
1. Detective and mystery stories, English—Dictionaries. 2. Detective and mystery stories, English—Bio-bibliography—Dictionaries. 3. Detective and mystery stories, American—Bio-bibliography—Dictionaries. 4. Detective and mystery stories, American—Dictionaries. 5. Spy stories, American—Bio-bibliography—Dictionaries. 6. Spy stories, English—Bio-bibliography—Dictionaries. 7. Spy stories, American—Dictionaries. 8. Spy stories, English—Dictionaries. 9. Crime in literature—Dictionaries. I. Winks, Robin W. II. Corrigan, Maureen.
PR830.D4M97 1998
823'.087209'03—dc21
[B] 98-36812
CIP

1 3 5 7 9 11 13 17 19 20 18 16 14 12 10 8 6 4 2

PRINTED IN THE UNITED STATES OF AMERICA

The paper used in this publication meets the minimum requirements of American National Standard for Information Sciences—Permanence of Paper for Printed Library Materials. ANSI Z39.48-1992.

Editorial and Production Staff

Project Editor
Jonathan G. Aretakis

Assistant Editor
Laura Kathleen Smid

Copyeditors
Sylvia J. Cannizzaro Gretchen Gordon
Carol Holmes Marcia Merryman Means
Dorothy Bauhoff Allen L. McDermid Ingrid Sterner

Proofreaders
Desne Border Catherine J. Langevin-Falcon
Vida Petronis Helen Wallace

Index
AEIOU Indexers

Manufacturing
Paul Wells, *Production Manager*
Judy Kahn, *Cover Design*

Executive Editor
Sylvia K. Miller

Publisher
Karen Day

Contents

VOLUME 1

Introduction xiii

Individual Writers

Margery Allingham / *Paula M. Woods* 1
Eric Ambler / *Peter Lewis* 13
Robert Barnard / *Jon L. Breen* 31
E. C. Bentley / *Thomas M. Leitch* 41
Nicholas Blake / *Thomas M. Leitch* 51
Lawrence Block / *Charles Ardai* 63
Jorge Luis Borges and the Metaphysical Mystery / *Michael Holquist* 83
John Buchan / *George O'Brien* 97
John Dickson Carr / *Michael Dirda* 113
The Nick Carter Stories / *J. Randolph Cox* 131
Raymond Chandler / *Joan Zseleczky* 143
Leslie Charteris / *Burl Barer* 169
G. K. Chesterton / *John C. Tibbetts* 181
Agatha Christie / *David Hawkes* 195
Wilkie Collins / *Audrey Peterson* 217
K. C. Constantine / *Jeffery Fraser* 233
Patricia Cornwell / *Ellen Bleiler* 243
Edmund Crispin / *Michael Dirda* 251
Freeman Wills Crofts / *Melvyn Barnes* 259
Amanda Cross / *Mary Rose Sullivan* 271
Carroll John Daly / *Rex Burns* 281
Colin Dexter / *Douglas G. Greene* 291
Arthur Conan Doyle / *Owen Dudley Edwards* 301
Daphne du Maurier / *June M. Frazer* 331
Mignon G. Eberhart / *LeRoy Lad Panek* 345
Stanley Ellin / *Marvin S. Lachman* 357
Ian Fleming / *Max Allan Collins* 367
Dick Francis / *Rachel Schaffer* 383
Émile Gaboriau / *Walter Albert* 399
Erle Stanley Gardner / *William F. Nolan* 409
Michael Gilbert / *B. A. Pike* 427

Sue Grafton / *Jean Swanson* 439
Anna Katharine Green / *Patricia Maida* 449
Graham Greene / *Brian Diemert* 459
Dashiell Hammett / *David Geherin* 473
George V. Higgins / *Erwin H. Ford* 491
Patricia Highsmith / *Noel Dorman Mawer* 503
Evan Hunter / *Dean A. Miller* 517
Michael Innes / *George L. Scheper* 527
P. D. James / *Dennis Porter* 541
Ronald A. Knox / *Susan Oleksiw* 559
John le Carré / *LynnDianne Beene* 569
Elmore Leonard / *Edward Gorman, Robert Skinner, and Robert Gleason* 589
Robert Ludlum / *Roy S. Goodman* 605
John D. MacDonald / *Lewis D. Moore* 615

VOLUME 2

Ross Macdonald / *Robert F. Moss* 633
Helen MacInnes / *Priscilla L. Walton* 651
Ngaio Marsh / *Bruce Harding* 665
Margaret Millar / *Mary Jean DeMarr* 679
John Mortimer / *Sharon Villines* 689
Sara Paretsky / *Margaret H. Kinsman* 699
Robert B. Parker / *Maureen Corrigan* 715
Edgar Allan Poe / *J. Gerald Kennedy* 733
Ellery Queen / *Francis M. Nevins* 757
Ruth Rendell / *B. J. Rahn* 773
Sax Rohmer / *R. E. Briney* 791
Dorothy L. Sayers / *Robert Allen Papinchak* 805
Georges Simenon / *George Grella* 829
Maj Sjöwall and Per Wahlöö / *Nancy C. Mellerski and Robert P. Winston* 853
Mickey Spillane / *Max Allan Collins* 869
Rex Stout / *David R. Anderson* 885
Julian Symons / *H. R. F. Keating* 901
Josephine Tey / *Alexandra von Malottke Roy* 911
S. S. Van Dine / *John Loughery* 923
Robert van Gulik / *Wilt L. Idema* 933
Edgar Wallace / *Richard Bleiler* 943
Donald E. Westlake / *Lawrence Block* 957
Cornell Woolrich / *Francis M. Nevins* 967

Themes and Subgenres
The Armchair Detective / *B. J. Rahn* 983
Black Detective Fiction / *Stephen Soitos* 995
Crime Noir / *Charles L. P. Silet* 1009
The Ethnic Detective: Arthur W. Upfield, Tony Hillerman, and Beyond / *Ray B. Browne* 1029
The Female Detective: From Nancy Drew to Sue Grafton / *Maureen T. Reddy* 1047
Gay and Lesbian Mystery Fiction / *Anthony Slide* 1069
The Historical Mystery / *Robin W. Winks* 1089
The Legal Crime Novel / *Jon L. Breen* 1103
The Police Procedural / *Jon L. Breen* 1117
Regionalization of the Mystery and Crime Novel / *J. K. Van Dover* 1139
Religious Mysteries / *William David Spencer* 1161
The Romantic Suspense Mystery / *Jennifer Crusie Smith* 1183
The Spy Thriller / *Wesley K. Wark* 1199
Women of Mystery: Helen McCloy, Doris Miles Disney, and Dorothy Salisbury Davis / *Robert Allen Papinchak* 1219

Appendix 1: Pseudonyms and Series Characters 1231
Appendix 2: Some Mystery and Suspense Subgenres 1241
Appendix 3: Major Prizewinners 1243
Contributors 1247
Index 1259

Introduction

Mystery, detective, and spy thriller fiction form a continuum and, taken together, are the most popular body of literature in the industrialized world today. In readership, sales, and name recognition, Agatha Christie alone outranks all authors who have ever lived, with the exception of William Shakespeare and, perhaps in their time, Joseph Stalin and Mao Tse-tung. Though statistics are inexact, it is said that every fourth book sold in the United States or Great Britain is a mystery. The body of literature dwarfs all other genres—including science fiction, the Western (now in serious decline), the romance novel, etc.—and has shaped that ubiquitous form of television entertainment, the crime film.

This extraordinary popularity arises, in part, from the readability of much of the literature. Character, place, incident, and plot drive most fiction, but all are intensified by the nature of the mystery, which often turns on a closely observed, yet cunningly concealed, detail. These books tell stories, chilling or horrific or, in the end, cathartic, but stories nonetheless. Readers are hungry for stories well told, and though many books in the genre are not, in fact, well told, many are very well told indeed.

This literature is, of course, formulaic and dismissed by some critics for that reason. One wonders why? Virtually all literature is in some measure formulaic: nature writing, popular science, current events, history. There are conventions to be observed, methodologies to apply, in virtually all disciplines. Popular culture is singled out for following a formula—unfairly, those who study it would argue, or fairly enough, others would say.

What is the formula? A mystery must have a puzzle, just as a detective story must have a detective. A spy thriller might have both, as well might a mystery, and though many scholars have written of significant and subtle distinctions between the types, most readers see them as unfolding one from another. The mystery should involve fair play; that is, clues—a term from Greek mythology referring to the thread by which one might hope to find one's way to the surface of the earth from a dark cave—must be fairly laid down for the reader to see, though they may be concealed behind language, or slipped in obliquely, or made to appear to have quite a different meaning than they actually do. Agatha Christie's greatest claim to fame might well be the skill with which she misdirects readers, entirely fairly (even in the much-discussed *Murder of Roger Ackroyd*), to confuse innocence and guilt.

In 1928, Monsignor Ronald Knox set out Ten Commandments of Detection, for even then some writers felt that the bounds of the formula were being broken in too cavalier a fashion. Knox's commandments look quite foolish today—that the detective must not commit the crime himself, for example. And the Detection Club, founded in Britain in the same year, looks positively unreal in its demand that "divine revelation, feminine intuition, coincidence, or the act of God" must play no role in the resolution of the story. Agatha Christie alone broke every one of Knox's commandments. John Buchan relied heavily on coincidence, Dorothy L. Sayers on acts of God, Sue Grafton on "gut feelings"—surely a more hard-boiled equivalent of intuition.

To be sure, many readers enjoyed pitting their wits against the writer and saw the mystery as a form of chess game. But few serious writers could commit themselves to a lifetime of writing in a straitjacket, and Christie, Dorothy L. Sayers, and others had, by the 1930s, rebelled against the stuffy strictures of

Knox and the Detection Club. Detective stories present a problem to be solved, just this and nothing more. To try to classify mystery and detective stories by the type of problem, the method of solution—psychological, procedural, accidental, etc.—is tedious and unhelpful. The poet W. H. Auden provided as clear a definition of the detective story as we need: "a murder occurs: many are suspected; all but one suspect, who is the murderer, are eliminated; the murderer is arrested or dies." Of course, this is no longer true: the murderer may succeed in evading detection or arrest; an innocent person may be convicted and executed for the crime. Some critics would argue that such a plot belongs to a crime novel, not a detective novel, but, again, these distinctions are of little help in understanding why mystery and detective books are so popular.

Why, then? Many reasons can be given. Readers experience vicarious travel through them, or learn arcane information about a trade, a practice, a profession. Mystery and detective books reflect our deepest fears and society's anxieties. They are subversive literature that may criticize society directly or, perhaps more often, obliquely, thus, as with the novels of James McClure, set in *apartheid*-era South Africa, avoiding the attention of the censors. Or they are conservative, helping to assure the reader that, however confusing life may seem, in the end all will be made right, will come clear, will return to stability and normalcy. Such stories confirm our suspicions that all is not what it seems, that people and states dissemble, that we must be on our guard, that friends may become or may even be at the moment of apparent friendship, deathly enemies. Descriptions of crimes may be cathartic, or titillating, making the reader a voyeur; when justice is meted out by the state, or a detective, or the community, or a great storm sent by God or Providence, perhaps we feel avenged. Possibly the fiction appeals far more to our emotions than to our intellects, gratifying and easing our sense of sin. Perhaps, we ought to remember, there are readers who like such fiction simply because it is entertaining.

Mystery and detective fiction, and on the whole spy fiction as well, has not often been produced outside the West, though Western books, often in translation, are widely read in India, China, Japan, and elsewhere. Of the seventy-odd writers discussed in individual essays in these volumes, all but six are from Great Britain or the United States. On the whole such fiction comes from capitalist, Protestant societies. Much ink has been spilled over ideological and psychoanalytic explanations for why this may be so, ranging from the simplistically Marxist to the equally simplistic Freudian. Literacy and leisure also account for the vast Western readerships.

Perhaps such fiction simply instructs us in the nuance of life. R. Gordon Kelly, in one of the most sensible of recent academic inquiries into *Mystery Fiction and Modern Life* (Jackson: University Press of Mississippi, 1998), suggests that the genre is closely linked to our perceptions of what constitutes modernity: "knowledge, trust, risk, and power" as they "arise in the course of everyday social interaction" (p. xi). James Joyce has suggested that all writing is about secrecy, exile, and cunning—and that so too is all life. Kelly emphasizes how the investigator of fiction must possess great skills of emotional management coupled with cognitive skills that can infer connections between the observable and the unobserved. Thus, he concludes, "Mystery fiction dramatizes the strategic value of the trained capacities demanded by conditions of modernity—making those capacities, in the final analysis, matters of life and death" (p. 197).

The academic study of this body of literature grew rapidly in the 1970s and 1980s, and there now exists a very substantial scholarly infrastructure. This growth owed a good bit to the popular culture movement in colleges and universities, which itself often stemmed from new interests developing in American Studies and English Literature departments. Teachers often turned to mystery, detective, and (less often) spy fiction because the clarity of writing and the plot-driven constructions were especially appealing to students who had neither the time nor the inclination to study closely woven texts, or who, often with their teachers, rebelled against the "classical canon" in English or American literature. Both editors of these volumes have taught courses on the use of detective fiction to teach inductive as well as deductive reasoning, and one editor has compared the way historians ask questions, seek evidence, and judge good answers to the methods of the fictional detective.

With spy fiction, the growth of the genre may also relate to the tensions of the Cold War, the desire to depict heroes and villains, and the growing sense, both feeding and feeding off of conspiracy theories, that the intelligence agencies of even one's own country were not to be trusted. Scholars compared "spy fiction" to "spy reality," and in Germany and elsewhere in Europe, there developed a substantial body of writing that drew upon the fiction of espionage to analyze societal fears.

Thus legitimized by academe, the genre was more widely accepted. No reader had any longer to hide a detective novel inside a mathematics textbook, and publishers less often had to draw attention to their wares with gaudy or violent dust jackets. Television and print reinforced each other, millions becoming acquainted with Colin Dexter's Inspector Morse through the small screen while thousands read Dexter's novels. University libraries now collect the manuscripts and letters of writers in the genre. Boston University's Mugar Memorial Library holds the papers of some three hundred writers of mystery, suspense, and espionage books and short stories; the University of Texas has acquired the papers of Ellery Queen; the Wheaton College library in Illinois has a key collection of Dorothy L. Sayers' manuscripts and letters. With primary research materials ever more abundantly available, more writers are providing critical interpretations and biographies, and more newsletters and quasi-scholarly journals are springing up, especially in Britain and the United States. Though there appears to be a slight decline in the number of college-level courses devoted to mystery fiction in recent years, scholarly attention remains intense, as the bibliographies to the essays in this volume attest.

But academic endorsement probably has relatively little to do with the recent growth in the genre, which is selling better than ever before. Certain varieties—the locked room mystery, for example, which poses the severest of puzzles and, most often, leads to the most rigidly logical and yet least realistically satisfying of solutions—appear to have gone into permanent decline, but other types, most particularly the psychological thriller and the technological thriller, appear to have no bounds. Paradoxically, readers appear to enjoy the formulaic quality of the fiction for what it teaches an ever more ethnically diverse readership about expectations and social mores within social subgroups, and yet readers also embrace Graham Greene's warning, put into the mouth of Beatrice Severn in *Our Man in Havana* (1958), "Beware of formulas. If there's a God, he's not a God of formulas."

Given the popularity of mystery, detective, and spy thriller fiction, and the productivity of so many of its practitioners, the editors have had a difficult task deciding which authors should be the subject of separate essays, and of what lengths. In the end the editors settled on sixty-nine writers (or teams) for full treatment, in essays ranging from 12,000 to 5,000 words in length, and on fourteen theme essays, each focussing on two or more authors and touching, typically, on forty or so. Still, readers no doubt will find a personal favorite omitted. The editors concluded that substantial essays on a smaller number of writers were to be preferred to short entries on many more, especially since several existing guides to this body of fiction already provide very brief statements.

The writers chosen for individual attention by the editors were felt to be particularly influential in shaping the genre, or markedly productive even in a prolific field, or so popular any reader ought reasonably to expect to find them discussed here. The theme essays were used where some genuine coherence existed, as with women detectives or historical mysteries, even though a given writer—such as Tony Hillerman, certainly an appropriate subject for a separate essay—might receive a bit less attention in a thematic essay (in this case, "The Ethnic Detective") than any comparative standard would suggest. A detailed index, helping the reader not only to locate authors discussed quite briefly, but also to see how a featured writer is invoked in other essays, is intended to further demonstrate how influence runs from one subgenre to another.

Other themes might well have been developed in separate essays. Medical mysteries and recent growth in environmental thrillers are two examples among many. Some writers contribute to two or even several themes in their work: Hillerman is discussed here for his Native American detectives, Joe Leaphorn and Jim Chee, but Hillerman's novels are also exercises in regionalism, are police procedurals, and have become increasingly concerned with environmental issues. "Detective fiction" is used too often, especially by individuals who have read little of it, to build walls around writers, though in fact, from Wilkie Collins and Sir Arthur Conan Doyle, the best writers have transcended genre. Sayers, like the American Amanda Cross, writes novels of manners and bears comparison to Jane Austen, while many writers who are preoccupied with describing crime and its consequences (George V. Higgins and Elmore Leonard come to mind) resemble Charles Dickens. Readers will be able to create their own categories to link the diverse authors discussed here.

How trite, banal, and just plain bad bald plot summaries make much of this literature sound! Poor writing and irresponsible editing occur in the genre, as they do in all literature and in nonfiction in abundance. Formulaic fiction pours out in vast quantities. Beginning writers often choose a mystery as their first effort. Many authors hide behind pseudonyms. A random sampling of thriller fiction in a bookstore or at airport stalls will reveal much that is execrable. But on the whole, the editors believe, the body of literature is getting steadily better: more logical, more in touch with reality, more ably written, more intriguing. Though the majority of writers singled out for individual treatment are deceased, there are many in the thematic essays who will, within a decade, be deserving of analysis of their own.

As daily life becomes less stable for many people, as words enter the daily vocabulary that, a generation ago, were banned from polite speech, as civility appears to erode in public settings, detective fiction becomes ever more democratic, more nearly the voice of the people. The English "cozy" continues to thrive, with little endorsement of familiar vulgarisms, in writers like Dorothy Simpson; at the same time, grittily demotic language direct from the streets, the locker room, and the tavern is honed by George V. Higgins or K. C. Constantine until it represents a truth about who we are and what we say that transcends judgments of good taste or acceptable language.

Perhaps the greatest achievement of American detective fiction, at least from Dashiell Hammett and Raymond Chandler forward, has been the full democratization of fiction, in contrast to the revealing class-oriented language and plots of the English Golden Age, when bodies were found in libraries, stabbed with antique Tunisian daggers, or were pushed overboard from deck chairs on grand transatlantic liners. Conversely, the great achievement of British contributors to the genre has been the moral weight, the complexity of ethical and moral responsibility, that a Sayers (as in *The Nine Tailors*) or a P. D. James brings to her work. Points of view blend, are no longer nationally distinctive, but there remains a residue of difference, in character, plot, and language, between the American and the British, or the French and the South African, voice. It is this diversity of voices that these volumes celebrate through the range of authors discussed here.

Robin W. Winks
Yale University
June 1998

Mystery and Suspense Writers

Margery Allingham
(1904–1966)

PAULA M. WOODS

Margery Allingham, Golden Age mystery writer, is usually associated with Dorothy L. Sayers, Agatha Christie, and Josephine Tey. Prolific author of more than thirty novels and collections of short stories, Allingham is best known for her mystery series featuring Albert Campion. In addition to five non-Campion mysteries, a "serious" novel, and a work of nonfiction, she published three novels under the pseudonym Maxwell March. She also published a number of articles and reviews, some anonymously. Critics have commented on the energy demonstrated in her work, the fantasy world she created, and the allegorical aspects of her novels.

Life

Born into a literary environment on 20 May 1904 to Herbert John and Emily Jane Hughes Allingham, Margery Allingham was educated at Endsleigh House School, Colchester; Perse High School for Girls, Cambridge; and Regent Street Polytechnic, London. The Allinghams lived in London until Margery was five and then moved to Layer Breton, Essex, near Colchester, returning to London during World War I. On 29 September 1927, she married Philip Youngman Carter (Pip), an artist and writer. They lived in London for a few years and then moved to Chappel in Essex in 1931. During the years at Chappel, Allingham established her early reputation as a novelist. Allingham's decision to write mysteries was apparently influenced by writers of the times. She was acquainted with the adventure stories of Edgar Wallace and P. G. Wodehouse and influenced by the American suspense novel, although she never commented specifically why she was attracted to formula fiction, nor did she draw clear distinctions among various genres or indicate that she had specific writers as influences. In 1935 the couple moved to D'Arcy House in the Essex village of Tolleshunt D'Arcy, where they resided until her death from cancer on 30 June 1966. These village residences provided inspiration for settings for a number of novels. Although the marriage at first seemed to be a casual one, it is evident from letters and from comments made by friends and family that theirs was a relationship built on understanding and respect, in spite of certain misunderstandings and strains. For some years Allingham was the primary breadwinner, supporting them through writing. They often collaborated, Allingham crediting Carter with supplying ideas for plots and characters. He finished *Cargo of Eagles* (1968), which she was writing at the time of her death, and wrote two novels from notes she left. Over the years Allingham and Carter sometimes maintained separate residences. He had a flat in London while she remained at Tolleshunt D'Arcy, an arrangement that caused considerable trouble with the Inland Revenue because of British income tax regulations.

Literary Career

Allingham's first published novel, *Black'-erchief Dick* (1923), was a promising venture for a nineteen-year-old. It was followed five years later by *The White Cottage Mystery,* a workmanlike novel, and her first venture into crime fiction. In 1929, *The Crime at Black Dudley* (U.S., *The Black Dudley Murder*) introduced Campion, the adventurer-detective who made Allingham's reputation. After ten Campion novels, Allingham made a break from the series with *Black Plumes* (1940), which introduced a new detective, Inspector Bridie. If Allingham intended to begin a new series featuring Bridie, she did not pursue this track, possibly because of a less than enthusiastic reception for the novel. In 1943 she published *The Dance of the Years* (U.S., *The Galantrys*), a novel about three generations of a family that bears a distinct resemblance to the Allingham family. Other non-Campion fiction includes *Wanted: Someone Innocent* (1946), *Deadly Duo* (1949), and *No Love Lost* (1954).

The Oaken Heart (1941) can best be described as a book-length personal essay detailing life in an English village during the early days of World War II. At the same time charming and thought-provoking, this nonfiction work contains themes that appear in Allingham's crime fiction, in particular, the village threatened by outside evil and rustic characters. Parts of *The Oaken Heart* obviously influence *Traitor's Purse* (1941; U.S., *The Sabotage Murder Mystery*) and *The China Governess* (1962).

Allingham is often compared with Sayers and Christie. Like Sayers she has a single series, with only one non-Campion novel. She was, however, more prolific than Sayers, writing over a longer period of time, and employing World War II and its aftermath prominently in her work. Allingham differs from Christie not only in that she has a single series, but also because she is concerned more with characterization and atmosphere. Her work, like Sayers', is often critiqued as novels as much as crime and mystery writing.

The best of Allingham's novels is *The Tiger in the Smoke* (1952), a highly atmospheric and symbolic novel of suspense. *The Fashion in Shrouds* (1938) has also garnered critical approval. *Traitor's Purse* (1941) presents an interesting character study set amid wartime tensions. *The Beckoning Lady* (1955) was her personal favorite.

Allingham's Campion novels demonstrate a number of strengths: complex plotting, development of both major and minor characters, concern with the psychology of the victims and supporting characters as well as the criminal, and strong sense of place and time. Her growth as a writer is evident if one reads through the series from *The Crime at Black Dudley* to *The Mind Readers* (1965), the last book she completed before her death. Including *Cargo of Eagles* in an assessment of Allingham's work is problematic since Carter completed it.

Plots

Allingham's plots are strong, often intricate, with unexpected twists not wholly unprepared for. She is concerned not only with the questions of who and how but also with why, exploring the motivations of perpetrator, sleuth, and supporting characters. The Campion novels include murder mysteries and thrillers or adventure stories, tales in which there is a puzzle to be solved but not necessarily a murder. In *Mystery Mile* (1930), the death is the suicide of a beloved character, and the search for the reason for his suicide becomes a subplot to the search for the identity of a criminal mastermind. What appears to be murder in *Police at the Funeral* (1931) is actually a suicide, while questions about the family's relationships become almost as important as the crime. The search for the perpetrator in *Flowers for the Judge* (1936; U.S., *Legacy in Blood*) is complicated by questions about the authenticity of a manuscript and the mysterious disappearance of a partner in the firm twenty years earlier. In *The Fashion in Shrouds* (1938), Allingham provides two deaths to solve, one three years old at the time of the action and the second occurring midway through the book. *The Fashion in Shrouds* in some senses operates like a novel of manners: Campion must negotiate his way through the mores of a group of the careless and pleasure-seeking wealthy to determine the identity of the perpetrator. In *The Tiger in the Smoke* (1952) the killer is known, and the mystery lies in finding him and discovering his motivation, which allows Allingham to create an almost allegorical story of the battle between good and evil. Perhaps the most interesting plot is the double mystery of *Traitor's Purse.* Suffering from amnesia, Campion must not only solve the mystery, he must also find out what the mystery is.

Campion and Family

Allingham uses the series to develop the character of Campion as he interacts with a supporting cast of continuing characters and numerous characters who make a single appearance. Over the course of the series, Campion ages, falls in love more than once and loses the object of his affections, marries, and has a son. He develops friendships, hones skills, and becomes a fully developed personality, evolving from the near caricature he is in *Black Dudley,* when he is isolated and embarked on an adventure of his own. Because the series covers more than thirty years, Campion ages at a natural rate, increasing the verisimilitude of the adventures.

Although Campion is a supporting character in *Black Dudley,* the protagonist being George Abbershaw, a physician/police consultant, Campion figures prominently in the action, an obviously capable figure in dangerous situations. In this novel Allingham establishes the characteristics that become part of Campion's persona as he develops over the course of the series: surface inanity, self-effacement, and the ability to blend in so that he is often overlooked. Adjectives such as "vacuous," "inane," and "inoffensive" are repeatedly used to describe him through the series. Physical descriptions support these qualities. In *Black Dudley,* he is characterized as a "fresh-faced young man with tow-coloured hair and . . . foolish, pale-blue eyes behind the tortoise shell-rimmed spectacles" (1979 ed., p. 11). Twenty years later, in *More Work for the Undertaker* (1948), he is said to have "the valuable gift of appearing an elegant shadow and was, as a great policeman had once said so enviously, a man of whom at first sight no one could ever be afraid" (1968 ed., p. 10). Late in the series, in *The Mind Readers,* he is a "thin man with pale hair and eyes and a misleadingly blank expression" (1972 ed., p. 46) who looks like "a civilized and essentially harmless person, his pale horn spectacles, larger in the lenses than is usual, making him appear owlish and rather helpless" (p. 178). Beginning with a chattering and frequently annoying individual, a "silly ass," given to patter worthy of a Gilbert and Sullivan operetta, Allingham develops her protagonist into a deadly serious adventurer who nonetheless never loses his ability to appear to be a silly ass, misleading those who underestimate him. The dramatic irony developed through third-person narrative of Campion's qualities is lost in *The Case of the Late Pig* (1937), when Allingham employs Campion as the narrator.

Campion not only cultivates disguises to mislead his enemies, he also hides his family identity: Albert Campion is a pseudonym, one of several he uses early in the series. In *Black Dudley,* Campion's social position and true identity are hinted at. He is obviously an aristocrat: "My own [name] is rather aristocratic, and I never use it in business" (1979 ed., p. 71), he tells Abbershaw. The second novel in the series, *Mystery Mile,* reveals that his real first name is Rudolph, while his last name is given only as "K——." Unlike Sayers' Lord Peter Wimsey, the young Campion believes it necessary to conceal his aristocratic connections, and his relationship with his family is strained. In *Mystery Mile,* he tells his brother in the course of a phone call that he can be disinherited only once. Caroline Faraday, the grande dame of the family in *Police at the Funeral,* knows who he is; in fact, she has maintained a long correspondence with his grandmother, "the dowager." She respects his desire to maintain his distance from his family: "I shall not expose you . . . after all, as long as that impossible brother of yours is alive the family responsibilities are being shouldered, and I see no reason why you shouldn't call yourself what you like" (1973 ed., p. 54). Later in the series the need to eschew family connections becomes less important. The name "Campion" seems to have become official. *Look to the Lady* (1931; U.S., *The Gyrth Chalice Mystery*) provides the best indication of Campion's social rank. In this novel Campion's aristocratic connections as well as his abilities as a detective are valuable, because he knows the symbolic and political importance of the Gyrth Chalice; he is obviously known to and employed by the unnamed but extremely important man, possibly the king himself, who appears in the last chapters to verify the authenticity of the chalice.

Campion's family includes a sister, Val, also something of a black sheep, who has become a noted fashion designer, and two clerical uncles, very different men of the cloth. Val figures importantly in *The Fashion in Shrouds.* Each of the uncles appears in more than one book. The Bishop of Devizes is deceased in both *Look to the Lady* and *Police at the Funeral* but is brought back to life in *Coroner's Pidgin (U.S., Pearls Before Swine)* in 1945. The saintly Canon Avril plays a prominent part in *The Tiger in the Smoke* and *The Mind Readers.* The wise and savvy Bishop is also a worldly wine expert. Canon Avril is the very pattern of the wise innocent, an apparently unworldly man who Police inspector Charlie Luke says is one of those who "[pick] their way like a drunk on a parapet, apparently obeying instructions which no one else can hear. They go barging into filth and it runs off them as if they were lead-glazed. They see all the dirt and none of it shocks them. They hand over all they've got and yet they never want" (*Tiger,* 1985 ed., p. 50). It is also said of him that "he believed in miracles and frequently observed them, and nothing astonished him. His imagination was as wild as a small boy's and his faith ultimate. In ordinary life he was, quite frankly, hardly safe out" (p. 23).

Although they are interesting, these relatives are not the most important of Campion's family connections. His nuclear family, which defines him as sleuth and person, consists of his valet/butler/partner in adventure, Magersfontein Lugg; his wife, Lady Amanda Fitton; and his son, Rupert, who appears only as a child. With Lugg, an ex-con whose contacts in the underworld prove valuable on a number of occasions, Campion maintains a somewhat casual relationship. Although the master/servant relationship informs their interaction, Campion and Lugg trade insults, and Lugg frequently questions his employer's sanity and intentions and periodically threatens to quit. The closeness of their relationship is nowhere more evident than in *Traitor's Purse* when Campion, suffering from amnesia and unable to confide even in Amanda, is willing to admit to Lugg that he has no idea who either of them is or what his mission might be. Lugg is important to Amanda and Rupert as well as to Campion. Lugg and Amanda establish an instant rapport in *Sweet Danger* (1933; U.S., *Kingdom of Death* and *The Fear Sign*), which matures to genuine affection. The continuing importance of Lugg to the family is underscored in *The Tiger in the Smoke* when Rupert, having heard about all the hairs on one's head being counted, is concerned that Lugg might not get into heaven because he is bald.

The relationship of Campion and Amanda, important in the action of several novels, reveals much about him as a person—his nobility, loyalty, and sense of duty. Nevertheless, Amanda was not Campion's first or only love. Although it is evident in *Mystery Mile* that he is in love with Biddy Pagett, he nobly steps aside when she falls in love with Marlow Lobbett. In subsequent novels he is painfully reminded of Biddy. At the end of the adventure in *Sweet Danger,* Amanda, suffering from a bullet wound acquired while aiding his scheme, asks, "I say, do you ever think about Biddy Pagett? You know—Biddy Lobbett." When he answers "Yes" in "one of his rare flashes of undisguised honesty," she essentially proposes: "I thought so. Look here . . . I shan't be ready for about six years yet. But then—well, I'd like to put you on the top of my list." His answer, "Is that a bet?" is his acceptance. The scene ends with Campion "looking down very tenderly at this odd little person who had come crashing through one of the most harrowing adventures he had ever known and with unerring instinct had torn open old scars, revived old fires which he had believed extinct" (1978 ed., p. 251).

This is not a "happily ever after" ending, though, for Amanda disappears from the series for about six years. In the meantime, Campion develops a passion for Linda Sutane in *Dancers in Mourning* (1937; U.S., *Who Killed Chloe?*), a married woman and mother, very feminine and "womanly," and almost the direct opposite of the independent and resourceful Amanda, who returns in *The Fashion in Shrouds* as an aeronautical engineer. Campion and Amanda pretend to be engaged and to split up in order to draw out the villain. At the end he proposes for real: "I'll be happy to marry you if you care for the idea . . . And then when I'm fifty, and feeling like a quiet life, you'll go and fall with a thud for some silly chap who'll give us both hell" (p. 255). This is what she calls "cake love," replying that "cake makes some people sick." In *Traitor's Purse,* the relationship endures Amanda's infatuation with Lee Aubrey as Campion, in his amnesiac state, finds the intensity of his emotion for her frightening: "His sense of possession was tremendous. It was the possessiveness of the child, of the savage, of the dog, unreasonable and unanswerable" (1983 ed., p. 42), and "Amanda was not only his: she *was* himself" (p. 65). At the end of the novel they are heading for marriage before he leaves for a highly secret mission on the Continent. Back from this mission in *Coroner's Pidgin,* Campion is delayed in his return to the family estate. When he finally arrives, the first person he meets is Rupert, whom Amanda introduces as "my war work."

From her first appearance Amanda is portrayed as a no-nonsense individual. As a teenager she engaged in unusual activities; she has built a dynamo at the mill at Pontisbright, and her expertise in things electronic is invaluable to Campion's scheme for discovering documents that will establish the Fittons' (Amanda's family) and England's claim to an oil-rich European principality; in *Sweet Danger* (1933), Amanda and Campion work to discover the claim. *More Work for the Undertaker* underscores Amanda's intelligence and skill at deduction when Campion reads the postscript to a letter from her, written before he solved the mystery, which suggests he consider the person who has indeed turned out to be the murderer. She has come to her conclusion only through newspaper accounts of the case. In *The Beckoning Lady* (1955; U.S., *The Estate of the Beckoning Lady*), back in her home territory of Pontisbright, she mildly scandalizes Campion when she "borrows" a battery from the car of a presumptuous visitor to power the garden lights: " 'Well, he was the one who wanted the lights,' said Amanda. 'Always see the right visitor pays. We're rather good at that in Pontisbright' " (1985 ed., p. 104).

Campion and Amanda's relationship is not a conventional one. It is a partnership; both maintain their independence. At the beginning of *More Work for the Undertaker* a "dowager with a name to conjure with," congratulating Campion on finally living up to his potential because of his impending appointment as a colonial governor, asks after Amanda: "She designs her own aeroplanes, doesn't she? How clever girls are these days," but she does not approve of the possibility that Amanda might not accompany him to his post. He makes the point that "her work is not unimportant," a point that does not impress the dowager (1968 ed., pp. 16–17). In *The Tiger in the Smoke,* Campion thinks: "It was not the only sort of marriage, but it was their sort" (1985 ed., p. 169).

Supporting Characters

In addition to a family, Allingham provides a number of supporting characters for Campion. They include "bright young people" and country gentry, any number of underworld contacts, and several Scotland Yard inspectors, most important among them, Stanislaus Oates and Charlie Luke.

Early novels feature the bright young people and country gentry. *The Crime at Black Dudley* employs a group of bright young people of the sort that figure prominently in much British fiction written between the world wars, assembled as cover for criminal activities of both murder victim and murderer. Their rescue is effected by that most English of country activities, a hunt, introducing the country gentry. Descendants of the bright young people, the London club set, who resemble the characters in the British writer Christopher Isherwood's Berlin stories in a certain edginess, appear most notably in *The Fashion in Shrouds* and *Coroner's Pidgin.* English country gentry figure in several novels. *Mystery Mile* features the Pagett siblings, who are trying to maintain their manor by renting it out. Another set of the gentry, the Gyrths, are threatened in *Look to the Lady.* Suspicion falls on country gentry as possible murderers of Pig Peters/Oswald Harris in *The Case of the Late Pig,* featuring Colonel Sir Leo Pursuivant, chief constable of the county, as a stereotypical country gentleman: gruff, softhearted, and given to uttering sentences without subjects. With the exception of *The Case of the Late Pig,* after *Sweet Danger* Allingham concentrates on urban settings, leaving behind country gentry as supporting characters until *The Beckoning Lady.*

Campion's numerous underworld contacts prove very useful in his adventures. Of course, Lugg often serves as a go-between, frequently passing judgment on the merits of his acquaintances. Most of these underworld contacts have minor parts or are merely mentioned in passing and do not actually appear. One exception is Thos T. Knapp, the "unspeakable Thos," electronic eavesdropper extraordinaire, who locates and helps rescue the kidnapped Biddy Pagett in *Mystery Mile* and reappears in *More Work for the Undertaker* when Campion solicits his knowledge and again years later, still eavesdropping, this time for a "respectable" operation, in *The Mind Readers.* An unusual underworld contact is the gypsy band in *Look to the Lady,* who cheerfully create mayhem at Campion's behest.

Campion's Scotland Yard associates are, of course, invaluable. Although not a regular member of the police, Campion works closely with them beginning in *Mystery Mile.* In the novels of the 1930s and 1940s, Stanislaus Oates is his primary contact, while Charlie Luke, introduced in *More Work for the Undertaker,* takes over that task in the novels of the 1950s and 1960s. Superintendent Yeo, that "most just if most policemanlike of policemen" (*More Work,* 1968 ed., p. 12) also appears in several novels but is overshadowed by Oates and Luke. Oates and Campion share a friendship; Campion is godfather to Oates's son, and they respect each other's abilities. Oates is described as dyspeptic and solemn, even gloomy looking. Having risen through the ranks from a constable walking a beat on the back streets of London, which he still knows well, in some ways he is still the man from Dorset. Luke is a Londoner, the son of a superintendent and grandson of a Criminal Investigation Division (C.I.D.) sergeant on his mother's side. Energetic, vital, charismatic, and intense, he is able to make a tale come to life, illustrating the qualities of the people he is talking about. At their first meeting Luke impresses Campion:

> Charlie Luke spoke without syntax or noticeable coherence but he talked with his

> whole body. When he described Doctor Smith's back his own arched. When he mentioned the shop front he squared it in with his hands. His tremendous strength, which was physical rather than nervous, poured into the recital, forcing the facts home like a pile-driver. (*More Work*, 1968 ed., pp. 22–23)

Luke and Campion's relationship suffers strains when, in *Beckoning Lady*, Luke falls in love with the Honorable Victoria Prunella Editha Scroop-Dory, an overbred, anachronistic aristocrat who ultimately proves a suitable mate in spite of Campion's misgivings. Luke continues as a vital force in the novels that succeed *More Work for the Undertaker*, especially in *Tiger in the Smoke*, *Hide My Eyes* (1958; U.S., *Tether's End*), and *The China Governess*. Indeed, he is a far more important figure in *Tether's End* than is Campion.

Antagonists

Opposing Campion's various contacts in the underworld and Scotland Yard are numerous antagonists. Since the series encompasses thrillers as well as murder mysteries, the antagonists are sometimes not criminals in the strictest sense of the term. *The Crime at Black Dudley* establishes Allingham's interest in "organized crime" with the introduction of the "Simister" gang, which also figures in *Mystery Mile*. In *Mystery Mile*, Campion meets and bests Simister himself. In *Look to the Lady*, the crime is the potential theft of a priceless relic by a well-organized gang employing a ruthless and desperate local horsewoman, Daisy Shannon (Mrs. Dick). This type of villain, ruthless and even charismatic, can be found in later novels also, but not necessarily connected to "organized" crime—people such as Brett Savanake in *Sweet Danger*, Lee Aubrey in *Traitor's Purse*, Jack Havoc in *The Tiger in the Smoke*, Gerry Hawker in *Tether's End*, and Lord Ludor in *The Mind Readers*.

Probably the best examples of Allingham's interest in the purely evil antagonist are Jack Havoc and Gerry Hawker. The usually practical Oates, who has preached against creating legend around criminals, astounds Campion, stepping "right out of character" by declaring that "Havoc is a truly wicked man . . . In all my experience I've met only three" (*Tiger*, 1985 ed., p. 58). Havoc is totally ruthless, a "born" killer who kills intentionally, not casually. He has escaped from prison by killing a distinguished doctor who became intrigued by his "neurosis." His killing spree continues through London, always, as Oates says, with purpose. He does not harm Amanda and Campion's cousin, Meg Elginbrodde, when they encounter him in Meg's dark house, nor does he harm Meg at the end of the novel when they recover the treasure that he has dedicated his life to finding, only to discover that it is a piece of religious statuary and not anything "valuable." Harming the women would have no purpose.

Havoc is one of Allingham's most interesting villains, a man who exudes a vitality not unlike Charlie Luke's. He has developed his own philosophy, the Science of Luck, which he believes works every time for him, a force that he has made no attempt to "humanize" and therefore "credit it with cruelty, or deliberated deception" (*Tiger*, 1985 ed., p. 224) and which he knows is "an impersonal force, vast as the slip stream of the planets, relentless as a river winding down a hill" (p. 225). Canon Avril calls it "The Pursuit of Death," and in the end it fails Havoc. Although Havoc is pursued by Campion and Luke, he is the true antagonist of Canon Avril, who knows his real identity and who understands the Science of Luck and what it is doing to Havoc: "The man who is with you when you are alone is dying. Fewer things delight him every day. If you attain the world, you cannot give him anything that will please him. In the end there will be no one with you" (p. 199). In the battle of Good against Evil represented by Avril and Havoc, Havoc is defeated when he fails to kill the old man.

Similarly, Gerry Hawker, another serial killer, is unable to let Polly Tassie die in the fire in her little museum in *Tether's End.* In both cases the power that defeats these conscienceless killers is love. For Havoc it is the pure, spiritual love of a man of God. For Hawker it is the intense love of an elderly childless woman for a man she has come to regard as her son. He returns to rescue her because, as he tells the police sergeant: "I need her" (1983 ed., p. 194). Luke knows why Hawker needs her: "She'll forgive him without question, whatever he's done to her and however high we hang him. *And he knows it.* It's no use you [the sergeant] blaming her. She can't help herself. She's only a vehicle. That's Disinterested Love, chum, a force, like nuclear energy. It's an absolute" (p. 196).

The other charismatic villains present a contrast to Havoc and Hawker, who are socially unimportant individuals. Savanake, Aubrey, and Ludor are all "captains of industry," high-profile men accustomed to ruling not only within their own spheres but nationally and internationally. All find their schemes thwarted by Campion, the seemingly inconsequential man they underestimate.

Eccentric Characters

One of Allingham's strengths is her creation of eccentric characters. Rural and urban, male and female, young and old, they are all delightful and sometimes frustrating to both Campion and his readers. Of course, Lugg and Canon Avril can be counted among the eccentrics, but Allingham is equally adept with the supporting characters in this category. Beginning with Mrs. Meade in *The Crime at Black Dudley,* a rural woman who, imprisoned by the Simister gang, is convinced her son will rescue her and teach the bad guys a lesson, Allingham progresses through a number of rural eccentrics. There are the brothers Willsmore, George and 'Anry of *Mystery Mile;* Scatty Williams and Dr. Galley of *Sweet Danger;* and Old Harry Buller of *The Beckoning Lady.* Urban eccentrics appear in a number of books in perhaps more variety and less individuality than the rural sort. In *Police at the Funeral* they are academic descendants, in *Flowers for the Judge* members of a publishing family, in *Death of a Ghost* (1934) artists, and in *Dancers in Mourning* musical artists.

The two novels most densely populated by eccentrics are perhaps *More Work for the Undertaker* and *The Beckoning Lady. More Work* features the Palinode siblings, children of Professor Palinode "who wrote the essays, and his wife the poetess . . . queer brainy people" (1968 ed., p. 13). In addition to the brainy and decidedly odd Palinodes, there are "Jas Bowels & Son (The *Practical* Undertakers)" (p. 18), a suitably repulsive pair who ship malefactors out of the country in coffins. Jas. Bowels just happens to be Lugg's brother-in-law; Lugg's choice words for him are "Bowels by name and Bowels by nature" (p. 19). *The Beckoning Lady,* reputed to be Allingham's own favorite novel, is set in Pontisbright, Suffolk, "a countryside which can boast the highest percentage of rare lunatics in the world" (1985 ed., p. 23). Scatty Williams, Amanda's helper in *Sweet Danger,* is mentioned, although he has little to do with the action, and "Uncle" William Faraday, who first appeared in *Police at the Funeral* and then in *Dancers in Mourning,* is memorialized. In addition to these characters who continue from earlier books, there are "Old Harry" Buller, whose chief claim to fame is his peculiar sense of smell, and Minnie and Tonker Cassands. Minnie is a celebrated artist and daughter of an artist, and Tonker is the inventer of the glübalübalum, a musical instrument as strange in construction and appearance as its name. The Cassands, who, although they are obviously devoted to each other, frequently live apart, are experiencing considerable trouble with the Inland Revenue over taxes. Minnie and Tonker perhaps represent the real Margery Allingham and Philip Youngman Carter, while Albert and Amanda Campion are the idealized version of author and spouse.

Of special note are a number of older female characters, many of whom can be considered eccentrics. Beginning with Caroline

Faraday, the iron-willed widow of a Cambridge master, in *Police at the Funeral,* these elderly women, often widows, play important roles in the plots of several novels. Belle Lafcadio, the widow and model of a prominent painter in *Death of a Ghost,* apparently a sweet little old lady keeping her husband's reputation intact, in reality is an astute critic of his work and very much aware of his weaknesses. Lady Carados in *Coroner's Pidgin* follows in the Caroline Faraday tradition of autocratic grandes dames. *More Work for the Undertaker* features Rene Roper, who first appears in *Dancers in Mourning,* and the Palinode sisters. "Decimal" Dot Warburton's role as caretaker of Canon Avril's and his church's financial affairs in *Tiger in the Smoke* and *The Mind Readers* is not as large as Caroline Faraday's role as caretaker of the family or Belle Lafcadio's role as caretaker of her husband's reputation, but it is crucial. Finally, Polly Tassie, in *Tether's End,* loves and believes in Gerry Hawker, even to the point of attempting to "procure" her niece for him to settle down with.

Psychology

This discussion of major and minor characters underscores Allingham's interest in the psychology of her characters. Of the nonvillains, Canon Avril is the most psychologically interesting. Allingham develops the picture of a truly spiritual man whose sense of right is equaled by his compassion. The artistic characters of *Dancers in Mourning* and *The Fashion in Shrouds* are a puzzle for Campion, who has difficulty relating to their egos. Probably the most obvious explorations of the minds of villains are *The Tiger in the Smoke* and *Tether's End,* both novels influenced by the aftereffects of World War II. As is to be expected, Allingham's exploration of the psychology of her characters matures over time; nevertheless, one of the most psychologically informed books is *Police at the Funeral,* the fourth of the Campion series. In this novel Allingham explores the relationship of Caroline Faraday and her dependent adult children. But more important, Campion wonders at what kind of hatred can have caused a man to take his own life, making it look like murder, and leave fatal booby traps for the rest of the family, trying not only to kill them but also to implicate them in his death and the deaths of their siblings. Naturally, Allingham also explores Campion's own psyche as he matures. The early need for disguise, as much personal as professional, disappears as he succeeds in his adventures and as his relationships develop.

Sense of Place

Allingham displays a keen sense of place in both urban and rural settings, a talent for which P. D. James has expressed admiration. She especially uses different areas of London, back streets and small squares, even in novels set primarily in rural areas. *Look to the Lady* begins in London, sending Val Gyrth into a cafe in an unsavory section of the city to connect with Campion. *Police at the Funeral* starts in London before moving to Cambridge, with Campion meeting Joyce Blount, Caroline Faraday's niece, in a back alley boiler room, Oates's former haunt. *Death of a Ghost* is set in Little Venice, the haunt of artists. *Traitor's Purse* finds Campion returning to London, a city stripped bare of metal fences and railings, selvaged for the war effort. *The Fashion in Shrouds* and *Coroner's Pidgin* are also basically London novels, as is *The China Governess.* Those novels that are the true London novels are *More Work for the Undertaker, Tether's End,* and *Tiger in the Smoke. More Work,* set in a neighborhood that has fallen on hard times after World War II, makes an implicit comparison of the past and present of London. *Tether's End* also relies on a neighborhood fallen on hard times but presents a larger view of the city, from the club that Hawker visits to the Dump, a desolate place where Hawker has disposed of his victims. In *Tiger in the Smoke,* London's back streets are again the setting, in particular, a small square dominated by St. Peter of the Gate Church. The "smoke" of the title refers to the fog that shrouds the city, adding to the uncertainty of the atmosphere as Campion and Luke grope their way both geographically and psychologically.

Allingham's rural settings show her equally deft hand with the pastoral. Employing such stereotypically charming English village names as Mystery Mile, Kepesake, Sweethearting, Sanctuary, and Pontisbright, she creates a pastoral fantasy world where innocence appears to be the norm but where, in reality, germinate the seeds of evil. In *Mystery Mile,* Campion uses an isolated village as refuge for an endangered American judge, but it is not surprising that outside evil penetrates, foreshadowed by the dangerous river muck that swallows its violators whole. The village of Sanctuary in *Look to the Lady* is home to the Gyrth Chalice, a mysterious relic that shadows the lives of the Gyrth men. Pontisbright, home of Amanda and seat of the "lost" earl of Pontisbright, is the setting for *Sweet Danger.* The picturesque Mill at Pontisbright, besides being "converted" by Amanda to generate electricity, hinting at a change in the pastoral innocence of the village, becomes the instrument of death for Brett Savanake. Although *Dancers in Mourning* is not a truly pastoral novel, it is set in a country house, and Allingham cleverly contrasts the simplicity of the setting with the sophisticated egos of the artists in residence. *The Beckoning Lady* returns the Campions to Pontisbright after several urban novels. Following the brooding *Tiger in the Smoke,* this novel revels in the quiet atmosphere of the countryside, which Charlie Luke, the city man, calls "terrifying . . . It's so beautiful that you don't notice for a bit that it's sent you barmy" (1985 ed., p. 26).

Changes in time are important in the series. Campion is part of that generation just too young to have experienced action in World War I and just too old for World War II, although, appropriately, he does embark on a secret mission just as World War II is breaking out. Therefore, the early Campion novels do not reflect the ravages of World War I, the war that nearly destroyed a generation of young men in England. The adventures of the novels of the 1930s reflect the concerns for the English middle class of the era between the wars—the decline of the landed gentry and a sense of uncertainty about the future as tensions increased in Europe. Those of the era after World War II reflect the changes wrought by the war, physically and socially.

These influences appear as early as *Mystery Mile,* in which the fiscal problems of the country gentry are evident. At the beginning of *Sweet Danger,* Campion is posing as the king of an obscure European principality in an attempt to locate the rightful earl of Pontisbright and secure the "ownership" of a tiny but strategic nation. *The Fashion in Shrouds* features the development of new planes and rumblings on the Continent in a general atmosphere of uneasiness. *Traitor's Purse* is based on the idea that England could be brought down by flooding the nation with counterfeit money. *Coroner's Pidgin* is set in Blitz-damaged London. The events of *The Tiger in the Smoke* had their seeds in a wartime conversation between Jack Havoc and Martin Elginbrodde, late husband of Heg Elginbrodde. The past of a character in *The China Governess* is rooted in the evacuation of children from London to the countryside during the Blitz, an event Allingham recounts in *The Oaken Heart,* and the setting of the book focuses on the rebuilding of London after the destruction wrought by these devastating German air bombardments.

Conclusion

Margery Allingham's status as one of the premier Golden Age mystery writers is assured. A skillful developer of puzzles, she does not allow the puzzle itself to overshadow the other elements of the works; her novels balance plots, characterization, and setting. Critics and ordinary readers alike have commented on her development of characters—both major and minor and those who appear once or who continue through the series. Of special interest are her settings, both physical and chronological, which she has developed through her skill with details. Readers report returning to Allingham's Campion series with pleasure, discovering details overlooked on previous readings that open up new ways of looking at the fantasy world she has created.

Selected Bibliography

WORKS OF MARGERY ALLINGHAM

NOVELS AND STORIES

Black'erchief Dick: A Tale of Mersia Island. London: Hodder and Stoughton, 1923; Garden City, N.Y.: Doubleday, Doran, 1923.

The White Cottage Mystery. London: Jarrolds, 1928.

The Crime at Black Dudley. London: Jarrolds, 1929; New York: Penguin, 1979. Also published in the United States as *The Black Dudley Murder.* Garden City, N.Y.: Doubleday, Doran, 1930.

Mystery Mile. London: Jarrolds, 1930; Garden City, N.Y.: Doubleday, Doran, 1930.

Look to the Lady. London: Jarrolds, 1931. Published in the United States as *The Gyrth Chalice Mystery.* Garden City, N.Y.: Doubleday, Doran, 1931.

Police at the Funeral. London: Heinemann, 1931; Garden City, N.Y.: Doubleday, Doran, 1932; New York: Manor, 1973.

Sweet Danger. London: Heinemann, 1933; New York: Penguin, 1978. Also published in the United States as *Kingdom of Death.* Garden City, N.Y.: Doubleday, Doran, 1933. Also published as *The Fear Sign.* New York: Macfadden, 1961.

Death of a Ghost. London: Heinemann, 1934; Garden City, N.Y.: Doubleday, Doran, 1934.

Flowers for the Judge. London: Heinemann, 1936; Garden City, N.Y.: Doubleday, Doran, 1936. Also published in the United States as *Legacy in Blood.* New York: American Mercury, 1949.

Dancers in Mourning. London: Heinemann, 1937; Garden City, N.Y.: Doubleday, Doran, 1937. Also published in the United States as *Who Killed Chloe?* New York: Avon, 1943.

The Case of the Late Pig. London: Hodder and Stoughton, 1937.

The Fashion in Shrouds. London: Heinemann, 1938; Garden City, N.Y.: Doubleday, Doran, 1938.

Black Plumes. London: Heinemann, 1940; Garden City, N.Y.: Doubleday, Doran, 1940.

Traitor's Purse. London: Heinemann, 1941; Garden City, N.Y.: Doubleday, Doran, 1941. New York: Bantam, 1983. Also published in the United States as *The Sabotage Murder Mystery.* New York: Avon, 1943.

The Dance of the Years. London: Joseph, 1943. Published in the United States as *The Gallantrys.* Boston: Little, Brown, 1943.

Coroner's Pidgin. London: Heinemann, 1945. Published in the United States as *Pearls Before Swine.* Garden City, N.Y.: Doubleday, Doran, 1945.

More Work for the Undertaker. London: Heinemann, 1948; Garden City, N.Y.: Doubleday, Doran, 1949; New York: Penguin, 1968.

Deadly Duo. New York: Doubleday, Doran, 1949. Published in the United Kingdom as *Take Two at Bedtime.* Kingswood, Surrey, Eng.: World's Work, 1950.

The Tiger in the Smoke. London: Chatto & Windus, 1952; Garden City, N.Y.: Doubleday, Doran, 1952; New York: Bantam, 1985.

No Love Lost. Kingswood, Surrey: World's Work, 1954; New York: Doubleday, Doran, 1954.

The Beckoning Lady. London: Chatto & Windus, 1955; London: Hogarth, 1985. Published in the United States as *The Estate of the Beckoning Lady.* Garden City, N.Y.: Doubleday, Doran, 1955.

Hide My Eyes. London: Chatto & Windus, 1958. Published in the United States as *Tether's End.* Garden City, N.Y.: Doubleday, Doran, 1958; New York: Bantam, 1983. Also published as *Ten Were Missing.* New York: Dell, 1959.

The China Governess. New York: Doubleday, Doran, 1962; London: Chatto & Windus, 1963.

The Mind Readers. London: Chatto & Windus, 1965; New York: Morrow, 1965; New York: Manor, 1972.

Cargo of Eagles. London: Chatto & Windus, 1968; New York: Morrow, 1968.

COLLECTED WORKS

Mr. Campion: Criminologist. Garden City, N.Y.: Doubleday, Doran, 1937.

Mr. Campion and Others. London: Heinemann, 1939.

Wanted: Someone Innocent. London: Pony Books, 1946. A novella and three stories.

The Case Book of Mr. Campion. Edited by Ellery Queen. New York: American Mercury, 1947.

Mr. Campion's Lady. London: Chatto & Windus, 1965.

The Mysterious Mr. Campion. London: Chatto & Windus, 1965; New York: Morrow, 1965.

The Allingham Case-Book. London: Chatto & Windus, 1969; New York: Morrow, 1969.

The Allingham Minibus: More Short Stories. London: Chatto & Windus, 1973; New York: Morrow, 1973.

The Allingham Casebook. New York: Carroll and Graf, 1992.

Mr. Campion's Lucky Day. New York: Carroll and Graf, 1992.

NONFICTION

The Oaken Heart. London: Joseph, 1941; Garden City, N.Y.: Doubleday, Doran, 1941.

BIOGRAPHICAL AND CRITICAL WORKS

Asbee, Sue. "Margery Allingham and Reader Response." In *Twentieth-Century Suspense: The Thriller Comes of Age.* Edited by Clive Bloom. New York: St. Martin's, 1990.

Cox, J. Randolph. "Miss Allingham's Knight: The Saga of Albert Campion." *Armchair Detective* 15, no. 1: 86–91 (1982).

Gaskill, Rex W. "Margery Allingham." In *And Then There Were Nine: More Women of Mystery.* Edited by Jane S. Bakerman. Bowling Green, Ohio: Bowling Green University Popular Press, 1985.

Huey, Talbott W. "Mr. Campion and the Survival of the Great Detective." *Clues* 3, no. 1: 90–104 (1982).

Mann, Jessica. *Deadlier Than the Male: Why Are Respectable Englishwomen So Good at Murder?* New York: Macmillan, 1981.

Martin, Richard. *Ink in Her Blood: The Life and Crime Fiction of Margery Allingham.* Ann Arbor: UMI Research Press, 1988. Bibliography includes non-mystery writings.

Panek, LeRoy. *Watteau's Shepherds: The Detective Novel in Britain 1914–1940.* Bowling Green, Ohio: Bowling Green University Popular Press, 1979.

Peters, Margot, and Agate N. Krouse. "Women and Crime: Sexism in Allingham, Sayers, and Christie." *Southwest Review* 59: 144–152 (1974).

Pike, B. A. *Campion's Career: A Study of the Novels of Margery Allingham.* Bowling Green, Ohio: Bowling Green University Popular Press, 1987. Includes descriptive bibliography.

Thorogood, Julia. *Margery Allingham: A Biography.* London: Heinemann, 1991.

Woods, Paula M. "The First Campion Novel." In *In the Beginning: First Novels in Mystery Series.* Edited by Mary Jean DeMarr. Bowling Green, Ohio: Bowling Green University Popular Press, 1995.

ERIC AMBLER

(b. 1909)

PETER LEWIS

ERIC AMBLER is one of the giants of twentieth-century mystery writing. In the 1930s he set out to transform the thriller from its status as the most intellectually despised of popular literary forms, and with the six novels he published from 1936 to 1940 he succeeded triumphantly. While retaining some conventions of the contemporary thriller, Ambler brought an unexpected sophistication to the genre. Stylistically and formally his early novels are much subtler than the standard thrillers of the time, which were ridiculed for their verbal banality, political crudity, and minimal characterization. Reviewers in the late 1930s were quick to recognize Ambler's originality, especially in his fifth novel, *The Mask of Dimitrios* (1939; U.S., *A Coffin for Dimitrios*), which for many readers remains his masterpiece. In this seminal book, now accepted as a major breakthrough in the history of mystery writing, Ambler dissolved the borderline between popular and serious, much as the slightly older Graham Greene was also doing.

The historical significance of Ambler's first six books is not in question. By redeeming the genre as a vehicle for serious ideas, he pioneered a type of thriller that was to exert a strong influence on a new generation of writers after World War II and during the Cold War. Ambler therefore helped to make possible the achievement of authors such as John le Carré. Ambler's own postwar career did not develop as might have been expected in that he did not jump on the Cold War bandwagon that sustained much thriller writing between 1950 and 1990. Indeed, Ambler took some time to recover the habit of novel writing after military service during World War II brought an abrupt end to the brief but prolific first phase of his fiction. When he began to publish again in the 1950s, he avoided the prevailing literary fashions of the time and went his own way. His postwar fiction has not had the impact of his first phase, but he has continued to be widely admired as a master of the genre and his influence continues to be acknowledged by later generations of writers.

Much of what has been written about Ambler is in the form of book reviews and journalistic interviews over about fifty years, while more academic approaches are usually found in books dealing broadly with spy fiction and the mystery genre. Very few books and essays focus on Ambler alone or on the whole of his oeuvre. The chronological arrangement of what follows reflects the way in which his career was so decisively bisected by World War II.

Earlier Life (to 1940)

Eric Ambler was born in London on 28 June 1909, the eldest of three children of Alfred

Percy Ambler and Amy Madeleine Andrews. During World War I the Amblers lived in a London suburb subject to German bombing, and such attacks provided Eric with some of his most memorable experiences of childhood. At school he did extremely well, gaining a scholarship to Colfe's Grammar School in Lewisham and subsequently winning a further scholarship to study engineering in London. In 1926 he joined the Edison Swan Electric Company as a trainee engineer, and when the company became part of Associated Electrical Industries, he moved to the publicity department. He continued to work in advertising, later for an independent agency, until he devoted himself to full-time writing in 1938.

Ambler's parents were stagestruck and became well-known for their musical performances in theatrical revues, even though they failed to break into the lucrative world of London's West End. They gave up the attempt in 1921, but their love of theatrical performance had a strong effect on the young Eric, who as a teenager was fascinated by the stage. While pursuing his studies and subsequent career with Edison Swan, Ambler was pushing ahead with his literary and theatrical ambitions. Under the impact of Henrik Ibsen and Luigi Pirandello, he decided to be a playwright, and by the 1930s he was writing avant-garde plays influenced by German Expressionism, a few of which were performed at London's Guildhall School of Music. On a lighter note, he followed his parents' example as a stage entertainer, being the pianist in a comedy double act. By 1935 he was uncertain about his direction as a dramatist and so decided to try something totally different. Always a voracious reader, he had already dabbled in novel writing but now set himself the daunting task of raising the thriller from the realm of pure pulp and giving it literary respectability.

The detective fiction of such Golden Age writers as Agatha Christie, with its strong puzzle element presenting an intellectual challenge to the reader, was considered vastly superior to the thrillers of writers like E. Phillips Oppenheim and "Sapper" (H. C. McNeile). Since John Buchan, the British thriller had become extremely formulaic and increasingly anti-Semitic, jingoistic, and xenophobic. To someone like Ambler in the mid-1930s, it was an anachronism. Yet he, like Graham Greene, realized that the genre possessed plenty of potential for exploring serious issues, especially the political crisis in Europe after the rise of Fascism in Italy and Nazism in Germany. Like many young intellectuals during the interwar years, Ambler was attracted by socialist ideas and supported the Popular Front, although he never became a Communist. During the 1930s he spent as much time as possible traveling in Europe and was fully aware of the nature of totalitarian regimes as well as the threat they posed to peace. What attracted Ambler to the thriller rather than the detective story was its ability to encompass international action and topical themes, such as the clash between capitalism and socialism, and the political battle between Right and Left. It could therefore transcend escapism. Detective fiction, on the other hand, had much less appeal for him because its cozy closed-world and upper-middle-class basis virtually prevented any engagement with the major issues of the day.

In 1938, only two years after launching his career as a novelist, Ambler took the risky decision to give up his job in advertising and become a full-time author, moving to France where it was cheaper to live. He immediately attracted the attention of film companies, translators working for foreign publishers, and newspapers keen to serialize his work. In Paris he met an American fashion correspondent, Louise Crombie, whom he married in October 1939, shortly after the war broke out. They visited America together before military service totally transformed Ambler's life in 1940.

Fiction: 1936–1940

In 1936 Ambler published his first novel, *The Dark Frontier,* which was not published in America until 1990. Inspired by *Cold Com-*

fort Farm (1932), Stella Gibbons' devastating parody of the English rural-romantic novel, Ambler set out to inflict the same comic treatment on the contemporary thriller. Burlesque of its standard elements is embodied in a distinguished British scientist, Barstow, who is transformed by an accident into an almost superhuman secret agent, Carruthers. Through the bizarre adventures of this double-sided character in an imaginary Balkan country called Ixania, Ambler has much fun at the expense of writers like Oppenheim, turning upside down their stereotypical plot devices and political values. Ambler further subverts the thriller by mocking its highly predictable idiom and clichéd language.

Yet as Ambler was writing it, *The Dark Frontier* outgrew its parodic intention and developed into something more than burlesque—an alternative form of thriller. The change of narrative viewpoint halfway through the story is symptomatic. The novel turns into a strange amalgam of science fiction and political fantasy, dealing with nuclear weapons some years before they became a practical possibility. At the same time, Ambler's fictional world is rooted in the political actualities of eastern Europe in the 1930s, where unbridled nationalism and fascism were becoming increasingly dominant. In his struggle to uphold civilized values against political thuggery and the unscrupulous arms trade, Barstow becomes much more than a burlesque figure. He eventually emerges as the hero of a new type of thriller. Because of its change of direction *The Dark Frontier* is a flawed work of art, but writing it was crucial to Ambler's development as he rethought the thriller's possibilities by inverting its conventions, so clearing the way for his next few novels.

In his second novel, *Uncommon Danger* (1937; U.S., *Background to Danger*), Ambler dispenses with the parodic structure of *The Dark Frontier* as well as its science fiction component and imaginary country in favor of sinister realism. In certain respects *Background to Danger* does provide what was expected of thrillers: it is an exciting adventure story involving murder, kidnap, intrigue, pursuit, escape, and a final shoot-out that thwarts a villainous political plot. The underlying structure resembles that of John Buchan's classic thriller, *The Thirty-Nine Steps* (1915), but critics immediately saw that Ambler's approach was refreshingly new and different.

First, the action is firmly embedded in the real-life political battleground of the 1930s: socialism against capitalism, Marxism against fascism, democracy against totalitarianism. Indeed, the Soviet military secrets around which the plot revolves relate specifically to an actual source of European tension, the oil-producing region of Bessarabia, controlled by Romania since 1918 but claimed by the Soviet Union. Ambler gives added credibility to his fictional conspiracy involving governments and big business by including references to contemporary politicians and organizations. Second, the central character, Nicholas Kenton, is an archetypal antihero rather than the conventional ultra-patriotic hero of thrillers. A cosmopolitan journalist, Kenton is the model for the typical Ambler protagonist in subsequent novels: an ordinary, unexceptional person who, by being in the wrong place at the wrong time, is suddenly involved in a network of political and criminal duplicity of which he was previously unaware.

Another aspect of Ambler's subversion of the standard thriller is the reversal of its characteristic ideological stance. His satire of big business and monopoly capitalism, represented by the multinational Pan-Eurasian Petroleum Company, as well as his very sympathetic treatment of a brother-and-sister pair of Soviet agents, Andreas and Tamara Zaleshoff, make this a left-wing thriller, which was an extraordinary novelty at the time. In broadly endorsing socialist values, Ambler attacks British insularity for its blindness to the political time bomb ticking away in continental Europe.

Ambler's fourth novel, *Cause for Alarm* (1938), is very much the successor to *Background to Danger,* even using Andreas Zaleshoff as a significant character again—something rare in Ambler, who normally avoids sequels and series characters. However, between these two books he brought out something substantially different, also in 1938: *Epitaph for a Spy*, not published in America until 1952 in a revised version with an introduction by Ambler. In England, the reception was most enthusiastic, critics praising it as one of the best books of its kind ever written. Structurally *Epitaph for a Spy* is closer to the classic English detective novel than to the fast-moving thriller, but Ambler handles the form in his own unique way so that his political concerns are never far from the surface. Having transformed the thriller in his two preceding novels, Ambler now puts a genuinely original spin on the detective story.

Ambler's variant of the whodunit takes place in the closed world of a hotel in the south of France—an appropriate setting for an English Golden Age mystery by Agatha Christie. Knowing that among the twelve people in the hotel is a spy gathering information about French naval secrets, the police pressure one of these, the first-person narrator Vadassy, to help them from the inside. Like Kenton in Ambler's previous novel, the ethnically Hungarian Vadassy is an ordinary person who has the bad luck to find himself in the middle of something sinister through no fault of his own. Yet as a stateless person without any family, very much a victim of the calamities and redrawn boundaries in eastern Europe after World War I, Vadassy is even more of an Amblerian outsider and loner than Kenton. The French police exploit Vadassy's vulnerability to make him cooperate, but Vadassy's efforts at detection prove to be extremely clumsy. Ambler's ironic comparison between his protagonist and S. S. Van Dine's fictional detective Philo Vance serves to distance his own realistic narrative from that of conventional detective fiction featuring such supersleuths as Christie's Hercule Poirot. Furthermore, it turns out that the police discovered the identity of the spy at the hotel early in their investigation, and that Vadassy's role as amateur detective was a subterfuge by the French police to help them round up an entire Italian spy ring rather than identify a single culprit.

Despite its quiet hotel setting, *Epitaph for a Spy* reaches out to embrace what was happening in Europe at the time. Ambler peoples the hotel with an extremely varied and cosmopolitan bunch, including Nazi agents and anti-Nazi Marxists. The hotel can thus be seen as a microcosm of the many tensions tearing Europe apart at the end of the 1930s. In *Epitaph for a Spy*, Ambler creates a totally unexpected blend of the spy novel and the classical detective story that turns out to be different from either. He plays with the Golden Age formula in such a way as to produce a political novel of considerable topicality. Published a year before World War II began, the novel is full of portents of conflict as European civilization trembled on the edge of an abyss.

With *Cause for Alarm* Ambler returned to the pattern of the alternative thriller he had developed in *Background to Danger*, but with more sophistication and subtlety. The main setting is Mussolini's Italy rather than central or eastern Europe, and the penultimate chapter in the British edition (dropped in the American edition) is a disturbing account of how a brilliant Italian scientist was gradually driven insane by his treatment under the Fascists. The narrative of pursuit and escape inevitably slows down for such discursive treatment of the history of Italian Fascism, but it does provide the novel with more historical breadth and political depth than it would otherwise have had.

Whereas the plots of Ambler's first two novels hinge on the familiar device of a quest for secret documents, that of *Cause for Alarm* involves an ingenious intelligence ploy by the Soviet agent Andreas Zaleshoff to plant information designed to cause a rift between his ideological enemies, Hitler's Germany and Mussolini's Italy. Any damage to their Berlin–Rome Axis would postpone, if only temporarily, the risk of war. Just as Kenton cooperates with Zaleshoff in *Background to Danger*, a young English engineer, Marlow, becomes his associate in *Cause for Alarm*, and most of the novel is told from Marlow's point of view. Like Kenton, Marlow is the antitype of the conventional thriller hero, but is more naive and insular in his liberalism. The opportunity to run his small company's Milan office proves to be his baptism of fire, bringing him face to face with the political nightmares of contemporary Europe and the moral incongruities of serving commercial interests by cooperating with tyrannical regimes.

Marlow's British company has lucrative contracts with the Italian navy for the production of armaments at a time when Mussolini's pact with Hitler is posing a threat to British strategic interests, including the possibility of military conflict. However, Ambler's treatment of the contradictions in capitalism is more complex in *Cause for Alarm* than in *Background to Danger,* where Ambler employs caricature to depict the leading figures of Pan-Eurasian Petroleum as moral monsters. Those associated with Marlow's company, on the other hand, are basically decent people who are trying to succeed within the capitalist system they have inherited. In Italy, Marlow soon finds himself caught between the mighty opposites of Fascism and Communism. On one side is General Vagas, a top Nazi spy who offers Marlow bribes to provide secret information about the Italian armaments industry. On the other is Zaleshoff with his Marxist analysis of the "gospel of King Profit" and his determination to do what he can to preserve European peace by undermining, at least to some extent, the Berlin–Rome Axis. Marlow sides with Zaleshoff and is able to feed Vagas intelligence about Italy's secret military airfields, information being deliberately concealed from Germany. Zaleshoff and Marlow do achieve their aim, but their success is much more muted than Zaleshoff's victory at the end of *Background to Danger.* The novel ends in midair with "But. . . ." The qualified optimism of the epilogue proved illusory, for within a year Europe was at war again.

Ambler's fifth novel, *A Coffin for Dimitrios* (1939) appeared in the week that World War II broke out. All of Ambler's novels so far had involved a transformation of the thriller genre, but in this novel he excels himself, going much further in bridging the divide between popular and literary fiction. At the same time he does not fail to create a gripping narrative of pursuit culminating in a dramatic denouement. Conscious that he was breaking new ground, Ambler struggled hard with this ambitious novel, and his efforts were rewarded by the critical acclaim he won. There was widespread agreement that Ambler, only just thirty, was the best living thriller writer and that he had redeemed the genre.

In *A Coffin for Dimitrios* Ambler requires his readers to piece together the story of Dimitrios between the early 1920s and the late 1930s from the various narrative fragments he presents: police archives, written statements, index cards, hearsay evidence, and interviews. Rather than a fixed viewpoint, there is a multiplicity of voices and perspectives. Two interwoven narratives provide the backbone of the novel; one follows the quest for Dimitrios and the other details the object of the quest himself. By making the questing figure, Charles Latimer, a successful English detective writer in the "cozy" Golden Age mold, Ambler introduces a self-reflexive element into the text that is highly unusual in mysteries. *A Coffin for Dimitrios* is partly about a writer and the nature of fiction. Throughout the novel there is a complex interplay between the reality of everyday life, the "reality" of English detective fiction, and the different "reality" of Ambler's alternative thrillers. He criticizes the classic English murder mystery of the interwar years for being so insular at a time of international danger and political atrocities, interpreting it as symptomatic of the tendency of the nation to bury its head in the sand when confronted by European fascism. Implicitly and explicitly Ambler endorses the thriller as a more adequate vehicle for exploring social, political, and economic realities than Golden Age detective stories, and in doing so makes a case for the thriller to be considered a literary form capable of high seriousness.

Abandoning the usual fast-moving and

chronologically linear basis of the thriller in favor of a complex narrative moving back and forth between past and present, Ambler covers virtually the entire period between the end of World War I and the start of World War II by tracing Dimitrios' career from 1922. Ambler offers a more comprehensive overview of the political upheavals of the period than in his earlier books, symbolizing in the figure of Dimitrios the nihilism and irrationalism unleashed during the interwar years by an amalgam of monopolistic capitalism and fascist ideology. As the title suggests, Dimitrios is the focal point of the novel, not Latimer, but it is through Latimer's research in different countries that the Greek's life story gradually unfolds. Latimer's obsession with Dimitrios begins in Istanbul in 1938 when a Turkish policeman tells him about a man whose corpse has been found—apparently Dimitrios. Unlike Kenton, Vadassy, and Marlow in the three preceding novels, Latimer does not become drawn into a nefarious world by chance. He deliberately chooses to enter that world as self-appointed detective because of his desire to learn the truth about Dimitrios. Even so, Latimer's fascination with Dimitrios puts him in increasing danger, especially since his quarry is not dead, as he pretends to be, but very much alive.

The portrait of Dimitrios that gradually emerges is that of a ruthless master criminal as successful entrepreneur and capitalist. Beginning in a small way in Smyrna, Dimitrios advances in his pursuit of money and power through blackmail and pimping in Sofia, attempted assassinations in various parts of Europe, espionage, international drug dealing, and the white slave trade on a global scale, becoming a wealthy, respectable businessman with a villa in Cannes and a seat on the board of an international bank based in Monaco. From the Marxist viewpoint pervading the novel, Dimitrios is presented not merely as a morally degenerate individual, but also as the symptom of a diseased society rooted in capitalist exploitation and the prioritizing of money at the expense of moral and spiritual values. Despite the reference to Hitler's autobiographical *Mein Kampf* in the novel, Ambler nowhere draws parallels between Dimitrios and Hitler, but these may have been at the back of his mind. Like Hitler, Dimitrios was born in 1889, began to attract attention in the early 1920s, was involved in a political coup in 1923, achieved outward respectability and a position of power in the early 1930s, and interfered in the affairs of other countries in the late 1930s.

In September 1939 Hitler precipitated World War II, which soon brought Ambler's career as a novelist to a standstill, but before it did so, he quickly wrote the sixth and last book of his first phase: *Journey into Fear* (1940). Although less ambitious than *A Coffin for Dimitrios*, it breaks new ground in one important respect: it is the most psychological of these early thrillers. In it Ambler undertakes a study in depth of one of his typical antiheroes, Graham, a scientist who initially seems an embodiment of English insularity: conventional, unimaginative, and politically unaware. A leading expert in the arms industry, Graham is capable of making a significant contribution to the war effort against Germany because of his knowledge of Turkey's secret military plans. He is consequently targeted by a Nazi assassination squad when on a mission to Turkey. Like Kenton and Marlow, Graham is an English innocent abroad who unexpectedly finds himself at the center of a nasty plot.

Mainly set on a ship in the Mediterranean with a small number of passengers, *Journey into Fear* is a closed-world narrative like the hotel-based *Epitaph for a Spy* and involves a similar range of cosmopolitan characters. Graham, having survived one attempt on his life in Turkey, is soon aware that his would-be assassin is also on board and has little difficulty in identifying him. As Graham struggles to find some way of outwitting his enemies, the tension gradually builds to an exciting climax, Ambler again proving to be a master of nail-biting suspense while also keeping the political dimension in the foreground. In *Journey into Fear* he does this more through introspection and psychological analysis than usual.

Finding himself in the equivalent of a death cell, Graham is forced to reassess his entire outlook on life, including politics, and experiences a kind of enlightenment. The boat journey becomes a journey of self-discovery, with fear being the necessary stimulus. Coming to terms with reality, Graham finds within himself the strength to resist what seems inevitable, his murder, and even finds the determination to fight back. In this way he personifies Britain's need to take on the Nazi threat. Whereas Kenton and Marlow experience a change of heart and mind through the influence of others and succeed by joining forces with Zaleshoff, Graham has to rely entirely on his own resources. Here, in the only novel Ambler wrote during wartime, his characteristic antihero, alone and under intense pressure, becomes positively heroic, a patriotic emblem of resistance to barbaric primitivism, a reluctant Saint George taking on the dragon of Nazism. Whatever the odds against him, Graham chooses not only to battle it out rather than submit fatalistically, but also, if possible, to win.

The note of patriotic triumph in Graham's eventual victory signals a shift in Ambler's political position following the outbreak of war. Ambler later admitted, in the introduction to *Intrigue* (1965), that he was still surprised he "should so readily have decided that the object of the reader's sympathy and concern in *Journey into Fear* could be an arms salesman." This would have been almost unthinkable in the earlier prewar novels, in three of which the company Graham works for, Cator and Bliss, represents the worst side of capitalism—heartless, money-grubbing, and warmongering. Ambler's satirical attitude to the military-industrial complex now gives way to an acceptance of its necessity since war is the only remaining means of resisting Nazi tyranny.

While completing *Journey into Fear,* Ambler rightly decided that, in the new circumstances of war, he would almost certainly not be able to finish another novel if he began it. However, for the only time in his life he indulged in a brief burst of short-story writing, a form he had previously decided was not for him after struggling with a few early efforts. Six of these stories, all dealing with a Czech policeman in London, mark an unexpected departure from Ambler's characteristic type of political thriller and are ingenious tales of detection in the Sherlock Holmes tradition. Ambler wrote these for newspaper publication under the collective title "The Intrusions of Dr. Czissar." Five years of war and six of peace would pass before a new Ambler novel was published.

Later Life (Since 1940)

In 1940 Ambler wanted to join the navy but ended up in the army. He was soon assigned to its film unit, and his war service consisted of writing and producing nearly one hundred training and propaganda films, including semidocumentary features. By the time he returned to civilian life in 1946, he was a senior figure in Army Kinematography with the rank of lieutenant colonel. During the war four of Ambler's six novels were made into movies by American companies: *Journey into Fear* (1942), *Background to Danger* (1943), *The Mask of Dimitrios* (using the British title, 1944), and *Hotel Reserve* (based on *Epitaph for a Spy,* also 1944). Plans to film *Cause for Alarm* came to nothing. Ambler's other early novel, *The Dark Frontier,* subsequently provided the basis for a British film scripted by Ambler himself, *Highly Dangerous* (1950). Another indication of American enthusiasm for Ambler was the publication as early as 1943 of an omnibus edition of the four novels already published in the United States, *Intrigue,* with an introduction by no less a Hollywood director than Alfred Hitchcock.

Hollywood was open to Ambler in 1946 and eventually did lure him away from England, but from 1946 until 1958 he devoted a great deal of creative energy to the British film industry and had a highly successful career as writer and producer. Twelve of his screenplays and one collaboration reached the screen, mostly adaptations of other writers' books. In addition he wrote magazine articles, collaborated with the Australian writer Charles Rodda on a series of novels issued under the name "Eliot Reed," and slowly returned to his own novel writing, publishing four books during the 1950s.

Ambler first visited Hollywood in 1957, when his marriage to Louise Crombie was coming to an end, and he received a number of tempting offers. He was soon established in California, where in 1958 he married Joan Harrison, an English TV writer and producer who had worked closely with Hitchcock for many years. In 1957 she produced Ambler's original TV drama "The Eye of Truth" for Hitchcock's *Suspicion* series, but it was another TV series that soon made Ambler's name known throughout America. With *Checkmate,* about private investigators in San Francisco, he created a series that had huge appeal and ran to seventy episodes between 1959 and 1962. After this initial success, Ambler's time as a Hollywood writer was largely frustrating, especially after his British experience. He worked on various screenplays, but only his first was made into a film, *The Wreck of the Mary Deare* (1959). The one cinematic compensation was the immense popularity of *Topkapi* (1964), based on his 1962 novel *The Light of Day,* although Ambler was not responsible for the adaptation.

The positive side of Ambler's California years was that he continued to write novels, publishing four more during the 1960s and gaining literary awards for them in both Britain and America. Even so, his novel writing was not without trauma. In 1961 his home in Bel Air, along with hundreds of others, was gutted by a brush fire. Most of what he owned was destroyed, including his library and the manuscript of the novel he was writing, *The Light of Day.* Undefeated, Ambler began it all over again.

In 1968 Ambler decided to return to Europe, and he and Joan moved to Switzerland in the following year, making extended visits to London throughout the 1970s. In 1982, with his wife's health deteriorating, Ambler settled in London, where he continued to live after Joan's death in 1994. While in Switzerland Ambler devoted himself largely to fiction, completing four more novels, and received prestigious accolades in Britain, America, France, and Sweden, notably the highest tribute of the Mystery Writers of America, its Grand Master Award. Although he has not published a novel since 1981, he has continued to write, notably a first volume of autobiography, *Here Lies* (1985). In 1986 he was the first-ever recipient of the British Crime Writers' Association's highest award, the Cartier Diamond Dagger for lifetime achievement. The long-awaited second volume of autobiography has not yet appeared, but an American edition of his collected stories, *Waiting for Orders,* was published in 1991 and was followed by an expanded British version, *The Story so Far: Memories and Other Fictions* (1993), which includes some new autobiographical material.

Until the publication of *Here Lies,* Ambler had not revealed a great deal of himself in either interviews or his writing, believing that an artist's work rather his life should be of prime interest to the public. Without strong encouragement from his British publisher, he might not have begun his autobiography when well into his seventies, and he did not find it an easy task. The first two-thirds of *Here Lies* cover the years up to the outbreak of World War II in 1939, when he was thirty. Most of the rest is devoted to his wartime experience, so there is very little about his involvement in the film industry. Nevertheless, *Here Lies* contains a fascinating account of his childhood and adolescence, including World War I and the problematic decade of the 1920s. It also describes his development as a writer during the 1930s, especially under the impact of foreign travel and conflicting political ideologies in Europe. Ambler has not yet given an account of his work for the cinema in Britain or of his time in Hollywood, although one of the autobiographical sections in *The Story so Far* does contain a vivid description of the 1961 fire in Bel Air that destroyed his house and possessions.

Postwar Fiction, 1950s

By 1940 Ambler, together with Graham Greene, had remade the English thriller. It would never be the same again. The Cold War provided the main stimulus for many postwar thriller writers up to about 1990, and Ambler himself was one of the first to exploit its potential. The first of his twelve postwar novels, *Judgment on Deltchev* (1951), is the type of book one would have expected of the author on the basis of his first phase. But immediately after completing this work, just as the fictional treatment of the Cold War was beginning to enjoy the great popularity that lasted for decades, Ambler took a different road. For the next thirty years, variety was what he aimed at.

Given his time-consuming involvement in British cinema immediately after the war, the wonder is not that Ambler took some years to return to writing fiction, but that he managed to do so at all. The "Eliot Reed" collaboration with Charles Rodda that began in 1949 may have helped, but even when Ambler was most involved in this, Rodda did much of the writing, Ambler being the idea man—feeding plots, situations, and characters to his coauthor. What saved Ambler from being totally devoured by the film industry was his love of the novel form and of its one-to-one writer–reader relationship. A factor in Ambler's difficulty in finding a way forward for his own fiction was that the political map had changed so much since the 1930s. His first six novels possess a certain coherence in that they were a response by a writer with socialist sympathies to the prewar European crisis and the threat of fascism. The defeat of Hitler and Mussolini meant that he had to rethink the possibilities of the political thriller, especially in the light of Stalin's despotic imperialism. The wartime alliance had collapsed into a new ideological conflict as the Soviet Union behaved increasingly like the defeated fascist powers.

Judgment on Deltchev, the eventual product of Ambler's struggle to find an answer to his creative problems and one of his most memorable books, is a sophisticated fusion of thriller and political novel. The complex narrative, with several interlocking sections, is woven around the treason trial of Yordan Deltchev in the unnamed capital of an imaginary Balkan country, which might almost be Ixania, from *The Dark Frontier,* fifteen years later. Several features are reminiscent of Ambler's early work: the Balkan setting, the lone Englishman out of his depth in continental politics, the sinister atmosphere of intrigue and violence. Like Latimer in *A Coffin for Dimitrios,* the Englishman is a successful writer—a dramatist called Foster—who accepts a journalistic assignment to report on the trial and finds himself dangerously involved in what he uncovers. As in the earlier novel, the nature of fiction becomes an important theme when the narrator, Foster, realizes that what is happening in court is a show trial planned as theatrically as one of his own plays. The evidence is patently fabricated and the verdict and sentence predetermined.

The stimulus for *Judgment on Deltchev* was provided by the spate of Stalinist show trials in Eastern Europe in the late 1940s designed to eliminate any organized opposition to the new Communist regimes by discrediting anyone of influence refusing to toe the Party line. Deltchev is a fictional counterpart of the many real-life liberals, democrats, and church leaders who were made out to be enemies of the people because of their pro-Western stance. Such non-Communist patriots had usually struggled against Nazism side by side with their Communist colleagues, but now they had to be presented as closet fascists, devious hypocrites motivated solely by self-interest. If doubts could be cast on someone as eminent as the charismatic Deltchev, not only a national hero but also virtual father of his country, then any possible opposition to the Communists could easily be subverted.

As the novel develops, the focus gradually shifts from Deltchev to the complex figure of Georghi Pashik, who runs a press agency and who has become a passionate defender of Western values. Pashik's desperate attempt to redeem the situation through an intricate plot sadly goes wrong, and like Deltchev he becomes a tragic victim of the new forces of darkness in control behind Stalin's Iron Curtain. The novel ends pessimistically with a lament for the fate of liberal democracy in eastern Europe and an indictment of the crimes committed in the name of socialism by Stalinists. Ambler's criticism of Soviet policy throughout the novel caused consternation among some devotees of his early work, who accused him of betraying socialism and encouraging virulent anti-Communism. Yet like George Orwell in the 1940s, Ambler was analyzing the repressive totalitarian reality behind Marxist-Leninist rhetoric.

For his eighth novel, *The Schirmer Inheritance* (1953), Ambler changed both his London publisher and his direction as a writer. While confirming his disillusionment with Communism, the novel is much less political than his previous work and springs other surprises. Until now, love and sex had been marginal in his fiction, but here he writes about intense and violent passion, in a relationship involving sadomasochism between the modern Franz Schirmer and the interpreter he falls for, Maria Kolin. This is also the first Ambler novel to be, at least partly, historical, since it opens during the Napoleonic wars and, although mainly set in the 1950s, keeps looking back to the nineteenth century. The original Franz Schirmer is a Prussian soldier who deserts in 1807, when badly wounded, and changes his name. This decision eventually gives rise to a major inheritance problem in 1938 when an eccentric American millionaire dies intestate. Ambler's narrative, partly based on some celebrated real-life cases, deals with the quest to find the missing heir to the fortune.

At first the aim of the quester in the 1950s, an American lawyer called Carey, is to establish that there is no rightful claimant, but as he trawls through the past, traveling widely to consult records and documents as well as to interview an extraordinary variety of people, he discovers that a similar investigative odyssey in 1939 was hot on the trail of the heir but was brought to a standstill by the war. Carey's detective work, as he follows clues around Europe, recalls Latimer's pursuit of Dimitrios, although his intention is different. All Carey needs is an answer to the simple question: Is the twentieth-century Schirmer alive or dead? Carey finally tracks down Schirmer in his Macedonian lair, where Schirmer's account of his experiences in World War II and the subsequent civil war in Greece, when Communists tried to take over, introduces a political analysis of Yugoslavia and Greece in the 1940s. As a tough professional soldier Schirmer is an intriguing and ambiguous figure, seemingly an outrageous opportunist but actually a man of integrity with a clear code of honor. For the maneuverings and rhetoric of politicians, especially Communists, he has nothing but contempt. Schirmer embodies a defiant individualism that is increasingly celebrated in Ambler's fiction. After the pessimistic ending of *Judgment on Deltchev,* the denouement of *The Schirmer Inheritance* is decidedly upbeat, with Schirmer and Maria making a successful getaway just as his great-great-grandfather and the woman who saved him, also Maria, did almost a century and a half earlier.

Until the mid-1950s Ambler's fiction had been firmly Eurocentric, despite the American element in *The Schirmer Inheritance,* but in his next two novels he followed Greene's example by employing more geographically remote third world settings. Both *The Night-Comers* (1956; U.S., *State of Siege*) and *Passage of Arms* (1959) are about southeast Asia and in different ways deal with the topical issue of decolonization. Like Greene, Ambler traveled to this part of the world in the 1950s and was drawing on first-hand experience. The story line of *State of Siege* is a variant of Ambler's characteristic device of dropping a political innocent into the center of a volatile and dangerous political situation. Steven Fraser, a Scottish engineer, has been working on a power and irrigation scheme on the island of Sunda, a fictional republic based on one of the islands in the Indonesian archipelago, formerly the Dutch East Indies. It is his bad luck, while waiting for a flight to London, to be staying in the building seized by rebels as their headquarters during an attempted coup against the government. Sunda's recent history is based on that of former European colonies in Asia occupied by Japan during World War II, making the process of liberation doubly difficult. The anticolonial struggle, with its accompanying atrocities against the Dutch landowners in the name of freedom, has been a great unifier for the Sundanese, but after independence the factions, united by their desire to get rid of the colonial power, fragment into rival, power-hungry groups.

Much of the novel is about the short period between Fraser's capture by the rebels, along with a Eurasian girl he befriends, and the ruthless suppression of the attempted coup. This experience proves to be a terrifying ordeal for the two of them since death seems the most likely outcome, but Fraser is sufficiently useful to the rebels to make their survival possible. By far the most interesting and complex character in the novel is Major Suparto, seemingly one of the rebels but in fact a double agent, a government mole in the rebel camp who is responsible for the failure of the coup. It is a pity that Ambler's choice of first-person narration through Fraser prevents Suparto, a patriot to some and a traitor to others, from being presented in more depth, since the moral problems confronting this enigmatic individual are at the heart of the political dilemmas facing new countries emerging from a colonial past. The fascination of Suparto, as of Pashik and Schirmer in the two preceding novels, lies in his profoundly ambiguous nature, embodying contradictions inherent in the concept of democracy itself.

The opening of *Passage of Arms,* set in the British colony of Malaya (shortly to become part of Malaysia), suggests that this, too, is a novel about political conflicts in Southeast Asia during the 1950s. However, it quickly turns into a different kind of novel, more comic than tragic, with the emphasis on human determination, cunning, and frailty rather than politics and power. The comedy is, however, more of character than situation, and the narrative includes some violent and brutal episodes. As in *State of Siege* the background for the main action is one of postcolonial civil strife, but Ambler now uses the actual situation in Indonesia where President Sukarno's Marxist-leaning government was under threat from a coalition of Islamic, anti-Communist, and secessionist elements. Where *Passage of Arms* differs not only from its immediate predecessor but also from all Ambler's earlier novels is in his replacement of a central character or two by a collection of characters roughly equal in importance, a formal feature of traditional comedy. Ambler's organization of the narrative is consequently unlike anything in his earlier work, where he favors a continuously unfolding sequence. Adopting cinematic montage, he now subdivides chapters into a large number of short narrative units, allowing rapid intercutting between one place or character and another.

The plot centers on a substantial cache of arms belonging to Communist guerrillas in Malaya, which is discovered by a clerk, Girija Krishnan. Determined to make money out of his find and eventually succeeding, Girija initiates the Byzantine and illegal processes by which the weapons are eventually destined for antigovernment Indonesian rebels. All sorts of people are involved in this frequently humorous "passage of arms," including several members of the Chinese Tan family; a politically naive American couple, the Nilsens; a crooked arms dealer posing as an English gentleman, Lukey; and a totally different type of British military man, Soames, intent on preventing damage to relations between Britain and Indonesia. Although the story ends fairly well for a number of the characters, especially Girija, the realism of the political context lends a bittersweet quality to the novel as a whole.

Postwar Fiction, 1960s

Comedy plays a part in *Passage of Arms,* but in his next novel, *The Light of Day* (1962), Ambler went much further in producing a true comedy thriller, for the first time creating a full-blown comic character, the narrator Arthur Abdel Simpson. *The Light of Day* is one of Ambler's most popular novels, and Jules Dassin's stylish film version, *Topkapi* (1964), is the best movie based on an Ambler novel. Whereas the style of Ambler's previous first-person narratives is neutral, focusing on the experiences undergone by the narrator rather than being a display of personality, that of *The Light of Day* is the style of the man himself, a flamboyant Falstaffian rogue whose life is built on lies, half-truths, and even the occasional truth. Stylistically, this is probably Ambler's most virtuoso performance. Over fifty and overweight, Simpson still retains attractive childlike qualities and inhabits a world of make-believe, dignifying his life by pretending to be what he is not. In reality, he lives by his wits in Athens, mainly as a parasite on tourists: a blend of chauffeur, guide, con man, tout, pimp, and petty thief. Possessing a certain innocence, he is neither vicious nor violent and is far too lacking in ambition to be a threat to society. Such a character might seem a pathetic wreck, but Simpson achieves genuine comic status by the sheer energy and inventiveness with which he always justifies himself, however inconsistently. He is a modern jester or anarchic outsider, capable of challenging conventional values by turning them upside down and quick to expose the humbug and hypocrisy of others.

As often happens in an Ambler novel, the central character inadvertently finds himself in major difficulties. Simpson's unfortunate encounter with a member of a highly professional criminal gang places him at their mercy, and he is blackmailed into cooperating with them without knowing what their plans are. As a result he is soon in serious trouble with the Turkish police, who suspect political terrorism, and is forced to cooperate with them as well, acting as an unofficial spy. There are plenty of twists and turns before Simpson reluctantly participates in the gang's daring plan to steal a priceless piece of "old Sultans' loot" from the Topkapi treasury in Istanbul. The mechanics of the robbery are described in detail, but despite its success there are more surprises in store. Simpson becomes the unlikely instrument of Nemesis, denying the thieves the fruits of their crime, although the gang manages to elude the Turkish police. As befits a comedy, no one is punished, and Simpson earns a modestly happy ending, receiving a reward for his part in recovering the stolen treasure.

After inventing such a memorably picaresque character as Simpson, Ambler thought of writing a trilogy about him, but his move to new publishers in both London and New York caused a change of plan. In 1963 he published his only collection of essays, *The Ability to Kill and Other Pieces,* and subsequently edited a collection of spy stories, *To Catch a Spy* (1964). He also brought out a new novel in 1964, *A Kind of Anger.* Only then did he return to "a further account of the life and adventures" of Simpson with *Dirty Story* (1967), the first Ambler novel to deal with Africa. Like most sequels, this is disappointing. The narrative is more episodic and less coherent than *The Light of Day,* and as Simpson travels from an urban environment to central Africa, the comic invention flags. However, a serious theme gradually comes to the fore—the multinational exploitation of third world resources. Aspiring to be a soldier of fortune, Simpson becomes a mercenary working for a large mining company involved with a rival company in a postcolonial border dispute between two fictional African countries. What is at stake is an extremely valuable mineral deposit, which is fought over. Simpson's Falstaffian account of the battle is in terms of grotesque comedy, but even he is morally shocked at the final outcome when crime perpetrated by multinational capitalism clearly pays. Not since his prewar novels had Ambler satirized the malpractices of big business in this way, and *Dirty Story* does actually point forward to his treatment of the proximity of business to crime in some later novels.

Between the two-part saga of Simpson came *A Kind of Anger,* different again, and one of Ambler's most disturbing novels, which explains its cool critical reception. Although the story line recalls elements in several earlier Ambler novels, both prewar and postwar, he now amalgamates these in unexpected ways to produce something new, especially as this is his first book in which a relationship between a man and a woman is central, determining the course of the action. The Dutch narrator of *A Kind of Anger,* Piet Maas, is Dostoevskian in conception and is perhaps the most conspicuous example of Ambler's debt to one of his favorite authors. At the outset, Maas is the most antiheroic of all Ambler's leading characters: loner, loser, and failed suicide. By the end he has undergone a transformation and remade himself, not for political reasons like Ambler's prewar protagonists, but as an existentialist assertion of individual identity. Like Graham in *Journey into Fear,* another psychological thriller, Maas has to turn himself into a hero—resourceful, inventive, and brave.

A journalist in Paris, Maas is sent on a seemingly impossible quest to find a missing person, Lucia Bernardi, who could be alive or dead. Because she is believed to be the only witness of a sensational murder in Zurich of an Iraqi political refugee, police throughout Europe have been pursuing her for weeks to no avail. The first part of the novel grippingly narrates Maas's successful pursuit of Lucia in the south of France. He then enters a world of extraordinary deviousness and intrigue in which little is what it seems. As Maas slowly uncovers the hidden agenda behind Lucia's disappearance, which concerns sensitive political documents about Iraqi Kurds, he undergoes a major crisis and changes from being her journalistic investigator to being her accomplice in a financial scam. Despite the many dangers surrounding them, Maas and Lucia eventually achieve their objective in the exciting and richly plotted final part of the novel. To arrive at a happy ending, Maas has to liberate himself from bourgeois inhibition by "a kind of anger," thus achieving a condition of anarchic individualism. He adopts a philosophy of individual enterprise that does not feel constrained by adherence to the law or principles of honesty when dealing with governments or big business, since politicians and multinational entrepreneurs employ deception and corruption as a matter of course. If *A Kind of Anger* is Ambler's most underrated novel, it is because its qualified endorsement of the anarchic impulse is not cushioned by comedy as in *Passage of Arms* or the Simpson novels. As a result it is even more morally subversive, but Ambler's ironic subversion is really at the expense of contemporary society dominated by corporate organizations of every kind.

The same might be said of the novel Ambler wrote after *Dirty Story.* Mainly set in Switzerland, *The Intercom Conspiracy* (1969) was his first novel after returning to Europe. The presence of characters from the intelligence world, including CIA and KGB agents, suggests a Cold War thriller, but espionage itself is incidental. In writing about the spy world Ambler is again very original, producing something quite unlike either Ian Fleming's swashbuckling James Bond adventures or John le Carré's hard-edged realism. The conspiracy is a scam of genius perpetrated by two senior NATO officers from small European countries, Colonels Brand and Jost, whose disillusionment prompts them to dream up a brilliant scheme to obtain an enormous amount of money from one intelligence organization or another. They see themselves as giant-killers, enterprising individuals taking on the might of both the United States and the USSR. Their plan is not to peddle secrets, the usual stuff of spy fiction, but to demand money for not releasing NATO or Soviet secrets to the world at large. They do this by secretly taking control of an eccentric international weekly newspaper, *Intercom,* managed in Geneva by Theodore Carter, a Canadian journalist. Carter is that familiar Ambler figure, an innocent in a web of intrigue, who

FRANKLIN REGIONAL
SENIOR HIGH
LIBRARY

in this case is the conspirators' unknowing instrument for carrying out their plan, with all its accompanying dangers. Because Brand and Jost get away with their scam, the final emphasis is not on their immorality but on their success. The anarchic implication is that in contemporary mass society the talents of inventive, imaginative men are likely to be frustrated by the conformist systems in which they have to function. It follows that outlets for enterprise and individuality may well tend toward the criminal. Ambler's dislocation of moral categories is a way of challenging unthinking assumptions about the modern world.

What is particularly fascinating about *The Intercom Conspiracy* is Ambler's oblique narrative method, perhaps the most innovative in all his fiction. The Ambler novel closest in technique is *A Coffin for Dimitrios,* with its documents, letters, and interviews; moreover, the detective novelist in pursuit of Dimitrios, Latimer, reappears in *The Intercom Conspiracy.* This time he has been on the trail of Brand and Jost with Carter's reluctant cooperation but vanishes in suspicious circumstances before he can complete his investigation. Ambler actually presents the novel as an unfinished first draft of Latimer's supposedly factual book about the conspiracy, an assortment of letters, statements, transcriptions of tape recordings, and Latimer's "narrative reconstructions," mainly based on Carter's testimony. Much of the novel is told from the perspectives of Carter and, to a lesser extent, his daughter Valerie, but since both of them are in the dark, the reader only gradually apprehends what is happening by deciphering the evidence and piecing together the mechanics of the conspiracy.

Fiction Since 1970

After completing *The Intercom Conspiracy,* Ambler visited Israel in 1970 to research the Middle East. His "Palestinian" novel, *The Levanter,* appeared in 1972, shortly before the massacre of Israeli athletes by Palestinian extremists at the Munich Olympics. The book could hardly have been more topical and was an instant best-seller. Not only are the setting and subject new for Ambler, but he also handles first-person narration differently from previous novels, even though the principal narrator, Michael Howell, the Levanter himself, is immediately recognizable as another of Ambler's trapped innocents. At the time, *The Levanter* was Ambler's longest postwar novel, and his leisurely treatment allows both the context and a number of minor characters to be presented in considerable detail. Despite his English heritage, Howell is very much a product of the eastern Mediterranean (the Levant), where he runs his family business from Syria with the help of his mistress, Teresa, one of the two minor narrators. Howell's retrospective account of events that have made him notorious and brought accusations that he contributed to terrorism, espionage, and murder is cast in the form of a public defense of himself and his company. Support comes not only from Teresa but also from an American journalist whose testimony frames Howell's own narrative.

Believing that he has been found guilty without having the opportunity to put his case, Howell does not tell his story for its own sake, as Ambler's narrators usually do, but to refute the charges leveled against him. Howell's problems arise because, unknown to him, one of his employees at a plant manufacturing batteries is a maverick Palestinian extremist, Salah Ghaled, who has secretly been using the factory as a base to prepare a terrorist attack on Israel. On discovering this, Howell falls into Ghaled's clutches and is forced to cooperate with him since he is unwilling to run for his life and abandon his business. Howell's position is impossible, but while seeming to collaborate he is desperately trying to find a way of defeating Ghaled, not because he is pro-Israeli and anti-Palestinian but because he rejects Ghaled's brutal authoritarianism. The battle is between two individuals, not political causes, and Howell's narrative gradually reveals how this particular David finally brings his Goliath of an opponent down. In the Middle East, however, Howell's personal victory is interpreted differently. Although he has done both the Palestinians and the Israelis a good turn, the Arab perception is that he is an Israeli agent provocateur, while in the West he is presented as being militantly pro-Arab and a virtual terrorist. Unlike Graham's comparable success in *Journey into Fear,* Howell's is severely qualified since there is no future in the Levant for the Levanter himself.

From the Middle East, Ambler turned to Central America and the Caribbean in *Doctor Frigo* (1974), one of his three or four finest achievements. He had begun but not finished a novel about Latin America in the mid-1960s, although a few years later part of it became a long story, "Blood Bargain." Ambler's choice of setting suggests the influence of Graham Greene, who had written several books about the region, but the Joseph Conrad of *Nostromo* (1904) and *Under Western Eyes* (1910) is a more appropriate comparison. In its treatment of Latin America and political exiles, as well as its leisurely creation of a fictional country, *Doctor Frigo* is Ambler's most Conradian novel.

After *Judgment on Deltchev* politics had become less central to Ambler's fiction, but *Doctor Frigo* marks a decided return to the political novel, and its pessimism contrasts with the upbeat tone of most intervening novels. In those Ambler celebrated the ability of individual enterprise to thwart powerful groups, whereas in *Doctor Frigo* the individual seems powerless in a world of high-level political intrigue. Ambler now foregrounds the sheer Machiavellianism of power politics and international intelligence operations as they bear down on the unnamed Central American country with all the intransigent problems typical of Latin America. The innocent at the center of this novel is Ernesto Castillo, nicknamed "Frigo," the son of an assassinated political leader who has become a national legend and martyr. Practicing medicine in exile in the French Antilles, Castillo is determined to keep clear of politics, but because of his name he is valuable to a conspiracy eager to restore his father's party to power in a bloodless coup, supposedly to improve the lot of the people. Yet the real reason for the coup is economic, having nothing to do with social justice. It is a way of creating a stable environment for a multinational consortium seeking to exploit the country's oil reserves.

Instead of Ambler's usual tactic of dropping an innocent into a dangerous situation, he concentrates on the elaborate process by which Castillo is manipulated, against his better judgment, into political activity, including the eventual coup. There is less action than usual in Ambler, the drama arising from the tension between characters and from Castillo's gradual discovery of the web being spun around him. Ambler achieves this drama brilliantly by employing a diary for first-person narration, so that the reader shares Castillo's struggle to apprehend what is at stake without any of the retrospection that is such a feature of *The Levanter.* The coup succeeds, but as Castillo abandons his country to pursue his medical career, the situation he leaves behind is ugly, with politicians and their factions exploiting the situation to their own advantage. Little has changed.

The ethics of free-market capitalism is one of Ambler's recurrent themes, but nowhere does he explore the gray area between legality and criminality as fully as in *The Siege of the Villa Lipp* (U.K., *Send No More Roses,* 1977). Although he touches on the pursuit of profit by multinational businesses regardless of moral or political consequences, his principal concern is white-collar crime, a major growth area in Western societies. To explore this criminal phenomenon Ambler creates one of his most complex narratives. The thriller-like elements of the murderous siege in the south of France, culminating in a dramatic climax, are intercut with flashbacks covering nearly forty years since 1938. The narrator, a suave and very clever Anglo-Argentinian millionaire who calls himself Paul Firman, is comparable to Howell in *The Levanter* in that his story is an exercise in self-justification, but whereas Howell is wrongly victimized, Firman is sinister and devious. What Firman is defending himself against is the charge made by a Dutch sociologist, Frits Krom, that he exemplifies the new breed of "Able Criminal." A master of casuistry and a cynical manipulator of language, Firman rejects the notion that he is engaged in anything criminal, insisting that he is a bona fide businessman—no more, no less. What makes Firman so disturbing is his insistence that the dividing line between legitimate commercial practices and criminal behavior is extremely flexible under modern consumer capitalism. Running through the novel is a debate between Firman and Krom about the uses and abuses of language in the areas of finance, business, law, and morality.

Firman began his career as an Able Criminal in Italy during World War II under the tutelage of a highly respected corporation lawyer, Carlo Lech. Together they devised a form of protection racket involving wealthy tax evaders whom they could blackmail after gaining power over them. Following Lech's death, Firman finds a new associate, Mat Tuakana, whose brilliance as an economist enables him to develop a financial empire using outwardly respectable forms of embezzlement and blackmail on a massive scale. Mat also has political ambitions. He wants to turn his homeland, a Pacific island approaching independence, into a major tax haven. When Krom's pursuit of Firman puts these plans in jeopardy, Mat attempts to eliminate both Firman and Krom by besieging the villa where they are meeting. For once Mat is unsuccessful, but it is revealed at the end of the novel that he has achieved his political goal by becoming his country's chief minister and de facto ruler. The Able Criminal triumphs over all.

Since *The Siege of the Villa Lipp* Ambler has published only one novel, *The Care of Time* (1981). In this superbly crafted story of intrigue and suspense, Ambler creates a tortuous plot packed with absorbing detail and containing sufficient surprises to keep the reader guessing throughout. However, it is a more conventional thriller than most of his postwar novels, especially the longer, exploratory ones of the 1970s, and in the later stages narrative excitement somewhat displaces serious social and political issues. This is partly because the "villain" at the center of the plot, one of the emirs of the United Arab Emirates known only as The Ruler, seems more like one of James Bond's movie adversaries than the complex and ambiguous figures of Ambler's preceding work. Obsessed with chemical weapons and established in a vast underground shelter in Austria that protects him from such warfare, The Ruler, a mixture of demented scientist and power maniac, is either mad or bad, a psychopathic lunatic or a personification of evil.

The American narrator, Robert Halliday, a journalist and ghostwriter, is an Amblerian innocent whose experience as a television interviewer and whose past involvement with the CIA make him useful to The Ruler in his scheme to set up top-secret negotiations with NATO. Throughout most of the novel Halliday is unaware of what is at stake: The Ruler will allow NATO to build a naval base in his country in exchange for nerve gases. Halliday is initially targeted by The Ruler's senior defense adviser, Karlis Zander, a European of many names who has served various radical Arab causes, often illegally. Yet in approaching Halliday, this fascinating adventurer and international entrepreneur also has his own secret agenda, which Halliday eventually discovers. Despite being elaborately tricked and virtually kidnapped by Zander, Halliday comes to sympathize with him as their involvement deepens, recognizing Zander to be a courageous individualist and great survivor. In the second half of the novel as The Ruler's bizarre intentions are gradually revealed, the power of television—its dangers and its benefits—becomes an important theme. In the end it is television that reveals The Ruler for the paranoid diabolist he is, but it is a close call since his hired assassins almost succeed in disposing of Halliday and Zander in the concluding shoot-out.

Since *The Care of Time*, Ambler has published only one work of fiction, "The One Who Did for Blagden Cole." This long story was written for *The Man Who* (1992), a Detection Club *Festschrift* edited by H. R. F. Keating to honor Julian Symons, the leading British historian of mystery writing and an important crime novelist in his own right. Like Symons, who also began to attract attention in the 1930s, Ambler has always upheld the role of the writer as entertainer and storyteller while maintaining high literary standards and confronting important themes in the tradition established by major Victorian novelists like Charles Dickens and Wilkie Collins. During the 1930s Ambler effected a virtual revolution of the thriller, making it a vehicle for thoughtful political fiction for the first time, and in this respect his influence on postwar writers throughout the long period of the Cold War has been immense. The influence of Ambler's postwar fiction has been less direct and conspicuous, but as a popular novelist devoted to excellence he has provided a model for serious writers using the mystery genre without being confined by its formulas. The sheer variety of subject and approach in his later work has also been invaluable since it has demonstrated that genre fiction is not nearly as restricted in scope as it is often said to be. Indeed one of Ambler's lasting achievements has been to erode the fiction categories employed by critics in the twentieth century. In successfully marrying the popular and the literary, Ambler is a true descendant of Dickens and Collins.

Selected Bibliography

WORKS OF ERIC AMBLER

NOVELS

The Dark Frontier. London: Hodder and Stoughton, 1936.

Uncommon Danger. London: Hodder and Stoughton, 1937. Published as *Background to Danger.* New York: Knopf, 1937.

Epitaph for a Spy. London: Hodder and Stoughton, 1938.

Cause for Alarm. London: Hodder and Stoughton, 1938.

The Mask of Dimitrios. London: Hodder and Stoughton, 1939. Published as *A Coffin for Dimitrios.* New York: Knopf, 1939.

Journey into Fear. London: Hodder and Stoughton, 1940; New York: Knopf, 1940.

Judgment on Deltchev. London: Hodder and Stoughton, 1951; New York: Knopf, 1951.

The Schirmer Inheritance. London: Heinemann, 1953; New York: Knopf, 1953.

The Night-Comers. London: Heinemann, 1956. Published as *State of Siege.* New York: Knopf, 1956.

Passage of Arms. London: Heinemann, 1959.

The Light of Day. London: Heinemann, 1962.

A Kind of Anger. London: Bodley Head, 1964; New York: Atheneum, 1964.

Dirty Story: A Further Account of the Life and Adventures of Arthur Abdel Simpson. London: Bodley Head, 1967; New York: Atheneum, 1967.

The Intercom Conspiracy. New York: Atheneum, 1969; London: Weidenfeld and Nicolson, 1970.

The Levanter. London: Weidenfeld and Nicolson, 1972; New York: Atheneum, 1972.

Doctor Frigo. London: Weidenfeld and Nicolson, 1974; New York: Atheneum, 1974.

Send No More Roses. London: Weidenfeld and Nicolson, 1977. Published as *The Siege of the Villa Lipp.* New York: Random House, 1977.

The Care of Time. London: Weidenfeld and Nicolson, 1981; New York: Farrar, Straus, & Giroux, 1981.

SHORT STORIES

Waiting for Orders. New York: Mysterious Press/Warner Books, 1991. Published in an expanded version as *The Story so Far: Memories and Other Fictions.* London: Weidenfeld and Nicolson, 1993.

AUTOBIOGRAPHY

Here Lies: An Autobiography. London: Weidenfeld and Nicolson, 1985.

OTHER BOOKS

The Ability to Kill and Other Pieces. London: Bodley Head, 1963. Published as *The Ability to Kill: True Tales of Bloody Murder.* New York: Mysterious Press, 1987.

Intrigue: Four Great Spy Novels of Eric Ambler. Introduction by Alfred Hitchcock. New York: Knopf, 1943. Includes *Background to Danger, Cause for Alarm, A Coffin for Dimitrios,* and *Journey Into Fear.*

Intrigue: Three Famous Novels in One Volume. London: Hodder and Stoughton, 1965. Includes *The Mask of Dimitrios* (British title for UK publication), *Journey Into Fear,* and *Judgment on Deltchev.*

To Catch a Spy: An Anthology of Favourite Spy Stories (editor). London: Bodley Head, 1964; New York: Atheneum, 1965.

"ELIOT REED" NOVELS (WITH CHARLES RODDA)

Skytip. Garden City, NY: Doubleday, 1950; London: Hodder and Stoughton, 1951.

Tender to Danger. Garden City, NY: Doubleday, 1951. Published as *Tender to Moonlight.* London: Hodder and Stoughton, 1952.

The Maras Affair. London: Collins, 1953; Garden City, NY: Doubleday, 1953.

Charter to Danger. London: Collins, 1954.

Passport to Panic. London: Collins, 1958.

ARCHIVES

The Eric Ambler Archive, Special Collections Department, Mugar Memorial Library, Boston University.

BIOGRAPHICAL AND CRITICAL STUDIES

Ambrosetti, Ronald. *Eric Ambler.* New York: Twayne Publishers, 1994.

———. "The World of Eric Ambler: From Detective to Spy." In *Dimensions of Detective Fiction.* Edited by Larry N. Landrum, Pat Browne, and Ray B. Browne. Bowling Green, Ohio: Popular Press, 1976.

Atkins, John. *The British Spy Novel.* New York: Riverrun, 1984.

Cawelti, John G., and Bruce A. Rosenberg. *The Spy Story.* Chicago: Chicago University Press, 1987.

"Confidential Agents." *Times Literary Supplement,* 20 July 1956: 434.

Davis, Paxton. "The World We Live In: The Novels of Eric Ambler." *Hollins Critic,* 8, no.1: 1–11 (February 1971).

Eames, Hugh. *Sleuths, Inc.* Philadelphia and New York: Lippincott, 1978.

Eue, Ralph, and Karl Heinz Wegmann. "Where Are We on That List of Questions?" *Filmkritik* 26, no. 12: 567–582 (December 1982).

Haffmans, Gerd, ed. *Über Eric Ambler.* Zurich: Diogenes, 1979.

Hertenstein, Walter. "Ambling with Ambler." *Tages-Anzeiger-Magazin,* 13 December 1975: 16–21.

Hopkins, Joel. "An Interview with Eric Ambler." *Journal of Popular Culture* 9, no. 2: 285–293 (1975).

James, Clive. "Eric Ambler." *New Review* 1, no. 6: 63–69 (September 1974).

Lambert, Gavin. *The Dangerous Edge.* London: Barrie and Jenkins, 1975.

Lewis, Peter. *Eric Ambler.* New York: Continuum, 1990.

———. "Eric Ambler and 'Eliot Reed'." *Durham University Journal* 87, no. 2: 379–383 (1995).

———. "Eric Ambler." In *AZ Murder Goes . . . Classic.* Edited by Barbara Peters and Susan Malling. Scottsdale, Arizona: The Poisoned Pen Press, 1997.

McCormick, Donald. *Who's Who in Spy Fiction.* New York: Taplinger, 1977.

Panek, LeRoy L. *The Special Branch: The British Spy Novel, 1890–1980.* Bowling Green, Ohio: Popular Press, 1981.

Symons, Julian. *Bloody Murder.* New York and London: Viking, 1985.

Robert Barnard

(b. 1936)

JON L. BREEN

Robert Barnard is a unique figure in the detective fiction of the last quarter of the twentieth century. No Golden Age nostalgic with a feeling for style could fail to appreciate Barnard, who is as unlikely to write a dull sentence or introduce a flat character as to withhold a vital clue or telegraph a surprise ending.

If crime fiction must be bifurcated into tough and cozy camps, writers like Barnard, whose settings run more to English villages, universities, theaters, and upper-middle-class suburbs than to street corners, brothels, nightclubs, and station houses, are generally consigned to the cozy school. But the biting wit and wicked satire of Barnard's novels, together with the hard and shocking endings that turn up in even the most pervasively comic of them, give his work a sense of bitter reality that shows up the inadequacy of such labels.

Biography

Barnard was born in Burnham-on-Crouch, Essex, on 23 November 1936, the son of a farm laborer turned writer. Barnard told interviewer Rosemary Herbert that his father, Leslie Barnard, "wrote cheap and awful women's romance stories, of the lowest kind. I mean sub–Barbara Cartland" (p. 253). Describing how boring, unremarkable, and humorless he was as a child, Barnard averred "that childhood days are the most irrelevant days of your life. Contrary to what Wordsworth said, the child is *not* the father to the man" (p. 254).

Following graduation from Oxford (Balliol College) in 1959, Barnard worked in London for the Fabian Society, which he describes in his article "Growing Up to Crime" as a "conservatively socialistic society dedicated to right thinking and good doing" (p. 9). After leaving his job for a promised post at the University of Mandalay, an appointment that fell through, he suffered three months of unemployment before taking a post as English lecturer at the University of New England in New South Wales, Australia, where he taught from 1961 to 1966. When his Australian wife, Mary Louise Tabor, whom he married in 1963, expressed a desire to move to Europe, Barnard took a post as senior lecturer at the University of Bergen, Norway.

His first effort at fiction writing, the beginning chapters of a satirical novel in which a Conservative politician patterned on Margaret Thatcher (well before her tenure as prime minister) visits Australia, lost impetus for lack of a plot. Then Barnard turned to the more standardized structure of detective fiction. His first completed novel, concerning Nazi looting of art, was extensively rejected. However, Collins Crime Club editor Elizabeth Walter urged him to send her something else, and Collins published his first novel, *Death of an Old Goat,* in 1974.

Although with few exceptions Barnard's novels are set in England, he spent his whole academic career in other countries. In 1976, after earning his doctorate during his ten-year stint in Bergen, he moved farther north to the University of Tromsø, where he remained as professor of English literature until 1983, when he decided to write full-time. He then returned to his native England and settled in Leeds. Although Barnard loved Norway and did not rule out returning there to live, he felt the need to update his knowledge of the home country he used as a background for his novels.

Author as Critic

An outstanding practitioner of detective fiction, Barnard is also among its most perceptive critics. His statements about other writers illuminate his own approach to the form. In *A Talent to Deceive: An Appreciation of Agatha Christie* (1980), Barnard counters the assumption that the hard-boiled school is more realistic than the classical:

> Books that concentrate their attention exclusively on gangsters, whores, and the corrupt superrich are every bit as partial in their scope and remote from the average reader's experience as books that concentrate on the genteel middle classes in the rural parts of Great Britain. . . . [I]f the average British policeman may blink at the goings-on of the investigators and the specimens of "detection" offered in the average Christie story, one wonders whether a real-life private eye in the Los Angeles or San Francisco area will really feel a shock of recognition when he reads of the doings of a Philip Marlow [*sic*] or a Lew Archer. (pp. 111–112)

Barnard concludes his Christie study with a direct answer to Raymond Chandler's criticism of classical detective fiction in "The Simple Art of Murder":

> [S]he brought murder into the home, where it belonged, seeing the murderous glint in the eye of the self-effacing bank clerk, the homicidal madness in the flutterings of the genteel lady companion. Chandler saw evil in the social organisms of which we are part; Christie saw it in our wives, our friends, the quiet circle of which we are a part. And perhaps thereby she made us sense it in ourselves. (p. 126)

Jacques Barzun has argued, in his introduction to the anthology *The Delights of Detection* (1961) and elsewhere, that detective stories are tales, a separate literary category with different intentions and expectations from those of the true novel. Barnard embraces this distinction, believing that to apply the standards of mainstream novels to detective fiction misses the point. Addressing Julian Symons' claim, most fully expressed in his history *Bloody Murder* (1972), that the detective story is evolving into the crime novel, Barnard told Herbert:

> It's funny that with the loss of religion we have embraced still further so many Puritan attitudes. The distrust of entertainment is quite pathetic. If you go from the detective story to the crime novel, you've got to be damned careful not to throw out the baby with the bath water. And the baby is entertainment. (p. 266)

In the essay "The English Detective Story," Barnard denies the assertion of some critics that the classical detective novel is dead. He claims that "probably half of the crime books published today still stick broadly to the . . . formula," but adds:

> What writers have learned is that the formula is adaptable, that it will take more realism, more humour, a wider class range, more psychological depth than the Golden Age writers used. But the basic formula is still very much alive and useful. The whodunit is not dead; it is hardly even dozing. (p. 36)

Early Novels

Barnard's academic post in New South Wales inspired his first novel, *Death of an Old Goat.* He introduces a likable and entertaining figure in Belville-Smith, an elderly visiting professor from Oxford, only to make him a murder victim less than a third of the way into the book. Before his throat is cut, Belville-Smith is received and treated quite poorly at Drummondale, a second-string Australian university. Barnard's satiric barbs have always been at their sharpest when aimed at his fellow academics; this venomous portrait of Drummondale's English department is no exception.

In "Growing Up to Crime" Barnard writes that his books are mostly improvisations. He begins them with no idea of who will kill whom, because too much planning in advance "constricts and irritates [him], and much of the zest goes out of the writing" (p. 13). Finding that the chosen victim in his first novel was his favorite character, he wanted to find ways to save him but could not. Meanwhile, the focal character for the remainder of the book is among the least likable figures.

Barnard freely acknowledges that the police detective, Inspector Royle, was inspired by Joyce Porter's obnoxious, bullying Chief Inspector Dover, who appeared in ten novels between 1964 and 1980. Called to the scene from a married woman's bed at the worst possible moment, Royle reluctantly lurches into action.

> The criminals of Drummondale—about twenty percent of the population—had a healthy respect for his fists and his boot, and none at all for his brain. But though he did not do a great deal to keep down crime, many people—and not just married women—were glad to have him around. For example he was well-known to the local publicans not only for his huge capacity with the beer glass, but also for his friendly readiness to ring them up before an after-hours raid. . . . He had a wife and two little girls in a weather-board house on the outskirts of the town, but mostly he tried to forget about them, and they in their turn tried not to think too much about him either. (p. 63)

Royle is aided by a would-be amateur sleuth, British lecturer Bill Bascomb, whom Barnard bases on himself. This combination of the vulgar Royle with the intellectual Bascomb echoes the team of Inspector Andrew Dalziel and Sergeant Peter Pascoe, a creation of Barnard's contemporary Reginald Hill.

For all the improvisation, the clues are fairly laid. A dramatic shock ending underscores the potential violence of a figure the reader has been laughing at. The comic tone of the novel makes this ending all the more powerful. This juxtaposition of humor and shock became a trademark of Barnard's early novels. Indeed, Barnard suggests in "Growing Up to Crime" that he shocked his prestigious English publisher, Collins Crime Club, into rejecting his next two novels:

> [T]here was my second book, set in the year 2000-odd, with the present queen, a distinctly Lady Bracknellish figure, finding her heirs and successors being knocked off one by one—rejected, I always thought, because Sir William Collins was hoping for a Life Peerage. Then there was *The Resurrection Men,* a blasphemous novella giving an account of what really went on between the first Good Friday and the first Ascension Day—rejected, I feel, because Collins are the official English publishers of the Bible, and they didn't want to put an alternative (and much funnier) version into circulation. (p. 14)

Barnard has been more highly valued in the United States than in his own country. (British writer Adrian Muller, assigned to do an interview with Barnard in 1996, admitted he had never even heard of his subject, nor had any British mystery readers of his acquaintance.) The enthusiasm of the lucrative American market eventually permitted Barnard to give up teaching and write full-time. Thus, it is surprising that the U.S. publication of Barnard's second novel, *A Little Local Murder*

(1976), was delayed for seven years. Perhaps the novel's humor, reminiscent of the character-based farces of playwright Alan Ayckbourn, struck American editors as too distinctively British. The story involves the efforts of various citizens to be included in a radio program prepared in the English village of Twytching for broadcast in its sister city of Twytching, Wisconsin.

Theatrical Settings

Barnard's third novel, *Death on the High C's* (1977), concerns Manchester's Northern Opera Company, where the jealousies and bickerings of singers set the stage for murder. Though Barnard insists the negative view of Australia implied in *Death of an Old Goat* did not reflect his real feelings, the widely hated first victim in this book is Gaylene Ffrench, a pretentious, promiscuous, and generally unlikable singer from Down Under. Barnard was developing a specialty in detestable victims. He told Muller, "I really love dreadful people" (p. 42).

The novel's second murder illustrates Barnard's pointed irony, human sympathy, and leftish political leanings:

> Thus died Sergeant Harrison of the Prince of Wales Theatre, formerly of the Royal Artillery, whose ancestors had fought for their Sovereign as soldiers of the line at Agincourt, Malplaquet and Waterloo, and for their class at Peterloo and factory gates throughout the grimier parts of the North of England. Their graves were unmarked lumps of foreign soil, or off-white tombstones of inferior stone and knobbly design. Sergeant Harrison's own immediate destination was the police morgue, where he lay side by side with Gaylene Ffrench, both fine figures, and a tribute to the care and feeding of their respective countries. (p. 83)

Apart from the droll narrative touches and well-realized opera house setting, *Death on the High C's* is not prime Barnard. He returned to a theatrical setting in a better novel, *Death and the Chaste Apprentice* (1989), set at the Ketterick Arts Festival. It is like one of Simon Brett's Charles Paris series in the fun it has quoting from bad reviews. The puzzle, the wit, and a surprising murderer make it a strong novel.

Religious Settings

The description of the unpublished *Resurrection Men* suggests an irreverent view of religion. Barnard told Herbert, "I'm one of those fairly rare people in my generation who hasn't even been christened. I've grown up in a totally unreligious environment" (p. 268). It is not so much religion itself as the people associated with religious practice that become the object of Barnard's satire in *Blood Brotherhood* (1977), in which a monk is murdered at a conference on the church's role in the modern world, held in an Anglican monastery in Yorkshire. Barnard depicts a variety of amusing clerical types and, as in a number of his early books, keeps the reader in suspense not only about the murderer's identity but about the detective's as well.

By comparison, Barnard's later return to a religious theme in *The Bad Samaritan* (1995), in which the wife of a Leeds vicar suddenly loses her faith, shows a less cynical and more sympathetic view of the human condition. Asked by Muller about his own religious views, Barnard replied,

> You have to imagine these things. People say that I am good at depicting children even though I haven't got any myself, but I've been a child, and I can imagine what it is like to be a child. It is similarly so with faith. I would very much like to have faith. I'm sure it is a very comforting thing and that it provides some sort of bedrock. So I can imagine what it must be like to lose your faith. (p. 43)

Literary Settings

In his fifth novel Barnard demonstrates the ability to satirize the formal detective story and exemplify it at the same time. The victim in *Unruly Son* (1978; U.S. title, *Death of a Mystery Writer,* 1979) is Sir Oliver Fairleigh-Stubbs, who rests solidly in the despicable tradition of Barnard corpses. He is based not on a real-life mystery writer but on English writer Evelyn Waugh. Some of the chapter titles ("Suddenly at His Residence," "Strong Poison," "Death Comes as the End") borrow or adapt those of famous detective novels. When confronted by Inspector Meredith, the fairly clued killer (maybe not least suspected by the experienced reader) provides a finish straight from the Golden Age of detection.

A subsequent literary satire, *Posthumous Papers* (1979; U.S. title, *Death of a Literary Widow,* 1980), includes one of British fiction's most venomously lampooned comic Americans, English professor Dwight Kronweiser, whose great work is to revive the reputation of working-class novelist Walter Machin. The parody of academic literary analysis is priceless. Dissecting Machin for the Payne's Great Authors series, Kronweiser writes,

> The major problem Machin confronts in *The Factory Whistle* is that of irrelation, which in its turn is his means of defining the absolute. The complementary, interpenetrating phenomena in proletarian life that the implied narrator confronts, and by confronting epiphanizes, are a means primarily of defining his own ambivalent relation both to the zeitgeist and to his own eternal validity. (pp. 46–47)

Other writers are featured in later novels, among them romancers in the latter-day tradition of the author's father in *Death in Purple Prose* (1987; U.S. title, *The Cherry Blossom Corpse*) and a well-meaning but pernicious historical biographer in *A Fatal Attachment* (1992).

Series Characters

Mystery fiction so thrives on series characters that even writers who prefer a fresh cast for each book are urged to create a continuing sleuth for the sake of brand loyalty. In the early part of his career, Barnard avoided series, though some of his police characters, such as Inspector Fagermo of the Norway-based *Death in a Cold Climate* (1980), would have been welcome in return engagements. Barnard's depiction of the bleakness of a winter above the arctic circle is chillingly effective. However, neither Fagermo nor the Tromsø setting of the novel recurred. Although many readers found it outstanding, Barnard was unhappy with it and has disparaged it in print.

The first Barnard character to appear in a series makes his debut in Barnard's favorite of his own works. In *Sheer Torture* (1981; U.S. title, *Death by Sheer Torture,* 1982), Scotland Yard's Perry Trethowan, who comes from a family of zany eccentrics (inspired by two British literary families famous for their quirkiness, the Sitwells and the Mitfords), must investigate the murder of his own father, a torture machine collector who dies in a strappado while wearing spangled tights. Perry, who is the first Barnard character to tell his story in the first person, is more embarrassed than grieved by the event. This first Trethowan novel has boundless charm and style.

If Barnard was impatient with series characters, the next two novels may illustrate why. *Death and the Princess* (1982), in which Trethowan protects an obscure British royal, has some nice satiric touches but a weaker than average plot. *The Missing Brontë* (1983; U.S. title, *The Case of the Missing Brontë*), allows Barnard to exercise a literary enthusiasm—he served as vice chairman of the Brontë Society from 1992 to 1995 and has fought the commercialization of Haworth. It is also a murderless novel, designed to foil his American publisher's insistence on putting the word "death" in every title. Still, overladen with local color, it is one of his weakest books.

Barnard returned to Trethowan in *Bodies* (1986), which satirizes the world of modeling and bodybuilding, and *Death in Purple Prose,* which has immense fun with a convention in Bergen of WARN (World Association of Romantic Novelists). Neither book fully satisfied its author, who believes the level of *Sheer Torture* was never again achieved because he felt obliged to stick to the first-person narration. Also, because a police detective normally enters the case after the crime has been committed, the victim in *Bodies* is already dead in the first chapter; this eliminates any pre-crime opportunity to develop the fascinating setting more completely.

Charlie Peace, a young black man who is a gym employee in *Bodies* and appears briefly as a newly hired cop at the end of *Death in Purple Prose,* becomes a series character on his own in *Death and the Chaste Apprentice.* Peace later appears in *A Fatal Attachment, A Hovering of Vultures* (1993), and *The Bad Samaritan.* In the last three, he is joined by Superintendent Mike Oddie, a policeman in the Yorkshire city of Sleate (that is, Leeds), who is first introduced in *A City of Strangers* (1990).

Barnard told Muller, "The reason I am not wedded to serial characters is that they dictate the tone of the books they appear in, and the thing I like about my own novels is that each one tends to be a bit different" (p. 42).

The Full-Time Writer

The tiring of a series character is not the only reason for the weakness of *The Missing Brontë.* Barnard had quit his teaching post and returned to Britain to be a full-time writer. Eventually, the reconnection with modern Britain benefited his work, but the short-term effect of going full-time was less desirable. Feeling he needed to step up production to two books a year, Barnard rushed the third Trethowan novel and the non-series *Little Victims* (1983; U.S. title, *School for Murder,* 1984). This resulted, by his own account, in "a dreadful book, absolutely my worst" (Muller, p. 42); *Little Victims* is much better than his scorn suggests. Set in a lesser English boarding school, it has among its cast of sharply drawn characters Hilary Frome, a delightfully despicable schoolboy villain. Hilary has the pretentious headmaster fooled to the extent of wanting to appoint him head boy, but the rest of the faculty, mediocre misfits though they are, are undeceived. The final line is a gem of irony.

Deciding that he was not required to produce two books a year (though in later years he often would), Barnard followed his two acknowledged duds with a personal favorite, *A Corpse in a Gilded Cage* (1984), about the effect on a working-class couple of a sudden and unexpected inheritance of a title and a stately home.

Politics

Though classical detective fiction, with its emphasis on restoring order, is generally considered the most conservative of mystery genres, a number of left-wingers have practiced it, usually leaving overt politics out of their novels. Barnard is unabashedly left of center in his sympathies—in his interviews, Margaret Thatcher is a constant target of derision. However, his one overt electoral satire, *Political Suicide* (1986), visits his authorial plague on both ends of the spectrum and everything in between. When Tory M.P. James Partridge drowns in the Thames—by suicide or murder—the resulting by-election produces jockeying among the three major parties for the vacant seat representing Bootham, South Yorkshire. Barnard noted with pride to Muller that he made "the Labour candidate quite as repellent, be it in a different way, as the Conservative candidate" (p. 43). Apart from these two and the Social Democrat candidate, several other parties put forth candidates:

> [T]he Communist Party decided that really they *ought* to show the red flag in depressed, industrial Bootham, though they knew they would have done infinitely better in, say, Hampstead; the National Front (which made token gestures toward respectability, rather

> as Charles II might appear on state occasions with his queen) thought the constituency was ripe for what they called radical thinking; and the Ecology Party, after much hesitation (for what, after all, had ecology ever done for Bootham?) decided that their ambitions to be a national party as successful as the German Greens obliged them to field a candidate.
>
> And then there were . . . the Home Rule for England candidate; the Women for the Bomb candidate; Yelping Lord Crotch, the Top of the Pops candidate; the Transcendental Meditation candidate (Ms. Humphrey Ward); the John Lennon Lives candidate; the Bring Back Hanging candidate; the Britain Out of the Common Market candidate; the Richard III Was Innocent candidate; and Zachariah Zzugg, the I'm Coming Last candidate. . . .
>
> This list . . . had by tradition to be read out every time the nation's television or radio broadcast coverage of the by-election. Shortly afterwards the government was to increase the amount demanded as deposit by electoral hopefuls, in order to discourage lunatic fringe candidates. The government had a very shaky grasp of psychology. (pp. 105–106)

As a mystery-cum-political-satire, the novel ranks with Edmund Crispin's classic *Buried for Pleasure* (1948), in which Crispin's Oxford professor and amateur sleuth Gervase Fen himself stands for Parliament.

A Change of Direction

Though he never completely deserted either the Agatha Christie–style puzzle or biting social satire, Barnard's career took a new turn with *Out of the Blackout* (1985). Not completely lacking in humor, the novel is more obviously serious at its core. The action ranges from 1941, when five-year-old London evacuee Simon Thorn turns up in the town of Yeasdon with no indication of where he came from, to 1982, when he puts the last piece to the puzzle of his own identity. A subsequent twentieth-century historical novel, *The Skeleton in the Grass* (1987), concerns a family of pacifist aristocrats whose politics cause them problems in 1936 England, where homegrown fascists are making inroads.

Both of these novels present contrasting happy and unhappy families, with the unhappy family at the center of *Out of the Blackout* and the happy one central to *The Skeleton in the Grass.* The subject of family life continues to occupy books like *A City of Strangers, A Fatal Attachment,* and *The Masters of the House* (1994), in which four children desperately try to go it alone after the death of their mother.

An Agatha Christie acolyte might be expected to better prepare the reader for the surprise ending of *A Fatal Attachment.* Still, the central situation is fascinating and original: a historical biographer specializes in wooing siblings away from their parents and has a possibly unhealthy influence on their lives. The multiple meanings of the title are fully appreciated only near the end of the book.

Discussing the frequent treatment of children in his later novels, Barnard told Herbert,

> I think really the modern age has invented its own way of making childhood horrifying. That includes child abuse. We do seem on the one hand to have stopped the hideous cruelties of the Victorian education system. . . . On the other hand we've filled childhood with new horrors and terrors. (pp. 260–261)

Pressed on whether his own experience led to this view of childhood, Barnard replied that it did, but would be drawn out no further.

Short Stories

Barnard is equally effective at shorter lengths, though he finds the short-story form more difficult than the novel. It is possible to write a full-scale whodunit in 4,000 to 5,000 words, but few attempt it. In appreciatively introducing a collection of Joyce Porter's Dover short stories, which he calls "mystery novels in miniature," Barnard notes,

> The problem, for most writers, is that the short-story length prevents them from using

> enough characters to provide suspense or from giving the characters the depth and vividness that alone could make the story interesting. (p. 5)

Thus, Barnard chose to specialize in the kind of domestic crime story exemplified by Alfred Hitchcock's television series, with a smaller cast of characters, usually a surprise twist, but rarely a whodunit. The stories have in common with the novels their ironic flavor. In *Death of a Salesperson and Other Untimely Exits* (1989), the satiric touch is especially deft in "Daylight Robbery" (about the art market and the stately home business) and "The Oxford Way of Death." New variations on overused suspense situations are achieved in "A Process of Rehabilitation" and "Happy Release." Sometimes the reader is subtly made aware of a coming disaster of which the characters in the story have no clue, as in "A Business Partnership" and "Little Terror."

The Bastable Historicals

The Victorian mystery *To Die like a Gentleman* (1993), written by Barnard a chapter or two at a time over a period of more than a dozen years, and finally published under the pseudonym Bernard Bastable, represents another departure. Briefer than most of his present-day works, and more pointed and economical than most historical novels, it is told primarily in letters and diaries. The period style is remarkably well achieved. With the customary wit and satirist's eye, the deftly plotted novel is generally lighter than his more recent novels with present-day settings. The victim, a household tyrant, is in the tradition of despicable Barnard corpses.

The two subsequent Bastable novels, more essentially comic, introduce Barnard's second first-person series character: Wolfgang Gottlieb (German form of Amadeus) Mozart. In the alternate universe of *Dead, Mr. Mozart* (1995) and *Too Many Notes, Mr. Mozart* (1995), the great composer does not die in 1791 but survives into old age in London of the 1820s and 1830s and serves as piano tutor to young Princess Victoria.

Barnard's Achievement

It is appropriate that the career of a writer who reveres Agatha Christie should be summed up in this way: while appearing to do one thing, Barnard was really doing something else.

Possibly no contemporary has been compared to Christie and the other Golden Age writers as consistently as Barnard. His customary progression from buildup to crime to investigation by police detectives to solution is superficially similar in structure to the Roderick Alleyn novels of Ngaio Marsh; but Barnard reveals in "Growing Up to Crime" that Marsh is not one of his favorite writers: "Marsh seemed to me a great and lively talent, but marred by her dreary and repetitive determination to establish precisely where everyone was at the stroke of 2:42" (pp. 8–9).

Much as he appreciates the structure of a formal detective novel, Barnard is not much concerned with the details of carpentry. He values spontaneity too much to be tied down by the timetables and other minutiae of a Freeman Wills Crofts. Although critics have praised his plotting, and he readily provides the reader with clues to his solutions, he is by his own admission not an outstanding builder of puzzles.

Barnard insists that looking for novelistic virtues from writers of detective fiction is as wrongheaded as looking for great acting skills from opera singers. He believes that detective novels for which critics make claims of mainstream literary value must be viewed with suspicion. He never gives up the effects of mystery and surprise to mimic the mainstream novel. He has resisted the malign tendency to mistake volume for substance and write mysteries longer and longer.

Determinedly unpretentious, Barnard writes in "Growing Up to Crime," "If I were advising a beginning writer . . . I would keep the advice severely practical: carry a notebook with you everywhere; learn about semicolons; leave a few spelling mistakes in your manuscript to make your editor feel good" (p. 22). But in the same essay, he scorns those who, in practicing an artificial form, refuse to approach it seriously. "Play it for real, write it for real. Do not apologize for the conventions: cherish them and renew them by new twists" (p. 16). He stresses how much more can be done within the conventions in today's detective novel than could be in years past; and for all his self-effacement and lack of pretension, his writings do, in their own way, expand the limits of detective fiction.

Robert Barnard's greatest strengths are the same ones that signal distinction in any kind of fiction: style, the ability to put words together on the page in ways that surprise, delight, enlighten, and sometimes assault the reader; characterization, the ability to delineate people who are more than just differentiated, more than just caricatures, who take on the dimensions of reality, however fanciful the story they inhabit might be; and social observations, whether humorous or serious, that augment the reader's understanding of a time, a place, a culture.

Barnard writes to entertain, not to challenge or impress his academic colleagues. So did Charles Dickens, the subject of his doctoral dissertation. No, Barnard is not Dickens, but he is a writer who can be read as a chronicler of the quirks and concerns of his times. The mystery, though, is not just a bonus; it is a framework, a superstructure, that allows all the felicitous phrases and social observations to be displayed to advantage.

Robert Barnard is as capable of bursting the limits of the detective novel, of (in that hateful phrase) "transcending the genre," as any living writer; but he realizes that the last way to achieve this kind of literary breakout is consciously to curry serious critical favor. All his protestations are designed to make sure he does not try to write literature and thereby spoil the recipe that permits him, within the bounds and conventions of a popular genre, to achieve it.

Selected Bibliography

WORKS OF ROBERT BARNARD

NOVELS

Death of an Old Goat. London: Collins, 1974.

A Little Local Murder. London: Collins, 1976.

Death on the High C's. London: Collins, 1977.

Blood Brotherhood. London: Collins, 1977.

Unruly Son. London: Collins, 1978. Published as *Death of a Mystery Writer.* New York: Scribners, 1979.

Posthumous Papers. London: Collins, 1979. Published as *Death of a Literary Widow.* New York: Scribners, 1980.

Death in a Cold Climate. London: Collins, 1980.

Mother's Boys. London: Collins, 1981. Published as *Death of a Perfect Mother.* New York: Scribners, 1981.

Sheer Torture. London: Collins, 1981. Published as *Death by Sheer Torture.* New York: Scribners, 1982.

Death and the Princess. London: Collins, 1982; New York: Scribners, 1982.

The Missing Brontë. London: Collins, 1983. Published as *The Case of the Missing Brontë.* New York: Scribners, 1983.

Little Victims. London: Collins, 1983. Published as *School for Murder.* New York: Scribners, 1984.

A Corpse in a Gilded Cage. London: Collins, 1984; New York: Scribners, 1984.

Out of the Blackout. London: Collins, 1985; New York: Scribners, 1985.

The Disposal of the Living. London: Collins, 1985. Published as *Fête Fatale.* New York: Scribners, 1985.

Political Suicide. London: Collins, 1986; New York: Scribners, 1986.

Bodies. London: Collins, 1986; New York: Scribners, 1986.

Death in Purple Prose. London: Collins, 1987. Published as *The Cherry Blossom Corpse.* New York: Scribners, 1987.

The Skeleton in the Grass. London: Collins, 1987.

At Death's Door. London: Collins, 1988; New York: Scribners, 1988.

Death and the Chaste Apprentice. London: Collins, 1989; New York: Scribners, 1989.

A City of Strangers. London: Bantam, 1990; New York: Scribners, 1990.

A Scandal in Belgravia. London: Bantam, 1991; New York: Scribners, 1991.

A Fatal Attachment. London: Bantam, 1992; New York: Scribners, 1992.

A Hovering of Vultures. London: Bantam, 1993; New York: Scribners, 1993.

To Die like a Gentleman. By "Bernard Bastable." London: Macmillan, 1993; New York: St. Martin's Press, 1993.

The Masters of the House. London: Harper Collins, 1994; New York: Scribners, 1994.

The Bad Samaritan. London: Harper Collins, 1995; New York: Scribners, 1995.

Dead, Mr. Mozart. By "Bernard Bastable." London: Little, Brown, 1995; New York: St. Martin's, 1995.

Too Many Notes, Mr. Mozart. By "Bernard Bastable." London: Little, Brown, 1995.

SHORT STORY COLLECTIONS

Death of a Salesperson and Other Untimely Exits. London: Collins, 1989.

The Habit of Widowhood. London: Harper Collins, 1996; New York: Scribners, 1996.

CRITICAL WORKS

Imagery and Theme in the Novels of Dickens. Oslo: Universitetsforlaget, 1974; New York: Humanities Press, 1974.

A Talent to Deceive: An Appreciation of Agatha Christie. London: Collins, 1980; New York: Dodd Mead, 1980.

A Short History of English Literature. Oslo: Universitetsforlaget, 1984. Revised as *A History of English Literature.* Oxford: Blackwell, 1994.

"The English Detective Story." In *Whodunit? A Guide to Crime, Suspense, and Spy Fiction.* Edited by H. R. F. Keating. London: Windward, 1982. Pp. 30–36.

Foreword to *Dover: The Collected Short Stories* by Joyce Porter. Woodstock, Vt.: Countryman, 1995. Pp. 1–6.

AUTOBIOGRAPHY

"A Murderer Confesses." In *Murder Ink,* rev. ed. Edited by Dilys Winn. New York: Workman, 1984. Pp. 198–201.

"Growing Up to Crime." In *Colloquium on Crime.* Edited by Robin W. Winks. New York: Scribners, 1986. Pp. 7–22.

INTERVIEWS

Herbert, Rosemary. In *The Fatal Art of Entertainment: Interviews with Mystery Writers.* New York: Hall, 1994. Pp. 250–275.

Muller, Adrian. *Mystery Scene,* January/February 1996: 32ff.

Cornwell, Bob. "The Questionnaire." *CADS,* October 1996: 79.

BIOGRAPHICAL AND CRITICAL STUDIES

Bell, Albert A., Jr. "Robert Barnard." In *Critical Survey of Mystery and Detective Fiction.* Edited by Frank N. Magill. Pasadena, Calif.: Salem, 1988. Pp. 82–87.

Breen, Jon L. "Robert Barnard." In *St. James Guide to Crime and Mystery Writers.* 4th ed. Edited by Jay P. Pederson. Detroit and London: St. James Press, 1996. Pp. 48–49.

E. C. BENTLEY

(1875–1956)

THOMAS M. LEITCH

THE LIFE AND WORK of E. C. Bentley are shaped by the deepest paradoxes of the Golden Age of the British detective novel. His memoir, *Those Days* (1940), confirms the evidence of his lifelong vocation in journalism as an active, extroverted man with wide-ranging interests while maintaining an unusual reticence about his private life. Despite his minute familiarity with British and European politics, Bentley achieved fame with *Trent's Last Case* (1913), a novel whose otherworldly country house setting seems to offer itself forthrightly as a retreat from the world of affairs. A model Englishman and the consummate professional writer, Bentley cherished that subversive sense of fun that so often provides a relief from British diffidence. Indeed, his sly sense of humor produced his most enduring literary creations, most of them amateur productions having virtually nothing to do with the journalism he saw as his life's work. Though *Trent's Last Case* was an immediate best-seller, it was nearly ten years before it established itself as the most influential detective novel between those of Arthur Conan Doyle and Dashiell Hammett; and its influence was exactly the opposite of what its creator might have predicted. Written as a joke, the novel turned instead into a joke on its creator, inaugurating a new era in the genre of detective fiction Bentley had originally set out to lampoon.

Life and Personality

Edmund Clerihew Bentley was born in Shepherd's Bush, London, on 10 July 1875. His Scottish mother, Margaret Richardson Clerihew, would lend her name to the distinctive form of light verse her son invented; his English father, John Edmund Bentley, was a barrister in the Lord Chancellor's Department whose exposure to crime and punishment provided the earliest background to Bentley's pioneering work in detective fiction. The eldest of four brothers, Bentley was sent to St. Paul's School, where he first met G. K. Chesterton, the lifelong friend whom he repeatedly identified as the formative influence on his life and work. It was at St. Paul's that Bentley, at the age of sixteen, devised a new verse form, a four-line mock "biography" whose effect depends on the way its improbable rhymes and trivial details satirize the pretensions of the public figure whose name gives each poem its opening line:

> John Stuart Mill
> By a mighty effort of will
> Overcame his natural bonhomie
> And wrote *Principles of Political Economy.*
>
> *The Complete Clerihews*, p. 90

The form's straight-faced burlesque made it a natural medium for collaboration between

Bentley and Chesterton, who contributed copious drawings to an early unpublished collection of these poems, and in 1905 to Bentley's first book, a collection of poems called *Biography for Beginners.* Instead of publishing the collection under his own name, Bentley issued it under the byline of "E. Clerihew," and the form he had invented became known as the "clerihew." It was a form whose distinctive tone of mock seriousness would characterize Bentley's most enduring fiction, though Bentley could hardly have realized it at the time.

In 1894, his final year at St. Paul's, Bentley won a history scholarship to the Oxford college of his choice. He selected Merton College, where he became friendly with John Buchan and Hilaire Belloc, excelled in debate and boating, and served as president of the Oxford Union before taking a second in Greats in 1898.

Although he was called to the Inner Temple bar in 1902, Bentley's vocation as a journalist promptly asserted itself. He had been contributing light verse and parodies to *Punch* for several years and had been writing for the *Speaker* for three years before he joined the *Daily News* staff as an editorial columnist in 1902, rising to the rank of deputy editor and beginning a remarkable string of five thousand editorial leaders for the *Daily News,* which he selected because of its outspoken opposition to the Boer War, and the conservative *Daily Telegraph,* where he served as foreign affairs editor from 1912 to 1934, when he retired.

Also in 1902 Bentley married Violet Alice Mary Boileau, the daughter of General Neil Edmonstone Boileau of the Bengal Staff Corps. The couple had three children, Neil, Betty, and Nicolas, Chesterton's godchild, who grew up to become a noted writer and illustrator.

The great work of Bentley's early years, and the book by which he will be remembered as long as detective stories are enjoyed, was *Trent's Last Case,* first published in America as *The Woman in Black.* Much to Bentley's surprise, the novel became not only a critical success but a commercial best-seller, frequently reprinted, translated, and filmed, and eventually paving the way for a long line of imitators. Bentley himself, remaining largely unaffected by its continued success, refrained from following the novel with a sequel for over twenty years.

Ironically, Chesterton's death in 1936 coincided with the beginning of a new chapter in Bentley's career. He collaborated with his friend H. Warner Allen on a new detective novel, *Trent's Own Case* (1936), and wrote "Greedy Night," his affectionate but stingingly effective parody of his disciple Dorothy L. Sayers. The following year he published the first of three collections of the short stories of Damon Runyon, the American humorist who had incongruously influenced Bentley's handling of American dialogue in *Trent's Last Case,* and whose inimitable style Bentley imitated in his preface. In 1938 Bentley edited *The Second Century of Detective Stories* for Hutchinson, the publishing firm whose *First Century* (1935) had been edited by Chesterton, and collected the detective short stories he had been publishing in the *Strand* and *Metropolitan Magazine* over the past quarter century as *Trent Intervenes;* the following year, he published *Baseless Biography,* the final collection of clerihews he was to see through the press. When Harold Nicolson was called up for service in World War II, Bentley came out of retirement to take his place as chief literary critic of the *Daily Telegraph,* and in 1940 his favorite of all his books, the autobiographical memoir *Those Days,* appeared.

In his own autobiography, *A Version of the Truth* (1960), Nicolas Bentley has left a brief but unforgettable portrait of his father as schooled by his parents in a kind of civilized aloofness that left him, as it seemed to his son, prematurely aged, shy, reticent, and prone to self-criticism—a habit perhaps compounded by his failure to achieve a first at Merton. Yet Nicolas Bentley describes his father as generous, open, and capable of great energy in volunteer work (he took a leading role in organizing wartime relief efforts for Belgian refugees). Despite his considerable cultural attainments, Bentley, according to his son, rarely went to concerts, films, or the theater, and never developed a taste for radio or television, instead growing gradually but distinctly more reserved as he grew older. However accurate this portrait may be, it is clear that his later years were distressing to Bentley. His house in London was bombed by the Nazis, sending him and his wife into the first of a long series of hotels; in 1949, two years after his second retirement from journalism, his wife died; and his final thriller, *Elephant's Work: An Enigma* (1950), failed to meet with the success of his detective stories; thereafter, the formerly athletic and extroverted Bentley retreated into his hotel room, and finally into his bed, until his own death on 30 March 1956.

Trent's Last Case

It was in 1910 that Bentley first unfolded to Chesterton his idea for a new sort of detective story that would stand the current conventions of the Sherlockian superman on their head. The story would conform broadly to every cliché of the genre by including a murdered millionaire, a plodding police detective outclassed by a gifted amateur sleuth, a suspiciously perfect alibi, some reckless derring-do with an automobile, a regulation crew of suspects (including not one but two personal secretaries to the murdered man), and the obligatory romantic interest.

But the novel would invert most of the clichés of the Great Detective—in particular, the two features that most troubled Bentley: his exaggerated peculiarities and his self-importance. Sherlock Holmes, who was still appearing regularly in the *Strand,* was a paragon of scientific reasoning; Bentley's detective would be a much more ordinary fellow, a cultivated humanist far less remote from the world of the audience. Holmes was noted for his ascetic aloofness; Bentley's detective would begin his investigation by falling in love with the chief suspect in the case. Holmes was paired with an amanuensis who remained constantly bewildered by each new revelation; the confidant to Bentley's detective would have a considerably more knowing relation to the mystery. Doyle mystified his readers by allowing Holmes access to material clues withheld from his readers or specialized knowledge beyond their capacities; Bentley would present his clues directly to the reader, making their import potentially available to anyone with a modicum of wit and common sense. Holmes's hallmark was his infallibility; Bentley's detective, equally meticulous in his reconstruction of the criminal's actions, would turn out to be completely wrong. Finally, in keeping with this last change, Bentley would shift the tone of the story from Dr. Watson's reverential awe to subtle parody, typified by the detective's own bantering self-deprecation, in keeping with his plan of producing what he would describe thirty years later in *Those Days* as "not so much a detective story as an exposure of detective stories" (p. 254).

Having spent some six or eight weeks plotting his story on his walks back and forth to the *Daily News* office and six months writing it at a standing desk in his home—he later observed that he did virtually all the work on the novel while he was on his feet—Bentley submitted "Philip Gasket's Last Case," the resulting deconstruction of the Sherlockian superman, to Duckworth toward the end of 1911 in competition for a fifty-pound prize for the best first novel. But when his friend Edward Garnett told him that the novel was not under serious consideration for the prize, Bentley, convinced by a chance conversation with Douglas Z. Doty of the New York publishing firm Century that a detective novel might well earn far more than fifty pounds in royalties, withdrew it from the competition and sent it with Doty to Century, which accepted it (despite a reader's report noting that "it is too distinctly *English* in several places") with one crucial proviso: that its hero be given a less silly name. Bentley obliged by christening his detective Philip Trent, a name whose associations were neutral and unexceptionably British; and the novel was published in March 1913 as *The Woman in Black,* its title presumably chosen to echo Wilkie Collins, the most formidable detective novelist in English. That same month, at the urging of John Buchan, Bentley's novel was issued by the British publisher Thomas Nelson under the title by which it became famous: *Trent's Last Case.*

The novel, which is dedicated to Chesterton (in return for *The Man Who Was Thursday,* Chesterton's own, far more radical deconstruction of the detective story, which he had dedicated to Bentley in 1908), begins with an elaborately Chestertonian set piece: an account of how the murder of towering, malignant American millionaire Sigsbee Manderson reduces financial markets around the world to terrified despair. "Men stabbed and shot and strangled themselves, drank death or breathed it as the air, because in a lonely corner of England the life had departed from one cold heart vowed to the service of greed" (p. 11), even though his death is fundamentally inconsequential: "To all mankind save a million or two of half-crazed gamblers, blind to all reality, the death of Manderson meant nothing" (p. 15). This first chapter, satirically oracular without ever quite crossing the line into farce, sets up the contrast between the catastrophically dehumanizing buccaneer capitalism of America's Gilded Age and the quiet reality of personal, apolitical, and quintessentially British intimacy into which the novel retreats as if into a hard-sought oasis.

The American, Manderson, whose most distinctive feature is "a complete absence of the sympathetic faculty" (p. 43), represents the first of these values; the English journalist Philip Trent, his opposite (and, it turns out, his double), represents the second. Trent, an accomplished painter whose "best aid to success had been an unconscious power of getting himself liked" (p. 55), is an amateur detective whose inquiries on behalf of Sir James Molloy's *Record,* a morning newspaper, are no more his proper vocation than his creator's foray into detective fiction. Arriving on the scene at Bishopsbridge, Trent immediately learns from his old friend Nathaniel Cupples, who happens to be Mrs. Manderson's uncle, that her late husband was universally detested—not only by his British secretary, John Marlowe, and his American secretary, Calvin Bunner, but particularly by Mabel Manderson, whom Trent spies at a nearby cliff stretching out her arms in a gesture of exultant freedom at her husband's death.

After considering the strange condition of Manderson's corpse—he was fully dressed, down to a necktie and pocket watch, yet without the false teeth he had left on his bedside table—and observing the telltale clues in a pair of Manderson's dress shoes and a pair of framed photographs in Marlowe's room, Trent suggests to Mabel Manderson that her husband's recent and widely remarked moodiness might have been caused by an affair between her and Marlowe. When she recoils weeping from his implication—an acknowledgment, he assumes, of her complicity—he withdraws from the case, leaving with her a copy of the letter he had intended to send to Sir James containing a detailed account of his reconstruction of the crime. This revelation comes little more than halfway through the novel—the same point as the climactic revelations of Doyle's *A Study in Scarlet* (1887) and A. E. W. Mason's *At the Villa Rose* (1910). But Trent's earlier proneness to light-hearted persiflage has been considerably chastened, and his sense of honor, more powerful than his desire for justice, keeps him from making his accusation public.

When he meets Mabel Manderson again the following year and realizes she cares nothing for Marlowe, who has recently become engaged to another woman, Trent impulsively proposes marriage to her, and she accepts. Now moved again to clear up the mystery of Manderson's death, Trent reopens the case, with results that have astonished readers ever since nearly as much as the detective himself. When the solution to the mystery is finally revealed, not by his own painstaking investigations, but by the genial, apparently inconsequential Cupples, Trent, stung by this "last revelation of the impotence of human reason" (p. 375), resolves that he will forswear criminal investigation; the Manderson affair will be Trent's last case.

The successive blows the novel deals to Trent's intellectual pride—first his suspicion of Mrs. Manderson's criminal complicity, then the hypothesis he develops for his dispatch to Sir James, and finally his eagerness to accept the theory one of his prime suspects offers, all turn out to be wrong—subvert not only the figure of the superhuman detective, but also the assumptions of rational order underlying that detective and his world. Despite Trent's accomplishments as a detective—which mirror Manderson's accomplishments as a financier—every rational plan he makes is undermined, generally for the better, by circumstance, whim, or emotional impulse. A world in which spontaneous emotion and expression repeatedly defeat reason is no place for a detective; it is no wonder that Bentley intended *Trent's Last Case* to be his sole contribution to the genre he thought he was bringing to its logical end.

Later Works

It was in the climate of Golden Age foolery and ingenuity, and the nostalgia for the imagined class-bound certainties of the prewar social order, that Bentley's later books appeared. Though all are written with urbanity and charm, none of Bentley's later works has enjoyed the influence of *Trent's Last Case.* The most successful are the stories collected in *Trent Intervenes* (1938), which, as Nicholas Blake acutely noted in his review of the collection, do not so much resolve as avoid the problem of how to keep the identity of the criminal secret. These stories, with few exceptions, are not whodunits of the sort favored in virtually all Golden Age detective fiction, short or long; they do not ask which of a small circle of suspects committed the crime, but rather how (and often whether) a crime was committed, and what to do about it.

Unlike such Golden Age masters of the detective short story as Agatha Christie and Ellery Queen, Bentley never focuses his mysteries on the revelation of personal identity because he is less interested in dramatizing the mystifying behavior of innocent suspects than in displaying Trent's easy mastery of the codes of conduct proper to the British professional class that reveal the malefactors and tell him how to deal with them: Trent knows what wine to order with fish, which words in a carefully composed letter stick out as a code, and how to steal a harmful narcotic from its unwitting victim without calling attention to the theft.

In emphasizing the detective's mastery of his professional tools over the deceptive behavior of the suspects, Bentley's short stories, like those of Sayers, abandon the whodunit in favor of the older, more comfortable Sherlock Holmes formula, though Trent remains considerably more self-effacing in his expertise than Holmes ever was. Instead of inviting admiration for the detective's mastery of scientific arcana, the stories celebrate the expressiveness of social and cultural codes within the reach of every literate reader. Particularly celebrated are "The Sweet Shot," the closest to a short whodunit Bentley ever came; "The Ordinary Hairpins," which traces the fate of a famous soprano who has disappeared following the deaths of her husband and child; "The Genuine Tabard," which spends more time unfolding than resolving a gentlemanly swindle; and "The Clever Cockatoo," perhaps the finest and most distinctive of all Bentley's short stories, in which the challenge to Trent is not only to solve the mystery but to determine how best to put his knowledge to use.

In fact, Bentley had never committed himself to the conventions of the whodunit as they would be developed by Christie and codified by Queen and John Dickson Carr; the most mysterious character in *Trent's Last Case,* after all, is the victim, who is never required to behave either innocently or guiltily for the detective. Bentley's only orthodox whodunit is the long-awaited sequel, *Trent's Own Case* (1936), which shares many features with its original: the hateful murdered millionaire; the earnest, ineffectual police inspector; the genial amateur detective Trent, who rises to every conversational difficulty with an amiably mangled literary allusion; the gratuitous excursion to the Continent; Trent's personal stake in the case (once again involving his concern for a lady's honor); the rich proliferation of episodes arising from each apparent clue; the dependence of the final unraveling on a series of accidents. These features would suggest the work of a gifted imitator if so many of them had not become clichés of Golden Age detective fiction.

Sir James Randolph is a philanthropist with a heart of iron who is shot to death the same evening that Trent, who has just finished painting his portrait, meets with him to ask him to cease his unwelcome attentions to the actress Eunice Faviell, Trent's friend. Another friend, the psychiatrist Bryan Fairman, comes under suspicion, as does Trent himself. The evidence in the case presents a fabulous array of red herrings—from the Tiara of Magabyzus to the history of a cork labeled "Felix Poubelle 1884," from Fairman's attempted suicide to Randolph's unexpectedly prodigious family tree—before Trent finally hires a double for Randolph who stalks Trent and his suspect through a golf match until the unnerved killer finally confesses after a climactic apparition on the thirteenth green.

Despite several hallmarks of Bentley's work, *Trent's Own Case* is less distinctive in every way than its illustrious predecessor, and not simply because it does not share its historical importance. Lacking both the innovative architecture of the earlier novel and its sly exposé of the genre's conventions, *Trent's Own Case* relies on a series of polished, amusing, essentially detachable anecdotes; it is no surprise that several early reviewers compared it to a seven-course dinner. Perhaps the most serious criticism to be leveled against the novel is that it is impossible to separate Allen's contributions from Bentley's own.

Elephant's Work (1950), Bentley's final novel, is unmistakably its author's own work; yet it shows him experimenting in a genre remote from his most distinctive gifts and interests. As Bentley relates in his memorial dedication to John Buchan, Buchan had advised him shortly after the publication of Buchan's *The Thirty-Nine Steps* (1915) to try his hand at a "shocker," a suspense thriller that was not bound by the proprieties and probabilities of the formal detective story. The novel, which traces the consequences of a railroad accident caused by an enraged circus elephant, demonstrates Bentley's peculiar inaptitude for the supposedly less demanding form.

Lord Severn, a passenger aboard the derailed train, is rescued from the scene by the entourage of "El Gatillo," General Justo Hernando de la Costa, of the Latin American country of Peligragua. Because Severn has amnesia and is found with the passport of one Dwight Philip Taylor, the General's men mistake him for a henchman of the General's sometime American colleague, Farewell Billy, who dispatched Taylor to the General to protect him against the schemes of the criminal mastermind Ketch. Severn, allowing himself to fall in with the General and his crew, finds them open, generous, and surprisingly well read. (On their first meeting, the General quotes Cardinal Newman.)

Despite an affecting climax when Severn suddenly recovers his memory, Bentley does not have Buchan's taste for improbability or impropriety: Ketch is a nefarious cipher; the details of his tireless succession of criminal plots are lamentably unclear; and the General and his raffish cohorts are sadly unconvincing as would-be English gentlemen. Lacking the well-bred mores of English society to constrain the behavior of Bentley's characters and to serve as the fulcrum of his satire, *Elephant's Work* produces instead the effect of unintentional comedy, while serving as a reminder that Bentley's best work depends on precisely the constraints Buchan identified as difficulties in writing detective fiction.

Legacy

Bentley's legacy rests not on the relatively derivative and unconvincing work of his later years, but on the singular achievement of *Trent's Last Case.* Yet his effect on the detective genre was precisely the opposite of what he had expected. Not only had Bentley failed to write the detective novel to end all detective novels; he had established, in spite of himself, a tone and style, and a set of new conventions, that would give the form he was seeking to explode unprecedented new life. Together with Mason's *At the Villa Rose* and the stories Chesterton had collected in *The Innocence of Father Brown* (1911), *Trent's Last Case* shifted the emphasis of the detective story away from awestruck admiration for the preternatural powers of the Great Detective to closer identification with the detective, as fictional sleuths revealed human frailties in place of bizarre eccentricities, together with a disarming talent for self-deprecation. All three of these books, but especially *Trent's Last Case,* published only a year before World War I, enshrined a world of gentlemanly, commonsensical values and class-bound moral certainties that the war would shatter. When the vogue for detective stories returned after the war, the humanistic, apolitical values Bentley had attached to Trent would be invoked again, but this time through an act of willful nostalgia, a longing for a world in which every gesture had its appointed meaning and reason reigned supreme once more in the closed communities—English villages and manor houses—whose serene moral order could be restored by the identification of a single criminal scapegoat.

The world of political history and public affairs appears just often enough in *Trent's Last Case*—in the opening chapter's straightfaced account of the markets' reaction to Manderson's death, for instance, and in Trent's attempt, in chapter 12, to forget Mabel Manderson by plunging himself into the role of roving newspaper correspondent—to counterpoint the world of Bishopsbridge as an unworldly retreat. By contrast, when Agatha Christie first introduces Hercule Poirot in chapter 2 of *The Mysterious Affair at Styles* (1920) as a Belgian refugee who has been housed by the charity of the local squire's wife, it is virtually the last time in Poirot's career when he is rooted in any particular historical situation; the international conspiracies Christie resurrected in novels from *The Big Four* (1927) to *Passenger to Frankfurt* (1970) are notable for their lack of historical actuality.

As he invoked the English country house as a willed retreat from history, Bentley's handling of the detective's investigations showed how the novel could become the dominant length of detective fiction. Sherlock Holmes is so omnicompetent that as soon as the facts of a case are presented to him, he is well on his way to its solution. It is therefore eminently logical that most of Holmes's exploits are recounted in short stories, or that most of Doyle's four Holmes novels, short as they are, cannot maintain their essential mystery for very long. Bentley made the detective likable enough, and catholic enough in his interests, to be engaging throughout the length and varied incidents of a novel, and (more important) fallible enough to require an entire novel to solve his greatest case. The resulting shift in the detective story's structure from a sleight-of-hand anecdote to a gradual revelation of character and motive, together with Bentley's nostalgic focus on the British professional class, effected a quiet but lasting revolution in the detective story.

The most important legacy of *Trent's Last Case,* therefore, is not the critical plaudits it received from Chesterton, R. Austin Freeman, Edgar Wallace, Agatha Christie, Freeman Wills Crofts, Ronald Knox, Dorothy L. Sayers, and other practitioners of the genre, but its decisive influence on the generation of detective novels that followed. The novel's first and most immediate influence was, appropriately, on Christie's *The Mysterious Affair at Styles,* which was written in 1916 but not published until 1920. Of all the Golden Age writers, Christie was most successful in domesticating Bentley's distinctively upper-class tone, making its language seem classless while preserving all the mechanisms (the closed community, the wealthy victim, the circle of domestic suspects, the series of wrong solutions casting suspicion on the lower classes before the denouement that plucked the culprit from the victim's own class) that maintained the reassuring insularity of the form.

Through the similar mediation of Sayers, Trent's witty banter, variously modulated, became the dominant note for Golden Age detectives from Lord Peter Wimsey to Albert Campion in Britain and from Philo Vance to Ellery Queen in the United States. At the same time the detective became more human and fallible, the mysteries their creators set became increasingly intricate, so that what critics like Sayers hailed as a new naturalism in the genre's tone was balanced by a formalizing of the mystery. Readers, assured by the "Challenge to the Reader" that Ellery Queen interposed before the revelatory chapters of his early novels that they were now in possession of every clue needed to solve the mystery, entered into its solution in a spirit of competition with the detective, ultimately transforming the detective story from a morality play to an intellectual puzzle. As this puzzle element became dominant, even Bentley's most fantastic innovations—the series of wrong deductions and the detective's final error—became regular features in the work of such Golden Age classics as Ellery Queen's *The Greek Coffin Mystery* (1932) and *Ten Days' Wonder* (1948) and John Dickson Carr's *The Arabian Night's Murder* (1935). Indeed, the detective novel to end all detective novels—a subgenre that could plausibly be traced back to Israel Zangwill's *The Big Bow Mystery* (1895)—flourished throughout the Golden Age in such exemplars as Agatha Christie's *Murder on the Orient Express* (1933), C. Daly King's *Obelists Fly High* (1935), and Cameron MacCabe's *The Face on the Cutting-Room Floor* (1937).

The formal detective novel, whose ingredients of gentility, ingenuity, self-deprecation, and self-parody Bentley had been so instrumental in establishing, was able to absorb so high a concentration of these qualities without shattering that the form Bentley had done so much to shape was not successfully challenged again until the advent of Dashiell Hammett and Raymond Chandler.

Selected Bibliography

WORKS OF E. C. BENTLEY

BOOKS

Biography for Beginners. By "E. Clerihew." London: Laurie, 1905.

Trent's Last Case. London: Nelson, 1913. Published as *The Woman in Black.* New York: Century, 1913.

Peace Year in the City, 1918–1919: An Account of the Outstanding Events in the City of London During the Peace Year. London: privately printed, 1920.

More Biography. London: Methuen, 1929.

Trent's Own Case (with H. Warner Allen). London: Constable, 1936; New York: Knopf, 1936.

Trent Intervenes. London: Nelson, 1938; New York: Knopf, 1938.

Baseless Biography. London: Constable, 1939.

Those Days: An Autobiography. London: Constable, 1940.

Elephant's Work: An Enigma. London: Hodder & Stoughton, 1950; New York: Knopf, 1950. U.S.: *The Chill.* New York: Dell, 1953.

Far Horizon: A Biography of Hester Dowden, Medium and Psychic Investigator. London and New York: Rider, 1951.

Clerihews Complete. London: Laurie, 1951.

Trent's Case Book. New York: Knopf, 1953. Includes *Trent's Last Case, Trent's Own Case,* and *Trent Intervenes.*

The Complete Clerihews. Oxford and New York: Oxford University Press, 1981.

The Scoop and Behind the Screen (with Dorothy L. Sayers et al.). London: Gollancz, 1983; New York: Harper & Row, 1983.

UNCOLLECTED SHORT STORIES AND ESSAYS

"Meet Trent." In *Meet the Detective.* London: Allen & Unwin, 1935; Harrisburg, Pa.: Telegraph Press, 1935. Pp. 98–105.

"Greedy Night." In *Parody Party.* Edited by Leonard Russell. London: Hutchinson, 1936.

"The Ministering Angel." In *To the Queen's Taste.* Edited by Ellery Queen. Boston: Little, Brown, 1946. Pp. 291–305.

"The Feeble Folk." *Ellery Queen's Mystery Magazine*, March 1953.

WORKS EDITED BY BENTLEY

Runyon, Damon. *More Than Somewhat.* London: Constable, 1937.

———. *Damon Runyon Presents Furthermore.* London: Constable, 1938.

———. *The Best of Runyon.* New York: Stokes, 1938.

The Second Century of Detective Stories. London: Hutchinson, 1938.

BIBLIOGRAPHY

Shibuk, Charles. "E. C. Bentley." In *Trent's Last Case.* Del Mar, Calif.: Publisher's Inc., 1977. Pp. 253–257.

BIOGRAPHICAL AND CRITICAL STUDIES

Baker, Isidore Lewis. *E. C. Bentley: Trent's Last Case.* Notes on chosen English texts. London: Brodie, 1956.

Barzun, Jacques, and Wendell Hertig Taylor. Preface to *Trent's Last Case.* New York: Garland, 1976. Pp. 1–2. Repr. in Barzun and Taylor, *A Book of Prefaces to Fifty Classics of Crime Fiction.* New York: Garland, 1976. Pp. 19–20.

Bentley, Nicolas. *A Version of the Truth.* London: Deutsch, 1960. Pp. 20–24.

Blake, Nicholas. "Trent and Others." *Spectator* 156, no. 5631: 992 (29 May 1936).

———. "A Dram of Poison." *Spectator* 161, no. 5747: 312–313 (19 August 1938).

Chandler, Raymond. "The Simple Art of Murder." *Atlantic Monthly* 174: 53–59 (December 1944).

Chesterton, G. K. "On Detective Story Writers." In *Come to Think of It . . . .* New York: Dodd, Mead, 1931. Pp. 33–38.

———. *Autobiography.* London: Hutchinson & Co., 1936.

Haycraft, Howard. *Murder for Pleasure: The Life and Times of the Detective Story.* New York: Appleton, 1941.

———. "Trent's Last Case Reopened." *New York Times Book Review,* 15 December 1963: 18–19. Repr. in *Trent's Last Case.* Introduction by Aaron Marc Stein. Del Mar, Calif.: Publisher's Inc., 1977. Pp. 266–268.

Hilfer, A. C. "Invasion and Excess: Texts of Bliss in Popular Culture." *Texas Studies in Literature and Language* 22: 125–137 (summer 1980).

Kermode, Frank. "Novel and Narrative." In *The Theory of the Novel: New Essays.* Edited by John Halperin. New York: Oxford University Press, 1974. Pp. 155–174.

Milne, A. A. "Books and Writers." *Spectator* 184, no. 6366: 893 (30 June 1950). Review of *Elephant's Work.*

Murch, A. E. *The Development of the Detective Novel.* New York: Philosophical Library, 1958. Pp. 203–204.

Panek, LeRoy. *Watteau's Shepherds: The Detective Novel in Britain, 1914–1940.* Bowling Green, Ohio: Bowling Green State University Popular Press, 1979. Pp. 29–37.

Partridge, Ralph. "The Murder of Nicholas Blake." *New Statesman and Nation* n.s. 11, no. 274: 807–808 (23 May 1936). Review of *Trent's Own Case.*

Priestman, Martin. *Detective Fiction and Literature: The Figure on the Carpet.* London: Macmillan, 1990. Pp. 115–123.

Redman, Ben Ray. Introduction to *Trent's Case Book.* New York: Knopf, 1953.

"The Return of Philip Trent." *Times Literary Supplement,* no. 1903: 495 (23 July 1938).

Review of *Trent's Last Case, Spectator* 110, no. 4419: 409–410 (8 March 1913).

Review of *The Woman in Black, Nation* 96, no. 2493: 361 (10 April 1913).

Reynolds, Barbara. "The Origin of Lord Peter Wimsey," *Times Literary Supplement,* no. 3919: 492 (22 April 1977).

Routley, Erik. *The Puritan Pleasures of the Detective Story: A Personal Monograph.* London: Gollancz, 1972. Pp. 119–123.

Sayers, Dorothy L. Introduction to *The Omnibus of Crime.* London: Gollancz, 1928. Pp. 9–47.

———. Introduction to *Trent's Last Case.* New York: Harper & Row, 1978. Pp. x–xiii.

Shenker, Israel. "Clerihews." *New Yorker* 59: 148, 151–152 (25 April 1983).

Shibuk, Charles. "E. C. Bentley." In *Twentieth-Century Crime and Mystery Writers,* 3d ed. Edited by Lesley Henderson. Chicago: St. James Press, 1991.

Stein, Aaron Marc. Introduction to *Trent's Last Case.* Del Mar, Calif.: Publisher's Inc., 1977. Pp. ix–xxv.

Symons, Julian. *Bloody Murder: A History from the Detective Story to the Crime Novel,* 3d rev. ed. New York: Mysterious Press, 1993.

Thomson, H. Douglas. *Masters of Mystery: A Study of the Detective Story.* London: Collins, 1931. Pp. 147–155.

Williams, Charles. "Letters to Peter—IV." *G.K.'s Weekly* 23, no. 585: 178–179 (28 May 1936).

Winton, Malcolm. "E. C. Bentley." In *Critical Survey of Mystery and Detective Fiction.* Edited by Frank Magill. Pasadena, Calif.: Salem Press, 1988. Pp. 112–117.

Nicholas Blake
(1904–1972)

THOMAS M. LEITCH

Despite Cecil Day Lewis' fame as a poet—a fame that reached millions when he was named England's poet laureate in 1968—little has been written about the detective fiction he wrote under the pseudonym Nicholas Blake. This neglect is unfortunate for several reasons. The phenomenon of celebrity authors who indulge in popular formulas has an obvious fascination. Despite Blake's offhand account of his plunge into detective fiction—it was the only honest way he could think of, he claimed, to earn the hundred pounds he needed to repair the leaking roof of his cottage—he was no mere dilettante in his chosen field. His detective novels were acclaimed as outstanding almost from the beginning. In 1939 John Strachey, in "The Golden Age of English Detection," pronounced him one of the leading figures in the genre. As a reviewer and theorist of detective fiction, Blake was thoughtful and articulate in defense of the genre. Finally, though Day Lewis' critics have followed his own lead in dismissing his detective novels as unimportant, the novels address many of the same problems that inform his poetry and continue to maintain at least as high a reputation within their field.

From Poetry to Detection

Cecil Day Lewis was born in Ballintubber, Ireland, on 27 April 1904, the only child of two Anglo-Irish parents, Frank Cecil Day Lewis, an Anglican clergyman, and Kathleen Blake Squires, a collateral descendant of the Irish author Oliver Goldsmith. Day Lewis' mother, who followed his father from Ireland to England in 1905, died when her son was four. Although her sister, Agnes Olive Squires (whom the poet called "Knos"), came from Dublin to join his father in raising the boy until the older man's remarriage in 1920, Day Lewis emphasizes in his memoir *The Buried Day* (1960) the unusual closeness he and his father shared throughout his childhood. As the curate, striving to be both mother and father to his only child, Frank Cecil Day Lewis became something of a playful older brother to him as well.

In 1909, when his father transferred to a parish in central London, Day Lewis enrolled in Wilkie's prep school nearby. He remained within the British school system for the next twenty-six years as both student and master. Although Day Lewis displayed little aptitude as a scholar, he won a scholarship in 1917 to the Sherborne School in Dorset, and in 1923, upon leaving Sherborne, he entered Wadham College, Oxford.

At Oxford, Day Lewis gravitated to the literary circles with which he would be widely associated for the rest of his life. In 1926, the year after *Beechen Vigil* (1925), his first book of poetry, appeared, he met the gifted, mercurial W. H. Auden, who, although he was three years younger, evidently stepped into the contradictory role of the playmate/authority figure Day Lewis' father had formerly assumed. Together with Auden, Day Lewis edited the anthology *Oxford Poetry 1927* and wrote its inflated, playfully self-mocking introduction. The note of playfulness is typical of Day Lewis' work, as is the device of hiding his own deepest convictions behind an assumed voice.

In 1927, after an undistinguished Third at Wadham, Day Lewis accepted a post at Oxford's Summer Fields School and, while preparing his second volume of poetry, *Country Comets* (1928), for publication, began work on his third, *Transitional Poem* (1929). At the same time, he made plans to marry Constance Mary King, the daughter of Rev. H. R. King, one of his Sherborne masters, after a long engagement. Because Summer Fields could not support another married master, Day Lewis found a new position at Larchfield School, in Helensburgh, Scotland, and he and Mary were married on 27 December 1928.

Initially, the marriage gave Day Lewis a welcome sense of the solidity and purpose displayed in the poetic sequence *Transitional Poem,* his first mature work. In 1930 Day Lewis secured his first (and essentially last) long-term position, at Cheltenham Junior School in Gloucestershire. Just as his scholastic performance at Wadham had been overshadowed by his passion for poetry, at Cheltenham he continued a diffident master more interested in writing than teaching. He marked the nine months leading to the birth of his first child, Sean, by writing a new poetic sequence, *From Feathers to Iron* (1931), which sets the spiritual barrenness of the contemporary world against the hope represented by a new life; two years later, the same year as his son Nicholas' birth, he completed the sequence *The Magnetic Mountain* (1933). The following year Day Lewis, who was identified with a well-known and influential circle of Oxford poets including Auden, Louis MacNeice, and Stephen Spender, published *A Hope for Poetry* (1934), the first book-length manifesto and analysis of the circle.

More explicitly than any of Day Lewis' earlier poems, *A Hope for Poetry,* which sets the rabidly committed Communist and the studiously anti-ideological bourgeois against each other as mutually canceling critics, makes a case for the return of political subjects to poetry. Like *The Magnetic Mountain,* this volume would have seriously compromised Day Lewis' position at Cheltenham if not for the comfortable assumption that poetry could not possibly have anything to do with real life.

For several years an anti-institutional bias had estranged him from the Church of England and inoculated him against any communion with Roman Catholicism. Yet, avid for membership in groups that would satisfy his need for social bonding, spiritual direction, and personal integration, Day Lewis, like several members of the Auden circle, had become a fellow traveler of the Communist Party of Great Britain. Fallen away from religious belief, disillusioned with old-fashioned liberalism, and sharply critical of the socioeconomic heresies of fascism and capitalism alike, Day Lewis sought

> a faith which would fill the void left by the leaking away of traditional religion, would make sense of our troubled times and make real demands on me. Marxism appeared to fill the bill. It appealed too, I imagine, to that part of me which from time to time revolted against the intolerable burden of selfhood and desired the anonymity of a unit in a crowd. (*The Buried Day,* p. 209)

Smothering in a stultifying teaching post, confronting a worldwide economic depression apparently without hope or direction, starving for a moral and spiritual authority that would replace his lost religious faith, chafing by now against the influence of a magnetic younger poet whose voice had long overshadowed his own, Day Lewis dared not declare his loyalties by joining the Communist Party openly for fear of endangering his family's income. And then the roof of his cottage sprang a leak.

Why the Detective Story?

Readers who find it difficult to recapture the strangeness of Day Lewis' second career now, when poets and poetry play an even more marginal role in public life than they did in 1935, might consider the shock they might feel if they discovered that Wallace Stevens or Robert Frost had written a score of mystery novels on the side. Out of all the kinds of writing he might have undertaken to make money, why did he choose the detective story? Day Lewis himself, in an introduction he wrote as Nicholas Blake to the British edition of Howard Haycraft's *Murder for Pleasure* in 1942, has provided a compelling rationale for his choice.

Blake's essay, excerpted as "The Detective Story—Why?" for its first American publication in Haycraft's 1946 anthology *The Art of the Mystery Story,* brushes aside the question of why people write detective stories—to earn money, to indulge their appetite for low experiences like murder and cruelty, to share their addiction with newcomers—and focuses instead on the question of why people read them, on why the formula had achieved such enduring popularity. Blake imagines a future anthropologist connecting the rise of the detective story with the post-Victorian decline in religious belief that leaves agnostics with no opportunity to rid themselves of their crippling sense of personal guilt. The detective story, argues Blake, translates the religious ritual of the scapegoat into acceptably secular terms by providing an original sin, a sacrificial victim, a high priest who executes the sacrifice, and, in the detective, an avenging power who purges the community of guilt by identifying and punishing the criminal in a climactic denouement recalling the Day of Judgment, the Christian apocalypse when the veil is rent and the world appears for the first time as it really is.

Blake borrows the final image from G. K. Chesterton's eschatological essays and Father Brown detective stories, but adds a new twist: the reader's identification with both the detective and the murderer, who represent conflicting impulses within his own divided nature. Describing the detective story as a contemporary folk-myth, a fairy tale for grown-ups, Blake identifies the figure of the detective as a fairy godmother whose magical powers are acceptable to modern scientific skepticism because they are either tempered with human eccentricities, as with Sherlock Holmes and Hercule Poirot, or cloaked in a purely institutional identity, as with the impersonal modern police detective.

Blake's ambitious claims for the therapeutic powers of detective fiction are grounded in social class. He ascribes the genre's popularity among the middle and upper classes to its bias toward protecting the established order and its values, in contrast to lower-class thrillers that are less interested in purging guilt through a ritual of transgression and punishment than in romanticizing the criminal as a heroic antiestablishment figure, a contemporary Robin Hood who challenges and undermines the status quo by successfully flouting its laws. Rooting the genre in fairy-tale fantasy, Blake contends that the central problem in detective fiction is to mix fantasy judiciously with reality. Authors who do not wish to stray outside the boundaries of the genre may either place unreal characters in realistic situations (as in the police investigations of Freeman Wills Crofts and his followers) or place realistic characters in fantastic or unlikely situations (as in the work of John Dickson Carr, Ngaio Marsh, and by implication Blake himself).

In plotting the development of the detective novel, Blake presciently isolates three trends that accelerated, particularly in his own work, in the years following the essay: the decline of high fantasy in the face of a more realistic representation of manners; the correspondingly nondescript images of recent detectives like Georges Simenon's Inspector Maigret; and the emphasis Simenon and others place on the unsparing representation of evil, which may end by making criminals so intent on delivering themselves to justice that they will take over the task of the detective. Taken together, these three developments heighten the ambivalent appeal of the detective story—of both crime and punishment, mystification and rationality, regressive fantasy and social reality—that Blake places at the heart of the formula.

The theorists most clearly influenced by Blake's sociological model of the detective story were Auden and Julian Symons. Indeed, Auden's 1948 essay "The Guilty Vicarage," which borrows much of its quasi-religious terminology from Blake, marks perhaps the only occasion when he is derivative of Day Lewis, rather than the other way around. Whatever its merits as a general analysis of detective fiction, Blake's emphasis on the power of the genre to assuage social guilt through ambivalent identifications goes to the heart of the genre's appeal for Blake himself. Characterizing the detective story as a secular ritual of sacrifice helps explain the strong element of ritual in Blake's novels—a ritual played out not in the game between author and reader, as in Ellery Queen and John Dickson Carr, but within the world of the characters, who repeatedly act with a fatalistic self-consciousness of their ordained roles.

The contradictory identifications of both heroes and villains in Blake's works are heightened because they operate not merely between the opposing figures of the criminal and the detective, but within nominal opposites. In Blake more than in any other contemporaneous writer of detective fiction, detectives and victims, criminals and innocent suspects alike are presented with keen ambivalence. Apparent victims in Blake's novels often turn out to be murderers; murderers are unmasked to reveal unexpectedly sympathetic depths; one character must often bear moral responsibility for a crime of which another is legally guilty; and the detective himself, who begins as a studiously unthreatening moral authority, gradually loses his redemptive powers over the thirty years of Blake's career.

Nigel Strangeways

Blake's sharp distinction between detective stories and thrillers is useful in analyzing his own fiction. However, this distinction does not prevent Blake's regular detective, Nigel Strangeways, from appearing in both genres. Featured in all but one of Blake's detective novels and in three thrillers, Strangeways makes his first appearance in the novel *A Question of Proof* (1935).

The first impression created by Sudeley Hall, the prep school setting of the novel, is of energetic literacy—in the opening scene the romantic lead, Michael Evans, quotes T. S. Eliot to himself while shaving—crossed with savage social conflict. Michael, carrying on an affair with Hero Vale, the headmaster's wife, has no hope that Percival Vale will divorce her, or that he will be able to get another teaching post if they marry. When Vale's nephew, a student at Sudeley, is discovered strangled in a haystack where Michael and Hero had just been trysting, suspicion falls on Michael. When Vale himself is murdered, Michael becomes the leading suspect.

In the meantime, however, a potential savior has arrived: Nigel Strangeways, nephew of the assistant commissioner. Strangeways, named after the Manchester prison, is firmly in the tradition of Golden Age detectives: an amateur with professional connections, intelligent and insouciant, with an obligatory bundle of eccentricities. His most distinctive note is his gaiety, which extends from his own battery of literary allusions and his abrupt departure from Oxford (he answered all his exam questions in limericks) to his incessant physical activity (the scene in which he is introduced rapidly turns into a car chase).

Although Day Lewis had hidden his authorship of *A Question of Proof* behind a pseudonym, he made no serious attempt to conceal his identity, and at least two reviewers of the book clearly knew who he was. So did the staff and the locals at Cheltenham Junior, who assumed, as Day Lewis recalled in

The Buried Day, "that the author of the book was having, or at any rate wished to have, an affair with the wife of Cheltenham College's new headmaster" (p. 202). The gossips were wrong in their particular charge but right in looking to the novel for snatches of autobiography. Throughout the Blake novels Day Lewis would freely adapt his own experiences—his stint in the wartime Office of Information in *Minute for Murder* (1947), his work in a publishing firm in *End of Chapter* (1957), his year at Harvard in *The Morning After Death* (1966). But Blake's novels do not simply recycle the events of his life as background for their stories; they use fictionalized characters and incidents as a means of working through—or more often playing with—the same sorts of insoluble problems Day Lewis made the subject of his poems.

Many of Strangeways' habits—the irrepressible high spirits, the flood of quotations, the ostrichlike lope—are clearly modeled on those of Auden. More generally, Strangeways, whose role is to rescue Michael Evans from the community that condemns him, plays the good father to Percival Vale's bad father. Vale—powerful, humorless, and married to Michael's love—represents authority at its most forbidding; Strangeways, the mildest authority figure imaginable, is, like Auden and Day Lewis' father before him, both father and brother to the hero. Indeed, the denouement proves Strangeways an unusually passive detective, since the criminal confesses his guilt on the vaguest provocation and then shoots himself with a revolver Strangeways has thoughtfully provided.

The repressed, colorless murderer is, in fact, as much an autobiographical figure as Michael, since his motive for murder is envious hatred sparked by a conviction that his worth is unappreciated at Sudeley—a feeling his author, well known but not well recompensed as a poet, surely shared at Cheltenham. By giving his hero a romance that makes his life at Sudeley passionate, links him to authority, and places him in danger, Blake expresses his ambivalence toward the cultural, social, and imaginative values the school represents. The overpowering longing the story expresses is not that Day Lewis consummate an affair with the Cheltenham headmaster's wife, but that the authority he loves and fears—whether vested in his father, in Auden, or in the Communist Party—chasten his most resentful impulses by punishing the envious murderer and miraculously deliver his better self from servitude.

As it turned out, *A Question of Proof* performed exactly these functions for its author. The novel's appearance, coinciding with a public talk Day Lewis imprudently gave on collective farming in Soviet Russia, both imperiled his position at Cheltenham and offered him escape. Rupert Hart-Davis, who had reviewed the novel for the *Spectator,* offered Day Lewis a contract to write three mainstream novels, and, confident that he could earn a living as a novelist, Day Lewis left Cheltenham. Free, moreover, of the official opprobrium that would follow such a step, he promptly joined the Communist Party, beginning a period of intense political activity that would last until 1938.

In the meantime, however, he began work on a new detective story, one whose attitude toward crime and punishment is even more contradictory. The new novel, *Thou Shell of Death* (1936; U.S. title, *Shell of Death*) is based on Cyril Tourneur's Elizabethan play *The Revenger's Tragedy.* Both concern a vengeful man's elaborate (and ultimately suicidal) attempt to kill each of the people responsible for the death of his beloved. Called down to Somerset to protect the life of Fergus O'Brien, who has received a series of floridly threatening letters, Strangeways joins a Christmas house party too late to protect the legendary Irish airman, who is shot dead on schedule. The choice of a Christmas party as the occasion for murder is thoroughly in keeping with the Golden Age convention of domesticity as a reassuring counterweight to the threats of violence, guilt, and mystery. But Blake complicates the polarities of violence and domesticity from the beginning by giving the heroic victim both homely domestic habits and associations with the wild. O'Brien is said to have flown bombing missions wearing carpet slippers (an echo of Auden's preferred footgear), and he spends his last days camped in an army hut on the grounds of Lord Marlinworth's opulent Chatcombe estate. And O'Brien's offhand literary allusiveness, apparently as playful as Strangeways', provides a sinister key to the motive for his death.

Although he is killed before chapter 4, O'Brien—based loosely on T. E. Lawrence (to whom Strangeways had been compared in *A Question of Proof,* and who had greeted Day Lewis' poetry with rapturous enthusiasm)—is clearly the dominant personality in the book, and the mystery of his death turns, as so often in Strangeways' later cases, into an inquest on his identity. Following a telltale clue from Tourneur to a decades-long quest for revenge, Strangeways dramatizes Day Lewis' ambivalence toward the magnetic, reclusive Lawrence, who had died only a year earlier, and his double cult status as the adventurer Lawrence of Arabia and the poet and classicist T. E. Shaw. Strangeways also meets Inspector Blount, the Scots police detective who will reappear in five later novels, and aviatrix Georgia Cavendish, to whom he is married at the beginning of his third case, *There's Trouble Brewing* (1937).

Although *There's Trouble Brewing* follows *Thou Shell of Death* in its characteristic confusion of killers and victims—Strangeways investigates the death of a dog, and subsequently that of his client, the dog's prissy, dominating, owner, both of whom die in a brewery vat—it is not otherwise remarkable. The novel that followed, *The Beast Must Die* (1938), is the most strikingly original of all Blake's detective stories. The story of Frank Cairnes's plan to find and kill the hit-and-run driver who ran down his son Martie takes a shockingly unexpected turn. When the driver, George Rattery, discovers the diary Frank has disguised as notes for one of the detective stories he writes under the pseudonym of Felix Lane, he realizes that Frank intends to kill him, and thwarts his plan in a dramatic confrontation—only to be fatally poisoned later the same day. Did Frank, threatened with exposure in the event of Rattery's death, kill him anyway, or is the murderer one of the other members of the household—all of them, even Rattery's young son, with powerful motives for murder?

More than any of Blake's earlier novels, *The Beast Must Die* plays with ideas of guilt and innocence (Frank Cairnes, even as he plots murder, remains wholly sympathetic; George Rattery, the nominal victim, is despicable) and transforms the whodunit formula (which of a limited number of possible suspects is the murderer?) to the did-he-do-it formula (is the obvious suspect guilty or not?). Reviewers of Blake who complained that he often revealed, or broadly foreshadowed, the identity of his culprits too early—it is only a slight exaggeration to say that if Agatha Christie's distinctive formula is the most unlikely suspect, Blake's is the most likely suspect—were missing the distinctive point of his novels: their status as psychological studies of guilt, actual as well as suspected. Blake's murderers may not always be the most sympathetic characters in his books—though they often are—but they are always the most interesting. Hence, it is no wonder that Strangeways is personally drawn to so many of Blake's murderers. His attachment to them is not only a ruse to make them seem less obviously guilty, but an acknowledgment of the lawgiver's unwilling complicity with the lawbreakers who are supposed to be his opposites. The psychological complexity of these lawbreakers makes them more memorable and the manifestation of their guilt more resonant, since the movement of the story is not so much to separate the guilty from the innocent as to explore the relation between the culprit's individual guilt and the communal guilt it expresses.

By 1939 Blake was widely acknowledged as one of the leading British writers of detective fiction. He had been reviewing detective stories for the *Spectator* since 1936. At the same time, the period of political activism during which Blake published his first four novels—

a period during which Day Lewis published his most overtly propagandistic work, including the poems in *A Time to Dance* (1935) and *Overtures to Death* (1938), the verse drama *Noah and the Waters* (1936), the essay *Revolution in Writing* (1935), and the counter-pacifist broadside *We're Not Going to Do Nothing* (1936)—had ended in 1938 when he moved to Musbury, Devon, far from any local Communist group, and drifted away from active membership in the Party (though he never formally terminated his membership). It was here that Day Lewis, his marriage already strained, began the first of several affairs, this one with Edna ("Billie") Currall, who bore him a son, William, in 1940.

These dramatic changes in Day Lewis' life had no obvious impact on the contemporaneous Strangeways novels. *Malice in Wonderland* (1940; U.S. title, *The Summer Camp Mystery*), like the preceding thriller *The Smiler with the Knife* (1939), is in fact marked by comparative lightness. *Malice in Wonderland* takes Strangeways to an oppressively organized summer camp called Wonderland (a woodlands version of Sudeley Hall) to unmask the so-called Mad Hatter, who is responsible for a spate of criminal mischief that never descends to murder. The following year, however, Blake published a much darker novel, *The Case of the Abominable Snowman* (1941; U.S. title, *The Corpse in the Snowman*), whose country house, like that of *Thou Shell of Death*, provides a Golden Age setting for the final act of a revenge tragedy whose origins lie years in the past. Alternating florid melodrama with scenes of high comedy and brooding suspense, the novel is a revealingly uneven piece of work. It shows once again Blake's fascination not only with deep-buried motives for murder, but with children as threatened innocents (atypically for the Golden Age), motives for murder, commentators on the action, and denizens and victims of the overregimented, Alice-in-Wonderland worlds of boarding school and summer camp.

In 1941 Day Lewis began a long affair with novelist Rosamond Lehmann, to whom his most highly regarded poetic cycle, *Word over All* (1943), is dedicated, and took a job as an editor for the Ministry of Information in order to spend more time in London with her. His association with communism was expunged from the popular mind by his activities over the next six years: his propaganda editing, his poetry—he followed his 1940 *Poems in Wartime* and his translation of Virgil's *Georgics* with *Poems 1943–1947*—and other work (delivering the Clark Lectures at Cambridge in 1946, beginning his long association as a reader at Chatto & Windus the same year). By this time the activist impulse had ebbed from Day Lewis' poetry, leaving predominant the contrary impulse it had obscured—a lyric, elegiac strain that marked Day Lewis' final independence from Auden. Freed from the polemics that had brought him to prominence before the war, Day Lewis emerged as a later, lesser Thomas Hardy whose verse was oriented toward the past rather than the future.

When he returned to the detective novel with *Minute for Murder* (1947), it was obvious that Blake had changed along with Day Lewis. The antic tone of the early novels is gone, along with Georgia Strangeways, who was killed in the Blitz (the author told friends he had grown tired of her). The puzzle is the soberest and most tightly focused of Blake's career: Who used Major Charles Kennington's brief visit to his brother-in-law, director of the Ministry of Morale, to sneak a poison capsule Kennington had taken from a captured German spy into the cup of Nita Prince, the director's personal secretary? Although Blake slyly satirizes his experiences at the Office of Information, the predominant tone is somber, and the action is arranged to reveal, as if by archaeological excavation, the seven suspects' hidden natures. Here as always, Blake prefers to uncover his characters' secrets through dramatic action rather than dialogue, and the story, widely regarded as Blake's masterpiece, builds steadily to a shattering scene in which the two leading suspects, their mutual hatred nakedly displayed, hurl accusations at each other until one of them is finally revealed as the murderer. Yet even here

Strangeways cannot abate his sympathy for the killer, who committed his crime in desperation and continues in a frenzy of grief. It is as if the identification of the culprit by name were only the cue for a deeper identification of his motive and true personality. Since the process of crime and detection simply agitates rather than resolves this personality, the detective is no longer a fairy godmother or a savior of a fallen but redeemable world but a detached observer of creatures who scheme to escape their tangled emotions by killing others and then continue to lacerate themselves until they are caught.

If *Minute for Murder* shows how a detective story can be both extroverted and claustrophobic, Blake's next novel, *Head of a Traveller* (1949), is one of his most tormentedly introverted. The central figure is the distinguished poet Robert Seaton, whose household is destroyed by the unexpected discovery of his vanished brother Oswald's decapitated corpse. The events of the fatal night remain obscure even after Strangeways' final explanation; the real interest of the novel is in its impassioned examination of the costs of poetry—the lengths to which poets and those who love them will go in pursuit of their craft. The story ends ambiguously, with Strangeways unable to decide whether to turn a confession he has received over to the police because he can see no clear correlation between criminal culpability and moral guilt, and because the guilt he has found is so fathomless. His agonized indecision represents a climactic defeat of the detective savior, who now appears not as the lighthearted master of the apt allusion but as the latest victim to be sacrificed to the guilt of a fallen world—and the cult of the poet.

Head of a Traveller clearly marks a crisis in Blake's development, since the endless complicity of the detective's world makes a mockery of his search for truth. Although he continued to write about Strangeways, Blake turned thereafter from the detective novel to periods of silence and to the thriller he had implicitly forsworn in 1942 as too subversive for his socially conservative tastes. The first novel to follow, *The Dreadful Hollow* (1953), is the tale of the staid village of Prior's Umborne, disrupted by a series of vicious poison-pen letters. It is the most cluttered of all Blake's novels, though it expands the narrow social realm of the English village mystery by introducing the financier Sir Archibald Blick as Strangeways' client and the murder victim. The main detective interest of the thriller that followed, *The Whisper in the Gloom* (1954; U.S. title, *Catch and Kill,* 1955), is that it gives Strangeways a new lover, sculptor Clare Massinger (presumably modeled on actress Jill Balcon, daughter of film producer Sir Michael Balcon, and Day Lewis' second wife since 1951, when he divorced Mary and broke off his affair with Rosamond Lehmann). Blake's next novel, *A Tangled Web* (1956; U.S. title, *Death and Daisy Bland,* 1960), is a crime novel in which Strangeways does not appear at all.

Strangeways does not return to form until *End of Chapter* (1957), in which the publishing house of Wenham & Geraldine (a thinly disguised version of Chatto & Windus, of which Day Lewis had become a director in 1954) is beset by acts of literary sabotage when some member of the firm repeatedly restores libelous passages marked for deletion from a retired general's memoirs. The pranks are shortly capped by the murder of a self-important actress who is also writing her memoirs. Since all the possible suspects are writers and editors, it is not surprising that the novel recalls the blasted poet of *Head of a Traveller.* More surprising are its echoes of the sympathetic killer of *Minute for Murder,* the victimized children of *The Case of the Abominable Snowman,* and the danger of the past repeating itself in the present of *The Beast Must Die.* The setting of a publishing firm, which allows so many characters to be both literate and unhealthily intimate, weaves all these subplots together in the elegiac mode characteristic of Blake's later work.

This mode deepens in the crime novel *A Penknife in My Heart* (1958) and the detective novel *The Widow's Cruise* (1959), which takes Strangeways and Clare Massinger on a cruise in the Greek isles along with an ill-sorted crowd of guests that includes a murderer and two victims. Again the mystery borrows motifs from Blake's earlier books, notably the repressed envy of *A Question of Proof* and the confusion of victims and killers, but in place of the energy and wit of those earlier stories, Blake adopts a chilly, detached tone that is lightened neither by the summer sun nor by the prominence of several children aboard the *Menelaos.*

In his next novel Blake exploits this monochromatic tone to produce his last important detective story. *The Worm of Death* (1961) is drenched in Greenwich fog, which contributes both an effectively sinister atmosphere and a figure for the pervasive sadness in the house of Dr. Piers Loudron, the surgeon who goes missing from his home shortly after a dinner with Strangeways and Clare Massinger and is later fished from the Thames. The leading suspects are the doctor's children; this becomes less and less surprising as Strangeways looks back into the family's dark history. Although the novel rises to a melodramatic denouement, with Clare saving Strangeways' life for the third time in their relationship, the epilogue—an excerpt from the doctor's diary, in which he sees his death approaching but, consumed by guilt, does nothing to avoid it—provides an appropriately grim conclusion.

Blake's next novel, *The Deadly Joker* (1963), is his only detective novel not to feature Strangeways; but the traditional formula of the English village mystery is all the more strictly observed for his absence. Another series of malicious practical jokes, this time in Netherplash Cantorum, leads to an audacious public poisoning in front of scores of witnesses before the narrator, amateur detective John Waterson, identifies the deadly joker by a telltale biblical allusion.

Following the publication of the Strangeways thriller *The Sad Variety* (1964) and his year as the Charles Eliot Norton lecturer at Harvard (1964–1965), Blake commemorated his American journey in the final Strangeways novel, *The Morning After Death* (1966). Strangeways settles into Boston's Cabot University only to find his research interrupted by crude jokes, American stereotypes, a fling with a graduate student, and murder. The tone is lighter than that of any of Blake's other postwar detective novels. Although Strangeways is less fairy godmother (as in the earlier novels) or chief elegist (as in the later) than bemused visitor from another world, it is pleasant to imagine that his valedictory appearance closes the circle of his career by speculating what happened to the boys of Sudeley Hall when they went to university.

Hybrids and Thrillers

Despite Blake's insistence that thrillers typically adopt an antiestablishment stance, his own thrillers—three novels featuring Nigel Strangeways as a subsidiary character and three from which he is completely absent—are slow to reach such a point. The series begins instead with several hybrid novels still on the side of the law and gradually moves toward a heightened ambivalence to authority.

The simplest of the series are the first two, *The Smiler with the Knife* and *The Whisper in the Gloom;* both read less like whodunits than like boys' adventure stories. The first pits Strangeways and his wife, Georgia (the novel's main character), against a group of British fascists. It concludes with an ingeniously extended series of woman-on-the-run set pieces (Georgia dresses up as Father Christmas, is arrested for shoplifting, and masquerades as one of the Radiance Girls) that anticipates the Hollywood style of the 1990s. The second, which subordinates Strangeways and Clare Massinger to young Bert Hale and his friends, is reminiscent of Alfred Hitchcock's film *The Man Who Knew Too Much.* In fact, the entire story, which begins when Bert unwittingly becomes privy to a dangerous scrap of information about a sinister group determined to block a vital European treaty, could have been titled *The Boy Who Knew Too Much.*

These novels, despite their aristocratic villains, use establishment heroes—Georgia is only pretending to be estranged from Strangeways, and Bert is eventually embraced by the authorities—to endorse establishment values. Blake returned to this formula in *The Sad Variety* (1964), in which Strangeways and Clare solve the espionage-related kidnapping of a physicist's daughter with the help of the precocious victim herself. In between, however, he published two far more subversive thrillers, both of them among his own favorite books.

A Tangled Web (1956) updates the celebrated Williams case—John Williams, a known burglar, was executed in 1912 for the murder of a police officer, despite the fact that none of the witnesses at the scene could identify him. The novel shows how its witless but charming hero, Hugo Chesterman, comes to be hanged for the murder of a policeman after he is lured into burglary and betrayed by his pathologically jealous friend Jacko Jaques with the unwitting help of Hugo's sweet but even dimmer lover, Daisy Bland. Blake grounds the novel in the pro-establishment moral polarities of the detective story—what crime could be more heinous than the killing of a police officer?—but thoroughly subverts them by divorcing Hugo's legal culpability from Jacko's moral responsibility and irradiating his guilty hero in the light of Daisy's love.

Blake's introductory note to the American edition of his next thriller, *A Penknife in My Heart,* acknowledges what many readers must already have known: the similarity of his plot to that of Patricia Highsmith's *Strangers on a Train* (1950), in which two strangers agree to exchange murders, each killing a relative the other would like to see dead. Blake's partnership is different from Highsmith's because Ned Stowe, though he is deceived by Stuart Hammer, agrees to the plan in advance; but both novels focus on the dynamics of guilt. In discovering the purgatorial sufferings of the wife he has allowed to be murdered, Ned Stowe, the fulcrum of Blake's novel, enters a purgatory of his own, from which there can be only one escape.

A Tangled Web and *A Penknife in My Heart* are Blake's most accomplished thrillers, but anyone interested in Day Lewis' life, and in the role of mystery fiction in his career, will find his final novel, *The Private Wound* (1968), his most provocative. The novel, cast in the form of a detective story without a detective, recalls its hero Dominic Eyre's doomed affair with Harriet Leeson, the bewitching wife of an IRA hero, back in the 1930s. When Leeson is murdered, Dominic is the obvious suspect of both the authorities and her vengeful widower. Blake's punning title indicates not only the connection between sex and death but the peculiarly self-lacerating nature of the novel, which is clearly based on Day Lewis' turbulent 1939 affair with Billie Currall—a resemblance the fictional epilogue to the novel broadly suggests. In the absence of a detective figure, the novel's cathartic revelations can come only from the killer's confession. This echoes the confessional status of the novel within Day Lewis' own work. Like *A Tangled Web* and *A Penknife in My Heart,* and indeed like most of Blake's postwar detective fiction, there is no possibility of a redemptive resolution at the hands of a therapeutic detective; given the decline in this figure's potency, there is only the elegiac expression of both the killer's and Dominic's own painfully unresolved guilt.

The intensely private nature of Blake's last novel contrasts ironically not only with the high public function he had earlier claimed for detective stories but with the venerable status Day Lewis had achieved by now. He had continued his translations of Virgil with the *Aeneid* (1952) and the *Eclogues* (1963). In 1950 he had been named a Commander of the British Empire; from 1951 to 1956 he served as Professor of Poetry at Oxford; in 1961 he had been appointed chairman of the Arts Council of Great Britain's poetry panel; and in 1968, as *The Private Wound* was in press, he was named poet laureate. His tenancy in this high ceremonial post was cut short by the cancer that was diagnosed the same year of his appointment. He died on 22 May 1972.

Selected Bibliography

WORKS OF NICHOLAS BLAKE

MYSTERY AND DETECTIVE NOVELS

A Question of Proof. London: Collins, 1935; New York: Harper, 1935.

Thou Shell of Death. London: Collins, 1936. U.S.: *Shell of Death.* New York: Harper, 1936.

There's Trouble Brewing. London: Collins, 1937; New York: Harper, 1937.

The Beast Must Die. London: Collins, 1938; New York: Harper, 1938.

The Smiler with the Knife. London: Collins, 1939; New York: Harper, 1939.

Malice in Wonderland. London: Collins, 1940. U.S.: *The Summer Camp Mystery* (New York: Harper, 1940); *Malice with Murder* (New York: Pyramid, 1964); and *Murder with Malice* (New York: Carroll & Graf, 1987).

The Case of the Abominable Snowman. London: Collins, 1941. U.S.: *The Corpse in the Snowman.* New York: Harper, 1941.

Minute for Murder. London: Collins, 1947.

Head of a Traveller. London: Collins, 1949; New York: Harper, 1949.

The Dreadful Hollow. London: Collins, 1953; New York: Harper, 1953.

The Whisper in the Gloom. London: Collins, 1954; New York: Harper, 1954. U.S.: *Catch and Kill.* New York: Bestseller, 1955.

A Tangled Web. London: Collins, 1956; New York: Harper, 1956. U.S.: *Death and Daisy Bland.* New York: Dell, 1960.

End of Chapter. London: Collins, 1957; New York: Harper, 1957.

A Penknife in My Heart. London: Collins, 1958.

The Widow's Cruise. London: Collins, 1959; New York: Harper, 1959.

The Worm of Death. London: Collins, 1961; New York: Harper, 1961.

The Deadly Joker. London: Collins, 1963.

The Sad Variety. London: Collins, 1964; New York: Harper, 1964.

The Morning After Death. London: Collins, 1966; New York: Harper, 1966.

The Nicholas Blake Omnibus. London: Collins, 1966. Includes *The Beast Must Die, A Tangled Web,* and *A Penknife in My Heart.*

The Private Wound. London: Collins, 1968; New York: Harper, 1968.

MYSTERY AND DETECTIVE SHORT STORIES

"A Slice of Bad Luck." In *Detection Medley.* Edited by John Rhode. London: Hutchinson & Co., 1939. Abridged ed. published as *Line-Up.* New York: Dodd Mead, 1940.

"The Assassins' Club." *Ellery Queen's Mystery Magazine,* March 1945. Repr. in *Murder for the Millions.* Edited by Frank Owen. New York: Fell, 1946.

"It Fell to Earth." In *Armchair Detective Reader.* Edited by Ernest Dudley. London: Boardman, 1948.

"A Problem in White" ["The Snow Line"]. *The Strand,* February 1949. Repr. as "A Study in White" in *Ellery Queen's Mystery Magazine,* May 1949; and in *The Queen's Awards,* 4th series. Edited by Ellery Queen. Boston: Little, Brown, 1949; London: Gollancz, 1949.

"Mr. Prendergast and the Orange." In *Great Stories of Detection.* Edited by R. C. Bull. London: Barker, 1960.

"Conscience Money." *Ellery Queen's Mystery Magazine,* January 1962.

"Sometimes the Blind." *Saint,* January 1964.

"Long Shot." *Ellery Queen's Mystery Magazine,* February 1964. Repr. in *Twentieth Anniversary Annual.* Edited by Ellery Queen. New York: Random House, 1965.

CRITICAL ESSAYS ON DETECTIVE FICTION

Murder for Pleasure: The Life and Times of the Detective Story. Introduction. London: Davies, 1942. Excerpted as "The Detective Story—Why?" In *The Art of the Mystery Story.* Edited by Howard Haycraft. New York: Simon & Schuster, 1946. Pp. 398–405.

"School of Red Herrings." In *Diversion: Twenty-Two Writers on the Lively Arts.* London: Max Parrish, 1950. Pp. 58–69.

WORKS OF CECIL DAY LEWIS

POETRY

Beechen Vigil and Other Poems. London: Fortune Press, 1925.

Country Comets. London: Hopkinson, 1928.

Transitional Poem. London: Hogarth Press, 1929.

From Feathers to Iron. London: Hogarth Press, 1931.

The Magnetic Mountain. London: Hogarth Press, 1933.

A Time to Dance and Other Poems. London: Hogarth Press, 1935.

Noah and the Waters. London: Hogarth Press, 1936.

Overtures to Death and Other Poems. London: Cape, 1938.

Word over All. London: Cape, 1943.

Poems, 1943–1947. London: Cape, 1948.

OTHER WORKS

Oxford Poetry 1927. Edited with an intro. by Day Lewis and W. H. Auden. Oxford: Blackwell, 1927.

A Hope for Poetry. Oxford: Blackwell, 1934.

Revolution in Writing. London: Hogarth Press, 1935.

We're Not Going to Do Nothing. London: The Left Review, 1936.

TRANSLATIONS

The Georgics of Virgil. London: Cape, 1940.
The Aeneid of Virgil. London: Hogarth Press, 1952.
The Eclogues of Virgil. London: Cape, 1963.

AUTOBIOGRAPHY

The Buried Day. London: Chatto & Windus, 1960.

BIOGRAPHICAL AND CRITICAL STUDIES

Auden, W. H. "The Guilty Vicarage," *Harper's,* May 1948: 406–411. Rpt. in *The Dyer's Hand and Other Essays.* New York: Random House, 1962. Pp. 146–158.

Bargainnier, Earl F. *Twelve Englishmen of Mystery.* Bowling Green, Ohio: Bowling Green University Popular Press, 1984. Pp. 142–168.

Barnes, Melvyn. *Murder in Print: A Guide to Two Centuries of Crime Fiction.* London: Barn Owl Books, 1986. Pp. 60–62.

Barzun, Jacques, and Wendell Hertig Taylor. Preface to *Minute for Murder,* by Nicholas Blake. London: Garland, 1974. Pp. 1–2. Repr. in their *A Book of Prefaces.* New York: Garland, 1976. Pp. 21–22.

———. *A Catalogue of Crime,* rev. and enlarged ed. New York: Harper & Row, 1989. Pp. 54–56.

Binyon, T. J. *"Murder Will Out": The Detective in Fiction.* Oxford: Oxford University Press, 1989. P. 36.

Broberg, Jan. "Conversation with Nicholas Blake." *Mystery Readers' Newsletter* 2, no. 3: 3–4 (February 1969).

Craig, Patricia, and Mary Cadogan. *The Lady Investigates: Women Detectives and Spies in Fiction.* New York: St. Martin's Press, 1981. Pp. 197–201.

Day-Lewis, Sean. *C. Day-Lewis: An English Literary Life.* London: Weidenfeld & Nicolson, 1980.

Dix, Winslow. "The Second Incarnation of C. Day Lewis." *Chronicle of Higher Education,* 19 March 1979: R13–R14.

Gindin, James. "Nicholas Blake." In *Twentieth-Century Crime and Mystery Writers,* 3d ed. Edited by Lesley Henderson. Chicago: St. James Press, 1991.

Hart-Davis, Rupert. Review of *A Question of Proof,* by Nicholas Blake. *Spectator* 154: 539 (29 March 1935).

Jayaswal, Shakuntala. "Nicholas Blake." In *Critical Survey of Mystery and Detective Fiction.* Edited by Frank Magill. Pasadena, Calif.: Salem Press, 1988. Pp. 136–143.

Lundin, Bo. "Poeten och deckaren [Poet and Detective]." *Jury* 1, no. 1: 21–23 (1972).

Miller, Tyrus H. "Cecil Day Lewis." In *British Writers Supplement III.* New York: Scribners, 1996. Pp. 115–132.

Oleksiw, Susan. *A Reader's Guide to the Classic British Mystery.* Boston: G. K. Hall, 1988. Pp. 94–101.

Riddel, J. N. *C. Day Lewis.* New York: Twayne, 1971.

Ross, Helaine. "A Woman's Intuition: Wives and Lovers in British Golden Age Detective Novels." *Clues* 2: 17–25 (spring/summer 1981).

Routley, Erik. *The Puritan Pleasures of the Detective Story: A Personal Monograph.* London: Gollancz, 1972. Pp. 179–180.

Strachey, John. "The Golden Age of English Detection." *Saturday Review of Literature* 19: 12–14 (7 January 1939).

Symons, Julian. *Bloody Murder: A History from the Detective Story to the Crime Novel.* 3d rev. ed. New York: Mysterious Press, 1993. Pp. 9, 131–132.

Lawrence Block
(b. 1938)

CHARLES ARDAI

SINCE 1958, when his first short story was published, Lawrence Block has produced one of the most varied and enduring bodies of work in the field of mystery fiction. Sometimes characterized as an author of "hard-boiled" or "noir" fiction because of his award-winning series of detective novels featuring alcoholic ex-cop Matthew Scudder and his very dark non-series crime novels, Block has also won a considerable following for his comic work, including eight adventure novels featuring agent provocateur Evan Tanner, four ribald capers featuring teenage Casanova-turned-sleuth Chip Harrison, and eight larcenous whodunits featuring self-effacing master burglar Bernie Rhodenbarr. Outside the mystery genre, Block has also experimented with supernatural fiction in *Ariel* (1980), mystical fiction in *Random Walk* (1988), historical military fiction in *Code of Arms* (1981), and erotic fiction in *Ronald Rabbit Is a Dirty Old Man* (1971) (as well as publishing more than one hundred pseudonymous novels). He has published several highly regarded works of nonfiction (particularly in the area of advice and instruction for writers) and numerous short stories.

While almost all of Block's fiction includes a crime element, many of his novels and most of his short stories are not mysteries in the classical sense of having the identification of the perpetrator of a crime as the focus of their plot. Even the Bernie Rhodenbarr novels, all but the first of which end with a traditional gathering of the suspects and unraveling of the book's tangled plot threads, concern themselves more with Bernie's pursuit of his criminal vocation, his narrow escapes and comic predicaments, than with the solving of the murder nominally at the book's core. By the time the final curtain is down, a killer is always unmasked, but until then Block occupies himself with a topic much dearer to his heart: the exploration of the criminal mind.

More than most mystery writers, Block demonstrates and compels sympathy for the criminal, both by presenting rational, well-argued defenses of criminal behavior and by providing convincing and intimate portraits of criminals' perspectives on the world they inhabit. Block's criminals are often sociopaths—even a comic hero like Tanner is more than slightly unhinged, as we will see—but they stake an enduring (and sometimes disturbing) claim to our affection and understanding.

The exceptions to this rule are Block's villains, who, when not terrifying, are contemptible. But not all villains are criminals in Block's universe, and not all criminals are villains. "There's honest and there's honest," one (dishonest) character says to Matt Scudder in the 1977 novel *Time to Murder and Create* (1983 ed., p. 9); and another character, in *The Devil Knows You're Dead* (1993), says of her life as a prostitute, "It's honest work. It may not be legal, but it's honest" (p. 119). In a world that seems by turns arbitrary and malicious, where God is absent and order is regularly subverted, criminality is sometimes the only path to justice; and in a world where law-abiding inhabitants often lead paralyzed, mechanical lives, defying the law can be a necessary element in exercising free will. In this regard, Block's characters have more in common with those of the European existentialists (such as Meursault in Albert Camus's *L'Étranger*) than with those of Arthur Conan Doyle or Agatha Christie.

Like his predecessors—hard-boiled detective novelists Raymond Chandler and Dashiell Hammett on one hand, noir suspense authors James M. Cain and Cornell Woolrich on the other—Block explores a dangerous terrain not just of mean streets and rundown hotels but also of psychological disaffection: rage and alienation, "deep, acidic sorrow" (*A Ticket to the Boneyard* [1990]), and feeling "unutterably alone" (*Out on the Cutting Edge* [1989]). It is a mental landscape more ravaged and scarred than the worst gin mill or back alley in which a Block character might find himself. Though Block conforms his work to the conventions of the mystery genre—his antagonists pose puzzles and his protagonists solve them—he never lets the reader forget that there are greater mysteries in his characters' lives. There are solutions in Block's novels, but no answers. In the face of the unanswerable, each character does what he has to do—perhaps what he cannot but do—one painful (or, in the case of Block's comic work, absurd) day at a time.

Life

Certain locations appear repeatedly in Block's work. One is Cleveland, Ohio, where the author appears never to have lived, although for three years he attended Antioch College near Dayton. (Perhaps because of the associations it has in the popular mind, Block uses Cleveland as a sort of foil to New York City; the former safe but banal, even comically so; the latter, although riddled with crime, the only place most Block characters could imagine living.) Another is Buffalo, New York, where Block was born. The elder of two children, Block was born on 24 June 1938 to Arthur Jerome Block, a lawyer, and Lenore Nathan Block Rosenberg. Block reports that he knew early on he wanted to be a writer: at age fifteen he received an encouraging comment on a high school essay, and before his twentieth birthday he had published his first short story, "You Can't Lose," in the February 1958 issue of *Manhunt* magazine.

Block attended Antioch in 1956 and 1957, and again in 1959, but left before completing a fourth and final year. During this period, Block gained his first work experience in publishing, first in the mailroom at Pines Publications, then as a manuscript reader at the Scott Meredith Literary Agency. Both positions brought him to New York City. In March 1960, Block married Loretta Kallet. His daughters, Amy, Jill, and Alison, were born in 1961, 1963, and 1970, respectively. In 1973, Block divorced his wife; ten years later, he married for the second time, to Lynne Wood.

Block's first mystery novel, *Babe in the Woods* (1960), was published under the name of then recently deceased William Ard and opens with two chapters of a manuscript Ard had left unfinished at his death. Between 1958 and 1960, Block published a dozen short stories in magazines with names like *Guilty Detective Story Magazine* and *Two Fisted Detective Stories Magazine,* as well as a half dozen erotic novels under pseudonyms. Around 1960 Block accelerated his writing of pseudonymous erotica to the rate of more than one book per month. He estimates that between 1960 and 1963 he averaged twenty novels per year. Block describes these books as "inferior work, categorically inferior, and [would] rather not be specifically linked to any of them" (*Contemporary Authors Autobiography Series,* vol. 2, p. 33). Accordingly, none of these books has been reprinted, although some dedicated collectors of Block's work have made a hobby of trying to identify them.

The first mystery novel Block published under his own name, *Mona* (1961; reissued as *Sweet, Slow Death* in 1986), was the first of many paperback originals Block saw published by Fawcett's prestigious Gold Medal imprint. The same year, Block published two other novels under his own name: *Death Pulls a Doublecross* (1961; reissued as *Coward's Kiss* in 1987) and *Markham* (1961; reissued as *You Could Call It Murder* in 1987), a tie-in with a television series of the same name. The next novel to carry Block's name, *The Girl with the Long Green Heart* (1965), was published four years later, after Block's standing order for one sex book per month dried up following a break with his literary agent.

The following year, Block published *The Thief Who Couldn't Sleep* (1966), which he has called "the first book that was uniquely my own" (*Contemporary Authors,* p. 34). What Block means by this is not entirely clear, but one thing is certain: this was the first of his books to become the basis for a series of novels about a main character "with a somewhat elastic approach to legal nicety" (*After Hours,* p. 97), who evolves from book to book. This is the dominant mode in which he has written ever since. The character in this case was a pathologically insomniac Korean War veteran named Evan Tanner who got himself embroiled in international intrigue largely to pass the time. Six more books about Tanner followed over the next four years: *The Canceled Czech* (1966), *Tanner's Twelve Swingers* (1967), *Two for Tanner* (1968), *Tanner's Tiger* (1968), *Here Comes a Hero* (1968), and *Me Tanner, You Jane* (1970). Block revived the series after a twenty-eight year hiatus with a new Tanner adventure, *Tanner on Ice* (1998).

Block's first hardcover publication, *Deadly Honeymoon* (1967), was also the first of his books to be adapted for the movies. (The 1973 film version, *Nightmare Honeymoon,* starred Dack Rambo and Rebecca Smith and was not memorable.) His second hardcover publication was *After the First Death* (1969), a pivotal novel in which he began exploring some of the major themes—including alcoholism—that would be central to the Matt Scudder series. In 1969 he also published *The Specialists* (which he originally planned to turn into a series, but never did) and *Such Men Are Dangerous,* the first of three especially violent crime novels published under the pseudonym Paul Kavanagh. The other two Kavanagh books, *The Triumph of Evil* and *Not Comin' Home to You,* were published in 1971 and 1974, respectively.

In the early seventies Block began writing more ambitious (and, in keeping with the times, more explicit) erotic novels, whose authorship he has since acknowledged. For five of the new books he revived one of his early pseudonyms, Jill Emerson, under which name he had previously written *Warm and Willing* (1964) and *Enough of Sorrow* (1965). Of the new Emerson books—*I Am Curious—Thirty* (1970), *Threesome* (1970), *Sensuous* (1972), *The Trouble with Eden* (1973), and *A Week as Andrea Benstock* (1975)—only *Threesome* was later reprinted, in a collector's edition published in 1997. Block also published *Ronald Rabbit Is a Dirty Old Man* (1971) under his own name and four books—*No Score* (1970), *Chip Harrison Scores Again* (1971), *Make Out with Murder* (1974), and *The Topless Tulip Caper* (1975)—under the pseudonym Chip Harrison. Of all these books, only the last two, in which Chip Harrison teams up with the Nero Wolfe–emulating detective Leo Haig, fall within the mystery genre.

In 1976 Block began the phase of his career for which he is best known, creating the dour and contemplative Matt Scudder, who appeared in thirteen novels in twenty years: *The Sins of the Fathers* (1976), *Time to Murder and Create* (1977), *In the Midst of Death* (1976—an error resulted in the third book in the series being published before the second), *A Stab in the Dark* (1981), *Eight Million Ways to Die* (1982), *When the Sacred Ginmill Closes* (1986), *Out on the Cutting Edge* (1989), *A Ticket to the Boneyard* (1990), *A*

Dance at the Slaughterhouse (1991), *A Walk Among the Tombstones* (1992), *The Devil Knows You're Dead* (1993), *A Long Line of Dead Men* (1994), and *Even the Wicked* (1996). One year after Scudder's debut, the witty and kleptophilic Bernie Rhodenbarr made his first appearance, and although an eleven-year hiatus intervened after the fifth book in the series—in many ways the best, and a hard act to follow—a total of eight books were published in twenty years: *Burglars Can't Be Choosers* (1977), *The Burglar in the Closet* (1978), *The Burglar Who Liked to Quote Kipling* (1979), *The Burglar Who Studied Spinoza* (1980), *The Burglar Who Painted like Mondrian* (1983), *The Burglar Who Traded Ted Williams* (1994), *The Burglar Who Thought He Was Bogart* (1995), and *The Burglar in the Library* (1997).

After 1976 the Scudder and Rhodenbarr books represented the majority of Block's output. For completeness, though, it is worth noting the handful of non-series novels, mostly experimental in nature, that Block published in the same period. *Ariel* tells the story of a young mother whose adopted daughter may or may not have smothered her infant brother in his crib under the influence of a malevolent ghost. *Into the Night* (1987) was the last novel written by Cornell Woolrich before his death in 1968; Block was hired by the Woolrich estate to complete the novel, since the manuscript lacked its opening and closing pages (as well as a handful of other pages throughout). Although Block's contribution totaled only a few dozen pages, there is no question that he left his stamp on the book. *Random Walk* (1988) dates from a period during which Block flirted seriously with New Age philosophy and tells of a group of strangers who pursue mystical enlightenment and healing by abandoning their lives and walking across the United States. Finally, *Hit Man* (1998), Block's only non-series novel in the 1990s, comprises ten novelettes about a lonely assassin, J. P. Keller, desperately trying to reconcile his cold and unfeeling profession with his intensely felt inner life. Keller's story is extremely violent and affecting, the sort of thing that, had Block written it twenty years earlier, might well have been the fourth book to bear the signature "Paul Kavanagh."

In 1983 Lawrence Block received his first award for mystery fiction, a Shamus Award from the Private Eye Writers of America, for *Eight Million Ways to Die.* Since then, he has been a regular nominee for and frequent recipient of awards in the genre, including three more Shamus Awards (for *The Devil Knows You're Dead* in 1994 and the Matt Scudder short stories "By the Dawn's Early Light" in 1985 and "The Merciful Angel of Death" in 1994 [both collected in *Some Days You Get the Bear*]); four Edgar Allan Poe Awards from the Mystery Writers of America (for *A Dance at the Slaughterhouse* in 1992, "By the Dawn's Early Light" in 1985, and the Keller short stories "Answers to Soldier" in 1991 and "Keller's Therapy" in 1994 [both collected in *Hit Man*]); the Nero Wolfe Award in 1980 for *The Burglar Who Liked to Quote Kipling;* two Maltese Falcons for *When the Sacred Ginmill Closes* in 1987 and *A Ticket to the Boneyard* in 1991; and the Marlowe Award for *The Burglar Who Traded Ted Williams* in 1995. In 1994 the Mystery Writers of America bestowed its highest honor on Block, naming him a Grand Master; the equivalent group in France subsequently did the same, awarding Block the "Grand Maître du Roman Noir."

Non-series Novels

In his first fifteen years of writing mystery novels, Block wrote many that were not part of any series, which is to say that the characters in a given book never reappeared in any other book. Since developing a character over the course of multiple novels is one of Block's strengths, his early non-series work lacks some of the richness that makes his later work (and even his contemporaneous work in the Tanner novels) so effective. However, the rest of Block's strengths—such as his lean and witty prose, naturalistic dialogue, compelling plots, and insight into the criminal mind—are all very much in evidence. There are also some compensating advantages that come with writing a non-series novel, which Block does not fail to take advantage of. For instance, there is no obligation to keep the protagonist alive at the end of the book. Significantly, none of these novels is comic. They often show great virtuosity, combining ingenious plot construction (which can be highly entertaining) and deft prose (which is frequently hilarious), but they are all quite serious in the end, a number of them darker, in fact, than even the bleakest of the Scudder novels.

Block's first four non-series titles anticipate much of his later work in a number of ways: all four are narrated in the first person; two are narrated by private detectives and two by professional criminals (in this case, confidence artists); and three of the four books take place partly or largely in New York City. They also have a good deal in common with one another. *Mona* and *The Girl with the Long Green Heart* are both about con men who, betrayed by the women they love, abandon dreams of escaping their criminal lives. *Coward's Kiss* and *You Could Call It Murder* are both about detectives who launch dogged homicide investigations after doing favors for their families or close friends, only to discover that those friends or family members are harboring shameful and deadly secrets. The lifelong fascinations that pervade Block's work get their first airing in these novels. Does a man choose the life he leads or does he lead the only life he can? Is con man Johnny Hayden right when he concludes, in *The Girl with the Long Green Heart,* that "a man must be what he is and do what he is geared to do" (1985 ed., p. 160), or can one change one's fate?

An even more central preoccupation for Block, which turns up in all his novels, is the problem of how to occupy one's time. "Figuring out what to do next is the chief challenge we're given in this life," Block has said (*After Hours,* p. 82). This issue operates both on a philosophical level—what activities give "the illusion of purpose" to a person's life? (p. 111)—and on a practical one. Characters watch a lot of movies in Block's novels; they take a lot of showers, eat a lot of meals, smoke a lot of cigarettes, and (perhaps most notably) drink a lot of alcohol. In short, they kill a lot of time—even in Block's most tightly plotted novels it is common to find passages of aimlessness, of characters not knowing what to do with their time or explicitly doing nothing. One of Block's goals in including such passages is presumably to increase the reader's sense that the stories he tells take place in the real world, since in the real world people do sleep and eat and shower and shave, and don't always know what to do with themselves. However, the consequence of his including them in such abundance is that he goes beyond establishing a realistic universe to establishing one characterized by a sort of existential monotony, a world in which those who seek purpose in their lives beyond the routine are routinely frustrated, if not destroyed.

These issues are given some consideration in the two detective novels (which also raise some questions about moral responsibility of the sort Block would treat more fully in the Scudder books), but they really come into focus in the crime novels. Joe Marlin, the main character in *Mona,* starts out content with his chosen method of getting through the days: he lives by seducing and then defrauding wealthy women. He also thinks of himself as having greater than average freedom because of his comfort operating outside the law and his mobility. (Marlin is the first of many Block wanderers, spontaneously abandoning his current life with just "a hundred bucks plus" in search of "money to spend and a new town to spend it in" [1986 ed., p. 2]. Block favors such rootless travelers—his fascination with the breed culminates in *Random Walk,* a novel entirely devoted to the therapeutic effects of leaving one's life behind and hitting the road on a moment's notice.)

However, when Marlin meets and falls in love with Mona Brassard, and together they decide to kill her gangster husband and get married, Marlin discards both his routine and his freedom. Once Joe has committed the murder, Mona deserts him for another gigolo; but even then Marlin is unable to break free of his own desire. His obsession with Mona is described in terms of addiction: he craves her, even when he comes to hate her.

Marlin is also the first of Block's remorseless killers, a man who, once determined to kill, feels himself "turning into a machine" who thinks "like clocks tick" (p. 64). The clockwork imagery is particularly telling; like Johnny Hayden's image of men being "geared" for a certain life, it suggests a vision of men as automata. How much freedom does Marlin really possess? Is it in his power not to pursue Mona at the end of the book, to avoid driving both of them (figuratively) into the abyss? Block seems to say no.

The two novels that follow *The Girl with the Long Green Heart* bring a new central theme into Block's universe: retribution. In *Deadly Honeymoon,* a newlywed couple, assaulted on their wedding night by a pair of Mob assassins, follow the killers back to New York, track them down, and take revenge. In *The Specialists,* six Vietnam veterans reassemble back home to punish criminals the law cannot touch. The difference, of course, is that David and Jill Wade are avenging a wrong perpetrated directly against them, while Colonel Roger Cross's team acts on behalf of others, a self-appointed guardian of the undefended. In effect, the Specialists opt to play God in a universe in which God would otherwise be silent and unrepresented. (It is no accident that the leader of the team is named "Cross.")

> You had to draw a line through mankind, a wavy line but a line, and on one side you had Good and on the other side you had Evil. There was good and bad in everyone, sure . . . and it was all well and good to know this, but when push came to shove it was just words; there was Good and Evil with no shades of gray and Judgment Day came seven days a week. (1985 ed., p. 13)

Of course, the Specialists also seek their own profit and are responsible for far more bloodshed in the course of the book than the mobsters they attack, so the team's moral position is somewhat tenuous. Still, they represent the first example in Block's work of a way of thinking that would later be central to the Scudder novels: an individual who wants to see justice done may have no choice but to make it happen himself, and doing so may require breaking the law.

After the First Death takes a similar point of view. The book opens with a classic noir scene: Alex Penn awakens from an alcoholic blackout in a Times Square hotel with a woman's savagely slashed body on the floor. Penn, only recently released from prison on a technicality, was jailed for an identical crime: murdering a prostitute during a blackout. As his memory returns he becomes increasingly certain that he didn't do it this time—but who will believe him? It is up to Penn to prove his innocence while on the run.

Apart from the mechanics of the plot (which are unusually clever even for Block), the novel is also notable for its mature treatment of Penn's coming to terms with how his universe operates. When he still thinks he is guilty, he expects the forces of law to punish him: "[I was] expecting to be met at the door by police . . . [the] inevitable moment of capture and surrender" (1984 ed., pp. 14, 37). But his is a lawless universe ("No police awaited me" [p. 14]), and in the absence of law, Penn is lost: twice he says, "I did not know where to go" (p. 15). His reaction is similar to that of the speaker in Robert Browning's poem "Porphyria's Lover," who strangles a woman and then is astonished to discover that "God has not said a word!" Penn comes to realize that he occupies a universe in which order and justice are human constructs: the order and justice one enjoys are the order and justice one makes.

Each individual is also responsible for constructing his or her own life and finding a purpose in it, or else coming to terms with its lack of purpose. Before the murder, Penn speaks of having constructed a daily routine to supply a "counterfeit purpose where none in fact existed. . . . I made myself busy although I had nothing to be busy about" (p. 27). The effort to clear his name suddenly gives Penn a genuine and urgent (if temporary) purpose. By the end of the book he has fallen in love, and that provides him with a new purpose. "We do not know quite where we are going," Penn acknowledges with newfound equilibrium. "But where you are going is less important, I think, than where you are" (p. 183).

This sort of equilibrium does not come easily to everyone, and indeed, the ending of *After the First Death* is atypically optimistic. By contrast, J. P. Keller in *Hit Man* struggles to gain even a small measure of comfort in a life with which he is increasingly uncomfortable. A professional killer since his youth ("I never set out to do this for a living . . . I did it once because someone told me to . . . and before I knew it it was what I did" [p. 103]), he now feels "desperately alone" (p. 51) and troubled that his "profit derives from the misfortune of others" (p. 60). He has a vital fantasy life that expresses itself in dreams and daydreams, and briefly he has companionship (first a beloved dog, then a girlfriend, but both soon leave him); outside of those short-lived relationships, he leads an isolated life in which his primary contact with other people involves killing them. Therapy fails, as do brief stints as a righteous retributor ("What did he think he was, some kind of avenging angel?" [p. 175]) and a government agent. In each case, the failure is due to an unscrupulous or incompetent individual's attempting to exploit or deceive Keller, and Keller emerges appearing ethical by comparison.

In the end, while he is able to come to terms with his need for fantasy—"Other lives make tempting fantasies . . . it was something to tease yourself with while you went on being the person you had no choice but to be" (p. 231)—it is not clear that he makes much progress toward being comfortable with what it is that he has "no choice but to be." He passes up the opportunity to retire and stays, willfully or not, on his path, just as Joe Marlin and Johnny Hayden do, but it is not clear whether Keller's fate will more closely resemble theirs or Alex Penn's.

By comparison, Miles Dorn, the protagonist of *The Triumph of Evil,* has a very clear path to redemption. Like Keller, Dorn is a professional assassin who has begun to question the life he has chosen for himself. ("I wonder how much a man can decide whether or not he wants the sort of life that has been his" [1986 ed., p. 5].) Recruited by a powerful underworld figure to help engineer a fascist coup in the United States, Dorn hesitates only briefly—then, having accepted the assignment, sets about fulfilling it in such a way as to achieve exactly the opposite result. As he acknowledges at the end of the novel, from the moment he was first contacted his "own death was inevitable" (p. 120); the question is whether he can foil the fascists' scheme before dying.

The Triumph of Evil was written in 1971 and is a document of its time. The political, racial, and generational turmoil the country was suffering comes through on every page. This is Block's only overtly political novel, and Dorn's dilemma is very different from Keller's. Yet they crave a similar absolution for their bloody lives, and one gets the impression that in the final moments of his life, Dorn achieves it.

The main characters in the other two books Block published under the pseudonym Paul Kavanagh are also questers after happiness, but they are both men so dangerous that society cannot long contain them. One rejects society; society rejects the other, exacting a fatal price for his antisocial ways.

The first, Paul Kavanagh in *Such Men Are Dangerous* (from which character Block took the pseudonym), is an ex–Green Beret who gets out of the service only to find himself turned down for intelligence work on the grounds that he isn't enough of a "robot" (1985 ed., p. 8) any more—like Keller, he has started to think for himself. Unsure of what to do with his time, Kavanagh lives aimlessly in New York for a while ("the one thing I wanted was something to do, and the one thing I didn't want was something to do" [p.

20]), then flies to a deserted island near Florida, taking nothing with him but a full money belt ("Wherever I went, I wanted to have everything with me. . . . If I couldn't carry it with me or throw it away, I didn't want it" [pp. 24, 32]). There he starts living an Edenic life, complete with a "decalogue" (p. 34) of his own contrivance, a list of ten commandments Kavanagh establishes for simplifying and regulating his life. Given his background, Kavanagh could have been a member of Colonel Cross's team; but rather than taking their approach of trying to fill the role of God in the godless universe of man, Kavanagh narrows his universe to one man, and fills the role of God only for himself.

A serpent intrudes in the person of George Dattner, the federal agent who rejected Paul earlier, now asking him to participate in a theft of nuclear weapons. Although Paul accepts and carries out the mission, when it is over he has an explosive confrontation with Dattner. He is unable, ultimately, to restrain his fury. It is not for being a killer or a traitor to his country that Kavanagh hates Dattner, nor for selling nuclear weapons, nor even for being a disloyal partner; it is for disrupting Kavanagh's pseudo-prelapsarian life and forcing him back into society.

Few characters in Block's fiction are more frightening than the psychotic and ruthless Kavanagh. Yet, in his way, he is also principled, and since all he craves is solitude, he is not a threat to society. For this reason, Kavanagh survives at the end of the book and even finds a kind of happiness back on his island. Kavanagh, like Penn, is able to establish a fragile but satisfying equilibrium: he does it by rejecting humanity and reverting to an almost animal existence, that of a noble savage only somewhat more savage than noble.

Not Comin' Home to You (1974), which fictionalizes the real-life Charles Starkweather/Caryl Fugate murder spree, has a different kind of animal to deal with. Starkweather (here "Jimmie John Hall") is an ignoble savage who has no desire to live in isolation, and in the end the society he disrupts—not just by the murders he commits but by his very nature—has no choice but to kill him.

Hall is not unprincipled or arbitrary, but he operates by one principle only: extreme self-interest. As portrayed by Block, Hall is a drifter (he first appears hitching a ride on the highway) who believes that he is more "real" and more in charge of his destiny than the people around him: "They all knew where they were going. It was all built into the drivers, stamped beneath the skin . . . he didn't know where he was going . . . yet he was something and they were nothing, nothing at all" (1986 ed., pp. 14–15). This can be read simply as a superiority complex, but it can also be viewed in light of Block's general existential concerns. Hall has an existentialist hero's horror of repetition, for instance, of being caught in a rut: at school he liked distance running but not sprinting because in sprinting one "did the same fool thing over and over again" (p. 62); he has contempt for the clerk at a motel in part because the clerk recites the motel's prices "as though he had been saying it twenty times a day for fifteen years" (p. 45). He recoils from any attempt to constrain him and lives as a radically uninhibited actor, a rampaging id.

Hall finds a kindred spirit in Betty Deinhardt, who hates both her parents for their automaton-like arguments ("The two of them took turns reciting familiar lists of the other's failings. It was all the same as always" [p. 50]), despises her father for wasting his life working on his cars ("They would never run properly. They would never be worth anything. They just occupied time that Frank Deinhardt had no better use for" [p. 35]), and dreams about a time when she will escape her stultifying small-town existence and "be alive and real" (p. 35). Until she meets Hall, she is just a dreamer; Hall initiates her in blood (both sexually and through the murder of her family, acts which Block explicitly links) and gives her the chance to join him, to be an individual rather than one of the mass, an actor rather than a spectator.

But Betty is not naturally an actor, and though she responds eagerly to Hall's philosophy, when Hall's influence diminishes, she reverts to type, craving a conventional domestic life and running to surrender when the police finally corner them. Betty's reward for returning to the fold is that she gets to live out her life in prison, while Hall is sent to the gas chamber. It is a reward that Hall—for whom all conventional life is a prison, actual prisons only more visibly so—could not have tolerated. He fights to the end, even with his last breath. His death may leave the world a safer place, but it is also in some important way an emptier place for his absence.

Interestingly, Hall is a great believer in predestination: despite the comment of a tendentious television psychologist who says that the attitude of rampaging youths like Hall is that "Nothing is established. Nothing is predetermined" (p. 48), Hall tells Betty that their future is "all written down somewhere. It's all planned" (p. 144). He thinks, though, that his destiny is to succeed, almost as if he were a reader of Block's other novels, in which nothing is easier than getting away with murder. Hall's misfortune is that he inhabits the one corner of Block's universe in which it is punishment that is inescapable. His destiny is to flare briefly and die—but because he lives with "both feet in the present instead of living in the past and dreaming on the future" (p. 43), all he can see is the brightness of the flare.

Chip Harrison

At the same time that Block was chronicling the doomed lives of psychotics as "Paul Kavanagh," he was also leavening his work with lighter fare as "Chip Harrison." The Chip Harrison novels began as erotic romps with no genre content at all (unless one counts the mere presence of a man with a gun at the start and end of the first book, *No Score*), and though they evolved into full-fledged mystery novels by the midpoint of the series, all four have a very light tone. Even when murder is involved it is just a plot element, not the human tragedy it is in Block's serious detective novels.

No Score and its sequel, *Chip Harrison Scores Again*, purport to be the true story, narrated in the first person, of a roaming, ambitious, and innocently lecherous teenage boy's sexual adventures. In the first book, Chip is a virgin and unhappy with his condition; by the end of the book he is a virgin no longer. In the second book, Chip goes south to escape a New York winter and comes close to settling down as manager of a small-town brothel. Whether any reader believed that the stories were true cannot be known, but for whatever it is worth, Block has said that even the publisher was kept in the dark by his agent about the fact that "Chip Harrison" was a pseudonym.

In the third book, *Make Out with Murder*, Chip answers a newspaper ad and enters the employ of Leo Haig, an eccentric New York City detective who breeds tropical fish and idolizes Nero Wolfe. In that novel and its sequel, *The Topless Tulip Caper*, Chip acts as Haig's Archie Goodwin, questioning each book's suspects, reporting what he has learned, and then rounding everyone up for a closing scene in which the Great Man theatrically reveals the killer's identity. Block has fun with Haig's eccentricities and Chip's continuing embarrassment in sexual situations, and despite the explicit goal being titillation ("I got a call from Joe Elder, who is my editor at Gold Medal . . . 'Not enough sex' " [*The Topless Tulip Caper*, p. 97]), Block manages to make them fair and engaging mysteries as well.

Evan Tanner

When Block began creating series characters, he tended to allot them each some quirks, a set of habits and traits that were to them as playing the violin and taking cocaine were to Sherlock Holmes. Chip Harrison, who is characterized solely by his libido, is the exception. When we meet Bernie Rhodenbarr, he never burglarizes a home without wearing latex gloves with the palms cut out. When we meet Matt Scudder, he tithes one-tenth of any income he receives to whichever church he happens to be nearest when the money is in his pocket. (Late in both series, when Block had grown more comfortable with his characters and less comfortable having them engage in odd bits of business, he had Bernie and Scudder give up their quirks. "After I sobered up I went on tithing for a while," Scudder says in *Out on the Cutting Edge,* "but it no longer felt right and I stopped" [1990 ed., p. 29].)

Evan Tanner, whom we meet first in *The Thief Who Couldn't Sleep,* was Block's first series character and, as such, received the greatest allotment of quirks. As the novel's title suggests, Tanner is unable to sleep; this has been the case ever since a piece of shrapnel destroyed the "sleep center" of his brain during the Korean War. Discharged from the army on a disability pension of $112 per month, Tanner uses his newfound spare time to learn foreign languages and join lost causes around the globe, ranging from the Flat Earth Society to the International Macedonian Revolutionary Organization. He makes ends meet by taking tests and writing papers for college students. After the first book he is a sometime employee of a government agency that has no name, getting assignments from "the Chief," a man whose name he does not know. After the third book his New York City apartment is also home to a little girl named Minna, a direct descendent of Mindaugas, the ancient king of independent Lithuania. And so on.

These quirks, and the novels' fundamentally preposterous nature (two of Tanner's favorite words to describe his adventures are "absurd" and "lunacy"), make it difficult to subject the Tanner books to serious analysis. They are picaresque shaggy-dog tales, written with an enjoyably haphazard quality, as though Block, like Tanner, made the adventures up as he went along.

However, it turns out to be fruitful to consider Tanner in light of Block's common themes. In Block's universe, where finding ways to spend one's time is a man's constant challenge, Tanner is the most cursed of men: instead of having to occupy himself only for part of each day, he has to fill his time without respite. ("I don't sleep," he says, ". . . so I had the special joy of being bored not sixteen hours a day . . . but a full twenty-four" [*The Thief Who Couldn't Sleep,* 1984 ed., p. 3]. In *Here Comes a Hero* he asks, "why waste eight hours a night sleeping when, with proper application, one can waste all twenty-four wide awake?" [p. 28].)

It is no wonder, then, that Tanner succumbs to a sort of madness, not to mention a powerful wanderlust that drives him to every corner of the globe. Robbed of the luxury of dreaming and compelled to occupy himself in some way, Tanner constructs a life for himself that permits him to "live out the fantasies other people use up in dreams" (*Tanner on Ice,* author typescript, p. 13). He starts a revolution and fathers a son in Macedonia, then drives out of Turkey with a carload of antique gold coins. He escapes from prisons and cages, and from being buried alive. He explores darkest Africa and smuggles dissidents out of the Soviet Union. He even gets to experience being cryogenically frozen and revived twenty-five years later.

Fantasies are not the only dreams Tanner gets to live, however. There is a dark side to the Tanner series as well: Block puts Tanner through a series of graphically described waking nightmares, ranging from illnesses, addictions, and riots in which people get torn limb from limb, to bloody massacres incited by none other than Tanner himself, who enthusiastically participates. These nightmare sequences culminate in the horrific scene in *Two for Tanner* when Tanner finds himself deep inside North Vietnam, lost and delirious, being strafed by American fighter planes. Scenes like this remind the reader that the Tanner novels were written in a country at war, during a time of national moral crisis. The Tanner books reflect their era in their violent mood swings, sometimes from slapstick comedy to shocking brutality within a single page. The comedy of the Tanner books is quite different from the light wit of the Bernie

Rhodenbarr books or Chip Harrison's raunchy carousing. It is comedy of the grotesque, a carnival of the absurd that mixes screams of horror in with the laughter.

As the reader's guide through this world that resembles a "painting by Salvador Dali" (*Tanner's Tiger,* p. 105), Tanner is an ambiguous hero. Though he takes lovers of all races, his attitudes are frequently racist and sexist. (Block has some fun at Tanner's expense in *Tanner on Ice,* when Tanner encounters the political correctness of the nineties for the first time.) By the eighth book he has eaten human flesh, tricked a jungle tribe into inhaling cyanide gas, tortured an old Nazi ("I never behaved more inhumanly before or since" [*Here Comes a Hero,* p. 34]), cut off a man's finger to make him disclose information and then killed him when he disclosed it, had sex with a fourteen-year-old girl, and given a passionate speech at a Nazi rally. Tanner has a sense of morality, but on foreign soil it sometimes lies strangely quiescent. It is not just that he blends in wherever he goes (in *Tanner's Twelve Swingers* he observes, "I have a touch of the chameleon about me" [p. 23]); he gets "carried away" (*The Canceled Czech,* 1984 ed., p. 100) and ends up rising to positions of leadership in the groups he joins, no matter how hateful. Like Jimmie John Hall in *Not Comin' Home to You,* Tanner is an actor, in the sense of being one who takes action where others can only support or follow. He is also a charismatic leader, and he sometimes chooses to act in ways and lead others in directions that make the reader cringe.

Why does Tanner do this? Because he has to do something. "Lost causes interest me," he says in *The Thief Who Couldn't Sleep* (1984 ed., p. 8): they are to be admired not because of their aims or chances of success, but simply because they give their adherents a sense of purpose and something to do from day to day. Though in *Two for Tanner* he says, "If you have to die, you might as well go thinking you're doing it for a good reason" (1985 ed., p. 180), in *Tanner's Tiger* he admits that "When one is in a revolutionary mood, any revolution will do" (p. 80). "One has to do idiot things from time to time," he says in *Tanner's Twelve Swingers,* "if only to assure oneself that one is a human being and not a robot" (1985 ed., p. 33). In his desire not to be a robot, Tanner expresses the feelings of many Block characters; but certain of the "idiot things" he is willing to do to demonstrate his free will are ones at which saner men might balk.

Such a character, unchanging over eight novels, might be hard to endure. Tanner is bearable because on one hand, when his adventures are funny they are very funny, and on the other hand, Block allows him to evolve as the series progresses. One of the strongest qualities of the Tanner series, and of Block's other long-running series, is that even at their most absurd they have the flavor of reality about them. Characters from previous books reappear in later books—not just major characters like Minna, but numerous minor characters as well. Characters remember events from book to book. Actions have consequences, and between books time passes: sex in one novel might produce a child in the next. One result is that the separate novels begin to take on the appearance of chapters in a much larger saga. Another is that Tanner is able to reflect on his conduct over time and change. In the fourth book, *Two for Tanner,* he has his first seriously reflective moment: "I wasn't entirely a carefree adventurer any more. I was a man with responsibilities" (1985 ed., p. 133). By the seventh book, *Me Tanner, You Jane,* he is actively considering whether he needs to "mature from youthful fanaticism to mature responsibility" (p. 107) and whether he should "begin setting my house in order and making some sort of logical pattern for my life . . . it was time I grew up" (1986 ed., p. 78).

Incrementally, over time, Tanner does grow up, changing from a heedless fanatic to a heedful one. His conscience is awakened (perhaps the conscience resides in a part of the brain near the sleep center and needed time to heal); and the element of the monstrous in his conduct gradually drops away. One is almost sorry to see it go—there is certainly a place in literature for the remorselessly amoral figure—but insofar as its departure is a sign of the recuperation of a character for whom the reader harbors a great deal of affection, it is welcome and deserved.

Bernie Rhodenbarr

Bernie Rhodenbarr is not a significantly less complex character than Evan Tanner, nor are the Rhodenbarr novels less important in Block's oeuvre—far from it—but they are somewhat less rewarding to scrutinize. The reason for this can be summed up with a single observation: Bernie Rhodenbarr is happy. He has moments of great anxiety, to be sure, such as any of the numerous occasions when someone sticks a gun in his face and demands that he turn over some object he does not then possess; he has moments when he feels undeservedly persecuted, such as the numerous occasions when he finds himself sought by the police for a murder he did not commit; he occasionally gets angry, as when his new landlord raises his rent from $875 per month to $10,500 per month; but overall the man is stable, sane, calm, self-deprecating, charming, pleasant, and happy.

It goes without saying that Bernie is a departure for Block, who might reasonably be said not to specialize in depictions of contentedness. And, to be fair, Bernie's contentedness has grown over the years. In the first two books in which Bernie appeared, he did not yet own Barnegat Books, the used bookstore that is a source of so much pleasure to him, nor had he met Carolyn Kaiser, the lesbian dog-groomer down the street who would become his drinking buddy, best friend, and occasional partner in crime. On the other hand, he was already a well-adjusted fellow, as New Yorkers go, and one who had already found the pursuit in life that gave him satisfaction.

Bernie lives to steal. His delight in breaking into other people's homes when they are not around and lifting their valuables is one of the most convincing depictions of gleeful criminality in the genre. "It's a little like a roller-coaster ride, and a little like sexual triumph . . . that little surge of excitement that's always there when I open a lock," he says in *Burglars Can't Be Choosers* (1983 ed., p. 10). "I know this is all morally reprehensible and there are days when it bothers me, but there's no getting around it," he says in *The Burglar in the Closet.* "My name is Bernie Rhodenbarr and I'm a thief and I love to steal. I just plain love it" (1997 ed., p. 19).

It is worth noting that Block has never chosen to depict a day when Bernie is bothered by the immorality of his actions. Comments like the following, which Bernie makes when stealing rare stamps from a collection, are the closest he has come: "A batch of pieces of colored paper would have changed ownership, and so would a batch of pieces of green paper, and no one on God's earth was going to miss a meal as a result of my night's activities" (*The Burglar Who Painted like Mondrian,* pp. 34–35).

Sounding more like the typical Block hero in the moodier-than-average *The Burglar Who Thought He Was Bogart,* Bernie describes his devotion to crime as follows: "I've tried to give it up and I can't. . . . Because it's who I am and what I do" (p. 4). This description echoes the feelings of fellow criminals like Keller or Joe Marlin or Johnny Hayden, but where those characters view their inability to leave a life of crime as a cause for despair, Bernie views it as a source of pleasure and pride, at worst deserving of a blush. Bernie enjoys what he does; he is very good at it, and he knows it: "[It's] what I do best. . . . It's a gift. Some guys can hit a curveball. Others can crunch numbers. I can open locks" (*The Burglar Who Traded Ted Williams,* p. 34). For him to give up crime and become, for example, a full-time antiquarian bookseller, would be to give up an important part of his identity and a major portion of the joy in his life.

But there is crime, and there is crime. Stealing from the wealthy is one thing; murder is another. Bernie is a fundamentally honest man ("There are different kinds of honest," he says in *Burglars Can't Be Choosers* [1983 ed., p. 153]) and a decent one ("I'm your basic nice guy" [*The Burglar Who Painted like Mondrian,* p. 87]), but somehow he repeatedly stumbles across, and is suspected of committing, homicides. In one case, a dead body is waiting in the bedroom of an apartment whose living room he is burgling; from then on he checks all the rooms in any apartment he enters. Another time, he hides in a closet when the tenant whose home he's burgling returns early with a date; when he gets out, he finds that the tenant has been killed. Much of the fun of the "Burglar" novels lies in watching Block devise a new way to get Bernie first embroiled in a homicide and then cleared of all charges. The deeper in a hole Block buries Bernie in the first half of a book, the harder he has to work to get him out again. Even when the solutions depend on the unlikeliest of coincidences or the most difficult-to-follow relationships among the characters ("everybody knows you can't tell the players without a scorecard" [*The Burglar Who Traded Ted Williams,* pp. 127–128]), the pleasure of watching Block (and Bernie) work is undiminished. In the end, it's never the solution that matters, anyway—it's the fun to be had along the way. As Block preaches in *Random Walk,* the reward is in the journey, not the destination.

One can divide the Rhodenbarr novels into three groups: the first two novels, which precede Bernie's acquiring the bookstore and meeting Carolyn, and in which Bernie is hired to steal ordinary objects (a blackmailer's papers in the first book, an ex-wife's jewelry in the second); the next three, which feature Carolyn and the bookstore, introduce the series' highbrow "celebrity" titles, and have Bernie pursuing objects of interest to collectors (an inscribed Kipling manuscript, a 1913 nickel of which only five were minted, an original Mondrian painting); and the last three, written ten years after the previous group, each of which has a background story against which the foreground mystery plays out. (In *The Burglar Who Traded Ted Williams,* it's Bernie's quest to keep from losing his bookstore when the rent skyrockets. In *The Burglar Who Thought He Was Bogart,* it's Bernie's nightly attendance at a Humphrey Bogart film festival and his adoption of "the Bogart on-screen persona" [p. 25]. In *The Burglar in the Library,* it's Bernie and Carolyn's trip to a snowbound English-style country house out of the pages of an Agatha Christie novel.)

As a character, Bernie neither ages nor changes much, although new elements are added to his life (for example, a cat, Raffles, in the later books). He is thus an even more fantastical creature than Tanner: the literate, clever, good-hearted burglar, leading an idyllic existence in an idealized New York of film festivals and penthouses, where crime periodically intrudes but justice always prevails, and where villains are punished but honest criminals can flourish in peace.

Matt Scudder

The Matt Scudder novels are by far Block's most celebrated work. Even more than the Tanner books, they form a single continuing saga, about a main character whose life changes dramatically over the course of the series. The early books contain some of Block's most clever plotting and puzzles; in the later books he trades genre pyrotechnics for novelistic technique and produces an increasingly impressive chiaroscuro portrait of a battered and damaged man slowly learning to bear the too-often unbearable world in which he lives.

This is not to say that the early books lack characterization or the later books plot; but as Block notes in *After Hours,* "You almost have to choose, if you're going to take this whole business seriously[,] between an intricate puzzle and a high level of reality" (p. 84). Even at their most puzzle-like, the Scudder novels have more depth than the average detective novel and are focused more on the why of a crime than the how and the who. But over time, as the puzzles fade increasingly into the background, other topics emerge as central:

the nature of friendship, the nature of evil, the distinction between crime and villainy. As Scudder's moral ontology develops, cruelty emerges as the greatest sin, followed by disloyalty—mere crime is not even on the list. It is fine to be friends with the dishonest; but one must never be dishonest with one's friends. As Mick Ballou (a killer and Scudder's best friend in the later books) sums it up, "You don't kill for no good reason. You don't make up reasons to give yourself an excuse to shed blood. And you don't . . . lie about it to them you shouldn't lie to" (*Out on the Cutting Edge,* 1990 ed., p. 199).

Like other Block heroes, Scudder spends a good portion of his time trying to figure out not only how to conduct his life from a moral perspective, but also what to do with his time from day to day. It is not until the later novels, when he starts to recover some of his self-esteem, that he comes up with something approaching an answer. Scudder's saga is the story of this rehabilitation, the journey from familiar Block cynic to a man with a sense of his worth and his purpose.

It is possible to divide the twenty years of Scudder's rehabilitation into five periods, a symmetrical structure containing two trilogies on either side of the seventh novel. Like all such analytical structures, this categorization is artificial and may not have been intended by the author, but the novels fall so naturally and usefully into this structure that it is hard to see them in any other way.

The first three books, which were all written in a single year in the seventies and have titles drawn from classical sources (*The Sins of the Fathers, Time to Murder and Create,* and *In the Midst of Death*), introduce us to a ragged antihero so traumatized by an encounter with the arbitrarily hurtful nature of Block's universe that he abandons his wife, his children, his career as a policeman, his home, his town, and his sobriety. The pivotal incident is an accidental homicide that occurs before the first book opens: when Scudder fires on a pair of robbers who are running out of a bar, one of his bullets ricochets and kills a young girl who happens to be passing by. For bringing down the robbers, he receives a commendation, but this just makes matters worse: he feels he can no longer be an agent of law in a world where righteous actions can produce horrible results, and horrible actions can produce commendations. "I did not want to be in a position where I could do wrong things for right reasons," Scudder says (*Time to Murder and Create,* 1983 ed., p. 112).

So Scudder resigns and embarks on several years of drinking bourbon with his coffee, doing favors for friends as an unlicensed P.I., and trying to make sense of a world that suddenly seems "senseless, pointless, hopeless" (*Eight Million Ways to Die,* 1983 ed., p. 213). There is a righteous fury to the early Scudder that goes well with the biblical-sounding titles: he acts as a conscience to the conscienceless and a punishing angel to the unjust, and, to the extent he can, plays God in a world desperately lacking God's attention. (Religious imagery permeates the books. In addition to tithing, Scudder goes to churches to find serenity and lights candles to the memories of people whose deaths he regrets. Interestingly, though, he has "no religion" [*The Sins of the Fathers,* 1982 ed., p. 61] and is undecided on the existence of God.)

Another thing the first three books have in common is that they were written before Block put an end to his own drinking, in 1977. The second three were written after, in the eighties, and perhaps not surprisingly they have Scudder's confrontation with alcoholism as their central theme. In the first book of the trilogy, *A Stab in the Dark,* an alcoholic lover, Jan Keane, sends Scudder to his first Alcoholics Anonymous meeting; the book ends with him fleeing angrily. In the second, *Eight Million Ways to Die,* he starts the book by attending a meeting and ends it by admitting, in tears, that he is an alcoholic. In the third, *When the Sacred Ginmill Closes,* he looks back on his years of drinking from the vantage point of the newly sober.

The next book, *Out on the Cutting Edge,* is the first in which Scudder is sober throughout. (In *When the Sacred Ginmill Closes,* brief scenes of Scudder's sobriety frame an extended flashback to events of ten years earlier—significantly, the year before the events of the first Scudder novel.) In this regard, *Out on the Cutting Edge* is not of a piece with the books that preceded it. Scudder inhabits a new world and occupies himself in new ways. Where previously he took a drink every few pages, now he attends an A.A. meeting every few pages. New major characters appear (in particular, Mick Ballou). Scudder's new environment begins generating his cases: where the earlier novels typically began with a client finding Scudder in a bar, *Out on the Cutting Edge* begins with one client finding Scudder at an A.A. meeting and another finding him over black coffee at a luncheonette. The book offers readers their first glimpse of a new Matt Scudder, one finally on the road to rehabilitation.

At the same time, *Out on the Cutting Edge* is also not of a piece with the three novels that follow it. The third trilogy, written and published around the same time that Thomas Harris' *Silence of the Lambs* became a huge success first as a novel (1988) and then as a film (1991), takes Scudder down a particularly dark path. Already troubled by having to confront the world without the protective filter of alcohol—"Whiskey . . . dimmed the lights and lowered the volume and rounded the corners" (*Eight Million Ways to Die,* p. 28). "It blurred the corners of the mind so that I couldn't see the bad dark things that lurked there" (*Sometimes They Bite,* p. 279)—Scudder now also has to pursue a new type of villain, the serial-killing sexual sadist. All three books (which again share a similarity of title: *A Ticket to the Boneyard, A Dance at the Slaughterhouse,* and *A Walk Among the Tombstones*) pit Scudder against villains who not only kill for pleasure, but dismember, rape, and torture for pleasure as well.

What is most disturbing, though, is not their conduct but Scudder's. In confronting the villains' cruelty and bloodshed, Scudder is forced to face his own taste for violence, and rather than recoiling from it, he embraces it. Now that he no longer drinks, he no longer has a way to keep himself numb to the horrors around and within him:

> I picked up the bottle and held it to the light, looking at the overhead bulb through the amber liquid the way you're supposed to view an eclipse through a piece of smoked glass. That was what whiskey was, I'd sometimes thought. The filter through which you can safely look upon a reality that's otherwise too vivid for the naked eye. (*A Ticket to the Boneyard,* 1991 ed., p. 241)

It is as if exercising restraint over his appetite for alcohol frees an even more unsavory appetite within Scudder, the appetite for blood: "Something was rising within me. . . . I felt it building in my body. . . . I wanted to kill him. I wanted to pound his face into the pavement. The wanting was physical, in my arms, in my legs . . ." (*A Ticket to the Boneyard,* p. 246). This passage ends with Scudder just barely holding back from killing a noxious but innocent man. At the end of the book, he faces the chief villain, a man who is the furthest thing from innocent, and this time he does not hold back. "I just don't want you to be alive anymore," he says to the unconscious villain before killing him. "And I want to be the one who sees to it" (p. 321).

In *A Ticket to the Boneyard,* Scudder at least has self-defense as an excuse: the villain is a vengeful psychopath with a grudge against him. In the second book of the trilogy, he pursues retribution against a husband and wife who admittedly are monstrous—they make pornographic films showing them killing young boys—but who are no threat to Scudder personally. And given the opportunity to kill or not to kill one of them at the end of the book, he chooses to kill: "I just plain wanted them dead. . . . And I just flat out wanted to be the sonofabitch who did it to them" (*A Dance at the Slaughterhouse,* p. 308). When the killing is over, he is not merely pleased with himself, he is elated: "I had never been more awake in my life" (p. 299).

However, by the time of the third book, Scudder has had a chance to reflect on what he wants to make of his life, and he backs away from the abyss. This time it is his client, drug dealer Kenan Khoury, who says of the villains, "I want [them] dead. . . . I want to do it, I want to see them die" (*A Walk Among the Tombstones,* 1993 ed., p. 35). When the time comes, Scudder does not participate:

> "You don't want to be here for it."
> "No."
> " 'Cause you don't approve?"
> "I don't approve or disapprove."
> "But it's not the kind of thing you would ever do?"
> "No," I said, "that's not it at all. Because I *have* done it, I've appointed myself executioner. It's not a role I'd want to make a habit of." (p. 282)

The fourth trilogy depicts Scudder's gradual recovery. As someone says of Keller in *Hit Man,* Scudder begins "turning human" (author typescript, p. 118). He marries again; he acts as a kind of surrogate father to a young protégé he befriended in the third trilogy; he finally applies for a P.I. license; and in *Even the Wicked* he even gives up the hotel room out of which he has conducted his life through all the previous books. The dominant theme of this trilogy is how one confronts mortality and prepares for death; but in Scudder's case, it is a matter of preparing for life and a return to normalcy. As Scudder puts it in *Even the Wicked,* it is a matter of "making amends, forgiving others and forgiving myself, systematically laying the ghosts of my own history" (1997 ed., p. 227).

Yet, as soon as he feels ready to rejoin the human race, Scudder begins to see signs of his own impending mortality. References to Scudder's age appear for the first time, and in abundance. (" 'Do you wear reading glasses, Mr. Scudder? . . . You're of an age to need them.' . . . I was the oldest man in the room by a considerable margin." [*The Devil Knows You're Dead,* pp. 153, 278].) Friends of Scudder's die. Characters in two of the books face terminal illnesses; the third book tells the story of a group of men who meet annually to mark the passage of time and recall those of their number who have died. This trilogy is about the development of a will, in every sense of the word: a will to live in the case of Scudder himself; a living will in the case of Jan Keane, who is dying; and a number of more conventional legacies, as in the case of Scudder's protégé, who "inherits" Scudder's hotel room.

In *A Long Line of Dead Men,* Mick Ballou notes that "man is the only animal who knows he'll die someday. And he's also the only animal who drinks" (p. 209). Perhaps Scudder's mortality is another of the "bad dark things" that he could not see clearly until he was sober. Or perhaps it is just the passage of time that is responsible for calling it to his attention. Either way, Scudder is suddenly conscious of his age, and just as suddenly, time is no longer something to kill, it's something to hoard—"Time's much too scarce to waste," Jan Keane reminds him (*The Devil Knows You're Dead,* p. 288). When at last he has something to live for, he finds himself "Fifty-five years old" and asking himself, ". . . what [have] I done with those years? And what [have] they done to me? And how many [do] I have left?" (*A Long Line of Dead Men,* p. 73). Even Scudder's recovery, then, has a tragic dimension. From a character with such a rich tragic history and an author still at the top of his form, one could expect no less.

Conclusion

Lawrence Block's contribution to the mystery field goes well beyond his considerable skill as a craftsman of plot and dialogue and the consistently high quality (and quantity) of his output. He created a number of the field's most memorable characters, put forth a consistent philosophical worldview and maintained it throughout a remarkably varied body of work, and kept alive a brand of crime fiction—not so much hard-boiled as uncompromising—which otherwise has grown scarce since around 1950.

In his comic work, Block delights the reader; in his serious work he compels compassion and consideration. He is his own anodyne, Bernie Rhodenbarr's New York serving to divert the reader who has had too long a stay in Matt Scudder's.

Most important, his work is fresh and intensely, compulsively readable. This is presumably the reason for its remarkable longevity (his work has the unusual tendency to remain in print) and popularity, and for the long list of awards and award nominations.

Selected Bibliography

WORKS OF LAWRENCE BLOCK

NOVELS

Babe in the Woods. By "William Ard." New York: Monarch, 1960.

Mona. Greenwich, Conn.: Fawcett, 1961. Repr. as *Sweet, Slow Death.* New York: Jove, 1986.

Death Pulls a Doublecross. Greenwich, Conn.: Fawcett, 1961. Repr. as *Coward's Kiss.* Woodstock, Vt.: Foul Play Press, 1987.

Markham: The Case of the Pornographic Photos. New York: Belmont, 1961. Repr. as *You Could Call It Murder.* Woodstock, Vt.: Foul Play Press, 1987. Tie-in to the television series *Markham.*

Warm and Willing. By "Jill Emerson." New York: Midwood, 1964.

The Girl with the Long Green Heart. Greenwich, Conn.: Fawcett, 1965; Woodstock, Vt.: Foul Play Press, 1985.

Enough of Sorrow. By "Jill Emerson." New York: Midwood, 1965.

The Thief Who Couldn't Sleep. Greenwich, Conn.: Fawcett, 1966; New York: Jove, 1984. Book 1 of the Evan Tanner series.

The Canceled Czech. Greenwich, Conn.: Fawcett, 1966; New York: Jove, 1984. Book 2 of the Evan Tanner series.

Tanner's Twelve Swingers. Greenwich, Conn.: Fawcett, 1967; New York: Jove, 1985. Book 3 of the Evan Tanner series.

Deadly Honeymoon. New York: Macmillan, 1967.

Two for Tanner. Greenwich, Conn.: Fawcett, 1968; New York: Jove, 1985. Book 4 of the Evan Tanner series.

Tanner's Tiger. Greenwich, Conn.: Fawcett, 1968. Book 5 of the Evan Tanner series.

Here Comes a Hero. Greenwich, Conn.: Fawcett, 1968. Book 6 of the Evan Tanner series.

The Specialists. Greenwich, Conn.: Fawcett, 1969; Woodstock, Vt.: Foul Play Press, 1985.

After the First Death. New York: Macmillan, 1969; Woodstock, Vt.: Foul Play Press, 1984.

Such Men Are Dangerous. By "Paul Kavanagh." New York: Macmillan, 1969; New York: Jove, 1985.

Me Tanner, You Jane. New York: Macmillan, 1970; New York: Jove, 1986. Book 7 of the Evan Tanner series.

No Score. By "Chip Harrison." Greenwich, Conn.: Fawcett, 1970. Book 1 of the Chip Harrison series.

I Am Curious—Thirty. By "Jill Emerson." New York: Berkley, 1970.

Threesome. By "Jill Emerson," New York: Berkley, 1970.

Ronald Rabbit Is a Dirty Old Man. New York: Bernard Geis Associates, 1971.

Chip Harrison Scores Again. By "Chip Harrison." Greenwich, Conn.: Fawcett, 1971. Book 2 of the Chip Harrison series.

The Triumph of Evil. By "Paul Kavanagh." New York: World Publishing Co., 1971; Woodstock, Vt.: Foul Play Press, 1986.

Sensuous. By "Jill Emerson." New York: Berkley, 1972.

The Trouble with Eden. By "Jill Emerson." New York: Berkley, 1973.

Make Out with Murder. By "Chip Harrison." Greenwich, Conn.: Fawcett, 1974. Book 3 of the Chip Harrison series.

Not Comin' Home to You. By "Paul Kavanagh." New York: Putnam, 1974; Woodstock, Vt.: Foul Play Press, 1986.

The Topless Tulip Caper. By "Chip Harrison." Greenwich, Conn.: Fawcett, 1975. Book 4 of the Chip Harrison series.

A Week as Andrea Benstock. By "Jill Emerson." New York: Berkley, 1975.

The Sins of the Fathers. New York: Dell, 1976; New York: Jove, 1982. Book 1 of the Matt Scudder series.

In the Midst of Death. New York: Dell, 1976. Book 3 of the Matt Scudder series.

Time to Murder and Create. New York: Dell, 1977; New York: Jove, 1983. Book 2 of the Matt Scudder series.

Burglars Can't Be Choosers. New York: Random House, 1977; New York: Pocket Books, 1983. Book 1 of the Bernie Rhodenbarr series.

The Burglar in the Closet. New York: Random House, 1978; New York: Signet, 1997. Book 2 of the Bernie Rhodenbarr series.

The Burglar Who Liked to Quote Kipling. New York: Random House, 1979. Book 3 of the Bernie Rhodenbarr series.

Ariel. New York: Arbor House, 1980.

The Burglar Who Studied Spinoza. New York: Random House, 1980. Book 4 of the Bernie Rhodenbarr series.

A Stab in the Dark. New York: Arbor House, 1981. Book 4 of the Matt Scudder series.

Code of Arms (with Harold King). New York: Richard Marek, 1981.

Eight Million Ways to Die. New York: Arbor House,

1982; New York: Jove, 1983. Book 5 of the Matt Scudder series.

The Burglar Who Painted like Mondrian. New York: Arbor House, 1983. Book 5 of the Bernie Rhodenbarr series.

When the Sacred Ginmill Closes. New York: Arbor House, 1986. Book 6 of the Matt Scudder series.

Into the Night. New York: Mysterious Press, 1987. Completion of an unfinished novel by Cornell Woolrich.

Random Walk. New York: Tor, 1988.

Out on the Cutting Edge. New York: Morrow, 1989; New York: Avon, 1990. Book 7 of the Matt Scudder series.

A Ticket to the Boneyard. New York: Morrow, 1990; New York: Avon, 1991. Book 8 of the Matt Scudder series.

A Dance at the Slaughterhouse. New York: Morrow, 1991. Book 9 of the Matt Scudder series.

A Walk Among the Tombstones. New York: Morrow, 1992; New York: Avon, 1993. Book 10 of the Matt Scudder series.

The Devil Knows You're Dead. New York: Morrow, 1993. Book 11 of the Matt Scudder series.

A Long Line of Dead Men. New York: Morrow, 1994. Book 12 of the Matt Scudder series.

The Burglar Who Traded Ted Williams. New York: Dutton, 1994. Book 6 of the Bernie Rhodenbarr series.

The Burglar Who Thought He Was Bogart. New York: Dutton, 1995. Book 7 of the Bernie Rhodenbarr series.

Even the Wicked. London: Orion, 1996; New York: Dutton, 1997. Book 13 of the Matt Scudder series.

The Burglar in the Library. New York: Dutton, 1997. Book 8 of the Bernie Rhodenbarr series.

Tanner on Ice. New York: Dutton, 1998. Citations in the text refer to author's original typescript. Book 8 of the Evan Tanner series.

Hit Man. New York: Morrow, 1998. Citations in the text refer to author's original typescript.

COLLECTED WORKS

Sometimes They Bite. New York: Arbor House, 1983; New York: Jove, 1984.

A/K/A Chip Harrison. Woodstock, Vt.: Foul Play Press, 1983. Containing *Make Out with Murder* and *The Topless Tulip Caper,* books 3 and 4 of the Chip Harrison series.

Like a Lamb to Slaughter. New York: Arbor House, 1984.

Introducing Chip Harrison. Woodstock, Vt.: Foul Play Press, 1984. Containing *No Score* and *Chip Harrison Scores Again,* books 1 and 2 of the Chip Harrison series.

Some Days You Get the Bear. New York: Morrow, 1993.

Ehrengraf for the Defense. Mission Viejo, Calif.: A.S.A.P., 1994.

UNCOLLECTED SHORT STORIES

"You Can't Lose." *Manhunt,* February 1958.

"A Fire in the Night." *Manhunt,* June 1958.

"The Way to Power." *Trapped Detective Stories,* June 1958.

"The Dope." *Guilty Detective Story Magazine,* July 1958.

"Murder Is My Business." *Off Beat Detective Story Magazine,* September 1958.

"Lie Back and Enjoy It." *Trapped Detective Stories,* October 1958.

"The Bad Night." *Guilty Detective Story Magazine,* November 1958.

"One Night of Death." By "B. L. Lawrence." *Guilty Detective Story Magazine,* November 1958.

"Ride a White Horse." *Manhunt,* December 1958.

"The Burning Fury." *Off Beat Detective Story Magazine,* February 1959.

"Look Death in the Eye." *Saturn Web Detective Stories,* April 1959.

"Bride of Violence." *Two Fisted Detective Stories Magazine,* December 1959.

"I Don't Fool Around." *Trapped Detective Stories,* February 1961.

"Package Deal." *Ed McBain's Mystery Magazine* 3 (1961).

"A Shroud for the Damned." *Keyhole Mystery Magazine,* April 1962.

"Frozen Stiff." *Manhunt,* June 1962.

"The Ehrengraf Affirmation." *Ellery Queen's Mystery Magazine,* March 1997.

"Three in the Corner Pocket." *Hot Blood* 10 (1997).

"Headaches and Bad Dreams." *The Best of the Best.* Edited by Elaine Koster and Joseph Pittman. New York: Signet, 1997.

"In for a Penny." Unpublished, commissioned for reading on BBC Four, 1997.

"How Far It Could Go?" *The Plot Thickens.* Edited by Mary Higgins Clark. New York: Pocket Books, 1997.

"The Burglar Who Smelled Smoke" (with Lynne Wood Block). *Till Death Do Us Part.* Edited by Jill Morgan. New York: Berkley, 1997.

"Looking for David." *Ellery Queen's Mystery Magazine,* February 1998.

NONFICTION

Swiss Shooting Talers and Medals (with Delbert Ray Krause). Racine, Wisc.: Whitman, 1965.

Writing the Novel from Plot to Print. Cincinnati, Ohio: Writer's Digest, 1979.

Real Food Places: A Guide to Restaurants That Serve Fresh, Wholesome Food (with Cheryl Morrison). Emmaus, Pa.: Rodale Press, 1981.

Telling Lies for Fun and Profit. New York: Arbor House, 1981.

Write for Your Life. Fort Myers Beach, Fla.: Lawrence Block, 1985.

Spider, Spin Me a Web. Cincinnati, Ohio: Writer's Digest, 1988.

LAWRENCE BLOCK

BIBLIOGRAPHY

Seels, James T. *Lawrence Block Bibliography, 1958–1993.* Mission Viejo, Calif.: A.S.A.P., 1993.

BIOGRAPHICAL AND CRITICAL STUDIES

Block, Lawrence. "Lawrence Block." In *Contemporary Authors Autobiography Series,* vol. 2. Detroit: Gale, 1989.

———, and Ernie Bulow. *After Hours: Conversations with Lawrence Block.* Albuquerque, N.Mex.: Univ. of New Mexico Press, 1995. Includes a bibliography.

Jorge Luis Borges and the Metaphysical Mystery

(1899–1986)

MICHAEL HOLQUIST

BORGESIAN," LIKE "KAFKAESQUE," has become a standard adjective in English. In both cases, the adjective conjures up a whole world and a range of sensibility associated with that world. In the case of Jorge Luis Borges, the associations his name conjures are those that derive from the tales that give new expression to the ancient tradition of philosophical storytelling. These stories have come to be called metaphysical mysteries because they put the most pressing questions about existence into narrative form. Like philosophers and religious prophets, authors of such tales wonder about the meaning of life, the quirks of personal destiny that call out to be explained, the mysteries of time and space, and the paradoxical nature of the truth. But unlike philosophers or prophets, the authors of metaphysical mysteries pose such questions in the form of stories, rather than in learned prolegomena or dry analects.

Any metaphysical mystery is always a parable insofar as it tells a story about particular characters in a specific setting, but what happens to such characters always has a second meaning above and beyond the specific events in the story. In a story such as Borges' "Death and the Compass," the manifest plot tells the story of a criminal's revenge on a detective who has killed the criminal's brother, but in the interstices of this tale is another. The latent story concerns Jewish mysticism, the nature of time, logic versus numerology, and the possibility of alternative universes.

Borges is not alone in writing such stories in the modern period; Vladimir Nabokov, Alain Robbe-Grillet, Witold Gombrowicz, Julio Cortázar, and others also played a role in creating this distinctively postmodern form. The American author Paul Auster has experimented with the genre of philosophically informed detective fiction (see his *New York Trilogy*, 1987, or *The Locked Room* [1986]). And James Sallis (*Death Will Have Your Eyes* [1997]) has extended the genre into subtle parodies of spy fiction. But it is in such stories as "The Garden of Forking Paths" or "Death and the Compass" that metaphysical mystery finds its most characteristic expression. This article concerns both a man and a genre. Because each is of exceeding complexity, it will perhaps be useful if we begin by looking at each in isolation before considering some of the ways they have become intertwined with each other.

The Genre of Metaphysical Mysteries

"Metaphysical mystery" is a term that covers many different kinds of narrative. In this essay, we shall concentrate on a subset of the larger genre, the metaphysical detective story, especially as it is exemplified in the work of the great Argentinean master, Borges. Borges experimented with other forms of metaphysical mystery, which we shall discuss here, but the quality in them that is most Borgesian is most fully elaborated in certain of the detective stories. In order to isolate the particular strands that are appropriate to this subject, we shall have to separate them from several others that might legitimately claim the same general title of metaphysical mystery.

"Metaphysical" in its normal usage refers to fundamental causes. It derives from the work Aristotle devoted to his meditation on the ultimate bases of reality in a volume that followed his researches in the more material domain of physics. Metaphysics, from this perspective, is the realm of speculation after, or beyond (in Greek, *meta*), physics. Insofar as metaphysics devotes itself to first principles, those things that lie behind material appearances, it must always be coupled with mystery. Conventional physics deals with problems that can be solved, but questions about the existence of God, the meaning of life, or what constitutes justice are never foreclosed. As the great Danish physicist Niels Bohr said, "The answer to a puzzle is an answer, whereas the answer to a mystery is another question."

Metaphysics has always been coupled with the mysterious insofar as it by definition engages the great unknowns. It is to be expected that narratives involving metaphysical themes should be enigmas of one kind or another. The paradoxes of the Greek stoic philosopher Zeno, the great questions at the heart of such tragedies as Sophocles' *Oedipus*, the dialogues between God and the devil and Job and his friends in the book of Job, the Midrash of the Hebrew interpretative tradition, the parables of Jesus, the koans of Zen Buddhism, Islamic wisdom literature, Hassidic tales about the Besht and other holy men, and eighteenth-century *contes philosophiques* have all dramatized the need to tell a story when speculating on final things. Socrates engages in rational disputation until he reaches the limits of what sheer unaided intellect can contain, at which point he invariably provides a myth, such as the great story of Er with which Plato's *Republic* concludes.

At the heart of the relationship between metaphysical tales, or wisdom literature, and detective stories is the central importance of plot. Most dictionaries give four meanings of plot: (1) an area marked off on a surface, usually the ground; (2) a chart, diagram, or map; (3) the plan of action of a play, novel, short story, etc.; or (4) a secret project or scheme, a conspiracy. All these definitions have in common an emphasis on borders, as is obvious in the first three of these definitions. But a conspiracy, too, is a thing set off: it excludes all those not in on the secret. In order to achieve this quality of boundedness, of being marked off, plots work by rules of exclusion; certain things must be left out. What plots leave out, of course, is contingency, the state in which events may occur by chance, accidentally, fortuitously.

This is the irrational against which Aristotle inveighs in the *Poetics,* in his famous definition of plot as that which has a beginning, a middle, and an end. Plots are products of culture, not nature; they are *made* things. A well-constructed plot stands against the messiness of brute nature, of ordinary lived experience, with its confusions, its half-finished sentences, its daily eruptions of the absurd.

In a very real sense, plots differentiate themselves as much by the specific nature of what they exclude as they do by the kind of thing they actually incorporate. Thus, the plot of tragedy requires that all petty or silly actions be avoided: if after Hamlet cries, "To be or not to be," he should belch, the borders of tragedy would be irreparably breached. It is just this type of border incident at the heart of so many ancient forms of wisdom literature. There are strong parallels between ancient forms of wisdom literature and modern detective stories. Each begins with a problem; false answers are provided in the middle, but at the end the true explanation is given. Just as in the classic detective story, there is a crime (or mishap), the wrong conclusion of the police (or rabbi), and finally the true answer provided by a superior investigator, be he Sherlock Holmes or, in the Midrash, Aha.

There are great differences between classic detective stories and wisdom narratives as well. The British novelist E. M. Forster once said that every novel has a clock, by which he meant that just as clocks organize time in our world, so does plot arrange time in the world of a novel. If we accept this way of putting things, it might be added that classic detective stories always contain not one clock, but two. There is a clock for the criminal and a clock for the detective. The action of the story consists in the synchronization of these two clocks. There are also two clocks in wisdom tales of the kind we have in the Midrash, but they tell different kinds of time.

Sherlock Holmes and other classic detectives (outside the subgenre of hard-boiled detective fiction) begin with human problems (who murdered whom); therefore human reason is enough to solve them, and such stories always end with a complete explanation of the riddles with which they began (often in the library of a country house, with the great detective saying, "No doubt you are all wondering why I called you here"). The detective story's rise can be related to the eighteenth-century Italian philosopher Giambattista Vico's principle for historians, *verum factum*—the axiom that says a human mind can always understand events that were determined by other human minds. The fact that the investigator of history is the same as the one who makes history is the condition that makes history possible.

But in the Midrash, and many other forms of metaphysical narrative, the one who would understand is a human being, whereas the one who creates is of a different, higher reality. The problem is a transcendent one; thus, the "answer" cannot be found through mere reason alone, and the "explanation," more often than not is that there is no purely logical explanation. One of the two clocks in the Midrash (as in many other forms of religious parable) tells human time, while the other paradoxically registers the timelessness of a higher sphere, where God dwells. There are two levels of reality; one belongs to God and does not change, and the other belongs to human beings and knows only change. The two levels represented by our immersion in time and God's timelessness represent as well two different levels of reality, the most real being that which is outside time and change.

The kind of "split level" reality of such tales continues to animate new versions of wisdom tales in our own time. Such parable-like structure is obvious in the works of the German writer Franz Kafka. But the close connection between manifest and latent levels of narrative is no less present in narratives necessitated by literally going beyond the conventional time and space of Newtonian physics, such as happens quite deliberately in the "thought experiments" of Albert Einstein in relativity theory or the conundrum of Schrödinger's cat in post-Einsteinian quantum physics.

This tradition is enriched in the nineteenth century by a new strain of narrative, the detective story. This is, of course, the genus from which the species "metaphysical detective story" derives. Detective stories as we now know them both belong to and struggle against the ancient traditions of metaphysical mystery stories. On the one hand, they are clearly centered on solving a problem and structurally resemble such older models as the riddle of the Sphinx in the Oedipus legends. Nevertheless, the emphasis in modern detective stories, even when the hero is a priest, as in G. K. Chesterton's Father Brown tales, is not on the deeper implications of puzzles involving life and death. It is rather the power of the human mind to overcome mystery. It is precisely this ambiguity in the classic tale of ratiocination as we get it in the stories of Sir Arthur Conan Doyle and Agatha

Christie that is exploited by the metaphysical detective story, which returns to the older tradition of meditating on the perplexities of existence.

There are, of course, disputes about the origin of the classic detective story. Some wish to push the date back to Sophocles' *Oedipus Tyrannos* or the story of King Rhampsinitus' treasure-house in Herodotus. Others see seventeenth-century rogue tales (such as Thomas Dekker's *The Belman of London* [1608]) or chapbooks about criminals hanged at Tyburn (such as Elkanah Settle's *The Complete Memoires of the Life of That Notorious Imposter Will Morrell*) as precursors.

We will not enter into these disputes in this essay. Suffice it to say that tales of crime are very old; detective stories, on the other hand, are of relatively recent origin, if for no other reason than that there were no detectives as such before the last century. It was only in the nineteenth century that the institution of the professional investigator was introduced in the police forces of France and England. In any case, to understand the rise of the metaphysical detective story, we shall have to spend a little time on the genre it defines itself against, the classic detective story.

That genre has an unusually distinct origin: we need go back only to the originating role played by Edgar Allan Poe in the history of the modern tale of ratiocination. Poe—probably influenced by the success of the *Mémoires* (1828) of François Eugène Vidocq, a founder of the French Sureté—published his "Murders in the Rue Morgue" in 1841. In one fell swoop, he invented most of the devices that became the hallmark of modern detective stories, including the use of the least likely person theme, the scattering of false clues by the real criminal, the locked room convention, deduction by putting oneself in another's position, the staged ruse to force the criminal's hand, the great detective's fondness for his pipe ("the twofold luxury of meditation and a meerschaum"), the masterly summary at the end of the story, and many more.

Even more important for the subsequent history of the metaphysical detective story, Poe invented the figure of the genius whose sheer powers of mind permit him to solve problems that baffle most of us, but particularly mere mortals of the kind found in most police departments. For it is the ideology the great detective embodies, whether he be Poe's C. Auguste Dupin, Conan Doyle's Sherlock Holmes, or Agatha Christie's Hercule Poirot, that provides the necessary ingredient needed to transform the ancient tradition of metaphysical speculation in narrative form into the postmodernist fable we associate with Borges. That ideology will be familiar to everyone who has ever read a classic detective story. It has several different components, but its chief attribute is faith in the absolute powers of reason. Poirot talks about his "little gray cells," and Holmes, of course, is so completely devoted to thought that even his old friend Dr. Watson feels that he is merely "the whetstone for [Sherlock's] mind."

Any number of devices have been introduced by classic detective story writers to emphasize that it is the sheer intellect of their heroes that solves the crime; there are, for example, blind detectives and detectives who never leave their premises. A brilliant (and very funny) example of this latter tendency is found in Borges' own parody of classic detective fiction that he penned with Adolfo Bioy-Casares (*Six Problems for Don Isidro Parodi* [1942; translation, 1981]), in which the hero solves crimes brought to him by others as he sits a prisoner locked in cell 273 of an Argentinean prison.

The most memorable metaphor for the power of reason in Poe is, of course, Dupin, the great detective of "The Murders in the Rue Morgue" and "The Purloined Letter." It is the detective, the instrument of pure logic, who is able to triumph because he alone in a world of credulous human beings holds to the Scholastic principle of *adequatio rei et intellectus,* the adequation of mind to things—the belief that the mind, given enough time, can understand everything. There are for such transcendent intellects no real mysteries; there is only ignorance and incorrect reasoning.

This celebration of reason, a high point of Enlightenment faith in the efficacy of the human mind to overcome all obstacles, reaches its apogee in nineteenth-century positivism, confident in the achievements of the natural sciences and optimistic about the future of technology. It is not by chance that Arthur Conan Doyle was trained as a medical man or that Sherlock was modeled on one of Doyle's professors at Edinburgh; the relationship between the great detectives of popular fiction and research scientists of the age of faith in the powers of the natural sciences to transform human life has been pointed out many times.

The detective story accurately reflects popular opinion about the power of the natural sciences and the ideology of reason on which the authority of science rested before World War II. But the unquestioned deference paid to science began to erode after Hiroshima. Several events conspired to raise new and disturbing questions about science and reason. The most obvious of these was the stunned reaction to the extraordinary destruction unleashed by atomic weapons. How was one to equate Enlightenment worship of reason with the achievement of the hydrogen bomb? As the horrors of places like the concentration camps at Dachau and Bergen-Belsen became known after the defeat of the Nazis, the German devotion to reason celebrated by Immanuel Kant began to take on another aspect: the world had to deal with the knowledge that a place like Buchenwald could operate in the outskirts of the Weimar of Friedrich von Schiller and Johann von Goethe.

Even eminent scientists began to have worries. Jacques Monod (a Nobel laureate in biology) claimed with some trepidation that "[science] wrote an end to the ancient animist covenant between man and nature, leaving nothing in place of that precious bond but an anxious quest in a frozen universe of solitude." Steven Weinberg, another Nobel Prize winner (in physics), makes the point with even greater clarity:

> The laws of nature are impersonal and free of human values. . . . We didn't want it to come out this way, but it did. . . . The whole system of the visible stars stands revealed as only a small part of the spiral of one of a huge number of galaxies, extending away from us in all directions. *Nowhere do we see human value or human meaning.*

As the English playwright Tom Stoppard has one of his characters say: "There is a straight ladder from the atom to the grain of sand, and the only real mystery in physics is the missing rung. Below it, particle physics; above it, classical physics; but in between, metaphysics."

The Metaphysical Detective Story

Long before scientists began to feel unnerved by their own success, artists had already turned for meaning in the new scientific age to old stories and inner feelings. The widespread feeling that perhaps reason and science had taken us into unknown and disturbing territory is reflected in many ways in literature; in high modernism it can be seen in the new dignity that became attached to myth, in such poets as W. B. Yeats or T. S. Eliot or in novelists such as James Joyce. And, of course, no myth is more powerful than Sigmund Freud's rereading of Oedipus; modernist texts swim in a psychoanalytical sea, where deep, symbolist probes into the unconscious are standard fare.

The metaphysical detective story, however, is an essentially postmodernist phenomenon; both Nabokov and Borges were dismissive of Freud. They represent another route back to the tradition of wisdom literature, the filiation in which the impersonality of the characters is guaranteed by the Aristotelian primacy of the plot over all other constituents in a tale's construction. Classic detective stories, too, emphasize plot over character (except for that of the Great Detective). But the plot they highlight is one that trivializes the great questions of life: classic detective stories exhaust the questions they raise in the solutions they provide. Their impersonality can be read as one of the ways modernism sought to negotiate its confrontation with a cosmos that seemed less and less a home to human beings: classic detective stories parallel the striving for pure form that dominates so much of modernist painting and architecture, the empty landscapes of Giorgio De Chirico, the inhuman geometry of Bauhaus buildings. Borges was always dismissive of surrealism, in particular.

The stage was set for the return of wisdom literature, this time in the hybrid form of the metaphysical detective story, in which plot once again is crafted with infinite ingenuity but with a telos that is completely at odds with that of the classic variant of Doyle and Christie. The end of the Borgesian detective story is not to close the (country house library) doors of inquiry but to open once again the gates of mystery—the library of Babel.

The artificiality and lifelessness of the well-crafted plot that characterizes classic detective stories is what metaphysical detective stories set out to oppose. Metaphysical detective stories are sometimes accused of a cold-blooded intellectualism. The whole purpose of their complexity, however, is to point to the life that has been excluded from telling. Each is an attempt to escape outside the formal requirements of narrative through the form itself. They perform this magic by subverting the clichés that are characteristic of what is arguably the most artificial narrative in modernism, the classic detective story. Robbe-Grillet makes this very clear when he focuses on old-fashioned detective stories in "For a New Novel," his manifesto for a different kind of fiction. He describes how in a classic thriller the evidence mounts up; you get fingerprints, photos, an overheard phrase. All these cry out for an explanation; they seem to exist only as a function of their role in an affair that is beyond them.

Things soon get complicated, however: the investigator is trying to establish a logical and necessary connection between the various clues, but the witnesses change their story, the suspects seem to have airtight alibis, new factors that had been overlooked turn up. The reader has to keep coming back to the recorded evidence: the exact position of a piece of furniture, the shape and frequency of a fingerprint, a word written in a message. The impression grows that nothing else is true. Whether they conceal or reveal a mystery, these elements that defy all systems have only one serious, obvious quality—that of being there.

In the great heyday of classic stories, the 1920s, The Detection Club of London, to which a dozen major authors belonged, required its members to take an oath: "Do you solemnly swear never to conceal a vital clue from the Reader?—Do you promise to observe a seemly moderation in the use of Gangs, Conspiracies, Death Rays, Ghosts, Hypnotism, Trap-doors, Chinamen . . . and utterly and forever to forswear Mysterious Poisons Unknown to Science?" The oath was meant to amuse, of course, but it did make clear certain fundamental principles, the most important of which was "never to conceal a vital clue from the Reader." This rule is significant because it reveals the underlying importance of puzzle and plot in the genre. You could no more leave out a clue than you could leave out a word in the design of a crossword puzzle. The reader plays at detective stories of the classic variety, interested mostly in putting together all the clues, less to solve the crime than to reconstruct the adventure of its plot, point by point. When readers come to the narrative end of the story, they have exhausted its teleological end as well.

Metaphysical detective stories, by contrast, keep separate the two levels of chronology and meaning that make up their antiplots. No matter how closely you attend the details and the sequencing of events in Robbe-Grillet's *Voyeur* (1958), it will never provide the key to the questions at the novel's heart, which is not who did it, but *why* he did it, a question that opens up the real mystery of evil that so preoccupied Fyodor Dostoyevsky's great detective in *Crime and Punishment* (1866), Porfiry Petrovich.

In the modern period there is, of course, a great flowering of hard-boiled detective fiction, characterized precisely by a moral universe in which the world is chaotic and dark.

Such writers as Raymond Chandler were reacting in their own way against the tidy order of the world presumed by those who wrote neat plots for detective stories in the 1920s. But that world has broken down in a different way for the great masters of the metaphysical detective story, and this is reflected in the formal play that always points to more questions, even when the crime is apparently "solved." This formal inversion is dramatized in different ways by different writers in the genre. In Cortázar's "Continuity of Parks," a man reading a mystery discovers too late that he is the murder's victim; in Gombrowicz's "Premeditated Crime," a son chokes the corpse of his dead father so as to provide the clues needed to solve the crime; in Robbe-Grillet's *The Erasers* (1956), a detective knows he must be at a certain place at a certain time in order to catch the criminal, but when he shows up it is he who commits the crime; and in Borges' "Death and the Compass," it is the detective who is the victim of the very crime he solves.

All these twists point to the affinity of metaphysical detective stories with the structure of parables, in which there are always two levels or, to return to our metaphor from E. M. Forster, two clocks—the literal (a man goes on a journey) and the figurative (the journey is his progress through life), as in John Bunyan's *Pilgrim's Progress* (1678). Corresponding to the parable's literal level is the detective story in metaphysical detective stories—the formulaic plot. The figurative level is present in the subversion of classic plot. Out of the friction between the two, whole new worlds of meaning can arise, and the most profound philosophical questions take on new urgency. Of all the postmodernists who turned to these possibilities, none did so with greater mastery than Borges.

The Man Borges

Jorge Luis Borges was born in Buenos Aires on 24 August 1899 to Jorge Guillermo Borges and Leonor Acevedo. His family was extraordinary on both his mother's and his father's sides; it was a family that might well have been invented to produce just the sort of writer Borges became. His mother and father both descended from families that had played an important role in South American history, and the house in which Borges grew up was filled with swords and musty uniforms commemorating the exploits of his forebearers. His paternal grandmother was a formidable Englishwoman, Frances Haslam, who had a powerful influence not only on Borges' father but on Borges himself. He was raised in a bilingual atmosphere in which English was as natural as Spanish. His first education was presided over by his English grandmother and an English governess, Miss Tink.

Borges' father, a lawyer and educator with wide political and philosophical sympathies, carefully explored the works of the Irish bishop and philosopher George Berkeley with his son and demonstrated the paradoxes of Zeno on a chessboard, thus gently directing Borges' first steps in his encounter with metaphysics. Living in a distant suburb of Buenos Aires, surrounded mostly by working-class Italians, many of whom spoke Spanish with difficulty, Borges spent much of his time with his beloved family behind the walls of their modest but well-appointed house. The two most important parts for Borges were the patio garden and his father's huge library. The garden with its palm tree was quintessentially Spanish; it was there he played extravagantly imaginative games with his younger sister, Norah. The garden was a first experiment with labyrinths, a key element in the later fiction, as are, of course, libraries. His father's library was English, consisting of thousands of volumes, including all the great English and American classics. As a very old man, Borges said, "If I were asked to name the chief event in my life, I should say my father's library. In fact, I sometimes think I have never strayed outside that library."

He fell in love with *Chamber's Encyclopedia* and the *Encyclopaedia Britannica,* the incongruity of whose alphabetically organized topics came to play a central role in such tales as "Tlön, Uqbar, Orbis Tertius." Borges read *A Thousand and One Nights* in the great translation by Sir Richard Burton (1885–1886) and most of the English (and, more surprisingly, American) classics. A fact that was to have profound influence on his literary career is that he also read many of the Spanish classics in English as well: "When later I read *Don Quixote* in the original, it sounded like a bad translation to me." This emphasis on English culture was rare in Argentina at the time; it was much more common to cultivate the French language, as did Borges' friend Victoria Ocampo.

Borges' early and lifelong immersion in Anglophone literature was to have two consequences for his literary output. The first was generic. Growing up on a diet of Poe, Robert Louis Stevenson, and Chesterton, he developed a taste for the detective story that led to his producing an anthology of tales in Spanish translation (1951) by such figures as Agatha Christie and Ellery Queen. And, of course, it was his deep knowledge of the classic variant that led Borges to experiment with metaphysical detective stories. A second effect of his Anglophone childhood is evident in his work: Spanish-speaking critics frequently remark on the unusual syntax of Borges' texts in that language, a trait they associate more with English prose. Borges himself was dissatisfied with much of his own production, feeling that it was too "lyrical" and "literary"; he renounced baroque experimentation in favor of a more austere, down-to-earth style he felt was more in the spirit of the Anglo-Saxons than the Latin peoples, a point he makes explicit in his preface to the collection of his stories he translated with Norman Thomas di Giovanni (*The Aleph* [1949; translation, 1970]).

Borges' father suffered from failing eyesight, a congenital condition that ultimately blinded not only him but his eminent son as well. Borges' father decided in 1914 to try doctors in Europe, and so the family moved to Geneva. Soon after their arrival, war broke out, and they decided to settle in Geneva, where Borges and his sister attended school. Through friends at the College Calvin, Borges discovered yet another world, the universe of the French Symbolist poets and of the German philosophers, especially Arthur Schopenhauer, whom he valued above all others. In 1919, the family moved again, this time to Lugano, and then on to Spain, where they moved about a great deal before more or less settling in Madrid. It is during these years that Borges first began to write seriously (although his version of a fairy tale by Oscar Wilde, which he had translated at the age of six, had already been published). Falling under the influence of the Andalusian poet Rafael Cansinos-Asséns, he joined a school called the "ultraists" in 1920. It was a period of unbridled youthful enthusiasm, and Borges in his later years came to despise the work he did during this period. Before leaving Spain to return to Buenos Aires in 1921, Borges burned two volumes of poems and essays he had written during this time of (for him) uncharacteristic excess.

Back in Buenos Aires, Borges plunged into various literary circles, finally publishing his first volume of poems in 1923, *Fervor de Buenos Aires.* The poems received a small, but enthusiastic, reception, even in Spain. Thus began a period of frantic activity that extended until roughly 1933. During these years, Borges founded or edited several literary magazines and published several new books of poetry. In 1929 one of these volumes won him a prize with which he immediately went out and bought a new edition of the *Encyclopaedia Britannica.* He dabbled in liberal politics, but finally left off when he became disgusted with this arena. He became a close friend of Victoria Ocampo, a remarkable woman who edited a journal called *Sur,* in which she published his works and further added to his reputation (one of Borges' greatest metaphysical detective stories, "The Garden of Forking Paths," is dedicated to Ocampo).

But as the 1930s began, Borges entered a dark period in which he again dismissed much of his most recent work, became even more disillusioned with Argentinean politics, and grew increasingly blind. He began to write about the cinema during these years and also published a number of sketches and stories devoted to populist subjects (sometimes under a pseudonym). In 1935 he published "The Approach to Al-Mu'tasim," considered by many to be the first work that is Borgesian in the sense that word now has. It is a review of a nonexistent book, an exercise in whimsy and deep learning that does indeed begin to suggest the fantastic universe Borges was about to create.

These years were unhappy as well because Borges was forced to work in a branch of the city library, surrounded by philistines who were unaware that among the books they were cataloging were some by their compatriot Borges. He was literally immured in the narrow but endless world of the library for nine years. During these years he made translations of important Anglophone writers, such as Virginia Woolf and William Faulkner.

In 1938 his father died, a great blow because the two had been unusually close. The tragedy was compounded in the same year when a minor accident resulted in septicemia, which brought Borges to the brink of death (as life sought to imitate the art of Leo Tolstoy's "Death of Ivan Ilyich" [1886]). After his recovery, in a kind of creative rebirth, Borges felt free to embark on a new literary path. Up until this point he had acquired a respectable reputation as a poet, translator, and essayist. Had he died in 1939, he would no doubt be remembered as one of the more important Argentinean poets and men of letters of his generation. He did not die and began to experiment with the short story form that was to bring him worldwide fame.

The first of the tales that came to define Borges' unique voice is "Pierre Menard, Author of *Don Quixote.*" As in another experiment of this period, "The Approach to Al-Mu'tasim," the skeleton of the story is less a tale as such than it is a scholarly commentary or review of another work: Menard, a French scholar and minor man of letters, aspires to write the novel *Don Quixote.* He wishes not to reproduce Cervantes' novel, but to produce it; what is more, he seeks to do so not by becoming Cervantes (studying seventeenth-century Spanish language and history) but by remaining Pierre Menard, a French citizen of the twentieth century. The conceit permits Borges an exquisite comparison between two identical passages: one from Cervantes' novel and the other from that of Pierre Menard. Menard's version is found to be superior (even though it is made up of the very same words as found in Cervantes' work) because in the twentieth century the meaning of the passage has taken on new layers of complexity. Cervantes talks about "truth, whose mother is history." Borges says of this:

> Written in the seventeenth century, written by the "ingenious layman" Cervantes, this enumeration is a mere rhetorical eulogy of history. Menard, on the other hand writes:
>
> ". . . truth, whose mother is history. . . ."
>
> History, *mother* of truth; the idea is astounding. Menard, a contemporary of William James, does not define history as an investigation of reality, but as its origin. . . . The final clauses . . . are shamelessly pragmatic. (*Ficciones,* p. 53)

Some of the key elements of Borges' metaphysical detective stories are already present in this story. Although Menard is not officially a detective, his relationship to Cervantes is that of, say, Lönnrot's toward Red Scharlach in "Death and the Compass," insofar as in each case the protagonist seeks to will himself into the mind and being of another. Menard is a literary scholar who acts like one of Borges' detectives; Lönnrot is a detective who acts like one of Borges' literary scholars. Menard hunts Cervantes by becoming him. In addition, the Menard tale has the typically Borgesian deadpan, scholarly style that describes the most outrageous events; a concentration on ideas for which the narrative form of the story is merely a vehicle; and an anxiety about belatedness that reflects itself in a preoccupation with libraries and mirrors. Neither of these plays a prominent role in "Pierre Menard" as such, but what is the confrontation of identical texts if not a mirroring? And is it not one of the foundational texts of Spanish literariness, of the Spanish library, that serves as the vehicle for what is—quite literally—speculation? And does this repetition of a classic text from the past not bespeak a certain uneasiness about the ability to say something new in the twentieth century? As the scholarly commentator of "Menard" says,

> There is no intellectual exercise which is not ultimately useless. A philosophical doctrine is in the beginning a seemingly true description of the universe; as the years pass it becomes a mere chapter—if not a paragraph or a noun—in the history of philosophy. (p. 53)

Borges explores metaphysical issues of time and reality in other stories that came tumbling from his pen. In "Tlön, Uqbar, Orbis Tertius," he invents a whole other universe based on an imaginary encyclopedia, but once again, the narrative turns around a set of recurring metaphysical preoccupations, announced in this story as a mot concerning belatedness again: "Mirrors and copulation are abominable, since they both multiply the numbers of man" (*Ficciones,* p. 17). At the heart of the story is a suspicion that reproduction in various kinds of systems devised to mirror a world outside the mind may have little claim to validity; they may, indeed, be no more than the word he used to give a title to the collection in which this story appeared: fictions. Captivated by the orderliness of the system of Tlön, "humanity forgets and goes on forgetting that it is the discipline of chess players, not of angels. . . . Now, in all memories, a fictitious past occupies the place of any other" (p. 34). The narrator has earlier said, "Tlön may be a labyrinth, but it is a labyrinth destined to be deciphered by men" (p. 34).

In several stories of this same period, the trope of a maze that needs to be disentangled is translated into a series of detective stories, in which ideas of labyrinthine complexity are turned into problems of deduction. At the simpler level, together with Adolfo Bioy-Casares, Borges published a number of short works with tongue in cheek: the anthology of stories published as *Six Problems for Don Isidro Parodi* had as its pseudonymous author H. Bustos Domecq. The sly humor of this volume can be gathered from the biographical sketch of Domecq (provided by "the schoolteacher Miss Adelma Badoglio") in its appendix:

> In 1907 [when Domecq was ten years old] the newspaper columns of Rosario accepted the early writings of this modest friend of the Muses without suspecting his age. . . . [I]n 1915 he published *Citizen!,* a work of sustained imagination marred, unfortunately, by certain Gallicisms which may be blamed on the author's youth and the shortsightedness of the times.

The tales are full of obscure jokes; the names of all the characters are arcane homages, such as the Golyadkin, who harks back to Dostoyevsky's minor fiction. But the chief characteristic feature of the metaphysical detective story is present throughout: each is a parody of the classic detective story insofar as each inverts syllogistic logic and the superhuman reason of the Great Detective's solution. The stories in *Six Problems* contain plots, for instance, in which a man seeks Parodi's help in solving a murder he himself has committed or in which a murdered man plots his own self-sacrifice.

But it is in two stories from this period published under his own name that the apogee of the metaphysical detective story genre is reached. "Death and the Compass" is a subtle variation on the two-clock structure of most classic detective stories. The detective is a compendium of all the great heroes of ratiocination. He has their contempt for the uninspired procedures of the police: when the commissioner provides a possible scenario for a crime, the detective says dismissively, such a scenario is "possible, but not interesting." He has a taste for the recondite and prefers to interpret the crime as part of an elaborate scheme based on the tetragrammaton, the four-lettered sacred name of the Hebrew god, and he delves into cabalistic mysticism instead of going through more conventional police work. His name is Lönnrot, after all, the name of the philologist/poet Elias Lönnrot, who created the great Finnish national epic Kalevala by piecing together fragments long scattered. He elaborates a complex theory based on the four letters of God's name, on a recurring pattern of four-sided lozenges, and the four points of the compass. Like a great scientist, he believes the truth of his deduction to be so profound that he can make predictions on its basis. He figures out when and where the next murder will occur, but when he shows up to prevent the crime, he is taken prisoner by Red Scharlach, a great criminal, who reveals that Lönnrot's scheme is based on a misreading of false clues left by Scharlach, who thus has succeeded in luring his enemy into a trap. Lönnrot is murdered, but not before the criminal says, "The next time I kill you, I promise you the labyrinth made of the single straight line which is invisible and everlasting" (*Ficciones,* p. 141). In other words, the linear logic that is the dream of Dupin and Holmes is precisely a labyrinth that will lead to their destruction. This conclusion not only provides an interesting twist to the narrative structure of the conventional detective story, it also opens up a number of metaphysical questions: It raises the question of whether each human has a particular destiny, or whether there are alternative paths by which he or she may play out his or her fate. Shall I live only once, or may I expect another life in some other time and place? These are questions that have been at the heart of wisdom literature, including the Cabala, which plays so important a role in the tale, since ancient times.

The second great exemplar of the metaphysical detective story from this period is "The Garden of Forking Paths." Once again, the story has (at least) two plotlines: the forking paths of the tale itself. The first plot, corresponding to linear time, may be thought of as a frame tale. It is a well-made spy story with a surprise ending as clever and unexpected as any in the classic canon: a Chinese agent during World War I reveals in the tale's last lines that he has succeeded in disclosing the location of a British artillery park to his superior in Berlin by murdering a man whose surname, Albert, is that of the city where the English have concealed their cannon. This story is presented as a gloss on Liddell Hart's *History of World War I,* and the temporal progression of its plot is appropriately "historical"—that is, it has a well-marked beginning (the spy's discovery that he has been unmasked), middle (the encounter with Stephen Albert), and end (the spy's capture, with the revelation of his motive for killing the sinologist, Albert).

But his story is merely a frame for another tale concerning a work on labyrinths written by an ancestor of the Chinese spy. This work causes Albert to ask the question, "How could a book be infinite?" It is also the question at the heart of *A Thousand and One Nights,* Borges' favorite book in his father's library and to which Albert alludes in this tale. Borges suggests a dizzying possibility in this very short story—not only in connection with the Chinese labyrinth but also in the play of repetitions within his own tale, such as the parallels between the Chinese spy working for the Germans and the Irish counterspy working for the British, the repeated use of the phrase, "happy soldier," and so on. Without the well-made plot of the frame tale, however, this speculation about plotlessness would not have signified; even endlessness, if it is to be understood, must be confined.

These stories brought Borges new fame and popularity. He left the branch library where he had been productive, but unhappy, and began a career as a lecturer that continued until his death. The regime of Juan Perón gave him a great deal of trouble in the 1950s (and his family as well—his sister was briefly imprisoned with prostitutes, and an attempt was made to bomb the house where Borges and his mother were living). In 1955, the Perón dictatorship fell, and Borges was appointed director of the National Library, noting: "I speak of God's splendid irony in granting me at once

800,000 books and darkness" (alluding to his now almost complete blindness).

In 1961 he shared the Prix Formentor with Samuel Beckett, the beginning of his vast fame abroad. From then until his death he began a series of visits to countries all around the world. On 4 August 1967 he married his old friend, the recently widowed Elsa Astete Millán, a relationship that lasted for less than three years. After the divorce, Borges moved back in with his mother. When the two traveled abroad, they were often taken for brother and sister or man and wife. In 1967 another important relationship developed; Borges began a period of intense collaboration with Norman Thomas di Giovanni. Although Borges ended the arrangement rather abruptly in 1972, the translations of Borges' works that resulted from this partnership brought him new fame in the English-speaking world. He turned the talents he had developed as a lecturer in Argentina into the fashioning of an extraordinary stage presence; witty, immensely erudite, elegant, and effortlessly flooding the auditorium with bon mot after bon mot, he was in great demand everywhere.

In 1970 he published his third collection of tales, *Doctor Brodie's Report* (translation, 1972), the eponymous story having obvious connections with the English satirist Jonathan Swift and Kafka, for all its originality. In 1973, Juan Perón was again elected president, and Borges resigned as director of the National Library. Despite his opposition to Perón (and later to the junta—he was particularly disgusted by the absurd Falklands War), many abroad felt his support of liberal causes was too ambiguous. This prejudice may help to explain why he was never awarded the Nobel Prize.

He began writing poetry again, and after a relatively small output in the 1960s, continued to pour out new volumes of verse as well as stories and essays. In 1975 he published another collection of stories, *The Book of Sand* (translation, 1975), and another volume of poetry, his seventh. In the same year, his mother died, a deep sorrow because she had been his constant companion and even at times his collaborator during the seventy-five years Borges spent with her. He began traveling even more feverishly. Among other places, he visited Japan, which had a special significance for several reasons, not the least being that his new secretary and constant companion, a former student named María Kodama, was an Argentinean of Japanese background. Together, they traveled around the world, producing in 1984 an account of their journey, with text by Borges and photographs by María Kodama. These were happy years for Borges, despite the fact that he was suffering from cancer of the liver. He was still traveling at the end. He died on 14 June 1986 in the city to which he had traveled on his first journey outside Argentina, Geneva.

Conclusion

Borges is a quintessential figure of his age. In his work the postmodernist plot against ideas about plot that had been abroad since the time of Aristotle is most deeply realized. As modernism waned, convictions about the world that had supported definitions of plot as having a well marked beginning, middle, and end became more tenuous. In the work of experimental writers on the Continent and in the United States, a number of self-conscious attempts were made to break out of linearity. In France, Marc Saporta's novel *Composition No. 1: Roman* (1962) came as a carton of unbound, unnumbered pages that the "reader" was supposed to shuffle from time to time as one would a deck of cards. In this attempt to mimic the I Ching, Saporta points to the factor that Aristotle and his disciples who wrote detective stories in the twentieth century were most anxious to suppress, the element of chance. In the United States, John Barth, another postmodernist heavily influenced by *A Thousand and One Nights,* experimented in the frame tale for his collection *Lost in the Funhouse* (1968) with a one-page story that required the reader to cut out and fold the sentence: "Once upon a time there was a story that began." What resulted was a Möbius strip, a topological figure that has two surfaces, but that also has the double-bowed appearance of the mathematical symbol for infinity. In another story, "Dunyaziad," Barth retells not "the story of Scheherezade, but the story of her stories." Once again, the emphasis is on escape from the closed universe of the linear plot; Barth "concludes" the tale by admitting, "I can't conclude it."

Borges clearly is obsessed by many of the same demons that drive Saporta and Barth (and Nabokov, Gombrowicz, Cortázar, and Robbe-Grillet, to name only a small number of other postmodernists). But his way of dealing with the issues is uniquely his. He returns to the ancient traditions of the wisdom tale and the parable, but he does so by stitching them into what appears, on the surface, to be a detective story. What results is not a typical postmodernist experiment. There are tricks in Borges, but he is not cute. His tales are a profound meditation on the very questions that have always been the subject matter of the great questions.

At the end of "The Garden of Forking Paths," the Chinese spy and the British sinologist are discussing the fine points of time and chance, the forking paths of a book written by the spy's ancestor, and forking paths in the labyrinth of history. The spy thanks Stephen Albert for unlocking the secret of the old manuscript, saying "[in all the times of the labyrinth] I deeply appreciate and am grateful to you for the restoration of Ts'ui Pên's garden." The scholar replies, "Not in *all*. . . . Time is forever dividing itself toward innumerable futures and in one of them I am your enemy" (*Ficciones,* p. 100). Of course, it is that particular labyrinth the two find themselves in, since it is fated that the spy will murder Albert.

What we have is a combination of a neat ending, but one that is more than a mere solution to a riddle or trivial puzzle. The spy, in the tale's last lines, reveals why he had to kill the scholar he so much admired, adding, "He does not know, for no one can, of my infinite penitence and sickness of the heart" (p. 101). This is the essence of Borges: a combination of conventionally well-made plot and a twist that calls into question the assumptions about time and knowing that attend all plots. In a world from which the sacred had been thought to have fled, we are once again plunged into mystery and wonder.

Selected Bibliography

There is no complete edition of Borges' works available in any language. The closest approximation is in French, which Borges felt he spoke badly, although it was in this language that he was first internationally honored with the Formentor prize. This edition is the *Oeuvres complètes,* edited by Jean-Pierre Bernès and published by Gallimard. The first volume was published in 1993, and a second volume is forthcoming. The first volume contains what I have assumed in this essay to be the quintessential Borges, certainly the Borges who is pertinent to metaphysical mysteries—everything he wrote between 1935 and 1953.

In Spanish, the situation is complicated, to say the least. Emecé, Borges' major publisher during his lifetime, is bringing out separate works as part of a projected *Obras completas.* Borges himself compounded the problem because he was constantly editing and reissuing different versions of his works. A joint uniform edition to be published by Emecé in Buenos Aires and by Alianza in Madrid is under way, but this undertaking, initiated in 1995, is a long way from being realized.

In English, the language Borges honored more than his own, there is not even a projected uniform edition. In this bibliography, I have listed only the major works that bear on Borges' relationship to metaphysical narrative in the best English translations, arranged chronologically. For Spanish bibliographies, I refer the reader to the texts by Emir Rodríguez-Monegal and James Woodall.

SELECTED WORKS

Ficciones. Edited, translated, and with an introduction by Anthony Kerrigan. New York: Grove Press, 1962. Includes "Death and the Compass," "The Garden of Forking Paths," "Tlön, Uqbar, Orbis Tertius," "The Approach to Al-Mu'tasim," and "Pierre Menard, Author of *Don Quixote.*"

Labyrinths: Selected Stories and Other Writings. Edited by Donald A. Yates and James E. Irby and with a preface by André Maurois. New York: New Directions, 1962.

Other Inquisitions, 1937–1952. Translated by Ruth L. C. Simms, with an introduction by James E. Irby. Austin: Univ. of Texas Press, 1964.

Dreamtigers. Translated by Mildred Boyer and Harold Morland, with an introduction by Miguel Eguidianos. Woodcuts by Antonio Frasconi. Austin: Univ. of Texas Press, 1964; rev. ed., 1985.

A Personal Anthology. Edited and with a foreword by Anthony Kerrigan. New York: Grove Press, 1967.

The Book of Imaginary Beings (with Margarita Guerrero). Revised, enlarged, and translated by Norman Thomas di Giovanni in collaboration with the author. New York: Dutton, 1969.

The Aleph and Other Stories, 1933–1969. Edited and translated by Norman Thomas di Giovanni in collaboration with the author. New York: Dutton, 1970. With commentaries and an autobiographical essay.

Doctor Brodie's Report. Translated by Norman Thomas di Giovanni in collaboration with the author. New York: Dutton, 1972.

The Book of Sand. Translated by Norman Thomas di Giovanni in collaboration with the author. New York: Dutton, 1975.

Six Problems for Don Isidro Parodi (with Adolfo Bioy-Casares). Translated by Norman Thomas di Giovanni. New York: Dutton, 1981.

Seven Nights. Translated by Eliot Weinberger, with an introduction by Alastair Reid. New York: New Directions, 1984.

BIBLIOGRAPHY

Foster, David William. *Jorge Luis Borges: An Annotated Primary and Secondary Bibliography.* New York: Garland, 1984.

BIOGRAPHICAL AND CRITICAL STUDIES

Alazraki, Jaime. *Borges and the Kaballah.* Cambridge, England, and New York: Cambridge Univ. Press, 1988.

Barnstone, Willis. *With Borges on an Ordinary Evening in Buenos Aires: A Memoir.* Urbana: Univ. of Illinois Press, 1993.

———, ed. *Borges at Eighty: Conversations.* Bloomington: Indiana Univ. Press, 1982.

Burgin, Richard. *Conversations with Jorge Luis Borges.* New York: Holt, Rinehart, and Winston, 1969.

Di Giovanni, Norman Thomas, ed. *The Borges Tradition.* London: Constable, 1995.

Irwin, John T. *The Mystery to a Solution: Poe, Borges, and the Analytic Detective Story.* Baltimore: Johns Hopkins Univ. Press, 1994.

Lindstrom, Naomi. *Jorge Luis Borges: A Study of the Short Fiction.* Boston: Twayne, 1990.

Read, Malcolm K. *Jorge Luis Borges and His Predecessors; or, Notes Towards a Materialist History of Linguistic Idealism.* Chapel Hill: Univ. of North Carolina Department of Romance Languages, 1993.

Rodríguez-Monegal, Emir. *Jorge Luis Borges: A Literary Biography.* New York: Dutton, 1978.

Sarlo Sabajanes, Beatriz. *Jorge Luis Borges: A Writer on the Edge.* Edited by John King. London and New York: Verso, 1993.

Sturrock, John. *Paper Tigers: The Ideal Fictions of Jorge Luis Borges.* Oxford: Clarendon Press, 1977.

Woodall, James. *The Man in the Mirror of the Book: A Life of Jorge Luis Borges.* London: Hodder and Stoughton, 1996.

Yates, Donald A. *Jorge Luis Borges: Life, Work, and Criticism.* Fredericton, Canada: York Press, 1985.

John Buchan
(1875–1940)

GEORGE O'BRIEN

An extraordinarily prolific author whose works range from a history of World War I to a work on taxation, and include a substantial number of novels in interestingly interrelated genres, John Buchan is best known for his thrillers—or "shockers," as he called them—the success of which overshadowed not only his other literary accomplishments but also the varied and prestigious work he carried out as a public servant of the British Empire. His most celebrated novels are the four spy-stories featuring Richard Hannay—*The Thirty-Nine Steps* (1915), *Greenmantle* (1916), *Mr. Standfast* (1919), and *The Three Hostages* (1924). Although his work in the genre is by no means confined to the Hannay quartet, these are the stories by which his name is primarily remembered, and Richard Hannay remains the prototypical Buchan hero. The popularity of the Hannay series may be due in part to the fact that three film versions have been made of *The Thirty-Nine Steps*, the first—directed by Alfred Hitchcock—in 1935, the second and third in 1959 and 1978 respectively. Buchan's work began to appear dated due to new departures and developments in spy fiction during the 1960s and 1970s. Recently, however, new editions of his best-known works, each complete with scholarly apparatus, together with a number of comprehensive biographical and critical studies and a keener intellectual appreciation of the genre to whose modern development he made a decisive contribution, have secured a prominent and permanent place for John Buchan's mystery writing.

Life

John Buchan was born on 26 August 1875 in Perth, Scotland, the eldest of a family of five born to Helen (née Masterton) and the Reverend John Buchan, a minister of the Free Presbyterian Church of Scotland. A year later, the family moved to the town of Pathhead in Fife, on the east coast of Scotland. Here young John Buchan's schooling began. He also attended school in nearby Kirkaldy. In 1888, Buchan's father became the minister of the John Knox Free Church, Glasgow. The Knox church was situated in the Gorbals, an area of the city notorious for its slums, heavy industry, and socialist politics. The Buchans did not live in the area, and the contribution that working-class Glasgow made to the formation of the author's worldview remains debatable.

Buchan's Scotland is very much a nonurban land of great natural beauty populated by a sturdy yeomanry and laborers who know their place, universally devoted to such outdoor pursuits as trout fishing, deer stalking, and rock climbing. Buchan was well versed in these activities, and the skills that derive from them recur throughout his fiction not merely as physical or technical accomplishments but as more complex measures of manliness, endurance, and a romanticized, though entirely cogent, vision of the providential interdependence between human nature and the natural environment.

This vision has its origins in numerous extended vacations that Buchan spent with his mother's family. The Mastertons farmed sheep in the valley of the Tweed, a river that forms part of the eastern border between Scotland and England. (The southern third of Scotland in which this valley is situated is known as the Borders and in addition to its numerous attractive rivers has a stretch of high country called the Southern Uplands.) It is also a region rich in literary and historical associations. The Masterton family farm was at Broughton Green, not far from the market town of Peebles, where both Mastertons and Buchans were prominent citizens.

After completing his secondary education at Hutchesons' Grammar School, Glasgow, Buchan won a scholarship to study at Glasgow University in 1892. Three years later, however, Buchan won a scholarship to read classics at Brasenose College, Oxford. By that time his literary career had already begun; his first book, an edition of the *Essays and Apothegms of Francis Lord Bacon* (1894), was published in 1894. Buchan's brilliant Oxford career included not only the presidency of the Oxford Union and a first-class degree, but also the rapid development of his literary interests. He wrote five books at Oxford, making a total of eight published before he was twenty-five. He won the prestigious Newdigate prize for poetry—the winning entry was entitled "The Pilgrim Fathers"—and he was also employed as a reader for John Lane, one of the most successful publishers of the day. Then as later, however, Buchan had no desire to become a full-time professional author. Instead, he decided to read for the bar, to which he was called—meaning that he was licensed to practice law—in 1901.

In the same year, Lord Alfred Milner, High Commissioner for South Africa, invited Buchan to join his staff as personal secretary. Buchan's two years in South Africa were spent supervising reconstruction after the Boer War. He traveled widely and found in his travels many landscapes and landowners that brought to mind the Tweed Valley. His challenging administrative tasks also meant firsthand exposure to the practicalities and rationale of Empire. The influence of this exposure can be detected in ideological positions of his fiction, beginning with the so-called boy's book, *Prester John* (1910), based on his South African experience. Returning to London in 1903, Buchan specialized in tax law and also continued to write, producing a regular flow of books and a spate of journalism. In 1906 he became chief literary adviser to the Edinburgh publishing house of Nelson, a position he held until 1929. In 1906 he also became engaged to Susan Grosvenor (a descendant of the duke of Wellington), whom he married in 1907. They had four children.

Because of the stomach trouble that plagued him throughout his life, Buchan was unable to serve as a combatant in World War I. His suggestion to Nelson that a history of the war be published serially became a massive assignment that Buchan himself undertook. This task made him fully conversant with all theaters of operations, a familiarity that lends impressive authenticity to the treatment of arms, strategy, foreign locales, and geopolitics in his thrillers. Other important wartime influences on his writing are an admiration for the pluck of enlisted men and a respect for the enemy. These influences were the result of periods at the front as a correspondent for the *Times* in 1915. More significant for his intellectual and creative development, Buchan acquired a great understanding of the interconnected realms of espionage and propaganda from his work for the Intelligence Corps in 1916, as director of information in 1917, and as director of intelligence in 1918 in the newly established Ministry of Information.

After the war, Buchan became a director of the news agency Reuters, and retired to Elsfield Manor, near Oxford, where he continued to write at the rate of more than a book a year. The range of his work covered, in addition to thrillers, historical romances and biographies. Honors began to come his way, beginning with his election to Parliament as the Tory member for the Scottish universities in 1927, a seat he held until 1935. The major universities of England, Scotland, the United States, and Canada awarded him honorary degrees. In 1933 and 1934 Buchan served in the honorary office of high commissioner to the General Assembly of the Church of Scotland. In 1935, he was created Baron Tweedsmuir—a name that reflects his attachment to the countryside of his boyhood—and was appointed governor-general of Canada. As a result of a head injury accidentally sustained at his official residence in Ottawa, Ontario, Buchan was taken for treatment to Montreal, where he died on 11 February 1940.

Buchan's Thrillers: An Overview

Buchan's thrillers may be grouped roughly into three sets: those with Richard Hannay as their protagonist, those featuring Sir Edward Leithen, and those concerning the adventures of Dickson McCunn. These groups do not account for all of Buchan's thrillers, but whether they belong to these groups or not, Buchan's work in this form has much in common with the rest of his fiction and, more indirectly but revealingly, with his historical biographies. Buchan's output as a whole is a body of work which is notably preoccupied with the attainment and maintenance of coherence. Although Buchan himself seemed not to take his thrillers too seriously, they can be profitably read as the expression of, or even as the fantasy life of, a man who found himself in the front line of the momentous social and political changes threatened—and to a considerable extent brought into being—by the historical events of the first thirty years of the twentieth century.

Buchan's thrillers occupy a distinctive place within the body of his fiction, and there are two main points of intersection between them and his other novels. One of these concerns content. All of Buchan's fiction centers around adventure. Early historical novels such as *Salute to Adventurers* (1915), set in colonial America, and more mature historical novels like *Witch Wood* (1927), set in seventeenth-century Scotland, have in common protagonists who find themselves plunged into dangerous, unfamiliar circumstances where physical survival and the preservation of a communal way of life are matters of the most urgent concern. Destructive forces must be confronted immediately. The daily round of invariably fulfilling and self-enhancing social engagement and social obligation is interrupted and threatened with extinction. The protagonist must now save the day instead of seizing it, the latter being his supposedly natural inclination. The narrative features periods of jeopardy, exhaustion, and stress, while throughout there is a constant undercurrent of hysteria.

In his thrillers Buchan gives these tense and demanding conditions a global context, a more immediate historical urgency, and a more narrowly defined set of time-space relations. Even though the specific action of the historical novels may take place over a brief period of time, it gains additional significance and loses a certain degree of tension from being an illustration of an overall epic historical sweep, the outcome of which the reader already knows. The thrillers, however, by being located in an immediate, open-ended present, have the sense of historical destiny implicit in epic sweep placed under severe stress. This critical state of affairs is signaled in the narrative by extremely demanding calendars and extremely troublesome physical circumstances often manifesting themselves in restricted interiors. Such circumstances, in turn, are complemented and exacerbated by excruciating problems of timing and an alarming shortage of room to maneuver. Buchan's thrillers subject the norms of adventure to a marked intensification of terms and conditions.

The second point of intersection concerns

the question of genre. Buchan freely acknowledged his indebtedness to such predecessors in the Scottish canon as Sir Walter Scott and Robert Louis Stevenson. A case could well be made that all Buchan's fiction constitutes an endless attempt to rewrite Stevenson's *Kidnapped*. But Buchan also draws consciously on not just the Scottish canon but on a broader tradition of the romance. Ultimately deriving from the picaresque—Buchan's first novel was *Sir Quixote of the Moors* (1895)—the romance, rather than dealing with man in society like the novel, emphasizes man beyond community and social usage, when all he has to rely on is his fortune.

Not surprisingly, chance, luck, coincidence, and fate play a large part in the consummation of the typical Buchan plot. And the vehicle of these plots is Buchan's version of the soldier of fortune. This generic type has undergone radical transformation since Buchan's day from carefree cavalier to malevolent mercenary.

For Buchan, the soldier of fortune is the modern knight-errant: dutiful, idealistic, hard-driving, chaste to a fault, his noble credentials are, if anything, too obvious. Richard Hannay may not be a knight of the realm, but many of the men crucial to the success of Hannay's various missions—Sandy Arbuthnot, Lord Clanroyden, Sir Archie Roylance—are indeed among the elite of the land. Their virtues and values may seem starchy and even laughably Victorian. Buchan is in no doubt, however, about the significance of preserving the imperial integrity that was the Victorian age's most notable historical accomplishment. This accomplishment's greatness is an ideal with which Buchan's operatives identify. The world which this ideal underpins is that of the white, Anglo-Saxon Protestant. Though snobbery may have played a part in Buchan's selection of titled defenders of the realm, it is preeminently their own realm that they attempt to save. Not surprisingly, breeding and privilege both fortify and justify their efforts. Hannay is the nonaristocratic exception who proves the entitled rule. Essentially errant, he requires an official mandate, and for the most part only functions alone in certain dramatic circumstances. But by his tenacity, strength of will, and feats of endurance, he attains knightly parity.

In addition to the social aspects of the knightly context, the existence of such high-minded warriors as protagonists gives Buchan's thrillers an impeccable literary pedigree. It would be an exaggeration to see these characters in, for instance, an Arthurian light. But such a light is a suggestion of the tradition which Buchan allows to inform his work. Yet his thrillers are far from being merely bookish or predictable, despite the many social and cultural stereotypes of Buchan's conservative imagination. What saves them is that the cause which engages the protagonists' chivalric attention—the outcome of World War I, the Empire, Anglo-American relations—is presented as not so much an ideal to be vindicated as an ideal under stress. Buchan adapts the adventure content of his thrillers to the pressing historical circumstances under which they were written, while retaining a strong awareness of adventure's generic lineage and tradition. By so doing, he provides not only rattling good yarns but also a revealing perspective on the twentieth-century thriller's cultural and literary gene pool.

The Hannay Quartet

The Thirty-Nine Steps (1915), which introduces Richard Hannay, has an economy and narrative drive which make it an acknowledged classic of works of its kind. In the novel's dedication—to his friend the publisher Thomas Nelson—Buchan acknowledges its origins in the American dime novel and defines his "shocker" as a "romance where the incidents defy probabilities, and march just inside the borders of the possible." *The Thirty-Nine Steps* is a convenient introduction to the world of the Buchan thrillers, the most substantial of which are the four Hannay novels.

The plot of *The Thirty-Nine Steps* consists

essentially of a sustained chase, one of Buchan's main imaginative standbys. For most of the novel, Hannay finds himself in a kind of no-man's-land. Only Hannay has any inkling of the dastardly plot by enemies whose object is to scupper the war effort of the British Navy by stealing its secret plans. But his knowledge leaves him isolated and vulnerable, a citizen pitting his wits against not only enemy powers but also against the police, who want Hannay as the prime suspect in the murder of an American journalist who has unearthed the plot. Hence his escape to Scotland and his pursuit there through country which Buchan knew like the back of his hand, and which he describes here, as throughout his work, with many a bravura touch in prose of great precision and verve.

Hannay, like anybody on the run, is very interested in his own survival. As events unfold, however, he sees that his own fate and even his identity is inextricably linked with the survival of the British fleet, and with the even larger issues of survival that depend on the fleet. In a sense, Hannay is empowered by the urgency of the position in which he finds himself. And this empowerment is something that he had needed.

Recently returned from a prosperous sojourn as an engineer in South Africa, Hannay is at loose ends in London, a condition which Buchan often uses as a preamble not merely to action and adventure for their own sake but to the possibility of self-renewal and commitment, which are the reward for action and adventure. It is all the more necessary for Hannay to demonstrate devotion to flag and fatherland because he feels something of an outsider. Having proved himself professionally and economically in the colonies is not enough. He must now attain a higher realm of value. Not surprisingly, the issue of identity recurs in various ways throughout *The Thirty-Nine Steps*, both in the number of times Hannay has to go incognito and, in a broader sense, because his survival is constantly in doubt.

Ultimately, Sir Walter Bullivant of the Foreign Office comes to Hannay's assistance. This development underlines the hero's earlier solitariness and the desperation that arose from it. But it also suggests that access to the corridors of power is an institutional and social ratification of Hannay's exclusively human resources of grit, improvisation, and foresight. Without this ratification, Hannay's effectiveness must remain open to doubt. The entry of Sir Walter—who remains a recurring presence in the Hannay quartet—enables the letter of the national interest to authenticate the spirit of adventure. Hannay cannot be seen simply as a freelancing individual. Indeed, he is not particularly individuated. Rather his role is that of a diagnostic probe, taking the temperature and if possible drawing the sting of the enemy.

In *The Thirty-Nine Steps*, Buchan sets the stage for most of his thrillers as far as theme and plot are concerned. One crucial theme to emerge is the character of power, and the nature of the Buchan thriller plot often addresses the uses and abuses of power, with particular emphasis on the international scene. The enemy is the one who abuses power, generally by desiring to acquire a monopoly of it. His violent, subversive, and clandestine maneuvers deliberately disregard the rules of the international power game. The rules are the code of honor and due procedure, which entitle one nation to the respect of another, and the game is the interplay of competing national interests. Civilization is built on the assumption that the rules can accommodate the game and is sustained on the practical implementation of that assumption. Violations of the rules—leading to manipulation of the game—are inevitably expressed in unscrupulous and amoral terms. The lack of institutional responsibility implied by such violations threatens anarchy and a collapse of the duly constituted, traditional power structure.

Greenmantle (1916) has the same basic thriller ingredients. This time the prolonged chase and undercover war has Germany directly in its sights, in particular German attempts to enlist the hordes of Islam in support of its war effort. Clearly, if this plot is successful it will be the end of civilization as Buchan and Hannay know it. Hannay's "hurried journey"—a narrative form for which Buchan expressed enthusiasm—takes him through wartime Germany, down the Danube and through the Balkans, to Constantinople and finally to the Near Eastern front of World War I, where the mission is successfully completed. Once again, and much more readily on this occasion, the forces of good and evil are clearly identified; the struggle between them is of the utmost national and international significance; the chase is the essential source of narrative momentum; local color makes a predictable but effective splash; and Hannay performs partly as a fool who rushes in and partly as an impressively quick thinking and physically courageous operative.

Broader geographical range—which from this point becomes another standard feature of Buchan's thrillers—is matched by other forms of enlargement in content and, consequently, in ideas. There is an increase in personnel; Hannay no longer works quite so alone. He is a member of a team consisting of Sandy Arbuthnot, Peter Pienaar from Hannay's South African days, and the American industrialist John S. Blenkiron. Peter Pienaar dies heroically in aerial combat in the next Hannay book, but the other two turn up intermittently in later Buchan thrillers. The group ethic which they embody is important not only for personal reasons and as a survival strategy, but also for its symbolic significance.

Sandy, a polyglot and a master of disguises, is a seasoned campaigner in "the Great Game," as British containment of czarist Russia's designs on India through Afghanistan and the North-West Frontier Province of British India was called—the phrase was coined by Rudyard Kipling, an important influence on Buchan's work and outlook. Blenkiron, on the other hand, Buchan's bulky and dyspeptic American, has ties to his home government which are rather nebulous. His presence, however, gives the character of the civilization that is under threat in *Greenmantle* a larger and clearer visibility. The implication is that British and American interests have much in common, not only because they are allies and imperial powers but also because they share cultural and moral heritage. Buchan's sketch of a North Atlantic *Anglophone* bloc here anticipates his postwar thinking on the subject. His view also functions as a racial foil—particularly noteworthy on account of the undertone of jihad in the plot—and as an expression of cultural solidarity in the face of German attempts to "madden the Moslem peasant with dreams of Paradise" (1993 ed., p.12) through manipulation of the one they call Greenmantle. Such a strategy is a blatant violation of the rules of the game.

The enemy's motivation and methods are another area in which *Greenmantle* is more elaborate than *The Thirty-Nine Steps*. Although the magnitude of the plot to overthrow the duly constituted world order by attacking not only the British Empire but also the Russian—"our side," as Sandy calls them when victory is assured—may seem preposterous, it does draw attention to Buchan's preoccupation with alliances, communities of interest, and systems. The enemy's methods are embodied by the impressive Hilda Von Einem. Here again a development in Buchan's approach is in evidence. Military tactics are secondary. First comes psychological control. Von Einem's job is to oversee the hearts and minds of her Islamic adherents. Her effectiveness is demonstrated as even Hannay finds himself rather overawed by this Teutonic Mata Hari, allured by her beauty, her iron will, and her gifts of command. More masculine than the lithe tomboys for whom the Buchan hero typically falls, Hilda Von Einem is also a reminder that the secret war that Hannay is recalled from active duty at the front to fight is in part "the big subterranean movement" characterized in *The Thirty-Nine Steps*. But Buchan enlarges his perspective to see the conflict as a mental and moral struggle, a struggle of reasonableness against excess and of rational policy against irrational mastery.

World War I also provides the context for *Mr. Standfast* (1919) while again opening fresh ground for another hasty journey. The nature of this ground is suggested by the novel's title. Mr. Standfast occurs in John Bunyan's *The Pilgrim's Progress*, and Buchan aligns Hannay's struggle with the pilgrim Christian's travail in the Bunyan classic. (The American title of Buchan's 1940 autobiography is *Pilgrim's Way*.) Such an alignment gives this Hannay novel an explicit cultural and intellectual focus, borne out by Hannay's contact with modern trends and by the fact that principle is shown to be as important an element as action.

With Hannay's visit to the Biggleswick community, Buchan quickly disposes of one version of the modern tendencies that veer much outside the novelist's beloved mainstream. The community's affectation of progressive views and controversial artistic taste and its general way of life are anathemas to Hannay, as to Buchan. A much more substantial form of engagement with a trend of the day is represented in Hannay's relations with the intellectual Launcelot Wake, who espouses pacifism. Hannay meets Wake because Wake's mission cover story is that he is an advocate for a prompt World War I ceasefire. The familiar plot—pursuit of a master spy, leading to revelations about world-threatening German skullduggery—is less significant in its own right than for the means it provides for Wake's redemption. Having endured much, with his dying breath Wake protests that all he has gone through has been for peace. In Hannay's eyes, however, what matters is Wake's willingness to fight for what he believes in. Wake ends up in the same moral category as Peter Pienaar, the stoic hunter and modern Mr. Standfast, whose suffering and self-sacrificial death counterpoints Wake's.

In a novel containing a greater than usual amount of physical discomfort and psychological duress, it becomes clear that suffering is the tribute which the agent pays to principle. Hannay implicitly accepts this formula tion of the moral economy of action. But *Mr. Standfast* suggests that its validity is confirmed by the willingness of others to embrace it. Here, behind the comings and goings of what Buchan called "my puppets," the sound of an earnest, secular sermon can be heard.

Although Richard Hannay appears in later Buchan novels, and also features in "The Green Wildebeest" (which appears in the short-story collection *The Runagates' Club*, 1928), his career effectively ends with *The Three Hostages* (1924), another race against time. But this novel also develops some of the ideological underpinnings introduced in its predecessors, casting its glance upon troublesome legacies of World War I.

The novel opens with Hannay ensconced in his life as lord of Fosse Manor—a country house first glimpsed in *Mr. Standfast*—and married with a son. These squirearchical circumstances are idyllic, but Hannay misses his old life of action, and besides, the peace is phony. Anarchists have just kidnapped the only daughter of the richest man in the world, Julius Victor, whose life's ambition is to bring about world peace. Soon afterward the children of two other prominent personages are taken hostage. The security of the next generation implicitly is at stake.

This state of affairs and the somewhat halting manner in which Hannay reenters the fray express the difficulty of characterizing the postwar world. During the war, the enemy and his dangers were eminently knowable and urgent action was obviously of the utmost importance. Now evil is no longer the external, and to some extent quantifiable, force it had been during the war. It has become more disguised, subterranean, amorphous. It exists behind the cultivated facades of the land of hope and glory. It exists behind the well-finished veneer of the villain Dominic Medina. The new war between good and evil is essentially a much more mental game, a war of nerves. Hannay's is the traditional mind-set, while Medina's—picking up on the perspective of *Mr. Standfast*—is modernistic, susceptible to false gods, lacking the hardheaded empiricism and stoical doggedness of the true Briton, and committed to the infiltration and manipulation of mentalities by acts of psychological terrorism such as kidnapping.

In contrast to the bland, unostentatious Hannay, Medina has mystique. This aura is one of the ways in which he is identified as being of a different breed. Part of the novel is devoted to the organization of a pan-Nordic front against what Medina represents. Not only does Hannay make a successful foray into Norway, but also his efforts depend on the contribution of a former German officer. As a confirmed imperialist, Buchan had very fixed views on the pecking order of the races. His attitude toward Africans in *Prester John,* Native Americans in *Salute to Adventurers,* and Jews in a variety of works are not only those of a man of his nation, class, and time but are also intrinsic to the world order that he valued and for whose preservation his "shockers" function as part parable, part sermon. And while Hannay is perfectly capable of admiring his enemy on an individual basis—as he does in the fatal Highland confrontation with Medina which concludes *The Three Hostages*—ultimately that is more to Hannay's credit as an officer and a gentleman.

Medina is wrong in principle. His evil issues from error. Service, exemplified by self-effacing Hannay, is more powerful than the mastery for which the flashy Medina conspires, being more in keeping with the norms of order, authority, and stability whereby continuity and its power structures are conserved. The world for which Hannay fought the war was a prewar world, obviously—not only a specific geography of political and economic interests but also a system of values, principles, motives, and beliefs. The perspective of *The Three Hostages* implies a certain unease about victory and a sharp sense that the struggle between good and evil may now be part of the fabric of national life, requiring more vigilance than ever.

In view of the threat posed by a villain like Medina, it is noteworthy that Buchan did not engage the postwar world with the consistent sense of urgency that characterized his wartime thrillers. Instead, his creative energies became more diffuse, much of them reserved for historical romances—*The Path of the King* (1921), *Midwinter* (1923), *Witch Wood* (1927), *The Blanket of the Dark* (1931), and *The Free Fishers* (1934)—the first of which, according to Buchan, was "my first serious piece of fiction." He also referred to the others as "serious works."

The Sir Edward Leithen Novels

Central as Richard Hannay is to Buchan's thrillers, Hannay's world and role are to some extent inspired by and reproduced in Buchan's novels featuring Sir Edward Leithen. Though much less well known than the Hannay quartet, the Leithen novels—*The Power-House* (1916; serial publication, 1913), *The Dancing Floor* (1926), *The Gap in the Curtain* (1932), and *Sick Heart River* (1941; U.S. title, *Mountain Meadow*)—similarly rehearse many of the major social pathologies which right-thinking men feel called upon to combat. Sir Edward also appears as one of a trio of eminent personages seeking to rid themselves not only of physical lassitude but also of spiritual sluggishness in *John Macnab* (1925). This novel is strictly an adventure story, with no political dimension, and is easy to relegate to the second rank of Buchan's works. But beneath its high jinks a well-integrated set of ideological positions are articulated regarding the social and cultural values of adventure.

As with the Hannay quartet, the Leithen series is more memorable for character than for plot. Sir Edward's title indicates his status as an insider. As a lawyer, he is much closer to the corridors of power than was Hannay. But although the law is a much more suggestive line of work for a prospective agent, Buchan uses Sir Edward's position to demonstrate more specifically how frail and vulnerable the powerful are, and how important it is that they be defended. This focus, as well as the timing of the publication of the Leithen novels, suggest that these works counterpoint the Hannay quartet.

Much of the agenda of Buchan's subsequent fiction is encapsulated in *The Power-House,* for instance, in a statement made by Lumley, head of the Power-House—a kind of consultancy for international anarchism—concerning Leithen's mistaken impression "that a wall as solid as the earth separates civilisation from barbarism" (1913 ed., p. 12). Leithen's reaction—"Now I saw how thin is the protection of civilisation" (1913 ed., p. 14)—is reinforced by his thought that if civilization's shield is so insubstantial, the fabric of everyday civic society can readily be torn. He imagines himself being spirited away in an ambulance, for example, without anybody being any the wiser. Such acts of subversion—sneaky, commonplace, intimate—not only eliminate the safety curtain between law and disorder, they also override the borders between national security and international menace. In contrast to Hannay, who effectively suspends his personality while on duty, Leithen acquires a more intensified sense of human nature through the medium of action.

The Dancing Floor is a case in point. Here, in addition to fighting the good fight, Leithen contends with the psychological mysteries of his nephew's Oxford friend Vernon Milburne, and with his own misguided belief that he is in love with a certain damsel in distress, Koré Arabin, ruler of the Aegean island of Plakos. Between unraveling Milburne's dreams and helping Koré to overcome her difficulties, Leithen exemplifies the nature of responsible action. The threat to Milburne's internal composure and the threat to the integrity of Plakos constitute a comprehensive model of fear. Leithen's defeat of that fear liberates his two young friends, who end up marrying each other, and the success rehabilitates Sir Edward's own flagging spirit so that he rediscovers his sense of mission and commitment. Again the survival of the coming generation is made viable. And the Greek background emphasizes the struggle for civilized values outlined by the broad brush strokes of the plot.

The Gap in the Curtain combines the emphasis on physical renewal that means so much to Leithen and his companions in *John Macnab* with the psychological insight contained in *The Dancing Floor*. As in *John Macnab*, the scene is a country-house weekend, and a good deal of flabbiness is in evidence. The physically depleted state of the guests has moral overtones and may, to some extent, represent Buchan's jaundiced and even somewhat fretful view of the spiritual atmosphere of the 1920s, particularly with regard to how that atmosphere affected the country-house set. The guests' exhaustion is a necessary precondition to availing themselves of the powers of Dr. Moe, the Swedish guru who permits them to see through "the gap in the curtain"—that is, into the future. Sir Edward does not see his future, but to the variety of guests who do—among them a capitalist, a politician, a soldier, and an explorer—the way ahead is far from certain, much less glorious. The narrative is a complicated cluster of motifs relating to disposition, temperament, character, survival, and fitness in various senses. Buchan shows Sir Edward to be engaged not only in contemporary struggles between good and evil but also in age-old struggles between faith and doubt.

Although much more of an adventure story than a thriller—it is, in effect, one long chase, or quest—*Sick Heart River*, Buchan's final novel, uses the character of Sir Edward to embody questions concerning personality and personal purpose. Leithen's search for Francis Galliard, a New York banker, in the wilderness of the Canadian north is obviously important for Galliard's sake. His abrupt disappearance to search for his roots is deeply unsettling, particularly to Blenkiron, Galliard's business partner and uncle by marriage, who entreats Leithen to undertake the search. International economic interests are also at stake. Leithen himself is in no doubt of the importance of those interests and of Galliard's affiliation with them, particularly since the interests are Anglo-American—Leithen gets his orders in New York—and Galliard is French-Canadian. The hegemony of the white nations of the North Atlantic is at stake.

What gives *Sick Heart River* its tension is not merely Leithen's sense of his mission's significance but his awareness that this is his last mission; he is dying of tuberculosis. His journey northward—the north being once again Buchan's place of final confrontation and resolution—offers a dual focus on survival whereby the personal becomes compatible with the public. These are the twin spheres in which the spirit of the quest—the core of adventure that is also the test of survival—makes its meaning. Here they finally attain unity.

The novel's title refers to a formerly mythical place of restoration, where sick hearts can find peace: "a strip of green meadowland by the waterside . . . while above it pine and birch had climbed in virgin magnificence to the crests" (1941 ed., p. 51). Despoiled by industry, however, it pushes Galliard and Leithen further north to Perrain where "there was no kindness" (1941 ed., p. 137) and where renewal is more troublesome. But, as Leithen and Galliard discover, renewal becomes more critical and more valuable in the frozen wastes. When Leithen finds Galliard and the place, it turns out to be a desolate and soul-destroying illusion. This discovery, together with the outbreak of World War II, spurs the dying Leithen to action among the demoralized local Native Americans, whose presence has been duly acknowledged throughout the Canadian section of the novel. Leithen thus becomes a symbol of the moral well-being that is most authentically attainable through struggle, that is best expressed in carrying out one's duty, that is most fruitfully encountered in nature, and that is fundamentally necessary to the preservation of things as they are.

The Adventures of Dickson McCunn

The Hannay and Leithen series together contain Buchan's most noteworthy work as a writer of thrillers. The Dickson McCunn books—*Huntingtower* (1922), *Castle Gay* (1930), and *The House of the Four Winds* (1935)—are more diffuse and are lacking in tension. They suggest an attempt to return to a simpler kind of adventurer and a more sunlit world of adventure. Perhaps they express the hope that the social and historical difficulties presented in, for example, *The Three Hostages*, can be bypassed and be "absorbed . . . into the ageless world of pastoral." Buchan expressed just such a hope regarding the traumatic events of World War I in his 1940 autobiography *Memory Hold-the-Door* (1950 ed., p. 177). Once again, character is to the fore. Now, however, it is Buchan's boyhood that the protagonist evokes, not his years of public service or his professional life. It is not only because McCunn is a respectable Glasgow grocer that he brings to mind the author's early years. His temperament—part Quixote, part Calvin—draws on two of Buchan's earliest influences.

The quixotic aspect of McCunn's personality may be readily seen in *Huntingtower*, as he casts aside the city and his grocer's role and takes to the countryside, where—his reading has convinced him—adventure is to be found. Instead of Hannay's band of resourceful professionals, McCunn has at his disposal an army of ragamuffins, the Gorbals Diehards. These spirited recruits to the ethos of adventure and its larger implications show in the course of the Dickson McCunn series the potential to mix with the highest in the land and to participate in the continuing war against international villainy. John "Jaickie" Galt is a case in point. By the time he appears in *The House of the Four Winds* he is a Cambridge-educated intimate of central European royalty.

As it happens, however, what McCunn finds in his quest for adventure is rather different from what he expected. It turns out not to be possible to turn a blind eye to the international political realities of the day. For every blithe McCunn, there is a victim of historical circumstances. Little thinking that he will find an actual princess in a tower in his travels, still less that her confinement will have a specific historical context, McCunn nevertheless rises to the occasion. Although the plot of *Huntingtower* revolves around the fate of Saskia, a Russian princess, and the band of evil-minded Bolsheviks who are on her trail, its fairy-tale aspects, with their ahistorical connotations of archetypes and recurring motifs, are difficult to overlook.

In *The House of the Four Winds*, the contemporary historical aspects of the story are similarly distanced. Set in the central European—or perhaps Balkan—state of Evallonia during the rise of a youth party which, though said not to be fascist, certainly seems to have strong leanings in that direction, the novel's historical context seems pretty clear. But action and setting persist in evoking fairy-tale and similar archetypal images with, for instance, the "great Schloss" of the novel's title a veritable Castle Perilous. Throughout the McCunn series, the house—a central structure, as the titles of the novels make clear—combines archetypal images of property, shelter, and settlement with more abstract historical concepts of dynasty, line, and, at the very least, local authority. Its role as a place of sequestration, which subverts such images (as in *Castle Gay*, where the kidnapped newspaper mogul Mr. Craw is held), must be rectified by the restorative intervention of McCunn the rescuer.

Lacking Hannay's insider status, and lacking also the official imprimatur of espionage that gives the Hannay quartet its dramatic pretext and justification, McCunn eventually—in *The House of the Four Winds*—becomes a marginal figure. He does not have the wherewithal to cross the geographical, social, and cultural border into the heart of the empire, where adventure intersects decisively with matters of high policy, principle, and power. Buchan has already made the desirability of complete assimilation abundantly clear in such characters as Sandy Arbuthnot, Lord Clanroyden, Sir Archie Roylance—a mainstay character of *The House of the Four Winds* as well as *John Macnab*—and even Hannay himself. And although Buchan views McCunn with affection and understanding, ensures that he is agreeable and diverting company, and avails of him to display his keen ear for the richness and variety of demotic Scottish speech, in critical ways he fails to be a knight-errant, a gentleman-warrior, and in general to make the imperial grade, thereby once more underlining the significance of doing so.

Other Works

Buchan wrote a number of thrillers that do not belong to any of his series but nonetheless contribute to a more complete sense of the range of the author's work in this form. These other thrillers also substantiate a sense of how frequently and with what commitment Buchan revisited the elemental struggle between good and evil and reiterated his fears and hopes for what he thought of as the civilized world. The books in question belong to different stages of Buchan's career, thereby adding to an appreciation of the focus and consistency with which he created fictional confrontations with the challenges and changes of his time. Even if, as he said of his thrillers in *Memory Hold-the-Door*, "I had no purpose in such writing except to please myself, and even if my books had not found a single reader I should have felt amply repaid" (1950 ed., pp. 205–206), it is striking that he returns again and again to the same preoccupations, or perhaps was led to them subconsciously. He recalls: "I never consciously invented with a pen in my hand; I waited until the story had told itself and then wrote it down" (1950 ed., p. 205).

Buchan's thriller-writing career began with *The Half-Hearted* (1900), an underdeveloped prototype of much that was to follow—exotic locale, self-sacrifice, sense of duty, arduous journey, and so on. Lewis Haystoun, wellborn, physically able, and socially well connected, is nevertheless a young man who lacks a convincing sense of purpose. This he eventually discovers on the way to the North-West Frontier, where he is drawn into "the Great Game." He dies defending the empire from a Russian invasion. This is a fate from which, revealingly, Buchan preserves future protagonists, survival regardless of the odds being very much part of the ethos of renewal that is one of the values of mold-breaking, risk-taking adventure.

Nevertheless, a career similar to Lewis Haystoun's is traced in *A Prince of the Captivity* (1933). Here again the theme of rehabilitation and renewal through action is developed. Adam Melfort volunteers to serve time in jail for an offense committed by his wife. As a consequence, his army career must come to an end. After his release, he reestablishes himself physically through a rigorous course of endurance tests. He then establishes his credibility through daring exploits of espionage behind enemy lines during World War I. A further challenge to his survival comes in the form of his Arctic rescue of an American millionaire. And Melfort is also involved in the defeat of a conspiracy for world supremacy. When he eventually meets his death in the Italian Alps, there is no doubt that he has successfully proven himself, and that through his refusal to shirk a life of action, he has indeed proven himself a man, morally as well as physically.

Two other novels that also help to complete a sense of the Buchan canon are *The Courts of the Morning* (1929) and *The Island of Sheep* (1936; U.S. title, *The Man from the Norland*). These novels are loosely connected. A villainous French aristocrat, Jacques D'Ingraville, one of the mercenaries on the losing side in *The Courts of the Morning*, turns up as the leading evil character in *The Island of Sheep*. And both novels have a Richard Hannay—now Sir Richard, M.P.—connection: *The Courts of the Morning* has a preface by him, and *The Island of Sheep* places his son Peter John directly in harm's way.

There is a distant but intriguing resemblance between *The Courts of the Morning* and Joseph Conrad's *Nostromo* (1904), as Sandy Arbuthnot, John S. Blenkiron, and newlyweds Sir Archie and Lady Janet Roylance strive to save the mines of the fictional South American country of Olifa. Their aim requires that a revolution be fomented, and much of the novel is taken up with an account of the tactics, strategies, terrain, and resources of the opposing sides. Sandy, in particular—operating under the nom de guerre "El lobo gris"—endures superhuman bouts of physical hardship, while showing himself to be a military mastermind and living proof—as if Buchan readers needed it—that fortune favors the brave. With Sandy's triumphant campaign, Buchan seemingly puts into action the theory of war of T. E. Lawrence—Lawrence of Arabia.

Military victory, to be entirely successful, must be accompanied by a revolution in outlook. In other words, there must be a substantial change of heart on the part of the dictatorial mining executive Castor. To bring this about, Castor is kidnapped. Slowly but surely, as he is exposed not just to the ideas but to the manners and sentiments of Sandy and his friends—especially Lady Roylance—Castor sees the error of his ways. His conversion to the type of allegiance suggested by the Arbuthnot-Blenkiron partnership complements the military victory—as a remark in the novel has it, "the difficulties even of Europe must be settled in the West" (1929 ed., p. 381). A more paradoxical but nevertheless crucial victory is exemplified by Castor's death, which takes place during a final desperate rush by the enemy, led by mercenaries who are all disaffected and unsettled World War I veterans. Castor dies by sacrificing himself for Lady Roylance, revealing himself not only to have crossed over to the right side politically and economically but also—equally important, and perhaps because of crossing over—to have become a gentleman as well. He finally was worthy of the civilization that fought for him.

The plot of *The Island of Sheep* also centers around a mining engineer, Magnus Haraldsen, and has its origins in Richard Hannay's early years in South Africa. A chance encounter with an acquaintance from those days named Lombard reminds him of a pledge they, together with Peter Pienaar, took to defend Haraldsen and his descendants from his sworn enemies. The plot begins to take shape with the kidnapping of Haraldsen's granddaughter, and many chases and narrow scrapes ensue, culminating in a climax on the cliffs of the Faeroe Islands. Together with Sandy Arbuthnot, Archie Roylance, and Peter John Hannay, justice is eventually done. The novel as a whole is a culmination of sorts, with its South African dimension, its focus on kidnapping and the fate of the coming generation, and not least its use of natural surroundings and natural phenomena in cracking the case. The inclusion of Arbuthnot and Roylance also makes *The Island of Sheep* the old firm's swan song.

John Buchan and the Thriller

For three main reasons, Buchan's thrillers occupy a pivotal position in the development of the genre. First, even if Buchan modestly downplayed his own thrillers, he was well aware of the genre's historic and cultural background in, especially, the "hurried journey," which, as he wrote in *Memory Hold-the-Door*, "in the great romances of literature . . . provides some of the chief dramatic moments, and since the theme is common to Homer and the penny reciter it must appeal to a very ancient instinct in human nature" (1950 ed., p. 203).

Second, Buchan had a keen knowledge of and appreciation for not only the nineteenth-century romances of Sir Walter Scott and Robert Louis Stevenson but also the diplomatic romances of Charles Lever (1806–1872)—*Tony Butler* (1865), for example—and the popular imperial adventures for boys of G. A. Henty. Buchan's sense of these works is not merely scholarly, however. His thrillers represent a critical engagement with these earlier representations of adventure and romance, by means of which he adapts their ethos and narrative structure to his own contemporary purposes.

The status of the contemporary in Buchan's thrillers is a third important reason for their significance. Not only does Buchan's experience as an insider give a sense of assurance and credibility to the action, the very fact that much of that action takes place in a historically conditioned here-and-now is noteworthy. If E. Phillips Oppenheim, contemporary master of the cloak-and-dagger school, was, in Buchan's words "my master in fiction" (quoted in Janet Adam Smith, p. 178), Buchan went on to modernize his master by infiltrating the thriller with the actual concerns, dangers, and challenges of his own generation. His use of the machinery of modern life—planes in *The Thirty-Nine Steps*, a car chase in *The Island of Sheep*, trains throughout—also helps to give his work additional excitement and a plausible worldliness, as does the detail of his natural landscapes and his relish for the material pleasures of clubland and the solidarities of male companionship. In his version of the principles and procedures of the male agent, Buchan also reveals a perhaps unwittingly modern train of thought.

For Buchan, the agent is a moral soldier, fortified not only by a mandate from political authority but also by inherited and unquestioned values of decency, tenacity, obedience, and so on. His orders are to maintain the world as it is; otherwise, mere anarchy will prevail. A good deal of his moral energy and unceasing physical activity derives from his willing acceptance of such a heavy responsibility. The modern note is struck, however, in the degree of doubt and insecurity that overshadows the mission, a sense of which is tellingly conveyed by the simple device of first-person narration. This same note, greatly amplified and with its dissonance frankly acknowledged, informs the imaginative landscapes of such illustrious successors as Eric Ambler, Graham Greene, and John le Carré, whose thrillers may be correctly seen, in part at least, as implicit correctives of Buchan. Victor Maskell, the protagonist modeled on Sir Anthony Blunt in John Banville's *The Untouchable* (1997), may regard Buchan as ridiculously old-fashioned. But the kind of material which his thrillers were the first to bring into focus—the conspiratorial shadow cast by contemporary history, the challenge to integrity and cohesion, the bleak vicissitudes of international power play—continue their complex existence in the genre, as shown in not only *Kumari* (1955) and *Helen All Alone* (1961) by Buchan's son, William, but also in *Heart's Journey in Winter* (1995) and *High Latitudes: A Romance* (1996), by James Buchan, John Buchan's grandson.

Selected Bibliography

WORKS OF JOHN BUCHAN

NOVELS AND SHORT FICTION

Sir Quixote of the Moors: Being an Account of an Episode in the Life of the Sieur de Rohaine. London: Unwin, 1895; New York: Holt, 1895.

John Burnet of Barns. London: John Lane, 1898; New York: Dodd, Mead, 1898; Edinburgh: B&W, 1994.

A Lost Lady of Old Years. London: John Lane, 1899; Edinburgh: B&W, 1995.

Grey Weather: Moorland Tales of My Own People. London: John Lane, 1899.

The Half-Hearted. London: Ibister, 1900; Boston and New York: Houghton Mifflin, 1900.

The Watcher by the Threshold and Other Tales. Edinburgh and London: Blackwood, 1902; enl. ed., New York: Doran, 1918; Edinburgh: Canongate, 1997.

A Lodge in the Wilderness. Edinburgh and London: Blackwood, 1906.

Prester John. London: Nelson, 1910; New York: Dodd, Mead, 1910. Edited by David Daniell. Oxford: Oxford University Press, 1994.

The Moon Endureth: Tales and Fancies. Edinburgh and New York: Blackwood, 1912; New York: Sturgis and Walton, 1912.

Salute to Adventurers. London: Nelson, 1915; Boston and New York: Houghton Mifflin, 1915.

The Thirty-Nine Steps. Edinburgh and London: Blackwood, 1915; New York: Doran, 1916. Edited by Christopher Harvie. Oxford: Oxford University Press, 1994.

Greenmantle. London: Hodder and Stoughton: 1916; New York: Doran, 1916. Edited by Kate McDonald. Oxford: Oxford University Press, 1993.

The Power-House. Edinburgh and London: Blackwood; New York: New York, 1916; Edinburgh: B&W, 1993.

Mr. Standfast. London: Hodder and Stoughton, 1919; New York: Doran, 1919. Edited by William Buchan. Oxford: Oxford University Press, 1994.

The Island of Sheep. London, 1919; Boston, 1920. Written by Buchan and his wife and published under the pseudonyms Cadmus and Harmonia. Republished as *The Island of Sheep.* London: Hodder and Stoughton, 1936. U.S.: *The Man from the Norlands.* Boston: Houghton Mifflin, 1936. Edited by Ian Duncan. Oxford: Oxford University Press, 1997.

The Path of the King. London: Hodder and Stoughton, 1921; New York: Doran, 1921.

Huntingtower. London: Hodder and Stoughton, 1922; New York: Doran, 1922. Edited by Ann F. Stonehouse. Oxford: Oxford University Press, 1996.

Midwinter: Certain Travellers in Old England. London: Hodder and Stoughton, 1923; New York: Doran, 1923; Edinburgh: B&W, 1993.

The Three Hostages. London: Hodder and Stoughton, 1924; New York and Boston: Houghton Mifflin, 1924. Edited by Karl Miller. Oxford: Oxford University Press, 1997.

John Macnab. London: Hodder and Stoughton, 1925; Boston: Houghton Mifflin, 1925.

The Dancing Floor. London: Hodder and Stoughton, 1926; Boston: Houghton Mifflin, 1926. Edited by Marilyn Deegan. Oxford: Oxford University Press, 1997.

Witch Wood. London: Hodder and Stoughton, 1927; Boston: Houghton Mifflin, 1927. Edited by James C. Greig. Oxford: Oxford University Press, 1993.

The Runagates' Club. London: Hodder and Stoughton, 1928; Boston: Houghton Mifflin, 1928; London: Sutton, 1996.

The Courts of the Morning. London: Hodder and Stoughton, 1929; Boston: Houghton Mifflin, 1929; Edinburgh: B&W, 1982.

Castle Gay. London: Hodder and Stoughton, 1930; Boston: Houghton Mifflin, 1930.

The Blanket of the Dark. London: Hodder and Stoughton, 1931; Boston: Houghton Mifflin, 1931; Edinburgh: B&W, 1994.

The Gap in the Curtain. London: Hodder and Stoughton; Boston: Houghton Mifflin, 1932; Edinburgh: B&W, 1993.

The Magic Walking-Stick. London: Hodder and Stoughton; Boston: Houghton Mifflin, 1932.

A Prince of the Captivity. London: Hodder and Stoughton, 1933; Boston: Houghton Mifflin, 1933; Edinburgh: B&W: 1996.

The Free-Fishers. London: Hodder and Stoughton, 1934; Boston: Houghton Mifflin, 1934; Edinburgh: B&W, 1994.

The House of the Four Winds. London: Hodder and Stoughton; Boston: Houghton Mifflin, 1935; London: Sutton, 1993.

Sick Heart River. London: Hodder and Stoughton, 1941. U.S.: *Mountain Meadow.* Boston: Houghton Mifflin, 1941. Edited by David Daniell. Oxford: Oxford University Press, 1995.

The Best Short Stories of John Buchan. 2 vols. Edited by David Daniell. London, 1980–1982.

BIOGRAPHY

Sir Walter Raleigh. London: Nelson, 1911; New York: Holt, 1911.

Montrose. London and Edinburgh: Nelson, 1928; Boston, Houghton Mifflin, 1928.
Sir Walter Scott. London: Cassell, 1932; New York: Coward-McCann, 1932.
Julius Caesar. London: Davies, 1932; New York: Appleton, 1932.
Oliver Cromwell. London: Hodder and Stoughton, 1934; Boston: Houghton Mifflin, 1934.
Augustus. London: Hodder and Stoughton, 1937; Boston: Houghton Mifflin, 1937.

HISTORY

Brasenose College. London: Robinson, 1898.
Nelson's History of the Great War. 24 vols. London: Nelson, 1915–1919. Rev. as *A History of the Great War.* 4 vols. London: Nelson, 1921–1922; Boston: Houghton Mifflin, 1922.
The History of the South African Forces in France. London: Nelson, 1920; London: Imperial War Museum, 1992.
The History of the Royal Scots Fusiliers (1678–1918). London: Nelson, 1925.
The Massacre of Glencoe. London: Davies, 1933; New York: Putnam's, 1933; London: Buchan and Enright, 1996.
The King's Grace, 1910–1935. London: Hodder and Stoughton, 1935. U.S.: *The People's King: George V.* Boston: Houghton Mifflin, 1935.

OTHER

Essays and Apothegms of Francis Lord Bacon. Edited by John Buchan. London: Walter Scott, 1894.
The African Colony. Edinburgh: Blackwood, 1903.
Poems, Scots and English. London and Edinburgh: Jack, 1917.
A Book of Escapes and Hurried Journeys. London: Nelson, 1922; Boston: Houghton Mifflin, 1923.
Homilies and Recreations: Essays. London: Nelson, 1926; Boston: Houghton Mifflin, 1926.
Memory Hold-the-Door. London: Hodder and Stoughton, 1940, 1950. U.S.: *Pilgrim's Way.* Boston: Houghton Mifflin, 1940; New York: Carroll and Graf, 1984.
John Buchan's Collected Poems. Edited by Andrew Lownie and William Milne. Aberdeen, 1996.

BIBLIOGRAPHIES

Hanna, Archibald, Jr. *John Buchan, 1875–1940: A Bibliography.* Hamden, Conn.: Shoe String Press, 1953.
Wilmot, B.C. *A Checklist of Works by and About John Buchan in the John Buchan Collection, Douglas Library, Queen's University.* Boston: G. K. Hall, 1961.
Cox, Randolph J. "John Buchan, Lord Tweedsmuir: An Annotated Bibliography of Writings about Him." *English Literature in Transition, 1880–1920,* 9, no. 5: (1966): 241–291; 9, no. 6: 292–325 (1966); 10, no. 4: 209–211 (1967); 15, no. 1: 67–69 (1972).
Blanchard, Robert G. *The First Editions of John Buchan.* Hamden, Conn., 1981.

ARCHIVES

The main holdings of Buchan manuscripts are in the National Library of Scotland and Queen's University, Kingston, Ontario. Collections of Buchan's extensive correspondence are at Brown University Library and the Houghton Library, Harvard University.

BIOGRAPHICAL AND CRITICAL STUDIES

Buchan, Anna. *Unforgettable, Unforgotten.* London: Hodder and Stoughton, 1945.
Buchan, William. *John Buchan: A Memoir.* London: Buchan and Enright, 1982.
Cawelti, John, and Bruce A. Rosenberg. *The Spy Story.* Chicago: Chicago University Press, 1987.
Daniell, David. *The Interpreter's House: A Critical Assessment of John Buchan.* London: Nelson, 1975.
Hart, Francis R. *The Scottish Novel from Smollett to Spark.* Cambridge, Mass.: Harvard University Press, 1971.
Himmelfarb, Gertrude. *Victorian Minds.* London: Weidenfeld and Nicolson, 1968; New York: Harper and Row, 1970.
Kruse, Juanita. *John Buchan (1875–1940) and the Idea of Empire: Popular Literature and Political Ideology.* Lewiston, N.Y.: Edwin Mellen Press, 1989.
Lownie, Andrew. *John Buchan: The Presbyterian Cavalier.* London: Constable, 1995.
Masters, Anthony. *Literary Agents: The Novelist as Spy.* Oxford: Blackwell, 1987.
Sandison, Alan. *The Wheel of Empire: A Study of the Imperial Idea in Some Late Nineteenth- and Early Twentieth-Century Fiction.* London: Macmillan, 1967.
Smith, Janet Adam. *John Buchan: A Biography.* London: Rupert Hart-Davis, 1965; Boston: Little, Brown, 1966.
———. *John Buchan and His World.* London: Thames and Hudson, 1979; New York: Scribners, 1979.
Turner, Arthur C. *Mr. Buchan, Writer.* London: SCM Press, 1949.
Tweedsmuir, Lady Susan. *John Buchan by His Wife and Friends.* London: Hodder and Stoughton, 1947.
Ridley, M. R. *Second Thoughts: More Studies in Literature.* London: Dent, 1965.
Usborne, Richard. *Clubland Heroes: A Nostalgic Study of Some Recurrent Characters in the Romantic Fiction of Dornford Yates, John Buchan and Sapper.* 2nd ed. London: Barrie and Jenkins, 1974.
Webb, Paul. *A Buchan Companion.* Stroud: Far Thrupp, 1994; Dover, N.H.: Alan Sutton, 1994.
Winks, Robin W. "John Buchan: Stalking the Wilder Game." In *The Four Adventures of Richard Hannay.* Boston: Godine, 1988.

The *John Buchan Journal,* dealing with all aspects of the author's life and work, has been in existence since 1980.

JOHN DICKSON CARR
(1906–1977)

MICHAEL DIRDA

UNQUESTIONABLY the greatest master of the locked-room mystery, John Dickson Carr nonetheless remains a slightly problematic figure in detective fiction. Some scholars—among them Jacques Barzun and Robin Winks—tend to regard his books as sterile exercises in ingenuity, with interludes of tiresome slapstick humor. Others—including the esteemed critic Anthony Boucher and the novelist Kingsley Amis—see Carr as the greatest detective story writer since G. K. Chesterton, or even since Arthur Conan Doyle.

Like most Golden Age novelists, Carr certainly wrote too much—more than seventy books, as well as scores of radio mysteries and suspense dramas. Yet his work is far more varied than is sometimes imagined, for he produced one superb example of "true crime" writing, *The Murder of Sir Edmund Godfrey* (1936); an important, indeed standard, biography, *The Life of Sir Arthur Conan Doyle* (1949); a fistful of swashbuckling historical novels of which the best is probably *The Devil in Velvet* (1951); some excellent criticism, chiefly the chapter titled "The Locked Room Lecture" in the novel *The Three Coffins* (1935; U.K. title, *The Hollow Man*) and "The Grandest Game in the World"; and several novels that are technical tours de force. To this last category belongs, most prominently, *The Burning Court* (1937), a thriller that blends most of Carr's strengths while ultimately turning the Golden Age mystery on its head. In its way, *The Burning Court* is as controversial a whodunit as Agatha Christie's *The Murder of Roger Ackroyd.* A more quietly impressive book is *The Judas Window* (1938), not only because knowledgeable critics view it as the finest locked-room mystery of all time, but also because Carr contrives to relate virtually the entire action as a courtroom drama.

Carr enthusiasts argue about which of this master's books is his best. For example, in *John Dickson Carr: A Critical Study,* S. T. Joshi dubs *The Arabian Nights Murders* (1936) the "greatest pure detective story ever written," while Robert E. Briney selected *The Crooked Hinge* (1938) as the Carr title for a library of classic mysteries. Historical novelist Lillian de la Torre choose *The Murder of Sir Edmund Godfrey.* Most informed readers would agree, however, that Carr wrote his most lasting books in the 1930s; and these will be the principal focus of the essay that follows. Let the reader be warned: I take care not to reveal the endings of most of the novels, but I do discuss the plot turns of *The Three Coffins* and the shocker twist in *The Burning Court.*

Starting Out

Though sometimes thought to be English, largely because of the settings of his books,

John Dickson Carr grew up in Uniontown, Pennsylvania, the city where he was born on 30 November 1906. His father, Wooda Nicholas Carr, was a moderately well-to-do lawyer and Democratic politico who was even elected to Congress for a term. His mother, Julia, appears to have been a formal, cold woman for whom her son reportedly felt little affection. A voracious reader as a boy, Carr was particularly fond of adventure fiction: Alexandre Dumas, Robert Louis Stevenson, the Sherlock Holmes stories. In school he proved an indifferent scholar, though the family maintained hopes that he might eventually attend an Ivy League university and become a lawyer.

To this end, young John was sent away to the Hill School, a highly regarded private academy (the man of letters—and notable disparager of detective fiction—Edmund Wilson was an alumnus from a previous generation). There the boy continued his spotty education, doing at best adequately in English and Latin and altogether dismally in mathematics (a subject frequently maligned in his subsequent fiction: "I do not think. I am a mathematician," asserts a character in *The Three Coffins*). While at the Hill School, Carr began to write his first serious stories, mainly swashbuckling tales of "Grand Guignol" adventure.

Because of his uninspired school record, Carr's parents abandoned hope of sending their only child to Harvard and were happy to see him admitted to Haverford College. There Carr blithely neglected his classes and continued to write "sensational" fiction. His tastes were clear from an early age: he reveled in mystery, adventure, and romance, and liked best of all to combine them.

In the years at Haverford the young Carr created his first important detective, Henri Bencolin, a French prefect of police who seems a first cousin to several suave Gallic masterminds: Edgar Allan Poe's detective Auguste Dupin; Maurice LeBlanc's gentleman-burglar Arsene Lupin; Pierre Souvestre and Marcel Allain's shadowy master of the underworld, Fantômas; and the reformed criminal turned detective, G. K. Chesterton's Flambeau. Henri Bencolin was to appear in a half dozen stories and five novels. In nearly all of them Carr took great pains to foster an atmosphere reminiscent of the *Arabian Nights,* a slightly cloying sense of the uncanny, menacing, and carnivalesque.

Carr failed to graduate from Haverford, yet somehow managed to persuade his family to finance a trip to Paris. There he wrote his first novel, a swashbuckler "filled with gadzooks and sirrahs" that he claims to have destroyed (parts may have been cannibalized for the seventeenth-century adventure novel *Devil Kinsmere* (1934), published under the pseudonym Roger Fairbairn). Thus, early in his career Carr reveals a deep attraction to the historical adventure story, and one cannot help but wonder whether he might have first seen himself as a successor to Rafael Sabatini rather than Sir Arthur Conan Doyle. Certainly the 1920s and 1930s are remembered not only as the heyday of the classic fair-play mystery, but also of grand historical adventure, the era of Samuel Shellabarger and Kenneth Roberts and Margaret Mitchell.

Upon his return from Paris, Carr settled down at home and produced, at age twenty-three, his first published novel, *It Walks by Night* (1930). This is a remarkably accomplished example of a macabre mystery (expanded from an earlier short story called, appropriately enough, "Grand Guignol"). A young woman is about to marry the Duc de Saligny, when her first husband, a homicidal maniac, escapes from an asylum and has his face reshaped by a plastic surgeon, whom he then murders. The unfortunate medico's head is eventually glimpsed floating in a jar of alcohol. Building on this gruesome background, Carr duly sets up an impossible murder: at his wedding party the duke goes into an empty room, and a short while later Bencolin discovers his decapitated body.

The book was well received, but it is noteworthy that the *London Spectator* wrote that "the story may be read either as itself or a burlesque of itself." Throughout Carr's work one often senses an inherent playfulness, a sense of author and reader engaged in a game of peekaboo. In truth, few of his novels truly frighten; Carr prefers to suggest an almost cozy sense of the uncanny. (He admired the antiquarian ghost stories of M. R. James.) Little wonder in this regard that the novelist set so many of his plots against backgrounds naturally rich in history and folklore—a wax museum, the Tower of London, a maze, a castle on the Rhine—or employed nearly all the usual elements of the classic ghostly tale: the crumbling manuscript, an Egyptian curse, the undead (and the non-dead), a witches' coven, ancient sorceries.

Certainly the tone of *It Walks by Night* is established by the book's epigraph, from a fifteenth-century manuscript, which talks of vampires and werewolves: "So I say to you, even you who live in the city of Paris, when your fire burns low by night, and you hear a gentle tapping of fingers at the window-pane, do not open your door to this supposed traveller. . . ." One can almost picture the young Carr, like the Fat Boy in Charles Dickens' *Pickwick Papers*, whispering: "I wants to make your flesh creep." And he manages to do it, too—in a cozy way, of course.

This same eerie atmosphere recurs in the next three Bencolin titles: *The Lost Gallows* (1931), *Castle Skull* (1931), and *The Corpse in the Waxworks* (1932). In this last—Carr's first masterpiece—the body of a young woman is found lying in the arms of a leering waxwork satyr inside the locked Musée Augustin, Collection of Wonders. In the course of solving the crime Bencolin and his sidekick-narrator Jeff Marle discover that the museum stands across the way from the Silver Key Club, a notorious and exclusive sex retreat operated by a criminal mastermind (with an advance degree in English literature!). The reason for this provocative murder ultimately turns on the knotty question of moral standards in a changing world.

Eerie Doings

What is the purpose of this slightly tongue-in-cheek Gothic atmosphere? First, John Dickson Carr simply liked such romantic touches. The real world could be a dishearteningly mundane place—especially for a kid from western Pennsylvania. How much more fun to engage in heart-pounding adventures, with slant-eyed beauties, secret societies, and uncanny means of murder.

> Here are three passports and an automatic pistol. You will proceed at once to Cairo, in whatever disguise you think fit; but take care that you are not followed by a man whose cufflinks take the form of a small black cross. Arrived in Cairo, you will proceed to the Street of the Seven Cobras, to a house you will identify by . . .(*The Four False Weapons*)

Throughout the 1930s the world hungered for such extravagance and mystery and found them in pulp magazines (*The Shadow*), serials (*Captain Marvel*), comics (*The Phantom*), and novels about captains from Castile or the insidious Dr. Fu Manchu. Over the drab world of the Great Depression the imagination could superimpose the exotic and alluring marvels of the *Arabian Nights*. In short, Carr fervently believed that fiction should be exciting.

Second, the locked-room mystery inherently evokes a witchy haze of the supernatural. The woman's body lies on the empty beach where she has been strangled, a single set of footprints—the victim's own—marks the silk-smooth expanse of sand. A man is suddenly shot at point-blank range in the middle of a cul-de-sac; three witnesses will swear that no one came near him—and the fresh fallen snow corroborates their testimony. Another man dives into a swimming pool and simply vanishes from the face of the earth. Stranger than science. Believe it or not. Impossible but true. From a novelistic point of view an eerie atmosphere also helps counter the locked-room mystery's tendency to dryness. Many "impossible crimes" involve precise timetables, elaborate stage machinery, improbable coincidence, room diagrams, the comparison of alibis, and so forth. Such inventorying can dull a story's edge, but after building an atmosphere of black magic, the mundane accumulation of facts may signal a welcome relief—the promise that sanity may eventually be restored to a world gone mad.

Third, Carr's particular trappings of the uncanny re-create a mood like that of a nightclub magic act. The reader agrees to surrender his doubts in order to enjoy the show that follows. We do not really think that the magician saws the lady in half, but it is fun to pretend we do. In that suspension of disbelief we prepare ourselves for the oohs and ahs of the final, unexpected trick that ends the show with a grand flourish.

Making His Mark

After the success of his first novel, John Dickson Carr moved to New York City, where he rented a house with two friends. In the late 1920s the writer established a pattern he would follow through much of his career: he would work intently on a book, sometimes for twelve hours at a stretch, for the weeks or months needed to finish it; then he would celebrate with heavy drinking and partying. Carr was a serious drinker and smoker most of his life, and his wife Clarice simply accepted this as the man's nature.

Carr met Clarice Cleaves in 1930 on a ship traveling to the United States from London. The young mystery novelist was returning from a holiday, and Clarice was hoping to make a life for herself in America. A shipboard romance blossomed, then grew serious in New York, and the couple married in 1932, without inviting either family to the wedding. Not long afterward, Carr and his new wife decided to move to London for a while. That while turned into a stay of some sixteen years. They were the years of his finest work.

In 1933 Carr produced *Hag's Nook,* the first exploit featuring his famous detective Dr. Gideon Fell. Despite the English setting, the general atmosphere of the novel is similar to that of the Bencolin continental shockers. There is a family curse, an ancient diary, a ruined prison, the evil Hag's Nook, the impossible crime. Instead of the saturnine and unsettling figure of Henri Bencolin, the detective this time out is an old lexicographer, part antiquarian, part Falstaff. Carr clearly modeled his new mastermind after the fat, genial creator of the Father Brown mysteries, G. K. Chesterton.

> [Dr. Fell] was very stout, and walked, as a rule with two canes. Against the light from the front windows his big mop of dark hair, streaked with a white plume waved like a war-banner. . . . His face was large and round and ruddy, and had a twitching smile somewhere above several chins. But what you noticed there was the twinkle in his eye. He wore eyeglasses on a broad black ribbon, and the small eyes twinkled over them. . . .

The old fellow drinks wine on top of beer on top of stout; he spills cigar ashes all over himself. Yet,

> he's one of the great institutions of England. The man has more obscure, useless, and fascinating information than any person I ever met. He'll ply you with food and whisky until your head reels; he'll talk interminably, on any subject whatever, but particularly on the glories and sports of old-time England. He likes band music, melodrama, beer, and slapstick comedies.

For years, it turns out, Fell has been at work on a history of the drinking customs of England.

The character of Dr. Fell evolved somewhat over the next twenty-five years, but basically he remained this wheezing, larger-than-life, Dickensian figure. His second adventure, *The Mad Hatter Mystery* (1933), firmly establishes the often madcap quality to the crimes he investigates. Consider the air of Wonderland in the novel's very title, or this opening paragraph:

> It began, like most of Dr. Fell's adventures, in a bar. It dealt with the reason why a man

> was found dead on the steps of Traitor's Gate, at the Tower of London, and with the odd headgear of this man in the golf suit. That was the worst part of it. The whole case threatened for a time to become a nightmare of hats.

A page or two later Fell appears:

> There was the doctor, bigger and stouter than ever. He wheezed. His red face shone, and his small eyes twinkled over eyeglasses on a broad black ribbon. There was a grin under his bandit's moustache, and chuckling upheavals animated his several chins. On his head was the inevitable black shovel-hat; his paunch projected from a voluminous black cloak. Filling the stairs in grandeur, he leaned on an ash cane with one hand and flourished another cane with the other. It was like meeting Father Christmas or Old King Cole. Indeed, Dr. Fell had frequently impersonated Old King Cole at garden pageants, and enjoyed the role immensely.

In Carr's early works the atmosphere of the unnatural, the forbidden, and the genuinely mysterious dominates the storytelling; with the Fell cases Carr mixes in a leavening of actual humor. As a result, the character of the mysteries lightens; they become more gamelike, more like "murder weekends" than murder cases. If the Bencolin books possess a genuinely dark and threatening atmosphere, like that of a haunted house in an M. R. James short story, the Fell novels more frequently resemble a carnival fun house, supplying equal measures of dizziness, illusion, marvels, and laughter.

After *The Mad Hatter Mystery* appeared, it was reviewed in the *Sunday Times* by one of the leading English mystery novelists, Dorothy L. Sayers:

> Mr. Carr can lead us away from the small, artificial, brightly-lit stage of the ordinary detective plot into the menace of outer darkness. He can create atmosphere with an adjective, and make a picture from a wet iron railing, a dusty table, a gas-lamp blurred by the fog. He can alarm with an illusion or delight with a rollicking absurdity. He can invent a passage from a lost work of Edgar Allan Poe which sounds like the real thing. In short he can write—not merely in the negative sense of observing the rules of syntax, but in the sense that every sentence gives a thrill of positive pleasure. This is the most attractive mystery I have read for a long time.

One could hardly argue with Sayers' general judgment, though her remarks about style may come as a surprise, since Carr's prose is usually regarded as merely adequate. Certainly, Sayers herself possesses a more polished and learned diction, a joy at its best if sometimes precious and distracting. Carr prefers plain, straightforward sentences that move with great swiftness. With a few phrases he sets up a tableau in the mind's eye; with another he suddenly instills a sense of something very queer: "A thief gets into a clockmaker's shop and steals the hands off a clock. Nothing else is taken or even touched; only the hands from a clock of no especial value. . . ." The words themselves may be common, but the situation, the idea, is striking, even poetic. In this evocative power lies Carr's most obvious stylistic gift.

Of course, given the nature of the crimes (and the need to keep up reader interest), Carr frequently indulges in melodramatic flourishes. Chapters end with a sentence in italics, with a whispered "blood," or with the sudden reappearance of a missing person. Many characters possess verbal tics, especially Fell with his "harrumphs" and trademark curses such as "Archons of Athens." Indeed, some characters approach the status of humors: the naive, young American who narrates the tale; the frustrated policeman (usually Inspector Hadley) who is intelligent, hardworking, and invariably wrong; the various interchangeable doctors, bankers, playboys, soldiers, and other standard dramatis personae of Golden Age mysteries.

Following the success of his Gideon Fell novels Carr decided to experiment further with his now usual mix of detection, spookiness, and humor. *The Eight of Swords* (1934) to some degree and *The Blind Barber* (1934) to an even greater one are intended as comic murder mysteries. In her review of the latter Dorothy L. Sayers claimed to have laughed uproariously; nearly thirty years later Anthony Boucher was still cracking up: "Who observes the clues while he's wiping his laughter-streaming eyes?" (1962 ed., preface). *The Blind Barber* takes place on a steamship and features a quartet of drunken revelers—a young American diplomat, his girlfriend, an old Norwegian sea captain, and a mystery writer named Henry Morgan—who attempt to solve a series of crimes, including a theft (of some reels of indiscreet movie film) and an apparent murder. There are pratfalls, drunken escapades, and stories told in broken English.

Such matters are subjective, but these humorous flourishes now appear lame, even downright embarrassing. Despite the claims of some admirers, Carr never approaches within hailing distance of P. G. Wodehouse's comic genius. Wodehouse depends on a deadpan style, brilliant similes, and razor-sharp plotting: Carr can manage the last, but the first two are utterly beyond him. His prose, though evocative, lacks the Wodehouse fizz. And his idea of humor seems to be far too broad for modern tastes—tipsy behavior, funny accents, cutesy lovers at odds. Happily, most of the Fell novels—excepting *The Case of the Constant Suicides* (1941), which overemphasizes alcoholic high jinks—add just a twist of humor. In fact, one reason Fell remains Carr's best detective is that he does not carry this burden of lackluster comedy.

In the 1930s the young detective novelist found himself competent enough to produce four or five books a year, but his publishers did not want more than two. What's a fast-working writer to do? Create a pseudonym. So was born Carter Dickson, hardly a secret identity to stymie even the most naive reader. In his first exploit, *The Plague Court Murders* (1934), Carter Dickson introduced his standard detective, Sir Henry Merrivale, known as H. M., or the Old Man.

If Gideon Fell is genial and Dickensian, Sir Henry Merrivale resembles an absentminded professor—blustery, childish, silly, and shrewd. Where Fell is modeled after Chesterton, Merrivale takes his inspiration in part from Mycroft Holmes, Sherlock's smarter brother (and later from the wartime Sir Winston Churchill):

> I thought of the extremely lazy, extremely garrulous and slipshod figure who sat grinning with sleepy eyes; his hands folded over his big stomach and his feet propped upon the desk. His chief taste was for lurid reading-matter; his chief complaint that people would not treat him seriously. He was a qualified barrister and a qualified physician, and he spoke atrocious grammar. . . . He was vastly conceited, and had an inexhaustible fund of bawdy stories. . . .

During the war Merrivale was apparently in charge of government intelligence operations, and he still maintains an office in Whitehall. On his door appear "enormous staggering letters: 'Busy!!! No Admittance!!! Keep Out!!!' and below the plate, as though with a pointed afterthought, 'This means You!' " Merrivale keeps liquor in his safe ("Important State Documents! Do Not Touch!!") and is usually napping at his desk.

Yet like all such men of genius, once stirred to action he is a veritable tiger on the scent. In *The Plague Court Murders*, "Carter Dickson" piles on the supernatural effects. Plague Court is a haunted run-down pile, cursed since the time of the great plague. One night a suave medium tries to exorcise its evil spirits and is found stabbed to death. Was Darworth killed by an ancient curse? Was the door to his little house locked to keep him in or to keep something out? Carr (as we will continue to refer to him) invents a seventeenth-century diary which concludes with a hideous curse on the family that still owns this ancient property. Of course, spiritualism is bunk—or is it? Why was Darworth so frightened at a seance a week before his murder when his own automatic writing produced the ominous message: "Only seven more days"? Of what or whom was Darworth so terrified? And, most important, how was the murder committed?

As it turns out, there is a woman in this case, a seductive and very dangerous woman. Though Carr's minor characters are generally as unmemorable as nickels, his young women tend to be surprisingly sophisticated. They are sensual beings; several have been divorced or had love affairs; most are basically nice but can be very naughty. The heroine of *The Judas Window* (1938) once allowed a caddish lover to take photographs of her in the nude—and in lascivious postures. H. M. predicts that her marriage will be a happy one. In later life, Carr was to use the term "ginch" (a portmanteau of girl and wench) to describe these liberated female moderns. That said, Carr's depiction of young love is nonetheless frequently saccharine, and many admirers of the novels simply learn to endure the gush for the sake of other genuine narrative pleasures.

Between 1935 and 1938 John Dickson Carr reached his creative peak. In these years he wrote *The Three Coffins, The Arabian Nights Murder, The Crooked Hinge, The Burning Court, The Peacock Feather Murders* (1937; U.K. title, *The Ten Teacups*), *The Judas Window,* and *The Murder of Sir Edmund Godfrey,* to mention only the unquestioned high spots. These are the books on which his reputation rests and are among the finest fair-play mystery novels ever written. Indeed, among Carr's contemporaries only Agatha Christie has composed as many first-rate puzzles. To gain a better sense of what a Carr whodunit, or howdunit, is like, let us look in some detail at three of those masterpieces.

The Three Coffins

There is always with John Dickson Carr a slight flavor of the novelette—a tendency toward histrionic ruffles and flourishes. If one allows for that quality—and some readers never do—his books are quite impossible to put down. Edmund Crispin became a mystery writer after a friend lent him *The Crooked Hinge,* and he found himself reading through the night. Kingsley Amis once remarked that the word "gripping" should be reserved strictly for Carr novels. Here, for instance, is the opening to *The Three Coffins:*

> To the murder of Professor Grimaud, and later the equally incredible crime in Cagliostro Street, many fantastic terms could be applied—with reason. Those of Dr. Fell's friends who like impossible situations will not find in his casebooks any puzzle more baffling or more terrifying. Thus: two murders were committed, in such fashion that the murderer must not only have been invisible, but lighter than air. According to the evidence, this person killed his first victim and literally disappeared. Again according to the evidence, he killed his second victim in the middle of an empty street, with watchers at either end; yet not a soul saw him, and no footprint appeared in the snow.

If a paragraph such as this fails to start your pulse racing, then John Dickson Carr will never be a writer for you.

Professor Grimaud, an antiquarian and author of a standard work on witchcraft, frequents a pub where he discusses sorcery, folk beliefs, and much else with a small circle of acolytes. One cold night a mysterious stranger unexpectedly accosts Grimaud: "You do not believe then . . . that a man can get up out of his coffin; that he can move anywhere invisibly; that four walls are nothing to him; and that he is as dangerous as anything out of hell?" As "Pierre Fley, Illusionist"—so his card reads—is about to leave, he asks a last enigmatic question of the professor: "Some one will call on you one evening soon. I also am in danger when I associate with my brother, but I am prepared to run that risk. Some one, I repeat, will call on you. Would you rather I did—or shall I send my brother?" End of chapter 1.

Note how Carr arranges his effects. His first paragraph establishes a tone of mystery and foreboding. Then he introduces the cozy, firelit pub atmosphere and the talk of ghosts and sorcery. The names are quietly suggestive: Grimaud recalls the French word *grimoire*—a book of magic spells; Fley echoes flay—as when you separate skin from a body. In the course of his unnerving ramblings the illusionist actually refers to a "hollow man," which is the British title of this novel. The references to three coffins, a mysteriously powerful brother, invisible revenants, and a dangerous forthcoming visit establish a thoroughly spooky atmosphere.

Chapter 2 shifts to Dr. Fell's house, where all is warmth and congeniality. Fell sits in a comfortable chair before a "steaming bowl of punch" (Old King Cole indeed). Ted Rampole, whose consciousness is the only one we enter during the narrative, "could see the firelight moving on crooked walls of books, and hear fine snow ticking the window panes behind drawn curtains." What could be more snug? To divert his friends Fell and Inspector Hadley, Rampole relates the pub incident, about which he has heard from a newspaper chum who is a member of Grimaud's discussion group; he then mentions what he learned from a visit to the theater where the enigmatic illusionist is performing. M. Fley is apparently very good, even uncannily good, at his art, and somewhat obsessive about coffins: "Three of us were once buried alive," he tells an associate. "Only one escaped." How did Fley escape? "I didn't, you see. I was one of the two who did not escape."

By this time Dr. Fell has begun to grow excited; he obviously sees or intuits more than his companions. Rampole then tells us that to protect himself from these threatening brothers Grimaud has gone out and bought . . . a painting, "a landscape of some sort, weird business showing trees and gravestones." At this point, Fell insists on hurrying to Grimaud's that very night. Just as Hadley's police car comes storming up to the house, a figure climbs out to the sill of a second-story window, hesitates, and leaps into the street. Our heroes nearly run him over, but instead Boyd—the newspaper friend of Rampole—leads the group into the house and up to Grimaud's room, where a shot had rung out just a few minutes previously. Boyd had been forced to jump from the window because he and Grimaud's daughter had discovered themselves locked in the front parlor. Fearing the worst, the men break open the locked door: "Nothing came out, although something was trying to come out." Grimaud, mortally wounded, is crawling toward them, but he soon stops and lies still.

Observe how much action Carr has packed into this evening, and it has only just begun. In fact, Carr generally comes close to preserving the three unities of time, place, and action. Usually, the first third of any novel will take place at the scene of the crime, and often a murder will be resolved within a day or two of its commission. Such focus gives these books their particular intensity; the mystery writer Nicholas Blake once commented that Carr's books possess "the mad logic and extravagance of a dream." One might only add: a dream from which one cannot awake. That mad logic is brilliantly suggested by Grimaud's choice of weapon to defend himself against the living dead: a painting. This may seem like madness, but we recognize instinctively that there must be method in it.

As Grimaud lies in his own blood, dying from a gunshot wound, he murmurs some strange words about a fox. Upon inquiry, members of the household recall a loud bump that preceded the pistol shot by a few minutes. Grimaud's secretary is revealed as a short, prissy, and docile man: "I am a mathematician. I never permit myself to think." The housekeeper, Ernestine Dumont, faintly suggests a woman in disguise. From these two we learn that a shadowy figure had knocked at the front door and demanded to see the professor. The housekeeper had temporarily closed and locked the door, then gone to inform her employer—only to discover the strange guest trudging slowly up the stairs behind her. "His hair had a dark painted shiny look, if you understand me, almost as though his whole head were made of papier mache." When Grimaud appeared on the threshold of his study, he invited the visitor in and locked the door. From that moment on the room remained under the close observation of the secretary and the housekeeper. The stranger never emerged. A short time later the gun was fired, and soon thereafter the dying Grimaud discovered. Naturally, all the windows are closed, and there is no sign of anyone in the room except the wounded antiquarian.

Carr is particularly adept at maintaining, indeed increasing, narrative excitement by his melodramatic knack for the unexpected event, phrase, or action. Why would a man who has just been shot make a superhuman effort to burn certain papers? What is the meaning of Grimaud's talk of a fox? What does the phrase "Seven Towers" suggest? At the hospital the surgeon notes the dying man's final words: "It was my brother who did it. I never thought he would shoot. God knows how he got out of that room. One second he was there, and the next he wasn't."

While Hadley questions the members of the household, Fell studies a few titles in Grimaud's library and deduces, with a Sherlockian flourish, that he was originally a Magyar and had been imprisoned in a notorious prison. Later, when Hadley is dumbfounded as to how the nightwalker could leave no footprints in the snow, Fell answers, "Oh that!, . . . You know, for a second I hoped you had something. But that part is obvious." Only, of course, to Gideon Fell.

As the investigation proceeds, an elderly hanger-on named Drayman explains how, many years earlier, he first met Grimaud in Transylvania. Drayman was riding on horseback near an infamous prison colony when he noticed three fresh graves. As he looked, the dirt began to move on one, and slowly a figure rose out of the ground and stumbled toward him. This living dead man was none other than Grimaud, who contrived to escape from the prison by pretending to be a victim of the plague that had claimed his two brothers. Naturally, Drayman hurried his escaped convict friend away across the border to freedom.

At this point, Hadley decides that it is time for a chat with Pierre Fley, though Fell and Rampole choose to call it a night. The chapter ends with a sword thrust: "They did not learn it until next morning; but Fley, as a matter of fact, was already dead. He had been shot down with the same pistol that killed Grimaud. And the murderer was invisible before the eyes of witnesses, and still he had left no footprint in the snow." What's more, he killed Fley almost immediately after shooting Grimaud. The headlines in the papers read, "Magician Killed by Magic."

Certainly, Carr has done all he can to suggest that Fley and his brother, whom the investigators dub Henri, have risen from their graves to seek vengeance on Grimaud. Did Henri then kill Fley too? Why? This pervasively uncanny atmosphere suffuses not only the mystery of the crimes themselves—the locked room, the murder at point-blank range before witnesses—but also the associated details: a peculiar painting, an exceptional magic act, odd antiquarian researches, suspicious household members, a romantic past, even a few suggestive hobbies: Drayman, for instance, possesses a passion for Guy Fawkes Day fireworks.

At this point, Carr slows his narrative pace to present a disquisition on the traditional ghost story:

> I will give you rules, sir. The ghost should be malignant. It should never speak. It should never be transparent, but solid. It should never hold the stage for long, but appear in brief vivid flashes like the poking of a face round a corner. It should never appear in too much light. It should have an old, an academic or ecclesiastical background; a flavor of cloisters or Latin manuscripts. . . .

Ghost stories, complains Fell, are not written much these days because modern writers "are afraid of the thing called Melodrama." Not a problem for John Dickson Carr.

This apparent digression keeps the reader's sense of the supernatural enflamed, while enriching the character of Dr. Fell: he is, we remember, an expert on all sorts of out-of-the-way subjects. There will be two more such digressions: in one a circus acrobat will discuss conjuring and the art of illusion; the other will be a full chapter in which Fell discourses on the shape and variety of locked-room problems. These disquisitions about ghost stories, magic shows, and locked rooms add to the winey flavor of *The Three Coffins,* making us feel as though we are sitting in a comfortable library or hotel bar listening to these witchy matters. We have been primed to see marvels, and we do. All London partakes of this air of menace:

> This eerie feeling of streets in hiding, or whole rows of houses created by illusory magic to trick you, had never deserted Rampole in his prowlings through London. It was like wondering whether, if you walked out your own front door, you might not find the whole street mysteriously changed overnight and strange faces grinning out of houses you had never seen before.

Not too surprisingly, Carr soon takes us to a room decorated with Turkish motifs in an Arabian Nights decor.

Meanwhile the clues accumulate and, as mystery fanciers, we wonder: Should we pay more attention to O'Rourke, the acrobat? How did the housekeeper come to be nicknamed the Pythoness? Why does Fell assert, suddenly, that an enigmatic remark "is, in fact, as enlightening as the church bells." What church bells? And what did Fley mean by saying he was going back to his grave?

In most of Dr. Fell's cases there is a touch of humor and usually a love affair between insipid young people. In this instance, the prissy secretary, Stuart Mason, serves as the chief target of Carr's humor: "You would have diagnosed a Physics B.Sc. with Socialist platform tendencies, and you would have been right." A Mr. Burnaby turns out to be a somewhat comical, somewhat pathetic character, who tries to be a Great Detective while also attempting to seduce Grimaud's daughter. Of course, her heart belongs to the intrepid journalist Boyd. But there are questions about the girl's ancestry. Who is her mother? With so many tantalizing questions and odd details, little wonder that Rampole and his wife construct a timetable, laying out all the information known about people's movements on the night of the murders.

In a neat touch Rampole's wife immediately suspects O'Rourke. Her husband replies, with the knowing air of a confirmed detective story addict:

> Yes, I'd thought of O'Rourke. . . . But you're picking him for just two reasons. First because he's a trapeze man, and you associate a flying escape of some sort with the way this thing was done. But, so far as I can see, it's impossible. Second and more important, you're picking him for the reasons that he doesn't seem to have any connection with this case at all; that he's standing around for no good reason, and that's always a suspicious sign, isn't that so?

This self-aware, slightly tongue-in-cheek quality—as though Carr were implicitly addressing his reader—stands out in the famous chapter "The Locked Room Lecture," Fell's analysis of the problems and permutations of murder committed within a "hermetically sealed chamber." In fact, Fell actually points out that he and his listeners are characters in a detective story, and that there's no point in being coy about it: the ludic or game-like character of the mystery is here unashamedly proclaimed. Much of the actual lecture is given over to a listing of the various generic ways of committing a locked-room crime (revealing, to those with eyes to see, the solution to *The Plague Court Murders*). Other sections are sharply formulated defenses of the Carrian mystery story:

> I like my murders to be frequent, gory, and grotesque. I like some vividness of colour and imagination flashing out of my plot, since I cannot find a story enthralling solely on the grounds that it sounds as though it might really have happened. . . . A great part of our liking for detective fiction is "based" on a liking for improbability. When A is murdered, and B and C are under strong suspicion, it is improbable that the innocent-looking D can be guilty. But he is. If G has a perfect alibi, sworn to at every point by every other letter

> in the alphabet, it is improbable that G can have committed the crime. But he has. . . .

After this didactic interlude, Carr brings us to the solution of this book's double murders. "Chance and circumstance made an even worse blunder," maintains Dr. Fell, in speaking of the Grimaud and Fley killings, "and they've combined to make a terrifying, inexplicable puzzle out of what is really only a commonplace and ugly and petty murder-case." Dr. Fell overstates this, for what was intended to have happened is hardly less complex than what did.

There is no need to reveal the solution to *The Three Coffins* here. Perhaps I might leave the curious with three hints: 1) Take carcful note of the semantic shifts in the use of the word "brother." 2) Why did it take two men to carry the wrapped painting up the stairs to Grimaud's room? 3) How did the witnesses know what time Pierre Fley was killed? Tantalizing, yes? What else would you expect from this great master of the impossible crime?

The Murder of Sir Edmund Godfrey

John Dickson Carr was passionate about seventeenth-century English history, and almost equally fascinated by real-life crime (his novels are dotted with references to infamous murderers such as Dr. Crippen and Madeline Smith). For many aficionados of this appealing subgenre, the case of Edmund Godfrey remains particularly tantalizing, in part because it nearly toppled a government. An unsavory character named Titus Oates appeared before Judge Edmund Godfrey and swore there was a conspiracy to put Charles II's brother on the throne. Soon thereafter Godfrey disappeared; five days later his body was found; he had apparently been strangled and stabbed. Was this then grisly evidence that Oates had been telling the truth about a popish plot? A government crisis ensued as the king struggled against the earl of Shaftesbury, who wished to exclude Charles' brother from succession to the throne. Caught in the cross fire, three innocent men were executed, while the true murderer was never discovered.

Carr decided to re-create the Godfrey case as though it were a detective novel, "a detective story built on facts." The result was one of the first full-length true-crime books, and still one of the best. Jacques Barzun and Wendell Taylor, in *A Catalogue of Crime,* call it a masterpiece, "rereadable indefinitely." (Such praise is particularly meaningful since this pair denigrate virtually all of Carr's fiction.) Indeed, the book is exceptionally gripping:

> Let there be a spice of terror, of dark skies and evil things—a pond by a blasted tree, and horsemen galloping by night. Let there be drums behind a great stage—of a nation caught with panic, of kings playing at chess, of fiddles in the drawing-room, and of ladies more fair than any this side the grave. And at intervals, over our pipes and glasses, let us discuss the evidence in a certain long library where we shall sit as the Society of Connoisseurs in Murder.

(This last phrase Carr borrows from De Quincey's checky essay, "On Murder Considered as One of the Fine Arts," the classic apologia for the importance of "design . . . grouping, light and shade" in the performance of a fine murder.) In fact, Carr actually interrupts his account and interpretation of the crime with "interludes" set in the society's imagined reading room.

In the first interlude, after dramatizing the events leading up to the discovery of the judge's body, Carr presents not one, not two, but twelve different solutions to the murder of Sir Edmund Godfrey. Each, he tells us, has had its adherents over the centuries. Later, after relating the aftermath of the crime, he returns to the Society of Connoisseurs of Murder, and methodically knocks down those solutions before proposing his own. In the end, he comes close to pointing the accusing finger at one of the least likely personages in the whole sordid story. As it happens, Carr's choice has become the canonical one, though some elements in his argument have been superceded in light of new medical knowledge about the murder. Still, *The Murder of Sir Edmund Godfrey* remains breathtakingly vivid, shrewd, and convincing. Alas, the book failed to sell as well as his fiction and Carr never undertook such historical detections again.

The Burning Court

In *The Burning Court,* John Dickson Carr again describes an impossible crime tinged with the supernatural. This time he leaves the reader suspended between belief and disbelief, amazed yet unsure of the story's true ending. Not only has someone poisoned old Miles Despard with arsenic, but his body has disappeared from a sealed mausoleum. What's more, the old man was seen talking to an unknown woman dressed in old-fashioned clothes just before his death—and that woman vanished from his locked bedroom.

At first the murderer appears to be Lucy Despard, married to the old man's nephew Mark Despard. However, suspicion shifts away from Lucy when the Despards' friend Ted Stevens, who works in publishing, discovers that a forthcoming book about women poisoners includes an account of the nineteenth-century Marie d'Aubray, who in a contemporary photograph looks exactly like his own wife Marie. What's more, his wife wears the same kind of bracelet as the thrill-poisoner. Later, it turns out that Marie d'Aubray is somehow linked with Madame de Brinvilliers, a seventeenth-century poisoner (mentioned in *The Murder of Sir Edmund Godfrey*) who had water forced down her throat with a funnel during torture. Ted Stevens' wife Marie is deathly afraid of funnels.

In spite of himself, Ted gradually begins to wonder whether his beautiful, loving wife may in fact be some kind of witch or ghoul, returned from beyond the grave. He grows more troubled when the accumulating evidence clears Lucy and points directly toward his own Marie. Then, at the eleventh hour, Gaudan Cross—the very author whose new book first sparked Ted's suspicions—appears and reinterprets the facts, clearing Marie and revealing the name, motive, and method of the actual killer. Just as Cross finishes his brilliant reconstruction of the crime, he sips from a glass of wine and drops dead of poison. What a shame! At least the guilty party has been identified and taken into custody.

At this point in *The Burning Court,* when everything has been resolved and the book appears quite complete, the reader discovers a two-and-a-half-page epilogue in which Carr enters the mind of Marie Stevens. Here the master plays his most stunning, mind-boggling narrative trick: Marie actually is a revenant, a member of a poison cult that has learned the art of reincarnation. She killed the old man and Gaudan Cross, who was himself one of her kind and will come back to life. In fact, she plans to make hubby Ted one of the "non-dead" soon: "He will be one of us presently, if I can transform him without pain. Or too much pain."

At the time, some traditionalists balked at this supernatural ending. It undercut the very rationale of locked-room murders: the crime should seem like the work of a supernatural fiend, but turn out to be merely fiendishly clever. Certainly, Carr himself demonstrates astonishing plotting skill by creating an impossible crime that seems to be committed by one person, turns out to be masterminded by another, and may really be the work of a third. *The Burning Court,* like *The Murder of Sir Edmund Godfrey,* probes the limits of the classical detective story.

Although the locked-room problem has often been judged little more than an exercise in logic and ingenuity, at its most profound it calls into question many of our assumptions about reality. If we are not a Dr. Fell, how do we know the truth about the events around us? The epilogue to *The Burning Court* suggests a dizzying corollary: no matter how persuasive the explanation of the Great Detective, might there not be yet one more account of the crime that is just a little more subtle, that reinterprets the same evidence to yield a quite different solution? After all, the murder of Sir Edmund Godfrey generated a dozen possible explanations. Is truth then only something we create? Perhaps the world that seems so substantial is in fact nothing but a theater, a waxworks, a Maskelyne magic show? Is it any wonder then that Carr's novels generate a feeling of mental vertigo? All that has seemed solid has vanished and left only illusion. When one considers these classic Carr works, or a comparable masterpiece like Anthony Berkeley's *The Poisoned Chocolates Case* (with its multiple solutions to the same murder), one cannot help but think of Piranesi's unescapable prisons, the infinite regress of M. C. Escher drawings, or the Japanese classic of ambiguous interpretations, *Rashomon.*

It is unlikely that many readers of John Dickson Carr actually take the trouble to check out the Rube Goldberg details of his impossible-seeming crimes. The solution does not really have to be workable; it merely needs to "seem" workable. In "Some Thoughts on Peacock Feet," E. F. Bleiler has shown that H. M.'s explication of *The Peacock Feather Murders* is built on a series of near impossibilities—given the angles and openings needed, the killer could not commit the crime. In "John Dickson Carr and the Aura of Genius," James Kingman proves that the device in *The Crooked Hinge*—a means by which a man may shrink his height at will—precludes his being able to perform other actions that occur in the story. Yet both these books remain masterpieces of the "miracle problem." The idea of how the murders might have been performed seems plausible, if unlikely, and that's enough. Douglas Greene once wrote, "We don't investigate the crime; we are fooled by it." That's exactly right. The pleasure of reading John Dickson Carr lies not in outguessing H. M. or Dr. Fell, but in being amazed.

Fresh Fields

In 1936 Carr was elected to England's prestigious Detection Club, whose members included Agatha Christie, Dorothy L. Sayers, Anthony Berkeley, Margery Allingham, and many other masters of the fair-play mystery. Allingham once inscribed one of her novels to the club's only American member: "To John Dickson Carr, the best mystery writer in the world, except me." Carr seems to have fit right in with his new friends, going so far as to collaborate with John Rhodes on a murder that takes place in an elevator, *Fatal Descent* (1939; U.K. title, *Drop to His Death*). Around this time the detective story critic E. Powys Mather, known as Torquemada, proclaimed John Dickson Carr one of the Big Five of mystery writing. Bear in mind that the novelist was then in his mid-thirties.

A restless spirit, Carr soon began to explore other media for his creative talents. For example, he sold some sensationalist short fiction to pulp magazines in America. From short stories—some featuring Col. March and the Department of Queer Complaints—he eventually moved into the writing of radio suspense dramas. During the late 1930s and through the 1940s Carr originated or contributed substantially to such famous radio series as *Appointment with Fear, Suspense,* and *Cabin B-13.* In one radio play, "The Dead Sleep Lightly," a man is frightened to death when he receives a phone call on a supposedly dead line, from a former mistress who has been in the grave for twenty years. In *Cabin B-13* a newly married woman boards a ship with her husband only to have him utterly disappear (the solution to this one is a variant of Chesterton's famous story "The Invisible Man"). In "Mr. Markham, Antique Dealer," Carr executes a brilliant tour de force involving only three characters, which leads up to the murder of the blackmailing Mr. Markham and his apparent return from the dead. In many respects, Carr's spooky radio dramas were the 1940s equivalent of Rod Serling's *Twilight Zone* television series. For many years these plays were presumed lost, but in the 1980s a score of them were made available in two volumes edited by Douglas G. Greene: *The Door to Doom* (1980) and *The Dead Sleep Lightly* (1983).

When the United States entered World War II Carr returned home with Clarice and their three daughters, only to be sent back to London to work in radio propaganda, contributing inspirational plays about freedom fighters in Europe and entertaining the British with mystery dramas. Of course, Carr continued to write novels as well, though no longer so quickly. His two best books of the 1940s are probably the Carter Dickson *Nine–and Death Makes Ten* (1940) and *He Who Whispers* (1946), published under his own name. Both are splendid, the former—murder on a ship crossing the Atlantic during wartime—was a favorite of Kingsley Amis; the latter has been included among the top locked-room problems in mystery fiction. But these two mysteries may be regarded as something of a last hurrah. Though Carr would continue to write detective fiction for the rest of his life, after 1948 his books never matched those of the 1930s.

Carr remained busy. In the late 1940s he embarked on *The Life of Sir Arthur Conan Doyle* (1949), with the support of the novelist's fractious son Adrian. The result is still the standard life of the creator of Sherlock Holmes, even if the book reads almost too dramatically: Doyle appears not only as the embodiment of chivalric virtues but also as the secret model for Holmes himself. In short, Carr approached his subject as a novelist looking for a good story. Following the success of the biography, Carr and Adrian Conan Doyle collaborated for a volume of so-so Holmes pastiches: *The Exploits of Sherlock Holmes* (1954).

In the midst of this varied work Carr suffered his first serious illness. Always prone to go off on a spree when drunk, he finally spun out of control, suffering a nervous breakdown and temporary writer's block. Other physical ailments also began to appear—a fistula, a stroke, eventually cancer—and for the last twenty years of his life John Dickson Carr was never quite well again.

Politically, Carr was deeply conservative; an instinctive Tory, a Stuart sympathizer, an admirer of Charles II. For Carr the postwar triumph of the Labour Party was an unmitigated disaster and he swiftly moved back to the States, eventually buying a house in Mamaroneck, New York—just down the street from Clayton Rawson, creator of the magician detective The Great Merlini, and not far from the home of Frederick Dannay, one half of the Ellery Queen writing team. In America, Carr hobnobbed with the Mystery Writers of America, was honored as a Grand Master, and happily talked shop about the various ways to commit murder. In these years, Carr even wrote two hilarious skits, parodies of Sherlock Holmes, for MWA functions: "The Adventure of the Conk-Singleton Papers" and "The Adventure of the Paradol Chamber." Carr could not quite settle down, however. When the conservatives returned to power he returned to England, but nothing was ever quite the same. Soon he was off to Tangier, then back to the States, then to Ireland, and eventually to Greenville, South Carolina.

At Work Till the End

Carr's best writing of the 1950s went into his historical thrillers. Their titles convey something of their gaudy power: *The Bride of Newgate* (1950), *The Devil in Velvet* (1951), *Fire, Burn!* (1957), *Captain Cut-Throat* (1955), *The Demoniacs* (1962). In *The Devil in Velvet* a modern-day professor sells his soul to the devil and finds himself in the body of his seventeenth-century namesake, Sir Nicholas Fenton. From his research the professor knows that somebody is poisoning Sir Nick's beautiful wife Lydia, but who? As the professor strives to save Lydia, he finds himself drawn to the saucy Meg, discovers to his surprise that he is an excellent swordsman, stands up to the machinations of the conniving earl of Shaftesbury, and ultimately resolves to change history. The novel is quite thrilling, and clearly demonstrates a resurgence of Carr's early passion for swashbuckling romance.

Carr's last novels—*Panic in Box C* (1966), *Dark of the Moon* (1967), *Papa Là-Bas* (1968), and *The Hungry Goblin* (1972)—are relatively weak efforts, and charity will assign their faults to Carr's deteriorating physical condition. In the 1970s he was treated for lung cancer and bounced back after chemotherapy, but eventually the cancer returned and he died in a hospice on 27 February 1977. He was seventy-one.

Still, John Dickson Carr went out writing. In the late 1960s he had begun to review mysteries for *Ellery Queen's Mystery Magazine* and continued in that position, with occasional intermissions, until his death. It is strange to think of the creator of Gideon Fell reading, with appropriate pleasure and admiration, the Matt Helm spy thrillers of Donald Hamilton, but so it was. Of course, "The Jury Box"—as Carr's feature was called—would often take time to praise reprints of the old masters, among them *The Father Brown Omnibus* by his old hero G. K. Chesterton.

In 1963 *Ellery Queen's Mystery Magazine* published Carr's longest work of criticism: "The Grandest Game in the World." This essay—originally intended as an introduction to an anthology of ten favorite whodunits—is an ardent defense of the fair-play mystery. "The fine detective story, be it repeated, does not consist of 'a' clue. It is a ladder of clues, a pattern of evidence, joined together with such cunning that even the experienced reader may be deceived, until, in the blaze of the surprise ending, he suddenly sees the whole design." At the writing of this kind of detective story John Dickson Carr remains very nearly without rival.

Selected Bibliography

Douglas G. Greene's biography—see below—contains an exemplary checklist of the works of John Dickson Carr. Many of Carr's books have been reprinted in various paperback editions, for example by International Polygonics and Carroll & Graf.

WORKS OF JOHN DICKSON CARR

NOVELS

It Walks by Night. New York: Harper, 1930.
The Lost Gallows. New York: Harper, 1931.
Castle Skull. New York: Harper, 1931.
The Corpse in the Waxworks. New York: Harper, 1932.
Poison in Jest. New York: Harper, 1932.
Hag's Nook. New York: Harper, 1933.
The Mad Hatter Mystery. New York: Harper, 1933.
The Blind Barber. New York: Harper, 1934; New York: Collier, 1962.
Devil Kinsmere. By "Roger Fairbairn." New York: Harper, 1934.
The Eight of Swords. New York: Harper, 1934.
Death-Watch. New York: Harper, 1935.
The Three Coffins. New York: Harper, 1935. U.K.: *The Hollow Man.* London: Hamish Hamilton, 1935.
The Arabian Nights Murder. New York: Harper, 1936.
The Murder of Sir Edmund Godfrey. New York: Harper, 1936.
The Burning Court. New York: Harper, 1937.
The Four False Weapons. New York: Harper, 1937.
To Wake the Dead. London: Hamish Hamilton, 1937; New York: Harper, 1938.
The Crooked Hinge. New York: Harper, 1938.
The Problem of the Green Capsule. New York: Harper, 1939. U.K.: *The Black Spectacles.* London: Hamish Hamilton, 1939.
The Problem of the Wire Cage. New York: Harper, 1939.
The Man Who Could Not Shudder. New York: Harper, 1940.
The Case of the Constant Suicides. New York: Harper, 1941.
Death Turns the Tables. New York: Harper, 1941; London: Hamish Hamilton, 1942.
The Emperor's Snuff-Box. New York: Harper, 1942.
Till Death Do Us Part. New York: Harper, 1944.
He Who Whispers. New York: Harper, 1946.
The Sleeping Sphinx. New York: Harper, 1947.
Below Suspicion. New York: Harper, 1949.
The Bride of Newgate. New York: Harper, 1950.
The Devil in Velvet. New York: Harper, 1951.
The Nine Wrong Answers. New York: Harper, 1952.
Captain Cut-Throat. New York: Harper, 1955.
Patrick Butler for the Defence. New York: Harper, 1956.
Fire, Burn! New York: Harper, 1957.
The Dead Man's Knock. New York: Harper, 1958.
Scandal at High Chimneys: A Victorian Melodrama. New York: Harper, 1959.
In Spite of Thunder. New York: Harper, 1960.
The Witch of the Lowtide: An Edwardian Melodrama. New York: Harper, 1961.

The Demoniacs. New York: Harper, 1962.
Most Secret. New York: Harper, 1964.
The House at Satan's Elbow. New York: Harper, 1965.
Panic in Box C. New York: Harper, 1966.
Dark of the Moon. New York: Harper, 1967.
Papa Là-Bas. New York: Harper, 1968.
The Ghosts' High Noon. New York: Harper, 1969.
Deadly Hall. New York: Harper, 1971.
The Hungry Goblin: A Victorian Detective Novel. New York: Harper, 1972.

OTHER WORKS

"The Dead Sleep Lightly." *Suspense.* CBS, 30 March 1943. The script of this radio play was reprinted in *The Dead Sleep Lightly.* Edited by Douglas G. Greene. New York: Doubleday, 1983. *Fell and Foul Play.* Edited by Douglas G. Greene. International Polygories, 1991.
"Mr. Markham, Antique Dealer." *Suspense.* CBS, 11 May 1943. The script of this radio play was reprinted in *Rogues' Gallery: The Great Criminals of Modern Fiction.* Edited by Ellery Queen. Boston: Little Brown, 1948.
"The Adventure of the Conk-Singleton Papers." A playlet parodying Sherlock Holmes, performed at the Mystery Writers of America annual meeting, April 1948. Script reprinted with some changes in *The Door to Doom.* Edited by Douglas G. Greene. New York: Harper, 1980.
"The Adventure of the Paradol Chamber." A playlet parodying Sherlock Holmes, performed at the Mystery Writers of America annual meeting, April 1949. Script reprinted with some changes in *The Door to Doom.* Edited by Douglas G. Greene. New York: Harper, 1980.
The Life of Sir Arthur Conan Doyle. New York: Harper, 1949.
The Third Bullet and Other Stories. New York: Harper, 1954.
The Exploits of Sherlock Holmes (with Adrian Conan Doyle). New York: Random House, 1954.
The Men Who Explained Miracles. New York: Harper, 1963. Short stories.
"The Grandest Game in the World." *Ellery Queen's Mystery Magazine,* March 1963.

POSTHUMOUS COLLECTIONS

The Door to Doom and Other Detections. Edited by Douglas G. Greene. New York: Harper, 1980. Expanded ed. as *The Door to Doom.* New York: International Polygonics, 1991. Short fiction.
The Dead Sleep Lightly. Edited by Douglas G. Greene. New York: Doubleday, 1983. Short fiction. Includes "The Grandest Game in the World."
Fell and Foul Play. Edited by Douglas G. Greene. New York: International Polygonics, 1991. Short fiction.
Merrivale, March, and Murder. Edited by Douglas G. Greene. New York: International Polygonics, 1991. Short fiction.

WORKS OF "CARTER DICKSON"

The Bowstring Murders. By "Carr Dickson." New York: Morrow, 1933.
The Plague Court Murders. New York: Morrow, 1934.
The White Priory Murders. New York: Morrow, 1934.
The Red Widow Murders. New York: Morrow, 1935.
The Unicorn Murders. New York: Morrow, 1935.
The Punch and Judy Murders. New York: Morrow, 1937. Published as *The Magic-Lantern Murders.* London: Heinemann, 1936.
The Peacock Feather Murders. New York: Morrow, 1937. U.K.: *The Ten Teacups.* London: Heinemann, 1937.
The Judas Window. New York: Morrow, 1938. Republished as *The Crossbow Murder.* New York: Berkley, 1964.
Death in Five Boxes. New York: Morrow, 1938.
Fatal Descent (with John Rhode). New York: Dodd, Mead, 1939. Published as *Drop to His Death.* London: Heinemann, 1939.
The Reader Is Warned. New York: Morrow, 1939.
And So to Murder. New York: Morrow, 1940.
Nine—and Death Makes Ten. New York: Morrow, 1940. Published as *Murder in the Submarine Zone.* London: Heinemann, 1940.
The Department of Queer Complaints. New York: Morrow, 1940.
Seeing Is Believing. New York: Morrow, 1941.
The Gilded Man. New York: Morrow, 1942.
She Died a Lady. New York: Morrow, 1943.
He Wouldn't Kill Patience. New York: Morrow, 1944.
The Curse of the Bronze Lamp. New York: Morrow, 1945. U.K.: *Lord of the Sorcerers.* London: Heinemann, 1946.
My Late Wives. New York: Morrow, 1946.
The Skeleton in the Clock. New York: Morrow, 1948.
A Graveyard to Let. New York: Morrow, 1949.
Night at the Mocking Widow. New York: Morrow, 1950.
Behind the Crimson Blind. New York: Morrow, 1952.
The Cavalier's Cup. New York: Morrow, 1953.
Fear Is the Same. New York: Morrow, 1956.

BIOGRAPHICAL AND CRITICAL STUDIES

Amis, Kingsley. "The Art of the Impossible." *Times Literary Supplement,* 5 June 1981.
Barzun, Jacques, and Wendell Hertig Taylor. "John Dickson Carr." In *A Catalogue of Crime,* rev. and enl. ed. New York: Harper & Row, 1989.
Bleiler, E. F. "Some Thoughts on Peacock Feet." *Mystery Fancier* 6, no. 3 (May/June 1982).
Briney, Robert E. Introduction to *The Crooked Hinge.* San Diego: University Extension, University of California, The Mystery Library, 1976.

———. Entries on John Dickson Carr and Carter Dickson in *1001 Midnights: The Aficionado's Guide to Mystery and Detective Fiction.* Edited by Bill Pronzini and Marcia Muller. New York: Arbor House, 1986.

Brittain, William. "The Man Who Read John Dickson Carr." In *Murderous Schemes: An Anthology of Classic Detective Stories.* Edited by Donald E. Westlake. New York: Oxford University Press, 1996.

Dirda, Michael. "The Houdini of the Mystery." *Washington Post Book World,* 26 March 1995. Review of Douglas G. Greene's *John Dickson Carr.*

Dove, George N. "The Locked Room Mystique." *Clues: A Journal of Detection* (fall/winter 1986).

Greene, Douglas G. "John Dickson Carr on British Radio." *Armchair Detective* 12, no. 1 (January 1979).

———. "Adolf Hitler and John Dickson Carr's Least-Known Locked Room." *Armchair Detective* 14, no. 4 (winter 1981).

———. "John Dickson Carr: The Magician of the Locked Room." In *The Fine Art of Murder: The Mystery Reader's Indispensable Companion.* Edited by Ed Gorman, Martin H. Greenberg, Larry Segriff, and Jon L. Breen. New York: Carroll & Graf, 1993.

———. *John Dickson Carr: The Man Who Explained Miracles.* New York: Otto Penzler, 1995.

Herzel, Roger. "John Dickson Carr." In *Minor American Novelists.* Edited by Charles Alva Hoyt. Carbondale and Evansville, Ill.: Southern Illinois University Press, 1970.

Joshi, S. T. *John Dickson Carr: A Critical Study.* Bowling Green, Ohio: Bowling Green State University Popular Press, 1990.

Keating, H. R. F. "The Hollow Man." In *Crime and Mystery: The 100 Best Books.* New York: Carroll & Graf, 1987.

Keirans, James E. "The Jury Box." *Armchair Detective* 24, no. 3 (summer 1991).

Kingman, James. "John Dickson Carr and the Aura of Genius." *Armchair Detective* 14, no. 2 (spring 1981).

Lachtman, Howard. "The Ideal Storybook Hero." In *The Quest for Sir Arthur Conan Doyle: Thirteen Biographers in Search of a Life.* Edited by Jon L. Lellenberg. Carbondale and Evanston: Southern Illinois Univ. Press, 1987.

Medawar, Tony, and James Keirans. "Suspense of the High Seas." *Armchair Detective* 24, no. 4 (fall 1991).

Nevins, Francis M. "The Sound of Suspense: John Dickson Carr as a Radio Writer." *Armchair Detective* 11, no. 4 (October 1978).

Panek, LeRoy. "John Dickson Carr." In *Watteau's Shepherds: The Detective Novel in Britain 1914–1940.* Bowling Green, Ohio: Bowling Green State University Popular Press, 1979.

Sayers, Dorothy L. Review of *The Mad Hatter Mystery. Sunday Times* (London), 24 September 1933.

———. Review of *The Blind Barber. Sunday Times,* 11 November 1934.

Symons, Julian. *Bloody Murder: From the Detective Story to the Crime Novel: A History.* New York: Viking, 1985.

The Nick Carter Stories

J. RANDOLPH COX

To a generation of boys at the turn of the century, the name Nick Carter was synonymous with the word "detective." The brightly colored cover illustrations on the publications containing his weekly adventures beckoned from the newsstands, promising an excursion into adventure. The appeal of the Nick Carter stories was heightened by the fact that they were all signed either by "the Author of Nick Carter" or by "Nicholas Carter" himself. The identification of the detective with his author was not new (Old Sleuth had told some of his own adventures a few years before), but Nick Carter's use of the device may have been one of the most successful. The tradition was continued some forty years later, in 1929, by Ellery Queen, whose name was also used for both author and detective. Beginning in 1886, one year before Sherlock Holmes, Carter's adventures were kept in nearly continuous production by a syndicate of writers. Translated into a dozen languages, the stories became an international success.

The original Nick Carter stories appeared in a sequence of publications: in the story paper, the *New York Weekly* (1886–1915); in three nickel weeklies—*Nick Carter Library* (1891–1896), *Nick Carter Weekly* (1897–1912), and *Nick Carter Stories* (1912–1915)—most of which were collected in two paperback series, *The Magnet Library* (1897–1907) and *The New Magnet Library* (1907–1933); in several pulp magazines, including *Detective Story Magazine* (1915–1927) and *Nick Carter Magazine* (1933–1936); and later in a long-running series of paperbacks (1964–1990).

The most significant parts of the series were the story paper serials (79), short stories (115), and dime novels (1,002 original stories) that appeared from 1886 to 1915. The pulp magazine stories (84) that followed were unsuccessful in retaining a steady readership, but a long-running radio drama (1943–1955), featuring actor Lon Clark, successfully recreated the Nick Carter formula for a new medium in 722 weekly episodes. The latest version of Nick Carter came in 1964 when the name of the character was used on the first of 261 paperbacks about a suave superspy (Nick Carter: Killmaster) in the James Bond pattern. This new Nick Carter had few of the characteristics of the original and never equaled the mass market appeal of his predecessors in print or on the air.

In many ways the character of Nick Carter never changed over the years except by degrees. He was never described in specific physical terms, but by his abilities. An early memorandum from the publisher (possibly from 1895) established the parameters within which writers on the series were to work. Nick is described as twenty-five years old, slightly below medium height (he is often referred to as the Little Giant), a thorough athlete, and possessor of a shrewd mind. He is skilled at languages and a master of disguise. It is emphasized that his disguises work so well because few people have ever seen his real face. (He maintains a public image that protects him from prying eyes, but still allows people to recognize him on the street.)

In the course of the series the world around Nick Carter changes, but he does not. Horse and carriage transportation is replaced by the automobile. Transatlantic travel by boat is commonplace, but it is supplanted by the airplane around 1910. There are new recurring characters introduced in the stories, new assistants pass through the pages, and new adversaries are defeated and locked away in prison.

Individual writers varied the point of view of some of their stories. Some even borrowed ideas from other writers like Arthur Conan Doyle. Nick was not present on every page of every chapter, but if he was not in the opening scene it was not long before a new client came to his door, Chick presented him with a new case, or the police chief called him on the phone.

While more than a hundred writers (37 in the dime novel version, over 70 in the Killmaster series) have written Nick Carter stories since 1886, only a few have made contributions significant enough to be singled out here.

John Russell Coryell

John Russell Coryell (1851–1924), the creator of Nick Carter, conceived him as a modern d'Artagnan and knight errant. Nick Carter has the ability to free himself from any difficulty he may encounter, no matter the odds, by his sharp wit, strength, and courage. The character Coryell created became so real to many readers that for years people wrote to the great New York detective for advice.

Coryell's life was filled with the sort of adventure that one might expect of the creator of Nick Carter. In 1869, at the age of seventeen, he quit the College of the City of New York, where he was studying law, to join his family in China, where his father was working in ship construction. The trip took him through a typhoon, which could have taken his life; instead it gave him some firsthand experience on which he could draw for many stories in the future.

While in China, Coryell served as consular clerk and as vice-consul at Canton and Shanghai, though he was only twenty years old. Following his years in China and Japan, he returned to the United States and settled in San Francisco, where he tried a career as a ship broker. Poor financial habits soon put him out of business, and he worked as a newspaper reporter for Harrison Gray Otis in San Francisco, Sacramento, and Santa Barbara. His experiences with Otis in Santa Barbara included dealings with crooked politicians and some traditional bad men. He was even challenged to a duel, which he won by sheer luck.

Coryell went back to New York in 1878 and began writing short juvenile stories for periodicals such as *St. Nicholas, Harper's Young People, Youth's Companion,* and the story paper *Golden Days.* They were a critical success, but the payment was not sufficient to support a growing family; in 1882 he had married Abby Lydia Hedge. Coryell approached the publishing firm of Street & Smith, whose president was his cousin, Ormond G. Smith, and offered to write a detective serial. The story, "The American Marquis; or, A Detective for Vengeance," appeared in the *New York Weekly* for more than twelve weeks early in 1885. Published over the pseudonym Milton Quarterly, it was sufficiently successful for the publisher to ask if Coryell could repeat his feat. The author confidently said he not only could but would.

Coryell's choice of the detective story as a fictional form might have been based on the popularity that detective stories enjoyed in the 1880s. Some of this was due to public familiarity with the cases of Allan Pinkerton and his detective agency as reported in the newspapers, but also with the accounts of their work that had appeared in a series of books signed by Allan Pinkerton and published between 1874 and 1885. The methods of the Pinkerton detectives (shadowing suspects, wearing disguises, and filing reports) were reflected in the methods of fictional detectives and especially the fictional detectives of the dime novels and story papers. Even the structure of the dime novel detective story was often in imitation of a Pinkerton report and it was frequently suggested that the story was based on fact.

Coryell's next serial was "The Old Detective's Pupil; or, The Mysterious Crime of Madison Square," published in the *New York Weekly* over the signature "Author of 'The American Marquis,' " a common form of pseudonym in those days. He was living in New Hope, Pennsylvania, in a house he wished to make his permanent home. Over a period of thirteen weeks, beginning 18 September and ending 11 December 1886, the serial introduced the world to the young Nick Carter on the brink of solving his first case, which involves finding the murderer of his detective father, old Sim Carter. By the end of the story Nick has also met and wooed Ethel Livingston and asked her to become his wife.

Shortly thereafter, Coryell wrote the sequel, "A Wall Street Haul; or, A Bold Stroke for a Fortune," which appeared in the *New York Weekly,* 12 March to 18 June 1887. The plot involves the theft of $3 million from the 15th National Bank on Wall Street; its solution is complicated by the rivalry between Nick and another detective, Matt Solomon. Solomon does not realize with whom he is dealing: throughout most of the story, Nick Carter is disguised as another detective named Harvey Jones. The only one who recognizes Nick Carter beneath the guise of Harvey Jones is his wife Ethel.

Coryell waited a few months before commencing his third and last Nick Carter serial, "Fighting Against Millions; or, The Detective in the Jewel Caves of Kurm," the longest and most fantastic of the three. Once again, the serial appeared in the *New York Weekly,* from 29 September 1888 to 19 January 1889, over a period of seventeen weeks. Nick and Ethel are now the parents of a baby boy named Ralph, who is kidnapped by someone who has previously arranged to discredit Nick's reputation as a detective. The quest for his son becomes the central element in the plot and leads Nick across a continent to the kingdom of Kurm, where he rescues the infant and justice prevails.

What sets Coryell apart from subsequent authors in the Nick Carter series is his style and the sense of fun he brings to the stories. He is not above satirizing the entire genre of nineteenth-century detective fiction, including the tradition of the use of disguise, to enliven his stories. Coryell later wrote more detective stories, for story papers and for pulp magazines, but he never wrote another Nick Carter story.

In 1900 Coryell left the world of dime novel and story-paper fiction and began writing satirical articles on social problems for Bernarr McFadden's magazines. He joined the staff of *True Story Magazine* and spent the rest of his life writing articles under the name Margaret Grant for that publication. He died in Mount Vernon, Maine, in 1924.

Frederic Merrill Van Rensselaer Dey

The first writer to make his living from writing Nick Carter stories, Frederic Merrill Van Rensselaer Dey (1861–1922), was the most prolific of all the writers on the series, the most imaginative, and the most tragic. Plagued early in his career with alcoholism, his work suffered and he had to withdraw from writing the stories. For a decade after he had written his last story for Street & Smith he continued to recreate his own history as the author of the Nick Carter stories. In an article for *The American Magazine* in 1920 he claimed authorship of a thousand stories for the series when the records indicate the number was less than half that figure. Perhaps after twenty years of writing them it seemed like a thousand. Unable to sell new stories, Dey took his own life in 1922. Five years later, Joseph Van Raalte, a writer for a national magazine who was as imaginative as his subject, left a fanciful portrait of Dey's life and last days that has colored most subsequent accounts. It is accurate in being the story of a man who dreamed beyond his means, but Van Raalte includes unsubstantiated incidents, is careless about dates, and assigns Dey the title of "Colonel." There is no evidence that Dey was ever called "Colonel" in his lifetime.

Frederic Merrill Van Rensselaer Dey was a graduate of Columbia University Law School (1883), practiced law for a time in Brooklyn, and joined William J. Gaynor's law firm as assistant corporation counsel. Dey was married twice, first in 1885 to Annie Shepard, by whom he had two children, then in 1898 to Mrs. Hattie (Hamblin) Cahoon. His second wife was a writer who used the pseudonym Haryot Holt (later amending it to Haryot Holt Dey).

In 1881, when he was twenty, Dey wrote a story ("Captain Ironnerve, the Counterfeiter Chief; or, The Gipsy Queen's Legacy") under the pseudonym Marmaduke Dey for Beadle & Adams; it appeared in their *Dime Library* series. Dey left the practice of law in 1887 to make a living at writing. In 1891, at the age of thirty, he was approached by Street & Smith and was offered the job of writing a weekly Nick Carter novelette of thirty-three thousand words for a new publication devoted exclusively to stories about the detective created by John R. Coryell. This was something of an innovation for the dime novel, since previous series had contained stories about a number of different characters even when the series, such as the *Old Cap. Collier Library* (1883) or the *Old Sleuth Library* (1885), was named for one of the continuing characters.

Confident in his ability, Dey accepted the offer and set to work. He had been given a deadline of ten weeks in which to write the first ten stories. Dey completed the first four stories within three weeks and sent the publisher a list of titles for all ten for advertising purposes. Later it would be the publisher who created the titles ahead of time, assigning writers to provide the stories to match.

Dey was then told the length of the stories should be twenty thousand words, not thirty-three thousand, so he cut his first three stories and finished the remaining seven stories within a month. By his own account, Dey wrote these first stories in longhand with a stub gold pen, and it would be years before he would be comfortable using a typewriter.

The first story, "Nick Carter, Detective: The Solution of a Remarkable Case," appeared in the first issue of the *Nick Carter Detective Library* dated 8 August 1891. As its plot involves a woman who is murdered by a cobra, it suggests a heavy influence from Poe's "Murders in the Rue Morgue." However, exotic settings, characters, and methods of murder were part of detective fiction tradition. The East Indian motif in Wilkie Collins' *The Moonstone* (1868) can be seen in many detective stories, including those published as dime novels. Examples include "The 'Eye of Jobu'; or, The Hunt for the Great Green Diamond," published in *Old Cap. Collier Library* no. 343, 22 April 1889, as well as Conan Doyle's second Sherlock Holmes novel, *The Sign of the Four* (1889). One of Doyle's most famous short stories, "The Speckled Band" (1892), continues the theme of a murderous reptile. Dey continued to write a story every week for the next twenty-eight weeks to fill the first thirty-eight issues of the publication. The series was sufficiently successful that toward the end of 1891, he was also asked to write a weekly serial installment of six thousand words about Nick Carter for the *New York Weekly.* The first of these, "Nick Carter and the Greengoods Men; or, The Great Detective's Thrilling Adventures in a New Field," began appearing in the issue for 2 January 1892.

The strain of such a schedule soon began to affect Dey's output; early in 1892 the publishers looked for alternate authors should Dey fall behind and fail to supply his weekly novelette and serial installment. New stories by other authors were scheduled so they would appear between those issues containing stories Dey had already completed. The publisher was thus never without a Nick Carter adventure on hand. Eventually reprints of Dey's old stories had to serve when the supply of new manuscripts from him had been exhausted. Among the writers who were drafted to write Nick Carter stories over the next five years were Eugene T. Sawyer, Edward Stratemeyer, Alfred B. Tozer, Charles W. Hooke, Eugene C. Derby, O. P. Caylor, R. F. Walsh, George Waldo Browne, William Wallace Cook, and Frederick Russell Burton. There were others later. Dey claimed to have recruited some of the substitute writers himself, but considering Street & Smith's editorial policy of closely directing their regular writers, this is unlikely. Early in 1893, Dey appears to have suspended writing the weekly novelettes altogether, having written only sixty-two of them, but he continued to write the weekly story paper serial installments until the end of 1894.

The writers who were assigned to fill in for Dey did not make any substantial contributions to the series but merely filled in with detective stories that might have been about any detective. Few of them produced a sizable number of new stories. Eugene T. Sawyer had written serials and novelettes for Street & Smith and provided occasional stories. Edward Stratemeyer, the creator of Nancy Drew, wrote about two dozen stories from 1892 to 1895, and those were often based on plot ideas provided him by the publisher. This method of working to an outline supplied by an editor was replicated by Edward Stratemeyer for the Stratemeyer Syndicate which, in 1906, he began for the purpose of producing juvenile series books.

The most regular contributors of new stories, which alternated with reprinted editions of Dey's earlier stories, were Frederick Russell Burton (1861–1909) and Weldon J. Cobb (1849–1922), a Chicago writer. Many of their stories were not about Nick Carter at all, but featured one of his assistants or the students in Nick Carter's detective school. Then, in 1902, Street & Smith purchased the rights to a series of detective stories that Norman L. Munro had published twenty years earlier in the famous dime novel series *Old Cap. Collier Library.* These were edited and rewritten by staff writers to fit the Nick Carter pattern.

Early in 1901, Dey returned to writing Nick Carter serials for the *New York Weekly;* three years later he resumed writing the weekly novelettes (his first novelette appeared dated 13 February 1904). For the next eight years Dey wrote most of the weekly novelettes (an estimated 328 stories) and twenty-seven story-paper serials about the great New York detective. He wrote his last Nick Carter story in May 1912 for publication early in 1913 in *Nick Carter Stories.*

Dey was not so much a writer as a storyteller, whose early Nick Carter stories involved fraud, murder, forgery, and revenge; eventually he replaced those traditional detective-story elements with plots as fantastic as those in any dime novel. His stories were incredibly imaginative, even bizarre, in terms of both their characters and situations. He contributed the recurring villain to a dime novel series. Nick Carter's archenemy was Dr. Jack Quartz, the man of many lives, who would seem to have died at the end of one story only to reappear, alive again, at the beginning of the next.

Dey may have been the first writer of a dime-novel series to consciously construct stories in sequence, in which the plots were linked together. Each story could stand alone, but there would be an element in the last chapter that he would develop further in the next story. When the publisher came up with the idea of publishing three of the stories together in a paper-covered book, it could often be done with a minimum of editing.

The stories Dey wrote after he returned to the series in 1904 are better constructed than those written in the 1890s. There are fewer examples of trying to tie up loose ends in the last three paragraphs and more examples of stories that flow from crisis to resolution, keeping the reader on the edge of his or her chair, wanting to know what will happen next.

While Nick Carter remained married in the series, Dey and other writers who followed him used Ethel sparingly. In one sequence of stories, the editors were caught napping and she is referred to as Edith for thirty-five weeks in 1901. One of the first things Dey did when he returned to writing the stories, in 1904, was to kill off Ethel. Dey may have felt he would have more freedom in plotting his stories if Nick did not have a wife to worry about, or to worry about him. There is no evidence the readers objected. This did not mean that Nick Carter was now free to become involved romantically with every new client. There were a few women who turned his head, but the relationships were never allowed to develop further.

Dey gave the series coherence through his use of established recurring secondary characters. These include not only Nick Carter's chief assistants Chick Carter and Patsy Murphy Garvan, but also the butler Joseph, the housekeeper Mrs. Peters, the female detective Ida Jones, and Ten-Ichi, son of the Mikado, who spends time in the United States learning from the great New York detective. These, plus frequent reminders of the earlier stories, establish parameters for Nick Carter's world and make it possible for readers to accept that world.

Dey often bases his stories on little things he observed while walking. He tells of watching a piece of paper float from the edge of a bridge to the deck of a boat that passed beneath, then going to his workroom and writing the first chapter of a Nick Carter story ("A Clew from the Clouds; or, Nick Carter's Mysterious Evidence," *Nick Carter Weekly* no. 499, 21 July 1906) around that incident. Dey relies on the repeated use of certain names for characters. His archvillain is named Quartz, and other villains often have names beginning with the letter "Q." He peoples his stories with characters named Madge: Mad Madge, Black Madge, Madge Morton, and Gypsy Madge. Dey sometimes inserts references to his own reading preferences. He was fond of Alexandre Dumas' *The Count of Monte Cristo,* the works of William Makepeace Thackeray, and the biblical books of Isaiah and Job. His favorite novel was Charles Lever's *Charles O'Malley: The Irish Dragoon* (he read it every year for 20 years), and he names an Irish detective whom Nick meets in France after the hero of the novel.

An example of a recurring theme in Dey's Nick Carter stories is to place the blame for the crimes upon a mad family. In *The Turn of a Card* (1913) the mad family is named Bulwer; there are six of them, three groups of nearly identical twin sisters. Some of the most interesting parts of the story are not the action scenes, but the verbal sparring matches between Nick Carter and one or another of the sisters. Asked to discover the identity of a masked vaudeville performer (a trick-shot artist) called "The Ace of Hearts," the detective watches their act, "The Turn of a Card," the hit of the Washington, D.C., theatrical season, with keen eyes. Five masked women, dressed in identical black costumes, differing only by the emblem of the card suit each represents on her chest, step out on stage. While Nick eventually unravels the mystery of their identity, he never explains the secret behind their act. How can the Ace of Hearts fire her automatic pistols so accurately that she produces a round hole in the center of the red hearts displayed on the chests of each of the others and not kill them? How deadly must her accuracy be as she tosses a set of dueling pistols in the air by their barrels, draws her automatics, and fires her last bullets to hit the triggers of the dueling pistols, producing two black bullet marks on her own chest? The curtain falls and the Ace and her assistants disappear until after the show. Nick may be curious about the method because of his own skill as a marksman.

From time to time Dey explains some of Nick Carter's skills to the reader:

> We all—who know Nick Carter—are aware of the two small pistols which he sometimes carries in the sleeves of his coat, fastened there by spiral springs of his own design—pistols which he can, by a single motion, throw into his hands and fire at the same instant; and we know, too, that no surer marksman ever lived than this famous detective. (*The Turn of a Card,* p. 319)

Dey does not depend on any single type of detective story. Some of his Nick Carter stories are classic drawing-room murder mysteries, others take the detective to the lowest dives and haunts in the city of New York, while others take him to lost cities to visit lost civilizations. Dr. Quartz is not the only recurring villain: there is gambler Dan Derrington, the burglar known as the Mocker, another known as the Unaccountable Crook because you can never tell what he may do next, and Captain Sparkle, the pirate, who owns a submarine with which he robs yachts.

Even while he was writing the Nick Carter stories, Dey wrote for other publications, including short stories for *The Black Cat* and serials for Beadle & Adams' story paper *The Banner Weekly;* did editorial work for Frank Tousey; and produced a remarkably successful little self-help and morality fable called "The Magic Story." Published in *Success Magazine* in 1900, it was republished as a small book and kept in print for decades. Its theme is that everyone has the seeds of success within himself. Having been the principal writer on the Nick Carter series for over twenty years, Dey switched easily to writing for the new pulp magazines and contributed a number of detective and crime serials to Frank A. Munsey's publications under the pseudonym Varick Vanardy. (The last name was constructed from his own name: Van R. Dey.)

Dey was a complex man who suffered from alcoholism for part of his life. Accounts differ and are not precise in regard to dates, but newspaper reports from about 1912 (just as he completed eight productive years as the chief writer of the Nick Carter stories) indicate that he was arrested in Denver for impersonating a law enforcement official; authorities said that when he had been drinking he had hallucinations and sometimes thought he really was Nick Carter. Whatever the truth of these accounts, Dey appears to have been a dreamer who lived in a world of his own creation, often far beyond his means. Perhaps he had spun so many dreams into stories that he did the same with his own life.

Dey embellished the story of his involvement with Nick Carter to the point where it is difficult to separate fact from fiction. When Alfred B. Tozer died in Battle Creek in 1916 and was referred to in newspaper accounts as the author of Nick Carter stories, Dey wrote a letter to the *New York Tribune* (4 January 1917) to set the record straight. Unfortunately some of his facts are incorrect (the date of the first story in the series that he wrote for Street & Smith) and others are suspect (he mixes the titles of Coryell's first two serials into one story), and he claims authorship of more stories than he wrote. In subsequent interviews Dey confuses dates and titles of his work for Beadle & Adams and expands the extent of his work for Frank Tousey on the "Handsome Harry" stories (he claims sole authorship of them). In one interview he claims that he gave Arthur Conan Doyle the idea for Sherlock Holmes's process of scientific deduction prior to the 1887 publication of *A Study in Scarlet.*

In 1920 Dey wrote an article for *The American Magazine,* "How I Wrote a Thousand 'Nick Carter' Novels," which added more elements to the myth of the creation, authorship, and character of Nick Carter. Behind his account we glimpse a confident author at work, systematically spending no more than eight hours a day for three or four days each month on a given story. He cannot have had much experience at such a schedule before this. His few stories for Beadle & Adams would have provided him limited opportunity for such a routine. Publisher's records indicate that Dey wrote less than half of the thousand stories he claimed and others later claimed for him. With a possible 44 serials and a definite 390 weekly novelettes, he can be credited with only 434 stories.

But no amount of imagination that went into the writing of Nick Carter and the life of his principal author can match the story of Dey's tragic death. Two years after the publication of the *American Magazine* article, Frederic Merrill Van Rensselaer Dey became despondent over the prospects for his future. He had not published a novel since 1920. Ironically, the title of that book (published under his Varick Vanardy name) is *Up Against It.* On Saturday, 22 April 1922, Dey rented a room in the Hotel Broztell on East Twenty-seventh Street. Late Tuesday evening, 25 April, he went up to his room on the seventh floor and put a bullet in his brain. Newspaper accounts vary as to the details, but the basic story is that he registered as "J. W. Dayer, of Nyack, New York," then wrote and mailed three letters, each of which indicated that things had "gone to smash" with him and he could not stand to be a burden on anyone.

Frederick William Davis

The next major writer of the Nick Carter series was a contrast in life and personality to the first two. He was neither adventurer nor lawyer-turned-writer, but a professional writer on whom his publishers could depend for neatly typed manuscripts, always turned in on time. Frederick William Davis (1858–1933) was a native of Massachusetts, born in his grandmother's home in Barnstable. He grew up in Chelsea and was graduated from Chelsea High School. His first job was as an employee for a local firm of crockery merchants, Clark, Adams & Clark.

So little is known of Davis' life that it is uncertain when or why he began to write fiction. Under the name Scott Campbell, he began publishing detective serials in the *Boston Globe* at least as early as 1890, when he was thirty-two years old; the earliest traced is " 'Green Goods'; or, A Victim of Circumstances," published from 1 to 21 February 1890. He produced about nineteen serials over the next decade before turning to Street & Smith in 1900. From then until his death he was a regular contributor of detective stories to a number of their publications.

These serials were all published in Street & Smith's *Magnet Library* of paperback detective fiction, many under his Scott Campbell pseudonym. He was also allowed to convert some of his *Boston Globe* serials into Nick Carter novels for the same series. The first was "Saved By a Sin; or, The Lost Diamonds of Delhi," from 1898, which he revised as "Nick Carter's Clever Ruse; or, Setting a Thief to Catch a Thief." After about two years he began writing novelettes, under the name Alden F. Bradshaw, about detectives Sheridan Keene and Steve Manley for a short-lived series called the *Shield Weekly* (1900–1901), and then original detective novels (as Scott Campbell) directly for the *Magnet Library* (1901). In 1902 his Sheridan Keene and Steve Manley stories were collected in the *Magnet Library* as Nick Carter stories. In 1903 he wrote his first original novelette for the *Nick Carter Weekly* and three years later he began writing Nick Carter serials for the *New York Weekly.* He contributed approximately twelve serials and 104 novelettes to the series, publishing his last, "Driven from Cover; or, Nick Carter's Double Ruse," on 25 September 1915.

While writing Nick Carter stories, Davis was also contributing a series of short stories about detective Felix Boyd to Street & Smith's *The Popular Magazine.* These were later collected and added to the *Magnet Library.* When the nickel weekly *Nick Carter Stories* was transformed in 1915 into the first pulp magazine devoted to detective fiction, *Detective Story Magazine,* one of the regular authors in the early issues was "Scott Campbell." Under this pseudonym, Davis continued to write original novels for the successor to the *Magnet Library,* which was named the *New Magnet Library.* Though signed by the pseudonym Nicholas Carter, many of these were about another detective named Harrison Keith.

Davis alternated between his home in Chelsea, where he lived with his sister, and his summer home in Onset until a fire destroyed the Chelsea residence. He then moved to New Bedford, where he lived the rest of his life. In 1907 he married Jennie B. Allen, daughter of Daniel B. Allen, a New Bedford tailor. His hobbies included boating and fishing.

His work was respected by his publishers, and Davis was considered unique among authors not only for being dependable and leading an exemplary life, but for living within his means, retiring around 1920 when he felt he could afford it. When Davis died in 1933,

Henry W. Ralston, vice president of Street & Smith, praised his writing as being of better quality than you would expect in a dime-novel series.

Davis began his career by imitating Arthur Conan Doyle's style, but soon developed one of his own. His Nick Carter stories have a more realistic basis than those of his predecessors. The characters are skillfully presented, the criminals have believable motives, and there is genuine suspense and uncertainty that Nick may not be able to solve the case without a lot of trouble. In a light, almost sophisticated style, Davis worked within the parameters set for him by his publishers. If he contributed little that was new to the series, he did not disappoint the readers who wanted a good story.

Samuel Charles Spalding

The last of the major writers of the series did little original work; his responsibility was to take stories written by others and adapt them to fit the Nick Carter series for the weekly *Nick Carter Stories* novelettes as well as the full-length novels in the *New Magnet Library.* Samuel Charles Spalding (1878–1962) was born in Leavenworth, Kansas, the son of the city clerk of Leavenworth. His mother died when he was eleven months old, his father and stepmother a few years after that, and he was raised by his Aunt Alice. Another aunt, Mrs. Charles B. Parkman, insisted they join her in Washington, D.C., where Samuel Spalding attended public school. He never graduated from high school but was admitted to the Unitarian Theological Seminary in Meadsville, Pennsylvania, and was graduated from there in 1903. That summer, he married a fellow seminary student, Jessie May Pulis, and the two were ordained as ministers. Spalding accepted a pastorate at Laconia, New Hampshire, in July.

On Christmas Eve, Spalding contracted typhoid followed by arthritis, a condition that forced him to resign his pastorate in 1905. The Spaldings lived with Jessie's family in Troy, New York, while Samuel tried a new career as a writer of short stories and stage adaptations of popular novels. He enrolled in the Page-Davis School in Chicago, a correspondence course in advertisement writing, which led to a job in New York as advertising manager with *Cosmopolitan Magazine* and other Hearst publications. By 1907 his arthritis made the daily trip to the office difficult, and he began looking for something he could do at home.

By chance he heard of an opening with Street & Smith writing Nick Carter stories for their *New Magnet Library.* Street & Smith had a reciprocal arrangement with the Amalgamated Press, publishers of the British weekly *Union Jack,* under which each publisher could use material published by the other. The most popular detective in the publications of the British counterpart to Street & Smith, the Amalgamated Press, in the early twentieth century was Sexton Blake. Created in 1893 by Harry Blyth (1852–1898) for the *Half-Penny Marvel,* by 1910 he was a weekly fixture in stories for boys produced by a syndicate of writers. Besides a weekly novelette in the *Union Jack,* he appeared weekly in small paperbacks under the collective title of the *Sexton Blake Library.* In many ways Blake was patterned after Sherlock Holmes. With his assistant, a boy named Tinker, and a bloodhound named Pedro, he had quarters in Baker Street where his landlady, Mrs Bardell, looked after his housekeeping and served his meals. In the 1920s and 1930s he drove a fast car called the Grey Panther. New stories were still being produced as late as 1978. It was not difficult for a writer to alter the names and settings of a Sexton Blake story to produce a Nick Carter story. The Amalgamated Press did not exercise their part of the agreement until the 1930s, when they published some of Street & Smith's popular novels about The Shadow in their weekly paper, the *Thriller.* Spalding was given copies of the Sexton Blake detective stories then appearing in the *Union Jack* and was told he could either rewrite them as Nick Carter novels at a fee of $100 a novel or write original novels for $125. From then until about 1915, by his recollection, he wrote or rewrote slightly more than one hundred Nick Carter novels (eighty-seven of these have been identified). His average rate was about two novels each month. He also recalled writing one novelette and several short stories directly for the pulp *Detective Story Magazine.* While working on the Nick Carter stories, Spalding made a brief appearance as the character and his author in a silent newsreel made by Jam Handy of Chicago, in which he was depicted in Nick Carter's den examining a stack of Nick Carter paperback novels.

Spalding moved to Chicago and the remainder of his career was spent editing business periodicals like the *Business Philosopher* and publishing sales magazines. In 1934, he and his wife moved to Gould Farm, a social service community near Great Barrington, Massachusetts, where they worked in various capacities. Mrs. Spalding died in 1954, Samuel Spalding in 1962 at the age of eighty-three.

Most of Spalding's Nick Carter stories were based on the original Sexton Blake stories, and they retain a decidedly British style; he never changed the settings sufficiently to lose that ambience. A good example of his own style of writing appears in one of his original novels for the series, *Bolts from Blue Skies* (1914). It is a lively story about a scientist who seems to have been blown up in the course of one of his own experiments, although Nick is not satisfied that it was an accident. The quality of the writing and the examples of Nick Carter's views on his own fame add to the enjoyment.

Following the demise of the dime novel, Nick Carter appeared in the pulp magazines. The first stories were published occasionally in *Detective Story Magazine* from 1915 to 1927. In 1933, Street & Smith introduced a new version of Nick Carter in stories by Richard Wormser (1908–1977) and others in *Nick Carter Magazine,* which lasted for only forty issues.

Nick Carter belongs to turn-of-the-century America as a representative of the detective story in its early form. His continuing success was based partly on shrewd marketing. Street & Smith knew how to keep their products looking fresh and up-to-date and in tune with current events. Some of the stories were actually based on real crime stories. In fact, Nick Carter had little real competition on the newsstand. His predecessors in the dime novels included Old Sleuth and Old King Brady, both advanced in years. Old Sleuth was a name used more often as an author than as a continuing central character. Old King Brady appeared only once or twice a month before 1899 when the stories began to appear in a weekly publication. Nick Carter, on the other hand, was a young man and his stories appeared every week, almost from the start. By his clear eye and strong jaw and the way he dressed in the cover illustrations, his appearance was unmistakable. The stories were presented in clear, readable type, a distinct improvement over the usual three columns of small print unrelieved by illustrations that had been common in dime novels prior to the 1890s.

In the confident years between the Civil War and World War I, Nick Carter was an appropriate hero for the age as well as a father figure to his young readers. Nick did the things boys aged eight to sixteen dreamed of doing and made it seem so easy. Young and clean-cut, his name had an American ring to it and was easily recognized and easily remembered. Practical and matter-of-fact, calm in the face of the worst perils, Nick Carter always won. Regular readers came to know what to expect when they picked up a new Nick Carter story. That this series lasted as long as it did suggests they were seldom disappointed.

Selected Bibliography

This bibliography of the Nick Carter novels is selective and limited to only some of those novels written by the four principal authors, John R. Coryell, Frederic Van Rensselaer Dey, Frederick W. Davis, and Samuel Spalding. More comprehensive lists of the more than seven hundred unique book titles (as well as reprints, weekly nickel novelettes, and story paper serials) will be found in the five bibliographies by J. Randolph Cox below and one by Allen J. Hubin. Unless otherwise noted, all Nick Carter novels were published by Street & Smith.

NICK CARTER STORIES

JOHN R. CORYELL

The American Marquis. New York, 1889. Coryell's first detective novel, but not a Nick Carter story.

The Old Detective's Pupil; or, On the Side of Law and Order. New York, 1889.

A Wall Street Haul; or, *A Bold Stroke for a Fortune.* New York, 1889.

Fighting Against Millions; or, The Detective in the Caves of Kurm. New York, 1892.

FREDERIC VAN RENSSELAER DEY

The Piano Box Mystery; or, Shipped by Freight. New York, 1892.

A Stolen Identity; or, A Beautiful Woman's Plot. New York, 1892.

The Great Enigma; or, Nick Carter's Triple Puzzle. New York, 1892.

The Gambler's Syndicate. The Story of a Great Swindle. New York, 1892.

Tracked Across the Atlantic; or, Nick Carter After the Smugglers. New York, 1894.

Nick Carter and the Green Goods Men. New York, 1899.

Gideon Drexel's Millions. New York, 1899.

From a Prison Cell. New York, 1906.

Dr. Quartz, Magician. New York, 1906.

Nick Carter's Close Call; or, A Dance with Death. New York, 1907.

The Disappearing Princess; or, Nick Carter's Royal Client. New York, 1910.

The Turn of a Card; or, Nick Carter Plays a Skillful Game. New York, 1913.

The Spider's Parlor; or, Nick Carter Bides His Time. New York, 1913.

FREDERICK W. DAVIS

Nick Carter's Clever Ruse; or, Setting a Thief to Catch a Thief. New York, 1900.

A Victim of Circumstances; or, "Green Goods." New York, 1900.

The Silent Passenger. New York, 1900.

The Man at the Window; or, The Girl from Cleveland. New York, 1901.

The Red Signal; or, The Malay Head Hunter's Crime. New York, 1902.

The Seal of Death. New York, 1903.

Playing for a Fortune. New York, 1905.

Harrison Keith's Double Cross; or, Against Heavy Odds. New York, 1909.

The Crimson Flash; or, When Rogues Lie Low. New York, 1912.

The Poisons of Exili; or, Nick Carter's Curious Mystery. New York, 1913.

The Wolf Within; or, Nick Carter's Coupon Clew. New York, 1914.

The Crook's Double; or, Crime and Concert Mixed. New York, 1917.

SAMUEL C. SPALDING

The Devil's Son. New York, 1911.

The Deadly Scarab; or, An Ingenious Criminal. New York, 1912.

A Moving Picture Mystery; or, The Call That Was Answered. New York, 1913.

Bolts from Blue Skies; or, Nick Carter's Chance Discovery. New York, 1914.

A Weird Treasure; or, A Keen But Mad Mind. New York, 1915.

The Yellow Label; or, The Drive Against Crime. New York, 1917.

Wildfire. New York, 1920.

COLLECTIONS

Nick Carter, Detective: Fiction's Most Celebrated Detective. Edited by Robert Clurman. New York: Macmillan, 1963. Includes "Nick Carter, Detective: The Solution of a Remarkable Case."

BIBLIOGRAPHIES

Cox, J. Randolph. *The Nick Carter Library.* Fall River, Mass.: Edward T. LeBlanc, 1974.

———. *New Nick Carter Weekly.* Fall River, Mass.: Edward T. LeBlanc, 1975.

———. *Nick Carter Stories and Other Series Containing Stories About Nick Carter,* 2 parts. Fall River, Mass.: Edward T. LeBlanc, 1977, 1980.

———. *Magnet Detective Library.* Fall River, Mass.: Edward T. LeBlanc, 1985.

———. *New Magnet Library.* Fall River, Mass.: Edward T. LeBlanc, 1991.

Hubin, Allen J. *Crime Fiction II: A Comprehensive Bibliography. 1749–1990.* New York: Garland, 1994.

ARCHIVES

The George Hess Collection, Children's Literature Research Collections, Walter Library, University of Minnesota, Minneapolis, Minn., and the Street & Smith Collection, George Arents Research Library, Syracuse University, Syracuse, New York, hold extensive collections of the Nick Carter publications. In addition, Syracuse holds internal records of the Street & Smith

Publishing Co. as well as unpublished manuscripts of Nick Carter stories.

BIOGRAPHICAL AND CRITICAL STUDIES

Coryell, John R. "Reminiscences of Nick Carter by His Creator." *Detective Story Magazine* 13 (5 March 1918).

Coryell, Russell M. "The Birth of Nick Carter." *The Bookman* (New York) 79. (July 1929).

Cox, J. Randolph. "Chapters from the Chronicles of Nick Carter." *Dime Novel Round-Up* 43 (May–June 1974):

———. "Dime Novel Reviews: The Coming of Dr. Quartz." *Dime Novel Round-Up* 45 (December 1976):

———. "Nick Carter in the Movies." *Dime Novel Round-Up* 47 (December 1978).

———. "The Detective-Hero in the American Dime Novel." *Dime Novel Round-Up* 50 (February 1981).

———. "Nick Carter, Fact or Fiction: The Historical Context of the American Dime Novel." *Dime Novel Round-Up* 54 (June 1985).

———. "The Dime Novel Detective and His Elusive Trail: Twenty Years of Dime Novel Research." *Dime Novel Round-Up* 54 (December 1985).

———. "Nicholas Carter, Detective?" *Dime Novel Round-Up* 59 (December 1990).

———. "Nick Carter Out West; or, The Great New York Detective in a New Setting." *Dime Novel Round-Up* 61 (February 1992).

———. "Nick Carter, Schoolmaster." *Dime Novel Round-Up* 62 (August 1993).

———. "A Syndicate of Rascals: The Men Behind Nick Carter." *Dime Novel Round-Up* 63 (February 1994).

Dey, Frederic Van Rensselaer. "Who Wrote Nick Carter?" *New York Tribune*, 5 January 1917.

———. "How I Wrote a Thousand 'Nick Carter' Novels." *The American Magazine* 89 (February 1920).

Murray, Will. "The Saga of Nick Carter, Killmaster." *The Armchair Detective* 15, no. 4 (1982).

———. "Nick Carter's Father." *Literary Digest* 46 (10 May 1913).

Leithead, J. Edward. "The Harrison Keith Stories." *Dime Novel Round-Up* 5 (November 1936).

———. "Nick Carter in Print." *Dime Novel Round-Up* 15 (October 1947).

———. "Nick Carter Detective Tales in *Magnet* and *New Magnet Library*." *Dime Novel Round-Up* 18 (May 1950).

———. "More About the Nick Carter Libraries." *Dime Novel Round-Up* 21 (February 1953).

———. "The Greatest Sleuth That Ever Lived." *Dime Novel Round-Up* 23 (May 1955).

———. "On Stage, Mr. Carter." *Dime Novel Round-Up* 26 (November-December 1958); 27 (January 1959).

———. "Nick Carter Reprints." *Dime Novel Round-Up* 28 (October–November 1960).

———. "Nick Carter in Another Man's Shoes." *Dime Novel Round-Up* 29 (November–December 1961).

———. "Doctor Quartz and Other Nine-Lived Villains." *Dime Novel Round-Up* 33 (May–June 1964).

———. "The Anatomy of Dime Novels: Nick Carter." *Dime Novel Round-Up* 33 (September–October 1964).

———. "Frederick [sic] Van Rensselaer Dey." *Dime Novel Round-Up* 35 (February 1966). "Supplement," *Dime Novel Round-Up* 35 (May 1966).

Spalding, Samuel Charles. *I've Had Me a Time!* (Great Barrington, Mass.: Friends of Gould Farm, 1961).

Van Raalte, Joseph. "Nick Carter: The Picturesque Career of the Man Who Made Him." *The Century Magazine* 115 (November 1927).

Raymond Chandler

(1888–1959)

JOAN ZSELECZKY

"The actual writing is what you live for," Raymond Chandler wrote his publisher Hamish Hamilton nineteen years into his literary career (*Selected Letters*, p. 289), and to judge by his work, he meant what he said. A man who came late to the craft after a midlife burnout in the oil business, he chose a genre (detective fiction) and a style (hard-boiled), then gave them all he had, creating convincing fictional worlds that left critics comparing him favorably with the literary lions of his time. "He made words dance," biographer Frank MacShane once wrote. Evelyn Waugh called him, in the era that published Hemingway, Faulkner, Fitzgerald, Nabokov, and Salinger, "the best writer in America," and W. H. Auden thought his books should be read as "works of art."

He went on to complete twenty-seven stories and seven novels, to work on the screenplays of seven films, and to charm the readership not just in English, but in twenty-nine other languages. He was regarded as a writer first, by both critics and readers, especially in Britain and France, and he often said his goal was to write good novels and not to be considered just a writer of detective fiction. (In this he succeeds half a century later.) He was blessed in his writing, if cursed in his life, by a deep and abiding romantic imagination, and his work reveals an emotional range that is staggering. He remained steadfast in his ambition to lift the mystery novel out of the subgenre into which most reviewers had tossed it, taking enormous risks with narrative, plot, and dialogue, and they all paid off. Clive James, in his essay "The Country Behind the Hill," wrote, "Auden was right in wanting him to be regarded as an artist. In fact Auden's tribute might well have been that of one poet to another."

He continues to attract even readers who disdain mainstream thrillers; he maintains a wide influence on writers even in other genres. His legacy of risk-taking directness is visible beyond the work of such mystery heirs as Ross Macdonald, Mickey Spillane, and Robert B. Parker, in novelists as diverse as J. D. Salinger (inventing plainspoken Holden Caulfield), Vladimir Nabokov (re-creating the American vernacular), and Joan Didion (injecting drama with black humor). Cinephiles are quick to emphasize the importance of his sensibilities in the birth of film noir. But of all his formidable talents, it is his style that most captivates. Whether he is describing love or death, a delicate beauty or a common thug, the enchantment of an Idle Valley dusk or the mystery of a car foundering in the surf off Lido pier, he somehow imbues his scenes with what he once said was the most difficult, most important thing a writer could hope to call forth: magic.

Raymond Thornton Chandler was born in Chicago on 23 July 1888 to Florence Thornton Chandler, originally of Waterford, Ireland, and Maurice Benjamin Chandler of Philadelphia, whose family roots stretched to Ireland and England. Both were of Quaker heritage, neither practicing. His father traveled often on railway business, and his mother frequently stayed with her sister and family in Plattsmouth, Nebraska. When Chandler was seven, after a separation brought on in part by his father's drinking and absences, and amid much bitterness, the Chandlers divorced and his father effectively vanished from his life.

Growing Up: Great Britain and the Continent (1896–1912)

Florence Chandler took her son back to Waterford to live with her mother and brother, Ernest Thornton. (Chandler changed residence more than a hundred times during his life.) When Chandler was eight, they moved in with an aunt and his maternal grandmother in South London, and he attended a local school. Summers were still spent in Waterford with his uncle, but otherwise Chandler grew up in female households. He developed a fervent loyalty toward his mother. He had seen enough class prejudice while in Ireland to develop strong opinions about class and religion, to which he freely admitted, as he admitted to being a snob, and in his youth he disdained any suggestion that he was Irish American.

When he was twelve the family moved to Dulwich, and he attended Dulwich College, an English public school which prepared its students to go on to university and boasted among its graduates a considerable group of literary stars, including P. G. Wodehouse and C. S. Forester. Chandler placed second among twenty-eight boys in his class, studying history, the classics, divinity, and languages in his first year, then moved to a course of study meant to be more practical and again excelled.

His constitution was not strong, and he was considered temperamentally high-strung. In his last year there, he took a course for those not intending to go on to university. The headmaster, A. H. Gilkes, placed emphasis on the development of his charges' character, but as a published novelist, also took pains to cultivate an interest in clear writing and had the class analyze passages read from novels and translate literature from the Latin and then back again. He also assigned short essays to his best students, including Chandler.

There was no money for further study. Chandler wanted to write, but his family pushed him toward the civil service, and thinking he might be able to hold down a simple job and write in his spare time, he went to France and Germany to study for the exams, after leaving school at seventeen before what would have been his final year. He mastered German and French, returned to Great Britain in 1907, and was naturalized. He placed third of six hundred candidates and first in classics. He took a clerical position at the Admiralty for which he was well qualified, hated it, and soon quit.

After teaching at Dulwich sporadically, he moved to Bloomsbury, where he again began to write. He published twenty-seven poems, all romantic but unremarkable. (The legendary literary denizens of Bloomsbury seem to have made no appearance in his writing or in his life.) He worked as a reporter at the *Daily Express* and at the *Westminster Gazette*, and wrote sketches for the latter. Then he began to write for the *Academy* (a magazine) and published a dozen articles and reviews there, many on literature. He also published his first story, "The Rose-Leaf Romance."

An ardent and accomplished fellow *Academy* contributor, Richard Middleton, had committed what Chandler considered "a suicide of despair" (*Raymond Chandler Speaking,* p. 24), and he began to wonder if the literary life could be pursued successfully without a separate income. The notion that he might have to consider giving up on writing began to take hold.

Years later, in 1932, he composed the long poem "Nocturne from Nowhere" about this period in his life, which is interesting not just in that it reveals the romantic young writer, but because it seems to indicate that his failure as a budding poet may have cost him an early love, the idealized girl with cornflower blue eyes who shows up in his fiction two decades later (notably in the figure of the "paralyzing" Eileen Wade, in *The Long Goodbye*).

He no longer had faith in his poetry, and he was worried about his future. In a last effort to write in England, he looked into the possibility of work composing newspaper serials, knew the writing would be "appalling" (*The Life of Raymond Chandler,* p. 22), and gave it up.

America and the War (1912–1918)

In 1912, with five hundred pounds borrowed from his uncle, Chandler went to New York. His illness shipboard induced Alma and Warren Lloyd, fellow travelers, to issue an invitation for him to recuperate in their vacation house in sunny Santa Monica, California. He first spent time in St. Louis and Nebraska, but finding the Midwest uncongenial, took up the Lloyds on their offer and went west. Warren Lloyd and a colleague helped him, after a short course and much self-teaching, get a bookkeeping job at the Los Angeles Creamery. He hated the work, but the Lloyds' Friday nights with a circle of clever friends proved stimulating enough to keep him socially engaged. By 1916 Florence Chandler had gone to California and after a time was boarding with Cissy and Julian Pascal, also friends of the Lloyds.

Within a year America was at war. Chandler set off for Canada to join the Canadian Army. He enlisted in the Fiftieth Regiment, the Gordon Highlanders, and in late November 1917, left Halifax for Liverpool when he was transferred to Seaford and the British Columbia Regiment. (He corresponded with Cissy Pascal throughout his term overseas.) The following March (1918) he was sent to France with the Canadian Corps. An artillery barrage left him with a concussion (he was the sole survivor of his unit) in June, and he returned to England. Chandler wrote it up but went on to block from memory most of his experience of war. (He did invoke it when he created a character critics felt reflected his sensibilities—veteran Terry Lennox, in *The Long Goodbye.*) He was promoted to sergeant and in July joined the Royal Air Force (a group he later named as the source of his learning to drink and drink heavily), but although he learned to fly, the war ended and he was never commissioned. He was discharged in February 1919.

Return to the American West (1919–1932)

Chandler chose to spend time in the Pacific Northwest, taking another fleeting stab at writing, then went to San Francisco, where he accepted a position working for an English bank. He left it soon after to move to Los Angeles.

The Dabney Oil Syndicate hired him as a bookkeeper, and after trouble was discovered in the firm's accounts, he was appointed assistant to John Ballantine, the man with primary responsibility for finance. But Ballantine died of a heart attack; Chandler, who had helped investigate a fiscal scandal, now witnessed the police work attendant to a death, became acquainted with procedure at the local morgue, and got firsthand experience watching an autopsy (a quartet of forensic episodes that can't have hurt when he turned to writing, and may in fact have influenced his choice of genre, since they all related to matters criminal). He was promoted to auditor and soon became a vice president, managing business, people, and office politics extremely well. (The oil industry later provided a background for events in his first novel, *The Big Sleep.*) He also continued to write poetry, especially for the woman who was to become his wife and lifelong muse.

Chandler had fallen in love with Cissy Pascal. In 1920 she divorced her husband, and just two weeks after the death by cancer of Florence Chandler (who had strongly disapproved of the union), she and Raymond Chandler were wed on 6 February 1924.

Pearl Eugenie Cecilia ("Cissy") Hurlburt, already twice married and divorced, was fifty-three but looked far younger. She listed her age when she wed Chandler as forty-three. He later wrote that she was "irresistible without even knowing or caring about it" (*Raymond Chandler,* p. 48), and he adored her.

Cissy was a sophisticated blonde beauty, a free spirit, and a highly independent woman given to drama (she pronounced his surname with a British accent and, crossing his name with Romeo's, referred to him affectionately as "Raymio"). An accomplished pianist, fond of music and literature and long walks, she was very intelligent, and she and Chandler could talk about anything. Her life, like his, was riddled with spells of illness. In time the difference in age began to matter: when she was sixty and ailing, Chandler was only forty-three and still handsome. But for the man with the erratic writing career who needed an inspiring and doting muse, she provided it as well as anyone could have.

The early years of their marriage were wonderful. Chandler was fond of Los Angeles in all its busyness and vulgarity. He and Cissy had more than enough money, their friendships were rewarding, their leisure was stimulating, and they loved each other. Chandler wrote out for friend and columnist Neil Morgan, years later, some rules for happiness in a marriage, for the inevitable day when "you will wish she would fall downstairs and break a leg, and vice versa," including:

> If the coffee is lousy, don't say so. Just throw it on the floor.
>
> In case of a quarrel, remember it is always your fault.
>
> Keep her away from antique shops.
>
> Never praise her girlfriends too much.
>
> Above all, never forget that a marriage is in one way very much like a newspaper. It has to be made fresh every damn day of every damn year. (*The Life of Raymond Chandler,* p. 241)

It seemed, in the beginning, as if they did indeed succeed in making it fresh every day. They were two against the world.

Chandler had risen rapidly to a position of responsibility as president of one oil company and vice president of another, handling legal matters and real estate transactions, but though he was considered extremely capable and astute, he never really liked the world of business. The strain under which he found himself in the 1930s began to tell. The devil-may-care social life that had begun with the Lloyds progressed (or perhaps more correctly got out of hand) to a point where he was drinking heavily. He and his wife fought so much about it that he moved into a hotel and sometimes disappeared for days. The liquor that had helped the ultra-shy Chandler socialize had become the instrument of his undoing.

He made what friends argue was a series of either suicide attempts or reckless cries for help. Several times, while drunk, he called to say he was going to jump out the hotel window. During this period he was said, while under the influence, to have pointed a loaded gun at his head in front of friend Milton Philleo after an altercation over a tennis date, and on another occasion, to have undone a seat belt and stood up cavalierly in a small plane they had taken up. There were frequent weekend binges in the company of a young female coworker, and sometimes Chandler did not manage to return to work until mid-week. He was admonished by his superiors to shape up. Some have said the Depression economy was as much or more to blame, but Chandler never hesitated to admit his drinking was a major factor that cost him, in 1932, his job.

Pulp Fiction

Chandler renounced alcohol and went to the Pacific Northwest to stay with friends. Eventually he returned, when his wife fell ill, and with her support, their savings, and a modest income of a hundred dollars a month (from friends he'd helped by providing them with information for a lawsuit involving an oil company), he began yet again to live the hopeful if insecure life of a beginning writer, taking a class and listing himself as a writer in the city directory. He had begun reading pulp magazines, deeming such fare more truthful in its storytelling than what fiction was to be found in other current periodicals, calling it, in a letter to Hamish Hamilton, "pretty forceful and honest, even though it had its crude aspect" (*Selected Letters,* p. 236), and he started to imitate writers he liked. (He always maintained that learning to write was best done through observation and imitation.) He rewrote several times a story by Erle Stanley Gardner, creator of Perry Mason, comparing his work to Gardner's and examining it for improvements and flaws, and studied Dashiell Hammett's writing, which he later said influenced him the most (though he came to dislike certain aspects of Hammett's work). After five months of perfecting his first detective story, he submitted it to the pulp magazine *Black Mask*. It was 18,000 words long and titled "Blackmailers Don't Shoot."

The editor of *Black Mask,* Joseph "Cap" Shaw, saw talent. "Blackmailers" was published in December 1933, and within a year it had become a frequent practice there to feature his stories first. America had 1,300 pulp writers, and *Black Mask* was foremost among magazines publishing in the hard-boiled school. He had risen fast to the top.

He published twenty-four stories in all. They were short and often cut to fit the space available, and at that time they paid a penny a word. The ever versatile Chandler, perhaps growing bored with a formulaic task, parodied the hard-boiled style in a couple of pieces that sailed into print as written, in spite of lines like, "Anything can happen. You can even get a full glass of beer at a cocktail lounge" ("Red Wind," *Dime Detective,* January 1938). Deft enough to slip past editors, the work had been initialed and set into type, broad laughs and all. (He carried this audacity into his full-length fiction, sometimes with mixed results.)

The stories from *Black Mask, Dime Detective,* and other magazines of this period show a neophyte learning to finesse plot and style and characterization. They also were cannibalized—borrowed and reshaped for use in Chandler's longer fiction. So much attention was paid to combining divergent plots that the minor flaws of these early stories as often as not survived in the novels, as when nobody seemed to know who had killed Owen Taylor, the Sternwoods' chauffeur, in *The Big Sleep*—not even the author.

Chandler liked what he was doing and it buoyed his confidence. This was not much of a living, though. He thought the mystery novel could be elevated to the status of literature. Five years after he had started in the pulps, he put together material from four of the stories and found his first long work.

Marlowe and Method

Chandler's earliest influences had been Henry James, of whose writing he had done a pastiche, and Saki (H. H. Munro), who had written for the *Westminster Gazette* and whose work he had been guided by in his writing of short sketches there. Besides Gardner and Hammett, he cited Ernest Hemingway, Theodore Dreiser, Sherwood Anderson, Ring Lardner, Jr., Carl Sandburg, and T. S. Eliot as his literary predecessors. (F. Scott Fitzgerald's influence should also be noted.) His solid education in language and the classics naturally buttressed everything he wrote, and the precise and demanding headmaster Gilkes hovered in memory, a distant sentinel.

Chandler borrowed heavily from his stories "Killer in the Rain" (1935) and "The Curtain"

(1936), and also took pieces from "Finger Man" (1934) and "Mandarin's Jade" (1937), to produce in just three months *The Big Sleep* (1939), his first novel, generally acknowledged as one of his best. He settled on a first-person narrative which, though it had its share of obvious limitations, put the reader inside the mind of the detective. It also provided a simple, logical answer to the problem of presenting a personal moral vision: let Marlowe say it.

If in the beginning they were not reviewed often enough (let alone well enough), Chandler's novels still made quite an impact. People who did not read the pulps had never heard of him, yet he read like a seasoned author, spoke in an original voice, wrote about one of the most memorable and engaging characters in crime literature (or in any literature, for that matter), and managed to make something truly new. His subject matter and chosen form were so wide ranging that characters from every echelon of California society wandered through his stories in one guise or another. He was not shy about passing along, with brutal candor, his unsparing opinions about fools, bad cops, women and their wiles, the idle rich, the stacked deck of class and privilege, and the ruthlessness of the greedy, whether they were after money, power, revenge, or the girl. At the same time he managed to get his complicated romantic sensibility (and thus in a sense himself) down on paper and to enliven the text with vivid language of the streets, often brilliant in its concision. He was also, in works of compelling drama leavened with wild comic business, impossible to put down.

But most of all he was authentic. He had come to know every side of Los Angeles, and he really was that rare creature Henry James said a writer must be "on whom nothing is lost." He was deeply intuitive, with a good eye and ear, and used an Olivetti typewriter fitted with keys that made it possible for him to record Spanish dialogue complete with diacritics. He kept a notebook filled with slang and another filled with possible titles, and listed in an address book names of potential characters. (Later, he gave characters pseudonyms that were significant by virtue of their initials—notably Paul Marston, in *The Long Goodbye.*) If he did not have a fix on what a seedy bar was like during the dinner hour, he was not above spending an afternoon "casing the joint," as Marlowe might have. In the beginning he did not talk to the police (he did not think they knew much), but he maintained a library of forensics works and avidly followed local scandals and murders. He was never averse to replotting, tossing out large sections of text if they didn't suit his purpose.

In spite of his earlier binge drinking, and his and Cissy's lifelong illnesses, he had no trouble adhering to a disciplined writing schedule. (He also wrote thousands of thoughtful letters to friends, publishers, agents, and others in the business—and later in life, to perfect strangers—and loved to discuss writing, though not his own.) In a personal formula for good writing, he typed his creation on half sheets and made himself get "magic" onto each one. He did not hesitate to refine his prose by discarding and beginning such short passages all over again, if they did not quite succeed, and the limitation on space made him learn to dazzle with dispatch.

Most of all, Chandler was capable of lifting the reader out of this world and setting him down in another. He achieved this in part by the sheer force of personality of his protagonist. Philip Marlowe grew as Chandler wrote—the detective of the early works is not so fully formed as Marlowe of *The Long Goodbye*—but he was always a handful, and in his revelations, whether he is keenly alert or sapped unconscious, tough skinned or passionately smitten, he is all there, and more than able to keep the reader captivated. Marlowe lives, and through his compelling narrative, Chandler sustains the dream.

That transporting vision is a rare form of literary magic, but the demands of the genre continue to cloud certain issues. In recent years, challenging Library of America's wisdom in deciding to republish Chandler in hardcover (an interesting challenge: Houghton Mifflin and Modern Library had done the same thing), critics like Joyce Carol Oates have questioned the writer's importance, chided him for "melodrama" (*New York Review of Books,* 21 December 1995), and criticized his use of certain street language and characterization, including those they claimed seemed to indicate in Chandler racism, misogyny, and anti-Semitism. Their sentiments are understandable, and the issue well worth raising, but Chandler was the wrong writer to skewer, for none of his alleged sins of language fails to meet the necessity test: all were required for authenticity. (Chandler is hardly alone in employing slang realistically in twentieth-century American fiction.) Such language was integral to his brand of storytelling, and the moods he managed to sustain were part of the formula. Marlowe is a ruthless judge of character, but also fair, and when he employs street lingo, using terms like "shine" and "wetback," he also takes pains to point out, for example in *The Long Goodbye,* that Mexican "doctors, technicians, hospitals, painters, architects are as good as ours. Sometimes a little better" (p. 375). There are "good" and "bad" characters among men and women, Jews and Gentiles, and people of every race. If anything, it is power and money he disdains, for the corruption they can sometimes produce.

Futhermore, in a genre where writing was filled with plot and street talk, and some characterization, but not much more, Chandler managed to create and sustain the illusion of another world to an uncommon degree. The writing of Fitzgerald, especially in later works like *Tender Is the Night,* had to have influenced him in this; there are glints of magical realism here and there among the dark forests of mystery, not to mention intimations of the same sort of impossible hope. He was an avowed Fitzgerald fan and displayed a romantic sensibility that filled his books with the same kind of troubled longing that is evident in *The Great Gatsby.* This is much like the romantic sensibility Dick Diver saw in the American actress Rosemary Hoyt, of whom he said, "her real depths are Irish and romantic and illogical" (*Tender Is the Night,* 1995, p. 164). Chandler was first and last, in life and in art, a romantic.

And a conjurer. *The Big Sleep* was the first indication of just what magic he could work: it is true, it is real, and it keeps the reader in thrall. But most of all, it provides an enduring hero, former Los Angeles Police Department and district attorney's investigator–turned-detective Philip Marlowe, who it is difficult not to like and like ardently. Chandler said Marlowe was a fiction: in life the average gumshoe had no moral sense, was not that intelligent, and could be just plain boring. Certainly he was not the fascinating creature Marlowe managed to be. Marlowe was his maker's mouthpiece, too, and nearly all the redemption that eventually finds its way into these novels gets there via the detective's sensibilities.

Philip Marlowe, with a straight nose, brown hair and eyes, and a jaw of iron, is a shade over six feet tall and capable of throwing a hard punch. An intellectual of sorts, never married, in his late thirties to early forties, he replays tough chess matches for his amusement, lives on next to nothing, has a deep fondness for women, smokes, drinks, refuses to do divorce work, and presents a quasi-romantic hero with a tough-guy mouth. His talk makes him a cynic but his actions make him an idealist and romantic, and many have called him "courtly." (He can also be sentimental in the extreme.) Women seduce him even as they disappoint him, and he fearlessly walks the meanest streets in his search for the truth. (He is as likely as not to be conned, grilled, manhandled, drugged, locked up, shot at, and even knocked unconscious in the process.) His self-deprecating humor acts as a foil to his moral sensibilities, making it easy for him to avoid sounding stiff or prissy, and it livens the text. (In *The Big Sleep,* he says he has several file cabinets "full of California climate" in his office and returns to it "to catch up on my foot-dangling" [p. 118].)

The detective's name may have been in part a nod toward Marlowe House at Dulwich. He was created from Chandler's pulp story detectives and characters, including one called Mallory and one called Marlow—these in homage to courtly poet Thomas Malory, a knight, who wrote of the "once and future king" in *Le Morte d'Arthur* (1485), and poet Christopher Marlowe, who wrote, "Come live with me, and be my love" ("The Passionate Shepherd to His Love," c. 1589). (He also wrote, "That was in another country; and besides, the wench is dead," in *The Jew of Malta,* c. 1589, which is a little closer in sentiment to some of the more fleeting relationships Philip Marlowe has with women.) Both poets had checkered histories. Malory was imprisoned for crimes of violence; Marlowe, also possessed of a violent temperament, was connected with acts of espionage and the forging of gold coins. (Gold coins both forged and real make an appearance in Chandler's third novel, *The High Window.*)

The Big Sleep (1938–1939)

Chandler completed *The Big Sleep* in the summer months of 1938, then submitted the manuscript to agent Sydney Sanders, and in 1939 it was published by Alfred A. Knopf in America and by Hamish Hamilton in Britain. Some reviewers considered the book too violent or too depraved, but there was also a groundswell of opinion that a brilliant new star had been discovered in the hard-boiled cosmos. (Chandler later wrote to Alex Barris that he would "never again equal [it] for pace," *Raymond Chandler Speaking,* p. 222.) The book sold more than three times as many copies as a typical mystery and went on to be reprinted in paperback and in a very inexpensive pulp edition, as most of his novels did. It was also used as the basis for two films of the same name.

Chandler took extreme risks in this work, in a formula that he kept throughout his novels. He admired the work of Dashiell Hammett, who he said "had taken murder out of the Venetian vase and dropped it in the alley" ("The Simple Art of Murder"), and in so doing, had made an art form more enduring and authentic than what one had commonly come to expect of detective fiction. "To accept a mediocre form and make something like literature out of it is in itself rather an accomplishment," he wrote (*Bloody Murder,* 1994, p. 164). He followed Hammett down that road, adopting the hard-boiled style. But he was far more demanding of himself: he wanted to make art. And the allure of his poetic narrative, the courtliness of his hero, brought something truly original to the genre. He has been imitated widely ever since, though never with the same success.

In *The Big Sleep,* Marlowe finds himself "calling on four million dollars" when the aging General Guy Sternwood retains him to investigate the blackmail over some gambling debts of his younger daughter, Carmen (this is just one of several mysteries to be solved). Before he has left the premises, her older sister, Vivian, grills Marlowe about his visit, without success.

In the complex plot—garnished with a wide array of unusually exotic elements, including hothouse orchids and laudanum, a naked and drugged girl posed on a throne, and an elite bookshop which is really a front for a pornography racket—Marlowe searches for answers. The dissolute Sternwood daughters take him to a gambling hall and to the fussy, fancifully decorated house of A. G. Geiger.

Marlowe cases Geiger's "rare book" emporium, which turns out to be a lending library of pornography. Tailing Geiger home, Marlowe hears shots, then witnesses a tableau—Carmen, naked, seated on a throne before a camera: he thinks the drugged girl has killed the smut peddler. He discovers Geiger's client list, takes Carmen home, and returns to Geiger's to find Geiger's body missing.

Geiger's murder draws Marlowe into the world of gambling club owner Eddie Mars. Marlowe learns that the blackmail has escalated from Vivian, who has received a letter and pictures of the naked Carmen. A man named Joe Brody turns out to have been behind the blackmail; he is shot by Geiger's lover, whom Marlowe turns in to the police.

Back at Geiger's house, the body has been returned, and Marlowe reports that as well.

Since his first encounter with Sternwood, Marlowe has had a suspicion about Vivian's ex-husband, Rusty Regan, and now realizes he should try to find him.

At home he finds Carmen in his bed (naked again and trying to seduce him) and manages to get her to dress and leave. He tears the bed apart in disgust (an act that has been interpreted many ways by critics). Carmen's behavior tips Marlowe off to the likelihood that she had also been unable to seduce Regan and had shot him. Along the way, a cold beauty named Mona Mars ("Silver-Wig") captures Marlowe's interest, after he finds himself in a jam and she undoes the ropes holding him captive. This is a neat reversal of the opening chapter's figure of a stained-glass knight, in the Sternwoods' hallway, trying to release a naked woman tied to a tree, itself a prologue to the Marlowe canon: he will always be rescuing somebody, or trying to.

Redemption comes when Marlowe tells Vivian to keep his fee, take Carmen away, and use the money to see that the girl gets well (the first of several courtly gestures—toward characters who usually don't deserve them—for Philip Marlowe). He ends his narrative with plaintive lines about how equal we are in death, and a sentimental word for Mona:

> What did it matter where you lay once you were dead? In a dirty sump or in a marble tower on top of a high hill? . . . you were not bothered by things like that. You just slept the big sleep, not caring about the nastiness of how you died or where you fell. . . .
>
> On the way downtown I stopped at a bar and had a couple of double Scotches. They didn't do me any good. All they did was make me think of Silver-Wig, and I never saw her again. (1939, pp. 215–216)

Unlike many other heroes in this genre, the detective of *The Big Sleep* is a three-dimensional character with real emotion and sexuality and a highly developed sense of moral purpose. (It is fine for him to want Mona; it is not fine for him to be seduced by the troubled young Carmen.) He is acting on his own initiative in searching for Regan and in looking after Carmen's interests beyond the blackmail, and his humanity is the best part of the story.

There is also a poetry to the language that had not been seen in mystery fiction: "At seven-twenty a single flash of hard white light shot out of Geiger's house like a wave of summer lightning. As the darkness folded back on it and ate it up a thin tinkling scream echoed out and lost itself among the rain-drenched trees" (p. 29).

Chandler had established many conventions for his fiction template besides poetic narrative. Time is the great leveler; the rich are sometimes dissolute; the law can end up causing more problems than it solves; and women can be a checkered lot. On a hunch, the detective starts looking for Rusty when it is not yet considered important to the case. Marlowe's encounter with the enticing Mona Mars brings out his sexual vulnerability and makes him reveal his sentimental heart, though he can't help but see through (a mite cynically) to her coldness. She is just the first in a line of devastating blondes who get away . . . but not before he manages to kiss her:

> Her face under my mouth was like ice. She put her hands up and took hold of my head and kissed me hard on the lips. Her lips were like ice, too.
>
> I went out through the door and it closed behind me, without sound, and the rain blew in under the porch, not as cold as her lips. (p. 185)

The book is also full of Chandler's similes and gibes, which have been disparaged as roundly as they have been praised, but some are enough to make one laugh out loud, as when he says of Vivian Regan, "Her black hair was glossy under a brown Robin Hood hat that might have cost fifty dollars and looked as if you could have made it with one hand out of a desk blotter" (p. 51).

Chandler was also a master of street talk (he filled his books with it), and some of the cleverest exchanges show up in this his first novel:

> "You're broke, eh?"
> "I been shaking two nickels together for a month, trying to get them to mate." (p. 83)
>
> . . .
>
> I grinned at her. "Did I hurt your head much?"
> "You and every other man I ever met." (p. 84)
>
> . . .
>
> "Geiger was living with the punk. I mean living with him, if you get the idea."
> Cronjager was staring at him levelly now. "That sounds like it might grow up to be a dirty story." (p. 100)

Marlowe has his own brands of vernacular and sarcasm, as in this exchange with tough guy Eddie Mars:

> [MARS] "I'm nice to be nice to, soldier. I'm not nice not to be nice to."
> [MARLOWE] "Listen hard and you'll hear my teeth chattering." (p. 108)

The Big Sleep, the exotic beauty of the septet of novels, has its particular charms. Many critics note Chandler's clever hand in interweaving the plots in this book (Chandler agreed) and say it is the best he ever did with his cannibalizations. It contains his protagonists' only kill; it introduces the language of the streets and returning characters like Bernie Ohls; it is in its language at turns poetic and biting, wistful and comic; and it summons brilliantly, through dialogue, gesture, and event, the complexity of one good man. The birth of Philip Marlowe was front-page literary news.

Farewell, My Lovely (1940)

The second novel, discarded once by Chandler in manuscript and rebegun, was finished in April 1940. Its title was also changed: originally *The Second Murderer,* it became, after the publisher asked for a change, *Farewell, My Lovely*. The book was cannibalized from "Try the Girl" (1937), "The Man Who Liked Dogs" (1936), and "Mandarin's Jade" (1937), and Chandler called it his favorite. It follows a woman's ascent from lounge singer to wealthy wife of an older man of power and influence, and through its characters, says much about the hypocrisy and greed of the venal and the corrupt in Bay City (meant to be Santa Monica).

As one result of the braiding of plotlines, the reader must suspend disbelief twice: first, when Marlowe walks right up to the case, in the person of just-out-of-jail Moose Malloy, by coincidence, and a second time, when he is contracted to help retrieve a stolen necklace (which, it turns out, belongs to Malloy's missing girl, who is rich and now consorts with high society). These are coincidences too large to swallow without complaint, except that the book is so good nobody seems to have cared. The reviews were an improvement over those he had received for *The Big Sleep,* and many agree with the author's assessment of this work as his best. While it may seem odd that so many readers and critics rated Chandler's first two books among the three favorites, Chandler had an explanation for it. He wrote, in a letter to Dale Warren (*Selected Letters,* p. 191), that writers became self-conscious as they saw reviews of books, and that early works were less likely to suffer from the effects of this, or to have "a loss of organic dash." He thought *Farewell, My Lovely* "less forced" than other works. He also felt he would never again be able to finesse such "plot complication" (*Raymond Chandler Speaking,* p. 222). Years later, Edmund Wilson, who had nothing but unkind words for mystery writers, wrote about detective fiction as a blot on American literature. Invited to sample fifty-two works, he said he thought Chandler was the only writer in the genre who knew how to tell a story, and that *Farewell* was the only mystery he enjoyed—and the only one he could finish.

In echoes of the book's original title, and paralleling the Velma/Helen dichotomy, the book is rife with disparate twins—white visitors to Florian's, people Marlowe plies with bourbon, redheads, ransom deliverers, Velma's photos, and the missing partners Marlowe's clients are seeking. There are two murderers, two exotics, and two "healers." And against all odds, Helen's last act takes two bullets (one that matters, and one that doesn't). (In the same way, she seems to have left us twice: once as Velma Valento, who ceased to exist when she married Lewin Lockridge Grayle—except for Malloy, who cannot forget her, and Marriott, who is blackmailing her—and then as Helen, the wealthy wife.) Finally, Malloy has a physical twin in the brawny immigrant tunneler Stoyanoffsky, whom Nulty had mistaken for him.

As with *The Big Sleep, Farewell, My Lovely* offers the reader exotic elements (rare jade, and jujus, and a gambling ship offshore), but it also presents a somewhat stymied Marlowe: he is forced to make his way past a number of hurdles—including one lazy cop, who arrests the wrong man, constant observation by other cops, and the fact that two of his clients end up dead.

Farewell is a tale of confounding separations. The one person who's been of enormous help, Anne Riordan, an affable and virtuous young woman who likes Marlowe, gets the courtly treatment, but it is also cold: she's too pure to besmirch, and her advances toward him are politely ignored. Though he admits candidly that her house would be a nice place "to wear slippers in," she is a virgin and too sweet for this tough guy. And he will always favor more experienced women. (Maybe they are safer—he can always leave them without much remorse, and rejection by them wouldn't cause him any real pain.)

In *Farewell, My Lovely,* Marlowe trips over trouble when he meets Moose Malloy in front of Florian's, a bar where Malloy is looking for lost love Velma Valento. Moose is a large guy—Marlowe later tells a cop, "He could wear you or me for a watch charm" (p. 17). Angry over getting no information about his girl, Malloy kills the manager. Later, Marlowe discusses the case with the cop Nulty, who wants him to investigate and go after Malloy. But Marlowe's instincts tell him to go after Velma.

In what seems a typical Chandler coincidence, Marlowe is offered a job as a bodyguard for the dandy Lindsay Marriott, who will pay a ransom for a rare jade necklace belonging to a friend. At the rendezvous, Marlowe is sapped when he gets out of the car with the money. He comes to twenty minutes later. A cop's daughter, redhead Anne Riordan, informs him Marriott has been killed. She helps Marlowe with the case, introducing him to a Mrs. Lewin Lockridge Grayle (Helen), whose necklace Marriott had been trying to retrieve. Helen Grayle, who at first seems to live up to her surname, comes on like a dream. She is another of the famous Chandler blondes, "a blonde to make a bishop kick a hole in a stained-glass window"—whose wealthy husband owns a radio station where she was once a singer.

Marlowe asks her about the night of the jewel theft: who knew she was wearing the necklace? As she rules out her servants, Marlowe says: "Well, where have we got to? No maid, no chauffeur, no butler, no footman. We'll be doing our own laundry next" (p. 124). She is with him all of ten minutes before they are kissing. She tells him to forget about the jewels, but asks him to meet her later at Laird Brunette's Belvedere Club.

Some jujus (Chandler's term for marijuana-laced cigarettes) were found on Marriott, containing the business card of a psychic, Jules Amthor. Marlowe sets up a meeting with him and ends up getting pistol-whipped there, then roughed up by the police and placed in a sanatorium, where he awakes in a stupor.

He investigates a gambling ship offshore and arranges for a message to be given to Moose Malloy. Later, Malloy visits him; when Helen arrives on the scene, Marlowe quickly hides him. Before the story has ended, Marlowe has brought the hopeful Malloy to truth . . . and death.

In this novel Chandler dived deeper into fearless writing of the streets, with his usual acerbic wit:

> "A nice quiet place Sam run, too . . . ain't nobody been knifed there in a month." (p. 23)
>
> . . .
>
> I poured her a slug that would have made me float over a wall. (p. 27)
>
> . . .
>
> It [the photograph] was Malloy, all right, taken in a strong light and looking as if he had no more eyebrows than a French roll. (p. 35)

Velma is described by Moose as "cute as lace pants" (p. 11), and a little later Marlowe calls the widow Jessie Florian "cute as a washtub" (p. 29).

The story furthers Chandler's ambitions in its poetic narrative, too, in lines most writers would never even try to get away with:

> A wedge of sunlight slipped over the edge of the desk and fell noiselessly to the carpet. (p. 40)

Marlowe speaks in states of extreme stupor in this novel, providing Chandler with an opportunity to show that he can, while maintaining a self-deprecating mood, do with interior monologue what he can do with everything else, even for a character who is just coming back from having been sapped into unconsciousness:

> Time passes very slowly when you are doing something. I mean, you can go through a lot of movements in a very few minutes. Is that what I mean? What the hell do I care what I mean? Okey, better men than me have meant less. (p. 61)

There is also a constant undercurrent of how things are not always what they seem (as with all those disparate twins) and of how one event can make all the difference. Velma becomes Helen because she married money, and in her new life she is blackmailed and ends up killing twice in her attempt to keep the persona intact, while protecting the tycoon who had lifted her out of her sorry life as a singer. It eventually takes her from this world into the next (with as much redemption as she can manage, considering), and Marlowe reflects on this in his conclusion:

> Maybe she saw a chance—not to get away—she was tired of dodging by that time—but to give a break to the only man who had ever given her one.
>
> . . .
>
> It was a cool day and very clear. You could see a long way—but not as far as Velma had gone. (p. 275)

It is difficult to read this passage (or to consider Moose Malloy) without recalling the end of *The Great Gatsby* and Nick Carraway's reflections on another man's long journey, and his yearning for a girl who in the end had succeeded only in bringing him to his death:

> I thought of Gatsby's wonder when he first picked out the green light at the end of Daisy's dock. He had come a long way to this blue lawn and his dream must have seemed so close that he could hardly fail to grasp it. He did not know that it was already behind him. (1995, p. 189)

The High Window and *The Lady in the Lake* (1941–1943)

Chandler considered his next novel, *The High Window* (1942), written at the same time as *The Lady in the Lake* and several short stories, his worst, but it was in its way an advance: no cannibalization, but an original new work. Perhaps its newness was what left Chandler lacking confidence.

The book is filled with elements previously encountered: singers, gamblers, and especially an innocent who needs the strong shoulder of Marlowe to cry on. It begins when Marlowe is asked by Mrs. Murdock to find a missing rare coin, possibly stolen by daughter-in-law Linda Conquest, a nightclub singer. Along the way, Marlowe is led to another situation, that of a man believed to have fallen through a window to his death, captured in a photograph, and the innocent secretary, Merle Davis, who has been conned into thinking that she is responsible.

Marlowe finds himself looking after the interests of the naive Merle. As with Carmen Sternwood in *The Big Sleep,* Marlowe quickly gets to the truth: the girl has been duped. Once again he sees to it (beyond anything one would normally expect of a detective, let alone a tough guy) that she is given the chance to straighten out her life. He ends up driving her home at the end of the book.

Critical reception was mixed, and although the book was the basis for a film adaptation (*The Brasher Doubloon,* 1947), it sold fewer copies than expected.

Chandler began *The Lady in the Lake* in 1939, but it was a work he left and came back to frequently, and he did not submit it for publication until 1943, after finishing several stories. The Chandlers had lived at Big Bear Lake, California, and he used it as the setting, now called Little Fawn Lake. The novel was cannibalized from "Bay City Blues" (1938), "No Crime in the Mountains" (1941), and the story "The Lady in the Lake" (1939), and nearly shares its title with the famous poem by Sir Walter Scott "The Lady of the Lake" (1810), in which the line "the will to do, the soul to dare" seems very much a sentiment in the tradition of Philip Marlowe (not to mention of his creator). Marlowe is, after all, a man of both conviction and resolve. The war, the vacationers at California resorts, and landscape and nature all add new elements for Chandler to write about.

Parfumier Derace Kingsley hires Marlowe. He is searching for his missing wife, Crystal, thought to have run off with her paramour, Chris Lavery. In searching for her, Marlowe discovers that Muriel, wife of the caretaker Bill Chess, is also missing. Dr. Albert Almore's wife has recently committed suicide, and his nurse has also disappeared. The four women are at the heart of the mystery.

Marlowe learns that Chess's wife found him in bed with Crystal; then both women disappeared. They are similar in appearance. A body found in the lake is thought to be Muriel's, and Chess is arrested. In the process of untangling the threads of several stories, Marlowe discovers that Dr. Almore's wife's "suicide" was really a murder covered up by the police. His nurse, Mildred Haviland, was responsible for setting up a situation that made it look as if Crystal had indeed run off. She also was responsible for the woman's death and subsequently emptied her bank account. In the search for answers, Marlowe finds a dead Lavery. It turns out that the body in the lake originally identified as Muriel's is really Crystal's, put there by someone who expected Chess to take the rap.

Jacques Barzun called *The Lady in the Lake* Chandler's best work, and Ross Macdonald included it in his list of favorites, too, but many see both this and *The High Window* as "transitional novels" (Marling, p. 104), in which Chandler both echoed earlier themes and tried to strike out into new territory, with mixed results. (In *Window,* the two plots—a stolen coin and a murder—do not intertwine as well as dual plots in the earlier books, and in *Lady,* the plot twists are too frequent and too tangled.)

The Lady in the Lake was the first of Chandler's novels to be reviewed widely in Britain. It sold more hardcover copies in America—14,000—than any of his previous novels. A twenty-five-cent edition of *The Big Sleep* was published in the United States by Avon and sold 300,000 copies, and Pocket Books followed with a similar edition of *Farewell, My Lovely* a few months later and broke the million-copy mark in sales. At this time, Norwegian and Dutch editions of *The Big Sleep* were also published. Chandler was at last getting the recognition he deserved.

Early Films (1941–1945)

Paramount producer Joe Sistrom had given director Billy Wilder a copy of *The High Window,* and Wilder read it and as a result decided he would cowrite his next picture, *Double Indemnity,* from the novel by James M. Cain, with Chandler. The Chandlers subsequently moved to Hollywood.

Hollywood studios had lured a number of writers, including Dashiell Hammett, F. Scott Fitzgerald, William Faulkner, and John O'Hara. The atmosphere, especially at Paramount (the only one of four studios Chandler spoke of with praise, and even that was qualified) was conducive to good work, especially for a man of Chandler's temperament: there was an easygoing quality to it, and the camaraderie of like-minded souls was heartening. Chandler constantly encouraged young writers and while at the studio got to hobnob with others whose work in fiction had led them there.

Chandler's writing had already excited interest in the film community. RKO had bought the rights to *Farewell, My Lovely*. The second film of Hammett's *Maltese Falcon* (1941) had had such a stunning success that sequels were in demand. Instead of introducing Marlowe to the world of film, *Farewell* was rewritten as *The Falcon Takes Over* and the movie was released in 1942. It was remade, with Dick Powell as the first Marlowe on film, in 1944. (Because a survey revealed that *Farewell, My Lovely* struck many as the title of a musical, the film was retitled *Murder, My Sweet* for American audiences.) Chandler's paperback sales soared as a result of the film's success.

Twentieth Century–Fox had bought the film rights to *The High Window* for $3,500; the film *Time to Kill* (1942) was based on it. (Chandler did not write it.) *The Brasher Doubloon* (1947), produced by the same studio, is based, some say more faithfully, on *The High Window.*

For *Double Indemnity* (1944), Chandler and Wilder worked together. (Chandler had come under the wing of Hollywood agent H. N. Swanson, who had represented both F. Scott Fitzgerald and William Faulkner there.) The pairing is notable for the effect it had on the novelist's confidence. Chandler insisted the Cain dialogue was terrible and remedied it remarkably. (He had never thought much of Cain and in print dismissed him.) He also wrote a voice-over filled with the Chandler incisiveness. At one point the claims manager, Keyes, talking about the two conspirators, says:

> They can't keep away from each other. They may think it's twice as safe because there are two of them. But it isn't twice as safe. It's ten times twice as dangerous. They've committed a murder. And it's not like a trolley ride together where they can get off at different stops. They're stuck with each other and they've got to ride all the way to the end of the line and it's a one-way trip and the last stop is the cemetery. (*Raymond Chandler in Hollywood,* p. 45)

In an interview Wilder said the two people he had known "with whom everyone is most interested are Marilyn Monroe and Raymond Chandler." He called them "enigmas" (*The World of Raymond Chandler,* pp. 54–55). Chandler, when they first met, warned him that he could not promise the script for another six days (to Wilder's amazement; films took months). He got $750 a week for the term of the writing. Wilder later paid him a mixed but awed compliment about the novels: "They weren't even as well plotted as Dashiell Hammett: but, by God, a kind of lightning struck on every page" (*The World of Raymond Chandler,* p. 47). "Lightning" was a great word for it, connoting as it did not just drama and sudden impact and nature, but electricity and danger and illumination.

Double Indemnity is about an insurance fraud centering on a murder: a housewife conspires with the agent who sold her the policy. It is taken from the 1944 James M. Cain novel that was among favorite hard-boiled novels of the time, but dialogue was never Cain's strong point, and it certainly did not lend itself to being used straight off the page in a film. Chandler, however, knew what was needed.

Wilder recalled that Cain was so happy with the resulting picture that he went over to the director at the premiere and gave him a hug and a kiss, saying "it was the first time somebody had done a good job on any of his stuff" (*Raymond Chandler in Hollywood*, p. 47). Wilder, while he found Chandler "acid, sour, [and] grouchy," still considered him extraordinary, since he was able to pick up the reins of a project and learn as he went. Chandler returned the compliment, saying Wilder had taught him as much as anyone could have about Hollywood and screenplays.

The film, though, is the best testament. Together with similar films, it helped guide Hollywood down a path on which it remains to this day. Later films like *Chinatown* (1974), *Body Heat* (1981), and *L.A. Confidential* (1997) induced a spate of reviewers to invoke Chandler, because that character of darkness and the tough but funny street lingo were unusual in American film, and singular enough to stand out in memory. (Writers and directors continue to work glimmers of homage to Chandler and the hard-boiled tradition into their art. James Ellroy's *L.A. Confidential* character Lynn Bracken is named in homage to Leigh Brackett, a screenwriter on *The Big Sleep* in 1946 [with William Faulkner and Jules Furthman] and *The Long Goodbye* in 1973. Ellroy's book, the screenplay by Bill Helgeland and Curtis Hanson, and the film contain numerous echoes of Chandler, among them a prominent constantly grinding oil well behind the scenes of sex and death at the Victory Motel; a raft of seamy episodes involving street drugs; the blackmail of a city official; a pornography racket; and Ellroy's character the homicide cop Bud White, who avenges wronged women with his fists, a modern-day Marlowe with his own "paralyzing" blue-eyed blonde.)

Double Indemnity was nominated for an Oscar, and Billy Wilder felt Chandler deserved the most credit for the screenplay's effectiveness. Chandler was already thinking about his next novel, but wooed to an easier task working on scripts in progress, he took on a job as cowriter, with Frank Partos, of the romantic film *And Now Tomorrow* (from the 1942 novel of that name by Rachel Field) at Paramount (1944), and then, with Hagar Wilde, cowrote *The Unseen* (1945), another mystery, based on the Ethel Lina White novel *Her Heart in Her Throat.* (White is more famous for her novel *The Wheel Spins* [1936], which was adapted for Hitchcock's *The Lady Vanishes.*)

Meanwhile, Swanson was finding bigger and better things for Chandler to consider. At one point there were plans for Chandler to write an adaptation of Fitzgerald's 1925 novel *The Great Gatsby* (sadly, nothing came of it). Knopf had sold the rights to the *The Big Sleep* to Warner Brothers, but Chandler's contract with Paramount precluded his working on the script. In 1945 he began a lucrative new contract. Swanson had managed to procure $1,000 per week for Chandler from Paramount, for a first look at anything he chose to write.

The Blue Dahlia and Later Films (1945–1947)

Paramount's John Houseman talked to Chandler about what work he had in progress, and the unfinished story "The Blue Dahlia" was selected. (Chandler got $25,000 for the completed typescript.) The picture began to be cast after the treatment had been completed, and then filmed around the clock as Chandler wrote the script. The star, Alan Ladd, had but three weeks until his return to the army when the first half of the script had been shot, and with nothing else to film, the studio panicked and offered Chandler $5,000 to finish writing it in time, but he was not impressed—in fact, he was upset at what he regarded as a lack of faith.

In a bizarre decision, he met with John Houseman and offered to do what they needed, on the condition he be allowed to work drunk, with cars in front of his house to carry medicine, liquor, and manuscript back and forth, a secretary to transcribe his work, and a direct line to the studio. He pulled it off, and the studio grossed $2.75 million (on a picture they had thought might not ever be finished). Chandler disliked having to rewrite clumsy love scenes between Alan Ladd and Veronica Lake (whom he nastily called "Moronica Lake"), but critical reception was so good that he was named in the reviews for his work, and the studio kept him on, raising his salary to $4,000 per week. He spent a month recovering from the long write. (A BBC radio play was subsequently written about Chandler's unusual method of finishing the script.)

The Blue Dahlia is a story about a returning soldier who discovers his wife has been unfaithful. When she is murdered and he comes to be considered the prime suspect, he must find the killer before the law finds him. With the help of her lover's wife, he does, and ends up falling in love with her.

Chandler received a second Academy Award nomination (this even with a plot that had been altered to acquiesce with Navy requests for changes concerning their image—they were not happy about a serviceman who was also a murderer—and production code requirements that lifted a lot of the liquor right out of the story, in spite of the fact that the protagonist was a drinker who had blackouts). Chandler later said that all the interference had made a "routine whodunit out of a fairly original idea," a murderer who is innocent of the knowledge of his crime (*The Life of Raymond Chandler*, p. 147).

Meanwhile, Chandler's newest plot about a murder, which later became *The Long Goodbye*, had begun to entice him. He had also been working on a screenplay of *The Lady in the Lake* with frustration and much argument with MGM studio heads. (It was finished by Steve Fisher, and Chandler had his name taken off it, he disliked the final product so much.)

Chandler published the essay "Writers in Hollywood" at the *Atlantic Monthly* in November 1945, offering his opinion that it was impossible to write film scripts there without becoming cynical. "Good original screenplays are almost as rare in Hollywood as virgins," he wrote. (A skirmish of letters for and against his position raged in the popular press.) He then worked on a screenplay of Elizabeth Sanxay Holding's 1946 novel *The Innocent Mrs. Duff*, but left it unfinished at Paramount.

Warner Brothers was making *The Big Sleep*. Chandler discussed the story with the screenwriters, Leigh Brackett and William Faulkner, director Howard Hawks, and star Humphrey Bogart, and even wrote a new ending (which they did not use). He was very happy with the film and liked the way Bogart could seem tough without saying anything. Lauren Bacall was in the tradition of smooth Chandler blondes, and she and Bogart sizzled.

That year the Mystery Writers of America awarded the Edgar to Chandler for the screenplay of *The Blue Dahlia*. The Chandlers moved, with their beloved cat Taki, a black Persian, to La Jolla, the one place they had loved while they lived there; they could now afford it.

In 1947 Chandler signed a contract with Universal to write at $4,000 per week plus a percentage of the profits. He produced the screenplay *Playback*, a story in which a girl, living in a hotel, gets involved with two politicos, one of whom ends up dead on her balcony. A detective from Canada risks everything to believe in her; his fondness for her is a complicating element. The girl cannot tell her story because to do so would put her under suspicion, though she has nothing to hide. The film was never made, but the story idea was resurrected when Chandler turned it into a novel of the same name in 1958.

In this era Chandler was a celebrity, but the rarefied air of "serious" literary criticism did not seem to have room for him in America. He was annoyed by a reference comparing his work with that of Graham Greene (*New Yorker*, Edmund Wilson), and by a piece denouncing Marlowe, insisting he made a good film detective but not much of a character in a novel (*Partisan Review*, R. W. Flint). Chandler thought the literati were only fooling themselves in a kind of self-perpetuating morass of highbrow sensibility and that some of the best fiction being written was springing up in the hard-boiled genre (the American public agreed, if sales are any indication). It did not matter what the American critics thought; his influence was beginning to be seen in other writers both within the genre and without. And in Britain, Bowen, Eliot, Maugham, Spender, Connolly, Burgess, and Priestley were all ardent Chandler fans.

He was also reviewing books at this time, and received royalties, between 1947 and 1951, from a successful radio program which broadcast scripts involving Marlowe (he did not write them but he was shown them for approval). It came to entice the then-largest radio audience in America—10.3 million.

The Little Sister (1948–1949)

Though Chandler had been diagnosed with a rare skin allergy that required him to wear gloves, and though his wife's condition (pulmonary fibrosis) grew steadily worse, the Chandlers kept busy. He maintained his many correspondences and wrote as much as he could, drinking little in his wife's presence. His novels by now had appeared in many languages. In France he was a modern hero and had been compared to Georges Simenon, author of the Maigret mysteries. Albert Camus had acknowledged a debt to Chandler in the creation of M. Meursault in *L'Étranger* (*The Stranger,* 1942).

Chandler had been working intermittently on *The Little Sister* (1949), which was lauded by some—one encyclopedia (H. R. F. Keating, *Whodunit?*) listed it as one of his three best and rated the plot more highly than that of *The Big Sleep*—but most reviews were more negative. Its sales, however, were excellent, possibly because film had brought Chandler to the attention of people who hadn't known about his books. Chandler said the plot of *The Little Sister* "creaked like a broken shutter" and called it the only one of his novels he actively disliked (letter to Hamish Hamilton, UCLA). It included his opinions about the studios, and his treatment of Hollywood types in the work is ruthless. (At one point he was fed up enough with the novel to avow that *Sister* would be the last of the Marlowe books.) *Cosmopolitan* paid $10,000 for first serial rights—he had come a long way from a penny a word—but the April 1949 abridgment did not please him; he had not expected to have material he had not written added to the work under his byline.

Chandler used the novel to expound on the sins of Hollywood and the still brilliant weirdness of his home: "California, the department store state. The most of everything and the best of nothing." He acknowledged that the book was one long diatribe against just about everything he hated about Hollywood and its denizens. The story bogs down with too many plot twists and turns, and one can't help but hear in the bored sigh of Marlowe the bored sigh of the writer. Chandler told James Sandoe, "It was written in a bad mood and I think that comes through." He vacillated between hating the work and merely feeling frustrated by it.

A collection entitled *The Simple Art of Murder* (eight stories and the essay of the title) was published in 1950. In the essay Chandler presented "the most powerful attack ever made on the classical detective story," according to Julian Symons (*Bloody Murder,* 1994, p. 164), who quickly adds that this terrain had already been widely explored, espcially by Philip Van Doren, in the essay "The Case of the Corpse in the Blind Alley." Both writers lamented the staleness of the genre's approach to story, which Chandler seemed to find rather two-dimensional. He blamed it in part on classical mystery fiction's unusually wide exposure and its publishers' lowered standards:

> The average detective story is probably no worse than the average novel, but you never see the average novel. It doesn't get published. The average—or slightly above average—detective story does. (1939, p. 4)

But he had little generosity of appreciation even for the better ones:

> the strange thing is that this average, more than middling dull, pooped-out piece of ut-

> terly unreal and mechanical fiction is really not very different from what are called masterpieces of the art. . . . Whereas the good novel is not at all the same kind of book as the bad novel. It is about entirely different things. (p. 4)

Chandler also worked on a treatment of Patricia Highsmith's novel *Strangers on a Train,* a story about two people who meet and agree to commit a murder apiece, each for the other. He was enthusiastic about cowriting with director Alfred Hitchcock, who went to La Jolla to work with him. Hitchcock did not like Chandler's script; Chandler found working on someone else's material distressing, because many things in Highsmith's story seemed illogical to him, while Hitchcock tended to keep implausibilities for the sake of mood or a great shot. At first Chandler was willing to go along, but after a bout with food poisoning, when Chandler voluntarily took himself off salary, things began to deteriorate. Hitchcock gave Chandler's writing to staff who changed it, Chandler felt used, and screenwriter Czenzi Ormonde rewrote the script at the end and shared the credit. Chandler later said that while he had wanted to work with the great director, Hitchcock always had to have things his way, and the stress and strain on a writer who submitted things only to have them changed wholesale, sometimes by staff assistants, was disheartening.

But he had an ace up his sleeve: a longer work of fiction in which he was going to do, for a change, what he wanted. *The Little Sister,* in all its disappointments, and the dispiriting experience he'd had writing *Strangers on a Train,* moved Chandler to search for a new voice. The great ambition had just got bigger. This would prove to be a much longer road. Despite setbacks and illness, Chandler was more steadfast than ever.

The Long Goodbye (1949–1953)

By 1952 he had completed 50,000 words of a work tentatively titled *Summer in Idle Valley.* Gravely unhappy about his last novel, he had broken all his rules. The resulting manuscript turned out to be his biggest leap between books. This was not just his longest work, twice the size of any of the others; it was also the one whose characters most revealed the inner Chandler, by way of revealing the inner Marlowe, and it was the truest in terms of emotion. The book had a new pace and a longer payoff to the plot, and a wider complement of writing skills was required. He described how he had planned to proceed in a letter to his new agent Carl Brandt's assistant, Bernice Baumgartner: "You write in a style that has been imitated, even plagiarized, to the point where you look as if you were imitating your imitators. So you have to go where they can't follow" (*Selected Letters,* p. 315).

Baumgartner and Brandt did not like where he had gone. To his first submittal of the manuscript they hastily replied from the heart—about their objections, especially to Marlowe's sentimentalism (Brandt found the character "Christ-like")—but Chandler, while allowing that he could err, stuck to his guns, saying he knew this was a book he could believe in. He did go on to make changes but determined that showing unfinished work to people was a mistake. (His publishers at Houghton Mifflin grew concerned, meanwhile, about his ability to complete another book.) He later broke with Brandt and Brandt, largely over their not having seen eye to eye with him on the work.

And on the new Philip Marlowe: for in his stripping Marlowe bare of many of his defenses, Chandler brought out the inner man, one who needed to be loved. In this book the story *is* Marlowe, and his friendship with a stranger whose life is placed in his capable hands. Terry Lennox is somebody he can drink with, somebody he will drive to the border to help escape a murder rap, somebody he will be jailed and roughed up for, and somebody who in the end lets him down and manages to make him disdain his sentimental heart. Moose Malloy had learned a great lesson during his loss of innocence in *Farewell,*

My Lovely. But for Marlowe *this* was the getting-of-wisdom novel, which allowed critics (finally) to say that a Chandler novel belonged in the mainstream American canon. Marlowe is a changed man at the end of the book—and one who has learned to take enormous chances with trust and friendship.

While he was revising *The Long Goodbye,* Chandler published "Ten Per Cent of Your Life" in the *Atlantic Monthly* (February 1952), a critical piece on Hollywood agents in which he skewered them roundly, and sent out a story called "A Couple of Writers," about a failed writer married to a failed playwright, which no one took. (Philip Durham labeled it "not in the Chandler vein.") His confidence would not be shattered, though; he knew what he had in *The Long Goodbye*. It would take much revising, but Chandler had always been a reviser.

Between the first draft and the last, the Chandlers went on an extended vacation to London, traveling via the Panama Canal. Chandler had always loved England. The "vulgarity" he found in California was nowhere in evidence there. He was fêted and felt himself an author in Britain, whereas, as pianist Natasha Spender wrote, in America he was regarded as "just a mystery writer" (*The World of Raymond Chandler*). Chandler visited many friends and people in the business of selling books and was heartened to see a new spirit in the working class that had developed since his days as a journalist and writer manqué. Penguin was issuing his earlier books in Britain in affordable paperback editions and had broken the half-million mark in sales.

In 1952, after they had returned, Chandler sent the revised and finished manuscript of *The Long Goodbye* to his publishers, who were happy to see they no longer needed to worry; but when it finally appeared in Britain in November 1953 and in America in the spring of 1954, the critical reception included the biggest raves he had known. Ralph Partridge, in *The New Statesman and Nation,* wrote of Chandler that "the rhythm of his prose is superb, and the intensity of feeling he packs into his pages makes every other thriller-writer look utterly silly and superficial" (*Down These Mean Streets,* p. 106). One *New York Times* review referred to it as a "masterpiece," critic Bernard DeVoto's review in *Harper's* called it "awesome," and Anthony Burgess wrote that no discussion of American fiction could fail to consider *The Long Goodbye.* (The Mystery Writers of America awarded him a second Edgar, for *The Long Goodbye,* in 1954.)

Unfortunately, not everyone agreed. The *New Yorker* thought *Goodbye* "hardly seems worth all the bother," and Anthony Boucher, in the *New York Times,* found the book "brooding" and said Marlowe here was "less a detective than a disturbed man of forty-two on a quest for some evidence of truth and humanity" (*Down These Mean Streets,* p. 102).

The Long Goodbye is a deeper vision, about a kind of innocence lost over the long course of the story by a more honest and forthright Marlowe. He is a man now capable of taking the leap of faith required to make a friend out of a casual acquaintance and to keep believing even when the distance and time separating them grow and grow. (It might have been called *The Long Awakening.*) Marlowe's faith in his friend is so strong that it takes forever for him to understand and believe what is really going on, even after clues begin to emerge, and to discover who the man really is. He is still questioning his own feelings at the end of the novel.

The story begins with Marlowe witnessing a drunk, Terry Lennox, leaving a club, taking him home, and soon after, rescuing him from an arrest for vagrancy. Lennox, rich and spoiled, is also a troubled soul, another heavy drinker for whom Marlowe has a sympathetic heart: he recognizes him to be a good man in somewhat reduced circumstances. Operating on instinct, Marlowe gives him the money he needs to go to Las Vegas to see about work. Lennox remarries his ex-wife Sylvia and repays the debt.

One day Lennox shows up needing serious help. His wife has been found dead, in her guest house, her head bashed in. He wants to be driven to Tijuana; Marlowe cautions him against revealing too much but takes him across the border. The police catch up with Marlowe, who will not betray his friend, and he is locked up but later released.

The detective is then hired to keep an eye on alcoholic novelist Roger Wade, married to an exquisite blonde named Eileen (a woman with cornflower blue eyes). Marlowe is smitten. Roger, who cannot finish his work and has recently developed suicidal tendencies (and who reminds us more than a little of his creator) is missing, and on a clue about a "Dr. V.," Marlowe sets out to find him. He learns that Eileen knew Sylvia Lennox. (It will later be revealed that they are sisters.)

Meanwhile, Marlowe has received a note from Lennox, and a $5,000 bill ("a portrait of Madison"). Following Lennox's request to have a drink for him at Victor's, Marlowe meets the unhappily married Linda Loring. He also begins to suspect that something deeper than his art is bothering Roger Wade, who has asked him to act as a kind of nursemaid. In a visit to the Wades', Marlowe tries to find clues to what lies behind Wade's deep unhappiness. A shot is fired out of Marlowe's view. Wade says he was trying to kill himself and the gun was fired into the ceiling, but Marlowe has learned to be suspicious of people's claims, especially in the Wade household.

In another visit, Wade is killed, apparently while Marlowe and Eileen Wade are drinking tea in the next room. Marlowe suspects Eileen. Later he manages to clear both Lennox and Wade of the suspicion of Sylvia's murder. Meanwhile, Marlowe and Linda Loring get to know each other better, and she invites him to run off to Paris with her, though Marlowe declines.

A Señor Maioranos (whose name echoes the Spanish for "better years") comes to see Marlowe, who quickly figures out it is a cosmetically altered Lennox. Invited to go out, Marlowe declines, but ends up wondering at the end of the book if his loyalties have been misguided. An important clue to the mystery, which some feel is more in the vein of a classic British whodunit than other Chandler novels, lies in Terry Lennox's past as Paul Marston.

Frank MacShane thought *The Long Goodbye* represented "the vision of a complete novelist" (Marling, p. 245). What is astonishing is how hard some reviewers found it to like this book, or Marlowe. The detective who has always insulated himself emotionally finally has a protracted friendship, with a very troubled man. It is only when he discovers how much the man has let him down that he turns him away at the end, but this caused reviewers to see Marlowe as a pontificating, self-righteous prig, when in fact he had come a long way from judgment to the element of trust where friendships were concerned. He has an affair with some substance to it: the one with Linda Loring. And he develops connections even with minor characters like Amos, the chauffeur who reads T. S. Eliot, sustaining a relationship over the course of the novel. (In a nod to the getting of wisdom, they discuss "The Love Song of J. Alfred Prufrock," just before Marlowe lets himself be seduced by Loring.) This is a warmer Marlowe, not a colder one. (The book is also much more revealing of Chandler, who shared characteristics here with both Lennox and Wade. Both were seen as "like Chandler," for their common predilection for alcohol. Lennox had been in the war in Britain, and Wade was a writer questioning the quality of his work as such. Not only was Marlowe newly complex; a new openness graced Chandler's work here.)

Marlowe's long and trusting relationship with Lennox, the most enduring in seven novels, indicated to some critics that a case for latent homosexuality could be made, either for Marlowe or for Chandler. Chandler's predilection for complete physical descriptions of male characters, especially those who are beautiful, shored up this opinion, as did the fact of Chandler's having married a woman seventeen years his senior, which coaxed them into using terms like "mother complex" by way of explanation.

While the exploration of Freudian theory is fascinating, interpreting it is a delicate matter. Although Chandler does give his male characters such as the dandy Lindsay Marriott in *Farewell, My Lovely* and Terry Lennox in *The Long Goodbye* equal time, describing them as fully as he does his female characters, it is fair to say that the dandy Marriott is just that. (Marlowe dislikes him and says so several times.) Lennox is Marlowe's friend and drinking buddy—but also someone he can help, and Marlowe has often helped others who are not love interests, like Carmen Sternwood in *The Big Sleep* and Merle Davis in *The High Window*. Like Wade, Lennox is an alter ego of Chandler's—and a buddy, not a love interest, of Marlowe's.

Chandler's biographers have turned up no evidence whatsoever of homosexuality, latent or otherwise (even if Marlowe did have a rough tone for certain ambiguous characters). He openly expressed dismay when reviewers broached the subject in reviews of *The Long Goodbye* (and some feel the later marriage of Marlowe to Linda Loring may have been devised in part in reaction to this). As to his relationship with Cissy, her age was unknown to him. Natasha Spender, in *The World of Raymond Chandler* and in subsequent interviews, said Chandler did not actually know his wife's age at the time of her death (*Raymond Chandler,* notes). Chandler was a man who loved women, and Cissy was the great love of his life.

A "long goodbye" is an interesting notion for a writer whose protagonist feels that, as the French say, "every goodbye is a little death." A long goodbye is a slow death. Chandler was not in the best of health, and in the years during which he finished the book, Cissy was slowly dying.

Widower

After many months in bed, heavily sedated and in terrible pain, and requiring oxygen at the end, Cissy Chandler died on 12 December 1954. Chandler was devastated. Not long after, in the *San Diego Evening Tribune,* he wrote, "Marriage is a perpetual courtship. . . . I always felt as if I had to win my wife every day as though we were meeting for the first time" (*Down These Mean Streets,* p. 105). It seemed no loss, however fundamental, ever really changed in him the attitude of the upstanding public school man who under duress can be counted upon to carry on.

After a stay at the sanatorium in late February (he had made another threat of suicide, and shots had rung out, but he later remembered nothing), he arranged to sell their house and most of their belongings. He sailed for England on 12 April 1955.

He met Jessica Tyndale, a banker, on board; they became close. In London he cut a wide swath, dining with publishers, writers, and friends. His melancholy had returned, and all were concerned. A bevy of younger women escorted him just about anywhere he wanted to go, in shifts, in a hedge against possible suicidal thoughts; they knew if he had an obligation to a woman, he would honor it, and the distraction would keep him occupied. He thanked them with jewels and extravagant bouquets. Women brought out his charm once more, but as much as he loved London, it reminded him of the days he and Cissy had spent there, which he considered among the happiest of his life.

In his loneliness, drink took over. He continued to play at being Galahad, especially to pianist Natasha Spender. Both ill, they went to Italy to recuperate. He also traveled with her and her husband, poet Stephen Spender, to Spain, where he contracted malaria. Malnourished as a result of his alcoholism, he took a cure in New York, and later another in California at the Chula Vista clinic, though these "cures" did not usually take, except briefly. He visited a fan to whom he had written, Louise Landis Loughner, fell in love with her, and asked her to marry him, but then they fought and broke up. He also realized the folly of his infatuation with Natasha Spender and broke with her in June 1957.

During this time he considered the possibility of playwriting and acquired some books on the subject. He also finished an old story called "The English Summer."

Playback and "Poodle Springs" (1957–1959)

Chandler used *Playback,* which he had written as a script for Universal, to make a romance. It had been cannibalized from "I'll Be Waiting" (1939) and "Guns at Cyrano's" (1936). (He had tried to work on it while finishing *The Long Goodbye,* but it was one of several projects during that time, and he had ultimately put it aside for later.) Helga Greene had become his literary agent, and they went to Palm Springs on vacation. After some research with local cops and a visit to the San Diego jail, Chandler finished the book, with Greene's help, at the end of 1957, three months early. (Chandler said it had been written "on Scotch and coffee.") It sold 9,000 copies in America but is usually considered one of the lesser works. It is of interest, however, that Marlowe here renews his affair with Linda Loring of *The Long Goodbye,* and she proposes to him. (He declines, not wanting to be a "kept man.")

Because Chandler had stayed in England too long, he became embroiled in a war with the British tax authorities. Meanwhile, Helga Greene's cousin, Maurice Guinness, had made the suggestion that Marlowe marry. It got Chandler to thinking, and he began to work on the short story "Poodle Springs" (meant to be Palm Springs), in which Marlowe and Loring have married and moved to the desert, the detective presaging a soon-to-be-announced engagement of his creator's. (The story was later extended into a novel by Robert B. Parker [1990], who also wrote a sequel to *The Big Sleep* entitled *Perchance to Dream* [1991]. In 1998 the playwright Tom Stoppard wrote a screenplay for *Poodle Springs,* which was made into a television movie for HBO by Bob Rafelson.)

Curtain

At the end of his life Chandler continued his friendships with women. Although he was ailing—often as a result of his alcoholism—he kept busy with travel, socializing, as much writing as he could manage, and writing to his numerous correspondents.

He hired an Australian secretary, Mrs. Jameson, a divorcée with children, and he supported them. He and Helga Greene were induced by Ian Fleming to travel to Capri, and to interview Lucky Luciano along the way in Naples, and Chandler did, in the sympathetic essay "My Friend Luco." (It was not published.)

By arrangement with Fleming, Chandler gave a talk on the BBC (the only known recording of his voice). He was invited to read poetry, and chose the work of W. H. Auden, Louis MacNeice, Stephen Spender, Cecil Day Lewis, and Jon Silkin, adding of his own work only one poem, an elegy he had written to Cissy, "Song Without Music" (it had appeared in the *San Diego Evening Tribune* shortly after her death). He also appeared on a television show, *Late Extra,* and after meeting former convict Frank Norman, wrote the foreword to the man's account of prison life, *Bang to Rights* (1958). He began work on a short story, "The Pencil," and wrote some columns for the *San Diego Evening Tribune,* at the behest of Neil Morgan.

Mrs. Kay West came to live with him as his secretary. He took another liquor cure, on the advice of a doctor. Upon leaving, he discovered the ménage at home was generating quarrels. Mrs. Jameson, whose ex-husband had died, had asked Chandler for money and been advised how hard it was now for him to fund her as generously as he had before. Even in his recurring illness he was managing to help women in need. It was next to impossible for him to say no to them.

In February of 1959, Helga flew to California. From his hospital bed he proposed marriage (he was almost seventy-one), and she accepted. She was an agent who had also helped him finish work, they had traveled together, and she made him very happy. He revised his will, which later resulted in much fighting among his women friends. He was elected president of the Mystery Writers of America for 1959, to his amazement, and attended a dinner in his honor in New York, giving a typically modest speech. It seemed a hopeful time.

Helga Greene introduced him to her father, who was taken aback to discover that his daughter's fiancé was his age. Instead of going to London as planned, Chandler returned that spring to California with a cold, staying in the house where he had stayed previously. On 23 March he went to the hospital with pneumonia, after a week alone in his cottage, and he never recovered. Three days before Easter he died at the Scripps Clinic, on the afternoon of Thursday, 26 March 1959, in La Jolla.

Now he is everywhere.

If sacrifice is part of the equation in art, the writer who in his last years tossed bijous and bouquets to young women, exchanging money for their happiness, was true to form. He had spent his life in art, creating and sustaining the illusion of a complicated man named Marlowe, and he had done it to his own impossible standards, in a genre he would forever alter. It was a grand ambition, even for the man who could make words dance, and Chandler's keen sense of effect and that literary fearlessness had served him well in it. The only thing more formidable than his conviction was his resolve.

And his enduring romance with American English, whom he courted anew each day, as if meeting her for the first time. (The places they went together!) He once told Bergen Evans, "I have more love for our superb language than I could ever possibly express."

But express it he did: all one has to do is look. Nobody wrote like Ray.

Selected Bibliography

WORKS OF RAYMOND CHANDLER

NOVELS

The Big Sleep. New York: Knopf, 1939; London: Hamish Hamilton, 1939; New York: Ballantine, 1939. Repr. New York: Vintage (Crime Series), 1992.

Farewell, My Lovely. New York: Knopf, 1940; London: Hamish Hamilton, 1940. Repr. New York: Vintage (Crime Series), 1992.

The High Window. New York: Knopf, 1942; London: Hamish Hamilton, 1943. Repr. New York: Vintage (Crime Series), 1992.

The Lady in the Lake. New York: Knopf, 1943; London: Hamish Hamilton, 1944. Repr. New York: Vintage (Crime Series), 1988, 1992.

The Little Sister. Boston: Houghton Mifflin, 1949; London: Hamish Hamilton, 1949. Repr. New York: Vintage (Crime Series), 1988.

The Long Goodbye. London: Hamish Hamilton, 1953; New York: Houghton Mifflin, 1954. Repr. New York: Vintage (Crime Series), 1988, 1992.

Playback. Boston: Houghton Mifflin, 1958; London: Hamish Hamilton, 1958. Repr. New York: Pocket Books, 1960; New York: Vintage (Crime Series), 1988.

Poodle Springs (unfinished). In *Raymond Chandler Speaking*. Boston: Houghton Mifflin, 1962; London: Hamish Hamilton, 1962. Completed by Robert B. Parker. New York: Putnam, 1989; Berkeley, 1990.

SHORT STORIES

"The Rose-Leaf Romance." Unlocated; can be found in *Chandler Before Marlowe*. See "Screenplays, Letters, and Other Writings," below.

"Blackmailers Don't Shoot." *Black Mask*, December 1933.

"Smart-Aleck Kill." *Black Mask*, July 1934, pp. 54–78.

"Finger Man." *Black Mask*, October 1934, pp. 8–38.

"Killer in the Rain." *Black Mask*, January 1935, pp. 8–33.

"Nevada Gas." *Black Mask*, June 1935, pp. 8–34.

"Spanish Blood." *Black Mask*, November 1935, pp. 38–64.

"Guns at Cyrano's." *Black Mask*, January 1936, pp. 8–37.

"The Man Who Liked Dogs." *Black Mask*, March 1936, pp. 10–33.

"Noon Street Nemesis." *Detective Fiction Weekly*, May 1936, pp. 36–62. Republished as "Pick-up on Noon Street," *Avon Story Teller*, edited by Jo Meyers and E. B. Williams, pp. 24–76.

"Goldfish." *Black Mask*, June 1936, pp. 10–35.

"The Curtain." *Black Mask*, September 1936, pp. 10–33.

"Try the Girl." *Black Mask*, January 1937, pp. 10–34.

"Mandarin's Jade." *Dime Detective*, November 1937, pp. 36–67.

"Red Wind." *Dime Detective,* January 1938, pp. 40–70.
"The King in Yellow." *Dime Detective,* March 1938, pp. 42–74.
"Bay City Blues." *Dime Detective,* June 1938, pp. 6–47.
"The Lady in the Lake." *Dime Detective,* January 1939, pp. 94–127.
"Pearls Are a Nuisance." *Dime Detective,* April 1939, pp. 68–96.
"Trouble Is My Business." *Dime Detective,* August 1939, pp. 42–76.
"The Bronze Door." *Unknown,* November 1939, pp. 90–106.
"I'll Be Waiting." *Saturday Evening Post,* December 1939.
"No Crime in the Mountains." *Detective Story,* September 1941, pp. 9–54. Repr. in *Great American Detective Stories,* ed. and with an introduction by Anthony Boucher. Cleveland and New York: World, 1945, pp. 49–95.
"Professor Bingo's Snuff." *Park East,* June–August 1951; *Go,* June–July 1951.
"Marlowe Takes on the Syndicate." *London Daily Mail,* 6–10 April 1959. Also published as "Wrong Pigeon." *Manhunt,* February 1960. Repr. as "The Pencil," *Argosy,* September 1965, pp. 126–159.
Two additional stories were published only posthumously: "A Couple of Writers" can be found in *Raymond Chandler Speaking,* and "The English Summer" can be found in *Notebooks of Raymond Chandler and "The English Summer"* (see under "Screenplays, Letters, and Other Writings," below).

COLLECTED SHORT STORIES

Five Murderers. New York: Avon, 1944.
Five Sinister Characters. New York: Avon, 1945.
Finger Man and Other Stories. New York: Avon, 1946.
Red Wind. Cleveland: World, 1946.
Spanish Blood. Cleveland: World, 1946.
The Simple Art of Murder. Boston: Houghton Mifflin, 1950; London: Hamish Hamilton, 1950. Repr. New York: Ballantine, 1950; New York: Vintage (Crime Series), 1988. Includes the title essay and "Spanish Blood," "I'll Be Waiting," "The King in Yellow," and "Pearls Are a Nuisance."
Smart-Aleck Kill. London: Hamish Hamilton, 1953.
Pearls Are a Nuisance. London: Hamish Hamilton, 1953.
Killer in the Rain. Edited and with an introduction by Philip Durham. Boston: Houghton Mifflin, 1964; London: Hamish Hamilton, 1953. Repr. Boston: Houghton Mifflin, 1964; New York: Ballantine, 1964. Eight stories.
The Smell of Fear. London: Hamish Hamilton, 1965. Fourteen stories, including "The Pencil," with an introduction by Chandler.

SELECTED ESSAYS

"The Simple Art of Murder." *Atlantic Monthly,* December 1944. Rev. version in *Saturday Review of Literature,* 15 April 1950. Unrevised version in *The Mystery Companion,* edited by A. L. Furman. New York: Gold Label Books, 1945, pp. 252–268.
"Writers in Hollywood." *Atlantic Monthly,* November 1945.
"Critical Notes." *Screen Writer,* July 1947.
"Oscar Night in Hollywood." *Atlantic Monthly,* March 1948.
"Ten Greatest Crimes of the Century." *Cosmopolitan,* October 1948.
"Ten Per Cent of Your Life." *Atlantic Monthly,* February 1952.
Foreword to Norman, Frank, *Bang to Rights: An Account of Prison Life.* London: Secker and Warburg, 1958.

SCREENPLAYS, LETTERS, AND OTHER WRITINGS

The Australian Love Letters of Raymond Chandler. Edited by Alan Close. Ringwood, Victoria: McPhee Gribble, 1995.
The Big Sleep: A Film Adaptation. Edited by George Garrett et al. Irvington (Film Scripts Series), 1989.
The Blue Dahlia: A Screenplay. Mattituck, N.Y.: Amereon, 1976. Reprint of Chandler's 1945 screenplay.
Chandler Before Marlowe: Raymond Chandler's Early Prose and Poetry, 1908–1912. Edited by Matthew J. Bruccoli. Foreword by Jacques Barzun. Columbia: Univ. of South Carolina Press, 1973. Includes "The Rose-Leaf Romance," twenty-nine poems, eight essays and sketches, and four reviews.
Double Indemnity. In *Best Film Plays.* Edited by John Gassner and Dudley Nichols. New York: Crown, 1946, pp. 115–174.
The Notebooks of Raymond Chandler and "English Summer: A Gothic Romance." Edited by Frank MacShane. New York: Ecco, 1976, 1991.
Raymond Chandler on Writing. Boston: Houghton Mifflin, 1962.
Raymond Chandler Speaking. Edited by Dorothy Gardiner and Katherine Sorley Walker. Boston: Houghton Mifflin, 1962, 1977. Contains excerpts from Chandler's letters, the surviving fragment of "Poodle Springs," and "A Couple of Writers."
Raymond Chandler's Unknown Thriller: The Screenplay of Playback. New York: Mysterious Press, 1985; London: Harrap, 1985.
Selected Letters of Raymond Chandler. Edited by Frank MacShane. New York: Columbia University Press, 1981.

FILMS

Double Indemnity (Paramount, 1944). Screenplay by Billy Wilder and Raymond Chandler. From the novel by James M. Cain. (Screenplay nominated for an Academy Award.)
And Now Tomorrow (Paramount, 1944). Screenplay by

Frank Partos and Raymond Chandler. From the novel by Rachel Field.

The Unseen (Paramount, 1945). Screenplay by Hagar Wilde and Raymond Chandler. Adapted by Hagar Wilde and Ken Englund from the novel *Her Heart in Her Throat* by Ethel Lina White.

The Blue Dahlia (Paramount, 1946). Original screenplay by Raymond Chandler. (Screenplay was nominated for an Academy Award and received the Edgar for 1946 from the Mystery Writers of America.)

Strangers on a Train (Warner Brothers, 1951). Screenplay by Raymond Chandler and Czenzi Ormonde. Adapted by Whitfield Cook from the novel by Patricia Highsmith.

COLLECTED WORKS

The Big Sleep and Farewell, My Lovely. New York: Modern Library, 1995.

Four Complete Philip Marlowe Novels. New York: Random House, 1986.

The Midnight Raymond Chandler. Edited and with an introduction by Joan Kahn. Boston: Houghton Mifflin, 1971. Contains *The Little Sister, The Long Goodbye,* and selected short works.

Raymond Chandler: Later Novels and Other Writings. Edited by Frank MacShane. New York: Library of America, 1995. Contains *The Lady in the Lake, The Little Sister, The Long Goodbye, Playback,* the screenplay for *Double Indemnity,* and selected essays and letters.

Raymond Chandler: Stories and Early Novels. Edited by Frank MacShane. New York: Library of America, 1995. Contains early magazine fiction, *The Big Sleep, Farewell, My Lovely,* and *The High Window.*

The Raymond Chandler Omnibus. New York: Random House, 1962. Includes *The Big Sleep, Farewell, My Lovely, The High Window,* and *The Lady in the Lake.*

The Second Raymond Chandler Omnibus. London: Hamish Hamilton, 1962. Includes "The Simple Art of Murder," *The Little Sister, The Long Goodbye,* and *Playback.*

BIBLIOGRAPHIES AND ARCHIVES

For critical studies from 1963 to the present, an international bibliography (updated quarterly) is available on CD-ROM from the Modern Language Association (205 Chandler entries as of this writing).

Bodleian Library (Modern Papers), Oxford University, Chandler files.

Bruccoli, Matthew J. *Raymond Chandler: A Checklist.* Kent, Ohio: Kent State University Press, 1968.

———. *Raymond Chandler: A Descriptive Bibliography.* Pittsburgh: University of Pittsburgh Press, 1979. The definitive bibliography of Chandler's work through 1979.

Bulletin of the New York Public Library, 26, pp. 555–628. Checklist of the library's Special Collections, including early editions and manuscripts of many authors in this genre.

Department of Special Collections, Research Library, University of California at Los Angeles. Contains manuscripts, notebooks, translations, and memorabilia.

BIOGRAPHICAL AND CRITICAL STUDIES

Auden, W. H. "The Guilty Vicarage." *Harper's,* May 1948.

Barzun, Jacques, and Wendell Hertig Taylor. *A Catalogue of Crime.* New York: Harper & Row, 1971. Rev. and enlarged, 1989.

Clark, Al. *Raymond Chandler in Hollywood.* London and New York: Proteus, 1982. Repr. Los Angeles: Silman-James, 1996.

Durham, Philip. *Down These Mean Streets a Man Must Go: Raymond Chandler's Knight.* Chapel Hill: University of North Carolina Press, 1963.

Fleming, Ian. "Raymond Chandler." *London Magazine,* December 1959, pp. 43–54.

Gross, Miriam, ed. *The World of Raymond Chandler.* Introduction by Patricia Highsmith. New York: A & W, 1978. Includes Clive James's essay "The Country Behind the Hill."

Hiney, Tom. *Raymond Chandler.* London: Chatto & Windus, 1997.

Keating, H. R. F., ed. *Whodunit? A Guide to Crime, Suspense, and Spy Fiction.* London: Winward, 1982; New York: Van Nostrand, 1982.

Luhr, William. *Raymond Chandler and Film.* New York: Ungar, 1982.

MacShane, Frank. *The Life of Raymond Chandler.* New York: Dutton, 1976.

Mahan, Jeffrey. "The Hard-Boiled Detective in the Fallen World." *Clues* 1 (Fall–Winter 1980): 90–99.

Marling, William H. *Raymond Chandler.* Boston: Twayne, 1986.

Nickerson, Edward A. "Crime Fiction: An Anatomy of Evil People." *Centennial Review* (East Lansing, Mich.) 25 (spring 1981): 101–132.

Oates, Joyce Carol. "The Simple Art of Murder." *New York Review of Books,* 21 December 1995.

Pendo, Stephen. *Raymond Chandler on Screen: His Novels into Film.* Metuchen, N.J.: Scarecrow, 1976.

Simpson, Hassell A. "So Long, Beautiful Hunk: Ambiguous Gender and Songs of Parting in Raymond Chandler's Fiction." *Journal of Popular Culture* 28 (fall 1994): 37–48.

Spicer, Christopher H. "A Hard-Boiled Philosophy of Human Nature." *Clues* (spring–summer 1983): 93–104.

Symons, Julian. *Bloody Murder: From the Detective Story to the Crime Novel.* London: Faber, 1972. U.S.: *Mortal Consequences.* New York: Harper, 1972. Rev. and updated as *Bloody Murder: From the Detective*

Story to the Crime Novel: A History. New York: Viking, 1985; London: Pan, 1994.

Thomas, Ronald K. "Style in American Photography and *Farewell, My Lovely*." *Criticism* (Detroit) 36 (summer 1994): 415–457.

Van Dover, J. K. *The Critical Response to Raymond Chandler*. Westport, Conn.: Greenwood, 1995.

Wolfe, Peter. *Something More Than Night: The Case of Raymond Chandler*. Bowling Green, Ohio: Bowling Green State University Press, 1985.

Leslie Charteris

(1907–1993)

BURL BARER

The adventures of Leslie Charteris' Robin Hood of modern crime, the Saint, have continually appeared since 1928, making Simon Templar the longest-running character in contemporary mystery fiction. Total Saint books in print worldwide exceed forty million. The novels and short stories chronicling the international escapades of Charteris' modern-day pirate have been translated into French, Spanish, Portuguese, Dutch, Italian, German, Hebrew, Arabic, Norwegian, Japanese, Danish, Finnish, Swedish, Chinese, and braille. From 1928 until his death in 1993, Leslie Charteris oversaw the Saint's exploitation in print, radio, film, and television. "I didn't want to be a writer," Charteris confessed to the *Sunday Express* in 1972; "I wanted to be one of the idle rich. As for writing, I hate writing. I hate the discipline. When I began to write I had much more enthusiasm and I thought practically every book was good when I wrote it. But you look back and think: Oh, God, that was bad" (p. 6).

Leslie Charteris was born Leslie Charles Bowyer Yin in Singapore on 12 May 1907, to Dr. S. C. Yin and Lydia Florence Bowyer. He learned Chinese and Malay from native servants before he could speak English. He was deeply inclined toward swashbuckling romanticism, and his favorite childhood tales were of plank-walking piracy in *Chums Magazine.* "My parents dragged me three times around the world before I was twelve," wrote Charteris in his capsule biography for *Twentieth Century Authors,* "and then they decided it was time I went to school. This was a mistake." Charteris was educated first at Falconbury prep school near Purley, England (1919–1922), then at Rossall public school (1922–1924), and finally at King's College, Cambridge, where he studied law, graduating in 1926. It was at Cambridge, the story goes, that young Charteris read *Trent's Last Case* (1912), by E. C. Bentley, and promptly decided he could write a better book himself and have it published. He was half right, and at seventeen he sold his first work of fiction. "It is worth noting," wrote Charteris (in *Twentieth Century Authors*), "that my teachers of English had no great opinion of my aptitude for this subject."

His first effort, *X Esquire,* was published by Ward Lock in 1927, the same year its youthful author legally changed his name. The decision to choose "Charteris" came when young Leslie learned of Colonel Francis Charteris—duelist, gambler, rake, and founder of the notorious Hellfire Club.

> By deed poll at the age of twenty, I adopted Leslie Charteris-Ian, the hyphenated tag being on the insistence of my father whose consent was necessary since I was a minor. But I never used the full name and even got it reduced to a footnote on my then British passport. Since 1927 I was known only as Leslie

> Charteris. When I was naturalized a U.S. Citizen in 1946 this was legalized as my entire and only name. (private letter, Boston University Collection)

With the publication of *X Esquire*, Charteris promptly quit school because he obviously did not need an education. His father disowned him, said Charteris, "because he thought artists and writers were rogues and vagabonds, nogoodniks" (Lofts and Adley, p. 16). "He confidently predicted I'd end up in the gutter somewhere" (*Sunday Express*, p. 6).

Charteris' income-producing activities, pursued to supplement the meager rewards of writing, provided experiences exceeding the robust daydreams of his contemporaries: world traveler, pearl diver, bridge player, and Malaysian tin-mine worker.

Early Novels: Foreshadowings of the Saint

The hero of Charteris' first novel is Terry Mannering, son of Sir John Mannering. Terry attended Cambridge, was an ace flyer in the war, studied medicine, and looks remarkably like his father. The plot, what there is of it, concerns a new form of tobacco slated for introduction into the United Kingdom under the brand name Spur Cigarettes. The whole consignment is mysteriously burned, and Spur's principal partners are assassinated by the mysterious "X Esquire." Mannering, the final chapter reveals, is the cowled Esquire saving England from a deadly delayed reaction to the new tobacco's poisonous properties—ten days following the first inhalation, the smoker dies after ten minutes of horrid agony. The evil plan, termed by Mannering "the most fiendish plot in all criminal history," was an absurd attempt to destroy Britain via both first- and secondhand smoke. *X Esquire*, according to critic William Vivian Butler, is "99½% derivative, and unpleasantly so." He would get no argument from its author. "Those first books were awful, frankly," Charteris told the *Miami News* in 1964; "they were immature and shallow and I was at a silly age. What the hell did I know about life then?"

Peter Lestrange, hero of Charteris' second novel, *The White Rider* (1928), is a more distinct Charteris creation. He has a disreputable background, spent a year in Sing-Sing prison, plays piano, has a tiny automatic strapped to his right forearm, and drives a red Furrilac. "His voice had the harshness of steel on chilled steel." Lestrange, an ex-buccaneer who lounges at the piano, is only a breath away from the full-blooded 1930s gentleman outlaw embodied in the Saint. "If there were to be any Saint books at all, obviously there had to be a first, and this is it," wrote Charteris in the introduction to the 1980 reprint of *Meet—The Tiger!* (1928; also published as *The Saint Meets the Tiger*). "I can't deny writing it . . . and I suppose that anyone who is interested enough in backtracking into Simon Templar's and my own adolescent beginnings has a right to access the awful truths."

Charteris was still younger than twenty-one when he wrote this first Saint novel, and in later years he was no more eager to have it paraded than any other youthful indiscretion. He found so much wrong with it that he claimed humble astonishment that it was published at all. "It was only the third book I'd written, and the best I would say for it is that the first two were even worse." True. Yet in the opening pages of *Meet—The Tiger!*, a character enters who is potentially everything that Charteris and his public had been waiting for—a unique blend of languidness and action, nonchalance and authority—a gentleman outlaw. The novel's plot is of minimal consequence, except that it allows us to meet the Saint (a mere foreshadowing of the self he later became) and for the Saint to meet Patricia Holm. "I've met the most wonderful girl in the world. . . . I shall kiss her very passionately in the last chapter. We shall be married" (p. 13).

Charteris, in reality, had no intention of marrying off Simon Templar. As he recalled in his essay "How I Created a Saint" (*Women's Mirror,* 12 June 1965):

> In nearly all the books I had studied, the nice guys married the nice girls in the end, it was a convention of the era, like the fade out kiss in the movies. I didn't feel that my projected long-playing character could be hampered by such bourgeois ties. . . . I could forget my hero's commitment to his first girl. I could play her down more and more; time would tell whether in the end, she would fade away.

Patricia Holm did not fade away until 1947. One of the best-drawn female characters in adventure fiction, she was bright, witty, self-reliant, and, considering Templar's many romantic entanglements, remarkably tolerant.

Neither Patricia's appeal and longevity nor the Saint's ultimate worldwide status as an international icon of adventure was planned or seriously anticipated in 1928. Charteris was simply trying to create another hero and sell another book. The Simon Templar of *Meet—The Tiger!* is an embryonic creation, and Charteris continued toying with the essential aspects that led Templar to evolve into the ultimate modern-day pirate in three other characters created between 1928 and 1929—the Duck, the Daredevil, and the Bandit.

The Duck, who was neither law enforcer nor lawbreaker, but rather an unusual romantic figure, appeared in "The Song of Bedivere," a short story published in the July 1928 edition of *Woman* magazine. "And there you have the Duck . . . the gay and debonair Duck, the irrepressible Duck, maddest and merriest, most sinning and most loved of all the Bright Young People." It was fate that governed the cheerfully inconsequential life of the Duck. The Duck's posture and demeanor, as fate would have it, predict and describe the exact stance of the haloed stick figure later used as the Saint's logo. "Hands on hips, the Duck flung back his head in silent laughter. His right hand waved a romantic gesture."

Christopher Arden, alias "Storm," hero of *Daredevil* (1929), combines traits displayed in Charteris' previous heroes. His "eyes were as cold and steady as chilled granite. His every least movement showed the supple grace of the born fighting man." Arden, like Lestrange, plays piano. He also had well-filled bookcases, fencing foils, boxing gloves, and sporting rifles. Storm is a friend of Terry Mannering (*X Esquire*) and Claud Eustace Teal of Scotland Yard. Teal later became the Saint's perennial foil and baited representative of the Establishment. Teal is the durable one in *Daredevil,* the character given the greatest exposition, the least hackneyed presentation, and the best dialogue. Storm, "the fighting daredevil with the Saxon hair and gunmetal gray eyes," gets the girl by the final page, but it is Teal who exits in a manner worth reprising. "Mr. Teal shook his head, shifting his gum to the other side of his mouth. 'Fat men didn't ought to drink' " (1954 ed., p. 256). Teal would repeat this exact line more than twenty years later at the conclusion of "The Talented Husband," the short story (in the *The Saint Around the World*) in which he retires from Scotland Yard.

Charteris' next hero, who appeared in *The Bandit* (1929), was not an Englishman—he was South American and an outlaw. "By profession, I am a bandit," he states. His name, the longest of any of Charteris' desperadoes, is Ramon Francisco de Castilla y Espronceda Manrique—a man with "muscles that normally were as swift and violent as freshly lubricated lightning." Ramon went to Cambridge on his father's money, wears Savile Row clothes, carries a slim gold cigarette case, and has "the speed and force of a compressed steel spring suddenly released."

As we see, certain aspects of the Saint's character evolve in novels characterized by his absence. The Simon Templar destined to emerge continues his embryonic development in *Daredevil* and *The Bandit,* two novels written after his debut in *Meet—The Tiger!* It was only after *Daredevil* and *The Bandit* that Charteris looked back and selected Simon Templar as the most durable of his desperadoes. As Charteris explained in a radio interview in Hawaii in 1960:

> They were all somewhat similar in many ways. I suppose I got lazy, or I got the idea that it was better to continue and build up one character than to spread yourself around among a dozen. I looked back over the characters I had created so far and picked the Saint, liked him the best, and decided to go on with him. The character, from that point on, has developed more than been created. Time went on, and more and more stories had to be written, and it was necessary to give him more depth and breadth and dimension than he originally had. I think the character is still growing, and I hope he will continue to grow because why should he stay still? He's not going to be the same age forever like Li'l Abner. He must age a little, very slowly and carefully of course, but as more and more things happen to him and he has more and more adventures, they must have an effect on his character, and must develop him. As I started to try to explain, the origin was just something that flew into my head one day, wherever these things fly from, and that's all there is to it. I decided that the Saint, the hero of my third book, was the least derivative, the one with the best growth potential, the one I could live with most comfortably for a long time. (Interview in Boston University Collection)

He had no idea how long that time would be, how extensive the exploitation, the number of countries in which such exploitation would bear fruit, or the diversity of media in which his character would be portrayed.

The Saint Evolves

It was only 1929, and Charteris had been commissioned by the controlling editor of Amalgamated Press, Percy Montague Haydon—midwife to the Saint, and the Toff, and several others—to write for *Thriller—The Paper of a Thousand Thrills.*

"The Toff," according to his creator, John Creasey, is "a rather heavy-footed Saint" and, in the opinion of William Butler, is "the diametric opposite of the self-sufficient Saint" (p. 148). The Toff appeared in 54 books over forty years. The Toff is knocked out, injured, and packed off to the hospital more often than any character in adventure fiction—and he is still a hero. While the Saint is remarkably self-sufficient, the Toff is not—which is to his credit. Were he more self contained, the Toff (an aristocrat) would have become a symbol of class dominance. Rather, he almost became the icon of interdependence.

Charteris debuted in *Thriller* with "The Story of a Dead Man," a non-Saint story later rewritten as a Simon Templar adventure. His second effort, "The Secret of Beacon Inn," was also a non-Saint story later rewritten as *The National Debt* for *Alias the Saint* (1931). *Thriller* first published "The Five Kings" on 4 May 1929, and Charteris revised it as *The Man Who Was Clever* for *Enter the Saint* (1930). In the process, he renamed the main characters. The original names were taken from a deck of playing cards, four kings and a joker in the middle as their logo. The joker is Simon Templar; the card logo became the stick figure with a halo.

Meet—The Tiger! was the first cold-start attempt to spark ignition on a new hero; here we have ignition and liftoff. A new power and energy surge through Simon Templar, derived from the greatest gift his creator could bestow—a sense of purpose.

> We Saints are normally souls of peace and goodwill towards men. But we don't like crooks, bloodsuckers, traders in vice and damnation. . . . We're going to beat you up and do you down, skin you and smash you and scare you off the face of Europe. We are not bothered about the letter of the law, we act exactly as we please, we inflict what punishment we think suitable, and no one is going to escape us. (*Enter the Saint,* 1930, p. 74)

The Man Who Was Clever began the Saint's new career and was Charteris' first story written as a novelette. "I don't think I'll ever lose my affection for it as a literary form," commented Charteris in his introduction to the 1941 edition of *The First Saint Omnibus*

(1939). "It is a nice length to read since it can be consumed completely at one sitting, in any idle hour, such as while lying in bed before going to sleep, or while waiting for the wife to put on her hat."

The Saint was not an instant sensation, but the factors that made Charteris unique as both writer and myth-creator were in full play—his effortless grasp of all things English and an unrelenting undercurrent of gentle, mocking derision about the British way of life. "I strongly suspect," notes William Vivian Butler in his classic work, *The Durable Desperadoes,* "a hidden sense of never quite belonging anywhere—except maybe with the swashbuckling gods of his childhood—enabled Charteris to make the Saint a romantic myth-figure powerful enough to mesmerize the English-speaking world" (p. 104).

What Butler terms "the most important thing about the Saint" (p. 129), and what sets Templar apart from such forerunners as Bulldog Drummond and Raffles, is that he is not a class hero in the traditional sense. He is neither working class nor upper crust—his background and upbringing are never disclosed—yet he passes with ease among both the leisurely sophisticated and the rough and tumble. The Saint has no old school ties and no financial means aside from piracy, is caustic and irreverent toward law enforcement, fosters South American revolutions, and takes violent action on behalf of struggling workers. In the conservative law-and-order world of detectives and crime fighters, Simon Templar was shatteringly piratical while remaining intrinsically moral and delightfully flamboyant. It is this deep, almost primal desire to experience life beyond convention and expectation that bonds Saint fans across generations and geography—the fantasy of having the best of all lives, interweaving the secure pleasures of the idle rich with the dangers of living under the shadow of the sword.

In 1930, the major publishing house of Hodder and Stoughton, whose roster included Sapper, Edward Phillips Oppenheim, Sir John Buchan, Edgar Wallace—the top names in the field—threw itself solidly behind the Saint. In addition, within eighteen months, the Saint was launched in the Yellow Jacket Library with the most lavish fanfare ever accorded a fictional hero. "The man who has never heard of the Saint is like the boy who has never heard of Robin Hood," declared Hodder's promotional department, cranking out exuberant prose touting Charteris' endearingly dangerous gentleman outlaw. "Stories of remarkable escapades," insisted the official press release, adding "the heroic achievements and marvelous adventures of the twentieth century's brightest buccaneer" (Butler, p. 116). Seven Saint books were published between 1930 and 1932 and five more between 1932 and 1934. Each appeared first in *Thriller* and then was rushed into hardback by Hodder and Stoughton.

Charteris' astonishing output between 1929 and 1932 may be directly attributed to his natural brilliance, a heavy dollop of financial incentive, and a burning desire to meet life on his terms. "I *had* to succeed," confessed Charteris in later years,

> because before me loomed the only alternative, the dreadful penalty of failure . . . the routine office hours, the five-day week . . . the lethal assimilation into the ranks of honest, hardworking, conformist, God-fearing pillars of the community. I was literally struggling for my life, that is, the only kind of life I could visualize worth living. (Barer, p. 17)

The young author dreamed of independent days and dissipated nights, of calling no man his boss, and of freedom to travel.

Charteris did not immediately throw himself behind his own creation with the same zeal as his publishers. He actually attempted to replace Templar with Lyn Peveril, a character he felt was an improvement on the Saint. Soon, however, he grasped the realities of successful marketing. Every reader who enjoyed one Saint adventure would soon be searching for earlier stories and looking toward the next. Potentially painful as this might be to a young writer's ego, Charteris' pride was not wounded so deeply that he did not swallow and cash in on it. If so many established masters had made it pay to enslave themselves to one character, so, too, could he.

Between 1929 and 1934, the Saint passed through two distinct stages and began a third. At first the Saint of *Meet—the Tiger!* is energetic, romantic, and piratical, but not a major hero. The *Thriller* Saint is very English—impudent, eccentric, outrageous, versatile, and prone to reciting absurd poetry and telling long stories. Subtle is not the best word to describe the early Simon Templar or the style of an even younger Leslie Charteris, yet it is in this rush of youthful exuberance and supreme self-confidence that Charteris defines for all time the essential aspects of the Saint's persona. As Charteris asserts in *The Policeman with Wings:*

> If Simon Templar had been a failure, he would have been spoken of pityingly as a man born out of his time . . . yet you didn't notice the anachronism, because he wasn't a failure. He made for himself a world fit to live in. . . . Simon Templar was a man who couldn't help spreading melodrama all around him like an infectious disease. (*Enter the Saint,* pp. 81–85)

Templar himself defines his basic creed in *The Holy Terror* (1932; U.S. title, *The Saint Versus Scotland Yard,* 1935). "To go rocketing around the world, doing everything that is utterly and gloriously mad—swaggering, swashbuckling, singing—showing all those dreary old dogs what can be done with life . . . robbing the rich, helping the poor, plaguing the pompous, killing dragons, pulling policemens' legs" (1935 ed., p. 191).

The third stage of the Saint's development became evident between 1932 and 1934. Templar is older, smoother, less flamboyant and outlandish, and markedly Anglo-American. This subtle transformation resulted from Charteris' honing of his craft—by 1932, Charteris was writing for both *Thriller* and the *Empire News,* delivering more than a story a week—and from his visit to the United States in November 1932.

Transatlantic Success

Despite the Saint's growing popularity in Great Britain, Charteris' income was remarkably meager. "I was glad to sell 25,000 word novelets for $150. On that kind of income, a thirty-five cent lunch was an economy. It was not until about 1934 [that] a few perspicacious editors began to tempt my genius with champagne money" (17 February 1964, letter to Miss Sally Raymond, *Gourmet Magazine.* Boston University Collection). The combined workload of *Thriller* and the *Empire News* put Charteris more under the gun than into the black. To earn five to six hundred British pounds (approximately $2,500 to $3,000) per year, an author had to produce the equivalent of a novel per month. No publisher would take more than four books a year from any one author, and most contracts insisted that writing for a competing firm required use of a nom de plume. Competition was intense; payment was low.

Well aware that American markets were more lucrative, Charteris visited New York. He had a dollar in his pocket for each of his twenty-five years; uncertainty crouched ahead; and surrounding him was Prohibition and the Great Depression. He had a marvelous time. "The elemental force of [New York] infected me," he wrote years later to his longtime friend Paul M. James, "spurred me to try to match the pace, dazzled me with the insane prospect of infinite horizons" (*Letter from the Saint,* July 1946, in Bodenheimer, pp. 15–16). *American Magazine,* slick-papered and well-respected, conceived the "reckless notion" that Charteris "might bring a new breath of something to American crime fiction with a 'British approach' " and paid him real American dollars. Charteris' first sale, "The Man Who Liked Toys," put him five hundred dollars ahead of his original grubstake. (The story was later changed to a Saint story and included in *The Saint Intervenes* [1934].) Sadly, he deposited his gains in the only New York City bank whose doors closed forever within hours of Charteris' transaction.

> In March, 1933, when I was literally down to my last borrowed nickel, I received my first offer from a Hollywood studio; and with no leeway to haggle about salary I found myself on my way within a couple of days, with my fare paid by Paramount and a few dollars to eat with on the train borrowed from an indulgent publisher. (Bodenheimer, pp. 15–16)

Charteris' initial Hollywood experience was, for him, remarkably unpleasant. He returned to England the same year (1933), where he wrote *The Saint in New York,* the Saint's first American adventure. However, by 1937 he was back in the United States for good, and he would become a naturalized American citizen in 1946. A truncated version of *The Saint in New York,* introduced as "A Short Short Mystery Novel," appeared in the September 1934 issue of *American Magazine.* The complete text was published by Hodder and Stoughton in Great Britain in 1935. The book became a worldwide sensation, making its author an international celebrity. Suddenly, Leslie Charteris had a best-seller, and RKO Radio Pictures acquired the movie rights, secured a tentative (but ultimately unfulfilled) commitment from Alfred Hitchcock to direct, and ultimately cast Louis Hayward in the starring role.

"That was a desperate move, actually," explained Charteris to the *St. Petersburg Times.* "The film company had sat on the story for three years waiting for Frederic March to take the part. They finally wound up with Hayward." George Sanders replaced Hayward in the second film, *The Saint Strikes Back,* and starred in several more Saint productions of varying quality. "He was even worse," continued Charteris; "I can't imagine anyone who less fitted the description of the Saint and he turned in constipated performances." Hugh Sinclair was the final RKO leading man to play the Saint, and Hayward returned for the independently produced *The Saint's Girl Friday* in the early 1950s. Two French films were also produced but have never been shown in any English-speaking country.

At the close of the 1930s, the Saint was a multimarket imperative. Simon Templar was a cult figure in Britain and a growing success in the United States thanks to RKO's films. Charteris, besieged by interviewers for personal details about the Saint, penned one of the most quoted statements a crime writer has ever made about his creation. He wrote in his introduction to *The First Saint Omnibus* (1939):

> I've been trying to make a picture of a man. Changing, yes. Developing, I hope. Fantastic, impossible—perhaps. Quite worthless, quite irritating, if you feel that way. Or a slightly cock-eyed ideal, if you feel differently. It doesn't matter so much, so long as you feel that you would recognize him tomorrow. . . . I have done this, frankly, because I love him. Over all these years, he has grown into me, and I have grown into him.

"All these years" had actually been fewer than eight years, but so much had transpired in both the outer world and the Saint in print that it must have seemed an eternity.

The 1940s brought Simon Templar to life in the marketplace in several versions, interpretations, and adaptations at the same time—books, movies, comic books, newspaper strip, and radio. The Saint debuted on the radio in 1940, when Terrance De Marney starred in six episodes, adapted from original Charteris stories, for Radio Athlone. These six episodes were later repeated on the British Forces Band.

In 1945 the Saint came to American radio. Edgar Barrier made thirteen episodes for NBC, and Brian Aherne starred in another thirteen for CBS. Vincent Price took over the halo in 1947, making fifty-one episodes for CBS. In July 1948, the show moved to the Mutual Broadcasting System, where Price recorded forty-seven programs. The show moved to NBC in 1950, where Price made a final batch of forty-four episodes. Barry Sullivan also starred as the Saint for two episodes while the show was at NBC. Tom Conway took over the role in May 1951 and starred in twenty-three episodes before the show finished in October of that year. In 1995, the Saint returned to British radio for the first time in more than fifty years when Paul Rhys starred as Simon Templar in three adaptations of original Charteris novels for BBC Radio 4.

The 1940s radio shows, comic books, and novels all shared the central character of Simon Templar, yet the characterizations were modified to suit the diverse media. The Saint was more than changing, he was mutating and proliferating. The most severe alteration came as the result of an event completely out of Charteris' creative control—World War II.

The Saint in Miami (1940) is the last Saint adventure of the third stage. He is as relaxed, carefree, and debonair as ever. The novel begins with impudence and familiar friends, but the plot involves the war in Europe coming to America's shores, and the final pages hint at different days ahead. The Saint's adventures, and Charteris' literary style, underwent major changes beginning in 1942. It was, in Charteris' opinion, impossible to portray the Saint as the twentieth-century's brightest buccaneer in wartime novels. The once outrageous outlaw had to be scaled down. "He had to lose some of the spurious grandeur I had endowed him with when the going was easy," confirmed Charteris in *The Second Saint Omnibus* (1951). "[The war] brought forth heroism that made everything I ever wrote about the Saint seem childish."

The Mature Saint

World War II gave us a new Saint, a streamlined version who is the next best thing to a G-man. Gone are the carefree days, the joyous impudence, Teal-baiting, and witty banter. Gone also are Patricia Holm and Templar's happy acquaintances. "The Saint's fingers combed through his hair. The piratical chiseling of his features looked quite old in a sardonic and careless way" (*The Saint Steps In* [1943]).

This new Saint was not completely devoid of the original's most endearing and enduring characteristics. There are sporadic moments when Charteris cannot resist reverting to the absurd elements of his earlier, more outlandish adventures. The most memorable of these sudden regressions is found at the climax of "The Sizzling Saboteur" (circa 1945) when the Saint and Olga Ivanovitch are, in classic thriller fashion, suspended by their wrists from boiler pipes. The Saint has a knife strapped to his leg. He frees himself by sliding off his shoes and socks, getting the knife wedged firmly between his big toe and the one next to it, and then swinging his knife-wielding foot while aiming the razor edge of the blade between his left wrist and the pipe. "I always knew all those years I spent in the Follies Chorus would come in handy," quips the Saint.

The war's end did not mean an immediate return to the good-old prewar days. The year 1946 was more like six decades, rather than six years, away from the 1930s. The 1930s had lent themselves to romance, wit, flamboyance, and elegance—a far cry from the crises-plagued and disillusioned postwar period. Charteris adapted old Saint radio scripts for *Call for the Saint* (1948) and seems to offer Templar back in full old-form glory complete with Patricia Holm, but there is something most assuredly askew. This is neither the prewar nor the wartime Saint, and it certainly is not the Patricia Holm from any previous novel or short story. In adapting the radio script to print, Charteris allowed the significantly different characterizations and relationships of the Saint radio program to invade and, in the opinion of some, corrupt the published saga.

The youthful pirate of the 1930s could not swashbuckle his way into the 1950s, nor could the Saint continue being a government functionary without Hitler or national security as an excuse. Perhaps it was time for the brighter buccaneer to retire. Numerous decades and innumerable changes after his debut, the Saint had become larger than fiction. The English outlaw created by the youthful

Leslie Charteris evolved into the mythic and, as private enterprise personified, became an industry unto himself. As Charteris wrote in *The Second Saint Omnibus,* "I still get royalties on all the books I have written. The Saint radio show is still on the air. The Saint comic strip is syndicated to an increasing list of newspapers from New York to Los Angeles, and also from Stockholm to Singapore. . . . I make no more promises."

And then something extraordinary happened. Leslie Charteris began writing with an astonishing new vitality, perhaps credited to his gloriously happy 1952 union with the dazzling movie beauty Audrey Long. "Getting through three wives was no problem," joked Charteris to the *Sunday Express*—his other unions included his first marriage, to Pauline Shiskin, with whom he had a daughter; four years with Barbara Meyer; and eight with Betty Bryant Borst. "I am astounded it wasn't more. I suppose I'm just susceptible. It's terribly easy to get married. Maybe I just learned very slowly, but I think I've learned the routine now. I know how to handle it."

For the next decade, Charteris gave readers the Saint in his most important phase—stage five. His adventures during those years are of validation and resolution—assuring followers of a history *with* the Saint rather than a history *of* the Saint. These were neither novels nor novellas, but exceptionally clever short stories playing upon the Saint's self-referential history.

> I gave up writing novels. I probably will never write another. I find the art of short-story writing much more exciting. The Saint appears only in short stories now. Any fool can sit down and write and write and if he writes long enough he'll come out with something. But it takes an artist to write a good short story. I have written, I believe, a few. (*Miami News,* 29 March 1964)

Charteris, to everyone's surprise, released a new novel, *Vendetta for the Saint,* that very year. Wrote Charteris in his *Saint Mystery Magazine* (1964):

> The hero of *Enter the Saint* cannot possibly be the same man as you find in my latest book, *Vendetta for the Saint,* nor would I want him to be, even though I have not let his age increase as openly as my own. But I believe if I had not let him grow along with me, such as some old-time readers still mourn his earliest phases, he might not have lived as long as this.

Vendetta for the Saint, co-written by Harry Harrison (who was not credited), was both a critical and financial success. "All the old vigor and color is still here," wrote Anthony Boucher of the *New York Times,* "all the grand sweep of adventurous narrative, all the humor . . . everything that makes Simon Templar such a superb hero of romance."

By the mid 1960s, Saint exploitation had extended into several international editions of the *Saint Mystery Magazine,* Scandinavian comic books, and what was at that time the final frontier, television. Approached throughout the 1950s by various television producers, Charteris refused to license the Saint to TV. Robert S. Baker broke through Charteris' wall of resistance in 1961, and the Saint finally came to television in 1962.

While Charteris thought the casting of the actor Roger Moore was acceptable, even if he was a bit too good-looking, he was less impressed with television's treatment of his original stories. As he lamented in an editorial for *Saint Mystery Magazine* in 1965:

> I have to suffer the humiliation of realizing that thousands of television viewers who do not read much . . . will justifiably assume that my published stories are as trite and plagiaristic as the televised distortions. This is a hurt which I did not allow for in the price that I accepted. I think that this resentment needed to be written into the permanent record.

The shows improved, and Charteris mellowed. As television produced a respectable, but not totally unrecognizable, Simon Templar, much the same product began to appear on bookstall shelves—a stage-six Saint. This new hybrid Saint, termed by William Vivian Butler "Assembly-line Saint" and by Charteris himself "synthetic Saint," appeared in teleplays adapted into print under Charteris' direct supervision.

It was, to be fair, only sensible to transform the best original episodes from the TV series into published adventures, and the authors selected for collaboration threw themselves into the task with admirable gusto. Fleming Lee, later a successful Florida attorney, was Charteris' first credited collaborator. Succeeding him were Peter Bloxsom, Graham Weaver, and Christopher Short. Short's *The Saint and the Hapsburg Necklace* (1976), unlike previous hybrids, was an original novel from start to finish. As such, it is the first Saint book to give full, single-author credit to someone other than Leslie Charteris.

Each and every "synthetic Saint" novel or short story contains a gem or two of classic, inimitable Charteris. The opening of *The Saint and the People Importers* (1971), although it is credited to Fleming Lee, is unmistakably written by the master. Conversely, *The Saint in Pursuit* (1970) is credited only to Charteris despite the fact that Lee did the initial fleshing out based on Charteris' continuity written for the *Herald-Tribune* Saint newspaper strip. One Lee/Charteris collaboration remains unpublished—"Bet on the Saint," also adapted from newspaper strip continuity. It was the only Saint novel rejected by Doubleday during Charteris' lifetime.

The first TV series ran until 1969; in all there were 118 hour-long episodes: seventy-one in black and white and forty-seven in color. A second television series, *The Return of the Saint,* starred Ian Ogilvy in twenty-four episodes and was broadcast internationally in the 1970s. Six two-hour movies made for television and starring Simon Dutton were produced by D. L. Taffner in the late 1980s as part of the syndicated barter package Mystery Wheel of Adventure. In addition, Taffner prepared a one-hour pilot starring Andrew Clarke for a proposed American-based television series, *The Saint in Manhattan.*

Charteris continued producing new Saint books, most of them pastiches, into the 1980s, concluding with *Salvage for the Saint* (1983), co-written by Peter Bloxsom. On 7 May 1992, the Crime Writers Association presented Charteris with the Diamond Dagger, their prestigious life achievement award. His statement on that date was similar to the introduction penned for the introduction to the 1980 Charter paperback reprint of *Meet—The Tiger!*

> I was always sure that there was a solid place in escape literature for a rambunctious adventurer such as I dreamed up in my own youth. I still cling to that belief—that there will always be a public for the old-style hero, who had a clear idea of justice, and a more than technical approach to love, and the ability to have some fun with his crusades. This is how and why the Saint was born, and why I hope he may eventually occupy a niche beside Robin Hood, d'Artagnan, and all the other immortal true heroes of legend. Anyway, on this date, I can say that I'll always be glad I tried.

Leslie Charteris passed away on 15 April 1993 in Windsor, England.

At present, the movie and television rights to the Saint rest with Paramount Pictures, with RKO holding remake rights on their original Saint movies. Val Kilmer starred in *The Saint* (1997), Paramount's first film in a proposed series. Edgar Award–winning author Burl Barer adapted the film's screenplay as a novel for worldwide publication the same year. Neither the motion picture nor the novel credited Leslie Charteris as creator of the character. Following Charteris' death in 1993, his estate authorized Barer to write new Saint adventures. The first, *Capture the Saint* (1997), was well received by both fans and critics. Ian Dickerson, friend and confidant of the Charteris family, is writing an authorized comprehensive biography of Leslie Charteris. And an award-winning web site is maintained on the Internet by bibliographer Daniel Bodenheimer.

Selected Bibliography

WORKS OF LESLIE CHARTERIS

NOVELS

X Esquire. London: Ward Lock, 1927.

The White Rider. London: Ward Lock, 1928.

Meet—The Tiger! London: Ward Lock, 1928; Garden City, N.Y.: Doubleday, 1929. Also published as *The Saint Meets the Tiger.* New York: Triangle Press, 1944.

Daredevil. London: Ward Lock, 1929; Garden City, N.Y.: Doubleday, 1929.

The Bandit. London: Ward Lock, 1929; Garden City, N.Y.: Doubleday, 1929.

The Last Hero. London: Hodder and Stoughton, 1930; Garden City, N.Y.: Doubleday, 1930. Also published as *The Saint Closes the Case.* Garden City, N.Y.: Sun Dial Press, 1941.

Enter the Saint. London: Hodder and Stoughton, 1930; Garden City, N.Y.: Doubleday, 1931. Includes *The Man Who Was Clever* and *The Policeman with Wings.*

Knight Templar. London: Hodder and Stoughton, 1930. Published as *The Avenging Saint.* Garden City, N.Y.: Doubleday, 1931.

Featuring the Saint. London: Hodder and Stoughton, 1931.

Alias the Saint. London: Hodder and Stoughton, 1931. Includes *The National Debt.*

She Was a Lady. London: Hodder and Stoughton, 1931. Published as *Angels of Doom.* Garden City, N.Y.: Doubleday, 1932. Also published as *The Saint Meets His Match.* Garden City, N.Y.: Sun Dial Press, 1941.

Wanted for Murder. Garden City, N.Y.: Doubleday, 1931. Combines *Featuring the Saint* and *Alias the Saint.*

The Holy Terror. London: Hodder and Stoughton, 1932; Garden City, N.Y.: Doubleday, 1932. Also published as *The Saint Versus Scotland Yard.* Chicago: A. L. Burt, 1935.

Getaway. London: Hodder and Stoughton, 1932; Garden City, N.Y.: Doubleday, 1933. Also published as *The Saint's Getaway.* Garden City, N.Y.: Sun Dial Press, 1943.

Once More the Saint. London: Hodder and Stoughton, 1933. Published as *The Saint and Mr. Teal.* Garden City, N.Y.: Doubleday, 1933.

The Brighter Buccaneer. London: Hodder and Stoughton, 1933; Garden City, N.Y.: Doubleday, 1933

The Misfortunes of Mr. Teal. London: Hodder and Stoughton, 1934; Garden City, N.Y.: Doubleday, 1934. Also published as *The Saint in London.* Garden City, N.Y.: Sun Dial Press, 1941.

Boodle. London: Hodder and Stoughton, 1934. Published as *The Saint Intervenes.* Garden City, N.Y.: Doubleday, 1934; New York: Triangle Books, 1940.

The Saint Goes On. London: Hodder and Stoughton, 1934; Garden City, N.Y.: Doubleday, 1935.

The Saint in New York. London: Hodder and Stoughton, 1935; Garden City, N.Y.: Doubleday, 1935.

The Saint Overboard. London: Hodder and Stoughton, 1936; Garden City, N.Y.: Doubleday, 1936. Also published as *The Pirate Saint.* New York: Triangle Books, 1941.

The Ace of Knaves. London: Hodder and Stoughton, 1937; Garden City, N.Y.: Doubleday, 1937. Also published as *The Saint Goes into Action.* Garden City, N.Y.: Sun Dial Press, 1937.

Thieves' Picnic. London: Hodder and Stoughton, 1937; Garden City, N.Y.: Doubleday, 1937. Also published as *The Saint Bids Diamonds.* New York: Triangle Books, 1942.

Prelude for War. London: Hodder and Stoughton, 1938; Garden City, N.Y.: Doubleday, 1938. Also published as *The Saint Plays with Fire.* New York: Triangle Books, 1942.

Follow the Saint. Garden City, N.Y.: Doubleday, 1938; London: Hodder and Stoughton, 1939.

The Happy Highwayman: Further Adventures of the Saint. Garden City, N.Y.: Doubleday, 1939; New York: Collier, 1939; London: Hodder and Stoughton, 1939.

The First Saint Omnibus. London: Hodder and Stoughton, 1939.

The Saint in Miami. Garden City, N.Y.: Doubleday, 1940; London: Hodder and Stoughton, 1941.

The Saint Two in One. Garden City, N.Y.: Sun Dial Press, 1942.

The Saint Goes West: Some Further Exploits of Simon Templar. Garden City, N.Y.: Doubleday, 1942; London: Hodder and Stoughton, 1942.

The Saint Steps In. Garden City, N.Y.: Doubleday, 1943; London: Hodder and Stoughton, 1944.

The Saint at Large. Garden City, N.Y.: Sun Dial Press, 1943.

The Saint on Guard. Garden City, N.Y.: Doubleday, 1944; London: Hodder and Stoughton, 1945.

Paging the Saint. Los Angeles: Jacobs Publishing, 1945.

Lady on a Train. Los Angeles: Shaw Press, 1945. Novelization of a screenplay.

The Saint Sees It Through. Garden City, N.Y.: Doubleday, 1946; London: Hodder and Stoughton, 1947.

Call for the Saint. Garden City, N.Y.: Doubleday, 1948; London: Hodder and Stoughton, 1948.

Saint Errant. Garden City, N.Y.: Doubleday, 1948; London: Hodder and Stoughton, 1949.

Arrest the Saint. New York: Permabooks, 1951.

The Second Saint Omnibus. Garden City, N.Y.: Doubleday, 1951.

The Saint in Europe. Garden City, N.Y.: Doubleday, 1953; London: Hodder and Stoughton, 1954.

The Saint on the Spanish Main. Garden City, N.Y.: Doubleday, 1955; London: Hodder and Stoughton, 1955.

The Saint Around the World. Garden City, N.Y.: Doubleday, 1956; London: Hodder and Stoughton, 1957.
Thanks to the Saint. Garden City, N.Y.: Doubleday, 1957; London: Hodder and Stoughton, 1958.
Señor Saint. Garden City, N.Y.: Doubleday, 1958; London: Hodder and Stoughton, 1959.
Concerning the Saint. New York: Avon, 1958.
The Saint to the Rescue. Garden City, N.Y.: Doubleday, 1959; London: Hodder and Stoughton, 1961.
The Saint Cleans Up. New York: Avon, 1959.
Trust the Saint. Garden City, N.Y.: Doubleday, 1962; London: Hodder and Stoughton, 1962.
The Saint in the Sun. Garden City, N.Y.: Doubleday, 1963; London: Hodder and Stoughton, 1964.
Vendetta for the Saint. Garden City, N.Y.: Doubleday, 1964; London: Hodder and Stoughton, 1965.
The Saint on TV (with Fleming Lee). Garden City, N.Y.: Doubleday, 1968.
The Saint Returns. Garden City, N.Y.: Doubleday, 1968; London: Hodder and Stoughton, 1968. Two adventures from television.
The Saint and the Fiction-Makers. Garden City, N.Y.: Doubleday, 1968. Original teleplay by John Kruse. Additional scenes by Harry W. Junkin. Adapted by Fleming Lee.
The Saint Abroad. Garden City, N.Y.: Doubleday, 1969.
The Saint in Pursuit. Garden City, N.Y.: Doubleday, 1970. Novelization of the comic strip.
The Saint and the People Importers (with Fleming Lee). London: Hodder Paperbacks, 1971; Garden City, N.Y.: Doubleday, 1971.
Saints Alive. London: Hodder and Stoughton, 1974.
Catch the Saint. London: Hodder and Stoughton, 1975.
The Saint and the Hapsburg Necklace (with Christopher Short). Garden City, N.Y.: Doubleday, 1976.
Send for the Saint. London: Hodder and Stoughton, 1977.
The Saint in Trouble. Garden City, N.Y.: Doubleday, 1978. Based on an original teleplay by Terence Feely and John Kruse. Adapted by Graham Weaver.
The Saint: Good as Gold. Roslyn: Ellery Queen Mystery Club, 1979.
The Saint and the Templar Treasure. London: Hodder and Stoughton, 1979.
Count on the Saint. Garden City, N.Y.: Doubleday, 1980.
The Fantastic Saint. Edited by Martin H. Greenberg and Charles G. Waugh. Garden City, N.Y.: Doubleday, 1982; London: Hodder and Stoughton, 1983.
The Saint: Five Complete Novels. New York: Avenel, 1983.
Salvage for the Saint. Garden City, N.Y.: Doubleday, 1983. Original teleplay by John Kruse. Developed and co-written with Peter Bloxsom.

SHORT STORIES

"The Song of Bedivere," *Woman,* July 1928 [not collected].
"The Story of a Dead Man," *Thriller* [no date, but after 1 January and before 4 May 1929].
"The Secret of Beacon Inn," *Thriller* [no date, but after 1 January and before 4 May 1929]; revised as *The National Debt* for *Alias the Saint.*
"The Five Kings," *Thriller,* 4 May 1929; revised as *The Man Who Was Clever* for *Enter the Saint.*
"The Man Who Liked Toys," [periodical not named], [no date, but circa 1933]; revised as "A Short Short Mystery Novel," *American Magazine,* September 1934.
"The Sizzling Saboteur," [no other information, circa 1945].

OTHER WORKS

"Charteris, Leslie." In *Twentieth Century Authors.* Edited by Stanley Kunitz. New York: H. W. Wilson, 1942.
"How I Created a Saint." *Women's Mirror,* 12 June 1965.
"Editorial." *Saint Mystery Magazine* (1965).

INTERVIEWS

St. Petersburg Times, 9 February 1964.
Miami News, 29 March 1964.
Sunday Express, 17 December 1972.

BIBLIOGRAPHY AND ARCHIVES

The Mugar Memorial Library at Boston University holds the manuscript papers of Leslie Charteris.

Bodenheimer, Daniel. *The Saintly Bible: An Exhaustive Bibliography of the Immortal Works of Leslie Charteris and His Saint Saga.* Sunnyvale, Calif.: Bodenheimer Publishing, 1993.

BIOGRAPHICAL AND CRITICAL STUDIES

Barer, Burl. *The Saint: A Complete History in Print, Radio, Film, and Television of Leslie Charteris' Robin Hood of Modern Crime, Simon Templar 1928–1992.* Jefferson, N.C.: McFarland, 1993.
Butler, William Vivian. *The Durable Desperadoes.* London: Macmillan, 1973.
Lofts, William Oliver Guillemont, and Derek Adley. *The Saint and Leslie Charteris.* Howard Baker, 1970.
Simper, Paul. *The Saint: From Big Screen to Small Screen and Back Again.* London: André Deutsch, 1997.

INTERNET RESOURCE

The Saintly Bible Web Page and Official Site of the Saint Club. http://www.saint.org.

G. K. Chesterton
(1874–1936)

JOHN C. TIBBETTS

JOURNALIST, ESSAYIST, POET, critic, broadcaster, and ideologue of religion and politics, Gilbert Keith Chesterton is probably best known today for his detective stories, especially the novel-length *The Man Who Was Thursday* (1908) and the series of tales featuring the Essex priest, Father Brown. Works like these played a significant part in his output during his entire writing career. Chesterton himself attracted public attention at the turn of the century as much for his flamboyant personality and outsized appearance (his three-hundred-pound bulk towered well above six feet) as for his first collections of verse and essays, including *The Wild Knight and Other Poems* (1900), *The Defendant* (1901), *Heretics* (1905), and *Orthodoxy* (1909). In a prolific writing career spanning thirty-five years, Chesterton published nearly one hundred books, contributed to two hundred more, traveled and lectured widely, and wrote thousands of articles and poems for over a dozen periodicals (two of which, the *New Witness* and *G. K.'s Weekly*, he edited himself). Since his death in 1936, many biographies, posthumous collections, and reprints of his works have appeared. His love of paradox and whimsy, his flashing wit and indomitable optimism, and his impassioned defense of spiritual values place him among the most beloved, oft-quoted literary figures of the twentieth century.

Life

On an early spring day in 1904, two men set out on a brisk walk across the Yorkshire moors of West Riding. They talked about their favorite things—wild, philosophical, and poetic things. In short, they discussed detective stories. The friends presented a study in contrasts: the tall, thirty-year-old man with a rumpled mop of reddish hair was Gilbert Keith Chesterton, a rising young journalist on holiday from what he described as "the hard drinking and hard thinking" of Fleet Street; the small, smooth-faced man struggling to keep up with him was his friend, Father John O'Connor, a curate (later monsignor) of the Roman Catholic Church.

It was a momentous ramble. O'Connor would find in Chesterton a future convert to the Church—he would hear Chesterton's first confession in 1922—and Chesterton found in O'Connor the model for a new literary character, the mild-mannered little Essex priest-detective, Father Brown. Chesterton later admitted he was astonished at O'Connor's knowledge of and insight into the criminal mind: "[I]t was a curious experience to find that this quiet and pleasant celibate had plumbed those abysses far deeper than I. I had not imagined that the world could hold such horrors."

Despite Chesterton's coy dismissal of his detective stories as only "innocent artifices," they are, as Jorge Luis Borges asserted in his essay "On Chesterton," a profound "symbol or reflection" of Chesterton's life. Moreover, they occupy a place in the first rank of crime fiction. In 1936 Ellery Queen declared that Father Brown "is one of the three greatest detective characters ever invented" (*Thirteen Detectives,* p. 8), on a par with Doyle's Sherlock Holmes and Poe's Auguste Dupin. More recently, Julian Symons, in *Bloody Murder,* placed the best of Chesterton's tales "among the finest short crime stories ever written."

Born into a conventional middle-class home on 29 May 1874 in Campden Hill, in the Kensington neighborhood of London, Gilbert grew up a dreamer. A moody and sometimes difficult child, he was described by one of his teachers as "a great blunderer with much intelligence." At the age of eighteen, after demonstrating only a desultory interest in his studies (but a lively facility for poetry and debate) at Colet House and St. Paul's School, he matriculated into University College, London, where he studied, among other things, Latin under A. E. Housman, and drawing at the Slade School of Art.

It was at this time, around 1893, as he recounts in his *Autobiography* (1936), that he fell into a late adolescent crisis of skepticism and depression. He dabbled in spiritualism and the occult, experimented with the Ouija board, and grew morbidly fascinated with diabolism.

Leaving University College without a degree in 1895, he gradually pulled himself out of his spiritual crisis. Coming to his rescue were a naturally buoyant optimism about life, his courtship of his future wife, Frances Blogg (whom he married in 1901), and a renewal of his Christian faith. The last was for him a moral victory that would shape the rest of his life (and, as shall be seen, influence the writing of his detective stories). Nowhere did he more eloquently express this affirmation than in his own personal apologia, *Orthodoxy,* a volume of loosely connected essays. Christianity, he declared, by contrast to the "topsy-turvy" attitudes of a skeptical age, is a "wild truth reeling but erect" (pp. 186–187). It "satisfies suddenly and perfectly man's ancestral instinct for being the right way up; satisfies it supremely in this; that by its creed joy becomes something gigantic and sadness something special and small" (p. 297). Central to this creed, he realized, was the felt machinations of a maker, a creator: "I had always vaguely felt facts to be miracles in the sense that they are wonderful," he wrote, "now I began to think them miracles in the stricter sense that they were *willful.* . . . I had always believed that the world involved magic: now I thought that perhaps it involved a magician" (pp. 109–110).

The roiling flamboyance of his creative energies unleashed, Chesterton quickly established himself as one of the most dazzling talents and colorful figures in the generation of young men of letters emerging before World War I. In periodicals and magazines like the *Speaker, Bookman,* the *Illustrated London News,* and the *Daily News,* he was a quick and witty pundit on the vagaries of the passing scene. His books, appearing in rapid succession, introduced various aspects of his protean talents: In *Greybeards at Play* (1900) he debuted as a poet; in *The Defendant* as a universal polemicist; in *Robert Browning* (1903) and *Charles Dickens* (1906), a literary biographer and critic; in *The Club of Queer Trades* (1905), a new voice in detective fiction; in *The Napoleon of Notting Hill* (1904) and *The Man Who Was Thursday* (1908), a novelist of fantastic vision and swashbuckling romance; and in *Heretics* and *Orthodoxy,* a Christian apologist. His slashing, hit-and-run prose style was peppered with the paradoxes and irrepressible wit that were becoming his trademarks.

Gradually, the legend emerged of the "jolly journalist" of Fleet Street (he referred to himself as an "accident" of Fleet Street). Brandishing a sword stick, wrapping a great cape about his towering frame, he wheezed his way in and out of taverns and cabs, scattering a trail of hastily scribbled articles, reviews, and essays in his wake. His eccentricities included a self-absorption and an absentmindedness so extreme he sometimes lost his way on the streets of his own neighborhood. Beneath such foolishness, however, was a very hardworking and passionate young writer—a man, as he himself put it, who could not help being a journalist because he could not help being a controversialist.

At the insistence of Frances, who loathed the frantic congestion of city life, the Chestertons left their Battersea flat in 1909 and relocated to Beaconsfield, a village twenty-five miles west of London on the Oxford road. For the next five years, his energies unabated, Gilbert continued to write, lecture, and travel. He discoursed on anything and everything, his prose as lithe and dazzling as a handspring by Douglas Fairbanks or a musical arabesque by Domenico Scarlatti. In his religious essays he donned the sword and buckler of a defender of the faith. If longtime friend and debating opponent George Bernard Shaw said that God was dead, Chesterton retorted that the Christian God was used to dying and rising from the dead. His political and social essays attacked the positivists and utilitarians, the atheists and the evolutionists, the capitalists and the socialists. By contrast, his occasional pieces, like "A Defence of Nonsense" (in *The Defendant*), were fraught with nonsense imagery: "A bird is a blossom loose from its chain of stalk; a man a quadruped begging on its hind legs; a house a gigantic hat to cover a man from the sun; a chair, an apparatus of four legs for a cripple with only two."

His strenuous schedule and excessive appetites and indulgences caught up with him late in 1914 when he suffered a physical and nervous breakdown. He collapsed into intervals of coma that lasted several months. No sooner had he recovered and returned to work, than he suffered another blow—the death of his younger brother, Cecil, in 1918. Although the heartbroken Gilbert never quite recovered his former ebullience, he still maintained a busy schedule, editing his brother's the *New Witness* and his own *G. K.'s Weekly;* penning apologies for the Catholic Church; and espousing the political movement known as distributism, which promoted decentralizing the economy in order to prevent concentrations of wealth and property ownership. Among his other urgent social and political concerns were a distrust of world government, evolutionary progress, secularism, eugenics, and the so-called New Theology and New World Order espoused by his colleagues H. G. Wells and George Bernard Shaw.

During his last years, despite illness and flagging energies, he managed three trips abroad, to Poland, Italy, and America; achieved an unexpected success as a BBC broadcaster; and wrote two of his greatest works, *St. Thomas Aquinas* (1933) and the *Autobiography* (published posthumously in 1936). At home in Beaconsfield, he enjoyed the quiet, loving support of his wife and the devoted services of his secretary, Dorothy Collins, who would manage his literary estate until her death in 1988. At last, suffering from chronic bronchial catarrh and various heart and kidney ailments, he sank into a coma and died at home in Beaconsfield at 10:15 in the morning of 14 June 1936. In an aptly improbable epilogue, his coffin, too big to be carried down the winding staircase, had to be lowered from the window to the ground.

He was buried in the Catholic cemetery in Candlemas Lane in Beaconsfield. His last written words, in *Autobiography,* renew the sense of the blessedness of life he had felt as a child and continued to honor the whole of his life: "Existence is still a strange thing to me; and as a stranger, I give it welcome" (p. 353).

Achievement and Philosophy

Few contemporary men of letters have aroused more divided critical opinion than Chesterton. Significantly, those who attack him do so for the same reasons as those who extol him. His prolific output, notorious paradoxes, unabashed patriotism, hearty optimism, reverence for the past, childlike whimsies, radically populist politics, and Catholic apologetics are easy targets for potshots and praises alike.

It is not the purpose of this essay to rebuke or confirm either his adherents or his detractors, except to note there is truth in both camps. If he ultimately seems, as commentator Garry Wills has suggested, a kind of jester playing hide-and-seek with meaning, reading his work likewise becomes a kind of chase between author and reader which, like the great chase that concludes *The Man Who Was Thursday,* is as soberly enlightening as it is delightfully confounding.

An important key to understanding Chesterton can be found in the little toy theater his father gave him as a child. "[S]o far as my memory is concerned," he recalled in the *Autobiography,* "this was the sight on which my eyes first opened in this world"; and which "I shall still remember . . . when all other memory is gone out of my mind" (p. 25). Truth may be found here; that is, in small things, in their edges, definition, and limitations. "You can only represent very big ideas in very small spaces," he argued in an essay entitled, aptly enough, "The Toy Theater" (in *Tremendous Trifles,* 1909); and he whimsically suggested that "the drama of wood and pasteboard" affords "glorious glimpses into the possibilities of existence."

However, he argued, after childhood we lose these clear outlines and limits in the engulfing, myriad details and chaotic shapelessness of living. Recovery of that lost clarity is a great thing; indeed, it is the only thing. For Chesterton it meant returning to the toy theater, as it were. Thus, speaking through the character of Innocent Smith in one of his finest works, the novel *Manalive* (1912), Chesterton says the true journey of life is simply finding a way to come back to where we began: "God made me love one spot and serve it and do all things however wild in praise of it" (p. 330). It is no accident that, in a very real sense, the toy theater was the only "home" Chesterton never left; putting it another way, it was the only home he took with him wherever he went. Even in his last years at Beaconsfield, he used it to enact miniature dramas to the delight of his children guests.

In a less exalted sense, Chesterton's return to first things was sometimes a short trip. It is said that one day the maid heard the sounds of a mighty splash issuing from his bathroom. In attempting to climb out of the tub, the great man had slipped and tumbled back into it again. "Dammit," he was heard to exclaim, "I've been here before!"

The Romance of Detective Stories

Drawing from the metaphor of the toy theater, as well as the religious affirmation he had experienced in his youth, the detective and crime stories that occupy a substantial portion of his work are metaphors for this ongoing search for—or return to—the primary instincts of man. Even subjects remote from standard detective formulas—a piece of chalk, a sermon by St. Francis, a tenet of distributism, a novel by Dickens, a fairy tale—are for him fantastic riddles of sin and redemption, scenes painted in exotic, heightened colors, populated by picaresque figures, and played out against the garish blaze of footlights. Recalling the aforementioned essays in *Orthodoxy,* what was required to extract a "wild, reeling, and erect" truth from seeming chaos was a champion of order, a figure who was no mere collector of clues but a master of paradoxes—a paradox monger, if you will.

The fact of the matter is Chesterton saw everything as a detective story. As early as his first essay on the subject, "A Defence of Detective Stories," he argued they embody "the whole romance of man." Alone among popular genres, the detective story "declines to regard the present as prosaic or the common as commonplace"; rather, it expresses "some sense of the poetry of modern life." The policeman or detective is a modern knight-errant protecting society from those "children of chaos," the criminals, inferring from the "hieroglyphs" of every stone, brick, and signpost the revelation of some great secret that will astonish the reader. But the secret must be more than a mere gimmick; it must be a revelation. "It is useless for a thing to be unexpected if it was not worth expecting," he insisted later in a 1925 essay, "How to Write a Detective Story": the climax "must not be only the bursting of a bubble but rather the breaking of a dawn" (pp. 4–6).

Chesterton also argued in another essay, "On Detective Novels" in *Generally Speaking* (1928), that the short story format is best suited to the detective formula. "The whole point of a sensational story is that the secret should be simple," he wrote. Such a story is like "a drama of masks," a "masquerade ball in which everybody is disguised as somebody else." The revelation, the "true personal interest" must be withheld until the moment that "the clock strikes twelve." Chesterton concludes: "We cannot really get at the psychology and philosophy, the morals and the religion, of the thing, until we have read the last chapter. Therefore, I think it is best of all when the first chapter is also the last chapter."

Father Brown

Father Brown, Chesterton's best-known detective, debuted in "The Blue Cross" in the *Storyteller* magazine in 1910; and his first twelve cases were collected in *The Innocence of Father Brown* a year later. "These stories are undoubtedly the most extraordinary work Mr. Chesterton has yet penned," the editor of the *Storyteller* enthused at the time; "Father Brown is a character destined to be long remembered in fiction." Indeed, Ellery Queen, in *In the Queen's Pastor* (1957), has ranked *The Innocence of Father Brown* among the four all-time finest collections of detective short stories, along with Poe's *Tales* (1845), Doyle's *Adventures of Sherlock Holmes* (1892), and Melville Davisson Post's *Uncle Abner* (1918). The rest of the Father Brown stories appeared in four subsequent collections: *The Wisdom of Father Brown* (1914), *The Incredulity of Father Brown* (1926), *The Secret of Father Brown* (1927), and *The Scandal of Father Brown* (1935). Two more uncollected stories, "The Vampire of the Village" in *The Father Brown Omnibus* (1951) and "The Donnington Affair," which first appeared in *Thirteen Detectives* (1987), bring the total to fifty-two stories.

Although it is clear that Father O'Connor was Brown's immediate inspiration, his literary antecedents are more elusive. While Chesterton always acknowledged Sherlock Holmes—"Everybody who has written a detective story has felt his long, angular shadow upon the page"—Father Brown's literary forebears in fact have little or nothing to do with the Master. Among the few literary precedents for a clergyman-detective is Silas Hocking's *Adventures of Latimer Field* (1903), a series of mystery and supernatural tales about an Anglican curate. More generally, Brown may also be regarded as an inversion of the archetypal comic Anglican curate of popular British farce—that is, a serious rather than a comic figure—a figure extending all the way back to Shakespeare.

Moreover, the priest's adventures can in no way be confused with the Holmes stories, or with the tales of other contemporaries—R. Austin Freeman, Melville Davisson Post, Baroness Orczy, or Ernest Bramah, to name just a few. Unlike the eccentric Holmes or the two-fisted Nick Carter, who usually occupy center stage in their adventures, Brown remains a passive, vaguely realized figure peripheral to the action, virtually anonymous until the moment he quietly steps forward with the final revelation. "In Father Brown it was the chief feature to be featureless," writes Chesterton in *Autobiography.*

> The point of him was to appear pointless; and one might say that his conspicuous quality was not being conspicuous. His commonplace exterior was meant to contrast with his unsuspected vigilance and intelligence; and that being so, of course I made his appearance shabby and shapeless, his face round and ex-

pressionless, his manners clumsy, and so on. (pp. 334–335)

Likewise, the stories' locations and atmospheres veil events in a sort of impressionist haze, reflecting Chesterton's fascination with the half-light of twilight and dawn. Here is a world where intuitively felt experiences supersede the mere accumulation of data. In "The Secret of Father Brown," the priest complains that the science of criminology is limited to "getting outside a man and studying him as if he were a gigantic insect; in what they would call a dry, impartial light; in what I should call a dead and dehumanized light" (in *The Secret of Father Brown*). In "The Absence of Mr. Glass," a story in *The Innocence of Father Brown,* he demonstrates how a weird aggregation of clues points not to a murderer but to a magician. Explaining that too often people tend to put "fantastic features into what are probably plain events," he advises "it is best to look first to the main tendencies of Nature." In "The Sign of the Broken Sword" (in *The Innocence of Father Brown*) he argues how a national hero can be a scoundrel and murderer. "I cannot prove it . . . but I am sure of it"; or, "I can't prove it, but I can do more—I can see it."

The central paradox in Father Brown, of course, is that he relies chiefly on his spiritual authority, coupled with his experience as a confessor, for insights into the vagaries of the human mind. Chesterton believes that the innocence and denial of experience symbolized by celibacy are negations that can lead to knowledge: it is the innocent, or humble man, who perceives things in the right perspective. Unlike Sherlock Holmes, who is an eccentric and therefore on the periphery of experience, Brown is equipped to comprehend human problems because he exists in the center of humanity. "Has it never struck you," Brown explains to the thief Flambeau in his first adventure, "The Blue Cross" (in *The Innocence of Father Brown*), "that a man who does next to nothing but hear men's real sins is not likely to be wholly unaware of human evil?" Thus, in "The Wrong Shape" he explains how he recognizes a killer who has arranged a fake suicide: "As one knows the crooked track of a snail, I know the crooked track of a man." And in "The Secret of Father Brown," he makes this startling admission: "I wait until I know I am inside a murderer, thinking his thoughts, wrestling with his passions; till I have bent myself into the posture of his hunched and peering hatred. . . . Till I am really a murderer."

Fortunately, however, knowing the worst of men, Brown is prepared to acknowledge the best of men. He seems less interested in proving the guilt of wrongdoers than in securing their redemption. His quarries are not villains so much as sinners ripe for conversion. Thus, Brown is capable of recognizing a human decency even in the servant who beheads his dead master in "The Honour of Israel Gow," or the guest who slits his host's throat in "The Vanishing of Vaudrey." In "The Flying Stars," after confronting the master thief Flambeau, Brown pleads with him to reconsider his life of crime and save his soul. Sure enough, the reformed Flambeau reappears in later stories, practicing as a private detective!

The Forgotten Detectives

Father Brown is by no means G. K. Chesterton's only detective. Less celebrated are other investigators whose cases are just as exotic and methods just as delightfully unconventional as his. To be sure, only a few are professional detectives or policemen; more significantly, most are what Chesterton cryptically calls "buoyant amateurs"—retired judges, civil servants, escaped lunatics, and accused felons. What unites them all is that, like Father Brown, they are insightful observers and diviners of paradoxical truths. They stand the world on its head. Sometimes, like Gabriel Gale—whose adventures will be discussed presently—they even stand on *their* heads. Their adventures, while wildly uneven in quality, are at their best every bit as good as Brown's. A few are even better.

The six stories in *The Club of Queer Trades* were serialized in the *Idler* in 1904, predating the first Father Brown story by six years. They were Chesterton's first attempt to put his theories of the detective story into practice. They are also among the most lighthearted of his stories, concerned not so much with violent crime as with the more mundane but equally startling mysteries encountered in everyday life.

Amid the crowded London of "perpendicular streets" and "flying omnibuses" figure two investigators, the brothers Rupert and Basil Grant (surely patterned after Gilbert and his brother, Cecil), who represent Chesterton's ideas of the worst and best in methods of detection. The red-haired Rupert is a private investigator cut from the standard mold. He dashes about London collecting the right clues and reaching the wrong conclusions. His gray-haired brother Basil, on the other hand, goes nowhere and knows everything. He is a retired English judge who became so disillusioned with English law that one day he "suddenly went mad on the bench" and fled the profession to live as a humble recluse in a Lambeth garret. Basil absorbs what he calls "atmospheres" and scorns a dependence on mere data. "Facts, how facts obscure the truth. I never could believe in that man—what's his name, in those capital stories?—Sherlock Holmes. Every detail points to something, certainly; but generally to the wrong thing" ("The Tremendous Adventures of Major Brown").

The stories revolve around a most unusual club, existing in a London notorious for its eccentric clubs. Membership demands that one must have originated one's profession and be able to earn a living by it. Basil Grant determines that a series of bizarre, sinister occurrences are actually the harmless actions of several prospective club members pursuing their preposterous trades. A case in point is the best of the stories, "The Tremendous Adventures of Major Brown." A case of mistaken identity leads to Major Brown's involvement in a series of bizarre events, including a death threat spelled out in flowers in a garden, an encounter with a woman who faces the sunset every afternoon at the stroke of six o'clock, and the unanswered question, "How did the jackal die?" The perpetrators of the crimes are revealed to be agents of a mysterious organization called the Adventure and Romance Agency (one of the "Queer Trades" of the book's title), which undertakes to inflict upon its clients "startling and weird events" so that they may return, in effect, to "that godlike time when we can act stories, be our own heroes, and at the same instant dance and dream." (By the way, neither Major Brown nor we ever learn the mystery of the jackal!)

Tales of the Long Bow (1925) links eight short stories about the activities of another of Chesterton's curious clubs, the League of the Long Bow, an organization of erstwhile but mild-mannered political revolutionaries: a retired lawyer, an Anglo-Indian colonel, a flying officer, an eccentric vicar, a young mathematics teacher, an aeronautical engineer, and an American millionaire. They are not detectives investigating crimes so much as curious citizens united in their pursuit of the real meanings behind several bizarre incidents. Why, for example, did Colonel Crane eat a hat-shaped cabbage; why did Owen Hood literally set a river on fire; how did Captain Hilary Pierce cause pigs to fly; and how did Commander Blair erect a castle in midair? "These things . . . are easily seen to be absurd," says one member in "The Exclusive Luxury of Enoch Oates," "but even after they are seen to be absurd, they are still there." It is characteristic of Chesterton that the irrational and miraculous events have entirely prosaic (if ingenious) explanations. Much of the reader's enjoyment proceeds from the way the author sets the powers of rationality and irrationality at each other's throats. However, the whimsical tone is sometimes forced and labored, and some passages of the book are marred by Chesterton's occasionally irritating tendency to inject agrarian Distributionist polemics into the proceedings.

The Paradoxes of Mr. Pond (1937) is Chesterton's last book, published posthumously and drawn from stories that had recently appeared in the *Storyteller.* Mr. Pond is a man who looks and behaves like a mild civil servant but is in reality a member of the Secret Service possessing considerable experience fighting crime and intrigue. (As Chesterton wittily puts it, Pond keeps the secret of his services.)

As we learn in the first story, "The Three Horsemen of Apocalypse"—lauded by Jorge Luis Borges as the best of all Chesterton's tales—Pond is like the placid little pool in his garden: "He was so quiet at all normal times, so neat in shape and so shiny. . . . and yet I knew there were some monsters in Mr. Pond also—monsters in his mind which rose only for a moment to the surface and sank again." Otherwise, Pond remains a quiet enigma, the still point between two colorful friends who serve as his foils, the stolid Sir Hubert Wotton and the swashbuckling Irishman, Sir Peter Patrick Gahagan.

Four tales are particularly fine. In "When Doctors Agree," Pond confronts the dilemma of two men who are in such complete agreement on things that one is forced to murder the other. "A Terrible Troubadour" is a curious retelling of Poe's "Murder in the Rue Morgue." "A Tall Story" presents a particularly striking setup involving a body that is found impaled in the ceiling by a large sword. Here the paradox, as stated by Pond, is: "The murderer was too tall to be seen." (And, indeed, Pond is right!) The fourth, "Pond the Pantaloon," benefits from some very clever allusions to the tradition of the Christmas pantomime.

The Paradoxes of Mr. Pond enjoys the dubious distinction of being the most maligned of Chesterton's mystery volumes, attacked by Kingsley Amis as a collection of "irresponsible and pointless" paradoxes and dismissed by Father Ian Boyd as containing "heavy-handed" irrelevancies. Martin Gardner, on the other hand, applauds their welcome return to the light hearted fancy of the early mystery stories; furthermore, he argues, because the presence of Catholic rhetoric is minimal here, they are better plotted "and less preposterous than most of his Father Brown yarns" (1990 ed., p. viii).

The five interlocking stories in *Manalive* revolve around the presumed crimes of a wild man named "Innocent Smith," a comically swashbuckling figure as likely to climb a tree as to dash across rooftops. Two investigators, Cyrus Pym and Michael Moon—cut from the same mold as Rupert and Basil Grant—sift through the facts in the case. Why did Smith fire bullets at his best friend; why did he steal property; why did he abduct a woman; and why did he commit polygamy? After sifting through the evidence and obtaining eyewitness accounts, Pym determines Smith is guilty and Moon concludes he is innocent. "We have come to think certain things wrong which are not wrong at all," Moon says. "In themselves they are not merely pardonable; they are unimpeachable." He explains that Smith's murder attempt was in reality a gesture to save a man's life; that his theft was merely the removal of items from his own house; that his acts of abduction and polygamy were complicit actions with his own wife. Far from being guilty of these crimes, declares Moon, Smith has merely acted to make himself and other people feel more keenly alive. As commentator Ian Boyd puts it, "The moral meaning of the crimes is concerned with an attempt to recover the lost sense of the wonder and glamour of everyday life." Smith is thus a virtuous soul, a capital fellow—a "man alive." Garry Wills describes *Manalive* as Chesterton's happiest book.

Four Faultless Felons (1930) comprises four novellas that were first published separately in two British periodicals, *Cassell's Magazine* and the *Storyteller,* in 1929 and 1930. For the book's publication, Chesterton added a prologue and an epilogue to tie them together. The "felons" of the title, John Hume, Dr. Judson, Alan Nadoway, and John Conrad, have in common the fact that they have been wrongfully accused of eccentric crimes. The detective work, as had been the case in *Manalive,* aims not to establish their guilt but to prove their innocence. "The truth is we have devoted ourselves to a new sort of detective story," one of the "felons" says, "—or detective service, if you like. We do not hunt for crimes but for concealed virtues."

There are two sets of investigators here, amateur and professional. The amateurs are the felons themselves, and they are usually correct in their deductions; the professionals, like Hayter in "The Moderate Murderer" and Harrington in "The Honest Quack," are invariably wrong in theirs. The titles capture the tone and the variety of paradoxes—"The Moderate Murderer," "The Honest Quack," "The Ecstatic Thief," and "The Loyal Traitor" (*Four Faultless Felons*). Of the four narratives, John Conrad's in "The Loyal Traitor" is by far the best. It concerns the disappearance of three men from a locked room, and the solution hinges on a spectacular feat of impersonation. But lest these formal puzzles get too complicated (as they undoubtedly do in the later work of Chesterton's literary disciple, John Dickson Carr), the detective, Harrington, admits his misguided deductions made too much of a criminal method: "That grand and bold artistic crime we dreamed of is, like many great things, too great for this world. Perhaps in Utopia, perhaps in Paradise, we may have murders of that perfect and poetical sort. But the real murderer behaves in a much more ordinary fashion. . . ."

In *The Poet and the Lunatics* (1929), drawn from stories published in *Nash's Magazine* in 1921, the lanky, fair-haired, and unpredictable Gabriel Gale is another in the long line of fool figures that fascinated Chesterton. Only his topsy-turvy sensibility can interpret and solve the mad crimes he encounters. In "The Yellow Bird," he describes his perceptions in words that recall Father Brown: "Perhaps you think I am as mad as [the criminal]. . . . And I have told you that I am at once like [the criminal] and unlike him. I am unlike him because, thank God, I can generally find my way home again." Furthermore, like Basil Grant, Gale prefers interpreting "atmospheres" and impressions to gathering physical clues: "Oh, proofs!" he scoffs, "I know the sort of proofs you want. The foot-prints of the remarkable boots. The bloody finger-print carefully compared with the one at Scotland Yard. The conveniently mislaid matchbox, and the ashes of the unique tobacco. Do you suppose I've never read any detective stories? Well, I haven't got any proofs—of that sort." Gale understands that a wild crime might be a merely commonplace event seen from a cockeyed angle; conversely, that a mild, innocuous incident might be an outrageous transgression of justice as seen from another angle.

These eight stories are among Chesterton's most evocative twilight tales, seen as if through smoky stained glass. Like Innocent Smith and the Faultless Felons, Gale even commits a crime of his own in "The Crime of Gabriel Gale"; and, like them, he is exonerated by his victim. Two other stories, "Shadow of the Shark" and "The Finger of Stone," present impossible crimes; the second has a delightfully outrageous solution worthy of Carr in his most deranged moments. It also contains a characteristically clever (and exceedingly wicked) commentary on the criminal as "artist."

The eight stories of *The Man Who Knew Too Much* (1922) are, collectively, the darkest in tone and theme of all Chesterton's mystery short stories. This is ironic in view of the fact that they were published shortly after Chesterton's conversion to the Catholic Church. But it must be remembered that he had recently suffered the disillusionments of the Great War, the death of his brother, and the growing realization that practical politics was a dangerous and corrupt game. Regarding the last, the stories may be construed as nothing less than dissections of the criminal activity at the top of England's social and political structure.

Horne Fisher, the lean, dour cousin and secretary of an important politician, is disillusioned and corrupted by his experience with the evil of the world. "I know too much," he says at one point,"—and that's what's wrong with me." What he knows are the things that aren't worth knowing—"all the seamy side of things, all the secret reasons and rotten motives and bribery and blackmail they call politics." Thus, too distrustful of the system to entrust the criminals he exposes to the machinations of civil justice, he allows them to go free, convinced they will bring about their own punishment. Two of the stories, "The Face in the Target" and "The Hole in the Wall," rank among Chesterton's finest achievements. The first is yet another variant of the murderer-as-artist theme; the second is concerned with a miracle crime—how can a drowned body disappear from a shallow pond? The scene painting and the rich sense of allegory here are quite stunning. It is this writer's favorite Chesterton detective story.

Virtually forgotten in Chesterton's oeuvre are four detectives who appear in one story apiece in an appendix to the 1922 British edition of *The Man Who Knew Too Much.* Inspector Traill, late of Scotland Yard, solves the problem of a murderous rose in "The Garden of Smoke." A Frenchman, Paul Forain, encounters a man who is murdered twice in "The Five of Swords." An aging red-haired hermit, Father Stephen (why do so many of Chesterton's characters have fair or red hair?), is slain by a most peculiar bullet during his investigations of a diamond theft in "The Tower of Treason." And, best of all, a veritable army of investigators tackles the problem of the disappearing squire in "The Trees of Pride." This story explains how a man can be "temporarily" murdered, and it is solved by the one man who has done his utmost to incriminate himself as the murderer! It is one of the most dazzlingly executed and richly atmospheric tales in all of Chesterton.

The Chestertonian Legacy

Chesterton played a major role in the development of the English detective story in its formal, or golden, age, during the period 1920–1940. His avowed (if not always rigorously followed) rules—to play fair with the presentation of clues, to battle wits with the reader, to conceal the identity of the criminal until the climactic moment (a relatively modern innovation, after all), to construct bizarre puzzles with purely rational solutions, and to encapsulate everything into a concentrated, short-story form—have long since been established as basic tenets of the classic detective story.

Chief among those younger contemporaries who acknowledged his influence are Agatha Christie (especially in *The Mysterious Mr. Quin,* 1930), Ellery Queen (in *The Adventures of Ellery Queen,* 1934), and John Dickson Carr. "Though my youth was much influenced by Conan Doyle and Sherlock Holmes," Carr declared late in life, "a still greater influence came from Chesterton. . . . Since so many of those concern impossible situations—locked rooms, incredible disappearances logically explained, and so on. . . ." (quoted in Greene, p. 313). Moreover, Carr's finest (and most outrageous) detective, Dr. Gideon Fell, is modeled after Chesterton himself.

Father Brown, meanwhile, has gained new generations of followers via the movies and television. He first reached the screen in *Father Brown, Detective* (Paramount, 1934), with Walter Connolly in the title role. Alec Guinness essayed the role in *Father Brown* (Ealing, 1954). Both were loosely adapted from the short story "The Blue Cross." In 1973 Kenneth More portrayed Father Brown in a series of teleplays produced by Sir Lew Grade's ATV Company.

Brown's example, meanwhile, has been taken up by several notable cleric-detectives, like Sister Ursula, who appears in two novels and short stories by Anthony Boucher; Rabbi Small, who figures in Harry Kemelman's well-known series; the Reverend Randolph, a Methodist minister in stories by Charles Merrill Smith in the 1970s; Father Koesler of Detroit, in novels by William X. Kienzle; Brother Cadfael, a twelfth-century monk in a series of novels by Ellis Peters; and Monsignor John Blackwood ("Blackie") Ryan, in Father Andrew Greeley's novel, *Happy Are the Meek* (1985).

The Maze Without a Center

The foregoing notwithstanding, it must be admitted that in certain other respects Chesterton's detective stories defy easy classification. Even the casual reader may notice that no matter how vigorously Brown, Gale, Fisher, Pond, and the other detectives work to affirm order and sanity—or, in the instance of Brown, secure redemption—an ominous quality persists, a dark tone that lurks beneath the plots' motley surfaces like a sustained pedal point. Take as an example one of the most obscure of all his detective tales, a late story, "The White Pillars Murder," which appeared in *English Life* in 1925 and then was promptly forgotten until it was resurrected by Ellery Queen in 1946. While hardly his finest detective story, it may be his most disturbing. Indeed, writing in *To the Queen's Taste* (1946), Queen declared it to be "the paradoxical detective story to end all paradoxical detective stories" because its detective, Adrian Hyde, does not solve the crime, he commits it. "[Detectives] get to know about criminals by being half criminals themselves," explains Hyde's assistant about his boss, "by being of the same rotten world, by belonging to it and by betraying it, by setting a thief to catch a thief . . ." (p. 308).

Once a champion of law and order, Adrian Hyde is now lost and damned. The obvious allusion to Robert Louis Stevenson's *Dr. Jekyll and Mr. Hyde* demands further attention. Chesterton thought the "supreme moment" in Stevenson's story occurred when, as a result of his experiments, Jekyll realizes he no longer has control over Hyde. Unexpectedly, without the use of the drug, Hyde reappears and usurps Jekyll's will. Jekyll has bought power from Hell, says Chesterton in *Robert Louis Stevenson* (1928), only to find there is a flaw in the bargain: "The whole point of it is that nothing is really secure, least of all a Satanist security. The moral is that the devil is a liar, and more especially a traitor; that he is more dangerous to his friends than his foes . . ." (pp. 55–56).

Can it be that in their flirtations with chaos and darkness Chesterton's detectives lay themselves open to a similar fate? "It was a risky business," admits Gabriel Gale in "The Crime of Gabriel Gale," "to walk on the edge of the precipice like that." In "The Chief Mourner of Marne" (in *The Secret of Father Brown*), Father Brown compares himself and his brethren to "vampires of the night" who feed off of the confessions of "the men who commit the mean and revolting and real crimes." (Indeed in "The Hammer of God," Brown discovers that the murderer is none other than a fellow priest who has fallen victim to overreaching pride.) The implication here, at the very least, is that the relationship between detective and criminal can be carried so far as to border on identity.

Moreover, the bizarre aspects and nightmarish designs of many of the crimes are not always so convincingly explained away by rational means. Father Brown once admitted that the most terrifying thing in the world was a maze without a center. And we recall a particularly unsettling moment in "The Honour of Israel Gow," when he regards the decapitated form of a recently exhumed corpse and murmurs, "Gentlemen, we have come to the end of the ways. . . . We have found the truth; and the truth makes no sense" (in *The Innocence of Father Brown*). Putting it another way, as Father Brown points out in "The Arrow of Heaven," even when the secret is revealed in broad daylight, "it's still a mystery."

Nowhere is this baffling ambiguity more apparent than in Chesterton's only novel-length detective story, *The Man Who Was Thursday* (1908). Gabriel Syme, poet and employee of Scotland Yard, infiltrates the Council of Days, a mysterious gang of anarchists so-called because the members have assumed the pseudonyms of the days of the week. After a series of confrontations, Syme, under the name "Thursday," discovers that each member is, in reality, a disguised detective. Behind the scenes, meanwhile, manipulating them all is the unfathomable "Sunday," who leads Syme and the others on a wild chase across the city. "Grinning like a goblin," Sunday mocks his pursuers, declaring that man is born to search, but not necessarily to understand, the world's secrets:

> You will understand the sea, and I shall be still a riddle; you shall know what the stars are, and now know what I am. Since the beginning of the world, all men have hunted me like a wolf—kings and sages, and poets and law-givers, all the churches, and all the philosophers. But I have never been caught yet. (p. 233)

The six men fall back in bewilderment, then awe and wonder.

There has been considerable debate over the novel's underlying meaning. Perhaps Gabriel Syme is the God-seeker and holy fool—like Job and Christ—a policeman bearing the name of an angel, who reaches the limits of logic as he confronts the undecipherable riddle of life. Ian Boyd, in *The Novels of G. K. Chesterton,* argues it can be interpreted "in terms of Chesterton's sacramental view of life, according to which nature both conceals and leads to the divine" (p. 44). Chesterton himself declared darker intentions in the foreword to *The Man Who Was Thursday: A Play in Three Acts* (1926): "I was not then considering whether anything is really evil, but whether everything is really evil."

What emerges from all of this, as Jorge Luis Borges has noted, is that while most mystery writers undertake to explain the merely obscure, Chesterton frequently tackled the inexplicable. In spite of all the curbs and restraints he built around his wild imagination, nightmares as decadent, even evil, as Poe or Kafka could not be denied. Perhaps Chesterton said more than he knew when he admitted in "The Three Temples" (1909) that his stories were like the gargoyles of some gigantic cathedral: "I have to carve the gargoyles, because I can carve nothing else; I leave to others the angels and the arches and the spires" (in *Daylight and Nightmare*). Maybe Chesterton's youthful victory over the temptations of diablerie and atheism was, as Borges claims, merely provisionary, the "precarious subjection of a demoniacal will." And it is likely that his detectives, priest, policemen, and lunatics ultimately realized, however reluctantly (or unconsciously), that they too must bow to secrets that are, in Borges' words, "secret, and blind, and central."

Selected Bibliography

WORKS OF G. K. CHESTERTON

DETECTIVE FICTION

The Club of Queer Trades. London and New York: Harper, 1905.

The Innocence of Father Brown. London and New York: Cassell, 1911.

Manalive. London and New York: Nelson, 1912.

The Wisdom of Father Brown. London: Cassell, 1914.

The Man Who Knew Too Much and Other Stories. London: Cassell, 1922; abridged ed. New York: Harper, 1922.

Tales of the Long Bow. London and New York: Cassell, 1925.

The Incredulity of Father Brown. London and New York: Cassell, 1926.

The Secret of Father Brown. London and New York: Cassell, 1927.

The Poet and the Lunatics: Episodes in the Life of Gabriel Gale. London and New York: Cassell, 1929.

Four Faultless Felons. London and New York: Cassell, 1930.

The Scandal of Father Brown. London and New York: Cassell, 1935.

The Father Brown Omnibus. New York: Dodd, Mead and Co., 1951.

ESSAYS ABOUT DETECTIVE STORIES

"A Defence of Detective Stories." In *The Defendant.* London: J. M. Dent and Sons, Ltd., 1901.

"Detectives and Detective Fictions." *Illustrated London News,* 4 November 1905.

"The Duties of the Police." *Illustrated London News,* 6 May 1911.

"Edwin Drood." In *Appreciations and Criticisms of the Works of Charles Dickens.* New York: E. P. Dutton and Co., 1911.

"The Divine Detective." In *A Miscellany of Men.* London: Methuen, 1912.

"On Political Secrecy," In *All Things Considered.* New York: John Lane, 1918.

"The Domesticity of Detectives." In *The Uses of Diversity.* London: Methuen, 1920.

"A Defence of Dramatic Unities." In *Fancies Versus Fads.* London: Methuen, 1923.

"How to Write a Detective Story." *G. K.'s Weekly,* 17 October 1925.

"The World of Sherlock Holmes." *Illustrated London News,* 15 January 1927.

"On Detective Novels." In *Generally Speaking.* London: Methuen, 1928.

"On Detective Story Writers." In *Come to Think of It . . .* London: Methuen, 1930.

Introduction to *A Century of Detective Stories.* London, 1935.

"The Best Detective Story." *Detection Medley.* London: Hutchinson, 1939.

"Sherlock Holmes" Part I and Part II. In Collins, Dorothy, ed. *A Handful of Authors.* London and New York: Sheed & Ward, 1952.

OTHER WORKS

Greybeards at Play. London: R. Brimley Johnson, 1900. Poems and sketches.

The Wild Knight and Other Poems. London: Grant Richards, 1900.

The Defendant. London: J. M. Dent & Sons, Ltd., 1901. Essays.

Robert Browning. New York: Macmillan, 1903. Criticism.

The Napoleon of Notting Hill. London: John Lane, 1904.

Heretics. London: John Lane, 1905. Essays.

Charles Dickens. London: Methuen, 1906. Criticism.

The Man Who Was Thursday: A Nightmare. London: Arrowsmith, 1908.

Orthodoxy. London and New York: John Lane Co., 1909. Essays.

Tremendous Trifles. London: Methuen, 1909. Essays.

Robert Louis Stevenson. New York: Dodd, Mead and Co., 1928. Criticism.

Generally Speaking. New York: Dodd, Mead and Co., 1929. Essays.

The Floating Admiral. London: Hodder & Stoughton, 1931; New York: Doubleday, Doran, 1932. Also includes contributions from Victor Whitechurch, Dorothy L. Sayers, and others.

St. Thomas Aquinas. London: Hodder & Stoughton, 1933. Criticism.

Autobiography. New York: Sheed & Ward, 1936; London: Hutchinson, 1937.

POSTHUMOUS DETECTIVE STORY COLLECTIONS

The Paradoxes of Mr. Pond. London and New York: Cassell, 1937; New York: Dover, 1990.

Daylight and Nightmare. Edited by Marie Smith. New York: Dodd, Mead and Co., 1986.

Thirteen Detectives. Edited by Marie Smith. New York: Dodd, Mead and Co., 1987.

BIBLIOGRAPHIES

Sprug, Joseph W., ed. *An Index to G. K. Chesterton.* Washington, D.C.: University of America Press, 1966.

Sullivan, John. *G. K. Chesterton: A Bibliography.* London: University of London Press, 1958. Updated in 1968 and 1980.

White, William. "G. K. Chesterton's Father Brown: A Bibliography." *The Armchair Detective* (summer 1983).

ARCHIVES AND STUDY CENTERS

A collection of Chesterton's papers is cataloged in the Robert John Bayer Memorial Chesterton Collection at the John Carroll University Library, Cleveland, Ohio. Another extensive collection, acquired from the Dorothy Collins estate after her death in 1988, is housed at the British Library in the British Museum. Its holdings, which include more than two hundred unpublished poems, plays, and short stories, numerous sketches and photographs, and many personal possessions and articles of apparel, are being cataloged at this writing. Study centers include the G. K. Chesterton Library, administered by Aidan Mackey, located in Westminster College in Oxford; and the Chesterton Institute, directed by Christopher Corkery, in Peterborough, Ontario.

BIOGRAPHICAL AND CRITICAL STUDIES

Barker, Dudley. *G. K. Chesterton: A Biography.* New York: Stein & Day, 1973.

Belloc, Hilaire. *The Place of Gilbert Chesterton in English Letters.* London and New York: Sheed & Ward, 1940.

Bogaerts, Anthony Mattheus Adrianus. *Chesterton and the Victorian Age.* Hilversum: Rozenbeek en Venemans, 1940.

Borges, Jorge Luis. "On Chesterton." In his *Other Inquisitions, 1937–1952.* New York: Washington Square Press, 1966.

Boyd, Ian. *The Novels of G. K. Chesterton: A Study in Art and Propaganda.* New York: Barnes & Noble, 1975.

Canovan, Margaret. *G. K. Chesterton: Radical Populist.* New York and London: Harcourt Brace Jovanovich, 1977.

Chesterton, Cecil. *Gilbert K. Chesterton: A Criticism.* London and New York: John Lane, 1909.

Clemens, Cyril. *Chesterton as Seen by His Contemporaries.* Webster Groves, Mo.: Mark Twain Society, 1939.

Clipper, Lawrence J. *G. K. Chesterton.* New York: Twayne, 1974.

Coates, John. *Chesterton and the Edwardian Cultural Crisis.* Hull: Hull University Press, 1984.

Conlon, D. J., ed. *G. K. Chesterton: The Critical Judg-*

ments. Antwerp: Antwerp Studies in English Literature, 1976.

———, ed. *G. K. Chesterton: A Half Century of Views.* Oxford and New York: Oxford University Press, 1987.

Corrin, Jay P. *G. K. Chesterton and Hilaire Belloc: The Battle Against Modernity.* Athens, Ohio: Ohio University Press, 1981.

Dale, Alzina Stone. *The Outline of Sanity: A Life of G. K. Chesterton.* Grand Rapids: Eerdmans, 1982.

Ffinch, Michael. *G. K. Chesterton: A Biography.* New York: Harper & Row, 1986.

Greene, Douglas G. "A Mastery of Miracles." In the *Chesterton Review,* August 1984.

Hollis, Christopher. *The Mind of Chesterton.* London: Hollis & Carter, 1970.

Hunter, Lynette. *G. K. Chesterton: Explorations in Allegory.* New York: St. Martin's, 1979.

Kenner, Hugh. *Paradox in Chesterton.* New York: Sheed & Ward, 1947.

O'Connor, John. *Father Brown on Chesterton.* London: Muller/Burns, Oates, 1937.

Pearce, Joseph. *Wisdom and Innocence: A Life of G. K. Chesterton.* San Francisco: Ignatius Press, 1996.

Queen, Ellery. *In the Queen's Parlor.* New York: Simon & Schuster, 1957.

———. *To the Queen's Taste.* Boston: Little, Brown and Co., 1946.

Rauch, Rufus William. *A Chesterton Celebration.* Notre Dame: Notre Dame University Press, 1983.

Titterton, W. R. *G. K. Chesterton: A Portrait.* London: Organ, 1936.

Ward, Maisie. *Gilbert Keith Chesterton.* New York: Sheed & Ward, 1943.

———. *Return to Chesterton.* New York: Sheed & Ward, 1952.

Wills, Garry. *Chesterton: Man and Mask.* New York: Sheed & Ward, 1961.

NOTE

Since 1974 the *Chesterton Review* has been published by Thomas More College, Saskatoon. Several Chesterton societies publish journals, including the American Chesterton Society's *Generally Speaking* and the Ottawa Chesterton Society's *All Things Considered.* In September 1997 they merged to form the journal *Gilbert!* published monthly. The Ignatius Press of San Francisco is in the process of publishing a multivolume series of Chesterton's complete works.

AGATHA CHRISTIE

(1890–1976)

DAVID HAWKES

AGATHA CHRISTIE RETURNED to the site of Ashfield, her beloved childhood home, in 1964. To her dismay, the old house had been demolished and replaced by a modern estate consisting of "the meanest, shoddiest little houses I had ever seen" (*An Autobiography,* 1977, pp. 518–519). It was a symbolic moment and one that recalls the unwelcome postwar encroachment of "the Development" on St. Mary Mead, Christie's anachronistic fictional village whose most prominent resident is Miss Jane Marple. Christie was among the last British writers whose formative experiences took place in the Victorian era, and she never stopped looking back to her childhood memories as inspiration for her writings. She was born in 1890, and though she lived until 1976, her work betrays a discomfort with modernity and a nostalgia for the comforts and certainties of an age in which a shared morality held sway, social problems seemed solvable, and Britain was confident of its imperial destiny. This, in fact, may be the secret of Christie's enormous popularity. Her work is characterized above all by a fear of the foreign, the different, the "other." The reader senses that she is writing from within a besieged culture, a society forever on the watch for enemies disguised as friends and obsessively policing its own standards of morality, reason, and normality. The appeal of Christie's novels lies in their message that disruptive and destructive influences can be identified, contained, and eliminated through the judicious application of logic, reason, and ethics. This was a message that biography and history made Christie particularly suited to convey.

Life, Background, and Influences

Christie was born Agatha Mary Clarissa Miller on 15 September 1890 in Torquay, England, to middle-aged parents; she had a brother and sister who were more than a decade older than her. Her father, Frederick Miller, was an American with a moderate private income, which allowed the family to live in genteel comfort in Torquay, a resort town on England's south coast. Agatha Miller had a quintessentially Victorian childhood. She enjoyed the love and attention of her nurse and various other servants as well as her immediate family and her "Auntie-Grannie," a formidable figure who, through an accident of genealogy, fulfilled both of these roles with regard to Agatha. She received no formal education, never attended school on a regular basis, and was instructed at home by a succession of governesses and tutors. Her education was completed at a French "finishing school." In her autobiography, Christie recalls with gratitude and enthusiasm the instruction she received in such then desirable feminine accomplishments as music, needlework, dancing, and drawing. Although this kind of education was by no means unusual for an upper-middle-class girl at the end of the nineteenth century, it was no longer the automatic course of events that it had been fifty years earlier. Feminist and enlightened liberal campaigners had convinced many families that girls should be educated on the same subjects, and with the same thoroughness, as boys. The method and substance of Agatha's education show that the Millers were not in the vanguard of progressive opinion on the issue, and throughout her life Christie remained happy to appear unintellectual. Her autobiography contains far more grousing over servant problems than reflection on the author's trade, and she is refreshingly unconcerned with intellectual pretensions. She recalls a holiday on which the menus were "written in Yugoslavian" (*An Autobiography,* p. 411) and remarks that after the success of her first novel, "Hercule Poirot . . . was hanging round my neck, firmly attached there like the old man of the sea" (p. 263). When she was awarded the Commander of the British Empire in 1956, she delightedly and accurately exclaimed, "One up to the Low-Brows!!" (Morgan, p. 305).

Christie was a self-sufficient child who conducted fanciful and solitary games with groups of imaginary friends, among them, the "Kittens" and the "Girls." Throughout her life she guarded her privacy closely; when, at the age of four, she overheard her nurse telling a maid about her "Kittens," the little girl was profoundly disturbed and vowed never to reveal her innermost thoughts again. Later on she played games that anticipate the concerns of her novels. Agatha and her sister, Madge, frightened each other with stories of their imaginary mad "elder sister," and Madge sometimes pretended to be that sinister figure in heavy disguise. Another of Agatha's childhood fantasies featured the malevolent "gunman," whom she suddenly seemed to recognize lurking beneath the appearance of a close family member:

> Some times, as we sat round a tea-table, I would look across at a friend, or a member of the family, and I would suddenly realize that it was *not* Dorothy or Phyllis or Monty or my mother or whoever it might be. The pale blue eyes in the familiar face met mine—under the familiar appearance. *It was really the Gunman.* (*An Autobiography,* p. 25)

The motif of a trusted intimate who suddenly is revealed as a hostile, dangerous stranger recurred frequently in Agatha Christie's life and work.

When she was eleven, Agatha's father died, and his death brought serious money worries to the Millers. It was the end of Victoria's reign, and the time when the haute bourgeoisie could live well on moderate private incomes was also drawing to a close. For a time, Agatha's mother considered selling Ashfield and was dissuaded from doing so only by the anguished protests of her children. They struggled on, keeping up appearances and economizing. In 1910, Agatha had to save expense by spending her "coming out" season in Egypt rather than London. Although she was not rich, she was attractive, and she relished the male attention that was lavished on her. Back in England, she considered and then abandoned a career as an opera singer; enjoyed the leisured social round of country house parties, hunts, and regattas; and turned down several marriage proposals. In her autobiography, Christie speaks with nostalgia of a time when there was "no worry about what you should be or do—Biology would dictate. You were waiting for The Man and, when The Man came, he would change your entire life" (Morgan, p. 42).

In 1912, Agatha met a handsome young aviator named Archibald Christie at a dance. Christie was a year older, an extroverted and popular man who was among the very first people to fly an airplane. The couple fell in love, and, impelled by the outbreak of World War I, they married in 1914. Like many women, Agatha moved into professional employment as a result of the war and spent the war years working in a hospital and then in a pharmacy. When, against the odds, her husband returned from the front alive, he became a stockbroker, and the couple settled in the commuter-belt suburban town of Sunningdale, where a daughter, Rosalind, was born in 1919. Two years later, the Christies made the daring and unconventional decision to accompany a certain Major Belcher on a tour of Australia, New Zealand, South Africa, and Canada, where Archie assisted the major in publicizing a forthcoming exhibition on the virtues of empire. It was their last extravagance. When they returned to England, Archie settled down to work in the City, London's equivalent of Wall Street, devoting his spare time to an increasingly compulsive commitment to golf, while his wife presumably looked forward to an eternity of uncomplicated domestic bliss.

It is ironic that of all the women of her generation, many of whom were deeply frustrated by the barriers that their gender placed in the way of their ambition, fame and success should descend so heavily on Agatha Christie, who never sought either. In her early twenties Christie began to compose poems and short stories in much the same spirit as she had taken up dancing and singing—as a diverting and improving amusement that would pass the short time before marriage and family intervened. On the advice of a family friend, she began submitting her work to journals and publishers until, in 1920, Bodley Head published her first novel, *The Mysterious Affair at Styles,* which Christie assumed would be her only book. But the novel sold so well that she quickly composed a follow-up, and it was with an eye to continued profits that her husband encouraged Christie to carry on with her writing.

The 1920s are often referred to as the Golden Age of British detective fiction, and the public seems to have been hungry for the certitude and resolution that this genre can offer. World War I was an unprecedented shock to the European psyche, and public taste was nostalgic for the safety and assurance of an earlier age. Christie's artful, gentle, conservative style answered these demands to perfection. Her work became hugely popular, especially following the innovative and intriguing mystery *The Murder of Roger Ackroyd* (1926). The pressure of fame on a naturally reclusive character must have been considerable, and it may have contributed to the most notorious incident of Christie's generally uneventful life: her disappearance for ten days in late 1926. At the time, Christie attributed the episode to temporary amnesia. There is no reason to doubt her nor to ignore the circumstances that must have contributed to its onset. Early in 1926, Agatha's beloved mother died, and, at the same time, Archie Christie announced that he had fallen in love with a younger woman, Nancy Neele. Whether or not she suffered a bout of clinical amnesia, it seems safe to assume that Agatha's disappearance was produced by the strain of these simultaneous tragedies. Her car was found abandoned near the house where, she knew, Archie and his lover were spending the weekend. When she was found ten days later, following a well-publicized manhunt, Christie was booked into a Harrowgate hotel under the name Mrs. Neele. No one can know the precise motives or pressures that caused her actions, but the facts allow a sympathetic observer to guess at her mental processes during that period.

After abortive attempts at reconciliation, the couple agreed to a separation and eventually to a divorce in 1928. Christie was profoundly affected by the experience, which seemed to recall her childhood fears that a known and trusted person should suddenly reveal himself as a hostile "gunman." In her autobiography she recalls her feelings when Archie arrived to announce that he wanted a separation:

> I think the nearest I can get to describing what I felt at that moment is to recall an old nightmare of mine—the horror of sitting at a tea-table, looking across at my best-loved friend, and suddenly realizing that the person sitting there *was a stranger.* (pp. 337–338)

Already established as an important theme, the idea of "the enemy within" became from this point on the dominant feature of Christie's work.

Christie did not allow the emotional crises of 1926 to interfere with her writing or with her travel. In following years she took the Orient Express to the site of Ur, in Iraq, to observe Sir Leonard Woolley's excavation of the site. At the dig, she encountered Max Mallowan, a budding archaeologist fourteen years her junior. They became close friends, but the difference in their ages and the fact that Mallowan was Catholic meant that Christie was shocked when Mallowan proposed marriage, and she was initially reluctant to accept. She was eventually persuaded, however, and the couple married in 1930 and remained happy until her death on 12 January 1976. Mallowan became one of the most prominent archaeologists of his generation, and Agatha frequently accompanied him on his digs, writing about them in her memoirs and using their exotic locations as the setting for many of her novels.

After her second marriage, Agatha Christie's personal life, or at least our knowledge of it, is subsumed beneath her writing. She had been severely wounded by the press attention paid to her following her disappearance, just as she had as a four-year-old when her nurse publicly revealed the existence of her "Kittens." In both cases her response was the same: she withdrew into a private sphere, protecting herself by refusing to appear in public or to grant interviews. Her novels nevertheless sold millions, and she also published short stories and a handful of psychological romance novels under the pseudonym of Mary Westmacott and, particularly after World War II, began to write plays. One of them, *The Mousetrap,* was produced in 1952 and continued to run until 1997, making it the longest-running drama in the world. Christie's work was first adapted for film in three 1930s British films about Poirot. *Witness for the Prosecution* (1957) and several films starring Margaret Rutherford as Miss Marple were successful in the 1950s, and in the 1970s, such novels as *Murder on the Orient Express* (1934) and *Death on the Nile* (1937) were made into highly lucrative movies. Nothing gave Christie more pleasure than to be awarded the C.B.E. or to be made a Dame of the British Empire; among her proudest achievements was to have been introduced to Queen Elizabeth II. This is, in part, the secret of Agatha Christie's appeal. She shares the same middlebrow values and aspirations of her audience; she understands her public instinctively, because she is herself a part of that public; and she expresses the hopes, regrets, and fears of the public in a form that resonates profoundly with them: the detective story.

Christie's Place in the Detective Tradition

It will be easier to understand Agatha Christie's work if we distinguish between the detective genre and crime fiction in general. English literature's concern with the criminal classes dates from the sixteenth century. A criminal urban subculture of displaced people flourished in Elizabethan London, and we find it depicted in the environment of Shakespearean characters such as Falstaff. The popular "cony-catching" (hustling) pamphlets of the Elizabethan pamphleteer Robert Greene celebrated the slang, or "cant," of the underworld and displayed an intimate knowledge of the tricks and conventions of the criminal element. This tradition continued after the rise of the novel in such picaresque narratives as Daniel Defoe's *Moll Flanders* (1722) and the sensationalistic *Newgate Calender,* which first appeared in 1773. A sustained interest in the customs and mores of London's capacious underworld runs through nineteenth-century fiction and provides the major selling point of such classics as Charles Dickens' *Oliver Twist* (1838).

The work of Agatha Christie has little in common with this tradition, with its neo-documentary reportage of the criminal life. She draws instead on the strain of detective fiction that examines crime from the outside, through the eyes of those whose job it is to prevent or correct it, and approaches crime as a logical rather than a social problem. The basic features of this genre are already visible in William Godwin's *Caleb Williams* (1794), in which the title character functions like a detective, uncovering the truth about a murder. But it is not until Edgar Allan Poe's tales that we meet the prototype of the modern fictional detective: C. Auguste Dupin. An aristocratic outsider, Dupin uses his superior intellect to solve mysterious crimes in stories such as "The Murders in the Rue Morgue" (1841) and "The Purloined Letter" (1845). In England, Wilkie Collins' *The Moonstone* (1868) introduced Sergeant Cuff in a similar role, and the figure of the eccentric, hyperrational sleuth reaches its apogee in Sir Arthur Conan Doyle's Sherlock Holmes novels of the 1890s.

We can thus identify two traditions of writing about crime, which are related but which also presuppose contradictory views of what crime is and how it may be counteracted. One is the tale of the underworld, which shows an almost sympathetic fascination with criminal culture and locates that culture in a realistic social setting. The other is the mystery, or detective story, which is not concerned with crime in general or as a social problem but with particular crimes, usually murders committed by and on people from far beyond the actual criminal classes. These two traditions vied with each other throughout the nineteenth century, but by the 1920s the mystery genre had gained a definitive ascendance. In the following decade, the popularity of this genre was underlined by the foundation of The Detection Club, which included such practitioners as G. K. Chesterton and Dorothy L. Sayers. Chesterton summarized the nature of such fiction's appeal: "By dealing with the unsleeping sentinels who guard the outposts of society, it tends to remind us that we live in an armed camp, making war with a chaotic world, and that the criminals, the children of chaos, are nothing but traitors within our gates" (Haycraft, p. 5). The reasons why such an appeal should be widespread are not hard to discern. World War I, and the ensuing depression and political instability, shattered the Victorian complacency of the British bourgeoisie. Middle-class audiences did not wish to be reminded of the mutinous, subterranean hordes coveting their wealth and privileges. Far more attractive was the idea that crime can be solved by the cool application of rational thought, that it is a problem susceptible to logical detection and redress. The fiction of Agatha Christie declares, in the face of mounting evidence to the contrary, that the world is ultimately comprehensible and orderly. It does so not only through the "little grey cells" of Hercule Poirot and the observatory powers of Miss Marple but also through the style, tone, and atmosphere that Christie painstakingly creates and which fulfills at least as vital a function in her work as the more immediately obvious features of plot and narrative.

Hercule Poirot: The Sleuth As Outsider

Agatha Christie's novels were successful partly because they were formulaic, and the essential elements of this formula are already present in her first book, *The Mysterious Affair at Styles* (1920). Significantly, the story takes place during World War I—the historical watershed that, more clearly than any other, heralded the end of Britain's imperial dominance. In this book, we are introduced to Christie's most famous creation: Hercule Poirot, the dandy with the egg-shaped head who is retired from the Belgian police and living in England as a war refugee. This was a topical reference. Germany's invasion of "plucky little Belgium" had spurred Britain's entry into the war, and Belgian refugees did take shelter near the Millers in Torquay. Their status as allies and victims won for the Belgians a provisional exemption from the casual xenophobia of many Britons. As the servant Dorcas comments in this first Poirot mystery, "I don't hold with foreigners as a rule, but from what the newspapers says I make out as how these brave Belges isn't the ordinary run of foreigners" (1975 ed., p. 249).

From the outset, then, Poirot represents the sanctioned outsider. He is manifestly different from the English upper classes with whom he mixes, in nationality, intelligence, and appearance ("absurd" is the adjective most frequently used to describe him), but he is tolerated because of his uncanny sleuthing powers. In *Styles*, the less sympathetic role of the unwelcome interloper is taken by Alfred Inglethorp, the second husband of the wealthy murdered widow and thus the prime suspect in the crime. As her son, John, comments, "The fellow is an absolute outsider, anyone can see that. He's got a great black beard, and wears patent leather boots in all weathers!" (p. 160). When the narrator, Poirot's friend Captain Hastings, first sees Inglethorp, the impression is confirmed: "He certainly struck a rather alien note. I did not wonder at John objecting to his beard. It was one of the longest and blackest I had ever seen" (p. 163). There is a note of gentle self-parody here: clearly it does not take much to be labeled an "outsider" in the social milieu that Christie depicts with such affectionate intimacy, and we are not surprised when the murderer turns out to be a much less obvious candidate.

There is also running through Christie's work a real, serious fear of outsiders, of people who are different from "us," of what post-modern literary theorists call "the Other." For a writer of her period, background, and education, the results could be unfortunate. Here are John and Mary, a sympathetic young couple, arguing over a male friend of hers:

> "I've had enough of the fellow hanging about. He's a Polish Jew, anyway."
>
> "A tinge of Jewish blood is not a bad thing. It leavens the"—she looked at him—"stolid stupidity of the ordinary Englishman." (p. 259)

When this character is later revealed as a German spy, Poirot mentions that he is "a very clever man—a Jew, of course" (p. 268), and much of Christie's fiction can be marred, for a late-twentieth-century reader, by this kind of casual, unreflective stereotyping. Rather than try to explain it away as an unfortunate lapse of taste, we would do well to consider this tendency as integral to the effect and power that Christie's work held for the middlebrow audience she addressed. In fact, the appeal of the Hercule Poirot stories lies in their exorcism of the Other by the Other—the defeat of the disguised, malevolent stranger by the openly foreign, amiably comic one. We recall here Christie's childhood phobias of the "older sister" and the "gunman"—sinister and hostile figures whose terror lay in their ability to appear as a familiar and trusted friend or family member. In almost every Christie book, there is a moment like that in *Styles* when John realizes that the murderer must be an intimate acquaintance: "There's no one else; no one, I mean, except—one of us" (p. 260). It is precisely the fact that Poirot is *not* "one of us" that gives him his unique perspective on the English upper classes and thus allows him to deduce the identity of the miscreant among them.

The pleasure that Christie's work invites us to share is that of the exposure and elimination of the alien presence by means of what is presented as rational, or "scientific," methodology. In a secular world whose last illusions about progress and civilization were floundering in the mud of the Somme, the notion that science and reason can discern an order beneath a chaotic appearance was deeply comforting. Poirot's method boils down to a doctrinaire empiricist positivism, an unshakable conviction that isolated bits of physical data—or "clues"—can be pieced together to reveal a consistent pattern of events. As he describes his procedure:

> "One fact leads to another—so we continue. Does the next fit in with that? A *merveille!* Good! We can proceed. This next little fact—no! Ah that is curious! There is something missing—a link in the chain that is not there. We examine. We search. And that little curious fact, that possibly paltry little detail that will not tally, we put it here!" He made an

extravagant gesture with his hand. "It is significant! It is tremendous!" (p. 184)

Most of the "clues" that fuel Poirot's deductive powers are pieces of purely physical evidence, and he perceives a semiotic significance in the objects around him that eludes less rigorous observers. But he also draws conclusions from observing people's conduct, and here again his outsider's perspective allows him to perceive what is hidden from the other characters. His interrogative technique is probing and suggestive, designed to bring out unconscious impulses and to establish a coherent pattern underlying seemingly random events. Here is a typical passage from *Styles:*

> "Shall I tell you why you have been so vehement against Mr. Inglethorp? It is because you have been trying to believe what you wish to believe. It is because you are trying to drown and stifle your instinct, which tells you another name—"
>
> "No, no, no!" cried Miss Howard wildly, flinging up her hands. "Don't say it! Oh, don't say it! It isn't true! It can't be true! I don't know what put such a wild—such a dreadful—idea into my head!"
>
> "I am right, am I not?" asked Poirot.
>
> "Yes, yes; you must be a wizard to have guessed." (p. 253)

Many of what became the conventional devices of Christie's fiction were already present in *Styles.* There is a concern with and close technical knowledge of poisons—the result of Christie's wartime experience in the pharmacy. There are the playful intertextual references, often connected to the "idiot narrator" figure of Captain Hastings, who mentions "a secret hankering to be a detective . . . Sherlock Holmes by all means" (p. 164). The humor springs from the reader's knowledge of the Holmes books, which tells us that Hastings approximates more closely the dimwitted Dr. Watson than the famous sleuth of Baker Street. Like Holmes, Poirot's character is an assemblage of various eccentricities—obsessive neatness, pomposity, a tendency to lapse into foreign idioms ("ah, triple pig," p. 213). The working classes are presented as cheerful idiots, and we usually encounter them in the guise of servants (although, significantly, the murderer is rarely a servant but almost always "one of us"). As in virtually all of Christie's novels, the main characters are united by class, nationality, and outlook. The dramatic tension arises from our knowledge that one of them is not the true insider—the "pukka sahib"—that he or she appears to be. And the catharsis at the book's end is produced by the sense that this interloper has been removed, restoring the homogeneity and equanimity that reigned before the unfortunate disruption.

The Murder of Roger Ackroyd is Christie's most formally accomplished and critically acclaimed work, though it was attacked by purist aficionados of the detective genre for not being "fair" to the reader by providing all the information needed to deduce the identity of the murderer. Credit for the idiosyncratic twist in the plot that caused the outrage—the murderer turns out to be the narrator, Dr. Sheppard—has been claimed by Lord Louis Mountbatten, who wrote a letter to Christie suggesting such a device in 1924. No matter whose idea it was originally, the device of the murderer-narrator is a perfectly logical development of Christie's persistent theme of the "secret adversary," or enemy within.

As usual, *Ackroyd* makes frequent ironic references to the generic conventions: "I played Watson to his Sherlock," Sheppard remarks (1943 ed., p. 165). Poirot himself enjoys a dual existence, as a character in the present work and also as a character in books—we gather that his previous adventures are known to the people among whom he lives in "real" life. At one point, Sheppard reveals to Poirot that he has been keeping a written record of the events as they unfold: "I've read some of Captain Hastings' narratives, and I thought, why not try my hand at something of the same kind?" (p. 270). Poirot then takes on the role of the reader: he studies Sheppard's narrative just as we do, but unlike us, he is able to deduce from it the identity of the murderer, thus demonstrating the truth of his conviction that "everything is simple, if you arrange the facts methodically" (p. 91). The fact that this is not strictly true—that it is actually very difficult to identify Sheppard through logical deduction on the basis of the evidence provided by the text—bothered many readers, who felt that making Sheppard the murderer was an underhand concession to bizarre modernist trickery. It also, however, serves the purpose of exalting Poirot above the reach of the common intellect. Having him read the same account of events as we do merely accentuates his consistent superiority of deductive power. We have the same evidence available to us as he does, and yet we are unable to reason our way to the correct conclusions.

Once again, Christie indicates his intellect by emphasizing his difference from the people around him: "Poirot became suddenly very foreign in manner, as he often did when excited over anything" (p. 147), comments Sheppard, and another character remarks that he is "just like a comic Frenchman in a revue" (p. 167). The xenophobia of the English characters often approaches the dimensions of camp, as when one character bemoans her encounters with debt collectors to Sheppard:

> "And then I got a letter from a Scotch gentleman—as a matter of fact there were two letters—both Scotch gentlemen, Mr. Bruce MacPherson was one, and the other were Colin MacDonald. Quite a coincidence."
>
> "Hardly that," I said dryly. "They are usually Scotch gentlemen, but I suspect a Semitic strain in their ancestry." (p. 170)

This prejudice impedes the rational faculties of the English and prevents them from evaluating the case on its merits. It also hinders them from taking Poirot seriously. Being free from their parochial assumptions, Poirot is able to penetrate their innermost thoughts. In passages such as the following one, the theme of the enemy within is internalized, through Poirot's psychological acumen:

> "Every one of you in this room is concealing something from me." He raised his hand as a faint murmur of protest arose. "Yes, yes, I know what I am saying. It may be something unimportant—trivial—which is supposed to have no bearing on the case, but there it is. *Each one of you has something to hide.* Come, now, am I right?" His glance, challenging and accusing, swept round the table. And every pair of eyes dropped before his. Yes, mine as well. (p. 155)

In *The Murder of Roger Ackroyd,* then, the enemy is "within" in two senses. First of all, it is the narrator, the one character whom the reader accustomed to realist conventions naturally expects to be trustworthy and reliable, who turns out to be the killer. This produces a disturbing effect on a reader who has learned to identify with the narrator of a novel. As a correlative, there is a greater stress here on psychology, on unconscious motivation, on the feeling that even within our own minds there lurks an unsuspected capacity for evil and destruction. The influence of Freudian ideas is discernible, but there is also an intensification of the generalized paranoia that characterizes Christie's presentation of the world.

The influence of psychology and psychoanalysis on criminology posed an obvious dilemma for writers of crime fiction. Since the time of Fyodor Dostoyevsky, writers had often suggested that murderers were frequently psychotic, motivated by unconscious fears and desires. And yet the classic detective story presupposes a rational motive for murder, one that can be logically deduced by the hyperreasonable sleuth. Christie examines this problem in *The A.B.C. Murders* (1936). By this stage in her career, she was confident enough with her familiar stock devices to begin to experiment with them. The narrator-as-character has disappeared, and the bizarre xenophobia of the British is presented at a distance, through an impersonal voice and, significantly, usually conveyed by looks and gestures rather than stated aloud. Of one character it is reported that on encountering Poirot, "his manner said: 'Really—these foreigners! All the same!'" (1977 ed., p. 65), while another is said to give the Belgian "an 'Oh, these foreigners' look" (p. 69). It is much clearer that Poirot's advantage lies precisely in the fact that he is so "foreign." This means that he is constantly underestimated by his prey and that he is able to use his outsider's perspective to reach a comprehensive understanding of the British psyche, not available to natives. At one stage Hastings asks Poirot why he didn't question a suspect directly. Poirot answers:

> No, *mon ami.* If I had "simply asked" as you put it, I should have got no answer at all to my questions. You yourself are English and yet you do not seem to appreciate the quality of the English reaction to a direct question. It is invariably one of suspicion and the natural result is reticence. If I had asked those people for information they would have shut up like oysters. (pp. 42–43)

There is a sense in which the outsider understands the culture better than the natives. When finally the murderer is revealed to be a character who has made several racist remarks during the story, Poirot is able to announce that he has become more British than the British: "You are full of a very insular superiority, but for myself I consider your crime not an English crime at all—not above board—not *sporting*" (p. 244). Christie implies that it is foolish to identify people as "one of us" on the basis of the way they *seem* to be. Again and again in her plots, the comically alien little Belgian is shown to be more truly "one of us" than the most outwardly "pukka" of "sahibs." Christie has been attacked for racism and anti-Semitism, but if one disregards certain automatic assumptions and usages of her background and era, the message of her books is that morality and virtue do not always reside in worldly status and cultural respectability.

The murderer in *A.B.C.* is not "English," not "sporting," because he has tried to frame an innocent man. The "A.B.C. murders" at first appear to be the work of a psychotic serial killer who is simply working his way through the alphabet, killing first anyone with the initial A, then B, and so forth. As Poirot remarks, this demands a departure from the traditional conventions of detective fiction:

> Always, up to now, it has fallen to our lot to work from the *inside.* It has been the history of the *victim* that was important. The important points have been: "Who benefitted by the death? What opportunities had those round him to commit the crime?" It has always been the "*crime intime.*" Here, for the first time in our association, it is cold-blooded, impersonal murder. Murder from the *outside.* (p. 103)

It is the apparently motiveless malignity of this murderer that puzzles Poirot. Circumstantial evidence foists suspicions on an eccentric character whose initials happen to be A.B.C., but the special nature of this case makes Poirot reluctant to accept the evidence of the facts without psychological corroboration. He raises this objection to Hastings, who begins to interrupt:

> "Of course, if you treat him like a psychological study," I began.
>
> "What else has this case been since the beginning? All along I have been groping my way—trying *to get to know the murderer.* And now I realize, Hastings, *that I do not know him at all!* I am at sea." (p. 19)

The lack of a motive, even the irrational motive of a lunatic, prevents Poirot from accusing the man indicated by the evidence. Eventually it turns out that the real murderer is someone quite sane, whose real target was one of the victims in particular, but who committed the other crimes in order to make the sequence appear to be the work of a psychopath. A rational motive is thus revealed beneath the apparently irrational pattern of events, and what appeared to be an anomalous case is shown to fit into the traditional detective pattern. It is a testimony to Christie's enormous influence, recently spread yet further by television productions of her Poirot stories starring David Suchet, and the Miss Marple television series, that this innovation has become a commonplace of detective fiction. Poirot draws from this the conclusion that rational logic and experience are the only elements necessary to solve a crime and that what seems irrational at first is only the incomplete manifestation of a deeper rationality:

> But what is often called an intuition is really *an impression based on logical deduction or experience.* When an expert feels that there is something wrong about a picture or a piece of furniture or the signature on a cheque he is really basing that feeling on a host of small signs and details. He has no need to go into them minutely—his experience obviates that—the net result is *the definite impression that something is wrong.* But it is not a *guess,* it is an impression based on *experience.* (p. 230)

Speeches like this one also represent Christie's stand against newer forms of detective fiction, such as the psychological thriller or the "hard-boiled,"gritty, and realistic school of American crime writing represented by Raymond Chandler and Dashiell Hammett. Her work remained determinedly formulaic, and when, as happened increasingly as her career progressed, she varied the location of her stories, she did so only in order to emphasize more strongly the familiar nature of the action described. In *Death on the Nile,* the cast of characters is simply uprooted from an English country house and placed on a tourist expedition in Egypt. They interact very little with the locals, and apart from the occasional visit to an ancient monument, the action could be taking place in Torquay. With Hercule Poirot an established figure in British popular culture, Christie was able to indulge her penchant for intertextual allusiveness. Poirot both is and is not a fictional character, as we discover from the other passengers' reactions to his presence:

> "That's Hercule Poirot, the detective. . . . That funny little man!"
>
> Tim said: "What on earth's he doing out here?"
>
> His mother laughed. "Darling, you sound quite excited. Why do men enjoy crime so much? I hate detective stories and never read them. But I don't think M. Poirot is here with any ulterior motive. He's made a good deal of money and he's seeing life, I fancy." (1965 ed., p. 43)

When Mrs. Allerton remarks that "men enjoy crime" she means, of course, that they enjoy crime fiction. We are not to suppose here that Poirot is a real detective about whom several nonfiction accounts have been written. He is a character from "detective stories." The appearance of an overtly fictional character signals that we are not to expect a realistic depiction of either the criminal act or the exotic setting. Agatha Christie's novels are morality dramas, with no need of detailed characterization or accurate description. As usual, Poirot's most pronounced characteristic is his foreignness, and this gives him the scientific perspective of an anthropologist on the English. The following exchange is typical:

> "You must understand that, though I am a foreigner, I know something of the English point of view. I know, for instance, that there are 'things which are done' and things which are 'not done'."
>
> Jim Fanthorp grinned.
>
> "We don't say that sort of thing much nowadays, sir."
>
> "Perhaps not, but the custom, it still remains." (p. 266)

Poirot's is a temporal as well as a geographical otherness—he is not only from another country but also from another time. Like her hero, Christie also began to view the present from the critical perspective of the past as she grew older, and larger themes begin sometimes to intrude into her work. Christie seems to be essaying an allusion to Dostoyevsky's *Crime and Punishment* (1866) when she gives an alienated young leftist a speech worthy of Raskolnikov:

> "What good has that woman ever been to anyone or anything? She's never worked or

> lifted a finger. She's just battened on other people. She's a parasite—and a damned unpleasant parasite. There are a lot of people on this boat I'd say the world could do without." (pp. 109–110)

Perhaps predictably, this young man does not turn out to be a murderer. But his position is countered by Poirot, who insists on the absolute sanctity of human life: "I believe it is the unforgivable offence—to kill" (p. 73). This will become a frequent saying of Poirot's, and even more so of Miss Marple's. Christie seems to be endowing her characters with a sense of purpose and higher mission. They frequently repeat that the taking of human life is never permissible. At one stage Poirot remarks that some murders have been committed out of "beneficence":

> Oh, yes, Madame. I have known of—shall we say A?—being removed by B solely in order to benefit C. Political murders often come under that heading. Someone is considered to be harmful to civilization and is removed on that account. Such people forget that life and death are the affair of the good God. (p. 89)

Of course, the paradox lying behind this affirmation of the sanctity of life is that Christie wrote, for the most part, at a time when the penalty for murder was death. In identifying the criminal, then, the detective inevitably causes the loss of another life. If we are to judge from her autobiography, this would have given Christie little concern. There she recalls the atmosphere of 1914, when "we had not then begun to wallow in psychology" and crime was a simple matter of right against wrong: "I was, like everyone else who wrote books or read them, *against* the criminal and *for* the innocent victim" (p. 424). Of one convicted of murder, Christie asks:

> Why should they not execute him? We have taken the lives of wolves, in this country; we didn't try to teach the wolf to lie down with the lamb—I doubt really if we could have. We hunted down the wild boar in the mountains before he came down and killed the children by the brook. Those were our enemies—and we destroyed them. What can we do to those who are tainted with the germs of ruthlessness and hatred, for whom other people's lives go for nothing? They are often the ones with good homes, good opportunities, good teaching, yet they turn out to be, in plain English, *wicked.* Is there a cure for wickedness? What can one do with a killer? . . . The best answer we ever found, I suspect, was transportation. A vast land of emptiness, peopled only with primitive human beings, where man could live in simpler surroundings. (p. 426)

But by 1977, when these words were published, there was little land peopled exclusively by primitives available for such measures, and Christie therefore considers an alternative:

> The only hope, it seems to me, would be to sentence such a creature to compulsory service for the benefit of the community in general; you might allow your criminal the choice between the cup of hemlock and offering himself for medical research, for instance. There are many fields of research, especially in medicine and healing, where a human subject is vitally necessary—animals will not do. At present, it seems to me, the scientist himself, a devoted researcher, risks his own life, but there *could* be human guinea pigs, who accepted a certain period of experiment in lieu of death, and who, if they survived it, would then have redeemed themselves, and could go forth free men, with the mark of Cain removed from their foreheads. (p. 426)

These are hardly unusual sentiments among people of Christie's class, age, and educational level. But they are interesting in a writer of detective fiction because they confirm many of the tendencies we have already noted in her work. First, there is a scornful disregard for the notion that social deprivation is a contributory factor to crime—killers "often" come from "good" backgrounds, and as in Christie's fiction they may be outwardly indistinguishable from other members of their milieu. Second, Christie dismisses "psychology," with its clinicalization of crime and consequent impulse to understand and help the criminal. Rather, she asserts, criminals are *naturally* wicked—they are predators analogous to wolves or (somewhat confusingly) child-killing wild boar. Finally, the criminal ceases, by his breach of the social contract, to be a fully human being. Any indignity, from death to the torture of forcibly being turned into a human subject for medical research, can legitimately be inflicted on those who take human life.

This remains the implicit position of Christie's work on matters of crime and punishment. The one significant exception to this rule is the most famous of all her works: *Murder on the Orient Express.* In this book, the mystery is that the clues seem to point in several different directions. Or rather, they seem to do so if the reasoning used is based upon stereotype and caricature. Thus, one official declares, "Depend upon it, it was a woman. Only a woman would stab like that" (1991 ed., p. 42), while another remarks, "That is the act of a man driven almost crazy with a frenzied hate—it suggests rather the Latin temperament" (p. 53). Poirot disagrees:

> "Do not Italians stab?"
>
> "Assuredly," said Poirot. "Especially in the heat of a quarrel. But this—this is a different kind of crime. I have the little idea, my friend, that this is a crime very carefully planned and staged. It is a far-sighted, long-headed crime. It is not—how shall I express it?—a *Latin* crime. It is a crime that shows traces of a cool, resourceful, deliberate brain—I think an Anglo-Saxon brain." (p. 137)

Poirot refuses the other characters' convictions that the crime must have been committed by a particular kind of person. He also rejects the notion that there is a particular kind of person who could *not* have committed the crime. At one stage, Colonel Arbuthnot speaks to him on behalf of a fellow passenger:

> "About Miss Debenham," he said rather awkwardly. "You can take it from me that she's all right. She's a *pukka sahib.*"
>
> Flushing a little, he withdrew.
>
> "What," asked Dr. Constantine with interest, "does a *pukka sahib* mean?"
>
> "It means," said Poirot, "that Miss Debenham's father and brothers were at the same kind of school as Colonel Arbuthnot was."
>
> "Oh!" said Dr. Constantine, disappointed. "Then it has nothing to do with the crime at all."
>
> "Exactly," said Poirot. (p. 124)

Poirot's intellectual superiority is now explicitly connected to his freedom from these blinkered Anglo-Saxon assumptions. When he first meets Arbuthnot, we're told that "Poirot, reading the English mind correctly, knew that he had said to himself: 'Only some damned foreigner' " (p. 8). The advantage thus gained enables him to deduce that every single passenger was involved in the crime—that it was a conspiracy for revenge on the victim, an evil child murderer named Cassetti. In this case, the sanctity of life does not seem to apply. Many characters observe of Cassetti that "Such a man wasn't fit to live!" (p. 79), and Poirot endorses their opinion when, having solved the case, he refrains from involving the police. It seems that it is not so much the taking of life that is wrong, nor the breaking of the law, but the condition of being what Christie calls "wicked." Having demonstrated his wickedness, Cassetti forgoes, in the eyes of Poirot and of his creator, the right to a legal trial and even the right to live. This is not, of course, a logically or legally respectable position. It is a visceral response to a fear of "crime" that springs from the sense that established values and moralities are being displaced by chaotic and alien forces. This was a fear shared by many people in the early and mid-twentieth century, and the novels of Agatha Christie give it one of its more representative expressions.

Christie's Other Detectives

Hercule Poirot was temporarily abandoned for Christie's follow-up to *Styles, The Secret Ad-*

versary (1922). This is her most explicitly political and topical work. The basic premise of the plot is stated early on:

> Bolshevist gold is pouring into the country for the specific purpose of procuring a revolution. And there is a certain man, a man whose real name is unknown to us, who is working in the dark for his own ends. The Bolshevists are behind the Labour unrest—but this man is *behind the Bolshevists.* Who is he? We do not know. (p. 226)[1]

Christie is writing in the panic-stricken aftermath of the war, when abortive revolutions were breaking out all over Europe, and in her book Britain seems about to undergo a similar fate. The leaders of the parliamentary Labour Party are specifically said to be working with the Bolsheviks, who are represented in the novel by the sinister Kramenin. A general strike is threatened, and "sensational hints of a Labour *coup d'etat* were freely reported" (p. 391). The job of uncovering the mastermind of the plot falls to Christie's least sympathetic protagonists, the winsome young couple of Tuppence Cowley and Tommy Beresford, whose burgeoning romance provides a rather distracting subplot. Tuppence, as her gender-neutral name suggests, is given few distinctively feminine characteristics, and she and Tommy seem more or less interchangeable. The essentials of their perspective on the world can be gathered from such expostulations as: "I know it's the fashion to run down the police. I rather believe in them myself" (p. 325) and "That's the worst of you foreigners. You can't keep calm" (p. 328).

The plot develops around the question of which of Tuppence and Tommy's two genial father figures, Julius Hersheimmer or Sir James Peel Edgerton, will turn out to be "Mr. Brown," the "secret adversary" of the title. The formulaic features of Christie's novels are here given an explicitly partisan coloring. The enemies within are leftist subversives and foreigners; one can never tell where they may be lurking, and their influence must be rooted out before they destroy everything that has made Britain great. This is the subtext that runs through most of Christie's work, but in *The Secret Adversary* these anxieties are made overt, as they also are in *The Secret of Chimneys* (1925). This book features an exiled Eastern European monarch in conflict with the "Comrades of the Red Hand," while England is in thrall to dubious financial interests, symbolized by the stereotypical Jew, Herman Isaacstein, whose name is constantly mispronounced by the Anglo-Saxon characters. This is casual prejudice rather than aggressive anti-Semitism, and although it is doubtless telling that Christie should repeatedly employ Jews to signify the alien, they, like Christie's other "outsiders," are apparent rather than real menaces—the serious threat is always from within.

The character of Miss Jane Marple is descended from Caroline, Dr. Sheppard's sister in *The Murder of Roger Ackroyd.* A spinster, she makes it her business to be aware of everything that happens in her village. With the assistance of her "Intelligence Corps," we are told, "Caroline can do any amount of finding out by sitting placidly at home" (p. 1). Christie has intuited that maiden ladies, with their leisure to observe and their aptitude for gossip, share much in common with the information-gathering sleuth, and she explored this insight at greater length in *The Murder at the Vicarage* (1930). Here we are introduced to Miss Jane Marple, an elderly spinster of modest independent means, who resides in a Disneyesque caricature of an English country village, St. Mary Mead. The stock characters of such an environment abound—vicars, yokels, squires, and numerous old ladies just like Miss Marple. In sharp contrast to Poirot, then, Jane Marple is the quintessential insider—a figure so absolutely typical of her surroundings that she blends into and becomes a part of them. Of course, it is just this identity as the stereotypical genteel old maid that makes her so atypical of fictional detec-

1. Page numbers refer to *The Mysterious Affair at Styles and The Secret Adversary: An Agatha Christie Omnibus* (1998).

tives. In *4:50 from Paddington* (1957), a police inspector has to fight back patronizing terminology as he reports Sir Henry Clithering's opinion of Miss Marple:

> "Just the finest detective God ever made—natural genius cultivated in a suitable soil. He told me never to despise the"—Dermot Craddock paused for a moment to seek for a synonym for 'old pussies'—er—"elderly ladies. He said they could usually tell you what might have happened, what ought to have happened, and even what actually did happen! And . . . they can tell you why it happened. He added that this particular—er—elderly lady was at the top of the class." (1984 ed., pp. 143–144)

Poirot, of course, stands out and attracts constant attention, both for his "foreign" appearance and for his fame as a detective. It is this quality of difference that makes possible his insights. In Miss Marple's case, the reverse is true: she never seeks, and rarely receives, credit for her sleuthing, which is successful because she is so much at one with her environment as to be practically invisible. Like Christie herself, Miss Marple's powers of observation are closely linked to her ability to identify and empathize with the people around her. As she explains in *The Murder at the Vicarage*:

> My hobby is—and always has been—Human Nature. So varied—and so very fascinating. . . . One begins to class people, quite definitely, just as though they were birds, or flowers, group so-and-so, genus this, species that. Sometimes, of course, one makes mistakes, but less and less as time goes on. And then, too, one tests oneself. (1958 ed., p. 252)

What this lifetime of observation has taught her is, above all, the ability to spot "a wrong 'un" at a great distance. "I'm afraid that observing human nature for as long as I have done, one gets not to expect very much from it" (p. 29), she tells the vicar, and her serene confidence in human depravity forms a comic contrast to the vicar's naive optimism.

The village of St. Mary Mead is not quite timeless, but change is always perceived as a negative development. After World War II, "the Development"—a modern housing estate—is constructed on the outskirts, though its proletarian inhabitants remain shadowy and anonymous. The maids, whom Miss Marple continues to employ in spite of her slender means, deteriorate in quality. The dominant tone of the Miss Marple books, even more than that of the Poirot stories, is one of nostalgia. Already in the second Marple novel, *The Body in the Library* (1942), a troubling breakdown in traditional order is suggested, when the body of a manifestly lower-class young woman is found in Colonel Bantry's library. Village gossip is quick to put the affair down to an illicit romance, but in fact the motive for murder concerns another perennial Christie theme: the acquisition of "old" money by the nouveau riche. The wealthy Conway Jefferson, having lost his immediate family in an airplane accident that has left him partly paralyzed, decides to adopt the eighteen-year-old working-class dancer Ruby Keene as his companion, nurse, and heiress. This disinherits his son and daughter-in-law, who are thus the most obvious suspects when Ruby is murdered. In this book, it is Miss Marple's explicitly feminine experience that allows her to make the breakthrough in the investigation by deducing the true identity of the dead body.

Although their main protagonist could not be more different from Poirot, the Marple books continue to employ many of the same stock devices. As Christie's career progressed, her self-referential jokes became more pronounced. In *The Body in the Library,* one character shows Miss Marple his autograph collection, which includes the signature of Agatha Christie, while Colonel Bantry tells his wife:

> You've been dreaming Dolly. It's that detective story you were reading—*The Clue of the Broken Match.* You know, Lord Edgbaston finds a beautiful blonde dead on the library hearthrug. Bodies are always being found in

libraries in books. I've never known a case in real life. (1988 ed., pp. 4–5)

The Marple books differ from the Poirot stories, however, in the relationship between the amateur detective and the police. Whereas Poirot enjoys the respect if not always the affection of Inspector Japp, Miss Marple is despised as an "interfering old pussy" by the representative of the police in St. Mary Mead, Inspector Slack. Whereas she is able to solve the case because of her feminine skill at watching and listening, Slack is blinded by his inability to observe: "Activity was always to Inspector Slack's taste. To rush off in a car, to silence rudely those people who were anxious to tell him things, to cut short conversations on the plea of urgent necessity. All this was the breath of life to Inspector Slack" (p. 40). The most desirable skills in a detective, Christie shows through Miss Marple, are the feminine ones of sensitivity and empathy, rather than the masculine ones of action and decisiveness. Christie would have been horrified to hear herself called a "feminist," but the Miss Marple books suggest that the heroine's uncanny deductive powers derive largely from the fact that she is a woman.

Drama and the Westmacott Novels

During World War II, Christie experimented by adapting one of her novels, published in Britain under the regrettable title *Ten Little Niggers* (1939), for the stage. Under the title *Ten Little Indians* it was a great success, and in subsequent years she produced several pieces written or adapted for the theater, including *The Mousetrap.* Christie's plays restate the essential themes and actions of her novels, but they do so in a starker, simplified form, avoiding the sometimes confusing plethora of similar characters who populate her longer works.

The premise of *Ten Little Indians* recalls the idea, expressed in *The Murder of Roger Ackroyd,* that everyone is guilty of something. As soon as all the characters are assembled in one room, the lights cut out, and a recorded voice is heard enumerating a list of terrible sins that each of them is said to have committed. One of them, Captain Lombard, soon admits that he is guilty as charged—he once abandoned his company of native soldiers to die in the jungle: "Not quite the act of a pukka sahib, I'm afraid. But after all, self-preservation's a man's first duty. And natives don't mind dying, you know. They don't feel about it as Europeans do" (p. 31). It soon emerges that all of these outwardly respectable characters have terrible sins on their consciences—sins that, for various reasons, earthly justice has failed to punish. At one point, two characters debate the possibility of divine retribution. One of them, Judge Wargrave, is skeptical and announces that "in my experience of ill doing, Providence leaves the work of conviction and chastisement to us mortals" (p. 40). This takes on deeper significance when Wargrave finally reveals himself as the murderer in a crazed speech:

> Silence in Court! If there is any more noise, I shall have the Court cleared. It's all right, my dear. It's all right. Don't be frightened. This is a Court of Justice. You'll get justice here. . . . You know . . . all my life I've wanted to take life,—yes, to take life. I've had to get what enjoyment I could out of sentencing the guilty to death. . . . I always enjoyed that—but it wasn't enough. I wanted more—I wanted to do it myself with my own hands. . . . But I'm a Judge of the High Court. I've got a sense of justice. . . . You were all guilty, you know, but the Law couldn't touch you, so I had to take the Law into my own hands. (p. 76)

A familiar theme of detective fiction is the conflict between the law and a higher sense of justice; in order to exploit this issue, most heroes of the genre, like Poirot and Miss Marple, are not cast as policemen. Poirot himself favors justice above the law in cases like the one in *Orient Express.* In this instance, however, Wargrave is clearly motivated by a psychotic pleasure in killing, which he has rationalized as fulfilling the demands of justice. Furthermore, he has made a mistake. Captain Lombard did not in fact abandon his troops to die. On the contrary, he turns out to share with Christie and Poirot the conviction that killing is the unforgivable sin: "I've broken most of the commandments in my time—and I'm no saint. But there's one thing I won't stand for and that's murder" (p. 75). In a departure from the novel, Lombard is absolved and survives to expose Wargrave and to marry another character. In this play, the character who expresses regard for sanctity of life defeats the figure who demands retribution on evildoers.

In *The Mousetrap* the motif of the alien is given a new twist by the introduction of two gay characters, Christopher Wren ("I always think that policemen are very attractive," p. 308) and Miss Casewell, "a young woman of a manly type" (p. 293). These figures are certainly played for laughs, but they are not unsympathetic. Neither of them is the murderer, who once again turns out to be the one character in whom the audience is encouraged to trust—the investigating Detective Sergeant Trotter. Before this is revealed, however, Trotter has succeeded in planting suspicions in the minds of other characters that the killer may be their own closest relation. As the young heroine Mollie Ralston cries when suspicion is thrown on her husband:

> I don't know what the Sergeant thinks. And he can make you think things about people. You ask yourself questions and begin to doubt. You feel that somebody you love and know well might be—a stranger. That's what happens in a nightmare. You're somewhere in the middle of friends and then you suddenly look at their faces and they're not your friends any longer—they're different people—just pretending. Perhaps you can't trust anybody—perhaps everybody's a stranger. (p. 335)

This is, in fact, the logical conclusion of Christie's fiction. If not even one's most intimate lovers and relatives can be trusted, then we are reduced to a Hobbesian "war of all against all," in which society splits up into mutually antagonistic atomic units. In the novels, there is always the reassuring presence of Poirot or Miss Marple, who can unfailingly perceive the rotter lurking beneath the benign facade. The plays, however, lack any such reliable authority. Indeed, the figures who might have been expected to play that role frequently reveal themselves to be the villains of the pieces. The result is that the audience is kept in a state of doubt and confusion throughout the action and is made to feel implicated in Trotter's ironically accurate remark that "one might almost believe that you're all guilty by the looks of you" (p. 351). Christie often seems to suggest that we are all guilty, but in *The Mousetrap* and *Ten Little Indians,* as in *Murder on the Orient Express,* the fact that all the characters carry some burden on their consciences does not detract from the exorbitantly evil nature of the killer—he or she who commits the unforgivable sin of murder.

The theme of *Witness for the Prosecution* (1954; produced 1953) concerns the attempt to assimilate the alien other into normative British codes of social, ethical, and legal conduct. The "witness" of the title is Romaine Heilger, a "foreigner" who is testifying against her husband, Leonard Vole, in a murder trial. His defense lawyer notices that the jury seems to dislike her: "To begin with, she's a foreigner, and they distrust foreigners. . . . And at the end of it all, she's not sticking to her man when he's down. We don't like that in this country" (p. 430). The idea that spousal loyalty is a peculiarly British phenomenon passes without demur, and Romaine's betrayal of her man clearly marks her as a continental. When, under cross-examination, she admits to having forged a letter in order to convict Leonard, the prosecutor cautions her in similar terms: "Being a foreigner you may not quite realize the responsibilities that lie upon you when you take the oath in an English court" (p. 444). As the twists of the plot intensify toward the denouement, it transpires that all along she has been testifying with the intention of ensuring her husband's acquittal by revealing her own perjury. The defense lawyer protests, "But couldn't you trust me? We believe, you know, that our British system of justice upholds the truth. We'd have got him off" (p. 448). Given the evidence against her husband, however, Romaine is skeptical. It seems that we are again being presented with the dilemma of the law being opposed to true justice. The "British system" in this instance would have executed an innocent man, and it took the intervention of the alien foreign presence to prevent this miscarriage. At this point, however, it is revealed that Leonard is actually guilty of the murder. Now the "British system" seems to have been subverted, and a guilty man has gotten away scot free. Finally, we discover that Romaine's husband has been deceiving her with another woman; in a fit of rage Romaine stabs him to death. He thus pays the penalty for his crime after all, and justice triumphs where the law had been defeated.

Christie's plays are notable for the conspicuous absence of Poirot or Marple and for a degree of formal freedom and thematic experimentation that suggest that the author was relieved to escape from the rigid generic constraints of the detective novel. Although her publishers tried to discourage her, Christie also wrote several nondetective psychological, autobiographical, and romance novels under the pseudonym Mary Westmacott. According to *An Autobiography,* these were Christie's own favorites among her works, which suggests that the habit of writing formulaic detective stories eventually began to pall. The Westmacott books are interesting in their own right and also because they throw new light on many of the features of Christie's better-known work.

The first Westmacott novel, *Giant's Bread* (1930), anticipates the theme of *The Body in the Library* with its depiction of "old" money in crisis. Here the story concerns a Jewish family, the Levinnes, who have purchased the country seat of Deerfield. County society initially ostracizes the newcomers, but the son of the family, Sebastian, is befriended by the scion of the neighboring estate of Abbots Puissants, Vernon Deyre, and his female cousin, Joe. Significantly, in this novel Christie's portrayal of Jews is largely sympathetic (though by no means free of what must appear to a modern reader as stereotyping). This suggests that the racist and anti-Semitic remarks of the Poirot volumes are intended to invoke a camp, exaggerated sense of a defensive Britishness, in accordance with Poirot's own endlessly emphasized foreignness. The Levinnes are eventually accepted into local society, largely because of ostentatious donations to charity, and Christie describes the process with subtle humor:

> People began to say: "of course they're impossible—but Mrs. Levinne is wonderfully *kind.*"
>
> And they said other things.
>
> "Oh, of course—*Jews!* But perhaps it is absurd of one to be prejudiced. Some very good people have been Jews."
>
> It was rumoured that the Vicar had said: "Including Jesus Christ," in answer. But nobody really believed that. The Vicar was unmarried which was very unusual—and had odd ideas about Holy Communion—and sometimes preached very incomprehensible sermons; but nobody believed that he would have said anything really sacrilegious. (1958 ed., p. 78)

There is a gentle, knowing, satirical tone here that is reminiscent of Jane Austen and suggests that Agatha Christie may not have been as much of a lowbrow as the creator of Hercule Poirot found it convenient to appear.

The plot of *Giant's Bread* suffers from the complexity and the convoluted, implausible twists that are assets in a detective story but unbecoming in serious realist fiction. The characters are vivid, however, and Christie gives a sympathetic portrayal of two independent "new women," Joe and Jane. These two are contrasted with the feminine, dependent, vain, and shallow Nell, whose superficial attraction the main male protagonist, Vernon Deyre, is tragically unable to resist. The author's sympathies are clearly with the assertive, active young women, and the book laments the various difficulties experienced by such women in the 1920s.

The novel opens with the performance of a new composition by the Soviet composer Boris Groen, which is promoted by Sebastian Levinne. As the audience files out, they complain about the "foreign" and "Bolshy" music and refer to Levinne as a "dirty foreign Jew" (p. 7): "The Bolshevists can boast they've produced one composer at last. . . . Too bad, Levinne, you've gone Bolshy. Collective Man. Collective Music too" (p. 10). Once again, parochial lowbrow taste is here being satirized from a superior perspective—a luxury Christie could never have permitted herself in her detective fiction. The rest of the novel traces the history of Levinne and particularly of his friend, Vernon Deyre. The latter's destiny as a composer is ironically prefigured in his childhood terror of a grand piano, which he thinks of as "the Beast" and which takes on much the same role in his life as the "gunman" evidently played in Christie's. We eventually discover that "Boris Groen" is none other than Deyre himself who, having lost his ancestral home, has indeed "gone Bolshy" and retreated to the Soviet Union to compose music under a pseudonym. He expounds his version of modernism in a letter to Levinne:

> It's the people who don't know machinery who see its soul and its meaning. . . . The "Nameless Beast" . . . My Beast? . . . I wonder . . .
>
> Collective Man—forming himself in turn into a vast machine. . . . The same herd instinct that saved the race of old coming out again in a different form. . . .
>
> Life's becoming too difficult—too dangerous—for the individual. What was it Dostoyevsky says in one of his books?
>
> *The flock will collect again and submit once more, and then it will be for ever, for ever. We will give them a quiet modest happiness.*
>
> Herd instinct . . . I wonder. (p. 303)

The allusion, which is one of several to Dostoyevsky in Christie's fiction, refers us to *The Brothers Karamazov* (1880) and the story of the Grand Inquisitor, who justifies tyranny on the ground that only through such measures can humans achieve a measure of earthly security. In *Giant's Bread* we are shown Vernon Deyre sacrificing happiness in love to his ambition to produce the new, impersonal, and collective music. The reference of the title to the nursery rhyme in *Jack and the Beanstalk* thus reveals its significance—the machine age is grinding Deyre's personal needs and individual character to force him to produce the "bread" of its accompanying music.

Several of the Westmacott novels evidently reflect incidents in Christie's own life, as they are described in various biographies and in her own autobiography. Her own favorite, *Absent in the Spring* (1944), which she apparently composed in three days, contains the reflections of a middle-aged woman stranded away from her family in the Middle East. *Unfinished Portrait* (1934) is a portrayal of the breakdown of her marriage, while *A Daughter's a Daughter* (1952) comments on her ambivalent relationship with her only child, Rosalind. *The Rose and the Yew Tree* (1948) is a topical novel, set during the 1945 general election, which seemed to many to herald a new age of socialism by decisively returning a Labour government. The theme of new money versus old returns here, and Christie shows a prophetic perspicuity by locating the conflict within the Conservative Party. In the 1980s the lower-middle-class leadership of Margaret Thatcher was to change the Party forever, taking it out of the hands of the genteel county "grandees" whose social environment Christie depicts with such affection. In *The Rose and the Yew Tree,* a conflict is waged over the Conservative nomination for the Cornish constituency of St. Loos, between Hugh Norreys, an archetypal old-school aristocrat, and John Gabriel, a middle-class arriviste who runs on his war record and a grasp of media manipulation that marks him clearly as one of the "new men." Perhaps the most consistent theme running through all of Agatha Christie's writing, whether fiction or nonfiction, serious or light, is a mistrust and suspicion of the coming "new" world, along with a fatalistic certainty that its advent cannot be long delayed.

At the selection meeting at which Gabriel is chosen, the upper-crust Tories are able to bear his "common" demeanor only "by reminding ourselves that it was necessary to get in touch with the People—the privileged classes were now so pitifully small!" (1978 ed., p. 18). These are words that might serve as an epitaph for the fiction of Agatha Christie. The world she left in 1976 was almost inconceivably different from the world she entered in 1890, and nothing was more changed than the position in the world occupied by a mildly genteel Englishwoman of conservative disposition. Throughout her career, Christie registers th[illegible] changes, evaluates them, and attempts to come to terms with them. She does so not through sophisticated reasoning or agonized soul-searching, but in an idiom that enables her to "get in touch with the People." In the writing of Agatha Christie the preoccupations, prejudices, and anxieties of "the People" are addressed with empathy and without condescension. If they are not removed, many of these concerns are at least ameliorated through the comforting recollection of a reassuring past and through the quiet assertion that beneath the chaotic innovation of the twentieth century, a logical, rational, and moral pattern of events can be discerned, if only with the eyes of a Poirot or a Marple.

Selected Bibliography

WORKS OF AGATHA CHRISTIE

NOVELS

The Mysterious Affair at Styles. London: Lane, 1920. Published as *Curtain and the Mysterious Affair at Styles.* New York: Dodd, Mead, 1975.

The Secret Adversary. London: Lane, 1922; New York: Dodd, Mead, 1922.

The Murder on the Links. London: Lane, 1923; New York: Dodd, Mead, 1923.

The Man in the Brown Suit. London: Lane, 1924; New York: Dodd, Mead, 1924.

The Secret of Chimneys. London: Lane, 1925; New York: Dodd, Mead, 1925.

The Murder of Roger Ackroyd. London: Collins, 1926; New York: Dodd, Mead, 1926; New York: Triangle Books, 1943.

The Big Four. London: Collins, 1927; New York: Dodd, Mead, 1927.

The Mystery of the Blue Train. London: Collins, 1928; New York: Dodd, Mead, 1928.

The Seven Dials Mystery. London: Collins, 1929; New York: Dodd, Mead, 1929.

The Murder at the Vicarage. London: Collins, 1930; New York: Dodd, Mead, 1930, 1958.

The Sittaford Mystery. London: Collins, 1931. Published as *The Murder at Hazelmoor.* New York: Dodd, Mead, 1931.

Peril at End House. London: Collins, 1932; New York: Dodd, Mead, 1932.

Lord Edgware Dies. London: Collins, 1933. Published as *Thirteen at Dinner.* New York: Dodd, Mead, 1933.

Why Didn't They Ask Evans? London: Collins, 1934. Published as *The Boomerang Clue.* New York: Dodd, Mead, 1935.

Murder on the Orient Express. London: Collins, 1934. Published as *Murder in the Calais Coach.* New York: Dodd, Mead, 1934; Harper, 1991.

Murder in Three Acts. New York: Dodd, Mead, 1934. Published as *Three Act Tragedy.* London: Collins, 1935.

Death in the Clouds. London: Collins, 1935. Published as *Death in the Air.* New York: Dodd, Mead, 1935.

The A.B.C. Murders. London: Collins, 1936; New York: Dodd, Mead, 1936, 1977. Published as *The Alphabet Murders.* New York: Pocket Books, 1966.

Cards on the Table. London: Collins, 1936; New York: Dodd, Mead, 1937.

Murder in Mesopotamia. London: Collins, 1936; New York: Dodd, Mead, 1936.

Death on the Nile. London: Collins, 1937; New York: Dodd, Mead, 1938, 1965.

Dumb Witness. London: Collins, 1937. Published as *Poirot Loses a Client.* New York: Dodd, Mead, 1937.

Appointment with Death. London: Collins, 1938; New York: Dodd, Mead, 1938.

Hercule Poirot's Christmas. London: Collins, 1938. Published as *Murder for Christmas.* New York: Dodd, Mead, 1939. Published as *A Holiday for Murder.* New York: Avon, 1947.

Murder Is Easy. London: Collins, 1939. Published as *Easy to Kill.* New York: Dodd, Mead, 1939.

Ten Little Niggers. London: Collins, 1939. Published as *And Then There Were None.* New York: Dodd, Mead, 1940. Published as *Ten Little Indians.* New York: Pocket Books, 1965.

One, Two, Buckle My Shoe. London: Collins, 1940. Published as *The Patriotic Murders.* New York: Dodd,

Mead, 1941. Published as *An Overdose of Death.* New York: Dell, 1953.

Sad Cypress. London: Collins, 1940; New York: Dodd, Mead, 1940.

Evil Under the Sun. London: Collins, 1941; New York: Dodd, Mead, 1941.

N or M? London: Collins, 1941; New York: Dodd, Mead, 1941.

The Body in the Library. London: Collins, 1942; New York: Dodd, Mead, 1942; Boston: G. K. Hall, 1988.

The Moving Finger. London: Collins, 1942; New York: Dodd, Mead, 1943.

Five Little Pigs. London: Collins, 1942. Published as *Murder in Retrospect.* New York: Dodd, Mead, 1942.

Death Comes As the End. New York: Dodd, Mead, 1944; London: Collins, 1945.

Towards Zero. London: Collins, 1944; New York: Dodd, Mead, 1944.

Sparkling Cyanide. London: Collins, 1945. Published as *Remembered Death.* New York: Dodd, Mead, 1945.

The Hollow. London: Collins, 1946; New York: Dodd, Mead, 1946. Published as *Murder After Hours.* New York: Dell, 1954.

Taken at the Flood. London: Collins, 1948. Published as *There Is a Tide. . . .* New York: Dodd, Mead, 1948.

Crooked House. London: Collins, 1949; New York: Dodd, Mead, 1949.

A Murder Is Announced. London: Collins, 1950; New York: Dodd, Mead, 1950.

They Do It with Mirrors. London: Collins, 1952. Published as *Murder with Mirrors.* New York: Dodd, Mead, 1952.

Mrs. McGinty's Dead. London: Collins, 1952; New York: Dodd, Mead, 1952. Published as *Blood Will Tell.* New York: Detective Book Club, 1952.

After the Funeral. London: Collins, 1953. Published as *Funerals Are Fatal.* New York: Dodd, Mead, 1953. Published as *Murder at the Gallop.* London: Fontana, 1963.

A Pocket Full of Rye. London: Collins, 1953; New York: Dodd, Mead, 1954.

Destination Unknown. London: Collins, 1954. Published as *So Many Steps to Death.* New York: Dodd, Mead, 1955.

Hickory, Dickory, Dock. London: Collins, 1955. Published as *Hickory, Dickory, Death.* New York: Dodd, Mead, 1955.

4:50 from Paddington. London: Collins, 1957. Published as *What Mrs. McGillicuddy Saw!* New York: Dodd, Mead, 1957; Bantam Books, 1984. Published as *Murder She Said.* New York: Pocket Books, 1961.

Ordeal by Innocence. London: Collins, 1958; New York: Dodd, Mead, 1959.

Cat Among the Pigeons. London: Collins, 1959; New York: Dodd, Mead, 1960.

The Pale Horse. London: Collins, 1961; New York: Dodd, Mead, 1962.

The Mirror Crack'd from Side to Side. London: Collins, 1962. Published as *The Mirror Crack'd.* New York: Dodd, Mead, 1963.

The Clocks. London: Collins, 1963; New York: Dodd, Mead, 1964.

A Caribbean Mystery. London: Collins, 1964; New York: Dodd, Mead, 1965.

At Bertram's Hotel. London: Collins, 1965; New York: Dodd, Mead, 1966.

Third Girl. London: Collins, 1966; New York: Dodd, Mead, 1967.

Endless Night. London: Collins, 1967; New York: Dodd, Mead, 1968.

By the Pricking of My Thumbs. London: Collins, 1968; New York: Dodd, Mead, 1968.

Hallowe'en Party. London: Collins, 1969; New York: Dodd, Mead, 1969.

Passenger to Frankfurt. London: Collins, 1970; New York: Dodd, Mead, 1970.

Nemesis. London: Collins, 1971; New York: Dodd, Mead, 1971.

Elephants Can Remember. London: Collins, 1972; New York: Dodd, Mead, 1972.

Postern of Fate. London: Collins, 1973; New York: Dodd, Mead, 1973.

Curtain: Hercule Poirot's Last Case. London: Collins, 1975; New York: Dodd, Mead, 1975.

Sleeping Murder. London: Collins, 1976; New York: Dodd, Mead, 1976.

SHORT STORIES

Poirot Investigates. London: Lane, 1924; New York: Dodd, Mead, 1925.

Partners in Crime. London: Collins, 1929; New York: Dodd, Mead, 1929. Repr. in part as *The Sunningdale Mystery.* London: Collins, 1933.

The Mysterious Mr. Quinn. London: Collins, 1930; New York: Dodd, Mead, 1930.

The Thirteen Problems. London: Collins, 1932. Published as *The Tuesday Club Murders.* New York: Dodd, Mead, 1933. Repr. in part as *The Mystery of the Blue Geranium and Other Tuesday Club Murders.* New York: Bantam, 1940.

The Hound of Death and Other Stories. London: Odhams, 1933.

Parker Pyne Investigates. London: Collins, 1934. Published as *Mr. Parker Pyne, Detective.* New York: Dodd, Mead, 1934.

The Listerdale Mystery and Other Stories. London: Collins, 1934.

Murder in the Mews and Three Other Poirot Cases. London: Collins, 1937. Published as *Dead Man's Mirror and Other Stories.* New York: Dodd, Mead, 1937.

The Regatta Mystery and Other Stories. New York: Dodd, Mead, 1939.

Double Sin and Other Stories. New York: Dodd, Mead, 1961.

13 for Luck! A Selection of Mystery Stories for Young Readers. New York: Dodd, Mead, 1961.

The Golden Ball and Other Stories. New York: Dodd, Mead, 1971.

Poirot's Early Cases. London: Collins, 1974. Published as *Hercule Poirot's Early Cases.* New York: Dodd, Mead, 1974.

Miss Marple's Final Cases and Two Other Stories. London: Collins, 1979.

NOVELS AS MARY WESTMACOTT

Giant's Bread. London: Collins, 1930; New York: Doubleday, 1930; Priam Books, 1958.

Unfinished Portrait. London: Collins, 1934; New York: Doubleday, 1934.

Absent in the Spring. London: Collins, 1944; New York: Farrar & Rinehart, 1944.

The Rose and the Yew Tree. London: Heinemann, 1948; New York: Farrar, 1948; Leicester: Ulverscroft, 1978.

A Daughter's a Daughter. London: Heinemann, 1952.

The Burden. London: Heinemann, 1956.

PLAYS

Black Coffee. London: Ashley, 1934; Boston: Baker, 1934.

Ten Little Indians. New York: French, 1946.

The Hollow. London and New York: French, 1952. Adaptation of the novel.

The Mousetrap. London and New York: French, 1952. Adaptation of the story "Three Blind Mice."

Witness for the Prosecution. London and New York: French, 1954. Adaptation of the story.

Spider's Web. London and New York: French, 1957.

Towards Zero (with Gerald Verner). New York: Dramatists Play Service, 1957; London: French, 1958. Adaptation of the novel.

Verdict. London: French, 1958.

The Unexpected Guest. London: French, 1958.

Go Back for Murder. London: French, 1960. Adaptation of the novel *Five Little Pigs.*

Rule of Three: Afternoon at the Seaside, The Patient, The Rats, 3 vols. London: French, 1963.

Akhnaton. London: Collins, 1973; New York: Dodd, Mead, 1973.

OTHER WORKS

The Road of Dreams. London: Bles, 1925. Verse.

Come, Tell Me How You Live. London: Collins, 1946; New York: Dodd, Mead, 1946. Travel writings.

An Autobiography. London: Collins, 1977; New York: Dodd, Mead, 1977.

The Mysterious Affair at Styles and The Secret Adversary: An Agatha Christie Omnibus. New York: Carroll & Graf, 1998.

BIOGRAPHICAL AND CRITICAL STUDIES

Bargainnier, Earl F. *The Gentle Art of Murder: The Detective Fiction of Agatha Christie.* Bowling Green, Ohio: Bowling Green State Univ. Popular Press, 1980.

Barnard, Robert. *A Talent for Detection: An Appreciation of Agatha Christie.* London: Collins, 1980.

Birns, Nicholas, and Margaret Boe. "Agatha Christie: Modern and Modernist." In *The Cunning Craft: Original Essays in Detective Fiction and Contemporary Literary Theory.* Edited by Ronald G. Walker and June M. Frazer. Macomb: Western Illinois Univ. Press, 1990. Pp. 120–134.

Day, Gary. "Ordeal by Analysis: Agatha Christie's *The Thirteen Problems.*" In *Twentieth-century Suspense: The Thriller Comes of Age.* Edited by Clive Bloom. New York: St. Martin's Press, 1990. Pp. 80–96.

DeMarr, Mary Jean. "The Comic Village." In *Comic Crime.* Edited by Earl F. Bargainnier. Bowling Green, Ohio: Bowling Green State Univ. Popular Press, 1987. Pp. 75–91.

Fitzgibbon, Russell H. *The Agatha Christie Companion.* Bowling Green, Ohio: Bowling Green State Univ. Popular Press, 1980.

Gill, Gillian. *Agatha Christie: The Woman and Her Mysteries.* New York: Free Press, 1990.

Grossvogel, David I. *Mystery and Its Fiction: From Oedipus to Agatha Christie.* Baltimore: Johns Hopkins Univ. Press, 1979.

———. "Death Deferred: The Long Life, Splendid Afterlife and Mysterious Workings of Agatha Christie." In *Art in Crime Writing: Essays on Detective Fiction.* Edited by Bernard Benstock. New York: St. Martin's Press, 1983. Pp. 1–17.

Hart, Anne. *The Life and Times of Miss Jane Marple.* New York: Dodd, Mead, 1985.

———. *The Life and Times of Agatha Christie's Poirot.* New York: Putnam, 1990.

Haycraft, Howard, ed. *The Art of the Mystery Story: A Collection of Critical Essays.* New York: Biblio and Tannen, 1976.

Irons, Glenwood, and Joan Warthling Roberts. "From Spinster to Hipster: The 'Suitability' of Miss Marple and Anna Lee." In *Feminism in Women's Detective Fiction.* Edited by Glenwood Irons. Toronto: Univ. of Toronto Press, 1995. Pp. 64–73.

Keating, H. R. F., ed. *Agatha Christie: First Lady of Crime.* New York: Holt, Rinehart, and Winston, 1977.

Klein, Kathleen Gregory. *The Woman Detective: Gender and Genre,* 2nd ed. Urbana: Univ. of Illinois Press, 1995.

Knepper, Marty S. "Reading Agatha Christie's Miss Marple Series: The Thirteen Problems." In *In the Beginning: First Novels in Mystery Series.* Edited by Mary Jean DeMarr. Bowling Green, Ohio: Bowling Green State Univ. Popular Press, 1995. Pp. 33–57.

Knight, Steven. *Form and Ideology in Crime Fiction.* London: Macmillan, 1980.

Maida, Patricia D., and Nicholas B. Spornick. *Murder She Wrote: A Study of Agatha Christie's Detective Fiction.* Bowling Green, Ohio: Bowling Green State Univ. Popular Press, 1982.

Mallowan, Max. *Mallowan's Memoirs.* New York: Dodd, Mead, 1977.

Morgan, Janet. *Agatha Christie: A Biography.* New York: Knopf, 1985.

Murdoch, Derrick. *The Agatha Christie Mystery.* Toronto: Pagurian Press, 1976.

Osborne, Charles. *The Life and Crimes of Agatha Christie.* London: Collins, 1982; O'Mara Books, 1990.

Ramsey, G. C. *Agatha Christie: Mistress of Mystery.* New York: Dodd, Mead, 1967.

Riley, Dick, and Pam McAllister, eds. *The Bedside, Bathtub, and Armchair Companion to Agatha Christie.* New York: Ungar, 1979; rev. ed., 1986.

Robyns, Gwen. *The Mystery of Agatha Christie.* Garden City, N.Y.: Doubleday, 1978.

Sanders, Dennis, and Len Lovallo. *The Agatha Christie Companion: The Complete Guide to Agatha Christie's Life and Work.* New York: Delacorte, 1984.

Shaw, Marion, and Sabine Vanacker. *Reflecting on Miss Marple.* New York: Routledge, 1991.

Slung, Michelle. "Let's Hear It for Agatha Christie: A Feminist Appreciation." In *The Sleuth and the Scholar: Origins, Evolution, and Current Trends in Detective Fiction.* Edited by Barbara A. Rader and Howard G. Zettler. New York: Greenwood Press, 1988. Pp. 63–68.

Symons, Julian. *Bloody Murder: From the Detective Story to the Crime Novel. A History.* New York: Viking, 1985; London: Pan, 1994.

Wagoner, Mary S. *Agatha Christie.* Boston: Twayne Publishers, 1986.

Winks, Robin, ed. *Detective Fiction: A Collection of Critical Essays.* Woodstock, Vt.: Countryman Press, 1988.

Wilkie Collins
(1824–1889)

AUDREY PETERSON

WILKIE COLLINS WAS an immensely popular Victorian author whose works were forerunners of the mystery novel as it developed in the twentieth century. *The Woman in White* and *The Moonstone* are enduring classics of the form, never out of print since their first appearance in the 1860s. Many other novels and short stories of Collins' are still read today, some for their qualities of suspense, others for their treatment of various social issues. He was in advance of his time in his concern for the rights of women; in more than one of his works he takes as his theme the need for compassion toward the "fallen woman," whose sexual history bars her from social acceptance. He deplored the Mrs. Grundys of the day who preached adherence to rules of morality and propriety without regard for human tolerance, and his private life was accordingly unorthodox. A bon vivant who loved French cooking and continental travel, he was a close friend of Charles Dickens, with whom he often collaborated on various literary enterprises. After the appearance of *The Moonstone* (1868) his work showed a marked decline in quality, but he continued writing to the end, still selling well and pleasing his contemporary readers.

Life

Wilkie Collins was born in London on 8 January 1824, the son of William Collins, a well-known and successful painter. Growing up in an artist's household might suggest a bohemian existence, but in fact, William Collins was a model of middle-class respectability, with firm religious principles and a practical eye for acquiring wealthy patrons who paid well for his work. He became a full member of the Royal Academy in 1820, giving him the right to add "Esquire" to his name, a distinction that raised his status above that of his own father. William Collins senior had been an art dealer, with a specialty in cleaning old pictures but with little talent for making money. He did, however, pass on to his grandson a gift for writing, having contributed to various magazines and published a novel and a biography of the painter George Morland.

In 1822 William Collins married Harriet Geddes, the daughter of a painter. They were, by all evidence, a devoted couple. Their first child was christened William Wilkie Collins, after the painter, Sir David Wilkie. Called "Willy" as a child, the son dropped the name "William" after the death of his father and became simply "Wilkie Collins." In 1828 his brother, Charles Allston Collins, was born. The two boys grew up in a secure household, Collins' chief complaint being that his father's deeply religious faith cast a gloom over their natural high spirits. The Sabbath was observed with attendance at endless sermons, and the boys were constantly instructed to pray and to copy passages in the Scriptures exhorting them to good behavior. At the same time, William Collins was not in the least a tyrannical father. He dearly loved his wife and sons and was for the most part kindly and affectionate.

Collins began attending school at the age of eleven, hating it, as boys generally did in that age when school meant boredom and beatings. At the end of a year, he was delighted when his father announced he was taking the family to Italy, where the painter could study the old masters. The two years spent on the Continent, chiefly in Italy, proved to be the highlight of Collins' childhood.

After nearly two years abroad, the family returned to England in August 1838. Collins again attended school until the age of seventeen. At that time, his father secured a place for him in the office of a tea importer in the Strand. Although Collins found the work dull, he was consoled by a lively social life. Despite his short stature, small hands and feet, and a forehead that bulged, his personal charm made him popular with young men and women alike. It was during this period that Collins began writing fiction. When his first short story, "The Last Stagecoachman," was published in 1843, he celebrated with a trip to Paris, where he developed a lifelong fondness for the fine wines and gourmet foods that appear throughout his work.

By 1846, William Collins' health was failing. Hoping for a better occupation for his elder son, he arranged for Wilkie to leave the Strand and enter Lincoln's Inn to prepare for the bar. Willing to please his father, but believing that writing was to be his life's work, Collins was even less attentive to the law than he had been to the importation of tea. He worked assiduously on what was to become his first published novel, *Antonina; or, The Fall of Rome* (1850), a historical romance that was only half finished when, after much suffering, William Collins died, in February 1847. The younger Collins set aside his novel and devoted himself to writing his father's biography. *Memoirs of the Life of William Collins, Esq., R. A.* was published by Longman, Brown, Green, and Longmans in 1848 and was well received.

William Collins' will gave his considerable estate to his wife Harriet, leaving his two sons dependent upon their mother's generosity until after her death. Once recovered from her loss, Harriet Collins' spirits revived and she warmly welcomed her sons' friends, including the young Pre-Raphaelite painters, John Everett Millais and Holman Hunt.

Meanwhile, Collins' writing career began to prosper. He finished *Antonina* and was delighted when it was published by Bentley in 1850, to reasonably favorable reviews. In 1851, *Rambles Beyond Railways,* an account of a walking tour in Cornwall, also received encouraging notices.

The year 1851 marked the beginning of Collins' long friendship with Charles Dickens. Amateur theatricals were all the rage throughout the nineteenth century, and no one was more stagestruck than Dickens himself. He invited Collins to join the cast of Bulwer-Lytton's *Not So Bad as We Seem,* which was performed in the presence of the Queen and the Prince Consort. The friendship grew rapidly, and Collins was soon a favorite of the Dickens household.

Inspired by the success of Dickens' Christmas books, Collins produced *Mr. Wray's Cash-Box* in 1852. Later that year, his first important novel, *Basil: A Story of Modern Life,* was published by Bentley, followed two years later by *Hide and Seek* (1854). In 1856 Collins joined the staff of Dickens' *Household Words,* the two authors often collaborating on pieces for the magazine. By early 1857, Collins' next novel, *The Dead Secret,* was running in the journal, and the friends were involved in theatricals again, this time a play written by Collins himself. *The Frozen Deep* was a drama of love and sacrifice, set on an arctic expedition, with Dickens, a brilliant actor, in the starring role. In his preface to *A Tale of Two Cities,* Dickens wrote that the theme of his novel was suggested by the Collins play.

In the following year, 1858, Collins began an unorthodox relationship. After his meeting with Caroline Graves, they lived together as man and wife, except for one interval, until his death. John G. Millais tells the dramatic, if apocryphal, story of their meeting, which suggests the opening scene of *The Woman in White* (1860), in *The Life and Letters of Sir John Everett Millais,* published in 1899, when the persons concerned were no longer living. The elder Millais claimed that after he had spent an evening at their home, the Collins brothers walked back with him to his home in Gower Street. Suddenly, they heard a piercing scream, and a young and beautiful woman emerged from a garden and seemed to float toward them, dressed in flowing white robes that shone in the moonlight. Millais merely remarked that she was a lovely woman, but Wilkie Collins said that he must see who she was and what was the matter. He then dashed off and did not return.

For many years after Collins' death, very little was known about his personal life. The friends who knew were not telling, at least not in print. It was not until the 1930s that the facts began to emerge, with the discovery of Collins' will, in which he divided his assets between Mrs. Caroline Graves and a Mrs. Martha Rudd and her three children, whom he acknowledged as his own.

Much new material about these two women has been uncovered since the late 1980s. In *The Secret Life of Wilkie Collins* (1988), William M. Clarke discloses many details about the lives of the two women. Through independent research, Catherine Peters came upon similar and new material, presented in her comprehensive work, *The King of Inventors: A Life of Wilkie Collins* (1991). It is now known that when Collins met her, Caroline Graves was a widow with a daughter about five years of age. In 1850 she had married George Robert Graves, a clerk. Within a year after the birth of their child, George Graves died of consumption, and Caroline was left destitute.

By 1858, Collins' income from his writing was at last sufficient to enable him to leave his mother's home, and in his new establishment Caroline lived with him, ostensibly as his "housekeeper." Collins adored the child Harriet, whom he called "Carrie." He treated her as his adopted child, and she returned his affection until the end of his life. Collins' male friends, including Charles Dickens, were in on the secret, and treated Caroline as their hostess. Respectable ladies, however, could not call, and Caroline could not be received at their homes. Collins' scorn for such social strictures appears throughout his fiction.

As for the other woman named in Collins' will, it is now known that Martha Rudd was a country girl from Norfolk who worked as a servant at a hotel near Yarmouth, where Collins had visited at various times. By 1868 Martha was living in London as Collins' mistress.

Now a curious series of events occurred. On 29 October 1868, Caroline left Collins and married a man named Joseph Clow. Both Collins and the daughter Carrie attended the wedding. At about this time, Martha became pregnant with Collins' first child, a girl born 4 July 1869. Within two years, Caroline had returned to Collins and nothing further was heard of Joseph Clow from that day to this.

Martha produced two more children, and Collins took pleasure in indulging the little ones. The two families lived only a short walk apart, an arrangement not unknown in Victorian circles. That Collins regarded Caroline as the "wife" and Martha as the "mistress" is clear in the wording of his will, where he stated that Caroline was to lie beside him in a joint grave in Kensal Green Cemetery.

In the beginning, Collins' life with Caroline must have been fulfilling, for it was during the first decade of their relationship that he produced his greatest work. By 1859 Dickens had left *Household Words* and was producing another periodical, *All the Year Round,* in which *A Tale of Two Cities* was coming to an end, and Dickens had arranged that as its last installment appeared on 26 November 1859, Collins' new novel, *The Woman in White,* would begin its run in the same number. The success of *The Woman in White* was phenomenal, surpassing even Dickens' sales. As the installments appeared, suspense built. Crowds gathered to get their copies. *Woman in White* perfumes appeared in the shops; cloaks, bonnets, waltzes, and quadrilles named for the novel were selling like hotcakes. Published by Harpers in America, it was equally a sensation across the Atlantic.

For the book publication, Collins made excellent terms with Sampson and Low, and his income, which had been steadily growing, now increased dramatically. In a letter to his mother he declared, with pardonable pride, that no one but Dickens had made more for his work, and that with future offers pouring in, he would be "at the top of the tree" before he was forty (Peters, p. 236).

The golden days rolled on for Collins, with the publication of *No Name* in 1862 and *Armadale* in 1866, culminating with *The Moonstone* in 1868. Unhappily, it was at this time that he began to suffer from the rheumatic pains and inflammation of the eyes that had afflicted both his father and his grandfather, complicated in his case by attacks of gout. After the completion of *No Name* he was unable to write for many months, trying various doctors and remedies, to no avail. Only laudanum, a form of opium, brought him relief, and for several years he used it freely, praising it as a godsend. Eventually, he did become addicted, but his attitude toward the drug was quite different from that of others like Thomas De Quincey or Samuel Taylor Coleridge. Collins never used it as a source of pleasure. In the early years, when the pains stopped, he simply stopped the laudanum. Even when he was aware of his addiction, he never suffered the pangs of guilt as others did. At times of great pain, he used it because he needed it. Nevertheless, its debilitating effects took their toll, as movingly described by the character of Ezra Jennings in *The Moonstone.*

After Collins' success with his novels of mystery and suspense, and particularly with *The Moonstone,* Dickens was inspired to try his hand at the genre and began work on *The Mystery of Edwin Drood.* Already ailing, he struggled on but left the novel unfinished at his death in 1870. The opening chapters are wonderfully atmospheric, but in over a century of speculation, no one can say whether his plotting would have matched that of his young friend and protégé.

In 1873, Collins left for a six-month tour of the United States, giving readings as Dickens had done. He met Henry Wadsworth Longfellow, Mark Twain, John Greenleaf Whittier, Oliver Wendell Holmes, and others, pronouncing his delight with the genuine friendliness of the Americans.

The final years of Collins' life were marked with spells of severe illness, relieved by periods of remission, but he never stopped writing. When he could not hold the pen, he dictated to daughter Carrie and others.

Collins died from a stroke on 23 September 1889. In keeping with his hatred of Victorian rituals, his will insisted upon a simple funeral and burial. Many close friends who had survived him gathered to attend, and the press paid tribute to his forty years of dedication to his craft.

Early Works

Like many beginning writers, Wilkie Collins felt his way through various forms and influences. In 1848, his *Memoirs of the Life of William Collins, Esq., R. A.* was praised for its clear, unaffected style and for its judicious portrait of the senior Collins, as artist and man.

The modest success of the *Memoirs* encouraged publishers to look with some favor on Collins' first novel, *Antonina; or, The Fall of Rome,* which was sold to Bentley in 1850. *Antonina* was written after the fashion of Edward Bulwer-Lytton, whose work was popular at the time. This tale of the sack of Rome by the Visigoths in the fifth century has little appeal to today's readers. Happily, Collins never reverted to the historical romance, addressing himself thereafter to the contemporary scene.

By the year 1850, the system of railways had spread over most of England but had not yet reached the county of Cornwall. To the average Londoner, Cornwall was a remote and little-known land of copper mines, fishing villages, and a wild, precipitous coastline. Collins and his friend, the artist Henry C. Brandling, set out on a walking tour and found the Cornish villagers friendly and hospitable, while the rugged scenery provided material for Collins in his subsequent fiction. *Rambles Beyond Railways; or, Notes in Cornwall Taken A-Foot* (1851) was successful enough to run into several editions.

The subtitle of *Mr. Wray's Cash-Box; or, The Mask and the Mystery* (1852) suggests that Collins was developing an interest in the mystery genre. Unfortunately, he fails to sustain the reader's suspense by giving away the solution in his introduction, where he announces that a stonemason did in fact take a cast from Shakespeare's bust and later learned his act was not criminal. Collins' desire to assure the reader that his work is based upon fact became a major concern throughout his career, with his unhappy compulsion to preface his works with explanatory remarks attesting to their accuracy.

Meanwhile, Collins had been working on a new novel, *Basil: A Story of Modern Life* (1852). Richard Bentley now saw that he had a promising young writer in Collins and paid him £350 (at that time about $1,700) for the novel. He also regularly accepted short stories, articles, and reviews from Collins for his successful journal, *Bentley's Miscellany.*

In the first edition of *Basil,* Collins included a "Letter of Dedication" to his friend Charles James Ward, declaring that the story was based upon "something real and true." In directing his characters toward the "light of Reality," he says, he may have "violated some of the conventions of sentimental fiction." However, since the business of fiction is to exhibit human life, no one can deny that "scenes of misery and crime must of necessity, while human nature remains what it is, form part of that exhibition." The label "sensation novels" was already beginning to be applied to works like *Basil,* and this is the first of many prefaces by Collins that challenge readers, and particularly reviewers, to accept scenes that may shock their sensibilities.

Collins particularly repudiated attitudes like those expressed in a review of *Antonina* in the *Athenaeum,* where H. F. Chorley had written: "We must warn Mr. Collins against the vices of the French school—against the needless accumulation of revolting details—against catering for a prurient taste" (Norman Page, ed., p. 41). While *Basil* was attacked as immoral in some circles, the novel that evoked all this reproach would scarcely lift an eyebrow today. As Dorothy L. Sayers remarked, in her unfinished *Wilkie Collins: A Critical and Biographical Study,* readers who took up *Basil* looking for another *Lady Chatterly's Lover* would be sadly disappointed (p. 86).

Basil is the story of a young man from an old and wealthy family who sees a beautiful young woman on an omnibus and falls in love with her at first sight. Learning that she is the daughter of a linen draper, he knows that his father, whose greatest pride is his ancient lineage, will never consent to such a misalliance.

The passages describing Basil's passionate love for Margaret have the unmistakable ring of personal experience. This is no sentimental fondness but a powerful physical attraction. He describes her in minute detail, not merely the beauty of her hair and face but the "dusky throat" and the "figure visible, where the shawl had fallen open, slender, but already well developed in its slenderness, and exquisitely supple" (Dover ed., p. 31). He thrills to each touch of her hand and to the occasional kiss he is permitted.

In this first novel of contemporary life, Collins shows a strong talent for character and setting. Basil's first meeting with Margaret Sherwin's father is a masterful picture of the nouveau riche shopkeeper attempting to raise his social status. In the drawing room at North Villa, everything appears oppressively new:

> The paper on the wall, with its gaudy pattern of birds, trellis-work, and flowers, in gold, red, and green on a white ground, looked hardly dry yet; the showy window-curtains of white

> and sky-blue, and the still showier carpet of red and yellow, seemed as if they had come out of the shop yesterday. (Dover ed., p. 61)

Mr. Sherwin boasts of having sent his daughter to a "most genteel school." He introduces his wife as his "better half" but treats her with contempt, and he offers Basil sherry that "cost six shillings a bottle."

The villainous Robert Mannion is equally well wrought. He is handsome in feature and build but severely inexpressive in manner, and because of his age, it never occurs to Basil to regard him as a rival. The night before Basil is to live with Margaret as man and wife, he sees her with Mannion, follows them to a hotel, and through an adjoining wall, listens to them engaging in sexual intercourse. This is the scene, with its depiction of the unmentionable, that sent the prudish critics into paroxysms of horror.

Significantly, Margaret must be punished. The "fallen women" Collins defends in later works are victims of poverty or ill-treatment, but because Margaret's betrayal has no redeeming cause, she is consigned to a lingering death. To today's readers these passages seem lengthy beyond endurance. Such stretching was in part due to that bane of all Victorian novelists, the demands of the lending libraries for three-volume novels. Mudie's, the most powerful of the lenders, kept a virtual stranglehold on authors for decades. The libraries made their money by doling out one volume at a time to their subscribers, and woe to the novelist who fell short of the required length. However, prolonged passages, particularly of death scenes, were adored by Victorian readers. Dickens was an expert in this field, and Collins often followed such popular trends.

The "violence" that some critics objected to in *Basil* occurs in the latter half of the novel, where Basil and Mannion quarrel after the seduction scene. They grapple, exchanging blows, and Basil throws Mannion to the pavement, disfiguring his face. Seeking revenge, Mannion follows Basil to Cornwall, where he falls to his death in a dramatic scene along the seaside cliffs that Collins remembered from his walking tour.

That Collins was feeling his way toward a mystery formula in *Basil* is apparent in the end, when the young hero enumerates a series of clues in Mannion's and Margaret's behavior that might, but for his innocence, have warned him of their intimacy.

In view of Collins' frequent defense of marriages between persons in different stations in life, it is useful to note that the rejection of Margaret Sherwin in *Basil* is due to her own reprehensible behavior, not to her inferior social standing.

Collins followed the intensity of *Basil* with a departure into a light and sometimes comic tone in *Hide and Seek; or, The Mystery of Mary Grice* (1854). The novel opens with six-year-old Zachary Thorpe being taken out of church in disgrace by his father and comforted by his affectionate mother, an attempt to make comedy out of Collins' own childhood resentments. As the subtitle suggests, Collins is lured by the desire to develop a suspenseful plot, but the devices rely heavily on coincidence and are distressingly transparent. More significant for Collins' development is the introduction of themes that recur throughout his subsequent fiction. Mary Grice, the unwed mother of the title, is the first of his sympathetic portraits of the fallen woman, and in her aunt Joanna Grice we see the first of the religious hypocrites whom Collins delights in condemning. The story recounts the death of Mary Grice, leaving an infant daughter who is cared for by a kindly couple connected with the circus. The child becomes a deaf-mute through an accident, is mistreated by the circus owner, and is adopted by Valentine Blyth, an artist of no talent but of limitless virtue.

The influence of Dickens is strong in this early novel. Mary's brother, Mat "Marksman" Grice, is a Dickensian eccentric in habits and speech, dedicated to finding his sister's seducer and having his revenge upon him. The deaf-mute child is the first of many physically handicapped characters in the Dickens mode.

The novel was well received, the *Athenaeum* reviewer noting with pleasure that in this novel "Mr. Collins has a genuine healthy sense of fun," without the "unwholesome odour" that hung over *Antonina* and *Basil* (Norman Page, ed., pp. 55–56).

At this period, Collins' obvious desire to write fiction of mystery and detection met with more success in his short stories than in his novels. A collection of stories that had previously appeared in Dickens' *Household Words* was published in 1856 under the title *After Dark.* While we have no evidence that Collins knew the work of Edgar Allan Poe, the parallels in these stories are suggestive. "A Terribly Strange Bed" is much in the manner of Poe's horror stories, and "A Stolen Letter" echoes the title if not the substance of "The Purloined Letter." Collins' detective in this story, unlike Poe's brilliant Auguste Dupin, is a kindly young lawyer who retrieves an incriminating letter for his client with the aid of a young lad whose cleverness in tailing a suspect while innocently loitering about eating pastries makes him a prototype for Sherlock Holmes's Baker Street Irregulars. The letter is not found in an obvious place, but, as in Poe's ending, a flippant message is left for the culprit to find in the place where it was hidden. In the same volume the well-crafted story, "The Lady of Glenwith Grange," contains a genuine mystery of identity, and the characters are handled with delicacy, with no attempt at Dickensian joviality.

Sustaining suspense for the length of a novel was a harder task. The reception of Collins' next attempt, *The Dead Secret* (1857), must have given him something of a jolt, for reviewers complained that the "secret" was discernible from the beginning of the book, as indeed it is. In a great house in Cornwall, a dying woman calls her maidservant to her side, making her swear to tell the secret they share to the woman's husband after her death. Except for a charming heroine in Rosamund Treverton, the novel is generally flat and unrewarding.

Again, it is in the short story form that Collins shows a growing aptitude for detective fiction. In a collection titled *The Queen of Hearts,* published in 1859, several are horror and ghost stories, but three stories advance Collins' skill in mystery technique. In "The Diary of Anne Rodway," two young seamstresses, Anne and her friend Mary, live in London in appalling poverty, described by Collins with deep concern. When Mary dies, Anne is certain that Mary was murdered, and her pursuit of a series of clues that disclose the identity of the guilty man have led some historians of detective fiction to name Anne as the first lady detective.

In the 1850s Collins shared Dickens' admiration for the recently formed London Detective Police, and the story "The Biter Bit" pays tribute to the professional efficiency of these men, who solve a robbery case that had been bungled by amateurs.

A more fully developed detective story, "A Plot in Private Life," features the ingenuity of Mr. Dark, a lawyer's clerk who solves a complicated case involving elements that have become familiar in twentieth-century mystery fiction: a disappearing husband, a blood-stained nightgown but no body, and a conclusion in which Dark gives a full account of the steps by which he unraveled the mystery, analyzing and explaining each clue. The character of Mr. Dark owes a good deal to Dickens' Inspector Bucket in *Bleak House* and forecasts the ingenuity of the incomparable Sergeant Cuff in *The Moonstone.*

By the year 1859, all the efforts Collins had made toward writing suspenseful mystery came to fruition in the superb quality of his first great success, *The Woman in White.*

The Woman in White

The enormous popularity of *The Woman in White* made Wilkie Collins an overnight celebrity. During its run in *All the Year Round,* the circulation rose even higher than it had for Dickens' *A Tale of Two Cities.* William Thackeray sat up all night to finish it, Edward Fitzgerald named his boat the *Marian Halcombe,* William Gladstone couldn't put it down, and Prince Albert adored it.

The initial idea for the novel came from a book that Collins picked up while strolling in Paris one day. In Maurice Méjan's *Receuil des causes célèbres,* Collins found an extensive account of French criminal cases. In one of these, the Marquise de Douhault was the victim of her brother, who seized her estates in 1787 and subsequently had her detained in an asylum under an assumed name. Although she escaped, she was never able to regain her legal rights. The account in Méjan mentions that the Marquise was wearing white when she left the asylum, clearly a source for the memorable scene near the opening of Collins' novel when Walter Hartright sees Anne Catherick on the night she escapes from the asylum: "There, in the middle of the broad, bright high-road—there, as if it had that moment sprung out of the earth or dropped from the heaven—stood the figure of a solitary Woman, dressed from head to foot in white garments" (Oxford ed., p. 15).

The novel that Collins fashioned from this source shows a remarkable leap in quality from his earlier works. The plot moves through its complications with absolute clarity and without the burden of taxing the reader's credulity. Collins introduced a technique of multiple narrators, each of whom gives an account of the events as they unfold.

The characters in the novel are superbly crafted. Marian Halcombe is the first and most admirable of Collins' strong women. Like George Eliot, whom Collins knew at this date, Marian has an excellent figure but a plain, even ugly, face, which is quickly forgotten as her charm and intelligence are felt. She deplores the limits society places on women, condemned to "patience, propriety, and petticoats." Devoted to her fragile young sister, Laura Fairlie, she sees the love developing between Laura and the young drawing master, Walter Hartright, but is helpless to prevent the previously pledged marriage of Laura to Sir Percival Glyde. Throughout the subsequent disasters, Marian is strong and resourceful. She is not above climbing on the roof to overhear conversations, and she is bold enough to rescue Laura from the asylum.

The incomparable Count Fosco is a brilliantly created villain, who plays tenderly with his birds and little white mice while concocting diabolical plots. The otherwise clear-headed Marian initially falls under the spell of his charm, with sexual overtones that Collins could only hint at. Marian's diary records that although Fosco is immensely fat and nearly sixty, he listens to her with such flattering attention that she has "sensations" that she "would rather not feel" (p. 197). Fosco has tamed his wife into a worshiping slave, and he skillfully controls the despicable Sir Percival Glyde. Although he is the mastermind of the evil plot against Laura, Fosco often expresses some of Collins' own attitudes. He has only contempt for the moral hypocrisies of society, and he scorns the time-worn belief that "murder will out," pointing out that only the failures are found out.

Marian describes her grudging admiration for Fosco at their early acquaintance, before her knowledge of him turns to passionate hatred:

> It seems hardly credible while I am writing it down, but it is certainly true, that this same man, who has all the fondness of an old maid for his cockatoo, and all the small dexterities of an organ-boy in managing his white mice, can talk, when anything happens to rouse him, with a daring independence of thought, a knowledge of books in every language, and an experience of society in half the capitals of Europe, which would make him the prominent personage of any assembly in the civilised world. (pp. 198–199)

For a novel of its length, *The Woman in White* is significantly without a subplot. Every character in the novel, as well as every incident, contributes to the whole. Mr. Fairlie, Laura's hypochondriacal uncle, surrounded by his art objects and unable to tolerate any form of distress, is not merely a caricature invented for comic relief, he is pivotal to the plot, for a healthy, normal uncle would have protected his niece from harm. Mrs. Catherick, with her obsession for propriety, having gained the distinction of a bow from the clergyman as he passes her window, inadvertently provides a clue to the "secret" she shares with Sir Percival. Even the garrulous old parish clerk, who opens the vestry for Walter Hartright, provides a vital clue, buried in what appears to be his interminable chatter. The timidity and confusion of Anne Catherick, whose appearance is a pale echo of Laura Fairlie's, are exhibited by Laura herself after her detention in the asylum and contribute to the failure of the servants and even her uncle to recognize her. Even the resemblance between the two young women, which may at first appear gratuitous, is accounted for when it is revealed that they are half sisters.

Collins' final stroke is the reappearance of Walter's little Italian friend, Professor Pesca. By the end of the novel, the reader has forgotten Pesca, whose role at the beginning was to obtain for Walter the position of drawing master at Limmeridge House and who now provides the means for exposing Fosco and leading him to his death.

Walter Hartright has often been seen as merely a conventional young hero, but it must be noted that in the second half of the novel he comes to life and takes vigorous action, performing the role of detective to uncover the mysteries and obtain Laura's right to her name and identity.

Collins' artistic achievement in this novel is matched, and some think surpassed, in *The Moonstone.* Yet, after a lifetime of writing, the words he elected to have inscribed on his tombstone were "Author of *The Woman in White* and Other Works of Fiction."

No Name and *Armadale*

Following the spectacular success of *The Woman in White,* Collins wrote in the preface to his new novel that *No Name* (1862) would be constructed on a different plan from the previous one, the only secret being revealed midway in the first volume. Attacking the English law that bars illegitimate children from inheriting property, he creates in Magdalen Vanstone a strong and resourceful young woman who stops at nothing to gain her ends. In the opening chapters, she is an eighteen-year-old beauty, her father's darling, the vivacious star of the amateur theatricals of country-house society. The security of this life is set against the utter degradation she feels on learning, on the death of their parents, that, as illegitimate children, she and her sister Norah are left penniless and virtually "nameless." While Norah passively accepts reality, Magdalen is obsessed with a desire for revenge against the uncle who inherits the estate and refuses to help the innocent girls. Magdalen sets forth alone, taking up with sleazy characters, using her dramatic talents to earn money through stage readings, adopting disguises and false names, and generally throwing propriety to the winds in her relentless passion for justice. Reviewers were typically dismayed at this flouting of convention, and readers were deliciously shocked at Collins' daring, while Mudie's, with an eye to profits, cheerfully issued the volumes one by one.

The influence of Dickens, which is at a minimum in *The Woman in White,* comes back in full force in *No Name.* Captain Wragge, with his one brown and one green eye and his jaunty roguishness, is Dickensian to the core. A small-time swindler who poses as Magdalen's "uncle," he becomes her accomplice in incomparable scenes of scheming. Wragge meets his match in the housekeeper, Mrs. Lecount, with her demure manner and her sharp practices. The simple-minded Mrs. Wragge, another eccentric in the Dickens manner, submits meekly to her husband as he shouts at her to put her cap straight or to sit up at the table.

Even today's reader may flinch a little when Magdalen actually marries Noel Vanstone, the weak invalid who has inherited the estate at the death of his father, although Noel's debilitated state may suggest that the marriage is never consummated. The marriage, however, represents an attack on a society that values outward appearance of respectability over genuine human feelings.

Magdalen cries out bitterly that once she has entered into a marriage, loveless or not, she will no longer be "Nobody's Child" and will become "Somebody's Wife."

Throughout his work, Collins revealed impatience with the artificial social barriers between servants and their employers. When Magdalen conceives the plan of exchanging places with her maid, Louisa, she asks the maid to sit down with her:

> "I ask you to sit near me," pursued Magdalen, "because I wish to speak to you on equal terms. Whatever distinctions there might once have been between us, are now at an end. I am a lonely woman thrown helpless on my own resources, without rank or place in the world. I may or may not keep you as my friend. As mistress and maid, the connection between us must come to an end." (Penguin ed., p. 495)

To satisfy the demands of propriety, Collins must condemn Magdalen's actions. She abjectly confesses her wickedness, endures a prolonged illness, and emerges purified, forgiven by everyone, before she can marry the faithful Captain Kirke. Collins has sailed as near the wind as convention would allow, and the final scenes, written during a particularly painful episode of illness, are the weakest in the novel.

In *No Name* Collins had to some extent downplayed the sensational elements in the novel, wishing to make Magdalen Vanstone a believable heroine who lived in the real world. In *Armadale* (1866) he abandons all such efforts and luxuriates in improbabilities. He treads the gothic line of the supernatural in Allan Armadale's elaborate dream, each prophecy being fulfilled with spine-tingling horror. At the same time, a logical explanation is offered, leaving the reader, as Collins states in an appendix, to believe or not, as he is so inclined. The character of Lydia Gwilt is so consistently evil and conniving that her brief attack of genuine love for Ozias Midwinter lacks conviction. The ancient theme of revenge visited upon the sons of wicked fathers is pushed to the limit and beyond. This is unashamedly the stuff of the "sensation novel," and Collins, evidently hoping to match again the wild success of *The Woman in White,* went too far. The result kept the reader turning the pages, but the literary quality suffered accordingly. T. S. Eliot damned it with faint praise when he wrote that *Armadale* "has no merit beyond melodrama, and it has every merit that melodrama can have," adding that "like most of Collins's novels it has the merit of never being dull" (*Selected Essays,* p. 468).

The character of Lydia Gwilt secures none of the sympathy the reader may have felt for Magdalen Vanstone. Lydia is a study in pure evil, fascinating because of her sexual charm but without the complexity of a Count Fosco. Today's readers may find a surfeit of scheming in the improbably lengthy entries in her diary, a device Collins was unduly fond of. Collins offers no apology for Lydia and treats with some scorn the revelation that she had been tried for murder and was released by the public outcry in her defense, an echo of a notorious contemporary case. In 1857, Madeleine Smith had been accused of poisoning her lover and was given the Scottish verdict of "Not Proven," calling forth cheers from the public, although the evidence strongly indicated her guilt.

The character of Ozias Midwinter adds merit to the novel. Having survived the appalling cruelties of his childhood, he emerges with sensitivity and intelligence, despite his obsessive fears that fate will cause him to bring harm to Allan Armadale. The "dark" and "fair" contrast, more traditional in fictional women, applies here to the dark-haired, serious Midwinter and the fair Allan, with his sunny nature.

The two Pedgifts, father and son, are among Collins' finest portraits of "good" solicitors. Although *Armadale* is not primarily a novel of mystery, the engaging younger Pedgift performs some amateur detective work, going to a cabstand in Bayswater, for example, and tracing the driver who had taken a fare to Pimlico, a device that was to become a staple for Sherlock Holmes. The elder Pedgift uses a method to elicit information, known to his acquaintance as "Pedgift's Postscript" and since immortalized by Lieutenant Columbo of television fame:

> Mr. Pedgift's practice had been the same throughout his life, on every occasion when he found his arts of persuasion required at an interview with another man. He invariably kept his strongest argument, or his boldest proposal, to the last and invariably remembered it at the door (after previously taking his leave), as if it was a purely accidental consideration which had that instant occurred to him. (Dover ed., p. 316)

The dramatic climax of the novel shows Collins borrowing from the "science" of the day, as he does increasingly in subsequent work, as Lydia pours liquid from a purple flask, sending poisonous fumes into the room where her presumed victim is sleeping. Anxious always to confirm the accuracy of his work, Collins' appendix assures his readers that he has consulted experts on all questions of law, medicine, and chemistry, and that he actually saw the apparatus and the chemical ingredients at work as they were described in the closing scenes of the book.

The Moonstone

For many readers, *The Moonstone* is Wilkie Collins' finest achievement. In her introduction to *The Omnibus of Crime* (1929), Dorothy L. Sayers paid the novel the ultimate tribute when she called it

> probably the very finest detective story ever written. By comparison with its wide scope, its dove-tailed completeness and the marvelous variety and soundness of its characterization, modern mystery fiction looks thin and mechanical. Nothing human is perfect, but *The Moonstone* comes as near perfection as anything of its kind can be. (p. 25)

As the novel ran in *All the Year Round* in 1868, the magazine's sales soared, as they had done for *The Woman in White,* and the public clamored for its copies. The question of who had stolen Rachel Verinder's diamond dominated the conversation at fashionable dinner tables and animated the talk of the servants below stairs. Contemporary reviewers praised the book for the absence of the "sordid" details they deplored in other Collins novels.

As a prototype for twentieth-century mystery fiction, *The Moonstone* introduces the "whodunit" formula sustained through the length of the novel. In *The Woman in White* the villains are known. All the questions begin with "how?" How did Count Fosco and Sir Percival do what they did? How can it be proved? How can justice be obtained? *The Moonstone* sets the pattern for the question "who?" by placing a group of suspects in an isolated setting, each of whom may have motive or opportunity to commit the crime. At a country house in Yorkshire, Rachel Verinder receives an enormous diamond left to her by an uncle for her eighteenth birthday. Before retiring, she places the diamond in a cabinet in her boudoir, in the presence of her mother, Lady Verinder, her cousins, Franklin Blake and Godfrey Ablewhite, and several of the servants. Hovering over this scene of domestic tranquillity is the exotic story of the Indian diamond and its violent history, with the threat of death to its owner.

The inimitable Sergeant Cuff, sent for from London to solve the disappearance of the diamond, shows his competence in contrast with the pompous local officer, Superintendent Seegrave, who heads a list of inept plodders serving as foils to great detectives in subsequent literature. Cuff was based in part on Inspector Whicher of the London Detective Police, an organization much admired by Dickens and Collins in the 1850s. Cuff shows his expertise as he examines some smeared paint with a magnifying glass and analyzes the time element in the drying of the paint. When he studies the household laundry-book, contemporary readers recognized at once the reference to the sensational murder case of Constance Kent in 1861. The girl was accused of murdering her three-year-old brother, largely because of evidence produced by Inspector Whicher, who showed that the "washing-book" listed a nightgown belonging to the sister that could not be accounted for, presumably because it was bloodstained and had been destroyed. When Constance was acquitted, Whicher was much criticized, only to be vindicated when the girl later confessed to the murder.

Unlike his successors in mystery fiction, Sergeant Cuff is not infallible. Despite his excellent methods, his first solution to the crime is wrong. He retires to the country to grow roses, prefiguring Sherlock and his bees or Hercule Poirot and his vegetable marrows, but unlike those sleuths, Cuff is not the central figure in the story. He disappears from the scene for a long segment of the novel, reappearing in the end to trace the diamond and reveal the fate of the perpetrator. Only with Conan Doyle and after did the detective become the chief focus of the novel.

Again, Collins used the technique of multiple narrators, each uniquely individualized. Gabriel Betteredge, the house steward and faithful retainer, begins the narration with his homely comments, citing texts from *Robinson Crusoe* in the manner of Bible quoters. Warmly humorous, he sets the generally cheerful atmosphere of the novel. The charming young hero, Franklin Blake, takes on the narrative duties, with his "French, German, and English" sides, reflecting Collins' preference for continental attitudes over straitlaced English ones. In contrast, the amusing character of Miss Clack, distributing her religious tracts, represents the evangelical bore whose cant Collins openly despised.

Unlike *The Woman in White,* where tragic events form the central plot and the tone is appropriately somber, *The Moonstone* moves in a peaceful world of wealth and ease. The young people, as Gabriel points out, having nothing useful to do, must find ways to amuse themselves. The jovial doctor who experiments with giving Franklin Blake the opium is merely playing a lighthearted prank. Even the loss of the diamond is regrettable but carries no hint of violence until the closing scenes of the novel.

Only the deformed and homely servant, Rosanna Spearman, recalls the reader to grim reality. Her neurotic obsession with the quicksands on the shore forecasts her tragic end. A short distance from the house, the sand hills run down to the sea, and between two spits of rock, Gabriel describes

> the most horrible quicksand on the shores of Yorkshire. At the turn of the tide, something goes on in the unknown deeps below, which sets the whole face of the quicksand shivering and trembling in a manner most remarkable to see, and which has given to it, among the people in our parts, the name of The Shivering Sand. (Penguin ed., p. 55)

Rosanna is the source for some social as well as moral commentary in the novel. Because of her background in a reformatory from which Lady Verinder had rescued her, she becomes an early suspect in the theft of the diamond, and her hopeless passion for Franklin Blake underscores the difference in class between them, contributing to her despair.

Similarly, the character of Ezra Jennings reflects the prejudice of society. A West Indian of mixed blood, he is a social outcast in spite of his intelligence and his competence as a doctor. Like Collins himself, Jennings has taken increasing doses of laudanum to ease the extreme pain of a chronic illness, and his account of its debilitating effects suggests that by this date, Collins is describing his own experience.

The novel begins with a prologue describing the storming of Seringapatam, where Rachel's uncle had ripped the famous diamond from a sacred Hindu shrine. The contrast is clearly implied between the Western view of the diamond as a means of wealth and power and the Eastern view of it as a spiritual symbol. Thus, the novel ends appropriately with the traveler Mr. Murthwaite visiting a remote region of India, where he sees the diamond again:

> There, raised high on a throne, seated on his typical antelope, with his four arms stretching toward the four corners of the earth, there soared above us, dark and awful in the mystic light of heaven, the god of the Moon. And there, in the forehead of the deity, gleamed the yellow Diamond, whose splendor had last shone on me in England, from the bosom of a woman's dress.

Last Works

While there is general agreement among twentieth-century readers that there was a marked decline in the quality of Wilkie Collins' works after *The Moonstone,* this view was not necessarily shared by his contemporaries. As a best-selling author whose name guaranteed a lively story, he was still paid well and remained popular with the public, although never at the level of his greatest success. His frequent bouts of extremely painful illness and the consequent increase in his use of laudanum inevitably contributed to the loss of his powers. At the same time, Collins became obsessed with writing novels of "purpose," where the tone became strident and polemical. In an essay on Collins in the *Fortnightly Review* (1889), the poet Algernon Charles Swinburne paraphrased a well-known couplet:

> What brought good Wilkie's genius nigh perdition?
> Some demon whispered—'Wilkie! have a mission.'
>
> (Norman Page, ed., p. 28)

Man and Wife (1870), the novel that followed *The Moonstone,* illustrates Swinburne's point. Collins attacks the marriage laws of Scotland, where an "irregular" marriage could be recognized without the intent of the parties. While Collins stretches credulity to place heroine Anne Sylvester at an inn where her seducer's innocent friend is mistaken for her husband, resulting in an assumed marriage, he vigorously defends the plight of women who are the victims of such illogical statutes.

Not content with one social problem in *Man and Wife,* Collins attacks a less convincing one: the tendency for young athletes, particularly at the universities, to engage in hooliganism. The extended passages condemning the "immoral" conduct of these young men makes for tedious reading.

The New Magdalen (1873), somewhat more readable today, presents a young woman, Mercy Merrick, formerly a prostitute, who successfully assumes the identity of a lady. When the truth is revealed, Mercy's tale of her life of poverty and abuse moves the minister, Julian Gray, to marry her, to the dismay of critics who protested against the impropriety of a clergyman marrying a fallen woman. In *The Fallen Leaves* (1879), a prostitute again achieves marriage. A novel whose chief characters are named Amelius Goldenheart and Simple Sally seems unpromising at best, but Collins' theme of compassion for the plight of the child Sally is persuasive. The attack upon vivisection in *Heart and Science* (1883), based upon a contemporary case of a doctor accused but acquitted of malpractice, serves to confirm Swinburne's couplet, as its fulminations tend to weary the reader.

In a more successful attack on a social problem, *The Evil Genius* (1886) presents a good case against the law in divorce that gave children to the father even though the mother was the innocent party. The Married Women's Property Act of 1882 had taken one step in the long battle for women's rights, but other protections were badly needed.

Collins made some attempts in the late works to recapture his earlier skill in mystery fiction. *The Law and the Lady* has some merit as a detective story. Valeria Macallan, one of Collins' admirably determined women, learns that her husband had been tried for murdering his former wife and had received the Scottish verdict of "Not Proven." She sets out to prove his innocence and clear his name, following clues that lead to the ultimate solution of the mystery.

For the most part, however, Collins seemed to have lost his ability to sustain suspense. Inspired by a visit to Venice, *The Haunted Hotel* (1879), a short novel with a murder and a ghost, combines the sensational and the gothic, but the mystery itself is too easily solved. Only the sinister aspects of the Venetian setting are effective. In *'I Say No'* (1884), Collins makes another attempt at a murder mystery. The resourceful schoolgirl, Emily Brown, uncovers the circumstances of her father's death, but the novel is a lightweight echo of earlier work.

The last novel, *Blind Love* (1890), was running serially when Collins suffered a stroke, and he asked Walter Besant to finish it, providing him with detailed notes for the final chapters. Based upon a case of insurance fraud, the book, while in no way the equal of Collins' best work, is remarkably coherent and holds the reader's interest more successfully than one would expect from the pen of a dying man.

Legacy

Wilkie Collins is best known today as the father of mystery fiction. *The Woman in White* is a masterpiece of suspense, while *The Moonstone* is the first full-length work using the "whodunit" formula, a pattern that became a staple of twentieth-century mysteries. His brilliant use of suspense and his depiction of detective skills lay a foundation for a major literary genre. To his contemporaries, Collins was known as a sensation novelist and a writer of social commentary. In this regard, all of his work makes a major contribution to scholars studying the society of Victorian England. In terms of literary quality, he never quite matched the genius of the Brontës, William Makepeace Thackeray, Anthony Trollope, George Eliot, or Thomas Hardy, but his best work places him well within the second rank of Victorian novelists. Perhaps Swinburne said it best, as cited by Norman Page, when he described Collins as a genuine artist who stands in relation to major genius as the minor Elizabethan dramatists stood in relation to Shakespeare.

Selected Bibliography

WORKS OF WILKIE COLLINS

INDIVIDUAL WORKS

(Dates of first editions in volume form.)

"The Last Stagecoachman." *Illuminated Magazine*, August 1843.

Memoirs of the Life of William Collins, Esq., R. A. London: Longman, Brown, Green, and Longmans, 1848.

Antonina; or, The Fall of Rome. London: Bentley, 1850.

Rambles Beyond Railways; or, Notes in Cornwall Taken A-Foot. London: Bentley, 1851.

Mr. Wray's Cash-Box; or, The Mask and the Mystery. London: Bentley, 1852.

Basil: A Story of Modern Life. London: Bentley, 1852; New York: Dover, 1980.

Hide and Seek; or, The Mystery of Mary Grice. London: Bentley, 1854.

After Dark. London: Smith, Elder, 1856. Stories; includes material by Dickens.

The Dead Secret. London: Bradbury & Evans, 1857.

The Queen of Hearts. London: Hurst & Blackett, 1859. Stories.

The Woman in White. London: Sampson Low, 1860; London: Oxford Univ. Press, 1975.

No Name. London: Sampson Low, 1862; London and New York: Penguin, 1994.

My Miscellanies. London: Sampson Low, 1863.

Armadale. London: Smith, Elder, 1866; New York: Dover, 1977.

The Moonstone. London: Tinsley, 1868; London and New York: Penguin, 1966.

Man and Wife. London: Ellis, 1870.

Poor Miss Finch. A Novel. London: Bentley, 1872.

The New Magdalen. London: Bentley, 1873.

Miss or Mrs? and Other Stories in Outline. London: Bentley, 1873.

The Frozen Deep and Other Tales. London: Bentley, 1874.

The Law and the Lady. London: Chatto & Windus, 1875.

The Two Destinies. London: Chatto & Windus, 1876.

The Haunted Hotel, a Mystery of Modern Venice: to which is added My Lady's Money. London: Chatto & Windus, 1879.

A Rogue's Life. From His Birth to His Marriage. London: Bentley, 1879.

The Fallen Leaves. London: Chatto & Windus, 1879.

Jezebel's Daughter. London: Chatto & Windus, 1880.

The Black Robe. London: Chatto & Windus, 1881.
Heart and Science. London: Chatto & Windus, 1883.
'I Say No.' London: Chatto & Windus, 1884.
The Evil Genius. London: Chatto & Windus, 1886.
The Guilty River. Bristol: Arrowsmith, 1886.
Little Novels. London: Chatto & Windus, 1887. Stories.
The Legacy of Cain. London: Chatto & Windus, 1889.
Blind Love. London: Chatto & Windus, 1890. Completed by Walter Besant.

COLLABORATIONS WITH DICKENS

The Holly-Tree Inn. New York: Dix & Edwards, 1855. First published in *Household Words,* Christmas 1855.
The Wreck of the Golden Mary. London: Bradbury & Evans, 1856.
The Two Apprentices. With a History of Their Lazy Tour. Philadelphia: Peterson, 1857.

BIBLIOGRAPHIES

Beetz, Kirk H. *Wilkie Collins: An Annotated Bibliography, 1889–1976.* Metuchen, N.J.: Scarecrow, 1978.
Sadleir, Michael. "Wilkie Collins, 1828–1889." In *Excursions in Victorian Bibliography.* London: Chaundy & Cox, 1922. Repr. 1974.

BIOGRAPHICAL AND CRITICAL STUDIES

Ashley, Robert. *Wilkie Collins.* New York: Roy, 1952.
Clarke, William M. *The Secret Life of Wilkie Collins.* London: Allison and Busby, 1988.
Collins, Phillip. *Dickens and Crime.* London: Macmillan, 1962.
Davis, Nuel Pharr. *The Life of Wilkie Collins.* Urbana: Univ. of Illinois Press, 1956.
Eliot, T. S. "Wilkie Collins and Dickens." In his *Selected Essays.* New York: Harcourt Brace, 1932.
Heller, Tamar. *Dead Secrets: Wilkie Collins and the Female Gothic.* New Haven, Conn.: Yale Univ. Press, 1992.
Hyder, C. K. "Wilkie Collins and *The Woman in White.*" *PMLA* 54: 297–303 (March 1939).
Lonoff, Sue. *Wilkie Collins and His Victorian Readers.* New York: AMS Press, 1982.
Marshall, William H. *Wilkie Collins.* New York: Twayne, 1970.
Millais, John G. *The Life and Letters of Sir John Everett Millais.* London: Methuen, 1899.
O'Neill, Philip. *Wilkie Collins: Women, Property, and Propriety.* Totowa, N.J.: Barnes & Noble, 1988.
Page, Norman, ed. *Wilkie Collins: The Critical Heritage.* London: Routledge & Kegan Paul, 1974.
Peters, Catherine. *The King of Inventors: A Life of Wilkie Collins.* Princeton, N.J.: Princeton Univ. Press, 1991.
Peterson, Audrey. *Victorian Masters of Mystery: From Wilkie Collins to Conan Doyle.* New York: F. Ungar, 1984.
Robinson, Kenneth. *Wilkie Collins. A Biography.* London: The Bodley Head, 1951.
Sayers, Dorothy L. Introduction to *The Omnibus of Crime.* New York: Payson and Clarke, 1929.
———. *Wilkie Collins: A Critical and Biographical Study.* Edited by E. R. Gregory. Toledo, Ohio: Friends of the Univ. of Toledo Libraries, 1977. Unfinished.
Taylor, Jenny B. *In the Secret Theatre of Home: Wilkie Collins, Sensation Narrative, and Nineteenth Century Psychology.* London and New York: Routledge, 1988.

K. C. Constantine
(b. 1934)

JEFFERY FRASER

The pseudonymous K. C. Constantine is the author of an acclaimed series of police procedurals set in the hard-bitten industrial town of Rocksburg, Pennsylvania. The series, launched in 1972 with *The Rocksburg Railroad Murders,* follows the career of Mario Balzic, an insightful, surprisingly compassionate, and sometimes vulgar police chief whose detective work is complicated by small-town politics, ever-shrinking resources, and the demands of being a father, a son, and a husband. By 1998 Constantine had published novels in the series. His books have been applauded by the *New York Times Book Review, Washington Post Book World, Publisher's Weekly,* and other major journals for their earthy dialogue, vivid characterization, and accurate and humane portrayal of life and crime in blue-collar America. The eighth novel of the series, *Joey's Case* (1988), earned him an Edgar Allan Poe Award nomination for Best Novel. For all of his critical success, however, the books did not sell well and several of his early novels are out of print.

Life

K. C. Constantine was born on 24 July 1934, in McKees Rocks Borough, Pennsylvania, an industrial town that borders Pittsburgh to the west along the Ohio River. It was his home for nearly thirty years and his experiences are reflected in the places, characters, and perspectives described in his books.

Constantine's family struggled throughout his childhood; at times they were desperately poor. His Russian-born father, a craftsman and artist, worked a variety of jobs, from restoring antiques and church statuary, to painting billboards, houses, and portraits of pets. He came to America in 1907, with instructions to earn a small fortune and return home, as his own father and three of his brothers had done before him; but in New York City, the only relative he could track down, an uncle, accused him of being an imposter and turned him away. He lived hand-to-mouth for ten years as an itinerant laborer until he enlisted in the U.S. Army during World War I. After his discharge, he moved to McKees Rocks, where he married Constantine's mother, whose father was one of the founders of the borough's Russian Orthodox church. An immigrant himself, her father owned retail businesses and apartments, which he later lost during the Great Depression.

Constantine was the youngest of four children, but only he and his older brother survived beyond their teenage years. Diphtheria claimed one of his sisters and another died of complications arising from a ruptured appendix. The family endured the deaths along with other hardships. In 1936, they lost everything when the Ohio River flooded their low-lying neighborhood. The Great Depression brought more misery. Unemployed for the better part of a painful decade, Constantine's father held one temporary job, an eleven-month assignment finishing the woodwork at Fallingwater, a millionaire's home designed by Frank Lloyd Wright and located forty miles southeast of Pittsburgh.

McKees Rocks was a melting pot of immigrant workers. In 1910, forty-one percent of the borough's population was foreign born—natives of England, Austria, Italy, Czechoslovakia, Poland, Russia, Hungary, Croatia, Germany, Lithuania, and Serbia. They worked in plants making railcars, enamelware, pulleys, springs, cans, wire, and steel bar. The work was hard and they earned little more than what they needed to keep a home. Injury and illness threatened financial disaster, as did recession, plant closings, and strikes. The borough was a melting pot more in appearance than in fact. Bigotry built walls that survived generations, as families settled according to their ethnicity. The Russians, Constantine's family among them, hugged the river with Ukrainians, Czechs, Croats, and a few Serbs in a place known as "The Bottoms." The Italians claimed the hills; blacks lived behind the Lockhart Iron & Steel plant; and the Poles lived in a place called Preston Village. Constantine knew the Polish neighborhood as "Hunky Town," and because he was Russian Orthodox, on Sundays he was forbidden to speak to schoolmates who filed into the Slovak Catholic church next door.

Education

For most McKees Rocks young men, public education was little more than an exercise in the rudiments of reading, writing, and mathematics, which they were obligated to endure before beginning their lives in the mills and factories. Many, in fact, began working second shift while in high school. Constantine was an exception. He was a good student who enjoyed reading, and often had to smuggle books past tough street-smart peers who disapproved.

Constantine's parents had not gone far in school. His father attended the equivalent of American elementary school in Russia, and Constantine's mother had finished only the third grade when her father sent her to work in a mill; but both placed a high value on educating their children. Constantine's mother taught him to read before he entered first grade. They wanted a college-educated son; they saved for it. Constantine's father took on extra work. When their oldest son chose to enlist in the U.S. Marine Corps after high school, they put their hopes on Constantine, but he had other ideas. He wanted to play baseball.

Constantine had set his sights on the major leagues at age twelve, after his uncle took him to watch the Pittsburgh Pirates at Forbes Field and explained to him that professional ballplayers made a living playing the game Constantine loved. In the sandlots around Pittsburgh he developed into a catcher skilled enough to catch the eye of a scout for the Pittsburgh club, but lacked the kind of star potential that buys more than a quick look in the minor leagues. On the day he was to sign a minor-league contract, he was in the hospital with a ruptured appendix; it cost him a slot on a minor league roster. He was left as a catcher on call, a spare part teams could borrow to plug into a lineup depleted by injury. The first call was from a Batavia, New York, team in need of a healthy catcher. Constantine played briefly, without distinction, and under the name of the injured player he had replaced.

Baseball failed to call back. In 1952, Constantine enrolled in Westminster College, a small Presbyterian school north of Pittsburgh, to pursue a degree in business administration. If he was going to spend his life in a plant, he would rather spend it in the office than on the factory floor.

Constantine's milltown education did not prepare him for college. He did not know how to use a library to research a topic. His accounting courses were a puzzle. He was overwhelmed by the classical literature he was assigned, and by the requirement of one humanities professor that he listen to the opera on the radio every Saturday night. He did not own a radio, nor did he have the money to buy one. He was also out-of-step socially. He was the only Russian Orthodox student on a campus where there were few Catholics, fewer blacks, and no Jewish students. Young men wore white bucks. Constantine had never known a man to wear white shoes. He lasted two years, surviving an arrest for stealing from the campus bookstore, but drawing an academic suspension for consistently poor grades. In 1954 he returned home, where more trouble was waiting.

Constantine's father, a union painter, had been badly beaten on his way to work at a downtown Pittsburgh department store where the Teamsters' Union was striking. He had been mistaken as scab labor. Constantine followed his father when he returned to work, picked out the teamster he believed did the beating, and dropped the man with a fist leaden with a roll of dimes. The sentencing judge gave him a choice: go to prison, or join the Marine Corps for the brand of discipline the judge felt he needed.

The boredom of serving in the peacetime military resulted in Constantine's first step toward becoming a writer. Driven by the words of a freshman composition professor who flunked him, twice—telling him, "You do not know how to make an English sentence" ("Writing About Balzic," p. 52)—Constantine wrote to fill idle hours. He also read more, over beers in a service club at Camp Lejeune, North Carolina. In the base library, he discovered by accident a copy of Eric Hoffer's *The True Believer* misfiled on the fiction shelves. He was impressed by Hoffer's prose, but more by the fact the author had not gone to school. He copied Hoffer's work longhand—sentences, paragraphs, and entire pages—replacing Hoffer's nouns and verbs with his own. "I was learning how to write from a guy who had never gone to school," he remarked (unpublished interview, 21 April 1997).

Constantine was readmitted to Westminster College under academic and social probation in 1958. As a condition of readmission, he was forbidden to set foot on campus for any reason other than to attend class. He took his writing seriously, his work improved, and his teachers began taking note. He earned a bachelor's degree in English in 1962, married, and began work on several novels. None was ever published. One examined life in the Marine Corps boot camp. All were "serious fiction," in Constantine's words, that reflected his training in classical literature (unpublished interview, 21 September 1997). In 1964, he was accepted into the University of Iowa Writers Workshop. The couple stayed in Iowa one year, long enough to have a son, and for Constantine to meet Robert V. Williams, who taught the only course he could afford to take. Williams convinced Constantine that he could, in fact, write an English sentence, but was not yet able to build a plot.

Constantine returned to McKees Rocks in 1965 after money for a teaching assistantship at the University of California at Hayward dried up. In McKees Rocks, he worked as a forklift operator and a substitute teacher of mentally handicapped children. In 1967, he was hired to teach English composition at a Catholic women's college in southwestern Pennsylvania. There he continued to write "serious fiction," ignoring the genre that embraces the kind of crime, characters, and psychology he was most familiar with.

Education in Crime

Constantine's youth was spent in a town notorious for public corruption, gambling, and pervasive organized crime. McKees Rocks residents viewed traditional authority, including the police department, with suspicion for good reason. It was common to see police at busy intersections soliciting money for a Police Athletic League that did not exist. As a teenager, Constantine witnessed the shooting of a man who posed no apparent threat to the police officer who gunned him down. In his essay "Writing about Balzic," he remembers how his neighbors became evasively dumb when cops came around:

> When I was very young, five at the oldest, some policemen came into our neighborhood and began to question people about something. If I knew what they were talking about then, I certainly don't remember it now; what struck me was that when the cops approached some people I knew, they suddenly couldn't speak English, or American as my father always called it. Now I knew that those people spoke American, because I heard them talking every day, yet there they were, seemingly unable to speak anything but the language they had learned as children. The immediate lesson was that cops were not to be trusted. (p. 46)

Local government officials were no better. One McKees Rocks burgess in the 1930s was convicted of murdering his wife and was himself murdered in prison. Local library files are thick with newspaper clippings of officials being indicted, convicted, or openly accused of corruption. Kickbacks were a way of doing business. Gambling joints and bars could not stay open all night without payoffs, and McKees Rocks clubs stayed lit like Las Vegas. The borough's most notorious public official, a burgess who ruled from the 1940s into the 1960s, survived two assassination attempts as well as indictments for allowing gambling and prostitution to flourish. An official of lesser weight, a street commissioner, was murdered in 1979 with cyanide-laced whiskey not long after being paroled for hijacking a truck laden with cheese.

The most prevalent illegality in McKees Rocks was gambling. Scores of social clubs were allowed to operate, providing places to drink and gamble after hours and on Sundays. Even churches were heavily involved in the gaming business. Lacking affluent members, they relied on the proceeds of gambling for operating funds—they organized elaborate raffles, bingo nights, and festivals featuring games of chance, some run by clergymen in collars.

The Rocksburg Railroad Murders

Budget cuts at the Catholic women's college claimed Constantine's job teaching English composition in 1969. He had moved his family to Westmoreland County, about thirty miles east of Pittsburgh, a place of affordable suburbs and shopping malls, farmland and struggling factory towns. Within a year, he was hired as a proofreader at a local newspaper, whose editor was a friend and a regular at the saloon where he drank. Constantine continued to write, but his writing was going nowhere. Agents and publishers were not interested in work they felt had no market. Mysteries, one agent told him, are what sell.

In line at a newsstand one morning, he noticed how mysteries by Carter Brown, Agatha Christie, Georges Simenon, and others were prominently displayed near the cash register. He asked if the books sold. The clerk said they sold so well he could not keep them in stock. Until then, the only such books Constantine had read were a few Mickey Spillane novels he bought in high school for their descriptions of sexual encounters. Driving past a neglected train station on his way home, he began to build a plot around a man found beaten to death near the tracks. From the idea came "Half Remembered Faces," a police procedural featuring a half-Italian, half-Serbian small town police chief named Mario Balzic. After a few rejections, the book was sold to Saturday Review Press and was published in 1972 as *The Rocksburg Railroad Murders.*

The book was well reviewed, earning praise for its straightforward plot and sympathetic characterization. Unfamiliar with the genre, Constantine created an unconventional protagonist in Balzic, a working stiff whose trump card is his insight into the psychology of his working-class neighbors. He carries no gun, and does not work alone, but with the state police and county detectives who share jurisdiction; he juggles his end of the investigation with the responsibilities of family, and has a capacity for compassion not often found in a character so exposed to the ugliest side of society. Newgate Calendar, in the *New York Times,* described *The Rocksburg Railroad Murders* as "one of the most sensitive crime novels of recent years."

Early Novels

Constantine's second book, *The Man Who Liked to Look at Himself* (1973), was widely ignored. Based on an actual case, the nasty story takes Balzic from the discovery of a sawed-in-half human femur to the kinds of sexually perverse secrets people sleep better not knowing. In *The Blank Page* (1974), Balzic is thrust into the world of academia to solve the murder of a coed found strangled, a blank sheet of paper on her belly. The chief suffers the pompous posturing of college professors, but demonstrates that when it comes to murder, an understanding of human nature, not book learning, is what counts. In *A Fix like This* (1975), a stabbing and a mobster's infidelity jeopardize Balzic's working arrangement with the gambling-supported underworld. The book, which shows Constantine's progress toward more complex plots and subjects, attracted little attention.

These first four books establish a sense of time, place, and character for the series. The stories reflect the times during which they were written, a period that encompasses the decline of mining and heavy industry that swept western Pennsylvania beginning in the mid 1970s, and later the emergence of conservative reformists in government, privatization, and family values. They are set in Rocksburg, a fictitious town in western Pennsylvania coal country, which emerges as an amalgam of the region's milltowns, places where jobs are blue-collar, minds are as narrow as the century-old streets, saloons and churches are filled, and high school football is king. Balzic, the central character, is surrounded by a colorful supporting cast: his old-world mother; enduring wife, Ruth; St. Malachy's poker-playing, wine-nipping priest, Father Marrazo; Myron "Mo" Valcanas, a formidable attorney even when half-sober; and an aging mafioso, Dom Muscotti, owner of Balzic's favorite tavern.

The novels are rooted in the realities of everyday, small-town police work. Homicides rarely involve complicated conspiracies. Most are crimes of passion, the results of repressed rage, a moment of insanity, or drug and alcohol use. Balzic's crime solving is not glamorous, thrilling, or violent, nor is it the result of clever genius. He works the phone, examines reports, and burns shoe leather walking the streets. Like the best detectives, both fictional and real, he recognizes conversation and observation as the arts of his trade.

Balzic keeps his department clean, unlike his predecessor who retired comfortably on the mob money he was paid to maintain an open town. Balzic's corruption is less hamfisted, more justifiable because his motive is not personal gain. In *A Fix like This,* Balzic's anger over what he thinks is a mob-related stabbing reveals the payoff he expects for steering clear of bookmaker Dom Muscotti's operation. "Dom, sixteen years ago next month, we made some rules, remember? No whores, no dope, and no muscle, right?" (p. 35). More subtle is his willingness to exploit the trust he has earned as friend and father to advance a case. In *The Rocksburg Railroad Murders,* he trades on friendship to pry from Father Marrazo words spoken by a suspect in the sanctity of a church confessional. When Balzic exploits the naïveté of his fourteen-year-old daughter to gain secrets about a schoolmate he suspects is a killer, he knows she is likely to be crippled with guilt if her innocent disclosures lead to an arrest.

Constantine tells his stories from Balzic's point of view, but in third-person narrative. He uses a conversational style of storytelling, relying on extensive tracts of working-class dialogue to build his plots and define his characters. *A Fix like This* demonstrates his willingness to buck tradition with plots that give as much weight to emotions, relationships, and personalities as they do to the nuts and bolts of solving the crime.

Constantine's short list of writers who had the most influence on his work includes Hoffer, Ernest Hemingway, E. B. White, and James Thurber. His early books were recognized as noteworthy examples of American naturalism, and his writing was compared favorably to such works as Stephen Crane's *Maggie, Girl of the Streets.*

Despite such praise, favorable reviews, and the progress Constantine felt he was making, his career soured after the publication of *A Fix like This,* which he considered the best of his first four books. Sales remained poor, the Saturday Review Press was bought and sold, and his editors kept changing. One editor, in response to Constantine's complaints about lousy sales, suggested he write cookbooks if it was money he wanted. Fed up, Constantine quit publishing.

Series Revived

Seven years passed before Mario Balzic was heard from again. He resurfaced in the Double Detective line of mysteries published by David R. Godine, Publishers, which repackaged Constantine's first four novels in two trade paperbacks. The deal was the result of a chance discovery by Robin W. Winks of *The Man Who Liked to Look at Himself* in a second-hand-book barn. Winks, a professor of history at Yale University and a reviewer of mysteries for the *Boston Globe,* was the general editor of the Double Detective series. He put Constantine in touch with an editorial director at Godine, William Goodman, who agreed to read new work. Rocksburg was back in business.

Constantine returned with a new perspective on his series. He had had a lot of time to think about Rocksburg during seven idle years and that thinking confirmed what those who had reviewed his books had suggested all along. What he had been writing dressed as a police procedural was, in fact, a social history of an American working-class enclave as seen through the eyes of a cop.

Steel and mining were in steep decline in western Pennsylvania when Constantine resumed writing, and Rocksburg returns in *The Man Who Liked Slow Tomatoes* (1982) as a city in distress. Industry is downsizing and so is city hall. Balzic's call to look into the disappearance of an unemployed miner is a welcome distraction from the stalled contract negotiations between the police union and city hall. Balzic takes his time investigating people who have been dealt a lousy hand as Constantine explores the emotional and financial toll the wholesale loss of jobs has on a community. The case converges on the missing man's father-in-law, a hard-headed retired miner named Mike Fiori, whose status as a working-class hero and reputation for growing sumptuous tomatoes hide a murderous heart. In drawing Fiori, Constantine conjured memories of his own grandfather, who had treated Constantine's father harshly throughout his life. Constantine despised his grandfather for it and celebrated his death by dancing a jig. *The Man Who Liked Slow Tomatoes* was published to strong reviews and sold nearly fifty thousand copies, the highest sales of any Rocksburg novel yet.

Meddling mayors and other small-time pols are a common source of irritation for Balzic, whose policy is to keep his nose out of party politics, remain neutral, and hope for the best. In *Always a Body to Trade* (1983), voter discontent sweeps scrubbed-clean Kenny Strohn into office to give Balzic a new boss. Constantine adds humor by allowing his characters to be themselves—Strohn's naïveté plays comically off Balzic's prickly patience with the reform-minded do-gooder. The case itself, a murder, takes Balzic to territories he rarely treads: drugs, rogue cops, and Rocksburg's black community. To accommodate all, Constantine introduces several plot lines and weaves them together as the story unfolds, a technique he came to use often.

In *Upon Some Midnights Clear* (1985) Balzic works three cases: the robbery of an old woman's Christmas Club money, a shooting, and an act of civil disobedience during which disgruntled Vietnam veterans stage a protest in the nude. Balzic's intuition allows him to see the old woman's robbery story for what it is: dubious, at best. Mary Hart, a pandering columnist for the *Rocksburg Gazette,* sees it as a Christmastime sob story ripe for picking, truth be damned. The subplot that results examines the press in unflattering light, finding it arrogant, ignorant, and abusive of its trust.

Joey's Case (1988), perhaps the most highly acclaimed Rocksburg novel, centers around a homicide based on the murder of a man Constantine knew and had been drinking with the night he was killed. Balzic's personal turmoil often intrudes on his police work, but never more so than here. Balzic is seeing a doctor for sexual impotence and dreads going home to face his wife. Meanwhile, the murder he's working has sex and guilt written all over it. The victim was killed by his ex-wife's boyfriend, and two chief witnesses, a teacher and her married lover, will not cooperate for fear of exposing their illicit romance. With every case, Balzic gains some morsel of understanding that sharpens his insight into the psychology behind the crime. In *Joey's Case,* the lesson is that hard-eyed meanness is a byproduct of feeling weak and powerless.

The job of living soon begins to demand as much from Balzic as his job as a cop. In *Sunshine Enemies* (1990) he is working a porn-store murder when he learns his mother has suffered a fatal heart attack. Balzic's work has always been complicated by distraction. Now grief, guilt, and questions of his own mortality are added to the baggage. The despair deepens for Balzic and Rocksburg in *Bottom Liner Blues* (1993). The economy is still on life support and the citizenry is showing signs of cracking, Balzic included. He has neglected his marriage and his lonely wife wants to negotiate a better deal. The Gulf War is raging and he has flashbacks of World War II combat in the Pacific. On the job, he is drawn to a disturbed woman's wild tale of a homicide waiting to happen, then allows himself to be distracted by Nick Myushkin, a malcontent so grating he has been kicked out of Muscotti's. Myushkin is a writer of police procedurals. He has published nine books, all favorably reviewed, yet lives below the poverty line. Not coincidentally, he holds a grudge against public libraries. Pistol in hand, he explains why:

> I'm supposed to get ten percent of retail, man, but not when libraries buy 'em by the hundreds, hey, my royalties go way down, like half. But once, man! Once, they pay for 'em. The rest of the time, all the time they're givin' 'em away until they fall apart, man, give 'em away once a week the first year, man, every two weeks every year after, until they fuck-ing fall apart, then they tape 'em up, and throw 'em on a table and sell 'em for a dime. And I don't get another goddamn penny outta that! (1994 ed., p. 180)

Constantine, an advocate for authors receiving at least a tax exemption for royalties lost through libraries, had copies of *Bottom Liner Blues* sent to members of the U.S. Senate and House subcommittees overseeing copyrights. He received three responses thanking him for his interest. The book itself attracted mixed reviews. "Mr. Constantine, who has a golden ear for dialogue, has not lost his Whitmanesque feeling for the voice of this forgotten region," Marilyn Stasio wrote in the *New York Times.* "Like his dispirited hero, however, the author seems to have given up on his job, which is not singing the blues, but telling stories."

Constantine's decision to write the series as a genre-wrapped social history came at a price. If a chronological pace demands that time march on, then so must Balzic, into the sunset. In *Cranks and Shadows* (1995), Balzic is sixty-five and tired. His wife is talking about Florida, city hall is in love with the notion of privatization, and police layoffs are imminent. He investigates strange reports of camouflaged commandos skulking around the city and learns, to his utter disbelief, they are public-spirited citizens who have organized their own Special Weapons and Emergency Response Team. For Constantine, it was a story ripped from the pages of his local newspaper. For Balzic, it is the end of the line. SWERT had been organized right under his nose—had even recruited one of his men—and Balzic had never picked up the scent. Realizing his most essential faculties are in decline, Balzic retires. "I remember my wife got bifocals long after I did," he tells a drinking pal, "and I told her, I said, hey, you gotta practice the posture, you know, throw the head back, the mouth drops open, and after you get that right you realize you just moved on to a new stage of life. You just went from a regular human being to a geezer" (p. 17).

Good Sons (1996) leaves the matter of Balzic's successor unsettled. Foot-dragging politicos will not commit; for the short term at least, the job falls to Detective Sergeant Ruggerio "Rugs" Carlucci. A single, better educated, and much younger man than Balzic, Carlucci first appeared in *Always a Body to Trade.* Constantine regretted writing Balzic as a man unwilling to play the game of politics, as it contradicts the reality of what a political appointee would have to do to survive as long as Balzic had; he corrects the error with Carlucci. Although *Good Sons* focuses on the forty-something detective's investigation of a rape-turned-murder, Balzic's shadow lingers as Carlucci relies on his mentor for access to Dom Muscotti and insight into how to be a leader. Balzic returns in *Family Values* (1997), eager to get out of the house and investigate a seventeen-year-old murder for the state's attorney general; it is an ugly case full of brutality and police corruption. As it unfolds Constantine explores the strains that retirement imposes on both retiree and spouse.

Brushback (1998) is Carlucci's book. As acting chief he works a thorny murder case, the baseball-bat beating of a local pitching phenom whose popularity has insulated him from well-deserved domestic-abuse charges. As Balzic had done through most of his career, Carlucci cares for an aging mother; but he emerges a more modern man. He is trained in criminology and crime-scene photography; does fingerprinting, but not well; and is computer literate enough that, by default, he oversees the department's transition from paper to microchip. By the book's end, Constantine reveals whether his new protagonist will work Rocksburg's toughest cases as a boss or as another man's subordinate.

Anonymity

Very little is written about Constantine and his work. His reviewers credited him with nudging the police procedural closer to literature, urged readers to discover his books, and wonder how a writer of Constantine's ability remained a missing person for so long. The answer to this question is that Constantine remained fiercely private—his contracts forbade publishers to disclose his identity, and he refused book tours and other marketing schemes that required public appearances. No photographs of him have been published. He granted few interviews, and when he did, insisted on strict conditions. Writers were required to put their questions to him over the telephone or in a letter. Even then, he was known to reroute return dispatches through his publisher to conceal their point of origin.

Constantine said he took the vow of anonymity after his brush with celebrity as a minor-league ballplayer. As small-time as it was, he was disturbed that fans would confront him in town and second-guess his pitch calls from the night before. He explains his anonymity another way on the dust jacket of *Upon Some Midnights Clear:*

> If a person is serious about observing others in order to write about them, he doesn't want them in disguise. A storyteller must remain ordinary, as inconspicuous as a shoplifter. Identified, he cuts himself off from the truths other people unconsciously, unpretentiously give to him. These gifts, without which he cannot succeed, would get lost behind all the camouflage people wear the moment they sense they have lost their immunity. And is there any doubt that a storyteller is society's stoolie?

In the late 1990s the man behind the pseudonym continued to write from western Pennsylvania, where the voices of Rocksburg were heard in the streets and saloons of steel towns dying along the rivers.

Bibliography

WORKS OF K. C. CONSTANTINE

ROCKSBURG NOVELS

The Rocksburg Railroad Murders. New York: Saturday Review Press, 1972.

The Man Who Liked to Look at Himself. New York: Saturday Review Press, 1973.

The Blank Page. New York: Saturday Review Press, 1974.

A Fix like This. New York: Saturday Review Press, 1975.

The Man Who Liked Slow Tomatoes. Boston: Godine, 1982.

Always a Body to Trade. Boston: Godine, 1983.

Upon Some Midnights Clear. Boston: Godine, 1985.

Joey's Case. New York: Mysterious Press, 1988.

Sunshine Enemies. New York: Mysterious Press, 1990.

Bottom Liner Blues. New York: Mysterious Press, 1993, 1994.

Cranks and Shadows. New York: Mysterious Press, 1995.

Good Sons. New York: Mysterious Press, 1996.

Family Values. New York: Mysterious Press, 1997.

Brushback. New York: Mysterious Press, 1998.

OTHER

Afterword to *The Man Who Liked to Look at Himself/A Fix like This,* Godine Double Detective, no. 3. Boston: Godine, 1983.

"Organized Crime." In *Murder Ink.* Edited by Dilys Winn. New York: Workman, 1984. Pp. 20–23.

"Writing about Balzic." In *Colloquium on Crime.* Edited by R. W. Winks. New York: Scribners, 1986. Pp. 41–61.

INTERVIEWS

Unpublished interview with Jeffery Fraser, 21 April 1997.

Unpublished interview with Jeffery Fraser, 21 September 1997.

BIOGRAPHICAL AND CRITICAL STUDIES

Albert, Walter. "K. C. Constantine." In *Twentieth-Century Crime and Mystery Writers.* Edited by John M. Reilly. Chicago: St. James Press, 1991.

Calendar, Newgate. Review of *The Rocksburg Railroad Murders. New York Times Book Review,* 11 February 1973: 30.

———. Review of *Always A Body to Trade. New York Times Book Review,* 21 August 1983.

Dowell, Pat. Review of *Cranks and Shadows. Washington Post Book World,* 19 February, 1995: 6.

———. Review of *Cranks and Shadows, Publishers Weekly,* 12 December 1994: 52.

Stasio, Marilyn. Review of *Bottom Liner Blues. New York Times Book Review,* 2 May 1993.

Stone, W. B. "K. C. Constantine." *Popular World Fiction.* Washington, D.C.: Beacham Publishing, 1987. Pp. 353–360.

Winks, R. W. Afterword to *The Rocksburg Railroad Murders / The Blank Page,* Godine Double Detective, No. 1. Boston: Godine, 1982.

Patricia Cornwell
(b. 1956)

ELLEN BLEILER

THE FIRST CRIME NOVEL Patricia Cornwell wrote featured a "walking wounded . . . poetic . . . handsome detective named Joe Constable" (Cantwell). It was rejected, but an editor who turned down the aspiring author's effort suggested, in effect, "Write about what you know." Cornwell followed the advice, incorporating not only principles gained from her experience working at a morgue, but also elements of her own personality. After several rejections, *Postmortem* (1990), the first of Cornwell's books featuring Dr. Kay Scarpetta, Chief Medical Examiner of the Commonwealth of Virginia, became a best-seller, and acquired numerous awards along the way: an Edgar for best first novel from the Mystery Writers of America, the Golden Dagger Award from the British Crime Writers Association, a Prix du Roman d'Aventure from France, and many others. It was the first time any mystery had been so acclaimed in a single year.

Postmortem also established the blueprint for succeeding Scarpetta novels: Scarpetta is called to the scene of a murder that may be the work of a serial killer; at some point she meets with an FBI profiler who outlines the murderer's probable personality traits; someone tampers with her computer or records; her political and professional enemies backstab her and attempt to oust her from her job; the criminal threatens her life; but Scarpetta, overcoming these and other obstacles, works out the solution and occasionally carries out its penalty, "executing" the evildoer herself. Despite such similarities, Cornwell's books continue to reach the best-seller lists, even when her heroine's adventures are so far-fetched as to bring the author dangerously close to self-parody.

Cornwell spent six years as a computer analyst in the office of the chief medical examiner of Virginia, where she observed much besides her screen, and has stayed in touch with former coworkers. Because of her in-depth knowledge, the most intriguing parts of her books are the realistic descriptions of postmortem procedure and the painstaking analysis of crime-scene evidence by skilled medical and forensic experts. Thus, despite endings that frequently strain belief, her readers seem irresistibly drawn to the grisly but ever fascinating details of the autopsy table and its environs.

Although the effects of violence—the bodies in Scarpetta's morgue—are graphically described, Cornwell does not wallow in the acts of violence that brought them there. Yet, the author does often achieve a creepy verisimilitude and immediacy with her precise descriptions of actual places, such as the New York City subway system's eerie interconnecting tunnels in *From Potter's Field* (1995); or the garbage-strewn hillside adjoining a deteriorating neighborhood in *Cause of Death* (1996).

No doubt the public's curiosity about the duties of a medical examiner, plus a taste for somewhat morbid sensationalism—perhaps mixed with genuine scientific curiosity—account in large part for Cornwell's popularity. In addition, there is enough "cyber-jargon" to appeal to those with technical computer expertise, although a nonspecialist may well skip such pages of exposition with no feeling of loss. Besides the technical computer jargon, there is a lot of gun talk. The author herself acknowledges carrying a revolver wherever and whenever she can, and has urged her staff to do the same. She knows a good deal about firearms and ammunition. Cornwell also speaks to feminist readers: Scarpetta frequently reminisces about the difficulties of having been a minority of one in her medical school classes. With few exceptions, her problems—professional as well as personal—are caused by men. A recurrent situation is her put-down of men who doubt her competence or question her authority.

Besides the arcane mysteries of the morgue and the intricacies of the computer, Cornwell writes admiringly about the FBI—the four main characters in the Scarpetta series are either Bureau agents or consultants. The author dedicated her sixth novel, *The Body Farm* (1994), to Utah's Senator Orrin Hatch for his efforts to increase Bureau funding. Cornwell is obviously familiar with the work of the FBI, though her descriptions of activities in Quantico, while laced with official-sounding acronyms, tend to reveal less procedure than topography.

The author's manuscripts are checked for medical and scientific accuracy by Dr. Marcella Fierro, a pathologist and deputy medical examiner with whom Cornwell worked at the morgue, and by Dr. David Wiecking, a forensic medical expert who is the actual chief medical examiner of Virginia. In addition, Cornwell depends on material she learned and on acquaintances she made while attending police academy and forensic science classes during her employment in the medical examiner's office. Certain news events also seem to have suggested ideas to her. In *Cause of Death,* for example, she describes, albeit not very convincingly, a religious cult that engages in terrorist activities; in *Unnatural Exposure* (1997) she explores the possibility of murder by means of a biologically engineered mutant virus.

Cornwell states that she has tried to deal in each Scarpetta novel with a particular kind of crime, such as the rape-strangulations of *Postmortem,* the erotomania that leads to murder in *Body of Evidence* (1991), or the killing of couples in *All That Remains* (1992). As she told Rosemary Herbert in *The Fatal Art of Entertainment,* Cornwell believes that because she writes about real social problems such as violence, her books are "crime novels" rather than mysteries, which, in any case, she claims not to read, considering them to be light entertainment without the gravity of her own subject matter. One might thus expect a realistic development, but aside from the scientific activities of Dr. Scarpetta and her fellow forensic experts, Cornwell's novels are not police procedurals. They make almost no mention of the repetitive, laborious routine that comprises so much of police investigation, even though the author herself spent three years as a police reporter with the *Charlotte Observer* and later served as a police volunteer, often accompanying officers to homicide scenes. Nor are the books really medical mysteries, in which the solution depends on clinical or biological factors, as in *Malice Aforethought* by Francis Iles (Anthony Berkeley Cox) or the earlier works of R. Austin Freeman or Arthur B. Reeve. *Postmortem* comes closest to a medical mystery in that the murderer is tracked by the identification of a glittery residue found on his victims' bodies, and is later recognized by an unusual physiological characteristic. A curiosity of hematology resolves a question in *All That Remains,* but only after the killer has already been identified by chance; and while a mutant virus does play a part in *Unnatural Exposure,* it has little to do with apprehending the malefactor.

Cornwell's books are essentially detective thrillers, with Dr. Scarpetta investigating the crime, always in tandem with the same police officer. While Scarpetta may seek help and information from other experts on her staff, it is she who finds the essential clues and follows them up, with her efforts eventually focusing the murderer's unwelcome attention on herself.

Perhaps in part because of her failure to detail police procedure, one of Cornwell's major shortcomings lies in the solutions to the crimes she otherwise so realistically describes. Motives may be weak and unconvincing, or the killer may be psychotic, thus making it unnecessary for the author to provide a comprehensible motive. In *All That Remains,* the murderer is a loner who seems to function normally enough in other respects, but kills couples because he is jealous of their ability to form relationships. The villain of *Unnatural Exposure* had an unhappy childhood and feels professionally slighted—understandable grounds for a certain amount of resentment, though hardly for the degree of effort involved in his crimes.

A criminal is often caught when he starts to "decompensate"—a word that appears frequently, although Cornwell never really defines it. Links between characters—for example, a rogue FBI computer analyst and the serial killer with whom she teams up—are sometimes unclear, explained only in terms of where the characters met. In *The Fatal Art of Entertainment* Cornwell admits that she often does not know how her stories will end until they do, and that she is frequently uncertain of her murderer's identity until the last few pages (except, of course, in *Cruel & Unusual* [1993] and *From Potter's Field,* two books that deal with a serial killer named Temple Gault). Because of Cornwell's uncertainty about her perpetrators, as well as an antipathy (acknowledged in her interview with Herbert) to entering too closely into a criminal's mind, the FBI profiles in her books are often vague and general: "a psychopathic individual who blends well enough with normal society that he did not draw attention to himself" (*Cause of Death,* 1997 ed., p. 262); "a loner. This doesn't mean he lives alone, however. He could be married because he's skilled at maintaining a public persona" (*Body of Evidence,* 1992 ed., p. 53). Cornwell told Herbert that she considers such evaluations remarkably "on target."

While Cornwell has secured a place for herself in mystery fiction because of the milieu about which she writes in such precise detail, elements in her books do occasionally recall other works. For instance, free samples sent through the mail are the means of spreading the deadly virus in *Unnatural Exposure.* This is a device reminiscent of Agatha Christie's *The Pale Horse* (1961), where a lethal substance is distributed via free samples given out by a marketing research worker. The work Cornwell's Scarpetta books are most often compared with, however, is Thomas Harris' *The Silence of the Lambs* (1988) and its film version (1991). Both authors describe sociopathic criminal characters who commit multiple murders and sleuths who work for the FBI. There are additional similarities, particularly in *Hornet's Nest* (1997), a non-Scarpetta novel for which Cornwell created another alter ego, an ambitious *Charlotte Observer* police reporter named Andy Brazil, who serves as a weekend police volunteer. Andy's father and the father of Clarice Starling in *The Silence of the Lambs* were both law enforcement officers who were killed while on duty. Transsexual killers figure in both works.

The most obvious feature Cornwell and Harris share, though, is a crazy mass murderer. Harris' deadly psychiatrist-savant Hannibal Lecter, undoubtedly as mad as anyone Cornwell has devised, is in fact so egregiously insane that he is recognizably fantastic. Cornwell, however, seems to believe in the reality of even her most lurid creations, notably Temple Gault. Harris' Hannibal Lecter, despite his fantasy aspect, is a vivid personality. Gault, although Cornwell reveals various facts about him—that he changes his hair color, that he attended the same college as the author herself—remains shadowy. Lecter interacts with the heroine throughout much of *The Silence of the Lambs* and remains at large at the book's end; prior to killing Gault at the conclusion of *From Potter's Field,* Scarpetta has met him face to face only once (before he flees at the end of *Cruel & Unusual*), and then so briefly that the meeting scarcely qualifies as an encounter. Cornwell herself presumably recognized affinities between her work and Harris'. An article in the London *Mail on Sunday* stated that Cornwell asked Jodie Foster, star of the movie version of *Silence of the Lambs,* to act the role of Scarpetta in a film, but Foster declined.

Recurring Characters

Several characters reappear in the Scarpetta books. Foremost among them is the narrator, Dr. Kay Scarpetta herself. A forty-year-old divorcée in *Postmortem,* and about the same age in the later works (in *Unnatural Exposure* she describes herself as "a middle-aged woman set in her ways," [hardcover 1997 ed., p. 78]) Scarpetta is a graduate of both Johns Hopkins University's college of medicine and Georgetown University's law school. In her interview with Rosemary Herbert, Cornwell denies basing Scarpetta on any single acquaintance but acknowledges that the character owes her Italian descent to Dr. Fierro, the pathologist and mentor with whom she worked in the Richmond morgue. (Scarpetta's name means "little shoe" or "dancing pump," an allusion, perhaps, to the leather industry in her ancestral city of Verona.) Reviewers of Cornwell's books have described Scarpetta as brainy, capable, and prickly. Despite her professional successes, though, her personal life seems rather dismal. Her mother and sister live in Florida. The former neither comprehends nor sympathizes with her daughter's demanding career; the latter is an often-married author of children's books who greatly resents Scarpetta's influence over her daughter. Scarpetta's sex life is patchy. A lover betrays her in *Postmortem.* A romantic interest from law school days resurfaces in *Body of Evidence,* but is subsequently killed by an IRA bomb in London, and Scarpetta remains without a love interest until *The Body Farm.*

Characteristics that Scarpetta shares with her creator include her Miami origin, her fair-haired good looks, her fondness for tennis, and her highly secured residence in Richmond. If Cornwell has acquired a skill, Scarpetta displays it. Cornwell learned scuba diving; when Scarpetta is summoned to the scene of a diving accident in *Cause of Death,* she just happens to have her own diving equipment in the trunk of her car, even though it is midwinter. If Cornwell has flown to England on the Concorde, Scarpetta follows.

Another major character in the Scarpetta books is former New York policeman Pete Marino, introduced in *Postmortem* as a sergeant in the Richmond force. At the start of the series, he is more than a little hostile toward Dr. Scarpetta and skeptical about her (or any woman's) ability to handle the chief medical examiner's exacting job. Marino is given to peculiar locutions: someone's house is a "crib"; a suspect is a "squirrel"; and so forth. By *Unnatural Exposure* he has become Captain Marino, commander of Richmond's homicide squad, and a close friend of Scarpetta's. Scarpetta worries about his health—he is overweight, smokes, and maintains an unwholesome diet—while he worries about her safety and tries to protect her from malefactors. After Marino's wife of thirty years decamps, Scarpetta, an avid cook when she has time, often invites him to her house for dinner. However, she still calls him "Marino"—never "Pete"—and he generally addresses her as "Doc." Their relationship remains platonic, although Marino clearly would like it to be otherwise. The author claims Marino is a composite of officers she came to know while serving as a police volunteer.

Scarpetta's niece Lucy makes her debut in *Postmortem* as a slightly neurotic ten-year-old computer genius. Later, while still a student, she helps the FBI to develop an important computer program for apprehending criminals. Lucy endures numerous tribulations, but from the time she is ten years old, her expertise proves invaluable in solving the electronic security violations that constantly plague her aunt. By *Unnatural Exposure,* Lucy has become Scarpetta's cosleuth and a full-fledged member of the FBI's Hostage Rescue Team. She is another of Cornwell's alter egos; her experiences reflect the author's own, particularly her difficult childhood and adolescent years and the serious automobile accident she had after drinking too much.

The fourth major character is Benton Wesley, a high school principal turned FBI profiler, who becomes Scarpetta's lover in *The Body Farm,* to Marino's chagrin. Wesley remains a somewhat shadowy figure; he is described as lean and silver haired, drives a BMW and uses Mont Blanc pens, but beyond these signs of rather upscale taste, Cornwell divulges little about him. Various scientific experts from Scarpetta's office also appear regularly, although Cornwell shows few qualms about killing off her staff members (*Cruel & Unusual, Cause of Death,* and *Unnatural Exposure*).

Cornwell is especially skilled at dialogue—the wry wisecrack, the quick repartee—as in *Cruel & Unusual* when Scarpetta arrives at the airport to meet her teenage niece from Florida:

> "Geez, this is a dinky airport," said Lucy, whose computer brain had formatting errors in the diplomacy sectors. "Why do they call it Richmond *International?*"
>
> "Because it has flights to Miami." (paperback 1993 ed., p. 81)

The author also creates quite vivid minor characters. Sometimes she uses them to flesh out her stories rather than forward the plot, as with Temple Gault's desperately genteel, deliberately obtuse mother in *From Potter's Field.* Other times, she makes them sufficiently likeable—as is Danny, the gentle, good-natured morgue assistant in *Cause of Death*—that the reader can comprehend Scarpetta's need to avenge them.

Scarpetta herself has the freshness of novelty in *Postmortem.* A prominent state official with dual areas of expertise in a male-dominated field, she arouses the reader's curiosity about her background, her somewhat troubled history, her personal and professional relationships. By the middle of the series, though, she has begun to display an uncomfortable degree of self-righteousness plus rather unbelievable omniscience. All her opponents seem to have personal grudges against her or political axes to grind (*Postmortem*); guilty secrets (*Cruel & Unusual*); or, if members of the police force, are in some way bent (*Cause of Death, Unnatural Exposure*). Any ideas or suggestions that hasten the solution of a crime are always hers.

Cornwell seems, in some degree, to think of her books as morality plays, pitting the forces of good against evil. Dr. Scarpetta considers the bodies on her autopsy table to be her "patients," and believes it is her task to avenge their untimely and cruel demise. To the author, Scarpetta represents decency, justice, and compassion. Thus, "It is my intense concern for the living that makes me study the dead," says Scarpetta in *Cruel & Unusual.* "What we learn from the dead is for the benefit of the living, and justice is for those left behind" (paperback 1994 ed., p. 385).

The Novels

Postmortem remains Cornwell's best effort. While each later book generally contains a number of interesting clinical, forensic, or criminological facts—the existence of the eponymous "body farm" (the University of Tennessee's Decay Research Facility where the rate of decomposition in human remains is studied); a chemical compound named "luminol" that can cause bloodstains to reappear on surfaces from which they were scrubbed long ago; and the fact that the FBI has an agent whose expertise is the identification of feathers (*Cruel & Unusual*)—in the later books especially, Cornwell's plots become increasingly formulaic and unrealistic, as do Scarpetta's exploits. The plots' diminished realism heightens the reader's awareness of other shortcomings. Scarpetta almost completely fails to delegate responsibility to her underlings, so that she spends an inconceivable amount of work time either driving or flying on errands that could perfectly well be accomplished by telephone or by a subordinate, or that are actually not her concern. For example, in *From Potter's Field,* she makes it her time-consuming chore to identify the provenance of a victim's army boots—a task that surely lies completely outside a medical examiner's sphere.

Cornwell's fear and outrage at the crimes she writes about are reflected in *Postmortem.* In her next book, *Body of Evidence,* this attitude has changed from a direct personal response to the crimes in her home city to a seemingly more deliberate effort at creating a thriller centered on a particular theme—"erotomania"—with numerous extra and often disparate elements added. The result is murky and overly intricate. There are plots within plots; Scarpetta's first love resurfaces, and she (but not necessarily the reader) wonders on whose side he is. As Marilyn Stasio wrote in the *New York Times Book Review,* Cornwell "burdens the narrative with red herring subplots, forcing her heroine into situations that compromise both her professionalism and her common sense. . . . frankly, it's more fun back at the morgue" (p. 31).

Cornwell's third book, *All That Remains,* also suffers from a certain density of personnel, as if Cornwell had somehow overpopulated it, but purely as a detective story, it has suspense and momentum. The story concerns the serial murder of several couples, whose remains are found only after they are too decomposed for the medical examiner to determine the cause of death by autopsy. "All that remains is . . . bones," Scarpetta says to a distraught parent. "When soft tissue is gone, gone with it is any possible injury . . ." (paperback 1993 ed., p. 4). Because of this, forensic anthropology plays a part in the story.

With *Cruel & Unusual,* the first book in the Temple Gault trilogy, Cornwell began turning her books into series. Temple Gault, who escapes in *Cruel & Unusual,* is barely tangential to the main plot in *The Body Farm,* and finally vanquished in *From Potter's Field.* A killer who dismembers his victims is mentioned in *Unnatural Exposure,* but although his work is imitated, he himself is not caught and might be expected to reappear in a later work. Unresolved incidents of this sort are presented with enough of a drumroll to notify readers that a sequel is on its way, almost as if the author hopes the next book will compensate for the present book's shortcomings and weaknesses.

Cruel & Unusual poses the questions: Was the right man executed in the electric chair? Had he been maltreated in prison? How could his fingerprints be connected with a crime committed after his execution? Reviewer Emily Melton said in the 15 April 1993 *Booklist* that Cornwell "takes so long to develop all the disparate plot pieces that the complicated climax, crammed into a few short pages, leaves the reader feeling slightly cheated and wondering why all the loose ends don't quite get tied up."

The Body Farm, second in the trilogy, gives the impression of having originally been conceived as an independent work. Much of it deals with Lucy's problems during her FBI apprenticeship, and has little bearing on the main plot except to provide a slender link to Temple Gault: Lucy is seduced by a fellow FBI trainee, who turns out to be Gault's "mole" in the FBI, and later his associate in crime. Lucy's electronic security clearance is ingeniously counterfeited in order to frame her for various violations of Bureau rules. She is to be the subject of an investigation. Scarpetta visits a senator friend in Washington, D.C., to ask him to use his influence to ensure a fair and thorough investigation. Aside from these digressions, *The Body Farm* is a reasonably good thriller containing elements of a southern regional novel.

From Potter's Field, the last volume of the Gault trilogy, is in many ways a potboiler. While it begins with a Christmas Eve shooting, the book is mostly about identifying Temple Gault's latest victim and finally trapping Gault himself. Writing for the *New York Times Book Review,* Elise O'Shaughnessy stated: "As Ms. Cornwell's nightmare world has become more lucrative, it has lost some [of its] gritty reality . . ."

In *Cause of Death,* Scarpetta continues her ascent into the realms of the superhuman, more or less single-handedly retaking a nuclear power plant from the lunatic-fringe religious cult that has seized it. Associated with the cult is its own private bible, a work apparently so horrible that it nearly maddens anyone who reads it; Cornwell divulges few further details about it. Readers of fantastic fiction may recall similar books in Robert W. Chambers' *The King in Yellow* and Stephen Vincent Benét's "The Minister's Books."

Hornet's Nest takes place in Charlotte, North Carolina, and features the young reporter Andy Brazil. Perhaps based on notes Cornwell kept from her service as a police volunteer, it contains none of the forensic and medical data that enliven her other books and received almost unanimously bad reviews. "It takes a far dimmer view of obesity than it does of criminality," wrote Donna Leon in the London *Sunday Times*; "comic-book like heroics, rescues, and solutions—always unbelievable," judged Peggy Deans Earle of the Norfolk *Virginian Pilot.*

Cornwell's descriptions of forensic science remain her best quality work. Even *Unnatural Exposure,* arguably the least tightly plotted and most weakly motivated Scarpetta book, contains an interesting exposition that may well be unique in fiction about surgical saws and how to tell whether a particular kind was used to dismember a body. Even at their weakest, Patricia Cornwell's books probably all make good airplane reading. Unfortunately, though, the later ones are apt to be left behind in the seatpocket.

Biography

Patricia Daniels Cornwell was born in Miami on 9 June 1956. Her father, Sam Daniels, a lawyer, and her mother, Marilyn Zenner Daniels, separated when "Patsy" was five years old—an event Cornwell claims she recalls with painful clarity. Two years later, her mother moved with Patsy and her two brothers to Montreat, North Carolina. By the time Patricia was nine, her mother was suffering from severe clinical depression. Unable to cope, she turned her children over to her Montreat neighbors, the Reverend and Mrs. Billy Graham. Mrs. Graham put the children into foster care with a missionary couple who had recently returned from the Congo. Patricia loathed her foster home and has remained bitter about it for more than thirty years, believing that because she was a girl, she had to endure various domestic indignities her brothers escaped. She did, however, remain friends with Mrs. Graham, who quickly recognized her writing ability and whose biography Patricia eventually published.

An undefeated member of her high school tennis team (as is Andy Brazil, the hero of *Hornet's Nest*), Patricia Daniels became anorexic when she was eighteen and was hospitalized, coincidentally, in the same facility where her mother had been treated. Eventually, Patricia attended Davidson College in North Carolina, where she majored in English. After graduating in 1979, Patricia went to work for the *Charlotte Observer,* and the following year married Charles Cornwell, a Davidson College professor of English, seventeen years her senior. Friends say the marriage was troubled from the start.

Patricia Cornwell's career with the *Observer* flourished—she was assigned to the police beat and won awards for investigative reporting—but in 1981 she and her husband moved to Richmond, Virginia, so that he could study for the ministry. In Richmond, Patricia initially occupied herself by expanding a newspaper profile she had written earlier into a full biography of Ruth Bell Graham, *A Time for Remembering,* published in 1983. Subsequently, she found work at the Richmond morgue, became a weekend police volunteer, and tried her hand at writing fiction. She and Charles Cornwell divorced in 1990, the year she hit her stride with the publication of *Postmortem,* in which she introduces Dr. Kay Scarpetta.

Cornwell owns to an especially strong and pervasive fear of omnipresent violence and assault. Not only does Richmond have one of the country's highest homicide rates, but at about the time she began writing, the city endured a number of serial killings. (One of the victims, a physician whom Cornwell observed at work in the morgue, was probably transmuted by her into the victim at the beginning of *Postmortem.*)

Cornwell makes no secret of her political preferences, working her personal opinions into some of her books to the point of editorializing. "You Democrats are responsible for the decommissioning of half the Navy's fleet," says a senator friend of Scarpetta's to the woman attorney general with whom they are traveling on a rescue mission in *Cause of Death* (paperback 1997 ed., p. 306). A physician at one of the Center for Disease Control and Prevention facilities where Scarpetta is quarantined in *Unnatural Exposure* claims, "We got salmonella in Orlando from unpasteurized orange juice, another potential cruise ship outbreak of E. coli . . . Botulism in Rhode Island, and some respiratory disease in an old folks' home. And Congress doesn't want to fund us" (hardback 1997 ed., p. 235). Cornwell seems to believe in the almost tangible reality of the evil she describes and claims she frightens herself to such an extent that she will not work on her books after dark. The author lives alone, as does Dr. Scarpetta. By mid 1996 her sense of evildoing plus her inside knowledge of Richmond's morgue garnered her a $24 million advance for her next three novels.

Selected Bibliography

WORKS OF PATRICIA CORNWELL

NOVELS

Postmortem. New York: Scribners, 1990; Avon, 1991.

Body of Evidence. New York: Scribners, 1991; Avon, 1992.

All That Remains. New York: Scribners, 1992; Avon, 1993.

Cruel & Unusual. New York: Scribners, 1993; Avon, 1994.

The Body Farm. New York: Scribners, 1994.

From Potter's Field. New York: Scribners, 1995; Berkley, 1996.

Cause of Death. New York: Putnam, 1996; Berkley, 1997.

Hornet's Nest. New York: Putnam, 1997.

Unnatural Exposure. New York: Putnam, 1997.

Point of Origin. New York: Putnam, 1998.

NONFICTION

A Time for Remembering: The Story of Ruth Bell Graham. New York: Harper, 1983.

BIOGRAPHICAL AND CRITICAL STUDIES

The Armchair Detective 25: 389–397 ff. (fall 1992).

Cantwell, Mary. "How to Make a Corpse Talk." *New York Times Magazine,* 14 July 1996, p. 15, col. 1.

Churcher, Sharon. "A Patricia Cornwell Mystery—Why Did Jodie Turn Me Down?" *Mail on Sunday* (London), 10 August 1997, p. 52.

Earle, Peggy Deans. Review of *Hornet's Nest. Virginian-Pilot* (Norfolk, Va.), 9 March 1997, Commentary Section, p. J2.

Fabrikant, Geraldine. "Talking Money with Patricia Cornwell." *New York Times,* 23 March 1997, Money and Business Section.

Herbert, Rosemary. *The Fatal Art of Entertainment.* New York: Hall, 1994.

Leon, Donna. Review of *Hornet's Nest. Sunday Times* (London), 9 March 1997, Features Section.

Melton, Emily. Review of *Cruel and Unusual. Booklist,* 15 April 1993. Quoted in *Book Review Digest 1994.* New York: Wilson, 1995.

O'Shaughnessy, Elise. Review of *From Potter's Field. New York Times Book Review,* 20 August 1995. Quoted in *Book Review Digest 1996.* New York: Wilson, 1997.

"Patricia Daniels Cornwell." In *Contemporary Authors New Revision Series.* Vol. 53. Edited by Jeff Chapman, Pamela S. Dear, and John D. Jorgenson. Detroit: Gale, 1997.

Pederson, J. P., ed. *St. James Guide to Crime and Mystery Writers.* 4th ed. Detroit: St. James, 1996.

Stasio, Marilyn. Review of *Body of Evidence. New York Times Book Review,* 24 February 1991. Quoted in *Book Review Digest 1991.* New York: Wilson, 1992.

Edmund Crispin
(1921–1978)

MICHAEL DIRDA

Compared with the ingenious Agatha Christie or the influential Dashiell Hammett, Edmund Crispin must seem a relatively minor mystery novelist. But are charm and wit to count for nothing? After all, one reads detective stories for many reasons, and there are few writers who can match Crispin's ratio of fun per page. Virtually all of Edmund Crispin's important fiction—eight novels and a collection of stories—appeared between 1944 and 1953. Just before his death, however, he did bring out one final novel, *The Glimpses of the Moon* (1977), which was followed by a posthumous collection of stories, *Fen Country* (1979). Both of these are relatively weak efforts, the first long and windy and the second a batch of unrevised short stories from newspapers and magazines. Crispin's first book, *The Case of the Gilded Fly* (1944), appeared when he was in his early twenties, and he produced all his major fiction as a very young man.

At his best, and that best is very good indeed, Crispin displays the buoyancy, humor, and high spirits of a young man. His novels—the most esteemed include *Holy Disorders* (1945), *The Moving Toyshop* (1946), *Love Lies Bleeding* (1948), *Buried for Pleasure* (1948), and *The Long Divorce* (1951)—are in fact models of breezy, comic fiction, as well as classic fair-play mysteries. As the poet Philip Larkin wrote in a letter, speaking of *The Moving Toyshop,* "Don't you think that all in all it's a charmingly lighthearted book?" The critic Anthony Boucher once described Crispin as a combination of Michael Innes, John Dickson Carr, M. R. James, and the Marx Brothers—and certainly his novels deftly blend witty erudition, complex whodunits, occasional antiquarian spookiness, and a taste for vaudevillian excess and farce.

To his detractors, though, Crispin's books can seem merely flippant and facetious, a dyspeptic view eventually espoused by his longtime friend Kingsley Amis. But to more sympathetic readers, who are legion, these same books possess a fizz and zest that make them quite irresistible. Crispin himself may look to Carr and Innes as his masters, but he also draws on the topsy-turvy whimsy of Lewis Carroll, P. G. Wodehouse's unrivaled flair for similes, and some of the madcap, tongue-in-cheek playfulness of Stella Gibbons' *Cold Comfort Farm* and Flann O'Brien's *At-Swim-Two-Birds.* Ultimately, the author of *The Moving Toyshop* possesses a gift that is denied some far greater novelists: while reading his sunny, perennially fresh and amusing pages, one finds oneself, for a while, quite indescribably happy.

Life

Edmund Crispin was the pseudonym of Robert Bruce Montgomery, who was born in

Chesham Bois, Buckinghamshire, on 2 October 1921. As a boy, Montgomery attended the Merchant Taylors' School in London. In 1943 he graduated from St. John's College, Oxford. There he studied modern languages, worked as an organist and choirmaster, and made himself into something of a local character. "As an undergraduate," wrote Larkin in a preface to *Fen Country,* "Bruce Montgomery habitually wore a suit and a handsome ring, both unusual among our contemporaries, and had the slightly intimidating air of one who knew what he was going to do." Owing to a congenital foot ailment—a tendency for his ankles to "go out"—the tall, red-haired Montgomery also used a stick or cane, and this combination of dandyism and self-confidence struck many in bleak wartime as a throwback to the golden Oxford of the 1920s. He was, to both Amis and Larkin, somewhat forbidding, though all three eventually became close friends.

"Edmund Crispin" was born in April 1942. As Montgomery recalled in an autobiographical sketch for *Armchair Detective:*

> I was with a genuinely bookish actor, in a pub in Oxford. We normally talked books. And we did so on this occasion. How the conversation got round to John Dickson Carr I can't quite remember, but I do remember the tone of mingled reproof, reproach and amusement with which my friend said, 'Oh, haven't you read John Dickson Carr?' I was a bit of an intellectual snob in those days, and thought the detective story rather beneath my notice. However, you didn't ignore advice about books from John Maxwell (my friend), and on our way back to my lodgings he called in at his, and he lent me a copy of "The Crooked Hinge."
>
> I went to bed with it not expecting very much. But at two o'clock in the morning I was still sitting up with my eyes popping out of their sockets at the end of one of the sections. . . . And of course I finished the book that night. It was to be a seminal moment in my career and to alter it entirely, for although subsequently I read and enjoyed other detective-story writers, in particular Michael Innes and Gladys Mitchell, it was Carr primarily who induced me to try my hand at one myself, thus creating Edmund Crispin.

Edmund Crispin and his detective, Gervase Fen, professor of English language and literature at Oxford, derive their unusual names from a character named Gervase Crispin in Michael Innes' *Hamlet, Revenge!* The figure of Fen is affectionately based in part on the Oxford professor W. E. Moore. Legend has it that in the ten days of the spring vacation of 1943, Montgomery sat down and dashed off his first mystery novel, *The Case of the Gilded Fly,* which was duly accepted by Gollancz. It was published while its author was still an undergraduate and received favorable reviews, even though Larkin complained that "it wasn't very good" and Amis groused, years later, about some flaws in the denouement.

Such gripes, hardly just, may be attributed to an altogether understandable envy. For during their Oxford years, Montgomery was both mentor and rival to his talented friends. (For instance, he introduced Carr's novels to Amis and Larkin, who became equally ardent fans.) Montgomery's boyishness, zest for living, lavish ways, and a weakness for drink by all reports made him an irresistible companion. He liked hotel bars and such underappreciated writers as Flann O'Brien, H. L. Mencken, and Wyndham Lewis. In their turn, Larkin and Amis taught him to appreciate jazz, or at least some jazz. For Bruce Montgomery was a young man gifted with a double genius. Not only could he write vivacious mysteries, he could also write serious music. He said in *Armchair Detective* that he had "learnt piano and organ and started to compose at the age of about 14." In due course, he attained modest celebrity as a composer of film music, being best known, alas, for the score to the slightly naughty *Carry On, Nurse.* With a libretto from Amis, the precocious Montgomery early on produced a Coronation anthem, "The Century's Crown," that was performed in Glasgow. Subsequent work included choral music, "An Ode to the Resurrection of Christ," "An Oxford Requiem," chamber pieces, and much background music for radio, film, and theater.

Because of his various extracurricular interests, Montgomery failed to earn the first-class degree everyone expected of him (he got a second) and soon took a job as a teacher at Shrewsbury School in Shrewsbury. As it happened, Larkin worked nearby, so the two would get together regularly for an evening of talk and drink. They also read each other's work. Larkin's biographer Andrew Motion asserts that "it was Montgomery who encouraged and directed him [Larkin] with more purpose than anyone else. By combining a devoted commitment to writing with a huge appetite for drinking and fooling around, he gave Larkin a model of the way in which art could avoid pretension." Montgomery critiqued Larkin's youthful novel *Jill,* while the poet offered sage counsel for Crispin's second production, *Holy Disorders* (an acknowledgment reads, "My sincere thanks are due to Mr. Philip Larkin for reading this book in manuscript and making a number of valuable suggestions"). Montgomery dedicated his third and most famous work, *The Moving Toyshop,* to Larkin, in part because the poet gave him the kernel of the plot.

Montgomery taught at Shrewsbury School from 1943 to 1945, imparting to his students his own passion for detective fiction and ghost stories. (One recalls the scene in *Love Lies Bleeding* where Gervase Fen instructs a group of boys about the spooky fiction of M. R. James, L. P. Hartley, and Walter De la Mare.) *The Moving Toyshop* appeared in 1946 and proved a great and deserved success; soon thereafter Montgomery started his professional music career as well. Not surprisingly, this gifted young man was soon in the money, drinking heavily, tipping lavishly, and entertaining extravagantly. Best of all, as Amis later remarked in his *Memoirs,* "He was said to move among starlets." A few years later, the author and composer built a bungalow in Devon (reportedly complete with bomb shelter) and settled down to a quiet country life. There he collected classical records, took an interest in church matters, played a little bridge, and worked the *Times* crossword puzzle. "He grew plump early," wrote Amis, "worried about his health, was not very attractive to women but found lovable by them, with beautiful manners when not falling down drunk, speaking often in a tone of jolly asperity, generous to a degree that would earn a hundred blessings."

As Crispin, Bruce Montgomery published a novel a year, and then his talent unexpectedly dried up. In the 1950s, he turned his attention increasingly to writing music, but he also began an important auxiliary career as one of Britain's leading critics of detective fiction, reviewing regularly for the Sunday *Times.* Like Amis, he was also an early advocate of science fiction and edited a half dozen superb anthologies as well as comparable volumes of supernatural and detective stories. By the early 1970s, however, Montgomery's drinking finally overwhelmed him. He started to have money problems and once needed to borrow a substantial sum from the notoriously stingy Larkin. He married late in life, and one might attribute to his wife, Ann, the existence of the final novel, *The Glimpses of the Moon.* In 1978, shortly before Larkin was to visit him, Bruce Montgomery died on 15 September at the age of sixty-six.

Crispin's Way

In a note for *Twentieth-Century Crime and Mystery Writers,* Edmund Crispin—as we will now call him—wrote, "I believe that crime stories in general and detective stories in particular should be essentially imaginative and artificial in order to make their best effect" (p. 269). Certainly any reader of Crispin's own fiction will agree about its imaginativeness and artificiality. Some of this strongly held viewpoint he must have acquired from Carr, whom Crispin described as that master of "the trickiest form of fiction humanity has so far devised." Speaking of the mystery in the introduction to *Best Detective Stories,* Crispin proclaimed: "We have come to demand of it not only a mystery with a plausible solution, but over and above that a mystery with a surprise solution, and over and above 'that,' a mystery with a surprise solution which by rights we ought not to have been surprised at all."

Because Crispin's humor is so much the most obvious quality in his fiction, the reader may sometimes overlook the art with which he structures his various puzzles. In this regard, the short-shorts collected in *Beware of the Trains* (1953) and *Fen Country* remind us more forcefully than the novels—which provide so many competing charms—that he was a firm believer in careful plotting, in setting forth a problem that really could be solved. Virtually all the stories, he wrote in the foreword to *Beware of the Trains,* "embody the nowadays increasingly neglected principle of fair play to the reader—which is to say that the reader is given all the clues needed to enable him to anticipate the solution by the exercise of his logic and his common sense."

In fact, Professor Gervase Fen himself at one point asserts that mystery stories are "the only form of literature which carry on the true tradition of the English novel." According to Innes, in *Holy Disorders,* Crispin makes an "attempt to lend to the highly specialized form of sensation fiction we call the detective story something of the prescriptive amplitude and bold variousness characteristic of the main stream of English fiction." Innes goes so far as to compare Crispin's second novel to Charles Dickens' *Mystery of Edwin Drood* in its "evocation of a cathedral town, its perception of the comedy latent in the English clerical character, and its cheerful acceptance of some of the broadest effects of the Gothic novel" (Introduction, *Swan Song,* 1980). Crispin was, by all reports, a deep believer in tradition and what one might call traditional English values. Gervase Fen himself sounds this conservative note: "I find it worth while to help clean up the mess made by malevolence and folly." For all his whimsicality, Fen can be quite formidable to evildoers, possessing "a kind of passionless sense of justice and of proportion, a deeply rooted objection to waste."

That said, Crispin is seldom a particularly tricky mystery writer. In at least two books—*Swan Song* and *Buried for Pleasure*—any half attentive reader should be able to figure out major elements of the solution, if not every detail. Yet these books' appeal is hardly dimmed by that fact. For as with the Sherlock Holmes stories or the exploits of Archie Goodwin and Nero Wolfe, we return to Crispin's books for their tone, their atmosphere, their wit—ultimately, for the inviting world they create on the page. As it happens, Crispin sets each of his novels against a backdrop that he knows well: Oxford (*The Moving Toyshop*), a boys' school (*Love Lies Bleeding*), a cathedral town (*Holy Disorders*), an opera company (*Swan Song*), a film studio (*Frequent Hearses*), a pretty country town (*The Long Divorce*). One might easily speculate that Crispin stopped writing mysteries when he ran out of new places in which to set them. Although these novels vary in character—*The Long Divorce* being, perhaps, the best classic whodunit, *The Moving Toyshop* certainly the zaniest, and *Holy Disorders* the spookiest—they all share that inimitable Crispin charm, his distinctive variety of intelligent and stylish comedy.

The Comedian as the Letter C

Crispin's unique lighthearted comedy draws on many elements: hilarious similes, broad farcical situations, funny names, puns, unexpected actions or statements, humorous characters, zany games, utterly inappropriate behavior, and tongue-in-cheek diction. Since these provide the distinctive flavor of a Crispin novel, they warrant extended attention. One should note, however, that the first half of a Crispin book is usually much funnier than the second, which is generally dominated by some threat to a sympathetic character and by Fen's deductions about the seemingly impossible crime.

Perhaps only Wodehouse exhibits a greater flair for the exaggerated, yet apposite, comparison. By juxtaposing the mundane with the fanciful, classical, learned, or unlikely, Crispin creates a slightly histrionic air, one of musical comedy and dandyish high spirits. Consider the following: "They passed a public house. 'I should like a Burton,' said Fen, gazing back at it with the lugubrious passion of Orpheus surveying Eurydice at hell-mouth." "Morose and mistrustful, Tuesday's dawn loitered in from the east, like a trade unionist contemplating a strike." The Superintendent "was a tall, burly, youngish man in plain clothes whose features some freak of heredity had assembled into a perpetual expression of muted alarm, so that to be in his company was like consorting with a man dogged by assassins." "'Men, of course,' said Elspeth with a worldliness Madame de Pompadour might have envied." Speaking of the police, Crispin notes, "their capacity for amazement makes Candide look like the most degenerate of urban sophisticates." "Said Humbleby with all the savagery of a cornered humanist."

Crispin is also the master of the farcical situation. *The Moving Toyshop* accelerates from one such farcical improbability to another. Richard Cadogan, a major English poet, arrives late at night in Oxford; glimpses a body in, of all places, a toy shop; is knocked on the head; escapes from a back room; and the next morning discovers that the toy shop has vanished. Soon Cadogan and his old chum Gervase Fen are pursuing an unknown girl because she matches a description from an Edward Lear poem. She leads them into a choir practice of the Handel Society, where Fen explains that Cadogan is actually the eminent German composer Dr. Paul Hindemith. Soon afterward, our heroes, along with an aged and tipsy professor named Wilkes, flag down a truck in order to pursue a kidnapper. The truck driver, a devout Lawrentian, preaches as they speed along that "industrial civilisation is the curse of our age. . . . We've lorst touch with Nachur. We're all pallid . . . We've lorst touch with the 'body.'" Near the novel's end, a group of undergraduate hearties, led by a decadent Brideshead-style dandy on a bicycle, pursue a very thin doctor through Oxford to the Parson's Pleasure bathing area. As the aesthete reaches the entrance to the swimming facilities, he presses "a pound-note confidentially into the gate-keeper's hand, with the remark: 'These are *all* my friends. Admit *everyone,* please.'" Similar extravagant moments can be found in virtually all the novels.

In this category of the farcical one must also place Fen's red sports car, Lily Christine III, which frequently refuses to start, makes ominous noises, and often loses body parts to minor accidents. For Fen is a terrible driver: "The three quarters of an hour which elapsed before they arrived at High Wycombe Adam occupied with repenting, in some detail, the moral imperfections of his past life."

Many of the names Crispin chooses for his characters possess literary echoes or humorous associations. Mr. Datchery honors a minor figure from *Edwin Drood,* Spode recalls Wodehouse's comical leader of the Black Shorts party, and the actress Gloria Scott takes her name from the Sherlock Holmes canon. One character signs a hotel register as "Major Rawdon Crawley," a name familiar to all fans of William Makepeace Thackeray's *Vanity Fair.* Then there are the broadly conceived minor characters: Mudge the policeman, a fellow named Snerd, the theater custodian Furbelow. We might be in a Dickens novel. At one surreal moment in *Buried for Pleasure,* Crispin produces a wall upon which is scribbled, "Down with Taft."

A musician in his other life, Crispin also proves to be an expert with accents and speech patterns. The Swiss pedant Peter Rubi in *The Long Divorce* has clearly learned English as a second language: "We must meet again. I would wish to talk a long time about the man Waugh." In each book we find that characters from various classes, whether policeman or truck drivers or shopkeepers, all speak with just the right nuances, slang, and turns of phrase characteristic of their social positions. Henry Higgins would be impressed.

Most fiction aims to maintain that "suspension of disbelief" which constitutes poetic faith. Crispin's makes no such claim. His novels constantly draw attention to their artificiality, a technique their author may have learned from Flann O'Brien. Sometimes Crispin will insert a footnote, informing us, for instance, that Furbelow's testimony is completely accurate. In nearly all the books there are coy parenthetical asides: "He was not aware that someone passing outside at the time observed and took note of the existence of the weapon." In one novel, Fen grouses because people talk of bringing in Sir John Appleby, the detective-hero of Innes' crime classics. In *The Long Divorce,* a journalist, planning a series on detectives, hopes to interview Sir Henry Merrivale, the creation of Carter Dickson. Characters in the novels frequently liken their actions to the far-fetched plot turns in the more sensational forms of detective fiction. Near the end of *The Moving Toyshop,* Crispin blithely mentions a somewhat bothersome undergraduate named Larkin, author of a paper on the influence of *Sir Gawain and the Green Knight* on Matthew Arnold's "Empedocles on Etna." When a truck driver needs to decide which way to go at an intersection, Richard Cadogan says, "Let's go left. After all, Gollancz [well known for its liberal sympathies] is publishing this book."

Similarly, Crispin glories in coincidence. Fen, resting in a coffee shop, loudly remarks to Cadogan, "I think we seek out Miss Alice Winkworth." At which point "a woman sitting at a nearby table got up and came over to them. 'You mentioned my name?' she said." Perhaps the funniest example of this almost postmodern self-awareness arises when Fen starts making up possible book titles for Crispin's use: "The Return of Fen," for instance, or "A Don Dares Death (A Gervase Fen Story)."

Fen and Cadogan play a game called "Unreadable Books" while they are tied up in a closet (*Ulysses, The Golden Bowl,* and *Clarissa* get the boot). At the end of *The Case of the Gilded Fly,* Fen announces that he is preparing a new anthology to be called "Awful Lines from Shakespeare" in which "'Alas, poor Gloster! Lost he his other eye?' will have pride of place." Near the opening of that same adventure, Fen sits impatiently on a train: "As his only distraction was one of his own books, on the minor satirists of the eighteenth century, which he was conscientiously rereading in order to recall what were his opinions on these persons, he became in later stages of the journey quite profoundly unhappy." In *Frequent Hearses* (1950), the good professor shakes himself "free of the stupor which the prose of Henry James invariably induced in him." In another investigation, an ardent admirer of Jane Austen's fiction turns out to be the murderer, about which Fen rudely comments, "One Janeite the less." When Fen uses a pseudonym, it is from Dickens; when he hears a voice in a bar paging "T. S. Eliot, Mr. T. S. Eliot," he jumps up and says, "That's me."

Although Crispin usually prefers a laugh-out-loud simile or a bit of learned allusion, he does not eschew the occasional pun. Explaining the prevalence of murder in his hometown, Fen notes that Oxford "is proverbially the home of lost corpses." In *Swan Song* we meet the Teutonic Miss Thorn—one of Crispin's best comic creations—who keeps house and guards the privacy of a famous composer: "The Master's brain is a highly delicate instrument; the least shock may unhinge it." Why should she be named Thorn? Almost certainly so that Fen might say, when he has assembled all the suspects at the end of the book, "Here is Miss Thorn," then add, with great severity, "in the flesh."

Crispin takes great delight in elaborate, rococo sentences, often expressed with a smack-your-lips gusto that the reader is intended to enjoy: "It proved to be Burns, the village Constable, a bright up-and-coming young man deficient in the conventions of slow rusticity which fiction commonly attaches to his office." During Oxford vacations "sung services, in the various chapels, degenerate with startling abruptness from a plethora to a definite scarcity, and the clergy are to be found droning away to exiguous congregations of surreptiously yawning devots." Where else but in Crispin (or possibly Innes) is one likely to find the word "suilline" (piglike)?

Donnish humor frequently leavens conversation with literary references or skewed allusions. As Fen gulps down a beer, he intones, "Oh, for a beakerful of the cold north," echoing John Keats's line about a "beaker full of the warm South." When Sir Richard Freeman, a police officer who writes literary criticism on the side (three books published), is first introduced, he "was holding a copy of Fen's *Minor Satirists of the XVIIIth Century* and was in the process of registering emphatic disagreement with the opinions of that expert on the work of Charles Churchill." Later, the disagreeable Wilkes tells a college ghost story, which the astute will recognize as an impressive homage to the antiquarian chillers of M. R. James. When Mr. Barnaby mentions a recruiting officer, he also remarks, "too Farquhar." (The eighteenth-century English comic dramatist George Farquhar wrote a play called *The Recruiting Officer.*) One needs to remember 1930s- and 1940s-style socialist realism to appreciate "one of those documentaries, so dear to the critics of the Sunday press, about the Earth and those who lead their simple lives in constant contact with It." The film company in *Frequent Hearses* is making a movie about the life of Alexander Pope. And *The Moving Toyshop* takes its title from a line of Pope's "Rape of the Lock": "the moving toyshop of their heart."

Occasionally, Fen will actually lecture to somebody: He tells us that Richard Wagner's opera *Die Meistersinger von Nürnberg* and Shakespeare's *Henry IV* convince one of the essential nobility of man, "as opposed to *Macbeth* [a curious choice] and the Ninth Symphony, which are really about the gods." At one romantic moment Richard Cadogan expounds, somewhat grandly, his theories about poetry—a passage largely written by the young Philip Larkin. Judd, the detective author in *Buried for Pleasure,* espouses some of the same doctrines as John Dickson Carr: "Characterization seems to me a very overrated element in fiction. . . . One's plots are necessarily *improbable* . . . but I believe in making sure that they are not *impossible."*

Fen's favorite expostulations "Oh, my paws!" and "Oh, my furs and whiskers!" derive from Lewis Carroll, a pervasive influence on the daydreamy feel of the books. The main clue in the mystery of *The Moving Toyshop* is based on rhymes from Edward Lear's limericks, with a nod to G. K. Chesterton's suspense story *The Man Who Was Thursday.*

Anybody who reads Crispin grows to appreciate certain recurrent figures and devices. For instance, by preference the novels open with descriptions of trains and train journeys. In several, the aging, drunken Wilkes appears, ever a welcome presence. Sir Richard Freeman and Inspector Humbleby are Fen's usual companions in detection. Who can forget the time when Sir Richard, learning that an attractive journalist specializes in crime, instinctively blurts out, "nasty subject"? In *Swan Song* we learn that the poet Richard Cadogan (of *The Moving Toyshop* adventure) has written the lyrics for an opera based on the *Oresteia* of Aeschylus. Such repetition helps bind the books together. Of course, Fen starts out with a rather plain wife and some children, but they gradually disappear. The same thing happened to that fellow academic, Carr's Dr. Gideon Fell.

Yet always with Crispin one returns to the style. When Inspector Mudge is methodically pointing out elements at the scene of a murder, another character is "momentarily overwhelmed by the illusion of being on a conducted tour." After Mudge explains something, he "paused, contemplating retrospectively, Adam fancied, the grammar of the sentence." Sometimes a phrase invests a description with delightful humor: "'There's a Providence watching over us, as I've always maintained.' And he gazed up at the ceiling, as though expecting actually to see this benignant spirit at its tutelary task." Those last half dozen words are sheer magic.

Ah, the language! Consider the subtle humor of the middle phrase in "Shorthouse explained to me, in confidence, that he was intending to kill his brother." The poison pen letters in *The Long Divorce* accuse "people of practices at which . . . Gomorrah would have looked slightly askance." And then there's the title to a late story, the savagely satirical and probably autobiographical account of a writer finally driven to murder by visitors constantly interrupting him while he tries to work: "We Know You're Busy Writing But We Thought You Wouldn't Mind If We Just Dropped in for a Minute."

Conclusion

Julian Symons once called Edmund Crispin the last of the farceurs, referring to the tradition of donnish humor represented by E. C. Bentley, Anthony Berkeley, and Innes. Certainly, Crispin's novels are obvious artificial constructs, designed to give pleasure. Yet unlike some other Golden Age figures, Crispin possesses a continued freshness, an unfaded youthfulness. For instance, compared with Crispin's similes, those of Raymond Chandler often sound corny and dated. Not that *Farewell, My Lovely* is not a far deeper and more complex book than *Frequent Hearses* or *Holy Disorders*. Yet insofar as the detective novel is recreation, a playful game between author and reader, the novels of Edmund Crispin will always merit a high place in the field. At the moment, harsh realism and gritty humor may be in the ascendant, but there remains to Crispin a civilized and compassionate comedy that is too rare, and valuable, to be dismissed as mere frivolity.

Selected Bibliography

WORKS OF EDMUND CRISPIN

NOVELS AND SHORT STORIES

Most of Edmund Crispin's books are available in paperback, mainly from Penguin.

The Case of the Gilded Fly. London: Gollancz, 1944. U.S.: *Obsequies at Oxford.* Philadelphia: Lippincott, 1945.

Holy Disorders. London: Gollancz, 1945.

The Moving Toyshop. London: Gollancz, 1946.

Swan Song. London: Gollancz, 1947. U.S.: *Dead and Dumb.* Philadelphia: Lippincott, 1947.

Love Lies Bleeding. London: Gollancz, 1948.

Buried for Pleasure. London: Gollancz, 1948.

Frequent Hearses. London: Gollancz, 1950. U.S.: *Sudden Vengeance.* New York: Dodd, Mead, 1950.

The Long Divorce. London: Gollancz, 1951. U.S.: *A Noose for Her.* New York: Spivak, 1952.

Beware of the Trains: Sixteen Stories. London: Gollancz, 1953.

The Glimpses of the Moon. London: Gollancz, 1977.

Fen Country. London: Gollancz, 1979. With a preface by Philip Larkin.

OTHER WRITINGS

Best SF: Science Fiction Stories, 7 vols. London: Faber, 1955–1970. Editor.

Best Detective Stories, 2 vols. London: Faber, 1959–1964. Editor.

BIOGRAPHICAL AND CRITICAL STUDIES

According to Douglas G. Greene (footnote in *John Dickson Carr: The Man Who Explained Miracles.* New York: Otto Penzler, 1995), David Whittle is currently writing a biography of Edmund Crispin.

Aird, Catherine, "Gervase Fen and the Teacake School." in *Murder Ink.* Edited By Dilys Wynn. New York: Workman, 1997.

Amis, Kingsley. *Memoirs.* New York: Summit, 1991.

Baird, Thomas. *"The Glimpses of the Moon"* and *"The Moving Toyshop."* In *1001 Midnights: The Aficionados Guide to Mystery and Detective Fiction.* Edited by Bill Pronzini and Marcia Muller. New York: Arbor House, 1986.

Barzun, Jacques, and Wendell Hertig Taylor. "Edmund Crispin." In *A Catalogue of Crime,* rev. ed. New York: Harper & Row, 1985.

Innes, Michael. Introduction to *Swan Song* by Edmund Crispin. New York: Walker, 1980.

Keating, H. R. F. *"The Moving Toyshop."* In *Crime and Mystery: The 100 Best Books.* New York: Carroll & Graf, 1987.

Larkin, Philip. Preface to rev. ed. of *Jill: A Novel.* New York: Overlook, 1976.

Montgomery, Robert Bruce. "Edmund Crispin." *Armchair Detective* 12, no. 1 (January 1979).

Motion, Andrew. *Philip Larkin: A Writer's Life.* New York: Farrar, Straus & Giroux, 1993.

Reilly, John. *Twentieth-Century Crime and Mystery Writers,* 3rd ed. Chicago: St. James Press, 1991.

Sarjeant, William A. S. "Obsequies About Oxford: The Investigations and Eccentricities of Gervase Fen." *Armchair Detective* 14, no. 3 (summer 1981).

Symons, Julian. *Bloody Murder: From the Detective Story to the Crime Novel. A History.* New York: Viking, 1985.

Thwaite, Anthony, ed. *Selected Letters of Philip Larkin, 1940–1985.* London: Faber, 1992.

FREEMAN WILLS CROFTS

(1879–1957)

MELVYN BARNES

AN ENGINEER WHO became one of the foremost exponents of the typically British detective story, Freeman Wills Crofts was in the 1930s and early 1940s regarded as one of the genre's "Big Five" and ranked with Dorothy L. Sayers, Agatha Christie, R. Austin Freeman, and H. C. Bailey. His output from 1920 to his death in 1957 consisted of thirty-four novels (including one for young adults), over fifty short stories, a stage play, and many radio scripts. He also collaborated with various eminent colleagues of The Detection Club in writing three detective novels and a volume of short stories.

While in recent years reprints of his works have been rare, he is still remembered as the master of the apparently unbreakable alibi that relied upon timetables and numerous other aspects of trains, boats, and planes. Above all, he is remembered as the creator of Inspector Joseph French.

Life

Crofts was born in Dublin, Ireland, on 7 June 1879, of an old County Cork family. His father, also named Freeman Wills Crofts, was a doctor in the British army who died while on service abroad. The young Freeman was brought up in Northern Ireland by his mother and stepfather, Archdeacon Harding of the Church of Ireland, and he was educated in the Methodist and Campbell Colleges in Belfast. The religious influences on his formative years were to show in the strong puritanical and moral flavor of his writing much later in life.

At the age of seventeen Crofts was apprenticed as a pupil in civil engineering to his uncle, Berkeley D. Wise, who was chief engineer of the Belfast and Northern Counties Railway. This set him on a successful career as a railway engineer, and his first appointment in 1899 as junior assistant engineer on the construction of the Londonderry and Strabane extension of the Donegal Railway was followed by further promotions. He became district engineer at Coleraine on the Belfast and Northern Counties Railway in 1900, and in 1923 moved to Belfast as chief assistant engineer.

Crofts was a keen musician. In particular, he was organist at Coleraine parish church and at least three other churches and an accomplished conductor who gained satisfaction from his success in the training of prize-winning choirs. He listed his other interests as driving, traveling, gardening, and carpentry, some of which were to prove useful to him in his stories.

In 1912 Crofts married Mary Bellas Canning, the daughter of a Belfast bank manager. It was a childless though mutually devoted marriage, with Mary staunchly supporting Freeman throughout his last seventeen years as a railway engineer and through almost four decades as a detective novelist. There was an overlap in Crofts's two careers; by the time of his early retirement from his original profession in 1929, he had written nine novels. He was not at that time in good health but had already become a highly successful writer, and it can therefore be assumed that the enforced choice was not difficult. A further immediate task remained, however, and he accepted the commission of the government of Northern Ireland to head an inquiry into the objections to the River Bann and Lough Neagh Drainage Scheme, some twenty-five miles west of Belfast.

At this crossroads of their life the Crofts moved across the Irish Channel to Guildford in Surrey, a locale that was to feature prominently in his novels. By then his fiction had not only brought him financial rewards, but also the high estimation of his peers in the field of detective fiction. In the latter respect he was recognized in 1930 by admission to the hallowed portals of The Detection Club, an exclusive organization just founded in London by Anthony Berkeley with the redoubtable G. K. Chesterton as its president. Further recognition of his talents came in 1938, when he was admitted as a Fellow of the Royal Society of Arts.

Crofts was forty years old at the outset of his writing career and did not become a full-time writer until he was fifty. He was therefore able to draw upon the experiences of a long working life and to put to good use the innumerable technicalities derived from his career in engineering. He continued to do so, with his books appearing at the rate of approximately one per year from 1920 until his death. In his later years he lived with Mary at Worthing in Sussex, and he died at a nearby nursing home on 11 April 1957. For some time his only publications had been volumes of short stories written earlier, but dogged by ill health he had been long engaged in producing what was to be his last novel. *Anything to Declare?* was published just a few weeks before his death.

The Cask

Following his move from Northern Ireland, Crofts was something of a celebrity in his adopted English town of Guildford. He was by then, after all, one of Britain's most applauded crime writers. In a 1939 article in the *Guildford City Outlook* entitled "I Found an Answer to Crime," he reminisced about the genesis of his career in the field. At an early age he had been an avid consumer of the Sherlock Holmes stories in *Strand Magazine,* which created a lasting impression. "I took them very seriously. . . . I noted the different things which could be learnt from the inspection of a briar pipe or spots of mud on garments. . . . The idea that I should one day write on similar subjects would then have seemed the last word in absurdity to me."

This early influence did not surface for many years. In 1919, while convalescing after a long illness, Crofts took a pencil and an exercise book and began to write a story. At first, he had no intention to publish the book and put it away for some time. Rereading it, he eventually appreciated its potential. Always the perfectionist, he revised it several times until he was satisfied with the final draft, but was nevertheless surprised when *The Cask* (1920) was accepted by the London publisher Collins.

Within twenty years *The Cask* sold some two hundred thousand copies. It launched a career that gave Crofts an international following, with his books translated into at least a dozen languages and with most of his titles published on both sides of the Atlantic in hard cover and paperback. Yet *The Cask* remained his masterpiece, and it became one of the major classics of the genre. In some respects an early example of the police procedural novel, it was influenced by the melodramatic plots and systematic detection found in the *romans policiers* of the nineteenth-century French writer Émile Gaboriau that were widely available in English translation.

Ellery Queen regarded *The Cask* as the first great modern police novel, while Rex Stout counted it among the ten best mystery stories in a list published in Vincent Starrett's *Books and Bipeds* (1947). Reviewing a 1967 reprint of *The Cask,* the American critic Anthony Boucher confirmed that the novel had lost neither its appeal nor its place in the history of detective fiction: "This book astonished me by being even better than I remembered it. Possibly the most completely competent first novel in the history of crime, it is the definitive novel of alibis, timetables and all the absorbing hairsplitting of detection." Particularly significant is the fact that it was published in 1920, the year in which Agatha Christie's *The Mysterious Affair at Styles* and H. C. Bailey's first volume of short stories, *Call Mr. Fortune,* were published. The entry on the scene of Crofts, Christie, and Bailey marked the advent of the Golden Age of detective fiction.

The Cask opens in sensational fashion. Several casks are damaged while a ship is being unloaded after a voyage from Rouen to London, and on closer inspection one of them reveals a grisly secret. It should contain statuary but instead it leaks gold sovereigns, and protruding from the coins are the fingers of a corpse. Inspector Burnley's first frustration, one of many, is that the cask disappears before he is able to investigate further. He pursues a complex trail until locating it again, complete with the body of an unidentified woman who has been strangled. What follows is the sort of international travelogue for which Crofts became renowned, with Burnley following the trail to Paris and the case being taken up at various points by the French police and by private detective Georges La Touche.

The solid and logical detective work, with scrupulous attention to detail, became Crofts's hallmark. He takes the reader along with the detective every step of the way and withholds no clues, sharing the detective's thoughts, the good and false leads, and the triumphs and frustrations exactly as they occur. In this respect Crofts dismissed the omniscient sleuth so often found in early detective fiction and rebelled against the tendency of other authors to spring unfair surprises that served only to display a detective's brilliance and flair. His use of conscientious police officers rather than gifted amateurs, and his narration of a painstaking inquiry involving the detailed analysis of the suspects' movements and alibis, marked *The Cask* as something new. It was indeed a cornerstone in the history of mystery fiction and rightly listed as such over twenty years later in *Murder for Pleasure* (1941) by Howard Haycraft, the American editor and mystery critic who later became president of the H. W. Wilson Company.

Early Works

Crofts quickly followed *The Cask* with another book in similar mold, *The Ponson Case* (1921). Inspector Burnley, never to appear again, was replaced by Inspector Tanner. Only the name was different, however; in all other respects Crofts showed again the dedicated professional with a systematic job to do. Tanner's investigation of the death of Sir William Ponson, found drowned in a river near his country manor, unearths such complications as bigamy, blackmail, and a marine disaster. It is, as always, a question of alibi busting, with Crofts typically displaying his knowledge of the main railway line to Scotland and the timetable from London to Lincolnshire.

With his third book, *The Pit-Prop Syndicate* (1922), Crofts adopts a new approach by combining elements of the thriller and the detective novel. This is achieved by showing how two amateur detectives get out of their depth after stumbling upon the activities of a villainous smuggling syndicate in France. Crofts brings matters back on his usual course by demonstrating that a competent professional—this time Inspector Willis—is needed to bring the case to a satisfactory conclusion. The investigation alternates between France and England, and there is more action than in most of Crofts's books, perhaps a reason that this book has been highly regarded by some commentators. Indeed, Julian Symons included it (rather than *The Cask*) in his list of the hundred best crime stories, which he compiled in 1959 for the London *Sunday Times*.

There was one more book before Crofts introduced the series detective who became his permanent protagonist. *The Groote Park Murder* (1923) opens with the discovery of a body in a railway tunnel in South Africa and an investigation conducted by Inspector Vandam. The action then moves to Scotland and involves Inspector Ross of Edinburgh. Crofts's knowledge of railways is again much in evidence, and the Scottish setting enables him to exercise his considerable skill in topographical description.

So the stage is set for the entrance of Inspector French. Crofts clearly knew the sort of investigating officer he was aiming for—diligent, thorough, deliberate, perhaps a trifle pedantic, and certainly unsensational. All that remained was to put a name to him and to build up his background in a succession of novels. That man is Inspector Joseph French of Scotland Yard, who is featured in every Crofts novel and most of his short stories from 1924 onward, with successive promotions to the eventual rank of Detective Chief Superintendent.

Inspector French

It is possible that Crofts might not have originally intended French to become a series character, particularly as his debut bore the title *Inspector French's Greatest Case* (1924). While that might have indicated that there were no more cases to come, French made an impact with the reading public, and Crofts must have immediately gained an affection for him.

He certainly gave some thought to French as a person, albeit quite deliberately an ordinary person. On his first appearance, he is described as

> a stout man in tweeds, rather under middle height, with a cleanshaven, good-humoured face and dark blue eyes which, though keen, twinkled as if at some perennially fresh private joke. His air was easy-going and leisurely, and he looked the type of man who could enjoy a good dinner and a good smoke-room story to follow. . . . Behind his back at the Yard they called him 'Soapy Joe' because of the reliance he placed on the suavity of his manners. (pp. 9–10)

Crofts also pays attention to French's happy home life, giving him a wife called Emily with whom he sometimes discusses his cases. Crofts makes frequent reference to French's fondness for good food, his enjoyment of traveling whether in the course of duty or on vacation, and his dislike of paperwork that encourages him to pursue leads well away from London rather than become tied to an office chair.

Beneath the pleasant exterior of French, however, Crofts was always at pains to demonstrate the traits that lead to his unfailing success. His patience, his endowment with Crofts's own knowledge of railways and timetables, his persistence when pursuing a quarry who has sought safety by concocting an elaborate alibi, all combine to make this mild-mannered man a formidable adversary. Crofts wanted to create a detective in whom his readers could believe, and he felt this required an official investigator who works within a code of conduct. The excesses of many of French's predecessors and contemporaries were to be avoided, and omniscience was to be replaced with the routine procedure of good police work, the precise analysis of all the data, the sorting of the relevant from the irrelevant, and the acceptance that a dead end required a fresh start. Above all, Crofts appreciated that in real life a detective could make mistakes and would then need to reconsider his position.

In all these respects French (and his predecessors in the Crofts canon) drew from Gaboriau's Monsieur Lecoq and Père Tabaret but improved upon them in terms of solid, unpretentious detection. He inspired others, notably Georges Simenon's Maigret (another detective with a listening wife), who first appeared in the 1930s. Crofts knew exactly what he was seeking to achieve. In *Meet the Detective* (1935), a volume edited by Cecil Madden, Crofts stated:

> Anyone about to perpetrate a detective novel must first decide whether his detective is to be brilliant and a "character," or a mere ordinary humdrum personality. When French came into being there seemed to be two good reasons for making him the second of these. One was that it represented a new departure; there were already plenty of "character" detectives, the lineal descendants, most of them, of the great Sherlock. The other reason was much more important. Striking characteristics, consistently depicted, are very hard to do. I tried therefore to make French a perfectly ordinary man, without peculiarities or mannerisms. Of course he had to have some qualities, but they were to be the ordinary qualities of ordinary fairly successful men. (p. 80)

Inspector French's Greatest Case opens with the discovery of a daring jewel theft in London's Hatton Garden and the murder of the firm's chief clerk. The case takes the Inspector to France, Holland, Switzerland, Spain, and Portugal before it is resolved on board a steamer bound for South America. *Inspector French's Greatest Case* established Crofts and French as major figures in the field of detective fiction. Its reputation also endured—the novel eventually was featured alongside *The Cask* as a "cornerstone" work in Howard Haycraft's 1941 *Murder for Pleasure* list.

French's second case, *Inspector French and the Cheyne Mystery* (1926; U.S. *The Cheyne Mystery*), is in many ways a return to the technique of *The Pit-Prop Syndicate.* It begins when young Maxwell Cheyne, country gentleman and author, is drugged in a Plymouth hotel and afterward finds his home has been burgled. He is then kidnapped, escapes, and is further attacked. The principal mystery is why all this has happened. At first Cheyne tries to outwit the aggressors on his own but soon finds that the professionals are better equipped to cope with such a mystery.

The faster action of this book might account for the fact that some critics rank it among Crofts's best work. Nevertheless, he returned to a more sedate pace with *Inspector French and the Starvel Tragedy* (1927; U.S. *The Starvel Hollow Tragedy*). French investigates a case of arson near York that involves triple murder, a love story (unusual for Crofts), a trip to France (usual for Crofts), and a meticulous buildup of evidence. A similarly sedate tone pervades *The Sea Mystery* (1928). The discovery of a decomposed body in a crate washed up on the Welsh coast takes French to Cornwall and back to London in his attempt to trace the crate back to its origin. There is a little more action when French investigates the serial killing of girls working in London movie houses in *The Box Office Murders* (1929; U.S. *The Purple Sickle Murders*).

Middle and Later Period

Sir John Magill's Last Journey (1930), in which French investigates the disappearance of a millionaire linen manufacturer who is on a trip to Belfast, has received considerable critical acclaim. It shows Crofts at his most ingenious, writing about a process for combining man-made silk and flax to make a cloth with the advantages of both, and drawing upon his personal knowledge of the topography of Northern Ireland.

This work was followed by four fairly weak stories: *Mystery in the Channel* (1931; U.S. *Mystery in the English Channel*), where French again indulges his passion for travel as he investigates an abandoned yacht with two corpses on board; *Sudden Death* (1932), in which French is faced with two seemingly impossible crimes in a country mansion; *Death on the Way* (1932; U.S. *Double Death*), a railway mystery set in Dorset where a track widening scheme gives rise to fraud and murder; and *The Hog's Back Mystery* (1933; U.S. *The Strange Case of Dr. Earle*), an undistinguished case of quadruple murder. These novels were followed, however, by one of Crofts's best works, *The 12:30 from Croydon* (1934; U.S. *Wilful and Premeditated*). This was his first full-length venture into the field of the "inverted" story in which the murderer's plans are described to the reader from the outset.

Charles Swinburn is an unusual Crofts murderer, a character with a creditable war record who can attract sympathy because he needs to acquire money to save his business and keep his staff employed. The reader follows every step of his plan to kill his rich uncle on the Croydon–Le Bourget flight, with topical and amusing insights into 1930s air travel. In the final chapters the focus shifts to French, who explains how he was able to solve the case. For Crofts it was a tour de force, a demonstration that he was the equal of other writers who specialized in the inverted form, through careful characterization and by getting inside the mind of a murderer. Furthermore, he showed that he could do so without sacrificing his series character; he used French to show how the murderer made fatal slips that only a trained investigator could identify.

Crofts might have been inspired by the 1930s vogue for inverted detective stories created by Francis Iles with *Malice Aforethought* (1931). It was, however, an experiment that he rarely repeated in a novel, at least in its purest form, although he later did so with considerable success in the short story format. Nevertheless, *The 12:30 from Croydon* ranks highly, and the American detective story aficionado James Sandoe selected it (with *The Cask*) for his "Readers' Guide to Crime" checklist that was included in Howard Haycraft's *The Art of the Mystery Story* (1946).

There followed two books of indifferent quality, *Mystery on Southampton Water* (1934; U.S. *Crime on the Solent*) and *Crime at Guildford* (1935; U.S. *The Crime at Nornes*), which were fortunately enhanced by Crofts's topographical knowledge and his ability to relate his plots to the Depression of the 1930s and its effect upon businesses. He rallied again, however, and followed with the excellent *The Loss of the "Jane Vosper"* (1936). This story opens dramatically as a cargo ship is rocked by explosions and sinks in the mid Atlantic, providing Crofts with ample opportunity to show his technical expertise. It is one of his best-known stories, with French investigating sabotage and murder.

The plot of *Man Overboard!* (1936) hinges on a formula to make petrol inert and thus fireproof, a revolutionary idea that gives rise to plotting and murder, while *Found Floating* (1937), which concerns a family poisoning and a disappearance during a Mediterranean cruise, demonstrates again Crofts's mastery of marine technicalities. *The End of Andrew Harrison* (1938; U.S. *The Futile Alibi*), a routine tale of the murder of a millionaire financier, was followed by one of Crofts's better books, *Antidote to Venom* (1938). Among several points of interest are its Birmingham setting, which is an unusual locale for Crofts; the zoo director who is the central character, and the fact that there is no attempt to conceal the identity of the murderer. It is also the book in which Crofts's religious beliefs are revealed most strongly, as the reader follows the conscience-stricken thoughts of the wretched protagonist.

In *Fatal Venture* (1939; U.S. *Tragedy in the Hollow*), Crofts created a novel idea of a floating casino that keeps within the law by cruising continuously around the British coast. French is faced with the murder of the ship's owner while on a trip to Northern Ireland, and this time Crofts not only displays his knowledge of shipping but also of photography.

In general, Crofts had produced his best work by the end of the 1930s. He continued to write novels that were craftsmanlike and competent, if not exceptional, though the mid-1940s saw two of particular merit. *Enemy Unseen* (1945) is notable for a most ingenious plot that takes the reader through a maze of suspicions until a well-kept secret is finally revealed. It also presents a well-drawn picture of wartime conditions in Cornwall and life in the Home Guard (a volunteer force that protected the English coast from enemy invasion). *Death of a Train* (1946), one of Crofts's major achievements, also features a well-drawn wartime atmosphere. It tells of a plot to sabotage a train carrying vital radio valves and combines a fast-moving story with fascinating details of how the train's derailment is effected. Erik Routley justly praises *Death of a Train:* "If you want the best example of the technique of arousing and holding a reader's interest in a specialized work situation, worthy to stand alongside the best middle-period Sayers, it would be in *Death of a Train,* one of his last books" (p. 126).

Until his death in 1957 Crofts wrote only three more novels, none bearing special distinction. There were lengthy gaps between them, as he was engaged in other work, including a book in which he took particular pride, *The Four Gospels in One Story* (1949). In this period he also wrote an Inspector French novel for young adults, *Young Robin Brand, Detective* (1947); a volume of short stories, *Murderers Make Mistakes* (1948), which he adapted from his BBC radio plays broadcast from 1943 to 1945; and many short stories for the London *Evening Standard* in the early 1950s, twenty-one of which were collected as *Many a Slip* (1955). The year before his death saw the publication of another volume of short stories bearing the title of the first short story he had ever written, *The Mystery of the Sleeping Car Express* (1956).

Assessment

Perhaps the most concise analysis of Crofts's work, as quoted by H. R. F. Keating in 1986 in the magazine *CADS* (*Crime and Detective Stories*), was the Detection Club salute to

> Freeman Wills (God bless him) Crofts
> Who held the banners high alofts
> Of alibis that test the brains
> And timetables for railway trains.

Indeed some may conclude that Crofts was just a reliable practitioner and talented storyteller, but this would be an underestimation of his contribution to mystery fiction.

In his time Crofts was highly regarded; H. Douglas Thomson afforded him more space in his *Masters of Mystery* (1931) than any other author, including Poe, Conan Doyle, Christie, and Sayers. Even earlier in America, in his introduction to the anthology *The Great Detective Stories* (1927), Willard Huntington Wright (later revealed as "S. S. Van Dine") had affirmed that Crofts's novels already stood "as the foremost representatives of their kind, as much as do the novels of Gaboriau and the Holmes series of Conan Doyle"; he went even further to suggest that "for sheer dexterity of plot Mr. Crofts has no peer among the contemporary writers of detective fiction."

Crofts was a detective novelist of the classical school, known to be an admirer in particular of R. Austin Freeman, who started writing earlier. He also admired the work of his contemporaries Agatha Christie, John Rhode, and Dorothy L. Sayers. All were mainstays of the Golden Age of British detective fiction, but Crofts differed from them in his use of the official police detective rather than the colorful character, the intuitive amateur, or the pseudoscientific expert. In this respect he influenced—but was never displaced by—countless others, most notably G. D. H. and M. Cole with their Superintendent Wilson and J. J. Connington with his Chief Constable Driffield. Indeed, by 1942 he was still inspiring Nicholas Blake, in his introduction to the British edition of Haycraft's *Murder for Pleasure,* to refer to "the classical *roman policier,* of which Freeman Wills Crofts is perhaps the most able living exponent."

Crofts was nonetheless aware of the attractions of some of the fictional detectives who were the antithesis of French, sometimes giving the latter the opportunity to draw comparisons as in *The Box Office Murders:* "In vain he longed for the skill of Dr. Thorndyke, who might have been able with his vacuum extractor to secure microscopic dust from its fibres which would have solved the problem" (p. 127).

In style, Crofts was described by H. Douglas Thomson as "the greatest apostle of the matter of fact" (1931 ed., p. 176). He presented facts systematically as his investigations proceeded, with clarity and authenticity. His method, succinct and to the point, led to Thomson's affectionate view of his writing as resembling "a well-informed newspaper article" (p. 177) and to Erik Routley's comment that "he writes like an educated clerk" (p. 125). The latter point can only have been intended as complimentary, given Routley's more telling suggestion that Crofts was "as regular and industrious in his methods as Trollope" (p. 124).

So what were the salient features of Crofts's work, distinguishing him from others at a time when detective novelists were legion? Primarily, there was the purity of his plot construction. Each minute detail fitted the jigsaw with the most satisfying logicality, and his books were the product of an intellect trained in engineering and mathematics. That may have made his stories mechanistic, perhaps too pedantic for the reader who requires a little more action, but they are nonetheless enjoyable as Crofts takes his readers along with his policemen and keeps nothing back. At an early stage in Crofts's career, E. M. Wrong, in his introduction to the anthology *Crime and Detection* (1926), stated that "almost the only detectives who take us fully into their confidence are those of Mr. Crofts" (p. xxvii), and this applied largely throughout Crofts's career.

Crofts's technique means that his stories are not a contest between reader and author, as is the case with so many other writers who hide the salient facts and introduce numerous red herrings. He nonetheless provides pleasure to countless readers who try to beat his detective to resolving how a murder was committed and how the murderer had covered his tracks. Crofts rarely set out to spring a surprise, but this did not mean that he failed to hold the attention of those who preferred the "whodunit" puzzle or wished to be astounded by the exposure of the "least likely person." Instead he engaged their interest in how the straightforward application of common sense and the meticulous analysis of data could result in an irrefutable case.

In short, Crofts considered that this approach more closely resembled real life. As Inspector French himself says in *The Sea Mystery:*

> There is this difference between a novel and real life. In a novel the episodes are selected and the reader is told those which are interesting and which get results. In real life we try perhaps ten or twenty lines which lead nowhere before we strike the lucky one. And in each line we make perhaps hundreds of enquiries, whereas the novel describes one. It's like any other job, you get results by pegging away. (p. 24)

This was, in one statement, the essence of Crofts.

In his essay "The Simple Art of Murder" (1944), Raymond Chandler called Crofts "the soundest builder of them all." He achieved this reputation largely because of his ability to demolish an alibi with clinical thoroughness. Just as John Dickson Carr was regarded as the master of the "locked room" murder from 1930, from 1920 forward Crofts proved himself to be the supreme exponent of the cast-iron alibi, which only a persistent detective armed with timetables could reduce to dust. When Crofts himself turned his attention to the "locked room" murder, as in *Sudden Death,* he approached the problem with his customary matter-of-factness rather than with Carr's touch of the bizarre:

> He returned to the question of the locked room. On his desk he made a model of it—rows of matches for the walls, squares of matches for the tables and chairs. He looked up books containing notes of all the ways in which locks could be tampered with. He put that phase of the problem aside. He concentrated on motives; who could have had a motive for doing what? He made lists of all the people in the case and of all the possible motives for the crimes and tried to connect the two. (p. 267)

Crofts relied predominantly on his knowledge of railways and other forms of transportation, and he described them in intricate detail. Of all his descriptions of life between the world wars, those related to transportation are the most graphic. They reveal not only his technical expertise but also his fascination for railway stations, docks and harbors, and airports. In most of his novels the salient feature is a journey by train, water, or air, and whenever this was based upon a real-life timetable, Crofts's accuracy could not be faulted, whether the journey was domestic or continental.

He was also, in spite of or perhaps because of his relentless factuality, a writer who could paint for his readers an interesting backdrop against which his plots could be explored. He set his novels, for the most part, in places that he knew—for example, the Northern Ireland of *Sir John Magill's Last Journey, Man Overboard!,* and *Fatal Venture,* or his home area of Guildford in *The Hog's Back Mystery* and *Crime at Guildford*—but he also ventured farther afield on occasion, into Wales, Yorkshire, the south coast, and Scotland. He was good at imparting local color, and when his detectives traveled across the English Channel the scenery was painted equally well. Indeed, he gave every impression of having identified, visited, and probably even photographed the various locations of his novels before he ever put pen to paper.

Crofts is also remembered for his devotion to the "inner man" of his central characters. In every book, whatever the state of play on a case, his detective must go through the daily ritual of breakfast, lunch, tea, and dinner. Everything stops for meals. Time after time, French or his associates suspend their deliberations in order to fortify themselves, and never allow the excitement of their discoveries to let them forget that it is time for food.

What stands out above all, however, is Crofts's moral position. He ranks with G. K. Chesterton and Ronald A. Knox among detective novelists who brought religious conviction to the tale of right versus wrong. His work carries the message that crime is abhorrent and criminals will be caught by the inexorable process of the law, and in this he appears old-fashioned when compared with many of the later crime novelists. Yet Crofts's approach was one to which his readers could relate, particularly in an age when even domestic murderers suffered the supreme penalty.

Sometimes he invites the reader to share in the tortured thoughts of a murderer whose victim is an unpleasant character deserving little sympathy, but in most cases he is completely unequivocal, with his murderers motivated by greed, committing the ultimate crime in the course of robbery or as part of a financial plot. Even when the harsh economic climate of the 1920s and 1930s drives a man to commit murder for the sake of his family or to keep his workforce from going under, Crofts takes the line that the law is paramount. It was a strongly held belief, probably stemming from the religiosity of his upbringing, and which led to Routley's description of him as "perhaps the greatest puritan of them all" (p. 124). He left his readers in no doubt that Inspector French would get his man, who would then be hanged.

All this—his writing technique, the nature of his plots, and his own morality—led some later commentators to regard Crofts as "humdrum." Most famously, Julian Symons suggested in his *Bloody Murder* (1972) that "Crofts was not just a typical, but also the best, representative of what may be called the Humdrum school of detective novelists" (p. 114). The Symons finger pointed also at John Rhode, R. A. J. Walling, J. S. Fletcher, and G. D. H. and M. Cole, though he could have added others such as J. J. Connington and E. R. Punshon.

This was perhaps an unfair description and certainly not a view shared by Crofts's many loyal readers. It must be accepted that he eschewed racy action and deep psychological analysis. Instead he achieved popularity by telling a story systematically and unsensationally, giving the reader a comfortable journey side by side with a detective whose very ordinariness was his principal appeal. His critics also overlook the fact that his writing, far from being dull, was exactly what many people required in the interwar years and that he accurately reflected the social mores of the time.

In fact, though many years have elapsed, there is little reason to qualify Haycraft's comment in *Murder for Pleasure:* "Whatever he may or may not produce in the future, Freeman Wills Crofts' permanent place in the history of detective fiction is already more than secure" (p. 124). In spite of the sad fact that Crofts is now out of print, it is a statement that still rings true.

Selected Bibliography

WORKS OF FREEMAN WILLS CROFTS

NOVELS

The Cask. London: Collins, 1920; New York: Seltzer, 1924.

The Ponson Case. London: Collins, 1921; New York: Boni, 1927.

The Pit-Prop Syndicate. London: Collins, 1922; New York: Seltzer, 1925.

The Groote Park Murder. London: Collins, 1923; New York: Seltzer, 1925.

Inspector French's Greatest Case. London: Collins, 1924; New York: Seltzer, 1925.

Inspector French and the Cheyne Mystery. London: Collins, 1926. Published as *The Cheyne Mystery.* New York: Boni, 1926.

Inspector French and the Starvel Tragedy. London: Collins, 1927. Published as *The Starvel Hollow Tragedy.* New York: Harper, 1927.

The Sea Mystery. London: Collins, 1928; New York: Harper, 1928.

The Box Office Murders. London: Collins, 1929. Published as *The Purple Sickle Murders.* New York: Harper, 1929.

Sir John Magill's Last Journey. London: Collins, 1930; New York: Harper, 1930.

Mystery in the Channel. London: Collins, 1931. Published as *Mystery in the English Channel.* New York: Harper, 1931.

Sudden Death. London: Collins, 1932; New York: Harper, 1932.

Death on the Way. London: Collins, 1932. Published as *Double Death.* New York: Harper, 1932.

The Hog's Back Mystery. London: Hodder, 1933. Published as *The Strange Case of Dr. Earle.* New York: Dodd, 1933.

The 12:30 from Croydon. London: Hodder, 1934. Published as *Wilful and Premeditated.* New York: Dodd, 1934.

Mystery on Southampton Water. London: Hodder, 1934. Published as *Crime on the Solent.* New York: Dodd, 1934.

Crime at Guildford. London: Collins, 1935. Published as *The Crime at Nornes.* New York: Dodd, 1935.

The Loss of the "Jane Vosper." London: Collins, 1936; New York: Dodd, 1936.

Man Overboard! London: Collins, 1936; New York: Dodd, 1936.

Found Floating. London: Hodder, 1937; New York: Dodd, 1937.

The End of Andrew Harrison. London: Hodder, 1938. Published as *The Futile Alibi.* New York: Dodd, 1938.

Antidote to Venom. London: Hodder, 1938; New York: Dodd, 1939.

Fatal Venture. London: Hodder, 1939. Published as *Tragedy in the Hollow.* New York: Dodd, 1939.

Golden Ashes. London: Hodder, 1940; New York: Dodd, 1940.

James Tarrant, Adventurer. London: Hodder, 1941. Published as *Circumstantial Evidence.* New York: Dodd, 1941.

The Losing Game. London: Hodder, 1941. Published as *A Losing Game.* New York: Dodd, 1941.

Fear Comes to Chalfont. London: Hodder, 1942; New York: Dodd, 1942.

The Affair at Little Wokeham. London: Hodder, 1943. Published as *Double Tragedy.* New York: Dodd, 1943.

Enemy Unseen. London: Hodder, 1945; New York: Dodd, 1945.

Death of a Train. London: Hodder, 1946; New York: Dodd, 1947.

Silence for the Murderer. New York: Dodd, 1948; London: Hodder, 1949.

Dark Journey. New York: Dodd, 1951. Published as *French Strikes Oil.* London: Hodder, 1952.

Anything to Declare? London: Hodder, 1957.

COLLECTED SHORT STORIES

Murderers Make Mistakes. London: Hodder, 1948.

Many a Slip. London: Hodder, 1955.

The Mystery of the Sleeping Car Express. London: Hodder, 1956.

DETECTION CLUB COLLABORATIONS

The Floating Admiral. London: Hodder, 1931; New York: Doubleday, 1932.

Six Against the Yard. London: Selwyn, 1936. Published as *Six Against Scotland Yard.* New York: Doubleday, 1936.

Double Death. London: Gollancz, 1939.

The Scoop and Behind the Screen. London: Gollancz, 1983; New York: Harper, 1983. Crofts contributed only to *The Scoop.*

OTHER WORKS

The Anatomy of Murder. London: Lane, 1936; New York: Macmillan, 1937. Nonfiction edited by Helen Simpson, with one Crofts contribution.

Inspector French. 1937. A stage play adapted from the 1932 novel *Sudden Death,* not commercially published but performed in Guildford, Surrey, England. An account of it is given in Tony Medawar (1990).

Great Unsolved Crimes. London: Hutchinson, 1938. Nonfiction with one Crofts contribution.

Young Robin Brand, Detective. London: Univ. of London Press, 1947; New York: Dodd, 1948. A novel for young adults.

The Four Gospels in One Story. London: Longmans, 1949.

BIOGRAPHICAL AND CRITICAL STUDIES

Chandler, Raymond. "The Simple Art of Murder." *Atlantic Monthly* (December 1944).

———. *The Simple Art of Murder.* Boston: Houghton, 1950; London: Hamilton, 1950.

Crofts, Freeman Wills. "I Found an Answer to Crime." *Guildford City Outlook* (February 1939).

Goodger, Martyn. "The Crime Novels of Freeman Wills Crofts." *Book and Magazine Collector* 101: 14–21 (August 1992).

Haycraft, Howard. *Murder for Pleasure: The Life and Times of the Detective Story.* New York: Appleton, 1941; London: Davies, 1942. Introduction by Nicholas Blake.

———, ed. *The Art of the Mystery Story: A Collection of Critical Essays.* New York: Simon, 1946.

Keating, H. R. F. "Freeman Wills Crofts." *CADS (Crime and Detective Stories)* 3: 3–6 (April 1986).

Keddie, James, Jr. "Freeman Wills Crofts." *The Armchair Detective* 2, no. 3: 137–142 (April 1969).

Madden, Cecil, ed. *Meet the Detective.* London: Allen & Unwin, 1935; Harrisburg, Pa.: Telegraph Press, 1935. Includes "Meet Chief Inspector French" by Crofts. Pp. 80–89.

Medawar, Tony. "Sudden Death on Stage." *CADS (Crime and Detective Stories)* 15: 7–14 (November 1990).

Routley, Erik. *The Puritan Pleasures of the Detective Story.* London: Gollancz, 1972.

Scott, Sutherland. *Blood in Their Ink: The March of the Modern Mystery Novel.* London. Paul, 1953.

Scowcroft, Philip L. "Transportation Themes in the Detective Fiction of Freeman Wills Crofts" *CADS (Crime and Detective Stories)* 25: 19–22 (March 1995).

Shibuk, Charles. "Freeman Wills Crofts." *CADS (Crime and Detective Stories)* 28: 17–20 (May 1996).

Symons, Julian. *Bloody Murder: From the Detective Story to the Crime Novel.* London: Faber, 1972. Published in the United States as *Mortal Consequences.* New York: Harper, 1972. 2nd. ed. published as *Bloody Murder.* London and New York: Viking, 1985.

Thomson, H. Douglas. *Masters of Mystery: A Study of the Detective Story.* London: Collins, 1931; New York: Dover, 1978.

Wright, Willard Huntington, ed. *The Great Detective Stories.* New York: Scribners, 1927.

Wrong, E. M., ed. *Crime and Detection.* London and New York: Oxford University Press, 1926. The introductions to the collections by Wright and Wrong were also reprinted in Haycraft's *The Art of the Mystery Story,* cited above.

Amanda Cross

(b. 1926)

MARY ROSE SULLIVAN

Amanda Cross is the name under which Carolyn G. Heilbrun, a professor of English literature and a feminist literary critic, writes detective fiction. Since 1964 she has published twelve novels and nine short stories that feature amateur detective Kate Fansler, a professor of Victorian literature at a New York City university. Heilbrun's style is reminiscent of that of Dorothy L. Sayers, while her subject matter focuses on academic ethics and women's issues. Among the many literature professors who also write mysteries, Heilbrun stands out for the interplay between her scholarly work and her fiction: she often uses her mysteries to illustrate aspects of her critical theory. She is also unusual in having attained eminence in both arenas—that of scholarship and that of popular culture—simultaneously. She served, for example, both as president of the Modern Language Association and as a member of the executive board of the Mystery Writers of America in 1984, and she has received recognition for both her research (Guggenheim and Radcliffe fellowships) and her fiction (an Edgar nomination and a Nero Wolfe award). Retired from teaching since 1993, Heilbrun continues to publish detective fiction as well as criticism and biography. Her feminist approach to mystery writing has influenced other writers, and her place in the history of detective fiction lies in her extension of the formula's boundaries to encompass the novel of ideas as well as feminist social critique.

Life

Carolyn G. Heilbrun was born in East Orange, New Jersey, on 13 January 1926, the only child of Archibald and Estelle (Roemer) Gold. Hers was a childhood of books; she describes, in *Writing a Woman's Life* (1988), how as a young girl she systematically read her way through all the biographies on the shelves of the New York Public Library. "I was profoundly caught up in biography," she says, "because it allowed me, as a young girl, to enter the world of daring and achievement" (1989 ed., p. 27). That world, she felt, was not available to her as a female. Her later attraction to the detective novel, as well as to the writing of women's biographies, apparently stems from a frustration at finding literary role models. Heilbrun acknowledges that the independent female protagonist she created—Kate Fansler—functions to some extent as her alter ego and is intended to serve as an example for contemporary women readers. She writes of her great admiration for her father, an immigrant to this country who financially helped other members of his family, and of her "sense of affectionate protectiveness"

(p. 119) toward her mother. We may glimpse a self-portrait in her description, in an essay titled "Sayers, Lord Peter, and God" (1968), of Dorothy L. Sayers—a writer with whom she always closely identified—as one who bore all her life "the attributes of an only child: inner resources, the security of one's unique position in an adult world, the loneliness that for strength or weakness, forever leaves its mark" (Repr., p. 459).

In 1947 Heilbrun graduated from Wellesley College, where she felt her solitariness, as well as her Jewishness, made her something of an "outsider"; this isolation may have turned her toward literary and social criticism. She earned a master's degree in 1951 and a doctorate in 1959, both from Columbia University where, after a brief stint at Brooklyn College (1959–1960), she began a teaching career that was to last for over three decades. She had married, in 1945, James Heilbrun, who would become a professor of economics, and they had three children, Emily, Margaret, and Robert. Her first scholarly publication was an essay in the *Shakespeare Quarterly* titled "The Character of Hamlet's Mother" (1957) that argued—signaling her move toward feminism—for a reassessment of Gertrude as a woman of penetration and sensitivity. Other scholarly works reflect a special interest in modern British writers: *The Garnett Family* (1961), the subject of her doctoral dissertation, and a critical monograph, *Christopher Isherwood* (1970).

In 1964 Heilbrun published her first mystery novel, *In the Last Analysis,* under the pseudonym of Amanda Cross. In *Writing a Woman's Life,* she reflects on the oddity of the choice for a woman who "had three children under the age of eight, a large dog, newly acquired, a husband who had gone back for his Ph.D. in economics, and a full-time job" (p. 112). She attributes the move to simply having run out of her favorite English detective stories, and thinking, "Why not try to write one?" (p. 113), although she sees in retrospect that the need for some "psychic space" and "another role" (p. 114) were at the time unacknowledged motives. As she was not yet tenured, she felt that a pseudonym was necessary, and that it protected her from colleagues who might find her choice of such a popular genre frivolous. At the same time, the anonymity gave her a sense of power, freeing her to re-create herself. (The pen name came from a road sign, MacCharles Cross, that her husband thought seemed a good name for a writer; an editor suggested she make it more feminine.)

In the Last Analysis was nominated for an Edgar by the Mystery Writers of America as best first novel, and it won an immediate audience. It features Professor Kate Fansler, willowy, soigné, and wealthy (a fantasy figure, as Heilbrun admits) who teaches Victorian literature at a large uptown university (rather like Columbia). As a sleuth she is adamantly an amateur, investigating only when called on by friends or when aroused by an injustice, a practice that assures her independence. In this work, she helps clear a psychiatrist friend of a murder charge after a patient is found dead in his office. The situation allows Kate to deliver strong opinions by way of witty literary allusions (her ability to quote appositely on every occasion becomes a hallmark of her style) while imaginatively reconstructing the murder scene. The outlines of Kate Fansler's character and mode of operation were immediately established, as was Amanda Cross's career. *The James Joyce Murder* (1967) followed, with Kate doing research in the country, when her young nephew is accused of killing a neighbor. Next came *Poetic Justice* (1970), in which Kate, back on campus in the midst of an academic dispute, investigates a colleague's death. It was quickly followed by *The Theban Mysteries* (1971), which finds Kate teaching a seminar on *Antigone* at her alma mater and uncovering the truth about the death of a student's mother.

During the five-year interval before her next mystery, Heilbrun published her first major work of literary criticism, *Toward a Recognition of Androgyny* (1973). The book's thesis, with which Heilbrun's name has become linked, is that only the condition of "androgyny"—defined as a refusal to accept socially dictated gender roles—can free the individual for full human potential. The book was controversial and Heilbrun was reproved for a lack of critical standards, but it is now generally regarded as a pioneering feminist challenge to the conventional ideals of the "masculine male" and "feminine female." Its thesis carried over into Heilbrun's mysteries, in plots increasingly focused on crimes against women, and in the character of Kate Fansler, who becomes more autonomous and more critical of the treatment of women by academic and literary institutions. In *The Question of Max* (1976), a graduate student is murdered because she threatens the male literary-critical hegemony. In *Death in a Tenured Position* (1981), Kate investigates the death at Harvard University of the first woman tenured in the women's studies program, with suspicion falling on the victim's faculty colleagues. This book caused a stir in academic circles, coming as it did amid heated debate about women's studies and complaints about the dearth of women on the Harvard faculty. Heilbrun, who had been a visiting professor at various other schools, denied any personal knowledge of conditions in the Harvard English Department (although the Cambridge setting in the novel may owe something to her time there as a Radcliffe Institute Fellow in 1976). Undeterred by the reaction, Heilbrun set her next mystery, *Sweet Death, Kind Death* (1984), on another New England campus, this time of an elite women's college, at which another woman professor is the victim of jealous colleagues.

Between these last two mysteries, Heilbrun had done some scholarly editing and had written *Reinventing Womanhood* (1979), in which she pursues her quest for examples of literary characters who could, by their refusal to sacrifice independence for the conventional "happy ending," serve as role models for contemporary women. Heilbrun sees a threefold failure in most "heroines": they fail to imagine themselves as autonomous, to bond with other women, and to resist the seductions of the male mainstream. These are all errors made by Janet Mandelbaum, the faculty victim in *Death in a Tenured Position,* who accepts the role of the "token woman" with fatal results.

In the next decade, Heilbrun's mysteries presented more positive role models. *No Word from Winifred* (1986) portrays a self-created woman who forms a strong friendship with another woman and whose voice is heard, if only through the journal she leaves behind. In *A Trap for Fools* (1989) Kate herself becomes the autonomous hero when, suspecting that she has been set up by the university, she investigates a faculty death amid an atmosphere of distrust and betrayal. In *The Players Come Again* (1990) Kate's persistence rescues a woman writer's work from oblivion, the sleuthing being an entirely literary enterprise of reconstructing a neglected manuscript.

As did *No Word from Winifred, The Players Come Again* shows Heilbrun's growing interest in the construction and transmission of women's biographies. She had just published a nonfiction work, *Writing a Woman's Life,* in which she argues the need to find new ways of telling women's life stories; she discusses how writing as Amanda Cross serves as both a way to re-write her own life and to dramatize an unconventional female destiny. Having long wanted to write a biography of a woman (in *The Question of Max,* Kate claims she, as a woman, is better qualified to write a woman novelist's biography than is the official biographer), Heilbrun undertook at this point just such a project, published as *The Education of a Woman: The Life of Gloria Steinem* (1995). The subject seemed a logical choice, combining a history of contemporary feminism with the life story of a high-profile, dedicated feminist. Nevertheless, as Heilbrun confessed in *The Last Gift of Time* (1997), it was the wrong choice: Steinem, for all her dedication to feminism, was too much the activist. Not introspective enough to exemplify Heilbrun's "autonomous woman," she was "a biographical subject lacking a subtext" (p. 50). Another nonfiction work of this period, *Hamlet's Mother and Other Women* (1990), a collection of essays on feminist theory and the teaching of literature, reprints three essays on detective fiction that illustrate the connection between her critical theory and her mystery fiction: "The Detective Novel of Manners" (1987), which praises Sayers' *Gaudy Night* for its portrayal of "the complex ambiguities of educating women" (p. 240); "Gender and Detective Fiction" (1986), which argues for formula fiction's effectiveness, despite its reputation for conservatism, in challenging stereotypes; and "Sayers, Lord Peter, and Harriet Vane at Oxford" (1986), which describes Sayers' protagonist in *Gaudy Night* as a "female hero coming to self-awareness and autonomy, and sharing equally with the male protagonist the perilous journey to self-development" (p. 257). All these observations shed light on the observable shift in Heilbrun's novels (those dating from the second decade) toward a more aggressive feminist stance: her detective is now almost exclusively occupied with disinterring the stories, lived and written, of silenced women.

In the same year as her Steinem biography, Heilbrun published another Fansler mystery, *An Imperfect Spy* (1995), in which once again a woman faculty member dies in suspicious circumstances, this time at a conservative law school; now, however, the stakes seem not so high and Kate's attitude is less uncompromising, developments that perhaps reflect Heilbrun's personal withdrawal from the academic scene. She had retired in 1993 from Columbia University, complaining that, as a feminist, she had received unfair and condescending treatment from her male colleagues. Despite her position as Avalon Foundation professor in the humanities and her numerous scholarly awards and honorary degrees, she had felt isolated on campus. In retirement, she brought out two new works in one year, representing both aspects of her long career: a book of personal essays, *The Last Gift of Time: Life Beyond Sixty* (1997), and *Amanda Cross: The Collected Stories* (1997). Both works seem to suggest a distancing from the conflicts that had so long engaged her. In the introduction to the stories, for example, she muses on her enjoyment in writing about her fictional detective, hoping only that "some people might enjoy her company and seek her out" (p. 5)—a sentiment that seems to suggest a step back from the urgent feminism of the novels. *The Last Gift of Time* describes pleasures of her new life—a house of her own, e-mail, old friends—and the discovery of lost relatives of her father's, who responded to newspaper reports of her retirement. In good health, enjoying grandchildren and a marriage of fifty years, she plans to write for as long as possible and suggests she has more left to say, especially as Amanda Cross. Indeed, within the year, she published another novel, *The Puzzled Heart* (1998), which reflects some of the personal themes and retrospective mood of *The Last Gift of Time.* Kate's husband, Reed, is kidnapped by a group opposed to her feminist stance, and the ensuing investigation forces Kate into an extended examination of her personal and professional relationships in an effort to uncover the motive behind what is clearly a crime of revenge.

The Amanda Cross Detective

Julian Symons, in *Bloody Murder,* describes Amanda Cross mysteries as "the kind of thing [Dorothy L.] Sayers might have written had she been an American professor rather than an English advertising copywriter," adding that "this might be taken as a compliment or the reverse" (p. 256). For Carolyn Heilbrun, it is unquestionably a compliment; she frequently expressed her admiration for Sayers and clearly took much of her inspiration for her Kate Fansler character from Sayers' Lord Peter Wimsey and Harriet Vane. Maureen Reddy, in *Sisters in Crime,* describes the early Kate Fansler as "nearly a female incarnation of Wimsey: wealthy, upper-class, somewhat eccentric, well-read, a believer in honor and justice" (p. 50). Reddy and other feminist critics object to Heilbrun's initial use of a male detective model and her acceptance of the genre conventions of classic detective fiction. Some of these conventions Heilbrun certainly embraced: a literate style, wit, and elegance all are important. Her model Sayers, she says in the essay "Sayers, Lord Peter, and God," "was never guilty of sloppy syntax, careless grammar or weak vocabulary; if her erudition was flamboyant, her command of the language was, in this age, dangerously near to deserving the epithet unique," and Lord Peter's conversation "is in the best tradition of the comedy of manners." What it comes down to, she concludes of the classic detective story, is that "intelligent people enjoy reading books about people at least as intelligent as they." Like Sayers, she will be accused of snobbishness, but Kate will nonetheless speak impeccable English, deplore rudeness in any form, and eschew gore and violence: she "has never fired a gun or been beaten up in the course of her work," even into the 1990s, as Heilbrun proudly points out in the introduction to her collected stories. But, style apart, Heilbrun obviously finds aspects of Golden Age mysteries, such as Detection Club rules of "fair play" or the "challenge" to the reader, unsuited to her detective's mode of operation, with its reliance on literary and psychological association of ideas, close reading of texts, and almost Holmesian leaps of imagination. There are no crossword puzzles, timetables, or room diagrams in Kate Fansler's terrain; the criminal's modus operandi is generally of small interest, and the "mystery" consists of hidden motives and buried secrets. The basic plot, played out in a variety of ways, can be summed up as "Who kills, and why?" Eventually, as Reddy points out in *Sisters in Crime,* the Cross metaquestion becomes " 'Who kills what kind of woman and why?' " (p. 54).

What impressed Heilbrun in Sayers' detective novels, even more than elegance of style, was the manner in which she allowed her detectives, Lord Peter and Harriet Vane, to grow and change. On the surface, Kate Fansler seems to change not at all. If not actually "frozen" at one age like some fictional detectives, Kate's aging is glacial at best: though in early middle age in the 1960s (as was her creator), in the 1990s she is still looking forward to reaching fifty. (Heilbrun, in *Writing a Woman's Life,* claims that Kate ages "less rapidly than do mortals, but inexorably" [p. 122]). She continues to drink socially—as much as any Golden Age detective—and smoke, long past the point of political correctness. Marriage changes her hardly at all: she keeps her name and financial independence and wears no ring. Nevertheless, she does change in notable ways, mainly in her raised gender-consciousness and in her increasingly skeptical view of the legal and academic establishments. Detection is no longer an adventure but a quest and a mission. She becomes less intellectual and more dedicated, takes up causes on principle rather than out of sympathy, and experiences self-doubt and deep anger. Although Heilbrun could hardly have anticipated that she would write about her creation for so many years, she did allow—perhaps with Sayers' example in mind—enough potential for growth in her initial characterization to make Kate's increase in moral purpose over the course of three decades seem entirely plausible.

The Early Novels (1964–1971)

In the Last Analysis introduces Kate Fansler as "a reader of detective stories" (p. 163) and a lover of literature.[1] The first paragraph begins with a quotation from T. S. Eliot and ends with one from William Butler Yeats, and the following pages invoke scores of writers. A phrase from the critic Lionel Trilling, a pun on a character's name ("Barrister"), and a scene from a D. H. Lawrence novel all provide clues to the killer's identity. Kate takes up, rather in a spirit of adventure, the case of her good friend (and former lover) Dr. Emanuel Braun after a graduate student is found murdered in his office; soon, however, she has to remind herself that "detective was not a game

1. All page numbers from Cross's novels refer to the paperback editions listed in the bibliography.

you played at because you admired Peter Wimsey, and had a friend in a fearful jam" (p. 106). Although she fastens quickly on the correct suspect, and even lights on his well-hidden motive, she is stymied by a lack of evidence to back up her suspicions, and she must rely on the footwork of her niece's fiancé, Jerry, and much more work from Reed Amhearst, the assistant district attorney with whom she is romantically involved. Amhearst, in fact, supplies the evidence, captures the suspect, and reports the conclusion to Kate, all in the last few pages, in an odd displacement of her as the protagonist.

Feminist critics particularly have objected to this male takeover and its repetition in the next novel, *The James Joyce Murder,* in which Reed's role expands: he solves the case, with almost no help from Kate, and rescues her when she has trouble with the police. This sidelining of the female protagonist, Reddy speculates, may be designed to present her in a temporary stasis "before the birth of a remade Kate" (p. 57) in the next novel. Others have seen it as an attempt to reproduce the equal-partner relationship of Sayers' Peter Wimsey and Harriet Vane (a reverse twist on that relationship can be heard, certainly, when Reed is introduced in *In the Last Analysis* as someone Kate had rescued "on the brink of disaster," thus putting him "forever in her debt" [p. 36]). A simpler explanation is that, in *The James Joyce Murder,* Heilbrun was not taking murder very seriously (how else can one explain the neighbors' consensus that the murdered woman's removal is "an act of sanitation"? [p. 75]). The author seems to be having fun at the expense of Joyce, that icon of modernism: each chapter uses the title of one of Joyce's stories in *Dubliners,* so that the reader's interest is less on the crime than on how the author is going to successfully use this device (the town is named "Araby" and a character "Evelina," and "Ivy Day in the Committee Room" becomes reading matter for the police, its concluding lines functioning as an ambiguous clue). Even Reddy concedes that Heilbrun is "poking gentle fun at herself and less-gentle fun at academe" (p. 57) in the portrayal of Padraic Mulligan, who writes best-selling novels under a pseudonym and mediocre scholarly work under his own name.

In *Poetic Justice,* the literary motifs still figure prominently—in homage to the poet W. H. Auden, who is quoted in chapter epigraphs and throughout—but the subject and tone are more political. Set on Kate's urban campus, amid student antiwar protests, the novel reveals her growing disillusionment with the university. A fierce faculty debate on the fate of an adult-education college within the university pits her against an older colleague once her idol (a figure apparently inspired by Lionel Trilling, who dominated the Columbia University faculty when Heilbrun was a student there and whose traditionalist viewpoint she came to resent). When another colleague involved in the debate is poisoned, Kate plays the role of assistant to Reed, who pinpoints the guilty party and even decides his punishment. By the book's end, Kate, having overcome her fear of marriage as a patriarchal invention, marries Reed.

In *The Theban Mysteries,* we see a rare example of Kate as teacher when she agrees to direct a seminar at her alma mater, the Theban School; the job requires putting aside her familiar role of graduate-school authority figure to guide a bright and irreverent group of prep-school girls through *Antigone*—a situation that allows Heilbrun to illustrate her developing theory of androgyny in the character of Antigone and others in the play. Kate's students learn about the contemporary relevance of Sophocles' play as they debate the Vietnam War. And Kate learns to pursue truth for its own sake (because the death of a student's mother is ruled accidental, no investigation is required). Critics have found it troubling that the dead woman is portrayed so unsympathetically—as an hysterical neurotic who is, in Kate's words, "absolutely better off dead" (p. 168). Jeanne Addison Roberts, for example, in "Feminist Murder," speculates that she, and the victim in *The James Joyce Murder,* represent "antiquated modes of female behavior" (p. 96) that must be eradicated.

The Second Decade (1976–1984)

In the novels that follow, the woman as victim becomes the focus. In *The Question of Max,* there are two such victims: a graduate student killed in pursuit of information about deceased British novelist Cecily Hutchins, about whom Max Reston is writing a biography, and the novelist's friend and correspondent Dorothy Whitmore (a feminist who somewhat resembles Sayers), whose private life is exposed. Kate does her own research on both but is led astray by her overactive imagination. Only when she tethers her romantic theorizing to the verification of objective facts, along with some close reading of the women's letters—leading her to tell-tale inconsistencies—does she uncover the plot by the biographer to appropriate the women's work. Reed's role here is new: present but silent during Kate's confrontation with the killer, he later steps in to rescue her, a development perhaps designed to show him now as a supportive minor partner.

The victim in *Death in a Tenured Position* is not, to be sure, sympathetic: Janet Mandelbaum, the first tenured woman in Harvard's women's studies program, was chosen by the male faculty because she will not rock the academic boat. But Kate must investigate her death by poison in the faculty offices because it represents institutional bias against women—and because Mandelbaum's husband, Kate's friend and one-time lover, has been wrongly accused of the crime. Reed is absent, Kate being on leave in Cambridge, and the solution to the mystery is wholly hers, a result of her recognizing clues in the readings the victim left behind.

Sweet Death, Kind Death (the title is from a Stevie Smith poem) has an entirely admirable woman victim, Patrice Umphelby, a professor and fiction writer whose apparent suicide (in the mode of Virginia Woolf's) conceals an ugly plot against her by a jealous colleague. Kate's invitation from the women's college to investigate the death, reminiscent of Sayers' novel ("It was just like *Gaudy Night,* if you really want to know," Kate says [p. 162]) contrasts with the administration's attitude in the preceding novel, and this time the victim's story will be told by way of a major biography. Kate's husband is in the background here, mulling a midlife change of job to teaching law, and she solves the elaborate mystery herself through a perceptive reading of the dead woman's life and writings.

The Later Novels (1986–1998)

No Word from Winifred makes the connection between detection and biography writing explicit. After reading the journal of Winifred Ashby, a woman who had carved out an unconventional life for herself and then disappeared, Kate concludes that she has been murdered. Her theory, that a jealous lover discovered Winifred's friendship with his wife, proves only partially correct, and the novel's conclusion leaves unresolved whether her disappearance constitutes another silencing of a threatening woman or, instead, a woman's victory by choosing exile and literally having the last word, her signature on a postcard.

On the other hand, *A Trap for Fools* (the title is from Kipling's poem "If"), which returns Kate to campus, is unambiguous in its condemnation of the university ethic. An investigation Kate is asked to undertake involves victims both male and female, faculty and student, black and white. Kate suspects betrayal by administrators, colleagues, and friends. No longer unflappable, she grieves over a second death she might have prevented. Faced with evidence of blackmail all about her, she even indulges in some herself, though for the most benign of purposes (increasing the number of minority scholarships).

The Players Come Again (the title is from Woolf's *The Waves*) puts academia aside to take on a literary establishment that has enshrined the modernist novel of Emanuel Foxx while ignoring his wife Gabrielle's role in its creation (a situation perhaps suggested by the James Joyce–Nora Barnacle relationship). Agreeing to do a biography of Gabrielle, Kate discovers the truth with the help of three women whose complex relationship ties them to Gabrielle and her buried manuscript. The biography goes unwritten; Kate settles for the mundane but necessary task of retrieving and arranging for publication an unrecognized work of art. A mystery without a corpse (the long-ago murder of Emmanuel Foxx is passed off cursorily in the last few pages), this novel treats the reclaiming of the dead woman's work as a symbol of the feminist cause.

An Imperfect Spy uses the motif of espionage, via allusions to John le Carré in the title and chapter epigraphs, as a metaphor for Kate's role and that of Harriet, a female staff member, in working at a conservative law school. They, along with Reed, operate "as moles in the best le Carré tradition" (p. 190) in monitoring the school's treatment of women. In a plot twist, however, Kate discovers that a woman teacher's suspicious death was an accident, not foul play; she then turns her efforts to helping a woman imprisoned for murdering her husband gain a retrial. Her misreading, and her reservations about the role of infiltrator ("I shall never be able to square with myself the thought of being a spy" [p. 208]) suggest a tempering of the reformer's zeal. After being tempted to have an affair with a colleague, she recommits herself to her marriage, establishing her freedom and fidelity at once. To some extent, Heilbrun comes full circle in this book, connecting literature with life: the imprisoned battered woman helped by Kate finds a lesson for herself in the fate of Thomas Hardy's Tess.

In *The Puzzled Heart,* Kate's commitment to her marriage and her doubts about her detective work are prominently on display. When Reed is kidnapped by a group of antifeminists, her initial shock is followed by a period of uncharacteristic passivity. The perpetrators of the kidnapping and a related murder are pursued by Reed's lawyer and their friend Harriet (of *An Imperfect Spy*); Kate is relegated to searching her past for what act of hers, beyond politics, might have incited the hate crimes—all the while berating herself for her failures as a detective. The book's title—a variation on Emily Dickinson's phrase about journeying to unfamiliar places with an "unpuzzled heart"—suggests that at this point Kate is negotiating, with some uncertainty, a new phase of her life.

The Short Stories

Of the nine stories in *Collected Stories,* eight were written for either the *Ellery Queen Mystery Magazine* or for feminist anthologies such as *Malice Domestic* or *A Woman's Eye;* one, "The George Eliot Play," was written especially for this collection of stories. "The Baroness," the only Heilbrun mystery not to use Kate Fansler, is also the only example of Heilbrun's use of a first-person narrator (although in some other stories Kate's niece Leighton narrates, Watson-style). The themes are those of the novels, with more focus on plot than on character development. In her introduction, Heilbrun explains that she much prefers full-length mysteries to short stories, and that these were written either in answer to requests or, when working on a nonfiction book, she had time only for a brief appearance of her detective.

In "Tania's Nowhere" and "The Disappearance of Great Aunt Flavia," Kate's understanding of female psychology helps her locate a missing woman; in "Once Upon a Time," she solves a baffling mystery in the present generation by uncovering a deep friendship between two women in an earlier one. "Murder Without a Text" reverses the usual Cross academic plot by having a woman professor accused of killing a student in her women's studies class; in "Who Shot Mrs. Boyd?" a jealous male author almost gets away with murder; and in "The George Eliot Play," Kate uses her knowledge of Victorian literature to uncover fraud in a "newly-discovered" manuscript. "The Proposition" and "The Baroness" both have to do with art theft, the first from a convent and the second from a New York City art museum; Kate recovers the convent's painting through clues from an art history book, and the museum's painting is surreptitiously returned by the woman narrator, on behalf of a friend. "Arrie and Jasper," about a little girl and her lost dog, is less typical of Amanda Cross than Conan Doyle (with a particular debt to "The Blue Carbuncle").

Conclusion

In the critical debate about detective fiction's suitability as a genre for feminists, most critics agree that the Amanda Cross mysteries, although conventional in form, are among the earliest and most effective at questioning, if hardly subverting, the established social order. In the introduction to her collected stories, Heilbrun claims that as a result of her detective's adventures "a small degree of order has been restored . . . but no institution has been profoundly changed" (p. 4). Reddy, in *Sisters in Crime,* finds Heilbrun the most influential creator of a female academic detective and Kate Fansler "the most complex and interesting detective" (p. 66) in this genre. Heilbrun's influence is not to be found in the most obvious characteristics of the modern female detective's universe, such as physical violence and graphic language, but rather in contemporary writers' increased concern with women's issues, in their use of a new kind of villain, symbolic of corporate or institutional guilt, and, above all, in their portrayal of women protagonists who can be observed to grow in self-knowledge and autonomy in the course of their detection.

Selected Bibliography

WORKS OF AMANDA CROSS

FICTION

In the Last Analysis. New York: Macmillan, 1964; New York: Avon, 1966.

The James Joyce Murder. New York: Macmillan, 1967; New York: Ballantine, 1982.

Poetic Justice. New York: Knopf, 1970; New York: Avon, 1979.

The Theban Mysteries. New York: Knopf, 1971; New York: Avon, 1979.

The Question of Max. New York: Knopf, 1976; New York: Ballantine, 1984.

Death in a Tenured Position. New York: Dutton, 1981; New York: Ballantine, 1982. Published in England as *Death in the Faculty.* London: Virago, 1981.

Sweet Death, Kind Death. New York: Dutton, 1984; New York: Ballantine, 1985.

No Word from Winifred. New York: Dutton, 1986; New York: Ballantine, 1987.

A Trap for Fools. New York: Dutton, 1989; New York: Ballantine, 1990.

The Players Come Again. New York: Random House, 1990; New York: Ballantine, 1991.

An Imperfect Spy. New York: Random House, 1995; New York: Ballantine, 1996.

Amanda Cross: The Collected Stories. New York: Ballantine, 1997.

The Puzzled Heart. New York: Ballantine, 1998.

NONFICTION

Note: The subject's nonfiction is published under the name Carolyn Heilbrun.

The Garnett Family. New York: Macmillan, 1961.

"Sayers, Lord Peter, and God." In *The American Scholar,* 37, no. 2: 324–334. (spring 1968). Repr. in *Lord Peter: A Collection of All the Lord Peter Wimsey Stories.* Edited by James Sandoe. New York: Avon, 1972. Pp. 454–469.

Christopher Isherwood. New York: Columbia University Press, 1970.

Toward a Recognition of Androgyny: Aspects of Male and Female in Literature. New York: Knopf, 1973. Published in England as *Toward Androgyny.* London: Gollancz, 1973.

Lady Ottoline's Album (as editor). New York: Knopf, 1976.

Reinventing Womanhood. New York: Norton, 1979.

The Representation of Women in Fiction (as editor, with Margaret R. Higgonet). Baltimore, Md.: Johns Hopkins University Press, 1983.

Writing a Woman's Life. New York: Norton, 1988; New York: Ballantine, 1989.

Hamlet's Mother and Other Women. New York: Columbia University Press, 1990.

The Education of a Woman: The Life of Gloria Steinem. New York: Dial Press, 1995.

The Last Gift of Time: Life Beyond Sixty. New York: Dial Press, 1997.

BIOGRAPHICAL AND CRITICAL STUDIES

Carter, Steven R. "Amanda Cross." In *Ten Women of Mystery.* Edited by Earl F. Bargainnier. Bowling Green, Ohio: Bowling Green State University Popular Press, 1981.

Cooper-Clark, Diana. *Designs of Darkness: Interviews with Detective Novelists.* Bowling Green, Ohio: Bowling Green State University Popular Press, 1983.

Knepper, Marty. "Who Killed Janet Mandelbaum and India Wonder? A Look at the Suicides of Token Women in Amanda Cross's *Death in a Tenured Position* and Dorothy Bryant's *Killing Wonder.*" *Clues: A Journal of Detection* 13, no. 1: 45–58 (spring–summer 1992).

Kress, Susan. *Carolyn G. Heilbrun, Feminist in a Tenured Position.* Charlottesville: University Press of Virginia, 1997.

Leonardi, Susan J. "Murders Academic: Women Professors and Gender Crimes." In *Feminism in Women's Detective Fiction.* Edited by Glenwood Irons. Toronto: University of Toronto Press, 1995.

Marshall, Denise. "Amanda Cross." In *Great Women Mystery Writers: Classic to Contemporary.* Edited by Kathleen Gregory Klein. Westport, Conn.: Greenwood Press, 1994.

Michie, Helena. "Murder in the Canon: The Dual Personality of Carolyn Heilbrun." *Massachusetts Studies in English* 9, no. 3: 1–12 (1984).

Reddy, Maureen T. *Sisters in Crime: Feminism and the Crime Novel.* New York: Continuum, 1988.

———. "The Feminist Counter-Tradition in Crime: Cross, Paretsky, and Wilson." In *The Cunning Craft: Original Essays on Detective Fiction and Contemporary Literary Theory.* Edited by Ronald G. Walker and June M. Frazer, with an afterword by David R. Anderson. Macomb, Ill.: Western Illinois University Press, 1990.

Roberts, Jeanne Addison. "Feminist Murder: Amanda Cross Reinvents Womanhood." In *Feminism in Women's Detective Fiction.* Edited by Glenwood Irons. Toronto: University of Toronto Press, 1995.

Symons, Julian. *Bloody Murder: From the Detective Story to the Crime Novel.* 3d ed. London: Pan Macmillan, 1992.

Wilt, Judith. "Feminism Meets the Detective Novel." *Clues: A Journal of Detection* 3, no. 2: 47–51 (fall–winter 1982).

Carroll John Daly

(1889–1958)

REX BURNS

Carroll John Daly's thirty-year writing career (1922–1955) lived and died with the phenomenon of the pulp detective magazine. Daly and his cohort, Dashiell Hammett, have been credited, separately and jointly, with creating the hard-boiled private eye, and both authors were among the earliest and most well-known contributors of crime stories to the *Black Mask* magazine. Some literary historians prefer to credit Hammett because of his greater realism and the much higher quality of his writing. Daly's claim is temporal—his was the earliest short story to present the first-person narrator who later developed into the hard-boiled detective ("The False Burton Combs," 1922) and the first novel to feature that figure in his full panoply, *The White Circle* (1927, serialized in 1926). Lacking the talent of Hammett, Daly nonetheless matched him in popularity during the 1920s and 1930s, and his influential creation has reappeared in various shapes and sizes ever since in print, movies, and television.

Life

Daly was born in Yonkers, New York, on 14 September 1889 of Irish parents, Joseph F. and Mary L. (Brennan) Daly. He attended Yonkers High School and the De La Salle Institute, studied for a short while both law and stenography, and then entered the American Academy of Dramatic Arts in New York City to try his hand at acting. It was not a career he wished to pursue, probably because it challenged him to step out of his comfortable reclusive life. He tried his hand unsuccessfully at sales, both stock and real estate, and business, as manager of a fire alarm company. And he worked temporarily as a "receiver" for a bankrupt company, a job awarded him by the Democratic political machine Tammany Hall as a favor to Daly's uncle, an influential New York City lawyer. Drawing on his experience first as an usher and then as an assistant manager of a motion picture theater, Daly—by then supporting his wife, Margaret C. Blakely, whom he had married in 1913, and their son, John, who eventually gained fame in the 1950s as a film and television actor—became owner of the first motion picture theater on the Atlantic City boardwalk. He later owned and managed theaters in Asbury Park, New Jersey, and in Arverne and Yonkers, New York.

His immersion in the cinematic styles and stories of the early twentieth century gave Daly a clear understanding of the lower- and middle-class audience who attended his movie theaters and of the storytelling techniques that appealed to that audience. The mixture of realism and melodramatic exaggeration found in reel after reel of the era's popular entertainment also characterizes, and eventually stultified, his fiction. Wanting to tell his own stories in print, Daly, at the age of thirty-three, sold his first short story to the pulp magazine *Black Mask.* It was a monthly periodical condescendingly founded by H. L. Mencken and George Jean Nathan and designed to fund their much more highbrow publication, the *Smart Set,* by milking cash from what Mencken called the "great booboisie." But whereas Mencken and Nathan had only contempt for their creation and its lower-brow readers, Daly's imagination and voice quickly found resonance in that mass audience.

During the heyday of the pulps, Daly's name and that of his series character on the cover meant a major jump in circulation—estimates range from 15 to 20 percent—for the issue that featured them. Three Gun Terry, Frank (Satan) Hall, Vee Brown, Clay Holt, and especially Race Williams were in popular demand by readers, even when the editors privately condemned their creator's writing style and literary awkwardness. Concerning his literary beginnings, Daly wrote that after his first two stories had been run by an associate editor, the senior editor, George F. Sutton, Jr., called him in and stated, "It's like this, Daly. I am editor of this magazine to see it make money. To see the circulation go up. I don't like these stories—but the readers do. I have never received so many letters about a single character before. Write them. I don't like them. But I'll buy them, and I'll print them." (quoted in Goulart, p. 29).

But by the 1950s both Daly and his medium were rapidly losing that popularity. The lurid romance of violence continued in its appeal, as Mickey Spillane's work testified after World War II and as numberless lone tough guys continue to demonstrate. Subject matter, however, is only one element of audience appeal; others include style, setting, and character. Spillane, who credited Daly for being a major influence, brought the hard-boiled private investigator into a mid-century setting, with modern language and greater sexual explicitness in *I, the Jury* (1947). Subsequent tough guys have changed costumes, from the tuxedo of James Bond to the sweaty headband of Sylvester Stallone to the black belts of various karate kickers. Daly did not change with his audience, and the result was that he became as old-fashioned as *Black Mask* itself. By the mid-1950s, Daly was unable to sell his Race Williams stories to an American public panting after Mike Hammer.

In 1953, his principal market lost and his health beginning to erode, he moved to Santa Monica, where he tried unsuccessfully to follow his son's example by establishing a career in the rapidly growing medium of television. The Santa Monica Writers Club made him an honorary member, but, as usual, honors of that sort did little to generate sales. Late in life, he moved to Montrose, California. It is not surprising to learn that his last work was written for comic books—where Mickey Spillane had begun his career. After a long illness, Daly died in the Los Angeles County Hospital on 16 January 1958.

Work and Times

The widespread disillusionment among American intellectuals following the butchery of World War I, the corruption generated by Prohibition, the popular sense of having been betrayed by society's leaders, the stunning and universal greed of the 1920s, and the disaster of the Depression were reflected by a number of American writers. F. Scott Fitzgerald, Ernest Hemingway, John Dos Passos, John Steinbeck, and other novelists continued and intensified, in their themes and styles of writing, the rejection of the Victorian authority that had been challenged by major literary figures early in the twentieth century and was finally destroyed by World War I. This same rebellion was shared by such minor authors as Daly, though with far less examination of self and of purpose in writing.

In addition, Daly, like other crime writers who preceded and followed him, made use of the popularly appealing archetypes who already existed in American literature. One such principal figure was the gunfighting hero of the Wild West, whose literary image was descended, as John G. Cawelti has demonstrated, from James Fenimore Cooper's Leatherstocking. The popularity of this western hero was established in the dime novels of the second half of the nineteenth century as well as in the new pulp magazines and silent movies of the early twentieth century. (It should be noted that along with detective stories, *Black Mask* featured Wild West yarns well into the 1930s, while pulp magazines devoted solely to cowboy adventure were still being published in the 1950s.)

"The False Burton Combs" appeared in the December issue of the *Black Mask* in 1922 (along with "The Road Home" by Dashiell Hammett writing as Peter Collinson). Daly's first story, "Dolly," had been printed in October, and, under the pseudonym John D. Carroll, he also published "Roarin' Jack" in the same issue as "The False Burton Combs." But the latter tale, with its nameless first-person narrator, urban setting, and casual shootings, pointed directly toward the character, action, tone, and ethics that defined the tough private eye who came to dominate American detective fiction—pulp and otherwise—in the era between the world wars. In this initial story, the protagonist is more of a bodyguard than a detective involved in a puzzle. Hired to protect the real Combs from gangsters, this "soldier of fortune," as he calls himself, impersonates his charge and then vanquishes the villains through his superior ability with pistols. Unfortunately for any potential series character, the protagonist's reward is straight out of Horatio Alger—a job, marriage, and a comfortable place in middle-class society.

In "It's All in the Game" (15 April 1923), Daly used another nameless narrator. This figure is more an avenging nemesis than a private detective. As with the narrator in "The False Burton Combs," this voice asserts the pragmatic toughness required to survive in a corrupt urban world of predators and callous authority. He creates among the villains a bloody mayhem that is justified in the name of doing whatever is called for to protect the weak and innocent from the evils of that fallen world.

Urged by the editor George F. Sutton, Jr., who saw series characters as a means of increasing his magazine's readership, Daly quickly developed narrators with names that were both virile and mnemonic. And he would not again commit the tactical error of marrying off his hero. His first series character, though not his most famous, made his debut in the *Black Mask* on 15 May 1923 as the title character in "Three Gun Terry." In psychology, language, and action, Terry Mack was the nameless named, but, of importance to literary history, he admitted to being—and was proud of it—a private eye tough enough to survive in an urban jungle and one who expected good pay for good work. As with Edgar Allan Poe's sleuth, C. Auguste Dupin, Three Gun Terry was born fully clothed in most of the characteristics that came to define the hard-boiled private investigator in countless future yarns. Insistently anti-romantic and debunking the more mannered and upper-class sleuths in the Golden Age detective fiction of the British tradition, he treated crime fighting as a business and rented out his pistols and his hard-earned knowledge of the streets. He told his story in rough and sometimes colorful language and managed to keep a battered sense of justice.

Like Poe in "The Murders in the Rue Morgue," Daly felt the need to introduce his protagonist to a world that might not recognize and appreciate his new characteristics. Unlike Dupin—and intentionally so—Mack is not a cerebral sleuth, but a man of reflexive action who, in Darwinistic fashion, relies on what he calls his "imagination" and what his only friend on the police force, O'Rourke, calls his "instinct": "You've got instinct. You feel danger before you see it. That's what keeps you alive" ("Just Another Stiff"). This difference between the Great Detective's book learning and Mack's natural talent is emphasized by the detective-narrator who speaks for—and like—an imagined everyday working stiff. Indeed, the ratiocination that had become a convention of most preceding detective fiction was seen by Daly as highbrow baggage that wasn't of much use in the real world of the fallen city.

"My life is my own," begins Mack in the opening line of his first adventure, "Three Gun Terry," "and the opinions of others don't interest me; so don't form any, or if you do, keep them to yourself. If you want to sneer at my tactics, why go ahead; but do it behind the pages—you'll find that healthier." Independent, self-confident, and aggressive, Mack defines his role in American life in slang and underworld jargon: "I have a little office which says 'Terry Mack, Private Investigator,' on the door; which means whatever you wish to think it. I ain't a crook, and I ain't a dick; I play the game on the level, in my own way. I'm in the center of a triangle; between the crook and the police and the victim." Using ungrammatical English, Mack's voice asserts his masculinity like a teenaged youth emphasizing his street smarts and lack of an effete formal education. Unlike that youth, Mack exists in fantasy, where daydreams of violent triumph are fulfilled without repercussion. Yet even as such fantasy is offered to the reader, Mack points out in vernacular that the life of hunting and combating evil is not a romantic quest but a pragmatic business at which he is the best. This mix of romantic fantasy and deflationary contemporary diction makes the fictional daydream more convincing by infusing a note of grimmer reality:

> Sometimes they gun for me, but that ain't a one-sided affair. When it comes to shooting, I don't have to waste time cleaning my gun. A little windy that; but you get my game.
>
> Now the city's big, and that ain't meant for no outburst of personal wisdom. It's fact. Sometimes things is slow and I go out looking for business. About the cabarets; in the big hotels and even along the streets I find it. It's always there. I just spot some well-known faces playing their suckers, and that's my chance. A bit of trailing; I corral the bird, offer my help, and then things get lively. Blackmail it is mostly, but it doesn't matter to me. And then the fee; a hard-earned but gladly paid fee—that's me!

After four paragraphs of orientation to Mack and his sinister urban world, the real action of the story begins; in Mack's words, "when I'm halfway down the block, a woman shoots out of a brownstone front." As earlier with Poe, it was not long before Daly gained an audience and the introductory material became unnecessary.

Daly's second series private investigator quickly became much more popular—and longer lived in print. On 1 June 1923, Race Williams made his appearance in the *Black Mask* in "Knights of the Open Palm," and characteristic of Daly's practice, the narrator is already a fixed type, as the story's second paragraph indicates:

> As for my business, I'm what you might call a middleman—just a halfway house between the dicks and the crooks. Oh, there ain't no doubt that both the cops and the crooks take me for a gun, but I ain't—not rightly speaking. I do a little honest shooting once in a while—just in the way of business. But my conscience is clear; I never bumped off a guy what [sic] didn't need it.

Slightly more articulate than Three Gun Terry, Williams is nevertheless a clone of that character. The story's title carries a double meaning that in blurring the distinction between good and bad, creates the morally gray region where Williams lives. Referring to the Ku Klux Klan members in the story, who are both vigilantes and grifters, "Knights of the Open Palm" also designates the paladin-for-pay who defines justice for a fee.

Like Mack, Williams is an expert—even superhuman—shootist living by a personal code of honor. An element of that honor is to demand pay to pursue a justice that is usually outside the law. Indeed, the law and its minions, like the leaders of the society dictating that law, tend to be vicious, incompetent, or corrupt. The urban frontier Williams inhabits, like the western frontier his forebears roamed, has little law and less justice. Race Williams brings frontier justice to the city setting, and it is probable that readers of the time found a nice mixture of novelty and familiarity in this urban cowboy. Indeed, the early Daly crime story was only one type among the varieties of fiction the *Black Mask* advertised. Other sub-genres showing up in its pages at various times included love stories, stories of the occult, adventures in exotic settings, detective yarns of the "great sleuth" variety, and, of course, tales of the Wild West.

Critical Evaluation

Much of Daly's work is melodramatic, emphasizing violent action and starkly defined characters. However, during the preceding century, American melodrama had developed a major realistic element. Focusing on the problems of middle-class domestic life (*Hazel Kirke,* for example) as well as dealing with social issues (such as slavery in *Uncle Tom's Cabin*), this realistic element of melodrama persisted well into the twentieth century and was found on the New York stages of the 1920s in plays such as *Abie's Irish Rose* (1922), by Anne Nichols, and a number of the works of Eugene O'Neill. It was also found in the new medium of film, whether in the *Birth of a Nation* or in countless horse operas of later years. Daly, with his knowledge of stage and cinema, applied the traditions of the melodramatic form to his new subject of urban crime. He felt that his stories, while heightened in dramatic tone, reflected actual life in America, and given the lurid newspaper headlines of the Prohibition era, there was some truth to his claim. He wrote in the opening paragraph of "City of Blood" (1936), "It's a well-known fact, of course, that a person is murdered every hour in the good old U.S.A." The "of course" emphasizes his and his audience's unquestioning acceptance of a widely perceived "fact."

American criminal life even invaded the world of the usually reclusive author. Daly's obituary in the *New York Times* (17 January 1958) features a case of mistaken identity that resulted in his arrest in the 1930s on suspicion of being a felon. A sheriff's deputy, looking for a swindler who had fled from California, came to the door of his home in White Plains accompanied by the local police. They had a warrant for a "John J. Daly" of 7 Concord Avenue and opined that Carroll J. Daly of 37 Concord Avenue was close enough. As Daly tells it:

> We went to New York on the train, I paying the fares. My captor suggested that we go to Cavanagh's restaurant on West Twenty-third Street for supper. I didn't have much of an appetite but the deputy made up for it. He ordered a steak, which he ate in cave-man style, then sharpened a match and used it for a toothpick. He told me not to give bail, because if I didn't I would be sent to the coast in his custody. He said that we would have a grand time. From the restaurant, he took me downtown . . . to play a game of pool.

Afterward, Daly was escorted to the Tombs and jailed until the affair was straightened out the next day by his friends and acquaintances.

The incident, reported as truth in his *New York Times* obituary, mimics scenes already published in Daly's tales and elsewhere. Daly himself described the event as "almost like fiction." In the deputy, the police, and the process, the reader can see a clear indication of the casual brutality and even corruption of the era's legal system. This type of police behavior became a marked characteristic of the new hard-boiled crime stories as well as of the era's realistic fiction. While Daly's writing makes use of melodramatic excess, it also has an infusion of the period's actualities.

Daly's style, admittedly limited, also owes much to the journalistic voices that gradually emerged in the latter half of the nineteenth century. Mark Twain, in *Life on the Mississippi,* praised the style of a New Orleans journalist for its compactness, lack of "gush," and absence of adjectives. He called the style "pemmican." Ernest Hemingway had this quality in mind when he made his famous statement that all American literature derived from *Huckleberry Finn.* Hemingway's own desiccated style gained its early impetus from his training in journalism. Daly did not go to school in the offices of an urban newspaper; however, he certainly read them, and in the Race Williams stories one can find indications of the terse, compact journalistic style that Hemingway was elsewhere developing into high art.

Generally, Williams' narrative voice emphasized short clauses, either independent or linked in a series by commas and coordinating conjunctions. The syntactical pattern for narrative passages is usually subject, verb, and object or complement:

> Ida Kranz stood close to a small piano and leaned against it. There was a curve to her thin lips and a cigarette hung from one corner of her mouth. I saw her half glance toward the window. That was when Iron-Man Nelson looked about the room, walked to a door, flung it open, closed it again and came back to the girl. ("Some Die Hard")

The effect on tone is one of factuality and immediacy—the syntax makes a stronger appeal to the reader's visual imagination than to the aural sense. And the use of the passive voice in the description of the woman gives a more palpable quality to the abstract meaning in her facial expression than would a more active portrayal. With far less sophistication than Hemingway, Daly tried to make his language physical through emphasizing nouns and through use of the passive voice to give a noun quality to adverbs and adjectives. However, Daly was far more interested in the effect of that diction and tone on readers than in any ontological reason for using it.

In an attempt to increase the pace of a story's action, Daly often—though by no means consistently—used a telegraphic style that approximates the compressed immediacy of action on film. This technique is usually found in dialogue, as in "Dead Hands Reaching" (1935):

> "I'm not interested in the Flame's psychic powers," I told him flat. "Talk real talk."
>
> Shoulders moved. He said: "You know me."

Or, from "Just Another Stiff" (1936), " 'So—'arched eyebrows went up—'you admit that others can be fast with a gun.' "

Daly also liked to use repetition of words and phrases for emphasis and irony. It is a technique that, overused and ill-handled, can—and often did—descend into flatulence. But like his protagonists, he was less concerned with nuance than with impact: "I took my drink straight and took it quick. Then I stared at myself in the mirror—and didn't like the dumb look that stared back. The dumb look went. A surprised one took its place, to fade to an angry one. I gulped, slapped a coin down on the bar, turned and walked out" ("Some Die Hard").

Williams' self-confessed "dumbness" indicates the major motif in these stories of rejecting the image of the more gentlemanly detectives so popular at the time. One of Daly's purposes, as with most literary movements proclaimed as new, was to declare the distance of this type of detective story from an established and more critically accepted form of crime fiction. Sherlock Holmes, Nick Carter, the Thinking Machine, Lord Peter Wimsey, Philo Vance, Hercule Poirot, and many other white-collar detectives—male and female—defined the genre at the time Daly began to write, and they remain popular today as period pieces. But as Williams states scornfully just after tossing down his drink, "I knew my stuff now. No more floundering in darkness, trying to be the dilly-dallying, pipe-smoking, deep-thinking detective. I was out for blood" ("Some Die Hard").

With a distrust of the intellect—for its lack of realism in crime fiction, for its glutinous effect on action, for its class associations—comes a lessening of intricacy of plot. Various critics have noted, since its first appearance, that the hard-boiled story tends to be simplified into a sequence of events no longer associated by cause but simply by proximity. Writing in *A Catalogue of Crime* (1989), the respected critic Jacques Barzun dismisses magisterially the hard-boiled style, arguing that it tends not to be a true detective story because it lacks the puzzle of an intricate plot.

However, reduction of plotting is found in the more serious literature of the period as well; the plots of Fitzgerald's *Great Gatsby,* of Thomas Wolfe's *You Can't Go Home Again,* or of Dos Passos' *Manhattan Transfer,* among other works, can be summed up in a few words or can even, in the last case, be labeled "anti-plot." For the more self-consciously artistic writers, the argument can be made that they reflect the cynical distrust prevalent in the 1920s and 1930s—distrust not only of social structures and value but also of the intellect.

A similar distrust of social values and intellect can be found in hard-boiled stories. In one widely promulgated explanation for the popularity of mystery and detective fiction, the reestablishment—through the detective's solution of the crime—of a disturbed social order appeals to the reader. Whereas this may be true in the English tradition of the mystery such as the "Cozy," this "reestablishment" in the hard-boiled genre is only temporal or very circumscribed. World War I left, for many writers and readers both, the feeling that out of the woven fabric of prewar literature, belief, and thought, only—as T. S. Eliot concludes in *The Waste Land*—"these fragments I have shored against my ruins."

Moreover, this skepticism toward intellect and distrust of human achievement can also be seen in earlier writers who accepted literary naturalism and its Darwinist equation of human with animal life, its belief in the inefficacy of individual will against the forces of environment and natural selection. Harold Frederick, Frank Norris, Hamlin Garland, and even T. S. Eliot, writing in "The Love Song of J. Alfred Prufrock," expressed, for various reasons, profound reservations about the glories of the human race and contemporary civilization. Like the coming generation of postwar writers, their plots tended toward chronological sequence rather than complex interrelationships of motive and accident.

Writers like Daly, intent more on selling than on seeing, were carried along in the tide of surrounding thought. His invention of the first hard-boiled detective reflected his times, and like the more talented writers of his period, he inherited the attitudes of literary naturalism, as defined in part by Stephen Crane and Theodore Dreiser, as well as the intensified disillusionment seen in Faulkner and Hemingway. And in his own limited way, Daly points toward the existentialism of Jean-Paul Sartre and Albert Camus.

Although Daly's protagonists, particularly Race Williams, have more importance historically than do their adventures, many of his themes have also become staples of the hard-boiled school. One dominant motif is the anti-romantic attitude. Again and again, Williams debunks the chivalric conventions of romantic adventure:

> Yes, I know. The right thing to do would be to blow off my face, tell the truth about Gentle Jim Corrigan, let the Flame go to jail, let Mary Morse close up her jewelry business, and go off to prison myself with head held high, knowing that I had served my country. But the truth is, I don't like jails any better than you do. Let the cops run their business. I'll run mine. ("Corpse & Co.")

The romantic heart, like the intellectual detective's head, was also suspect in Daly's tales. One reason delineated by critics is that affection for a woman could entrap the archetypal figure of the male lone ranger. A second cause is the literary realism and naturalism that Daly embraced, a genre that rejects romantic styles and beliefs. Yet Daly's anti-intellectualism left his hero relying for survival on his instincts (or "imagination"). The consistent result was a deep suspicion of love as an aspect of romanticism and of thought as the result of education. Instead, both feeling and thought derived, in the terms of social Darwinism, from the human animal.

The Flame, a femme fatale who attracts all men, including Race, like moths to a candle, has a long literary history as the virgin/whore: "There were times when [the Flame] was young and lovely, the sparkle of youth in her eyes—and times, too, when she was hard, cold, cruel, a woman of the night" ("Just Another Stiff"). The attraction between the Flame and Williams added tension to the stories, but Williams always managed to keep from being burned. Williams' violence, too, carried a hint of anti-romanticism, occasionally in its factual delineation but, more important, in its justification. Creating fear served two purposes for Williams, both anti-romantic in their practicality. First, it aided survival: "It's fear that makes a man's hand slow . . . when he has to draw to make his kill. And the creating of fear is my stock in trade" ("Corpse & Co."). Second, it advertised his business: "One [newspaper] did its stuff and wouldn't hurt my business any. Yep, the blazing banner I liked best read—'Race Williams Does It Again' " ("Just Another Stiff").

Very seldom did Daly show a self-conscious humor that rose above the level of sardonic wisecrack and sneer. Once in a while, however, the reader is given a glimmer of antic action and timing that is straight from cinematic burlesque. When Williams kills an assassin, Race's employer, the wealthy Frank Morse, wants to hide the slaying from the police. Race has to push Morse away before he can call his contact on the force:

> And while I waited for my connection, Uncle Frank spouted how impossible it was to have the police in, spouted about the good name of Morse, the firm—and what have you."Listen, Mr. Morse," I gave him straight talk. "I don't know exactly what your method is for moving undesirable bodies. It may be excellent. But this is my corpse and . . ."
>
> "Hello, O'Rourke? I've got a stiff for you." ("Dead Hands Reaching")

Characteristic of the times, Daly shared the tendency of pulps to give villains, especially the great villains who threatened wide destruction, a non-British lineage: Lutz, the Gorgon Brothers, Count Jedho, and—Daly wasn't above a pun—One Man Armin. Specific to Daly's Irish heritage, the names of Race Williams' police acquaintances reflect historical animosity: the honest cop and Race's friend, O'Rourke, versus Williams' sadistic police nemesis, Nelson.

One of the longest-lived salient traits of the hard-boiled detective should not be omitted, that of the soft heart under a tough shell. In a world of moral chaos, in a literary tradition where the heart is untrustworthy, virtuous action becomes suspect and even embarrassing. Without deep examination, Race does follow the promptings of his heart even though that same heart and its feelings are suspect and described by the hero as probably false and sentimental: "When I reached Conklyn Lee's old brownstone front, I like to think there was something else besides [a challenge] urging me—something of the crusader if you want to go DeMille on me" ("Just Another Stiff").

In character, point of view, tone, diction, setting, values, and rebellion against earlier styles of detection, Daly was an initial and major contributor to the development of the hard-boiled detective. In addition, his popular fiction provides a touchstone for larger movements in the literary history of his time.

Selected Bibliography

WORKS OF CARROLL JOHN DALY

NOVELS

Two-Gun Gerta. With C. C. Waddell. New York: Chelsea House, 1926.
The White Circle. New York: Clode, 1927.
The Snarl of the Beast. New York: Clode, 1927.
The Man in the Shadows. New York: Clode, 1928.
The Hidden Hand. New York: Clode, 1929.
The Tag Murders. New York: Clode, 1930.
Tainted Power. New York: Clode, 1931.
The Third Murderer. New York: Farrar and Rinehart, 1931.
The Amateur Murderer. New York: Washburn, 1933.
Murder Won't Wait. New York: Washburn, 1933.
Death's Juggler. London: Hutchinson, 1935. U.S.: *The Mystery of the Smoking Gun.* New York: Stokes, 1936.
Murder from the East. New York: Stokes, 1935.
Mr. Strang. New York: Stokes, 1936.
Emperor of Evil. London: Hutchinson, 1936. New York: Stokes, 1937.
Better Corpses. London: Hale, 1940.
The Legion of the Living. Toronto: Popular Publications, 1947.

Murder at Our House. London: Museum Press, 1950.
Ready to Burn. London: Museum Press, 1951.

SELECTED SHORT STORIES

"Dolly." *Black Mask,* October 1922.
"The False Burton Combs." *Black Mask,* December 1922. Repr. in *The Hard Boiled Detective: Stories from Black Mask Magazine (1920–1951).* Edited by Herbert Ruhm. New York: Vintage, 1977.
"Roarin' Jack," *Black Mask,* December 1922.
"It's All in the Game." *Black Mask,* 15 April 1923.
"Three Gun Terry." *Black Mask,* 15 May 1923.
"Knights of the Open Palm." *Black Mask,* 1 June 1923. Repr. in *The Great American Detective.* Edited by William Kittredge and Steven M. Krauzer. New York: New American Library, 1978.
"Some Die Hard." *Dime Detective,* September 1935.
"Dead Hands Reaching." *Dime Detective,* November 1935.
"Corpse & Co." *Dime Detective,* February 1936.
"Just Another Stiff." *Dime Detective,* April 1936.
"City of Blood." *Dime Detective,* October 1936.

COLLECTED STORIES

The Adventures of Satan Hall. New York: Mysterious Press, 1987.
The Adventures of Race Williams. New York: Mysterious Press, 1989. Includes "City of Blood," "Corpse and Co.," "Dead Hands Reaching," "Just Another Stiff," and "Some Die Hard."

BIOGRAPHICAL AND CRITICAL STUDIES

Barson, Michael. " 'There's No Sex in Crime': the Two-fisted Homilies of Race Williams." *Clues* (fall/winter 1981).
Barzun, Jacques. "Introductory." In his *A Catalogue of Crime.* Rev. ed., New York: Harper & Row, 1989.
Benstock, Bernard, ed. *Art in Crime Writing: Essays on Detective Fiction.* New York: St. Martin's Press, 1983.
Cawelti, John G. *Adventure, Mystery, and Romance: Formula Stories as Art and Popular Culture.* Chicago: Univ. of Chicago Press, 1976.
Collins, Jim. *Uncommon Cultures: Popular Culture and Post-modernism.* New York and London: Routledge, 1989.
"Daly, Carroll John." In *Contemporary Authors,* vol. 112. Edited by Hal May. Detroit: Gale Research.
"Daly, Carroll John." *Twentieth-Century Crime and Mystery Writers,* 3d ed. Edited by Leslie Henderson. Chicago: St. James Press.
Docherty, Brian. *American Crime Fiction: Studies in the Genre.* New York: St. Martin's Press, 1988.
Gardner, Erle Stanley. "Speed Dash." *Atlantic Monthly* (June 1965).
Geherin, David. *The American Private Eye: The Image in Fiction.* New York: Ungar, 1985.
Goulart, Ron. *The Dime Detectives.* New York: Mysterious Press, 1988.
Grella, George. "The Hard-Boiled Detective Novel." In *Detective Fiction: A Collection of Critical Essays.* Edited by Robin W. Winks. Woodstock, Vt.: Countryman Press, 1988.
Gruber, Frank. *The Pulp Jungle.* Los Angeles: Sherbourne Press, 1967.
Hamilton, Cynthia S. *Western and Hard-Boiled Detective Fiction in America: From High Noon to Midnight.* Iowa City: Univ. of Iowa Press, 1987.
Layman, Richard. "The Changing Face of Crime Fiction: *The Black Mask.*" *Bookman* (5 May 1986).
Nolan, William F. *The Black Mask Boys: Masters in the Hard-Boiled School of Detective Fiction.* New York: Mysterious Press, 1985. Includes a bibliography of Daly's *Black Mask* stories.
O'Brien, Geoffrey. *Hard-Boiled America.* New York: Van Nostrand, 1981.
Panek, Leroy Lad. *Probable Cause: Crime Fiction in America.* Bowling Green, Ohio: Bowling Green State University Popular Press, 1990.
Pettengell, Michael John. "Naturalism in American Hard-Boiled Fiction: The First Four Decades." Ph.D. diss., Bowling Green State University, 1990.
Pronzini, Bill. *Gun in Cheek: A Study of "Alternative" Crime Fiction.* New York: Coward, McCann & Geoghegan, 1982.
Willett, Ralph. *Hard-Boiled Detective Fiction.* BAAS Pamphlets in American Studies, no. 23. Halifax, England: British Association for American Studies, 1992.
Zhang, Quan. "Behind 'Black Mask': The Marketplace and 'Black Mask' Fiction of the 1920s and 1930s." Ph.D. diss., University of Maryland, College Park, 1993.

Colin Dexter
(b. 1930)

DOUGLAS G. GREENE

Colin Dexter created one of the most popular fictional detectives in the history of the mystery genre. Inspector Morse and Sergeant Lewis appeared in twelve novels, five short stories (with a cameo appearance in a sixth), and more than thirty television episodes over a period of twenty-two years. The television adaptations have been described as the most successful of all British television series, and in 1990 Morse was chosen by Britain's Crime Writers Association as the most famous British detective.

The success of Morse and his creator seems, at least at first glance, an anomaly. The action in the books is cerebral; the telling is intellectual; the stories pay little heed to modern social, economic, or gender issues; sex and violence, though major themes, are never graphic; the puzzle, with elaborate clues, multiple solutions, and unexpected twists and turns, seems more reminiscent of Golden Age writers of the 1920s and 1930s than of Dexter's contemporaries. Yet, Dexter is able to combine this byzantine plotting with a modern sensitivity toward character and the unpredictability of life. Although Morse solves his cases intellectually ("He has an A brain," says his creator [quoted in Miller, p. 78]), the ultimate point of the books may be the limitation of human reason—indeed, of human desires and ambitions. This bleak view of the human condition distinguishes the stories from those of the 1930s. In some ways, Dexter's stories read as though the novels of Agatha Christie or John Dickson Carr have been infused with a modern sense of *noir*—they are angst-laden puzzle stories.

In fairness, it should be added that Dexter himself always denied that his novels explore the human condition. "The idea that I'm analyzing or explaining anybody's dark abyss of the soul is silly," he said in a 1997 interview reported in the *Pittsburgh Post-Gazette;* his main purpose is to make the reader continually turn the page. In fact, he once said, tongue in cheek, that the success of his books is due to their short chapters. "I'm just a whodunit writer," Dexter concludes. But, as successful as his novels are as puzzle stories, they also do say something about our times, even about "the dark abyss of the soul."

Life

Born in Stamford, Lincolnshire on 29 September 1930, Norman Colin Dexter came from a Methodist home. His father was a taxi driver. He served in the Royal Corps of Signals from 1949 to 1950. He then studied classics for four years at Christ's College, Cambridge, receiving his bachelor of arts degree in 1953 and his master of arts in 1958. He was married in 1956 to Dorothy Cooper; they had two children. He taught Latin and Greek for thirteen years, and while doing so wrote three textbooks under the name "N. C. Dexter," to help students enter Oxford or Cambridge—two volumes on liberal studies (1964) and one on politics (1966). His effectiveness as a teacher, however, was more and more limited by his increasing deafness—he eventually lost all of the hearing in his left ear and required a hearing aid in his right. In 1966 he moved to Oxford and became assistant secretary to the Oxford Delegacy for Local Examinations, where he remained until his retirement in 1987. Though he rooted for Cambridge in the annual boat race, Dexter became very much an Oxfordian, and all his Morse stories are set there.

In the early 1970s Dexter went to Wales on vacation with his wife and children. It rained most of the time; the children were fussy; Dexter read several novels to pass the time; he was particularly disappointed in a detective story. Much as Arthur Conan Doyle had done after reading Fergus Hume's *The Mystery of a Hansom Cab,* Dexter decided that he could do better, and wrote four or five pages of the first chapter of *Last Bus to Woodstock* (1975). Six months later, he picked up the pages again and completed the manuscript. The typescript—Dexter wrote his novels and short stories by hand and hired a typist to prepare the final copy—went off to the publishing house of William Collins, who made the mistake of keeping the book for six months, then returning it with six pages of criticism. Rather than rewriting for Collins, Dexter sent *Last Bus to Woodstock* to Macmillan, who published it in 1975. St. Martin's published the American edition.

Dexter wrote each of his early books, *Last Bus to Woodstock, Last Seen Wearing* (1976), and *The Silent World of Nicholas Quinn* (1977), between the end of the broadcast of the long-running radio show *The Archers* and his trip in the evening to the pub for a pint of ale. Reviews were generally positive, but critical recognition came more quickly than popular success until the Crime Writers Association awarded the Silver Dagger (second place for best mystery novel of the year) to *Service of All the Dead* (1979) and *The Dead of Jericho* (1981). Two more novels, *The Riddle of the Third Mile* (1983) and *The Secret of Annexe 3* (1986), appeared before the television series was broadcast and made Inspector Morse and his creator famous.

Television Series

Around 1984, Ted Childs, Central Television's Controller of Drama, wanted to develop an Independent Television series that would rival the BBC's *Miss Marple,* featuring Joan Hickson. Childs brought the matter up to a producer, Kenny McBain, who had been reading Dexter's novels and liked the idea of a television series set in Oxford, where Central Television is located. John Thaw was cast as Inspector Morse, and Kevin Whately as Lewis. The first series, broadcast in January 1987, contained three adaptations of Dexter's novels. The next series, December 1987–March 1988, presented four programs, only one of which was based on a Morse novel. By this time, the difficulty of turning Dexter's cerebral plots into the visual medium of television had become apparent, and the other three programs were based on new scenarios written by Dexter but made into full-length scripts by other writers. One of the programs plotted by Dexter, "The Wolvercote Tongue," became the basis (but with a different denouement) of his Morse novel *The Jewel That Was Ours* (1991). Later episodes of the series occasionally adapted Morse novels, but most used original scripts.

Unlike some writers who cannot abide the screen or television versions of their characters, Dexter was very pleased with Central Television's series. "I think television did me very proud," he says. "I think John Thaw was a wonderful choice" (Miller, p. 78). Dexter himself appeared in a cameo in every program. The success of the series was based on the quality of the writing, acting, and cinematography, but also on the fact that even with new storylines, it remained faithful to the Morse novels. Although the clues are often visual rather than literary, they remain intellectual, and most important, the world-weariness, the angst of the books remains intact. This excursion into the television series is important; as will be pointed out later, the video portrayal of Morse and Lewis greatly influenced the later Dexter novels and short stories. In the context of Dexter's career, the recognition brought by television resulted in best-seller status for his books. *The Wench Is Dead* (1992) and *The Way Through the Woods* (1996) both won the Crime Writers Association's Gold Dagger, and Dexter became a member of the most prestigious organization of mystery writers, The Detection Club.

Inspector Morse

Dexter admits that Morse is "a semiautobiographical character" (quoted in Sanderson, p. 14). Morse shares with his creator an expertise in crossword puzzles, a love of the music of Richard Wagner and the poetry of A. E. Housman, a fondness for cask-conditioned beer and Glenfiddich Scots whisky, and an addiction to *The Archers.* Dexter himself was a judge for the Best Brews in Britain competition, and won the Ximenes clue-writing contest for crosswords many times. He also set crosswords for the *Oxford Times.* Like Dexter, Morse's religious training was Methodist, his father was a taxi driver, and he served in the Royal Corps of Signals. Dexter took Morse's name from Sir Jeremy (C. J.) Morse, the chairman of Lloyd's Bank, who was famous for setting crosswords. Lewis' name came from Mrs. B. Lewis, the pseudonym of Dorothy Taylor, also a crossword expert. In *Last Bus to Woodstock,* Morse, like Dexter at the time, is in his mid-forties. He is lightly built, with dark, thinning hair. He drives an old Lancia. Sergeant Lewis, a grandfather, is older than Morse and in all the books preceding the television series he is placid, thickset, and slightly awkward looking, and has a Welsh wife.

Dexter was especially fond of the novels of Agatha Christie and John Dickson Carr, and he gave Morse some characteristics of a 1930s detective: "I wanted him to be very clever . . . [with] a cerebral quickness and the ability to come to an immediate conclusion—even if it's the wrong one—without hesitation. I always liked John Dickson Carr's detectives, Gideon Fell and Sir Henry Merrivale, because of this" (Sanderson, p. 14). Morse is like a Golden Age sleuth in his love of puzzles for their own sake. In *The Wench Is Dead,* we learn that "Ever since he had first come into contact with problems, from his early school-days onwards—with the meanings of words, with algebra, with detective stories, with cryptic clues—he had always been desperately anxious to know the answers." Throughout the novels Morse is frequently seen working on *The Times* crossword puzzle, which he finishes in only a few minutes.

Apart from this love of puzzles, Morse is quite different from the detectives invented by Carr and Christie. The sex life, if any, of Dr. Gideon Fell and Sir Henry Merrivale, of Hercule Poirot and Miss Marple, plays no role in their cases. Indeed, going back to Sherlock Holmes, any carnal relationship with the opposite sex is seen as a weakness in the classic puzzle solvers—which is one reason that when her character Lord Peter Wimsey was married, Dorothy L. Sayers said that *Busman's Honeymoon* (1937) was a love story with detective interruptions. Morse, however, wants a relationship with a woman desperately, even despairingly at times. In *Last Bus to Woodstock* he is described as lustful, and almost becomes the detective-as-dirty-old-man. "He always seemed to dream of women" (1977 ed., p. 35). In several books, Morse spends time reading pornographic magazines in the homes of suspects. He attends strip-tease shows first to gather information, but returns for his own enjoyment. In *The Dead of Jericho* he worries about his failure to be aroused by a stripper, and remarks that given the opportunity he would have been a peeping tom. But, though always attracted to women, Morse is too melancholy, too much a loner to form a long-term relationship. In a self-defeating way, he is drawn to women with whom there can be no permanence—in one book he daydreams about an affair with a woman who becomes the victim; in others he lusts after the murderer. Dexter often points out (for example, in *Service of All the Dead*) that women are attracted to Morse, as they find his attention and intensity flattering, but Morse is usually too hesitant and uncertain to respond until the moment has passed.

This combination within Morse of a man who is a frustrated voyeur, yet hopes for a genuine relationship with a woman, a man who enjoys the lowest form of pornography as well as Wagner and Housman, leads Dexter to remark that the crude and the cultured are combined in Morse—as symbolized by the fact that he takes both the establishment *Sunday Times* and the scandal-mongering *News of the World.* In *The Riddle of the Third Mile,* Morse remarks that his mind is "mainly motivated by booze and sex" (New York ed., p. 211). Morse's sometimes prodigious consumption of cask-conditioned ale and Glenfiddich is as important a part of his character as his usually frustrated lust. Morse gets most of his lunchtime calories in liquid form—four-pint lunches are not uncommon—and he is quite certain that alcohol helps him to think more clearly. Morse's other weaknesses include fear of heights, difficulty in viewing corpses, and meanness with money. Almost invariably, though he makes perhaps one-third of Morse's salary, Lewis has to pay for the round of drinks. "I think one of the great crimes," Dexter says, "is a reluctance to pay your round" (quoted in Sanderson, p. 14). Even worse, Morse can be mean-spirited, criticizing colleagues in public, or venting his frustration on whoever happens to be near (usually Lewis). His ingratitude can be striking, especially when he calmly appropriates other people's ideas and claims them as his own. He can be overwhelmingly conceited: he says, in *The Dead of Jericho,* "I happen to be blessed with the best brain in Oxford" (1983 ed., p. 11).

Yet, in spite of these weaknesses, Morse remains an immensely likable character. His melancholy attitude is not self-indulgence; it is a recognition, Dexter says, that the world has gone awry. Morse has lost his childhood religious faith—Dexter describes him as "a low-church atheist" (Miller, p. 79)—and has found nothing to replace it. But his straightforward facing of the void has a kind of nobility, as when in *The Daughters of Cain* (1994), he comforts a colleague who has lost his wife to cancer by saying that the pain will always be there. His own vulnerability, his pain, can result in an unexpected sympathy for others that makes Morse himself sympathetic. In short, he is as much a genius as the great detectives of the past, but he is also fallible, with the weaknesses that distinguish humans from gods. At the end of the twentieth century, he became a hero for readers and television viewers in an age that wanted its heroes to have the foibles and flaws that most of his audience has.

Unlike the classic detectives of the past who live in an ageless never-never land, Morse grows older from book to book. He becomes more stocky, develops a bald-spot, and his once dark hair turns gray. Moreover, his abuse of alcohol and his addiction to cigarettes—he tries to give them up in almost every book, but lapses whenever a character offers him a smoke—result in serious health problems. In *The Wench Is Dead* Morse is hospitalized with a stomach hemorrhage, and is diagnosed with an enlarged liver. He is again hospitalized with a bleeding ulcer in *The Daughters of Cain,* and in *Death Is Now My Neighbour* (1996) he develops diabetes, brought on by alcohol. In an interview, Dexter remarked, "I think it's only proper [Morse] should get a little bit of comeuppance for his disregard of all the rules of physical health" (Miller, p. 78). It is worth noting that the amount of alcohol consumed by John Dickson Carr's Dr. Gideon Fell and Raymond Chandler's Philip Marlowe had no effect on their health—their creators were not as fortunate. As Morse ages, he loses the harsh edges of his character. The drinking does not stop, but the love of pornography is less evident, and he treats his colleagues with more sensitivity. In the otherwise unremarkable short story "Morse's Greatest Mystery" (1987), Morse investigates the theft of four hundred pounds collected by patrons of a pub to benefit a charity for mentally handicapped children. When he fails to solve the case, Morse removes four hundred pounds from his own savings to replace the stolen money.

Sergeant Lewis

The centerpiece of the novels is the relationship between Inspector Morse and Sergeant Lewis. In many ways Lewis is the antithesis of Morse—a good family man, happily married, who sees nothing intriguing about pornography. A religious man, he tells Morse that he does believe Jesus rose from the dead. Lewis is content with life; his soul holds no abyss. His weaknesses include a love of fast driving, and a diet made up almost exclusively of eggs and chips. He is not primarily a foil to Morse's erratic brilliance. The sergeant is a competent, reasonably intelligent policeman, who lacks Morse's imagination but adds to the partnership a straightforwardness that often puts Morse on the right scent. In *The Secret of Annexe 3* (1986), Lewis is described as younger rather than older than Morse—perhaps a precursor to the almost father-son relationship developed in the television series; in later novels Dexter's Lewis moves closer to Kevin Whately's Geordie portrayal; as Dexter commented, "the differentiated accents, as opposed to two vaguely southern ones, are more interesting" (Sanderson, p. 20). Like Whately's portrayal, the Lewis of the books becomes more willing to respond to Morse, and to act independently of him. Above all, Dexter says quite directly that Lewis is a good man, and this characteristic is obvious whether he is the Lewis of the novels or of television.

When Lewis first appears in *Last Bus to Woodstock,* Morse is quick to find him dull and pedantic in his questioning of a witness, and soon Lewis is muttering about "that bloody man Morse" (1977 ed., p. 102). Through most of the novels Morse treats Lewis ungraciously. Even his compliments are double-edged: "Don't underestimate yourself, Lewis," he says in *The Riddle of the Third Mile;* "let me do it for you" (New York ed., p. 200). But Morse becomes more and more dependent on Lewis' common sense, sometimes demanding of Superintendent Strange that only Lewis work for him. "Exactly why he enjoyed Lewis's company so much," Dexter writes, "Morse had never really stopped to analyse; but perhaps it was because Lewis was so totally unlike himself. Lewis was placid, good-natured, methodical, honest, unassuming, faithful, and (yes, he might as well come clean about it!) a bit *stolid,* too" (p. 70).

Despite his frequent anger with Morse, Lewis finds their relationship brings meaning to his policework. In the middle of a case, Lewis fantasizes that a plaque might someday appear in a pub recording that he and Morse solved a case there. In the novelette "The Inside Story," collected in *Morse's Greatest Mystery* (1995), Morse thunders at Lewis: "I need help—*your* help, Lewis. For Chrissake get on with it!" (p. 153). Lewis's response demonstrates the satisfaction he finds in working with Morse:

> Far from any annoyance, Lewis felt a secret contentment. In only one respect was he unequivocally in a class of his own as a police officer, he knew that: for there was only one person with whom the curmudgeonly Morse could ever work with any kind of equanimity—and that was himself, Lewis. (p. 153)

In *The Wench Is Dead,* when Morse is in the hospital, he actually wants to apologize to his sergeant for his ungraciousness. "When was that, sir?" Lewis asks. "I thought you were always ungrateful to me" (1990 ed., p. 94). Morse feels content when Lewis forgives him, and Lewis is happy that Morse needs him. In *Death Is Now My Neighbour,* Morse presents Lewis with his most personal gift. In the early novels, Morse has no first name (although in *The Dead of Jericho,* he is "E. Morse"). Throughout the books, Morse refuses to reveal his given name until, as a touching indication of what can only be called his love for Lewis, he presents it as a gift at the end of *Death Is Now My Neighbour.*

The relationship between Inspector Morse and Sergeant Lewis reflects one of the major themes of Dexter's novels—the search for human connectedness. Morse and Lewis find it; many of the other characters do not, or if they do it is almost a reflection of failure, as in the description of the relationship between husband and wife in *The Secret of Annexe 3:* "Even the disappointments and the quarrels and the boredom . . . all seemed to form a strangely binding sort of tie between them" (p. 105). The ambivalent emotional meanings of sexual relationships are a major motivating force for Dexter's characters. For some, like Morse himself, sexual desire reflects a need for a relationship with another human being. For others sex is something to beg for; one man gives a woman a checklist to determine whether she will go to bed with him. Sex may be just a whim; in the opening of *Last Seen Wearing,* a teenager suggests to a man "I wish we could be naughty together" (St. Martin's ed., p. 11), and his acceptance turns out to drive much of the plot. Sex may connect power and desire, as in *Service of All the Dead:* "She hated the man and the power he had come to wield over her—yet she needed him, needed the virility of his body" (1980 ed., p. 141). Sometimes, sex has a crude religious connotation, as when a women opens her legs "like the arms of a saint in holy benediction" (p. 38). The solution of *The Riddle of the Third Mile* depends on the murderer's trust that each of three distinguished scholars will find the offer of the fulfillment of any sexual fantasy too enticing to resist. In all of these examples, and many others, sex becomes a metaphor for our estrangement from each other. Whether Dexter's characters are voyeurs or married couples in quiet desperation, whether they use sex for power or simply for physical gratification, they rarely find human connectedness in sex. Only Lewis' happy marriage stands in contrast to this bleak view of human relationships.

Solving the Puzzle

In plot and structure, Dexter's novels are puzzle stories. The mystery always remains in the foreground, and Dexter frequently reminds the reader that the novel is no more than a story. In *The Riddle of the Third Mile,* for example, Dexter heads each chapter with teasing comments separating the narrator from the events; the heading of chapter seven is "In which those readers impatiently waiting to encounter the first corpse will not be disappointed, and in which interesting light is thrown on the detective, Morse" (New York ed., p. 49). In other novels, Dexter introduces the chapters with quotations from literature (or other sources) and the game for the reader is to work out their relevance to unraveling the mystery. Moreover, Dexter often points out to the reader where Morse has gone wrong: "Unfortunately, the item of far greater importance she'd just imparted was completely lost on Morse. At least for the present" (*The Dead of Jericho,* 1983 ed., p. 91). (Of course, Dexter hopes it will be completely lost on the reader as well.) Sometimes, Dexter uses almost a "had I but known" approach (a school of mystery fiction made famous by Mary Roberts Rinehart), as in such sentences as, "Had he but realised it, he was now within a few yards of a clue that would smash his previous hypotheses to smithereens" (*Service of All the Dead,* 1980 ed., p. 170).

Borrowed from the 1930s detective story is an emphasis on word play, anagrams, crossword puzzle clues, and literary references. The anagram appears frequently in Dexter's books: in *Service of All the Dead,* where it is misleading, in *The Riddle of the Third Mile,* where it is wrong, and in *The Wench Is Dead,* where it confirms Morse's solution. "The Inside Story" (collected in *Morse's Greatest Mystery*) presents Dexter himself as "Rex de

Lincto"—described as "short, fat, balding, slightly deaf" (1995 ed., p. 154). The major clue is a crime story written by the victim for a competition. In *The Way Through the Woods,* an anonymous poem sent to a newspaper indicates where the body of a missing woman is hidden, and various solutions are suggested in the Letters to the Editor. In *The Dead of Jericho,* the solution seems to lie in the similarity of the victim's life with that of Jocasta in *Oedipus Tyrannus.*

The novels and short stories also involve more straightforward clues—timetables, physical objects, and so on, but Morse tends to misread them: "Morse had got it wrong of course," Dexter points out early in *The Daughters of Cain.* "Morse nearly always got things hopelessly, ridiculously wrong at the start of every case" (New York ed., p. 18). Dexter has explained in a *Boston Herald* interview that his plots, and Morse's unraveling of them, are like double-entendre word clues in crossword puzzles: "If you pick the wrong word for the first answer, everything else will fit in, until you get to the last word. Then you must start all over again. That's rather a good metaphor for how Morse proceeds." Dexter has also compared Morse's method to a horse race. At the beginning of the novel, Morse chooses a horse, and gallops furlongs ahead of the rest of the field. The problem is that he is in the wrong race. Morse tries to find a pattern to explain everything, the more complicated and fanciful the pattern, the better. No coincidence is too outlandish for Morse; in fact he sometimes prefers solutions that depend on coincidence. When in *Service of All the Dead,* Morse finally relinquishes a complicated explanation, the narrator comments:

> Here it all was, then—in front of him. It was all so very simple, too—so childishly simple that Morse's mind, as always, had refused to believe it and had insisted instead on trying to find . . . the weirdest, most complex solutions. Why, oh why, just for once in a while was he not willing to accept and come to terms with the plain, incontrovertible facts of any case—the facts that stared him point-blank in the face and simply shrieked out for a bit of bread-and-butter common sense and application? (1980 ed., pp. 201–202).

Morse eventually decides "it would be no bad idea to have a quiet look at the problem itself before galloping off to a solution," but Lewis still has to tell Morse, "You can't just make up these things as you go along, sir" (p. 110).

Morse's ability to create one imaginative solution after another allows Dexter to use other major tools of 1930s detective novelists he admires. Carr, Christie, and many others delighted in having the detective make cryptic comments which seem just beyond the reach of the reader. Morse makes them frequently, asking questions no one expects, making comments that seem out of context. This pattern, of course, goes back to Sherlock Holmes, and Morse has committed a good number of passages of Holmesian dialogue to heart, including Holmes's classic remark about the curious incident of the dog in the nighttime. In addition, since Morse is so frequently wrong, Dexter can play with the 1930s technique of following a false solution (or solutions) at last with the truth. In *Last Seen Wearing,* for example, Morse reaches five successive solutions before returning, finally, to the second. In *The Secret of Annexe 3,* he develops an elaborate theory, alters it with further information, then discovers that he has been partly wrong. Lewis agrees that Morse has explained much of the mystery, but says some of the inspector's theory does not hang together. Morse comes up with another explanation, and appropriates Lewis's theory without giving the sergeant credit. He then arrests a suspect on the basis of yet another pattern he has discerned, but when this explanation turns out to be wrong he has to release the suspect. The final solution proves that his first arrest was correct after all.

Dexter's most revealing example of the multiple solutions technique is not a Morse novel but the short Sherlock Holmes pastiche, "A Case of Mis-Identity" in *Morse's Greatest Mystery.* The story begins as a retelling of Sir Arthur Conan Doyle's "A Case of Identity," in which, having deduced that a young woman's suitor, who has disappeared, is actually her stepfather, who wants to control her income, Holmes threatens the stepfather with a hunting-crop. In Dexter's version, however, Holmes's brother Mycroft points out the flaws in Sherlock's theory, especially the assumption that a woman would not be able to recognize her disguised stepfather, with whom she is living. Instead of depending only on imaginative reconstruction, Holmes tells his brother, he should have confirmed a few facts. Mycroft suggests that the young woman invented much of the story herself. This explanation, however, turns out to be as fanciful as Sherlock's, for Watson has proof that the woman was telling the truth and that the suitor does indeed exist. "A Case of Mis-Identity" ends with Holmes preparing for legal action from the man whom he had threatened to thrash with his riding-crop. In this story, Dexter shows that Holmes (and by extension the other cerebral detectives of fiction) were much like Morse; each needed his Watson or Lewis to make him face reality.

It is, therefore, not a paradox that Dexter combines the elaborate puzzle story of the 1930s with a flawed detective and a noir view of the world of the last quarter of the twentieth century. The literary clues and byzantine solutions not only demonstrate Morse's brilliance; they also show his fallibility. Morse is a loner in a world in which chance and fate (though Morse refuses to believe in fate) have as much influence as reason and imagination. Morse's attempts to form relationships with women show how difficult it is to make connections between human beings in the modern world; his association with Lewis provides hope that humans can connect with each other.

Selected Bibliography

WORKS OF COLIN DEXTER

INSPECTOR MORSE NOVELS

Last Bus to Woodstock. London: Macmillan, 1975; New York: St. Martin's Press, 1975; London: Pan, 1977.

Last Seen Wearing. London: Macmillan, 1976; New York: St. Martin's Press, 1976; New York: Bantam, 1989.

The Silent World of Nicholas Quinn. London: Macmillan, 1977; New York: St. Martin's Press, 1977.

Service of All the Dead. London: Macmillan, 1979; New York: St. Martin's Press, 1979; London: Pan, 1980.

The Dead of Jericho. London: Macmillan, 1981; New York: St. Martin's Press, 1981; London: Pan, 1983.

The Riddle of the Third Mile. London: Macmillan, 1983; New York: St. Martin's Press, 1983.

The Secret of Annexe 3. London: Macmillan, 1986.

The Wench Is Dead. London: Macmillan, 1989; New York: St. Martin's Press, 1990.

The Jewel That Was Ours. London: Macmillan, 1991; New York: Crown, 1991.

The Way Through the Woods. London: Macmillan, 1992; New York: Crown, 1993.

The Daughters of Cain. London: Macmillan, 1994; New York: Crown, 1994.

Death Is Now My Neighbor. London: Macmillan, 1996; New York: Crown, 1996.

SHORT STORIES

Morse's Greatest Mystery and Other Stories. London: Macmillan, 1993. Contains four Morse short stories, one in which Morse appears briefly, and five others. Two, "The Inside Story" and "Neighborhood Watch," appeared earlier in 1993 in separate editions. Repr. as *As Good as Gold and Other Stories.* London: Pan, 1994, with the addition of the title story which features Morse. The U.S. edition, published as *Morse's Greatest Mystery and Other Stories,* includes "As Good as Gold." New York: Crown, [1993] 1995.

OTHER

Liberal Studies: An Outline Course 1–2 (with E. G. Raynor). Oxford: Pergamon Press, 1964; New York: Macmillan, 1964. 2 vols.

Guide to Contemporary Politics (with E. G. Raynor). Oxford: Pergamon Press, 1966.

INTERVIEWS

Behe, Rege. "Dexter, Morse Puzzle Readers Again with 'Death.' " *Pittsburgh Tribune-Review,* 1 February 1997.

Brown, David. "Morse Decoder." *Christian Science Monitor,* 5 March 1997.

Corrigan, Maureen. "Decoding Inspector Morse." *Newsday,* 2 March 1997.

Devine, Lawrence. "Morse Decoder." *Detroit Free Press,* 15 March 1997.

Herbert, Rosemary. "Race to Brookline and Hear Sleuth's Mysteries Revealed." *Boston Herald,* 13 February 1997.

Miller, Ron. In *Mystery! A Celebration.* San Francisco: KQED Books, 1996.

Montgomery, M. R. "Inspector Morse's Genial Twin." *Boston Globe,* 25 February 1997.

Williams, Jane. "Brief Encounter." *A Shot in the Dark* (September 1996).

Smith, Tim. "Mystery Man." *Fort Lauderdale Sun-Sentinel,* 19 February 1997.

BIOGRAPHICAL AND CRITICAL STUDIES

Benstock, Bernard. "Colin Dexter." In *Dictionary of Literary Biography,* 87. Detroit: Gale, 1989.

Olsen, Anda. "(Norman) Colin Dexter." In *Twentieth-Century Crime and Mystery Writers.* Edited by John M. Reilly. New York: St. Martin's Press, 1985.

Sanderson, Mark. *The Making of Inspector Morse.* London: Macmillan, 1990. A study of the television series.

Spurrier, Ralph. "(Norman) Colin Dexter." In *Twentieth-Century Crime and Mystery Writers.* Edited by John M. Reilly. Chicago: St. James Press, 1991.

ARTHUR CONAN DOYLE

(1859–1930)

OWEN DUDLEY EDWARDS

SIR ARTHUR IGNATIUS CONAN DOYLE was born in Edinburgh, the capital of Scotland, on 22 May 1859, to Charles Altamont Doyle and Mary Foley Doyle. His father, a skilled draftsman and artist of the fantastic, was the youngest son of John Doyle, who, under the pseudonym HB, was the great British political cartoonist of his day. John Doyle was born in Ireland, as was Mary Foley, each descended from over a thousand years of Irish Catholicism (although Mary's mother, Catherine, may have been of Protestant origin). Charles Doyle settled in Edinburgh in 1849, as clerk in the civil service under the surveyor for Scotland; his assignments included the restoration of the old Stuart Palace at Holyrood, unused by British rulers for two centuries. Charles Doyle's first Edinburgh landlady was Catherine Foley, whose daughter he married in 1855. Arthur was their third child and first boy.

Scottish and Irish Roots

Conan Doyle's famous detective, Sherlock Holmes, and his narrator-friend, Dr. Watson, are so symbolic of England in the international imagination that their creator's Scots birth and Irish origin may be more of a shock now than to the Victorians who first welcomed them. Conan Doyle retained a strong Scots accent to his death, and he peppered his pages with Irish names—McCarthy, Doran, Prendergast, Murphy, Blessington, Sutton, Kirwan, Moriarty, Moran, Slaney, Hayes, Carey, Cairns, Mount-James, Staunton, Croker, Lucas, Barrymore, West, Von Bork (derived from "Burke"), Merville, Gibson, Joyce, and Cummings, to draw a list only from the Sherlock Holmes stories, leaving out the Irish-populated *Valley of Fear* (1915). Even "Sherlock" was the name of a Dublin lord mayor, a Liberal MP, and a popular biographer of the Irish nationalist leader Charles Parnell; and "Holmes" is an Anglicization of the Irish MacThomáis—Killmacthomáis being the barony adjoining the lands of Conan Doyle's Irish cousins, whom he visited in the early 1880s. But there are many other possible inspirations for Sherlock and Holmes, including cricketers, schoolmates, doctors, clerics, and the elder Oliver Wendell Holmes.

Similarly, much of Conan Doyle's Englishness clarifies itself when seen from a Scottish perspective. The recovery of the lost Stuart crown in the Holmes story "The Musgrave Ritual" was prompted by his father's work at Holyrood and his love from boyhood for the works of Sir Walter Scott, who supervised the rediscovery of the lost Scots regalia in 1818. A non-Holmes story of 1908, "The Silver Mirror," also stems from boyhood journeys to see his father's restoration of the Holyrood mantelpiece, above which Conan Doyle imagined a mirror haunted by the reflection of the murder in 1566 of the secretary David Riccio before the eyes of his horrified employer, the then pregnant Mary Queen of Scots. Sherlock Holmes in *The Valley of Fear* describes a painting in the possession of the archcriminal Professor Moriarty, by Jean-Baptiste Greuze: it was in fact made part of the Scottish National Gallery's collection in 1861, where the boy would have seen it on visits with his father. More generally, Conan Doyle's mixture of outspoken British patriotism and objective analysis of English attitudes, manners, and customs is a legacy of his non-English heritage. He wrote one of his most throat-catching stories, "A Straggler of '15'," about an aged English soldier's fading memories of Waterloo, but he also wrote an unrivaled series of historical short stories around the personality of Brigadier Gerard, a fanatical follower of Napoléon.

In short, Sherlock Holmes and Dr. Watson were quintessentially English because their creator was not: Englishness was a quality he studied scientifically and mapped artistically. He was conscious of another great Scots presenter of Englishness, James Boswell, who immortalized Dr. Samuel Johnson in an unmatched biography by appreciation of his Englishness with a perspective an English writer could never have achieved. Conan Doyle used the Boswell principle of a modest narrator winning audience identification; Holmes in the first short story calls Watson "my Boswell."

Holmes's London owed almost everything to a diligent reading of maps, for Conan Doyle came to settle there only in 1891, five years after first creating Holmes, Watson, and their Baker Street apartment. Much of the actuality comes from Edinburgh. Conan Doyle's native city was unusual in being so residential at its center, almost all of the main institutions standing within short walks of one another. A few splashes of different shades of mud could be distinguished by a very fine observer and attributed to different streets in the heterogeneous city center, but Holmes's similar achievement for the huge metropolis of London would be impossible. The effect was important. Many of Holmes's readers were deracinated immigrants to the big city, glad to think of its control by a scientific observer, regardless that such techniques derived from a much smaller and more compact community. The stories' quick changes of neighborhood in terms of social standards would apply much more to Edinburgh than to London; the Scottish capital is famous for its wynds, stairs, and closes, through which the traveler can move from opulence to squalor with far more speed than a Londoner might manage save in the pages of Conan Doyle.

Early Life

Charles and Mary Doyle were the parents of nine children, six of whom survived beyond childhood. Charles gradually developed alcoholism and epilepsy. In early boyhood, Arthur was for a time domiciled with a sister of the eclectic Scottish historian John Hill Burton, the man who gave him a lifelong taste for book collecting and history. The winds howled over the hills and dales of the Burtons' Liberton, an Edinburgh suburb, where he took rural walks and caught his first fish by kicking it out of a stream. The Holmes stories suggest an oddly open space for the weather in Baker Street. When the Doyles found a home together in Newington, nearer central Edinburgh, the rapidly growing and pugilistic Arthur found himself the leader of a tough Catholic street gang; as their champion he fought the local Baptist minister's boy. Holmes's street urchin helpers, the Baker Street Irregulars, are a memory of those days. So, too, may be the air gun in "The Empty House," with which Colonel Sebastian Moran attempts to assassinate Holmes by firing across Baker Street; it would have been fired more naturally across the narrow Sciennes Hill Place in Edinburgh, where the boys brawled. But Conan Doyle claimed never to have seen the street he made the most famous London thoroughfare in literature.

To get him away from the spectacle and example of his father's drinking, Arthur was sent in 1868 to the Jesuits at Hodder, the preparatory school of Stonyhurst College, near Preston in Lancashire, England. The famous Catholic religious order prided itself on training powers of mental retention, and Conan Doyle's hold on his reading was reported to be prodigious. Indeed, it had its dangers. He was sometimes accused of plagiarism, having all too well assimilated some details from another work he was innocently regurgitating. The very first Holmes story, *A Study in Scarlet* (1888), owes the first description of Holmes investigating to Émile Gaboriau's similar description of Père Tabaret in *L'Affaire Lerouge* (1866). The subplot's account of Mormon persecution was probably inspired by *The Dynamiter* (1885), one of whose episodes, by Robert Louis Stevenson's wife, Fanny, turned on similar data of Utah vigilance. Stonyhurst provided its own memories. The facade of the formidable main building, the dark corridors of the interior, the yew alley, and the observatory all did duty in *The Hound of the Baskervilles* (1902); one history of Stonyhurst even has a chapter entitled "Baskerville Hall." "The *Gloria Scott*," which touches on Holmes's college career, speaks of "college chapel" in contexts reminiscent of Stonyhurst. Holmes's friend Trevor in that story becomes a tea planter in Terai; Conan Doyle's closest friend at Stonyhurst, James Ryan of Glasgow, similarly became a tea planter in Ceylon.

Stonyhurst in his time also included two boys named Moriarty, one of whom won phenomenal distinction as a junior boy in mathematics, while the other combined piety of demeanor and cynical contrivance: the qualities of both Moriartys reappeared in Holmes's formidable opponent, their namesake. But the Jesuits themselves later gleefully noted that Holmes's account of Professor Moriarty's "soft, precise fashion of speech," leaving "a conviction of sincerity which a mere bully could not produce," perfectly described the manner of the Reverend Thomas Kay, S.J., prefect of discipline. As a schoolboy, Conan Doyle frequently fell afoul of Kay, above all for illicit pipe smoking. Moriarty's sardonic rebuke on first meeting Holmes—"It is a dangerous habit to finger loaded firearms in the pocket of one's dressing-gown"—might well have derived from an observation made by Kay about lighted pipes plunged into dressing-gown pockets. Father Kay may also take credit not only for Conan Doyle's remaining a pipe smoker for life but also for the comparable addictions of Holmes and Watson.

Although Conan Doyle was happier at Stonyhurst than his autobiography, *Memories and Adventures* (1924), suggests, it was there that he lost his belief in the Roman Catholic faith. The Jesuits seem to have been tactful about it, forgave the financially embarrassed parents at least some fees, and enabled the boy to win a year at their Austrian school at Feldkirch. This attitude encouraged a mutual courtesy, which in due course resulted in Sherlock Holmes being twice described as undertaking cases for the Pope and in his creator's successful campaign for the removal of anti-Catholic sentiments in the official coronation oath of the British monarchs. (But when Pope Pius X condemned Spiritualism, the faith to which Conan Doyle was increasingly drawn, he became more strongly hostile to the church of his birth.) The vestigial effects of Catholicism on his detective stories were most marked in the priestly character of Sherlock Holmes: he forgives criminals and refuses to turn them over to the police, in several instances, in the manner of a priest granting absolution. This is true of Holmes's entire career from "The Adventure of the Blue Carbuncle" to "The Adventure of the Veiled Lodger." In *The Hound of the Baskervilles,* Watson protects a murderer's relatives, who aided his jailbreak, nor will he shoot the unarmed fleeing murderer who has just attempted to brain him with a rock. G. K. Chesterton, as a convert to Catholicism, was Conan Doyle's bitter opponent in the war of Spiritualism and Catholicism, but as detective story writer he was his disciple, and Father Brown's forgiveness for repentant criminals only echoes Holmes's. Even Chesterton's celebration of the priest's obligation to forgive repentant sinners, however ugly their crimes, in "The Chief Mourner of Marne" (*The Secret of Father Brown,* 1927) holds as true of Holmes's forgiveness in "The Blue Carbuncle" for Ryder, who had deliberately framed an ex-criminal for his own profit. Brown absolves in the name of Christ; Holmes, in that story, in the name of Christmas.

For all of their future conflict, both Catholicism and Spiritualism in Conan Doyle's life strengthened his inherent hostility to materialism, and the great tension in his intellect lay between spirituality and his scientific training as he turned to medicine. The year at Feldkirch (1875–1876) assisted his growth of perspective and gave future strength to some of his finest historical fiction—"How the Brigadier Played for a Kingdom" on the rise of German nationalism against Napoléon and "The Lord of Chateau Noir" on French resistance against the Germans in 1870. In detective fiction it provided real, human Germans for the only Sherlock Holmes story about the outbreak of World War I, "His Last Bow," as well as the confidence that allowed Holmes to detect a German-speaking royal client in "A Scandal in Bohemia."

Back in Edinburgh in 1876, young Arthur found the household dominated by the new lodger, Bryan Charles Waller, a student in pathology who quickly persuaded the family that the boy needed to follow in his footsteps. Waller opened an exciting vista of real-life literary associations to his chosen disciple; he was named for his uncle, Bryan Waller Procter, who as "Barry Cornwall" was the dedicatee of William Makepeace Thackeray's *Vanity Fair* (1848) and Wilkie Collins' *The Woman in White* (1860). *Vanity Fair* became a powerful influence on Conan Doyle's historical fiction, while Wilkie Collins proved to be the only significant English detective-story writer whose work midwifed Conan Doyle's own genius. Collins' *The Moonstone* (1868) gave Doyle specific inspiration, in its Indian origin, for his first novel, *The Mystery of Cloomber* (1888). His second Sherlock Holmes story, *The Sign of the Four* (1890), received its stimulus from the same book, in its brilliant and brusque detective Sergeant Cuff and in the youthful sleuth Gooseberry, precursor to the Baker Street Irregulars. Gooseberry was also the inspiration for the district messenger Cartwright, recruited by Holmes in *The Hound of the Baskervilles.* (And, in its turn, Cartwright prompted the surname "Carter" for the youthful collaborator also known as "Tinker" henceforth assigned by the Amalgamated Press's multiplicity of authors to that obvious clone from Holmes, Sexton Blake.) Even more than *The Moonstone, The Woman in White* brings to unrivaled perfection the use of multiple narration, including that of a tombstone that proves to be the most complete liar in the book. From the first, Conan Doyle worked on the possible variations of his narrators' personalities and the clues these characters might provide. Dr. Watson was only the latest of many experiments in the first person. The overbearing Bryan Waller established from 1876 a collaboration as the boastful but knowledgeable man of experience patronizing the more down-to-earth and silently resentful auditor. Watson's irritation at the know-it-all Holmes he first encounters seems to be drawn from Waller's impact on Conan Doyle. Waller graduated, undertook doctoral research, and proclaimed himself a "consulting pathologist," as Holmes later styled himself a "consulting detective." Moreover, the Pathology Department at Edinburgh University was in the hands of an ailing professor whose subordinates, struggling for the succession, turned to Waller while according him little credit for his successes. It is thus that Watson discovers Holmes's relationship to the rival Scotland Yard men who consult him. Holmes's early confident manner, quick to dismiss objections and peppering itself with ha's and hum's, is also derived from the personality of Waller; these characteristics rapidly diminish over the course of the series.

Sources for Sherlock

The creation of Sherlock Holmes received many other stimuli at the University of Edinburgh Medical School, where Conan Doyle studied from 1876 to 1881. In particular, there was Joseph Bell, the senior surgeon at the Edinburgh Royal Infirmary who made Conan Doyle his outpatient clerk, required to prepare his patients. The ordeal was made much worse by Bell's technique of deducing firm facts from appearances: the method was clearly designed to intimidate both patients and students. One day, recorded Clement Gunn, a fellow student of Conan Doyle's:

> a woman silently entered and, without speaking, handed to Dr Bell a small vial, stoppered with a plug of soft paper, around which was wound some black thread. Joe immediately said, "Well, ma'am, so your man's a tailor? And how long has he been ill?" The woman looked surprised and confirmed the information. (Liebow, p. 129)

Not until she had left did Bell condescend to enlighten the goggle-eyed students: "It was quite evident that this woman was not the patient; she was too well. She wore a wedding ring, but was not dressed as a widow. The vial was plugged with some of those stoppers of paper on which tailors wind their threads when in use." Another outpatient was recalled by Charles Watson MacGillivray as having been confronted with the words " 'Of course I know you are a beadle and ring the bells on Sundays at a church in Northumberland somewhere near the Tweed.' 'I'm all that,' answered the startled patient, 'but how do you know? I never told you.' " Once again, the patient was left in wonder forever but the ringside students were informed on his departure:

> Ah, of course, gentlemen, you all know about that as well as I did. What! You didn't make that out! Did you not notice the Northumbrian burr in his speech, too soft for the south of Northumberland? One only finds it near the Tweed. And then his hands. Did you not notice the callosities on them caused by the ropes? Also, this is Saturday, and when I asked him if he could not come back on Monday, he said he must be getting home to-night. Then I knew he had to ring the bells tomorrow. Quite easy, gentlemen, if you will only observe and put two and two together. (Liebow, p. 135)

But this prototype of Sherlock Holmes at his most instructive delivered his judgments in a rich Scots accent. The deductions were even more helpful in winning command of patients and students liable to undervalue so unreconstructed a Scots accent. Bell was also given to teaching by paradox or epigram, much as his own great teacher, the master microsurgeon James Syme, had worked. Once again this was fundamental to Holmes, whose teaching manner clearly impressed itself on Watson. Many Holmesisms, whether original to Syme, Bell, or Conan Doyle, are valuable in countless fields, among them, "You should never lose sight of the alternative," "There is nothing more deceptive than an obvious fact," and "Circumstantial evidence is occasionally very convincing, as when you find a trout in the milk, to quote Thoreau's example."

Joseph Bell was only one of the formidable and fascinating figures made for an artist's inspection in Conan Doyle's medical school. The Scottish Enlightenment persisted longest in the medical field, and Sir Robert Christison, the great toxicologist, offered the spectacle of a venerable giant from the palmiest of days still in full possession of his powers. He retired in 1877, at the end of Conan Doyle's first year as a student, promptly climbing the towering volcanic eminence at the heart of the city, Arthur's Seat, to show that his departure at eighty years of age betokened no diminution of his powers. He had been fifty-five years in two successive chairs and went back to the old body-snatching days: he had investigated the two famous Irish murderers Burke and Hare, who smothered sixteen persons in 1828 to obtain the anatomists' fees for subjects. The case would naturally interest a medical student from the same ethnic group; Conan Doyle's library of criminology soon included a rare report of the trial of Burke and his mistress, and Christison's visibility sharpened the psychological involvement.

Christison as Professor of Medical Jurisprudence and Police had sought to discover whether the only extant body supplied by Burke and Hare to the surgeon Robert Knox, that of Mary Docherty, in fact showed evidence of murder. Burke said he had received it as a dead body to be resold (initially he had implied that he had not even known he was receiving it when it was handed over in a box) and explained bruises on the old woman's corpse as the product of packing. Christison assembled a number of bodies of dead persons and dogs and hit them at various intervals to see whether bruises could be produced after death. Ten years after entering Edinburgh Medical School, Conan Doyle wrote a similar scene in *A Study in Scarlet.* Before meeting Holmes, Dr. Watson is warned by his friend Stamford, who is to introduce them:

> "He appears to have a passion for definite and exact knowledge."
>
> "Very right too."
>
> "Yes, but it may be pushed to excess. When it comes to beating the subjects in the dissecting-rooms with a stick, it is certainly taking rather a bizarre shape."
>
> "Beating the subjects!"
>
> "Yes, to verify how far bruises may be produced after death. I saw him at it with my own eyes."

The young Conan Doyle was by then a successful short-story writer for English magazines, but, like many Scots, his opinion of English medical attainments was low; he clearly assumed that a Scots experiment of 1828 would shock English practitioners in the 1880s. Christison's report to the authorities and to the scientific public appeared in the *Edinburgh Medical and Surgical Journal* in 1829 and was entitled "Murder by Strangling [typographical captioning error for "Suffocation"], with some remarks on the excess of External Violence on the Human Body soon after Death," very much the title style of Holmes's monographs. His verdict was that he believed Mary Docherty had been murdered, but he could not prove it. Christison passionately held that doctors should not give evidence for either side of a court trial, criminal or otherwise; they should testify as amici curiae, their evidence being what scientific truth demanded, with no inclination toward any party to the proceedings. Here again the principle of investigative independence asserted by Holmes stems from Christison. Priest and scientist were facets of his calling, and each, whatever their mutual antipathies, required his independence. As Holmes puts it in "The Problem of Thor Bridge," one of his final cases (in speaking to a multimillionaire client whom he begins by proving a liar), "When I have seen this young lady, it is very possible that I may be of more use to you in the matter, though I cannot promise that my conclusions will necessarily be such as you desire."

Christison's refusal to push his evidence beyond its limits meant that the Crown, avid for a conviction to meet public demand, obtained a verdict of guilty against Burke only by granting immunity to his equally guilty colleague, Hare. This also fascinated Conan Doyle, who used the idea of an informer as guilty as those he helped to hang in his crude pre-Holmes story "My Friend the Murderer" and, much more artistically, in the Holmes adventure "The Resident Patient." In 1911, "The Disappearance of Lady Frances Carfax" used a villain partly based on Burke whose mistress meets Holmes in words similar to those in which Burke's lady answered the investigating police. Even the two German spies in "His Last Bow" are Von Bork and Von Herling.

Stamford also tells Watson:

> Holmes is a little too scientific for my tastes—it approaches to cold-bloodedness. I could imagine his giving a friend a little pinch of the latest vegetable alkaloid, not out of malevolence, you understand, but simply out of a spirit of inquiry in order to have an accurate

> idea of the effects. To do him justice, I think that he would take it himself with the same readiness. (*A Study in Scarlet*)

Holmes, of course, does exactly this under our horrified eyes when he subjects both Watson and himself to investigation of the reason-destroying properties of *Radix pedis diaboli* ("The Adventure of the Devil's Foot," 1910). When Watson saves them Holmes acknowledges that it was "an unjustifiable experiment even for oneself, and doubly so for a friend. I am really very sorry." But by now Watson is far too devoted to Holmes to concur: "It is my greatest joy and privilege to help you." The antecedent is once again Christison. Not only does his monograph "On the Ordeal Bean of Old Calabar" (*Edinburgh Medical Journal,* 1855) obviously anticipate "The Devil's Foot" (the burning noxious root is an ordeal poison of West Africa), but Christison nearly lost his own life when trying the properties of the bean at home. The principle of autoexperiment was particularly honored at Edinburgh. Christison's life on this occasion was saved when he got a message to his neighbor and frequent antagonist Sir James Young Simpson, who had pioneered the use of chloroform in childbirth by self-exposure to its application, with consequent loss of consciousness.

The most famous example of autoexperiment to emerge from the Edinburgh Medical School was recorded—fictionally—not by a doctor but a lawyer with medical connections, in Robert Louis Stevenson's *Strange Case of Dr. Jekyll and Mr. Hyde* (1886). Conan Doyle did not know Stevenson, but throughout the 1880s he was fascinated to find himself as a fictionist treading so clearly in the footsteps of this contemporary (who was actually his senior by nine years). In *Memories and Adventures,* Conan Doyle writes:

> Stevenson's last year at Edinburgh University must have just about coincided with my first one [Stevenson was called to the bar in 1875 but was in town in 1876–1877 seeing his old university friends], and [Sir James Matthew] Barrie must also have been in that grey old seat of learning about the year 1876 [he entered in 1878]. Strange to think that I probably brushed elbows with both of them in the crowded portal. (p. 302)

This was an elegant if sardonic allusion to the proximity of "Rutherford's historic bar" (as Conan Doyle described it in "His First Operation"), where, unknown to each other, Conan Doyle and Stevenson were fellow drinkers and Barrie was not. Rutherford's had a set of closed cubicles shielding customers from sight but not sound of one another, no doubt with some unforeseen eavesdropping from interested parties. Holmes describes a similar circumstance in "The Adventure of the Solitary Cyclist" to explain his battle-scarred condition to Watson after the foul-mouthed Woodley has overheard his inquiries in the country pub.

Stevenson in Samoa became a pen-friend of Conan Doyle's and detected Bell behind Holmes's science of deduction. But before he knew Stevenson's name, Conan Doyle was his disciple. "How well I remember the eagerness, the delight with which I read those early tales in *Cornhill* [magazine] away in the late seventies and early eighties. They were unsigned, after the old unfair fashion, but no man with any sense of prose could fail to know that they were all by the same author" (*Through the Magic Door,* p. 270). And he put Stevenson's method to practical use.

> Surely John Silver, with his face the size of a ham, and his little gleaming eyes like crumbs of glass in the centre of it, is the king of all seafaring desperadoes. Observe how the stong effect is produced in his case: seldom by direct assertion on the part of the story-teller, but usually by comparison, innuendo, or indirect reference. (*Through the Magic Door,* p. 261)

It was Conan Doyle's own greatest disciple, P. G. Wodehouse, who pointed out a comparable but not similar obliqueness of vision:

> Taking Moriarty as the pattern villain, don't you see how much stronger he is by being an inscrutable figure and how much he would

> have been weakened if Conan Doyle had switched off to a chapter showing his thoughts? A villain ought to be a sort of malevolent force, not an intelligible person at all. (*Performing Flea: A Self-Portrait in Letters*)

As for Barrie, he collaborated with Conan Doyle in a musical comedy, *Jane Annie* (1893), wrote one of the best parodies of Holmes, and drew on Holmes's authoritative if unorthodox practicality for a variety of characters, from Peter Pan to the admirable Crichton. Wendy is also a natural development of Watson, with her domesticity, restraints on self-indulgence, consciousness to vulnerability in adventure, and so forth. But no derivation from Holmes has equaled Wodehouse's famous manservant Jeeves, and no derivation from Watson has matched his Bertie Wooster.

Many others in the embattled, exotic Edinburgh medical faculty involuntarily played artist's model to the young Conan Doyle; no doubt he mixed character traits and mannerisms in many creations, as he did with Holmes and Moriarty. He studied zoology with the great Wyville Thomson and found another facet of the future Holmes in his assistant, John Murray, previously the best student in endless courses with no clear ultimate intent of graduation—this is Holmes as Stamford knew him at the time of Watson's introduction. Murray's apparently aimless pursuits of knowledge ended very suddenly when Thomson, about to lead his expedition on the ship *Challenger* to chart the flora and fauna of the Atlantic from the Arctic to the Falklands, suddenly found himself bereft of a key man, and an interested colleague pitched Murray into the ship with virtually no time for second thoughts. Holmes's hospital researches end when Watson enters his life. There is no explicit statement to this effect, but Watson, if only by offering a foil, gave Holmes coherence, and would certainly wean him of his drug addiction.

The sea plays an important, if peripheral, part in several Holmes stories, a natural result of Conan Doyle's acceptance of a post as ship's doctor on a Greenland whaler for seven months from March through October 1880. Something of the loneliness, the passions, the hatreds, the quirks of fate, and the mutual exploitations of that world are hauntingly glimpsed in the Holmes story "The Adventure of Black Peter," with its harpooned corpse and clues in sailor tobacco and rum. After his graduation from medical school in 1881, Conan Doyle took another turn as doctor at sea, this time in the steamer *Mayumba* sailing to the West African coast, where he spent three days with the dying United States minister to Liberia, the black former antislavery leader Henry Highland Garnet, with whom he discussed history and literature and heard firsthand accounts of the race struggle leading to the American Civil War. Garnet directly inspired two fine Holmes stories, "The Five Orange Pips" and "The Yellow Face," illuminating the Ku Klux Klan and interracial marriage from a black perspective. Garnet also inspired a horrific mystery story, "J. Habakuk Jephson's Statement," offering a solution to the mysteriously empty sailing ship *Mary Celeste* sighted on 5 December 1872: in the story an American black, thirsty for revenge against the white race who had enslaved his people and outraged his womenfolk, ends a long career as a mass murderer by hijacking the ship, taking her to African waters, and leaving her adrift after massacring the white passengers and crew. The incidents on the real ship remain a mystery, but the story, published in *Cornhill,* was so convincing in tone that many readers took its author for an escaped passenger. The ship has ever since been popularly known by the name it bears in Conan Doyle's story: the *Marie Celeste*. Conan Doyle's new tone of authenticity proved to be one of his greatest strengths, with the unwanted side effect of eliciting innumerable readers' belief that Watson's narratives were true stories.

Early Writings

Conan Doyle had been striving for authenticity. He began his literary career as a student, unsuccessfully offering a ghost story to *Blackwood's* when he was about nineteen and winning his first commercial print in *Chambers's Edinburgh Journal* in September 1879, for "The Mystery of Sasassa Valley," duly claimed to be a "true" story. The execution of Sasassa firmly dates it subsequent to the unpublished "Haunted Grange of Goresthorpe—A True Ghost Story," which sat, unused and unnoticed, in *Blackwood's* files for the next century. But the unprinted story had ambitions of plot outstripping its successful stablemate, and its character development, while crude, was much superior. Both involved a simpler narrator admiring the resource and zeal of a more adventurous friend. Bryan Charles Waller was still irritating Conan Doyle, all the more because he dominated the Doyle family; paid for their lodgings; helped treat the epileptic, alcoholic, and unemployed Charles Doyle; and was growing increasingly attentive to Conan Doyle's female relatives. He was obviously, however, one origin of the capable, forceful friend. Another was a more disreputable figure, George Turnavine Budd, scion of a great Devonshire medical family, who drew Conan Doyle to Plymouth early in 1882 for a partnership that seems, in fact, to have been cover for a plot to ruin him. Conan Doyle, driven out to make a fresh start in Portsmouth, built a medical practice from nothing. The cases began to come in, some of them maritime. And while the initial stories exploiting public ignorance of Australia, Africa, and America had small value, Conan Doyle found his first real success in mysteries of the sea. "That Little Square Box" is a hilarious tale with a poltroonish narrator who convinces himself that two other passengers plan to blow up the ship, only to find that their terror box houses two racing pigeons released at sea for a contest. It was the first tale that stayed in print until his death, and it testified to one of the most important, if least noticed, aspects of his mystery fiction—its wit and humor. He was one of the most amusing writers of his time.

There was little humor in his next great work, "The Captain of the *Pole Star,*" a beautifully delicate account of a temporarily ice-bound whaler under a captain haunted by his dead love, whom he ultimately follows across the snow to his own death. The explanation of her fate mentions the woman's death in Cornwall "under circumstances of peculiar horror" during the captain's absence at sea, an additional plot unrealized for almost thirty years, finally brought to fruition in "The Devil's Foot." Next followed "Jephson," with a much more chilling humor, turning on the narrator's failure to realize obvious signs of homicidal intent from a fellow passenger:

> I never saw such emotion in a man's face as when, on rushing out of the cabin with the smoking pistol in his hand, he met me face to face as I came down from the deck. Of course he was profuse in his apologies, though I simply laughed at the incident.

It is the reverse of the ploy of "That Little Square Box," and from time to time Conan Doyle played contraries to his advantage. In the Holmes story "The Adventure of the Abbey Grange," an innocent woman throws suspicion for her husband's murder on nonexistent burglars, and the non-Holmes "B.24" is told by the burglar on whom a wife plants the blame for her murder of her husband. In a way, we see here the doctor as author examining alternative hypotheses in diagnosis.

Sometime about 1882–1884, Conan Doyle wrote his first novel, *The Mystery of Cloomber,* not destined to be published until 1888. It follows Wilkie Collins as a quest by Indian mystics to avenge their master, murdered by a British general, and also in the use of the multinarrator form (one chapter being in pure Scots). The plot is absurd, but the homicidal mystic Ram Singh is impressively pre-Holmesian: what in Holmes are deductions, from him are predictions. His discourse has the amusing conceit of expressing with scientific precision claims that are dependent upon the most extreme forms of spiritual transcendence of nature. This is consistent with many protodetectives in Conan Doyle's early fiction, from the unpublished "Haunted Grange" onward. In that story the protagonist is frequently both scientific in manner and spiritual in matter. But in Sherlock Holmes, Conan Doyle wanted to portray the scientist's method in opposition to the spiritual. Holmes does not deny the existence of God—in a famous passage in "The Naval Treaty" he specifically deduces the existence of a benevolent deity from that of the rose. But he scouts any supernatural explanation for crime in an excellent sardonic manner, as in *The Hound of the Baskervilles:*

> "In your opinion there is a diabolic agency which makes Dartmoor an unsafe abode for a Baskerville—that is your opinion?"
>
> "At least I might go the length of saying that there is some evidence that this may be so."
>
> "Exactly. But surely, if your supernatural theory be correct, it could work the young man evil in London as easily as Devonshire. A devil with merely local powers like a parish vestry would be too inconceivable a thing."

As Conan Doyle's finest literary critic, W. W. Robson, pointed out, Holmes loses his flippancy on the question as the case proceeds. He disproves any question of a ghost, but he admits an exaltation of evil. The point, in a sense, is spiritual without being supernatural: the Baskervilles may not be haunted by a devil hound, but the evil passions bringing the legend into existence wreak destruction down to the latest generation. The fact that the human agency causing the pseudo-supernatural epiphanies is a Baskerville makes the excellent moral that our bogeymen arise from the sins to which we are most inclined ourselves. The Jesuits cast long shadows.

The Holmes Oeuvre

Any future development of spiritual appreciation, or even literary sophistication, in Holmes is sharply absent from *A Study in Scarlet,* the story that launched him. This first version makes great play with Holmes's ignorance of the Copernican theory or of the work of Thomas Carlyle, although in its sequel, *The Sign of the Four* (1890), Holmes cites Carlyle's debts to the German writer Jean Paul Richter, and in "The Musgrave Ritual," mostly set well before *A Study in Scarlet,* the relationship of sun to earth is vital to the case. In first drawing the character, Conan Doyle quickly threw together a composite of medical specialists and students known to him and added caricaturish touches on the ignorance that specialization seemed to breed. Music he could permit to Holmes from the first—Christison and others were noted enthusiasts for it. Otherwise, Holmes was so scientific as to be what his creator called a calculating machine. It was in Watson that medical humanity was to be celebrated. He was naturally a product of Edinburgh medical prototypes as well, the most obvious being a namesake, Bell's old friend and rival Patrick Heron Watson. Bell's cold-blooded readiness to mystify his patients with deductions never explained to them contrasted with Watson's constant solicitude for the feelings of sufferers under his care. It was said of him that nobody in Scotland was prepared to die until they had first seen Watson. In a medical story, "Behind the Times," the scientific young narrator-doctor turns in his own illness to the old-fashioned humanitarian rather than to his equally scientific contemporary:

> I felt that I should have medical advice without delay. It was of Patterson naturally that I thought, but somehow the idea of him had suddenly become repugnant to me. I thought of his cold, critical attitude, of his endless questions, of his tests and his tappings. I wanted something more soothing—something more genial.
>
> "Mrs Hudson," said I to my housekeeper, "would you kindly run along to old Dr Winter and tell him that I should be obliged to him if he would step round."
>
> She was back with an answer presently.
>
> "Dr Winter will come round in an hour or so, sir, but he has just been called in to attend Dr Patterson."

The name of Holmes's housekeeper, Mrs. Hudson, is suggestive here: the Holmes-

Watson distinction is also in Conan Doyle's mind. The detective stories were so successful partly because they were founded on the medical life he knew so well and because he had seen where the craft of the doctor and that of the detective were essentially the same. The medical "case study," as they learned to lay it out in Edinburgh Medical School, is behind the classic Holmes story, beginning with *A Study in Scarlet*. First the case is presented and then we receive erroneous theories, preliminary investigations are made along the right lines, the critical diagnosis is achieved, the treatment is commenced, and the case is rounded up with a final statement as to the operation of the cure and with the new information concerning the origin of the disease. The Holmes stories offered many modifications, but Conan Doyle's origins as a doctor writing up and occasionally even publishing medical case histories conditioned the making of the Great Detective stories. Christison, as editor of the *Edinburgh Medical and Surgical Journal,* had established the principle of clear enunciation of each case in absorbing and simple English.

Holmes and Watson quickly stood on their own, after initially depending on originals. Singularly enough, they seem to have begun in different stories. As far as we can now deduce, Conan Doyle was simultaneously working on a detective story and on a play, called "A Tangled Skein," and "Angels of Darkness," respectively. The story acquired a young man called Sherrinford Holmes with a medical friend called Ormond Sacker. ("Ormond" is Anglicized Gaelic for eastern Munster, whence came Conan Doyle's maternal ancestors, the Foleys, whose surname Anglicizes the Irish-Gaelic word for a devastator—a Foley was one who sacked Ormond; hence the name was a disguised matronymic.) The play related a girl's flight from Mormons who wished to add her to their harems, her rescue by a doomed hero named Jefferson Hope, and her consignment by the dying Hope to a devoted English doctor named Watson. The Watson of "Angels of Darkness" is not particularly like his namesake who took Ormond Sacker's place in "A Tangled Skein," renamed *A Study in Scarlet*. (In self-sacrifice he resembles the Watson of *The Sign of the Four* and later.) Sacker had been given the biography of Dr. Patrick Heron Watson: medical service in war, wounding on the battlefield, convalescence and subsequent fever, and dispatch home with health presumed irretrievably ruined. (Patrick Heron Watson's war had been the Crimean, but otherwise the particulars are the same.) Then Conan Doyle hit on the play's plot to supply the criminal's motivation in the detective story, and the name of Watson was transferred to the detective's somewhat critical companion, who already embodied the previous history of a genuine Watson. It also explains why the story is laid out as it is: the Mormon chapters have no clear narrator, and the Watson chapters read like reminiscences. The memoirs of Patrick Heron Watson would have been extensive beyond the days of his convalescence; of course, Dr. John H. Watson would never have a career to merit memoirs outside his friendship with Sherlock Holmes. But for the first novel, that was no certainty. *A Study in Scarlet* was obviously influenced in structure of its detective plot by the C. Auguste Dupin stories of Edgar Allan Poe, but the Mormon elements recall flashbacks in Gaboriau. In method Holmes virtually announces that it blends the intellect of Poe with the energy of Gaboriau—by dismissive comments contrasting with Watson's admiration.

Conan Doyle's practiced talents as a storyteller, in use since his schooldays, had hitherto produced three short stories of the first rank and a good portfolio of other work for such magazines as *Belgravia, Temple Bar, All the Year Round,* and *London Society.* In particular, he had experimented with a variety of narrators, female and male, child and adult, poltroon and philanthropist, snob and cabman, doctor and anchorite. But the birth of the narrator, and of the hero that narrator would bring within reach of his audience, was a singularly copper-bottomed performance with which to inaugurate the most famous detective duo in literature. Watson's adult life is described in terms close to that of Patrick Heron Watson. He meets a Stamford telling of a Christison-like Holmes with dashes of Murray; he meets a Holmes variously resembling Bell, Budd, and Waller; and then we move into the murder with a vision of the detective in action very close to Père Tabaret. No work from Conan Doyle up to then had grounded itself so firmly. Did he know instinctively the task he performed must have the stuff of endurance? The models were quickly discarded, and the music of the dialogue became that of Socrates' expositions to his young friends in Plato's works, with incursions from ruder acquaintances like Thrasymachos in *The Republic* or like Athelney Jones in *The Sign of the Four,* more roughly handled than the Glaucons or Watsons:

> "Ha! I have a theory. These flashes come upon me at times.—Just step outside sergeant, and you, Mr Sholto. Your friend can remain. What do you think of this, Holmes? Sholto was, on his own confession, with his brother last night. The brother died in a fit, on which Sholto walked off with the treasure! How's that?"
>
> "On which the dead man very considerately got up and locked the door on the inside."
>
> "Hum! There's a flaw there."

As that passage indicates, Conan Doyle intended to keep the humor as well as the pace moving. The Holmes-Watson duality is established in *A Study in Scarlet* on the convention that Watson is the most splendidly human narrator since Boswell. The neophyte reader is meant to accept Watson's first idea of Holmes as a mixture of the boastful and the fantastic to be quickly discredited. We expect Falstaff to be shown up; we expect Don Quixote to be proved wrong. The friction born of Conan Doyle's resentment over Bell's patronizing, Christison's elite status, Waller's egocentricity, and Budd's intrigues is the grit to make the pearl in the oyster. Similarly, in F. Scott Fitzgerald's *The Great Gatsby* (1925), Nick Carraway, like Watson, is the narrator chronicling his own mistakes. He, too, begins by expecting Gatsby to be exposed and is thunderstruck to discover how true his claims prove. And Carraway's last word to Gatsby—"You're worth the whole damn bunch put together"—echoes Watson's close to "The Final Problem" when he thinks Holmes dead—"the best and the wisest man whom I have ever known"—which is itself the last word of Plato's *Phaedo* on the death of Socrates. Watson's admiration for Holmes is built on the ruins of his initial skepticism. He still retains the Boswell enjoyment of his great man's little follies, such as his vanity or his taste for the theatrical, and he can still be irritated. Conan Doyle achieved a masterpiece of self-reference by having Holmes begin *The Sign of the Four* with a denunciation of *A Study in Scarlet:*

> He shook his head sadly.
>
> "I glanced over it," said he. "Honestly, I cannot congratulate you upon it. Detection is, or ought to be, an exact science, and should be treated in the same cold and unemotional manner. You have attempted to tinge it with romanticism, which produces much the same effect as if you worked a love-story or an elopement into the fifth proposition of Euclid."
>
> "But the romance was there," I remonstrated. "I could not tamper with the facts."
>
> "Some facts should be suppressed, or, at least, a just sense of proportion should be observed in treating them. The only point in the case which deserved mention was the curious analytical reasoning from effects to causes, by which I succeeded in unravelling it."
>
> I was annoyed at this criticism of a work which had been specially designed to please him. I confess, too, that I was irritated by the egotism which seemed to demand that every line of my pamphlet should be devoted to his own special doings.

There is a private joke here. Holmes insists the story should have remained "A Tangled Skein" and discusses it with that useful but humdrum metaphor in play; Watson has made it *A Study in Scarlet* with the artistry and aesthetics—and audience appeal—that his title implies. It is Plato's joke: demanding that imaginative literature be banned, in his *Republic,* which is one of the finest pieces of imaginative literature in political science. In *Through the Magic Door,* Conan Doyle remarked of Dr. Johnson: "If Boswell had not lived I wonder how much we should hear now of his huge friend? With Scotch persistence he has succeeded in inoculating the whole world with his hero worship" (pp. 48–49). This is a far truer verdict on Watson than Conan Doyle's own deprecating references to Watson as a humorless figure.

In *The Sign of the Four,* for instance, Watson, asked by Holmes what he thinks of inspector Athelney Jones's whirlwind investigation, answers, "I think that we have had a close shave ourselves of being arrested for the crime." Agatha Christie rightly makes her detective Hercule Poirot say in *The Clocks* (1963), "The pleasure of the language, the creation above all of that magnificent character, Dr Watson. Ah, that was indeed a triumph." Watson, as Ronald Knox noted, embodies much of the technique and the duties of the Greek chorus. He becomes an entity into which the reader may be self-realized, and as the stories continued and Watson married after *The Sign of the Four,* the identification is easier. What more universally recognizable person was there than the family doctor? And here is one of the most sympathetic—he will rescue a patient from an opium den, or cure a railway guard who then sends passengers in medical need to him, or stand in for a neighboring medico who will naturally reciprocate. "Folk who were in grief came to my wife like birds to a lighthouse." The doctor's only peculiarity is his friendship for a reclusive figure of singular attainments, and thus we gain access to Sherlock Holmes.

Conan Doyle's decision to combine his detective story and his Mormon story meant that Holmes's part even in the tale that introduces him is severely limited. He is not present in nine of the fourteen chapters, and while *The Sign of the Four* shows him in all, the love interest and the narratives of Mary Morstan, Thaddeus Sholto, and Jonathan Small silence or distance him for part of the story. As Conan Doyle began, so he went on. In the other two long Holmes stories, Holmes himself is offstage for almost all of six of the fifteen chapters of *The Hound of the Baskervilles* and for eight of the fifteen of *The Valley of Fear.* The structure, though not the proportions, of most of the short stories follows *A Study in Scarlet,* so that Holmes is almost silent for the client's enunciation, the criminal's confession, and so on. It greatly heightens his effect. In the interval, Holmes, for all of his cold-blooded manner, converses with a dry pungency after the manner of surgeons waiting for the chloroform to take effect before operation. The talk on the trail of Small in *The Sign of the Four* is an excellent example, with occasional practical intrusions much as Bell would no doubt check on his clerk Conan Doyle's having the equipment in hand.

The totality of the sixty Holmes stories looks in retrospect like a carefully orchestrated progression, for all of the trivial inconsistencies. Holmes and Watson meet in the first story, Watson marries in the second, Holmes remains severely impervious to female charm but acknowledges defeat by a woman in the third ("A Scandal in Bohemia"), Holmes first speaks of his college career in the nineteenth and twentieth, Watson first meets Holmes's brother in the twenty-fourth, Holmes apparently dies in the twenty-sixth but returns in the twenty-seventh causing Watson momentarily to lose consciousness, Watson has cured Holmes of drug addiction by the thirty-eighth, Watson saves his own and Holmes's sanity in the forty-third, Holmes weeps in fear of Watson's death in the fifty-third. It takes twenty years in time within the cycle, nearly forty over time of publication, for Holmes and Watson to realize how much they mean to each other:

> "You're not hurt, Watson? For God's sake, say that you are not hurt!"
>
> It was worth a wound—it was worth many wounds—to know the depth of loyalty and love which lay behind that cold mask. The

clear, hard eyes were dimmed for a moment, and the firm lips were shaking. For the one and only time I caught a glimpse of a great heart as well as of a great brain. All my years of humble but single-minded service culminated in that moment of revelation.

"It's nothing, Holmes. It's a mere scratch." ("The Adventure of the Three Garridebs," 1924)

The progression is one of growing mutual regard and ultimately love (as Conan Doyle was careful to call it), but it is also a progress in Holmes's humanization. It also reflects a deepening of his spirituality, which his creator, for all of his own beliefs, never made Spiritualism. Holmes's absolution is curt in the early stories; it becomes far more considered in the later. The penultimate case, "The Veiled Lodger," contains a beautiful instance of the hopes and limits of priestcraft as well as medicine when Holmes tries to prevent a lion-mangled murderer from committing suicide:

"Yes," said the woman, "the case is closed."

We had risen to go, but there was something in the woman's voice which arrested Holmes' attention. He turned swiftly upon her.

"Your life is not your own," he said. "Keep your hands off it."

"What use is it to anyone?"

"How can you tell? The example of patient suffering is in itself the most precious of all lessons to an impatient world."

The woman's answer was a terrible one. She raised her veil and stepped forward into the light.

"I wonder if you would bear it," she said.

It was horrible. No words can describe the framework of a face when the face itself is gone. Two living and beautiful brown eyes looking sadly out from the grisly ruin did but make the view more awful. Holmes held up his hand in a gesture of pity and protest, and together we left the room.

Two days later, when I called upon my friend, he pointed with some pride to a small blue bottle upon his mantelpiece. I picked it up. There was on it a red poison label. A pleasant almondy odour rose when I opened it.

"Prussic acid?" said I.

"Exactly. It came by post. 'I send you my temptation. I will follow your advice.' That was the message. I think, Watson, we can guess the name of the brave woman who sent it."

And yet Conan Doyle seriously contemplated ending the series at least ten times. The evidence cuts two ways: there were frequent impulses for termination, whose undertones suggest a shadowy strategy for survival. The first Holmes story was completed in 1886 and offered unsuccessfully to several publishers; it was on the recommendation of Jeanie Gwynne Bettany, to whom her husband, Ward Lock's science editor George T. Bettany, had shown it, that the publishers offered £25 for the complete copyright, that is to say, she recommended the acceptance, and the publishers demanded the rights. It eventually appeared in *Beeton's Christmas Annual* for 1887, where it was noticed and applauded principally by the Edinburgh *Scotsman* and the *Glasgow Herald,* possibly encouraged by friends of Charles Doyle, who was by then institutionalized. This ensured a book publication, for which drawings by the author's father were commissioned. An American magazine publisher, S. S. McClure, read it with interest but took no immediate action. The Philadelphia magazine *Lippincott's* sought an English edition; Ward Lock was approached, Bettany was signed up as editor, and Conan Doyle and Oscar Wilde were invited to a meal whose ultimate results were *The Sign of the Four* and *The Picture of Dorian Gray,* appearing in the magazine in February and July 1890, respectively.

Wilde had expressed admiration for Conan Doyle's work and may have known *A Study in Scarlet;* as editor of *Woman's World, Beeton's* would have crossed his desk, he knew Bettany's assistant Coulson Kernahan, and he shared Conan Doyle's admiration for Poe. Whether or not it was Wilde who suggested a sequel to *A Study in Scarlet,* he was an influence on Holmes's development. Holmes's aesthetics improved markedly between the two books while his drug addiction emerged; Wilde was no drug addict, but it accorded with Dorian Gray's experiments. Thaddeus Sholto in *The Sign of the Four* had touches of Wilde, and "A Case of Identity," the next story but one, opens with Holmes refuting what is in fact Wilde's "The Decay of Lying" on life as imitation of art, on the plea that in a legal case under discussion

> the husband was a teetotaller, there was no other woman, and the conduct complained of was that he had drifted into the habit of winding up every meal by taking out his false teeth and hurling them at his wife, which you will allow is not an action likely to occur to the imagination of the average story-teller.

Wilde would have been delighted by this Platonic method of refutation; "The Decay of Lying" is very much a neo-Platonic dialogue. But one of the charms of the Holmes stories for the next forty years would be hilarious throwaway lines. Even the deeply tragic "Veiled Lodger" commences with Watson's complaint about attempts to destroy his case notes:

> The source of these outrages is known, and if they are repeated I have Mr Holmes' authority for saying that the whole story concerning the politician, the lighthouse and the trained cormorant will be given to the public. There is at least one reader who will understand.

It was the *Strand* magazine that made Holmes a household word when H. Greenhough Smith, editor of George Newnes's recently founded monthly family publication, accepted "A Scandal in Bohemia." Conan Doyle, his wife, and their children had moved to London in 1891; his success as a Portsmouth general practitioner he sought to transfer to eye specialization, but he received no clients and began the Holmes short stories, which first appeared in the *Strand* in July 1891. Holmes made the *Strand,* and the *Strand* made Holmes. Six stories were quickly followed by six more. And the topics were immediate to their readers. In place of vengeance stalking the Mormon ravishers and the pursuit of Indian treasure, we are much more firmly in England: a potentate faces threats from a discarded mistress, a plumber's daughter is courted by her stepfather to freeze her fortune, a pawnbroker's premises are cleared to enable a bank to be robbed, a bushranger retired to an English estate murders his blackmailer, an English heir to an American fortune is killed by his benefactor uncle's former colleagues, a beggar maintains a fine villa in Kent. The antecedents may derive from overseas horrors, but the initial hold of the stories was the credibility of their characters in the *Strand*'s recruitment area. It was also their quiet force in social comment: late Victorian England was the seat of some very dubious fortunes and ugly petty extortions.

Conan Doyle's fears as to the fate of his sisters as governesses—three of them had gone to Portugal—or for the dangers of women marooned with drunken husbands or fathers had an immediacy when recast in fictional form to tell of Dr. Grimesby Roylott's serpentine murders of his stepdaughters ("The Adventure of the Speckled Band") or Jephro Rucastle's deployment of an innocent governess so as to keep hold of his daughter's fortune ("The Adventure of the Copper Beeches"). The stories were not escapist; Holmes might solve the mystery, but he could not wipe out the wrongs of Irene Adler ("A Scandal in Bohemia"), or expose James Windibank to the stepdaughter he had deluded with the connivance of her mother ("A Case of Identity"), or reverse the ill fortune of the redheaded pawnbroker ("The Red-Headed League"), or return the stolen money on which bushranger Turner grew rich ("The Boscombe Valley Mystery"), or even preserve the life of his client John Openshaw hunted down by the Ku Klux Klan ("The Five Orange Pips"). Holmes suggested order and professionalism and the means for making more sense of an increasingly bewildering city, but the very fact that so few of his cases involved formal crime, far from reassuring, warned of the gray area at the heart of Victorian moral complacency. The stories entertained, but they did not lie. The moral balance might shift more in the direction of the murderer Jefferson Hope than of his victims, and even of the more heinous homicide of Jonathan Small than of the gallant Major who swindled him and his Indian comrades.

The stories were rightly captioned "Adventures of Sherlock Holmes" by the *Strand*. They are mysteries, but they are not puzzles in the sense of inviting the reader to measure wits against the author. A close reading of *A Study in Scarlet* may turn suspicions against the cabman—indeed the much-underrated Watson asks what had become of him—but our place is to follow, not to anticipate. At times Conan Doyle firmly cautions against an excess of detection. When the much purer reasoner enters the series in the shape of Holmes's brother Mycroft, his passion for research and indifference to its dangers directly results in the death of Paul Kratides and—had it not been for his more humanitarian brother Sherlock—would have accounted for that of his client, Melas, as well ("The Greek Interpreter"). Conan Doyle seems to have been thinking here of eminent medical specialists famous for embodying the adage that the medical case was solved, though the patient died. Sherlock Holmes sins a little in similar fashion when his failure to give Openshaw a couch on a foul night results in the client's death. Similarly, in *The Hound of the Baskervilles,* his anxiety to trap Stapleton results in his client, Sir Henry Baskerville, almost losing his life or (as Mrs. Stapleton had forewarned the baronet) his reason.

If the stories involve social protest against ill-deserved wealth and poverty, or against police railroading of convenient suspects to jail, or against male exploitation of women under their guardianship, there is also a subtext of the humane against the scientific medical emphasis:

> "Our inquiries led to no result; and from that day to this no word has ever been heard of my unfortunate father. He came home with his heart full of hope, to find some peace, some comfort, and instead—"
>
> She put her hand to her throat, and a choking sob cut short the sentence.
>
> "The date?" asked Holmes, opening his note-book. (*The Sign of the Four*)

The success of the Holmes stories, with increased payments for the second six and still more for the second twelve, ensured that Conan Doyle would thenceforth be a professional writer rather than a literary medico, all the more when McClure syndicated his work in North America. But Conan Doyle realized that he was in danger of being trapped by a formula. Already one or two of the stories were open to the criticism that he might have made more of them without Holmes; he acknowledged a few errors on the supposedly infallible detective's part, again in an amusing use of Holmes for adverse commentary on his own literary success:

> I made a blunder, my dear Watson—which is, I am afraid, a more common occurrence than anyone would think who only knew me through your memoirs. ("Silver Blaze")
>
> That one word, my dear Watson, should have told me the whole story had I been the ideal reasoner which you are so fond of depicting. ("The Crooked Man")

This use of Holmes as the severest critic of his own saga is deliciously deconstructionist, but it testified to Conan Doyle's unease that in some cases a good story might require a less successful protagonist. This self-doubt is stronger in the second group of twelve short stories, published in book form as *The Memoirs of Sherlock Holmes* (1893, minus "The Cardboard Box," whose alcoholic wife murderer may have come too close to home for contemplation, especially when Charles Doyle died between magazine and book publication). "The Yellow Face" is frankly a failure for Holmes, though a wonderful defense of interracial marriage as a story and almost incredible as a product of the racialist 1890s. The deductions in "The Stockbroker's Clerk" are not only elementary but would have prevented a murder had they been made when the client first stated the case to Holmes: in other words, the story would make more sense had the investigators been ordinary mortals like you and me. On the other hand, Conan Doyle certainly was not rejecting Holmes. The Philistine (save for music) of *A Study in Scarlet* had fully given way to the aesthete.

The philosopher of the rose also inquires:

> What object is served by this circle of misery and violence and fear? It must tend to some end, or else our universe is ruled by chance, which is unthinkable. But what end? There is the great standing perennial problem to which human reason is as far from an answer as ever. ("The Cardboard Box")

The Holmes stories derived much of their strength because they came so naturally from Conan Doyle's mind, being written often as if he spoke through Holmes as well as through Watson. His decision to end Holmes was not taken out of any hatred of his creation, however irritated he might have become at the assumption that Holmes was all the literary work for which he was really fit, and by this point he had written *Micah Clarke* (1889), on the Monmouth Rebellion, and *The White Company* (1891), on fourteenth-century chivalric warfare. But he had to work harder with those books, taking time on historical research and hence valuing them more than the Holmes stories he threw off so easily. Eventually, he decided on Holmes's death while himself visiting Switzerland to help his tubercular wife, Louisa, to live.

"The Final Problem" (1893), supposedly concluding with Holmes and Moriarty plummeting to their deaths down the Reichenbach Falls, was not final: the postfinal—and insoluble—problem is whether Conan Doyle took out insurance in favor of a possible resurrection. The most suspicious circumstance is in a fragment of dialogue unexplained in its text:

> "Have you any objection to my closing your shutters?"
>
> The only light in the room came from the lamp upon the table at which I had been reading. Holmes edged his way round the wall, and flinging the shutters together, he bolted them securely.
>
> "You are afraid of something?" I asked.
>
> "Well, I am."
>
> "Of what?"
>
> "Of air-guns."
>
> "My dear Holmes, what do you mean?"

But while Holmes then enters upon a fascinating description of the career and attainments of Professor Moriarty, he never tells Watson what he means until his return three years later or, from the point of view of his contemporary readers, ten years later, *The Hound of the Baskervilles* coming out in 1901 as an untold pre-Reichenbach adventure, and "The Adventure of the Empty House" revealing his survival at Reichenbach. It is in the latter that the air gun is explained:

> You remember at that date, when I called upon you in your rooms, how I put up the shutters for fear of air-guns? No doubt you thought me fanciful. I knew exactly what I was doing, for I knew of the existence of this remarkable gun, and I knew also that one of the best shots in the world would be behind it.

Did Conan Doyle, like Sherlock Holmes, know exactly what he was doing when he had Holmes close Watson's shutters? On balance it would seem he had an alternative plan if his public and his aesthetic priorities dictated a return. "The Empty House," after all, turns entirely on the air gun both for the murder with which it commences and for the attempted murder of Sherlock Holmes with which it climaxes.

Historical Novels and Other Stories

It was for historical fiction that Holmes was silenced, and in his absence Conan Doyle produced an entrancing series of historical short stories, *The Exploits of Brigadier Gerard* (1896) and their successor *The Adventures of Gerard* (1903). The stories do contain mysteries, but in a characteristic Conan Doyle inversion of earlier methods, they are mysteries whose true solution is perfectly plain to the audience and obscure only to the protagonist. Napoléon in the very first adventure works out a scheme that entirely depends on the Brigadier detecting its imposture, as he wholeheartedly fails to do. But the strength of the series vindicates Conan Doyle: as good historical fiction should, these works touch the past in the places formal history cannot reach. He had been playing with other forms of mystery fiction, sometimes involving a supernatural plot. His "Lot No. 249" is an insidiously frightening mummy reanimation story. Two of his historical novels, *Rodney Stone* (1896) and *Uncle Bernac* (1897), turned on mysteries, but the necessary tension fails when real historical figures, such as Nelson and Napoleon, bring the plot to a standstill by giving individual performances. It does not prevent some splendid work when matters are going full tilt.

The real substitute for Holmes emerged in 1898 with a *Strand* series published in book form as *Round the Fire Stories* (1908), essentially mystery stories without detectives. Two of them involve parodies of Sherlock Holmes. "The Lost Special" includes a letter to the *Times* "over the signature of an amateur reasoner of some celebrity at that date" opening in fine Holmesian fashion: "It is one of the elementary principles of practical reasoning . . . that when the impossible has been eliminated the residuum, *however improbable,* must contain the truth."

But this proves to be a prooemium to a ludicrous notion that a vanished special train had been eliminated by a "secret society of colliers, an English *Camorra,* which is capable of destroying both train and passengers." Similarly, in "The Man with the Watches," a letter to the *Daily Gazette* "over the signature of a well-known criminal investigator" makes fine sub-Holmesian preliminary pomposities only to explain the disappearance of three railway passengers and the appearance of a fourth, ticketless and dead, by the assurance that the latter must have been in a slow train running parallel to the other:

> He opened the door of his carriage, stepped from the footboard of the local train to the footboard of the express, opened the other door, and made his way into the presence of these . . . people. . . . My theory stands or falls upon one point, and I call upon the railway company to make strict inquiry as to whether a ticket was found unclaimed in the local train through Harrow and King's Langley upon the 18th of March.

The refutation might be Holmes replying to a Scotland Yard bungler:

> To this elaborate and plausible hypothesis the answer of the police, and of the company was, first, that no such ticket was found; secondly, that the slow train would never run parallel to the express; and, thirdly, that the local train had been stationary in King's Langley Station when the express, going at fifty miles an hour, had flashed past it.

Conan Doyle was evidently enjoying himself by showing that the brilliant amateur might not always have the best of it. He had indeed satirized the Bell-Holmes method of deduction in one of his stories of medical life, "A False Start," as early as 1891 (and sent a skit on his Holmes stories, "The Field Bazaar," to the Edinburgh *Student* to help his old university raise money for a cricket pavilion in 1896).

Would Holmes have improved the *Round the Fire Stories*? Probably not: the "amateur reasoner" is essentially minor in those two stories, whose focus is elsewhere. The mystery element is much stronger without Holmes and Watson to keep our attention, and the psychology of its perpetrators is in deeper study. "The Man with the Watches" concludes with a crooked gambler accidentally killing a youth he has corrupted and then rescuing and being rescued by his victim's vengeful brother:

> "I guess I couldn't leave you," said he. "I didn't want the blood of two of you on my hands in one day. You loved your brother, I've no doubt; but you didn't love him a cent more than I loved him, though you'll say that I took a queer way to show it. Anyhow, it seems a mighty empty world now that he is gone, and I don't care a continental whether you give me over to the hangman or not."

This is Conan Doyle entering into the world of Dashiell Hammett's *The Glass Key* (1931), with its questions of love and honor among crooks. In *The Valley of Fear* he introduced the hard-boiled undercover detective Birdy Edwards of Pinkerton's: Hammett joined Pinkerton's in Baltimore, while *The Valley of Fear* was being serialized in the *Baltimore Sun* and, after leaving Pinkerton's, launched his first full-length Pinkerton-style novel, *Red Harvest* (1929), with significant debts to its predecessor. "The Lost Special" owes its character to the case of Alfred Dreyfus, an officer in the French artillery who was accused and wrongly convicted of betraying military secrets. The false evidence was beginning to break open as Conan Doyle was writing. In his story Conan Doyle assures an audience clearly alert to the contemporary symbolism that special interests will go to any lengths to suppress the truth and cover up for privilege. The solution is put into the mouth of an utterly unscrupulous agent blackmailing a French elite for whose protection he had destroyed the train and its dangerous inhabitants:

> You will remember that Gomez threw his bag of papers out of the window, and I need not say that I secured that bag and brought them to my employers. It may interest my employers now, however, to learn that out of that bag I took one or two little papers as a souvenir of the occasion. I have no wish to publish these papers; but, still, it is every man for himself in this world, and what else can I do if my friends will not come to my aid when I want them? Messieurs, you may believe that Herbert de Lernac is quite as formidable when he is against you as when he is with you, and that he is not a man to go to the guillotine until he has seen that every one of you is *en route* for New Caledonia. For your own sake, if not for mine, make haste, Monsieur de ——, and General ——, and Baron —— [you can fill up the blanks for yourselves as you read this]. I promise you that in the next edition there will be no blanks to fill.

The story is admirably told in de Lernac's cynical, clinical narrative of the means by which the train was destroyed with virtually no trace and the horror of the victims as they foresaw their fate, but the end is double-edged, cutting to the bone. Conan Doyle's magazine audience knew perfectly well why a landed gentleman, a general, and an aristocrat, however unidentified, are singled out by de Lernac (whose own name betokened a gentleman assassin in his own right). These are the classes from whom the anti-Dreyfus forces were made. De Lernac's earlier description of why they needed him to kill Caratal, the passenger in the special, suggests above all the caricaturist's grandson eyeing the French elite then visibly engaged in concealing the forgeries that had sent Dreyfus to Devil's Island:

> The honour and careers of many of the chief men in France were at stake. You have seen a group of ninepins standing, all so rigid, and prim, and unbending. Then there comes the ball from far away and pop, pop, pop—there are your ninepins on the floor. Well, imagine some of the greatest men in France as these ninepins and then this Monsieur Caratal was the ball which could be seen coming from far away. If he arrived, then it was pop, pop, pop for all of them. It was determined that he should not arrive.

Émile Zola's protest letter to President Faure, published as *J'accuse* (1898), and his consequent prosecution probably sparked the story off. Ironically, "The Lost Special" appeared at the beginning of August 1898, which ended with the arrest and suicide of one of the forgers, Colonel Henry.

Many of this collection's other stories require that investigation or discovery lie in the hands of an utter innocent, however reprehensible his own life. Denouement is out of control, where with Holmes some control is at least probable. It increases the fear and diminishes the security. One of Conan Doyle's finest efforts in this or any other collection, "B.24," is the declaration of a man obviously doomed to life imprisonment, unless the reader is prepared to be very optimistic indeed about what the inspector of prisons to whom it is addressed may do and discover. In fact, the force of the story is in part that we are a chorus to make up our own minds as to the outcome. We are intended to accept the story, but we are not encouraged to believe that officialdom will do so. It has rejected the prisoner's statement at every point, and there is no Holmes to go to.

The most interesting contrast of all between Holmes and non-Holmes stories can be found by comparing "The Brazilian Cat" with *The Hound of the Baskervilles,* which followed it three years later. Both appear in the *Strand* and turn on the same principle: a young heir to wealth and property is marked down for murder by a cousin, whose Latin American wife ineptly tries to warn the victim. The murder weapon is a wild animal all the more fearsome for *its* domestic cousins. A few obvious variations are made: the Brazilian cat is known to belong to its owner, the Baskerville hound is not; the cat-menaced heir is destitute and unaware of his imminent inheritance, the hound-threatened heir has come into his own; the cat murderer's wife tries to scare the victim away by rudeness, the hound murderer's by urgent, yet civil warning anonymous and otherwise. But above all, the cat, as W. W. Robson pointed out, is almost erotic in its hunting of a victim increasingly mesmerized by it; the hound acts out the role of an infernal emissary—punitive, remorseless, and deficient in all emotion except scent, pain, and (apparently) hunger. The killer with the cat makes affectionate parade with his pet, all the more terrifyingly; but who could imagine games with the hound?

Holmes and Watson are the keys to what makes theirs completely different stories: they ensure that *The Hound of the Baskervilles* is given its grandeur of space, of time, of distance. It is in fact critical to "The Brazilian Cat" that the victim is, as his murderer's wife tells him, a fool, empty of head, of pocket, and of heart; the reader is surely on the alert for foul play, at least once warning has been given. The murderer can succeed only by unveiling his hypocrisy and homicidal hostility to his victim. The *Hound* is unusual among Holmes stories in offering a wealth of suspects, among whom both Holmes and Watson make very intelligent progress. Sir Henry Baskerville may not be bright, but he has put himself in capable hands—Watson's, as it turns out, being safer than Holmes's. And his murderer cannot let the victim know what earthly agency has marked him down; his alibi is, in fact, Hell, whence the victims will assume the hound has come. (The story was published a few years after Francis Thompson's "Hound of Heaven.") The murderer himself is trapped by the evil to which he has surrendered himself—the family cruelty, rapacity, lechery, and autocracy; he wants to use his wife as bait to entrap his cousin, and yet he becomes convulsed with jealousy when he succeeds. It is sound psychology: the great political scandal of Conan Doyle's time, the Parnell divorce case, seems to have broken because Captain W. H. O'Shea was divided between using his wife to gain Parnell's patronage for him and resenting her success. And the longer range gives the *Hound* much greater strength, for all of the power and force of "The Brazilian Cat": the moor, the mist, the cries, the convict, even the unidentified figure of Holmes himself on the tor hold the reader in a symphony of ebbing and flowing fear. Apparently, Conan Doyle originally dreamed of a *Hound* without Holmes, but the animal evil required the scientific and emotive forces of good on a comparably heroic scale. Had Holmes entered the story of "The Brazilian Cat," there could have been no story; it all depends on the narrative of the hideous night as the cat's prey—lost to us if the victim dies, eliminating the need for Holmes if he lives.

The Return of Holmes

The *Hound* ensured the return of Sherlock Holmes. The public, enraged at Holmes's demise, had sought comfort in many imitations, including the converse principle when Conan Doyle's brother-in-law Ernest William Hornung created the amateur burglar Raffles and his former school fag (i.e., gofer), Bunny, dedicated "To ACD This Form of Flattery." Raffles, too, had supposedly perished, with even greater ambiguity about his chances of survival, and returned to life three years later, in 1900. Conan Doyle had his doubts about making a thief a hero, however sympathetic he had made some of his own murderers (most, up to the end of the *Return*). But he was prepared to imitate the imitation, particularly when the American *Collier's* offered $45,000 for a series of thirteen. It was appropriate; his former syndicator McClure was now heading the muckraking pack, as the investigative journalists of the time were called, and such figures as Lincoln Steffens, Ray Stannard Baker, and Ida M. Tarbel were already following Holmes's methods in the magazines that had printed him, as they exposed crooked politics, sharp industrial practices, labor racketeering, and racial discrimination. *Collier's* in a few years' time would print an investigation that ultimately split the Republican Party between William Howard Taft and Theodore Roosevelt, thus electing that detective-story enthusiast Woodrow Wilson to the White House in 1912. But Theodore Roosevelt had already been avid with enthusiasm to bring Conan Doyle to the White House in 1903, when a rumor circulated that *The Return of Sherlock Holmes* (1905) would require research in America. It was premature; Conan Doyle had made a very successful lecture tour in 1894 and only returned in 1914, with his second wife, Jean Leckie, whom he married in 1907, fourteen months after the death of his long-invalided Louisa. It was not until 1917 that "His Last Bow" offered the spectacle of an Americanized Holmes, even sporting what Dr. Watson termed "that horrible goatee," a beard "giving him a general resemblance to the caricatures of Uncle Sam" (another reminder of Conan Doyle's cartoonist grandfather). Holmes described it as "the sacrifices one makes for one's country." The Americanization was necessary to pass as an Irish-American terrorist ("He seems to have declared war on the King's English as well as on the English King.") so as to penetrate a German spy ring.

When Conan Doyle was convalescing in Cornwall in 1909, he found himself on board a local craft whose boatman told him Holmes might not have been killed when he fell down the waterfall (albeit "The Empty House" denied he had fallen down it), but he was never the same man afterward. Conan Doyle responded to this by writing "The Devil's Foot," a marrow-freezing study of Celtic sibling rivalry and vengeance. The description of the ordeal is heavy enough:

> I had hardly settled in my chair before I was conscious of a thick, musky odour, subtle and nauseous. At the very first whiff of it my brain and my imagination were beyond all control. A thick, black cloud swirled before my eyes, and my mind told me that in this cloud, unseen as yet, but about to spring out upon my appalled senses, lurked all that was vaguely horrible, all that was monstrous and inconceivably wicked in the universe. Vague shapes swirled and swam amid the dark cloud-bank, each a menace and a warning of something coming, the advent of some unspeakable dweller upon the threshold, whose very shadow would blast my soul. A freezing horror took possession of me. I felt that my hair was rising, that my eyes were protruding, that my mouth was opened, and my tongue like leather. The turmoil within my brain was such that something must surely snap. I tried to scream, and was vaguely aware of some hoarse croak which was my own voice, but distant and detached from myself.

Thus Conan Doyle replied to Cornwall with his individual Celtic twilight. The tale reflected, as he perpetually stressed, his obligations to Edgar Allan Poe, whose scientific basis to horror was serious while not professional; here Conan Doyle takes it a stage further, using the detective as patient and as investigator on the Edinburgh principle. It is Watson who detects in this passage, and we have moved into medical mystery. This violates our conventions, which may explain some of the dislike felt for the story by the great Holmes-lover T. S. Eliot, whose *Murder in the Cathedral* (1935) borrows from "The Musgrave Ritual" in the Second Tempter's questions derived from the catechism of the Ritual itself. But it betokens Conan Doyle's readiness to meet a new world in its more naturalistic terms and its demands for revolution. The *Return,* stories written in 1903–1904, reworked the old methods in a pattern of the widowed Watson back in Baker Street. The individual stories that followed, however, reflected a darkening prewar world where the case-study formula was frequently swept aside, and Conan Doyle's own preoccupations shadowed episodes where Holmes was often at fault. "The Adventure of the Wisteria Lodge" is partly metaphorical for the huge compensation granted King Leopold of the Belgians after the exposure of his slave empire in the Congo under his personal rule. The murderous ex-potentate in the story escapes partly because of Holmes's friendly rivalry with a clever local policeman. Submarine plans vital to the developing Anglo-German naval rivalry are reported stolen, and Mycroft Holmes promptly rules off-limits the higher civil servant in whose family the spy is ultimately found. The collection published as *His Last Bow* (1917) reveals a set of milestones to World War I.

Simultaneously, other mystery stories chartered the disintegration of the old world. "How It Happened" is a short piece born of Conan Doyle's growing Spiritualism, in which the reader suddenly discovers the narrator has been killed in the car accident he describes (founded on one in which the author was pinned underneath his own motorcar for several hours). "The Horror of the Heights" may be the first mystery story turning on death, mutilation, and disappearance in the air; it is explained by a recovered manuscript diary, remotely inspired by Poe's "Ms. Found in a Bottle" but with its own personal terror induced by the diarist's fatal decision to return to the perilous airspace where he had been attacked by monsters. The diarist, Joyce-Armstrong, is a hardheaded investigator winning our identification, where Poe's doomed writer is essentially a creature of Fate. And it is another sign of the real-life horror to come; the closing sentences are in fact prophetic of air combat in the ensuing war. The manuscript editor speaks after the close of the fragmented last diary pages:

> Such in its entirety is the Joyce-Armstrong Statement. Of the man nothing has been seen. Pieces of his shattered monoplane have been picked up in the preserves of Mr Budd-Lushington upon the borders of Kent and Sussex, within a few miles of the spot where the note-book was discovered. If the unfortunate aviator's theory is correct that this air-jungle, as he called it, existed only over the south-west of England, then it would seem that he had fled from it at the full speed of his monoplane, but had been overtaken and devoured by these horrible creatures at some point in the outer atmosphere above the place where the grim relics were found. The picture of that monoplane skimming down the sky, with the nameless terrors flying as swiftly beneath it and cutting it off always from the earth while they gradually closed in upon their victim, is one upon which a man who valued his sanity would prefer not to dwell. (*Complete Sherlock Holmes and Other Detective Stories,* p. 1172)

The aftermath of war brought the final Holmes stories, written in a harsher, bleaker world, retrospective of the decade 1896–1906 but exhibiting both the unrestrained frankness of the 1920s and its disillusionment. Criticism ready to regurgitate the commonplace and cliché has been dismissive of these stories, collected as *The Case-Book of Sherlock Holmes* (1927), as though the Cornish boatman had finally been vindicated. In fact, many of the finest qualities of the Holmes cycle are still visible, and almost half the group—"Thor Bridge," "The Adventure of the Sussex Vampire," "The Three Garridebs," "The Adventure of the Illustrious Client," and "The Veiled Lodger"—may be accorded vintage status. Conan Doyle was really experimenting with the stories. After he had received Ronald A. Knox's analysis of the cycle in 1912, Conan Doyle, appreciatively but self-critically, seems to have reworked the principle of their anatomy. The very next story, "The Adventure of the Dying Detective," broke most of the rules Knox had so ably classified as to the pattern of development; instead of being a case in which Holmes unmasks a deception, the deceiver is Holmes, and the supposed ally he makes Watson bring to him is a murderer whom he traps. This was followed by the last Holmes novel, *The Valley of Fear,* in which Conan Doyle originally thought of dropping Watson's narrative for a third-person voice and actually did so for all scenes save those in which Watson appears. The non-Holmes part of the story features an extremely ambiguous protagonist whose role as an accessory or agent provocateur to the crimes he ultimately exposes is never wholly resolved. Significantly, the crime Holmes investigates is concluded by this other detective's account of events, in which his profession of innocence seems less plausible than the likelihood that he maneuvered his old enemy into a murder trap (and Holmes pointedly does not express his acceptance of the story, his usual custom after hearing such statements). *The Valley of Fear* ends with a stark epilogue recording the ultimate fate of the dubious ex-detective Birdy Edwards: his pursuers finally kill him, an implication that society could not protect the man who broke its laws to end otherwise indestructable tyrannies. It also plays with the possibility of the fugitive Edwards' co-conspirators, his wife and his friend, being simultaneously in love with each other while wholeheartedly supportive of him. It makes suspicious figures of them in the early stages of the Holmesian investigation, but its unresolved status at the conclusion is realistic fiction if unusual mystery fare.

The wartime story "His Last Bow" is a third-person narrative, since to reveal its German spymaster in action Holmes and Watson must first be offstage. So, too, is the weak transposition from a play, "The Adventure of the Mazarin Stone," with which the stories were resumed. "The Adventure of the Blanched Soldier" and "The Adventure of the Lion's Mane" are both told by Holmes himself, the former rather weakly save for the narratives of the client and of his fugitive friends, which climax powerfully in a leper hospital in South Africa. "The Lion's Mane" originally had more rational use for a Holmes narrative, since canceled material in the manuscript indicates Conan Doyle's intention to have Holmes chronicle his own defeat. It is not clear what was the wrong solution for which he was to have opted, but the right one (that espoused by him in the final text) was originally ascribed to a naturalist excluded from the ultimate version. Conan Doyle had never intended to project Holmes as infallible—even in *A Study in Scarlet* he is brilliantly outwitted by a friend of the murderer, in the guise of an old lady, and he is close to defeat in a few. But this would have been the first case in which another investigator succeeds where he fails. It seems likely that Conan Doyle would have preferred to maintain the idea—there was something gallant in Holmes's acknowledging his better in at least one instance—but his wife, secretary, editor, or all three may have ensured a change of plan. The naturalist Dr. Mordhouse never reached print, but as the last line even in its present form indicates, he "very nearly avenged Scotland Yard." The group of six stories, of which these two Holmes-narrated episodes formed part, were the last to appear. Conan Doyle formally took leave of him in the preface to the *Case-Book,* and himself died of heart failure on 7 July 1930.

Conclusion

He died at home in Crowborough, Sussex, where he had lived since his second marriage and had seen his second family—Denis, Adrian, and Jean—grow up. Of his first family, his son Kingsley was killed in World War I, and his daughter Mary survived him. He had lived in Hindhead, Surrey, for the health of his first wife in her final years; for all of his Holmes stories being synonymous with late Victorian London in popular estimation, he lived there for only half a decade. Neighbors in Hindhead included George Bernard Shaw, who drew on Holmes, Watson, and the fearsome homicidal stepfather Dr. Grimesby Roylott of "The Speckled Band" to inspire Professor Henry Higgins, Colonel Pickering, and the philosophical dustman Alfred Doolittle in *Pygmalion* (1913), later the basis of the musical *My Fair Lady* (1956). The terrifying moment when, in the wake of Holmes's client Helen Stoner's intimations of mortal danger, the probable threat to her life makes his entrance (fortunately, after her departure) may be compared with Shaw's use of an equally, if contrastingly, dubious paternal figure.

> "Which of you is Holmes?" asked this apparition.
>
> "My name, sir, but you have the advantage of me," said my companion quietly.
>
> "I am Dr Grimesby Roylott, of Stoke Moran."
>
> "Indeed, Doctor," said Holmes blandly. "Pray take a seat."
>
> "I will do nothing of the kind. My stepdaughter has been here. I have traced her. What has she been saying to you?"
>
> "It is a little cold for the time of the year," said Holmes.
>
> "What has she been saying to you?" screamed the old man furiously.
>
> "But I have heard that the crocuses promise well," continued my companion imperturbably.

> DOOLITTLE (*at the door, uncertain which of the two gentlemen is his man*) Professor Higgins?
>
> HIGGINS. Here. Good Morning. Sit down.
>
> DOOLITTLE. Morning, Governor. (*He sits down magisterially*) I come about a very serious matter, Governor.
>
> HIGGINS (*to Pickering*) Brought up in Hounslow. Mother Welsh, I should think. (*Doolittle opens his mouth, amazed. Higgins continues*) What do you want, Doolittle?
>
> DOOLITTLE (*menacingly*) I want my daughter: thats what I want. See?
>
> HIGGINS. Of course you do. You're her father, arn't you? You don't suppose anyone else wants her, do you? I'm glad to see you have some spark of family feeling left. She's upstairs. Take her away at once.
>
> DOOLITTLE (*rising, fearfully taken aback*) What!
>
> HIGGINS. Take her away. Do you suppose I'm going to keep your daughter for you?

The interaction of literary economics is instructive. Conan Doyle wants Grimesby Roylott to be menacing, although tactically defeated in the encounter; hence Holmes leaves aside his usual overawing reassuring of clients and intruders and blocks Roylott by simple refusal to betray his daughter. Shaw wants the encounter to be funny, so Higgins uses a usual Holmes trick and then discomfits Doolittle by reversal of Holmes's method, threatening to produce the daughter. Holmes declines to accept Roylott as solicitous parent; Higgins insists on accepting Doolittle as such. This is but one case of the omnipresence of Holmes in subsequent English literature.

Another instance of Conan Doyle's effect is that on another Hindhead neighbor, Grant Allen (1848–1899). Allen produced some remarkable mystery stories, beginning with "The Great Ruby Robbery" in the *Strand* for September 1892, only thirteen months after the first Holmes story, but here the detective is unmasked as the criminal by a maidservant. In 1896 the *Strand* ran *An African Millionaire* (1897), Allen's series on the swindling of a crooked millionaire and his contemptible narrator—the man's secretary and brother-in-law—by a criminal master of disguise. The purpose is to question the law by which the lesser crook is ultimately sent to jail while his much more guilty victims go free. The social purpose of Allen's work may account for Conan Doyle's coolness to the Raffles created by his own brother-in-law a year or so later. Allen also created series of women detectives in such books as *Miss Cayley's Aventures* and *Hilda Wade* (1900), but he died while the last was running in the *Strand* with its final episodes unwritten. It was finished by Conan Doyle from Allen's deathbed instructions; the last installment (February 1900) was all too appropriately entitled "The Episode of the Dead Man Who Spoke."

Such cases of intertextuality remind us that Conan Doyle was a creative star in a galaxy, throwing out and receiving influences. If he is the father of the modern detective story in its series form, he indignantly denied any attempt to rob Edgar Allan Poe of his place as its grandfather. His own desire to win an audience for his other fiction prevented his taking Holmes beyond the sixty stories, and the figure was about right. The one Holmes story against which a convincing charge of dullness has been raised is the last, "The Adventure of Shoscombe Old Place." But our admiration for Holmes, and perhaps the still greater admiration due to Watson, too easily distracts attention from his non-Holmes mystery stories, particularly the *Round the Fire Stories*. He put the short story on a scientific basis no less than did his most famous character with his detection. He peopled his fiction with figures often worthy of a place beside the best of Sir Walter Scott's or Charles Dickens' favorites, not simply Holmes, but also Watson, Moriarty, Inspector Lestrade, and Holmes's female adversary Irene Adler ("A Scandal in Bohemia"), whose success partly lay in making both Holmes and Watson thoroughly ashamed of themselves. Detective stories cannot afford the luxury of multidimensional figures, since exploration of human minds undercuts the distribution of suspicion. But because Conan Doyle was much more concerned to make the people play their part in his drama than to divert the reader's doubts and questionings from the main quest in hand, he could enjoy himself with miniature portraits. Some of the sharpest of these are deflations of aristocracy or, in later stories, plutocracy. The English detective story of the early twentieth century made much of nostalgia or, to be rude, snobbery: the stately home or big house was much exalted, even if few mystery writers reached the level of Dorothy L. Sayers, whose detective is a duke's younger son with his pedigree announced at the start of later adventures, thus conveniently reminding readers of his and their place. By contrast, the Holmes stories agree with the works of Shaw and Grant Allen in being antiaristocratic, and are usually more hostile than Shaw's. Holmes's comments are quickly alive to the contemptible patronizing of aristocrats, for example, in "The Adventure of the Noble Bachelor": "It is dated from Grosvenor Mansions, written with a quill pen, and the noble lord has had the misfortune to get a smear of ink upon the outer side of his right little finger." And elsewhere in the same story:

> "I understand you have already managed several delicate cases of this sort, sir, though I presume that they were hardly from the same class of society."
> "No, I am descending."
> "I beg pardon?"
> "My last client of the sort was a king."
> "Oh, really! I had no idea. And which king?"
> "The King of Scandinavia."
> "What! Had he lost his wife?"
> "You can understand," said Holmes suavely, "that I extend to the affairs of my other clients the same secrecy which I promise to you in yours."

The delicacy but firmness of the portraits of the self-serving Lord Holdhurst in "The Naval Treaty," fast with patronage for his own family and faster to drop an embarrassing member of it; or of the Duke of Holdernesse in "The Adventure of the Priory School," ready to endanger an innocent legitimate son to protect a guilty bastard; or of Lord Mount-James in "The Adventure of the Missing Three-Quarter," screaming abuse at the thought of losing a fraction of his wealth, speak to the family skill in depiction very close to dissection.

Conan Doyle disclaimed originality and even portrayed himself in fiction as "a plodder" in "A False Start," where he satirizes Bell's method by showing it fail in apprentice hands. His genius lay in drawing together the methods, techniques, ideas, skills, economics, and such of great predecessors. Poe might be his great exemplar in detective fiction, with such additions as Gaboriau, Wilkie Collins, and Stevenson might supply. But the economics of the short story he learned from Christison as editor of the *Edinburgh Medical Journal* and from Guy de Maupassant as artist. Dialogue he worked out from Plato, Cervantes, Boswell, and Oscar Wilde. Style he drew from Thomas Macaulay, Sir Walter Scott, and a variety of classical sources, including the Bible (Catholic Douay as well as Authorized King James). His ability to transform an inspiration was endless. The plot of "The Noble Bachelor," when one thinks about it, is simply the song "Young Lochinvar" from Scott's *Marmion* (1808), and the fate of the butler in "The Musgrave Ritual" seems an inversion of that of Marmion's mistress, just as the motive of the odious Jonas Oldacre in "The Adventure of the Norwood Builder" inverts that of the Black Dwarf in Scott's eponymous novel. Conan Doyle could draw from very high sources.

Holmes becomes a Christlike sacrificial figure in "The Final Problem" when he accepts death to ensure that the personification of evil in Moriarty and his organization perish. He is the resurrected Christ in "The Empty House," especially in Mary Magdalene's taking Christ for a gardener (one of the books used by Holmes as camouflage in his bookseller disguise is *The Origin of Tree Worship,* which recalls both the gardener and the medieval use of "tree" as a synonym for Christ's cross). He is Christ fasting as preliminary to an encounter with the devil in "The Dying Detective" (Watson taking him off to eat at the conclusion thus becomes a ministering angel, as he frequently was). Too much is sometimes made of Conan Doyle's intellectual obligations; his generosity of heart led him to give excessive credit. Thus the journalist Fletcher Robinson interested him in stories of a ghostly hound on Dartmoor and even told Cambridge friends that he was helping Conan Doyle write the story. In fact, Conan Doyle seems to have paid him to encourage his own talents. Robinson went on to write detective stories, several of whose plots develop from the previously published *Return of Sherlock Holmes.* As for the *Hound,* we have already noted its affinities with "The Brazilian Cat," predating his acquaintance with Robinson. *Micah Clarke,* his first historical novel, features pursuit across the Salisbury plains by ghostly dogs. "The Copper Beeches" had already included a predatory family mastiff used to discourage threats to the villain's attempts to defraud his own daughter. Cramond in Conan Doyle's native Edinburgh was haunted by the howling of a hound originally belonging to a crusader. Even the topography of Dartmoor was evidently known to Conan Doyle from his days in Plymouth, as we may judge from the Holmes story "Silver Blaze." Probably Robinson did write some chapters of a hound story, which Conan Doyle rewarded and discarded. No line of *The Hound of the Baskervilles* could be the work of another hand, and why on earth should it be? The old proverb about there being no point in buying a dog and barking oneself may be happily reversed in this case.

We do have some cases of revisions of his stories by Conan Doyle in the process of composition. "The Norwood Builder" evidently was originally conceived with a larger role given to the housekeeper, whose sexual relations with Jonas Oldacre appear to have been much more explicit at that stage. "The Solitary Cyclist" required some reworking. Later on, "The Lion's Mane," as we have noted, discarded a character on whom its denouement originally turned. The third-person draft of *The Valley of Fear* survives. But there is, for the most part, amazingly little sign of reworking in any extant manuscript. Conan Doyle, significantly using language of his medical training, spoke of the conception and writing of the detective stories as "organic." His historical fiction, on the other hand, required continual research and checking on his part, though Napoleonic times and campaigns seem to have become instinctively familiar to him once he was well embarked on his Gerard series. But the Holmes stories above all streamed from his pen. It is probably not true that he undervalued them—although he did not agree with Sherlock Holmes in refusing to count modesty among the virtues—but he may have worried a little about excessive attention to them. He wrote them so rapidly that he put a great deal of himself and his family into them, and the withdrawal of "The Cardboard Box" from inclusion in the *Memoirs* and from general consumption for a quarter century illuminates one instance of an uneasiness aroused from time to time. He wrote to his mother in 1903 that to preserve his "ideal of art," he had suffered financial loss, including that from "my refusal to republish in a book the Round the Fire series of stories" (Green and Gibson, p. 152). When one considers the stories included certification of a lunatic (as he had had to ensure for his father) in "The Beetle Hunter"; discovery of an alcoholic in "The Japanned Box"; protection of a family member stealing official property in his possession in "The Jew's Breastplate"; opening of a long-locked room, which reveals the dead body of a vanished father in "The Sealed Room"; and paternal protection of a fugitive outlaw son in "The Story of the Latin Tutor," it is easy to discern his euphemism to his mother.

As a critic, Edmund Wilson has the admirable quality of constructive inspiration, whether he is right or wrong. His *Classics and Commercials: A Literary Chronicle of the Forties,* reprinting his famous denunciation of mystery stories, also included the *New Yorker* essay (17 February 1945) with which he followed his two diatribes:

> My contention is that Sherlock Holmes *is* literature on a humble but not ignoble level, whereas the mystery writers most in vogue now are not. The old stories are literature, not because of the conjuring tricks and the puzzles, not because of the lively melodrama, which they have in common with many other detective stories, but by virtue of imagination and style. They are fairy-tales, as Conan Doyle intimated in his preface to his last collection, and they are among the most amusing of fairy-tales and not among the least distinguished.
>
> The Sherlock Holmes stories, almost as much as the Alice books or as Edward Lear's nonsense, were the casual products of a life the main purpose of which was something else, but creations that in some sense got detached from their author and flew away and had a life of their own. . . .
>
> You see the force of his imagination exemplified in a curious way in some of those stories in which the dénouement is inadequate or disappointing. A young woman goes to work in a country house where she will be extravagantly overpaid if she will consent to have her hair cut short, to wear a dress of electric blue, to sit in certain places at certain times and to allow herself to be made to laugh uproariously at a succession of funny stories told by the master of the house; a professional interpreter of Greek finds himself suddenly shanghaied in a cab and taken to a stuffy London house with velvet furniture, a high white marble mantelpiece and a suit of Japanese armor, where a man who wears glasses and has a giggling laugh compels him to put questions in Greek to a pale and emaciated captive, whose face is all crisscrossed with sticking plaster. Neither of these stories—"The Copper Beeches" or "The Greek Interpreter"—quite lives up to its opening evocation. The way of accounting for the sticking plaster seems, indeed, entirely unsatisfactory, and since Watson tells us that this "singular case" is "still involved in some mystery," we are almost inclined to suspect that the affair concealed something else which the detective had failed to penetrate; but the images have exercised their power—a power that is partly due to their contrast with, their startling emergence from, the dull surface of Victorian London.

Here Doyle is exploiting a device quite remote from the suave story-spinning of Stevenson: he is working in the familiar tradition—in which the English art of fiction has excelled since the days of *Robinson Crusoe*—of the commonplace and commonsense narrative which arouses excitement and wonder. He can make us feel the presence of the "sinister"—to use one of his favorite words—even in a situation which does not include any fantastic ingredient. . . . (pp. 267, 269–270)

To turn a little of Wilson on himself, the wonder of this passage is not so much its perceptions as the atmosphere it exudes, in its way almost as miraculously tangible as Conan Doyle's atmosphere and both as potent and as apparently impenetrable as the cloud in the ordeal climaxing "The Devil's Foot." It is our induction into magic, the magic of Wilson's delight in reading Conan Doyle. It is as though Wilson, no less than Conan Doyle, is operating so close to the surface that he had no realization of doing something more remarkable than any of his other work. Wilson will perpetually yield results from depth analysis of his material, but here, for once, we are allowed to see him in the process of being enchanted, almost watching the flow of prose below his finger, before his eye, within his brain. This is important because it is ultimately beyond any analysis. It is to see ourselves among the audience of one of the greatest storytellers in the stream whose source goes far beyond the dawn of writing. Conan Doyle began as a storyteller in the oral tradition, entertaining his fellow schoolboys at Stonyhurst, and as such he was in the old Irish and Scottish mode still in use in the remoter Celtic firesides of his time, but long abandoned throughout the civilized world for all of its reading of Homer. Nor did Edmund Wilson's touch fail him in titling his piece. He caught the classic magic from a chapter-ending phrase: "Mr Holmes, They Were the Footprints of a Gigantic Hound!"

Selected Bibliography

WORKS OF ARTHUR CONAN DOYLE

The extraordinary success of the Sherlock Holmes stories began with their serialization in the *Strand* magazine of London from 1891 onward. For details of original publication in the *Strand* and other magazines, the reader is referred to Green and Gibson's bibliography. British publication alone has been noted for magazines or books; Green and Gibson supply details of contemporary serialization and publication in British, American, British colonial, and some European venues.

SHERLOCK HOLMES NOVELS

A Study in Scarlet. London: Ward, Lock, 1888.
The Sign of the Four. London: Spencer Blackett, 1890.
The Hound of the Baskervilles: Another Adventure of Sherlock Holmes. London: George Newnes, 1902; New York: McClure, 1902.
The Valley of Fear. London: Smith, Elder, 1915; New York: Doran, 1915.

SHERLOCK HOLMES STORIES

The Adventures of Sherlock Holmes. London: George Newnes, 1892; New York: Harper and Brothers, 1892.
The Memoirs of Sherlock Holmes. London: George Newnes, 1894.
The Return of Sherlock Holmes. London: George Newnes, 1905; New York: McClure, 1905.
His Last Bow: Some Reminiscences of Sherlock Holmes. London: John Murray, 1917; New York: Doran, 1917.
The Case-Book of Sherlock Holmes. London: John Murray, 1927; New York: Doran, 1927.

SHERLOCK HOLMES COLLECTIONS

Sherlock Holmes: His Adventures, Memoirs, Return, His Last Bow, and the Case-Book. The Complete Short Stories. London: John Murray, 1928.
Sherlock Holmes: A Study in Scarlet, The Sign of the Four, The Hound of the Baskervilles, The Valley of Fear. The Complete Long Stories. London: John Murray, 1929.
The Oxford Sherlock Holmes, 9 vols. Edited by Owen Dudley Edwards, with Richard Lancelyn Green, W. W. Robson, and Christopher Roden. Oxford: Oxford University Press, 1993. A revised version of this edition was issued in the World's Classics series, 1994.
The Complete Sherlock Holmes and Other Detective Stories. Introduced and selected by Owen Dudley Edwards. Glasgow: HarperCollins, 1994.

OTHER MYSTERY NOVELS

The Mystery of Cloomber. London: Ward & Downey, 1888.

The Firm of Girdlestone: A Romance of the Unromantic. London: Chatto & Windus, 1890; New York: Lovell, 1890.

The Doings of Raffles Haw. Cassel, 1892.

The Parasite. London: Constable, 1894.

Rodney Stone. London: Smith, Elder, 1896; New York: Appleton, 1896.

Uncle Bernac: A Memory of the Empire. London: Smith, Elder, 1897; New York: Appleton, 1897.

The Lost World, Being an Account of the Recent Amazing Adventures of Professor George E. Challenger, Lord John Roxton, Professor Summerlee, and Mr. E. D. Malone of the "Daily Gazette." London: Hodder and Stoughton, 1912; New York: Doran, 1912.

The Poison Belt, Being an Account of Another Adventure of Prof. George E. Challenger, Lord John Roxton, Prof. Summerlee, and Mr. E. D. Malone, the Discoverers of "The Lost World." London: Hodder and Stoughton, 1913; New York: Doran, 1913.

OTHER MYSTERY SHORT STORIES

Mysteries and Adventures. London: Walter Scott, 1889; Leipzig: Heinemann & Balestier, 1893. Also published as *The Gully of Bluemansdyke and Other Stories* (London: Walter Scott, 1892) and as *My Friend the Murderer and Other Mysteries and Adventures* (New York: Lovell, 1893). This collection was made against Conan Doyle's wishes by James Hogg, editor of *London Society*, the magazine of first publication. The New York and Leipzig editions add Conan Doyle's first published story "The Mystery of Sasassa Valley," which originally appeared in *Chambers's Edinburgh Journal* on 6 September 1879, and four others, bringing the original seven up to twelve.

The Captain of the "Polestar" and Other Tales. London: Longmans, Green, 1890.

Round the Red Lamp, Being the Facts and Fancies of Medical Life. London: Methuen, 1894; New York: Appleton, 1894.

The Exploits of Brigadier Gerard. London: George Newnes, 1896.

The Green Flag and Other Stories of War and Sport. London: Smith, Elder, 1900; New York: McClure, 1900.

The Adventures of Gerard. London: George Newnes, 1903; New York: McClure, 1903.

Round the Fire Stories. London: Smith, Elder, 1908; New York: McClure, 1908.

The Last Galley: Impressions and Tales. London: Smith, Elder, 1911; New York: Doubleday, Page & Co., 1911.

Danger! and Other Stories. London: John Murray, 1918.

The Land of Mist. London: Hutchinson, 1926; New York: Doran, 1926.

OTHER MYSTERY COLLECTIONS

The Ring and the Camp, Pirates and Blue Water, Terror and Mystery, Twilight and the Unseen Adventure, and Medical Life Tales of Long Ago. 6 vols. London: John Murray, 1922. The original six volumes are incorporated almost entirely in one volume, *The Conan Doyle Stories*. London: John Murray, 1929.

The Professor Challenger Stories: The Lost World, The Poison Belt, The Land of Mist. London: John Murray, 1952.

The Complete Brigadier Gerard: The Exploits of Brigadier Gerard, The Adventures of Gerard. Edited and introduced by Owen Dudley Edwards. Edinburgh: Canongate Classics, 1995.

The Unknown Conan Doyle: Uncollected Stories. Edited by John Michael Gibson and Richard Lancelyn Green. London: Secker & Warburg, 1982.

OTHER FICTION

Micah Clarke. London: Longmans, Green, & Co., 1889; New York: Harper and Brothers, 1889.

The White Company, 3 vols. London: Smith, Elder, 1891. Also published in one volume. New York: Lovell, 1891.

Jane Annie; or, The Good Conduct Prize (with J. M. Barrie). London: Chappell, 1893; New York: Novello Ewer, 1893.

NONFICTION

Through the Magic Door. London: Smith, Elder, 1907. A critical appreciation of major authors who influenced Conan Doyle's development as a mystery writer, including Sir Walter Scott, Thomas Babington Macaulay, James Boswell, Samuel Johnson, Edgar Allan Poe, Thomas Carlyle, and Herman Melville.

Memories and Adventures. London: Hodder and Stoughton, 1924; Boston: Little, Brown, 1924. Contains amusing if not always accurate information on the making of Sherlock Holmes.

The Uncollected Sherlock Holmes. Edited by Richard Lancelyn Green. Harmondsworth, Eng.: Penguin, 1983. Invaluable collection of Conan Doyle's major writings on Sherlock Holmes, with a superb introduction.

BIBLIOGRAPHIES

De Waal, Ronald Burt. *The World Bibliography of Sherlock Holmes and Doctor Watson*. New York: Bramhall House, 1974.

Green, Richard Lancelyn, and John Michael Gibson. *A Bibliography of A. Conan Doyle*. Oxford: Clarendon Press, 1983; New York: Oxford University Press, 1983. The Soho Bibliographies, vol. 23. The most valuable book on Conan Doyle, apart from his own.

ARCHIVES

"The Haunted Grange of Goresthorpe." Edinburgh: National Library of Scotland. MS 4791, written c. 1878.

"Angels of Darkness." Toronto, Ontario: Toronto Metropolitan Library. Written c. 1886. A play, probably an early draft of *A Study in Scarlet,* featuring Dr. Watson but not Sherlock Holmes.

BIOGRAPHICAL AND CRITICAL STUDIES

Carr, John Dickson. *The Life of Sir Arthur Conan Doyle*. London: John Murray, 1949. Reverential and conversationally fictional.

Edwards, Owen Dudley. *The Quest for Sherlock Holmes: A Biographical Study of Arthur Conan Doyle*. Edinburgh: Mainstream Publishing, 1982; Totowa, N.J.: Barnes and Noble, 1983. The biography ends in 1882. Establishes Conan Doyle's Edinburgh, Irish, and Catholic antecedents, to which it relates the corpus of his writing.

Higham, Charles. *The Adventures of Conan Doyle: The Life of the Creator of Sherlock Holmes*. London: Hamish Hamilton, 1976. The most widely ranging biography to date, but sensationalist and unreliable except when supported elsewhere.

Lellenberg, Jon L., ed. *The Quest for Sir Arthur Conan Doyle: Thirteen Biographers in Search of a Life*. With a foreword by Dame Jean Conan Doyle. Carbondale: Southern Illinois University Press, 1987. Studies by different analysts of the biographies of Sir Arthur Conan Doyle.

Liebow, Ely. *Dr Joe Bell Model for Sherlock Holmes.* Bowling Green, Ohio: Bowling Green University Popular Press, 1982.

Nordon, Pierre Weil. *Sir Arthur Conan Doyle: L'Homme et l'oeuvre*. Paris and Brussels: Didier, 1964. Translated by Frances Partridge as *Conan Doyle*. London: John Murray, 1966. Biographically thin, but contains useful critical insights using evidence from family manuscripts.

Pearson, Hesketh. *Conan Doyle: His Life and Art*. London: Methuen, 1943. Readable and sometimes shrewd, but inaccurate.

Roden, Alvin E., and Jack D. Key. *Medical Casebook of Doctor Arthur Conan Doyle: From Practitioner to Sherlock Holmes and Beyond*. Malabar, Fla.: Robert E. Krieger, 1984. An excellent grounding of Conan Doyle's work in his medical background, with minor inaccuracies.

Symons, Julian. *Portrait of an Artist—Conan Doyle*. London: Whizzard Press/Andre Deutsch, 1979. A brief work that confines Conan Doyle too closely to Holmes and Watson personalities.

Wilson, Edmund. *Classics and Commercials: A Literary Chronicle of the Forties*. New York: Farrar, Straus, 1950; London: W. H. Allen, 1951.

Wodehouse, P. G. *Performing Flea: A Self-Portrait in Letters*. London: Jenkins, 1953; New York: Simon & Schuster, 1962.

ACD: The Journal of the Arthur Conan Doyle Society, edited by Chrisopher and Barbara Roden, is published annually in Ashcroft, British Columbia. It reports on scholarly developments and publishes biographical and critical essays.

DAPHNE DU MAURIER
(1907–1989)

JUNE M. FRAZER

BEST KNOWN AS a writer of Gothic tales and historical romance, Daphne du Maurier was also the author of plays, scholarly biographies, essays, and a travel book. She was familiar to millions of readers through her highly popular fiction and to moviegoers through the many successful adaptations of her tales into film. Although critical success and academic attention always eluded her, she died in 1989 covered with honors: Fellow of the Royal Society of Literature; Dame Commander, Order of the British Empire; and 1977 winner of the Mystery Writers of America Grand Master Award.

Family Background and Life

Daphne du Maurier was born on 3 May 1907, in London, England, to Gerald and Muriel (Beaumont) du Maurier, an affluent, very cosmopolitan couple. Du Maurier wrote memoirs, biographies, and novels based on her family history and modeled characters in her fiction upon members of her family. An early important ancestor, and the titular character of her novel *Mary Anne* (1954), was her notorious great-great grandmother Mary Anne Clarke, the mistress of the duke of York, second son of King George III. Despite Clarke's scandalous reputation, du Maurier admired her cleverness and strength, which inspired many a daring female du Maurier character. Mary Anne Clarke's daughter, Ellen, in 1831 married Louis-Mathurin Busson du Maurier, whose father, a master glassblower, had emigrated from France to England in 1789 and invented a fictional aristocratic past for himself, adding "du Maurier" ("Maurier" was the name of his farm in France) to the family name of Busson. Du Maurier's *The Glass-Blowers* (1963) is a novel about the Busson family, though with fictional names. Ellen Clarke du Maurier's son, George du Maurier, was famous as the author of *Peter Ibbetson* (1891) and *Trilby* (1894). Daphne's family biography, *The du Mauriers* (1937), is primarily about George du Maurier, and in 1951 she published *The Young George du Maurier: A Selection of His Life and Letters, 1860–1867.* She greatly admired her grandfather and his fiction, employing some of his motifs, like time travel, in her own, and identifying with him as a writer loved by readers but scorned by critics. In "The Young George du Maurier" (published in *The Rebecca Notebook* in 1980), she comments that *Peter Ibbetson* and *Trilby*

> somehow found their way into the hearts of his contemporaries in a way few novels have done before or since. The word "hearts" is used intentionally, because the critical mind cannot admit that George du Maurier was a great novelist, in the sense of a Dickens or a Thackeray. . . . Yet these two stories sounded

> such an echo in the emotions of the men and women of his day . . . that they were read, and reread, and thumbed again, year after year, down to our own time; and not only read, but in some inexplicable fashion deeply loved. (1980 ed., p. 224)

The most important ancestor to her was George's son, her father Gerald du Maurier, a famous actor-manager. She wrote about him in a biography, *Gerald: A Portrait* (1934), and in a 1973 essay "The Matinee Idol," she wrote that "scarcely a day passes without some reminder [of Gerald], from the photographs and mementoes round the house down to his signet ring, which I wear upon my finger . . ." (*The Rebecca Notebook,* p. 245). His powerful personality can be seen in many of the male characters in her fiction, most notably Pappy, famous singer and patriarch of "the fabulous Delaneys," in *The Parasites* (1949). Du Maurier shows Gerald's charismatic impact on her as both beloved role model and dominating parent by splitting herself into two daughter-characters—Maria, rising actress who emulates his single-minded professionalism, and Celia, dependent homebody who sacrifices her own talent and independence to make a home for Pappy and bask in his charmed presence.

Du Maurier grew up in luxurious surroundings, equally at home in London, where she attended Miss Tullock's Day School, and in Paris, where she completed her education in 1926 at the Camposena School, a finishing school just outside Paris. An avid and eclectic reader, she lived from a young age in imaginary worlds, wishing that she could be a boy and even at age thirteen inventing a male alter ego for herself—Eric Avon, champion cricketer at Rugby School, who "just shone at everything" (*Myself When Young* [1977], p. 56). Reflecting later in life on her choice of a male rather than female alter ego, she noted that Eric Avon emerged again as the male narrator of five of her novels: *I'll Never Be Young Again* (1932), *My Cousin Rachel* (1951), *The Scapegoat* (1957), *The Flight of the Falcon* (1965), and *The House on the Strand* (1969), each of these (unlike Eric Avon) inadequate men who "depended, for reassurance, on a male friend older than himself," while her three female narrators—Honor Harris of *The King's General* (1946), Sophie Duval of *The Glass-Blowers,* and the narrator of *Rebecca*—were women who "depended upon no one but themselves" (*Myself When Young,* p. 58).

Although her female narrators were more like Eric Avon than her male narrators, du Maurier nevertheless observes that she identified with the inadequate male narrators. She does not attempt to reconcile this oddity—she simply dismisses it as role-playing like her father's acting—but it appears to reflect both her recognition of the limitations placed on women and her pride in those who, like Mary Anne Clarke, dared to achieve excitement and adventure within those limitations. In "This I Believe" she called "the greatest problem of our time" the question of how women were "to preserve, to maintain the family," their "first purpose in life," and still find scope for their own ambitions and desires (*The Rebecca Notebook,* p. 267). She does not resolve this problem either here or in her fiction, where she deals with it by such devices as allowing the heroine to have her romantic adventure outside marriage, then relinquish it for her family, as Dona St. Columb does in *Frenchman's Creek* (1941), or marry an adventurous male, as Mary Yellan does in *Jamaica Inn* (1936).

Du Maurier herself was happily married to Major Frederick Arthur Montague Browning for thirty-three years; they had three children, all named after characters from fiction: Tessa from Thomas Hardy's *Tess of the D'Urbervilles,* Flavia from Anthony Hope's *The Prisoner of Zenda,* and Christian from John Bunyan's *Pilgrim's Progress.* Du Maurier was able to preserve and maintain her family and still pursue a highly successful career because she did both in the same place—her beloved Menabilly, a beautiful Elizabethan house in Cornwall, England's westernmost county, on the southwest coast, where du Maurier lived most of her life and set much of her fiction. In *Vanishing Cornwall,* published in 1967 with photographs by her son, Christian, she described the moment at age nineteen when Cornwall claimed her: "There was a smell in the air of tar and rope and rusted chain, a smell of tidal water. Down harbour, around the point, was the open sea. Here was the freedom I desired, long sought-for, not yet known. Freedom to write, to walk, to wander, freedom to climb hills, to pull a boat, to be alone" (Doubleday ed., p. 14).

Not long after going to live in Cornwall she discovered Menabilly and experienced the same instant affinity she had felt for Cornwall itself. The house filled her with such awe, she writes in "The House of Secrets" (1945), that on her second visit, at sunrise, "Some instinct made me crouch upon my belly and crawl" toward it. (*The Rebecca Notebook,* p. 36). It made her feel a "trespasser in time," evoking images of "Doublet and hose. Boot and jerkin. Patch and powder. Stock and patent leather. Crinoline and bonnet" (p. 36). The empty house seemed to her "like the sleeping beauty of the fairy tale, until someone should come to wake her," willing to yield her secrets "to one who loved her well" (p. 37). Du Maurier explored Menabilly, researched its history, and finally moved herself and her family into it in 1943, there to remain for twenty-six years. She concludes "The House of Secrets," written two years after moving to Menabilly, with a reverie connecting the house to her fiction: "And at midnight, when the children sleep, and all is hushed and still, I sit down at the piano and look at the panelled walls, and slowly, softly, with no one there to see, the house whispers her secrets, and the secrets turn to stories, and in strange and eerie fashion we are one, the house and I" (p. 41).

Judith Cook writes in *Daphne* that in du Maurier's last years she was chronically depressed, often confused, and unable to write; of her actual death, she writes:

> On the morning of 19 April 1989, Esther Rowe [du Maurier's housekeeper/secretary for over thirty years] went in to wake Daphne as usual, to find she had died in her sleep. No-one who loved her or knew her as she used to be would have wished her to linger on; the last years must have proved extremely distressing, particularly for her family. (p. 300)

Gothic Fiction

It is not surprising, given this powerful affinity between du Maurier and this "house of secrets," that her best works were Gothic tales, for a Gothic tale is set in a house of secrets. Manderley, the setting for *Rebecca,* was modeled on Menabilly—"Menabilly . . . Menabilly . . . Manderley . . . 'On the road to Mandalay, / Where the flyin'-fishes play . . .' " (*Vanishing Cornwall,* Doubleday ed., p. 15)—whose scarlet rhododendrons lining the drive are the first ominous portent for the timid heroine as she approaches the beautiful house haunted by the guilty secrets of the beautiful, evil Rebecca. Typical of the Gothic heroine, the narrator of *Rebecca* is young, orphaned, and friendless when, visiting the Riviera as paid companion to the rich, vulgar American Mrs. Van Hopper, she meets Maxim de Winter, the typically Gothic older and more sophisticated man. She describes herself then as "hopeful and eager, handicapped by a desperate gaucherie and filled with an intense desire to please" (p. 18), while Maxim, in contrast, reminded her

> of a portrait seen in a gallery, I had forgotten where, of a certain Gentleman Unknown.[1] Could one but rob him of his English tweeds, and put him in black, with lace at his throat and wrists, he would stare down at us in our new world from a long distant past—a past where men walked cloaked at night, and stood in the shadow of old doorways, a past of narrow stairways and dim dungeons, a past of whispers in the dark, of shimmering rapier blades, of silent, exquisite courtesy. (p. 22)

Despite the hint of cloaks, shadows, dun-

1. All quotations from *Rebecca* and *My Cousin Rachel* are taken from the omnibus edition published by Heinemann (New York, 1980).

geons, and whispers of blades, the narrator marries this "Gentleman Unknown," as Gothic heroines do, on very short acquaintance and knowing little about him.

Asked why she never gave the young narrator a Christian name, du Maurier explained in *The Rebecca Notebook* that "I could not think of one, and it became a challenge in technique . . ." (p. 3). It also supports the plot, for the narrator is trying to gain a name, to displace Rebecca as Mrs. de Winter, a daunting task, since Rebecca was thought by all to have been greatly loved by Maxim, and to have been as efficient and exquisite a mistress of Manderley as she was beautiful in person and style. The heroine's task is made the harder by the devotion to Rebecca of Mrs. Danvers, the housekeeper, who has kept Rebecca's room as a shrine, all her beautiful clothes and possessions intact. The room, in fact, serves as a secret, "forbidden room," a requisite in Gothic fiction, though, ironically, Mrs. Danvers would like the heroine to go there, see Rebecca's beautiful room and possessions, recognize herself as an interloper, and leave; Mrs. Danvers almost mesmerizes the narrator into leaping to her death from the window of Rebecca's room. Doubling the forbidden room formula, the boathouse, Rebecca's hideaway, is also forbidden; the narrator goes there too, against Maxim's orders, searching for string as a makeshift leash for the dog Jasper.

The boathouse, as is characteristic of the Gothic forbidden room, holds the solution to the mystery: Rebecca did not drown as reported—Maxim killed her there, shot her through the heart when she taunted him with the announcement that she was bearing an illegitimate child who would be heir to Manderley. The narrator now learns that Rebecca used her role as the perfect mistress of Manderley as a cover for her own secret licentious life and that Maxim hated her for it. His remoteness from the narrator was not, as she had feared, because she could not measure up to Rebecca but because he felt she could not love a man so much older than she, that he had taken advantage of her youth and friendless situation. Du Maurier's handling of the Gothic hero's exoneration from complicity in the dark secrets of the house is ingenious: Rebecca was not pregnant but had instead been diagnosed with incurable cancer, information that leads the court to a verdict of suicide and Maxim and the reader to the conclusion that Rebecca had deliberately provoked Maxim to kill her. Manderley does not survive the yielding up of its secrets; Mrs. Danvers burns it to the ground. But the narrator now has an identity; the epilogue shows her with Maxim in middle age, living quietly in a modest hotel in the south of France, confident that she is now Mrs. de Winter.

In *Literary Women,* Ellen Moers observes that for Ann Radcliffe, the great founder of the Gothic novel by and for women, the Gothic novel allowed women to have excitement and adventure "without offending the proprieties. . . . indoors, inside Mrs. Radcliffe's castles, her heroines can scuttle miles along corridors, descend into dungeons, and explore secret chambers without a chaperone, because the Gothic castle, however much in ruins, is still an indoor and therefore freely female space" (p. 126). The Gothic formula allowed du Maurier to reconcile her understanding of the female yearning for an adventurous life with her belief that a woman's sphere is the home.

Yet another appeal of the Gothic tale for du Maurier was that it was the form for *Wuthering Heights.* Du Maurier identified closely with Emily Brontë, and believed that Emily and her novel were somehow shaped, like herself, by Cornwall; she observes in *Vanishing Cornwall* that both Emily's "mother and her aunt [Branwell] had on their own doorstep, through childhood and adolescence, the wild moorland scenery, the stories and the legends, of West Penwith," in Cornwall (Doubleday ed., p. 158). Du Maurier did extensive research on the Branwell-Brontë family, which culminated in 1960 with the publication of *The Infernal World of Branwell Brontë,* in which the relationship between Emily and her brother is closely studied. In her earliest writing, du Maurier had wanted to write like Katherine

Mansfield; as a child she had lived near Mansfield and her husband, John Middleton Murry, in Hampstead and as a very young woman had laid flowers on Mansfield's grave. Du Maurier's early short stories reflect this Mansfield influence, but in maturity she felt a greater kinship to Brontë, which she explains in "Death and Widowhood": "I am a writer too. Neither a poet nor a great romantic novelist like Emily Brontë, but a spinner of webs, a weaver of imaginary tales" (*The Rebecca Notebook,* p. 272).

Rebecca still stands as du Maurier's masterpiece, but she had served her apprenticeship in writing Gothic tales with *Jamaica Inn,* also inspired by an old structure in Cornwall. On a riding expedition to Bodmin Moor, du Maurier and Foy Quiller-Couch, daughter of Arthur Quiller-Couch (whose novel *Castle Dor* [1962] du Maurier completed after his death), stayed at a wayside inn, Jamaica Inn, which, she wrote, "would later grip my imagination almost as much as Menabilly." She gives its history: "A temperance house in 1930, it had been a coaching stop in old days, and I thought of the travellers in the past who must have sought shelter there on wild November nights, watched by the local moorland folk. No temperance house then, but a bar where the little parlour was, the drinking deep and long, fights breaking out, the sound of oaths, men falling" (*Myself When Young,* p. 185). Although the inn was peaceful enough when she visited it, du Maurier's imagination leaped to Jamaica Inn's violent nineteenth-century past, and to a young heroine—much like Mrs. Radcliffe's own Emily in *The Mysteries of Udolpho*—under the control of a dark and mysterious uncle.

Mary Yellan, another orphaned girl, at twenty-three leaves her native farm country at Helston to obey her dying mother's wish and join her Aunt Patience and her aunt's husband, Joss Merlyn, at Jamaica Inn. If *Rebecca* doubles the convention of the forbidden room, *Jamaica Inn* doubles the convention of the sinister male who holds power over the friendless girl, for Mary is first in the power of her brutish and violent uncle, who has turned the pretty and lighthearted aunt she remembered from childhood into a tremulous, bedraggled old woman, and then, in a mistaken bid for assistance and sanctuary, in the power of the strange albino, Francis Davey, the vicar of Altarnun, whose once sincere Christianity is now a cover for his fanatic worship of the ancient pagan gods of Cornwall, his gentle demeanor masking the soul of a rapacious wolf.

Both men's houses have guilty secrets. The forbidden room at Jamaica Inn is a way station for smuggled goods, the sinister men Mary sees entering and leaving it on her nightly vigils are not only smugglers but breakers who use false beacon lights to lure ships onto the rocks of the nearby coast and then beat to death all souls trying to escape the sinking ship. Forced to accompany her uncle on one such horrible expedition, Mary is attacked and almost raped by her uncle's closest associate, the loathsome Harry the Pedlar. When Mary's aunt and uncle are murdered and she goes to Davey for help, she finds that his house, too, hides a secret; in her room she finds a hidden drawing, executed by Davey himself, of his congregation with heads of sheep, himself, preaching to them, with the head of a wolf. Knowing that exposure is imminent, he tells Mary that he is the real head of the smuggling ring and the murderer of her aunt and uncle and forces Mary to accompany him in his attempted escape. Saved in turn from Davey by his suicide leap from the rocks when the pursuing Squire Bassat closes in, Mary decides to return to Helford and resume the quiet life of the farm country. But she is overtaken on the road by Jem Merlyn whom she had fallen in love with earlier; Jem is the younger brother of Joss and, though a horse thief, more respectable. She chooses wifehood and adventure at the same time by marrying a man with the "tainted Merlyn blood," and the novel closes as she sets off with Jem to the Midlands to begin a new life. Readers loved *Jamaica Inn,* and it became du Maurier's first popular success.

Du Maurier's third wildly popular Gothic tale, *My Cousin Rachel,* appeared in 1951. Du

Maurier did not cause quite as much furor as Agatha Christie caused with *The Murder of Roger Ackroyd* over the issue of fair play in having the narrator be the murderer, but she did cause a sensation by leaving it unclear whether Rachel was a murderer—whether, indeed, there even was a murder. Young Philip Ashley, the narrator, almost dies of a wasting illness with symptoms similar to those of his cousin Ambrose, his protector and father figure who had married the mysterious cousin Rachel in Italy, where he had gone for his health. Ambrose was said to have died of a brain tumor, as well he might, for his own father had died by that cause. He might, on the other hand, have been poisoned by Rachel, an expert in herbal medicine, which she applied to Ambrose, she tells Philip, when she tried to soothe him from the angry and paranoid fits brought on by his brain tumor. Similarly, the tea Rachel brews for Philip during the peaceful idyll between his suspicions of her could be poison as well—or it could be just what she says it is, a particularly delicious and innocent blend of tea.

There are many reasons to find Rachel suspicious. Ambrose's letters home after meeting her turn rapidly from joyful love to trepidation to anguish and fear, finally culminating in calling her "Rachel my torment" (p. 662) and begging Philip to come at once. When Philip arrives Ambrose is already dead and Rachel suspiciously away. Once in England and visiting Philip, Rachel is alternately loving and aloof, sensible and wildly extravagant. She has a suspicious Italian friend, confidant, and business adviser named Rainaldi, whose company she seems to prefer to Philip's. Furthermore, on the eve of his twenty-fifth birthday, when Philip gives her his inheritance and all the family jewels along with an offer of marriage, she accepts the money and the jewels and seemingly his proposal, then the next morning says that he misunderstood her about the marriage. However, she does return the jewels, and his offer of marriage was more implicit than explicit. Ambrose's suspicions and fears could have been paranoia, caused by a brain tumor and by his inability, as with Philip, to comprehend the ways of a sophisticated European woman.

Poisonous laburnum seeds found in a search of Rachel's room, however, so deepen Philip's suspicion that, on the Sunday when she is about to return to Italy, he lets her go to her death by failing to warn her that the bridge over the ravine in the new garden is unsafe. Thus, the identity of murderer and victim, normally quite clear in either of the mystery forms of detective and Gothic fiction, is left here so unclear as to allow for opposite readings: Rachel may be a murderess who deserves her death, or she may be the innocent victim of Ambrose's and Philip's paranoia, and Philip, the narrator-hero, may be the murderer. Du Maurier was equally unwilling outside the novel to resolve the readers' quandary: her friend and biographer, Judith Cook, relates that Daphne was always being asked, " 'Was she or wasn't she a poisoner?' and Daphne would always reply, 'Sometimes I think she did, sometimes I didn't—in the end I just couldn't make up my mind' " (p. 213). The novel subverts the Gothic mystery formula in other ways: the sophisticated, sinister older figure is a woman, the younger, naive figure a man. The suspicious, sinister figure's house, Rachel's villa in Italy, is not the setting for the novel; the house of Philip, the naive, innocent one, is. When Rachel comes to visit, her room becomes a suspicious place, a sort of forbidden room to Philip, but when he invades it to find its guilty secrets, the evidence is inconclusive. Du Maurier thus enjoyed tantalizing readers by playing with the conventions of the Gothic formula, but it was her best and most successful form, and on it her popularity and reputation chiefly rest.

Historical Romance and Family Saga

If Menabilly, the "house of secrets," led du Maurier to the Gothic tale, it also led her to the historical, costume romance, to "Boot and jerkin. Patch and powder." She followed the highly successful *Jamaica Inn* and *Rebecca,* both made into films in 1939–1940 by the rising director Alfred Hitchcock, with *Frenchman's Creek* in 1941 and *The King's General* in 1946, both costume romances. *Frenchman's Creek,* set in the eighteenth century, is the more light-hearted of the two, as Dona, Lady St. Columb, bored with her marriage and her frivolous London life, returns to Cornwall and, masquerading as a boy, engages in great feats of derring-do with a handsome and poetic French pirate of secret aristocratic birth who, Robin Hood fashion, robs the rich English landlords to assist the poor of the countryside. When Dona's husband and the other landlords have him almost in their grasp and, barely escaping hanging, he returns to France, Dona does not go with him, for despite their passionate love, they have long agreed that eventually Dona would accept the more important claims on her as wife and mother and remain with her family, cherishing her memories to cheer her in matronhood.

The King's General is both more historical and less an entertainment. Set during the parliamentary wars of the English seventeenth century, it is told by Honor Harris, one of the three female narrators du Maurier referred to as self-sufficient women. It is also part of the story of Menabilly, for Honor Harris lives there for much of the novel, du Maurier making the ravishment of Menabilly by the parliamentary forces stand as a microcosm of the destructiveness of the whole war. The King's General is Honor's lifelong lover, Richard Grenvile, like the French pirate Jean-Benoit Aubéry of *Frenchman's Creek* a handsome, swashbuckling hero of great daring. Honor retains the respect of family and friends despite her scandalous love with Richard because her strength and courage sustain the Rashleigh family (her sister Mary is married to John Rashleigh, ancestor of the Rashleigh from whom du Maurier rented Menabilly) throughout the long ordeal of the war.

The novel ends with the Restoration in sight, Richard—too outspoken for the king's political advisers—living in obscurity in France, Honor living quietly with her brother Robin, knowing she will not live to see the Restoration, writing her story for no one but herself. Although single and childless, Honor Harris fits the du Maurier pattern of women who find their adventure in the domestic sphere. She acts as surrogate mother to Richard's unloved son Dick, and she sustains the household at Menabilly, but she also performs great acts of courage, even though confined to a wheelchair, paralyzed from a riding accident on what would have been her wedding day. Chiefly a historical, costume romance, the novel also has its Gothic touch—a secret room. Researching Menabilly prior to leasing it, du Maurier came across a story of the discovery of a secret room with a skeleton dressed in the clothes of a cavalier and worked the skeleton into the story. Honor discovers a concealed room next to her own being used as a storage place for the king's supply of gold and then uses it herself as a hiding place for Richard and for Dick—who becomes the skeleton of the legend when he commits suicide alone in the secret room, expiating his shame for betraying his father.

In between the two historical romances du Maurier turned, in *Hungry Hill* (1943), to another form of historical novel, the family saga. Set in Ireland, across the water from Cornwall, *Hungry Hill* traces the Brodrick family through four generations, beginning with Copper John Brodrick starting the first copper mine on Hungry Hill in 1820 and ending in 1920 with the mines already closed and sold and John Henry Brodrick, the last descendant, salvaging all the remnants he can from the burnt remains of the family mansion, Clonmere. What seems to have chiefly interested du Maurier in writing their story was the way Copper John's modern goal of progress through entrepreneurship was undermined and finally defeated by the untameable land itself and by other, more ancient manifestations of the human spirit: the stubborn will of the Donovan tribe to reclaim the land they had anciently owned, and the different ideals of the dreamers who infiltrated the Brodrick family through marriage and bred heirs more interested in love and beauty than in the price of copper. *Hungry Hill* is not as good as du Maurier's first novel and family saga, *The Loving Spirit* (1931), perhaps because du Maurier did not have the feel for Ireland that she had for Cornwall, and perhaps because its themes did not interest her as much. *The Loving Spirit* takes its epigraph from Emily Brontë:

> Alas—the countless links are strong
> That bind us to our clay,
> The loving spirit lingers long,
> And would not pass away.

The novel was the first working out of a theme that was to become more and more insistent in du Maurier's fiction of the later 1950s and onward: the idea of the human spirit existing outside time, establishing links between people of similar aspirations in different time periods.

In *The Loving Spirit* du Maurier traces one hundred years and four generations of the shipbuilding Coombe family, based on the Slade family of Cornwall, who had fascinated du Maurier, much as Menabilly had, when she first moved to Cornwall. Her boat, the *Marie-Louise,* was made by a member of the Slade family, who gave du Maurier the figurehead of the *Jane Slade,* the family-built boat named for his grandmother. Du Maurier kept the figurehead at her house (then Ferryside), using it as a binding motif in the novel as the figurehead of Janet Coombe, the first of the many women in her novels who longed for adventure but accepted wife- and motherhood, sending her spirit through successive generations, "handing down this strain of restlessness and suffering, this intolerable longing for beauty and freedom . . . bound by countless links that none could break, uniting in one another the living presence of a wise and loving spirit" (1971 ed., p. 320).

It was in this period of historical romance and family saga novels that du Maurier revisited her own family history in *Mary Anne,* the fictionalized biography of her scandalous ancestress (referred to earlier), and in *The Parasites,* a novel based on her family (also discussed earlier). In the late fifties and sixties the idea of the human spirit transcending time, a theme found in her grandfather George du Maurier's fiction and which she explored in *The Loving Spirit,* became insistent in her thinking again. She had also explored the use of the alter ego, or double in her early work—first in the invention of her own teenage alter ego Eric Avon and later in *My Cousin Rachel,* as Philip Ashley reenacts Ambrose Ashley's experience with Rachel and comes to feel that he and Ambrose are one person, a notion reinforced when the dying Rachel calls him Ambrose. Both these motifs—of the human spirit transcending time and the alter ego, or double—inform three novels of the fifties and sixties: *The Scapegoat, The Flight of the Falcon,* and *The House on the Strand.*

Alternate Time Worlds, Alternate Selves

The Scapegoat (1957) combines the motif of the double, or doppelgänger, familiar to du Maurier and to readers from such works as Robert Louis Stevenson's *Dr. Jekyll and Mr. Hyde* and Joseph Conrad's *The Secret Sharer,* with the motif of the imposter, which may remind some mystery readers of Josephine Tey's *Brat Farrar.* Set in twentieth-century France, *The Scapegoat* tells the story of John, university lecturer in French history, bachelor with no intimate relations or friends, dissatisfied with the emptiness of his life, wishing, as he motors through the French countryside on his annual holiday tour, that he could connect with the French people whose history he knows so much about but whose lives are so remote from him. Stopping to eat, he meets his exact double, Jean, the impoverished Comte de Gué, head of a large and deeply troubled household. When Jean gets John drunk and changes identities with him while he is unconscious, John, with no connections to require his presence elsewhere, and no life of his own, goes to Jean's chateau and assumes his life and identity. No one at the chateau spots the imposture, and within a week John has connected with Jean's family and has many of their problems, caused by Jean's greed and neglect, on the path to a solution. But Jean's rich wife, Françoise, falls to her death from a window in the chateau and Jean returns to claim her fortune.

John is saved from killing Jean by the intervention of the local curate, but he cannot resume his old identity because Jean has obliterated it—resigned from the university, given up his apartment, and sold his car. Denied both the new identity and the old, John goes for comfort to Béla, Jean's mistress (and his during the imposture). She tells him that all may yet be well, that all he has brought to the family will survive, and John realizes that his newfound capacity for love will remain. As the novel ends he is driving toward the Abbaye de la Grande Trappe, perhaps to remain there. The improbability of the imposter plot is less troublesome than the ending, since nothing in the the novel supports Béla's confidence that Jean will reform and continue the process of healing John began. Du Maurier's point, however, is clear: through the shared identity both men gain—John learns to connect with other lives, Jean learns something of John's benevolence—and society (the household) benefits from both kinds of men. Jean's gregarious self-confidence creates a household that John, the fastidious loner, could not have created, but John's steadiness and benevolence is needed to correct the mistakes of the more charismatic double and to hold society on a steady course.

This theme is worked out more systematically in *The Flight of the Falcon,* du Maurier's most symbolic novel. Set in contemporary Italy about twenty years after World War II (about the same time *The Scapegoat* was set in France), the novel studies two brothers who need each other for completion, like Jean and John in that one is charismatic but potentially evil, the other self-effacing but benevolent. Doubling the double motif, Aldo and Armino are not only alter egos of each other but also modern avatars of fifteenth-century brothers: the evil Duke Claudio, the falcon of the novel's title, and his benevolent younger brother Carlo, duke after Claudio died in his attempted flight over the city of Ruffano, seat of the ducal palace. As a child Armino had worshiped the older Aldo, who, acting out his theory that Christ and the devil are the same, alternately (as Christ) overwhelmed Armino with love and (as devil) stabbed him with a kitchen fork. Armino had thought Aldo dead, a pilot shot down in World War II, but when Armino returns to Ruffano to pursue the mystery of an old servant's murder he finds Aldo astonishingly there, alive and the powerful head of the city Arts Council. Armino falls into the old disciple role again, though troubled by Aldo's insistence that the evil falcon was really a force for good (both Christ and devil) and by Aldo's apparent intention, in imitation of the falcon, to terrorize the city in order to purge it.

When Aldo replicates the falcon's flight over the city, the awesome flight is at first successful, but Aldo fails to pull the cord of his parachute, crashes into the hills, and dies. At the moment of success of his soaring flight, Armino concludes, Aldo felt like a god, and he comes to think of him as Icarus, who flew too close to the sun. After his death Armino and others learn that Aldo's good work with orphans and other less privileged students had been more extensive than anyone had imagined, and he has succeeded in bringing the Commerce and Economics students into acceptance in the community and stripping the conservative Arts and Education powers of their entrenched hold. In du Maurier's scheme Aldo is Duke Claudio, the falcon, with potential for both great good and great evil, Armino (who, in childhood, was nicknamed Beo, the blessed), is the beneficent younger brother, Duke Carlo; he continues Aldo's good work without Aldo's propensity for violence and disorder.

The use of the double motif in *The Scapegoat* to suggest that the timid force for good must embrace the more charismatic force for evil is thus worked out in *The Flight of the Falcon* with more complexity and with a richer texture of symbolism; it is perhaps du

Maurier's most ambitious work. Mystery subplots in both novels take second place; the mystery of the servant's murder in *The Flight of the Falcon,* for example, ends lamely when the man the police have been holding confesses to the murder. Du Maurier seems less interested in mystery now than in the thematic possibilities of characters in different times working out their destinies as alter egos, or doubles, of each other. Her third doppelgänger novel, *The House on the Strand,* continues to work out these themes, returning as well to the earlier idea that helped shape her Gothic fiction—that houses continue to hold the spirits of those who lived in them. The house in *The House on the Strand* is Kilmarth, the six-hundred-year-old house du Maurier moved into when she left Menabilly.

Dick Young, staying in the house on the Strand as the guest of his biophysicist friend Magnus Lane, actually travels back to the fourteenth century with the aid of potions supplied by Magnus, who has induced him to be his guinea pig in an experiment. Like John in *The Scapegoat,* Dick is a bookish sort of man, dissatisfied with the emptiness of his life, not really in love with his American wife, Vita, who is pressing him to take a job with her brother in New York. Arriving at the house a few days before Vita and his stepsons, he begins the experiment, swallowing some of the potion B that Magnus has left for him in the basement laboratory. This begins a series of trips back to the 1320s, Dick feeling more alive and vital in that time than in his own, ever more in love with the Lady Isolda and identified in sympathy with the brave men who love her, Otto Bodrugan and the steward Roger Kylmerth. Magnus comes for a visit but walks into the path of a train, himself on a journey to the 1320s when there was no train in that spot, and Dick's supply of potion B is cut off. He has enough for one more journey, which finds Isolda and Roger at Roger's house, where she has gone for protection from the evil Joanna, and Dick realizes that the house they are in is Kilmarth, the one he is staying in, Magnus' house. For the first time he enters the action of his alternate world, becoming so protective of Isolda and Roger and so enraged at Joanna that he lunges for her and strangles her, waking to realize that he is strangling a terrified Vita.

The doctor called in to tend both Vita and himself gives a good psychological explanation—Dick has created alter egos in Roger and Otto as a relief from stress—and recommends a holiday in Ireland. Dick eludes Vita and the boys at the airport and returns for one last journey, using some potion C that he had secreted in the head of a cane inherited from Magnus. He finds Isolda dead and Roger dying of the bubonic plague; he is saying the prayers for the dead for Roger to ease his dying when he returns to the twentieth century, is overcome with paralysis, and dies—but peacefully, because he has found love and connected with people in a way he never could in his life in the present. It is interesting that Dick, the novel, and apparently du Maurier herself reject the doctor's psychological explanation; instead, the novel suggests, Isolda, Roger, and the others are still existing somewhere in time, available to Dick through a commonality of temperament and desire, what du Maurier first called "the loving spirit."

The House on the Strand also reflects du Maurier's interest in a new phenomenon of the 1960s, the use of hallucinogenic drugs, which she saw as a possible entry to the sixth sense, an idea that had always intrigued her. In a way all du Maurier's fiction is linked by this idea, from her family saga novels; to the idea of Menabilly as a "house of secrets," which led her both to Gothic tales and to historical romance; to the motif of the alter ego or double; to the hope, in *The House on the Strand,* that hallucinogenic drugs could be a source of help, healing, and community as they allowed people entry to the collective unconscious. Greatly interested in the theories of the psychologist Carl Jung, she wrote in "This I Believe" that there "is a faculty amongst the myriad threads of our inheritance that, unlike the chemicals in our bodies and in our brains, has not as yet been pinpointed by science, or even fully explained. I like to call this faculty the sixth sense."

She describes it as "a sort of seeing, a sort of hearing, something between perception and intuition, an indefinable grasp of things unknown," acknowledged by psychologists as "Unconscious Mind, the Superego, the Psyche, the Self" but not yet acknowledged by science except as some sort of "memory storehouse, connected to the brain." Whatever it be, she argues, "it is also a storehouse of potential power . . . [which] can act as guide, as mentor, warning us of danger, signalling caution, yet also urging us to new discoveries. This untapped source of power, this strange and sometimes mystical intuitive sense, may come to be, generations hence, mankind's salvation" (*The Rebecca Notebook,* p. 268).

Short Fiction: the Macabre

This sense of the permeability of the boundary between the conscious and the unconscious, the normal and the paranormal, informed much of du Maurier's short fiction, the form her writing mostly took in the last phase of her life. Although she saw in access to the paranormal the potential for many improvements for the future of the race, she recognized the terror for human beings at those moments when normal reality is broken through by the unknown and unexpected. Most of her late short stories portray these sinister moments in what she called "the macabre." The emergence of this new quality in her writing was first strongly evident in the collection of stories called *The Apple Tree,* published in 1952. Readers are familiar with the most famous of the stories from that volume, "The Birds," through the film made by Alfred Hitchcock in 1963. Du Maurier did not like this film, partly because it shifted the locale from Cornwall to America and introduced a love interest, but it captured well the terror in du Maurier's story, the breakthrough into the unknown, when the birds, usually under the control of humans, become their relentless attackers.

Du Maurier wrote so much short fiction that discussing it all would take a volume in itself. Its flavor, what she meant by "the macabre," can perhaps be conveyed by looking at one of the late stories, which may be her best, "Don't Look Now," from the collection *Not After Midnight* (1971; published in the United States as *Don't Look Now*). The story returns to the time-displacement technique of *The House on the Strand,* though in this story John, the character with the sixth sense, has a natural gift for the paranormal without the aid of drugs. On a holiday in Venice he and his wife, Laura, encounter two elderly ladies, one of whom is blind and psychic and tells them that she can see their recently dead little daughter sitting beside them and warns them to leave Venice immediately because there is danger. John does not believe in psychic phenomena and thinks her a fraud, but her prophecy comes true when they return to the hotel to find a telegram from their son Johnnie's school saying that he requires an emergency appendectomy. Laura starts back immediately by air, John plans to follow the next day; but as John is leaving Venice he sees Laura in her unmistakable red coat and accompanied by the two ladies passing him in the other direction on the canal. After a frantic and fruitless search for Laura he finds that she had arrived in England before he saw her on the canal, and he goes to the police to call off the search he has instituted for her. On the way back to the hotel, in an unfamiliar part of the city, he sees a small child in a coat with a pixie hat running in terror for her life, and he follows her to save her, into a house, up the stairway, into a room where she bolts the door and takes off her coat—to reveal that she is not a little girl but an insane dwarf. He realizes in the moment before her knife pierces his throat that he had seen Laura in the boat on the canal, returning, the day after tomorrow, as a result of his death. A 1973 film made from "Don't Look Now" by the director Nicholas Roeg added to the long string of successful adaptations of du Maurier's fiction into film, the medium through which many admirers worldwide know and enjoy her work.

"In my end is my beginning," du Maurier wrote in "This I Believe" (*The Rebecca Notebook*, p. 262). Despite the great magnitude and variety of her work, there is a remarkable continuity to it, the sense of the macabre in the final period of short fiction being but a variation on the early idea of the human spirit's capacity to break through its temporal limitations—the theme of the first novel, *The Loving Spirit.*

Selected Bibliography

WORKS OF DAPHNE DU MAURIER

NOVELS

The Loving Spirit. London: Heinemann, 1931; Garden City, N.Y.: Doubleday, 1931; Cambridge, Mass.: Bentley, 1971.

I'll Never Be Young Again. London: Heinemann, 1932; Garden City, N.Y.: Doubleday, 1932.

The Progress of Julius. London: Heinemann, 1933; Garden City, N.Y.: Doubleday, 1933.

Jamaica Inn. London: Gollancz, 1936; Garden City, N.Y.: Doubleday, 1936.

Rebecca. London: Gollancz, 1938; Garden City, N.Y.: Doubleday, 1938.

Frenchman's Creek. London: Gollancz, 1941.

Hungry Hill. London: Gollancz, 1943; Garden City, N.Y.: Doubleday, 1943.

The King's General. London: Gollancz, 1946; Garden City, N.Y.: Doubleday, 1946.

The Parasites. London: Gollancz, 1949.

My Cousin Rachel. London: Gollancz, 1951.

Mary Anne. London: Gollancz, 1954; Garden City, N.Y.: Doubleday, 1954.

The Scapegoat. London: Gollancz, 1957; Garden City, N.Y.: Doubleday, 1957.

Castle Dor (by Arthur Quiller-Couch, completed by du Maurier). London: Dent, 1962; Garden City, N.Y.: Doubleday, 1962.

The Glass-Blowers. London: Gollancz, 1963; Garden City, N.Y.: Doubleday, 1963.

The Flight of the Falcon. London: Gollancz, 1965; Garden City, N.Y.: Doubleday, 1965.

The House on the Strand. London: Gollancz, 1969; Garden City, N.Y.: Doubleday, 1969.

Rule Britannia. London: Gollancz, 1972.

Rebecca. Jamaica Inn. Frenchman's Creek. My Cousin Rachel. New York: Heinemann, 1980.

SHORT FICTION

The Apple Tree. London: Gollancz, 1952. Published in the United States as *Kiss Me Again, Stranger.* Garden City, N.Y.: Doubleday, 1953.

The Breaking Point. London: Gollancz, 1959; Garden City, N.Y.: Doubleday, 1959.

Not After Midnight. London: Gollancz, 1971. Published in the United States as *Don't Look Now.* Garden City, N.Y.: Doubleday, 1971.

Echoes from the Macabre. London: Gollancz, 1976.

The Rendezvous and Other Stories. London: Gollancz, 1980.

PLAYS

The Years Between. London: Gollancz, 1945.

September Tide. London: Gollancz, 1949.

BIOGRAPHY AND AUTOBIOGRAPHY

Gerald: A Portrait. London: Gollancz, 1934.

The du Mauriers. London: Gollancz, 1937; Garden City, N.Y.: Doubleday, 1937.

The Infernal World of Branwell Brontë. London: Gollancz, 1960.

Growing Pains: The Shaping of a Writer. London: Gollancz, 1977. Published in the United States as *Myself When Young.* Garden City, N.Y.: Doubleday, 1977.

ESSAYS

"Faces to the Sun." *Good Housekeeping* 112: 19 (April 1941).

"Menabilly: The Most Beautiful House I Have Ever Seen." *House and Garden* 92: 92–97, 113, 114, 118 (August 1947).

"The Place Has Taken Hold of Me." *Saturday Evening Post* 249: 48–50 (December 1977).

OTHER NONFICTION

The Young George du Maurier: A Selection of His Life and Letters, 1860–1867. London: Peter Davies, 1951.

Vanishing Cornwall. London: Gollancz, 1967.

The Winding Stair: Francis Bacon, His Rise and Fall. London: Gollancz, 1976; Garden City, N.Y.: Doubleday, 1967.

The Rebecca Notebook and Other Memories. Garden City, N.Y.: Doubleday, 1980. Includes "Death and Widowhood," "The House of Secrets," "This I Believe," "The Matinee Idol," and "The Young George du Maurier." Also contains some reprinted short stories.

Enchanted Cornwall: Her Pictorial Memoir. Edited by Piers Dudgeon. Photographs by Nick Wright. London: Joseph, 1989; New York: Viking Penguin, 1989.

BIOGRAPHICAL AND CRITICAL STUDIES

Auerbach, Nina. "Daphne Du Maurier." In *British Writers, Supplement III.* New York: Scribner, 1996.

DAPHNE DU MAURIER

Cook, Judith. *Daphne: A Portrait of Daphne du Maurier.* London: Bantam, 1991.

Forster, Margaret. *Daphne du Maurier.* London: Chatto & Windus, 1993.

Kelly, Richard. *Daphne du Maurier.* Boston: Twayne, 1987.

Leng, Flavia. *Daphne du Maurier: A Daughter's Memoir.* Edinburgh: Mainstream Publishing, 1994.

Moers, Ellen. *Literary Women.* Garden City, N.Y.: Doubleday, 1976.

Shallcross, Martyn. *The Private World of Daphne Du Maurier.* London: Robson Books, 1991.

Stockwell, LaTourette. "Best Sellers and the Critics: A Case History." *College English* 16: 214–221 (January 1955).

Mignon Good Eberhart
(1899–1996)

LEROY LAD PANEK

Mignon good eberhart was born on 6 July 1899 in University Place, Nebraska, the daughter of William Thomas Good and Margaret Hill Bruffey Good. From 1917 to 1920 she attended Nebraska Wesleyan University, a Methodist institution barely thirty years old when she enrolled. While she left without a degree, after she later achieved considerable popularity her college in 1935 awarded her an honorary doctorate. Three years after leaving college, she married Alanson C. Eberhart, a civil engineer. It is probably not coincidence, then, that a number of romantic male leads in her books are civil engineers, including the mysterious and impulsive Jim Gainsay in Eberhart's first novel. There is some confusion about when Eberhart began to write. The jacket on the Crime Club edition of *The White Cockatoo* (1933) states that "she began writing murder stories three days after she was married." In Eberhart's entry in Howard Haycraft's *Twentieth Century Authors* (1945), she says "I began to write in 1930," a patently inaccurate statement given that her first novel was published in 1929. There is some agreement, however, that Eberhart began to write to occupy herself when she accompanied her husband on his frequent business trips.

After the publication of her first novel, *The Patient in Room 18* (1929), Eberhart entered her second book, *While the Patient Slept* (1930), in one of the many detective story writing contests of the late 1920s and early 1930s, and it received the $5,000 Scotland Yard Prize. Indeed, Eberhart became something of a celebrity almost overnight. Until *Speak No Evil* in 1941, when Eberhart moved to Random House, all of her novels were Doubleday Crime Club selections and were published simultaneously by Lane, Collins, or Heineman in Britain. In addition to first publication by top-flight houses, beginning in 1935 Eberhart's novels regularly appeared as serials in *Ladies' Home Journal, The Saturday Evening Post,* and *Collier's.* Also in the mid 1930s, Eberhart's short stories were published in *The Delineator* and *The American Magazine* (including one, "Murder in the Garden," written with Grantland Rice), two other very popular periodicals. In 1946 Eberhart divorced her husband and was married briefly to John Hazen Perry. She divorced Perry and remarried Alanson Eberhart in 1948.

Longevity and, one assumes, industrious habits made Eberhart an extremely productive writer. While book and magazine publishers took to her almost immediately, Eberhart has received little notice from critics or genre historians. Most histories and handbooks ignore everything she wrote except her Nurse Keate books, and many accounts of her work contain factual errors. The reason for this is clear: in the early 1930s Eberhart chose to straddle genre fences, to write both mystery stories and love stories. So sometimes the covers of her books proclaim her as "the American Agatha Christie" and sometimes they picture storm-tossed and terrified young women in the arms of ruggedly handsome men. This dichotomy put Eberhart beyond the pale for most students of mystery and detection. Judging from her output, from the frequent reprints, and from the number of her books still in print, this had the opposite effect on her readers.

Early Works

Eberhart's first detective, Lance O'Leary, appears in four novels: *The Patient in Room 18, While the Patient Slept* (1930), *The Mystery of Hunting's End,* and *From This Dark Stairway* (1931). In all four he joins Eberhart's best-known character, Nurse Sarah Keate. As he develops, O'Leary appears to grow partly in opposition to the character of the flamboyant detective genius associated with Arthur Conan Doyle's Sherlock Holmes. O'Leary is young, dapper, and understated: as described in *While the Patient Slept,* "He was no magician; he did not turn rabbits out of his pockets as a conjurer does. . . . Neither did he possess that quite marvelous faculty of distinguishing at a glance between things that were clues and things that were not, as do certain fictional detectives" (p. 60). O'Leary's idiosyncrasies are small—he fidgets, for instance, with the stub of a pencil. And he approaches solving crimes in an analytical manner: in the first novel he says, "It is just logic, reason, the physical, material quality of cause and effect. There isn't anything mysterious about it. It is just the—the arithmetic of analysis" (p. 220). If this sounds like Edgar Allan Poe's "calculus of probability," it is. O'Leary fits conventions old and new.

In his immaculate dress, and possessing "a manservant with the most discreet and secretive voice I ever heard" (*While the Patient Slept,* p. 61), O'Leary is cast in the same mold as Peter Wimsey, Philo Vance, and many of the other male detectives of the 1920s. His relationship with Nurse Keate—deferential, modest, and collegial—might have made him memorable had Eberhart chosen to develop this aspect of his character. But as she had formulated him, O'Leary could not serve the increasing emotional elements in Eberhart's novels. So while Nurse Keate continues, O'Leary is replaced by another detective, Jacob Wait, who briefly serves those elements more effectively.

Eberhart began writing during the heyday of the "fair play" detective story. By 1928 E. C. Bentley's *Trent's Last Case* (1912) had become something of a classic, Christie had published *The Murder of Roger Ackroyd* (1926), and S. S. Van Dine's *The Greene Murder Case* (1928) reached fourth place on the U.S. best-seller list. That same year Van Dine codified the rules of the detective-story game in a list of twenty "do's and don't's" published in *The American Magazine,* one of Eberhart's short-story outlets. According to these rules, the most prominent (although perhaps not the most important) feature of the detective story of this period was the creation of a number of conventions that purported to "play fair" with readers, giving them the opportunity to solve the crime along with the characters in the story. So novels and short stories inserted maps, architectural drawings, timetables, lists, and documents to permit readers to "play along."

Eberhart used many of these conventions in the O'Leary books. She includes, for instance, a schematic drawing of the lodge at Hunting's End, and there are lists of facts and persons galore (including the characteristic dramatis personae). O'Leary routinely compares solving a crime to fitting together the pieces of a puzzle. Indeed, even the much maligned "had I but known" feature of Eberhart's novels serves the ends of fair play, calling the reader's attention to facts and events relevant to the outcome of the story. These are, however, simply the appurtenances of the fair-play story.

Many of Eberhart's early novels, including several that do not involve O'Leary, feature some of the more essential plot devices of the fair-play book. In several, her detective outlines the motives for murder, thereby setting forth a set of ground rules much as Christie often did. Eberhart is also fond of the closed circumstance, or "locked room" murder. No one apparently can enter the Federie house in *While the Patient Slept,* or the Thatcher residence in *Murder by an Aristocrat* (1932). At Hunting's End, "there is no one concealed in the lodge. Doors and shutters and windows are bolted. And moreover the storm itself prohibits the possibility of anyone's making his way to or away from the lodge" (*The Mystery of Hunting's End,* p. 97). With the setting thus limited, the detective and the reader sift the evidence and shift their attention from one to another of the limited cast of characters. Moreover, Eberhart keeps her plotting options open and responds to the rules by warning her readers to suspect everything, as in *While the Patient Slept:*

> "Do you think it possible that someone—some outsider—a thief or housebreaker—could have got into the house?" He looked at me oddly.
>
> "Anything is possible, Miss Keate." (p. 157)

Readers should also not forget the women present. Hence, in the same novel Lance O'Leary explains that he employs male pronouns only "in a rhetorical sense," and asks "why don't you include the women, Nurse Keate?" (p. 152).

Having provided readers certain aids and having alerted them to significant facts, events, or acts, obfuscation becomes the principal task of the fair-play writer. This is where much of the zaniness of this kind of mystery story appears. In several cases Eberhart's victims are done to death in multiple ways: in *The White Cockatoo,* for example, the first victim appears to be stabbed. Then there is a suspicion that he was shot, and it later turns out he was poisoned. In *Fair Warning* (1936), there are arsenic, the dandelion knife, and the paperweight—potential murder weapons all. But Eberhart uses other conventions more prominently. Invariably there is tampering with the evidence. One of Nurse Keate's defining characteristics is her tendency to hide important bits of evidence from the authorities. Indeed, in her early books, Eberhart almost always plays a kind of game with the evidence. Thus, the radium appears and disappears in *The Patient in Room 18,* as does the jade elephant in *While the Patient Slept,* and the Chinese snuff bottle in *From This Dark Stairway.* All of this, of course, has little to do with what the evidence really means. More essentially diverting, however, is that in Eberhart's fair-play books everyone, for one reason or another, has visited the scene of the crime. They come in through doors and windows, down stairs and corridors. As the detective in *Danger in the Dark* (1937) says, "Good God, it looks as if you'd have needed traffic signals to keep from running over each other" (p. 266).

Nurse Keate

Characteristic of Eberhart's early fair-play books is a lightness of tone provided by the character of Nurse Sarah Keate and her first-person narration. Nurse Keate appears in all of the O'Leary novels and by herself in *Murder by an Aristocrat, Wolf in Man's Clothing* (1942), and later in a return engagement in *Man Missing* (1954). She is the amateur detective who assists in the solution of the crimes, even as she attenuates the problems by hiding evidence. She also adds the comic element that is a feature of many of the best-known fair-play books. The lighter side of Nurse Keate is revealed by her observations about her person, character, and situation in life. Thus, she muses on her person by observing that "Nancy having slim hips and no stomach, whereas there are times when I feel that I am practically all stomach" (*From This Dark Stairway,* p. 27). About her character, in *While the Patient Slept,* Nurse Keate tells the reader, "It is true that while I hope I'm not snoopy, you understand, nor meddlesome, still there's no use denying the fact that I do have a lively and inquiring mind" (p. 56). Finally, she is always quite frank about her station in life: "I had read somewhere that thin old maids were pathetic and fat old maids gross and all old maids sentimental, and had resolved to be none of the three myself" (*The Patient in Room 18,* p. 21). Keate's self-deprecating humor, along with her down-to-earth pluck, contributes considerably to the ambience of Eberhart's early novels, which are in some ways very much like those of other fair-play authors of the 1920s and 1930s. But there is more to Nurse Keate than this.

Throughout her works, Eberhart portrays men as rational and women as intuitive. The relationship between Susan Dare, Eberhart's only female detective, and her associate Jim Byrne, for example, demonstrates that women have unique abilities that are not connected with facts and reason: "And she must herself this time, without Jim's help, confirm with hard fact the findings of the queer divining rod of her own consciousness" (*The Cases of Susan Dare,* p. 225). This contention appeared earlier in the character of Sarah Keate. To begin with, Nurse Keate bases her judgments of guilt and innocence on sentimental impulses, as in *From This Dark Stairway,* where she cannot think Ladd guilty because of her "moments of romantic fancy" (p. 191). For her, reason is not a sufficient guide. In *While the Patient Slept,* she tells readers, "I accepted the explanation because it seemed the only rational one to accept, but I felt in my heart a kind of instinctive repudiation of it" (p. 135). Both instinct and "a sixth sense" frequently guide her thoughts and actions. Indeed, Eberhart makes an effort to delineate these psychic phenomena. In *From This Dark Stairway,* they represent the persistence of primal qualities: "I saw nothing and shrugged away that sixth sense which was trying to warn me. Strange how we civilized people fight our impulses: call them nerves and such like" (p. 139). Eberhart comes back to the same point about behavior in her later works, where the term "atavistic" invariably accompanies the concept.

While Nurse Keate's intuition is almost at odds with the primarily rational procedures expected of the fair-play novel, her other emotions edge these early works toward another kind of fiction. "Even I," says Nurse Keate in *From This Dark Stairway,* "who am as a rule, the most prosaic and unimaginative of women, felt very clearly and definitely the danger in the silent old hospital" (p. 34). From the very first novel, she feels that "something evil and loathsome near at hand was creeping over me" (*The Patient in Room 18,* p. 34). In each succeeding book, Eberhart displays Nurse Keate's ability to feel the malaise attending crime and the unease that precedes and follows the commission of violent acts.

In addition to this sensitivity, which can have rational grounds—after all, the passions that lead to crime and the apprehension and guilt of suspects are very real things—in these novels Eberhart gives Nurse Keate access to the spirit world, the same realm that fascinated both Arthur Conan Doyle and Harry Houdini. In *The Patient in Room 18,* Nurse Keate senses the paranormal: "The room was quite empty of human presence, though to my tired nerves it seemed that there might be other presences" (p. 258). This moves her to suspect that there was "some power of evil at work in that silent old house whose gifts transcended purely human ability" in *While the Patient Slept* (p. 150). And in *From This Dark Stairway,* suspicion becomes conviction when Keate reflects "that any number of policemen could not get their clutches on the impalpable thing that actually did seem to brood over the hospital" (p. 132). In fact, in that same novel one of the complications is a patient's sighting of her dead father in her room: "A visitor. From another world" (p. 191). Though not a serious introduction of spiritualism, this brief brush with the spirit world indicates Eberhart's impulse to move away from the rational, somewhat playful world of the fair-play detective story and toward something else. An initial move in that direction came in her creation of her second recurring detective character.

Jacob Wait

Jacob Wait is Eberhart's second, and last, continuing detective character. He appears first in *Fair Warning* and then in *Danger in the Dark, The Pattern* (1937), and *Hasty Wedding* (1938). Wait is exotic. Wait is emotional. Wait is scary. Eberhart first tried out the character type in Detective Crafft, the detective in *The Dark Garden* (1933): "He was a secretive, incalculable, little brown man who knew too much. She was never to discover just how and where he learned all that he knew. He was like a djinn, very old in evil wisdom, very sly, diabolically crafty" (p. 98). In Jacob Wait, however, this type of character is much more fully developed. First, he is not the stereotypical detective hero. Wait has "a small, warm strain of Jewish blood in him" (p. 86), and this makes him exotic. "Thus," Eberhart tells us in the continuation of the passage from *Danger in the Dark,* "he was deeply imaginative and perceptive" (p. 86). Eberhart develops this trait as a dark passion. So, in *Fair Warning,* she gives us this passage:

> And an investigation—any investigation—was likely to give him now and then moments of horror when he looked, with that inconvenient sensitiveness, out of the eyes of other people—the people he was pursuing. That was dreadful, and he hated that, too, and thus more than anything he hated those people. (p. 71)

Because of his intelligence and passion, and because Eberhart's principal characters always hide something to protect themselves and others, Wait is frightening: "Dorcas did not speak. She was suddenly very much afraid of a little, sallow-faced man who walked like a cat and had somber dark eyes . . ." (*Hasty Wedding,* p. 132).

But Detective Wait did not last long. Neither Wait nor Lance O'Leary was indispensable to Eberhart. Indeed, after Wait there are no more detectives in her series, indicating Eberhart's loss of faith in the detective character. In the foreword to *The House on the Roof* (1935), Eberhart comments that "I have long been troubled by a strong suspicion that, no matter how ingenious the fictional solution of a fictional crime might be, real and living police would make short work of it." So, from the mid-1930s onward, Eberhart simply assures readers that there are police and they are very, very efficient: "There was no way to gauge the potential power of the police; they did things, found things, reasoned from bits of evidence which the layman did not know existed" (*Danger in the Dark,* p. 67). But detectives and police officers—as characters—have no place in her stories. After Jacob Wait, then, the police do two things. They come in at the end to deliver an official version of guilt or innocence, a deus ex machina role almost anticipated by O'Leary's role in *From This Dark Stairway.* More important, they represent various real or perceived threats to characters, especially the innocent characters.

Sensation Novels

It is worth noting that at the same time that two of S. S. Van Dine's fair-play novels (*The Greene Murder Case* and *The Bishop Murder Case*) climbed to the best-seller lists, another American writer possessed the kind of broad public appeal that makes blockbuster books. From 1909 to 1930 Mary Roberts Rinehart beat all of the fair-play writers hands down: during that period ten of her books reached the best-seller lists. And Rinehart represents a very different branch of the mystery story than that made popular by Van Dine. Her books, in fact, should be classified more as "sensation" novels than as detective stories.

The sensation novel began in Britain in the 1860s and brought together elements of gothic fiction, Victorian melodrama, and detective work. The most important sensation writer was Wilkie Collins, known today largely for *The Moonstone* (1868), but during his own time his *Woman in White* (1860) was equally popular. Indeed, the first detectives to appear in American novels appeared in sensation novels—first in Seely Register's *The Dead Letter* (1866), and then in Anna Katharine Greene's *The Leavenworth Case* (1878). Mary Roberts Rinehart worked in this tradition, and so did Mignon G. Eberhart.

The first requisite of the sensation novel is the creation of atmosphere—scary, oppressive, threatening atmosphere. This was one of Eberhart's specialties. First, there is nasty weather. Rain, along with thunder and lightning, is a feature of *The Patient in Room 18* and *The House on the Roof.* Remorseless heat bears down on the hospital in *From This Dark Stairway.* Chicago's fog plays a major role in *The Dark Garden* and *The Glass Slipper* (1938). Eberhart does a great deal with meteorology, summoning snow, high winds, even a hurricane. Foul weather accompanies foul deeds, but Eberhart also uses weather to fray characters' nerves and to heighten the hysteria that mounts during the investigation of the crimes in the novels.

Much as the weather is always gloomy in sensation novels, they also have spooky, gothic settings. And here Eberhart moved into the sensation novel tradition rather quickly. She began by using the hospital, with its elevator and nurses stations, pretty much as a complicated fair-play setting for the murders in *The Patient in Room 18.* But two years later, the dark stairway becomes the hospital's most important attribute. Eberhart quickly left the hospital, though, and moved into the big, rambling, old house. So in her second novel, *While the Patient Slept,* Eberhart transports Nurse Keate to Federie House: "It was not a cheerful place. There is a kind of morose secretiveness about the narrow shuttered windows and iron gate and rearing chimneys and blind tower" (p. 2). This kind of gothic setting becomes the ideal site for another of the sensation novel's motifs: the hidden stranger. Eberhart includes hidden characters in *While the Patient Slept* and in *The White Cockatoo,* where she takes her readers to the disused wing of a second-class hotel in a region of France subject to mistral winds. She gets the same kind of double effect with the penthouses in *The House on the Roof* and *Never Look Back* (1951), where she introduces both isolation and dizzying vertigo.

With locale, in fact, one can observe Eberhart's increasing use of the motives and motifs of the sensation novel. In her first six books, Eberhart purposely makes the locale anonymous. Nurse Keate's hospital is located in "B——," a city somewhere in the Midwest. Even though she moves her readers to France with *The White Cockatoo,* it is to the town of "A——." In *The Dark Garden,* however, the action takes place in rain-lashed and fog-shrouded Chicago. Following this, Eberhart wrote a series of books set in that city: *The House on the Roof, Hasty Wedding, The Glass Slipper,* and five of the six stories in *The Cases of Susan Dare* (1934). There is, of course, the thrill of Chicago, its "sheer energy and power, epitomized in the roar of sounds that engulfed them in the street" (*The Dark Garden,* p. 12), so different from Eberhart's girlhood Nebraska. In Chicago there are strange tenants in apartment houses, tenants who may be (and sometimes are) gangsters. In the city, as well, the efficient and faceless officialdom of the police becomes a hovering threat. There is also a primal fear associated with the city, expressed in *Wings of Fear* (1945): "The cities [Chicago and Saint Louis] that marked that journey were modern, hedged and protected by police and Federal agents, by law and order and safe, sane, comforting custom—all of which suddenly failed to operate" (p. 62).

In the sensation novel, and in Eberhart's books, the creation of threatening atmosphere and gothic setting—the empty old house on a dark and stormy night—serves to heighten the principal objective of the narrative: the involvement of the reader with the plight of a worthy but helpless character. This became the focus of Eberhart's fiction from the early 1930s onward. Traditionally, in crime fiction and elsewhere, women characters are the helpless victims. With only a few exceptions (*The White Cockatoo* and *Another Man's Murder* [1957], which have male heroes), the principal focus of Eberhart's books is on women. To them she applies techniques, both ancient and modern, which make them helpless. First of all, they are alone. Either one or both of their parents are dead, usually their fathers. Were they alive, the heroines' fathers probably would not be of much help: in fact, in several cases (*The Unknown Quantity* [1953] and *Nine O'Clock Tide* [1977]) Eberhart made her heroines' deceased fathers English professors, an archetype of well-meaning ineffectuality. Similarly, older women, especially in the novels of the 1930s, are infirm, hypochondriacal, or ineffectual. And they are not the heroines' mothers. While many of her female leads live with a family (a circumstance dictated by Eberhart's choice of writing mysteries that take place in mansions), they are only distantly related or vaguely connected to it, and thus do not have anyone to whom they can turn. Eberhart created even more excruciating isolation in novels like *The Glass Slipper* and *Another Woman's House* (1947), where the heroine lives in a place that emphatically belongs to her husband's former wife.

In addition to making her women characters essentially orphans, Eberhart employs other means of emphasizing their helplessness. Sometimes roles are imposed upon them which they neither desire nor for which they are fit: the role of ornamental wife, for instance, in *Fair Warning, The Glass Slipper,* and other novels. Eberhart sometimes makes the heroine the victim of a conspiracy. She first uses this convention in *The White Cockatoo,* where a number of people devise plots, including the introduction of a double, to get their hands on Sue Tally's inheritance. Eberhart uses the double again in *The Unknown Quantity* (1953); in the intervening years she employs disguised intent and false witness as conspirators' techniques.

Fundamentally, however, it is the crime that makes Eberhart's female characters helpless. Eberhart's heroines are frequently present when the first crime of the novel is committed. The car Katie Warren drives runs over Charlotte Weinberg in *The Dark Garden;* Marcia Godden clasps the knife in her husband's chest when her sister-in-law appears in *Fair Warning;* and Deborah Cavert visits Mary Monroe when she is shot in *The House on the Roof.* And this is only a sampling. Frequently, too, the heroines are the first ones to discover the bodies: Daphne Haviland finds her murdered fiancé in *Danger in the Dark;* Dorcas Whipple finds Ronald Drew in *Hasty Wedding;* Serena March finds a body in her closed-up house in *Escape the Night* (1944). All of this makes them prime suspects. In fact, near the end of many novels the police are about to arrest the heroine. This plays to readers' sentiments, because readers know that she is innocent.

To increase the tension on the female victim, Eberhart adds another twist. Her heroines have something to hide, something unconnected with the actual crime, but something that might be construed as incriminating by strangers and the police. Thus, for instance, in *Fair Warning* Marcia Godden cannot reveal that she had been spooning with Rob Copley, and Deborah Cavert in *The House on the Roof* will not tell that Anthony Wyatt was also at the scene of the crime. Both they and Eberhart's other heroines suffer multiple threats. While they are innocent, the circumstances of the crime may lead others to believe them to be guilty, so they must protect themselves. Additionally, the circumstances may also lead others to believe that someone with whom the heroine is emotionally involved may be guilty, and she must protect him by remaining silent about details of the crime that may be falsely incriminating. So the heroine's actions may spring both from self-protection and the nobler motive of love.

The Love Romance

It is difficult to separate motifs from the sensation novel from those of the love romance. Clearly, however, in the 1930s Eberhart moved closer and closer to the love story intended for a female audience. From 1934 until the mid-1940s her fiction was a regular feature of American women's magazines. This began with her short stories written for the *Delineator,* a periodical founded by Ebenezer Butterick and sold wherever Butterick sewing patterns were sold. The *Delineator* featured fashions but also published well-known authors, along with articles on divorce, marriage problems, suffrage, and education. And it was very, very popular: in 1930 Tebbel and Waller-Zuckerman in the *American Magazine* tell us that the *Delineator*'s circulation was 2,450,000. More important, the *Ladies' Home Journal* published ten serialized versions of Eberhart's novels, from *The House on the Roof* in 1935 through *The Cup, the Blade, or the Gun* in 1961. Indeed, the appearance of Eberhart's first novel coincided with the *Journal*'s revitalization as it became the largest selling women's magazine in the world. And when Eberhart's pieces were not appearing in the *Ladies' Home Journal,* they appeared in *The Saturday Evening Post* (Mary Roberts Rinehart's magazine) or in *Collier's.*

Magazines like these had as much to do with creating and broadening the audience for the detective story in America as did the pulp magazines of the same era. At the turn of the century, *Harper's Weekly, McClure's,* and *Collier's* magazines brought the Sherlock Holmes stories to American readers for the first time, and the detective story became a standard ingredient in the so-called slick magazine well past the 1940s. While most popular magazines occasionally carried detective stories, under editor George H. Loring *The Saturday Evening Post* made them a regular feature and attracted most of the well-known detective story writers of the 1920s and 1930s: the *Post* carried pieces by Agatha Christie, Mary Roberts Rinehart, Earl Derr Biggers, Leslie Ford, Rex Stout, and J. P. Marquand. The appearance of serial versions of two of Eberhart's novels in *The Saturday Evening Post* in 1936 was a definite sign of her having joined the genre's elite. It also exposed her work to a very large audience, for as Frank Mott notes (*A History of American Magazines,* vol. 4, p. 696), the *Post* sold three million copies a week in 1937. Eberhart's move to the *Ladies' Home Journal,* where the majority of her serialized novels appeared after 1936, may have been occasioned by the appointment in 1935 of fellow Midwesterners Bruce and Beatrice Blackmar Gould as editors of the *Journal* and their successful revitalization of the magazine. This was based, in part, on Mr. Gould's experience as an associate editor of *The Saturday Evening Post,* owned, as was the *Journal,* by Curtis Publishing. This move brought Eberhart's works to a somewhat larger audience—in 1942 *The Ladies' Home Journal* sold four million copies per week (p. 554)—to an audience composed largely, although not exclusively, of women.

While the *Post* was a bit ahead of its time in its portrayal of women—in its pages women occasionally smoked, drank, and, in Katharine Bush's serialized novel *The Red Headed Woman* (1931), had affairs—all of these magazines promulgated the traditional roles of women as wives and mothers. Granted, they carried features on education, divorce, religion, and domestic economy, but in their fiction they most frequently carried the message that love was a woman's highest attainment.

Eberhart's fiction fit the context of the 1930s women's magazine. When Eberhart's female characters work, for instance, they have traditional, subsidiary jobs. From the Sarah Keate books to Rue Hatterick (*The Glass Slipper*) and Drue Cable (*Wolf in Man's Clothing*), they are nurses. Serena March (*Escape the Night*) and Sarah Travers (*The Unknown Quantity*) are typists. Even well into the 1980s, with Emmy Brace in *Alpine Condo Crossfire* (1984), Eberhart's women characters work at lower-level support jobs, which serve as training for the marriages into which they all rush: " 'you should know that Emmy and I intend to marry—' He looked down at Emmy. 'Right, Emmy? Can you give up one job—but take me for another?' " (p. 228).

In Eberhart's novels, of course, some men are more of a job than others. And some are just not worth the effort. From *The White Cockatoo* onward, the dark plots of villains complicate the lives of Eberhart's female heroes. Ronald Drew, for instance, in *Hasty Wedding,* woos Dorcas Whipple in order to get his hands on the Whipple fortune. This character type persists in Eberhart's fiction: twenty-three years later in *The Cup, the Blade, or the Gun,* Lucien marries Sarah so he can lay hands on her inheritance. Eberhart's first *Saturday Evening Post* novel was *Fair Warning,* a title with more than one meaning. Here she introduces another type of evil male, the husband who has money, position, superficial charm, and, a heart of stone. As with the roué, Eberhart continues to use this character well up into the 1970s.

In Eberhart's works, female characters, too, can complicate the heroine's job of finding a man and marriage. From Alicia Pelham in *The Glass Slipper* onward, Eberhart introduces female rivals. Beautiful, experienced, socially connected, often older and downright voracious, they lay claim to the heroine's love interest. Through intimidation, bearing false witness, and threats, they seek to both defeat the heroine and win her lover—not necessarily to marry him, but to possess him. In *Escape the Night,* Eberhart applies the label to this type of woman familiar to everyone who had seen or heard of the actress Theda Bara: "Johnny is perfectly crazy about Amanda and she won't let him go. She doesn't want him; she's just a—like a vampire" (p. 24).

Relationships, the focus of the love romance, play an increasingly important, almost dominating role in Eberhart's novels from the mid-1930s onward. Given the times, relationships mean marriages, and Eberhart builds novels around a variety of them. First of all, originating in the sensation novel, there is the forced marriage. One of these almost occurs in *Danger in the Dark,* where Daphne Haviland agrees to marry Ben Brewer in order to save her family's business. Equally ancient, but appealing to readers during the Depression, is the marriage of convenience, a type of arrangement Eberhart features as a motivating force in *Fair Warning, Murder by an Aristocrat, The Glass Slipper, Nine O'Clock Tide,* and elsewhere. Here women marry men with whom they are not familiar because they offer affluent, comfortable, and seemingly romantic lives. Then there is the hasty wedding, featured in the novel of that title as well as in *The House on the Roof.* Here a masterful man hurries the heroine into marriage in order to protect her (and himself) from the rigors and dangers of a criminal investigation. Indeed, it seems at times that Eberhart tried to work in every nuptial permutation that she could imagine. There are elopements, annulments, separations, and divorces aplenty. Starting with *Fair Warning,* Eberhart builds any number of books around a married woman who meets a man from the past and at the same time discovers that her marriage is hollow. "She had been married to Sam Havlock now for three years; she was still not certain of his reactions to anything" (*Nine O'Clock Tide,* p. 9). It is a relationship without intimacy or romance. It is a relationship that is destroying her:

> And I hate meddling. But I've seen you change, Marcia—from a healthy, normal girl to a—white-faced, nervous, hunted looking woman. . . . You have one life to lead. Just one. . . . You are what those tender young tulip sheaths would be if I walked on them. You are beaten down. Crushed. Your body, your initiative, even your common sense isn't functioning. . . . (*Fair Warning,* p. 8)

So the heroine of necessity must consider divorce but cannot undertake it because, again from *Fair Warning:* "Oh—I can't. It's all wrong. I'm married to him. . . . Marriage—it lasts, Rob. Till death do you part" (p. 27).

Which, of course, was the whole point to begin with: these characters for the most part wind up dead. In the first two "bad husband" novels, *Murder by an Aristocrat* and *Fair Warning,* they are murdered because they are bad husbands. Later on, in books like *The Unknown Quantity* and *Nine O'Clock Tide,* their deaths come about because of unrelated sinister or criminal activities they had undertaken in the past.

So what is the alternative for Eberhart's women? As she puts it in *Wings of Fear,* they want a life where "all the confusion and chaos [falls] into place and everything [is] orderly and [has] a reason and motive and a truth about it" (p. 118). And in Eberhart's novels there is only one kind of person who can offer this—the man who takes charge, like Anthony Wyatt in *The House on the Roof:* "She [Deborah Cavert] obeyed Anthony Wyatt blindly—because she was confused, terrified; because he had made her obey him. Because he had been so direct, certain, altogether compelling" (p. 39). Or because he is somebody who can say

> "You've had a hideous experience, you can't think or—or plan for yourself. Will you do as I tell you Daphne, my darling?"
>
> "I—What, Dennis, Why?"
>
> "Because you are in danger, Daphne." (*Danger in the Dark,* p. 59)

None of these heroes, however, is a detective. From early on, Eberhart articulates the ancient theme of "murder will out." Of murderers she says, "That secret loosing of bestiality. Of ruthlessness. Surely such an experience would leave its mark forever upon the murderer; stamped as if in letters upon his face" (*Danger in the Dark,* p. 142). This is very much like Dickens' observations about Jonas Chuzzlewit as he slouches off to murder Tigg. But murderers do not wear murder on their visages in Eberhart. Nevertheless, while it is not brought about by the hero, their exposure is both inevitable and providential. Thus, after the travail they have suffered during the investigation, the answer comes from outside. What Eberhart's heroes offer, then, are their eagerness to protect the heroine and their willingness to share her peril. And in so doing, they provide that "word of affection, of mutual faith" the heroine longs for in *The Unknown Quantity.*

Conclusion

Without a doubt, Eberhart has been ignored or condemned by critics of the mystery genre, largely due to her combination of the murder mystery with elements of suspense and love. Jacques Barzun and Wendell Taylor, for instance, say with some restraint that "In her output since the days of Nurse Keate and Susan Dare, there has been little to entice the discriminating reader" (*A Catalogue of Crime,* p. 185). Even H. R. F. Keating, who thinks well of her later books, concedes that Eberhart is not much of a writer. And this is evident in her casualness, even sloppiness, about details, especially scientific details. Indeed, some of her plots tax even the most credulous readers. Then, too, she can write some very stupid prose: she says there are "incredibly swift bullets" (*The House on the Roof,* p. 222) and that "the moment my eyes reached her foot with its nice instep I knew she was an American" (*The White Cockatoo,* p. 11).

Eberhart's usual adroit plotting along with, no doubt, her persistence in writing mysteries over fifty years of her life brought her any number of awards, including being named a Grand Mistress of the genre by the Mystery Writers of America. A greater tribute to her, however, resides on page 39 of the copy of *Wolf in Man's Clothing* in the Rockingham Public Library of Harrisonville, Virginia, and on page 71 of *Another Woman's House* in the Hoover Library of Western Maryland College. On both of these pages a reader has left the impress of her rouged lips.

Selected Bibliography

WORKS OF MIGNON GOOD EBERHART

NOVELS

The Patient in Room 18. New York: Doubleday, 1929.
While the Patient Slept. New York: Doubleday, 1930.
The Mystery of Hunting's End. New York: Doubleday, 1930.
From This Dark Stairway. New York: Doubleday, 1931.

Murder by an Aristocrat. New York: Doubleday, 1932.
The Dark Garden. New York: Doubleday, 1933.
The White Cockatoo. New York: Doubleday, 1933.
The House on the Roof. New York: Doubleday, 1935.
Fair Warning. New York: Doubleday, 1936.
Danger in the Dark. New York: Doubleday, 1937.
The Pattern. New York: Doubleday, 1937.
The Glass Slipper. New York: Doubleday, 1938.
Hasty Wedding. New York: Doubleday, 1938.
Brief Return. New York: Collins, 1939.
The Chiffon Scarf. New York: Doubleday, 1939.
The Hangman's Whip. New York: Doubleday, 1940.
Speak No Evil. New York: Random House, 1941.
Strangers in Flight. New York: Bantam, 1941.
With This Ring. New York: Random House, 1941.
Wolf in Man's Clothing. New York: Random House, 1942.
The Man Next Door. New York: Random House, 1943.
Unidentified Woman. New York: Random House, 1943.
Escape the Night. New York: Random House, 1944.
Wings of Fear. New York: Random House, 1945; Popular Library, 1945.
Five Passengers from Lisbon. New York: Random House, 1946.
The White Dress. New York: Random House, 1946.
Another Woman's House. New York: Random House, 1947.
House of Storm. New York: Random House, 1949.
Hunt with the Hounds. New York: Random House, 1950.
Never Look Back. New York: Random House, 1951.
Dead Man's Plans. New York: Random House, 1952.
The Unknown Quantity. New York: Random House, 1953.
Man Missing. New York: Random House, 1954.
Postmark Murder. New York: Random House, 1956.
Another Man's Murder. New York: Random House, 1957.
Melora. New York: Random House, 1959.
Jury of One. New York: Random House, 1960.
The Cup, the Blade, or the Gun. New York: Random House, 1961.
Enemy in the House. New York: Random House, 1963.
Run Scared. New York: Random House, 1963.
Call After Midnight. New York: Random House, 1964.
R.S.V.P. Murder. New York: Random House, 1965.
Witness at Large. New York: Random House, 1966.
Woman on the Roof. New York: Random House, 1967.
Message from Hong Kong. New York: Random House, 1969.
El Rancho Rio. New York: Random House, 1970.
The House by the Sea. Pockettes, 1972.
Two Little Rich Girls. New York: Random House, 1972.
Murder in Waiting. New York: Random House, 1973.
Danger Money. New York: Random House, 1975.
Family Fortune. New York: Random House, 1973.
Nine O'Clock Tide. New York: Random House, 1977; Fawcett Popular Library, 1980.
The Bayou Road. New York: Random House, 1979.
Casa Madrone. New York: Random House, 1980.
Family Affair. New York: Random House, 1981.
Next of Kin. New York: Random House, 1982.
The Patient in Cabin C. New York: Random House, 1983.
Alpine Condo Crossfire. New York: Random House, 1984; Warner Books, 1989.
A Fighting Chance. New York: Random House, 1986.
Three Days for Emeralds. New York: Random House, 1988.

SHORT STORIES

The Cases of Susan Dare in *The Delineator:* "Introducing Susan Dare" (April 1934), "The Spider" (May 1934), "Easter Devil" (June 1934), "The Claret Stick" (July 1934), "The Man Who Was Missing" (August 1934), "The Calico Dog" (September 1934).
"Dead Yesterday." *The Pictorial Review,* September 1934.
"The Wedding Dress." *The Delineator,* April 1935.
"Flowering Face." *The Delineator,* May 1935.
"Pastiche." *The Delineator,* August 1935.
"Feather Heads." *The Delineator,* October 1935.
"Murder by Proxy." *The Delineator,* May 1936.
"Murder in a Storm." *The Delineator,* October 1936.
"Bermuda Grapevine." *The American Magazine,* October 1938.
"Express to Danger." *The American Magazine,* February 1939.
"Deadly Is the Diamond." *The American Magazine,* June 1942.
"Murder Goes to Market." *The American Magazine,* July 1943.
"Murder in the Garden" (with Grantland Rice). *The American Magazine,* May 1935.
"House of Storm." *Ladies' Home Journal,* April 1949.
"Witness for My Love." *Ladies' Home Companion,* June 1950.
"The Crimson Paw." *The American Magazine,* October 1952.
"Murder in Waltz Time." *The American Magazine,* May 1953.
"Terror Trap." *The American Magazine,* December 1955.
"The Wagstaff Pearls." In *The Best Detective Stories of 1953.* New York: Dutton, 1953.
"Mr. Wickwire's Gun Moll." In *A Choice of Murders.* Mystery Writers of America, 1958.
"Mr. Wickwire's Widow." In *With Malice Toward All.* Mystery Writers of America, 1968.
"Murder on St. Valentine's Day." In *Alfred Hitchcock's Stories That Go Bump in the Night.* New York: Random House, 1977.
"Murder at the Dog Show." In *Fifty Years of the Best from Ellery Queen's Mystery Magazine.* New York: Carroll & Graf, 1991.

SERIALIZED NOVELS

The House on the Roof. Ladies' Home Journal, 1935.
Fair Warning. Saturday Evening Post, 1936.
Danger in the Dark. Saturday Evening Post, 1936.
The Pattern. Ladies' Home Journal, 1937.
The Glass Slipper. Collier's, 1938.
Hasty Wedding. Ladies' Home Journal, 1938.
The Chiffon Scarf. Ladies' Home Journal, 1939.
The Hangman's Whip. Saturday Evening Post, 1940.
Speak No Evil. Ladies' Home Journal, 1941.
With This Ring. Ladies' Home Journal, 1941.
The Man Next Door. Ladies' Home Journal, 1943.
Wings of Fear. Collier's, 1945.
The White Dress. Ladies' Home Journal, 1946.
Another Woman's House. Ladies' Home Journal, 1947.
The Cup, the Blade, or the Gun. Ladies' Home Journal, 1961.

COLLECTIONS OF SHORT STORIES

The Cases of Susan Dare. New York: Doubleday, 1934.
Five of My Best. Collins, 1949.
Deadly Is the Diamond. New York: Random House, 1958.
The Crimson Paw. Hammond, 1959.

MANUSCRIPTS

Eberhart's manuscripts are collected at Mugar Memorial Library, Boston University.

BIOGRAPHICAL AND CRITICAL STUDIES

Barzun, Jacques, and Wendell Hertig Taylor. *A Catalogue of Crime.* New York: Harper & Row, 1971.
Keating, H. R. F. *Crime and Mystery: The 100 Best Books.* New York: Carroll & Graff, 1987.
Mott, Frank Luther. *A History of American Magazines, 1885–1905.* 5 vols. Cambridge, Mass.: Harvard University Press, 1957.
Tebbell, John, and Mary Ellen Waller-Zuckerman. *The Magazine in America, 1741–1990.* New York: Oxford University Press, 1991.

Stanley Ellin

(1916–1986)

MARVIN S. LACHMAN

Gaining immediate recognition with his first published short story, "The Specialty of the House" (1948), probably the most famous story in twentieth-century crime fiction, Stanley Ellin became the most renowned short story writer in his field. During his long career he also became well known for his often controversial novels. When he was selected for the Grand Master Award given by the Mystery Writers of America (MWA) in 1981, it was the only time a writer whose fame in the short story field equaled (and possibly exceeded) that for his novels was so honored.

More than other great mystery short story writers, Stanley Ellin demonstrated versatility, writing almost every type of story. Like John Collier and Roald Dahl, he was able to combine the macabre and the humorous, even in writing about marriages about to end in murder. He was perhaps best known for his stories of the psychologically disturbed, but he also wrote about the social issues of his day, including urban unemployment and pollution. Ellin's underrated fair-play detective novellas, though few in number, are comparable to that more prolific, present-day master of plot ingenuity, Edward D. Hoch. Whatever Ellin's subject matter, he sustained reader interest with suspenseful storytelling reminiscent of Cornell Woolrich. Beginning with his first story, a surprise ending that logically flowed from what had gone before was his hallmark.

Early Life

Stanley Bernard Ellin was born in Brooklyn, New York, on 6 October 1916 and graduated from Brooklyn College in 1936 with a bachelor of arts degree. Ellin read widely, especially Edgar Allan Poe, Guy de Maupassant, Ernest Hemingway, William Faulkner, F. Scott Fitzgerald, and Ring Lardner. However, he admitted being indifferent to the Sherlock Holmes detective stories of Sir Arthur Conan Doyle. Ellin wanted to be a writer, but like many of his generation, graduating from college during the Depression, he had to look elsewhere to earn a living. In 1937 he married Jeanne Michael; they had one daughter, Susan. He briefly worked for a newspaper and wrote for radio, and he also taught and was a farmer and an ironworker in a boatbuilding and repair yard, becoming foreman in charge of hull construction on tugboats before he entered the United States Army in 1944. Although he wrote in his spare time, he had nothing published while he was in the service.

On discharge from the army, in 1946, Ellin

expected to resume his trade as an ironworker, but he was encouraged by his wife to devote himself full-time to writing. While she worked, he took advantage of a weekly stipend of twenty dollars that, after World War II, the United States government provided veterans for one year, to aid them in adjusting to careers in civilian life. When he assumed the presidency of the MWA in 1969, he looked back on the time when his wife was "paddling furiously to keep us financially afloat" (*Mystery Writers Annual,* 1969, p. 2).

Ellin received many pro forma rejection slips from magazines before the idea for "The Specialty of the House" occurred to him. He and his wife, discouraged, were trying to cheer themselves up by dining at Gage and Tollner's in Brooklyn, a restaurant known for its nineteenth-century ambience. A waiter took their order but never returned, leaving the Ellins to speculate on his fate. The result was a famous story, albeit one that was at first rejected by the *New Yorker, Esquire, Harper's,* and other magazines. Ellin recalled, "Jeanne remarked that a curious publication titled *Ellery Queen's Mystery Magazine* [*EQMM*] seemed to have a taste for the criminously unusual and a tenderness for unripe talent which could be in my favor" (*The Armchair Detective,* p. 195). He submitted the story to *EQMM* in 1946, but it was a year and a half before it was published in their May 1948 issue.

First Story and First Novel

Once, "The Specialty of the House," like Dahl's "Lamb to the Slaughter," was so well known that critics considered it acceptable to disclose its ending. The fact that there is now at least one generation of readers probably unfamiliar with the story compels one to avoid telling too much about it. Laffler, a gourmet, takes his assistant, Costain, for dinner at Sbirro's, a gaslit restaurant of great atmosphere, after making it sound more like a cathedral than a place to eat. The restaurant has a small, exclusive clientele, and the menu allows no choice. Diners eat whatever Sbirro chooses to prepare, though lamb Amirstan is the most eagerly awaited dish, albeit it is seldom served. The opportunity for a diner to visit the kitchen is rare, but one for which Laffler longs; he finally gets his wish in the story's shudder-provoking climax. "The Specialty of the House" was considered by the pre-eminent mystery critic of his time, Anthony Boucher, the best first story he had ever read.

At the time "The Specialty of the House" was published, *EQMM* was the most prestigious publisher of American short crime fiction. It remains so, though there is no longer the anticipation that once awaited the publication of the winners in the magazine's annual contest. Frederic Dannay, the bibliophile on the team of cousins writing as "Ellery Queen," was instrumental in establishing the magazine in 1941 as one receptive to unusual crime stories. Probably the most demanding short story editor ever, he asked Ellin for many changes in the story, including its title, which was originally "The Kitchen at Robinson's." He also asked Ellin to hold the story and submit it for the 1948 contest, which Ellin did, winning the award for best first story. Ellin credited Dannay with having changed the course of his life and being responsible for his career.

Dannay's interest encouraged Ellin so much that he quickly completed *Dreadful Summit,* a novel that was published in March 1948, two months before his first short story. At this stage in his career, Ellin was not certain that he wished to be a genre writer. He later claimed, in "Writing a Mystery Novel" (*The Writer's Handbook,* p. 291), that his first mystery novel sold "because I had no idea while I was writing it that I was writing a mystery novel. . . . [I was] innocently writing what I conceived to be a serious novel which dealt with murder." *Dreadful Summit* is a poignant coming-of-age novel in which the action is telescoped into twenty-four hours. Sixteen-year-old George LaMain obtains a gun to have his revenge on the man who humiliated his father by beating him savagely.

Although Ellin was New York born and bred, his work, because of his reliance on characterization and dialogue, does not always try to capture the city. *Dreadful Summit* is an exception, with good scenes of Manhattan's West Side, especially around Madison Square Garden, which was then at Fiftieth Street and Eighth Avenue.

Early Short Stories

There were occasional years in which Ellin submitted two stories to *EQMM* (and the rare year in which, mired in writing a novel, he did not submit any), but usually the magazine publicized his "annual" story, and these were greeted enthusiastically. "Robert," in the October 1958 issue of *Sleuth,* a short-lived magazine sponsored by MWA, was the only story not written for *EQMM,* and it was one of Ellin's weakest. Ellin won a prize in every *EQMM* contest he entered, eleven in all. (Since thirty-nine of Ellin's forty short stories were written for *EQMM,* the dates following titles discussed herein refer to the initial publication in that magazine.)

To paraphrase Calvin Coolidge, the business of many of Ellin's protagonists was business. Ellin's second short story, "The Cat's-Paw" (June 1949), is about Crabtree, hired by the mysterious George Spelvin (his name is an inside theater joke, a pseudonym used by actors who wish to keep their identities secret) to run an office called Crabtree's Affiliated Reports. It is a perfect job for Crabtree, who has the necessary clerical skills and attention to detail, and he has never been happier. Then, in one of the surprise endings characteristic of Ellin, he learns that if he is to keep his position, committing murder may be part of his job description. Arthur, in "The Best of Everything" (September 1952), wants to rise above his humble origins to impress his boss's daughter. He finds an ideal person to teach him how the wealthy behave, with considerable risk to the teacher as well as the pupil in one of Ellin's typical endings in which the biter is bitten. Charles, in "The Seven Deadly Virtues" (June 1960), is equally ambitious and thinks he has a job with a company that will teach him how to become expert at conniving.

Ellin's protagonists are often fanatics. "The Orderly World of Mr. Appleby" (May 1950) is his antique and curio shop, the most important thing in his life. His wife's lack of sympathy for Appleby's interest causes him distress but may be more dangerous to her. In "Fool's Mate" (November 1951), George Huneker, after being given a handsomely carved chess set, becomes addicted to the game, ignoring all else as he plays games against an imaginary foe, "White," each evening. When Huneker's wife derides his chess playing, "White" sows the seeds of violence in George, who has become increasingly schizophrenic.

Early Novels

Unlike colleagues who were so prolific that they required pseudonyms (because most publishers were reluctant to issue more than one book yearly under a single name), Ellin used only his own name. Even though Ellin's short stories were often compared to those of de Maupassant, his well-known writing habits were closest to two other slow-working French writers: Flaubert and Proust. He took at least a month for a short story and frequently more than a year for a novel, revising and rewriting constantly before he was satisfied. He did not publish his second novel until four years after his first and published only four short stories in the interim.

In *The Key to Nicholas Street* (1952), Ellin was able to explore, at greater length than in the story format, the psychology, especially the obsessions, of the members of the Ayres family and their neighbor, Kate Ballou, an artist whose actions prove catalytic and lead to her own murder. In this tour de force, there are five alternating narrators, and the reader is not sure until the end who is the detective in the case, let alone the killer. In addition to skilled characterization, this book has far more detection, including clues, than Ellin's other novels, partly satisfying the demanding critics Jacques Barzun and Wendell Hertig Taylor, devotees of classic puzzles who were, however, disappointed that the solution was revealed by the murderer's confession.

Ellin's early work was popular with filmmakers. *Dreadful Summit* was filmed by Joseph Losey as *The Big Night* (1951), with John Barrymore, Jr., as the young protagonist. An eminent French director, Claude Chabrol, directed *The Key to Nicholas Street* (retitled *Leda,* 1959), with Jean-Paul Belmondo. Ellin was unhappy with Chabrol's adaptation, in which a husband leaves his wife not because she is self-seeking and incapable of love, but because she is aging and losing her beauty.

Moments of Decision

Choice, with the risks and consequences of a mistake, is often an important element in Ellin's stories. Although he has no direct proof, Robert in "The Betrayers" (June 1953) is sure that his next-door neighbor is a wife killer. Is Robert prepared to face the consequences if he calls the police and he is wrong? Aptly titled, "The Moment of Decision" (March 1955) is one of Ellin's most famous stories and won first prize in *EQMM*'s annual contest. A dispute between neighbors leads to a dare in which Raymond, a magician, bets Hugh he can leave a locked stone cellar closet. When Raymond appears to be dying inside the closet, Hugh thinks it could be a ruse to gain release, but if he is wrong, he will be responsible for a man's death.

By the time he published his third novel, in 1958, Ellin had won two MWA Edgar Allan Poe awards for Best Short Story of the Year. The first, "The House Party" (May 1954), is, on the surface, a suburban story of a troubled marriage, with elements of conflict, jealousy, and murder, but it includes an intriguing note of fantasy that was rare for Ellin. "The Blessington Method" (June 1956) won a Special Award of Merit from *EQMM* before receiving an Edgar. It was the first of many stories in which Ellin uses a crime plot to explore social issues, in this case aging. Mr. Treadwell is unhappy because his elderly father-in-law lives with him and his wife. Mr. Bunce from the Society of Gerontology calls on him. He claims that the very existence of the elderly is the problem, since they are "neither producers nor consumers, so they are only barriers to continued progress" (p. 11). Bunce proposes a solution that requires a deceptively attractive choice by Treadwell, with far-reaching implications.

Edgar-Winning Novelist

The Eighth Circle (1958) earned Ellin his third Edgar in five years, this time for best novel. Boucher felt that it defied easy categorization, wondering in the *New York Times Book Review* whether it was a suspense story or the first serious novel about a private detective. Murray Kirk is very different from the marginally successful, knightlike, idealistic private detectives of Raymond Chandler and Ross Macdonald, walking down their "mean streets." He lives in a first-class hotel suite and makes no apology for his interest in money, claiming that "if you're paid well enough for lifting a rock you don't get too queasy at the sight of whatever is crawling underneath it" (1959 ed., p.15). Because he is willing to do whatever is necessary to gain success, he derides idealists nostalgic for the 1930s: "the jolly band of middle-aged intellectuals who got through the Depression with their pride in one piece and wistfully look back on it now as THE great adventure . . . when ideas not money was the common currency" (p. 208).

Hired to find evidence to absolve a policeman charged with a crime, Kirk hopes to find proof of his guilt because he has fallen in love with the accused's fiancée. Even the cynical Kirk begins to have self-doubts. The title, *The Eighth Circle,* derived from Dante's *Inferno,* refers to the dwelling of, among others, the liars, hypocrites, thieves, and pimps. Ellin's novel, more than almost any other private detective novel, is an examination of morality and lost idealism.

Although he continued to write crime short stories, Ellin sought a wider audience with his next novels. *The Winter After This Summer* (1960) and *The Panama Portrait* (1962) each has elements of suspense, though neither is a crime novel. The former is another of Ellin's family- and psychology-oriented books, focusing on wealthy Daniel Egan and his guilt feelings at having allowed a roommate to perish in a fraternity fire. In the second book, Ben Smith, a grown-up version of Egan, is sent to the fictional South American island of Santo Stefano to close a deal and quickly becomes a pawn of its ruling families, whose wealth is contrasted to the poverty and hopeless lives of the island's natives. Neither book was especially successful with critics or readers.

More Adaptations

After his unsuccessful dip into the literary mainstream, Ellin waited five years before publishing his next novel. Sales to other media of options on his work or rights to them removed some of the economic pressures to produce. Between 1956 and 1962, eight Ellin stories were aired on the *Alfred Hitchcock Presents* television program, including a relatively faithful version of "The Specialty of the House" (1959), with Robert Morley ideally cast as the gourmet Laffler. Starring Alan Bates as the social climber, *Nothing but the Best* (1964) was a well-received British film version of Ellin's short story "The Best of Everything."

A More Prolific Novelist

Introducing "Death of an Old-Fashioned Girl" in the June 1966 issue of *EQMM,* Ellery Queen called Ellin "the man who, many critics believe, is the Number One writer of mystery short stories actively producing today" (p. 6). At that time, despite his Edgar for *The Eighth Circle,* Ellin was primarily known for his short stories. He had published only five novels from 1948 through 1966, but he produced nine more between 1967 and 1984. With the virtual disappearance of television anthology programs such as Hitchcock's after 1965, a reliable market for selling ancillary rights to short stories was gone. Novels were a wiser choice economically. They also gave Ellin, in the 1970s, room for experimentation without leaving the crime genre, where his reputation had been earned.

Ellin wrote three relatively conventional crime novels in what for him was quick succession. In the first, *House of Cards* (1967), Reno Davis, an American ex-boxer and now a hopeful novelist, takes a job as tutor to the heir of a wealthy family in Paris, only to discover a secret regarding a right-wing group, which then pursues him throughout Europe. This secret, what Hitchcock would have called a "MacGuffin" (a dubious plot device to move the story forward), and the subsequent chase made the book quite cinematic; *House of Cards* was filmed in 1969 and stars George Peppard, Inger Stevens, and Orson Welles. It was the last of Ellin's work to be made into a movie. Boucher compared the book to Ellin's short stories, noting that its plot was far too limited for its length (336 pages) and likening Ellin to a miniaturist attempting a gigantic canvas. *The Valentine Estate* (1968) earned Ellin an Edgar nomination, though it was not generally well received by newspaper reviewers, who commented on its contrived plot, in which Elizabeth Jones, in order to inherit a million dollars, must marry. She chooses Chris Monte, a has-been tennis player, placing him in jeopardy from those to whom the estate would go if she remained unmarried. Ellin's setting was a well-limned Miami Beach, a locale he used increasingly, presumably because the Ellins were then spending their winters in the Miami area.

Ellin was one of the earlier writers to set books outside New York or California. He again used Florida in his next novel, *The Bind* (1970). Jake Dekker is a private detective of sorts, a freelance operative for insurance companies. His job is to find out whether a heavily, but only recently, insured man has died accidentally in a car crash. No more idealistic than Murray Kirk, Dekker knows that keeping Guaranty Life Insurance from having to pay will bring him a generous contingency fee. As interesting as is Dekker's detective work, more complex is his relationship with the woman whom he hires to pose as his wife so that he can insinuate himself into wealthy Miami society.

Testing the Boundaries of Censorship

Ellin's prior work did not prepare his readers for *Mirror, Mirror on the Wall* (1972). *EQMM*'s editorial policy prohibited sex scenes and more than mild obscenity. In his earlier novels he had not found a subject to test censorship guidelines, which had been rapidly changing since the late 1960s. In his message as outgoing president of MWA in *Mystery Writers Annual* (1970, p. 2), Ellin worried about "the right of the author to put down on paper whatever he wishes to, the right of the publisher to present these words to the public." In *Mirror, Mirror on the Wall,* Ellin made sex and four-letter words an integral part of a psychological detective story. It begins with Peter Hibben standing over the dead body of a woman in his Greenwich Village apartment and flashes surreally back through his life and, in a virtual Freudian index, his sexual history. Waiting for the police, in his mind he "converses" with a psychiatrist, Dr. Ernst, who tells him (though it is by no means clear that Hibben is the killer): "A murderer must at least know the motive for his crime or there is no more peace for him on earth. And in your depths you believe I am the one to unearth the motive for your crime" (p. 47). Seldom, if ever, has there been a mystery in which psychological, as opposed to physical, clues are so important to the denouement.

Mirror, Mirror on the Wall proved to be Ellin's most successful novel. Francis M. Nevins said in the *Mystery Fancier* (p. 36), "No more powerful modern crime novel has been written by an American." H. R. F. Keating selected it in 1987 for his list of the one hundred best crime novels. When it was published in France, it received the Grand Prix de Littérature Policière for 1975.

Ellin was an elder of the Quaker meeting in Brooklyn and a foe of capital punishment. His religious beliefs form the background for his next book, *Stronghold* (1975). In Lake George, New York, four gunmen, led by James Flood, imprison the family of wealthy banker Marcus Hayworth. Their plan is to hold the family hostage while Hayworth goes for a ransom of four million dollars. The book is narrated alternately by Flood and Hayworth, who, as a Quaker, is a believer in nonviolence and rules out enlisting the help of the police because it could lead to violence and death. This crisis tests his philosophy that "every man has the right to die for his beliefs. No man has the right to kill for them" (p. 283). There are no easy answers in this, Ellin's most suspenseful and thought-provoking book.

After a disappointing thriller, *The Luxembourg Run* (1977), about the revenge of a wealthy American smuggler whose Dutch girlfriend has been killed, Ellin finally created his first (and only) series character, a well-off New York private detective, John Milano. In another book strong on Florida atmosphere, *Star Light, Star Bright* (1979), Ellin has Milano, as a favor for an "old flame," act as bodyguard to a religious cult leader against whom there have been death threats.

The second Milano book, *The Dark Fantastic* (1983), is Ellin's most heatedly debated book, one that was turned down by even his longtime publisher (and several others) until Otto Penzler's Mysterious Press, then a relatively small company, agreed to bring it out. If *Mirror, Mirror on the Wall* is about sex and abnormal psychology, *The Dark Fantastic* is about race and sex and abnormal psychology. Again, Ellin uses alternating narrators: Milano, his detective, and Professor Kirwan, a racist madman dying from cancer. Kirwan's words are full of the vilest racial invective, the reason publishers were loath to accept it and some readers were appalled by it. Still, it was clear to most readers that the hate-filled thoughts are those of the character, not the author. Added to the racial passages are explicit descriptions of Kirwan's sexual abuse of a teenage black girl. The girl and her family live in an apartment building occupied mostly by blacks in Brooklyn's Flatbush (where Ellin grew up), and Kirwan, its landlord, plans to blow up the building at a time when most tenants will be home. Milano becomes involved when he has a love affair with the teenager's older sister, and considerable suspense is generated by the question of whether Milano will discover Kirwan's plan in time to prevent the bombing.

Ellin's last novel, *Very Old Money* (1984), is surprisingly low-key, considering the attention created by two of his earlier books, but it is one of his more subtle and sophisticated works. Told at a leisurely pace, it is about Mike and Amy Lloyd, husband and wife and unemployed teachers, who go into domestic service for a wealthy New York family, where they befriend a reclusive blind woman who, surprisingly, has recently become interested in paintings. They discover that their employers have many secrets in this book, which has been likened to a suspenseful version of *Upstairs, Downstairs.*

Abnormal psychology always interested Ellin and had been part of his work from the beginning, culminating in the emphasis he placed on it in his later novels. The minds he explored in his shorter work were varied, including the businessman who suspects his wife of infidelity in "Broker's Special" (January 1956) and the reclusive young woman who must cope with rape and identification of the culprit in "You Can't Be a Little Girl All Your Life" (May 1958). A schoolteacher nearing retirement finds her sanity threatened by a small boy in "Robert," and the compulsive Mr. Willoughby, in "Unreasonable Doubt" (September 1958), goes on vacation because he is suffering from stress, only to hear a crime story in a railroad club car that exacerbates his condition. A disturbed patient selects a psychotherapist even sicker than he in "The Other Side of the Wall" (August 1972).

Before Hannah Arendt wrote of "the banality of evil" in connection with the trial of Karl Adolf Eichmann, Ellin had explored it in two notable stories. Mr. Keesler of Brooklyn is "The Nine-to-Five Man" (November 1961), a methodical family man who commutes to "work" daily like any other businessman but who has a criminal secret that he keeps even from his wife. The attitude of the state "electrocutioner" in "The Question My Son Asked" (November 1962) toward his work is critical and makes it a strong story, one that underscores Ellin's feelings about the death penalty.

Ellin generally eschewed classic puzzles because, as he says in "Writing a Mystery Novel" (p. 293), "Their whole emphasis is on the ingenuity which goes into the manufacturing of a plot rather than the creativity which breathes life into it." Yet, in two novellas, he shows that adroit plotting and believable characterization are not mutually exclusive. In the Edgar-nominated "The Crime of Ezechiele Coen" (November 1963), a vacationing New York police detective, Noah Freeman, is asked by Coen's daughter to disprove the shameful allegation that he, a Jew, collaborated with the Nazis in Rome during the war. A physical clue, a seemingly impenetrable gate, adds the element of an impossible crime. In another novella set in Rome, "The Twelfth Statue" (February 1967), a hated producer disappears from a guarded stage during the filming of a historical epic. This was the closest Ellin came to the true impossible crime story, even offering a false solution in the Ellery Queen tradition while having a diverse cast of characters worthy of a far longer work.

The Short Story of Social Problems

Increasingly, during his last twenty years, Ellin used the problems of urban living, confronting fictionally in his short stories the question of whether cities like his beloved New York were still livable. (He returned to Brooklyn from Florida each spring.) "The Day the Thaw Came to 127" (March 1965) is about an apartment building inadequately heated by its owner in winter. The difficulty of obtaining medical treatment impels "The Corruption of Officer Avakadian" (December 1973). Urban noise and graffiti are at the heart of "A Corner of Paradise" (October 1975) and "Graffiti" (March 1983), respectively. The latter was another Edgar-nominated story. Before the term "downsizing" became so commonly used, Ellin, in "Reasons Unknown" (December 1978), demonstrated its psychological effect with Morrison, who is convinced he will lose his job in a reorganization of middle-level management and not be able to obtain another because he is over forty.

By the 1980s issues of environment and economic development had become frequent motives in crime fiction, and in his last story, "Unacceptable Procedures" (December 1985), Ellin tackled the latter, using a criminal plot that is a variation on Henrik Ibsen's *An Enemy of the People.* Dr. Jodl of Switzerland has established a medical research center in Huxtable Falls, New Hampshire, that is proving a boon to the town's economy. Can the local political leaders continue to ignore the disappearances of outsiders near the town when they may be connected to Jodl's clinic?

There was a lighter side of Ellin, as seen in his Gallic trilogy, three consecutive, relatively lighthearted Parisian stories, beginning with the Edgar-nominated story of wine vintages, "The Last Bottle in the World" (February 1968). "Coin of the Realm" (February 1969) is about an American tourist shopping for coins in Paris. "Kindly Dig Your Grave" (November 1970) is one of several Ellin stories to use painting as background. It features Madame Lagrue, "The most infamously successful dealer in bad art" (p. 6), and O'Toole, an expatriate American painter. "Just Desserts" (6 October 1980), about an outstanding Paris chef, is a cooking story that is full of fun and has a highly unusual victim.

Ellin's first nine stories were collected in 1956 as *Mystery Stories,* one of the landmark volumes in crime fiction. Julian Symons and H. R. F. Keating considered it the finest collection of twentieth-century crime stories. At a time when much mystery fiction had become predictable, Symons said about Ellin in *Mortal Consequences,* "the great quality he has brought back to the crime short story is imagination" (p. 174). In 1968 Ellery Queen added *Mystery Stories* to *Queen's Quorum,* a listing of the "125 Most Important Books of Detective-Crime-Mystery Short Stories."

Ellin's Legacy and the Future

Stanley Ellin died of a heart attack on 31 July 1986 in Brooklyn. Despite the short time that has elapsed since his death, Ellin seemed in danger of being forgotten, his work already out of print, until one of the smaller publishers, Foul Play Press, reprinted two novels in 1996. Militating against reprint, Ellin's work does not fit the major trends in mystery publishing in the 1990s, some of which began before his death. Most publishers were promoting series and encouraging their writers to create continuing characters. Ellin's only series character appeared but twice. While Ellin provided many insightful views of New York City (especially Brooklyn) and Florida, he was not primarily a regional writer. By the mid-1980s it seemed that almost every American crime novel had a strong regional component.

It was in magazines that Ellin got his start and achieved his short story success. By the 1990s, there were few major mystery magazines, and they seldom published reprints. Even though there has been a great increase in the number of short story collections in book form, most feature original stories by currently popular writers. Some collections do include reprints, but they are generally theme-oriented, for example, stories about animals (especially cats) or holidays. Ellin's hard-to-classify work does not fit easily into most of these collections and is not reprinted nearly as often as its quality merits. Yet, rereading his work shows that while some of his novels are specific to period, most of his short stories have a timeless quality, raising the hope that new generations will be introduced to the ingenuity and painstaking craft of "The Specialty of the House" and other Stanley Ellin stories.

Selected Bibliography

WORKS OF STANLEY ELLIN

NOVELS

Dreadful Summit. New York: Simon & Schuster, 1948. Repr. as *The Big Night.* New York: Lion, 1950.

The Key to Nicholas Street. New York: Simon & Schuster, 1952.

The Eighth Circle. New York: Random House, 1958; Dell, 1959.

The Winter After This Summer. New York: Random House, 1960.

The Panama Portrait. New York: Random House, 1962.

House of Cards. New York: Random House, 1967.

The Valentine Estate. New York: Random House, 1968.

The Bind. New York: Random House, 1970. Repr. as *The Man from Nowhere.* London: Cape, 1970.

Mirror, Mirror on the Wall. New York: Random House, 1972.

Stronghold. New York: Random House, 1975.

The Luxembourg Run. New York: Random House, 1977.

Star Light, Star Bright. New York: Random House, 1979.

The Dark Fantastic. New York: Mysterious Press, 1983.

Very Old Money. New York: Arbor House, 1984.

COLLECTED WORKS

Mystery Stories. With an introduction by Ellery Queen. New York: Simon & Schuster, 1956. Repr. as *Quiet Horror.* New York: Dell, 1959. Includes "The Specialty of the House," "The Cat's-Paw," "The Best of Everything," "The Orderly World of Mr. Appleby," "Fool's Mate," "The Betrayers," "The Moment of Decision," "The House Party," and "Broker's Special."

The Blessington Method and Other Strange Tales. New York: Random House, 1964. Includes "Robert," "The Seven Deadly Virtues," "The Blessington Method," "You Can't Be a Little Girl All Your Life," "Unreasonable Doubt," "The Nine-to-Five Man," and "The Question My Son Asked."

Kindly Dig Your Grave and Other Wicked Stories. Edited and with an introduction by Ellery Queen. New York: Davis, 1975. Includes "Death of an Old-Fashioned Girl," "The Other Side of the Wall," "The Crime of Ezechiele Coen," "The Twelfth Statue," "The Day the Thaw Came to 127," "The Corruption of Officer Avakadian," "The Last Bottle in the World," "Coin of the Realm," and "Kindly Dig Your Grave."

The Specialty of the House and Other Stories: The Complete Mystery Tales, 1948–1978. With an introduction by Stanley Ellin. New York: Mysterious Press, 1979.

UNCOLLECTED STORIES

"The Ledbetter Syndrome." *Ellery Queen's Mystery Magazine* 74, no. 7: 6–15 (17 December 1979).

"Just Desserts." *Ellery Queen's Mystery Magazine* 76, no. 4: 5–13 (6 October 1980).

"Graffiti." *Ellery Queen's Mystery Magazine* 81, no. 3: 7–18 (March 1983).

"Mrs. Mouse." *Ellery Queen's Mystery Magazine* 82, no. 5: 137–156 (October 1983).

"Unacceptable Procedures." *Ellery Queen's Mystery Magazine* 86, no. 6: 3–16 (December 1985).

OTHER WRITING

"Writing a Mystery Novel." In *The Writer's Handbook.* Edited by A. S. Burack. Boston: The Writer, Inc., 1967.

"Stanley Ellin Talks About Himself and His Writing." *Mystery Lover's Newsletter* 2, no. 3: 13–14 (February 1969). An unsigned interview.

"From Our New President." *Mystery Writers' Annual.* New York: Mystery Writers of America, Inc., 1969.

"From Our Former President." *Mystery Writers' Annual.* New York: Mystery Writers of America, Inc., 1970.

"Options, Anyone?" *Mystery Writers' Annual.* New York: Mystery Writers of America, Inc., 1971. Ellin writes about the filming of *The Key to Nicholas Street.*

"Specialty of the House: Edwardian Style." *Mystery Writers' Annual.* New York: Mystery Writers of America, Inc., 1976. Ellin writes about the 1975 Crime Writers International Congress in London.

"The Destiny of the House." *Armchair Detective* 12, no. 3: 195 (summer 1979). Ellin's fiftieth anniversary tribute to Ellery Queen and his discussion of how "The Specialty of the House" was written and published.

"The Specialty of the Shipyard." *Mystery Writers Annual.* New York: Mystery Writers of America, Inc., 1983. Ellin's shipyard work experiences.

ARCHIVES

The Mugar Memorial Library at Boston University holds the manuscript collection of Stanley Ellin.

BIOGRAPHICAL AND CRITICAL STUDIES

Baker, Robert A., and Michael Nietzel. *Private Eyes 101 Knights: A Survey of American Detective Fiction, 1922–84.* Bowling Green, Ohio: Popular Press, 1985. "The Big City Knights of Stanley Ellin," pp. 192–197.

Briney, Robert E. *1001 Midnights.* Edited by Bill Pronzini and Marcia Muller. New York: Arbor House, 1986. Evaluations by Briney of *The Dark Fantastic, The Key to Nicholas Street, The Specialty of the House, and Other Stories: The Complete Mystery Tales, 1948–1978,* and *Star Light, Star Bright* (the last named by John Lutz and Briney), pp. 231–235.

Keating, H. R. F. *Crime and Mystery: The 100 Best Books.* New York: Carroll & Graf, 1987. Essay regarding his inclusion of *Mirror, Mirror on the Wall,* pp. 161–162.

Nevins, Francis M. *The Mystery Fancier* 1, no. 1: 36 (January 1977). In an untitled review of *Kindly Dig Your Grave and Other Wicked Stories,* Nevins also refers to *Mirror, Mirror on the Wall.*

Queen, Ellery. *Mystery Stories.* New York: Simon & Schuster, 1956. Introduction.

———. Queen, Ellery. *Kindly Dig Your Grave and Other Wicked Stories.* New York: Davis, 1975. Introduction.

Symons, Julian. *Mortal Consequences.* New York: Harper & Row, 1972. Discussion of Ellin's work, pp. 174–175.

IAN FLEMING
(1908–1964)

MAX ALLAN COLLINS

JAMES BOND AND Ian Fleming are as intertwined in the public consciousness as are Tarzan and Edgar Rice Burroughs or Mickey Mouse and Walt Disney—popular-culture icons who transcend their status as fictional characters and their creators. The pop-culture phenomenon that is James Bond, however, has become far more famous than his creator, Ian Fleming, whose first-rate escapist fiction is today overshadowed by the films it spawned. More than thirty years after the death of the gifted British author, his character is still fighting evil in novels as well as in the longest-running, most financially successful series in the history of motion pictures—not bad work for a character who started as a lark, a vacation diversion, for Fleming, a journalist. In 1952, while on holiday at Goldeneye, his retreat in Jamaica, Ian Fleming wrote his first novel, *Casino Royale* (1953).

"Horrified by the prospect of marriage and to anesthetize my nerves," Fleming later said, "I sat down, rolled a piece of paper into my battered portable and began" (Zeiger, Popular Library ed., p. 78). Those pages witnessed the birth of James Bond, Agent 007—the British spy with the "license to kill" who has gone on to become one of the most renowned characters in modern escapist fiction.

Early Life and Wartime Experiences

Ian Lancaster Fleming was born in London on 28 May 1908 to a well-to-do family that believed deeply in service to country. His father, Valentine Fleming, gave up his post at the prestigious family banking house in order to run for and win a seat in Parliament in 1910. With the outbreak of World War I, Valentine joined the army and crossed the English Channel to fight the Germans; he was killed at Gillemont Farm in France in 1917 and posthumously awarded the Distinguished Service Order for valor. Ian Fleming grew up idolizing his war-hero father and the patriotic roots of his family, which may help explain why, upon leaving Eton and finishing his early education at a tutorial college in London, young Fleming chose to enter Sandhurst, the British equivalent of West Point, rather than follow his brother, Peter, to Oxford. Loathe to speak of his youth, Fleming's only comment about his childhood was that it was "overprivileged." He went on to say that since all writers seemed to be neurotic, he must be, too, describing himself as "rather melancholic, and probably slightly maniacal as well" (Zeiger, p. 29).

After resigning from Sandhurst in 1927, and despite the fact that his decision infuriated his mother, Fleming chose to leave the army, deciding that his future lay with the Foreign Service. He studied languages at the Universities of Geneva and Munich and became fluent in both French and German, while also learning some Russian. After two years of study, Fleming took the Foreign Service exam. There were five openings at the time, and though Fleming finished a respectable seventh in the examinations, he found himself at twenty-three without a career.

The year was 1931 and the Great Depression had the world in its grip. Fleming, luckier than most, was able to land a job with Reuters News Service through the kindness of Sir Roderick Jones, a family friend and, at the time, the chairman of Reuters. Fleming started in the editorial office and eventually became a reporter. He always spoke highly of the time he spent there, saying, "It was in Reuters that I learned to write fast and, above all, to be accurate, because in Reuters if you weren't accurate you were fired, and that was the end of that" (Zeiger, p. 29).

Fleming was still working as a reporter, though no longer with Reuters, when World War II broke out. Owing in part to his facility with languages, Fleming was recruited to join Naval Intelligence as personal assistant to the director, Admiral John H. Godfrey. Respected and well liked by Fleming, Godfrey served as the model for James Bond's commanding officer, "M." While traveling with Godfrey in Lisbon—an open city in 1941, making it a haven for spies, counterspies, and double agents—Fleming saw high-ranking members of the German intelligence community playing a high-stakes game of chemin de fer in the casino at Estoril. Fleming believed that his Nazi counterparts were using the game as a way to raise money for their war chest; he thought that with his fifty pounds of travel money he, an experienced gambler, could throw a monkey wrench into the Germans' plans. In less than half an hour the Germans relieved Fleming of his money, but one good thing came out of the episode for the novice British agent: this incident became the central scene of *Casino Royale.* In the fictional version, however, James Bond vanquishes the villain, a Russian agent named Le Chiffre, in a similar high-stakes game of chemin de fer.

Another event from his service with British Intelligence that later fueled his fiction was a training exercise during which Fleming had to swim underwater and attach a limpet mine to the underside of a derelict tanker; this act, when performed by Agent 007, became one of the most exciting sequences and set up the climax of *Live and Let Die* (1954). According to Fleming, his wartime experience also included killing a man—although, unlike the cool Bond, Fleming said the event made him ill.

As was true with Dashiell Hammett and his detective characters, Fleming and Bond seemed to carry more credence with readers because there was deemed to be a sense of "truth" in these books—in Hammett's case because he had been a Pinkerton detective and in the case of Fleming because he had been a spy during World War II. Readers seemed to think that because Hammett and Fleming had once held the same type of exciting, dangerous jobs about which they wrote, their characters, and hence their stories, were more realistic than those of their contemporaries. Since several episodes from Fleming's life became part of his fiction, there was a kernel of truth in what Fleming wrote—but these were, after all, novels, and fanciful ones at that. James Bond is, in small part, the man that the author was; even more, however, he is the man Fleming wished himself to be.

Bond descends from a family tree of fictional adventurers that includes Leslie Charteris' Simon Templar (the Saint), Sapper's Bulldog Drummond, and Sir John Buchan's Richard Hannay. Like his fictional forebears, Bond is dashing, with a devil-may-care attitude and a real taste for what he is doing. When Fleming was a young man, these characteristics were often attributed to him, but by the time *Casino Royale* was published, Fleming was forty-three, married, and father to a new son. He had left Naval Intelligence at the end of the war and returned to the newspaper business as foreign manager for the Kemsley newspaper chain. The days when he and Bond could have been considered counterparts had already passed him by.

One trait they did share was a seeming unwillingness to settle down or treat the women in their lives with any compassion. Fleming's marriage on 24 March 1952 to Anne Geraldine Charteris (formerly Lady Rothermere) was a passionate, if somewhat stormy association; his only other serious relationship seems to have been with a woman who served as a dispatch rider during the war—she was killed in her flat by a bomb fragment during the Nazi air raids on London. She seems to have been a precursor to the many Bond heroines who are dispatched quickly and without mercy. In *Casino Royale,* Bond's feelings about the opposite sex are summed up thus: "Women were for recreation. On a job, they got in the way and fogged things up with sex and hurt feelings and all the emotional baggage they carried around" (1954 ed., p. 27). In his younger days, Fleming's reputation as a ladies' man had been very similar to Bond's. With marriage and family, Bond became the author's surrogate, enjoying the rakish life that Fleming was reduced to writing about.

Bond inherited Fleming's ideals of patriotism and service to country—he is every bit as devoted to his duty as Fleming and his own father before him—and he also inherited Fleming's predilections for tobacco and alcohol. Despite not smoking in several of the later movies, Bond has a three-pack-a-day habit in the novels. Until his death at fifty-six, and despite having already had one heart attack, Fleming refused to give in to his doctor's request that he quit smoking. Agent 007 is quite particular that his martinis be "shaken, not stirred"; Fleming's own tastes ran to the quarter bottle of gin per day that he admitted to drinking.

One of the few major differences between author and character was in their sense of humor. Although the author was known to have enjoyed pulling the odd practical joke on his friends, Bond is relatively humorless, particularly in the early books. (The story of how 007 got his name is itself amusing: struggling to decide what to call his hero, Fleming settled on the dullest name he could find—that of the author of one of his favorite books, *Birds of the West Indies,* by an American ornithologist named James Bond.) By *You Only Live Twice* (1964), the twelfth novel, Agent 007 is finally beginning to show a sense of humor. Perhaps by then Fleming was being influenced by the movie versions of his books, because Bond's humor is closer to the characterization of Sean Connery's sardonic nonchalance than the cold, ruthless automaton who first appears in *Casino Royale.*

The style that Fleming maintained for most of the Bond books began with that first novel. The plot was driven inexorably forward by the author's ability to hurtle the reader from chapter to chapter; Fleming always thought the author's chief responsibility was to keep the plot moving. The use of detail, considered a Fleming staple, was infused to heighten the realism, to make the action, no matter how preposterous, believable. The menus of meals, the expensive brand-name products, and the descriptions of gambling incidents give the books their color and offer readers a vicarious entrance into a jet-set world much more exciting than their mundane existences.

First Bond Novels

In *Casino Royale,* Fleming set up what became the basic structure for most of the Bond books. The first third of the novel includes a a teaser in the first chapter, depicting Bond already on the case, followed by a second-chapter flashback showing 007 being ordered on assignment by M. The remainder of the first third follows Bond as he searches for clues, encounters the villain and his henchmen, and cultivates the female romantic interest of the story. The middle third of the Bond stories usually portrays Bond tracking the villain to his lair and almost inevitably being captured. Then, in the final third, 007 dispatches the villain, saves the world, and gets the girl (though he seldom holds on to her for long).

Casino Royale introduces readers to an unemotional, pitiless, humorless Bond whose only saving graces are his conviction about his job and his vulnerability in falling for that very first "Bond girl," Vesper Lynd; once Vesper dies, however, Bond reverts to his previous callousness. The violence is explicit in the novel, with a torture sequence that Fleming never topped for sheer sadism. This is the darkest portrait of Bond in the series, and the writing style is nearly as clipped as the Hammett school of hard-boiled fiction. The introduction of Bond's Central Intelligence Agency cohort, Felix Leiter, gives 007 a friendly, easy-to-like foil and also sets up Leiter as the "cavalry," who frequently rides to Bond's rescue. Leiter, in part, is an obvious attempt to cater to the wide American audience.

The use of gambling, both at the tables and in Bond's high-rolling lifestyle, is a theme that recurs throughout the series, along with the series' main theme of Good versus Evil. *Casino Royale* provides an entire chapter on the nature of Good and Evil, in keeping with Fleming's updating of the adventure novel; that a good man like Bond must stoop to evil means is at least superficially explored throughout the series.

When Fleming sat down to write that first book, he had no idea the sort of phenomenon he was about to create. In fact, with the book finished and his holiday over, he flew back to London with the manuscript in his luggage, thinking he would take the thing home and stick it away on a shelf. Then he had lunch with his friend William Plomer, and everything changed. (Plomer was a poet and novelist who had worked with Fleming in Naval Intelligence and now served as literary adviser to the publisher Jonathan Cape.) During that meal, Fleming innocently asked how one would have cigarette smoke come out of a woman after she had inhaled. He liked neither the terms "exhaled" nor "puffed it out." Plomer studied his friend and said, "My God, you've written a book" (Pearson, 1966, p. 200). Certain that Plomer would tell him the unvarnished truth about his manuscript, Fleming allowed his friend to read it. Plomer loved the story and persuaded Fleming to send it to a publisher; in 1953, Jonathan Cape published *Casino Royale.*

Although the book sold out its initial 4,750-copy British printing, when Macmillan published the American version in 1954, the first Bond adventure went virtually unnoticed. Popular Library published the first American paperback in 1955, changing the title to *You Asked for It;* the reprint's performance was poor. Reviews were mixed. The *Times Literary Supplement* said, "Mr. Fleming's first novel is an extremely engaging affair," while Anthony Boucher's critique in the *New York Times Book Review* stated that Fleming "pads the book to novel length leading to an ending that surprises no one but Bond himself" (Benson, pp. 7, 8).[1]

In late 1954 James Bond also made his first appearance in another medium with the television production of "Casino Royale," starring Barry Nelson, for an anthology series called *Climax.* The plot of the novel remained mostly intact, but Felix Leiter, Bond's friend and cohort with the CIA, was made to be the British agent, while Bond was portrayed as an American spy. Even changing Bond's nationality didn't seem to help—the show garnered a small audience and was soon forgotten.

When *Live and Let Die* appeared earlier that same year, it sold out its initial British printing of 7,500. Again, the American edition, published in 1954, did not fare well, selling only slightly better than its predecessor. Anthony Boucher, continuing to express what came to be a long-standing distaste for Fleming's books, wrote "high spots are all effectively described . . . but the narrative is loose and jerky" (Benson, p. 15). The *Springfield Republican,* on the other hand, said, "The narrative moves at a headlong pace, there is sheer terror enough for a month of comic books, and

1. Raymond Benson's *The James Bond Bedside Companion* (1984) quotes various reviews of Fleming's work that were originally published in other sources.

a climax that is truly exciting. Don't read it unless your nerves are in pretty good shape" (Benson, p. 11).

With *Live and Let Die,* Fleming grew as a writer. Although the second book is marginally less violent than the first, in one suspenseful scene one of Mr. Big's henchmen breaks the little finger of Bond's left hand, an incident so vividly written that when the finger finally cracks, readers not only feel Bond's pain, they can practically hear the finger snap. Fleming's keen attention to detail helped flesh out the story, and his use of the "Undertaker's Wind"—one of the prevailing winds in Jamaica, which "blows all the bad air out of the island at night" (Macmillan ed., p. 121)—as symbolic of Bond's mission on the island gives the book an overriding metaphor.

Friendship also becomes more important in this book. Bond and Leiter spend long stretches of time together, allowing their relationship to grow. In this regard Fleming helps make Bond more human than he was in *Casino Royale;* their friendship also makes the moment much more dramatic when Bond finds out that although Leiter has lost half an arm and half a leg to a shark attack, he will live. The Bond girl in this novel, Solitaire, also receives kinder treatment from the hero. When the young woman is so obviously attracted to Bond that she protects him from harm in their very first meeting, 007 almost instinctively begins to trust all she says despite his suspicion about her true allegiance.

In the spring of 1955, the producer Gregory Ratoff paid Fleming six thousand dollars for the film rights to *Casino Royale;* unfortunately, Ratoff died before the project could move forward. April of that year saw the publishing of *Moonraker,* the third book in the series, a departure for Fleming in that he focuses more on character than plot. Although it is fast-paced, the book does not move at the breakneck speed of the previous Bond books. Reviews were mixed. *Moonraker* is a different sort of Bond book, with fewer action scenes and less location-hopping. The reader for the first time settles into Bond's head and is made privy to his innermost thoughts as he investigates the villain Hugo Drax. More a mystery than an action-adventure yarn, *Moonraker* allows the reader to ride with Bond in his Bentley and visit his flat in Chelsea—James Bond becomes a more three-dimensional character.

When Perma Books released the paperback version of *Moonraker* in America in 1956, however, the title was changed to *Too Hot to Handle.* This edition featured a cover comment characterizing Fleming as "a writer whom the Associated Press calls 'super-special . . . with blows below the belt the way Mickey Spillane delivers them.'" The comparisons to Spillane seemed inevitable. Both men dealt with sex and violence on a more superficially realistic, visceral level than did most other genre writers of their time. Their wartime experiences had taught them both that soldiers returning from the front were looking for more graphic entertainment than had previously been popular. Bond and Mike Hammer, Spillane's detective hero, find no shortage of women to satisfy their emotional and sexual needs; neither is ready to settle down with one woman when so many desirous women are available to them. Both characters were viewed by readers and reviewers as cold-blooded and ruthless, as were the popular heroes of Hammett, Raymond Chandler, and other hard-boiled mystery writers. But these two were different. Where Hammett's Sam Spade is willing to turn in a lover to the police for murder because it is the morally acceptable thing to do, he seems to be little more than a cog in the system. Hammer, though, is willing to commission himself as judge, jury, and executioner when it comes time to dispatch the femmes fatales who have done him wrong; he works beyond the judicial system, serving more as an avenging angel.

Bond is a mixture of the two, passionately patriotic and yet nearly remorseless when it comes to killing. He considers himself part of the system, and his license to kill, which he uses with little compunction, is merely a tool in his battle to do what is right for God and for country. Fleming liked to describe Bond as a knight—a sort of a modern-day Saint George doing battle with the dragons that threatened the peace and tranquillity of his beloved British Empire. In fact, Fleming alludes to that metaphor no fewer than three times in the course of the series. Significantly, Spillane makes the same comparison concerning Hammer, particularly in *The Girl Hunters* (1962).

In *Diamonds Are Forever* (1956), the fourth Bond adventure, the author returned to the breakneck pacing of the first two books. This location-jumping, hair-trigger tempo was already being called "the Fleming sweep" by some reviewers. The trip-hammer tempo keeps things moving fast enough that some of the more contrived elements end up being overlooked. The story also features the return of Felix Leiter. The friendship between Bond and Leiter provides insights into both men. When the book was released in America in October 1956, Boucher wrote, "Fleming's handling of America and Americans is well above the British average; as before he writes excellently about gambling; and he contrives picturesque incidents and a moderately believable love story" (Benson, p. 15).

Having at least partially won over his harshest critic, Fleming was disappointed again when American sales lagged behind those of his homeland. This may explain to some extent why Fleming was growing disenchanted with Bond. In a letter to Raymond Chandler at about this time, Fleming confessed that he didn't think much of his own books. Chandler replied that Fleming was being too hard on himself, although Philip Marlowe's creator did admit that he felt *Casino Royale* was still Fleming's best book. During this period Fleming checked himself into a clinic, Enton Hall, seeking relief from his sciatica. The visit helped relieve his pain, but doctors there advised him to cut back on his intake of cigarettes and alcohol—advice he virtually ignored. One of the doctor's reports noted that already Fleming's heart was showing signs of the onset of serious problems. (The stay probably inspired Bond's similar visit to a clinic in *Thunderball*.)

Together, all these circumstances led Fleming to a monumental decision. In the fifth book, *From Russia, with Love* (1957), the story ends when SMERSH agent Rosa Klebb kicks Bond with a poisoned-tip blade hidden in the toe of her shoe. (SMERSH is the conjunction of two Russian words and means roughly "death to spies.") Klebb is hauled away as the cold numbness creeps over Bond's body; then, "Bond pivoted slowly on his heel and crashed headlong to the wine-red floor."

From Russia, with Love: Bond's Popular Success

From Russia, with Love was an experiment, and a highly successful one. Instead of relying on his usual formula, Fleming did not allow 007 to appear until the eleventh chapter—nearly a third of the way into the book, after introducing Rosa Klebb and a "Russian James Bond," Red Grant, whose training is the focus of the first section. Coupled with the cliff-hanger ending, this approach gave the novel a different structure from that to which Bond fans were accustomed. Many of the familiar elements were tweaked to a higher level in a suspenseful narrative that features well-crafted characterizations mixed with Fleming's usual lush detail, the pacing flying along on the famous Fleming sweep. In *From Russia, with Love,* the reader glimpses Bond's self-doubt, the feeling of boredom that makes him believe he may be "becoming soft." Another humanizing detail about 007 the man is revealed: he is afraid of flying. This more three-dimensional Bond has become a person with whom the reader can identify. No longer simply an inhuman figure bent only on accomplishing his mission, Bond expresses feelings of awkwardness, foolishness, and even guilt (for having almost gotten his friend Darko Kerim killed). This novel is also more sexually provocative than its precursors, not only in the scenes between Bond and the heroine, Tatiana Romanova, but in Fleming's graphic and lusty descriptions of a fight between two women at a gypsy camp, with details that capture even the sweat and smell of the wrestling women. And finally, *From Russia, with Love* served to introduce readers to the gadgetry that became a staple of the film series. Bond is given an attaché case containing secret compartments for money and ammunition as well as two hidden throwing knives, one of which ends up saving the hero in his confrontation with Red Grant, the assassin sent to kill him.

Fleming's readers were left to ponder whether 007 was dead, and the ending gave Fleming time to decide how, or even whether, to continue the series. Whether Spillane's previous abandonment of Mike Hammer in *Kiss Me, Deadly* (1952) influenced Fleming is unknown, but Spillane had left Hammer apparently dying in a burning building at the conclusion of the popular novel.

In the spring of 1956, Fleming started selling his novels to be adapted for a comic strip. He received fifteen hundred pounds per novel and retained script approval; the strip began with *Casino Royale* and was highly successful. At the same time, Fleming was asked to contribute to a series of articles for London's *Sunday Times,* for which he still worked, on diamond smuggling. Fleming's flair for drama helped make the series successful; the articles were published in the autumn, not long after the publication of *From Russia, with Love.* The book, which came out on both sides of the Atlantic almost simultaneously, was an immediate hit. With the publication of his diamond-smuggling series in book form in November 1957, Fleming proved to himself that he could write about something besides Bond. Even though *The Diamond Smugglers* received uneven reviews, Fleming felt less pressure to push himself. *From Russia, with Love* was a hit: sales figures were on his side, and the reviews were generally favorable. Fleming felt vindicated to go on with the series.

Transitional Work and Films

When *Doctor No* was published in England in March 1958, Fleming found himself under attack once again. Writing in the *New Statesman,* the conservative British columnist Paul Johnson called *Doctor No* "the nastiest book I've ever read." He concluded by saying, "Fleming deliberately and systematically excites, and then satisfies the very worst instincts of his readers." In *Twentieth Century Magazine,* Bernard Bergozi cited the "sex, snobbery, and sadism" in the novel (quoted in Benson, p. 17).

With this controversy as an attention-gathering backdrop, *Doctor No* began outselling all the previous Bond novels. When the book arrived in America in June, James Sandoe of the *New York Herald Tribune Book Review* termed it "the most artfully bold, dizzyingly poised thriller of the decade" and stated, "You'd much better read it than read about it" (quoted in Benson, p. 17). *Doctor No* reverted to Fleming's previous plot structure with an opening teaser followed by a scene where Bond receives his assignment from M. Bond, who was lying on a hotel room floor, presumably dying, at the end of *From Russia, with Love,* is resurrected simply through the device of a phone call from M to the physician caring for 007. When the doctor gives Bond a clean bill of health, Fleming has him off and running again.

Beginning with a simple investigation into the disappearance of Commander Strangways and his secretary from their station in Jamaica, Fleming leads Bond into the most fantastic plot of any of the novels to date, pitting the secret agent against one of the best villains of the series. Using a radio beam he has developed, Dr. No intends to deflect U.S. test missiles from their projected course. While it may sound relatively tame in light of the forty years that have passed since its publication, *Doctor No* could easily be viewed as Fleming's first leap into the realm of science fiction. The author also used this book as an opportunity to examine the meaning of power or, as Bond tells Dr. No, the illusion of power. The villain boasts of his own power, but in the end Bond buries him, literally, to prove his point about such a megalomaniacal illusion. And with the return of the Cayman Islands native Quarrel—who had worked previously for British Intelligence and with Bond in *Live and Let Die*—Fleming again demonstrates how highly Bond values friendship; when Quarrel is killed by the tank known as the "dragon," Bond feels a deep sense of loss.

Again Fleming makes the sexual aspect of his tale openly erotic. Honeychile Rider, the novel's love interest, is the most sexually provocative of any of the Bond girls so far. The scenes between Honeychile and Bond are charged with an animal electricity that lifted the sexual tension to new heights, providing an interesting emotional undercurrent to a character so cold that his author attached a number to him.

Although the American reviews, like Sandoe's, were generally more kind than their British counterparts, Boucher was, once again, a voice of negativity: "[*Doctor No*] is 80,000 words long, with enough plot for 8000 and enough originality for 800" (quoted in Benson, p. 17). Boucher's opinion notwithstanding, the James Bond phenomenon was taking off. Fleming and his friend Ivar Bryce began thinking about making their own Bond film. Toward that end, they set up meetings with writer-director Kevin McClory to discuss making 007 a film star as well. The spring of 1959 saw the release of the seventh Bond novel, *Goldfinger*. Sales were brisk, and this time even Boucher jumped on the bandwagon: "The whole preposterous fantasy strikes me as highly entertaining." James Sandoe also praised *Goldfinger*, calling it "a superlative thriller from our foremost literary magician" (quoted in Benson, p. 18).

Goldfinger is less suspenseful than previous entries, but it served as another excavation of the character of James Bond. Agent 007 spends more time reflecting than in previous books, revealing his feelings on women and death. Bond also exhibits more of a sense of humor, constantly taking funny jabs at Goldfinger's henchman, Oddjob. The familiarity of a series has begun to set in, with the tongue-in-cheek attitude of the author more openly displaying itself through increasingly larger-than-life characters and situations drifting ever farther afield from the underpinnings of reality that Fleming's own espionage experiences had previously provided.

Like *Moonraker*, the story is divided into three parts. The three section titles refer to the ways in which Goldfinger encounters Bond: "Happenstance," "Coincidence," and "Enemy Action." This division gives the book a more episodic feel, which may further explain why the suspense level was not up to Fleming's usual standard. Although there is a certain cat-and-mouse quality to the relationship between 007 and Goldfinger, the tension of that relationship is undercut by the fact that Goldfinger's true plan, Operation Grand Slam, a scheme to rob Fort Knox, is only featured in the final third of the book. *Goldfinger* also features the most outrageous (and outrageously named) Bond heroine, Pussy Galore. An ally of Goldfinger's, and presumably a lesbian, Pussy Galore seems an impossible goal for the seducer Bond, yet she winds up in his arms—another example of Fleming's move into knowing self-parody.

A transitional book that marks the end of the early stage of Fleming's writing, *Goldfinger* establishes a style that remained thenceforth essentially the same; while the famous sweep and rich use of detail was left intact, the later books showed a more mature, aware writer who gives the reader stronger characterizations and slightly different themes with which to deal, merging increasingly detailed, loving, descriptive writing with a lighter, self-mocking tone.

With *Goldfinger* selling well and the next book, *For Your Eyes Only*, due to be an anthology of short works subtitled "Five Secret Occasions in the Life of James Bond," Fleming, Bryce, McClory, and Fleming's cohort and friend Ernest Cuneo set about planning the Bond movie. The film was to be directed by McClory and scripted by Fleming and McClory from an original idea, not one of the novels brought to the screen. The four men collaborated, each bringing ideas to the story; in the original version, the Russians were cast as the villains. McClory, however, suggested the idea of an international group of terrorists that was eventually given the name Special Executive for Counterintelligence, Terrorism, Revenge, and Extortion, or SPECTRE (countless Fleming imitators later seized upon a similar use of acronyms). Cuneo added the idea of a massive underwater battle for the climax of the film, and over the next month the group waded through ten different versions in the form of outlines, treatments, or actual scripts. As 1959 drew to a close, however, the film project began to languish, and Fleming took off on a five-week tour to conduct research for a series of stories to be published in the *Sunday Times* on the most impressive cities in the world. The travelogue was eventually turned into the book *Thrilling Cities* (1963), which featured Fleming's impressions of such cities as Hong Kong, Macao, and Monte Carlo; included in the collection was a short story, "007 in New York," which offered James Bond's views on the Big Apple.

Where the 1950s had witnessed the birth of James Bond, the 1960s saw him rise to heights even Fleming had never dared imagine. In the spring of 1960, a collection of five short stories, *For Your Eyes Only,* was released. Reviews of those stories—"From a View to a Kill," "Risico," "The Hildebrand Rarity," "Quantum of Solace," and the title story—were mixed. Fleming's writing was praised, but the story lines were generally considered weak.

"From a View to a Kill" features a female character, Mary Ann Russell, who saves Bond's life, the first time a woman is able to do what Bond could not. "For Your Eyes Only" highlights the relationship between M and 007 and deals with a theme familiar to Bond readers, justice beyond the scope of the law. Agent 007 volunteers to kill the assassins responsible for the murders of some friends of M. Since the killers have escaped to the United States, the British police are of no help—nor are the American authorities. It falls to M, using Bond as his instrument, to take the law into his own hands. "Quantum of Solace" is another experiment for Fleming in that it explores the relationship between a couple whose marriage is falling apart. Bond's only real function in the story is to serve as listener for the governor of Jamaica, who is telling Bond the story in the form of an anecdote. "Risico" is not one of Fleming's better efforts. The author tries to jam too much story into too limiting a vehicle; expanded to a novella, it might have succeeded better. The only point of interest is that for the first time Bond finds himself going to battle with drug smugglers. "The Hildebrand Rarity" features a well-drawn, compact version of the Bond villain: Milton Krest, a perverted, sadistic weakling who buoys his power by beating his wife. Not a true secret-agent tale, "Rarity" allows readers to see Bond's temper come to the fore. Krest is so completely disgusting in his actions that it is all 007 can do not to attack him. When Krest is murdered on his yacht, Bond does little to find out who killed him and later even assists the killer, who is never named, by dropping Krest's body over the side of the boat to a watery grave.

In December 1960, while on a skiing holiday in the Alps with his wife, Fleming met Harry Saltzman, a Canadian film producer who secured a six-month option on all existing and future Bond books, with the exception of *Casino Royale* (that book, originally sold to the late Gregory Ratoff in 1955, had since been sold by Ratoff's widow to a man named Charles Feldman). Bond's status as a pop-culture entity was accelerating on every front. When *Life* magazine printed the list of President John F. Kennedy's ten favorite books in March 1961, *From Russia, with Love* ranked ninth in a group made up primarily of biographies and nonfiction. The impact of being mentioned on that list was immediate. Fleming's sales in the United States skyrocketed.

The same month that Fleming's stock was rising in America owing to President Kennedy's endorsement, *Thunderball* (1961), the ninth book in the series, was published in Great Britain. *Thunderball* was based on the screenplay ideas that Fleming had been batting around with Kevin McClory and screenwriter Jack Whittingham. McClory, who had read an advance copy of the book and seen no acknowledgment of himself or Whittingham, immediately filed for an injunction to keep the book from being shipped, pending resolution of who actually had rights to the story. A judge ruled that the book could be published but that publication should not be seen as slanting the upcoming trial in favor of either Fleming or McClory. It was two more years before the dispute was finally resolved.

None of this wrangling mattered to readers, who flocked to the book, or to reviewers, many of whom had fallen into a pattern of resigned faint praise for Bond and his creator. In *Thunderball,* Fleming imbued Bond with a greater sense of his own mortality and an awareness that as he got older, his body was not what it had once been. This may have been the author's way of confronting his own failing health or simply of bringing Bond to maturity. In any event, *Thunderball, On Her Majesty's Secret Service* (1963), and *You Only Live Twice* (1964), the three books that make up what is commonly referred to as the Blofeld Trilogy, are the most introspective and darkly lugubrious books of the series while retaining Fleming's love for descriptive writing and tongue-in-cheek self-parody. The real world of espionage, at this point, has been left far behind. (Ironically, however, *Thunderball*'s "far-fetched" plot, concerning terrorists stealing nuclear weapons, anticipates a threat that in today's world is only too real and grim a possibility.)

In Ernst Stavro Blofeld, the head of SPECTRE, Fleming finally gave Bond a villain of equal scale, a Moriarty to Bond's Sherlock Holmes. If Bond represents all that is good, then Blofeld is surely the personification of evil. A shrewd, ruthless man, Blofeld has always been successful at his treachery, until he meets Bond, an adversary able to match his own cunning. Whether it is a joke or a subliminal commentary, no one can say, but Blofeld's birthday, 28 May 1908, is the day Ian Fleming himself was born.

The popularity of Bond was blossoming, and the stress and tension of managing that growing "property" got the better of Fleming. On 12 April 1961, he had a major heart attack and spent the next month in the London Clinic. Again his physician warned him to cut down on tobacco and alcohol and to get plenty of rest; again Fleming ignored the doctor's advice, telling his friends he had no intention of spending his life in a manner that he could not enjoy.

During this hospital stay, to battle the doldrums, Fleming wrote the only children's book of his career, *Chitty Chitty Bang Bang* (1964), the story of a magical car, the eccentric family that owns it, and the adventures they have in it. A film followed in 1968. Interestingly enough, Fleming's American counterpart, Mickey Spillane, also dabbled in writing children's books late in his career. Perhaps the element of boyhood adventure displayed in both authors' writing for adults made it inevitable that they would one day write directly for children. While Ian Fleming recuperated in France, Saltzman, his film-option time running out, joined in partnership with another man interested in bringing 007 to the big screen. Albert ("Cubby") Broccoli had more connections in the film industry than did Saltzman, but Saltzman had the options. From that dilemma Eon Productions was born, and by summer the pair had a deal with United Artists for six films, the first of which would be *Thunderball.*

Richard Maibaum, a former collaborator of Broccoli's, was hired to write the screenplay. The project became bogged down owing to McClory's injunction, and the substitute first production became *Doctor No.* By October, the struggling actor (and former Mr. Universe) Sean Connery beat out a thousand hopefuls for the role of James Bond. Connery lacked the scar on the right cheek, the comma of black hair over his right eyebrow, and the cruel blue eyes that had become synonymous with Bond, but he did have charisma, and his portrayal gave Bond something he had often lacked in the novels—a sense of humor. Fleming's initial reaction to the casting of Connery was negative, but once he saw the actor in action he changed his mind—so much so that Bond, who had merely been a British secret agent in the early novels, eventually was given Scottish heritage like the actor who was portraying him. In fact, at the end of *The Man with the Golden Gun* (1965), Bond rejects the opportunity for knighthood because he is "a Scottish peasant, and will always feel at home being a Scottish peasant" (New York ed., p. 157). Other Bonds, including Roger Moore, George Lazenby, Timothy Dalton, and Pierce Brosnan, limned the role successfully, but Connery's singular, masculine charisma forever branded him "the real James Bond" to most film (and Fleming) fans.

The Spy Who Loved Me (1962), the tenth book in the James Bond series, represented another experiment for Fleming. Bond doesn't even enter until two-thirds of the way through the novel, and the story is told from the point of view of Vivienne Michel, the female character (in the British edition, Vivienne Michel was listed under Fleming's name as co-author). In a foreword to the American edition, Fleming wrote that he had found the manuscript on his desk with a note from Vivienne claiming that every word was "the purest truth." This Bond novel seems to be the one in the series that has the least middle ground where Fleming's fans are concerned; it tends to be either loved or hated. Because the story is told from Vivienne's point of view, the novel is perhaps more popular with women readers; there has even been speculation that Fleming wrote the book in that manner to cultivate a larger female following for his sexist hero.

However slight its narrative, *The Spy Who Loved Me* presents Fleming's best female characterization. Since Vivienne tells the story, readers are finally allowed inside the head of one of the Bond girls, to better understand the psyche of such a creature and to better understand Bond's irresistible appeal to women. As a spy story, however, the novel makes a good Harlequin romance. Fleming expected mixed reviews and was not disappointed. He was, however, disappointed by the violent attacks hurled his way by critics who called some episodes from Vivienne's early life "pornographic." Female critics seemed to be less harsh, but most criticism was so biting, and so widespread, that the book was eventually banned in several countries and suffered a long delay in publication of the paperback edition in England.

In October 1962, with his health again in question, Fleming attended the world premiere of *Doctor No.* "Those who've read the book," he said, "are likely to be disappointed, but those who haven't will find it to be a wonderful movie" (Benson, p. 24). The spring of 1963 saw the publication of *On Her Majesty's Secret Service,* including a limited edition of 250 that were numbered and signed by Fleming. The cover featured the Bond family coat of arms complete with the motto The World Is Not Enough. This time Fleming captured both the critics and the book-buying public. When New American Library released the American version, it topped the *New York Times* best-seller list for more than six months.

Further insight was given into Bond's character in this novel. It opens with a disgruntled and bored Bond drafting a letter of resignation. Although he is stoic and even grim in the early books, depression is never in the character of 007. Bond's resignation is put on hold, however, while the superspy once again tracks down Ernst Stavro Blofeld. In the course of his efforts to find the villain, Bond encounters La Comtesse Teresa di Vicenzo, known as Tracy, and falls in love with her. Tracy is a wounded human being, a "bird with a wing, perhaps two wings down," (New York ed., p. 29) as Bond notes, but something about her fascinates him. When Blofeld's stronghold is destroyed, Blofeld himself escapes, and Bond takes the biggest step of his life by marrying Tracy. They both seem truly happy, until their bliss is shattered by gunfire. Before he passes out, Bond spies Blofeld in the passing assassination car, and then he turns his head to see his beloved Tracy dead. What had been the basis of the usual Bond thriller—lots of action, loving description, fast-paced plot, lovely women, and high adventure—comes to a sad, bloody end, leaving the reader to contemplate whether true happiness is something that a man like Bond can ever find.

In May 1963, the American film version of

Doctor No was released to good reviews and solid box office sales. James Bond finally had a secure foothold in the United States. The second film, *From Russia, with Love,* premiered to favorable reviews in London in October of the same year. November 1963 was a busy month for Fleming. A Bond short story, "The Property of a Lady," appeared in *The Ivory Hammer: The Year at Sotheby's,* a story Fleming had been commissioned to write for the famous auction house. "The Property of a Lady" went on to be published in *Playboy* magazine as well as in the anthology *Octopussy* (1966). Fleming's travel book, *Thrilling Cities,* was finally released in both Great Britain and the United States, and on 19 November his legal battle with Kevin McClory over the ownership of *Thunderball* finally went to court.

The case was settled out of court the next month, when McClory was granted the film rights to *Thunderball* in exchange for allowing the novel to revert back to Fleming. A small proviso stated that the title page would carry the line "This story based on a screen treatment by Kevin McClory, Jack Whittingham, and the author." McClory was also granted rights to the material that he, Whittingham, and Fleming had worked on. This material, known as "the Film Scripts," eventually became the basis for McClory's own Bond film, *Never Say Never Again.*

January 1964 found Fleming entrenched at his Jamaican home, Goldeneye, writing *The Man with the Golden Gun* and feeling uneasy. The book wasn't progressing to his satisfaction; he wrote to his old friend William Plomer that he was running out of steam and that the novel needed massive rewriting. In March 1964, possibly aware that his health wasn't good, Fleming sold 51 percent of his stock in Glidrose Productions, the company that owned James Bond, to Booker Brothers, a company run by a golfing chum, Lord Campbell, for an estimated $280,000.

Agent 007's adventure in Japan, *You Only Live Twice,* was published that same month. Many reviewers ranked it among the best Bond novels, which now numbered twelve. *You Only Live Twice* opens with James Bond depressed, lamenting the loss of Tracy. In order to help him snap out of it, M orders him to Japan to negotiate the acquisition of the new Japanese Magic 44 secret cipher system. The Japanese emissary, Tiger Tanaka, informs Bond that he will hand over Magic 44 if Bond will perform a service for Japan. The Japanese government needs Bond to assassinate a certain Dr. Shatterhand, who profits by catering to Japanese suicidal traditions. As the mission unfolds, Bond discovers that Dr. Shatterhand is really his old enemy Ernst Stavro Blofeld. In the end, Bond gains his revenge by strangling Blofeld, but when the mountain fortress explodes, 007 is struck in the head by a piece of debris and loses his memory. He is fished from the sea by Kissy Suzuki, with whom he lives for the next year. Then, after noticing the name of a Russian city in a newspaper, Bond decides to go there to track down his identity. When he leaves, Kissy is there to see him off, never telling him that she is carrying his baby. This was a cliff-hanger that rivaled that of *From Russia, with Love.*

The Bond Legacy

April 1964 saw favorable response from both critics and the public to the film version of *From Russia, with Love.* Bond was rolling along now, a pop-culture juggernaut that seemed unstoppable, even in the face of its creator's demise. On 11 August, Ian Fleming had his second major heart attack, and it was fatal. By the time of Fleming's death, the *New York Times* estimated, he had already earned $2,800,000 from his books alone. But surprisingly, and even ironically, it was after Fleming's death that Bond's popularity truly skyrocketed. Spies were starting to turn up everywhere in books, television, and movies. Ignited by the success of Agent 007, a sort of secret-agent groundswell began. Television shows like *The Man from U.N.C.L.E., I Spy, Secret Agent, The Avengers* (which actually began in 1961 in response to Fleming's popularity at home), and *Mission Impossible* sprang up regularly over the next couple of years. Dean Martin starred in a series of amiably awful movies featuring Donald Hamilton's spy hero, Matt Helm. James Coburn made two films as superspy Derek Flint, and Michael Caine portrayed the more realistic working-class spy Harry Palmer, the antihero of a series by author Len Deighton, in the films *The Ipcress File, Funeral in Berlin,* and *The Billion Dollar Brain.*

As for Bond himself, next to the Beatles, he had become Britain's biggest export. Lines of toys, games, puzzles, and even a 007 magic set found their way to the marketplace. Consumers were snapping up 007 collector cards, toiletries, clock radios, and even lingerie. James Bond, the fictional lark Ian Fleming had begun a dozen years before, was a full-blown pop-culture phenomenon. He and spies like him seemed to be taking over the world. Shirley Eaton, who portrayed Jill Masterson in the film, appeared on the cover of *Life* magazine covered in gold paint to publicize the impending release of *Goldfinger.* The film became a major box office hit, and Bond's success for the future was guaranteed.

In April 1965, *The Man with the Golden Gun,* finished by Fleming's literary executors, was published posthumously. Kingsley Amis, who in 1968 wrote the next Bond novel, *Colonel Sun,* under the pseudonym Robert Markham, described *The Man with the Golden Gun* as "a sadly empty tale, empty of the interests and effects that for better or worse, Ian Fleming made his own" (quoted in Benson, p. 30). The reviews were only slightly more flattering when the book was released in the United States the following August. Despite the tepid reception from critics, the book went on to become a best-seller on both sides of the ocean.

The novel opens with a riveting, if somewhat abrupt, scene in which Bond, brainwashed while in Russian custody after traveling there at the end of *You Only Live Twice,* attempts to assassinate M. After the brainwashing is reversed, Bond is presented with the difficult assignment of terminating a KGB-controlled assassin, "Pistols" Scaramanga. It is M's conclusion that the mission will either prove Bond fit to resume his duties or kill him. After several somewhat dubious encounters with the villain, a shoot-out erupts on a train. Bond's trusty ally, Felix Leiter, is there to bail out 007, but Scaramanga manages to jump from the train and escape into the jungle, where he and Bond have a final showdown.

Easily the weakest book in the series, *The Man with the Golden Gun* begins well, but the Bond of this book is a throwback to the humorless robot of *Casino Royale.* Whether this was a failed experiment by Fleming or the fault of his literary executors is unknown. Possibly the book is a rough draft, never given its author's final polish; it reads more like a detailed synopsis or treatment than a finished work. Perhaps had Fleming been able to properly complete it, the novel would be a less sad farewell to this classic character of escapist fiction.

Double O Seven, James Bond: A Report, by O. F. Snelling, published in 1964, had been the first book to deal with the writings of Ian Fleming. In 1965 Jonathan Cape published the first "official" Fleming study, *The James Bond Dossier,* by Kingsley Amis. In the same year, a double bill featuring *Doctor No* and *From Russia, with Love* was released to movie theaters in America and abroad, and the films made more money than they had upon their original release. Near the end of the year, *Thunderball* became the highest-grossing Bond film to date.

In 1966 *Octopussy,* a collection containing two of Fleming's Bond stories, was released to a mediocre response. "Octopussy" is a morality story about a villain, Major Dexter Smythe, in which Bond serves only as a catalyst to start Smythe on a path that culminates in the man's suicide. "The Living Daylights" finds Bond in Berlin to cover the escape of a British agent who is the target of an assassin known as Trigger. For three days Bond watches the building he is sure Trigger will be shooting from when the agent tries to escape from the East. As a diversion, Bond begins watching a blonde woman carrying a cello case who passes the building every day. On the night the British agent finally attempts his escape, Trigger leans out a window to shoot. Bond has the killer in his sights when he realizes Trigger is the blonde woman he has been watching. Although the British agent escapes unharmed, 007's hesitation keeps him from killing Trigger, only wounding her instead.

The story is of interest in that it shows Bond considering the morality of his career. After the incident, when he is chastised for only wounding Trigger, Bond's comeback is, "Okay. Maybe it will cost me my Double-0 number" (New York ed., p. 92). Complacency is a new emotion for Bond, an unexpected insight into the secret agent's psyche. In later editions of *Octopussy,* a third story, "The Property of a Lady," was added to the set. This story, the one Fleming had originally written for *The Ivory Hammer: A Year at Sotheby's,* was not one of his best, and its inclusion in this collection can be seen only as an afterthought to fatten the volume. The plot is limited, and the resolution occurs with hardly any effort made by Bond.

Since Fleming's death the series has pressed on in books by other authors and, of course, the films. *Tomorrow Never Dies,* released in December 1997, became the eighteenth official Bond film. *Never Say Never Again,* the film finally made by Kevin McClory, which marked the return of Sean Connery as Bond, and *Casino Royale,* the completely absurd comedy version of Bond, are not among those on the "official" list flowing from the Broccoli-Saltzman production team and their heirs. After Amis did *Colonel Sun,* John Gardner took over the Bond novels, retiring from the series after a long run.

In James Bond, Ian Fleming created a superhero for the last half of the twentieth century. Sophisticated, smart, and coldly ruthless when he had to be, 007 has become a major entry in the pop-culture lexicon. Fleming's "pleasant diversion" easily outlasted the mimics and fakes, and James Bond, as absurd as he may be, still stands tall as the best-known spy in the world. The underlying realism that Fleming was able to bring to his stories because of his experience as a spy turned out to be exactly what the public was looking for. Like his contemporary Mickey Spillane, Fleming raised the stakes on sex and violence in a postwar society that seemed starved for the sort of grittiness that these men brought to their prose. Although not destined to be remembered as a great writer, Fleming has to be acknowledged as a superior storyteller. His ability to keep readers turning pages with ever-increasing urgency is a gift delivered to few writers, and Fleming made fine use of his gift in his relatively short fiction-writing career. By numbers of books, Fleming's output was not large, but his twelve novels and two collections make up an enviable legacy.

At the author's funeral, his friend William Plomer, who had been the first to encourage Fleming to seek publication for *Casino Royale,* referred to Fleming as "on top of the world, with his foot on the accelerator, laughing at the absurdities, enjoying discoveries, absorbed in his many interests and plans, fascinated and amused by places and people and facts and fantasies, an entertainer of millions, and for us a friend never to be forgotten." And as an epitaph, Fleming himself probably said it best in Bond's obituary in *You Only Live Twice,* given by the secretary (and Bond girl) Mary Goodnight: "I shall not waste my days trying to prolong them. I will use my time" (New York ed., p. 152). Those few words go far in explaining the life of Ian Fleming.

Selected Bibliography

WORKS OF IAN FLEMING

NOVELS

Casino Royale. London: Jonathan Cape, 1953; New York: Macmillan, 1954. Published as *You Asked for It.* New York: Popular Library, 1955.

Live and Let Die. London: Jonathan Cape, 1954; New York: Macmillan, 1954.

Moonraker. London: Jonathan Cape, 1955. U.S.: *Too Hot to Handle.* Perma Books, 1956.

Diamonds Are Forever. London: Jonathan Cape, 1956.
From Russia, with Love. London: Jonathan Cape, 1957; New York: Macmillan, 1957.
Doctor No. London: Jonathan Cape, 1958.
Goldfinger. London: Jonathan Cape, 1959.
Thunderball. London: Jonathan Cape, 1961; New York: Viking, 1961.
The Spy Who Loved Me. London: Jonathan Cape, 1962.
On Her Majesty's Secret Service. London: Jonathan Cape, 1963; New York: New American Library, 1963.
You Only Live Twice. London: Jonathan Cape, 1964; New York: New American Library, 1964.
Chitty Chitty Bang Bang: The Complete Adventures of the Magical Car. Illustrated by John Burningham. London: Jonathan Cape, 1964.
The Man with the Golden Gun. London: Jonathan Cape, 1965; New York: New American Library, 1965; Wilmington, Del.: Swan, 1966.

COLLECTED WORKS

For Your Eyes Only. London: Jonathan Cape, 1960. Includes "From a View to a Kill," "Risico," "The Hildebrand Rarity," "Quantum of Solace," and "For Your Eyes Only."
Octopussy. London: Jonathan Cape, 1966; New York: New American Library, 1966. Includes "Octopussy," "The Living Daylights," and "The Property of a Lady."

OTHER WORKS

The Diamond Smugglers. London: Jonathan Cape, 1957.
Thrilling Cities. London: Jonathan Cape, 1963. Includes "007 in New York."

BIOGRAPHICAL AND CRITICAL STUDIES

Amis, Kingsley. *The James Bond Dossier*. London: Jonathan Cape, 1965.
Bennett, Tony, and Janet Woolacott. *Bond and Beyond: The Political Career of a Popular Hero*. London: Macmillan, 1987.
Benson, Raymond. *The James Bond Bedside Companion*. New York: Dodd, Mead, 1984.
Brosnan, John. *James Bond in the Cinema*. London: Tativy Press, 1972.
Eco, Umberto. "Narrative Structure in Fleming." In *Gender, Language, and Myth: Essays on Popular Narrative*. Edited by Glenwood Irons. Toronto: University of Toronto Press, 1992. Pp. 157–182.
Pearson, John. *The Life of Ian Fleming*. London: Jonathan Cape, 1966; New York: McGraw Hill, 1966.
———. *James Bond: The Authorized Biography of 007*. London: Sidgwick and Jackson, 1973; New York: Morrow, 1973.
Pelrine, Eleanor, and Dennis Pelrine. *Ian Fleming: The Man with the Golden Pen*. Wilmington, Del.: Swan, 1966.
Snelling, O. F. *Double O Seven, James Bond: A Report*. New York: New American Library, 1964.
Tanner, William. *The Book of Bond; or, Every Man His Own 007*. London: Jonathan Cape, 1965; New York: Viking, 1965.
Van Dover, J. Kenneth. *Murder in the Millions: Erle Stanley Gardner, Mickey Spillane, Ian Fleming*. New York: Ungar, 1984.
Zeiger, Henry A. *The Spy Who Came In with the Gold*. New York: Duell, Sloan, and Pearce, 1965; New York: Popular Library, 1965.

Dick Francis

(b. 1920)

RACHEL SCHAFFER

TWO MAJOR THREADS weave through Dick Francis' life and work: riding horses and writing about horses. From a childhood spent schooling and showing horses through service as an airplane fitter and pilot during World War II, a distinguished career as a steeplechase jockey in England from 1946 to 1957, and a second career after retirement as a racing columnist and writer of mystery novels set in the racing world, Francis' life experiences and inherent talents have made him one of the most popular authors of mystery fiction in the world. He once said that the novel he was at work on in the late 1990s, *10-Lb Penalty* (1997), his thirty-sixth mystery and thirty-eighth book, would be his last, but he considered retiring earlier in his career without making good on his threat. Whenever he does retire, readers around the world will be very sorry indeed to see an end to the publication of a new Dick Francis mystery each year.

The Early Years

Richard Stanley Francis was born on 31 October 1920 on his maternal grandfather's farm in Pembrokeshire, Wales, near the town of Tenby. His mother, Catherine Mary Thomas, and father, Vincent Francis, were both Welsh, and a love of horses descended to him from both sides of his family. His father and paternal grandfather were both jockeys, his father also managed a hunting stable during Francis' childhood, and his maternal grandfather rode to hounds and bred hunters. During summers and holidays, Dick and his brother, Douglas, were sent to their grandfather's farm, where they rode the resident donkey bareback, a technique their father believed was the best way for riders to learn balance.

Francis has often described the moment when he first considered himself a professional horseman (for example, in *The Sport of Queens,* pp. 13–14). When he was five years old, Douglas challenged him to ride the donkey backward over a small fence. Although he took several falls, he persevered until he accomplished the feat and thus earned sixpence, his first riding fee. He says in *Sport,* "In my heart, from that moment, I became a professional horseman" (p. 14).

Francis always detested going to school, attending Maidenhead County Boys' School in Berkshire on average only three days a week; he considered it a waste of time and much preferred helping his father school horses, in the process learning to ride by trial and error, rather than through formal lessons, and with shouted instructions from his father and overheard advice from the resident riding master as guidance. As he gained in skill and experience, he began showing ponies and horses, winning a variety of pony and riding classes, including a drawerful of rosettes for "Best Boy

Rider." The love of his young life, however, was hunting, not for the killing of the fox but for "the glorious freedom of making my way across country as fast as I could and as boldly as I dared," at the same time "making it a point of honour never to go through a gate if it could be avoided" (*Sport,* p. 25).

Francis says that he does not remember ever making a conscious decision to become a jockey; it was simply something that he knew from childhood he was going to do. He was short enough to consider becoming a flat jockey during his early years, but he eventually grew eighteen inches in less than four years and redirected his interest toward steeplechasing, where greater height and longer legs for gripping the horse's sides are advantages in staying seated over jumps.

Francis finally left school for good at the age of fifteen and continued to help train and show the horses from the yard his father managed. After a year, he renewed his efforts to become an apprentice jockey at a racing stable and begin riding as an amateur, but the trainer who had agreed to take him on when he turned seventeen died, and he had no luck with other trainers. Then his parents decided to start their own stable, and Francis was needed to help them run it, which he did until the outbreak of World War II.

As the war progressed, the family business declined to the point where Francis had little to do. In 1940 he attempted unsuccessfully to join the cavalry and decided the next best choice was to become a pilot. This wish, too, was denied as the ranks were full when he applied, but on the advice of a deceptive recruiting officer, he joined up as an airframe fitter with the intention of remustering later, only to be laughed at for his naïveté when he tried to change assignments. Demonstrating the persistence that would characterize so many of his novels' protagonists, he continued to submit an application for flying school every month, even while chasing the enemy back and forth across Egypt, servicing Royal Air Force airplanes.

Finally, worn down by Francis' persistence, the RAF reassigned him to fighter pilot training in 1943 where he learned to fly a Tiger Moth—and loved it. But by that time, the war was drawing to an end, and no new fighter pilots were needed. Instead, Francis was assigned to fly a Wellington bomber, whose sluggishness, compared with the single-engined aircraft on which he had learned to fly, reminded him later in life of "some weary old three-mile steeplechasers" (*Sport,* p. 43). He was also trained to fly a glider to drop soldiers across the Rhine but again was not needed for actual duty and finished out the war escorting surrendering German ships into British ports.

When the war ended, Francis was twenty-five years old, quite an advanced age to become an apprentice jockey, but he refused to give up his dream. He resumed work at his father's stable and contacted every trainer he had any connection with, finally finding a place as secretary to the retired jockey George Owen in Cheshire, England, straightening out his paperwork and riding horses in races when the owners did not mind having a novice jockey in the saddle because of their low expectations for the horses' chances. Thus began Francis' years as an amateur jockey.

The Riding Years

Francis' first ride as an amateur for Owen was in a novice steeplechase on Russian Hero (later winner of the Grand National, the only major steeplechase Francis never won); they came in a respectable fourth. He rode fairly often after that on horses whose owners did not expect much from them—"the bad horses, the green horses, and the tired old horses," as Francis called them in *Sport* (p. 59)—gaining valuable experience but not winning a single race. It was not until the next spring, after thirty-nine tries, that he won his first race, and later the same day he won his second. By the end of the season, he had won nine races of a total of sixty-two, which placed him respectably in the middle of the amateur jockeys list. In his last race of the season, he broke his collarbone. Soon after, he was married, on 21 June 1947, to his fiancée, Mary Margaret Brenchly, with his arm in a sling. He and Mary eventually had two sons, Merrick, formerly a horse trainer who became owner of a horse transport business, and Felix, a onetime high school physics teacher who left his job to become Francis' business manager.

Toward the end of his second season as a jockey for Owen, Francis had become so successful as an amateur that the National Hunt Committee, the governing body of British steeplechasing, gave him an ultimatum: in the future, he must restrict himself to amateur races or turn professional. He chose the latter. In 1948 Lord Bicester, owner of some of the best chasers in England, asked Francis to become his second-string jockey and ride for him when his regular jockey was unavailable. Eventually, as he gained experience and a reputation for excellence, he was asked to ride regularly for two additional stables, an arrangement that continued for three seasons, until, in 1953, Peter Cazalet, trainer of the Royal horses, asked Francis to ride regularly for him, an extremely prestigious career move for a British jockey. From then until his retirement, Francis primarily rode the Queen Mother's horses.

Two high points mark Francis' riding career. The first was being named Champion Jockey for the 1953–1954 racing season, when he won 76 of 331 races ridden, more than any other jockey for that year. The second came in the 1956 Grand National, when he rode the Queen Mother's great steeplechaser, Devon Loch. What happened as they jumped the final fence and headed up the straight in first place has become one of the most famous stories in British racing history. From one stride to the next, Devon Loch's hindquarters apparently collapsed underneath him, and he sprawled spread-eagled on the course, unable to finish the race, though completely unhurt. Francis never had another chance at winning the Grand National, and his loss on Devon Loch proved to be one of the greatest disappointments of his life.

By that time in his racing career, at the age of thirty-six, Francis had accumulated an impressive record of injuries from racing falls: twelve broken collarbones of a total twenty-one broken bones (not counting ribs, which do not usually interfere with riding), five broken noses, and an assortment of concussions, contusions, and dislocations. During most of his career, he had been able to bounce back from an injury with all the flexibility and speed needed by a top jockey, but that ability began to decline with age. The owners he rode for, anxious that he not get hurt, did not refuse to let him ride their good horses but withheld the difficult ones, the ones that might cause him injury. To Francis, this was a sure sign of the beginning of the end: when trainers start trying to protect a jockey from injury, the rides soon become more and more limited until the jockey is eased out of competition entirely.

A respected friend urged Francis to retire while he was still at the top of his profession, advice that he reluctantly followed. He officially retired in February 1957 with a career total of 345 wins, 285 seconds, and 240 thirds of 2,305 races—and with no idea what to do next. Within two weeks, however, he received invitations to become a race judge (a rare honor for a jockey) and a race commentator, both of which he accepted. He was also asked by the *London Sunday Express* to lend his name to four articles on racing, to be ghost-written by staff members. Francis had been made the same kind of offer a couple of years earlier, to let a ghostwriter pen his "autobiography"; he had insisted on writing it himself and had finished most of it by the time he was told that professional jockeys could not be published, and he put the manuscript aside. Still, the experience had shown him that he could, in fact, write, and with the same kind of insistence on honesty and integrity that appears in his novels' protagonists, he accepted the *Express*'s invitation and wrote the first few articles himself, which were followed by a regular column written as the *Express*'s racing correspondent. The column appeared for the next sixteen years (1957–1973).

The Writing Years

After his retirement from racing, Francis finished writing his autobiography, *The Sport of Queens,* which appeared in 1957, sold out its first printing within a week, and is still in print. It presents a detailed picture of his early years, his war experiences, his career path and the motivation that drove him to excel, and the nature of a jockey's life, with its technical requirements, its hard work and boring routine, and its ultimate joys and rewards. The 1981 revised edition also contains an afterword covering his retirement, subsequent jobs, and the development of his career as a novelist.

The style of this nonfiction work is quite different from that of his later novels; it is more journalistic and unvarnished, with little of the dramatic and poetic language that highlights his fiction, but when he discusses racing, there are flashes of his later trademark humor and eloquence. Many of the themes and autobiographical details that he incorporates into his novels also appear here, especially the values of determination, hard work, personal integrity, and modesty.

For several years after his retirement, Francis and his family managed to live on a reduced income in the house they had built near Blewbury, England, but eventually he concluded that in order to take care of "the threadbare state of a carpet and a rattle in my car" (*Sport,* p. 239), he needed a more lucrative job. Since, according to J. Madison Davis, "he had always liked mystery thrillers" (p. 14) and had so much experience in racing to draw on, he decided to try writing a racing mystery. The result, *Dead Cert* (1962) was favorably received, and with its publication, Francis began a thirty-five-year pattern of producing one new mystery approximately every year.

The method Francis used in writing his autobiography has proved over the years to be the only one that works for him, and he has continued to use it for each novel. He says in *Sport* that he knew nothing about rough drafts and stages of editing or that editors existed and would help polish his prose before publication. He believed "that a book as first written was what got (or didn't get) published, and I wrote accordingly. The first shot had to be the best I could do" (p. 240). His description of his writing process reveals the discipline, patience, and attention to detail that appear as regular character traits in his mystery protagonists:

> When I write any one sentence, I think first of all of what I want it to say. Then I think of a way of saying it. Usually at this point I write it down (in longhand, in pencil, in an exercise book) but if I think that the form my thought has taken is a bit dull or pompous I just sit and wait, and after a while a new shape of words drifts into my head, and I write that down instead. Sometimes I rub bits out and try again, but once the sentence looks all right on paper I go on to the next one and repeat the process, and so on. It's all pretty slow as one sentence can sometimes take half an hour. (p. 241)

The next day, he reads what he has written and perhaps adds a sentence or makes minor changes in wording or grammar, but whenever he has tried more extensive rewriting, he has felt that "although what I'm attempting may be different, it won't be *better* and may well be worse, because my heart isn't in it" (p. 240–241). After he has written a couple of chapters, he types them out (nowadays on a word processor), and they are essentially finished. He summarizes the overall process: "I start consequently at Chapter 1, page 1, and plod on to THE END; and although by page 1, I have a fair idea of what the book is going to be about in general, I never know exactly what is going to happen. The story grows while I write it" (p. 241). He used to take the entire process for granted, he says, but now he finds it "increasingly mysterious" (p. 241), a satisfyingly ironic comment from a mystery writer.

Francis acknowledges two main influences on his writing process: his experience writing for a newspaper, which, he says, taught him discipline and economy of language, and his wife, Mary, who initially enouraged him to start writing and who provides feedback on grammar and phrasing. Francis has said, "She's my only editor, really" (Gleick, p. 140) and "we write as a team" (Cooper-Clark, p. 239). Mary has also done much of the research for the nonracing content of Francis' novels, such as learning to fly a small plane when he needed information for *Flying Finish* (1966) and taking up photography for *Reflex* (1981).

One further influence on Francis' writing, suggested by Paul Bishop, among other critics, is his experience as a jockey: "His pacing [in his novels] is impressive, and perhaps it isn't too farfetched to suppose that he is able to pace a novel so well because of what he learned about pacing a horse through a race" (p. 146). Francis himself compares his ability to balance action with description in his novels to riding a race:

> You keep your high moments until the last furlong and then you produce your horse to win. When you're jumping the big fences, you're placing your horse to meet that fence. When you're writing your story, you're placing your words so that the reader will be excited at the right moment and, then, easing off after you've jumped the fence. ("Dick Francis: An Interview," p. 10)

Francis' reliance on his firsthand experience with riding to strengthen the authenticity of his novels and avoid making technical mistakes is a principle he extends to every aspect of his writing. Perhaps more than most writers, he writes strictly from experience. He will not write about a place unless he has seen it himself or about specialized information outside his areas of expertise unless he or his wife has done extensive research into it. Thus, during the seven months of each year when he is not writing, Francis and his wife travel and do research in preparation for each new book. Robert Cantwell says that "Francis' imagination is strictly literal; when he describes a scene he duplicates some place he knows" (p. 87) and gives an example. A scene in *Blood Sport* (1967) in which a horse is led along a mountain path comes from horseback riding in the mountains of Wyoming. Cantwell quotes Francis as saying, "I couldn't have written that if I hadn't been there" (p. 81). He has also lived and worked in Florida and the Cayman Islands.

Many of the other details that make Francis' novels feel completely authentic also come from his real-life experience. In fact, he has incorporated much of his life history, as well as his insider's knowledge of horses and racing, into his novels. Various novels explain the minutiae of how jockeys go about earning a living and advancing their careers (*Nerve* [1964], *Enquiry* [1969]); how to plan and ride a winning race (*Dead Cert, Nerve, Break In* [1986]); how the jockeys' valet system, pension fund, and racing fees work (*Nerve*); and much more. Several novels also make use of Francis' experience with racing injuries and their effects on the human body, including the pain, the jockey's unique ability to heal rapidly and ride while injured, and the loss of those abilities with age. The details of the dislocated shoulder that causes ex-jockey Jonah Dereham so much pain in *Knockdown* (1974) as well as the method needed to put it back in place and the webbing strap that helps keep it there come from Francis' own experience with this type of injury. So does the description of the iron lung (and the accompanying emotional turmoil) in which James Tyrone's wife must spend her days in *Forfeit* (1969): Francis' wife herself contracted polio fairly soon after their marriage and was temporarily confined to an artificial respirator. *Forfeit* also makes use of Francis' experience at the *Sunday Express:* Tyrone is a racing correspondent for a newspaper.

However Francis writes his novels, the results are works that have been very well received by the reading, reviewing, and rewarding public. His books have been translated into more than two dozen foreign languages, published in many different formats, and dramatized on radio and television (Sid Halley of *Odds Against* [1965] was the inspiration for six episodes of a British series called "The Racing Game"). *Dead Cert* was filmed twice, in British and Russian movie versions. According to Daisy Maryles, his recent titles have been printed in enormous quantities—295,000 copies of *Wild Horses* (1994) and 303,000 copies of *Come to Grief* (1995), for example—and all of his titles are still available in print. Book reviewers consistently praise his latest effort, and according to Bishop, "Most critics agree that even a subpar Francis novel is still superior to those of many other thriller writers at the top of their form" (p. 146). William L. DeAndrea summarizes his writing career succinctly: "He became one of the finest, most acclaimed, and most popular mystery writers in history" (p. 126).

Several of Francis' novels have received prestigious awards in the field of mystery fiction. *For Kicks* (1965) won a Silver Dagger (second place) from the British Crime Writers Association in 1965; *Forfeit* won the Edgar (Allan Poe) award from the Mystery Writers of America for 1969; *Whip Hand* (1979) won both the Edgar and the Gold Dagger (first place) for 1979 and 1980, respectively; and *Come to Grief* won Francis a third Edgar in 1996. Francis also received the Cartier Diamond Dagger for lifetime achievement from the British Crime Writers Association in 1989 and the Grand Master Award for lifetime achievement from the Mystery Writers of America in 1996. He was named an Officer of the Order of the British Empire in 1984.

In addition to his autobiography and mystery novels, Francis has also written a biography of jockey Lester Piggott, several short stories, the screenplay for the British film version of *Dead Cert,* and a variety of articles for horse-related publications.

The Mysteries

Within the mystery genre, Francis is generally classified with hard-boiled mystery writers, but while he does share many traits with such authors as Raymond Chandler and Dashiell Hammett, his British sensibility and personal aesthetics carry his novels well beyond the hard-boiled tradition, with their greater range of themes and characterizations. Francis himself prefers to call them "adventure stories" rather than detective novels (Cooper-Clark, p. 225). Marty Knepper believes that Francis "has taken the risk of violating the conventions of the genre, even challenging the assumptions on which it is based" (p. 242), and therefore "is more interesting and challenging because his work both follows and critiques the hard-boiled detective fiction formula" (p. 231). His treatment of plot, character, and theme together with his use of language result in the unique blend of content and style that Davis calls the "Francis formula," a formula that has kept his works popular with readers and critics alike for more than thirty years.

The plots of Francis' mysteries are essentially hard-boiled, focusing on corruption and its effects on the innocent, though many plot elements reach far beyond the hard-boiled formula, delving into a broader range of crimes, motivations, and professions. The crimes vary in nature; murder does not always play a part, and the motivations range from greed to jealousy, from power lust to flat-out psychosis. Francis has said that each of his stories begins with "a dirty deed," which he bases on actual events (Carr, p. 219). In his earliest novels and the majority of those that follow, the dirty deed affects the area that Francis knows best: horse racing. In each case, horses, the people who work with them, or the racing game itself (or all of them) is threatened in some way: in *Dead Cert,* horses are being tripped during races in order to predetermine the outcomes; in *Nerve,* the careers of promising jockeys are being ruined by a jealous psychopath; in *Odds Against,* a wealthy land developer has designs on a racecourse; and so on. In developing the criminal plot elements, Francis has also explored every aspect of working with racehorses: riding them as a jockey in *Enquiry,* training them in *Bonecrack* (1971), buying and selling them as a bloodstock agent in *Knockdown,* racing them as an owner in *High Stakes* (1975), transporting them professionally from place to place in

Driving Force (1992), and solving crimes against them and/or racing as professional investigators in *The Edge* (1988), *Slayride* (1973), and *Come to Grief*, among others.

With his fifth novel, *Flying Finish*, Francis begins to broaden the ways in which he integrates horses and racing into his plots: while horses still appear in a variety of roles in the stories, as breaks from the mystery-related action or as background color, the mysteries themselves may not concern racing directly. In *Flying Finish*, for example, the air transport company for shipping horses that protagonist Henry Grey works for is actually cover for the transport of another kind of cargo entirely. Similarly, Charles Todd of *In the Frame* (1976) paints horses for a living, and scenes at racetracks are included in the novel, but the mystery itself centers around a burglary ring using art galleries as fronts and paintings of horses as bait. *To the Hilt* (1996) focuses on an embezzlement scheme aimed at a brewery; horses and racing figure in the plot only because the protagonist's stepfather owns a steeplechaser and sponsors a race.

Prominently featured or not, horses are always present in Francis' novels in one way or another, an immutable element of his formula that his readers expect and look forward to. (Knepper [p. 248] refers to a novel in Amanda Cross's mystery series in which protagonist Kate Fansler comments that she still reads Dick Francis "because she liked him and to discover how he would work the horse in this time" [*The Question of Max*, p. 117]. Kate is not alone.) Because he knows them intimately, he can write realistically and vividly about the animals themselves and every aspect of the racing world. The racing scenes he integrates into most of his novels bring their own brand of excitement and enjoyment to the plot, whether or not they are related to the mystery. When Francis describes Kit Fielding's races in *Break In* or Rob Finn's in *Nerve*, readers become vicarious participants and experience as closely as they ever will what it feels like to hurtle "over large jumps on semi-wild half-ton horses at thirty miles an hour" (*Come to Grief*, p. 34).

Another typical plot element in Francis' novels, one that on the surface connects him closely to the hard-boiled tradition, is putting the protagonist in danger to show how tough he is and how well he handles physical abuse. Each novel, with rare exceptions, contains at least one action scene that results in damage to the hero. In several, those with jockey protagonists, there are injuries from racing falls, which are usually unconnected to the central mystery, a difference from most hard-boiled novels. In others, the damage results when the protagonist gets too close to the villain(s) and becomes a threat, as in the typical hard-boiled mystery. Francis' protagonists, like hard-boiled detectives, never go looking for a fight, but unlike their hard-boiled colleagues, a few admit they do not even know how to fight (Steven Scott of *High Stakes*, for one). Even so, most do acquit themselves well when given the chance, exhibiting extreme courage and some skill even while taking a beating.

However, as Knepper points out, the vast majority of Francis heroes "suffer a great deal of violence but administer very little" (p. 238). Sooner or later, whether they fight back or are captured too quickly or sneakily to struggle, almost every protagonist is inevitably subjected to the "pain set piece," in which the villain inflicts severe physical and sometimes mental punishment—at times nothing less than the most sadistic torture—on the undeserving hero (Schaffer, "The Pain"). In *Nerve*, for example, the twisted villain hangs protagonist Rob Finn by his arms from a bridle hook, douses him with cold water, and leaves him to freeze to death. In *Flying Finish*, a sadistic young punk tortures Henry Grey by shooting parallel lines along his ribs. In *Smokescreen* (1972), the villain handcuffs Edward Lincoln to the steering wheel of his car and abandons him to die in the sweltering African wilderness. In each case, the hero's mental and physical suffering is described in explicit first-person detail so that readers are forced to identify with him, suffer with him, and eventually triumph over the pain with him. There is nothing titillating or romantic about the violence inflicted in Francis' novels, as Knepper carefully points out, a "significant difference," she says, between Francis and other hard-boiled writers (p. 240).

The most graphic and moving scenes of this type are those featuring private investigator Sid Halley, who appears in three Francis novels, *Odds Against, Whip Hand,* and *Come to Grief.* Sid is an ex-jockey, forced to retire when a racing fall cripples his left hand, which he refuses to have amputated and keeps hidden in his pocket, a source of much grief and embarrassment to him. In all three novels, the villains pinpoint Sid's hands as his greatest weakness and the means for coercing him to abandon the cases he is investigating.

In *Odds Against,* Sid is asked by his ex-father-in-law, Charles Roland, to investigate the attempted takeover of Seabury racecourse by wealthy Howard Kraye. In a quintessential Francis torture scene, Sid is tied to a chair while Kraye tries to force him to reveal the location of incriminating information. In spite of his fear, Sid continues to withhold the information, so Kraye smashes his wrist with a poker:

> He used all his strength and with that one first blow smashed the whole shooting match to smithereens. The poker broke through the skin. The bones cracked audibly like sticks.
>
> I didn't scream only because I couldn't get enough breath to do it. Before that moment I would have said I knew everything there was to know about pain, but it seems one can always learn. Behind my shut eyes the world turned yellow and gray, like sun shining through mist, and every inch of my skin began to sweat. There had never been anything like it. It was too much, too much. And I couldn't manage any more. (Pocket ed., pp. 211–212)

But, of course, he does manage more, remaining silent when Kraye "put the tip of the poker on my shattered bleeding wrist and gave a violent jerk" (p. 212) and telling him "where to go" only when Kraye threatens to do it again. Even then, "where to go" turns out to be where a colleague is spending the night and can initiate a rescue. Sid never has any intention of telling Kraye the truth, but he knows Kraye will not believe him unless he is convinced he has broken Sid.

Sid's encounter with Kraye results in the amputation of his left hand, leaving him with one good hand and a new fear: losing it, too, and with it, his independence. Francis explores this threat to Sid's courage in two more mysteries, each with its own pain and fear set piece. In *Whip Hand,* the villain threatens to blow Sid's right hand off with a shotgun, and Sid, restrained and helpless, describes his reaction: "All the fear I'd ever felt in all my life was as nothing compared with the liquefying, mind-shattering disintegration of that appalling minute. It broke me in pieces. Swamped me. Brought me down to a morass of terror, to a whimper in the soul. And instinctively, hopelessly, I tried not to let it show" (Pocket ed., p. 108). Although Sid gives in to his fear and temporarily flees the country, his integrity will not allow him to close his eyes to the villain's continuing wickedness, and he exposes him. When the villain returns to exact his revenge with the shotgun, Sid refuses to give him the satisfaction of showing the fear he feels, and the villain backs down because of the inevitable public reaction against him for turning a former jockey-hero into a helpless cripple. "I'd be better off killing you," he says to Sid. "I thought numbly that I wasn't so sure, either, that I wouldn't rather be dead" is Sid's unspoken reply (p. 314).

Sid's final confrontation with the fear of losing his one good hand takes place in *Come to Grief* when the villain tightens a wrench around his right wrist as a form of physical and mental torture. Sid says:

> I tried to dislodge myself from the wrench but my hand was too numb and the grip too tight. I found it difficult to think. My hand was pale blue and gray. Thought was a crushed wrist and an abysmal shattering fear that if the damage went on too long, it would be permanent. Hands could be lost.
>
> Both hands. Oh, God. Oh, *God.* (pp. 289–290)

These pain set pieces serve a number of functions in Francis' novels. At the most visceral level, they increase the dramatic impact of the story and force readers to identify with the protagonist's suffering—and with his reasons for suffering. They also allow Francis to explore two aspects of the protagonist's character: the ability to bear pain in a good cause and recover rapidly, a jockey's stock in trade, which Francis knows well from personal experience, and the willingness of a single man to sacrifice himself for the greater good of society. The first trait may well be a matter of personal pride, for Francis himself was injured many times and rode races more than once with a broken bone or other injury. The second trait goes deeper than mere pride, however: the determination to defeat evil and protect the innocent is a fundamental part of the moral code that all of Francis' protagonists share.

Francis' cast of characters is another familiar component of his formula and, like his plots, blends hard-boiled traditions with his personal vision. Primary among his players are his protagonists, whom Elaine Bander considers "neither hard-boiled nor soft-boiled (I think of them as six-minute heroes)" (p. 11). They are certainly as tough and stoic as any hard-boiled detective and often as lonely, but unlike the typical hard-boiled hero, their personalities are fully developed and multidimensional. Unlike the true loners, they crave love, tenderness, and close personal relationships in their lives, and usually, by novel's end, they have found them.

Francis' use of protagonists who are, for the most part, amateur detectives and his use of a different protagonist in almost every novel (the exceptions being Sid Halley in three novels and Kit Fielding in two) are two large departures from the serial hard-boiled professional detectives of Raymond Chandler or Mickey Spillane. Francis has said that the professionals he knows often have minds too much like the criminals they pursue, and since he is writing in the first person, essentially conveying his own personality to the reader, and believes that he himself has no criminal tendencies, he prefers to make his protagonists amateurs (Cooper-Clark, p. 233). He varies his protagonists rather than creating a series character for an equally pragmatic reason: he finds that creating a new protagonist each time helps him "to fill the book up" (Cooper-Clark, p. 232). Knepper points out that it also allows the protagonists more freedom to change over the course of each novel, becoming fully dynamic rather than exhibiting the same character traits throughout a series (p. 227), and it allows Francis to explore different facets of his own personality as well.

Francis has sometimes been accused of writing about the same protagonist in all of his novels, although they go by different names, come from different social backgrounds, have a variety of professions, and, to a certain extent, display different personality traits and outlooks on life. He himself has said, "My heroes are all very similar. They are the sort of chaps I'd like to meet" (Weeks, p. 12). What all Francis protagonists have in common, and what gives them their core similarity to each other and, to a certain extent, to hard-boiled detectives in general, is their shared moral code emphasizing integrity, honor, decency, self-sacrifice, perseverance, courage, and an ultra-heroic stoicism in the face of pain and suffering. Francis acknowledges that his protagonists reflect aspects of himself (Cooper-Clark, p. 229), especially since they embody values and character traits that he considers essential in a good man, but, he admits, "I'd like to think I was as good as the heroes I create, but I'm not" (Weeks, p. 12).

The worth of the protagonist is at some point tested in each novel through a personal threat to his safety or the safety of someone or something he cares about, whether a person, horses, or racing. Sooner or later, he must choose between giving in to the villain's demands in order to save his own skin or risking himself or others in order to defeat evil and restore order, the recurring theme of mystery fiction. In every case, readers can rely on him to do the right thing, even at the expense of extreme physical and mental suffering. Sid

Halley's actions illustrate the true heroism of the typical Francis protagonist. He cannot be bribed or beaten into submission. Time after time he asks himself why he is exposing himself to danger, and time after time the response is the same: because it is the right thing to do. He cannot just stand by and do nothing while innocent parties are being hurt.

Francis' protagonists share other characteristics as well. The majority are loners, without wife, children, or parents and with serious doubts about their ability to resolve the problems they face. Like hard-boiled detectives, they distrust authority and avoid going to the police whenever possible, preferring to handle criminal matters in their own way. They are often emotionally reserved, keeping the depth of their feelings to themselves to such an extent that others often consider them cold. They are also modest to a fault and cultivate their underestimation by others, especially the villains. It is other "good" characters—usually mentors, bosses, and surrogate fathers—who recognize their true excellence and eventually offer some form of reward and recognition.

The vast majority of Francis' protagonists also bear a variety of emotional or physical burdens of some kind, private fears and tragedies, such as injuries, handicaps, a damaged or dead loved one, a painful divorce, or scars left by a painful childhood. They have taught the men who must cope with them sympathy, understanding, and tolerance for others' weaknesses. For example, Halley's crippled hand makes him take a special interest in Zanna Martin, a minor character in *Odds Against* who was badly disfigured in a fire. He encourages her to overcome her embarrassment about her scars and rejoin society, and in the process he himself undergoes a degree of healing and personal growth.

Francis' villains, unlike his heroes, have no moral code to govern their behavior. They are driven by greed, jealousy, or the lust for power, and many are as sadistic as Howard Kraye of *Odds Against*. Like the protagonists, they come from a variety of backgrounds, though they are mostly well-to-do, even aristocratic, in order to throw readers off the scent, Francis says (Carr, p. 214). Barry Bauska points out that several villains in earlier novels had telltale hyphenated or foreign names (p. 244). Davis considers Francis' villains "exaggerated, less human than demonic" (p. 114), total contrasts to the incorruptible, multidimensional protagonists. And John Welcome comments, also in direct contrast to the protagonists' reverential and protective attitude, "[For the villains] the racing game is an instrument for social revenge, or a means to an illegal fortune" (Gunton and Stine, eds., p. 152). In general, the villains complement the heroes as perfect foils in character and behavior.

Francis' treatment of women characters in his novels is rarely hard-boiled, but neither are they as fully developed as his male protagonists. He has never attempted a female protagonist because, he says, "I can't really place myself in a woman's mind" (Weeks, p. 12), and since he restricts himself faithfully to writing about what he knows, he does not simply assume the same kind of knowledge about women that he does about his male protagonists, who are, after all, reflections of himself. Davis believes that Francis has an essentially chivalrous and nonsexist attitude toward women. They are rarely harmed in his novels, and they are never stereotyped as evil vixens or femmes fatales. Likewise, there are very few female villains, and those who are involved in crimes have only minor roles. His women characters are usually the protagonists' love interests or supporting players—family members or workers in the racing industry. Many female characters are professionals—trainers (Annie Villars in *Rat Race*, [1971]), an air traffic controller (Sophie Randolph in *Knockdown*), even a jockey (Alessia Cenci in *The Danger* [1984]). Professionals or not, most share a desire for independence and economic self-sufficiency as well as equality in their romantic relationships.

Francis has been criticized for the lack of development of his female characters, many of whom are basically no more than stock foils for the male leads, there to support them emotionally, provide romantic interest, and occasionally play a small role in helping resolve the mystery. Davis criticizes him for making many of the love interests emotionally dependent on the hero, but that relationship is usually reciprocated: the hero himself also becomes emotionally dependent on his love, finding something that has been missing from his life and growing as a person because of her. For example, Henry Grey of *Flying Finish* and Matt Shore of *Rat Race,* both described (and describing themselves) as emotionally reserved to the point of coldness, return to full, feeling humanity when they fall in love.

Knepper, on the other hand, praises Francis' characterizations of women "as human beings as they exist in the real world" (p. 234). In some of his earlier novels his women do seem static and one-dimensional—noted primarily for their attractiveness or their need of rescuing. By his later works, they come to display more interesting and unique personalities. For example, Rob Finn's mother, in *Nerve,* is described as "not a motherly person in any way" (Pocket ed., p. 23). Alexander Kinloch's mother, in *To the Hilt,* at first seems to be just the same, but by the end of the novel, Al realizes that "her ultra-controlled outer face" (p. 256) does not in fact hide a lack of love; like so many of Francis' protagonists, she simply prefers to keep her emotions private. Moreover, while in Francis' early novels any love interest who initially hesitates to enter a relationship with the protagonist inevitably capitulates by novel's end, in later books, such as *Decider* (1993) and *To the Hilt,* it is the protagonists who often compromise what they want in accepting admittedly imperfect relationships with their wives for the sake of the women's happiness.

One other category of characters must be included in any discussion of Francis' writing because they play such integral roles in his novels. Like the cowboy heroes of the American West (just one similarity among many), Francis' protagonists have a strong attachment to horses in general and to those they work closely with in particular. Beyond the motivation they offer the villains as targets and the heroes as innocent victims in need of protection, horses also offer clues to the solution of the mystery and, more important, often function as full-fledged personalities in their own right. To the jockeys who ride them, horses are partners—admired, respected, and, in most cases, beloved colleagues as individually unique as any human. Their jockeys work to understand their personalities and quirks and what it takes to get the best performance from them in races. The best horses offer their riders the most fulfilling moments of their lives, when horse and rider become one and winning is their shared goal. Kit Fielding of *Bolt* (1987), with all the eloquence Francis can muster, says, "The result was racing at its sublime best, an unexplainable synthesis at a primitive level and undoubtedly a shared joy" (Fawcett ed., p. 64). Even difficult horses with troublesome personalities are admired and respected as long as they exhibit the will to win, as does the difficult Template in *Nerve.* His jockey, Rob Finn, has mixed feelings about him: "He was not a kind horse: there was no sweetness in his makeup and he inspired admiration rather than affection; but I liked him for his fire and his aggressiveness and his unswerving will to win" (p. 194).

Thematically, Francis begins at the same point as classically hard-boiled writers like Chandler and Hammett, that is, the "dirty deed," and explores the struggle between good and evil, right and wrong, honesty and corruption. But he also brings to his novels a very British sensibility, that of an honorable gentleman in the most chivalrous sense of the term, so that, as Francis himself says, " 'Right' must come out in the end in my stories" (Cooper-Clark, p. 233)—there are no morally ambiguous endings in his novels.

Also in the tradition of hard-boiled themes, many Francis protagonists lack families: a number are orphans, or have only one parent, or are estranged from their parents. However, a key difference from the hard-boiled tradition is that missing, estranged, or on good terms, parents play a large role in the protagonists' lives, and family relationships form an ongoing theme in Francis' novels, especially that between father and son, as Albert Wilhelm (1991), Davis, and many other critics have noted. Fathers have a powerful influence on the protagonists' character development. When they are absent, the protagonists often seek out surrogate fathers. When they are present, the fathers are often remote or stern (as Francis' own father was), reluctant to praise but quick to criticize. Francis says in his autobiography that he learned a great deal from being raised this way (*Sport*, pp. 20–21), as do several of his protagonists with similar parents; nonetheless, the themes of father-son conflicts and the search for an accepting, emotionally accessible father figure are common in Francis' novels, as in *Bonecrack* or *Proof* (1985). As a result, the sons have to come to terms with their unsatisfactory relationships and look for validation within themselves, a part of the growth and maturation of the protagonist that is another recurring theme.

Other themes in Francis' novels are even less typical of hard-boiled stories; they are more the stuff of "serious" literature. For example, coming from a still very class-conscious society, Francis often includes class observations and conflicts in his novels. His protagonists vary widely in their social backgrounds, some very poor, others middle class, and a few very wealthy. Their different backgrounds allow Francis to explore the frictions between members of different classes from varying points of view, emphasizing that class and money themselves do not determine the worth of the man. More important is what he does with his life. In *Odds Against,* for example, Halley remembers how his lower-class, illegitimate birth and working-class profession of jockey at first made his wealthy father-in-law suspicious of him, but when the older man discovers that Sid can play chess and actually challenge him, he learns that intelligence is not necessarily linked to class, occupation, or even education. The class conflict from the protagonist's point of view is reversed in *Flying Finish,* where wealthy Lord Henry Grey is the victim of lower-class Billy's sadistic animosity toward the upper class. As Francis shifts the social status of his protagonists, he forces his readers to identify with a variety of class positions and face their own stereotypes of what makes a man. However, sympathetic though he is to members of all classes and aware of their struggles and aspirations, Francis' deep respect for the nobility and overall approval of the social status quo are revealed in his protagonist's attitudes and actions, which are unlike those of the typical hard-boiled hero.

As well as Francis handles plot, characters, and theme, for some readers his use of language is their main source of enjoyment. His style, tone, wit, humor, and phrasing skills show an innate talent for writing that is all the more surprising in a man who left school at age fifteen. The writer and critic Anthony Boucher's review of *Nerve* has often been quoted by other critics to capture the unlikely transition between Francis' careers—and his excellence in both of them: "One's reaction is not, 'How can a great jockey write such a good novel?' but rather, 'How can such an excellent novelist know so much about steeplechasing?' " (Bauska, p. 244). Francis is the first to give credit to his wife for her editing help, but it is his unique voice that emerges from the process.

The tone and style of Francis' writing are not particularly hard-boiled: British reserve and understatement, plus frequent self-deprecating irony, predominate over toughness and wisecracks. This approach works especially well when his first-person narrators describe their bouts with pain and suffering, whether from racing injuries or villainous punishments. Davis remarks that the contrast between their cruel suffering and the cool tone Francis uses to describe it highlights the stoic nature of the heroes and increases the impact on the reader (as in Sid Halley's ordeal, quoted earlier). On the other hand, Francis on occasion does use a more hard-boiled style, especially when his protagonists are the most alone, depressed, or even suicidal, as in *Blood Sport* and *Rat Race.* For example, the short, staccato sentences and grim tone of the very first paragraph of *Blood Sport,* featuring the suicidal British government agent Gene Hawkins, could have been written by Raymond Chandler:

> I awoke with foreboding. My hand closed in a reflex on the Luger under the pillow. I listened, acutely attentive. No sound. No quick surreptitious slither, no rub of cloth on cloth, no half-controlled pulse-driven breath. No enemy hovering. Slowly, relaxing, I turned half over and squinted at the room. A quiet, empty, ugly room. One third of what for want of a less cozy word I called home. (Pocket ed., p. 7)

Matt Shore of *Rat Race* is similarly depressed and similarly hard-boiled in his language, for example, when he describes a not very honest horse owner: "The next time I saw him, he was holding a well-filled glass and adding substantially to his paunch, while muttering belligerently to a pasty slob who housed all his brains in his biceps" (Pocket ed., pp. 106–107).

But this style is relatively rare in Francis, and he uses language in other ways, too. His economy with words and his ability to phrase things just right provide him with extremely sharp tools for his social and psychological insights. In one social observation from *Blood Sport,* Hawkins notices a woman sunning herself by a swimming pool in Las Vegas, "inviting heat-stroke and adding to a depth of suntan which would have got her reclassified in South Africa" (p. 173). A psychological observation from the same novel, in which Gene comments on the naïveté of a minor character: "Like most law-abiding citizens, she had not grasped that a criminal mind didn't show, that an endearing social manner could coexist with fraud and murder. 'Such a *nice* man,' the neighbors say in bewilderment, when Mr. Smith's garden is found to be clogged with throttled ladies. 'Always so pleasant' " (p. 165). Here word choice ("endearing social manner," "clogged with throttled ladies") and a puckish sense of humor combine to produce language that is very British and totally Francis—and certainly not hard-boiled.

This example illustrates that Francis can also be extremely funny as well as witty, and he incorporates a great deal of humor of different types in his novels. He uses black humor as comic relief during and after his pain set pieces or whenever things become too serious, and he sometimes includes comic characters for the same reason. One example is Chico Barnes in *Odds Against,* who asks Halley—who has been shot and is lying in a hospital bed—"Haven't you got a telly then? Cheer you up a bit, wouldn't it, to see some other silly buggers getting shot?" (p. 12). He can also be downright whimsical at times, showing a degree of lightheartedness that might surprise some readers. In *The Edge,* for example, the protagonist, working undercover on a train as a waiter named Tommy, signs himself in when he visits the horse car as "Tommy Titmouse" (p. 105); one of the lightest scenes Francis has ever written occurs in his first novel, *Dead Cert,* during a poker game between the protagonist and the young children of his best friend, who has recently been killed. First, one of the children chides him for not paying attention to the game, and they discuss what it means to be in love:

> "What's in love?" said William, who was playing tiddly-winks with his chips, to Henry's annoyance.
>
> "Soppy stuff," said Henry. "Kissing, and all that slush."
>
> "Mummy's in love with me," said William, a cuddly child. (Pocket ed., p. 84)

Then William picks up his hand:

> His eyes and mouth opened wide. This meant he had at least two aces. They were the only cards he ever raised on. I saw Henry give him a flick of a glance, then look back at his own hand. He discarded three and took three more, and at his turn, he pushed away his cards. I turned them over. Two queens and two tens. Henry was a realist. He knew when to give in. And William, bouncing up and down with excitement, won only four chips with three aces and a pair of fives. (p. 84)

Francis' wit, sharp eye for physical and psychological detail, and way with words combine to excellent effect in one of his writing fortes: thumbnail sketches of characters, both major and minor. In one to four sentences, he can capture the essence of people—how they dress and think, their social backgrounds, their attitudes toward people and life, and much more. For example, Rob Finn of *Nerve* describes a taxi driver: "He was a big sturdy man of about fifty, weather-beaten like a sailor, with eyes that looked as if they had seen everything and found most of it disappointing" (p. 172).

Conclusion

Dick Francis has had two careers in his life and has reached the pinnacle in both of them, gaining recognition and awards as jockey and as writer. He has made lasting contributions to the hard-boiled mystery genre, expanding the formula to highlight the racing world and develop his own vision of what it means to be a moral man in an often corrupt world, clinging to a code of honor that often brings him pain and suffering, but also great satisfaction and the gratitude of those who recognize and benefit from his excellence. Francis' protagonists consistently exhibit honorable behavior and express values that reflect those of their creator. Francis provides role models for his readers, not just escapist entertainment, and raises serious moral issues for their consideration. He says in *Sport:* "I've found that moving everywhere simultaneously in two different worlds—horses and books—has given me perhaps wider understandings of humanity than either might have done on its own" (p. 247), and he has used those understandings to make lasting contributions to the mystery field. Bauska credits him with continuing growth as a writer, claiming that he "is becoming less a writer of thrillers and more a creator of literature—while remaining, as he always has been, splendidly readable" (p. 244). Francis has had a far greater effect on the world through his novels than through his racing career, but it is the latter that will always be most precious to him. The conclusion of *Sport* (p. 247) puts his many achievements into perspective—*his* perspective: "I was a jockey for a little over ten years . . . and despite all the satisfactions that have come my way since, those years, in retrospect, were the special ones. The first growth; the true vintage. The best years of my life."

Selected Bibliography

WORKS OF DICK FRANCIS

NOVELS

(American paperback editions of Francis' novels are published by Harper & Row [through *Whip Hand*] and Pocket Books [through *Come to Grief*]. Selected page references from those editions are noted in the text.)

Dead Cert. New York: Harper & Row, 1962; Pocket Books, 1975.
Nerve. New York: Harper & Row, 1964; Pocket Books, 1975.
Odds Against. New York: Harper & Row, 1965; Pocket Books, 1975.
For Kicks. New York: Harper & Row, 1965; Pocket Books, 1975.
Flying Finish. New York: Harper & Row, 1966.
Blood Sport. New York: Harper & Row, 1967; Pocket Books, 1975.
Forfeit. New York: Harper & Row, 1969.
Enquiry. New York: Harper & Row, 1969.
Rat Race. New York: Harper & Row, 1971; Pocket Books, 1978.
Bonecrack. New York: Harper & Row, 1971.
Smokescreen. New York: Harper & Row, 1972.
Slayride. New York: Harper & Row, 1973.
Knockdown. New York: Harper & Row, 1974; Pocket Books, 1976.
High Stakes. New York: Harper & Row, 1975.
In the Frame. New York: Harper & Row, 1976.
Risk. New York: Harper & Row, 1977.
Trial Run. New York: Harper & Row, 1978.
Whip Hand. New York: Harper & Row, 1979; Pocket Books, 1981.
Reflex. New York: Putnam, 1981.
Twice Shy. New York: Putnam, 1982.
Banker. New York: Putnam, 1982.
The Danger. New York: Putnam, 1984.
Proof. New York: Putnam, 1985.
Break In. New York: Putnam, 1986.
Bolt. New York: Putnam, 1987; Fawcett Crest, 1988.

Hot Money. New York: Putnam, 1987.
The Edge. New York: Putnam, 1988; Fawcett Crest, 1988.
Straight. New York: Putnam, 1989.
Longshot. New York: Putnam, 1990.
Comeback. New York: Putnam, 1991.
Driving Force. New York: Putnam, 1992.
Decider. New York: Jove, 1993.
Wild Horses. New York: Jove, 1994.
Come to Grief. New York: Jove, 1995.
To the Hilt. London: Michael Joseph, 1996.
10-Lb Penalty. London: Michael Joseph, 1997.

NONFICTION

The Sport of Queens: The Autobiography of Dick Francis. New York: Otto Penzler, 1957. Reissued by the Armchair Detective Library, 1993.
A Jockey's Life: The Biography of Lester Piggott. New York: Putnam, 1986. Published in Great Britain as *Lester: The Official Biography.* London: Michael Joseph, 1986.

SHORT STORIES

"Carrot for a Chestnut." *Sports Illustrated,* 5 January 1970: 48–59. Repr. in *Stories of Crime and Detection.* Edited by Joan Berbrick. New York: McGraw-Hill, 1974; *Ellery Queen's Faces of Mystery.* Edited by Ellery Queen. New York: Davis, 1977; and *The Dick Francis Treasury of Great Racing Stories.* Edited by Dick Francis and John Welcome. New York: Fawcett Crest, 1989.
"The Day of the Losers." *Ellery Queen's Mystery Magazine,* 9 September 1981: 6–16.
"A Day of Wine and Roses." *Sports Illustrated,* 7 May 1973: 106–112, 116–119. Repr. as "The Gift" in *Winter's Crimes 5.* Edited by Virginia Whitaker. London: Macmillan, 1973. Also repr. as "The Big Story" in *Ellery Queen's Crime Wave.* Edited by Ellery Queen. New York: Putnam, 1976.
"Nightmare." In *Ellery Queen's Searches and Seizures.* Edited by Ellery Queen. New York: Davis, 1977. Pp. 141–149.
"Twenty-one Men Good and True." In *Verdict of Thirteen: A Detection Club Anthology.* Edited by Julian Symons. New York: Ballantine, 1978. Pp. 44–59. Repr. in *Best Detective Stories of the Year: 1980.* Edited by Edward D. Hoch. New York: Dutton, 1980.

INTERVIEWS

Cooper-Clark, Diana. "Interview with Dick Francis." In her *Designs of Darkness: Interviews with Detective Novelists.* Bowling Green, Ohio: Bowling Green University Popular Press, 1983. Pp. 225–239.
"Dick Francis: An Interview." *Writer* 103, no. 7: 9–10 (July 1990).
Frances, Dick. *CBS News Sunday Morning,* 27 April 1997.

BIOGRAPHICAL AND CRITICAL STUDIES

Axthelm, Pete. "Writer with a Whip Hand." *Newsweek,* 6 April 1981: 99–100.
Bander, Elaine. "The Least Likely Victim in Dick Francis's Banker." *Clues* 13, no. 1: 11–19 (spring/summer 1992).
Barnes, Melvyn P. *Dick Francis.* New York: Ungar, 1986.
Bauska, Barry. "Endure and Prevail: The Novels of Dick Francis." *Armchair Detective* 11, no. 3: 238–244. (July 1978).
Bishop, Paul. "The Sport of Sleuths." *Armchair Detective* 17, no. 2: 144–149 (spring 1984).
Cantwell, Robert. "Mystery Makes a Writer." *Sports Illustrated,* 25 March 1968: 76–88.
Carr, John C. "Dick Francis." In his *The Craft of Crime: Conversations with Crime Writers.* Boston: Houghton Mifflin, 1983. Pp. 202–226.
Cross, Amanda. *The Question of Max.* New York: Ballantine, 1987.
Davis, J. Madison. *Dick Francis.* Boston: Twayne, 1989.
DeAndrea, William L. "Francis, Dick." In his *Encyclopedia Mysteriosa.* New York: Prentice Hall, 1994.
DeKoven, Marianne. "Longshot: Crime Fiction as Postmodernism." *Lit: Literature Interpretation Theory* 4, no. 3: 185–194 (1993).
Fiscella, Joan B. "A Sense of the Under Toad: Play in Mystery Fiction." *Clues* 1, no. 2: 1–7 (fall/winter 1980).
"Francis, Dick." In *Current Biography Yearbook.* Edited by Charles Moritz. New York: H. W. Wilson, 1981. Pp. 152–156.
Gleick, Elizabeth. "As Easy as Falling off a Horse." *People,* 23 November 1992: 139–140.
Gould, Charles E. "The Reigning Phoenix." *Armchair Detective* 7, no. 4: 407–410 (fall 1984).
Gunton, Sharon, and Jean C. Stine, eds. "Francis, Dick." In *Contemporary Literary Criticism,* vol. 22. Detroit: Gale Research Company, 1982. Pp. 150–154.
Harvey, Deryck. "A Word with Dick Francis." *Armchair Detective* 6: 151–152 (1973).
Hochstein, Mort. "Dick Francis, Odds-on Favorite." *Writer's Digest,* August 1986: 32–34.
Knepper, Marty S. "Dick Francis." In *Twelve Englishmen of Mystery.* Edited by Earl F. Bargainnier. Bowling Green, Ohio: Bowling Green University Popular Press, 1984. Pp. 222–248.
Maryles, Daisy. "Jockeying for Position." *Publishers Weekly* 241, no. 40: 15 (3 October 1994).
———. "More Winners for Francis." *Publishers Weekly* 242, no. 40: 20 (2 October 1995).
Newcombe, Jack. "Jockey with an Eye for Intrigue." *Life,* 6 June 1969: 81–82.
Schaffer, Rachel. "Dead Funny: The Lighter Side of Dick Francis." *Armchair Detective* 26, no. 2: 76–81 (spring 1993).
———."The Pain: Trials by Fire in the Novels of Dick

Francis." *Armchair Detective* 27, no. 3: 348–357 (summer 1994).

———. "A Jockey's Best Friend: Horseplay in Dick Francis Mysteries." In *The Dog Didn't Do It!* Edited by Mary Jean DeMarr and Sharon Russell. Bowling Green, Ohio: Bowling Green University Popular Press, forthcoming.

Stanton, Michael N. "Dick Francis: The Worth of Human Love." *Armchair Detective* 15, no. 2: 137–143 (1982).

Strauss, Gerald. "Dick Francis." In *Beacham's Popular Fiction in America: 1950–1986.* Edited by Walton Beacham. Washington, D.C.: Beacham Publications, 1986. Pp. 466–473.

Wagner, Elaine. "The Theme of Parental Rejection in the Novels of Dick Francis." *Clues* 18, no. 1: 7–13 (spring/summer 1997).

Weeks, Brigitte. "Writing Mystery Novels." *Writer,* August 1983: 11–12. Reprinted from *The Washington Post (Book World),* 27 March 1983: 10.

Wilhelm, Albert E. "Fathers and Sons in Dick Francis' *Proof.*" *Critique: Studies in Contemporary Fiction* 32, no. 3: 169–178 (spring 1991).

———. "Finding the True Self: Rites of Passage in Dick Francis's *Flying Finish.*" *Clues* 9, no. 2: 1–8 (fall/winter 1988).

Zalewski, James W., and Lawrence B. Rosenfield. "Rules for the Game of Life: The Mysteries of Robert B. Parker and Dick Francis." *Clues* 5, no. 2: 72–81 (fall/winter 1984).

ÉMILE GABORIAU
(1832–1873)

WALTER ALBERT

"Have you read Gaboriau's works?" I asked. "Does Lecoq come up to your idea of a detective?"

Sherlock Holmes sniffed sardonically. "Lecoq was a miserable bungler," he said, in an angry voice; "he had only one thing to recommend him, and that was his energy. That book made me positively ill. The question was how to identify an unknown prisoner. I could have done it in twenty-four hours. Lecoq took six months or so. It might be made a text-book for detectives to teach them what to avoid."

Sir Arthur Conan Doyle, *A Study in Scarlet* (1886)

HOLMES'S ALLITERATIVE SNIFFING is met with silent indignation by Dr. Watson, who clearly admires the French detective. If he had wished to press the point, Watson might have pointed out to his supercilious friend that Holmes was inaccurate in his assessment of the length of time it took for Lecoq to identify the prisoner in Émile Gaboriau's *Monsieur Lecoq* (1869), the novel to which Holmes refers. Holmes's dismissal is unworthy of him and certainly does not excuse the fact that he is five months "or so" off the mark.

Holmes is equally dismissive of Edgar Allan Poe's C. August Dupin (whom he calls "an inferior fellow"), and while some of this attitude may be ascribed to typical British wariness of anything French, it is undoubtedly also territorial. Holmes, whose vanity was legendary, is carving out for himself, consciously or not, a niche as the "world's greatest consulting detective," and he appears to consider historical precedent only as something he comes on the scene to correct. He might have reflected that a modern metropolitan police force was not established in Great Britain until 1829, almost two decades after the founding in 1811 of the French Sûreté by François Eugène Vidocq. Vidocq, a reformed convict, recruited many of his detectives from the criminal class, correctly assuming that with proper supervision, their experience would give them an insight into and an edge on the activities and reasoning of the criminals they would seek to apprehend.

Gaboriau, however, had almost no fictional prototype of the professional policeman to draw on when he came to create Monsieur Lecoq, an agent of the French Sûreté, but he was familiar with Vidocq's *Mémoires* (1828–1829), a four-volume work that was almost certainly ghostwritten in part. Honoré de Balzac based his charismatic character Vautrin (the protagonist's nemesis in his celebrated novel *Le Père Goriot,* 1834) on Vidocq. But when Gaboriau turned to Vidocq as the source for his Sûreté detective thirty years later, he carefully laundered the character of Vidocq's sinister criminal background, which Balzac had emphasized in Vautrin, to make Lecoq a hero suitable for the serial novel–reading public.

Étienne-Émile Gaboriau was born on 9 November 1832 to Charles-Gabriel Gaboriau, a minor public official in Saujon, a little town north of Bordeaux, and Marguerite-Stéphanie Gaboriau (née Magistrel), daughter of a notary. Gaboriau's father moved only eight months after the child's birth to a post at Saint-Pierre d'Oleron and then in 1837 to La Rochelle, where Émile's sister, Amélie, was born on 11 September 1838. In 1842, after an unfavorable report was submitted on his work, the chronically dissatisfied elder Gaboriau was sent to an inferior post at Tarascon-sur-Rhône. Here Émile entered the community secondary school, where he was a classmate of Alphonse Millaud, a nephew of the publisher who was instrumental in Gaboriau's later success as a novelist. In 1843 he was enrolled briefly in a Parisian school, living with his uncle Charles Roux, but the arrangement proved to be unsatisfactory, and the child was soon enrolled as a boarder at a small seminary in Aix-en-Provence. In September, Charles-Gabriel was nominated to a post in Saumur, and his son transferred to a local secondary school, somewhat to the regret of his family, who were unhappy with the school's mediocre reputation. His years there, except for signs of proficiency in Latin, were undistinguished, and there is no record of his having completed his studies and received a degree. He did show signs of literary talent (a poem written to his aunt survives), but there is little documentation of these years.

Gaboriau presented himself for military service in 1851 but had served only until the end of December 1853—as a second-class infantryman in the Fifth Regiment, which was stationed at Vendôme—when his father purchased a replacement to serve out the remaining years of his seven-year commitment. Gaboriau appears to have followed his father's wishes and apprenticed himself to a notary, but by 1856 he was in Paris and soon (perhaps as early as 1857) published a volume of poetry that, predictably, did not sell. It did, however, provide something of a boost for a journalistic career, and he began to collaborate on the weekly journal *La Vérité* (The Truth), whose name had only recently been scaled down from its original designation of *La Vérité pour tous* (The Truth for Everybody). Gaboriau's first contribution was, not unsurprisingly, a poem signed "Émile G.," but he soon began writing a column, "Échos de la Semaine" (Weekly Echoes). The newspaper did not long survive its name change, and Gaboriau moved from rag to rag, dabbling in the theater (a lifetime passion that influenced the creation of Lecoq) and writing on a wide variety of current events. Then, in 1861, he began publishing his first books (three in 1861 alone), which included historical studies, a volume of biographies of famous actresses, and, more important, several fictional works that followed in the steps of Balzac and constituted a series of studies of contemporary customs.

Gaboriau's output during this first decade in Paris was prodigious if not particularly distinguished. If it did not bring him fame or fortune, it was a productive period and an apprenticeship that undoubtedly made him the consummate craftsman he shortly showed himself to be. His name was, however, hardly one that meant much to the serial novel public when *L'Affaire Lerouge* (1866) began to appear in installments in the Parisian daily *Le Pays* late in 1865. Its success there, although not the sensation that his work subsequently became, did catch the eye of the enterprising Moïse Millaud. Millaud, who had come to Paris in 1836 from his native Bordeaux, published his first newspaper, *L'Audience,* in 1839. After a series of business undertakings that saw him making, and losing, more than one fortune, in 1863 Millaud created *Le Petit Journal* and, in 1865, *Le Soleil,* both dailies that were to play important roles in Gaboriau's career.

L'Affaire Lerouge, the first of Gaboriau's *ro-*

mans judiciaires (judicial novels), was published in installments in *Le Pays,* from 14 September to 7 December 1865. The novel caught the eye of Millaud and was reprinted in *Le Soleil,* from 18 April to 2 July 1866, with book publication by Edmond Dentu in October 1866. *Le Soleil* boasted an impressive list of collaborators and contributors, among them Alexandre Dumas *père* and Victor Hugo, whose novel *Les Travailleurs de la mer* (1866; translated as *Toilers of the Sea*) ran serially in *Le Soleil* from April to July 1866, even as the newspaper was running almost concurrently the previously published *L'Affaire Lerouge.* This was heady company for the journeyman columnist and novelist Émile Gaboriau, but his meteoric rise came to justify Millaud's sharp publisher's eye. Both the serial reprinting and the book publication were enthusiastically received, and *Le Crime d'Orcival* (1867) was quickly published in serial form in *Le Soleil* (15 October to 20 December 1866) and then in Millaud's most prestigious daily, *Le Petit Journal,* which had a circulation that by 1866 was approaching two hundred thousand copies at a time when the next closest rival (*Le Figaro*) had an average press run of thirty-three thousand. The novel's serial run concluded in *Le Petit Journal* on 6 February 1867, with a book contract concluded with Dentu on 3 February. Gaboriau's next novel, *Le Dossier no. 113* (1867), began its serial run on 7 February, with *Les Esclaves de Paris* (1868) following on 9 July. *Les Esclaves* was a massive novel in three parts, and its serialization was not completed until 3 March 1868. Finally, *Monsieur Lecoq,* the last of this accelerating cascade of novels, was serialized beginning on 27 May 1868; the average issue with one such installment showed an increase of forty thousand copies in sales. By the time *Monsieur Lecoq* was published by Dentu in February 1869, the earlier novels were already being reissued in magazine serial and book form, including illustrated editions that began with the reappearance of *L'Affaire Lerouge* in 1869. Foreign contracts for the books were signed as early as 1868, and by 1870 German, Italian, and British translations were under way for all of Gaboriau's works. His international success speedily duplicated his domestic reception.

In spite of Lecoq's prominence as Gaboriau's signature character, he played a major role in only three of the novels: *Le Crime d'Orcival, Le Dossier no. 113,* and *Monsieur Lecoq.* Whoever the principal investigator might be, the narrative patterns were already firmly in place in *L'Affaire Lerouge,* where the investigator is "le père" (old) Tabaret, also known as "Tirauclair" (the one who clears things up). In *L'Affaire Lerouge,* Tabaret recalls how he began as a collector of books but soon found himself gathering only materials that "intimately or more distantly" dealt with the police:

> Reminiscences, reports, pamphlets, speeches, letters, novels, everything was good to me, and I devoured it. Thus little by little I felt myself drawn toward that mysterious power that, from the depths of the rue de Jérusalem, watches over and protects society, sees through everything, raises the heaviest curtains, studies the underside of every web, guesses at what people don't confess to, knows the exact worth of men, the price of consciences, and amasses in its files the most fearful as well as the most shameful secrets. (p. 50)

This fascination drew him inexorably toward the French police bureau, the Sûreté, to whom he became an invaluable consultant and investigator. He never accepted a sou for his services and worked for the "pleasure" of the chase. The mention of his name came to generate "convulsions" in Gévrol, the archetypal police drudge, devoid of imagination and jealous of the inspired work of Tabaret and Lecoq. It is, in fact, Lecoq who slyly advises Daburon, the magistrate, to call in Tabaret, advice that Daburon immediately accepts in spite of Gévrol's warning that Tabaret, like the scientist who reconstructs lost animals from a single bone, claims that he can reconstruct the scenario of a murder from a single fact. "He is," adds the inspector, "too passionate, like an author" (p. 21).

This comment, although it is meant to be critical, undoubtedly recommends Tabaret to Daburon, whose power cannot be overestimated:

> Society's representative, vested with discretionary powers that derive from his conscience and the law, the magistrate controls a most formidable machinery. Nothing gets in his way, nobody can give him orders. Administration, police, armed force, everything is at his disposal. At a word from him, twenty agents, a hundred if need be, turn Paris upside down, spread throughout France, explore Europe. He has only to think that somebody might shed light on an obscure point, and that man, cited to appear in his office, will come, from whatever distance he may be. That's the magistrate. (*Monsieur Lecoq,* vol. 1, p. 266)

Thus, Gaboriau points out that Daburon, "skillful at deducing from the known to the unknown, . . . excelled in organizing facts." His only shortcoming, it appears, is a lack of "daring" for those "risky theatrical manoeuvres that bring out the truth like a bombshell" (p. 7).

Tabaret is also a master at deduction, and he quickly displays this skill with Sherlockian flair after his examination of the cottage where the widow Lerouge's battered body was found. "The widow . . . knew her murderer. . . . He was, then, admitted without difficulty. He's a still young man, a little above the average in height, and elegantly dressed. That evening he wore a top hat, carried an umbrella, and smoked a fine cigar" (p. 37). Gévrol exclaims in disbelief ("But that's a novel!"), while Lecoq barely hides his enthusiastic admiration and the magistrate seems enchanted with the report.

This initial phase of the investigation, the on-site interviewing and examination of the crime scene, is followed by the withdrawal of Daburon to his chambers in Paris. He continues to direct the investigation even as his interviews lead inevitably to the apprehension of a probable suspect. And that identification leads, also inevitably in Gaboriau, to an extended flashback. "You will see," Lecoq confides in *Le Dossier no. 113,* "how far into the past you must sometimes go to find the roots of a crime. Everything comes together and connects there" (1985 ed., p. 328). Gaboriau's narratives are invariably rooted in family and social relationships, and they are dramas that may have festered for years before they explode in the murder that sets in motion an investigation.

This history is particularly enveloping in *L'Affaire Lerouge,* for it involves secrets in the lives of both the chief investigator and the magistrate, personal connections to the accused and his family that taint their impartiality almost from the beginning. The man eventually arrested for the murder is Albert de Commarin, raised as the legitimate son of the Comte de Commarin and cared for in his infancy by the widow Lerouge. Documents point to Noël Gerdy, a young Parisian lawyer, as the legitimate heir, victim in his infancy of a secret exchange of the children of the count's wife and mistress carried out by the widow Lerouge at the instigation of the count's mistress. Tabaret lives in the same building as Noël and his "mother" and has come to love the young man as if he were his own son, a fact he does not admit to Daburon. Daburon's secret is equally damaging, for he once loved the young woman to whom Albert is engaged, and his hatred for the young man is "burned" into his heart. In spite of feelings that would appear to make it impossible for them to act fairly, the passion of Tabaret and Daburon for truth and justice outweigh their private feelings. Tabaret and Daburon cannot reveal, let alone share, their personal involvement without publicly compromising their professional roles and leading to grounds for having their participation in the investigation challenged. These two profoundly compromised characters set a pattern for a certain distancing of major characters from the most potentially dramatically charged confrontations in Gaboriau's judiciary fiction. The secondary characters, the illegitimate children and wronged wives, the melodramatic staples of serial fiction, take up their predestined and familiar roles center stage. But the powerful magistrates and their gifted investigators play out their more complex roles in relative silence.

Their active careers nonetheless are profoundly affected by this troubling case. Tabaret becomes disillusioned, and his belief in the infallibility of justice is shaken by the dramatic and unsettling reversals of the Lerouge case; thenceforth he devotes much of his time to fighting for the abolition of the death penalty and the establishment of an organization dedicated to the support of the poor and innocent who have been accused of crimes. Daburon retires to Poitou and is not heard from again. Tabaret, although he does not again conduct an investigation in the series, returns, most notably in *Monsieur Lecoq,* which establishes Lecoq as the preeminent agent of the Sûreté. Lecoq's role in *L'Affaire Lerouge* is limited to a brief appearance at the Lerouge cottage as a subordinate to the unimaginative Gévrol. There he is described as "an ex-convict who has served his time, clever in his profession, as subtle as amber, and jealous of his superior, whom he considered to be modestly endowed" (p. 22). His major contribution is the suggestion to Gévrol that Tabaret might be consulted for the investigation.

In the rapidly published succession of Gaboriau's judicial novels, the superficially deferential and lightly sketched Lecoq of *L'Affaire Lerouge* appears in *Le Crime d'Orcival* as the chief investigator for whom Gévrol is a "master" and a "rival," but no longer an active presence in the investigation. Moreover, Paris, the site of the Sûreté's headquarters on the rue de Jérusalem, now belongs, Lecoq declares, to him and his colleagues. "All Paris is under the magnifying glass of the rue de Jérusalem like an anthill under the naturalist's microscope" (p. 344). This grandiose vision of his power is undoubtedly an echo of the cry of Balzac's ambitious protagonist Rastignac, who, in *Le Père Goriot,* challenges the city: "Paris, it's between us!" Lecoq, at the beginning of his career, issues the same challenge in *Monsieur Lecoq:* "Now, it's between you and me!" (p. 26). His challenge, however, is to the crime he has been charged with investigating. Lecoq's powers, as formidable as his intelligence may be, are multiplied by the power of the Sûreté. In an extended poetic discourse to the little band of associates (Doctor Gendron and Plantat, the civil judge of Orcival) with whom he works closely during the Orcival investigation, he traces his career, which began when he was advised by his employer, a noted astronomer, to make more salubrious use of what appeared to be natural gifts for a criminal career. "Fearing I would become a thief, I became instead a police officer" (*Le Crime d'Orcival,* p. 124). In that job, he was able to deal with the true "theater," society, with its "real" dramas:

> A crime is committed, that's the prologue.
>
> I arrive, the first act begins. With a single glance, I take note of the slightest details in the setting. Then I try to understand the motives, I group my characters, I link the events with the main plot, I group all the circumstances. That's the exposition.
>
> Soon, the plot thickens, the thread of my inductions leads me to the guilty party; I see into his mind, I arrest him, I deliver him up.
>
> Then, the big scene arrives, where the criminal argues, schemes, tries to throw me off the track, but . . . the magistrate overwhelms him. . . .
>
> My last act is the trial. . . . If the jury says "no!" that's it. My play was bad, I'm booed. If they convict, however, it's because my play was good; I'm applauded. I triumph. (pp. 125–126)

This remarkable tirade, an exercise in pure theater, reveals Lecoq's conception of his role as playwright and is also remarkably consistent with the structure of Gaboriau's judicial novels.

As a principal actor in his plays, Lecoq is a master at disguise. "His mobile face lends itself to strange metamorphoses [as] he molds his face at will just as the sculptor molds modeling clay. He changes everything in himself, even his eyes" (pp. 53–54). This trait undoubtedly derives from François-Eugène Vidocq's use of disguise. The professional rivalries, the skillful art of disguise, the checkered past, all these elements entered into Gaboriau's fashioning of Lecoq, but he quickly excised Lecoq's criminal past to make him a potential rather than an actual criminal. This suppressed link between the detective and the criminal may have survived in the detective novel as the uncanny ability of the detective to enter into the criminal's mind. But Gaboriau, after flirting with the compromised investigator and magistrate in *L'Affaire Lerouge,* quickly understood that his protagonists must demonstrate the same passion for integrity in their character as they did in their pursuit of justice.

Lecoq, even as he proclaimed his singular strengths, confessed to a weakness. "Like every man, I have my Achilles' heel. I overcame a weakness for gambling, I have not overcome a weakness for women" (p. 126). And for one woman in particular: "Yes, I, the Sûreté policeman, the terror of robbers and murderers . . . I who know everything, have seen everything, heard everything, I, Lecoq am for 'her' simpler and more naive than a child" (p. 127). This weakness, proclaimed in *Le Crime d'Orcival,* is put to rest in *Le Dossier no. 113.* In this novel, Lecoq is at first "a man of a certain age, of distinguished appearance, wearing a white tie and spectacles with gold frames" (p. 47), but later he is described as "this today and that tomorrow; now dark-haired, now blond, sometimes quite young, at other times so old that you would say he is a hundred years. . . . Anybody could be him. If you were to tell me that you were Lecoq, I would answer, 'It's quite possible'" (pp. 65–66).

Le Dossier is the slightest (if not the shortest) of the series. A safe in a locked room to which only two men have a key is opened, and a deposit of three hundred thousand francs is taken. Because the employer is manifestly innocent, his chief clerk is charged with the crime. The investigation is marked by chases, a melodramatic confrontation in an isolated house during a thunderstorm, and a colorful and imaginative masked ball as a centerpiece. Uncovering an elaborate blackmail scheme that has the guilty appear to be innocent and the innocent guilty, Lecoq exposes the blackmailer and allows the members of a family whose secrets threatened to destroy them to begin a process of reconciliation and healing. Once the case has been laid to rest, Lecoq then closets himself with the woman he had once loved and who had surfaced during the case as the mistress of the man whose innocence he has established. It's typical of Gaboriau that what would, in another novel, be one of the great scenes, takes place offstage.

Lecoq surfaces only briefly in Gaboriau's novel *Les Esclaves de Paris.* This is an intriguing combination of romance fiction in the development of its several interlocking relationships and an almost Dickensian look at the underbelly of a Parisian crime world that seems to reach into every household of the bourgeois nouveaux riches and still powerful noble families. Gaboriau completely abandons his usual narrative structure to move freely along the great avenues where the rich live in seclusion and in the shabby ghettos of the desperately poor. The novel is dominated by one of Gaboriau's greatest creations, the master criminal Mascarot, proprietor of an agency that furnishes servants to the best families in Paris, servants whose task is to gather information that Mascarot uses for his blackmail operations. The entire city seems subject to his control, until he conceives a plan for a financial scam that will make him and his associates independently wealthy. This plan is thwarted by Lecoq, who, of course, sees, hears, and knows everything that goes on in Paris. Lecoq's role is only to resolve the plot, but Mascarot can be seen as a criminal version of Lecoq, a master of disguises whose downfall occurs when Lecoq unmasks his triple persona. Gaboriau's sense of theater was never more acute than in this novel.

In April of 1868 the walls of Paris and the principal provincial cities were, as Roger Bonniot puts it, covered with "immense multicolored posters" that displayed the words "MONSIEUR LECOQ!" repeated in enormous letters "in four lines arranged diagonally" (p. 148). This was the first wave of a carefully planned publicity campaign announcing the imminent publication of *Monsieur Lecoq,* which would, claimed Millaud, "surpass in interest everything that [Gaboriau] has published" (p. 148).

In spite of the fact that *Monsieur Lecoq* is the last published of the Lecoq series, it presents the detective on the threshold of a career he has already established in the earlier *Le Dossier no. 113* and *Les Esclaves de Paris.* Bonniot, Gaboriau's biographer and exhaustive researcher into the tortuous trail of the novelist's serial and book publications in these crucial years, believes that the order of publication of the *romans judiciaires* departs from their order of composition. Noting the discrepancy in Lecoq's status in the novels published between *L'Affaire Lerouge* and *Monsieur Lecoq,* Bonniot cites two letters, of 27 December 1864 and 16 January 1865. Gaboriau refers to his starting work—after the first magazine publication of *L'Affaire Lerouge*—on a second, "long" novel that would be published if *L'Affaire Lerouge* proved to be "successful." Bonniot believes this novel was *Monsieur Lecoq* and attributes the delay in its completion to the "length and complexity" of the second part. Bonniot's hypothesis is a reasonable one, and the internal evidence is certainly compelling in its own right. It also offers an explanation for the structural anomaly of *Les Esclaves de Paris,* which Millaud called a new direction for Gaboriau's work, one that removed the criticism that Gaboriau was content to repeat himself endlessly with a formula whose success was already proved.

Lecoq's triumph in *Monsieur Lecoq* does not come easily to the young detective, although the case's resolution earns him the promotion that he covets and lays the foundations of the career that made him a legend among the agents of the Sûreté. Bleiler, even as he defends his preference for the novel, bases it on the first volume ("The Investigation") and in the Dover edition, which his fine essay prefaces, abridges the novel. This editing may move the work closer to the novel Bleiler would like it to have been, but it is less true to the novel that Gaboriau wrote and whose structure is perfectly consistent with the earlier novels in the series.

The modern reader may certainly find the novel-length flashback of the second volume, "The Honor of the Name," a quite different animal from the intellectual game of cat and mouse that characterizes Lecoq's pursuit of the enigmatic criminal "Mai" in the first volume. It is not a narrative that one can fault for lack of criminal action—what with several deaths (including one of Gaboriau's favorite devices, murder by poisoning), a daring prison escape, and flight from France to escape criminal prosecution—but Lecoq is not physically present. The reader does, however, understand that the information is recorded as the result of Lecoq's investigation, and its narrative density and superb plot momentum are as compelling as the pursuit in the first volume. Like all of Gaboriau's flashbacks, it is rich in detail on the setting and on the social structures that always involve members of the landed aristocracy, and the characterizations are focused and often memorable.

Sir Arthur Conan Doyle uses this narrative structure in his first Holmes story, the short novel *A Study in Scarlet.* He returns to it in his other Holmes novels, and his most effective use of it may be in *The Hound of the Baskervilles* (1888), which remains the most popular of the novels. In spite of Holmes's critical comments about Lecoq to Watson in *A Study in Scarlet,* Conan Doyle's own opinion of Gaboriau seems to have been more positive and thus more like Watson's. R. F. Stewart has observed that in his autobiography, *Memories and Adventures* (1924), Conan Doyle confesses that he had "rather been attracted" by Gaboriau's "neat dove-tailing of his plots" (p. 256).

This attraction to Gaboriau's plotting is one that few of the more impatient modern readers of the detective novel would share. Conan Doyle's limited use of the flashback looks backward, not forward. Only two decades separate the publication of the first Holmes novel from Gaboriau's last Lecoq investigation; Holmes's success marks the ascendancy of the consulting detective over the professional policeman. And it was to be decades before the modern police procedural challenged the private detective.

The 1860s were years of great professional success for Gaboriau, but he confessed in a letter that there was no "prisoner . . . no slave as constrained, attached, bound and chained-up" as he was. "I can't," he further complained, "as long as a serial continues, separate my thoughts from that fiction to which I struggle to give life" (Bonniot, p. 237). He worried about his father's health even as his own condition gave cause for concern, but his obligations kept him in Paris, allowing him only brief escapes from the city that had all but become his prison. After the success of *Monsieur Lecoq,* Gaboriau published a series of social chronicles that captivated readers with their picturesque details of life in the French capital. A crime novel, "Le Filou et l'agent de police" (The Rogue and the Police Detective), was never completed, and proposed projects began to outnumber the completed ones. A promising series of stories that were to feature the reminiscences of a retired Sûreté agent, J.-B. Casimir Godeuil, was launched in *Le Petit Journal* in July of 1870 with "Le Petit Vieux des Batignolles" (The Little Old Man of Batignolles). The Watson-like narrator, a "public health" student, is befriended by a Sûreté detective, and the brilliant, concise plotting of the short story makes the reader regret that the series did not continue.

Gaboriau was confined to Paris during the Franco-Prussian War of 1870–1871, but with the return to normalcy, he published three novels between 1871 and 1873. One of them, *La Corde au cou,* returned to the cycle of crime novels. In this novel, published in 1873, Gaboriau ironically completes the dramatic scenario described in *Le Crime d'Orcival.* For the first time, the case is followed through to the Cour d'Assises (criminal court), where an innocent man, wrongly accused of arson and attempted murder, is convicted and sentenced to twenty years of hard labor. But the conviction is overturned by the skill of Gaboriau's last detective creation, Goudar. Goudar, who is persuaded to take a leave from his post in the Préfecture (police headquarters) and, disguised as an itinerant street musician, tricks the real culprit into confessing.

Gaboriau married Amélie Rogelet, his companion of eleven years, on 24 July 1873, but he died suddenly on 28 September 1873 from what was diagnosed as "une apoplexie pulmonaire" (pulmonary apoplexy). Amélie survived him by only three years, dying of consumption, with the rights to his literary properties willed, according to her husband's wishes, to his sister, Amélie Coindreau.

Gaboriau's Lecoq is largely forgotten today, except by specialists in genre fiction, and it might seem that history has shown the same dislike for the Sûreté detective that Holmes expressed to Watson. New editions of Gaboriau's work in the original French and in translation continued to appear for several decades after his death, but international enthusiasm for Lecoq waned after the appearance of Sherlock Holmes. The economy and conciseness of the short-story form favored by Conan Doyle was more to the "modern" taste than Gaboriau's massive novels, whose adoption of lengthy flashbacks employing the devices of romantic adventure fiction diluted the appeal of the detection and investigation talents of the detectives who captivated his readers during Gaboriau's lifetime.

With his distrust of policemen and his belief in his own superiority, the private detective was the legacy of Conan Doyle. These attitudes came to dominate the detective fiction of the so-called British Golden Age and in that quite different model, the hard-boiled detective that was the legacy of the 1920s and 1930s. The police procedural, with the canonization of police department routine, was a development of the 1950s, but it bears a tantalizing trace of Gaboriau's judicial novels. The modern detective, working doggedly to solve his cases and often hampered by the opposition of incompetent superiors and jealous colleagues, is an unlikely conflation of Gaboriau's departmental hack, Gévrol, and his imaginative rival, Lecoq. Lecoq may often have been at odds with his less gifted colleagues, but he demonstrated a darkly poetic, even sinister infatuation with the Sûreté unlike Sherlock Holmes, who had only contempt for England's Sûreté, Scotland Yard. In Gaboriau's fictional world, Lecoq triumphed over Gévrol, but it was the descendants of Gévrol, the plodding, routine-minded employee, and not those of the brilliant, eccentric Lecoq, who became the heroes of the modern procedural. Holmes's contemptuous dismissal of Lecoq has carried the day, and Watson's embarrassed silence echoes literary history's verdict.

Selected Bibliography

WORKS OF ÉMILE GABORIAU

L'Affaire Lerouge. Paris: Edmond Dentu, 1866. Variously translated as *The Lerouge Case, The Widow Lerouge,* and *Old Tabaret, the Self-made Detective; or "Piping," the Lerouge Case.*

Le Crime d'Orcival. Paris: Edmond Dentu, 1867. Variously translated as *The Orcival Crime, The Mystery of Orcival,* and *Crime at Orcival.*

Le Dossier no. 113. Paris: Edmond Dentu, 1867; Éditions Encre, 1985. Variously translated as *File Number 113, Dossier No. 113,* and *The Blackmailers* (abridged).

Les Esclaves de Paris. Paris: Edmond Dentu, 1868. Translated as *Slaves of Paris.*

Monsieur Lecoq, 2 vols. Paris: Edmond Dentu, 1869. The two volumes have been published in two different English translations under the same title as the French edition.

La Corde au cou. Paris: Edmond Dentu, 1873. Variously translated as *Rope Around His Neck, Within an Inch of His Life, In Deadly Peril,* and *In Peril of His Life.*

Le Petit Vieux des Batignolles. Paris: Edmond Dentu, 1876. Translated as *The Little Old Man of the Batignolles.*

BIOGRAPHICAL AND CRITICAL STUDIES

Bleiler, E. F. Introduction to *Monsieur Lecoq* by Émile Gaboriau. New York: Dover, 1975. The bibliography established by Bleiler is not limited to Gaboriau's judicial novels.

———. "Émile Gaboriau." In *St. James Guide to Crime and Mystery Writers.* Edited by Jay P. Pederson. Detroit: St. James Press, 1996. Bleiler's entry on Gaboriau includes dates of publication of English translations that are not given in the Dover volume.

Bonniot, Roger. *Émile Gaboriau ou la naissance du roman policier.* Paris: Ed. J. Vrin, 1985. The volume includes an index that gives limited access to the information, but there are no notes and no bibliography of primary sources. The organization is chaotic.

Curry, Nancy L. *The Life and Works of Émile Gaboriau.* Ph.D. diss., Univ. of Kentucky, 1970.

Doyle, Sir Arthur Conan. *The Complete Sherlock Holmes,* vol. 1. New York: Doubleday, n.d.

Stewart, R. F. *And Always a Detective: Chapters on the History of Detective Fiction.* North Pomfret, Vt.: David & Charles, 1980.

Vidocq, F. E. *Les Vrais Mémoires de Vidocq.* Edited by Jean Savant. Paris: Éditions Corres, 1957. This may be the authentic version of Vidocq's text, which has a tortuous publishing history. It is difficult to determine what part—if any—Vidocq had in the actual writing.

Erle Stanley Gardner

(1889–1970)

WILLIAM F. NOLAN

CONSIDER THE STATISTICS: in a career that spanned five decades, Erle Stanley Gardner sold more than seven hundred fictional works, including 127 novels (82 of them featuring his fighting lawyer, the global icon Perry Mason). Adding in four hundred articles and more than a dozen travel tomes, his overall creative total climbs past eleven hundred, embracing 155 published books in thirty-seven languages around the world. Media totals for Perry Mason alone include six motion pictures, 3,221 radio episodes, 271 television episodes, and more than twenty made-for-television movies. No updated figures are available, but it is estimated that some 325 million of Gardner's books have been distributed globally, making him one of history's all-time best-selling mystery writers. At the height of his popularity (in the mid-1960s), his novels were being sold at an average of twenty-six thousand copies per day! No other author came close to this amazing sales record.

Yet writing was only one facet of Gardner's complex life. He spoke fluent Chinese, worked as a professional attorney for twenty-two years, and was an ardent sportsman (boxing, fishing, archery, tennis, and golf), a constant traveler (China, Baja California, and the desert country of the American Southwest), a working rancher (raising horses, dogs, and cattle), founder of and activist in the Court of Last Resort (established to aid prisoners who maintained that they had been unjustly convicted), an enthusiastic wildlife photographer (illustrating his own travel books), and an amateur explorer and criminologist—with an in-depth knowledge of geology, archaeology, engineering, astronomy, forensic medicine, natural history, and the breeding habits of the California gray whale.

Early Life

Erle Stanley Gardner was born to Charles W. Gardner and Grace Adelma Waugh Gardner on 17 July 1889, the second of three sons, in Malden, Massachusetts, a modest community boasting a strong New England heritage. Speaking of his ancestors (as quoted in *The Black Mask Boys*), Gardner declared that his roots extended back to the *Mayflower* on his mother's side and that he was "descended from hardy New England stock. My forebears were the captains of windjammers, whalers . . . out of Nantucket" (Nolan, p. 94).

At age ten, he had just completed the fourth grade when his father moved the family west to Portland, Oregon, where the elder Gardner intended to pursue a career in engineering. Three years later they were headed into the Klondike, where Charles Gardner found employment as a mining engineer. Shortly after the turn of the century, the author's family settled in the small mining town of Oroville, in northern California, where Charles Gardner became an expert in gold-dredging placer mining. His son was a natural rebel who chafed under authority. By 1906, at age seventeen, after lampooning his school's officious principal, he was suspended from Oroville Union High School. He transferred to Palo Alto High School, in the San Francisco Bay Area, where he managed to graduate in June of 1909.

Erle Stanley Gardner's father wanted him to become a lawyer. Following high school, in pursuit of this goal, he went to work in a law office in Willows for twenty dollars a month. By that autumn, however, he was attending Valparaiso University in Indiana, where he lasted less than a month. During a fistic encounter in Gardner's dorm (which he had converted into a boxing ring), a professor was knocked down. Eventually, a warrant for Gardner's arrest was issued by the university. (He later claimed to have skipped town just "one jump ahead" of the sheriff.)

After a brief stint on a railroad construction crew in Eugene, Oregon, the youth headed back to California, where he obtained a job in the law office of E. E. Keech in Santa Ana. He spent fifty hours a week in lawyers' offices, and when he was not working or studying, he was boxing. In 1911, with both eyes blackened from an amateur match, he passed the California bar exam. That same year, at age twenty-one, Gardner opened his own one-room law office in Merced, a farming town in California's San Joaquin Valley. Business, however, was dismal. When he was offered the chance to work for I. W. Stewart, a corporation attorney in the southern California town of Oxnard (in Ventura County, some fifty miles up the coast from downtown Los Angeles), he quickly accepted.

Oxnard was a raw, brawling young town then, notorious for its brothels and saloons—and with its own bustling Chinatown. An early champion of the underdog, Gardner soon determined that the Chinese were not receiving fair legal representation in American courts. They were victims of severe, quasi-official prejudice and were being used as scapegoats, pawns in dirty local politics. Gardner took on their cause, brilliantly defending them in court against gambling charges, learning to speak their language, and becoming affectionately known to the residents of Chinatown as "t'ai chong tze" (the big lawyer).

During this period a young woman from Mississippi, Natalie Frances Talbert, began work in Stewart's law office. She and Gardner met, fell in love, and were married in April of 1912. A year later their daughter (and only child), Natalie Grace Gardner, was born. At the age of twenty-three, the young lawyer became a father. His law practice was experiencing problems. In defending the Chinese, he had alienated the district attorney, the local police, and the city council. A fresh opportunity soon presented itself. He was invited to join in partnership with Frank Orr, a respected young attorney in Ventura, the nearby county seat. Realizing that he was a pariah in Oxnard, he happily took a position in the newly established law firm of Orr and Gardner.

But as a "compulsive rover," he grew restless. This roving spirit may have been what prompted him to leave the firm in 1917 to try his luck as a salesman. He spent the next three years as a rep for Consolidated Sales of San Francisco, crisscrossing the continental United States as he hawked automotive products to manufacturing plants. In later years he cited his experience as a sales rep as the foundation for his sales career as a writer. However, by 1921 the company had foundered, and Gardner was "dead broke."

He was grateful for the opportunity to resume his full-time law practice with Frank Orr in Ventura. Yet he hated the office routine, much preferring what he termed "the good old rough-and-tumble of a courtroom fight in front of a jury" (Hughes, p. 57). It was in court that he felt mentally challenged, and according to his biographer Dorothy B. Hughes, he was proud of his exceptional memory: "I could listen to the testimony of witnesses by the hour and recall almost verbatim what each witness had said" (p. 67).

In *Erle Stanley Gardner's Ventura*, by Richard L. Senate, Gardner's daughter, Grace, recalled their life together in these years: "[My father] believed in exercise and began each day with an outdoor workout. . . . Noon was the main meal of the day and he always came home for lunch. [We ate] good, wholesome food" (p. 51). Despite his insistence on "good, wholesome food," Gardner was also a fervent meat-and-potatoes man. As Senate recalled: "When Mason wins a tough case, he and his staff go out for a thick steak (medium rare), garden salad and a baked potato. When Gardner won a case, he would go to Ventura's Pierpont Inn and enjoy a thick steak (medium rare), a garden salad and a baked potato" (p. 3).

Concerning his courtroom performances, the *New York Times* reported that Gardner

> radiated self-confidence . . . his voice was resonant . . . [and] his way with a hostile witness was plain wizardry. . . . In behalf of his clients, he nosed about in forgotten statutes . . . to find just the right precedents . . . [and] at the proper dramatic moment he would spring the precedent on judge and jury. No one who had known him as a lawyer ever had to look far . . . to find where Perry Mason came from. (Hughes, pp. 62–63)

In 1921, however, Gardner was still a dozen years away from the creation of his legendary character; Mason would have to wait in line behind a host of other fictional heroes. However, Gardner did break into print that year with a fifteen-dollar sale to the rough-edged pulp magazine *Breezy Stories.* "Nellie's Naughty Nighty," printed in the August 1921 issue, so upset his conservative mother that she refused to read a word beyond the title. How could a good Methodist boy end up in such a shocking publication?

Pulp Fiction

Gardner needed additional income to supplement what he was earning as a lawyer and attempted to start a mail-order law course. When it failed, he turned to pulp writing. The cheap-paper pulp magazines had begun to flourish during the 1920s and grew to become a huge open market for writers over the next two decades. Gardner was determined to tap into this burgeoning market. There was one big catch. His first sale had been a fluke, since he knew absolutely nothing about the techniques of professional writing. Over the course of the following two years his manuscripts were consistently rejected. Out they would go, and back they would come. This did not surprise or discourage him. "I wrote the worst stories that ever hit New York," he later admitted (Hughes, p. 77). "My stories were terrible. . . . I didn't know how to plot [and] I had no natural aptitude as a writer" (Nolan, p. 96).

Gardner refused to give up. By 1923 he was using the pen name Charles M. Green on all of his fiction, and it was under this appropriate byline that he had mailed a luridly melodramatic novelette, "The Shrieking Skeleton," to *Black Mask* magazine. The circulation manager, Phil Cody, read it and sent a blistering in-house note to the editor, George Sutton: "This story gives me a pain in the neck . . . it's pretty near the last word in childishness, and the plot has whiskers like unto Spanish moss on an old oak." Cody went on to say that the characters "talked like a dictionary" and that the story was "puerile, trite, obvious, and unnatural" (Fugate, p. 44). Cody added several other strong negative comments, and the manuscript was quickly returned to "Green." By mistake, Cody's note was included with the story. To Gardner, it was a welcome revelation. Up to that time he had never received any editorial criticism.

Using Cody's rejection note as a guide, he rewrote the entire manuscript page by page, word for word. It took three long nights of typing to finish the revision. Then he mailed it back to the magazine. "Sutton was so embarrassed by the whole incident that he bought the story . . . [for] a hundred and sixty dollars. That did it. I was launched on a literary career" (Hughes, p. 79). Actually, it was *Black Mask*'s assistant editor, Harry North, who saw potential in this new writer. Gardner called him "a patient cuss with something of a sense of humor. . . . [He'd give me] coaching on the margin of rejection slips and in short personal letters" (Hughes, p. 79).

In 1924 Gardner had nine short stories and three novelettes printed in the pulps, but only one really meant much to him: his first appearance in *Black Mask* under his real name that September with a story featuring series character Bob Larkin, who fought crime armed only with his ready wit and a pool cue. The following year, for *Black Mask,* Gardner created Ed Jenkins, the "Phantom Crook," who operated between the law and the underworld and was hunted by both. Jenkins became the author's longest-running series character, starring in a total of seventy-four adventures. Two other long-running series characters made their debut that year: western rider Black Barr, "Fate's Gunslinger," and the improbable Speed Dash, dubbed the "Human Fly" for his ability to scale tall office buildings.

Gardner's sales at *Black Mask* were by then a steady source of income. He had become one of the magazine's most popular contributors and had made a good friend of Phil Cody. It was Cody who convinced him that he needed an agent and lined him up with Robert Hardy in New York. Gardner told Hardy: "I've never been mediocre in anything I've done yet, and I want to either go to the top in the fiction game or quit it altogether" (Hughes, p. 88).

Indeed, with Hardy opening several new pulp markets for him in 1926, Gardner notched an amazing twelve-month total of ninety-seven sales, including twenty-six to *Black Mask* alone. His fiction was, however, still wildly melodramatic, as reflected in the overtly flamboyant series characters he created for the pulps: Lester Leith, the "Gentleman Rogue"; Sidney Zoom, "Master of Disguise" (with his police dog, Rip); Soo Hoo Duck, "King of Chinatown"; Dan Seller, the "Patent Leather Kid"; Señor Arnaz de Lobo, "Soldier of Fortune"; Paul Pry, the "Crime Juggler"; J. Keen, "Alibi Fixer"; Dane Skarle, the "Carny Crimefighter"; El Paisano, the "Roadrunner"; Ben Harper, the "Man Who Couldn't Forget"; and Ed Migrane, the "Headache."

And, along the way, came the Old Walrus, Fish Mouth McGinnis, Hard Rock Hogan, and Go Get 'Em Garver and his detective duo, Jax Bowman and Big Jim Grood, billed as the "Avenging White Rings" (from the black masks they wore with white rings circling the eyes). Gardner's "Man in the Silver Mask" reflected period melodrama at its most lurid, and the author's description is darkly menacing:

> There was a suggestion of grim, sinister firmness about the mouth, a suggestion which was heightened by the firm chin. The eyes were a peculiar slate gray. The upper part of the face was concealed by a mask of metallic silver, modeled to conform to the contours of the nose, but not entirely concealing the cheek bones and the lower forehead. From behind the mask, the gray eyes seemed to take on the metallic glint of the silver. (Goulart, pp. 180–181)

The pulp historian Ron Goulart elaborates on Gardner's mysterious protagonist:

> Aided by a seemingly sinister Oriental named Ah Wong, the Masked Man was headquartered in a secret hideaway and was fond of kidnaping gangsters and threatening to torture them. His war against crime was basically psychological and he and the deaf-and-dumb Chinese never actually followed through on their threats. Sometimes merely a look at the Masked Man was enough to scare the average crook into talking. (p. 180)

These unsubtle, larger-than-life characters were featured in more than forty different pulps, from *Fighting Romances* through *Clues, Gang World, Air Adventures, Rapid Fire Detective, Three-Star Western, Ace High, Top Notch,* and a host of others equally lurid. Recalled Gardner: "It's a wonder I didn't kill myself with overwork. If I finished one story by twelve-thirty . . . I couldn't go to bed without starting another" (Hughes, p. 83). Indeed, he was a one-man fiction factory, pounding out well over a million words a year, including a full novelette every three nights, and at the same time running a law firm by day and trying cases in court. Gardner held an extremely pragmatic, down-to-earth view of his writing talent and often spoke of marketing his stories in much the same way cookies and cakes are sold by a grocer. Each year he tried to improve his product, making his material more salable.

By June of 1931 Gardner and his wife had embarked on a six-month tour of China at the invitation of a prominent mandarin family in Canton. This was a period of serious unrest for China, caught between aggression from Japan on one hand and the threat of a civil war on the other. Out of this seething intrigue, Gardner created a new pulp hero for *Argosy:* Major Copely Brane, "International Adventurer." The author's own adventures in China rivaled those of his new hero. He was accused of being an American spy and placed under arrest, he was pursued by river pirates, he was caught in a typhoon in Macao, and he came very close to being kidnapped when he walked the streets of Canton without an escort. Yet through it all, Gardner kept the "fiction factory" at full boil, completing eight novelettes each month he was in China and scribbling "a mountain of notes" for future stories.

The year 1932 proved to be a major turning point in Gardner's career. He found that replacing his typewriter with a Dictaphone not only increased his output but also eliminated the strain of typing each manuscript. Gardner began to dictate his stories on wax cylinders, turning them over to his secretary for transcription. He would then make hand corrections on the typed copy before sending it out to market. By this time Gardner was in his forties, and with a dozen years of short fiction behind him, he was determined to try a novel. Dictation made this longer form much easier, and in just five days he completed a seventy-thousand-word work, "Reasonable Doubt." Then he quickly dictated a second full-length novel titled "The Silent Verdict." The protagonists in both, Ed Stark and Sam Keene, were lawyers—tough, wisecracking characters presented in the typical pulp tradition.

Both novels were rejected by several New York publishers before finding a home with Thayer Hobson, president of William Morrow and Company. Gardner's agent wrote to him quoting Hobson's editorial opinion: "The lawyers in your two books are quite different . . . he thinks you might combine their qualities to advantage [and] use the same character over and over again a la Sherlock Holmes" (Fugate, p. 176). Hobson followed up with a personal letter to Gardner in which he expressed concern over some of the pulpish aspects contained in both works. "Make your lawyer . . . more subtle and a little less hard-boiled" (Fugate, p. 177). He also asked Gardner to come up with a name that would be more acceptable to a book audience. Stark and Keene were too much in the pulp mode. As a boy, Gardner had subscribed to a magazine called the *Youth's Companion.* The publisher's logo was printed in bold letters on the cover of each issue: "PERRY MASON AND COMPANY, Boston, Mass." The perfect name had been found—and one of the most famous characters in crime fiction was born.

Perry Mason

There was still the matter of titles. Ideally, the title of one novel should provide a link to the next. Gardner harked back to a series of 1920s Speed Dash novelettes printed in *Top Notch* as "The Case of the Misplaced Thumbs," "The Case of the Candied Diamonds," and "The Case of the Crushed Carnation." He decided to use this same title pattern for the new Perry Mason series. "Reasonable Doubt" became *The Case of the Velvet Claws* (1933), and "The Silent Verdict" became *The Case of the Sulky Girl* (1933).

Gardner worked hard to eliminate the taint of pulp; he refined his lawyer-protagonist and toned down his overall writing style. Della Street, Mason's ever-loyal secretary, was originally characterized (in "Reasonable Doubt") as being nearly as tough as her boss:

> "She's got that snobby complex."
> Stark grinned at her. "You're jealous," he said.
> Della Street's face flushed. "The hell I am," she said, and slammed the door behind her as she flounced back into the outer office. (Fugate, p. 187)

Contrast this scene with its revised version (as published in *The Case of the Velvet Claws*):

> "She's got that snobby complex."
> "Lots of people are like that, Della."
> "I know, but she's different. . . . She'd turn on you in a second if it would be to her advantage."
> Perry Mason's face was thoughtful. "It wouldn't be to her advantage," he remarked, his voice preoccupied.
> Della Street stared at him for a moment, then softly closed the door and left him alone. (Fugate, p. 187)

In a letter to his publisher, Gardner explained just what he wanted to do with Mason. "The character I am trying to create for him is that of a fighter who is possessed of infinite patience. He tries to jockey his [legal] enemies into a position where he can deliver one good knockout punch" (Hughes, p. 103). In *The Case of the Velvet Claws,* Mason describes himself as "a paid gladiator. I fight for my clients. . . . I have to shoot square with them [but] I can't always expect them to shoot square with me" (Fugate, p. 186).

Mason was not the first of his fictional attorneys. Gardner was, however, for a number of years, reluctant to use a lawyer as a series protagonist, feeling that (as a fiction writer) he was too close to the material. In 1932, for *Black Mask,* he decided he was ready for a series on Ken Corning, the character many critics point to as the prototype for Perry Mason. Corning was a young fighting attorney from New York. He first appeared in November 1932 in the pages of *Mask* and was featured in five more issues into August of 1933. By then, Perry Mason was established in *The Case of the Velvet Claws,* and Gardner dropped the Corning series. Gardner was forty-three when *Velvet Claws* was published and had been a practicing lawyer for twenty-two years. In 1933, after the release of his first book, he finally stepped back from the profession, making himself available only on a consulting basis.

After being confined for so many years in a law office, Gardner yearned for an active outdoor life. In line with this interest, he had a camp wagon custom-built to his specifications, stocked it with equipment and food supplies, and happily took off for the high desert, accompanied by Rip, his German shepherd. For the pulps, Gardner wrote a series of modern westerns, which he dubbed his "Whispering Sands" series. His deep feelings for the terrain surfaced in a lyrical description quoted in his collection *Pay Dirt* (1983): "There it lies, miles on miles of it, dry lake beds, twisted mountains of volcanic rock, sloping sage-covered hills, clumps of Joshua trees, thickets of mesquite, bunches of giant cactus. It has the moods of a woman, and the treachery of a big cat" (p. 11).

Gardner claimed that the desert shaped character better than any other thing on earth. "The spell of the desert will grip you [as you] drift off to sleep, lulled by the sound of sand whispering to sand" (*Pay Dirt,* pp. 12–13). His daughter recalled that her father loved sleeping under the stars, that he felt "confined" indoors. A roof over his head was not natural to him—he wanted the sky for his roof. Relaxing under this open sky, Gardner was able to dictate up to fifteen thousand words a day. And having "refined" his prose, he finally achieved a breakthrough into the "slicks" (the higher-paying slick-paper magazines) when *Liberty* bought three of his Mason novels to run as serials.

Besides Mason, Gardner established several other running characters in the series to back up his fighting lawyer. His office at Seventh Street and Broadway in Los Angeles was presided over by secretary Della Street. Private eye Paul Drake, who did Mason's investigative work, had an office in the same building. Mason's antagonists were Hamilton Burger, the district attorney who constantly lost to Mason in court, and Police Lieutenant Arthur Tragg, who was often the arresting officer. Although he did not entirely abandon pulp writing until 1943, Gardner began slowing his production of pulp tales in favor of Mason and other writing projects.

Early in 1935 Gardner's marriage to Natalie ended. There was no divorce and no bitterness; he continued to send her money for the remainder of her life, but their close relationship was over. Gardner admitted that he had never been meant for marriage and family. By this point, Warner Brothers had acquired motion picture rights to several of Gardner's novels, and the studio was busily cranking out Perry Mason films. Three were released in 1935, with two more appearing in theaters in the following year. On-screen, Gardner's lawyer was portrayed by the dapper Warren William in the first four Masons and by the Latin lover Ricardo Cortez in the fifth. Neither actor pleased Gardner, and the liberties taken with his books roused him to outright anger.

The critic Joan Kotker, reviewing *Perry Mason* in the spring 1997 issue of the *Armchair Detective,* cites the fact that "the success of the film version of Dashiell Hammett's *The Thin Man* affected the Perry Mason movies. . . . The result was that in *The Case of the Curious Bride* Mason is introduced 'recovering from a drinking binge . . . on his office floor,' showing that just like Nick Charles, Mason can down them with the best" (p. 236). Additionally, instead of operating out of his small office, he heads up a huge law firm with an army of partners and secretaries. After a sixth film in the series, Gardner refused to license any more of his Mason novels to Hollywood. (He declared that he didn't need the money, and he certainly didn't need the grief.)

From the beginning of the Mason series, readers began to speculate on the exact relationship between Perry and Della. What was going on between them? Was it *more* than a boss/secretary relationship? Were they in love? Were they sleeping together? Would they marry? Gardner enjoyed this kind of speculation and often teased his readers by setting up emotional scenes that promised more than they delivered. In *The Case of the Lame Canary* (1937), Mason proposes to Della, but she gently rejects him with the comment that he is not the marrying kind. Perry won't take "no" for an answer. He asks her again in *The Case of the Substitute Face* (1938), and again she refuses, telling him that he does not really want a wife. He tries a third proposal in *The Case of the Drowsy Mosquito* (1943), but once again she declines his offer.

Actually, from the outset of the series, Gardner had determined that Perry and Della would never wed, despite reader demand to the contrary. In an essay for the *Atlantic* in January of 1965, he recalled giving in to such a demand when he was writing the Ed Jenkins stories for *Black Mask.* Ed became involved with a rich socialite, Helen Chadwick. She wanted him to marry her, and *Black Mask* readers agreed. They pressured Gardner into allowing Ed to marry Helen. Right away, he knew the marriage wouldn't work. The Phantom Crook just couldn't operate with a wife in tow. "So I . . . killed Helen off," Gardner stated. "My daughter [who was a Jenkins fan] wouldn't speak to me for a month." He went on to talk about the Mason series. "I'm in love with Della Street, [and] I'm not going to kill her off . . . better authors than I am find themselves unable to cope with the problem of a married hero, [so] I'm not going to paint myself into that corner again" (p. 75).

Della knows her place in Mason's life, not as his wife but as a secretary who was willing to go to jail for him. Della does, in fact, get arrested five times. She suborns a witness and conceals evidence to aid her boss. Furthermore, on at least four occasions, she risks death by physical violence. In other words, she will do anything for Perry—except marry him, which is just the way Gardner wanted it.

As Gardner's writing style matured over the years, Perry Mason matured too. In the early novels, the lawyer was cast very much in the pulp tradition; Gardner admitted that "smash-bang action" was really the basis of Mason's exploits. Certainly, in these early novels, Mason was much closer to a *Black Mask* private eye than to the calculating courtroom attorney he later became. In his first novelistic adventure, he actually carried a gun and was not averse to punching someone in the jaw. From his behavior in the early books, Mason could have been convicted of assault and battery, bribery, illegal wiretapping, fleeing a warrant, breaking and entering, reckless driving, and withholding and destroying evidence; his illegal misdeeds were numerous.

Ironically, critics later took Gardner to task for his *lack* of action and for the author's dependence, almost wholly, on dialogue. Francis Nevins, a longtime Mason fan, came to Gardner's defense in *Twentieth-Century Crime and Mystery Writers:* "What vivifies these novels is the sheer readability, the breakneck pacing, the involuted plots, the fireworks displays of courtroom tactics (many based on gimmicks Gardner used in his own law practice), and the dialogue, where each line is a jab in a complex form of oral combat" (p. 358).

Gardner was not always happy with his own efforts. In the mid-1930s, after more than a dozen Mason novels had been printed, including *The Case of the Lame Canary,* he became frustrated over what he saw as a mounting lack of realism in the series. In the future, he planned to keep "a tighter rein" on his formula-driven plots. Critic Russel B. Nye analyzed the Gardner novels in his comprehensive study, *The Unembarrassed Muse:* "Each Mason plot is divided into seven recognizable sections," he noted, "as formalized as Japanese Noh drama" (p. 255). He listed the seven sections:

1. The case is introduced.
2. Mason investigates.
3. His client is wrongly accused.
4. Mason investigates further.
5. The trial begins.
6. Mason reverses the case by introducing new evidence.
7. The true culprit is exposed in court.

Of course, Nye was correct—but he did not mention the diverse complications and fresh twists Gardner brought to this basic formula to maintain pace and suspense. He never bored or disappointed his loyal readers.

"The Mason of these novels," declared Nevins, "is a tiger in the social-Darwinian jungle, totally self-reliant, asking no favors, despising the weaklings who want society to care for them, willing to take any risk for a client no matter how unfairly the client plays the game with him" (*Twentieth-Century Crime and Mystery Writers,* p. 358). The Mason formula found a strong advocate in mystery master Raymond Chandler. In a 1946 letter to the author, he comments on Gardner's "artistic performance" and "intensity":

> That intensity may be a matter of style, situation, character, emotional tone, or idea. . . . It may also be a perfection of control over the movement of a story similar to the control a great pitcher has over the ball. That is to me what you have more than anything else and more than anyone else. . . . Every page throws the hook for the next. I call this a kind of genius. (*Selected Letters,* p. 69)

Retreat to Nature

In the autumn of 1937, roaming through California's back country, Gardner discovered his "ideal retreat," set outside Temecula amid rolling hills one hundred miles southeast of Los Angeles. It was here, in an area between ocean and desert, that he established his Rancho del Paisano—eventually adding twenty-seven new buildings on land encompassing three thousand acres. Gardner hated telephones, considering them a noisy distraction. For many years he refused to have one installed at his ranch. As the actor Ralph Bellamy explained, "If you wanted to get hold of Gardner, you had to call a Standard station in Temecula. When one of Gardner's crew drove past the station, the attendant would flag him down and relay the message. If Gardner thought it important, he would come down to the station and make a call from the telephone there" (Tuska, p. 102).

Gardner was far too restless to settle in a single location, and during the years he owned the ranch in Temecula he also traveled to a variety of other "hideouts" at scattered locations: to Paradise Camp in the timber country of northern California, to a desert retreat in Yucca Valley, to a house in Palm Springs, to another in Oceanside, to a cabin at Shasta Lake north of the San Francisco Bay, to a date ranch outside Indio, to a house in Portland, Oregon—and to a place he called "Camp Hood," on the Hood Canal in Washington State. Where he went, his "girls" went with him to handle his continuous stream of dictation. Their number increased as he built his mountain of prose, and he eventually employed six full-time secretaries. He came to depend on them as part of his essential team.

Writing, to Gardner, remained an exacting business. Far from the popular notion that he casually whipped out his novels, improvising each scene out of thin air at his Dictaphone, he actually spent many hours on each of them. Before beginning dictation, he worked out all of his plots in longhand with painstaking care in a variety of notebooks over a period of days or weeks. He would never start to dictate until every plot problem had been solved, every character fully delineated—and with the final courtroom fireworks laid out in detail. Letters to Thayer Hobson, Gardner's publisher and longtime friend, attest to the hard work he put into each book. Hobson pointed out that Gardner had a great appreciation for his readers and that he did not ever want to let them down. He did not write for a publisher; he wrote for the people.

Gardner loved animals, and the ranch at Temecula gave him the opportunity to fulfill his bigheartedness. He began by taking in a number of stray dogs (one neighbor called the place "dog heaven") and added horses, a baby coyote, a chipmunk—and even a pet mouse. He delighted in the fact that wild birds would wing down to eat from his hand. Nature was sacred to Gardner. Everything living, including the land and the rocks and the trees, were interchangeable to him, all part of a mysterious universe.

By September of 1937, Gardner's career had taken another upward turn when *The Saturday Evening Post* (a market he had been courting for years) serialized his eleventh Mason novel, *The Case of the Lame Canary.* (Over the next two and a half decades the *Post* serialized another fifteen Mason stories.) A second major slick, *Country Gentleman,* contacted Gardner, asking him to come up with a new series character that they could feature in their pages. He responded by creating the small-town district attorney Doug Selby (who appeared outside the pages of *Country Gentleman* in nine books over the next twelve years). In writing about Selby, Gardner crafted a fictionalized projection of himself, reflecting his early Oxnard days.

Late Writings and Multimedia Success

Despite the money earned from his pulp and slick sales (and from the Mason novels), Gardner was low on funds by the fall of 1938. His annual cost-of-living expenses had climbed to thirty thousand dollars, and he was forced to ask his publisher for an advance against future royalties. In an effort to provide additional income, he decided to create a new series under a pen name; he chose A. A. Fair. The series featured the adventures of an oddball pair of private investigators, Bertha Cool and Donald Lam.

Robin Smiley best described the pair (in his "Collecting Erle Stanley Gardner," from the November 1992 issue of *Firsts* magazine):

> Bertha Cool . . . is big, crude, and stingy. Bertha is adorned with a large tonnage of gold jewelry and likes physical exertion only a little better than spending money—that is, not at all. Her brightest operative (later in the series, her partner) is Donald Lam, a lawyer whose frank trickiness has run him afoul of

> the powers that be in the bar association, causing him to change his profession to private eye. Lam is tiny, weighing maybe 120 pounds. Bertha carries nearly that much weight around in the form of her gold jewelry alone. Donald is bright, fearless, and treads always on the edge of the law in the service of his clients. He also likes his female clients a little too much, and not necessarily platonically. Bertha finds his womanizing dangerous, if endearing. It has been argued that Donald Lam is the Gardner character who comes closest to the author's own personality and experience as a young lawyer in Oxnard. The Bertha Cool/Donald Lam books rank with the best Masons; some readers like them better. (p. 28)

When Morrow editors complained about Bertha's profanity, Gardner refused to tone down her salty dialogue, claiming that he swore as much as Bertha and telling Hobson that the publisher would just have to accept Bertha as he portrayed her. Readers did just that. The Cool and Lam duo detected their way through twenty-nine novels into 1970, achieving solid popularity with mystery buffs. (Although critics linked Fair to Gardner, the author kept his real name off the books until 1952, when he allowed Morrow to use the byline "by Erle Stanley Gardner, writing as A. A. Fair.")

Gardner often incorporated his experiences as a lawyer into his novels, using real-life cases in which he had been involved as the basis for many of his plots. One of these actual cases centered around the death of William Magby. He was found in a closed garage with the motor of his car running. Since he had attempted suicide earlier, it was assumed in this case that he had taken his own life. His family hired Gardner to prove that Magby's death was accidental, and he did so by citing the fact that the day was very windy and that this wind had blown the garage door shut while Magby was working on his car. Gardner won—and he used this same court argument in his A. A. Fair mystery *Double or Quits* (1941), in which the real Magby case took up a third of the novel.

Gardner often conducted extensive research for his fictional cases, once firing a gun at a tub full of water in his bathroom to see exactly how long it would take for the water to run out of the bullet hole. (He ruined the bathroom floor, but he found out what he needed to know for the book.)

When Gardner launched his Mason series in the 1930s, the mass-market paperback did not exist, but by 1940, with the emergence of Pocket Books, he had found a lucrative new outlet for his novels. At a quarter apiece, readers eagerly gobbled them up, and over the next two decades Pocket Books sold more than one hundred million Masons, with a company guarantee to Gardner of one hundred thousand dollars per year. With the paperback revolution in full swing, Perry Mason seemed to be everywhere, and Gardner's financial future was secure.

During the early 1940s into the mid-1950s, Gardner also covered certain major trials as a reporter for the *New York Journal-American*, the *Denver Post*, and the *San Francisco Examiner*. Additionally, he found time in 1955 to turn out twenty-eight articles for *American Weekly* in a series headed "The Casebook of True Crime." The Mason novels, however, were the center of his career: "Regardless of the market I plan to reach, Perry Mason . . . must deal with character conflicts, human emotions and situations which flow out of the relationships, rather than characters used merely to support the situations. Menace and suspense must flow naturally from what the people do and what they do must be logical" (Fugate, p. 75).

As Gardner turned away from the pulps, he was publishing as many as five books a year. His readers were insatiable; they could not get enough of Gardner. A Mason radio series was inevitable. In this era before television, millions of avid listeners tuned in each week to their favorite shows. In October of 1943, when radio drama was at its peak, "The New Adventures of Perry Mason" made its debut on CBS. (During the show's twelve-year run, Mason was played over the airwaves by Bartlett Robinson, Santos Ortega, Donald Briggs, and John Larkin.) Unlike Dashiell Hammett, who cared only about the money and had no creative interest whatever in the radio shows based on his characters (Sam Spade and the Thin Man, among others), Gardner carefully monitored the Mason series; he listened intently to every episode, reviewed scripts, and made detailed notes that he passed along to the show's producers. After his unhappy experience with Warner Brothers, he wanted to be sure that the radio world of Perry Mason accurately reflected the world of his novels.

Gardner's final *Black Mask* tale was printed in September of 1943, the year he quit writing for the pulps. His total of 104 stories exceeded that of any other *Black Mask* writer. Add to this another 450 tales (most of them long novelettes) penned for the rough-paper markets beyond *Black Mask,* and Gardner must be rated as one of the most prolific writers in pulp magazine history. It must also be noted that all through the pulp years, and increasingly thereafter, Gardner was writing articles by the score for such markets as *Sports Afield, Popular Photography, Desert Magazine, Life, Popular Science, Field and Stream,* and *Writers Digest* as well as numerous pieces on the use of bow and arrow for *Ye Sylvan Archer.*

With extra funds at his disposal, he was finally able to indulge his passion for travel and exploration on a much larger scale. In 1947 he mounted an expedition into the heart of Mexico's Baja California peninsula, over twelve hundred miles of dirt and sand roads, mountains, and dry washes. This trip resulted in the first of five books on Baja, *The Land of Shorter Shadows* (published by Morrow the following year). In all, he wrote thirteen travel books. Gardner had added yet another facet to his ever-expanding career.

His greatest challenge as a writer and humanitarian lay just ahead, a project that involved him deeply with the nation's criminal justice system. On a trip to New York early in 1948, Gardner stopped by the offices of *Argosy* to visit his old friend, the editor Harry Steeger, who was actively seeking fresh, offbeat material for the magazine. Gardner proposed an ongoing series of investigative pieces exposing unjustly convicted men and women who had become victims of the court. Steeger liked the idea and approved it for *Argosy.*

Of course, Gardner needed to have solid evidence to support his claims. For this purpose, in 1948 he formed a board of investigators made up of experts in various fields of criminology to review these special cases. This board became known as the Court of Last Resort. In all, over a ten-year period, Gardner wrote more than seventy-five articles for *Argosy* in this series, as well as a book, triggering the release of many unjustly imprisoned individuals. Along the way, the author became a self-taught authority in scientific crime detection. Dorothy Hughes paid tribute to Gardner's delving into these new areas of expertise: "He studied forensic medicine, polygraph work, and criminal psychology [and could] hold his own in discussions of the subjects with professionals in the field" (p. 266). Gardner's book on this subject, *The Court of Last Resort,* was published in 1952, winning him an Edgar the following year from the Mystery Writers of America in the "best fact-crime" category. It was a hard-earned and well-deserved honor. The impact Gardner made in this decade on the administration of justice cannot be overemphasized, and what he accomplished in prison reform was truly notable.

Paisano Productions

Perry Mason rolled onward. Beyond his success in hardcover and paperback and on the airwaves, Mason was destined to gain a vast new audience. His television debut was on the horizon. By the mid-1950s, radio drama was rapidly giving way to television. Network executives were well aware of Gardner's immense popularity, and they knew that a Mason television show would attract a very large viewing audience. The author, however, proved to be a hard sell, flatly turning down an offer of one million dollars for television rights to Perry Mason. The executives were stunned; what did this man want? What he wanted was creative control. He decided that the best way to obtain it was to produce the new series through a company of his own. Thus, in 1956 Paisano Productions was born, named after his ranch in Temecula.

From the outset, Gardner played watchdog on every Mason story or script; the early submissions roused his ire, and he fired off an angry letter venting his frustration to his old friend Hobson. Attacking the writers whose work he had reviewed, he declared that "each and every one of [them] wants to change Perry Mason. [They call it] 'adapting the character to television.' . . . It is the god-damndest assortment of crap. . . . Mason becomes a smart aleck, a wisecracker, a man who looks upon murder only as an opportunity for a new quip" (Hughes, pp. 165–166). It took Gardner a full year to prepare the show to his satisfaction. He personally chose dark-eyed actor Raymond Burr to portray Mason (and to this day, owing to constant reruns into the 1990s, Burr—who died in 1993—is still strongly identified with the role). Barbara Hale was signed to play steadfast Della Street, with actor William Talman as D.A. Hamilton Burger, who always lost his cases to Mason.

To Gardner, this was the way it had to be. Perry Mason could not lose in court. He must always win for his clients. Gardner pointed out that his public had not tired of this basic approach in twenty-five years. He explained exactly how he saw the concept: "This is the vision of the knight charging to the aid of the damsel in distress. It is the fairy godmother touch of Cinderella, in which justice is brought to the downtrodden. And it also has something of Robin Hood because Mason's mind is about the same as Robin's bow and arrow" (Fugate, p. 99).

Perry Mason made its debut on CBS in late September of 1957, becoming one of the most successful shows in television and running into the spring of 1966. Individual "Movies of the Week"—starring Burr as Mason—kept the series alive in subsequent decades. Gardner reviewed every story, from original presentation to final script. "I . . . know something about what the public wants," he declared, "and a hell of a lot about what the public *doesn't* want" (Hughes, p. 248).

Although it failed to attract a large viewing audience, Gardner's *Court of Last Resort* also debuted on television in 1957, running to twenty-six half-hour shows. Actor Lyle Bettger portrayed the chief investigator for a seven-man court that sought to free wrongfully convicted prisoners. Meanwhile, Gardner kept turning out books, publishing a new Mason novel every four months through the 1950s and into the mid-1960s, along with his travel tomes and the Cool and Lam adventures. In the 1960s, with one hundred books to his credit, he received a second Edgar from the Mystery Writers of America, in recognition by his peers of his status as a Grand Master of the genre.

By then in his seventies, he was still active and decided to take off for a new Baja adventure (and another travel book) as proof to his publishers and readers that he was not slowing down. In a gesture of farewell to his legendary pulp character Ed Jenkins, Gardner penned a final story about the Phantom Crook for *Argosy* in 1961—eighteen years after his last Jenkins story for *Black Mask.* Short fiction no longer occupied a place in his career. His main strength resided in the novel—and it is worth noting that of the 151 mystery novels that appeared on best-seller lists from 1895 to 1965, Gardner was responsible for 91. The law profession remained a dominant force in Gardner's life; it was always with him. As Hughes pointed out: "No matter his success as an author, no matter the world fame, he thought of himself always as a lawyer who had left the law to write stories" (p. 267).

Final Years

Thayer Hobson began to suffer rapidly failing health; his death in October of 1967 of a ruptured appendix proved to be a shattering blow to Gardner. It was followed, in February of 1968, by the news that his long-estranged wife, Natalie, had succumbed to a heart attack. Gardner was badly shaken, and he admitted that Natalie's passing was "a great shock." Their love for each other had never dimmed. Although they had been separated some thirty years, Gardner had always stayed in touch with her. After her death, Agnes Jean Bethell took center stage in his life. She had been an integral part of Gardner's career since his early days in Ventura, when she had first worked for him as a secretary. She traveled with him, supervised his work, protected his privacy, and was the real-life model for Mason's ever-loyal Della Street.

Gardner had promised that he would never marry anyone else so long as Natalie was alive. He had kept that promise. Now that his first wife was gone, however, he was finally free to marry Jean. The wedding took place on 7 August 1968 in Carson City, Nevada. Jean became his second wife despite the fact that she knew he was dying of cancer. Gardner battled the disease with the same energy and dedication he had devoted to his books, but this time, unlike his always-victorious lawyer, he was destined to lose. In a 1969 letter he admitted: "I have been making trips to the hospital. . . . I can't stand and I can't sit. I'm doing all my work these days lying down" (Hughes, p. 298).

His friends and neighbors at Temecula arranged a surprise party at the ranch to celebrate Gardner's eightieth birthday that July. He was in good spirits and thoroughly enjoyed himself. By October, however, Gardner was back in the hospital, undergoing severe cobalt treatments in an attempt to slow the cancer's progress. The treatments were ineffective. Back home, he worked on galleys for his latest novel, sending along a note to the publisher to explain why he had made some cuts, "to keep the pace fast and furious." Narrative drive was still a high priority with Gardner.

He endured more hospital treatment in January and February of 1970. Then came the dark news: his doctors told him that they could do no more to prolong his life. The end was very near. He asked Jean to take him home; he wanted to spend his final days in familiar surroundings. Erle Stanley Gardner died at Rancho del Paisano on 11 March 1970. The eulogy was delivered by Marshall Houts, who had worked with the author on the Court of Last Resort. Houts read from a book he had dedicated to his deceased friend: "To Erle Stanley Gardner, lawyer, author, citizen, friend—who contributed more to the cause of justice than any man of his generation" (Hughes, pp. 304–305). Gardner's cremated ashes were scattered over his beloved Baja Peninsula.

Conclusion

During the course of the two decades following his death (1971–1991), more than a dozen of his books were posthumously published under the supervision of Jean Gardner. Five of them feature Perry Mason—two novels (completed shortly before his death) and three collections—bringing the total volumes of Mason tales to eighty-six. Six other collections of his early pulp stories highlight such flamboyant characters as Lester Leith, Paul Pry, and Ed Jenkins, and two other volumes assemble the best of his "Whispering Sands" series.

What is Erle Stanley Gardner's legacy? His books continue to sell at a steady rate, and Perry Mason still wins court cases in endless television reruns; Gardner's credentials as one of the century's most successful mystery writers are firmly in place. But there is a broader picture to consider. Marvin Lachman, writing in the July 1970 issue of the *Armchair Detective,* sums up Gardner's ultimate achievements, placing him within the context of his times:

> Gardner's life and work was not so far removed from the turbulence of the United States in the 1970s. Erle Stanley Gardner's literary career spanned almost half a century (1921–1970)—a violent era in American history. He wrote during the time of Sacco-Vanzetti, the depression of the 30s, bitter (and bloody) labor-management disputes, World War II and its aftermath of Korea, the Cold

> War, and McCarthyism. He was still writing actively through the 1960s as violence and political assassination seemed to become a way of life in this country.
>
> In his personal life, Gardner was never a man to shirk the problems of his day. . . . He was interested in nature and active in helping to preserve the natural resources of North America . . . long before ecology became fashionable.
>
> However, even if Gardner had not been the activist he was, his contribution would still have been great. He gave enjoyment and a measure of needed relief to literally hundreds of millions of readers. Howard Haycraft has reported the importance of the mystery as a means of relaxation to weary Londoners during the days of the Blitz. It is not an exaggeration to point out that Gardner, as our most popular writer, has played a similar role in this country during the troubled days of the last 50 years.
>
> Perhaps skillfully disguised within the innocent pleasure of the Perry Mason books there is hidden a lesson. That lesson may be that those who commit violence will be ultimately punished as are the criminals in the Mason series. More importantly, the innocent (who are often poor in these books) can change their condition by the exercise of the kind of courage, honesty, resourcefulness and ingenuity which Mason demonstrates—and still remain within our system. Perry Mason's career has always been a search for justice, and if there were more Perry Masons in real life seeking justice, we could all sleep a bit more soundly at night. (p. 272)

The critic Jon Tuska ranks Gardner as "one of the most important authors of detective fiction in the Twentieth century," declaring that "his Perry Mason novels are sober and concerned with the interpretation of circumstantial evidence; his A. A. Fair books are filled with delightful humor; and his Doug Selby stories successfully capture the atmosphere of a small town in the middle decades of this century" (pp. 142–143).

In sum, Gardner, more than any other writer, popularized the law profession for a mass-market audience, melding fact and fiction to achieve a unique blend; no one ever handled courtroom drama better than he did. Gardner poured a lifetime of experience into his fiction, becoming expert in a dozen fields. He knew about mining and guns and terrain; he could discourse by the hour on police procedures, prison management, and forensic medicine. His books, however imaginative, were *authentic*. He took justifiable pride in that. As man and writer he was truly one of a kind, "a product of his era, a bold knight of rare calibre that our age no longer seems to produce" (Senate, p. iii). At Gardner's death, the doors of the fiction factory closed forever. But what was created there continues to entertain and instruct multitudes around the world.

Selected Bibliography

WORKS OF ERLE STANLEY GARDNER

NOVELS

The Case of the Velvet Claws. New York: Morrow, 1933.
The Case of the Sulky Girl. New York: Morrow, 1933.
The Case of the Lucky Legs. New York: Morrow, 1934.
The Case of the Howling Dog. New York: Morrow, 1934.
The Case of the Curious Bride. New York: Morrow, 1934.
The Clew of the Forgotten Murder. By "Carleton Kendrake." New York: Morrow, 1935.
This Is Murder. By "Charles J. Kenny." New York: Morrow, 1935.
The Case of the Counterfeit Eye. New York: Morrow, 1935.
The Case of the Caretaker's Cat. New York: Morrow, 1935.
The Case of the Sleepwalker's Niece. New York: Morrow, 1936.
The Case of the Stuttering Bishop. New York: Morrow, 1936.
The D.A. Calls It Murder. New York: Morrow, 1937.
The Case of the Dangerous Dowager. New York: Morrow, 1937.
The Case of the Lame Canary. New York: Morrow, 1937.
Murder up My Sleeve. New York: Morrow, 1937.
The Case of the Substitute Face. New York: Morrow, 1938.
The Case of the Shoplifter's Shoe. New York: Morrow, 1938.
The D.A. Holds a Candle. New York: Morrow, 1938.
The Case of the Perjured Parrot. New York: Morrow, 1939.

The Case of the Rolling Bones. New York: Morrow, 1939.
The D.A. Draws a Circle. New York: Morrow, 1939.
The Case of the Baited Hook. New York: Morrow, 1940.
The D.A. Goes to Trial. New York: Morrow, 1940.
The Case of the Silent Partner. New York: Morrow, 1940.
The Case of the Haunted Husband. New York: Morrow, 1941.
The Case of the Turning Tide. New York: Morrow, 1941.
The Case of the Empty Tin. New York: Morrow, 1941.
The D.A. Cooks a Goose. New York: Morrow, 1942.
The Case of the Drowning Duck. New York: Morrow, 1942.
The Case of the Careless Kitten. New York: Morrow, 1942.
The Case of the Smoking Chimney. New York: Morrow, 1943.
The Case of the Buried Clock. New York: Morrow, 1943.
The Case of the Drowsy Mosquito. New York: Morrow, 1943.
The D.A. Calls a Turn. New York: Morrow, 1944.
The Case of the Crooked Candle. New York: Morrow, 1944.
The Case of the Black-Eyed Blonde. New York: Morrow, 1944.
The Case of the Golddigger's Purse. New York: Morrow, 1945.
The Case of the Half-Wakened Wife. New York: Morrow, 1945.
The D.A. Breaks a Seal. New York: Morrow, 1946.
The Case of the Backward Mule. New York: Morrow, 1946.
The Case of the Borrowed Brunette. New York: Morrow, 1946.
Two Clues. New York: Morrow, 1947.
The Case of the Fan Dancer's Horse. New York: Morrow, 1947.
The Case of the Lazy Lover. New York: Morrow, 1947.
The Case of the Lonely Heiress. New York: Morrow, 1948.
The Case of the Vagabond Virgin. New York: Morrow, 1948.
The D.A. Takes a Chance. New York: Morrow, 1948.
The Case of the Dubious Bridegroom. New York: Morrow, 1949.
The Case of the Cautious Coquette. New York: Morrow, 1949.
The D.A. Breaks an Egg. New York: Morrow, 1949.
The Case of the Negligent Nymph. New York: Morrow, 1950.
The Case of the Musical Cow. New York: Morrow, 1950.
The Case of the One-Eyed Witness. New York: Morrow, 1950.
The Case of the Fiery Fingers. New York: Morrow, 1951.
The Case of the Angry Mourner. New York: Morrow, 1951.
The Case of the Moth-Eaten Mink. New York: Morrow, 1952.
The Case of the Grinning Gorilla. New York: Morrow, 1952.
The Case of the Hesitant Hostess. New York: Morrow, 1953.
The Case of the Green-Eyed Sister. New York: Morrow, 1953.
The Case of the Fugitive Nurse. New York: Morrow, 1954.
The Case of the Runaway Corpse. New York: Morrow, 1954.
The Case of the Restless Redhead. New York: Morrow, 1954.
The Case of the Glamorous Ghost. New York: Morrow, 1955.
The Case of the Sun Bather's Diary. New York: Morrow, 1955.
The Case of the Nervous Accomplice. New York: Morrow, 1955.
The Case of the Terrified Typist. New York: Morrow, 1956.
The Case of the Demure Defendant. New York: Morrow, 1956.
The Case of the Gilded Lily. New York: Morrow, 1956.
The Case of the Lucky Loser. New York: Morrow, 1957.
The Case of the Screaming Woman. New York: Morrow, 1957.
The Case of the Daring Decoy. New York: Morrow, 1957.
The Case of the Long-Legged Models. New York: Morrow, 1958.
The Case of the Foot-Loose Doll. New York: Morrow, 1958.
The Case of the Calendar Girl. New York: Morrow, 1958.
The Case of the Deadly Toy. New York: Morrow, 1959.
The Case of the Mythical Monkeys. New York: Morrow, 1959.
The Case of the Singing Skirt. New York: Morrow, 1959.
The Case of the Waylaid Wolf. New York: Morrow, 1960.
The Case of the Duplicate Daughter. New York: Morrow, 1960.
The Case of the Shapely Shadow. New York: Morrow, 1960.
The Case of the Spurious Spinster. New York: Morrow, 1961.
The Case of the Bigamous Spouse. New York: Morrow, 1961.
The Case of the Reluctant Model. New York: Morrow, 1962.
The Case of the Blonde Bonanza. New York: Morrow, 1962.
The Case of the Ice-Cold Hands. New York: Morrow, 1962.
The Case of the Mischievous Doll. New York: Morrow, 1963.
The Case of the Stepdaughter's Secret. New York: Morrow, 1963.
The Case of the Amorous Aunt. New York: Morrow, 1963.

The Case of the Daring Divorcee. New York: Morrow, 1964.
The Case of the Phantom Fortune. New York: Morrow, 1964.
The Case of the Horrified Heirs. New York: Morrow, 1964.
The Case of the Troubled Trustee. New York: Morrow, 1965.
The Case of the Beautiful Beggar. New York: Morrow, 1965.
The Case of the Worried Waitress. New York: Morrow, 1966.
The Case of the Queenly Contestant. New York: Morrow, 1967.
The Case of the Careless Cupid. New York: Morrow, 1968.
The Case of the Fabulous Fake. New York: Morrow, 1969.
The Case of the Fenced-In Woman. New York: Morrow, 1972. Published posthumously.
The Case of the Postponed Murder. New York: Morrow, 1973. Published posthumously.

NOVELS BY A. A. FAIR

The Bigger They Come. New York: Morrow, 1939.
Turn on the Heat. New York: Morrow, 1940.
Gold Comes in Bricks. New York: Morrow, 1940.
Spill the Jackpot. New York: Morrow, 1941.
Double or Quits. New York: Morrow, 1941.
Owls Don't Blink. New York: Morrow, 1942.
Bats Fly at Dusk. New York: Morrow, 1942.
Cats Prowl at Night. New York: Morrow, 1943.
Give 'em the Ax. New York: Morrow, 1944.
Crows Can't Count. New York: Morrow, 1946.
Fools Die on Friday. New York: Morrow, 1947.
Bedrooms Have Windows. New York: Morrow, 1949.
Top of the Heap. New York: Morrow, 1952.
Some Women Won't Wait. New York: Morrow, 1953.
Beware the Curves. New York: Morrow, 1956.
You Can Die Laughing. New York: Morrow, 1957.
Some Slips Don't Show. New York: Morrow, 1957.
The Count of Nine. New York: Morrow, 1958.
Pass the Gravy. New York: Morrow, 1959.
Kept Women Can't Quit. New York: Morrow, 1960.
Bachelors Get Lonely. New York: Morrow, 1961.
Shills Can't Cash Chips. New York: Morrow, 1961.
Try Anything Once. New York: Morrow, 1962.
Fish or Cut Bait. New York: Morrow, 1963.
Up for Grabs. New York: Morrow, 1964.
Cut Thin to Win. New York: Morrow, 1965.
Widows Wear Weeds. New York: Morrow, 1966.
Traps Need Fresh Bait. New York: Morrow, 1967.
All Grass Isn't Green. New York: Morrow, 1970.

SHORT STORY COLLECTIONS

(All but the first collection were published posthumously.)

The Case of the Murderer's Bride and Other Stories. Edited by Ellery Queen. New York: Davis, 1969.
The Case of the Crimson Kiss. New York: Morrow, 1971.
The Case of the Crying Swallow. New York: Morrow, 1971.
The Case of the Irate Witness. New York: Morrow, 1972.
The Amazing Adventures of Lester Leith. Edited by Ellery Queen. New York: Dial Press, 1980.
The Human Zero: The Science Fiction Stories. Edited by Martin H. Greenberg and Charles G. Waugh. New York: Morrow, 1981.
Whispering Sands: Stories of Gold Fever and the Western Desert. Edited by Charles G. Waugh and Martin H. Greenberg. New York: Morrow, 1981.
Pay Dirt and Other Whispering Sands Stories of Gold Fever and the Western Desert. Edited by Charles G. Waugh and Martin H. Greenberg. New York: Morrow, 1983.
The Adventures of Paul Pry. New York: Mysterious Press, 1989.
Dead Men's Letters. New York: Carroll & Graf, 1990.
The Blonde in Lower Six. New York: Carroll & Graf, 1990.
Honest Money. New York: Carroll & Graf, 1991.

NONFICTION

The Land of Shorter Shadows. New York: Morrow, 1948.
The Court of Last Resort. New York: Morrow, 1952.
Neighborhood Frontiers. New York: Morrow, 1954.
Hunting the Desert Whale. New York: Morrow, 1960.
Hovering over Baja. New York: Morrow, 1961.
The Hidden Heart of Baja. New York: Morrow, 1962.
This Desert Is Yours. New York: Morrow, 1963.
The World of Water. New York: Morrow, 1964.
Hunting Lost Mines by Helicopter. New York: Morrow, 1965.
Off the Beaten Track in Baja. New York: Morrow, 1967.
Gypsy Days on the Delta. New York: Morrow, 1967.
Mexico's Magic Square. New York: Morrow, 1968.
Drifting down the Delta. New York: Morrow, 1969.
Host with the Big Hat. New York: Morrow, 1970.
Cops on Campus and Crime in the Streets. New York: Morrow, 1970.

ARCHIVES

The Gardner Papers (probably the most extensive single-author collection extant) is housed at the Humanities Research Center at the University of Texas, Austin. This huge collection includes *millions* of items—from manuscripts, notebooks, letters, and books to a full-scale replica of Gardner's working study from Temecula.

BIOGRAPHICAL AND CRITICAL STUDIES

Bounds, J. Dennis. *Perry Mason: The Authorship and Reproduction of a Popular Hero.* Westport, Conn.:

Greenwood Press, 1996. A study of Gardner's world-famous character, with emphasis on radio, television, and film adaptations.

Chandler, Raymond. *Selected Letters of Raymond Chandler.* Edited by Frank MacShane. New York: Columbia University Press, 1981. Includes several letters to Gardner.

Fugate, Francis L., and Roberta B. Fugate. *Secrets of the World's Best-Selling Writer: The Storytelling Techniques of Erle Stanley Gardner.* New York: Morrow, 1980. Includes charts, diagrams, outlines, with several appendices on plotting, characters, backgrounds, method, and theory. Quotes heavily from Gardner's notebooks.

Goulart, Ron. *The Dime Detectives: A Comprehensive History of the Detective Fiction Pulps.* New York: Mysterious Press, 1988. Contains detailed analysis of many of Gardner's early crime-solving characters.

Hughes, Dorothy B. *Erle Stanley Gardner: The Case of the Real Perry Mason.* New York: Morrow, 1978. With the most extensive bibliography extant of Gardner's books, stories, articles, and media works, compiled by Ruth Moore. With seventy-three photos.

Johnston, Alva. *The Case of Erle Stanley Gardner.* New York: Morrow, 1947. The first book-length study of Erle Stanley Gardner.

Nolan, William F. *The Black Mask Boys: Masters in the Hard-Boiled School of Detective Fiction.* New York: Morrow, 1985. Gardner is profiled as one of eight major *Black Mask* authors, with a checklist of his work for the magazine, and with one of his *Black Mask* pulp stories reprinted.

Nye, Russel B. *The Unembarrassed Muse: The Popular Arts in America.* New York: Dial Press, 1970. An all-inclusive study of popular culture containing a section on Gardner and Perry Mason.

Reilly, John M., ed. *Twentieth-Century Crime and Mystery Writers,* 2nd ed. New York: St. Martin's Press, 1991. Contains a lengthy bibliography/biography of Erle Stanley Gardner.

Senate, Richard L. *Erle Stanley Gardner's Ventura: The Birthplace of Perry Mason.* Ventura, Calif.: Charon Press, 1996. Includes a checklist of Erle Stanley Gardner's books.

Tuska, Jon. *In Manors and Alleys: A Casebook on the American Detective Film.* Westport, Conn.: Greenwood Press, 1988. Includes a lengthy section, "Perry Mason," within the chapter "The Master Detectives."

Van Dover, J. Kenneth. *Murder in the Millions: Erle Stanley Gardner, Mickey Spillane, Ian Fleming.* New York: Ungar, 1984.

Michael Gilbert
(b. 1912)

B. A. PIKE

Michael Francis Gilbert was born on 17 July 1912, in Billinghay, Lincolnshire, the son of Bernard Samuel Gilbert and Berwyn Minna Cuthbert Gilbert. He attended St. Peter's, Seaford, and Blundell's School, and received a bachelor of laws degree from the University of London in 1937. He worked as an articled clerk from 1938 to 1939, before joining the Honourable Artillery Company. He served in North Africa and Italy during World War II. Captured in January 1943, he was held in an Italian prisoner of war camp until his escape in September 1943. In 1947 he joined Trower, Still and Keeling, a firm of solicitors in Lincoln's Inn, in which he later became a partner. Also in 1947, he married Roberta Mary Marsden. They have seven children. In 1980 he was appointed a Commander of the Order of the British Empire (CBE) by Her Majesty Queen Elizabeth II.

Gilbert is one of the most versatile of mystery writers, with several strings to his bow. In 1951, Eric Forbes-Boyd of the *Sunday Times* described him as "equally able to summon up suspense with wig and gown or cloak and dagger," and he has himself identified the number of "promising pools" into which he has "dipped": the detective story or whodunit; the adventure story or thriller; the whydunit, concerned with motive rather than motion; and the spy story and the police procedural. To these should be added the revenge story, where getting even is the mainspring of the action. This has been something of a speciality of Michael Gilbert, especially in the shorter form.

Among earlier mystery writers, he most admires Margery Allingham and Dorothy L. Sayers, "the two best detective writers of the century" (Michael Gilbert, letter to author, 17 May 1997), and he allows that his work owes something to their example. He has been widely praised throughout his career, often by those best in a position to judge him, his crime-writing peers: among them Eric Ambler, Francis Iles, Edmund Crispin, Anthony Boucher, Julian Symons, and Amanda Cross. Eudora Welty is quoted admiring "that old Gilbert expertise." He holds the Diamond Dagger of the Crime Writers Association and is a Grand Master of the Mystery Writers of America.

Throughout his career, Gilbert's primary concern has been to entertain the reader: to stimulate, to amuse, to intrigue, and to satisfy. He also contrives, without lecturing, to inform and even to educate, not only in the legal expertise of his own professional life but in many other fields of specific criminal investigation and general human experience: ballistics, forensics, tide tables, archaeology, genetic codes, the specifics of how bombs are made and how bodies float. Implicit in all he writes is a firm faith in an ordered society, in "the old bastions" of civilization: "religion, family life, the rule of law" (*Anything for a Quiet Life*, 1990, p. 112). He shows continually his belief in the basic human right to life without fear in all its forms and in the need to check, control, and punish those who disregard the law and disrupt and even destroy the lives of others.

Early Novels, 1947–1953

Gilbert began to establish a significant reputation with his first book, *Close Quarters* (1947). For devotees of well-bred detection this remains a key title, satisfying in several ways—in its cathedral close setting; in the vitality of its closed circle of suspects; in the challenge of a complicated puzzle, enhanced by the lure of a crossword; and in the comforting demonstration that from chaos, order may be restored. From the same mold is *Smallbone Deceased* (1950), a fruit of the author's early experience as a solicitor in Lincoln's Inn. It keeps its place among the elite of legal detective novels, with an intricate action arising from certain defects of character and certain subtleties of law. The narrative makes felicitous use of the rhythms of a legal office, at once defined and dissected by the patient investigation of Henry Bohun, a recent recruit to the firm, with above-average thinking time, since he is a noctambulist.

Between the early detective novels Gilbert published two thrillers, not necessarily to show his versatility but undoubtedly with that effect. *They Never Looked Inside* (U.S. title, *He Didn't Mind Danger*) appeared in 1948 and *The Doors Open* in 1949. Both are action stories in the grand tradition, with rackets to be smashed and action men to tackle the tougher assignments; their being so palpably of their time, however, gives them an individual savor. They inhabit a postwar world of hope and recovery but also of uncertainty, disappointment, and continuing privation. They dramatize the opportunities for crime created by instability and press into service "the restless dissatisfaction of the demobbed soldier" (*They Never Looked Inside*, 1964 ed., p. 131).

With *Death Has Deep Roots* (1951), Gilbert added the courtroom novel to his bag, admirably combining the formal grace of the detective puzzle with the forward thrust of the thriller. The narrative includes a detailed account of a murder trial at the Old Bailey, with much court procedure and a gratifying climax. *Death in Captivity* followed in 1952 and drew on the author's own experience as a prisoner of war in Italy. Again the formal processes of the detective novel provide the fundamental appeal of the story, while the prison camp setting gives it its distinctive character. This book was filmed as *Danger Within*, from its American title. The U.S. edition omits the two closing chapters, based on the hazardous walk "along the backbone of the Appennines" undertaken in 1943 by the author and two other escaped prisoners.

Fear to Tread (1953) returns to the territory of the earlier thrillers, the dodgy, dangerous London of thugs, racketeers, and organized crime. The doughty head of a tough South London school becomes involved with a lucrative black market in food, still flourishing ten years after the war. Mr. Wetherall puts himself in the position of the "small boy who thought it was *such* fun fiddling with the detonator of the ten-thousand-pound bomb" and emerges bloody but unbowed.

All the novels to 1953, excepting only *Death in Captivity*, benefit from the reassuring presence of Chief Inspector Hazlerigg, the first of Gilbert's series policemen and a stalwart of what might be called the old school. He is shrewd and experienced, thorough, sane, and dependable, with the humanity of a seasoned campaigner and acknowledged, unquestioned authority. Although far from the omniscient, inviolable detectives of the great tradition and with nothing fanciful about him, he yet shares with them the power to shape events and impose order on chaos. Adept at pulling strings and picking up pieces, he does not himself run into danger; rather, he asserts by his very presence a guarantee that all will eventually be well.

Novels, 1955–1980

Sky High (1955; U.S. title, *The Country-House Burglar*) presents an enterprising villain, who gives us a run for our money before his unmasking. One of the most endearing of Gilbert's novels, it is at once a lively thriller, with a bomb in a lavatory cistern, and a beguiling whodunit, set amid the rural decorum of whist drives and choir practice. *Be Shot for Sixpence*, which followed in 1956, breaks new ground, moving from familiar London streets to the Austro-Hungarian border and on into Yugoslavia (though it opens in Kent with an engaging self-portrait of the author: "the mildest of men . . . writing thrillers [in a] converted rectory . . . [with] a wife, a small, resolute woman with the spirit of a grenadier and four fat daughters" [p. 9]). It is defined by its British dust-jacket blurb as "a thrilling fast-paced story of international intrigue" and the action is launched in time-honored fashion with an advertisement in the personal column of the *Times*. What begins as a quest for a vanished friend ramifies into something altogether more demanding. *After the Fine Weather* (1963) is cut from the same cloth, an edgy thriller set in the Tyrol, with a climax "in the tradition of high adventure," according to its publisher. The hapless witness of an assassination is caught up in the dangerous sequel to the killing. She survives to show her mettle, in the approved manner of heroines worthy of the name.

Between these action thrillers Gilbert published his first full-fledged police procedural novel, *Blood and Judgement* (1959), which remains a prime achievement. The police protagonist is no longer Hazlerigg, but a younger man, still with his way to make. Patrick Petrella first appeared in stories published in the British fiction magazine *Argosy* during the 1950s (and did not feature in another novel until 1993, when *Roller-Coaster* appeared). This case is important for him in that it brings him into direct conflict with a superior officer, whom he disobeys by conducting an independent investigation beyond his orders. He is made aware that sometimes "the police stink" and are concerned only with "cobbling up" a case—here by withholding from a coroner's court evidence that might help the defense. The outcome is sufficiently a triumph for him to make it expedient for his superiors to disregard his stepping out of line. Justice, in fact, is served by his action.

The Crack in the Teacup (1966) takes its title from a poem by W. H. Auden, where the mundane details of domestic life are seen as veiling the darker extremes of existence: "The crack in the teacup opens / The lane to the land of the dead." The detective is a young solicitor in a small seaside town bedeviled by the abuse of power in local government. His curiosity is prompted by a display of violence, which he himself witnesses: a warning sign of a deeper corruption, there for anyone who will read it. The novel benefits immeasurably from the author's presentation of small-town government and his canny manipulation of its procedures. The reader is drawn into a crusade and committed from the outset by moral indignation and eagerness to see wrongs righted, yet the narrative is always buoyant, and no sermons are in evidence.

Flash Point (1974) is akin to *The Crack in the Teacup* in that it, too, questions the integrity of those who wield civic power, but it inhabits a wider territory, taking in government, the press, and the law at a national level. The prime target of the campaign that occupies the narrative is a popular and gifted Member of Parliament, invaluable to his party and, potentially, to the nation. A charge against him, maintained implacably by the lawyer who brings it, sets events in motion, prompting an intricate sequence of attack and counterattack, controlled by the author with characteristic aplomb. The significant issue addressed by the narrative is the "hard, inescapable fact that those who govern are irked by the fetters of the law" (p. 179). Among much else to provoke thought, we encounter "an agency of the Government . . . prepared to break the law in order to protect its own people, if they're important enough" (p. 131).

The Etruscan Net (1969; U.S. title, *The Family Tomb*) is set in postdiluvian Florence and evidently draws on the author's experience in Italy. The narrative is buttressed by a learning lightly worn, necessary because the action hinges on dubious Etruscan artifacts and the English protagonist is a distinguished Etruscologist, imprisoned falsely on a hit-and-run charge. A picturesque English colony contributes richly to the action, particularly in defense of its ill-used compatriot. It is, however, the Italians who dominate and largely make the narrative. The novel derives much of its effect from the contrast between the age-old decorum of a great center of civilization and the tension induced by fears of injustice and violence.

The Body of a Girl (1972) offers a powerful account of the effects of greed and violence on a small community: "the power of money and the power of fear." It sounds from the outset a warning note, in the voice of a senior Home Office official, who fears that "a total breakdown of law and order" may be at hand. The action is set in a town high on the Thames and moves from the discovery of a well-hidden corpse to a violent climax in a safe deposit vault surrounded by water. Besides murder, it encompasses suicide, blackmail, intimidation, and organized crime. The investigation is conducted jointly by the local force and a newcomer, the equivocal Chief Inspector Mercer, a new kind of policeman, attuned to the tougher times in which he operates. A long way from Hazlerigg and some way, even, from Petrella, he is both ruthless and unscrupulous, a valuable ally but a dangerous enemy. His colleagues resent and mistrust him, so much so that his conduct is officially questioned. At the end, he risks his career for a brutal personal revenge (and acknowledges that he and the killer are men of the same stamp).

Death of a Favourite Girl (1980) is an even finer achievement, recognizably from the same mold, but richer and deeper and with a more powerful resonance. It is equally effective as police procedural and whodunit, persuasive and absorbing with a staggering surprise held in reserve for the closing pages. The favorite girl is a TV celebrity who gives her name to the American edition, *The Killing of Katie Steelstock*. She continues to live in the community in which she has grown up, that of a Thames-side village, more focused and close-knit than its counterpart in *The Body of a Girl*. An early sequence defines the community in some detail, by way of a dance at which key figures are present. This is traditional Gilbert country, reminiscent of *Sky High*, but the disruption is harsher and the tensions run higher and reach further. Katie's death brings into the open much that is dark and disturbing, not least her own need to dominate through emotional cruelty; she has been a "bitch" with "a saw-edged tongue," scheming and unscrupulous, with a liking for "the whip hand" and a wish to "have people on the end of a string" (p. 116). Her death is investigated by Superintendent Charles Knott, a practical policeman displaying "a hard professionalism." Even though he "is not an intellectual man," he is able, from an instinct combining shrewdness and experience, to "grasp the shape and outline of any crime he was called on to investigate." Like Mercer, he represents a threat: to the suspects in the case, to the rural colleagues he regards as "swedes," even to justice itself. Together, "the narrowness of his vision" and "the weight of his personality" make him formidable, implacable in pursuit, and impossible to deflect from his chosen course. He lacks integrity, claiming that it is "for the opposition to prove him wrong" (p. 144) and suppressing part of the evidence to make it harder for them to do so. Since, in this case, he *is* wrong, his power is seriously abused.

By contrast, *The Ninety-Second Tiger* (1973) is one of the lightest of Gilbert's novels, a slick, swift thriller set in the Persian Gulf and a fruit of the author's own experience as legal adviser to the ruler of Bahrain. The Tiger of the title is the hero of a long-running television series, in the course of which he has "rescued ninety-one beautiful girls and knocked out ninety-one villains" (p. 13). When the series ends, he is recruited as military adviser by the ruler of Umran, "a student of television" unable, it seems, to distinguish between a figure of fantasy and the actor who plays him. Events, however, support the view that they are interchangeable. The actor takes the job and the Tiger enters a dangerous world of assassins and private wars, smuggling arms and mineral rights. Of course, he enhances his television status in the process, and the novel ends with a wry reflection prompted by the making of the ninety-second *Tiger*: "If life went on at its present rate, writers of this sort of stuff were going to have to run fast to keep up with it."

The Night of the Twelfth (1976) draws traditional strengths from the details of police procedure and the false trails of the whodunit but gains its particular force from its resort to abnormal psychology. The narrative makes potent use of the claim that "for ninety-nine per-cent of the time the pure sadist acts perfectly normally," and we see, at the end, the disintegration of "an apparently agreeable man" (p. 151), revealed as "hollow and black and vicious," suddenly less than human, reduced, appallingly, to a "thing" (p. 217). The setting is a high-grade preparatory school in Sussex, an enclosed and privileged world, linked by sudden shocking evidence to a series of sadistic murders of prepubescent boys. The school setting intensifies the fear that we feel, a mounting anxiety as to who may suffer and what may be revealed. Small privacies are invaded, and defects of personality seem as if they might turn monstrous; even so serious a matter as an attempted abduction appears mild in comparison with the hideous threat that pervades the action. The indications of the truth are set scrupulously before us, but so cunning is the manipulation of character and incident that the outcome brings a considerable shock.

The Empty House (1978) is a political thriller, centered on a deadly discovery in the field of biological warfare. The scientist responsible is assumed to have died when his car goes over a cliff in north Devon, but he proves to have insured himself first, so that suspicion is properly aroused. The action develops into a quest for the vanished boffin, (expert), conducted principally by an astute young insurance investigator with an exceptional visual memory and a capacity for survival. He has, too, the advantage of knowing the territory, with friends at court from his time at Blundell's, John Ridd's school in Tiverton: the narrative ranges with ease and authority over the Exmoor landscape. The action is vigorous and various, a complicated sequence of move and countermove involving the British secret service and an assortment of dangerous imposters, aliens programmed to political ends and ruthless in their pursuit. Their activities are invoked by the title of the novel, a quotation from a poem by William Butler Yeats, brought into focus in the closing chapters.

Novels, 1982–1997

End Game (1982; also published in the U.K. as *The Final Throw*) is a thriller, conforming admirably to Gilbert's own description of certain of his later works: "a straight adventure story with criminal or legal trimmings." The action is meticulously organized and amply provides "trimmings" of both kinds: dubious continental coach tours; a dangerous East End "fixer"; section 54 of the Finance Act; and a series of phone calls, recorded and transcribed by the recipient. The pattern of the narrative mirrors a game of snakes and ladders (from which a complex police operation is named). One player, despite his quick wits, seems "destined to descend," while another moves up, with equal inevitability. At the top of the board is the "Genghis Khan of the business world," who collects companies "like cigarette cards" (*The Final Throw*, p. 16); at the bottom is the educated tramp with whom the story starts, a wretched, wasted ruin almost destroyed by heroin.

The Long Journey Home (1985) is likewise

an ambitious action thriller, founded partly on the link between money and the abuse of power and partly on revenge as a motive. It offers Gilbert's most extended treatment of a favorite theme and forcefully displays the singleness of purpose of the committed avenger. From the first there is the threat of violence, realized as the narrative progresses in a series of extreme events. In early scenes set in Italy, an entire neighborhood suffers brutal abuse, and even in a high-level English boardroom an undercurrent of violence makes itself felt. No fewer than nine of the characters die hideously: four by fire, three in a Dartmoor quicksand, one in a lift that cuts him in half, and one on a wheel, tortured most cruelly before his end. The action is launched in Rome, where the future avenger allows his plane to leave without him, so entering the charmed life that sustains him, in true action hero fashion, throughout the dangers that lie ahead. His engineer's eye has registered the defects that cause the plane to crash on the first lap of its journey. He goes on to avoid death by fire in an Appennine farmhouse and turns the tables on a contract killer in Nice—the former simply by luck, the latter through a timely warning and inspired quick thinking. He achieves, spectacularly, a double revenge—of reciprocal fire for the man who burned to death his Italian friends and of Devonshire mud for those who tortured and murdered his English ally. The narrative is saved from any sense of facile heroics by the precision of the writing and its intensity of feeling; both the European scenes and the boardroom power game are finely achieved. Beyond the pristine zest of action and adventure is a heartfelt awareness of how dreadful life can be for those who become its victims.

Between these vigorous thrillers came *The Black Seraphim* (1983), a gentler book set, like *Close Quarters*, in Melchester, but more like *The Crack in the Teacup* in that civic corruption is a dominant theme and the author's legal and financial expertise is well to the fore. There is civil war in the city, with church and state at odds; two newspapers foment the dissension, and those with feet in both camps are destroyed. Dean and Archdeacon fail to agree, each aware of his powers and resolute in invoking them. Both are intransigent men, the Dean awesomely so and the Archdeacon more irksomely. It is the latter who dies during a cathedral service, having been set up, in time-honored fashion, as the least popular denizen of the close. Motives for eliminating him proliferate, lengthening the odds and intensifying interest. A young pathologist investigates, pursuing elusive forensic evidence with due caution and concern.

Trouble (1987) is a metropolitan thriller in the line from *Fear to Tread* and *Flash Point*, but far more dangerous than either. The novel displays an impressive relevance to the modern world and its more violent preoccupations; even the dust-jacket blurb contains a reference to today's headlines. It may properly be deemed explosive, since the smuggling of supplies for the Irish Republican Army is a major issue. Terrorism and racial tensions carry equal weight within the narrative, converging as the action progresses, so that what has seemed to be advancing on two fronts becomes concentrated to a single powerful surge toward the close. Child pornography and professional rivalries also contribute to the pattern, one of the most intricate of Gilbert's devising. He shows himself as adept with public anxieties as with personal tragedies, with schoolboy bravado as with extremes of adult ruthlessness. A vicious terrorist is a key figure, and one of the many reasons for continuing to read is the desire to see him brought low. To defeat the enemy requires cooperation among "the judicial, the executive and the advisory" powers: "If trouble came, things would go smoothly only if all parts of the machine meshed together" (p. 93). The action demonstrates how the meshing is achieved, with eleventh-hour luck and despite many difficulties. The resolution restores a sort of stability, but the cost has been high, and the peace is unlikely to be permanent. The summing-up is simple and heartfelt: "What a mess."

Paint, Gold, and Blood (1989) is an engaging thriller in a lighter vein. Despite a strong leavening of brutality, it displays much of the zest and allure of the traditional adventure story. The hero—and the old-fashioned word is appropriate—is a "beautiful young man" who looks "just . . . hatched from the egg" (p. 254). He is still at school when the action opens, on holiday in France and about to begin his sentimental education with a chambermaid when violence supervenes. The narrative embraces a multitude of sins: fraud at a public school, a cynical trade in astrology, the bombing of a Parisian restaurant, art forgery and a traffic in stolen pictures, the laundering of ill-gotten gains, and a series of ruthless political murders. The pictures range from a supreme masterpiece by Titian to the dreadful daubs of Beatrice Oldfield (dispatched, with amazing frequency, to South America). The action is sufficiently complex and varied to atone for an uninhibited resort to coincidence, and beyond all the foreground fireworks is an implicit account of an unspoken rivalry between the *jeune premier* and his closest friend (who is astute and ambitious, lacking in scruple, and as likely to figure at Westminster Abbey as at the Old Bailey).

The Queen Against Karl Mullen (1991) is described in its blurb as "a novel about the games lawyers play." It shows that those engaged in the service of the law are resourceful people, adept at the side step and usually with another shot in the locker. It acknowledges that some solicitors are known to "fabricate evidence," that "a lot of criminal procedure is unethical," that sufficiently eminent persons may legally attempt to evade the consequences of their actions, and that the object of a criminal trial is not to establish truth but to "demonstrate whether convincing proof can be adduced of the guilt of the man charged." In favor of English law is the fact of its being "old enough and steady enough to stand up for unpopular people" and also that it allows for the occasional intelligent jury, such as that which determines the fate of Karl Mullen. He is a colonel in the South African military police, a harsh, uncompromising man with a reputation for unspeakable brutality. His arrival in London to extradite a terrorist provokes extreme reactions among those for whom "hatred of the South African regime" is "a religion," their cause "a fight against evil." Feeling against him runs high and is intensified by the newspaper coverage of his case. We are made grimly aware of the power of the press to influence public feeling and of the double standards inherent in much journalism. The journalists involved are cynically determined that "the pot . . . be kept on the boil" and are intoxicated by "dangerous and exciting possibilities." The action is crowded and various, the narrative rich and provocative. Explosive material is handled with impeccable judgment and to persuasive effect.

Roller-Coaster is Gilbert's farewell to Patrick Petrella, his clever, unorthodox policeman, now the Superintendent in charge of No. 2 Area East, north of the Thames, "full of tough people and criminal possibilities" (p. 11). It is an exhilarating police procedural, worthy of Petrella on his final appearance. It takes us confidently through the routines and responsibilities that make up this particular policeman's lot, and we come to understand why he regards his work as "the roller-coaster on which he was a captive passenger." We are made aware that, merely by occupying the office he holds, he releases hostile forces, having always to watch his back and stay ahead of his enemies. The action involves him with murderous thugs, with wage snatches and boat thefts, with a trade in child pornography, with a self-righteous investigative journalist, with a priest's suicide, with a potentially rogue sergeant, with an actually corrupt senior colleague, with a disciplinary inquiry into his own conduct, and with a final confrontation in time to prevent a murder. It also brings him up against "the idiotic rules we've made, to wrap criminals up in cotton wool," and the fact that, in certain cases, police action "doesn't depend on the rights and wrongs of the case. It depends on the nature of your quarry." The members of "the criminal class" are hounded with all the power at the law's command, but those of superior status often are not.

Ring of Terror (1995) is unexpected: a departure from Gilbert's accustomed treatment of contemporary life and crime. It is the first of an intended trilogy of novels set in the earlier part of the century, all involving a new series detective, Luke Pagan. He is a boy of fifteen when the story opens but is soon established as an ambitious constable in the Metropolitan Police force.

Uncharacteristically for Gilbert, whose usual method has been to weave a pattern from interlocking strands of dialogue and incident, the narrative here is virtually linear to the halfway point, following Luke and his perception of people and events: thereafter, the familiar modus operandi prevails. The action centers on a ring of Russian immigrants, bent on civic disruption and willing to kill policemen in the process. The Tsar's first minister has "undertaken to promote a campaign of terror in London," to force the British government to "send back to Russia all recently arrived emigrés" (p. 141). Winston Churchill is home secretary, and he and the siege of Sidney Street figure in the action; the Clapham Common murder is also invoked. The authorities are handicapped, then as now, by "our well-known tolerance" (p. 90), limited powers, public hostility, and human fallibility. At the end, Luke is co-opted into MO5, the "Home Security section," founded in 1909 and destined to become "one of the most important outfits in the country" (p. 216) at the time of World War I.

In *Into Battle* (1997), Luke is an established secret agent, posing as a waiter in a Portsmouth hotel in pursuit of a German spy well established in an English identity: a dangerous, constant presence, patient, resilient, and ruthless. The second stage is set in London, where Scotland Yard and MO5 combine to defeat Operation Asgard, a German conspiracy to weaken British defenses, complicated by Irish thugs with "a very adequate motive for supporting the Germans" (p. 102). For the final stage we move to Le Touquet, where a British military encampment is bedeviled by internal treacheries and the threat of a hostile army assembling in secret nearby. The narrative achieves an effect of sober truth, recording historical events and featuring such eminent contemporaries as Basil Thomson, head of the Criminal Investigation Division at Scotland Yard, and Bernard Spilsbury, a leading pathologist of his day. At the same time, it has the lively appeal of a traditional adventure thriller, in which Luke and his associates survive against heavy odds and, eventually, rout the opposition. As always, the author makes us aware of the problems of keeping order in a country where a subversive journalist may operate unchecked, where local police are suspicious of secret agents, and where a magistrate can thwart the course of justice. His admiration for Vernon Kell, the head of MO5, is always apparent and entirely persuasive. A third and final Luke Pagan novel is planned, to be entitled *Over and Out*.

Short Stories

Besides his novels, Michael Gilbert is the author of nearly one hundred collected stories and more than seventy uncollected stories, published in newspapers, magazines, and anthologies. The collected stories are assembled in nine volumes.

Game Without Rules (1967), *Mr. Calder and Mr. Behrens* (1982), and a reprint collection, *The Road to Damascus* (1990), are remarkable for a fusion of elegance and violence; the same might be said for their protagonists, a pair of omnicompetent senior spies, Joseph Calder and Samuel Behrens. Both are formidably clever and accomplished—civilized men living quietly in the country, one with a noble dog and the other with an agreeable aunt. Yet both are also ruthless secret agents, resourceful and implacable in the fight against treason and subversion, ready for anything and murderous when necessary.

Young Petrella (1988) and *Petrella at Q* (1977) show Patrick at different stages of his career; moving from Detective Constable to Detective Sergeant in the former and from Detective Inspector to Detective Chief Inspector in the latter, which also carries a brief biography of him. The Petrella stories are clever and unpredictable, dealing in the main with unpretentious people and delighting in the details of small-scale urban life. Besides charm and humor, they display considerable ingenuity and broad human sympathies. They range from lighter items, in which no one gets hurt—"The Night the Cat Stayed Out" and "The Coulman Handicap"—to more somber, deeper pieces—"Lost Leader" and "Why Tarry the Wheels of His Chariot?"

Anything for a Quiet Life appeared in 1990 and was conceived as a whole. All nine of its stories feature Jonas Pickett, newly decamped to the coast from a solicitor's practice in London. They are characteristically Gilbertian—varied, inventive, intriguing, amusing—but they also demonstrate how, even "in retreat" from urban pressures, the modern world persists in proving "perilously difficult" (p. 112). Gilbert also wrote three mixed volumes: *Stay of Execution* (1971), *Amateur in Violence* (1973), and *The Man Who Hated Banks* (1997). The contents of *Stay of Execution* are "stories of legal practice," ranging from a wry opening shot—"Back on the Shelf"—to the substantial title story, in which a condemned man escapes from police custody and sets about proving his innocence. Some of Gilbert's choicest stories appear here: "Modus Operandi," in which Hazlerigg justifies the low esteem in which he holds forensic evidence; "Xinia Florata," in which an unconventional will is destroyed by its undeserving beneficiaries; and "The Blackmailing of Mr. Justice Ball," which begins irresistibly: "'So Popsy is dead at last,' said Mr. Rumbold. 'Extreme senility, coupled with fits. Excellent!' " *Amateur in Violence* is named from a powerful story of revenge (the most anthologized of all Gilbert's shorter fictions). The collection was assembled by Ellery Queen, who observes in his introduction that "Mr. Gilbert . . . is in complete command of his material, in complete control of his storytelling." He comments, too, on the "fertile imagination that never fails him," his "subtle and ingenious designs," and his writing "often with a droll, dry wit, and always with compassion." The long title story of *The Man Who Hated Banks*, featuring Petrella, also offers a revenge—a particularly choice example, likely to arouse the widest sympathy. The collection draws on the work of four decades: early stories with Hazlerigg and Henry Bohun and, from 1979, a notable triad in which William Mercer, the enigmatic tough from *The Body of a Girl*, runs true to form.

The uncollected stories include many that merit revival and a wider fame. "A Corner of the Cellar" is a grim little domestic tragedy, startling in its intensity. "The Cork in the Bottle" and "Basilio" feature a subtle South American police chief, Colonel Cristobal Ocampos. "The Seventh Musket" is remarkable both for its setting—Spain during the Peninsular War—and its detective—the Duke of Wellington. "Somebody" and "The Smiler" offer chilling portraits of psychopaths, whom it becomes necessary to stop in their tracks. A notable group of avengers includes "The Cabinet Maker," a victim of political brutality who achieves a consummate revenge; the army gunners in "Five on the Gun" and "The Man Who Sold Out," who employ to devastating effect the tools of their trade; "Judith," who proves herself every whit as dangerous as her Old Testament prototype; and "Grandmother Clatterwick and Mr. McGuffog," who conspire to pervert the course of oenophily. In "The Inside Pocket," a veteran soldier contrives the extermination of a blackmailer with the precision and daring of a complex military operation.

In the late 1990s, Gilbert's work included a series featuring the legal firm of Fearne and Bracknell, from which three stories appeared in *Ellery Queen's Mystery Magazine*: "The Mathematics of Murder," "Tiger Country," and "The Lord of the Book." They deal, respectively, with a serial killer murdering City men on suburban trains, the revenge of a grieving widow on her husband's destroyer, and the contrivance of the downfall of the leader of a dishonest religious cult; they also demonstrate clearly that their author was not running out of steam. The fertility of his creative imagination was up and running in his ninth decade.

Selected Bibliography

WORKS OF MICHAEL GILBERT

CRIME NOVELS

Close Quarters. London: Hodder and Stoughton, 1947; Uniform edition, 1964; New York: Walker, 1963.

They Never Looked Inside. London: Hodder and Stoughton, 1948. U.S.: *He Didn't Mind Danger*. New York: Harper, 1949.

The Doors Open. London: Hodder and Stoughton, 1949; New York: Walker, 1962.

Smallbone Deceased. London: Hodder and Stoughton, 1950; New York: Harper, 1950.

Death Has Deep Roots. London: Hodder and Stoughton, 1951; New York: Harper, 1952.

Death in Captivity. London: Hodder and Stoughton, 1952. U.S.: *The Danger Within*. New York: Harper, 1952.

Fear to Tread. London: Hodder and Stoughton, 1953; New York: Harper, 1953.

Sky High. London: Hodder and Stoughton, 1955. U.S.: *The Country-House Burglar*. New York: Harper, 1955.

Be Shot for Sixpence. London: Hodder and Stoughton, 1956; New York: Harper, 1956.

Blood and Judgement. London: Hodder and Stoughton, 1959; New York: Harper, 1959.

After the Fine Weather. London: Hodder and Stoughton, 1963; New York: Harper, 1963.

The Crack in the Teacup. London: Hodder and Stoughton, 1966; New York: Harper, 1966.

The Dust and the Heat. London: Hodder and Stoughton, 1967. U.S.: *Overdrive*. New York: Harper, 1968.

The Etruscan Net. London: Hodder and Stoughton, 1969. U.S.: *The Family Tomb*. New York: Harper, 1969.

The Body of a Girl. London: Hodder and Stoughton, 1972; New York: Harper, 1972.

The Ninety-Second Tiger. London: Hodder and Stoughton, 1973; New York: Harper, 1973.

Flash Point. London: Hodder and Stoughton, 1974; New York: Harper, 1974.

The Night of the Twelfth. London: Hodder and Stoughton, 1976; New York: Harper, 1976.

The Empty House. London: Hodder and Stoughton, 1978; New York: Harper, 1979.

Death of a Favourite Girl. London: Hodder and Stoughton, 1980. U.S.: *The Killing of Katie Steelstock*. New York: Harper, 1980.

End Game. New York: Harper, 1982. U.K.: *The Final Throw*. London: Hodder and Stoughton, 1982.

The Black Seraphim. London: Hodder and Stoughton, 1983; New York: Harper, 1984.

The Long Journey Home. New York: Harper, 1985.

Trouble. London: Hodder and Stoughton, 1987; New York: Harper, 1987.

Paint, Gold, and Blood. London: Hodder and Stoughton, 1989; New York: Harper, 1989.

The Queen Against Karl Mullen. London: Hodder and Stoughton, 1991; New York: Carroll and Graf, 1991.

Roller-Coaster. London: Hodder and Stoughton, 1993; New York: Carroll and Graf, 1993.

Ring of Terror. London: Hodder and Stoughton, 1995; New York: Carroll and Graf, 1995.

Into Battle. New York: Carroll and Graf, 1997; London: Hale, 1997.

SHORT STORY COLLECTIONS

Game Without Rules. New York: Harper, 1967.

Stay of Execution. London: Hodder and Stoughton, 1971.

Amateur in Violence. New York: Davis, 1973.

Petrella at Q. London: Hodder and Stoughton, 1977; New York: Harper, 1977.

Mr. Calder and Mr. Behrens. London: Hodder and Stoughton, 1982; New York: Harper, 1982.

Young Petrella. London: Hodder and Stoughton, 1988; New York: Harper, 1988.

Anything for a Quiet Life. London: Hodder and Stoughton, 1990; New York: Carroll and Graf, 1990.

The Road to Damascus. Helsinki: Eurographica, 1990. Stories from earlier collections, in English.

The Man Who Hated Banks and Other Mysteries. Norfolk, Va.: Crippen and Landru, 1997.

SELECTED UNCOLLECTED STORIES

"The Smiler." *John Bull*, 9 August 1952.

"Five on the Gun." *Evening Standard*, 7 April 1953.

"The Seventh Musket." *Argosy*, August 1954.

"A Corner of the Cellar." *Argosy*, March 1955.

"The Cabinet Maker." *Reveille*, 26 April 1955.

"The Man Who Sold Out." *Adventure*, June 1955.

"Somebody." *Argosy*, May 1958.

"Basilio." In *Winter's Crimes 1*. Edited by George Hardinge. London: Macmillan, 1969; New York: St. Martin's Press, 1969.

"The Cork in the Bottle." *Ellery Queen's Mystery Magazine*, October 1969.

"Grandmother Clatterwick and Mr. McGuffog." *Accent on Good Living*, May/June 1970.

"The Inside Pocket." In *Crime Wave*. London: Collins, 1981.

"Judith." *Ellery Queen's Mystery Magazine*, April 1993.

"The Mathematics of Murder." *Ellery Queen's Mystery Magazine*, March 1995.

"Tiger Country." *Ellery Queen's Mystery Magazine*, October 1995.

"The Lord of the Book." *Ellery Queen's Mystery Magazine*, December 1997.

EDITED WORKS

Crime in Good Company: Essays on Criminals and Crime-Writing. London: Constable, 1959.
Best Detective Stories of Cyril Hare. London: Faber, 1959; New York: Walker, 1961.

BIBLIOGRAPHY

Pike, B. A. *The Short Stories of Michael Gilbert: An Annotated Checklist, 1948–1997*. South Benfleet, England: CADS, 1998.

MANUSCRIPT COLLECTIONS

Michael Gilbert's papers are held by the University of California, Berkeley, and Mugar Memorial Library, Boston University.

BIOGRAPHICAL AND CRITICAL STUDIES

Denton, Frank. "Michael Gilbert." In *Twentieth Century Crime and Mystery Writers*, 3rd ed. Edited by John M. Reilly. Chicago: St. James, 1991.
Dove, George N. "Michael Gilbert." In *Twelve Englishmen of Mystery*. Edited by Earl F. Bargainnier. Bowling Green, Ohio: Bowling Green State University Popular Press, 1984.
Gindin, James, and Joan Gindin. "Michael Gilbert." In *British Mystery and Thriller Writers Since 1940*. Edited by Bernard Benstock and Thomas F. Staley. Detroit: Gale, 1989.
"Michael Gilbert." In *Contemporary Authors New Revision Series*, vol. 54. Edited by Jeff Chapman and John D. Jorgenson. Detroit: Gale, 1997.
Queen, Ellery. Introduction to *Amateur in Violence*. New York: Davis, 1973.

Sue Grafton
(b. 1940)

JEAN SWANSON

Sue Grafton transformed the American mystery novel in the 1980s with her depiction of hard-boiled female private eye Kinsey Millhone. She was not the first author to create such a heroine, and she did not lead the revolution by herself—writers like Sara Paretsky, P. D. James, Eve Zaremba, Marcia Muller, and Maxine O'Callaghan were also producing mysteries with women private eyes—but Grafton's books became such best-sellers that she may have had the biggest impact on readers' perceptions and expectations of the genre. As the decade wore on, more and more writers, especially women writers, began to write about female private eyes, and the groundbreaking work of earlier authors fueled a publishing phenomenon. Critics and readers called the 1980s and 1990s a second Golden Age of the mystery and identified the female protagonist as the hottest of trends. Sales of books by women mystery writers boomed, reflecting the increasing percentage of mystery readers who were women. Grafton, Paretsky, Linda Barnes, Karen Kijewski, Muller, Liza Cody, and many other talented writers brought a new approach to mystery fiction that reflected the rapid and immense changes in women's roles and in society. Thus, a great American art form of the twentieth century was altered forever.

Life

Sue Taylor Grafton is the daughter of Vivian Harnsberger and lawyer and mystery writer Cornelius Warren Grafton, who was perhaps best known for his book *The Rat Began to Gnaw the Rope* (1943). (Coincidentally, Sue Grafton's first mystery novel, *"A" is for Alibi*, was published in the same year that her father died.) Born on 24 April 1940, Grafton grew up in Louisville, Kentucky, and in 1961 she received a bachelor of arts degree in English from the University of Louisville. Twice divorced, Grafton is now married to Steven Humphrey, with whom she collaborated on several teleplays. They live in Santa Barbara and have a second home in Louisville. Grafton has two daughters and a son from her previous marriages. Before turning to writing mysteries, she worked as a medical secretary; she then spent fifteen years writing teleplays for Hollywood productions, including several adaptations of Agatha Christie mysteries. In an interview with the *New York Times*, she noted that she wrote the first Kinsey Millhone novel as a way to get out of Hollywood and away from the television executives who often ruin a writer's work.

Grafton won many awards for her mystery novels, including the Shamus Award for best novel, given by the Private Eye Writers of America, for *"B" Is for Burglar* and *"K" Is for Killer*; the Anthony Award for best novel, given by the membership of Bouchercon, the World Mystery Convention, for *"B" Is for Burglar*, *"C" Is for Corpse*, and *"G" Is for Gumshoe*; and both the Anthony Award and the Macavity Award for best short story for "The Parker Shotgun." She also served as president of the Mystery Writers of America and the Private Eye Writers of America.

Early Works

Set in 1939, Grafton's first novel, *Keziah Dane* (1967), opens with a dark and difficult scene in which a poor rural family must shoot their beloved old dog to put him out of his misery. Keziah Dane is a widowed mother of six, who lost her husband and oldest son in a flood two years earlier. The family is caught in a downward spiral of poverty; they live in a small, squalid boat on the dry bed of the river that has already killed their menfolk. A drifter and con man, Web, arrives one day and changes their wretched lives forever. In spite of its almost unrelenting darkness, *Keziah Dane* is a thoughtful, poetic novel; however, some critics decried its lack of action, and the novel was not a commercial success.

Grafton produced another story of poverty-stricken rural families with her second novel, *The Lolly-Madonna War* (1969), but this time she wrote plenty of action scenes. Two feuding families, the Feathers and the Gutshalls, live on a mountain in what appears to be Appalachia. The fathers in these families have been quarreling for years, and the acrimony now extends to their children. The Feathers kidnap a girl they assume is the mail-order bride of a young Gutshall. The long-simmering feud erupts into a war, and even the young men who are reluctant to join in and who realize the futility of it all are caught up in the fighting. Published at the height of the Vietnam War, the political implications of this novel are impossible to ignore.

The Alphabet Series

After many years of writing teleplays, Grafton decided to write a mystery novel. She has often said in interviews that, during a bitter custody dispute with her ex-husband, she would lie in bed at night and invent ways to murder him. She poured her anger and imagination into writing *"A" Is for Alibi* (1982), in which she devised a suitably devious method of murder (death from ingesting poisonous oleander) for her fictional victim, the womanizing divorce lawyer Laurence Fife. Grafton spent five years writing *"A" Is for Alibi.* She had to learn thoroughly what investigators do before she could write a private eye novel. She wants her books to be realistic, and she does all her own research. She owns the guns that her series heroine uses, for example, and she reads extensively about forensics, poisons, and other tools of the trade.

The series that developed from "A" was phenomenally successful. Although *"A" Is for Alibi* sold only six thousand copies, by the late 1990s Grafton's books had sold millions of copies and were published in twenty-three languages. Seven of her mysteries were *New York Times* best-sellers; some, like *"L" Is for Lawless* (1995), moved to number one on the list as soon as they were published. *"M" Is for Malice* (thirteenth in the series) debuted in 1996 with a million-copy first printing.

Grafton's protagonist in the alphabet series is Kinsey Millhone, whose biographical details emerge as the series progresses. Kinsey was born on 5 May 1950 in Santa Teresa, California; her mother's maiden name is her given name. When she was five, her parents were killed in a car crash and she went to live with her mother's sister, Aunt Gin, in a mobile home in Santa Teresa. Her mother's family lives just an hour away in Lompoc, but until *"J" Is for Judgment* (1993) she knows nothing of them. Aunt Gin died when Kinsey was in her twenties, so she is twice-orphaned and alone in the world.

In an interview on her web page (www.sue

grafton.com), Grafton describes Kinsey as a blue-collar worker. Kinsey makes enough money to support herself, but she is not wealthy. Sometimes she makes mistakes in her cases; she is an ordinary human—neither an ideal woman nor a feminist stereotype of any sort. Perhaps this very quality of being average conveys to readers that it is perfectly normal for a woman to do a job that men had always done, and to do it competently and without fuss. Kinsey takes care of herself, by herself, without seeing anything especially significant in her status as a single woman. She often takes on cases that a typical reader can identify with: a waitress distressed over her daughter's mysterious death; a man cheating his insurance company; a badly injured young man trying to prove that the car accident in which he was injured was deliberate malice and not an accident after all. In some of the novels, Kinsey physically fights people and shows that women can defend themselves effectively. A stubborn, persistent private eye, she brings villains to justice; she is the hero readers might want to be, yet she sees herself as an ordinary person doing her job as well as any investigator, male or female, might do.

Kinsey has a continuing group of friends, acquaintances, and useful contacts in the novels. Her landlord is Henry Pitts, a sexy retired baker in his eighties, whom Kinsey adores guardedly. He entertains her with his bread, the crossword puzzles that he devises, and his occasional companionship. Kinsey eats regularly at a funky neighborhood restaurant owned by Rosie, who is something more than an acquaintance and something less than a close friend. In the early novels, Kinsey has a loose working relationship with California Fidelity, a local insurance company, and she is friendly with Vera Lipton, a claims adjuster for the company. She has an occasional romantic fling, most notably with police detective Jonah Robb, and later with another private eye, Robert Dietz; but for the most part she is a loner, as are the classic male private eyes of American fiction.

> I'd spent two years as a cop and another two years amassing the four thousand hours required to apply for my private investigator's license. I'd been duly photographed, fingerprinted, bonded, and credentialed. Since my principal means of employment involved exposure to the underside of human nature, I tended even then to keep other people at a distance. I have since learned to be polite. I can even appear friendly when it suits my purposes, but I'm not really known for my cute girlish ways. (*"K" Is for Killer* [1994], pp. 20–21)

Kinsey drives a beat-up old Volkswagen, wears jeans and turtlenecks, and cares little about fashion or interior decorating. She lives in a small apartment (formerly Henry's garage) with just enough room for the few material goods she possesses. She owns one dress. No domestic goddess, she eats junk food, usually has an empty refrigerator, and loves peanut butter and pickle sandwiches. She runs for exercise every day, although she does not particularly enjoy it, because she knows she must stay fit in order to do her job well. When she is under stress, she cleans house. Order and tidiness are important to her, especially in the small, enclosed spaces that she prefers. Lying comes easily to her, but she disapproves of small infractions like overdue library books or parking tickets. Kinsey is a workaholic, always thinking about her cases, and intensely observant of the people she encounters while working on a case.

Kinsey does not age in real time; *"M" Is for Malice*, published in 1996, is set in 1985. Each book takes place shortly after the previous adventure. In *"A,"* Kinsey is thirty-two; in *"M,"* she is thirty-five. This timing allows Grafton to show Kinsey's growth as a character. In the early books, Kinsey tries to keep emotion out of her life and out of her cases, but it cannot always be done. She struggles, after *"A,"* with the knowledge that she has killed a human being and with what that has meant to her emotionally. Each novel tells us a bit more about her and about the gallery of vividly drawn secondary characters with whom Grafton surrounds her. In the first few books, Kinsey is a somewhat dour, intense figure, who doggedly pursues villains until the end of each story. As the series progresses, she sharpens her repartee and becomes more deft with her wit, which grows out of the absurdities of her daily life.

The early novels begin and end in the form of a report written by Kinsey at the conclusion of the case. This literary device serves to frame the story and provide some distance, for both narrator and reader, from the violence and emotional distress of murder and its aftermath. The novels are written in the first person in a terse prose that lends itself well to the development of suspense. Grafton sets out her stories cleanly and fairly; they are easy to read, engaging, and suspenseful. Each of Kinsey's reports (thus each novel) ends with the same words: "Respectfully submitted, Kinsey Millhone."

Often the mystery in a Grafton novel is centered around a family secret. The families are generally dysfunctional, as they are in the classic tales of Raymond Chandler, Ross Macdonald, and other hard-boiled writers. Grafton says in an interview with Susan Morgan that she likes to write about domestic murders, because, as Kinsey says, all families are dysfunctional. But one twist in Grafton is that often family members are physically ill: in *"A,"* the father of a murder victim is wheelchair bound; Bobby Callahan in *"C" Is for Corpse* (1986) is severely disabled after a car crash; both parents of Bailey Fowler in *"F" Is for Fugitive* (1989) are very ill. If the standard detective novel opens with a state of disorder that the detective's investigations eventually turn into a state of order and peace, then Grafton violates that tradition by creating characters whose internal disorders will be put right only by death.

Grafton sets her novels in the fictional town of Santa Teresa, with a population of eighty-five thousand. It is no coincidence that she uses the same name for her fictional "home" as did Ross Macdonald. Just as in Macdonald's novels, Santa Teresa is a thinly veiled version of Santa Barbara; the reader could easily match Kinsey's standard routes around town to a map of Santa Barbara. Grafton plays with the contrast between the colorful opulence of her wealthy city and the minimalist existence of her detective. She likes Santa Barbara as a setting because it is so beautiful and genteel that it seems an unlikely spot for murder. A far cry from the mean streets so beloved of many private eye writers, it is a setting reminiscent more of the cozy subgenre of mysteries than of the hard-boiled school. Grafton takes her detective on the road, too; she often sends Kinsey to some of the odder corners of southern California, like the sand dunes of Imperial County or the drab beach towns of the central coast.

Grafton is often lauded for never writing the same book twice. Many mystery writers, when they establish a series character, also settle the kind of books they will write throughout the series: humorous mysteries, light cozies, or dark psychological suspense novels. The stories that feature Kinsey's exploits as a private eye are remarkably varied. Some are dark, hard-boiled tales, like *"K" Is for Killer;* some are caper novels, like *"L" Is for Lawless;* some are wrenchingly emotional stories of devastating family tragedies, like *"C" Is for Corpse;* some are inverted mysteries, in which the villains are known to the reader at the outset, like *"H" Is for Homicide* (1991), and some are straight puzzle mysteries, like *"A" Is for Alibi.* As she progresses through the series, Grafton reaches for new ways to showcase Kinsey's capabilities and to tell suspenseful and thoughtful narratives. By varying the format of her novels, Grafton takes chances with her character that many writers of long-running series avoid. Perhaps she can afford to take such chances because her books have proved so popular with readers, but authors of popular series usually avoid playing such risky games with the fickle affections of the public.

Perhaps one of Grafton's most clever ideas has been to use an alphabetical sequence in naming her books. The device sets up a continuing level of suspense and entertainment as readers try to guess what the next book's "title will be: Q is for Query? Quarry? Quarrel? And what will she do about X?" Readers of mysteries love puzzles; this ongoing title puzzle is a delight for them. It makes it easy for readers to remember which book they read last and to know which one to buy next. In short, it's a savvy marketing trick. It also matches the style of Kinsey's case reports: terse, practical, and smart. The initials of major characters, often Kinsey's clients, match the initial of the title: Bobby Callahan in *"C,"* Bailey Fowler in *"F,"* Lorna Kepler in *"K,"* and so on.

It may be difficult to remember now the excitement engendered by the appearance of women as powerful detectives in private eye novels. In the early 1980s several writers garnered attention for their attempts to change this popular and established fictional form and address social and gender issues in their mysteries. Sue Grafton, Sara Paretsky, Marcia Muller, P. D. James, and Barbara Wilson are often cited as major figures of the time. Indeed, Paretsky's first V. I. Warshawski novel and the first Kinsey Millhone novel both appeared in 1982. However, fifteen years later, Grafton has become the best known and perhaps most influential of the group. Paretsky has written fewer novels, and her later, more politically oriented mysteries did not meet with the critical acclaim given to her earlier efforts. Muller's long series of mysteries featuring Sharon McCone has become increasingly respected and admired in the mystery world, but she has yet to crack the best-seller lists and gain a mass audience. James, although a famous and best-selling author and a dame of the British Empire, has so far produced only two books featuring her understated private eye Cordelia Gray. And Wilson has written some fine feminist mysteries, but they are published by a small press and have not been widely distributed and read.

Critics and readers alike have debated whether or not Kinsey Millhone is a feminist character. Perhaps the most distinguished scholar of feminist mysteries, Kathleen Gregory Klein, thinks that Kinsey has feminist inclinations but is not precisely a feminist. Perhaps this echoes Grafton's own opinions. Grafton tells Bruce Taylor in the *Armchair Detective*, "[I] chose the classic private eye genre because I like playing hardball with the boys. I despise gender-segregated events of any kind." She also says that Kinsey is her own alter ego, with identical sensibilities. So it may be that Grafton is not particularly interested in writing about feminist issues in her novels, but her alter ego, Kinsey, the dispassionate observer, can disclose her point of view with sardonic comments about gender inequities.

Kinsey is often compared to V. I. Warshawski, the private eye heroine of Sara Paretsky's crime novels. Although both are tough, smart detectives, V. I. is a former lawyer, very much involved with women's issues and groups, while Kinsey, orphaned at an early age, had a few semesters in junior college and remains much more of a loner than V. I., with a more minimalist lifestyle. Perhaps the key difference in the two series is that Kinsey's cases tend to be pure mysteries, often centered on family secrets, with few direct social implications. The cases are usually neatly solved (unlike some of V. I.'s), and as a character, Kinsey is not generally concerned about politics or current affairs. Both women have had their share of violent encounters, and both have been injured. Kinsey is definitely a Californian, with an awareness of the beauty of the California coast and a sense of irony about how nature's beauty contrasts with the potential for evil in people. V. I. lives and works in a gritty Chicago setting, which mirrors the darkness of the villains she unmasks. Both Kinsey and V. I. may be hard-boiled private eyes, but they are very different women.

In the end, the debate over the extent of Kinsey's feminism is not the crucial issue in reading Grafton. What matters is that Grafton has, in effect, changed the face of American crime fiction while telling memorable stories in a unique voice.

Individual Works

The opening book in Grafton's series, *"A" Is for Alibi,* takes place in 1982. Kinsey is hired by Nikki Fife to find the real murderer of her divorce-lawyer husband, Laurence Fife. Nikki has spent the last eight years in prison, after being convicted of poisoning Laurence. Kinsey is intrigued by the idea of looking into this old crime, and she begins her investigation methodically. She discovers that Laurence had many affairs around town, and she meets some of the embittered women he left behind. She also meets Charlie Scorsoni, Laurence's former law partner, and she is so attracted that she goes to bed with him. Eventually, she realizes it is a bad idea to have sex with a suspect, and breaks off their affair. In the closing scene of the novel, she kills the murderer when he chases her onto the beach and corners her as she hides in a trash can. In a throwback to her childhood, she has taken refuge in a small contained space when a crisis occurs. Grafton told Susan Morgan in an interview that she wanted to turn around the convention in male hard-boiled novels where the private eye shoots the murderess, his former lover, in the last scene of the book. It comes as no suprise, then, that *"A"* is a distinctly angry and dark novel.

The opening of *"B" Is for Burglar* (1985) is typical of Grafton's early works: "My name is Kinsey Millhone and most of my reports begin the same way. I start by asserting who I am and what I do, as though by stating the same few basic facts I can make sense out of everything that comes afterward" (p. 1). Kinsey is hired by Beverly Danziger to find her missing sister, in a scene that echoes many a classic private-eye novel and film: a beautiful, elegant woman comes into the (usually male) detective's office and asks him to search for a lost relative. Kinsey digs into the life of the missing woman, even after her client fires her and tells her to stop investigating. The plot twists and turns in a highly satisfactory way, reminiscent of traditional puzzle mysteries as much as of hard-boiled private-eye novels. Homicide detective Jonah Robb, to whom Kinsey is attracted, appears here for the first time.

"C" Is for Corpse includes some fairly graphic autopsy sequences, prefiguring a device that became popular with such later mystery writers as the best-selling novelist Patricia Cornwell. Kinsey becomes more sardonic and wisecracking, in the manner of a typical private-eye hero. Bobby Callahan has been badly injured in a car accident some months earlier. He is making a slow recovery when he hires Kinsey to look into the incident that maimed him. The police have ruled it an accident, but he thinks someone deliberately tried to kill him. Bobby has a severely dysfunctional family, including a stepsister with anorexia and a grasping stepfather, but his mother is depicted sympathetically. Kinsey grieves for Bobby when he dies in a second incident, and she is able to forge a genuine emotional connection to his mother. One of Grafton's best books, *"C"* is a memorable and riveting story, with finely drawn secondary characters.

"D" Is for Deadbeat (1987) is a less satisfying novel than its predecessor. Kinsey's client is an ex-con, John Daggett, who asks her to find someone and give him a check for $25,000. Kinsey's doubts about her client and his large check are confirmed when she discovers that a drunken Daggett had been responsible for the deaths of several people in a car crash. Daggett turns up dead shortly after hiring Kinsey, and everyone she interviews about his mysterious death seems to have a reason for hating this unsavory man.

In *"E" Is for Evidence* (1988), Kinsey must work for herself. She has been implicated in an arson plot and is accused of insurance fraud. California Fidelity suspends her from her affiliation with them, and she must clear her own name. By now, she is having an affair with Jonah Robb, who cannot choose between Kinsey and his wife and kids. Kinsey is as close as she ever gets to admitting loneliness. Another dysfunctional family, the Woods, commands center stage here and causes Kinsey to reflect on how much she cherishes her unmarried state. Kinsey's second ex-husband, Daniel Wade, reappears after eight years saying he is clean and sober, and he asks her to do a favor for him. It turns out that he left her for a man, who now has persuaded Daniel to help set up Kinsey for information about this case. *"E"* has a convoluted and confusing plot. Grafton has abandoned the enclosing structure of a report here; the story is told as a straightforward narrative.

In *"F" Is for Fugitive,* (1989), Kinsey is hired to look into a murder that occurred seventeen years earlier in Floral Beach, a town just up the coast from Santa Teresa. Bailey Fowler had pled guilty to voluntary manslaughter for the crime, then escaped from prison and disappeared for many years. Now he has been caught after living a clean life in Los Angeles, and he denies murdering his former girlfriend. Bailey's dying father hires Kinsey to find the real killer. Kinsey not only investigates the old crime, but also explores the hidden life of a small, dilapidated beach town.

Kinsey's life is threatened so seriously in *"G" Is for Gumshoe* (1990) that she reluctantly hires a bodyguard, Robert Dietz. A private eye himself, Dietz teaches her about guns and investigative techniques. Cast in the role of potential victim and protected by a more experienced detective, Kinsey comes close to ceding some of her independent spirit in this installment of the series. She goes out to The Slabs, a poor desert community near the Salton Sea, to find her client's mother, who has not been heard from in some time. Kinsey arranges for the senile mother to be brought up to Santa Teresa to be near her daughter, and this innocent solution sets in train a series of terrifying and lethal events in the town. Kinsey also begins an affair with Dietz.

As part of her loose affiliation with California Fidelity, Kinsey agrees to look into a fraudulent insurance claim in *"H" Is for Homicide*. This brings her into contact with Bibianna Diaz, the claimant, who has run away from her lethal boyfriend in Los Angeles. Kinsey goes undercover, punches a cop, and goes to jail just in order to stay close to her suspect. The plot is flimsily constructed and frankly unbelievable. It is unlikely that Kinsey would risk losing her license by committing a felony. The biggest problem with *"H"* is Grafton's uncharacteristic use of stereotypical Hispanic gang members as villains. The best aspects of the novel are the descriptions of fake auto accidents set up to cheat insurance companies, and of Kinsey's friendship with Bibianna. *"H"* is often considered the weakest novel in the series.

"I" Is for Innocent (1992) is set in December 1983. Kinsey has been fired from her loose affiliation with California Fidelity and must go out on her own. She meditates on how getting fired has tested her self-confidence: "I wanted to feel like the old Kinsey again . . . talkin' trash and kickin' butt. Being cowed and uncertain was really for the birds" (p. 221). She rents an office from her lawyer, Lonnie Kingman, and does some detective work for him. In her first job, she investigates the murder of Isabelle Barney. Her estranged husband has been acquitted of the murder, but everyone believes that he did it, and Isabelle's family is suing him in a civil trial. Kinsey says:

> In most investigations I'm hired for, the object of the exercise is to flush out culprits: burglars, deadbeats, embezzlers, con artists, perpetrators of insurance fraud. Occasionally, I take on a missing-persons search, but the process is much the same—like picking at a piece of knitting until you find a loose thread. Pull at the right point and the whole garment comes unraveled. This one was different. Here, the quarry was known. The question wasn't who, but how to bring him down. (p. 62)

"J" Is for Judgment deals more directly and intensely with the conflicting emotions that families can arouse. Kinsey is asked by a friend at California Fidelity to help him find Wendell Jaffe, who apparently committed suicide some years ago after being caught perpetrating an illegal pyramid scheme. The insurance company has paid out a huge claim

to his widow, when Jaffe is sighted alive. Kinsey finds him in Mexico, then loses the trail; but he shows up in Santa Teresa when his son is arrested. Then Kinsey, the orphaned loner, suddenly develops family troubles of her own. She is dumbfounded when she discovers that she has relations only an hour away, some of whom knew of her existence but never contacted her. Stunned and angry, she refuses to meet them. Meanwhile she wonders, has Jaffe put himself in harm's way to help his son, or has he just come back for the money he left behind? The ultimate resolution of the intricate plot hinges, as in so many of Grafton's books, on family tensions and resentments.

In *"K" Is for Killer,* Kinsey discovers life on the nightside, and this dark novel turns out to be one of the best in the series. She is hired by Janice Kepler to investigate her daughter Lorna's death. Janice first talks to Kinsey late one cold February night; this establishes the pattern of night work that Kinsey follows throughout the book. "I've always been a day person. . . . Tonight, yet again, I was nudged by restlessness. Some long suppressed aspect of my personality was being activated, and I could feel myself respond" (p. 95). As it turns out, Lorna Kepler was a high-class call girl at night; she hid this from her parents by working a legitimate job during the day. Especially notable are the first two paragraphs of the book, in which Kinsey talks, gracefully and evocatively, about her personal need to find the murderers of the dead.

Perhaps Grafton was inspired by her admiration for Elmore Leonard and his joyfully offbeat caper novels when writing *"L" Is for Lawless*. The story begins when Kinsey does a favor for Henry Pitts by checking the veteran's eligibility status of a neighbor. Thus begins a tale that takes her on the road to Texas and onward to Louisville, Kentucky (Grafton's home town), in search of money that is still missing from a forty-year-old bank heist. This is almost a caper novel; it is fast, funny, and engrossing. While evading a ruthless killer, Kinsey careens about the country with an ex-con and a thief, trying to retrieve the loot they have been waiting for all those years. She even performs a memorable masquerade as a hotel maid.

"M" Is for Malice is the story of the Malek family, especially Guy Malek, the black sheep of the family. Guy disappeared from his home when young, and Kinsey is hired to trace him after his father's will names him as an heir along with his three brothers. There are many heated family arguments in the big old house outside Santa Teresa, and it comes as no surprise when murder strikes. Although supposedly Guy was a drug addict and a thief when he was a teenager, he is now a gentle, born-again Christian, and Kinsey surprises herself by liking and respecting him. *"M"* is distinctly mystical and much more emotionally wrenching than most of the earlier novels. Robert Dietz, from *"G,"* returns unexpectedly and Kinsey must decide if she wants to risk exposing herself to abandonment again by reviving their affair. In the final paragraph of the novel, Kinsey deals with her grief for the murder victim and for her family:

> In the end, I set him free, not in sorrow, but in love. It wasn't for me. It was something I did for him. When I woke, I knew that he was truly gone. The tears I wept for him then were the same tears I'd wept for everyone I'd ever loved. My parents, my aunt. I had never said good-bye to them, either, but it was time to take care of it. I said a prayer for the dead, opening the door so all the ghosts could move on. I gathered them up like the petals of a flower and released them to the wind. What's done is done. What is written is written. Their work is finished. Ours is yet to do. (p. 300)

After the atmospheric and masterly *"M,"* the matter-of-fact tone of *"N" Is for Noose* (1998) comes as something of a shock. Kinsey is on the road again, and most of the book is set in the fictional town of Nota Lake, perched on the eastern slope of the Sierra Nevada. The widow of a local sheriff's deputy hires Kinsey to find out what was troubling her husband in the last weeks before he died of a heart attack. Kinsey is attacked and beaten up in this novel, and she seems uncharacteristically frightened in the aftermath of the assault. The tough, self-reliant Kinsey is eclipsed by fear and melancholy, and she revives only when she is fed a hallucinogenic drug and attacked again by a killer. As in many of the earlier novels in the series, Kinsey must sort through the problems of a dysfunctional family to find the key that will allow her to solve the case.

What do the coming years hold for Sue Grafton and her alter ego, Kinsey Millhone? Grafton is elusive when asked about the remainder of her series, although readers may anticipate successive adventures for Kinsey until she reaches *"Z" Is for . . .* Zero? As Kinsey arrives at her last case sometime in the twenty-first century, readers will have had a chance over the years to sample many varieties of the classic mystery novel in the works of Sue Grafton.

Selected Bibliography

WORKS OF SUE GRAFTON

NOVELS

Keziah Dane. New York: Macmillan, 1967.
The Lolly-Madonna War. London: Owen, 1969.
"A" Is for Alibi. New York: Holt, 1982.
"B" Is for Burglar. New York: Holt, 1985.
"C" Is for Corpse. New York: Holt, 1986.
"D" Is for Deadbeat. New York: Holt, 1987.
"E" Is for Evidence. New York: Holt, 1988.
"F" Is for Fugitive. New York: Holt, 1989.
"G" Is for Gumshoe. New York: Holt, 1990.
"H" Is for Homicide. New York: Holt, 1991.
"I" Is for Innocent. New York: Holt, 1992.
"J" Is for Judgment. New York: Holt, 1993.
"K" Is for Killer. New York: Holt, 1994.
"L" Is for Lawless. New York: Holt, 1995.
"M" Is for Malice. New York: Holt, 1996.
"N" Is for Noose. New York: Holt, 1998.

SHORT STORIES

Kinsey and Me: A Collection of Short Stories. Santa Barbara: Bench Press, 1991. Includes "The Parker Shotgun."

NONFICTION

Writing Mysteries: A Handbook by the Mystery Writers of America. Edited by Sue Grafton. Cincinnati: Writer's Digest Books, 1992.

SCREENPLAY

Lolly-Madonna XXX (with Rodney Carr-Smith). 1973.

TELEPLAYS

"With Friends Like These." CBS, 1975. Episode in the series *Rhoda.*
"Walking Through the Fire." CBS, 1979. From the book by Laurel Lee.
"Sex and the Single Parent." CBS, 1979. From the book by Jane Adams.
"Nurse." CBS, 1980. From the book by Peggy Anderson.
"Mark, I Love You." CBS, 1980. From the book by Hal Painter.
"Seven Brides for Seven Brothers" (with Steven Humphrey). CBS, 1982. Pilot TV episode.
"A Caribbean Mystery" (with S. Humphrey). CBS, 1983. From the novel by Agatha Christie.
"A Killer in the Family" (with S. Humphrey and Robert Aller). ABC, 1983.
"Sparkling Cyanide" (with S. Humphrey and Robert M. Young). CBS, 1983. From the novel by Agatha Christie.
"Love on the Run" (with S. Humphrey). NBC, 1985.
"Tonight's the Night" (with S. Humphrey). ABC, 1987.

BIOGRAPHICAL AND CRITICAL STUDIES

Cassidy, Bruce, ed. *Modern Mystery, Fantasy, and Science Fiction Writers.* New York: Continuum, 1993.
Christianson, Scott. "Talkin' Trash and Kickin' Butt: Sue Grafton's Hard-Boiled Feminism." In *Feminism in Women's Detective Fiction.* Edited by Glenwood Irons. Toronto: University of Toronto Press, 1995.
DellaCava, Frances A., and Madeline H. Engel. *Female Detectives in American Novels: A Bibliography and Analysis of Serialized Female Sleuths.* New York: Garland, 1993.
Geherin, David. "Grafton, Sue." In *St. James Guide to Crime and Mystery Writers.* Edited by Jay Pederson. Detroit: St. James Press, 1996.
Goodman, Susan. "Sue Grafton, Tony Hillerman." *Modern Maturity,* July 1995: 74–82.
"Grafton, Sue." *Current Biography Yearbook 1995.* New York: Wilson, 1995. Pp. 219–224.
Herbert, Rosemary. *The Fatal Art of Entertainment: Interviews with Mystery Writers.* New York: Hall, 1994.
Irons, Glenwood. "New Women Detectives: G Is for Gender-Bending." In *Gender, Language, and Myth: Essays on Popular Narrative.* Edited by Glenwood Irons. Toronto: University of Toronto Press, 1992.
Johnson, Patricia E. "Sex and Betrayal in the Detective Fiction of Sue Grafton and Sara Paretsky." *Journal of Popular Culture* (spring 1994): 97–106.
Jones, Louise Conley. "Feminism and the P.I. Code: or 'Is a Hard-Boiled Warshawski Unsuitable to Be Called a Feminist?' " *Clues* (spring/summer 1995): 77–87.

Kaufman, Natalie Hevener, and Carol McGinnis Kay. *"G" Is for Grafton.* New York: Holt, 1997.

Klein, Kathleen Gregory. *Great Women Mystery Writers.* Westport, Conn.: Greenwood Press, 1994.

———. *The Woman Detective: Gender and Genre.* 2d ed. Urbana: University of Illinois Press, 1995.

Morgan, Susan. "Female Dick." *Interview* (May 1990): 152–153.

Munt, Sally R. *Murder by the Book? Feminism and the Crime Novel.* London: Routledge, 1994.

Nemy, Enid. "A Is for Alter Ego." *New York Times,* 4 August 1994, sec. C.

Nichols, Victoria, and Susan Thompson. *Silk Stalkings: When Women Write of Murder.* Berkeley, Calif.: Black Lizard, 1988.

Rabinowitz, Peter J. " 'Reader, I Blew Him Away': Convention and Transgression in Sue Grafton." In *Famous Last Words: Changes in Gender and Narrative Closure.* Edited by Alison Booth. Charlottesville: University Press of Virginia, 1993.

Reddy, Maureen T. "The Feminist Counter-Tradition in Crime: Cross, Grafton, Paretsky, and Wilson." In *The Cunning Craft: Original Essays on Detective Fiction and Contemporary Literary Theory.* Edited by Ronald Walker and June Frazer. Macomb: Western Illinois University, 1990.

———. *Sisters in Crime: Feminism and the Crime Novel.* New York: Continuum, 1988.

Taylor, Bruce. "G Is for (Sue) Grafton." *Armchair Detective* (winter 1989): 4–13.

Tomc, Sandra. "Questing Women: The Feminist Mystery After Feminism." In *Feminism in Women's Detective Fiction.* Edited by Glenwood Irons. Toronto: University of Toronto Press, 1995.

Walton, Priscilla L. " 'E' Is for En/Gendering Readings: Sue Grafton's Kinsey Millhone." In *Women Times Three: Writers, Detectives, Readers.* Edited by Kathleen Gregory Klein. Bowling Green, Ohio: Bowling Green State University Popular Press, 1995.

ANNA KATHARINE GREEN

(1846–1935)

PATRICIA D. MAIDA

WITH THE PUBLICATION of *The Leavenworth Case* in 1878, Anna Katharine Green launched her career, earning the title Mother of Detective Fiction. In this book, she introduced her serial detective Ebenezer Gryce, a member of New York's Metropolitan Police Force who made his way up the ladder to become a detective inspector and win the hearts of faithful readers. At the time, Green was thirty-two years old, single, and a college graduate. A quiet but determined woman, she had been writing since childhood, trying her hand at poetry and drama before finding her metier in detective fiction.

Although the romantic "women's fiction" that flooded the literary market in the late nineteenth century would have been a likely medium for her, Green chose a bolder course. Detective fiction had become a man's field, but Green sought her place there, creating her serial detective—Inspector Gryce—a decade before the appearance of Arthur Conan Doyle's Sherlock Holmes. Ultimately, she published thirty-five novels, four collections of short stories and novelettes, a book of poetry, and a drama.

Life

A combination of positive factors helped spawn Green's writing career: a supportive family, an education, good connections, and a gift for storytelling. Born in Brooklyn, New York, on 11 November 1846, a block from Henry Ward Beecher's Plymouth Church, young Anna was raised in a middle-class home with an older sister (Sarah Elizabeth) and two older brothers (James and Sidney). Her parents, Katherine Ann Whitney Green and James Wilson Green, an attorney, were from Connecticut, with roots going back to early New England settlers. After the death of her mother in 1849, Anna's family left Brooklyn and eventually settled in Buffalo, New York, where she attended public schools. Although opportunities for higher education were limited for women of her generation, she graduated from Ripley Female Seminary in Poultney, Vermont, in 1866, becoming one of a small cadre of American women to earn the baccalaureate degree.

Green had always been a writer. As a schoolgirl, she filled her notebooks with poems and stories. At Ripley, she became president of the Washington Irving Society and hosted a lecture by Ralph Waldo Emerson. Afterward she sent him some of her poems, asking for a critique and encouragement. Emerson responded in a letter dated 30 June 1868, praising her work generally but challenging the notion that writing poetry should become "a profession" for her (*Letters of Ralph Waldo Emerson,* pp. 22–23). A tenacious young woman, Green continued to seek a place for herself as a professional writer despite Emerson's reservations. (Eventually, George Putnam published a collection of her poems, *The Defense of the Bride and Other Poems,* in 1882; however, her poetry did not receive the acclaim of her novels.)

After graduation from college and while she was living with her family back in New York City, Anna began to write detective fiction. But she had to conceal her manuscript from her father, who did not think detective fiction was an appropriate medium for a woman, much less his younger daughter. However, with Grace Green, her stepmother, encouraging her efforts, Anna covertly wrote *The Leavenworth Case.* When it was finished, she showed the 145,000-word manuscript to her father. After he read it, he had to admit that she had written well. And despite the "indelicacy" of the genre, once he was convinced that his daughter had talent, James Green used his connections to help her get published. She often recounted how she read the manuscript of *The Leavenworth Case* to the literary agent Rossiter Johnson at his Manhattan hotel, an ordeal that took two days. George Putnam then agreed to publish the novel, which eventually sold more than a million copies and was reprinted in the United States and Europe. With the start of her career, Green changed her middle name from "Catherine" to "Katharine" as an indication of her new persona.

If her success was surprising, so was Green's private life. The unassuming and rather plain woman living in Brooklyn made news in 1884 when she married a handsome actor; at the time she was thirty-seven years old—long past her prime. Eight years her junior, Charles Rohlfs, the son of German immigrants, had been introduced to Anna by the minister of South Park Congregational Church, where both regularly attended services. Her father begrudgingly gave his consent to the match only when Rohlfs promised to give up the stage and develop a trade to support his future wife. Since he had been trained as an artisan at Cooper Union in Brooklyn, Rohlfs began to design furniture in the mission style, eventually achieving recognition in the United States and England for his fine craftsmanship. Although his works are now highly valued museum pieces, during their marriage he was not the primary wage earner. And despite his promise to his father-in-law and his commitment to his craft, love of the theater occasionally led him to pursue opportunities on stage. In fact, Anna and Charles Rohlfs put their talents together to produce a dramatic version of *The Leavenworth Case* in 1891 with Charles cast in the role of the murderer. While critics did not give the drama glowing reviews, the popularity of the novel ensured an enthusiastic audience.

Green continued to pursue her career as a professional writer while raising three children: Rosamund (born in 1885), Sterling (born in 1887), and Roland (born in 1892). After her marriage, she published her work as Mrs. Charles Rohlfs, establishing her new status in the public eye. (Consequently, today her works can be listed under either Green or Rohlfs.) When the Rohlfs family moved to Buffalo in 1888, Charles designed and assisted in building their home at 156 Park Street. There they established roots and pursued individual careers for the next thirty-four years. To local residents, many of whom did not know of her fame, "Mrs. Rohlfs" was a typical homemaker, who could often be seen tending her garden or serving on church committees. However, she was also a disciplined writer who sat down every day in the writing chair that Charles designed for her—a comfortable high-backed chair with a wide right arm to accommodate her notebook. Green wrote in pencil in school-style notebooks, producing the equivalent of a novel a year; her last novel, *The Step on the Stair* (1923), was published when she was seventy-seven years old.

Novels

The contrast between the well-run, middle-class lifestyle of Green and the chaotic lives of her fictional heroes and heroines is a testament to both her imagination and her understanding of social issues. Green had a sense of the times, of the pivotal concerns of people of her generation. Money and status motivated the burgeoning middle class and nouveaux riches of New York City—Green tapped into these forces in her plots. The majority of her fiction involves money—the loss of it, the need for it, the crime that comes from greed.

The Leavenworth Case depicts two cousins suspected of murdering their guardian for a large inheritance. Horatio Leavenworth is found in the locked library of his Fifth Avenue home, shot to death. The most likely suspects are his two nieces, who stand to inherit his fortune. As readers clamored to discover whether one or both of the young ladies were guilty, they also understood the implications of their plight. The futures of both women were at stake, for not even a Fifth Avenue address would guarantee good marriages if scandal should tarnish their reputations. With a romantic brush, Green paints the fair Eleanore and the dark Mary, reinforcing the light and dark imagery with mysterious tensions between the two women. The reader knows that Mary is covering up a secret, that she is protecting Eleanore, but not until Ebenezer Gryce gets to the heart of the puzzle are the secrets revealed.

Although the characterization of the young women reflects elements of the sentimental style, the romantic treatment of the characters is tempered by realistic features of the detective novel. The crux of the novel is a complicated puzzle, the pieces to be fitted by the plainclothes detective named Gryce. He is an ordinary man who is so self-effacing that he often looks downward or over the shoulders of people he interrogates: "Mr. Gryce was a portly, comfortable personage with an eye that never pounced, that did not even rest—on you. If it rested anywhere, it was always on some insignificant object in your vicinity, some vase, inkstand, book or button" (p. 7). A young attorney, Everett Raymond, recognizes Gryce as soon as he arrives at the murder scene—Gryce is renowned for his skill. Raymond becomes an unofficial assistant to Gryce, playing a role much like Sherlock Holmes's helper Dr. Watson. Raymond is also the first-person narrator who speaks to the reader as a naive but interested party. The reader is able to identify with Raymond and is further able to participate in solving the crime when provided with diagrams of the house and the scene of the crime.

Details of the crime scene are rendered scientifically, even though forensic science was just developing at the turn of the century. Green describes the inquest into the crime and also provides a detailed ballistics report on the fatal bullet, tracing the markings on the casing and evidence of gunpowder. An expert witness testifies: "That faint line of smut on the edge of one of the chambers, is the telltale, sirs. A bullet passing out, always leaves smut behind. The man who fired this, remembering the fact, cleaned the barrel, but forgot the cylinder" (p. 51). Green may have absorbed a measure of her technical information about criminology from her father. No doubt she had many opportunities in her family's social circle to become acquainted with knowledgeable people. On one occasion, she disclosed in an interview, she accompanied her father on a trip to Long Island, she seated in the back seat of a horse-drawn carriage, her father seated up front with the Chief of the Metropolitan Police Force ("Why Human Beings Are Interested in Crime," p. 84). One can picture the young Anna sitting quietly, tuning in to their conversation.

The Leavenworth Case helped set the standard for classic detective fiction. Detective Gryce has a unique style—cerebral in his detective methods but thoroughly human, from his unassuming behavior to his encroaching arthritis. With Raymond providing social entrée to the Fifth Avenue social set and doing some of Gryce's legwork, the case develops slowly and methodically. The pursuit of the murderer is complicated by a host of red herrings, most likely suspects, and plentiful clues. But once Gryce discovers motive and method, he sets up what was later to be termed a "confrontation drama," where all the suspects are brought together and the guilty party is finally unmasked.

Green's own reading provided models for her fiction. Although she had an interest in a wide range of literature, in detective fiction her mentors were Edgar Allan Poe and Émile Gaboriau. Poe had set the standard in mystery fiction with his short stories featuring C. Auguste Dupin, an effete French detective. Gaboriau, whose *L'Affaire Lerouge* was published in France in 1863, developed the novel of detection with his French detectives, Monsieur Lecoq and Père Tabaret. However, unlike Poe, Green chose the novel rather than the short story as her primary genre, and unlike both Poe and Gaboriau, she created an American detective working in New York City. In doing so, Green became one of the first American women to publish a nonserialized novel of detection.

Like Poe and Gaboriau, Green was adept at constructing puzzles. For example, *The Leavenworth Case* is complicated by sets of doubles: two murders (Horatio Leavenworth and Hannah Chester), two likely suspects (Eleanore and Mary Leavenworth), and two disparate venues for the crimes (Manhattan and a resort area in upstate New York). Green complicated these structures to increase the difficulty of her puzzles. We see doubles in a number of Green's puzzles, including *A Matter of Millions* (1890), where a multimillion dollar inheritance is left to a girl named Jenny Rogers—Gryce must determine which of two possible girls with the same name is the intended heiress. (Later, Agatha Christie, a reader of Green's work, increased the level of difficulty in her own fiction by tens in *Murder on the Orient Express* and *Ten Little Indians*.)

Impersonation and disguise as well as unexplained disappearances, devices used by criminals as well as by detectives, also increase the difficulty of Green's puzzles. In her classic short story "The Staircase at the Heart's Delight" (in *A Difficult Problem and Other Stories*, 1900), the young Ebenezer Gryce impersonates a well-to-do young man at a tavern at 5 South Street in lower Manhattan, where wealthy men have mysteriously disappeared only to be found later in the murky Hudson River. Gryce presents himself as a wealthy man-about-town in order to become a potential victim and discover the mystery of the infamous staircase. In another short story, "Midnight in Beauchamp Row" (in *A Difficult Problem and Other Stories*), a young wife, Letty Chivers, is terrorized by an intruder who is after the two thousand dollars in payroll money that her husband has hidden in their cottage. Her husband is a trusted employee responsible for depositing company money, but he is called away before he can get to the bank. A tramp's intervention "saves" her and unmasks the intruder, who, to her horror, turns out to be her husband in disguise. In *Hand and Ring* (1883) Mr. Gryce assumes the role of a hunchback as a cover for sleuthing. In *The Mystery of the Hasty Arrow* (1917), Caleb Sweetwater, an assistant to Gryce, successfully impersonates a debilitated old man living in a Brooklyn tenement in order to infiltrate a murder suspect's home territory.

Green's plots were often inspired by current news stories, for bodies were found daily in the Hudson River, and people disappeared—sometimes through violence and frequently to escape debts, the consequences of their crimes, or marriages. Bigamy, for example, threatens the reputation of the heroine in *The Mayor's Wife* (1907). Olympia Packard, who was forced into marriage when she was a young girl living out West, ran away immediately after the ceremony; shortly thereafter she heard that her husband had killed himself. She has since remarried, this time to a man who is mayor of the city. Now she is being blackmailed by John Silverthorn Brainard, the husband she thought was dead. The plot is complicated by doubles, for John Brainard has also remarried, willfully committing bigamy. However, he is without scruples, using his current wife and even his elderly aunts to finance his lifestyle. Although Green's fictional account is cunning and enthralling, in reality, Olympia Packard's plight was not uncommon. Men also faced the disappearance of their wives, such as the situation Roger Ransom recounts in *The Chief Legatee* (1906): "I was married to-day in Grace Church. At the altar my bride. . .wore a natural look, and was in all respects, so far as any one could see, a happy woman, satisfied with her choice and pleased with the eclat and elegancies of the occasion. . . . I had absolutely no idea that she meant to leave me" (pp. 9, 11). Disappearances and reconstructed identities were facts of life at the turn of the century in a society without social security numbers and the various methods of identification we have today.

New York City was a logical choice as the environment for most of Green's fiction; it was fashionable and exciting—and appealing to readers. Even though she did not move in the same circles as the noted author and socialite Edith Wharton or the wealthy Mrs. Astor, Green captured the lifestyles of the rich and powerful. Caroline Schermerhorn Astor, the wife of millionaire capitalist William Backhouse Astor, developed a select list of four hundred New York socialites—said to be limited by the number of people who could fit into her ballroom. Tales of gala balls and delightful escapades of "the Four Hundred" were regular features of the daily press. And even though Ebenezer Gryce was not from the upper class, his clients were, and he entered their homes as a keen observer. In 1897, when she presented Amelia Butterworth, an aristocratic dowager, as her new detective, Green gave her a Fifth Avenue address and society connections. With Butterworth, the reader was whisked into the inner circle. And in 1915, with the creation of Violet Strange, the debutante sleuth, Green reinforced her hold on New York society—this time featuring the younger generation.

That Affair Next Door (1897) introduces Amelia Butterworth, an older, unmarried, upper-class woman with a keen mind and an eye for detail who lives in a fashionable brownstone on Gramercy Park. Thus, she is the person to alert the police to the presence of a strange woman in the brownstone next door, owned by the Van Burnham family. She explains why she took an interest in the case: "First: because the house was empty, or supposed to be so, the family still being in Europe; and secondly: because, not being inquisitive, I often miss in my lonely and single life much that it would be both interesting and profitable for me to know" (p. 1). Her suspicions lead to the discovery of the body of a woman crushed beneath a weighty bookcase. Butterworth then insinuates her way into the police investigation by providing an insider's view of New York society. Butterworth also tells the readers that she is a woman of "strict Presbyterian training" who believes in the influence of Providence (*Lost Man's Lane,* 1898, p. v); it is often the providential moment that gives her an edge in perceiving the truth.

Green also chose to make Butterworth the first-person narrator, thus giving her the strongest voice in the novel. When Gryce enters the scene, she has already assessed the situation and fills him in on details. Her voice is assured, but leavened by wit and humor. When Mr. Gryce suggests that they work together to solve the murder, she thinks, "I am as sly as he, and though not quite as old—now *I* am sarcastic—have some of his wits, if but little of his experience" (p. 57). She knows that her observations on the house and the behavior of its occupants are worth something. It is Butterworth who recognizes that a hat pin is the actual murder weapon. With her knowledge of fashion, she can trace which hatmaker designed the hat the murdered woman was wearing—this leads to critical information about the identity of the victim. Since this puzzle, like that of *The Leavenworth Case,* is complicated by sets of doubles (two sisters, Caroline and Isabella, and two brothers, Franklin and Howard—each with wives), Butterworth has to ferret out family secrets and make fine distinctions before she deduces who the murderer is. And she succeeds, much to the chagrin of the official police investigator, Inspector Gryce.

Lost Man's Lane, however, reveals that Butterworth and Gryce have become friends despite their earlier rivalry. He asks her to assist him in solving a case of missing persons—four people have disappeared, each last seen entering a remote lane in the rural village of

Sibley, New York. At first Butterworth is reluctant to leave the city, but Gryce is persuasive; he sends her a telegram: "Do not let anything that I have said last night influence you to leave your comfortable home. The adventure offers too many dangers for a woman" (p. 24). Naturally, Miss Butterworth takes the bait, believing firmly in her ability as a woman to cope with any dangers she might encounter. She is also interested in the case because the children of a deceased friend, Althea Knollys, live in the village. Green injects humor into this caper with Butterworth facing her greatest fear—dogs; ironically, she is blind to the real threat to her life, a human being. This case presents haunting escapades in a country house, including possible evidence of vivisection as well as some realistic scenes with a psychopathic killer who threatens Butterworth's life. Green constructs a clever whodunit with a most unlikely suspect. (The ending of this novel may remind readers of Agatha Christie's *Sleeping Murder*, where Miss Marple almost becomes the murderer's final victim.)

Although Manhattan was the primary locale for her novels, Green also used other settings. The upstate New York country village became a fertile environment for detection, as in *Lost Man's Lane*. But Green did not limit herself to one area of the nation; her vista extended beyond New York, from New England to the far West. For example, *Agatha Webb* (1899) features the New England seacoast, *A Matter of Millions* (1890) is set in New Mexico, the action of *Miss Hurd: An Enigma* (1894) takes place in California and Connecticut, and *The Filigree Ball* (1903) highlights life in Washington, D.C.

Green developed connections between her sleuths that encouraged readers to follow their adventures in subsequent novels and short stories. When Amelia Butterworth makes her first appearance in *That Affair Next Door*, she is the central sleuth in the novel, but Ebenezer Gryce assists her as the official police representative. The upper-class Miss Butterworth and the stolid middle-class Detective Gryce are foils for each other, engaging in banter and lively discussions. As Gryce ages, Green introduces Caleb Sweetwater, a new recruit to the Metropolitan Police whose boundless energy complements Gryce's more cogitative style. As they work together, a father/son relationship develops. Sweetwater is first introduced in *A Strange Disappearance* (1880), where he plays a minor role, but he is subsequently developed as a more fleshed-out character in *Agatha Webb*. This novel provides a life history for Sweetwater; it takes place in Sutherlandtown on the New England coast, where he was raised. The reader learns that Sweetwater is a talented violinist who gives up a musical career to become a detective and, more important, that he is a trusted and dutiful young man who offers his services to a patron in repayment of past kindness. A maturing Sweetwater continues to work with Gryce in *One of My Sons* (1901), *The Woman in the Alcove* (1906), *Dark Hollow* (1914), and *The Mystery of the Hasty Arrow* (1917). By forging these relationships among her detectives, Green made them more real and human to a wide readership—men, women, the upper class, the middle class, Americans, Europeans.

Special conundrums in her fiction are among Green's trademarks, including sophisticated mechanical devices, such as the pulleys that controlled the deadly settle in *The Filigree Ball*, a device that causes the inexplicable murder of a prominent Washington man. "The Little Steel Coils" (in *Masterpieces of Mystery*, 1913) describes how poison was given to the victim by coating the steel coils of a puzzle with a rare poison. The uniquely constructed staircase in "The Staircase at the Heart's Delight" provides a cunning means of dumping unsuspecting young men into the murky waters of New York City's harbor. With the advent of electricity, Green engaged readers' interest in the powers of this new technology. (Broadway was first wired in the 1890s.) Thus, the focus of "The Bronze Hand" (in *A Difficult Problem and Other Stories*) is a secret electric signaling device that is set off whenever a ring is placed on the bronze hand of a sculptured figure. *The*

Circular Study (1900) presents a locked-room mystery, where the victim is found murdered in his futuristic study—a room with a unique system of colored electric lights used to send coded signals to those outside the room.

Green's fiction is most provocative in her depiction of the unfair treatment of women and their children. Although she was not active in the suffragist organizations of her day, by focusing on the tight social constructs that undercut a woman's power, she voices her protest. Money is a basic issue, for Blackstone's law—which guided American jurisprudence through the beginning of the twentieth century—held that once she was married, a woman lost her individual identity under the law, and thus her right to own personal property in her own name. Although New York State was the first to enact legislation to protect women's interests under the Married Women's Property Act, other states were slow in taking up the cause. It was not until women later gained the right to vote that their right to hold property was protected. Green portrays repeated situations where young, marriageable women become vulnerable to men who marry them for their money. We see this situation in such novels as *Cynthia Wakeham's Money* (1892), *The Mystery of the Hasty Arrow, The Step on the Stair,* and "The Gray Madam" (in *A Difficult Problem and Other Stories*).

Green also shows how married women are subject to physical abuse, for example, in *Miss Hurd: An Enigma.* In this novel, Vashti Murdoch becomes the object of an obsessive and homicidal husband who pursues the terrified Vashti from a ranch in California across country to New England, where she tries to escape from him by changing her identity. Abandonment and bigamy are the themes of *That Affair Next Door* and *The Mayor's Wife.* The dramatic denouement of *That Affair Next Door,* for example, depicts a debutante being escorted down the aisle on her wedding day only to be confronted by a second bride—heavily veiled—who emerges from a side aisle. The mysterious figure reveals herself to be the groom's legal wife, whom he had married years before and abandoned.

The double standard that allowed men greater freedom fostered bigamy and other abuses. While men were expected to pursue their fortunes by any means necessary—often at the expense of women—the unmarried woman had few respectable opportunities for independence. In *The Mill Mystery* (1886), Green portrays Constance Sterling, a single woman who has to work in order to support herself, yet some men and other women look down on her because they consider work outside the home "unfeminine." The young man who assists Miss Sterling affirms his admiration for her daring: "In this age and in this country a woman like yourself forfeits nothing by maintaining her own independence. On the contrary, she gains something, and that is the respect of every true-hearted man that knows her" (p. 105). Ermentrude Taylor, the heroine of *The Mystery of the Hasty Arrow,* is abandoned by her opportunist husband while she is expecting their first child. As best she can, she raises their daughter by herself, living on the edge of poverty. Meanwhile her husband remarries—this time to a wealthy, well-placed woman. Not only a bigamist but also a murderer, this man will stop at nothing to conceal his first marriage and protect his new life.

Violet Strange, the amateur sleuth that Green introduced in 1915, is forced to work on the sly because her father, Peter Strange, does not approve of upper-class women in the work force—especially his debutante daughter. (Violet may well have been modeled after Green's own daughter, Rosamund, who would have been close in age to the character.) Although she lives in a mansion on Fifth Avenue and enjoys the services of a chauffeur, Miss Strange needs much more money to finance a secret project. *The Golden Slipper* (1915) is a collection of nine short stories featuring Violet Strange—the last story, "Violet's Own," reveals why she needs the money. Violet gets her name from the flower: she is little and appears delicate, but she has a strong character and a mathematical mind. Although murder does enter into Strange's cases, for the most part she solves problems, such as recovering stolen or lost property, protecting a family from scandal, and restoring the good name of her fiancé, Roger Upjohn ("The Grotto Spectre").

In one case, for example ("The Doctor, His Wife and the Clock"), Violet works from a written report to analyze the sequence of events that has stumped the police and put a husband and wife's good name in jeopardy. Using her powers of deduction, Violet solves the puzzle. In another case ("The Golden Slipper"), Miss Strange is employed by the father of a debutante to discover if his daughter is the thief who has been stealing from within her social circle. In order to protect his family's good name, he dares not go to the police. However, the thief has become so daring and strikes so close to home that he desperately needs help. Violet easily becomes part of the group and sets a trap, unmasking the guilty party—and preventing scandal. In each case, her ability to move in upper-class circles gives her entrée to situations too delicate for the police. Ultimately, the reader learns that Violet's desire for her own money has not been a selfish one; she has been secretly assisting a disowned older sister to pursue a career in music ("Violet's Own").

In the 1920s, detective fiction was entering its Golden Age, and other women in England and the United States had begun to establish careers as writers of detective fiction. For these writers, the legacy of Anna Katharine Green was particularly significant. Among them was Agatha Christie, who acknowledges in her autobiography that she read Green and was particularly affected by the two young women, Mary and Eleanore, of *The Leavenworth Case.* Mary Roberts Rinehart also refers to Green in her autobiography, revealing that she derived the title of her first mystery, *The Circular Staircase,* from Green's novel *The Circular Study.* Although the extent of Green's influence on specific authors is difficult to assess, certain elements can be seen in the works of later writers. For example, characters similar to Amelia Butterworth are found in Christie's Jane Marple and Rinehart's Hilda Adams—each of these female sleuths is an older, single woman with an uncanny ability to solve mysteries. Considering the development of the genre, writers of detective fiction—male and female, American and European—all share in Green's legacy, for the classic form she helped establish became the model for the writers who followed her.

A woman who had a successful professional career, Anna Katharine Green not only was skilled at her craft, she also provided a voice for society's victims in her fiction. When she died at her home in Buffalo on 11 April 1935, she had achieved fame for fiction that challenged readers to think, to reconsider social conditions, and—most of all—to enjoy the thrill of a good mystery. In his review of *The Leavenworth Case,* Wilkie Collins provides some insight into Green's achievements:

> Her powers of invention are so remarkable—she has so much imagination and so much belief (a most important qualification for our art) in what she says. . . . Dozens of times in reading the story I have stopped to admire the fertility of invention, the delicate treatment of incident—and the fine perception of event on the personages of the story. (*The Critic,* p. 152)

Selected Bibliography

WORKS OF ANNA KATHARINE GREEN

NOVELS

The Leavenworth Case. New York: Putnam, 1878.
A Strange Disappearance. New York: A. L. Burt, 1880.
The Sword of Damocles: A Story of New York Life. New York: Putnam, 1881.
XYZ. New York: Putnam, 1883.
Hand and Ring. New York: Putnam, 1883.
The Mill Mystery. New York: Putnam, 1886.
7 to 12. New York: Putnam, 1887.
Behind Closed Doors. New York: Putnam, 1888.
The Forsaken Inn. New York: R. Bonner's Sons, 1890.
A Matter of Millions. New York: R. Bonner's Sons, 1890.
Cynthia Wakeham's Money. New York: Putnam, 1892.
Marked "Personal." New York: Putnam, 1893.

Miss Hurd: An Enigma. New York: Putnam, 1894.
Dr. Izard. New York: Putnam, 1895.
The Doctor, His Wife and the Clock. New York: Putnam, 1895.
That Affair Next Door. New York: A. L. Burt, 1897.
Lost Man's Lane. New York: Putnam, 1898.
Agatha Webb. New York: American News, 1899.
The Circular Study. New York: R. F. Fenno, 1900.
One of My Sons. New York: Putnam, 1901.
Three Women and a Mystery. New York: New York Leisure Hour Library, 1902.
The Filigree Ball. Indianapolis: Bobbs-Merrill, 1903.
The Amethyst Box. Indianapolis: Bobbs-Merrill, 1905.
The House in the Mist. New York: New York Book, 1905.
The Millionaire Baby. Indianapolis: Bobbs-Merrill, 1905.
The Chief Legatee. New York: Authors and Newspapers Association, 1906.
The Woman in the Alcove. Indianapolis: Bobbs-Merrill, 1906.
The Mayor's Wife. Indianapolis: Bobbs-Merrill, 1907.
A Woman of Mystery. London: Collier, 1909.
Three Thousand Dollars. Boston: R. G. Badger, 1910.
The House of the Whispering Pines. New York: A. L. Burt, 1910.
Initials Only. New York: A. L. Burt, 1911.
Dark Hollow. New York: Dodd, Mead, 1914.
To the Minute, Scarlet and Black. New York: Putnam, 1916.
The Mystery of the Hasty Arrow. New York: A. L. Burt, 1917.
The Step on the Stair. New York: A. L. Burt, 1923.

SHORT STORY COLLECTIONS

The Old Stone House and Other Stories. Freeport, N.Y.: Books for Libraries Press, 1891. Includes "The Old Stone House," "A Memorable Night," "The Black Cross," "A Mysterious Case," and "Shall He Wed Her?"
A Difficult Problem and Other Stories. New York: F. M. Lupton, 1900. Includes "A Difficult Problem," "The Gray Madam," "The Bronze Hand," "Midnight in Beauchamp Row," "The Staircase at the Heart's Delight," and "The Hermit of —— Street."
Masterpieces of Mystery. New York: Dodd, Mead, 1913. Includes "Midnight in Beauchamp Row," "Room No. 3," "The Ruby and the Caldron," "The Little Steel Coils," "The Staircase at the Heart's Delight," "The Amethyst Box," "The Grey Lady," "The Thief," and "The House in the Mist."
The Golden Slipper and Other Problems for Violet Strange. New York: Putnam, 1915. Includes "The Golden Slipper," "The Second Bullet," "The Intangible Clew," "The Grotto Spectre," "The Dreaming Lady," "The House of Clocks," "The Doctor, His Wife and the Clock," "Missing: Page Thirteen," and "Violet's Own."

OTHER WORKS

The Defense of the Bride and Other Poems. New York, 1882.
Risifi's Daughter: A Drama. New York, 1887.
"Anna Katharine Green Tells How She Manufactures Her Plots." *Literary Digest* 58: 48 (13 July 1918).
"Why Human Beings Are Interested in Crime." *American Magazine* 87: 38–39, 82–86 (February 1919).

ARCHIVES

The Library of the University of Texas at Austin holds manuscripts and letters.

BIOGRAPHICAL AND CRITICAL STUDIES

Collins, Wilkie. "Wilkie Collins on *The Leavenworth Case.*" *Critic* 22: 52 (28 January 1893).
Emerson, Ralph Waldo. *The Letters of Ralph Waldo Emerson.* Edited by R. I. Rusk. New York: Columbia University Press, 1939.
Maida, Patricia D. *Mother of Detective Fiction: The Life and Works of Anna Katharine Green.* Bowling Green, Ohio: Bowling Green State University Popular Press, 1989.
Maio, Kathleen L. "Anna Katharine Green." In *American Women Writers,* vol. 3. Edited by Lina Mainiero. New York: Ungar, 1981: 498–500.
Mooney, Joan M. "Best Selling American Detective Fiction." *Armchair Detective* 3: 98–100 (1970).
Murch, Alma E. *The Development of the Detective Novel.* Westport, Conn.: Greenwood, 1981.
Woodward, Kathleen. "Anna Katharine Green." *Bookman* 70: 168–170 (October 1929).

GRAHAM GREENE
(1904–1991)

BRIAN DIEMERT

ONE OF THE most prolific writers of the twentieth century, Graham Greene earned both popular and critical acclaim in a literary career that ran from the mid-1920s to his death in 1991. By the late 1930s he was seen as one of the finest English novelists of his generation, and by the late 1940s he had acquired an international reputation. When serious critical attention began to be paid to his work in the 1950s, it focused on the religious aspects of his writing, particularly in what were called his Catholic novels (*Brighton Rock* [1938], *The Power and the Glory* [1940; published in the United States as *The Labyrinthine Ways*], *The Heart of the Matter* [1948], *The End of the Affair* [1951], and, later, *A Burnt-Out Case* [1961]).

Yet long before this, Greene had proved himself a successful and increasingly popular writer with a number of books (*Stamboul Train* [1932; published in the United States as *Orient Express*], *It's a Battlefield* [1934], *England Made Me* [1935; published in the United States as *The Shipwrecked*], *A Gun for Sale* [1936; published in the United States as *This Gun for Hire*], *The Confidential Agent* [1939], and *The Ministry of Fear* [1943]) that to varying degrees transformed the genre of the thriller as it was passed down from Erskine Childers, John Buchan, Edgar Wallace, and others. Indeed, Greene's "elevation of the form of the thriller into a medium for serious fiction" (Sharrock, p. 12) is his great technical achievement.

At one time, Greene chose to call several of his books "entertainments," a label that tended to discourage serious analysis of some of his best work. Any distinction between his thrillers and his other novels, between entertainments and novels, is, however, finally untenable, for all of Greene's novels end up being thrillers.

Life

Beyond certain basic facts, the particulars of Greene's life were until recently largely unknown. Since the publication, however, of the first volume of Norman Sherry's authorized three-volume *Life of Graham Greene* in 1989, a more detailed portrait has emerged. Sherry's sympathetic biography, two volumes of which have appeared to date, has been joined by two more biographies that take in the whole of Greene's life: Michael Sheldon's rather unflattering *Graham Greene: The Man Within* and Anthony Mockler's *Graham Greene: Three Lives.* And people who knew Greene, such as Leopoldo Duran and Michael Korda (the nephew of Alexander Korda, who produced the films *The Fallen Idol* and *The Third Man*) have begun to record their impressions of the man.

What emerges is a complicated, often contradictory portrait of a writer who took great pains to construct a public image of himself that concealed many of the essential details of his life while teasingly revealing others, with the total effect confirming the sense of the man that we get from his novels. Greene tells us in *A Sort of Life* (1971), for instance, that some of his earliest memories are of "sitting in a pram at the top of a hill with a dead dog lying at my feet" (p. 13) and of seeing a man break from a crowd, run into a house, and slit his own throat in full view of those outside (p. 14). Such "memories" are the very stuff of Greene's fiction, yet his autobiographical writings largely keep our attention fixed on the literature and its production. Seldom are the important people in his life or his relationships with them mentioned, much less discussed. Furthermore, when facts related to his own development are offered, their veracity is almost always suspect.

A case in point involves Greene's often circulated report that he played Russian roulette as an adolescent. The subject of undergraduate verse and a 1946 essay, "The Revolver in the Corner Cupboard," the story is repeated in *A Sort of Life* (pp. 92–96). Evidence uncovered by Greene's biographers, however, casts doubt on the truthfulness of the tale. For Sheldon, who refers to "The Revolver in the Corner Cupboard" as a "story," the narrative may have been constructed in order to confer dignity upon an actual, and embarrassing, suicide attempt in a potting shed. For Sherry, who calls the document an "essay," the Russian roulette story recounts one of many suicide attempts made by Greene as a young man, which eventually led him to psychoanalysis in 1921. Whatever the facts of the case, there can be little doubt that after a relatively happy childhood, Greene's adolescence was troubled.

Born on 2 October 1904 in Berkhamsted, England, Graham Greene was the fourth of six children of Charles Henry Greene and Marion Raymond Greene. In 1910, his father became headmaster at Berkhamsted College, and at thirteen, Greene was moved out of the family residence into the boarders' residence, spending vacations at home. Since these two abodes were, in fact, part of the same building, Greene found himself in an uncomfortable position. Confined to student life on the other side of the "green baize door" (*A Sort of Life,* p. 46) that separated the school from the family's residence, Greene was miserable because he saw himself as outside his family but, because of his relationship to the headmaster, never accepted and often persecuted by the other boys (p. 54). For Greene, student life was marked by torment and betrayal, but it was also the source of a rich personal mythology that surfaces in many of his books and of his thematic preoccupations with trust, loyalty, and betrayal.

Greene's miseries at school and his reading of *The Viper of Milan* by historical and children's writer Marjorie Bowen are credited by him in his autobiographical essay "The Lost Childhood" with profoundly shaping his vision of the world. Identifying his chief tormentor, a boy named Carter, with Bowen's villain, Visconti, Greene discovered that "human nature is not black and white but black and grey." Bowen, he wrote, gave him his "pattern . . . perfect evil walking the world where perfect good can never walk again, and only the pendulum ensures that after all in the end justice is done" (*Collected Essays,* 1969, p. 18).

Greene's days as a boarder ended in June of 1921, when a nervous breakdown prompted his parents to send him to London to undergo psychoanalysis with Kenneth Richmond. The following six months were some of the happiest in Greene's life, and at the end of 1921 he returned to Berkhamstead as a day boy.

In 1922, at the age of 18, Greene entered Balliol College at Oxford University to study history, and in 1925, despite a tendency toward heavy drinking, he graduated with a Second in History. Unemployed, he took a job in Nottingham to work on the *Nottingham Journal,* which he left in March 1926 in order to return to London, for it was also in 1925 that Greene met and fell in love with Vivien Dayrell-Browning, a Catholic. In order to marry her, he converted to Catholicism in 1926; the two were married in 1927 and had two children, Lucy (born in 1933) and Francis (born in 1936). Marriage, however, did not dampen Greene's taste for other women, and the couple finally separated in 1948. From 1926, Greene worked as a subeditor at the *Times,* leaving in 1930 to devote himself to a career as a writer after the publication and relative success of his first novel, *The Man Within* (1929).

The next ten years fully shaped Greene as a writer. Spurred by financial necessity and overwhelming ambition, between 1929 and 1940 he published nine novels, two travel books, a collection of short stories, scads of book reviews, and, once a week from 1935 to 1940, film reviews for the *Spectator* and the short-lived *Night and Day,* of which he was an editor. He also wrote a biography of Lord Rochester, not published until 1974, and edited a collection of essays on public school life, *The Old School* (1934), to which he contributed. In no other period was he so prolific.

The 1930s shaped Greene in several other ways as well. As with most writers of his generation—Christopher Isherwood, W. H. Auden, Louis MacNeice, Stephen Spender, Cecil Day Lewis, and George Orwell among others—Greene was acutely aware of his place in history: "I think of those years between 1933 and 1937 as the middle years for my generation, clouded by Depression in England . . . and by the rise of Hitler. It was impossible in those days not to be committed . . . as the enormous battlefield was prepared around us" (*Ways of Escape,* 1980, p. 37). In *England Made Me,* his generation's position is expressed in Anthony Farrant's and Minty's desire to believe in something—"in the old country, in the king, in 'shoot the bloody Bolsheviks,' in the comradeship of the trenches" (p. 180)—but they are too old to do so.

In the political and economic climate of the Depression years, "moral seriousness" and a reaction to high modernist aesthetics took hold among several of the younger writers. Many of them espoused explicitly leftist political views, and Greene, though less declarative than some, such as Day Lewis or Spender, was affected by the leftist political atmosphere around him. Orwell later described him in a letter to T. R. Fyvel (the author and journalist who was the literary editor of the *Tribune*) to be "a mild Left with faint CP [Communist Party] leanings" and drew attention to "the usual left-wing scenery" in books like *A Gun for Sale, England Made Me, The Confidential Agent,* and others: "The bad men are millionaires, armaments manufacturers etc. and the good man is sometimes a Communist" (p. 496).

Greene's fiction in the 1930s displays a sharp political critique, but nowhere is he dogmatic in his assertion of an alternative to the present order. Because he saw the problems of the period as rooted in deeper causes than economics or politics, he rejected party allegiances and declared his "distrust of any future based on what we are" (*Journey Without Maps,* 1936, p. 20). In his mind, and he was not alone in thinking this, the period could end only in destruction because only violence could "satisfy that moral craving for the just and reasonable expression of human nature left without belief" (*Collected Essays,* p. 334). In this context, an ambivalence in Greene's thinking is revealed. On the one hand, political change seems insignificant because it is ineffective beside the larger spiritual forces at work in the world (Pinkie in *Brighton Rock,* for instance, is apparently a spiritual force of evil), but on the other hand, social and economic conditions demand that the writer possess a political consciousness (Pinkie's background of poverty in a crowded tenement is frequently emphasized). Greene seems to be trying to have things both ways.

For some critics, the fact of this seeming contradiction, coupled with Greene's failure to take a public stance on the Spanish Civil War, has aroused suspicions about the degree of his commitment to the Left in the 1930s. Was he merely an opportunist parroting the popular sentiments of the time, or did he possess a genuine commitment to the Left (even if, as Judith Adamson argues, it emerged later in his career)? Or perhaps, as Sheldon suggests, Greene's championing of the Left and its leaders had another, darker purpose? Such questions are difficult to answer with certainty, but I suspect that Greene's commitment to the Left grew as the 1930s progressed. Like Arthur Rowe in *The Ministry of Fear,* Greene came to the place where he realized that one "couldn't let things stay as they were, with the innocent struggling in fear for breath and dying pointlessly" (p. 180). Indeed, it is one of the particular features of Greene's work that his fiction in the following decades seems wholly consistent with the political perspective of the earlier work.

During the war, Greene was recruited into the Special Intelligence Service (SIS), later called MI6, and assigned to Sierra Leone, where he reported on shipping along the West African coast, searched Portuguese vessels for contraband diamonds (which were destined for Germany), and learned what he could about enemy activities, including efforts to repair French naval vessels, in the neighboring Vichy colony of French Guinea. For all of this, Greene found that his duties left him with time to write *The Ministry of Fear* and to gather material for *The Heart of the Matter.* At SIS he met and became friends with Kim Philby, who was his superior. Although all of the facts are not yet known, there is some evidence to suggest that Greene's abrupt resignation from SIS on the eve of D-day in June 1944 may have been motivated by the knowledge, or at least the suspicion, that his friend was a double agent. Whatever the case, Greene remained friends with Philby, publicly defending him and visiting him in Moscow. Like many writers, Greene threw nothing away, and his understanding of and friendship with Philby later found expression in the character of Maurice Castle in *The Human Factor* (1978).

Although Greene left his position with SIS, Paul Fussell and others have speculated that Greene never wholly relinquished his ties to the "old firm." Sherry suggests that Greene's visits to Vietnam in the early 1950s brought Greene into renewed contact with MI6, while Sheldon goes further to argue that Greene's involvement with MI6 never really ended. In this context, Greene's public admiration for leftist leaders, from Castro to Ho Chi Minh to Salvador Allende, is for Sheldon yet another example of Greene's duplicity. Certainly, the exact degree to which Greene maintained ties to British Intelligence is unclear, but the evidence points to at least periodic contact over the years.

In any case, readers have often been struck by the uncannily prophetic elements in Greene's fiction. In *Our Man in Havana* (1958), for example, Wormold's fictional reports describe the construction of missile installations in Cuba some four years before the 1962 crisis. As a world traveler, Greene often found himself in situations and locales on the eve of or during periods of political instability—besides Vietnam, we see him in Kenya covering the Mau Mau uprisings, in Cuba and the Congo in the late 1950s, and in Latin America in the 1960s and 1970s. And frequently such visits provided material for his books, such as *The Quiet American* (1955), *Our Man in Havana, A Burnt-Out Case, The Comedians* (1966), *The Honorary Consul* (1973), and *The Captain and the Enemy* (1988), which often seemed to foreshadow future events. Speaking figuratively, Greene wrote in *A Sort of Life,* "every novelist has something in common with a spy" (p. 103). It is a metaphor he often used in his career, going back to *Stamboul Train,* in which the character Quin Savory, a popular writer patterned on J. B. Priestley, observes: "A novelist depends on other men; he's an average man with the power of expression. ''E's a spy,' . . . 'E 'as to see everything and pass unnoticed" (p. 61). Recent disclosures, however, suggest that in Greene's case he may not have been entirely metaphorical.

Greene's many travels no doubt contribute to the generally menacing atmosphere that pervades these novels, though the "Greene" stamp is clearly evident in all of his novels and stories. Their allegedly stylized milieu has caused critics since Arthur Calder-Marshall coined the term in 1940 to describe the world of Greene's fiction as "Greeneland." Understandably, Greene objected to this label (as he did to other labels—a Catholic novelist, a political novelist, or a man of the thirties—that were fixed upon him): "Some critics have referred to a strange violent 'seedy' region of the mind . . . which they call Greeneland, and I have sometimes wondered whether they go round the world blinkered. 'This is Indo-China,' I want to exclaim, 'this is Mexico . . .' carefully and accurately described. . . . But I know that argument is useless. They won't believe the world they haven't noticed is like that" (*Ways of Escape,* p. 60). As David Lodge notes, however, Greene's objections to "Greeneland," ostensibly motivated by "a feeling that it impugns the veracity of his account of the world," have a great deal to do with his suspicion of literary criticism (pp. 127–128).

In the later years of his life, Greene continued to travel widely and to write, albeit at a slower pace. In the 1960s he became a tax exile and left England to live in Antibes, France, where he remained until December 1990, when ill-health forced him to move to Vevey in Switzerland, where he could be close to his daughter, doctor, and hospital. He died there on 3 April 1991 of a blood disease; he was eighty-six.

Works

The decades between the world wars are almost universally described as the Golden Age of Detective Fiction by the genre's historians because many of its most famous practitioners began publishing then. Greene said he was very interested in the detective story in the twenties and thirties, and a cursory view of his fiction and comments in *Ways of Escape* reveals a continuing engagement with the form. Although the entertainments particularly are usually identified as Greene's thrillers, even those books not called entertainments bear the marks of the genre: *Brighton Rock, The Quiet American,* and *The Power and the Glory* all utilize elements of the thriller in the structuring of their narratives. Yet Greene's texts also depart from the formulas he inherited. Indeed, if we can credit his comments in *Ways of Escape,* we see him deliberately trying to alter the form in order "to create something legendary out of the contemporary thriller" (p. 68).

This desire was realized in books such as *A Gun for Sale, The Confidential Agent, The Ministry of Fear,* and *The Third Man* (1950), but Greene's early fiction, besides betraying his strong attraction to the melodramatic adventure stories he enjoyed as a youth, shows a young author groping for popular success. Some of this struggle is described in *A Sort of Life,* but an early short story, "Murder for the Wrong Reason" (1929), shows us Greene working within the conventions of the classic detective story, in this case a locked-room mystery. The story, in which Detective Inspector Mason investigates the murder of Hubert Collinson, is undistinguished but revealing, both of Greene's familiarity with the genre (there are several allusions to Arthur Conan Doyle's works) and of his preoccupation with a divided self pursued by what Mary McCarthy later called "the Eumenides of conscience" (p. 220), which haunt all of Greene's protagonists. Mason, we see, proves to be the murderer, so his investigation is ultimately an exploration of himself and his past. First seen here, the portrait of the divided man (perhaps a legacy of Greene's distant but often evoked relation Robert Louis Stevenson?) is everywhere in Greene's fiction.

The combination of criminal investigation and self-investigation in detective stories, as descended from Oedipus' story, can be found in most of Greene's books. *The Quiet American,* for example, shows us Thomas Fowler, a British journalist, probing his memory to recall his motivations, his past, and his relationship with the murdered American Alden Pyle, whose death is being investigated in the narrative's frame by Vigot, a French police inspector.

Characteristically, the story is dotted with self-conscious references to other detective stories, in this case, because of Vietnam's status as a former French colony, to Georges Simenon's Maigret stories. Fowler, unlike Mason, is not a murderer, but he bears responsibility for Pyle's death at the hands of the Communists (Fowler sets Pyle up), and his motives, though ostensibly political (he fears Pyle's innocence may exacerbate the conflict), are clouded with personal jealousies (Fowler's mistress, Phuong, left him for Pyle). In some ways, Fowler, like Mason, has committed murder for dubious reasons, for, as Greene says, sexual passion is one of the most likely motives for murder among those who are not members of the so-called criminal classes (*Ways of Escape,* p. 73). Mason, we understand, has killed Collinson not out of jealousy, but out of the fear that Collinson will blackmail him, and a repentant Fowler attempts to justify his actions on political grounds.

After three relatively weak novels, *Stamboul Train,* Greene's fourth published novel, marks a distinct shift in his early development toward a more economical style enhanced by a cinematic technique that became a feature of his writing. Less ambitious than the earlier books, *Stamboul Train* follows a collection of mostly English characters traveling on the Orient Express to Istanbul. Greene described the book as a kind of "Grand Hotel" on wheels, with the train trip, a common setting in novels and films in the thirties, providing the narrative with its rapid pace and relatively taut structure. Again, melodramatic elements abound: Dr. Czinner, a Communist revolutionary leader returning out of exile to Belgrade, is intercepted, summarily tried, and executed at a border station; a chorus girl, Coral Musker, is seduced and has a brief affair with a wealthy investor, Myatt; and a ruthless armed thief, Grünlich, is seen escaping from his latest crime.

Stuffed with the elements of popular fiction—murder, romance, seduction, revolution—*Stamboul Train* was a deliberate and relatively successful attempt to achieve widespread appeal so as to make some money. Later, after he published *A Gun for Sale,* Greene called *Stamboul Train* an entertainment, and most critics discuss it in the context of the other texts he chose to call entertainments: *A Gun for Sale, The Confidential Agent, The Ministry of Fear, The Third Man, Loser Takes All* (1955), and *Our Man in Havana. Stamboul Train,* however, like the novella *Loser Takes All,* is different from the other five books, which are clear variations of the thriller's formula. To be sure, there are elements of the thriller in *Stamboul Train,* but the overall pattern of investigation and pursuit that we see elsewhere is only marginally employed. Indeed, the basic structure of the thriller is not only superbly developed in the later books but also comes to dominate many, if not most, of Greene's subsequent novels. Ultimately, the entertainment label that Greene employed raises fundamental questions about his intentions and his texts.

In *Ways of Escape,* Greene said he initially used the word "entertainment" in 1936 to distinguish his less serious from his "more serious work" (p. 78), which, presumably, carried a "message" (Donaghy, p. 39); however, after *The Ministry of Fear,* he said, the two types of texts came to resemble each other more and more until he gave up the distinction in 1969, when he published *Travels with My Aunt.* For many critics of Greene's work the label has caused no end of trouble as they struggle to distinguish novel from entertainment. A particularly influential point of view, first proposed by R. W. B. Lewis in the 1950s, is that Greene used his entertainments as preparation for the more serious novels that followed: *A Gun for Sale* readied him for *Brighton Rock, The Confidential Agent* for *The Power and the Glory, The Ministry of Fear* for *The Heart of the Matter.*

The schema is richly suggestive of thematic parallels, yet these very parallels should signal us to the essentially untenable nature of the distinction, and certainly Greene's own comments about how and where he used the label suggest this as well. That is, *Brighton Rock* was initially called an entertainment in its first American edition but not in its British edition; drafts of *The Quiet American* refer to it using this term; "The Fallen Idol" is called an entertainment, but the identical story, published as "The Basement Room" in Greene's short story collections, is not; *England Made Me* is not termed one either, although Greene said he "let himself go" in the form of "the pot-boiler, the adventure story" for the first time with this novel after discovering how much he liked the form when writing *Stamboul Train.* Still, several critics continue to see a distinction and use the word to discuss such books as *The Human Factor* and *Doctor Fischer of Geneva* (1980).

Relatively late in his career, Greene condemned what he viewed as a double standard in literary judgment that saw the "hard to read" as great and the "readable" as not so great. At other times, however, he seemed to encourage this double standard by arguing that the entertainments privileged action over character, which was the primary interest in the novels. Of course, one could argue that the difference seemed more apparent in the 1930s than it does now, but comments of this sort are ultimately belied both by the fiction and by Greene's unabashed admiration, amply demonstrated in reviews, of what G. K. Chesterton and Orwell called "good bad books"—such as those by Buchan, H. Rider Haggard, Wallace, Conan Doyle, and others. The reasons for the label, then, must lie elsewhere.

Perhaps a hint of what these might be is found in a 1949 interview with Père Jouve and Marcel Moré:

> MARCEL MORÉ: You have sometimes been criticized for using the form of the detective novel to express the metaphysical anxiety and anguish in the world today. On the contrary, I think it is excellent that you write in a form comprehensible to the masses and not reserved for the elite.
>
> GRAHAM GREENE: Let's say my favourite form is the "thriller" rather than the detective novel, strictly speaking. Isn't the shrewd little Father Brown . . . a little old-fashioned today? What we're interested in discovering in the middle of the twentieth century isn't who the criminal is, but rather to what state of abandon a man hunted down for a crime can be reduced. . . . It's [the old detective novel in the manner of Agatha Christie] "honest" work. That's all there is to say. Read Eric Ambler instead. (Donaghy, pp. 24–25)

Two ideas come to the foreground here: the first is the notion that Greene deliberately used a popular form because he was writing accessible literature for the masses, not the elites, and the second is that he found the old-fashioned, classic detective story as exemplified by the work of Chesterton, Christie, or Dorothy Sayers out of place in the modern world. Greene's use of the entertainment label, then, arises out of a desire, shared by many of the younger writers in the 1930s, to turn away from the esoteric experiments of the high modernist writers, such as James Joyce or Virginia Woolf, and write "seriously" for a larger audience who could then be presented with new ways of seeing and thinking about politics, economics, and the established social order: "If you excite your audience first," Greene wrote in 1936, "you can put over what you will of horror, suffering, truth" (*The Pleasure Dome,* 1972, p. 94).

Greene's transformation of popular literature involved reworking the thriller as it was passed on by writers such as Wallace and Buchan, whom Greene admired but whose vision he wrote in *Ways of Escape* no longer seemed suited to the new age:

> More than the dialogue and the situation had dated: the moral climate was no longer that of my boyhood. Patriotism had lost its appeal, even for a schoolboy, at Passchendaele . . . it was difficult, during the years of the Depression, to believe in the high purposes of the City of London and of the British Constitution. . . . It was no longer a Buchan world. (p. 54).

Buchan, Greene wrote elsewhere, taught that "death may come to any of us . . . by the railing of the Park or the doorway of the mews" (*Collected Essays,* p. 169)—a valuable lesson in 1941—but the intellectual content of Buchan's fiction, emphasizing the values of empire and the ideology of capitalism, repelled Greene in 1941: "the materialism" and the "enormous importance" Buchan placed on individuals could no longer be justified in the late 1930s and early 1940s (*Collected Essays,* p. 168).

Instead, Greene's and Ambler's thrillers develop what Michael Denning has called an "anti-fascist aesthetic," which manifests itself as an ironic approach to the genre, a reversal of earlier codings of heroes and villains, and a realistic approach to violence that discredited the antiseptic treatment accorded it in earlier thrillers and detective novels (Denning, pp. 65–66). In *England Made Me, A Gun for Sale,* and *The Confidential Agent,* fascism is identified with the forces of international capitalism and corporate interests, while in *The Ministry of Fear* the obvious enemy is Nazi Germany.

In Greene's books, however, the fascistic is also characterized by individuals such as Fred Hall in *England Made Me,* Pinkie in *Brighton Rock,* K. in *The Confidential Agent,* Hilfe in *The Ministry of Fear,* and, earlier, Grünlich in *Stamboul Train* and Jules in *It's a Battlefield.* Many of these characters are brutal in their language or in their actions or in both, but they are also curiously childish—arrested in their development and lacking empathy. Raven, too, in *A Gun for Sale* is brutally violent, but circumstance and Anne Crowder, whom Raven takes hostage, conspire to raise his and our consciousness of Sir Marcus' villainy. (Sir Marcus, the head of Midland Steel, employed his underling Davis to hire Raven to assassinate the Czech Minister of War so as to precipitate an international crisis and war, which would bolster the sagging fortunes of the steel industry.) Raven's heritage of poverty and physical deformity, as well as his position as a victim of others' treachery (Davis pays him with stolen currency), renders him a sympathetic figure; his vengeful hunt for Davis and then Sir Marcus becomes for us the pursuit of justice, while Mather's search for Raven is merely the pursuit of law.

In Mather, the police inspector, and his assistant, Saunders, we see Greene invoking the familiar paradigm of the master detective accompanied by his less able companion: one thinks of Edgar Allan Poe's C. Auguste Dupin and his unnamed companion, Conan Doyle's Sherlock Holmes and Watson, or Christie's Hercule Poirot and Hastings. A stock element in detective fiction, it first occurs in Greene's oeuvre in "Murder for the Wrong Reason," in which Mason coaches a slow-witted constable in the investigation. In *A Gun for Sale,* however, Mather's intellectual and imaginative limitations, typified by his horror of uncertainty, help debunk the myth of the detective as an all-powerful superhuman capable of penetrating the deepest mysteries of human behavior and criminal action with absolute authority. Indeed, with a few notable exceptions, such as E. C. Bentley's *Trent's Last Case,* the detective in the classic British detective story is always right and usually able to fill in the gaps in the chain of causality. His or her reasoning powers render all things visible: the criminal will be discovered, and the social order will be restored through his or her elimination.

In the 1930s, however, such individual certainty as that possessed by the detective is profoundly suspect because of its perceived associations with authoritarian and totalitarian forms of governance. Similarly, guilt cannot be so locally confined to a single individual. Hence, figures such as Raven and Pinkie are caught within a complicated social and political network that mitigates their apparent guilt and leaches it into the larger society. The same can be said of Jim Drover, the bus driver in *It's a Battlefield,* who is awaiting execution for the killing of a policeman at a political demonstration. (The dead man was about to club Drover's wife.) Jim Drover does not appear as a character in the novel, but his situation is the catalyst for Greene's interrogation of the issues of the murderer's guilt, the law's punishment, and human justice.

In *A Gun for Sale,* Mather is the reversal of the Holmesian detective and so represents a challenge to the detective's claim to authority. In Greene's work, motives are always complicated—no single person can accurately interpret or read the complicated social, political, and cultural events of the 1930s and beyond. In this respect, his thrillers bear some resemblance to the hard-boiled novels of Dashiell Hammett and Raymond Chandler, which emerged contemporaneously in the United States and also sought to undermine the interpretive authority of the detective. The satisfying fiction of a Sherlock Holmes or of a Lord Peter Wimsey, who can reassure readers that guilt will be uncovered and justice prevail, that the social order is basically fine if only the deviant element is removed, no longer finds the same kind of acceptance in the middle of the Depression.

To be sure, the classic detective story enjoyed immense appeal between the wars as escapist reading in both Britain and the United States, but it also became increasingly mannered, separating itself off from life outside the text both in its thematic content and in its formal conventions. In "The Guilty Vicarage," W. H. Auden read the form as religious allegory, arguing that the Christ-like detective restored the fallen world to Edenic purity; readers, he felt, suffered an acute sense of sin and sought to expiate their guilt through the literature. In this light, the fundamentally conservative impetus of the genre is apparent.

Greene shared Auden's religious perception of the form—"Murder, if you are going to take it seriously at all, is a religious subject" (*The Pleasure Dome,* p. 192)—but not Auden's enthusiasm for the classic detective story. Preferring the thriller, Greene viewed the detective story as too often mired in details and lacking in realism: "There were too many suspects and the criminal never belonged to what used to be called the criminal class" (*Ways of Escape,* p. 73). He characterized its readers as "the perpetually immature," tired intellectuals and crossword puzzlers who refused to allow authors to treat their subject realistically.

Consequently, Greene wrote, "We are driven back to the 'blood,' the thriller. There never was a school of popular English bloods. We have been damned from the start by middle-class virtues, by gentlemen cracksmen and stolen plans and Mr Wu's. We have to go farther back than this, dive below the polite level, to something nearer the common life" (*Reflections,* 1991, pp. 65–66). Greene's thrillers sought to convey a "sense of life," which involved a recognition that motives are never clearly discerned and mysteries are never wholly solved. In *A Gun for Sale,* Mather and Saunders are puzzled by the "successful" outcome of their investigation, while Raven's death prevents him from fully understanding his role in the plot. Only Anne is able to glimpse something like truth: "Men were fighting beasts, they needed war" (p. 182).

Mather's bewilderment is shared to varying degrees by most of Greene's protagonists; such diverse figures as D., Rowe, Martins, Wormold, and even Bendrix in *The End of the Affair* all stand puzzled before a complexity they can never fully comprehend. Characters who make a pretence to certainty, on the other hand, such as Ida Arnold in *Brighton Rock* or the Assistant Commissioner in *It's a Battlefield,* are clearly presented as limited and ultimately incapable of fully grasping the nature of events. For Greene's investigators, the willingness to accept doubt ensures survival; as D. in *The Confidential Agent* notes, "You could trust nobody but yourself, and sometimes you were uncertain whether after all you could trust yourself" (p. 10).

Ida Arnold, Arthur Rowe, Rollo Martins, and Wormold are all amateurs working independently of or in opposition to established authorities. On one level, they represent the tradition in detective fiction of the amateur sleuth, but on another they subvert that tradition through their confused and haphazard methodologies. In *The Ministry of Fear,* for example, Arthur Rowe seeks to discern the reasons for an attempt on his life, but, as in Buchan's *The Thirty-Nine Steps,* his investigation moves from the personal into the larger arena of international intrigue and confusion that is the war. Rowe's outwardly moving investigation finds a correspondence in a more inward search for self that is made explicit in the fact that an explosion induces amnesia in him and erases twenty years of his memory. His struggle to remember his past, including his name, intimately involves him in an exploration of his motives in the mercy killing of his wife: "Mercy to her or mercy to me. They didn't say. And I don't know myself" (p. 37). The question hangs unanswered. Rowe, like Mason and Raven, is another of Greene's guilty investigators.

Ultimately for Greene, all of humanity finds itself in this situation. An inner spiritual condition, the result of "some aboriginal calamity," manifests itself in the larger sociopolitical world. (The phrase is Cardinal Newman's, taken by Greene as an epigraph for *The Lawless Roads,* 1939.) This condition is then represented in the imagery of the frontier, the revolution, and the battlefield. When the war finally came, Greene viewed it as the external manifestation of a psychological and spiritual state. What had been a metaphor for many writers became the reality; hence, in *Ministry of Fear,* Rowe argues in a dream that "thrillers are like life. . . . The world has been remade by William Le Queux" (p. 65). (Le Queux, a journalist and British Secret Service agent, became a prolific writer of spy stories, many of which sought to publicize the need for British preparedness for war.) Life during wartime became the stuff of thrillers. Notions of guilt, betrayal, deception, the puzzling search for meaning and for self-knowledge dominate *The Ministry of Fear,* as they did British life.

The conflation of thrillers and life that *The Ministry of Fear* asserts is, of course, greatly facilitated by the circumstance of the war, yet it also draws our attention to the self-reflexive nature of many of Greene's texts. *The Ministry of Fear* recapitulates and stretches the thriller's formula. Rowe, like Raven, is a further updating of Buchan's Richard Hannay, while Scotland Yard's Prentice seems like a figure patterned after Holmes. Greene unmasks and then explodes the conventions of detective fiction through a series of allusions to contemporary crime fiction and film and to nineteenth-century adventure stories and adolescent romances by Charlotte Yonge, Captain Gilson, and others. Their work, though it had once provided comfort, no longer satisfies: Rowe "learn[s] that adventure stories didn't follow the literary pattern, that there weren't always happy endings" (p. 180). Such is the modern world of political, social, and textual instability.

Later, in *Our Man in Havana,* the dichotomy between life and fiction is comically explored when Wormold's fictitious reports, appropriately sent through a book code, are taken for the real thing, and so the textual becomes real. Fundamentally, then, critical reading and skilled interpretation are necessary qualities that must be fostered and encouraged. In Greene's books, his investigators are, as is often the case in classic detective stories, engaged in the actual and metaphorical task of reading texts and constructing narratives. Examples of this abound in his fiction, but I need list only a few to make the point: Ida Arnold reads the Ouija board, D. is a professor of Romance languages who has written on the *Song of Roland,* Martins writes westerns, Bendrix is a novelist, Fowler is a journalist, and the Assistant Commissioner is writing a report on the political reaction to Jim Drover's execution. These characters and more are all readers and interpreters of texts. Greene's thrillers, like all detective stories, are stories of reading that teach us how to read critically. They also teach us that no reading or interpretation can be final; authority is always suspect, and texts are always mysterious.

Greene's influence on the thriller has been enormous (one thinks of John le Carré's work), but his achievement as a writer extends far beyond his work within the genre. Given his extraordinarily long career and the volume of material he produced, any attempt to categorize him as one kind of writer or another is destined to be misleading and an injustice to the author. Nonetheless, to read Graham Greene's thrillers is to read some of his finest work.

Selected Bibliography

WORKS OF GRAHAM GREENE

AUTOBIOGRAPHY

In Search of a Character: Two African Journals. London: Bodley Head, 1961; Harmondsworth, Eng.: Penguin, 1980.

A Sort of Life. London: Bodley Head, 1971; Harmondsworth, Eng.: Penguin, 1974.

Ways of Escape. London: Bodley Head, 1980; Harmondsworth, Eng.: Penguin, 1981.
"While Waiting for a War." *Granta* 17: 11–32 (autumn 1985).

ESSAYS AND CRITICISM

"The Seed Cake and the Love Lady." *Life and Letters* 10, no. 56: 517–524 (August 1934).
Why Do I Write? An Exchange of Views Between Elizabeth Bowen, Graham Greene, and V. S. Pritchett. London: Percival Marshall, 1948; New York: British Book Centre, 1948.
"The Lost Childhood" and Other Essays. London: Eyre and Spottiswoode, 1951. Pp. 173–176.
Collected Essays. London: Bodley Head, 1969; Harmondsworth, Eng.: Penguin, 1981. Includes "The Lost Childhood."
The Pleasure Dome: Collected Film Criticism, 1935–1940. Edited by John Russell Taylor. London: Secker and Warburg, 1972. Reprinted as *Graham Greene on Film.* New York: Simon & Schuster, 1972; Oxford: Oxford University Press, 1980.
"The Virtue of Disloyalty." In *The Portable Graham Greene.* Edited by Philip Stratford. New York: Viking, 1973. Pp. 606–610.
Reflections. Selected and introduced by Judith Adamson. London: Reinhardt Books, 1991.

NOVELS AND STORIES

The Man Within. London: Heinemann, 1929; Harmondsworth, Eng.: Penguin, 1980.
"Murder for the Wrong Reason: An Unusual Thriller in Three Installments." *Graphic* 126: (5, 12, 19 October 1929). Repr. in *"The Last Word" and Other Stories.* London: Reinhardt Books, 1990. Pp. 110–137.
The Name of Action. London: Heinemann, 1930.
Rumour at Nightfall. London: Heinemann, 1931.
Stamboul Train. London: Heinemann, 1932; Harmondsworth, Eng.: Penguin, 1979. U.S.: *Orient Express.* Garden City, N.Y.: Doubleday, Doran, 1932.
It's a Battlefield. London: Heinemann, 1934; Harmondsworth, Eng.: Penguin, 1980.
England Made Me. London: Heinemann, 1935. Harmondsworth, Eng.: Penguin, 1981. U.S.: *The Shipwrecked.* Garden City, N.Y.: Doubleday, Doran, 1935.
A Gun for Sale. London: Heinemann, 1936; Harmondsworth, Eng.: Penguin, 1984. U.S.: *This Gun for Hire.* Garden City, N.Y.: Doubleday, Doran, 1936.
Brighton Rock. London: Heinemann, 1938; Harmondsworth, Eng.: Penguin, 1988.
The Confidential Agent. London: Heinemann, 1939; Harmondsworth, Eng.: Penguin, 1980.
The Power and the Glory. London: Heinemann, 1940; Harmondsworth, Eng.: Penguin, 1977. U.S.: *The Labyrinthine Ways.* New York: Viking, 1940.
The Ministry of Fear. London: Heinemann, 1943; Harmondsworth, Eng.: Penguin, 1982.
The Heart of the Matter. London: Heinemann, 1948; Harmondsworth, Eng.: Penguin, 1980.
"The Third Man" and "The Fallen Idol". London: Heinemann, 1950; Harmondsworth, Eng.: Penguin, 1973. U.S.: *The Third Man.* New York: Viking, 1950.
The End of the Affair. London: Heinemann, 1951; Harmondsworth, Eng.: Penguin, 1980.
The Quiet American. London: Heinemann, 1955; Harmondsworth, Eng.: Penguin, 1980.
Loser Takes All. London: Heinemann, 1955; Harmondsworth, Eng.: Penguin, 1977.
Our Man in Havana. London: Heinemann, 1958; Harmondsworth, Eng.: Penguin, 1977.
A Burnt-Out Case. London: Heinemann, 1961; Harmondsworth, Eng.: Penguin, 1973.
The Comedians. London: Bodley Head, 1966; Harmondsworth, Eng.: Penguin, 1980.
Travels with My Aunt. London: Bodley Head, 1969; Harmondsworth, Eng.: Penguin, 1977.
Collected Stories. London: Bodley Head and Heinemann, 1972.
The Honorary Consul. London: Bodley Head, 1973; Harmondsworth, Eng.: Penguin, 1974.
The Human Factor. London: Bodley Head, 1978; Harmondsworth, Eng.: Penguin, 1978.
Doctor Fischer of Geneva; or, The Bomb Party. London: Bodley Head, 1980; Harmondsworth, Eng.: Penguin, 1981.
Monsignor Quixote. London: Bodley Head, 1982; Harmondsworth, Eng.: Penguin, 1983.
The Tenth Man. London: Bodley Head and Anthony Bland, 1985; Harmondsworth, Eng.: Penguin, 1985.
The Captain and the Enemy. London: Reinhardt Books, 1988.

PLAYS

Collected Plays of Graham Greene. Harmondsworth, Eng.: Penguin, 1985.

TRAVEL WRITING

Journey Without Maps. London: Heinemann, 1936; Harmondsworth, Eng.: Penguin, 1983.
The Lawless Roads. London: Heinemann, 1939; Harmondsworth, Eng.: Penguin, 1979. U.S.: *Another Mexico.* New York: Viking, 1940.

INTERVIEWS

Allain, Marie-Françoise. *The Other Man: Conversations with Graham Greene.* New York: Simon & Schuster, 1983.

Burgess, Anthony. "Monsieur Greene of Antibes." In his *But Do Blondes Prefer Gentlemen? Homage to Quert Yuiop and Other Writings.* New York: McGraw-Hill, 1986. Pp. 20–25.

Donaghy, Henry J. *Conversations with Graham Greene.* Literary Conversations Series. Jackson: University Press of Mississippi, 1992.

Kermode, Frank. "The House of Fiction: Interviews with Seven English Novelists." *Partisan Review* 30: 61–82 (1963).

BIBLIOGRAPHIES

Cassis, A. F. *Graham Greene: An Annotated Bibliography of Criticism.* Scarecrow Author Bibliographies, no. 55. Metuchen, N.J.: Scarecrow Press, 1981.

Wobbe, R. A. *Graham Greene: A Bibliography and Guide to Research.* New York: Garland, 1979.

BIOGRAPHICAL AND CRITICAL STUDIES

Adamson, Judith. *Graham Greene: The Dangerous Edge: Where Art and Politics Meet.* New York: St. Martin's Press, 1990.

Alley, Kenneth D. "*A Gun for Sale:* Graham Greene's Reflection of Moral Chaos." *Essays in Literature* 5, no. 2: 175–185 (fall 1978).

Allott, Kenneth, and Miriam Farris Allott. *The Art of Graham Greene.* New York: Russell and Russell, 1951.

Auden, W. H. "The Guilty Vicarage." 1938. In *The Dyer's Hand and Other Essays.* London: Faber, 1963. Pp. 146–158.

Bergonzi, Bernard. *Reading the Thirties: Texts and Contexts.* Pittsburgh: University of Pittsburgh Press, 1978.

Bloom, Harold, ed. *Graham Greene.* Modern Critical Views. New York: Chelsea House, 1987.

Calder-Marshall, Arthur. "The Works of Graham Greene." *Horizon* 1: 367–375 (May 1940).

Couto, Maria. *Graham Greene: On the Frontier. Politics and Religion in the Novels.* New York: St. Martin's Press, 1988.

Cunningham, Valentine. *British Writers of the Thirties.* Oxford: Oxford University Press, 1988.

Davis, Elizabeth. *Graham Greene: The Artist as Critic.* Fredericton, New Brunswick: York Press, 1984.

Denning, Michael. *Cover Stories: Narrative and Ideology in the British Spy Thriller.* London: Routledge and Kegan Paul, 1987.

De Vitis, A. A. *Graham Greene.* Twayne's English Authors Series, no. 3. Rev. ed., Boston: Twayne, 1986.

Diemert, Brian. *Graham Greene's Thrillers and the 1930s.* Montreal: McGill-Queen's University Press, 1996.

Duran, Leopoldo. *Graham Greene: Friend and Brother.* Translated by Euan Cameron. New York: Harper Collins, 1994.

Evans, Robert O., ed. *Graham Greene: Some Critical Considerations.* Lexington: University of Kentucky Press, 1963.

Fussell, Paul. "Can Graham Greene Write English?" In his *The Boy Scout Handbook and Other Observations.* Oxford: Oxford University Press, 1982. Pp. 95–100.

Gransden, K. W. "Graham Greene's Rhetoric." *Essays in Criticism* 31, no. 1: 41–60 (January 1981).

Hynes, Samuel, ed. *Graham Greene: A Collection of Critical Essays.* Twentieth Century Views. Englewood Cliffs, N.J.: Prentice-Hall, 1973.

Kelly, Richard. *Graham Greene.* New York: Ungar, 1984.

———. *Graham Greene: A Study of the Short Fiction.* New York: Twayne, 1992.

Korda, Michael. "Life and Letters: The Third Man." *New Yorker,* 25 March 1996: 44–51.

Kunkel, Francis L. *The Labyrinthian Ways of Graham Greene.* Mamaroneck, N.Y.: Appel, 1959; rev. ed., 1973.

Lambert, Gavin. "The Double Agent: Graham Greene." In his *The Dangerous Edge: An Inquiry into the Lives of Nine Masters of Suspense.* New York: Grossman-Viking, 1976. Pp. 132–170.

Lewis, R. W. B. "Graham Greene: The Religious Affair." In his *Picaresque Saint: Representative Figures in Contemporary Fiction.* Philadelphia: Lippincott, 1959. Pp. 220–274.

Lodge, David. *Graham Greene.* Columbia Essays on Modern Writers, no. 17. New York: Columbia University Press, 1966. Reprinted as "Graham Greene." In his *The Novelist at the Crossroads and Other Essays on Fiction and Criticism.* London and New York: Ark Paperbacks, 1986. Pp. 87–118. Reprinted and updated in *Six Contemporary British Novelists.* Edited by George Stade. New York: Columbia University Press, 1976. Pp. 1–56.

———. "What There Is to Tell." *Write On: Occasional Essays, 1965–1985.* London: Secker and Warburg, 1980. Pp. 125–130.

Macleod, Norman. " 'This Strange, Rather Sad Story': The Reflexive Design of Graham Greene's *The Third Man.*" *Dalhousie Review* 63, no. 2: 217–241 (summer 1983).

Malamet, Elliott. "The World Remade: The Art of Detection in the Fiction of Graham Greene." Ph.D. diss., University of Toronto, 1990.

McCarthy, Mary. "Graham Greene and the Intelligentsia." *Partisan Review* 11: 228–230 (1944).

McEwan, Neil. *Graham Greene.* Macmillan Modern Novelists. New York: St. Martin's Press, 1988.

Melada, Ivan. "Graham Greene and the Munitions Makers: The Historical Context of *A Gun for Sale.*" *Studies in the Novel* 13, no. 3: 303–321 (fall 1981).

Meyers, Jeffrey, ed. *Graham Greene: A Revaluation. New Essays.* New York: St. Martin's Press, 1990.

Miller, R. H. *Understanding Graham Greene.* Columbia: University of South Carolina Press, 1990.

Mockler, Anthony. *Graham Greene: Three Lives.* The Guynd by Arbroath, Scotland: Hunter Mackay, 1994.

O'Prey, Paul. *A Reader's Guide to Graham Greene.* Worcester: Thames and Hudson, 1988.

Orwell, George. "Letter to T. R. Fyvel. 15 April 1949." In *In Front of Your Nose,* vol. 4 of *Collected Essays, Journalism, and Letters of George Orwell.* Edited by Sonia Orwell and Ian Angus. London: Secker and Warburg, 1968. Pp. 496–497.

Phillips, Gene D. *Graham Greene: The Films of His Fiction.* Studies in Culture and Communication. New York: Teachers College Press, 1974.

Pryce-Jones, David. *Graham Greene.* Writers and Critics. Edinburgh: Oliver and Boyd, 1963; rev. ed., 1967.

Rosenberg, Bruce A. "At a Crossroads: Eric Ambler and Graham Greene." In *The Spy Story.* Edited by John G. Cawelti and Bruce A. Rosenberg. Chicago: University of Chicago Press, 1987. Pp. 101–124.

Scott, Carolyn. "The Urban Romance: A Study of Graham Greene's Thrillers." In *Graham Greene.* Edited by Harry J. Cargas. The Christian Critic Series. St. Louis: Herder, n.d.

Sharrock, Roger. *Saints, Sinners, and Comedians: The Novels of Graham Greene.* Notre Dame, Ind.: University of Notre Dame Press, 1984.

Sheldon, Michael. *Graham Greene: The Man Within.* London: Heinemann, 1994. U.S.: *Graham Greene: The Enemy Within.* New York: Random House, 1995.

Sherry, Norman. *The Life of Graham Greene.* Vol 1: 1904–1939. Toronto: Lester and Orpen Dennys, 1989.

———. *The Life of Graham Greene.* Vol. 2: 1939–1955. New York: Viking, 1994.

Silverstein, Marc. "After the Fall: The World of Graham Greene's Thrillers." *Novel* 22, no. 1: 24–44 (fall 1988).

Smith, Grahame. *The Achievement of Graham Greene.* Sussex, Eng.: Harvester, 1986.

Spurling, John. *Graham Greene.* Contemporary Writers. Edited by Malcolm Bradbury and Christopher Bigsby. London: Methuen, 1983.

Stratford, Philip. *Faith and Fiction: Creative Process in Greene and Mauriac.* Notre Dame: University of Notre Dame Press, 1964.

Thomas, Brian. *An Underground Fate: The Idiom of Romance in the Later Novels of Graham Greene.* Athens: University of Georgia Press, 1988.

West, W. J. *The Quest for Graham Greene.* London: Weidenfeld and Nicolson, 1997.

Wolfe, Peter. *Graham Greene: The Entertainer.* Carbondale: Southern Illinois University Press, 1972.

———, ed. *Essays in Graham Greene: An Annual Review,* vol. 1. Greenwood, Fla.: Penkevill, 1987.

Woodcock, George. *The Writer and Politics.* London: Porcupine Press, 1948. Repr. Folcroft, Pa.: Folcroft Press, 1970.

Dashiell Hammett
(1894–1961)

DAVID GEHERIN

There is little evidence in Dashiell Hammett's early years to suggest that he would ever become a writer, let alone such an important one. It could also be argued that in light of the literary silence that marked the final twenty-seven years of his life, there is little evidence in his later years to suggest that he was a writer then. But in a remarkable period of intense creativity between 1923 and 1934, he wrote five novels and dozens of short stories that revolutionized the mystery genre and helped transform American prose.

Early Life

Samuel Dashiell Hammett was born on 27 May 1894 in his grandfather's house on a farm in St. Mary's County, Maryland. He was the second of three children born to Richard Thomas Hammett, a farmer who later worked at a variety of jobs, including local postmaster and justice of the peace, and Annie Bond, whose mother's family name was De Chiell. When Hammett was six, the family moved first to Philadelphia and then, a year later, to Baltimore. Young Sam, as the boy was called, was bright and industrious and an avid reader. His formal education, however, ended at the age of fourteen, when his father became ill and was no longer able to work. Sam was forced to quit Baltimore Polytechnic Institute and take a job as a messenger boy for the Baltimore and Ohio Railroad. For the next several years, he worked at a variety of odd jobs—freight clerk, stevedore, nail machine operator in a box factory—in the Baltimore area.

In 1915, at the age of twenty-one, Hammett answered an ad that led to a job with Pinkerton's National Detective Agency, at that time the largest private law enforcement agency in the United States. The Baltimore office was located in the Continental Building, which gave Hammett the name for the fictional detective agency where his first great literary creation, the Continental Op, worked. His boss and mentor at Pinkerton's, James Wright, became the model for the Op.

Hammett quickly learned the skills of his new trade—especially shadowing suspects without being spotted—and the rules of the game: be loyal to your client, maintain your integrity, and never become emotionally involved with the case. His work eventually took him cross-country and exposed him to a variety of useful experiences. Among his first successes was locating a stolen Ferris wheel. His duties also educated him in the harsh ways of the world. For example, he was sent to Butte, Montana, where the Pinkertons were hired by the Anaconda Copper Company as strike breakers against the Industrial Workers of the World. The lynching of a union organizer while he was there had a strong influence on his later political views.

In June 1918, Hammett enlisted in the army. He trained as an ambulance driver at Camp Mead, Maryland, but he spent much of his military duty in the hospital. First he contracted the Spanish influenza that was sweeping the country in 1918; later, it was determined that he had also contracted tuberculosis. His health was permanently damaged, and he was declared disabled and discharged from the army in 1919 with the rank of sergeant. He rejoined the Pinkerton Agency, eventually moving to the Spokane, Washington, office. His poor health, however, caused him to be hospitalized often. During an extended hospitalization in Tacoma, Washington, he met and fell in love with Josephine (Jose) Dolan, a young nurse from Montana. In 1921, Hammett was transferred to a hospital near San Diego to take advantage of the better climate. After his discharge, he moved to San Francisco, where, on 7 July 1921, he married Jose (who was at the time five months pregnant with their first child, a daughter).

When his health permitted, he continued to work part-time for Pinkerton's in San Francisco, tracking down counterfeiters and searching for missing daughters. He even worked gathering evidence for the defense in the famous Fatty Arbuckle case of 1921. (Arbuckle, a film comedian, was charged in the rape and murder of a young actress named Virginia Rappe. Arbuckle was eventually acquitted of the charges, but his career was ruined.) Hammett's health problems continued (his weight dropped to 126 pounds), and he was forced to quit his work with Pinkerton's in 1922.

By then supported entirely by military disability payments, Hammett began taking classes in stenography and writing at Munson's Business College in San Francisco, with an eye toward learning newspaper reporting. He also spent considerable time in the public library, reading widely and voraciously. Although his previous writing experience was limited to hammering out case reports for Pinkerton's, Hammett decided to try his hand at writing. He began composing freelance advertising copy for local businesses. And he started to write fiction. His first published story, a 100-word sketch entitled "The Parthian Shot," appeared in the *Smart Set* (22 October 1922), a popular sophisticated magazine founded by George Jean Nathan and H. L. Mencken. At the age of twenty-eight, Sam Hammett, ex-Pinkerton detective, began publishing short stories under the name of Dashiell Hammett.

Hammett soon began drawing upon his Pinkerton experiences in his writing. For example, in the March 1923 issue of *Smart Set,* he published a series of brief vignettes under the title "From the Memoirs of a Private Detective." These twenty-nine numbered entries, some no longer than a sentence, not only give the reader a glimpse into the real-life experience of a private detective, they also reflect an ironic view of the world that one suspects might also be a legacy of that experience. Entries like these—"I was once falsely accused of perjury and had to perjure myself to escape arrest" and "A man whom I was shadowing went out into the country for a walk one Sunday afternoon and lost his bearings completely. I had to direct him back to the city" (Johnson, pp. 44–45)—evoke a view of life that philosophers a decade or two later termed "absurd."

Continuing to draw upon his Pinkerton experience, Hammett began to write short stories for the mystery pulp markets. One such pulp, *Black Mask,* had been started by Nathan and Mencken, the owners of *Smart Set.* Apparently not entirely convinced that this was the direction he wanted to pursue as a writer, Hammett published his first stories in *Black Mask* (the first, "Arson Plus," appeared on 1 October 1923) under the pseudonym Peter Collinson ("Peter Collins" was carnival slang for a nobody; thus, "Peter Collinson" was "nobody's son"). By the time his third story appeared in *Black Mask,* Hammett had dropped the pseudonym and begun to use his real name. By the end of 1923, Hammett had published fourteen stories, seven of them in *Black Mask.*

The Continental Op Stories

In the early 1920s, the most popular and influential mystery writer was Arthur Conan Doyle, whose Sherlock Holmes stories dominated the genre. Two of Holmes's most famous descendants, Agatha Christie's Hercule Poirot and Dorothy L. Sayers' Lord Peter Wimsey, made their first appearances at this time—Poirot in 1920 and Wimsey in 1923. Magazines on both sides of the Atlantic were filled with imitations of the brilliant deductive genius. Things were about to change dramatically, however, especially in the pages of *Black Mask.* On 1 June 1923, four months before Hammett's first story appeared in the magazine, a New York writer, Carroll John Daly, introduced in its pages a radically new kind of detective, a tough-talking, trigger-happy character named Race Williams. Unlike all those amateur detectives like Sherlock Holmes, who solved crimes by using their brains, Race Williams relied on his blazing guns rather than his dim wits to fight crime. His philosophy was simple—"I never bumped off a guy what didn't need it"—and so were his methods; he chose to shoot first and ask questions later. The early Race Williams stories represent a refreshing change from the effete intellectual detectives that held sway at the time. But Daly was a clumsy writer who relied on melodramatic effects, and Race Williams was little more than a boastful braggart.

Thus, when Hammett decided to try his hand at mystery writing, his models were limited to either the clever amateur intellectual sleuth, on the one hand, or the new kind of detective created by Daly, on the other. But as an experienced detective himself, Hammett was put off by the unreality of both models. Although he had little experience as a writer, what he could bring to the genre that he felt was then lacking was a convincing sense of realism. In a 1944 essay entitled "The Simple Art of Murder," Raymond Chandler (whose first stories began appearing in *Black Mask* a decade after Hammett's) honored his predecessor for introducing realism into the mystery story. "Hammett took murder out of the Venetian vase and dropped it into the alley," Chandler wrote. He also praised Hammett for giving "murder back to the kind of people that commit it for reasons, not just to provide a corpse; and with the means at hand, not hand-wrought dueling pistols, curare and tropical fish" (p. 16). While Chandler is certainly correct in his assessment of Hammett's contribution, it is unlikely that Hammett deliberately set out to do anything as dramatic as transform a genre. All he sought to do was to create a detective whose personality and methods were modeled on real life.

Like Race Williams, the Continental Op narrates his stories in the first person, but he has none of the boastful bravado of Daly's larger-than-life hero. (His anonymity is emphasized by his lack of a name; he is identified only as an operative for the Continental Detective Agency.) The Op speaks in straightforward, unadorned, matter-of-fact prose. Even his toughness is of a different sort than Race Williams'. He is usually on the receiving rather than the delivering end of violence in the early stories, where he is beaten up, shot at, and even knocked on the head and dumped overboard into San Francisco Bay. He seldom uses his gun, and when he does it is usually to fire a warning shot at a fleeing suspect rather than to plug him between the eyes like Williams.

Nor is he a brainy sleuth like Sherlock Holmes. His success is due not to his wits but to slow, deliberate plodding. And so he is depicted patiently interviewing witnesses and tracking down leads, most of which go nowhere. He shadows suspects all day long and into the night, and when he can't do it all himself, he doesn't hesitate to call upon the assistance of fellow Continental operatives. His solution to the case comes not because he is lucky, or a crime-solving genius, or a crack shot; it's simply because he knows how to do his job and works hard at it.

In the early Op stories, Hammett's emphasis is largely on the Op's procedures rather than on his character. Often drawn from

Hammett's Pinkerton experiences, these early tales read like case reports. They have the ring of truth because of Hammett's emphasis on authenticity (they contain enough insider details about investigative procedures to serve as an instructional manual for budding detectives), but they show little in the way of literary merit. In fact, two of the early Op stories were rejected by *Black Mask* in 1924, prompting a letter from Hammett to the magazine apologizing for his lapses. He acknowledged that he had allowed the Op to degenerate into a meal ticket: "When I try to grind out a yarn because I think there is a market for it, then I flop." He publicly thanked the editors for "jolting me into wakefulness" and vowed to stick to "the stuff I enjoy writing" (Johnson, p. 53).

The first of Hammett's early stories to show how seriously he began to take his work and to reveal the direction he was to take the Op (and the mystery story) are "The House in Turk Street," published in *Black Mask* in April 1924, and its sequel, "The Girl with the Silver Eyes" (June 1924). In the first story, the Op methodically goes from house to house on Turk Street, seeking information about a missing man who has reportedly been seen in the neighborhood. Without warning, in the middle of a quiet conversation in the home of a kindly elderly couple, the Op is surprised to find himself held at gunpoint by a trio who have been hiding in the house. Tied up and gagged, he tries to figure out what is going on. Gradually, he pieces together the story; the trio—a man named Hook, a red-haired woman called Elvira, and Tai, a fat Chinaman who speaks with a British accent—had stolen $100,000 in bonds and, with the cooperation of the elderly couple, were using their house as a hideaway. As the story unfolds (in a situation that prefigures the situation Hammett later used in *The Maltese Falcon*), we watch as the trio engages in a series of deadly double crosses. Elvira, whom the Op quickly assesses as dangerous, deliberately stirs things up between her partners so that she can steal the bonds while they are distracted. Then Tai leaves behind a gun, knowing the Op will use it to shoot Hook when Hook returns to kill the Op. Things turn even more violent when the elderly couple, who were being duped out of their share of the loot, return and are shot by the Chinaman. The Op manages to disarm Tai, but Elvira escapes.

In "The Girl with the Silver Eyes," the Op is hired to find a local poet's missing girlfriend. When he eventually tracks her down, he is surprised to discover that she is the missing Elvira, disguised as a woman named Jeanne Delano. While Hammett, as usual, pays close attention to the details of the Op's investigation, the focus of the story shifts to reveal new insights into the Op's character. For one thing, he finds himself in situations where he must rely more on violence: he shoots one man and, when an informant double-crosses him and begins shooting at his car, the Op runs the man over. He also must resist the provocative charms of the beautiful Elvira, who tries to dissuade him from turning her in. The Op listens to her story, all the while struggling to keep his emotions under control; then he turns her over to the cops. In the end, Elvira moves close and whispers into his ear "the vilest epithet of which the English language is capable" (*Continental Op,* p. 178).

Hammett began turning out stories that were longer (many running ten thousand to twelve thousand words) and better developed, more imaginative, and less reliant on his Pinkerton experiences. He started to pay more attention to characterization, not just of the Op but of the supporting characters in the stories. And most significant of all, he began to pare down his prose into a new hard-edged brilliance. But in 1926, with his wife pregnant with their second child, Hammett felt the need for a more reliable source of income than his writing was producing. He accepted a job as advertising manager for a chain of San Francisco jewelry stores owned by Albert S. Samuels (to whom he later dedicated *The Dain Curse*). However, ill health continued to plague Hammett, and he was forced to quit his job after only a few months. Meanwhile, a new editor, Joseph T. Shaw, had just taken over at *Black Mask.* Shaw admired Hammett's Op stories and encouraged him to resume the series. Hammett responded enthusiastically to Shaw's invitation (prompted in part, no doubt, by Shaw's offer of a raise in the rate he would pay for Hammett's work); after an eleven-month absence, the Op returned to *Black Mask* in a pair of lengthy novellas, *The Big Knockover* (February 1927) and its sequel, *$106,000 Blood Money* (May 1927), together known as *Blood Money,* the longest and most complex Op story to date.

Although he is often given credit for doing so, Shaw did not himself create what became known as the "hard-boiled" mystery story. What he did do was nurture and popularize it by encouraging a group of talented writers (Raymond Chandler among them) to follow Hammett's lead in combining authenticity and immediacy in writing. The term hard-boiled implies both an attitude and a style. The hard-boiled character is not an individual devoid of emotion, but rather one who resists its temptation by knowing how to control it. Thus, the Op does what he must do, unswayed by emotion. ("Emotions are nuisances during business hours" is his motto.) If he must question a suspect at a bad time, he'll do it; if he must turn in a beautiful woman, even though he is tempted by her attractiveness, he'll do it. As he tells the beautiful Russian woman who thinks she can use her beauty to walk away from a crime, in "The Gutting of Couffignal," "You think I'm a man and you're a woman. That's wrong. I'm a manhunter and you're something that has been running in front of me" (*The Big Knockover,* p. 33). When she begins to leave, confident that no man would ever shoot her, the Op stops her with a shot in the leg.

Corresponding to the hard-boiled character was a major shift in prose style away from the polished and ornate to the concrete and laconic. Credit for this radical shift must be shared by Hammett and Ernest Hemingway. Both writers began experimenting with the effects that could be derived by stripping language of the false and artificial that had weighed it down. Hemingway, then living in Paris, was turning out stories written in bare concrete prose that eventually appeared in a collection entitled *In Our Time* (1925). By that time, Hammett had already published seventeen stories in *Black Mask* in which he had begun to develop a similar economical style perfectly suited to the no-nonsense Op. In his hands, dialogue became as pungent and hard-hitting as its speakers—"One chirp out of you and I'll tie a knot in your neck" (*Continental Op,* p. 225); descriptions of action became as stripped down as haiku—"There was a grinding sound. A crash. The noise of metal folding on itself. The tinkle of glass" (*The Big Knockover,* p. 19).

Blood Money represents a new direction in Hammett's fiction. Working on a larger canvas (thirty-five thousand words), Hammett was able to depict violence on a much more elaborate scale than heretofore. The story opens with 150 gangsters converging on San Francisco for a daring daylight robbery of two banks. In the ensuing shootout with the outnumbered police, sixteen cops, five robbers, and twelve innocent spectators are gunned down. Shortly afterward, bank robbers' bodies start piling up, fourteen in one house and six in another—all victims of execution. Themes of deceit and betrayal also feature more prominently. Not only are the bank robbers betrayed by their leader, but the Op is also duped into letting a scared old man walk away during a roundup of the gang. Too late he learns that the "scrawny little bozo" (*The Big Knockover,* p. 401) he let go was a man named Papadopoulos, the brains behind the bank heist. Worst of all, the Op discovers that Jack Counihan, a promising young fellow op, has succumbed to the charms of a female ringleader and has sold out to the crooks.

The story also allows Hammett to focus on the Op's character in a significant new way. More of the Op's private life is revealed (he plays poker regularly with friends); more important, we witness the Op becoming involved in morally questionable activities. For example, he shoots one of the crooks in the back and then feigns concern and acts as his nurse, hoping the wounded man will lead him to his henchmen. And he arranges things in such a way that Counihan, the traitor, is gunned down, thus sparing the agency the embarrassment of having to admit his treachery. All of this suggests that the Op might be well on his way to the condition of his boss, the Old Man, who has become so cold-blooded because of his work that "he could spit icicles in July" (*The Big Knockover,* p. 355). At the end of the story, the Op decides to take a few weeks off from work, and the story concludes with a rare (for him) personal confession: "I felt tired, washed out" (*The Big Knockover,* p. 451).

Red Harvest

With the continuing encouragement of Shaw (who urged him to produce longer Op stories), Hammett turned out his most ambitious work to date, a four-part serial whose first installment, "The Cleansing of Poisonville," appeared in the November 1927 issue of *Black Mask.* In February 1929, under the title *Red Harvest,* it appeared in hardcover as Hammett's debut novel.

The Op travels to the remote Western mining town of Personville (known locally as "Poisonville") at the request of Donald Willsson, the reform-minded editor of the town newspaper. Within hours of the Op's arrival, Willsson is murdered. Elihu Willsson, the dead man's father, who for forty years has owned the town "heart, soul, skin and guts"—and who also owns "a United States senator, a couple of representatives, the governor, the mayor, and most of the state legislature" (p. 8)—hires the Op to find out who killed his son as well as to clean up the town. "I want a man to clean this pig-sty of a Poisonville for me," he declares, "to smoke out the rats, little and big" (p. 42). The Op takes the job, and even though Elihu later tries to fire him, he refuses to leave town until the bloody cleanup is completed.

Shaw wanted action, and Hammett delivers plenty of it in *Red Harvest.* But while the violence exists on a scale unmatched even in *Blood Money* (before the dust settles, more than two dozen characters are killed), what is significant in the novel is not so much the extent of the violence but Hammett's attitude toward it. The violence often erupts unexpectedly: a man steps out of his house, puts his fingers to his mouth, whistles, and is gunned down; a boxer, his arm raised in the middle of the ring in victory in a match he was paid to lose, suddenly drops to the canvas, dead from a knife thrown into the back of his neck. Throughout, however, the Op's description of the bloody incidents remains characteristically detached and understated: "The bullet smacked blondy under the right eye, spun him around, and dropped him backwards," he reports. He fires at the killer, misses him, and then adds almost in passing, "My slug crumpled the red-faced man behind him" (p. 105). This deadpan description of violence embodies an almost casual attitude toward it. But, whereas in his previous appearances this detached, unemotional code enabled the Op to function efficiently as a detective, in *Red Harvest,* Hammett explores the dangerous consequences of that code.

In *Blood Money,* the Op first begins to be tainted by the violence in his world. In *Red Harvest,* his worst fears about himself are realized. Initially, he finds it all too easy to bend the rules: "When you're out on a job you've got to do it the best way you can," he tells fellow op Mickey Linehan. "And anybody that brings any ethics to Poisonville is going to get them all rusty" (p. 117). Eventually, his own behavior begins to bother him so much that he refuses to submit reports to the Old Man, knowing just how difficult it would be to defend his actions to his boss. "The Old Man will boil me in oil if he ever finds out what I've been doing," he confesses (p. 157). Later, during a night of heavy drinking with Dinah Brand, a local woman he has been using in his various schemes to play one side against the other, he openly expresses his concerns. He complains that he has become "poisoned" by the town and that after some sixteen murders in less than a week, he worries that "if I don't get away soon I'll be going blood-simple like the natives" (p. 154).

His worst fears seem to be confirmed the next morning when, waking up after he has passed out from drinking laudanum-laced gin, he discovers Dinah Brand's dead body beside him. An ice pick is stuck in her left breast, and his hand is tightly gripping the blade. Registering neither surprise nor panic, the Op carefully examines the body, systematically removes all traces of his fingerprints from the scene, and leaves. Since we see things only through the Op's eyes, and since he himself is unsure what happened, the question of his guilt in her death is left up in the air. That the reader must consider the very real possibility that the Op has become a cold-blooded killer indicates just how much he has changed.

Eventually, thanks to the Op's skill in stirring things up, the ringleaders of the town kill each other off, the murderer of Dinah is identified, and the town is placed under martial law. But in the process, the Op himself has been tainted: "twenty years of messing around with crime" have left him with "hard skin all over what's left of my soul" (p. 157). The Op has always placed loyalty to his job above all else. But taken to its logical extreme, as it is in *Red Harvest,* this single-minded attitude leads him into morally murky waters; in order to do *this* job, he allows the ends to justify his means. The line between the good guys and the bad guys becomes blurred. The Op admits that he could go after the crooks legally, but, he confesses, "It's easier to have them killed off, easier and surer, and now that I'm feeling this way, more satisfying" (p. 157). No longer simply an efficient crime-solver, the Op has allowed himself to become a one-man vigilante force whose actions lead directly to several deaths. Not only does he enjoy himself, he also proudly announces that what he calls the "very un-nice part" (*Red Harvest,* p. 115) he has been playing in the bloodbath doesn't prevent him from getting his twelve solid hours of sleep at night.

When fellow op Dick Foley, who frequently appears in the stories, begins to display uneasiness over his colleague's actions, the Op sends him packing back to San Francisco. In the end, the Op himself returns to San Francisco, but no amount of creative fudging in his reports can fool the Old Man. The novel concludes with the Op's admission, "He gave me merry hell" (p. 216). The reader can only speculate what (if any) kind of "merry hell" the Op might have to give himself after his visit to Poisonville.

Red Harvest represents Hammett's most deliberate attempt at social commentary. Moving the action from San Francisco to an isolated locale with the suggestive name of Poisonville gives Hammett an opportunity to create a symbolic locale, a microcosm of urban America. The Op's first impression of Personville paints the symbolic landscape in almost Dickensian terms: he describes "an ugly city of forty thousand people, set in an ugly notch between two ugly mountains that had been all dirtied up by mining. Spread over this was a grimy sky that looked as if it had come out of the smelters' stacks" (p. 4). To some degree, the depiction of Personville was inspired by Hammett's own experiences a decade earlier as a Pinkerton detective sent into the middle of the miners' strike in Butte, Montana. In *Red Harvest,* however, Hammett isn't interested in the causes of the strike or in the political issues involved; he's interested in the consequences. Elihu Willsson has broken the backs of striking workers in his mine by importing a bunch of hired thugs. After the strike ends, however, Willsson finds he can no longer control his hired hoodlums. His desire to have the Op clean up the town is not inspired by any civic concern; he simply wants to regain control of the town for himself. (Nor is the Op himself motivated by any idealistic concerns; he takes great pleasure simply in causing trouble.)

Personville is a town consumed by widespread corruption, where the police are in cahoots with the crooks and where everything and everyone has a price. Thanks to the Op's skill in stirring things up, the forces of evil are thrown out of balance, and the bad guys end up destroying each other. But the cleansing of Personville offers little cause for celebration.

The crooks are dead, but the town has not been returned to its good and decent citizens (there don't seem to be any); there is only a vacuum ready to be filled by the next wave of opportunistic thieves. Order is restored, though the situation is only temporary. As the Op tells Elihu Willsson, the city is "all nice and clean and ready to go to the dogs again" (p. 203).

The nightmarish portrait of corruption and bloodshed in *Red Harvest* reflects conditions that were becoming widespread in many American cities in the late 1920s. Prohibition, which began in 1919, transformed millions of law-abiding Americans into lawbreakers every time they took a sip of bootleg whiskey. It also touched off a wave of violence throughout the country as rival gangs engaged in bloody battles for control of cities corrupted by gangsters, bootleggers, cops on the take, and greedy politicians. America's social fabric was being rent, and *Red Harvest* captured it in striking terms.

Although the novel shows telltale signs of having been conceived originally as four separate but related episodes, the story remains fast-paced and action-packed. Yet it is much more than a blood-drenched gangster thriller. Hammett used the larger dimensions of the novel to combine fast and furious action with social commentary and an insightful portrait of his heretofore largely anonymous hero. Hammett obviously felt comfortable with the novel form. He wrote only three more Op stories after *Red Harvest.* But in a burst of creative activity, he published three novels in the next two years.

The Dain Curse

Published just five months after *Red Harvest, The Dain Curse* also features the Op and also appeared in *Black Mask* as four separate installments prior to publication as a novel. Hammett, however, was unable to duplicate the success of his first novel. *The Dain Curse* is generally regarded as one of his weakest novels. The story begins in San Francisco, where the Op is hired to investigate the theft of several diamonds from the home of Edgar Leggett. The investigation proceeds routinely until the case takes a surprising twist when Leggett turns up dead. Leggett leaves behind a lengthy suicide note that exposes several dark family secrets. It is revealed that his twenty-year-old daughter, Gabrielle, when she was a child of five, had been used in a bizarre plot to shoot her own mother. Further, it was Leggett's second wife who engineered the plot, and the two wives were sisters. Gabrielle, convinced that she suffers from the "Dain curse" (her mother's name was Lily Dain), has found refuge in morphine addiction.

The Op's role shifts from sleuth to savior in the second section when he is hired to rescue Gabrielle. She has fallen under the spell of a pair of religious charlatans who operate the Temple of the Holy Grail. The Op moves into the temple, and the action of the novel turns increasingly gothic and melodramatic: the Op is gassed and begins seeing ghosts, Gabrielle's doctor is found stabbed to death on the temple's altar, and Gabrielle is discovered drenched in blood, grasping the bloody dagger that was used as the murder weapon.

In the third section, the Op receives a telegram from Eric Collinson, Gabrielle's husband, summoning him to the small coastal town of Quesada, eighty miles from San Francisco. Gabrielle's welfare has become something of an obsession to the Op. Shortly after arriving in Quesada, he takes a walk and stumbles upon Collinson's dead body in the surf beneath a cliff. More puzzles arise, including the disappearance of Gabrielle, who has been kidnapped and once again must be rescued by the Op. In the final section, the Op fully assumes the role of savior as he devotes himself to convincing Gabrielle that the Dain curse is a "lot of hooey" and to curing her of her drug addiction. While insisting that this is simply a job ("I'm only a hired man with only a hired man's interest in your troubles" [p. 182], he declares), it is obvious that his feelings for the young woman run deep. Only when he has nursed her through her addiction can he rest easy. Readers who recall the Op's bloody activities in *Red Harvest* might be surprised to hear Gabrielle tell her rescuer, "You're the nicest man in the world" (p. 222).

Hammett himself called *The Dain Curse* a silly story. Its weaknesses are many. The action is often melodramatic—the Op is attacked by dagger, gun, gas, and bomb. And even more than its predecessor, it breaks down into four separate episodes that resist being integrated into a coherent whole; whereas *Red Harvest* was held together by continuing characters, a common setting, and a unifying theme, this novel lurches from one location to another, keeps introducing new characters, and is held together only by the presence of Gabrielle Leggett, the helpless damsel in distress who is less a character than an organizing device. In addition to its structural weakness, the novel is also uncharacteristically talky. Too much of the novel is given over to lengthy exposition of past events (e.g., a suicide letter that goes on for four pages) and offstage action. And without the colorful underworld characters the Op usually encounters, there is little of the pungent dialogue that flavors Hammett's best stories.

The Dain Curse is far from a total failure. It includes several exciting scenes and interesting stylistic experimentation. For example, when the Op is chloroformed and begins hallucinating, Hammett trades his usual understated prose for several paragraphs of stream-of-consciousness writing. There is also a hint of rare playfulness in the novel. Hammett's physical description of Owen Fitzstephan, a novelist friend of the Op's, mirrors his own appearance. He also gives Eric Collinson, Gabrielle's husband, the same last name he himself had used as a pseudonym for his early published stories.

Fitzstephan, the novelist, and the Op, the detective, conduct a provocative discussion about the parallels between their respective professions: both are engaged in fitting pieces together into a coherent pattern, both construct "reality" in their own ways, and both acknowledge the arbitrariness of the truth of what they do. Their similarities are underscored by the Op's recollection that "we used to drink out of the same bottle" (p. 13). These discussions serve to make a point about the elusiveness of truth and the limitations of all attempts at interpreting reality. That Fitzstephan himself turns out to be the evil manipulator behind most of the murders in the book (and, though he kept it a secret, a Dain himself and thus something of a rebuke to the Op's argument to Gabrielle that the Dain curse was "hooey") only adds to the irony of the novel.

Having brought the Op to a major crisis of self-identity in *Red Harvest,* it appears that Hammett wasn't entirely sure what to do next with his detective. The role of knight in shining armor he assumes in *The Dain Curse* never seems to fit him comfortably. It isn't surprising that Hammett would use the Op in only three more short stories. Having exhausted his possibilities as a character, he felt it was time to try his hand at a new kind of hero.

The Maltese Falcon

For his next novel, *The Maltese Falcon* (written in 1929, while he was revising *The Dain Curse* for book publication, and published in 1930), Hammett drew upon character types and plot situations from his earlier stories. But he created a new detective and employed a new narrative approach, which resulted in his crowning achievement and one of the finest American detective novels ever published. Samuel Spade, of the Spade and Archer Detective Agency in San Francisco, is hired by a young woman, who gives her name as Miss Wonderly, to rescue her sister from a man named Floyd Thursby. Spade's partner, Miles Archer, eying the attractive woman, volunteers to handle the assignment. A few hours later, both Archer and Thursby are dead, and Spade, who is having an affair with Archer's wife, finds himself a prime suspect in his partner's murder. Spade tracks down Miss

Wonderly, who gives her name as Miss Leblanc and then again changes it to Brigid O'Shaughnessy. She convinces Spade that she is in danger from Thursby's friends. Shortly afterward, one of those friends, an effeminate, perfumed man named Joel Cairo, offers Spade $5,000 to recover the statue of a black bird that Thursby supposedly had. Spade soon learns that Cairo and Brigid, along with Casper Gutman, a fat man with an overly formal manner of speaking, are all looking for the same object—a jewel-encrusted gold statue of a falcon. Spade finds himself in the middle of a deadly game of deceit, double cross, and murder.

Hammett had employed many of these elements in his previous Op stories. The explanation for how an experienced detective like Miles Archer could be murdered at close range comes from "Who Killed Bob Teal?" An international trio of thieves who are double-crossed by their beautiful female partner first appeared in "The Whosis Kid." In "The Girl with the Silver Eyes," the Op has to struggle to resist the temptations of an alluring femme fatale in order to turn her over to the police (as Spade does with Brigid O'Shaughnessy). But for the first time unhampered by having to write for magazine serialization, Hammett molded his material into a fast-paced story full of unexpected twists and turns.

The key to the novel's originality is the character of Sam Spade. Though Spade resembles the Op in certain ways—both are resourceful, pragmatic detectives who live and work in San Francisco—the differences between them are significant. No longer an anonymous employee of a large organization, Hammett's new detective is given a name (the first words mentioned in the novel) and his own agency. After his partner's death in the opening chapter, he's entirely on his own. In physical appearance, he is also distinguished from the fat, balding Op. Described as looking "rather pleasantly like a blond Satan" (p. 3), Spade, unlike the Op, is attractive to women. The Op managed to resist the rare sexual temptation that came his way. Spade, on the other hand, is something of a womanizer. He is carrying on an affair with Iva Archer, his partner's wife, and sleeps with Brigid O'Shaughnessy (and then uses the opportunity to search her apartment while she is deep in postcoital sleep). Spade's sexuality adds a dimension to his character that Hammett exploits nicely in the novel.

The effectiveness of Spade's character derives in part from Hammett's decision to employ a third-person narrative point of view instead of the first-person voice he had used for the Op stories and novels. First-person narration establishes an intimacy between narrator and reader. The reader becomes privy to the narrator's thoughts, speculations, fears, and so on. Thus, for example, the reader knows how deeply the violence in Personville is affecting the Op because he speaks about it, even though he is never fully forthcoming about the degree to which he is being contaminated. Third-person narration, by contrast, offers a camera-eye perspective that portrays all the characters objectively and none subjectively. As a result, the character of Spade himself becomes one of the key mysteries in the novel.

By hiding Spade's thoughts about the case and his feelings about the other characters, Hammett ensures that the reader is never entirely sure how to respond to Spade. How crooked is he? Has he succumbed to the same intense greed for the falcon that Brigid, Gutman, and Cairo share? Does he really love Brigid? Could he actually be the murderer of Miles Archer, as the police suspect? One never knows for sure because Spade reveals so little of his inner self. Hammett does, however, provide some important clues to his character. For example, when Spade is awakened at 2 A.M. by a phone call announcing Archer's death, Hammett describes him systematically and deliberately rolling a cigarette. We don't know what Spade is thinking, but we sense we are watching a character who has developed a discipline for maintaining careful control of his emotions.

Spade also tells Brigid a revealing story about a man named Flitcraft he once met. Flitcraft was a Tacoma businessman who mysteriously disappeared one day, leaving behind a wife and two children. Spade located him five years later, living in Spokane with a new wife and young baby. Flitcraft tells Spade that a falling beam from a building under construction narrowly missed hitting him, shocking him into a sudden awareness of the haphazardness of life. Instead of the "clean orderly sane responsible affair" (*The Maltese Falcon*, p. 64) he had previously assumed existence to be, he suddenly understood it to be random and irrational. He took off. The interesting thing to Spade is how closely Flitcraft's new life mirrors the one he left behind. Spade concludes that "he adjusted himself to beams falling, and then no more of them fell, and he adjusted himself to them not falling" (p. 64). Brigid listens politely to Spade's lengthy anecdote and then quickly changes the subject, ignoring the point. But an alert reader can sense how much this story means to Spade, how it comes as close as we get in the novel to a statement of his philosophy. Spade lives his life in full awareness that beams often fall, and though one cannot control external events, one can at least control oneself.

Beneath Spade's inscrutable surface is a character with depth and complexity, unpredictable and capable of surprise. We are, for example, surprised to learn at the end of the novel that Spade knew all along that Brigid had killed Archer. We might also be surprised that although he appeared to be in league with Gutman and his gang, Spade turns over to the police the money Gutman paid him to find the falcon. He also turns Brigid over to them for the murder of Miles Archer. "Don't be too sure I'm as crooked as I'm supposed to be" (p. 215), he tells her. Spade details his reasons for resisting Brigid's charms. For one thing, she killed his partner, and "when a man's partner is killed he's supposed to do something about it. It doesn't make any difference what you thought of him. . . . When one of your organization gets killed it's bad business to let the killer get away with it" (p. 213). And even though he admits he might be in love with Brigid, that's not enough: he knows she is using him, and he doesn't like it. "I won't play the sap for you" (p. 213), he tells her.

The Maltese Falcon is a brilliant study in greed and deceit. In pursuit of the priceless falcon, the various characters who get swept up in its wake stop at nothing, including murder, to have it for their own. That the bird turns out to be fake—like so many other things in the novel—only exposes the futility of their sordid quest. Gutman has been on the trail of the falcon for seventeen years. Only his death at the hands of one of his own henchmen finally puts an end to his obsession.

In *Red Harvest* and *The Dain Curse*, the Op faces many dangers, most of them physical. The trick is to dodge the bullets and bombs headed his way. For Spade, the dangers are more subtle, but no less deadly. In his world, nothing is certain, not even the names of his client. Everyone (including Spade himself, who is sleeping with Iva Archer behind his partner's back) is out to deceive or betray everyone else. In such a world, only the toughest and shrewdest survive. That Spade survives without becoming contaminated, as does the Op in *Red Harvest*, is a measure of his toughness—and his integrity. In the end, Spade doesn't necessarily "solve" the mystery. The location of the real falcon, if in fact there is one, remains a mystery. The murder of Miles Archer is explained, though questions remain about other killings. In the new kind of mystery story that Hammett was writing, there are no tidy answers to all the riddles. One does the best one can; survival is more important than solutions.

The Maltese Falcon was an immediate success and introduced Hammett to an audience far beyond the pulps. The novel spawned three Hollywood film versions: the first was released in 1931; the second, under the title *Satan Met a Lady*, came out in 1936; the third, and most famous, was John Huston's 1941 version that featured Humphrey Bogart as Sam Spade. Huston had the good sense to retain much of Hammett's original dialogue, and Bogart's performance as Spade was so compelling that he became the model for an entire generation of film private eyes. Hammett's novel was the first crime story to appear as a Modern Library edition in 1934. *The Adventures of Sam Spade* also became one of the most popular radio series in the late 1940s.

The Glass Key

In the fall of 1929, Hammett's personal life was undergoing upheaval. His marriage to Jose had broken up, and he had fallen in love with a writer named Nell Martin. He and Nell decided to leave San Francisco and move to New York. This change in his personal life was mirrored by a related shift in his writing. In his next novel, *The Glass Key* (completed in early 1930 and published in 1931), Hammett abandoned the private detective heroes that had proved to be so successful in his previous work, and though he did not forsake the mystery entirely, he attempted in his new novel to expand beyond the generic limitations of the mystery novel.

The murder of Taylor Henry is the incident from which the action of *The Glass Key* develops. Henry is the son of Senator Ralph Henry, who is facing a tough reelection battle. The senator needs the backing of Paul Madvig, a powerful local political boss, which he gets because Madvig has fallen in love with his daughter, Janet (whom the senator has used to lure Madvig). When suspicion falls upon Madvig in the murder of Taylor Henry (someone has been sending anonymous letters to individuals all over town implicating Madvig), he calls upon his friend and trusted associate, Ned Beaumont, for help. Madvig eventually confides to Beaumont that he killed Taylor, but Beaumont doesn't believe him. He digs up evidence that proves that Senator Henry actually killed his own son during an argument; Madvig, who was there, was willing to take the blame to protect the senator out of misguided love for his daughter. Then, in a surprising final twist, Janet Henry declares her love for Beaumont, which strains the friendship between the two men. The novel ends with the couple planning to move together to New York.

In the picture it paints of a corrupt society, *The Glass Key* resembles *Red Harvest*. However, Hammett's worldview has grown increasingly more cynical. There are no good guys in this novel. The senator, described as "one of the few aristocrats left in American politics" (p. 9), is a murderer. The owner of the local newspaper is deeply in debt and prints whatever his creditor tells him to print. The two most powerful behind-the-scenes forces in town are Paul Madvig, whose political machine is fueled by bribery and patronage, and Shad O'Rory, a gangster who boasts that "half the coppers in town are buying their cakes and ale with dough they're getting from me and some of my friends" (p. 68). Ned Beaumont, Madvig's right-hand man, is part of the same corrupt system; unlike the Op, an outsider who seeks to clean up Personville, Beaumont is an insider unmotivated by any sense of justice. He wants only to save his friend's skin. Although he is not a detective (he's a gambler on a losing streak). Beaumont does a creditable job getting to the bottom of the murder mystery. But the murder investigation exists largely as a way for Hammett to expose the nature of big-city power politics.

Beaumont is no hero. He's tough and cynical ("I don't believe in anything, but I'm too much of a gambler not to be affected by a lot of things" [p. 177]) and clever and loyal to his buddy, whose reputation he's trying to salvage. But he stoops to planting evidence and threatening blackmail. Hammett also includes scenes that serve little purpose other than to reveal an unpleasant side to his character. Sam Spade is a womanizer who is sleeping with his partner's wife, but it doesn't cause his death. Beaumont seduces the wife of the newspaper publisher, which promptly drives the publisher to commit suicide once he finds out. In yet another disturbing scene, Beaumont sits coolly by and watches a man snap the neck of another man and does nothing to stop it.

The title of the novel comes from a dream

Janet Henry relates to Beaumont in which the two of them are walking in a forest. Tired and hungry, the pair come upon a house filled with good things to eat. They find a key and open the door, only to discover hundreds of snakes slithering all over the floor. They quickly slam and relock the door, shutting the snakes inside. Janet later admits to Beaumont that her dream actually had a very different ending: the key they used to open the door was made of glass and shattered in the lock, allowing the snakes to escape and swarm all over them. The symbolism of Janet's dream has been interpreted in various ways. On a purely psychological level, the snakes might have an erotic overtone related to Janet's guilt at feeling sexual desire for Beaumont when it is his best friend with whom she is supposedly in love. On the other hand, the dream can be seen simply as underscoring the notion that once a particular door is opened, it can't always be closed. One must be prepared, as Hammett's heroes usually are, to deal with whatever consequences arise from one's actions.

Critical opinion about *The Glass Key* is mixed. Hammett reportedly completed the novel in one thirty-hour marathon writing session, which might account for the loose ends and unanswered questions, including several about Beaumont himself. The novel also lacks the strong sense of place Hammett created in *Red Harvest* and *The Maltese Falcon.* In the latter novel, for example, San Francisco was depicted in precise detail, from specific streets and familiar landmarks to local atmospheric details like the Alcatraz foghorn. In *The Glass Key,* by contrast, the city is never even identified specifically (though it likely is based on Baltimore, where Hammett lived as a child). Perhaps Hammett, who had just moved to New York, was unfamiliar with the new urban setting he was using. Or perhaps he simply wished to downplay the specifics of place in order to create a more universal setting for his tale of political corruption. In any case, setting plays a minor role in this novel compared with his previous ones.

As in *The Maltese Falcon,* however, Hammett once again demonstrated that unhampered by having to conceive of his novel as separate episodes, he could spin a fast-paced plot. He also once more took advantage of the objective third-person narration he had employed to such effect in his previous novel. We are perhaps less uncertain about Ned Beaumont's motives than about Sam Spade's, but thanks to Hammett's objective perspective, the reader is kept guessing about Beaumont's feelings concerning events and other characters.

Despite the success he enjoyed in *Black Mask,* Hammett was never entirely satisfied with being considered simply a pulp writer. He had more serious ambitions, and *The Glass Key* showed him trying to stretch beyond his pulp origins. Unfortunately, such an attempt to break away from familiar territory ultimately had devastating consequences on his writing career.

The Thin Man

In the span of just two years, Hammett had gone from a struggling pulp writer to a writer in demand. In 1930, he sold the film rights to *Red Harvest, The Maltese Falcon,* and, even before it was published, *The Glass Key.* In the summer of that year, he was also offered a contract by Paramount Pictures to write original film stories and moved to Hollywood (without Nell Martin). His first Hollywood experience brought mixed results. Only one of his stories made it to the screen (*City Streets,* a 1931 film that starred Gary Cooper and Sylvia Sidney). He also spent much of his time drinking heavily and getting into trouble (he was assessed $2,500 in damages in response to an assault charge brought by an actress who claimed she was injured resisting his advances). But it was also during this time, on 22 November 1930, that he met an aspiring writer named Lillian Hellman, with whom he spent the rest of his life.

Thanks to the many distractions in Hollywood, Hammett's writing suffered. Offers from the higher-paying "slick" magazines enticed him to turn out three Sam Spade stories in 1932—two for *American Magazine,* one for *Collier's*—but they are inferior efforts, designed only to cash in on Spade's popularity. He also wrote a novella entitled *Woman in the Dark,* published in *Liberty* in 1933. Alfred Knopf kept pressuring him to complete the novel he had promised, one he had begun writing in 1930 but had put aside. Profligate in his ways, Hammett was, as usual, in need of money, and so, in 1933, he determined to complete the unfinished novel, entitled *The Thin Man.* He intended it to be his last detective novel, though certainly not, as it turned out to be, his final novel.

In Hammett's original version, the main character was a San Francisco private detective named John Guild. When Hammett resumed the project, Guild's character was changed to a New York City police detective, and he was relegated to a minor role. The hero became Nick Charles, a retired private detective married to Nora, a lumber heiress. Nick has traded sleuthing for managing his wife's business interests, trying to ensure "that you don't lose any of the money I married you for" (p. 16). He gets involved in the search for the missing Clyde Wynant, an eccentric inventor who is suspected in the murder of his secretary, Julia Wolf, only because of his wife's nagging. He'd much rather spend his time doing what he does best—drinking and partying.

Hammett sustains the mystery of the missing Clyde Wynant quite effectively. (The exceptionally slender Wynant is the "Thin Man" of the title; in the films based on the novel, the Thin Man came to refer to Nick Charles himself.) Wynant's shifting whereabouts are hinted at by reports of sightings, telephone calls, telegrams, and so forth. His possible involvement in the murder of another character also arises. Nick Charles eventually gets to the bottom of things, including the shocking revelation that Wynant has been dead all along, murdered by his attorney Herbert Macaulay, Nick's old army buddy with whom he has been working on the case. However, the solution to the mystery is somewhat forced. Nick Charles ends up sounding like one of those armchair detectives Hammett had diligently avoided creating earlier. Hammett prided himself in the early Op tales on getting the details of the actual investigation exactly right; now Nick Charles simply spins an elaborate theory to account for all the mysteries without ever really doing much in the way of investigating.

The Thin Man is disappointing not so much for its lack of merit (its cleverness and breezy pace made it extremely popular) but in comparison with Hammett's earlier work. For example, where in his previous novels Hammett set the mystery against the backdrop of, say, political corruption in *The Glass Key;* or placed it in the context of an examination of obsession, as in *The Maltese Falcon;* or used it to explore the values of the detective himself, as in *Red Harvest,* in *The Thin Man* the background to the mystery is of an entirely different sort. Here the larger context is having a good time. Hammett, the realist of crime, became Hammett, the social comedian. Hammett makes no pretense at seriousness in *The Thin Man.* Instead of taking a critical view of society, he is satisfied with giving us glimpses into the sophisticated party-going scene in New York. Instead of underworld slang and tough talk, we hear jokes and clever remarks. Instead of questions aimed at ferreting out the truth, most of Nick's questions refer to imbibing: "How about a drop of something to cut the phlegm?" (p. 10), "How about another drink?" (p. 35), or "How about shaking up a drink?" (p. 92).

Nick Charles's character also lacks the depth of Hammett's previous protagonists. There is no sense of mystery about him, no suggestion of a darker side to his personality. He drinks heavily, but Hammett never exploits this as a character weakness, as he does in the case of the Op's encounter with the dehumanizing effects of violence in *Red Harvest.* Nick is an ex-detective, but Hammett chooses not to make much of his lack of a job to give meaning to his life (which was a key point in the portrayal of the Op and Spade). Unlike his predecessors, Nick isn't even a tough guy: he assaults one gunman by throwing a pillow at him, and his lone wrestling match is with a woman. He suffers a bullet wound, but it fails to prevent him from going to a dinner party that evening. And, significantly, he does almost no actual investigating. He solves the crime from a distance, simply by coming up with a theory that he insists is right because "it doesn't click any other way" (p. 194). Nick and Nora are ultimately superficial characters; aside from their playful banter and shared interest in party-going, there is little depth to the pair (whom Hammett himself later described as being insufferably smug).

The Thin Man obviously celebrates Hammett's new relationship with Lillian Hellman (to whom he dedicated the book). The lively and affectionate banter between Nick and Nora reflects that between Hammett and Hellman. The cleverness of the dialogue reveals a surprising side to Hammett, who previously had limited himself largely to matter-of-fact prose and, especially in the Op stories, terse dialogue. In its sexual suggestiveness, some of the dialogue in *The Thin Man* even pushes the limits of what was considered acceptable at the time. For example, when Nick goes off to question the attractive Mimi Jorgensen, Nora advises him to "keep your legs crossed" (p. 93). Later, after he has tussled with the provocative Mimi, Nora asks, "Tell me the truth: when you were wrestling with Mimi, didn't you get an erection?" (though in many editions of the novel, Hammett's original line was bowdlerized to read "didn't you get excited?" [p. 151]). "Oh, a little," replies Nick.

The Thin Man was published in January 1934, a year in which the money began pouring in, though Hammett earned little of it from his fiction writing. The first film version of *The Thin Man,* starring William Powell and Myrna Loy, was released in 1934 and became enormously successful, and Hammett was promptly hired to write a sequel, which was called *After the Thin Man.* Eventually there were six Thin Man films (as well as a radio and a television series), though aside from *After the Thin Man,* none involved Hammett's participation. It has been estimated that Hammett earned close to a million dollars from all the Thin Man projects.

Hammett also earned five hundred dollars a week to write story and dialogue for a comic strip entitled *Secret Agent X-9,* illustrated by Alex Raymond, creator of Flash Gordon. Agent X-9 was designed to compete with the popular Dick Tracy comic strip. X-9 is an efficient crime-fighter who, like the Op, is given no name. Hammett was eventually fired for missing deadlines, though the strip continued without his contribution. Hammett also wrote three stories for *Collier's* in 1934: "Two Sharp Knives," a crime story; "His Brother's Keeper," a boxing story; and "This Little Pig," a Hollywood satire. They proved to be the last original works he published during his lifetime.

The Long Silence

The mystery of why Hammett wrote nothing between 1934 and his death twenty-seven years later, in 1961, can never be fully explained. Theories abound: he drank too much to write, success spoiled him, he had earned so much money that he no longer had any incentive to write, his creative energies were sapped by his collaborative work with Lillian Hellman, he became consumed by political activities, he suffered from a severe case of writer's block, or once he stopped writing mysteries, he simply had nothing more to say. Whatever the reason, Hammett remained silent as a writer, though he remained a very public figure. It is true that his success brought rich financial rewards that exacted a severe toll. He lived (and partied) at an extravagant level. He became one of the highest-paid writers in Hollywood, employed by several of the big studios, though his heavy drinking caused him to be fired frequently for irresponsible behavior. His excessive drinking also resulted in more than one hospitalization. Only a doctor's stern warning in 1948 that his drinking would soon kill him eventually persuaded him to stop.

It is also true that he worked actively with Hellman in helping her write her first plays. In 1933, he encouraged her to write a play based upon a true story he had read about a girls' school in Scotland that was rocked by rumors that the owners were lesbian. He served as critic and editor, helping Hellman shape the material into *The Children's Hour,* which enjoyed enormous success on Broadway and launched her career as an important American dramatist. In 1941, he worked with her on a screenplay for the film version of another of her plays, *Watch on the Rhine.* Hammett also became actively engaged in leftist political activities. He supported the antifascist republican cause during the Spanish Civil War in the 1930s. He spoke at Communist-sponsored anti-Nazi rallies during the 1940s. He served as chairman of the Committee on Election Rights and the Motion Picture Artists Committee and was president of the League of American Writers in 1941. Eventually, as the Cold War hysteria of McCarthyism began sweeping the country, Hammett's political activities brought him to the attention of the authorities. In 1951, he was a trustee of the Civil Rights Congress, an organization that provided bail for some Communists who had been arrested. Hammett was subpoenaed to testify about the whereabouts of four of the Communists who had jumped bail. He refused to answer questions and was found guilty of contempt of court; he spent five months in prison.

There is evidence that during these years Hammett made sporadic attempts at writing. In 1939, he began one novel, variously titled "My Brother Felix" and "There Was a Young Man," though only a few pages survive. According to his biographer Diane Johnson, Hammett even joked about his failure to write: "It's swell having a new novel not to do. I was getting pretty bored with just not working on that half a dozen or so old ones" (p. 218). In September 1942, at the age of forty-eight, Hammett enlisted as a private in the army and was assigned to the remote volcanic island of Adak in the Aleutian Islands, hundreds of miles from the Alaska mainland. There he founded and edited the camp newspaper, the *Adakian.* He also began planning a novel about a man who comes home from the war and finds he no longer likes his family, but nothing came of the idea. Ten years later, in 1952, he made one last serious attempt to write a novel. Entitled "Tulip," the largely autobiographical novel featured a writer who served a jail sentence for his political views. However, this effort, too, was abandoned after Hammett had managed to write about twelve thousand words. Hammett's final years were spent quietly in Katonah, New York. He had long been in ill health when he died of lung cancer on 10 January 1961, at the age of 66. Following his wishes, he was buried in Arlington National Cemetery.

Hammett's Legacy

The figure of the tough-talking, hard-boiled private eye has enjoyed a long and illustrious career in American crime fiction. It is difficult to imagine, however, that there would have been a Philip Marlowe or a Lew Archer or a Spenser, or any one of a hundred others, were it not for Dashiell Hammett. For while he did not himself originate the figure of the private eye, he was the first writer to realize the literary potential of this new kind of fictional detective. Thanks to his experience as a Pinkerton detective, he brought honesty and realism to the depiction of this new hero. Thanks also to his deliberate avoidance of artificial and flowery language, he developed a hard-edged, economical style of writing. Combined with the authentic sound of colorful slang and convincing dialogue, this hard-boiled style helped bring about a transformation of American prose. Hammett was a true original whose characters the Continental Op, Sam Spade, and Nick and Nora Charles continue to live on, not just in his stories and novels but also in radio, television, and films, long after he prematurely laid his pen aside.

Selected Bibliography

WORKS OF DASHIELL HAMMETT

NOVELS

Red Harvest. New York: Grosset and Dunlap, 1929.
The Dain Curse. New York: Grosset and Dunlap, 1929.
The Maltese Falcon. New York: Knopf, 1930.
The Glass Key. New York: Knopf, 1931.
The Thin Man. New York: Knopf, 1934.

SHORT STORIES

The Adventures of Sam Spade and Other Stories. Edited by Ellery Queen. New York: Spivak, 1944. Includes "His Brother's Keeper."

The Continental Op. Edited by Ellery Queen. New York: Spivak, 1945.

The Return of the Continental Op. Edited by Ellery Queen. New York: Spivak, 1945.

The Art of the Mystery Story. Edited by Howard Haycraft. New York: Simon & Schuster, 1946. Includes "The Memoirs of a Private Detective."

Hammett Homicides. Edited by Ellery Queen. New York: Spivak, 1946. Includes "The House in Turk Street," "The Girl with the Silver Eyes," and "Two Sharp Knives."

Dead Yellow Women. Edited by Ellery Queen. New York: Spivak, 1947. Includes "Who Killed Bob Teal?"

Nightmare Town. Edited by Ellery Queen. New York: Spivak, 1948.

The Creeping Siamese. Edited by Ellery Queen. New York: Spivak, 1950.

Woman in the Dark. Edited by Ellery Queen. New York: Spivak, 1951. Includes "Arson Plus."

A Man Named Thin and Other Stories. Edited by Ellery Queen. New York: Ferman, 1962.

The Big Knockover: Selected Stories and Short Novels. Edited and with an introduction by Lillian Hellman. New York: Random House, 1966. Includes "The Gutting of Couffignal," "The Big Knockover," and "$106,000 Blood Money."

The Continental Op. Edited by Steven Marcus. New York: Random House, 1974. Includes "The House in Turk Street," "The Girl with the Silver Eyes," and "The Whosis Kid."

ARCHIVES

The Hammett Manuscript Collection is at Humanities Research Center, University of Texas, Austin.

BIOGRAPHICAL AND CRITICAL STUDIES

Chandler, Raymond. *The Simple Art of Murder.* New York: Ballantine, 1950.

Dooley, Dennis. *Dashiell Hammett.* New York: Ungar, 1984.

Gregory, Sinda. *Private Investigations: The Novels of Dashiell Hammett.* Carbondale: Southern Illinois University Press, 1985.

Johnson, Diane. *Dashiell Hammett: A Life.* New York: Random House, 1983.

Layman, Richard. *Shadow Man: The Life of Dashiell Hammett.* New York: Harcourt Brace Jovanovich, 1981.

Madden, David, ed. *Tough Guy Writers of the Thirties.* Carbondale: Southern Illinois University Press, 1968.

Marling, William. *Dashiell Hammett.* Boston: Twayne, 1983.

———. *The American Roman Noir: Hammett, Cain, and Chandler.* Athens, Ga: University of Georgia Press, 1995.

Mellen, Joan. *Hellman and Hammett: The Legendary Passion of Lillian Hellman and Dashiell Hammett.* New York: HarperCollins, 1996.

Metress, Christopher. *The Critical Response to Dashiell Hammett.* Westport, Conn: Greenwood Press, 1994.

Nolan, William F. *Hammett: A Life at the Edge.* New York: Congdon and Weed, 1983.

Skenazy, Paul. *The New Wild West: The Urban Mysteries of Dashiell Hammett and Raymond Chandler.* Boise: Boise State University, 1982.

Symons, Julian. *Dashiell Hammett.* San Diego: Harcourt Brace Jovanovich, 1985.

Wolfe, Peter. *Beams Falling: The Art of Dashiell Hammett.* Bowling Green, Ohio: Bowling Green University Popular Press, 1980.

George V. Higgins

(b. 1939)

ERWIN H. FORD II

Since he emerged on the American literary scene in 1972 with his first published novel, *The Friends of Eddie Coyle,* George Higgins has been a subtle and pervasive influence in American literature. He is the author of twenty-seven novels, two books of political journalism, a collection of short fiction, numerous articles in the scholarly and popular press, book and television criticism, newspaper columns, and book reviews for the *New Republic,* the *Chicago Tribune,* the *New York Times,* the London *Times,* and the *Washington Post.* He has written for the *Providence Journal,* the Boston *Herald American, Boston Magazine,* the *Boston Globe,* the *Wall Street Journal,* and the *Atlantic Monthly,* among others. *The Friends of Eddie Coyle* was a finalist for a National Book Award and was selected in 1985 as one of the twenty best American novels since World War II by the British Booksellers Association. The New York Public Library named him "Literary Lion," and he has been celebrated in the House of Lords for his contribution to literature. His oeuvre is noted for its arcane, authentic dialogue; his intimate knowledge of the criminal underworld; and the classical purity of his novelistic form.

Higgins' nonliterary careers contributed vastly to his fiction. He was a noted assistant attorney general for the Commonwealth of Massachusetts and an assistant United States attorney for the District of Massachusetts. He was a premier member of the Boston criminal bar; as president of the law firm George V. Higgins, Inc., in Boston, he became a trial lawyer of national stature. He has worked as a New Journalist alongside Tom Wolfe, Hunter S. Thompson, and Joan Didion, and in 1988 he became a professor of English at Boston University. As a journalist, he has championed honesty and morality in the media. As an attorney, he has condemned corruption in American participatory democracy. His lifelong concern with transgression has won him the respect of his fellow writers as the natural heir to the Calvinism of Nathaniel Hawthorne and Henry James, his Irish-Catholic origins notwithstanding.

Life

George Vincent Higgins was born on 13 November 1939, in Brockton, Massachusetts, of mixed Irish and Yankee stock. His father, John Thompson Higgins, was an English teacher and schoolmaster from Boston's South Shore; his mother, Doris Montgomery Higgins, also a teacher, came of old Vermont farming stock. Higgins grew up in working-class Rockland, Massachusetts, where his grandfather Charles Higgins had been a banker and where his father was the high-school principal.

Higgins was an energetic child who spent his boyhood in a household frugal except in the matter of literacy. Omnivorous in their reading tastes, John and Doris Higgins let their son read what they read: the *Atlantic Monthly, The Saturday Evening Post,* and the works of Ernest Hemingway, Sir Arthur Conan Doyle, J. P. Marquand, and John O'Hara. George Higgins brought home *Field and Stream, Saga,* and *True.* When the local librarian stopped the boy from reading Hemingway, which she considered too adult for him, Doris Higgins called the library and ordered her to let him read what he wanted. As a result, Higgins developed a sense of his future profession early in life. With his parents' encouragement, he began to write fiction on a broken-down Smith Corona portable that John Higgins had cast aside. He wrote late at night, but no one complained about the pounding and clacking that issued from his room. What justified keeping one's mother awake late at night by pounding on typewriter keys, he said, "is that what I am doing is important work. It has to be done *right now,* and it doesn't matter how selfish you or any one else choose to think I am, because I am going to do it. Right now."

Although his parents placed few restrictions on what he read, Higgins' upbringing was sternly Catholic—of what he terms the "old-fashioned" Jansenist subspecies. Each Sunday the Higginses went to Holy Family Church in Rockland and, after church, had Sunday dinner with the family. John Higgins gave what money he felt he could afford to the church, though he refused to tell his priests how much he gave. When envelopes were distributed and parishioners were instructed to write their names on the envelopes along with the amount enclosed, John Higgins refused to sign them. On the basis of those tithe envelopes, the pastor discriminated among applicants competing for scarce seats in the parish school. Catholics whose children did not get in to what were called "Sisters' schools" were considered fractious, out of grace, or too poor to afford the minimum prescribed offerings. As a result, George Higgins was not permitted to attend Catholic schools. His father, however, thought it appropriate, since he was the local high-school principal and knew how it would appear if he sent his son to a parochial school. But by his own admission, Higgins never strayed from his religious roots. "I have no quarrel whatsoever with the faith," he has said, and his Irish-Catholicism played a vital part in the formation of his literature.

At fifteen he wrote his first novel, called "Operation Cincinnatus" (which he destroyed in 1973 or 1974). It concerned Lucius Quinctius Cincinnatus, the Roman general who left his farm to fight against invaders. He got the idea from his school Latin text. Elements of the story appealed to Higgins: a sense of patriotism, a duty stronger than personal desire, and the idea of leaving one's pastoral origins to go to war. Higgins edited the school newspaper and fished for pickerel in Reed's Pond. He played sandlot baseball at Rockland's Memorial Park, managed the high-school basketball team, and lettered in baseball all four years at Rockland High. Despite his youthful interest, the idea that he might spend his adult life writing stories seemed distant; John Higgins wanted his son to become a doctor.

Higgins graduated from Rockland High School in 1957. Declining a scholarship to Harvard University, he entered the premedical program at Boston College. His premed studies, however, were short-lived—he found science tedious and distasteful. He changed his major to English and fell under the influence of the youthful and charismatic Boston College English faculty, among whom were Leonard Caspar, the biographer of Robert Penn Warren; Ed Hirsch; John Maloney; Pierre Duhamel; and the Jesuit Francis Sweeney. Higgins' aspirations were clearly literary, and his reading in college was eclectic: Joseph Conrad, Graham Greene, Mark Twain, Henry James, Gustave Flaubert, and Fyodor Dostoyevsky. He disliked Milton immediately; blindness, he quipped, was God's punishment for *Areopagitica.* The Boston College English faculty taught him Saint Thomas Aquinas,

Saint John of the Cross, and even Pierre Teilhard de Chardin, who was, at the time, proscribed by the Vatican.

In 1960 Higgins submitted a short story entitled "There Are No Gods Beneath the Bridge" to the *Atlantic Monthly*'s fiction contest and won first place. He graduated from Boston College with a bachelor's degree, and on the strength of his success writing fiction—but against John Higgins' strenuous objections—he entered Stanford University in 1961 to study creative writing in a graduate program directed by the novelist Wallace Stegner. He attended Stegner's creative-writing courses and courses in American literature taught by critic Irving Howe. But Higgins was uncomfortable in Stanford's radical climate. He felt singled out by Howe, a former Trotskyite. Higgins felt that Howe disliked his Irish face and surname, and he claimed that Howe associated his Irishness with the anti-Communist demagogues Joseph McCarthy and Pat McCarran.

The liberal moral climate in California at the time offended the boy's conservative sensibilities. The sexual revolution had begun, and drug use was prevalent. Higgins was appalled by both. Not inclined to withhold his views, Higgins sat silently, unhappily, far from home. His Stanford studies were, as a result, unsuccessful. He developed a bleeding ulcer and returned to New England in 1962 without completing his master's degree, traumatized by what he felt to be Stegner's disregard for students and Howe's anti–Irish Catholic, anti–New England sentiment. He completed his Stanford master of arts in absentia in 1965 but gave up thoughts of an academic career.

Returning home to New England with few career prospects, Higgins applied to the J. Walter Thompson advertising agency, the Federal Bureau of Investigation, and the Central Intelligence Agency for jobs. John Higgins obtained a waiver of teaching credentials that would have allowed his son to teach English in Massachusetts public schools, but Higgins declined, taking instead a job as a reporter in Rhode Island. From 1962 to 1966 he worked as a reporter and journalist for the *Providence Journal* and later for the Associated Press in Springfield and Boston. During his early years as a reporter, he interviewed John Forbes Thompson, Speaker of the Massachusetts House of Representatives—a political carnivore who later appeared in various forms in Higgins' fiction. Thompson, who was eventually indicted on numerous counts of corruption and bribery, came to symbolize for Higgins the essential nature of democratic politics: amoral, pragmatic, given of necessity to ethical compromise, but withal effective in meeting community needs. In 1963, after covering a series of organized-crime cases in Springfield, Massachusetts, for the Associated Press, Higgins decided that he wanted to become a trial lawyer. He was drawn by the courtly manners and exaggerated courteousness in what he termed "the last blood sport." He felt he had found an outlet for his competitive nature. He entered Boston College Law School in 1965.

Higgins was a mediocre student. His strengths lay in rules of evidence and trial procedure, which made up only a minor portion of his studies. It was to be a pattern thoughout his life: the desire to be in the thick of things rather than on the sidelines, a preference for the *vita activa* over the *vita contemplativa.* And his interests were divided. While in law school, Higgins met Elizabeth Mulkerin, a student at the Harvard School of Education. She, too, was Irish-Catholic, and they were married on 4 September 1965. The next year, in September of 1966, John Higgins died of a heart attack. Newly married, still grieving at his father's death, in 1967 George Higgins received his law degree and went to work as a deputy assistant attorney general for the Commonwealth of Massachusetts under Attorney General Elliot Richardson.

A law career that began without distinction soon brought Higgins renown, owing to his natural energy and combative personality. Higgins' years as an assistant attorney general were hugely formative. Attorney General Richardson had a brilliant legal mind with a highly developed sense of social responsibility, and in working for Richardson, Higgins lost the fear of Yankee anti-Irish bigotry that had been ingrained by several generations of Irish-Catholic forebears to whom "NINA" (No Irish Need Apply) signs were a fresh memory. In this context, Higgins also began to gather material for his fiction; here he encountered the policemen, criminals, and attorneys whose speech he later re-created with the ruthless, spectacular veracity that came to characterize his fiction.

Higgins left the attorney general's office in 1970 to become a federal prosecutor and later a criminal attorney in private practice. In the meantime, he continued to write fiction. In 1972, at thirty-three years of age, he published his first book, to immediate public recognition. *The Friends of Eddie Coyle* was a compact novel written in six weeks while Higgins had a grand-jury sitting. The novel dealt with the Boston criminal underworld and immediately caught the attention of crime and mystery readers because of its harsh and authentic dialogue. But *The Friends of Eddie Coyle* also intimated a concern that outlived Higgins' interest in crime and mystery: it dealt at a deeper level with the economy of friendship and community. If, as Higgins' Irish-Catholicism held, sin had wages, virtue had an economy of its own, particularly the virtues of friendship and fidelity to one's community.

Within a year *The Friends of Eddie Coyle* was adapted as a Paramount film starring Robert Mitchum and Peter Boyle, and Higgins soon produced two more novels of the criminal underworld: *The Digger's Game* (1973) and *Cogan's Trade* (1974). *Cogan's Trade*, praised by fellow novelist John Gregory Dunne as "an almost flawless novel" (p. 25), was harsh, symmetrical, and predictable in the best tradition of classicism and rationalism.

Although his acclaim as a writer was growing, Higgins continued to practice criminal law. He found himself unable to limit his expenditure of energy, at times to his detriment. Between 1973 and 1980 he defended numerous clients against criminal charges; as president of George V. Higgins, Inc., he represented such diverse and infamous figures as the Watergate conspirator G. Gordon Liddy and the Black Panther Eldridge Cleaver. But his production of novels accelerated until, in 1980, he gave up the practice of law to devote himself to fiction writing and journalism.

Higgins' marriage to Betty Mulkerin throughout these years was fraught with tension. They differed on the use of birth control, family planning, and the ritual of confession. Betty felt threatened by his success, and her hostility toward his various careers worsened. After publication of *The Digger's Game*, she developed obvious symptoms of mental illness, rages, paranoia, and alcoholism. Though Higgins remained a devout Catholic, he, like many, disagreed with the papal ban on divorce. In 1973 Higgins and his wife separated: Higgins moved out of their home, filed for divorce, and began "six years of real blood-on-the-floor hair-on-the-wall court fighting" to gain custody of their two children, John and Susan, who meanwhile remained with Betty. A judge awarded Higgins custody some years later. In the interim, Betty underwent repeated psychiatric treatment, while Higgins sought financial stability for himself and the children.

In 1975 Higgins published a work of political reportage, *The Friends of Richard Nixon*, a particularly cogent analysis of the Watergate proceedings, in which Higgins analyzes Nixon's actual criminal offense and portrays the hypocrisy of the press in the "feeding frenzy" that surrounded Watergate. That same year he also produced *A City on a Hill*, a novel of the democratic system inspired by Henry Adams' social and political satire *Democracy* (1880). In 1976 Higgins published *The Judgment of Deke Hunter*, a classic bildungsroman in its purity of form and dialogue, perhaps his greatest literary achievement. In 1979 *A Year or So with Edgar* adapted his criminal vernacular and his Puritan-Jansenist view of human transgression to the world of lawyers and journalists. *Kennedy for the Defense* (1980), *A Choice of Enemies* (1984), and *Penance for Jerry Kennedy* (1985), marked a new ascent in his popularity. *The Rat on Fire* (1981), which deals with the community's selection of a sacrificial victim, was inspired by stories he had heard from state policemen while working under Elliot Richardson. It is a story of arson and insurance fraud set amid Boston's racial strife over busing. *The Patriot Game* (1982) casts a cold eye at the Irish-American nostalgia for Ireland and American financial support of the Irish Republican Army, toward which Higgins had no sympathy. Higgins wrote that his father had "devoutly approved of the United States" ("Witness," p. 596), which became for George Higgins, too, a type of New Jerusalem. Years later, considering Ireland, the IRA, the Dail (or Assembly of Ireland, created in opposition to British rule), and the hold of the Roman Catholic Church on Ireland, Higgins said he was glad that his ancestor Arthur Higgins had emigrated in the mid–nineteenth century. He would not, he knew, have been happy in Ireland.

While researching *The Friends of Richard Nixon,* Higgins met Ed Cubberley and his wife, Loretta, who worked in the Washington office of Senator Edward Kennedy. When Ed Cubberley died of cancer several years later, Higgins and Loretta Cubberley began a romance that continued while Higgins fought for custody of his children from the increasingly unstable Betty Higgins, and then through his divorce. In 1980 he and Loretta Cubberley were married.

Higgins' forays into newspaper journalism were as energetic as his fiction writing, if less single-minded. Shortly after the publication of *Cogan's Trade,* Higgins began to write a column for the counterculture newspaper the *Boston Phoenix.* It was the first of a number of news columns for Higgins. Between 1974 and 1987 he wrote for the *Chicago Tribune,* the *New York Times,* the *Times* of London, the *Washington Post,* the Boston *Herald American, Boston Magazine,* the *Boston Globe,* the *Wall Street Journal,* and the *Atlantic Monthly.* If Higgins' fiction style was brief, concise, and Senecan, the literary style of his columns was what Raymond Sokolov of the *Wall Street Journal* termed "vicarish." Higgins mastered, the journalist noted, prose styles ranging from "Bean-town thug" to "Churchillian rhetorician."

In 1987 he was appointed professor of creative writing at the State University of New York at Buffalo, his first venture back into the academy since his unhappy tenure as a graduate student at Stanford. Arriving in Buffalo to teach, he was greeted by news headlines and cocktail parties in his honor. Nevertheless, the next year, when he was offered a permanent position at SUNY Buffalo, he declined. New England—specifically Boston—was his home. In 1988 a longtime friendship with Boston University president John Silber paid dividends in the form of an offer of a teaching position at Boston University. (Some years earlier, Higgins had defended an acquaintance of Silber's on criminal charges.) Silber appointed Higgins to an English department that already boasted the presence of Saul Bellow and Derek Walcott.

While teaching creative writing at Boston University and living in Milton, Higgins continued to produce one novel per year, as well as a book of political history (*Style Versus Substance,* 1985), a nonfiction book on baseball (*The Progress of the Seasons,* 1989), and a widely used writing text (*On Writing,* 1990). In later novels, *The Mandeville Talent* (1991), *Defending Billy Ryan* (1992), and *Bomber's Law* (1993), Higgins continued to explore the nature of community, the economy of virtue, Irish-Catholicism, and the changes that occurred in the Irish-Catholic consciousness with its ascent to affluence. Higgins' fascination with human transgression is fruitfully mingled with the Puritanism of Jonathan Edwards, Cotton and Increase Mather, and Nathaniel Hawthorne: his Irish-Catholicism notwithstanding, Higgins seemed destined to carry on the great gloomy tradition of predestination and inescapable sin espoused by his Protestant New England forebears.

Early Crime and Political Novels

The Friends of Eddie Coyle, The Digger's Game, and *Cogan's Trade* form a loose trilogy of crime novels inspired by Higgins' contact with the criminal underworld while he was working as assistant attorney general for Massachusetts and as a U.S. attorney. His fiction was strongly influenced by Elliot Richardson's stern Yankee political and social philosophies. The novelist Norman Mailer praised his skills at reproducing dialogue, and the critic J. D. O'Hara of the *New Republic* said of Higgins' work that "one thinks of Shaw on *Ulysses:* A fidelity so ruthless that it is hardly bearable," thus linking Higgins in the public eye with what later became a central concern of his fiction, his Irish-Catholic heritage. In these three novels, Higgins deals with the question of evil—which he defines variously as faithlessness to one's community—and with community as the center of consciousness. Crime in his early novels is a search for an answer to the question "Am I free?" The answer Higgins' protagonists give to the question of individual freedom is a Calvinist-Jansenist "No!" Eddie Coyle is a habitual criminal and gunrunner who faces prison unless he gives evidence against his criminal companies. He seeks to avoid breaking faith with his underworld "friends," only to be killed by them. Higgins' next novel, *The Digger's Game,* concerns a character closer to Higgins' origins. Jerry "Digger" Doherty is a charming rogue and Irish villain, a "hard Harp," in Higgins' words, who owes a debt to Shakespeare's Falstaff and to Boston Irish politician James Michael Curley. In *The Digger's Game,* Higgins shows a mistrust of the Irish-Catholic community that prevents Digger Doherty from growth and learning. In *Cogan's Trade,* Higgins explores the underworld's notion of justice within its own community and the way criminal communities enforce codes of behavior. His central figure, mob enforcer Jackie Cogan, is Mephistophelian, a sociopath prescient of Sam Tibbets of *Outlaws* (1987)—diametrically opposed to the romanticized mob figures of Mario Puzo and Gay Talese, who had achieved popularity at the time. Higgins' dialogue re-creates human speech under stress, a vernacular full of elision, fractured tenses, and mangled syntax. The reading public immediately appreciated the novelty of the dialogue novel, but the significance of Higgins' variations on the traditional central figure of the detective novel did not become apparent until later.

The Friends of Eddie Coyle and *Cogan's Trade* limited Higgins' dialogue to a criminal milieu, and Higgins chafed under the appellations "crime novelist" and "popular writer." He maintained that he wrote stories of transgression and the reactions of "characters under stress" and was influenced, he said, by Hemingway, Stendhal, and John O'Hara. With *A City on a Hill, Dreamland* (1977), and *A Year or So with Edgar,* Higgins began to explore the possibility that his dialogue and his sense of the inevitability of transgression might apply to a wider setting. *A Year or So with Edgar* applies his vernacular to the world of journalists and attorneys with nominal success. *A City on a Hill* deals with the inner workings of the Massachusetts political system and how the democratic process induces responses like the criminal milieu. Each isolates the individual in pursuit of freedom; personal crisis results when that freedom proves illusory. *Dreamland* explores a community Higgins' Irish parents and grandparents had found hostile: New England WASP society. Attempting the mannered style of John O'Hara's characters, Higgins failed to capture his characters' Yankee speech. *Dreamland* is, however, a novel of the secret life, of what Rudyard Kipling called the "Great Game," a reflection of what Higgins admired about WASP culture: its sense of social responsibility and willing self-sacrifice.

With *The Judgment of Deke Hunter* it became apparent that Higgins was producing something with the significance of James Joyce's stream-of-consciousness fiction. Higgins had begun to show speech to be as unwilled and uncontrolled as thought, yet equally revelatory. *The Judgment of Deke Hunter* concerns a young state police corporal torn between his needs for sensual fulfillment and fidelity to his family and career. Hunter has a dissatisfied wife, a police sergeant who wants him to move upward in the ranks, and a sexual liaison with a mob-connected young woman. Unlike central figures in popular crime novels who remain static while they solve crimes, Deke Hunter is a dynamic character who solves no crimes. *The Judgment of Deke Hunter* concerns Hunter's search for his place in community and his moral education. If the full significance of Higgins' work and of *The Judgment of Deke Hunter* was missed by the reading public, it was because he was branded early in his career as a writer of crime novels and thrillers.

Higgins' personal fortunes had waned and waxed between 1973 and 1980, with predictable effect on his fiction. He published one novel per year, generally having to do with crime or transgression of various sorts.

Exploring the Nature of Justice

With his marriage in 1980 to Loretta Cubberley, a new period in Higgins' literature began. With the tranquillity and fulfillment his marriage offered, he began a series of novels that were broader in scope and less obviously Puritan-Jansenist in outlook. They dealt with the Boston criminal bar and the individual's struggle with what the theologian Cornelis Jansen called "an original state of justice," as opposed to human justice. Higgins defined evil in *The Friends of Eddie Coyle* and *Cogan's Trade* as faithlessness to one's community, but in *The Patriot Game* transgression takes the form of the Irish-American's nostalgia for the violence of the revolutionary political organization Sinn Fein and the IRA. *A Choice of Enemies* is his closest look at political corruption. The central figure, Bernie Morgan, was patterned after John Forbes Thompson, a former Speaker of the Massachusetts House of Representatives. Accused of corruption, in 1965 Thompson declared: "If I be a rogue, then I am a delightful one" (Higgins, "Old Pro"). Bernie Morgan, Higgins' avatar of Thompson, is a "man of appetites" who advances democracy by the strength of his own desires. Morgan is democracy's mover as well as its sacrificial victim and Paraclete. In revealing Morgan's sins as well as his charms, Higgins shows himself influenced by Hawthorne and James and by the pragmatism of William James, Charles Sanders Pierce, and Oliver Wendell Holmes.

In a trilogy of novels concerning a Boston criminal attorney, Higgins sought a middle ground between his harsh early novels and his less successful political novels. In *Kennedy for the Defense* and *Penance for Jerry Kennedy,* and later in *Defending Billy Ryan,* Higgins—inspired by his experiences as a criminal defense attorney—examines the effects of crime and the workings of fate on the just man. The Kennedy books deal with crime from the perspective of an attorney defending criminal clients while attempting to keep his own community free of transgression and disruption. The books owe a debt to the biblical Jeremiah, since each chronicles the disruptive effects of affluence on the Boston Irish and each is at heart a lament for the dissolution of ad hoc constraints on human behavior. In that, Higgins' novels differ from formulaic crime novels, which, as more than one critic has pointed out, seek to restore faith in the social order.

The Kennedy novels were comedic to the extent that Jerry Kennedy is static in nature and generally able to mediate between justice and his clients' needs. In his next two books, however, Higgins returns to dynamic central figures enmeshed in circumstances beyond their control and struggling to find grace despite their own foibles. *Impostors* (1986) is a fictional study of corruption and hypocrisy in the press, inspired by his experiences covering Watergate. Although Higgins was less concerned with goodness than with evil in earlier novels, in *Impostors* he defines goodness in a fashion that recalls the themes of Shakespeare. Goodness, he demonstrates, resides in the reunification of community once the criminal has been expelled and in successful heterosexual love. *Outlaws* (1987) combines factual events—the 1976 Brinks robbery by student radicals and the famed Boston Blackfriars' murder case—with Higgins' notion of evil as arrested human development, a topic of perennial interest to him. *Outlaws* is anti-biographical. It presents an alternative life to Higgins' own in the figure of Sam Tibbets, a student radical and New Englander who comes under the pernicious influence of drugs and political radicalism on the West Coast, away from his stabilizing New England roots.

In his later novels, Higgins looks backward toward his youthful ideas of marriage, community, New England, and the dark pastoral of his early novels. In *Wonderful Years, Wonderful Years* (1988), he reexamines his fragile Catholic notions of marriage and morality and addresses his marriage to Betty Higgins, which he had previously refused to do because of the pain he feared it would inflict on his children. *Wonderful Years, Wonderful Years* reconciles his earlier view of marriage as impoverished and tension-fraught with his later view of traditional marriage as the answer to crime and the divided community. *Trust* (1989) and *Victories* (1990) alter his earlier view of New England away from Boston as a dark pastoral where evil befalls his characters. An opinion formed early in his life that Boston provides light and safety, while rural New England is the origin of confusion and bleak knowledge, as in Hawthorne and Herman Melville, changes with *Trust* and *Victories*. Rural New England does have charms for his fictional characters, and a virtuous life is possible there.

Fictional Re-creation of New England

In *The Mandeville Talent, Defending Billy Ryan,* and *Bomber's Law,* Higgins continued a process he had begun with *The Friends of Eddie Coyle* and *The Digger's Game:* the fictional re-creation of New England. New England is not just a literary setting for Higgins, but a theoretical construct where universal moral laws play themselves out. With Higgins' increasing artistic sophistication, crimes in his later novels are more complex than the murder, theft, and brutality of his early novels: they include computer theft, child pornography, murder, fraud, bribery, and fixed bids on state contracts. In addition, Higgins extended the definition of "economy" from the monetary into the moral realm. His characters expend energy to maintain stability and to reunite communities disturbed by crime and transgression; the rewards are commensurate with the energies they expend. Although his early novels move toward a just reckoning and the *dies irae,* or day of wrath, fundamental to his Irish-Catholicism, in later novels Higgins sought to redress his reputation as a crime novelist by extending his dialogue beyond anything he had produced previously. These last novels are virtuoso works, designed to prove to a critical audience that his early novels were scarcely transient pieces of pop literature, but rather were serious experiments in narrative, diction, and plot. His ostensible concerns remained fixed: fate, human transgression, the effect of affluence on the Irish-American community, and the antagonism between Irish Boston and Yankee New England. But in *The Mandeville Talent* and *Bomber's Law,* respectively, Higgins alters the way information is transmitted through dialogue and the way human speech reflects self-knowledge, as his characters become aware of their corrupt natures.

Higgins produced variations on the formulaic novel of crime and detection while presenting his vernacular in a variety of settings. *Sandra Nichols Found Dead* (1996) is an unusually lurid novel based on the murder of Nicole Brown Simpson by her former husband, Orenthal James Simpson, and the prosecution's failure to convict the murderer. The body of the beautiful socialite Sandra Nichols is discovered in a swamp, murdered and stuffed into a garbage bag. Her husband, the wealthy, womanizing sportsman Peter Wade, has an iron-clad alibi. Nichols' life has been far from pristine; she sought an avenue into the moneyed classes by sexually servicing men behind the restaurant where ultimately she met Peter Wade. Sandra Nichols' relentless desire for wealth is itself venal, and her children are left behind to bear the scars of her life and her death. The state police cannot acquire enough evidence to bring Wade to trial. At the heart of the novel is the impotence of law to deal with crime among the moneyed social classes.

In *Sandra Nichols,* a divorced, reflective, aging Jerry Kennedy takes on a wrongful death suit against Peter Wade, on behalf of the murdered Sandra Nichols and her children. As a fictional character, Kennedy remains static within the novels, though he ages and his circumstances change with each work. How does community punish a sociopath who cannot be convicted, who leaves heartbreak and murder in his wake? *Sandra Nichols Found Dead* has the wit and brilliant dialogue of Higgins' earlier works. His insights into the economy of virtue and retribution are familiar from *Kennedy for the Defense* and *Penance for Jerry Kennedy,* and there is a biblical ring to his solution of the problem of insoluble evil. To punish the murderer financially remains the closest thing to the Old Testament law of "an eye for an eye" left in our humane age.

A Change of Gravity (1997) concerns the changing nature of American politics, corruption, friendship, virtue, family, and devotion to duty. It is one of Higgins' more reflective efforts before a return to genre novels and a further addition to his fictional re-creation of New England. Set in the chambers of Massachusetts Superior Court Judge Barrie Foote, the plot concerns a hearing on the indictment of State Representative Danny Hilliard and Ambrose Merrion for bribery and corruption. Higgins carries the reader back and forth through time, across a period of twenty years, before returning to the present day. Danny Hilliard, a former high-school science teacher in the fictional New England town of Canterbury, met Ambrose Merrion years earlier. Hilliard had just entered state politics in his home town of Canterbury. Merrion worked behind the parts counter at the local Ford dealership. Together Hilliard and Merrion move from one election to another, bringing jobs, justice, growth, and prosperity to Canterbury.

Much of *A Change of Gravity* is Hilliard's history as state representative, his friendship with Merrion, his devotion to his constituents, his priapism, and, finally, his indictment in late middle age for crimes that, when he set out upon a career in state politics some twenty years earlier, were not crimes at all. The moral poles have shifted in the intervening years. There is a heavier earth to contend with now, a change of gravity. Higgins' fascination with politics as the arena of tricksters and con men began with *A Choice of Enemies,* where his central figure, Massachusetts pol Bernie Morgan, was ruthless and avaricious: Morgan made deals, and his henchman Frank Costello punished those who reneged on them. *A Change of Gravity* views politics from a kinder perspective. Danny Hilliard is a devoted public servant with a weakness. He is a womanizer who takes care of his constituents. Merrion is his friend, adviser, and hatchet man. As in earlier works, Higgins is still concerned with the redemptive power of friendship and fidelity to community. Friendship is the only thing stronger than the justice that calls Higgins' central figures to account. Hilliard and Merrion have achieved a kind of grace that exists over and above changing social mores.

By the time Higgins wrote *A Change of Gravity,* his long effort to produce serious literature had proved costly to his finances and his readership. In his forthcoming novel, *The Agent,* Higgins returns to commercial fiction of the crime and mystery genre, in a story that centers on the death of a high-profile bisexual sports agent. Higgins' central figure is a police detective who, by means of his deductive powers, searches out the murderer while making philosophical observations on American popular culture. The novel adds nothing new to the crime genre, but it may return Higgins to the public eye.

Conclusion

Despite Higgins' immense productivity, his single-minded pursuit of traditional themes has been detrimental to his general popularity. He is a writer against whom other writers compare their talents. Elmore "Dutch" Leonard, David Mamet, John Gregory Dunne, Mordecai Richler, and Ward Just each cite Higgins as influential to their work. The quality of his dialogue is nearly unmatched in twentieth-century literature. He has brought about a renewed interest in New England's customs, history, and people. Yet, since his early novels, Higgins has never attained the broad readership that would have made his oeuvre part of the literary canon. There remains to his literary concerns an essential conservatism, a dwelling on human constants—sin, damnation, virtue, redemption, and ineluctable fate—that is out of style and out of keeping with the moral relativism of the late twentieth century. Nonetheless, his body of work stands as a significant, even monumental individual achievement.

Selected Bibliography

WORKS OF GEORGE V. HIGGINS

NOVELS

The Friends of Eddie Coyle. New York: Knopf, 1972.
The Digger's Game. New York: Knopf, 1973.
Cogan's Trade. New York: Knopf, 1974.
A City on a Hill. New York: Knopf, 1975.
The Judgment of Deke Hunter. Boston: Little, Brown, 1976.
Dreamland. Boston: Little, Brown, 1977.
A Year or So with Edgar. New York: Harper & Row, 1979.
Kennedy for the Defense. New York: Knopf, 1980.
The Rat on Fire. New York: Knopf, 1981.
The Patriot Game. New York: Knopf, 1982.
A Choice of Enemies. New York: Knopf, 1984.
Penance for Jerry Kennedy. New York: Knopf, 1985.
Impostors. New York: Holt, 1986.
Outlaws. New York: Holt, 1987.
The Sins of Their Father. London: Deutsch, 1988.
Wonderful Years, Wonderful Years. New York: Holt, 1988.
Trust. New York: Holt, 1989.
Victories. New York: Holt, 1990.
The Mandeville Talent. New York: Holt, 1991.
Defending Billy Ryan. New York: Holt, 1992.
Bomber's Law. New York: Holt, 1993.
Swan Boats at Four, New York: Holt, 1995.
Sandra Nichols Found Dead. New York: Holt, 1996.
A Change of Gravity. New York: Holt, 1997.
The Agent. San Diego: Harcourt Brace, forthcoming.

SHORT STORIES

"Mass in Time of War." *Cimarron Review,* September 1969.
"Dillon Explained That He Was Frightened." *North American Review* 255 (fall 1970): 42–44.
"The Habits of the Animals, the Progress of the Seasons." *North American Review* 256 (winter 1971): 56–58. Repr. in *The Best American Short Stories 1973.* Edited by Martha Foley. Boston: Houghton, Mifflin, 1973.
"Two Cautionary Tales: 'Donnelly's Uncle' and 'The Original Water Course.'" *North American Review* 258 (winter 1974): 40–43.
"A Place of Comfort, Light, and Hope." *North American Review* 262 (spring 1977): 35–37.
"Warm for September." *North American Review* 262 (spring 1977): 31–34.
"Adults." *Playboy,* December 1982: 146.
"All Day Was All There Was." *Arizona Quarterly* 19 (spring 1983): 23–36.
"Devlin's Wake." *Playboy,* December 1983: 126 et seq.
"Ducks and Other Citizens." *Hudson Review* 36 (1984): 677–687.
"Mother's Day." *Playboy,* March 1985: 84 et seq.
"The Balance of the Day." *Gentleman's Quarterly,* November 1985: 262.
"The Devil Is Real." *Playboy,* March 1986: 58 et seq.
"Sins of the Fathers." *New Black Mask Quarterly* 4 (1986): 50–59.
"Intentional Pass." *Playboy,* April 1987: 88.
"A Small Matter of Consumer Protection." *Playboy,* May 1988: 112.
"Landmark Theater May Shut Down." *North American Review* 282 (March 1997).

NONFICTION

The Friends of Richard Nixon. Boston: Little, Brown, 1975.
Style Versus Substance: Boston, Kevin White, and the Politics of Illusion. New York: Macmillan, 1985.
The Progress of the Seasons: Forty Years of Baseball in Our Town. New York: Holt, 1989.
On Writing: Advice for Those Who Write to Publish (or Would Like To). New York: Holt, 1990.

ARTICLES

"Old Pro Keeps Grip in Bay State." *Providence Journal,* 9 February 1963.
"Witness: Something of a Memoir." *Massachusetts Review* 10 (summer 1969): 596–602.
"The Private Eye as Illegal Hero: How Philip Marlowe Got to Be Dirty Harry." *Esquire* 78 (1972): 348, 350–351.

"The Friends of Richard Nixon." *Atlantic,* November 1974: 40–52.
"Professor Richardson et al.: A New England Education." *New England Journal of Public Policy* (summer/fall 1985).
"A Letter to the Copy Editor." *Sewanee Review* 104 (summer 1996): 433.

INTERVIEWS

George V. Higgins: A Documentary. Hosted by Melvyn Bragg. The South Bank Show, London Weekend Television, n.d.
Interview with Terry Gross. National Public Radio, Philadelphia, Pa.: 11 November 1986.

BIOGRAPHICAL AND CRITICAL STUDIES

Adams, Phoebe Lou. "Review of *On Writing.*" *Atlantic,* July 1989.
Anderson, Roger. "Devouring Higgins' Novel Should Leave You Satisfied." *Houston Chronicle,* 6 December 1992.
Boot, Max. "Police-Beat Writer Spins City Tales." *Christian Science Monitor,* 11 December 1992: 12–13.
Campbell, Robert, "A Perfect Sales Pitch." *Washington Post,* 22 October 1989.
Connelly, Sherryl, "The Best of Crimes." *Daily News,* 18 October 1992.
Doyle, Brian. "My Lunch with George." *Boston College Magazine* 50 (spring 1991): 27–45.
Dretzka, Gary. "The Crimes of Their Lives." *Chicago Tribune,* 20 September 1987.
Dunne, John Gregory. "Hearing Voice." *Esquire,* May 1977: 25–28.
Dyer, Richard. "Gee George Higgins Is Good. . . ." *Boston Globe,* 3 November 1989.
Ford, Erwin H. "Expiation Ritual in the Crime Novels of George V. Higgins." Ph.D. diss., SUNY Buffalo, 1988.
———. "Higgins' Trades." *Buffalo News,* 24 January 1988: E-1.
Galligan, Edward L. "Getting It Right: The Novels of George V. Higgins." *Sewanee Review,* spring 1982.
Gowrie, Grey. "Profanity Behind the Tea Parties." *London Daily Telegraph,* 12 November 1989: 18.
Hayes, Michael J. "Very nearly GVH: Savoring the Texts of George V. Higgins." In *American Crime Fiction: Studies in the Genre.* Edited by Brian Docherty. New York: St. Martin's Press, 1988. Pp. 115–130.
Jacoby, Susan. "Of Love and Loyalty Among Boston's Irish." *Newsday,* 3 October 1989.
Jones, Malcolm, Jr. "Our Most Underrated Writer." *Newsweek,* 13 December 1993: 62.
Kaminsky, Stuart M. "A True George Higgins Hero, Trapped in a Shadowy World." *Chicago Tribune,* 11 December 1988.
Kelly, Ed. "Higgins' 'Trust' Is a Feast of Talk." *Buffalo News,* 14 January 1990.
Krogh, Thomas, and Isak Rogde. "Higgins' Bransje." *Samtiden: Tidsskrift for Politik, Litteratur og Samfunnssporsmal* 93, no. 5 (1984): 68–70.
Levanston, E. A. "The Literary Dialect of George V. Higgins' *The Judgment of Deke Hunter.*" *English Studies* 62 (August 1981): 358–370.
Lisheron, Mark. "The 40,000 Friends of George Higgins." *Milwaukee Journal,* 15 September 1992: 1–2.
Lochte, Dick. "The Talk of the Boston Irish." *Los Angeles Times,* 1 January 1989.
Matthews, Christopher. "The Other National Pastime." *New York Times Book Review,* 24 February 1991.
McCaffrey, Lawrence. *Textures of Irish America.* Syracuse, N.Y.: Syracuse University Press, 1992.
Nolan, Tom. "High Crimes and Misdemeanors." *Wall Street Journal,* 30 June 1995.
———. "Up Against the Law." *Wall Street Journal,* 22 September 1992.
O'Briant, Don. "Dialogue with a Novel Difference." *Atlanta Journal Constitution,* 16 December 1990.
O'Hara, J. D. "Review of *Cogan's Trade,* by George V. Higgins." *New Republic,* 30 March 1974: 26–27.
Prescott, Peter. "Talking Shop in the Mob." *Newsweek,* 25 March 1974: 99.
Richardson, Elliot Lee. *The Creative Balance: Government, Politics, and the Individual in America's Third Century.* New York: Holt, Rinehart, and Winston, 1976.
Shragg, Peter. "The Long Arc of Years." *Nation,* 21 August 1989.
Skow, John. "The Man with the Golden Ear." *Time,* 26 November 1990.
———. "Solve It Again, Sam." *Time,* 15 November 1993.
Sokolov, Raymond. "Mystery in Berlin and Boston." *Wall Street Journal,* 20 December 1988.
———. "Two Class Acts." *Wall Street Journal,* 26 December 1989.
Symons, Julian. "Number One with a Bullet." *Washington Post Book World,* 23 August 1987.
Vesterman, William. "Higgins's Trade." *Language and Style* 20, no. 3 (summer 1987): 223–229.
Walker, Walter. "Something's Rotten in the State of Massachusetts." *Washington Post Book World,* 2 October 1988.
Wolitzer, Hilma. "A Jailbird's Scheme." *New York Times,* 21 January 1990.

Patricia Highsmith
(1921–1995)

NOEL DORMAN MAWER

PATRICIA HIGHSMITH, an only child, was born Mary Patricia Plangman on 19 January 1921, in Fort Worth, Texas. Her parents, Jay Bernard Plangman and Mary Coates Plangman, both commercial artists, separated before her birth and divorced soon thereafter. Three years later, her mother married Stanley Highsmith, who adopted Patricia. For much of her early life Highsmith was cared for by her maternal grandmother, whom she loved, but her memories of these years were not pleasant, because of the perpetual strife between her mother and stepfather. Patricia Highsmith disliked her mother and did not see her at all during the last twenty years of her mother's life. When Highsmith was six, the family moved to New York City. In 1942 she graduated from Barnard College, where she had edited the college literary magazine. After graduation she supported herself by writing scenarios for comic books and television scripts for Alfred Hitchcock. Highsmith took extended trips to Mexico and Europe during the ensuing years, and finally settled for good in Europe in 1962. She died in a Swiss hospital on 4 February 1995. Although Russell Harrison gives a combination of lung cancer and aplastic anemia as the cause of death, other sources give leukemia, and it is interesting to note that a character in Highsmith's *Ripley's Game* (1974) has a curious kind of leukemia that goes into remission for years.

Early Period

Patricia Highsmith's early novels include her most famous and acclaimed works and illustrate her beliefs, as she described them in a 1981 interview in the journal *The Armchair Detective,* that murder is either the product of anger or of mental derangement, and that there is "something in" the bad-seed theory: "I happen to believe more in heredity than I do in environment," she told Diana Cooper-Clark (pp. 314–317). By 1981 Highsmith had broadened her view to include, even to emphasize, social and cultural influences on behavior, but the views quoted here dominate her early novels.

After six rejections of her first novel, Highsmith took advantage in 1948 of a stay arranged for her by Truman Capote at the writer's colony at Yaddo, near Saratoga. (Capote's 1965 true-crime novel *In Cold Blood* portrays of a pair of sociopathic killers whose relationship suggests the pairings of "mismatched friends" portrayed by Highsmith in her early works.) The revised manuscript was published in 1950 as *Strangers on a Train,* and the novel remains Highsmith's best-known work, thanks largely to Alfred Hitchcock's 1951 film version. The familiar plot, in which two strangers agree to commit murders for each other, has also been filmed in 1969 by Robert Sparr as *Once You Kiss a Stranger,* where the two men become a man and a woman; in 1996 by Tommy Lee Wallace as *Once You Meet a Stranger,* where all roles are gender reversed; and in 1987 by Danny DeVito in the parodic *Throw Momma from the Train.*

The novel illustrates Highsmith's obsession with a theme that she describes in her 1966 how-to book, *Plotting and Writing Suspense Fiction,* as "the relationship between two men, usually quite different in makeup, sometimes obviously the good and evil, sometimes merely ill-matched friends" (p. 145): here, as in later works, the apparently "ill-matched" men nonetheless seem, to other characters as well as to the reader, to have an erotic attachment. This first novel also illustrates Highsmith's characteristic use of a dual point of view, here alternating between the two protagonists, Charles Bruno and Guy Haines.

Like Henry James, Highsmith never uses first-person narration. She prefers a limited third-person omniscience, as she says in *Plotting,* because third-person narration gives the reader less opportunity to see what "nasty schemers" her characters are (p. 81). Highsmith's deliberate use of point of view to obscure her characters' motives has elicited much critical censure. Without James's authorial commentary, the reader is often left confused: Is the protagonist deliberately deceptive, or only deceiving himself? Is Highsmith emulating Agatha Christie's duplicitous narrator in *The Murder of Roger Ackroyd,* or perhaps one of the protagonists of John Franklin Bardin (whom Highsmith reviewed for the *Times Literary Supplement* in 1976), who are in doubt of their own sanity? In her first two novels characters compare themselves to Dostoyevsky's Raskolnikov, suggesting self-deception rather than villainy.

The two protagonists of *Strangers* share a family pattern that resonates throughout Highsmith's work and, indeed, echoes her own familial experience. In Highsmith's paradigm there is an authoritarian father (or, more often, a father figure, of either gender) and a weak, overindulgent, often fanatically religious mother. One or both parents are frequently absent, their places taken by one or more relatives. In *Strangers,* Bruno has the authoritarian father and overindulgent mother, while Guy has the absent father and religious mother. Both protagonists seek figures to replace the unwanted or missing parent. Bruno seeks to supplant his hated real father by having a kinder, more appealing father figure (Guy) kill the father and take his place in Bruno's life. Guy, on the other hand, seeks both a father figure and a stronger, more worldly version of his mother (to replace his first wife, who has much in common with Bruno).

Bruno, the sociopath, attempts to arrange the murders of the inconvenient wife and father. In his crusade to convince Guy to fulfill his part of the bargain, Bruno is clearly ill-matched with Guy, but Highsmith reveals the truth beneath the paradigm: such pairs are two sides of the same person, the two sides which Highsmith illustrates in virtually all her fiction. These sides are variously labeled civilized and primitive, good and bad, light and dark, overcontrolled and impulsive. Each member of the pair is attracted to the repressed or unrealized self that he sees in the other. Bruno thinks of himself and Guy as two supermen, equal in their superiority; Guy's strongest wish is to deny kinship with the "lesser" side of himself, yet time after time he identifies with Bruno.

Bruno's murder of Guy's wife finally wears down the initially horrified Guy, and Guy completes the bargain by killing Bruno's father. Then, prompted by the internalized religion of his mother, Guy actively embraces punishment. He is now aware of the primitive, the Bruno, within himself, but sees no way to integrate this with his idealism. His only solution is to give himself over to the retribution of his mother's god, as embodied in the legal system.

After the success of *Strangers,* Highsmith turned to another project: a lesbian novel, which she published in 1952 under the pseudonym Claire Morgan. (Highsmith did not openly acknowledge writing the novel until 1990, when it was published in the United

Kingdom as *Carol;* a U.S. edition bearing Highsmith's real name, but retaining the original title, appeared in 1991.) *The Price of Salt* is not a crime novel, but rather a suspenseful romance, in which two women, after various difficulties, find happiness together (and are depicted in what are Highsmith's only love scenes). The book was groundbreaking in 1952, having, as Highsmith noted in her afterword to the 1991 edition, perhaps the first happy ending in the genre. The positive portrait of two psychologically normal people who find love and apparently live happily ever after was never repeated in Highsmith's work, which otherwise portrays a world of ill-matched couples, not only of men, but frequently of men and women. *The Price of Salt* is also her last novel until *Edith's Diary* (1977) to focus on a woman character.

Highsmith's 1954 *The Blunderer* (also published as *Lament for a Lover,* 1956) reverts explicitly to the ill-matched friends pattern by having one of the two major characters, Walter Stackhouse, keep a notebook illustrating his conception of "unworthy friends," mismatched, symbiotic pairs. The masochistic Stackhouse is embroiled in a marriage with a sadistic woman whom he fantasizes about murdering. He takes his inspiration from a newspaper clipping describing a man, Melchior Kimmel, who apparently murdered his wife and got away with it. Stackhouse's wife, however, commits suicide by jumping from a cliff, so that Stackhouse appears to have killed her.

Kimmel, this novel's sociopath, does not understand why Stackhouse is drawn to him. He engages in a protracted struggle with Stackhouse, who, more like Guy Haines than like Bruno, has identified with the Kimmel side of himself, but has attained no resolution of his two sides, and seems to welcome the death he suffers at Kimmel's hands. The first of several Eastern Europeans Highsmith depicts, Kimmel is a refugee from fascism and has little understanding of his own sadomasochistic urges. He abjectly accepts the punishment he is about to receive for killing Stackhouse, yet never identifies with him.

In 1955 Highsmith took an extended trip to Mexico and during that trip wrote the first of a series of five novels about a charming sociopath, Tom Ripley. The popularity of this character in Europe is suggested by the number of Ripley novels made into films by René Clément, Wim Wenders, Claude Autant-Lara, Claude Chabrol, and Claude Miller. Highsmith herself expressed great fondness for Ripley, even suggesting that Ripley was doing the writing for her. In all the Ripley novels Highsmith confines the point of view chiefly to Ripley, promoting the reader's identification with Ripley and leaving herself open to the charge of immorality. In a 1957 *Times Literary Supplement* review of *The Talented Mr. Ripley* (1955), the anonymous reviewer compared Ripley to André Gide's Lafcadio in *Les Caves du Vatican* (1914), a comparison set forth again by Anthony Hilfer in 1984. This particular Gide novel attained notoriety in 1961 with the publication of Wayne Booth's *The Rhetoric of Fiction* (1961), in which Booth condemns Gide's apparent approval of immorality as indicated by his luring the reader into identification with Lafcadio. Marghanita Laski and others point to Highsmith's narrative practice, just as Booth might, as an example of authorial immorality. Highsmith herself equivocates: while condemning murder generally, Highsmith, in a 1982 television interview, asserted that Ripley is "neither good nor bad"—that he usually "kills when he absolutely has to and kills reluctantly."

In his first incarnation, Ripley is an orphan who was raised by an authoritarian aunt who humiliated him and bound her to him with meager handouts. As is the norm in Highsmith's works, Ripley escaped this reality first by creating a fantasy world. He then projects his fantasies onto an expatriate American acquaintance, Dickie Greenleaf, when he is sent by Dickie's parents to retrieve their son from Italy. Not only does Ripley fail to bring Dickie home, he falls under the spell of his fantasy of becoming Dickie's soulmate and sharing the apparent glamour of Dickie's life of wealth. Dickie, however, fails to respond, and Ripley, in the anguish of rejection, drowns

Dickie, and then takes his money, clothes, possessions, and name. In his self-contempt, Ripley has already acquired Dickie's voice, mannerisms, and interests, through imitation. In "becoming" Dickie, Ripley takes on not only Dickie's personality, but also his self-assurance, and he is so aware of the duality he has created that he can separate Ripley's guilt from "Dickie's." Convinced of his innocence, Ripley as Dickie finally evades detection completely.

When this novel was filmed by René Clément (as *Purple Noon,* 1961), the French director rearranged the story so that Ripley was caught. But Highsmith preferred to leave Ripley free to reappear in later novels. These later novels show Ripley, no longer dependent on being "Dickie," married, living in France, and thriving as the mastermind behind various confidence games. In *Ripley Under Ground* (1970) Ripley both masquerades as a dead painter and kills an art collector, to protect an art-forgery scheme. In *Ripley's Game* (1974, filmed in 1977 by the German director Wim Wenders as *The American Friend*), Ripley revenges himself upon a man who has slighted him by exploiting that man's illness, leukemia. He convinces the man that, to provide for his family after his death, he must accept Ripley's offer of money in return for helping Ripley kill some mafiosi.

The final Ripley novels, *The Boy Who Followed Ripley* (1980) and *Ripley Under Water* (1991), continue the pattern of crime and no punishment, although Ripley seems less and less a criminal and more a vigilante, a defender of the innocent or of himself from others more unbalanced than he. *Ripley Under Water* was the last novel published by Highsmith before her death, and confirmed her 1982 prediction in the television interview "Profile of a Writer" that Ripley would never be caught. She also asserted that, for Ripley as for herself, the "sanctity of life" was "just a mental attitude."

The Talented Mr. Ripley was followed by a return to the sadomasochistic marriage theme. In *Deep Water* (1957) Victor Van Allen, another son of an authoritarian father, has made an ill-matched marriage: while he is rich and intellectual, his wife, Melinda, is neither. Melinda, humiliated by Victor and his friends, retaliates by engaging in a string of affairs with men for whom Victor has nothing but contempt: by his standards, they are crude and uneducated. As Melinda increasingly flaunts these relationships, Victor's pose of amused indifference becomes strained. Highsmith, who is sparing in her use of symbols, here uses the image of trees blowing in a storm, an image Victor associates with his father's scorn for his weakness, to signal Victor's increasingly tenuous hold not only on his emotions, but also on his sanity. After killing more than one of Melinda's boyfriends, Victor finally disintegrates. In a frenzy he kills Melinda and seems virtually unaware of what is actually happening when the police take him away.

Transitional Period

In her next work, Highsmith begins to turn from an exclusive focus on psychopathology toward an examination of relatively normal human beings, initiating a gradual movement from a psychological to a more sociocultural perspective. *A Game for the Living* (1958) is her only whodunit. In it the use of an unreliable narrative consciousness not only maintains the mystery until the very end but also allows the protagonist, as in earlier works, to reveal more about himself than about anyone else. Set in Mexico, the novel takes the point of view of a naturalized German Mexican, Theodore Schiebelhut, more an observer than a participant in the action, and an outsider in the society as well. Theodore's misinterpretations of native Mexicans and their culture render him no more privy than the reader to the actual occurrences surrounding the murder and lead him to the wrong conclusion about who committed the murder. Theodore is not mentally unbalanced, but simply lacking in self-knowledge. In using the consciousness of a European in a third-world society,

Highsmith may lead most of her (presumably first-world) readers to trust Theodore's perceptions, which are revealed as a tissue of stereotypes and misapplied cultural norms. Theodore sees himself as the overcontrolled, rational ("civilized") German, and his friend Ramon Otero, whom he believes guilty of the murder, as the typical impulsive, superstitious ("primitive") Mexican Catholic.

Through his interactions with Ramon, Theodore discovers his own emotionality and irrationality. Ramon is in no way responsible for the murder, yet he blames himself and even confesses to the murder. The Mexican police and a psychiatrist, familiar with this pattern of behavior, realize that Ramon is simply trying to atone for having had an affair with the victim and that this reaction is common in a culture and religion where a sense of guilt is ubiquitous.

Two major changes occur in Highsmith's familiar pattern: Ramon and Theodore, neither of whom is mentally unbalanced, gain understanding of themselves and each other. Theodore has some similarities to Ripley, but the contrast is more telling: Theodore can think of murdering while never seriously considering it; and Theodore is a genuine artist, not the dilettante that Ripley is. Although Theodore may see himself as an awkward outsider, he never goes to the extremes, either of self-loathing or of grandiosity, that Ripley does. In addition, Theodore's relationship to Ramon is based on fondness and curiosity; in no way is it symbiotic or sadomasochistic. The relationship between the two men is mutually beneficial: they learn from one another.

Theodore's learning process introduces the second major innovation in this work: increasing self-questioning of one's own cultural biases and their effect on one's perceptions. Ramon, who is a professor, is not primitive; the policeman who sees through Ramon's confession is not the stupid and brutal functionary that Theodore expects, but rather a humane and enlightened man who not only sees that Ramon is innocent but also sends him to a psychiatrist rather than to jail. This policeman also is a superior detective who finds the real murderer (a friend of Theodore and Ramon's whose role in the story is largely peripheral) relying on reason rather than on emotion—unlike the "rational" Theodore, whose emotions convince him that the distraught Ramon must be guilty.

A Game for the Living is not a model whodunit—we are given no clues that would enable us to solve the crime, and by the last pages we are so caught up in the development of Theodore and Ramon that the mystery is forgotten. Nor is it a typical ill-matched-friends story: the characters reach a better understanding of themselves and each other and come to appreciate both their differences and similarities. No longer is Highsmith confining herself to the mutually destructive effects of complementary pathologies, but rather is portraying the mutual misunderstandings of two essentially rational, humane people who have contrasting cultural backgrounds. Theodore's introspection and self-questioning enable him to see how cultural differences affect the behavior and perceptions of both himself and Ramon. This development away from psychopathology and toward the exploration of cultural influences becomes dominant in Highsmith's later works.

Highsmith's next two novels, *This Sweet Sickness* (1960) and *The Cry of the Owl* (1962) are both set in rural towns in the United States. The novels were written during a period when Highsmith made a number of trips to Europe, and just before she settled there permanently. Both novels initiate the development of her portrait of Americans functioning in groups—a phenomenon which seems to allow individuals to indulge their buried sadism and primitivism.

This Sweet Sickness reprises the "mentally unbalanced son of authoritarian father figures" (aunt and uncle). Like Victor in *Deep Water,* David Kelsey is both eager for approval and contemptuous of most people, whom he considers his inferiors. Overcontrolled and isolated, he constructs a fantasy world to inhabit: his former sweetheart will leave her husband and child, marry David, and live in the house he is literally constructing for her.

David has idealized the ordinary Annabelle and convinced himself that she will come to him as soon as she can escape her husband. No amount of rejection on Annabelle's part makes any impression on David.

As with Victor, in the face of perpetual rejection and humiliation David's stoicism eventually begins to disintegrate. As David descends into a psychosis, his fantasies become virtual hallucinations. After having been implicated in two deaths, David flees from the police to New York City, where he lives a fantasy life with an imagined Anabelle, conversing with her even in public. When his capture is imminent, David, aware at least that he is trapped, jumps from a window ledge toward a figure that "could be Annabelle" (p. 249). Beneath him, in the minutes preceding his suicide, a heckling mob—Americans in a group—urges David to jump.

In *This Sweet Sickness,* as in *Deep Water,* confining the point of view to a single character serves to obscure that character's pathology, at least for a time. Both David and Victor seem initially to be credible and reliable. In *The Cry of the Owl,* Highsmith varies this pattern: the sane one of her two male protagonists, Robert Forester, leads us to believe that he must be unbalanced: we first encounter him as a Peeping Tom, apparently compulsively drawn to one particular woman. But Forester, though he is depressed, is one of the new breed of Highsmith characters whose involvements with the truly unhinged lead them, however painfully, to self-knowledge. We belatedly learn that the other characters Forester is involved with are all either sociopaths or psychotics. With the sadomasochism, addiction, and mob violence that infest the rest of the novel, Highsmith sets the tone for her portrayal of American society in the 1970s and 1980s.

Forester's voyeurism is actually a temporary reaction to a marital breakup and its attendant depression. In peeping, Forester feels he is in touch with normal people who have normal relationships. His chief weakness seems to be lack of judgment: the son of an alcoholic himself, he married a sadistic alcoholic, and he becomes involved with the unbalanced and the sociopathic. What seemed ideal looking in from the outside turns out to be something quite else. Jenny, the girl in the window, becomes pathologically attached to Forester, who does not have the will to end the relationship. By the time Forester becomes aware of his errors in judgment and extricates himself from Jenny, her boyfriend Greg has joined with Forester's wife, Nickie, in an alcohol-soaked plot to destroy Forester. The plot backfires, Greg kills Nickie, and Forester is now aware enough to save himself from implication in her death. Forester also suffers the condemnation and overt attack of a mob that perceives him as a voyeur and murderer. Highsmith here presents the civilized-primitive dichotomy through the contrast of the injudicious but kindly and reasonable Forester with the vengeful and irrational mob, which Highsmith develops much more fully than she had the crowd that taunts David in *That Sweet Sickness.*

In her next novel, Highsmith revisits Greece, reprising the ill-matched-friends theme to develop even further the character who gains insight from his encounter with his opposite and uses that insight to remake his life. The protagonist of *The Two Faces of January* (1964) never commits any crime (though he had been punished as a youth for an alleged rape), but engages in a journey through experiences that will prove overwhelmingly beneficial to him. Crime becomes increasingly peripheral in Highsmith's works; in *The Two Faces of January* the story's criminal element is embodied in a con man, Chester McFarland, whom Rydal Keener meets in Greece. To Rydal, Chester is the reincarnation of his recently deceased authoritarian father (whose funeral he refused to attend), and Rydal will alternately pursue and be pursued by Chester. Rydal is obsessed with the shame and humiliation which continue to be inflicted on him by his internalized father. Objectifying that internalized father in Chester and then interacting with that now demythologized human being gives Rydal the opportunity to relive his formative experiences with new insight and detachment. Rydal is even aware when he switches roles—playing the contemptuous father to Chester's humiliated son—and thereby experiences the revenge he had wished to inflict on his actual father.

While these things are happening, Rydal works out his insights in a journal, finally confronting and expelling his demons and freeing himself from the past. Highsmith's protagonist transcends family and personal pathology through the medium of his "other" self, the objectified, internalized father. As Rydal sees himself take on his father's characteristics with Chester, enlightenment comes. Rydal sees and accepts his own authoritarianism, so like that he had despised in his father. Highsmith, too, seems to have exorcised the ill-matched-friends theme, which plays less and less a role in her fiction.

Mature Period

In the novels of her next period, Highsmith seems to lose all interest in psychopathology, focusing almost exclusively on the psychology of normal individuals as they react to social and cultural phenomena. *The Glass Cell* (1964), is the work which she analyzes at length in *Plotting and Writing Suspense Fiction.* As in *Game for the Living,* where she elevates the setting—Mexico and its culture—to a place of prominence, in *The Glass Cell* the dominant setting, a prison, is a determinant of behavior and attitudes that eclipses familial and other influences. In *Plotting,* Highsmith asserts that her purpose in *The Glass Cell* was to "show the deleterious effect of exposure to brutality in prison, and how this can lead to antisocial behavior after release" (pp. 104–105). In attempting to show the dominance of cultural influences in determining behavior, Highsmith again uses, as in *Game for the Living,* a "normal" protagonist. Here, however, her protagonist both lacks insight and is subject to malignant cultural influences. Hence he moves from ignorance not to self-knowledge, but rather to cynicism, the unreflecting person's "realism." That cynicism enables the protagonist to survive, as Ripley's belief in his own innocence ensures his survival. Highsmith's early portrayals of guilt and innocence anticipate the relativism that becomes the dominant theme in later works.

The protagonist of *The Glass Cell,* Philip Carter, is an engineer on a construction project who becomes an unwitting accomplice in his employer's scheme to overcharge for building materials. Carter, whose only crime, says Highsmith in *Plotting,* is being "overtrustful" (p. 105), is found guilty by a jury that assumes that anyone who participates in an illegal scheme must do so knowingly. Highsmith suggests that such cynicism and corruption are endemic in the American society in which this work is set. Carter thinks of himself as irresponsible, a judgment which his highly critical aunt and uncle who raised him have often made and he has accepted. Though his view alters, his insight does not. He merely replaces one superficial view with another, seeing himself progressing from naïveté to his cynical version of realism.

Carter is no criminal, nor is he a sociopath or psychotic. Highsmith seems to see Carter much as she sees the later Ripley: he becomes a criminal, but only in response to the real criminals of this world. The prison, seen only through Carter's eyes, is a Kafkaesque world where the innocent are punished for breaking laws of which they never have been told, and the most corrupt are rewarded. Philip breaks a rule by trying to help a fellow prisoner who, like his former employer, has set him up. His punishment is to be consigned to a Poe-like dungeon—dark, bare, metal-walled—and then to be hung by his thumbs until they are permanently dislocated. Philip is left crippled and in intractable pain—an easy prey to morphine addiction.

Prison has a single redeeming factor for Philip: there he meets Max, a soulmate who also was led to prison through bad luck and naïveté. However, Philip's growing friendship with Max is cut off when Max is killed in a prison riot. At this point Philip commits his first real crime, murdering the man who may have caused Max's death, and he abandons all faith in humanity: no one is to be trusted, not even his wife, upon whom he is dependent.

When he gets out of prison, Philip discovers that his wife has been having an affair. This does not affect his dependence on her or his need to preserve the marriage, but it helps confirm his conviction that the whole world operates by an ethic of corruption and betrayal. He accepts his addictions to his wife and to morphine, and accepts that he can now commit any crime, including the murder of his wife's lover. He lies so convincingly that he is not arrested for the murder and concludes that, where his ignorance sent him to prison, his "realism"—cynicism—will enable him to survive.

Carter learns to survive in a corrupt society by himself becoming corrupt. In *A Suspension of Mercy* (1965; U.S. title *The Story-Teller*), the protagonist learns the same lesson. Sydney Bartleby is the writer of a successful television adventure show, *The Whip,* the titular hero of which is very like Tom Ripley: the Whip is a successful (probably sociopathic) criminal who is never caught. Sydney is himself a would-be Ripley, if only in fantasy, and he uses the opportunity offered by his wife's leaving him to imagine—and write about in his journal—murdering her. He goes so far as to act out the murder, removing the imaginary body from the house in a real rolled-up rug and burying it in the woods. When his wife fails to return and is finally classified as missing, Sydney's diary becomes evidence used by the police to accuse Sydney of her murder.

Alicia, Sydney's wife, has in fact simply gone off with a boyfriend, and, as her absence and affair have become protracted, she has become ashamed to come home. In a drunken escapade she falls from a cliff—or is pushed by her boyfriend. When her death is discovered, Sydney, now addicted to seeing his own actions as fodder for the exploits of the Whip, kills Alicia's boyfriend. Then he discovers that he feels no guilt for this murder and is, like the Whip, thereby insulated from punishment.

In *A Suspension of Mercy,* Highsmith again risks censure by giving the predominant point of view to a charming villain, and one who finally apparently becomes invulnerable. She also moves into a new mode of character development, one which parallels and extends the ill-matched-friends pattern. Here, and in later works, the protagonist creates his own alternative self in writing. He then proceeds to change in response to what he has written, in this case to become more like the Whip. Later works offer variations on this method.

Those Who Walk Away (1967) is little more than a repetition of earlier themes and situations. The setting, Italy, is the scene of Ripley's early escapades, suggesting that this story belongs to an earlier period in Highsmith's career. This is again the tale of two men, this time a young man and his former father-in-law, who alternate as pursuer and pursued. The young man, whose wife has committed suicide, feels guilty and seems to invite punishment. The father-in-law, who perhaps bears some responsibility for his daughter's death, not only feels innocent, but also blames his son-in-law. The novel is a series of chase scenes and murder attempts, culminating in the father-in-law's attempted murder of his son-in-law. Nobody dies, everybody goes free, and the novel ends with little learned or resolved.

Two years later, in *The Tremor of Forgery* (1969), Highsmith makes another leap forward in her development. As in *A Suspension of Mercy,* the protagonist, Howard Ingham, is a writer of fiction who creates another self in a novel, but rather than simply modeling himself after the character in the novel, as Sydney does, Ingham initially sees his fictional character as bearing no relation to himself—the character is just a self-deluding, flawed, and foolish man. However, as Ingham develops new insights and behaviors through his contact with the alien North African culture, his fictional creation mirrors his changing views.

As Rydal Keener in *The Two Faces of January* was able to acquire a new understanding of himself and his dead father through his contact with a father figure, so Ingham comes to a new understanding of himself and his culture through the experience of living in Tunisia. The novel's cast includes two other Americans, who are offered in contrast to Ingham: Francis Adams, a right-wing fundamentalist superpatriot; and Ina Pallant, Ingham's fiancée, initially an open-minded liberal, like Ingham himself.

Adams, Highsmith's paradigm of ignorance and intolerance, is impervious to anything but the differences between his values and lifestyle and those of the foreign, hence inferior, culture. Ina, on the other hand, comes to North Africa ready to open herself to the new culture, and initially takes an adversarial position with Adams on such issues as the Vietnam War. However, as both the alien culture and Ingham's changing attitudes and behavior remain incomprehensible to her, Ina begins to seek out Adams, to talk of the American way, and even to attend a Christian church—not her usual practice.

Ingham, too, is at first disoriented by the unfamiliarity of Tunisian society and tries to fit what he encounters into the stereotypes he brings with him. When he thinks he may have fatally injured an intruder, he is at first sure that he should go to the police. As his concern over the incident fades, Ingham finds himself seeing his actions with the fatalistic perception of a native Tunisian. As this change is occurring Ingham sees himself more and more at odds with Adams and Ina, and more in accord with Anders Jensen, a gay painter who lives among the Tunisians and who can see both their differences and their humanity.

As Ingham moves toward this new understanding of himself and the world, he also returns to thoughts of his former wife, Lotte, who once seemed to him inferior to the cultivated Ina, but who was much more attuned to him emotionally. What had once seemed of lesser importance to Ingham now becomes just one of several equally indispensable parts of himself. As Rydal Keener's new awareness enables him to accept the father in himself, so Ingham now can accept both the Lotte and the Ina ("primitive" and "civilized") as essential aspects of being human. And seeing what the rejection of an essential part of themselves has done to Adams and Ina, Ingham finally feels compassion for them, as he returns to his own world ready to seek out Lotte and to rewrite his novel.

Return to America

Though Highsmith was still living in Europe in 1970, she was increasingly concerned about the apparent deterioration of American society. In addition to writing two more Ripley novels during this period, Highsmith also produced her most horrifying portrait yet of American urban culture in *A Dog's Ransom* (1972). Here New York City has become a vision of hell, crawling with raving street people, drug- and alcohol-crazed muggers and murderers, and resurrections of some of her most appalling character types from earlier works: a naive, masochistic protagonist who disintegrates under the pressure of sadistic villains—another Eastern European and a policeman—and who is abandoned by both his idealized girlfriend and a father figure who is himself unable to reconcile his own warring selves. Here the cast and setting of *The Blunderer* are juggled, with the well-meaning but inept protagonist, the policeman Clarence Duhamell, being attracted not to the Eastern European sadist but rather to the rejecting father figure.

Duhamell meets Ed Reynolds (whose daughter has recently been murdered) and his refugee wife, Greta, after their beloved dog has been stolen. Duhamell dedicates himself to finding the dog, becoming more and more obsessed with this task as he becomes increasingly dependent on the approval of Ed, who finds Duhamell oppressive. Ed's response to Duhamell initially echoes that of Guy Haines to Bruno in *Strangers on a Train:* he sees himself in Duhamell (particularly when Duhamell, erupting in fury, kills the dognapper). Yet he ultimately rejects Duhamell and the more emotional, fallible side of himself that Duhamell embodies, preferring to retreat into his familiar cynical, overcontrolled self.

Highsmith's New York is rife not only with vice and violence but also with class and ethnic hatred. Kenneth Rowajinski, the unemployed and disreputable dognapper, despises the Reynolds for their wealth and culture; the sadistic policeman who torments and finally kills Duhamell hates Duhamell because he is a college graduate and seems comfortable with people like the Reynolds. This society, like the prison in *The Glass Cell,* produces anger, violence, and madness. In all of the remaining novels published before her death, Highsmith portrays what seems an obsessional, perhaps partly film- and television-induced, view of America. As Highsmith passes fifty, she seems increasingly fixated on her former homeland, both the New York City she grew up in and the more westerly regions that may recall her native Texas. Indeed, Highsmith's editor at Knopf once described her as "a Texan until the . . . end" (quoted in Peters, p. 150).

In 1977 Highsmith produced what is generally considered her last major work, *Edith's Diary.* After this work her novels, largely condemnations of American society, appeared less frequently. Nonetheless, *Edith's Diary* shows that Highsmith was still developing. Although the short story collection *Little Tales of Misogyny,* first published in England the same year as *Edith's Diary,* is a catalog of vicious stereotypes of women, and although in the 1966 *Plotting and Writing Suspense Fiction* Highsmith asserts that she writes chiefly about men because they are more interesting than women, in *Edith's Diary* Highsmith departs radically from her apparent misogyny, though she still allows some of her most sympathetic characters to make derogatory remarks about both feminism and affirmative action. (The latter concern, however, seems primarily racial, and Highsmith is guilty of such gestures as portraying the only black policeman in *Dog's Ransom* as engaged in reading a comic book.)

The publication of *Edith's Diary* at least partially repaired Highsmith's reputation among feminists. The Edith of the title is Highsmith's first woman protagonist since *The Price of Salt,* and her story is a devastating portrait of a woman in the America of McCarthyism, the Cold War, the Vietnam War, and Watergate. Edith Howland, who is honest and uncompromising, watches as the hypocrisy resulting from the climate of paranoia and megalomaniac colonialism transforms all her friends, most especially her allegedly liberated but essentially patriarchal and authoritarian husband, into agents of the establishment, who finally attempt (unsuccessfully) to silence and tame Edith by having her committed to a mental institution.

As her nation descends into madness and all those around her self-protectively retreat from earlier radical views, Edith appears (largely for her refusal to retreat) to descend into madness. The most persuasive evidence of Edith's madness is her diary, in which she has, in now predictable Highsmith fashion, created an alternate self whose life increasingly diverges from that of the actual Edith. As the life in the diary becomes more and more a fantasy, and as Edith increasingly takes refuge in creating that fantasy, so the reader may be led to believe that Edith is, as many reviewers assume, becoming insane. Other critics, however, see Edith's creation of a fantasy world as very much conscious and controlled, as an attempt to preserve her sanity in the face of an increasingly insane society.

Last Period

In her final years, Highsmith abandoned character development almost entirely, and her novels became virtual tracts for illustrating the social and economic phenomena—capitalism, abortion, street crime, fundamentalism—that Highsmith saw corroding American society. In *The Boy Who Followed Ripley,* Highsmith sends Ripley to an America where unbridled capitalism has become synonymous with crime. In *People Who Knock on the Door* (1983), capitalism, fundamentalist religion, and right-wing politics have become synonymous with hypocrisy and are now ubiquitous, at least in the Midwest portrayed in the novel. Actual criminals have long since been largely peripheral figures in Highsmith's novels, but the society itself makes all its members complicit in its culture of crime—the crimes of violence, greed, oppression, and political irresponsibility.

In *People Who Knock on the Door* (referring to tract-bearing evangelists), that malignant American culture destroys a small-town Indiana family, first by estranging its members from one another, finally by provoking a son, in righteous zeal, to kill his father. When the patriarch of the Alderman family, Richard, becomes a born-again fundamentalist, his intolerance results in his banishing his liberal eldest son, Arthur, who has assisted his girlfriend in aborting their child. When Richard's own adultery is revealed, however, Robbie, the younger son, becomes enraged at his father's hypocrisy and kills him. Robbie is convinced that Richard deserves to die for his sins. Throughout the novel not only Arthur but also various minor characters voice, sometimes quite improbably, Highsmith's views on various social concerns. While Edith held the same views as Arthur and his friends, Edith was a fully developed character. Arthur, however, is perhaps the most wooden and unconvincing of Highsmith's creations, apparently existing primarily to voice the author's opinions.

Found in the Street (1986) is Highsmith's final portrait of New York City, and the atmosphere is unremittingly threatening: random violence, barbaric gangs, and crazy people all menace the few sane inhabitants. Among the many things found in the street by the chief protagonist, Jack Sutherland, is Ralph Linderman, an eccentric misanthrope with a dog named God, who is fixated on a teenaged and apparently naive newcomer to the city, Elsie Tyler, whom Ralph believes he must protect (mostly from men). Jack, too, becomes obsessed with Elsie, but not sexually: it is his wife, Natalia, who becomes Elsie's lover, while the apparently asexual Jack fantasizes giving up his bed to them. The reprise of the sexually ambiguous male figure (who has the familiar oppressive childhood) is accompanied by the introduction of a large number of gay and lesbian characters, the first time such people have taken center stage since *The Price of Salt.* The novel ends with Elsie's murder by a jealous, drug-addicted lesbian. As one of the characters comments, "That's what this city has, what this city does" (p. 267).

Five years later, in 1991, Highsmith published *Ripley Under Water,* the final Ripley adventure, and the last work she published before her death. Ripley, who has become tame and almost virtuous, is pursued by an American who is a greedy, demented version of Ripley himself. Ripley lets the American drown, refusing to rescue him only because he fears for his own life if the American lives. *Small G: A Summer Idyll* (1995), published shortly after Highsmith's death, is a slight tale of intrigue, jealousy, and romance in a "partly gay" (the "small g" of the title refers to the designation in a tourist guidebook) bar in Zurich and is filled with characters, mostly gay or bisexual, who are worlds away from the earnest and desperate protagonists of *The Price of Salt.* In *Small G* the protagonists, a man and a woman, both settle for casual, open relationships. The society of the 1990s (and this is Zurich, not small-town Indiana) has made it so acceptable to indulge in homosexual behavior that sexuality no longer need be the characters' chief preoccupation, as it was in the earlier novel. Here Highsmith portrays characters who are primarily interesting human beings who happen to be homosexual.

Short Stories

Highsmith's seven volumes of short stories offer a broader view of her talents than do the novels. The first, *Eleven* (1970; U.S. title *The Snail-Watcher*), contains stories that were originally published as early as 1945 and, like her later collections of stories, is not primarily concerned with crime. Highsmith performs in a variety of genres, including horror (in two of the stories in *Eleven* characters are killed by snails, anticipating *The Animal Lover's Book of Beastly Murder* [1975], in which animals revenge themselves upon oppressive humans); fantasy–science fiction (in "The Empty Birdhouse" an imaginary creature, a "yuma," moves in with a couple); symbiotic, sadomasochistic relationships (two old women, longtime companions, endlessly torment one another, but cannot break the bond that ties them together); and character development (or the lack of it) along the lines of her novels.

The theme of fantasies taking over one's life, as in *This Sweet Sickness*, is a persistent theme, from *Eleven*'s "The Heroine" (Highsmith's first published story, which appeared in *Harper's Bazaar* in 1945), in which a young servant's fantasy of saving the family she works for becomes so obsessive that the young woman burns down her employers' house in order to have the opportunity to rescue them; to "The Romantic" in *Mermaids on the Golf Course* (1985), where a young woman prefers imaginary lovers to the men she actually meets, to the point of avoiding real encounters in order to stay home with her fantasies.

The ill-matched-friends theme also appears in a number of ingeniously varied stories, as in the haunting "The Terrors of Basket-Weaving" (in *The Black House* [1981]). Here the protagonist, again a young woman (Highsmith is much more egalitarian in her stories, giving women many central roles), discovers talents within her that seem to connect her to a racial past and to qualities within herself that both intrigue and frighten her—so much so that she destroys the ancient wicker basket (the surrogate ill-matched friend, representing the primitive she has repressed) that had evoked these feelings. A related theme, the need to be part of an "us" that defines itself in contrast to "them," is explored in such tales as "The Network" (in *Slowly, Slowly in the Wind* [1979]), where a group of New Yorkers gathers together for mutual protection against the less acceptable and more dangerous members of society—the "civilized" once again banishing the "primitive."

In her final collection, *Tales of Natural and Unnatural Catastrophes* (1987), Highsmith emphasizes the political and social concerns that appear in her late novels. Such titles as "Rent-a-Womb vs. the Mighty Right" and "President Buck Jones Rallies and Waves the Flag" sufficiently indicate her focus.

Conclusion

The most common designation given to Patricia Highsmith's novels is "suspense fiction." In that genre she succeeded so well as to receive the highest praise from a number of readers. Graham Greene, in his introduction to *Eleven*, calls her "the poet of apprehension" (p. 10), and others compare her to Dostoyevsky and Henry James. That her reputation and popularity in Europe are so much greater than in the United States (where she is chiefly known as the author of the book on which Hitchcock based *Strangers on a Train*) is attributed variously to her unflattering portraits of middle-class Americans, to her European tastes and attitudes, to her relegation in America to genre categorization rather than to that of "straight" fiction, or even to her being a woman in a field formerly dominated in America by men.

Strangers on a Train and *The Talented Mr. Ripley*, with their complex, suspenseful plots and their symbiotically (and perhaps erotically) joined, mismatched friends, remain Highsmith's best-known and most esteemed novels. Graham Greene praised the subtler *Tremor of Forgery*; others prefer the feminist awakening of *Edith's Diary*. There is a drastic decline in the quality of the novels after *Edith's Diary*; message overwhelms plot and character. Essentially, in her best works, Highsmith emerges as a novelist of character, and her most memorable creations—Ripley,

Guy and Bruno, David in *This Sweet Sickness,* and Philip in *The Glass Cell*—convincingly embody her concern with the possibilities of individual development in a world where the quest for self-knowledge and personal integrity is so easily defeated by the circumstances of one's birth and life.

Selected Bibliography

WORKS OF PATRICIA HIGHSMITH

First editions are listed immediately after the title. Most titles published first in the United States were published simultaneously or shortly thereafter by Heinemann, London. Penguin and Hamlyn have published a number of Highsmith's works in paperback; more recently, in New York, both Penzler/Mysterious Press and Atlantic Monthly Press have printed or reprinted in hardcover a number of titles. All citations in the text are from the last-listed edition.

NOVELS AND SHORT STORIES

Strangers on a Train. New York: Harper, 1950; Harmondsworth, Middlesex: Penguin, 1974.

The Price of Salt by "Claire Morgan." New York: Coward-McCann, 1952. U.K.: *Carol* by Patricia Highsmith. London: Bloomsbury, 1990; Tallahassee: Naiad, 1991.

The Blunderer. New York: Coward-McCann, 1954; Feltham, Middlesex: Hamlyn, 1978. U.S.: *Lament for a Lover.* New York: Popular Library, 1956.

The Talented Mr. Ripley. New York: Coward-McCann, 1955; Harmondsworth, Middlesex: Penguin, 1976.

Deep Water. New York: Harper, 1957; Harmondsworth, Middlesex: Penguin, 1974.

A Game for the Living. New York: Harper, 1958; Feltham, Middlesex: Hamlyn, 1978.

This Sweet Sickness. New York: Harper, 1960; Harmondsworth, Middlesex: Penguin, 1972.

The Cry of the Owl. New York: Harper, 1962; Harmondsworth, Middlesex: Penguin, 1973.

The Two Faces of January. Garden City, N.Y.: Doubleday, 1964; Feltham, Middlesex: Hamlyn, 1966.

The Glass Cell. Garden City, N.Y.: Doubleday, 1964; Harmondsworth, Middlesex: Penguin, 1973.

A Suspension of Mercy. London: Heinemann, 1965; Harmondsworth, Middlesex: Penguin, 1972. U.S.: *The Story-Teller.* Garden City, N.Y.: Doubleday, 1965.

Those Who Walk Away. Garden City, N.Y.: Doubleday, 1967; Feltham, Middlesex: Hamlyn, 1979.

The Tremor of Forgery. Garden City, N.Y.: Doubleday, 1969; Feltham, Middlesex: Hamlyn, 1978.

Ripley Under Ground. Garden City, N.Y.: Doubleday, 1970.

Eleven. London: Heinemann, 1970; Harmondsworth, Middlesex: Penguin, 1976. U.S.: *The Snail-Watcher.* Garden City, N.Y.: Doubleday, 1970.

A Dog's Ransom. New York: Knopf, 1972; Harmondsworth, Middlesex: Penguin, 1975.

Ripley's Game. New York: Knopf, 1974; Harmondsworth, Middlesex: Penguin, 1974.

The Animal Lover's Book of Beastly Murder. London: Heinemann, 1975; Harmondsworth, Middlesex: Penguin, 1979.

Edith's Diary. New York: Simon & Schuster, 1977.

Little Tales of Misogyny. London: Heinemann, 1977; New York: Penzler, 1986.

Slowly, Slowly in the Wind. London: Heinemann, 1979; New York: Mysterious Press, 1985.

The Boy Who Followed Ripley. New York: Lippincott, 1980; Harmondsworth, Middlesex: Penguin, 1981.

The Black House. London: Heinemann, 1981; Harmondsworth, Middlesex: Penguin, 1982.

People Who Knock on the Door. London: Heinemann, 1983; Harmondsworth, Middlesex: Penguin, 1984.

Mermaids on the Golf Course. London: Heinemann, 1985; Harmondsworth, Middlesex: Penguin, 1986.

Found in the Street. London: Heinemann, 1986; New York: Atlantic Monthly, 1987.

Tales of Natural and Unnatural Catastrophes. London: Bloomsbury, 1987; New York: Atlantic Monthly, 1989.

Ripley Under Water. New York: Knopf, 1991.

Small G: A Summer Idyll. London: Bloomsbury, 1995.

SELECTED NONFICTION

"New York Revisited." *New Statesman,* 26 February 1965: 311–312.

Plotting and Writing Suspense Fiction. Boston: The Writer, 1966.

"The Power of Fear." *Times Literary Supplement,* 15 August 1975: 912. Review.

"Galahad in L.A." *Times Literary Supplement,* 18 June 1976: 733. Review of Raymond Chandler biography.

"A Glint of Madness." *Times Literary Supplement,* 24 December 1976: 1601. Review of *The John Franklin Bardin Omnibus.*

"Murder in Space City." *Times Literary Supplement,* 22 April 1977: 481.

"The Talented Mr. Poe." *Times Literary Supplement,* 23 December 1977: 1492.

Introduction to *The World of Raymond Chandler.* Edited by Miriam Gross. London: Weidenfield & Nicolson, 1977.

"Deadly Innocents." *Times Literary Supplement,* 6 September 1985: 967.

"The Mystery of the Juice." *Washington Post,* 26 June 1994: C1, C4.

INTERVIEWS

Cooper-Clark, Diana. "Patricia Highsmith—Interview." *The Armchair Detective* 14: 313–320 (spring 1981).

Hamilton, Ian. *New Review* 4: 31–36 (August 1977).

Supree, Burt. *Voice Literary Supplement,* August 1982: 7.

"Profile of a Writer." London Weekly Television. British Broadcasting Corporation, 1982. Videotaped interview.

BIOGRAPHICAL AND CRITICAL STUDIES

Becker, Mary Helen. "Patricia Highsmith." In *Twentieth-Century Crime and Mystery Writers.* Edited by John M. Reilly. New York: St. Martin's, 1980.

Brophy, Brigid. "Bartleby the Scriptwriter." *New Statesman,* 29 October 1965: 664–665.

Cavigelli, Franz, and Fritz Senn, eds. *Über Patricia Highsmith.* Zurich: Diogenes, 1980.

Evans, Odette L'Henry. "A Feminist Approach to Patricia Highsmith's Fiction." In *American Horror Fiction.* Edited by Brian Doherty. New York: St. Martin's, 1990.

Greene, Graham. Foreword to *Eleven,* by Patricia Highsmith. Harmondsworth, Middlesex: Penguin, 1972.

Harrison, Russell. *Patricia Highsmith.* New York: Twayne, 1997.

Hilfer, Anthony C. " 'Not Really Such a Monster': Highsmith's Ripley as Thriller Protagonist and Protean Man." *Midwest Quarterly* 25: 361–374 (1984).

———. *The Crime Novel: A Deviant Genre.* Austin: Univ. of Texas Press, 1990. Discusses Highsmith in chapter 6.

Keating, H. R. F., ed. *Whodunit?: A Guide to Crime, Suspense, and Spy Fiction.* New York: Van Nostrand, 1982.

Klein, Kathleen Gregory. "Patricia Highsmith." In *And Then There Were Nine . . . More Women of Mystery.* Edited by Jane S. Bakerman. Bowling Green, Ohio: Bowling Green State University Popular Press, 1985.

Laski, Marghanita. "Long Crimes, Short Crimes." *Listener,* 20 November 1975: 684–685. Review of *The Animal Lover's Book of Beastly Murder.*

Lesser, Wendy. *Pictures at an Execution: An Inquiry into the Subject of Murder.* Cambridge, Mass.: Harvard Univ. Press, 1993. Highsmith is discussed in chapter 3.

Mahoney, Mary Kay. "A Train Running on Two Sets of Tracks: Highsmith's and Hitchcock's *Strangers on a Train.*" In *It's a Print!: Detective Fiction from Page to Screen.* Edited by William Reynolds and Elizabeth Tremblay. Bowling Green, Ohio: Bowling Green State University Popular Press, 1994.

Martin, John W. "Humor and Malevolence in Wenders' *The American Friend.*" *Michigan Academician* 13: 145–153 (1980).

Mawer, Noel Dorman. "From Villain to Vigilante." *The Armchair Detective* 24: 34–38 (winter 1991).

Peters, Brooks. "Stranger Than Fiction." *Out,* June 1995: 70, 72, 150.

Richardson, Maurice. "Simenon and Highsmith." In *Crime Writers.* Edited by H. R. F. Keating. London: British Broadcasting Corporation, 1978.

Scholz, Christian. "Dramatik des Lebens." *Basler Magazine* (Switzerland), 12 January 1991: 1–3.

"Seeking Adventure." *Times Literary Supplement,* 18 January 1957: 33.

Symons, Julian. *Bloody Murder.* New York: Viking, 1985.

Szogyi, Alex. "The Magic Realism of Patricia Highsmith." *Village Voice,* 15 August 1977: 37, 39.

"The Talented Miss Highsmith." *Times Literary Supplement,* 24 September 1971: 1147–1148.

Tolkin, Michael. "In Memory of Patricia Highsmith." *Los Angeles Times Book Review,* 2 February 1995.

Evan Hunter
(b. 1926)

DEAN A. MILLER

UNDER BOTH of his best-known pen names (and he has used four others at one time or another), the extremely durable Evan Hunter has managed both to interpret and to affect the crime mystery and the novelistic scene of the past forty years in North American fiction. As Ed McBain, he can take most of the credit for the invention of the police procedural "team" genre in his 87th Precinct crime novels. There are now fifty of these books in the series, which is a considerable achievement that also presents certain obvious problems. McBain is not in the same league as the French writer Georges Simenon, but then no one is, while only the Englishman Michael Gilbert, operating in *his* own special niche in the mystery-suspense field and commencing his authorial activity after the end of World War II, has had anything like the continuous run McBain can point to. It can be claimed that McBain should share credit for the police team novel with the British Maurice Procter (1906–1973), whose first Inspector Martineau novel, *Hell Is a City,* appeared in 1954. Procter, however, had a creative span of a quarter century and has been dead for almost that long; in any event, the British police procedural novel needs its own space and analysis. One Swedish critic, K. A. Blom, lays out a series of possible root starts for the police procedural: Lawrence Treat's *V As in Victim* (1945), Hillary Waugh's *Last Seen Wearing* (1952), and Sidney Kingsley's play *Detective Story* (1949). Credit for the American team procedural certainly belongs to McBain, however, and to the impact and influence of his long-running and successful series.

What McBain invented was a crime novel form that owed its existence to several factors, both referent to shifts in technique and nuances of genre but also to social and even political actualities present in the United States in the mid-1950s. On the most basic level he adapted the format of the World War II war film, where the protagonists are a team of soldiers (one city boy—Italian preferred—one rube or Southerner, and one Polish-American, possibly a Jew) who rub along together, learn from one another, take casualties, get the Big Job done. This problem-solving, eventually cooperative team concept goes back at least to the nineteenth century and Jules Verne and to the casts Verne assembled for *The Mysterious Island* (1870) or *Journey to the Center of the Earth* (1864). The recent war experience was, however, also germinative in another way: in the midst of the self-congratulatory middle-class perfections of the easy Eisenhower years, crime, even in fiction, now required something like a "war" mentality and a quasi-military team effort in order to solve new and increasingly more barbarous assaults on civil (civilian) life. Finally, the new genre took something from the hard-boiled tradition, in terms of the use of street speech, the frequency and intensity of violence, and an overall darker coloration.

It is also true that as the pseudonymous McBain was constructing his new police team and tactics, introducing his characters—Carella, Hawes, Kling, Meyer Meyer, Parker, and all the rest—and putting them to violent work in a cityscape he also invented, Evan Hunter was creating his own assault on the verities of the bland decade; *The Blackboard Jungle* (1954) showed where the good times and the prosperous dreams had not reached at all, and how what were then called slums bred antiauthoritarian and uncontrollable, anarchic violence, revealing an educational nightmare completely untouched by Dick, Jane, and Spot. Hunter's revelations, drawn from his own teaching experience, were greeted with outraged disbelief by the boosterish establishment of the 1950s: clearly he had gone too far. The general public, however, ate him up.

Early in his career McBain experimented with other pseudonyms. As Curt Cannon, he pursued the first-person narrative of the hard-boiled and harder-drinking private investigator (as advertised in the title of a collection of short stories, *I Like 'em Tough,* published in 1958); Cannon is so poor that he isn't even able to rent a ritually shabby private eye's office. As Hunt Collins, the author published *Cut Me In* (in 1954), and as Richard Marsten, he wrote six crime-suspense novels from 1954 to 1959, which have mostly been reprinted under the Ed McBain name; as Marsten, he also wrote several children's books. As Ezra Hannon, the author published one book, *Doors* (1976), but he now flies only the flags of Hunter and McBain and has been known to remark that when he makes restaurant reservations, Ed McBain gets the prime table, while Evan Hunter gets the table by the kitchen.

Life

Salvatore A. Lombino was born in upper Manhattan on 15 October 1926. He was born into Italian-American tenement, if not slum, life. McBain himself called the area a ghetto (Carr, p. 3) and holds the latter-day opinion that life on 120th Street was tough but not brutal or gang-ridden; everyone was largely in the same socioeconomic boat. In 1944 he joined the U.S. Navy to avoid the draft, with the reasoning that those being drafted into the army at that time "were being sent to Italy, to get their asses shot off" (Carr, p. 3). He went to sea, saw the world, was discharged in 1946, and went back to school at Hunter College in New York City, where he received a bachelor's degree in 1950. He has been married and divorced twice, has married a third time, and has three sons from his first marriage and a stepdaughter from his second. Other than some secondary school (vocational) teaching and a short stint at the Scott Meredith literary agency in the 1950s, he has supported himself and his family as a professional writer of fiction. An ordinary biographical type of entry for McBain/Hunter is, then, to some degree beside the point: he is above all and after all a writer, and is defined by his always difficult if sometimes rewarding occupation.

Observers, critics, and other writers (prone to a personal curiosity that McBain says he himself is free from, except in the way of research) have perpetuated small urban legends about this author, the first being to derive his Anglo-Saxon pen name Evan Hunter from his alma maters, Evander Child High School in the Bronx and Hunter College; in fact, this derivation is disputed by the author. Another matter in dispute has to do with his invented scene, the city of Isola with its surrounding *banlieues* of Majesta, Calms Point, the rivers Harb and Dix, and so on; the received wisdom is that this construction simply is New York City, with its boroughs, rotated clockwise ninety degrees. McBain insists that this is only partly true, for he exercises the option to invent details and apply them to Isola itself and its surround. There is what McBain calls a "piece of disinformation" (repeated in several sources) that he received the Mystery Writers of America Edgar Award in 1957 (in fact, Charlotte Armstrong and Donald Mc-

Nutt. Douglas won the award in 1957). Finally, there is the occasionally vexing question of the author's own ethnicity and his reaction to it. McBain's central character, the "good cop" Steve Carella, is Italian but doesn't "look" Italian (not in the same way that his confrere Meyer Meyer is made to look and act Jewish); Carella is not a churchgoer, rarely falls into the bosom of his parents and family, is not overtly part of the pasta-and-pizza culture, and doesn't use the Italian expressions that often appear on the lips of both real and fictional Italian-Americans, but occasionally—in the earlier novels—he is known to fall into a fugue where he meditates on the state of being an Italian-American. For all that, McBain insists that he is comfortable with and within his tribe. Of course, it is much too late to change names now. He has legally been Evan Hunter, as he notes, since 1952.

None of these sidelights have much to do with McBain the writer, and it is likely that he is more concerned with maintaining his strict, if not rigid, writing schedule and with his sales here and overseas, where, for example, the French and the Japanese are especially keen on translations of the 87th Precinct series. The French enthusiasm is clearly evident in the fact that the most recent edition of *Les livres disponibles* has seventy-nine Hunter/McBain titles in French—twenty-three more than are listed in *Books in Print* in the United States (the current Italian equivalent lists twenty-nine McBain titles). According to Blom, the Swedes are also enthusiastic about McBain, whose *Cop Hater* (1956), published in Sweden in 1957, was the first police procedural to appear there. We can accept that McBain has an international reputation and audience.

As for McBain as a political being, we have the remarks he himself made to go on, as well as the admitted resemblance of the author to his main character, Steve Carella. From the first, we get the impression that McBain is an urban liberal; in a 1983 interview with Carr, he admitted his loathing of Richard Nixon, and he was responsible for a rather ham-handed riff on the Nixon phenomenon, in *Hail to the Chief* (1973). If McBain resembles the fictional Carella in character, he is open-minded and uncomfortable with bigotry (of which Carella encounters a good deal, both on and off the job). This is not to say that Carella is not subject to fits of social philosophizing, because he is; in fact, as the series has gone on, the author's view of urban life and urban policing has grown darker, more sober, and more pessimistic.

Crime Writing

Ed McBain seems to be most comfortable in the arena of his work. Aside from his novelistic career, McBain has had a solidly successful relationship with film and film-making. One of his first 87th Precinct books, *The Mugger* (1956), was filmed early on; Evan Hunter wrote the screenplay for the 87th Precinct novel *Fuzz* (1968) as well as for the novel *Walk Proud* (1979) and, earlier, for *Strangers When We Meet* (1958). Perhaps predictably, 87th Precinct novels have also been filmed by the Japanese (*King's Ransom,* 1959; retitled *High and Low,* directed by the master Akira Kurosawa and released in 1962) and the French (*Ten Plus One,* 1963; filmed as *Without Apparent Motive,* 1972); a French-Canadian company filmed *Blood Relatives* (1975), released in 1977. Hunter's big, violent, and sensational novel *The Blackboard Jungle* reached the screen in 1955; McBain has said that there was not a line of dialogue in the film that came from the book, but that it was a good movie nevertheless. His *Buddwing* (1964), a clever expedition into what was finally revealed to be the supernatural, received a good critical reception and was filmed as *Mr. Buddwing* to a similar response, while his western novel *The Chisholms: A Novel of the Journey West* (1976) gave birth to its own television series in 1978–1979. A TV series, *87th Precinct,* had its debut in 1961 and ran to 1963. Another Hunter novel, the "caper" novel *Every Little Crook and Nanny* (1972), was turned into a film starring Victor Mature in one of his last appearances on film and the roguish Lynn Redgrave.

McBain's best-known film credit began a long sequence in which one idea has been recycled. In 1917 Arthur Machen, the Welsh mystic and supernaturalist, published a short story called "The Terror," in which the animal world (including the insects) turns against a war-crazed mankind. This was the likeliest inspiration for Daphne du Maurier's story "The Birds," a study of the evil of utter anomaly, first published in 1953. The story was then made into a cult-classic film by Alfred Hitchcock, released in 1963. "Evan Hunter" wrote the screenplay for this film, and on McBain's own evidence Hitchcock had Hunter remove every trace of du Maurier from the script—that is, any trace of the subtlety of evil. Whatever sort of cinematic genius he presented, Hitchcock was never subtle—his birds are simply avian muggers. McBain has made the film or his involvement in it a recurring theme; in *Jigsaw* (1970), Meyer Meyer admits to not liking the film (McBain says that he didn't like it, either—nor *Fuzz,* for that matter), and in a late 87th Precinct novel, *Nocturne* (1997), the point is made that plenty of people still think that Hitchcock himself wrote the screenplay. In fact, the scenario of *The Birds* is still in curious view; a pop-science theory has been propounded that a "bloom" of seaborne toxic microorganisms *could* have made seagulls and other seabirds, at least, crazy enough to turn on human beings.

By publishing fifty books in the 87th Precinct series, McBain has given himself to the reviewers to gnaw on many more than fifty times, and the results have varied according to the perceptive and literary skills of these reviewers. McBain may or may not read his reviews; one gets the impression that if he does, he has never changed his style to suit, any more than he will admit to borrowing—or even learning—from his colleagues in the genre. Some writers, however, he does admire, and his choices are sometimes strange. McBain may give credence to critics who are also writers. The great Julian Symons, in *Bloody Murder,* admitted to a liking for McBain's flair for realistic dialogue, while noting "the characteristic McBain weakness of sentimentality" (p. 233). Symons has critical words about the police procedural genre itself, where elaboration of plot, he thinks, wars with the realism essential to the genre. He says, however, that McBain is "the most consistently skillful" (p. 232) of the genre's practitioners. James McClure (South African author of the Kramer and Zondi police procedural novels) did an appreciation of him for *Murder Ink* ("Carella of the 87th") that is friendly and certainly intelligently perceptive, though he credits McBain with a skill at irony that would seem to conflict with Symons' depiction of him as sentimental (in an interview with John Carr, McBain calls himself "a softy" [p. 19]). McClure points to McBain's skill with cliché; "If the field that engrosses him is knee-deep in clichés, so be it, " he says, and goes on to point out that "the very essence of McBain is that he embraces his clichés with . . . loving enthusiasm" (p. 305). Is McClure game-playing here? Almost certainly it is *he* who is the ironist in describing how "a strong leaning toward grass-roots kitsch" (p. 305) and a cheerfully Norman Rockwellesque sensibility are to be read as McBain's strengths, not his weaknesses, and that the taste and feel and reality of the police officer's life must be encased in the world of cliché.

McBain has had a turbulent relationship with the main mystery writers' organization in this country, the Mystery Writers of America; in his interview with Carr, he said that he had dropped his membership because he found that awards (the Edgars) were being arranged to bolster an author's chance for increased sales. The rift seems to have been healed by 1985, when he was awarded Grand Master status by the group. At present, McBain's books (both the 87th Precinct stories and the Matthew Hope novels) can count on book club nominations by the Literary Guild, the Mystery Guild, and the Doubleday Book Club; whether either McBain's or Hunter's books reach so-called best-seller status depends on who commands the count, but writing under either name (and McBain specifically), he can pretty much count on a dedicated, tried-and-true readership, a readership confident that they will not be disappointed when a new book appears. McBain also controls the copyrights (and reprint options) of the 87th Precinct books through his own creation, the HUI Corporation; thirty-four titles in the series are at present in print.

Before taking up the 87th Precinct books in critical detail, it should be noted that McBain began another series in 1977 with the publication of *Goldilocks.* Like John D. MacDonald before him and Elmore Leonard afterward, McBain moved to Florida; in his Matthew Hope books he has shifted the scene to Calusa, a fictional small city on the Gulf side of the peninsula. Hope is a lawyer, and so the series involves more detection than crime solving, though he deals extensively with private investigators and the local police; each of the books has a title with a fairy-tale association, and, as usual, McBain twists and maneuvers his plotting through the title's nuances. Ten of the Matthew Hope books have been published, of which all but one are in print.

87th Precinct Novels

In drawing up a detailed critical analysis of McBain's work, we can begin with space and time, as constrictions or as aids in forming the fictional world he creates. McBain announces his invention of the place where the 87th Precinct team operates, has its victories and its defeats—all the streets, squares, neighborhoods of Isola and the adjacent communities, and in detail. That, in reality, this is New York City, with its two rivers and the boroughs, is never quite clear, but the better question is what McBain gains by his construction. Other writers have often exercised their ingenuity in inventing place or retagging the literal details of the detective game; Rex Stout, for example, plays with us and with his "Marley" (or "Bowdoin") .38 and .32 caliber pistols, "Manson" locks, even a "Stenophone" (for a Dictaphone) cylinder—and the egregious "Heron" automobile. But Stout's Nero Wolfe is emplaced in a recognizable New York City—and, more, Stout was not required to hold to the dictates of a realistic genre, since he wrote in the Great Detective mode. Probably the worst that can be said for McBain's urban illusion is that it breaks even, gaining or holding as many readers—presumably fascinated by the puzzle-solving potential in this device or just enjoying the game—as it loses readers who may find the device boring or irritating.

The question of *time* comes in simply because it has been forty years since McBain started this successful series of police procedurals. Carella, Hawes, and Kling are identified as veterans of various branches of the service in World War II; they would have been slightly older than McBain himself. As a pitiless secular chronology runs, they would all be coots and codgers now, and long retired. But, obviously, normal time does not run in Isola. Time, in McBain's world, is flexible; note the fact that Carella's twins, who are nine years old in *Bread* (published in 1974) are ten in *Heat* (published in 1981); they are still ten in *Romance* (published in 1995). The twins were born at the very end of *'Til Death,* published in 1959. But Lieutenant Byrne is still a lieutenant forty years on, and the other characters still hold their old places. This sort of temporal sleight of hand can become a problem, as we will see.

A McBain 87th Precinct novel has, first, its cast of recognizable characters working the precinct. Villains and evildoers are then added; only one of the latter has appeared more than once (if one doesn't count Richard M. Nixon), and that is the Deaf Man. Carella is married to a deaf-mute (in his overview of McBain reflected in Carella, McClure noted, and rejected, the idea that Teddy Carella, the wife, is a caricature created from the masculine wish-fantasy of possessing a beautiful but dumb mate). Carella is known to stray. Bert Kling is perpetually unhappy in love, losing his women either to violence or to other men. Cotton Hawes is forever on the prowl for love or its equivalent. Then we have the balding and reflective Meyer Meyer, the family man, and another family man in Art Brown, who is black; McBain integrated the squad early on. All these detectives are more or less competent and effective (or lucky); we also have Andy Parker, who is lazy, corrupt, and, in general, a foul human being—and, usually, a bad (but at least an experienced) cop—and Fat Ollie Weeks, of the 83rd Precinct, who is physically repulsive and bigoted but also a committed, streetwise, and, often, competent detective. It is not difficult to recognize something of Fat Ollie in Andy Sipowicz, of the very successful television series *NYPD Blue;* McBain has had more than his share of influence on the police procedural shows appearing on the small screen. McBain has even promoted to detective (on the basis, brilliantly, of his quite accidental solution of a crime) a patrolman, Richard Genero, who began as that archetypal cop who can't spell—a jape that must go back at least to Sir Robert Peel's Peelers, the first urban (London) police force.

The 87th Precinct detectives are then caught up in the plot web that McBain weaves, and here the author is almost too ingenious. McBain is fond of a good, convoluted plot, sometimes led off by a title with a sort of elbow-in-the-ribs coyness or Halloween ghoulishness (as in *Give the Boys a Great Big Hand,* 1960, or *Let's Hear It for the Deaf Man,* 1973). McBain is also fond of ambiguous titles: *Heat* refers to an urban summer hot spell and to sexual passion, and it is also a street term for a firearm. If there is a central plotline, it ought to be brought to a conclusion, but McBain will spin off subplots unmercifully if the mood is on him—and, as in the case of his drawn-out dialogue sequences, readers have to stick with it, or him, because we can't know when a seemingly dead-end conversational line of infuriating prolixity is going to develop purpose and direction. In *Hail, Hail, the Gang's All Here!* (1971), McBain pulled off a coup de théâtre by detailing one day's harvest of crime in the precinct, from minor to major—all of which were solved or the cases closed, which, as one critic wrote, probably strains the "realistic" claim of the police procedural to its limit.

The clichés of which McClure spoke with admiration were, it must be said, in many cases not clichés when McBain began to use them. Two of them ought to be mentioned here: the matter of police procedural realism and McBain's development of demotic or "street" dialogue, again as an extension of the hard-boiled school of detective fiction. The details of the policeman's or detective's life are put right into McBain's pages: a filled-in report, the process of identification (or Identikit) drawing, applications for a search warrant, notes used in the trail of evidence, even photographs. Formulas for determining the progress of rigor mortis are detailed, as is the chemical composition of a fingerprint. How will the reader take this? A great many obviously take the realistic detailing positively, and, in fact, most police procedurals today follow at least the general pattern of reference to normal police routine, reports, and other paperwork; forensic evidence and its interpretation; the logging of evidence; and the rest. The reverse of the coin is perhaps less clear. The illustrated details can be taken to be an unsubtle form of padding. More seriously, the injection of realism may lead to an unfulfillable demand by the reader for *complete* realism—which could be deadly to any hope for a fast-paced plot. In *Eighty Million Eyes* (1966), Captain Grossman, the forensic pathologist of the series, who is performing an autopsy of the prominent, possibly murdered victim, identifies a rare toxin in the corpse in a manner of minutes. The likelihood of this occurring in the real world of police routine is extremely remote, but the plot, which is advancing swiftly and inexorably, demands it. We must, here as elsewhere, suspend belief—and modify our expectations concerning police procedural "realism."

As to realism in dialogue, again McBain tantalizes us. On first exposure (or re-exposure) to McBain, the reader is likely to pick up on the brisk, almost syncopated pacing of the dialogue—where McBain jabs us with much of his humor, and he is a writer with a serious bent toward humor, low and otherwise. We must follow along and be patient, because McBain will use seemingly inane exchanges to briefly impede the flow of the plot—and try our patience—when it is in his interest to do so. He almost obsesses on dialogue, using it to suddenly introduce peripheral characters, seemingly for their own sakes—characters extraneous to the action but brilliantly drawn in a few lines of dialogue. The playful aspect of McBain and his writing is not to be missed. He may borrow from elsewhere for his repertoire of tics and tricks: he segues into a *Dragnet* mode in *'Til Death,* while in *Heat* he constructs a phone conversation between a pitiable and frustrated caller and an obdurate operator that owes a great deal to Mike Nichols and Elaine May and their comic dialogues of the 1950s. McBain had to struggle initially with his black street talk (in *Bread,* for example); in later narratives he does a much better job of transcribing black dialect.

Finally there is the action. McBain shows his deep roots in the hard-boiled school and is not squeamish. Long skeins of conversation may be interrupted by bursts of furious violence, occasionally gratuitous; McBain likes guns (though he knows less about them than a realistic writer of cop dramas should), and the toll of gunshot victims in his novels is considerable, if not Spillanesque. As for other forms of mayhem, McBain seemed to have his own Hitchcockian McGuffin (or gimmick) in his early novels; his version of the Chandler formula ("Have a man come through the door with a gun") was to have one of his detectives knocked out as he came through a door, often by means of a gun.

It makes sense to examine, with some degree of thoroughness, a few of McBain's novels, taking one each from the early, middle, and late decades in which the series has run, and look for strengths and weaknesses. *'Til Death* (1959) caught Julian Symons' attention for what he called McBain's "sentimentality"; Symons also liked the novel's dialogue, in that it displays the author's deadpan comedic skills. The story core of *'Til Death* has to do with the very Italian-American wedding of Steve Carella's sister; the central suspense in the novel turns on whether or not a psychopath will succeed in killing the bridegroom and therefore casting a pall over the proceedings. Two red herrings are interjected, in the shape of others who might wish the groom ill; one of these herrings proves to be, in fact, dangerous, but his passion (he counted himself an old flame of the bride's) and his plots are clumsily rendered. One of McBain's formulaic but usually interesting *femmes très fatales* is put into the plot. All in all, we have in hand a galloping narrative; genuine, if sometimes artificially invoked and described suspense; good and realistic dialogue—and, on the other hand, padded and occasionally unlikely verbiage—"realism," improbabilities connected to firearms, and crude plot twists. One conclusion would be that this is not McBain at his best, but, even so, he can almost always pull us willy-nilly into the toils of his narrative, lead us past his smaller gaffes, and bring us breathless to his neatly, if obviously crafted conclusion (no, nobody, psychopath or not, manages to kill the groom).

About twenty years into the series, McBain wrote *Long Time No See* (1977) with another heavy-humored title (the victims in the series of murders are all blind). By that time, McBain's powers were fully developed and deployed, and there is even a more than faint hint of world-weariness or perhaps fatigue, if not of writer's burnout. The plot, however, is as high voltage as ever. A blind beggar and his blind wife both have their throats cut on successive days. The beggar is black, and his wife white, but the developing key to the investigation seems to lie in the blind man's U.S. Army career: he had been blinded by a grenade fragment in Vietnam ten years earlier. Another blind woman is killed, or butchered, in the same manner. Carella, with a little help from Meyer, is the principal investigator in the case, which develops several false trails before ten-year-old psychiatric evidence (interviews and a dream reported by the blinded vet) begins to point Carella in the right direction. A final murder attempt on another blind man, fended off by the man's Seeing Eye dog, followed by a copy of a blackmail letter found in the first victim's safe-deposit box, and the villain is revealed—a villain who was using the old device of extending his killing spree beyond his original target in order to mislead the investigation. Along the way, McBain gives Ross MacDonald a gratuitous jab (referring to "murder brewed in a pot for half a century" [*Long Time No See,* p. 116] and solved by a private investigator) and bounces another rock—a hard-boiled rock?—off deluded enthusiasts for murders concocted and solved by "little old ladies in Sussex" (p. 232) rather than by hardworking police detectives in Isola. In sum, McBain again can talk us past the improbabilities (here, for instance, how exactly one chloroforms a large and alert Seeing Eye dog and how the killer manages to avoid the blood from his butchered victims) and presents case closure in the very last, pell-mell pages. He even dabbles, successfully, in the murky pool of psychiatric evidence. In other words, McBain's reputation as a first-class wordsmith is still, in this novel published at the midpoint of the series, intact.

Romance, the penultimate title to date, in the 87th Precinct series, was published in 1995. At the outset of the novel, McBain shows the fancy plotting footwork for which he is well known; from a long passage in which Bert Kling is trying to get a date with a woman, we segue into what seems to be an identifiable New York: an NYPD detective writing up a report on threatening telephone calls. This turns out to be a play—a play about a crime in New York City—with the neat reversal that has McBain's fictional setting (Isola et al.) surrounding a "fictional" setting that is, in fact, real. The romance of the title is also the name of the play, a real turkey whose subtalented "star" is knifed three times—once as part of the play, once in an attempt faked by her and her agent to hype the play and her part, and the third time for keeps. The action of the novel is essentially generated by actors, and established police procedure thus comes up against all sorts of artifice, acting skill, ego, and ambition. In the midst of all this, Kling is falling in love—more romance—and I fear that McBain's temporal sleight of hand already mentioned comes a cropper here. Kling mentions "a war" in which he was involved, but the earlier books identify this as World War II. By a clearly delineated 1995, Kling would be worried not about romance with a beautiful woman of whatever color, but about his prostate, his hearing, his eyesight, and the obituary page (to be fair, Fat Ollie Weeks now has reading glasses). If readers ease past this little, but literal, contretemps, they will find more complex plotting, more sex (interracial and homosexual), more violence, and a believable conclusion. The reader will also encounter a neat self-reference when an actor in the play proudly identifies his movie roles; he has played a cop in all of the movies made from McBain novels—including the Japanese one directed by Kurosawa.

Before encapsulating and summing up McBain's writing career and his impact on the crime novel, it is wise to take a glance at his "new" (since 1978) Matthew Hope series. The Hope novels would seem to allow McBain to step out of the 87th Precinct, police procedural routine, to clear ground in a new environment and develop new novelistic strategies and tactics. The old McBain plotting talent is clearly visible in *There Was a Little Girl* (1994), which begins with the protagonist being shot down; as he lies in a semicoma, his private investigator and police friends, and his lover (who is an assistant district attorney), try to retrace his movements up to the moment of the shooting. Hope's own actions and conversations before the shooting are then crosscut with those of his friends following, later, in his track. A real-estate deal turns into an involvement with a small circus and its bizarre denizens. We meet a couple of McBain's Fatal Women. An old suicide turns out to have been murder, a new "suicide" that definitely is murder, and finally a drug ring are revealed. The book's conclusion turns back to the 87th Precinct ambience, with police interrogations and a brisk round of plea bargaining. McBain cannily refuses to bring his main character back in the last pages; he remains comatose, but there is hope for Hope. In sum, this is a cleverly and almost too intricately plotted novel, crossing between the crime procedural and the crime suspense genres. There is plenty of gaudy variation in the characters presented, along with lots of conflict and little deep characterization. McBain neatly picks up the plentiful opportunities presented by circus routine, speech, and mores.

Conclusion

In terms of a study of mystery writers and their craft, Ed McBain is, of course, Evan Hunter, but Evan Hunter has received little attention here. In the Hunter persona he is a novelist, and if crime and criminality intrude into his novels, it is as a plot element or perhaps as a *moral* problem. McBain displays and forms up the solid achievement of this writer in the crime mystery scene and set of genres. What has kept him—Hunter-as-McBain—afloat for so long is his preternatural gift for devising complex and ingenious plots. Given the format of the police procedural novel (a format he helped set), McBain is able to weave any number of new and usually convincing plot elements through his narrative, in and around his stock of characters (or stock characters); clichés are reversed or stood on their heads or outrageously emphasized, twists of plot arrive from well out in left field, and the sheer brio of the performance carries us along. If other writers now create a better, sharper, more allusive, better-tuned dialogue than does McBain, they necessarily build on his foundation. If McBain's novels seem padded and puffy, the humor pawky, the formulas a little worn, it is still true that the master can, at any time he wishes, whistle the reader right down that garden path or put a new spin on an old, old story. McBain knows his craft, and he makes us believe that he knows it.

Selected Bibliography

WORKS OF ED MCBAIN

THE 87TH PRECINCT NOVELS

Cop Hater. New York: Permabooks, 1956.
The Mugger. New York: Permabooks, 1956.
The Pusher. New York: Permabooks, 1956.
The Con Man. New York: Permabooks, 1957.
Killer's Choice. New York: Permabooks, 1957.
Killer's Payoff. New York: Permabooks, 1958.
Lady Killer. New York: Permabooks, 1958.
Killer's Wedge. New York: Simon & Schuster, 1959.
'Til Death. New York: Simon & Schuster, 1959.
King's Ransom. New York: Simon & Schuster, 1959.
Give the Boys a Great Big Hand. New York: Simon & Schuster, 1960.
The Heckler. New York: Simon & Schuster, 1960.
See Them Die. New York: Simon & Schuster, 1960.
Lady, Lady, I Did It! New York: Simon & Schuster, 1961.
Like Love. New York: Simon & Schuster, 1962.
Ten Plus One. New York: Simon & Schuster, 1963.
Ax. New York: Simon & Schuster, 1964.
He Who Hesitates. New York: Delacorte Press, 1965.
Doll. New York: Delacorte Press, 1965.
Eighty Million Eyes. New York: Delacorte Press, 1966.
Fuzz. Garden City, N.Y.: Doubleday, 1968.
Shotgun. Garden City, N.Y.: Doubleday, 1969.
Jigsaw. Garden City, N.Y.: Doubleday, 1970.
Hail, Hail, the Gang's All Here! Garden City, N.Y.: Doubleday, 1971.
Sadie When She Died. Garden City, N.Y.: Doubleday, 1972.
Let's Hear It for the Deaf Man. Garden City, N.Y.: Doubleday, 1973.
Hail to the Chief. New York: Random House, 1973.
Bread. New York: Random House, 1974.
Blood Relatives. New York: Random House, 1975.
So Long As You Both Shall Live. New York: Random House, 1976.
Long Time No See. New York: Random House, 1977.
Calypso. New York: Viking Press, 1979.
Ghosts. New York: Viking Press, 1980.
Heat. New York: Viking Press, 1981.
Beauty and the Beast. London: Hamish Hamilton, 1982.
Ice. New York: Arbor House, 1983.
Lightning. New York: Arbor House, 1984.
Eight Black Horses. New York: Arbor House, 1985.
Another Part of the City. New York: Mysterious Press, 1986.
Poison. New York: Arbor House, 1987.
Tricks. New York: Arbor House, 1987.
Lullaby. New York: Morrow, 1989.
Vespers. New York: Morrow, 1990.
Widows. New York: Morrow, 1991.
Kiss. New York: Morrow, 1992.
Mischief. New York: Morrow, 1993.

And All Through the House. New York: Warner Books, 1994.

Romance. New York: Warner Books, 1995.

Nocturne. New York: Warner Books, 1997.

THE MATTHEW HOPE NOVELS

Goldilocks. New York: Arbor House, 1977.

Rumpelstiltskin. New York: Viking Press, 1981.

Jack and the Beanstalk. New York: Holt, Rinehart, and Winston, 1984.

Snow White and Rose Red. New York: Holt, Rinehart, and Winston, 1985.

Cinderella. New York: Holt, 1986.

Puss in Boots. New York: Holt, 1987.

The House That Jack Built. New York: Holt, 1988.

Three Blind Mice. New York: Arcade, 1990.

Mary, Mary. New York: Warner Books, 1992.

There Was a Little Girl. New York: Warner Books, 1994.

WORKS OF EVAN HUNTER

The Evil Sleep! N.p., Falcon, 1952.

The Big Fix. N.p., Falcon, 1952.

Don't Crowd Me. New York: Popular Library, 1953.

The Blackboard Jungle. New York: Simon & Schuster, 1954.

Strangers When We Meet. New York: Simon & Schuster, 1958.

A Matter of Conviction. New York: Simon & Schuster, 1959.

Buddwing. New York: Simon & Schuster, 1964.

A Horse's Head. New York: Delacorte Press, 1967.

Nobody Knew They Were There. Garden City, N.Y.: Doubleday, 1971.

Every Little Crook and Nanny. Garden City, N.Y.: Doubleday, 1972.

The Chisholms: A Novel of the Journey West. New York: Harper & Row, 1976.

Walk Proud. New York: Bantam, 1979.

Lizzie. New York: Arbor House, 1984.

Criminal Conversation. New York: Warner Books, 1994.

Privileged Conversation. New York: Warner Books, 1996.

BIOGRAPHICAL AND CRITICAL STUDIES

Blom, K. A. "Polis! Polis!" In *Murder Ink.* Edited by Dilys Winn. New York: Workman, 1984.

Carr, John C. "Ed McBain." In *The Craft of Crime. Conversations with Crime Writers.* Boston: Houghton Mifflin, 1983.

Dove, George N. "McBain, Ed." In *St. James Guide to Crime and Mystery Writers,* 4th ed. Edited by Jay P. Pederson. Detroit: St. James Press, 1996.

McGlure, James. "Carella of the 87th." In *Murder Ink.* Edited by Dilys Winn. New York: Workman, 1984.

Priestman, Martin. In his *Detective Fiction and Literature.* New York: St. Martin's, 1991.

Symons, Julian. In his *Bloody Murder: From the Detective Story to the Crime Novel,* 3d rev. ed. New York: Mysterious Press, 1992.

MICHAEL INNES

(1906–1994)

GEORGE L. SCHEPER

MICHAEL INNES was the pseudonym of John Innes Mackintosh Stewart, the author of forty-five volumes of mystery and thriller entertainments and an Oxford don of distinguished career as both literary historian and, in his later years, novelist and short-story writer under his own name. By critical consensus, it is as a "donnish" narrator and, specifically, as an evocator of Oxonian ambiance, both in the Innes mysteries and the Stewart novels and stories, that the author was and continues to be best known. Although Stewart had been an undergraduate at Oxford and subsequently came to know Oxford as well as anyone, in his career from 1949 to 1973 as Student (i.e., senior fellow) of Christ Church, there was always, he once admitted, "a species of naive nostalgia . . . at work" in his evocations, the "compelling fascination" that traditional English life and manners had for one who was an expatriate ("John Appleby," p. 13). For Stewart had been born and raised a Scot, and his first academic posts after graduation were in Leeds, Adelaide, and Belfast. Thus, what Stewart says about his detective John Appleby is also, in a manner, true of himself as a writer, both as Innes and as Stewart: "He is within a society remembered rather than observed—and remembered in terms of literary conventions which are themselves distancing themselves as his creator works. His is an expatriate's world" ("John Appleby," p. 13).

It is what critics have consistently noted as perhaps the chief thing about all the fictions of Stewart—that they are written in a highly literate and mandarin prose reminiscent especially of Henry James and that they evoke an Edwardian zeitgeist that has become politically and socially, and now academically, rather obsolete. It is also widely conceded, even among his detractors, that within his chosen mode, Stewart is a master stylist and humorist and a compelling raconteur. As Erik Routley has said with reference to the mystery narratives, "The impression you always get is that of a first-class senior common-room raconteur with a sense of humour, to whom you listen just for the pleasure of hearing it happen" (Routley, p. 158). The reputation and legacy of Stewart the mystery writer in his field have and undoubtedly will continue to surpass and outlast the reputation and legacy of Stewart as a novelist outside the mystery genre, as the author himself once acknowledged in an interview, conceding that he supposed "Innes is rather better at what *he* does than Stewart is at what *he* does" (Scheper, 1986, p. 12). On the other hand, the stature of Stewart as a student of literature, based especially upon his major work, *Eight Modern Writers* (1963), the final volume of the Oxford History of English Literature, is modest but secure, and his life's work as a don, lecturer, and tutor bears whatever invisible legacy is granted to the dedicated and admired teacher.

Life and Career

John Innes Mackintosh Stewart was born in Edinburgh on 30 September 1906, the son of John Stewart and Elizabeth Jane (née Clark) of Nairn, and raised in the genteel environment of the outskirts of the Georgian New Town. Although his father, a lawyer, was chief executive officer of the Edinburgh School Board, including its flagship high school, young Stewart was enrolled instead at the New Town's Edinburgh Academy, an eleven-year period he remembered mostly for its grim, unadorned philological pedagogy, a spartan routine broken only by equally spartan and "disagreeably muddy games" ("An Edinburgh Boyhood," p. 67). These experiences were reflected in Stewart's fictional quintet, *A Staircase in Surrey* (1974–1978). Aesthetic relief from the austerity of the academy was provided by the Scottish National Gallery, in rooms with "Italian light on Scottish walls" ("An Edinburgh Boyhood," p. 68), evincing the early responsiveness to art that served Stewart well in his various fictional endeavors.

Upon leaving the academy, Stewart persuaded his parents to approve a cross-border move to England, enabling him to apply for and accept a scholarship to Oriel College, Oxford, in 1925, at age nineteen. Although it was on the edge of radical transformation, Oxford between the wars, in the mid-1920s, was a vastly traditional institution still governed, as Stewart noted, by most "antique conventions" (*Myself and Michael Innes* [1987] p. 57). Stewart amply drew on these conventions, above all in the Oxford Quintet and in a whole series of Oxford-related mysteries. Among Stewart's undergraduate contemporaries were Christopher Isherwood and Wystan (W. H.) Auden. His moral tutor, the philosopher W. D. Ross, delivered to Stewart what he remembers as his most memorable lesson:

> Ross told me at some brief beginning-of-term interview, when I had no doubt been talking pretentiously about my reading and opinions, that it seemed to him that a great deal of nonsense was written about literature. Because he said this at once diffidently and with authority . . . , I received it as a maxim at once, and have applied it with great benefit in my dealings with critical expatiation ever since. (*Myself and Michael Innes,* pp. 38–39)

After achieving his first in English Language and Literature in 1928, followed by a sort of postgraduate grand tour to Germany and Austria (with some study of psychoanalysis in Vienna), Stewart found himself essentially unemployed, although he kept his oar in by winning, in 1929, a literary competition for which Oxford graduates were invited to compete, the Matthew Arnold Memorial Prize. Then, through a chance encounter with Francis and Viola Meynell, founders of the Nonesuch Press, Stewart secured the job of editing John Florio's translation of Montaigne, which in turn garnered him a postgraduate fellowship as Bishop Fraser's Scholar at Oriel, the base from which he launched his academic career.

Stewart's first full-time academic post was as Lecturer in English at the provincial University of Leeds. It was there, in his Leeds boardinghouse, that he met his future wife, Margaret Hardwick, a medical student; they married in 1932. The relatively uneventful five years he spent at the university (1930–1935) nevertheless provided fertile comic material for Innes' pair of "redbrick" (that is, Non-Oxfordian) academic mysteries, *The Weight of the Evidence* (1943) and *Old Hall, New Hall* (1956; U.S. title, *A Question of Queens*). When an opportunity presented itself of accepting a post as Jury Professor of English at the University of Adelaide in South Australia, Stewart and his wife carefully weighed their unpromising prospects (his as underpaid assistant lecturer and hers as medical worker in postnatal clinics) against the solemn advice to "let nothing except penury take you into exile" and opted for antipodean exile (*Myself and Michael Innes,* p. 97). The move was momentous in one unforeseen way, for it was during the voyage to Australia in

1935 that both Michael Innes and John Appleby were born:

> John Appleby came into being during a sea voyage from Liverpool to Adelaide. Ocean travel was a leisured affair in those days, and the route by the Cape of Good Hope took six weeks to cover. By that time I had completed a novel called *Death at the President's Lodging*. . . . I was simply writing a yarn to beguile a somewhat tedious experience—and in a popular literary kind at that time allowable as an occasional diversion even to quite serious and even learned persons, including university professors. ("John Appleby," p. 11)

Stewart later portrayed his mystery-writing regimen in unassuming terms: "For nine months of the year, and between six and eight o'clock in the morning, the South Australian climate is just right for authorship of this sort. . . . Sometimes I lie on the beach and wonder if I mightn't some day write something else" (Kunitz and Haycraft, p. 1348). Innes continued a regular output during the years in Australia, resulting in some dozen titles published between 1936 and 1946, including two—*Lament for a Maker* (1938) and *What Happened at Hazelwood* (1946; U.S. title, *What Happened at Hazlewood?*)—with significant Australian connections. Many years later, Stewart reflected:

> This suggests more application than, I fear, actually went into the activity; one is rather freely inventive when one is young, and the stories seemed to get themselves on the page out of odd corners of my mind at odd times and seasons. I never brooded over them as I was to brood over ordinary "straight" novels later; and here I was only being faithful to that first *ethos* of the "classical" English detective story as a diversion to be lightly offered and lightly received. ("John Appleby," p. 13)

At Adelaide, Stewart lectured and represented the university at various local cultural endeavors, although he never quite shook the fact that he was, as he memorably puts it, "a provincial dropped in among colonials" (*Myself*, p. 104). Thus, at the close of World War II, when the cessation of hostilities in the Pacific enabled his family to book a steamer back to the British Isles, Stewart allowed himself to be rescued from Australia to a post at Queen's University in Belfast. There the Stewarts enjoyed a quiet and contented two years (1946–1948), notable for the richly comedic use of Irish setting and ambiance in a subsequent thriller, *The Journeying Boy* (1949; U.S. title, *The Case of the Journeying Boy*). While he continued writing at the pace of a book a year, on the academic side of the ledger, Stewart experienced some unease from wondering whether Queens indeed "marked the end of a road" (*Myself*, p. 121).

Stewart had, however, by then written *Character and Motive in Shakespeare* (1949), confirming his scholarly credentials and leading directly to an invitation to do the final volume of the *Oxford History of English Literature*. Stewart spent ten years on the project, and the resultant *Eight Modern Writers* stands as his paramount academic contribution. The securing of this project coincided with Stewart's appointment in 1949 as Student of Christ Church, Oxford, the position he held for the rest of his professional life until his retirement in 1973. From 1969 to 1973, he also held the position of Reader in English Literature of Oxford University. Upon retirement, he became professor emeritus.

Stewart's twenty-five years at Christ Church were outwardly uneventful; as he himself noted, referencing British author Samuel Johnson, "An academic life puts one little in the way of extraordinary casualties" (*Myself*, p. 156). Such small academic drama as might transpire became, however, grist for Stewart's fictional mill, as, commencing with *Mark Lambert's Supper* in 1954, he embarked on a sort of third career, as mainstream fiction writer. Stewart's characteristic output for the next thirty years then became one Innes mystery a year and one Stewart work of fiction every sixteen months or so, along with a continuous production of academic monographs, editing, and periodical writing. As one *Times*

Literary Supplement reviewer commented, "The quite Trollopian productivity of Mr. J. I. M. Stewart commands our respect and gratitude. High-powered university teaching, high-fantastical thrillers, urbane, neo-Jacobean social comedies, lit. crit. for the Sundays—this industrious juggler can keep his eye on all these balls at once as they twinkle in the air above a pair of remarkably safe hands" (p. 313).

The Stewart fictions were given a generally favorable, if not always enthusiastic, critical reception. For one thing, many reviewers noted the similarity between the oeuvres. Richard Mayne, for example, in a review of Stewart's *Acre of Grass* (1965), noted that there has

> obviously always been a novelist inside the writer of whodunits, and the retort comes pat—isn't there also a whodunit writer inside the novelist? To say this, however, is only to restate the point that Stewart is a traditional writer. Clues, climaxes, suspense, mystery and surprise are the tried ingredients of the classic novel. . . . Mandarin prose may be lying down, but it isn't dead—Stewart himself, indeed, is a witness to what it can still achieve. (*New Statesman*, p. 206).

Similarly, in a review of Stewart's *Bridge at Arta and Other Stories* (1981), A. N. Wilson, in emphasizing the old-fashioned conservatism and "innocent" snobbery of the Stewart milieu ("the reassuring impression that art stopped short somewhere during the leisurely reign of George V"), goes on to note that "the division between Michael Innes and J. I. M. Stewart, has, over the years, become so slight as to be inconsiderable" (p. 22).

Stewart's academic writing during this period included, besides *Eight Modern Writers*, separate biocritical monographs on James Joyce (1957), Thomas Love Peacock (1963), Rudyard Kipling (1966), Joseph Conrad (1968), and Thomas Hardy (1971). Among various introductions and edited volumes, special interest attaches to Stewart's introduction to the Penguin edition of Wilkie Collins' *Moonstone* (1966) for his comments on Collins' attempts to blend detective fiction with the concerns of the novel proper, the central concern of Innes' own essay on his craft, "Death As a Game" (1965). Stewart retired in 1973. His wife, Margaret, died in 1979, and for a time he continued to live in their home at Fawler Copse, outside Wantage in Oxfordshire, with his youngest son, Angus, who was himself a novelist. The year 1986 saw the publication of the last Innes mystery, *Appleby and the Ospreys*, and the final work of fiction by Stewart, *Parlour 4 and Other Stories*; the next year his collection of autobiographical reminiscences, *Myself and Michael Innes*, was published. After some years of declining health, Stewart died on 12 November 1994, at the age of eighty-eight, survived by three sons and two daughters.

Curtain-Raisers: The First Four Innes Mysteries

With such a prolific corpus of writing and with such strongly perceived interconnections, both stylistic and thematic, between the two bodies of fiction (and, indeed, between both of these and the academic writing as well), it is necessary to attempt some sort of periodization and thematic taxonomy of Stewart's corpus. The first four mysteries stand out as notable, even exceptional, contributions to the mystery genre, each after its own fashion: *Death at the President's Lodging* (1936; U.S. title, *Seven Suspects*) as a highly complex closed-environment or limited-circle-of-suspects puzzle in an academic setting; *Hamlet, Revenge!* (1937) as an academic cum country-house mystery on the occasion of a private theatrical; *Lament for a Maker* as a brooding, Stevensonian experiment in Scottish atmosphere and the device of multiple narrators; and *Stop Press: A Novel* (1939; U.S. title, *The Spider Strikes*), as its subtitle implies, as an attempt at combining country-house detective business with comedy of manners of a highly literary and whimsical sort.

Death at the President's Lodging was an impressive debut. In a *Spectator* review, Nicholas Blake (the mystery pseudonym of the British poet C. Day-Lewis) pronounced it "the most brilliant first novel I have had the luck to read. . . . But Mr. Innes commands such a battery of wit, subtlety, learning and psychological penetration that he blows almost all opposition clean out of the water" (p. 770). Some reviewers, however, found the plot simply too fantasticated for credibility. Stewart himself, in his autobiography, remarks, after having reread the book for the first time in the half century since its composition, "I am chiefly struck by the sheer hard work that must have gone to slogging out an orthodox and extremely intricate plot" (*Myself*, p. 115). And in an earlier essay, writing as Michael Innes, he had characterized the story as "an immensely complicated murder" in which "Appleby is kept so busy getting it straight that he has very little leisure to exhibit himself in any point of character" ("John Appleby," p. 11). This may have been too harsh, for Appleby does present himself as quite a distinct, even innovative detective hero; a recent graduate himself of the fictional Saint Anthony's, he is quite capable of holding his own with the learned dons and is utterly unfazed by their academic abracadabra. He is what Innes calls "a highly assimilative person, who moves, or has learned to move, with complete assurance in any society" (p. 14).

In the novel itself, Innes offered a memorable characterization of Appleby as something more than the product of a long discipline of careful and technical study: "A contemplative habit and a tentative mind, poise as well as force, reserve rather than wariness—these were the tokens perhaps of some underlying, more liberal education. It was a schooled but still free intelligence that was finally formidable in Appleby" (1962 ed., p. 11). In later chronicles, Appleby perhaps moves a bit away from this carefully constructed persona, as Innes admits: "Later on he is hazardously given to flashes of intuition, and to picking up clues on the strength of his mysteriously acquired familiarity with recondite artistic and literary matters" ("John Appleby," p. 12). But in this first narrative, Appleby is clearly defined as an agent of retributive justice acting on behalf of a threatened but still viable academic ideal. The solution, which seems at first to be a matter of calculating times and movements in the manner of the traditional puzzle story, in fact comes to Appleby in the form of a literary/philosophical clue. It is about turning upside-down something British essayist Thomas De Quincey, in the essay "Murder Considered As One of the Fine Arts," attributes to Immanuel Kant. As Professor Titlow, a prime suspect in *Death at the President's Lodging,* paraphrases De Quincey: "in no conceivable circumstance could it be justifiable to lie—not even to mislead an intending murderer as to the whereabouts of his victim." Professor Titlow, the source of the anecdote, explains how he acted on the converse imperative: "If the cunning of a murderer could only be defeated by a lie, then a lie must be told—or acted" (1962 ed., pp. 256–257).

Innes' second mystery, *Hamlet, Revenge!* was, in terms of sheer literary quality, a further advance. Even Ralph Partridge, never a keen enthusiast of Innes, conceded, "There is an aroma of Miss Dorothy L. Sayers about Mr. Innes which many will find agreeable. Powerful, fluent, well-educated prose almost condescending, as it were, to act as vehicle for detection—that is the force at Mr. Innes' disposal" (1937, p. 225). Here the murder occurs in the context of a private theatrical performance of *Hamlet* at a ducal palace, and the key document in the case proves to be Shakespeare's play itself—along with sundry other Elizabethan texts.

The mysterious clues are provided in the form of a series of messages consisting of fragmentary quotations from a variety of Elizabethan texts, and the attempt to reconstruct the murder itself, which occurs during the course of the performance, hinges on competing and fundamentally conflicting interpretations of the play and its staging. The production, under the direction of Giles Gott, an Oxford don, is mounted strictly according to the principles of the so-called historical school, and Gott has faithfully re-created an Elizabethan stage in the palace's great hall, thus unwittingly creating, as one character remarks, "a perfect material setting for a mystery: upper stage, rear stage, trap-doors and what-not" (1962 ed., p. 54). Stewart would point out with pride how years later he learned "that Sir Walter Greg, the most eminent Shakespeare scholar of the time, had read *Hamlet, Revenge!* again and again, submitting it to 'the same kind of scrutiny he gave to the variants in the first quarto of *King Lear*' " (*Myself*, p. 119).

Of course, all this academic matter about Shakespeare was in the foreground of the author's attention as a university lecturer and is reflected in Stewart's *Character and Motive in Shakespeare.* As if to demonstrate Michael Innes' own continued concern with *Hamlet* criticism, two of Innes' radio plays about Hamlet were presented on the BBC's *Third Programme* in 1948 and 1949: "The Hawk and the Handsaw" and "The Mysterious Affair at Elsinore" (both published in 1950 in *Three Tales of Hamlet,* by Innes and Rayner Heppenstall).

Innes' third mystery, *Lament for a Maker,* is a richly textured tale of a much hated, guilt-ridden, and death-obsessed Scottish laird found hurled to his death at the foot of his snowbound ancient tower on a Christmas morning. Stewart has noted that it is "a heavily Stevensonian story, set in Scotland and drawing upon the sort of people I came from" (*Myself*, p. 118). Early reviewers, such as Nicholas Blake, considered it his best book to date, and later critics have reaffirmed this judgment. Melvyn Barnes noted that it "is generally considered as his supreme achievement," adding his own assessment that "This must surely rank as one of the most beautifully written detective novels of all time" (p. 63). Many will agree with Erik Routley that there must be many readers who, however long ago they first read *Lament for a Maker,* "have found it impossible to forget" (p. 159). Stewart himself testifies to being one of them: "I regard this novel as leaving something in the mind . . . which is a quality not owned by the numerous Innes stories all too often" (*Myself,* p. 124). Routley went on to offer the following tribute:

> Despite the long run of excellent stories he has produced since, I still think this was the profoundest plot he ever constructed. In many ways it achieved things which Innes never came near again. . . . The sheer beauty of the long narratives of Ewan Bell, in faultless Scottish prose, the powerful evocation of the presbyterian grimness of a Scottish castle, the quite distinguished communication of the narrator's integrity and moral agony, are all at a level which the author doesn't seem to have wanted or tried to repeat. (pp. 158–159)

Routley may be precisely right, because Innes himself explains in "Death As a Game" why he thinks the exploration of character and motive in the true novel is incompatible with the artificial conventions of detective fiction, a "world in which everybody is liable to murder anybody else" (p. 55) and in which "anybody in the story must be capable of acting under any motive and to any end" (p. 56). He concludes, "Here is the main obstacle to achieving what, following Miss Sayers, I've had a shot at often enough: blending the detective story with 'straight' fiction, so as to achieve a distinct kind with some literary substance. It doesn't work. As soon as I start *caring*—or even just exploring in a disinterested way—the thing goes wrong" (p. 56). Whether Innes is necessarily right in this general self-assessment, it is certainly true that after *Lament for a Maker,* he decisively returned to what he calls here his more characteristic "mannered and wholly artificial approach" (p. 56) to crime in virtually all of his subsequent mystery entertainments.

Certainly that helps explain why his very next book, *Stop Press,* while retaining a certain novelistic ambition, does so distinctly in the mode of comedy of manners, influenced more by Jane Austen and Anthony Trollope than by Edgar Allan Poe and Sir Arthur Conan Doyle. The setting is one of those quintessentially British long weekends in a country-house environment, where the plot, as Julian Symons (who judged this "perhaps the best" of all Innes' work) put it, is "balanced on little jets of unfailingly amusing talk" (*Mortal Consequences,* p. 127). The book is, in fact, a perfect example of the genre that Hanna Charney and others have come to call "the detective novel of manners," self-consciously literary and full of bookish talk and quotations and of self-referential comments about writing, particularly the writing of detective fiction. One character even delivers herself of an Innes-like disquisition on the artificial conventions of detective fiction. The protagonist is a would-be scholar of the poet Alexander Pope, who has, however, made his fortune as a mystery writer and has in a very real sense fallen into the grip of his own creation—as plots he has thought of, but never yet written down, start to enact themselves among his family and acquaintances. This theme of the boundary between art and life coming undone proved to be a recurrent preoccupation for Innes; it can also be found in such other works as *Appleby's End* (1945) and *Appleby's Answer* (1973).

Thrillers and Fantasias

Innes never drew upon the realities of World War II or the ensuing Cold War in his strictly detective fictions, but he did so in a group of stories of the 1940s and 1950s that are better classified as thrillers, that is, flight-and-pursuit stories and anxiety tales of mistaken identity and impersonation. Unlike the traditional formal detective novel, which is backwardly plotted and aimed at reconstructing, in Robert Champigny's phrase, "what will have happened," thrillers and anxiety tales are forwardly plotted, unfolding a tale of ever-heightening suspense that attempts to maximize the reader's vicarious emotional involvement. Unlike the formal detective novel of manners, premised on an essentially innocent world temporarily blighted by an intrusion of evil and a general atmosphere of suspicion—which are, respectively, expelled and dispelled by the Prospero-like detective hero—the world of the thriller, as Ralph Harper has argued, is existential, a world where no one and nothing is what it seems, where guilt and suspicion are never finally dispelled, and where the protagonist, and even the reader, seem to remain implicated rather than vindicated. Innes' thrillers, however, are never quite that dark—in fact, he is the virtual inventor of a whole new hybrid genre, the comic thriller, or thriller-fantasia.

Stewart traces the ancestry of his thrillers to two of his own countrymen: Sir John Buchan and Robert Louis Stevenson. In an anecdote Stewart related in 1942, his headmaster at the Edinburgh Academy had, in a tone of "mild censure," once predicted that what Stewart might write someday would be a *Kidnapped* or a *Treasure Island* (Kunitz and Haycraft, p. 1348); nearly fifty years later, Stewart remembered the incident as having a bit more bite:

> Having been obliged to read the essays with which I had competed for prizes, he had formed, and expressed to me, the opinion that I might one day manage a *Coral Island,* but that a *Treasure Island* would be beyond the twitch of my tether. The point of this very just remark was that both R. M. Ballantyne and Robert Louis Stevenson had been Academy boys. (*Myself,* p. 29)

Innes' first foray into the romantic adventure mode was *The Secret Vanguard* (1940), a spy thriller within a World War II and Nazi fifth column context, but almost wholly focused on the relentless pursuit of an innocent girl who happens to overhear and understand the encoded intelligence messages being passed back and forth in a railway carriage. (It's done through spouting lines of poetry back and forth, and Sheila recognizes some bogus lines; as she explains, "If you happen to know about Swinburne, of course they stick out a mile" [1982 ed., p. 51].) The chase sequence across the Scottish moors is the main thing, and it is evoked by Innes with a masterly sense of topography and an exquisitely heightening tension. Ralph Partridge's grudging tribute in *New Statesman* is that in this novel "Innes' talent for pastiche serves him faithfully, even gloriously. . . . Every step of *The Thirty-Nine Steps* he treads again with the punctiliousness of a don and the fidelity of a Scotsman" (p. 392). Stewart's self-assessment is that this chase sequence over the moor is,

> I judge, the most empathetic writing I have anywhere achieved. . . . The juxtaposition of [the blind fiddler's] crazy imaginings and the closely-worked minute-by-minute account of Sheila's flight has the felicitousness that does sometimes drop unbidden into a writer's grasp. Here—to vary the figure—it lands me on a perch from which I descend clumsily enough. The closing chapters of *The Secret Vanguard* are a huddle of spy-and-detective stuff much lacking in clarity and credibility. (*Myself*, p. 125)

The "straightest" thriller Innes ever wrote was *The Man from the Sea* (1955), presided over, as Stewart has put it, by "the hovering presence of Joseph Conrad" (*Myself*, p. 128). Although he draws on the overworked Cold War plot of a scientist with knowledge crucial to civilization, the narrative itself is crisp and compelling, conveyed in a prose that is correspondingly lean and hard. In the opening scene, two naked men warily confront each other on a moonlit Scottish beach, and their subsequent relationship—reminiscent of that of the narrator and his doppelgänger in Conrad's story "The Secret Sharer"—involves them in another of Innes' patented chase scenes through territory he knows so well. "What I recall with some satisfaction in the novel," he says, "are certain vignettes of Scottish life and character: that and a fairly authentic command of demotic Scotch in the simpler characters" (*Myself*, p. 129).

In contrast are a pair of early comic thrillers, *Appleby on Ararat* (1941) and *The Daffodil Affair* (1942), which represent what Stewart himself calls "extravaganzas, . . . my principal attempts to bring a little fantasy and fun into the detective story" (*Myself*, p. 118). The former is a bit of straight imperial romancing in the South Pacific, a Rule Britannia parable about good English form finally overcoming native savagery and Nazi brutality. The latter is a more sophisticated fantasia about a nefarious plot by a transnational secret organization to dominate the postwar world by cornering the market in psychic phenomena; the idea is to take advantage of the Götterdämmerung occasioned by World War II in order to gain control over the new world order through manipulation of the resurgent spiritualism certain to follow upon the collapse of rationality.

Underlying the bizarrerie of *The Daffodil Affair* are matters of genuine political and philosophical concern to which Innes repeatedly returns. In particular, the idea of the exploitation of the chaos of war-torn Europe, under the pretext of "preserving" its threatened art treasures, is the driving Mephistophelian idea behind the villainous forces of *From "London" Far* (1946; U.S. title, *The Unsuspected Chasm*). After an opening sequence that plunges the unassuming protagonist, Richard Meredith, a fiftyish, mild-mannered academic, into a wild Buchanesque chase sequence, the novel pits Meredith in philosophical debate with the mastermind of the Society for the Diffusion of Cultural Objects, whose argument is that

> Everywhere public order perishes, and civil polity has become but a historical phenomenon. . . . For the populations of Europe will be no more than a peasantry and a wandering banditti. And thus when these works of art are brought forth from their half-century of seclusion men will no more think to inquire of their former owner's rights than they do of tom-toms and totem-poles in some museum of Polynesian anthropology. (1981 ed., p. 170)

Meredith is able to see through this rehash of the German philosopher Oswald Spengler and perversion of the English essayist Walter Pater, and the latter part of the novel is an essentially comic encounter with the superrich American magnate who is the buyer behind the whole operation. His dirty little secret, and why he keeps his finest oil painting acquisitions in a locked collection, is that he is, to his everlasting chagrin, color-blind.

In structural terms, Innes' next two thrillers, *The Journeying Boy* and *Operation Pax* (1951; U.S. title, *The Paper Thunderbolt*), are similar to *From "London" Far:* all three begin with a Buchanesque chase sequence, and all three end at a sort of "castle perilous." The former Innes regards as the favorite among his mysteries, and it is notable for the most extensive use of Irish ambiance in any of his books; it is, he says, "a Donegal as real as I can make it" (*Myself,* p. 127). Before, however, we get to "the philosophical republic of Mr. De Valera" (1964 ed., p. 145), the book presents a lurid crime perpetrated in a West End cinema, a freakish rail journey through England, and a brief satirical portrait of Belfast, "grimly utilitarian and shrouded in rain" (p. 136). The plot itself, involving a scientist with a crucial formula, is hackneyed enough (for another Innes variation on the theme, see *Hare Sitting Up,* 1959), but the "hunted man" aspect is effectively sensational and effective as moral allegory as well. The immediate object of the hunt, the scientist's son, experiences an archetypal rebirth in the womblike caves of the Irish coast and becomes a man, while his tutor and protector, though a man "almost irrationally determined to deny that the universe holds anything dangerous or surprising" (p. 160), is for all that "a very good man indeed" when placed in "a *very* tight place" (p. 238). Reviewer Will Cuppy, in the New York *Herald Tribune Weekly Book Review* judged this "the best mystery story in years," a work that obliterated any distinction between mystery novel and novel proper: "Too good to be true, but here it is" (p. 12).

Innes' other most ambitious thriller sequence occurs in the opening section of *Operation Pax,* but here the hunted man is not one of Innes' unassuming, mild-mannered academics, but a weasily crook inadvertently caught up in the machinations of yet another group bent on exercising social and political control by way of a "secret formula." The chase itself is a tour de force of thriller topography, a hare-and-hounds chase through all manner of environments and by all manner of vehicles, ending up in Oxford, where the final stage of the pursuit takes place round the massive catalog of the Bodleian Library's Upper Reading Room. This and much of the rest of this neglected Innes masterpiece best places it in the next category, that of the academic mystery.

Murder in the Great Good Place

As Auden argued, the classic detective story, as opposed to the thriller, is premised on a closed and closely related society that appears to be in an innocent state of grace until murder, presumably from within, precipitates the crisis. For Innes, the university, the art gallery, and the country house are the embodiments of that formula. The country house has been used in too many Innes mysteries to enumerate. As do other practitioners of "the Mayhem Parva school" of genteel and formulaic mystery fiction, Innes first of all uses the country house and the country-house weekend as microcosms of English society (the designation "Mayhem Parva school" for the formal British detective story was coined by Colin Watson [pp. 165–175]). In such settings, representative types of the whole social tapestry may conveniently be brought under one roof—and, as a character in an Ivy Compton-Burnett novel has said, "Roofs seem to give rise to situations" (quoted by Gill, p. xxi). Moreover, Innes has taken the familiar device of the great country house as a complex physical setting and given it a further shove, so that architecture itself becomes a genuine plot factor. *The Open House* (1972), *Appleby's Other Story* (1974), and *Appleby at Allington* (published in the United States as *Death by Water,* 1968) could well be denominated as "Palladian thrillers," the latter actually being an instance of murder by Palladian symmetry.

As for the university, "It is a sound instinct," Auden said, "that has made so many detective story writers choose a college as a setting," where the violation of the cloistered academy and the academic ideal "is a sign that some colleague is not only a bad man but also a bad professor" (Winks, p. 18). It is a point that had been made, less facetiously, by Marjorie Nicolson in her 1929 *Atlantic Monthly* essay "The Professor and the Detective"—and has been roundly critiqued by critics of the Golden Age formulates, such as Colin Watson in *Snobbery with Violence.* For Innes, of course, the academic ideal is intact, and Oxford is the Great Good Place par excellence, except that his portraits of academics tend to reflect the "humours" characters of Ben Jonson, as he made explicit in his prologue to *Death at the President's Lodging:*

> The senior members of Oxford and Cambridge colleges are undoubtedly among the most moral and level-headed of men. They do nothing aberrant; they do nothing rashly or in haste. Their conventional associations are with learning, unworldliness, absence of mind, and endearing and always innocent foible. . . . They are, as Ben Jonson would have said, persons such as comedy would choose; it is much easier to give them a shove into the humorous than a twist into the melodramatic; they prove peculiarly restive to the slightly rummy psychology that most detective stories require. (1962 ed., p. 5)

Innes' novels with a significant Oxford connection include, in addition to that first title, *Stop Press, A Family Affair* (1969; U.S. title, *Picture of Guilt*), *Appleby Plays Chicken* (1957; U.S. title, *Death on a Quiet Day*), and, of course, *Operation Pax,* with its two great sequences, "Bodley by Day" and "Bodley by Night," which take us into the veritable holy of holies of the university. It is not just that the Bodleian serves as an eerie Piranesian labyrinth perfect for physical mystification, but that it is, as the repository of intellectual tradition, an emblem of Western civilization and its values.

And what is true of books is also true of paintings, another emblem of cultural values for Innes' formal detective novels. In *A Private View* (1952; U.S. title, *One-Man Show*), the Duke of Horton is perturbed over the theft of a Vermeer from his private galley not so much because of any personal financial or even aesthetic loss to himself as because of his sense of failed stewardship: "Upbringing you know. I was taught that we simply held all those things in trust. Not for the nation. My father disapproved of nations, whether his own or any other. But for civilization in general. So in losing the Vermeer I feel I've fallen down, rather, on the job" (1975 ed., p. 53). Thus, all the bookish talk in Innes' academic mysteries or such tales as *The Long Farewell* (1958) or *The Ampersand Papers* (1978), and all the connoisseurship in such titles as *A Connoisseur's Case* (1962; U.S. title, *The Crabtree Affair*), *Christmas at Candleshoe* (1953), *Silence Observed* (1961), or the comic art thrillers involving the DaVinci Gallery (*A Private View; Money from Holme,* 1964; and *A Family Affair*), or the more recent Honeybath series (*The Mysterious Commission,* 1974; *Honeybath's Haven,* 1977; *Lord Mullion's Secret,* 1981; and *Appleby and Honeybath,* 1983)—all that cultural literacy and allusiveness are not mere show-off erudition, affectation, or elitist snobbery. Rather, the literate detective's recourse to book learning and art history are intended as touchstones of his ability to distinguish the genuine from the bogus, as playful reminders of what, after all, is our shared sense of the best that has been known and thought in the world, and of what, finally, we set store by. Innes, we might say, does for his readers what the best sort of don might do: as readers we are in conversation with someone who is gracious enough to expect us to bring the best of ourselves to the encounter.

Selected Bibliography

WORKS OF MICHAEL INNES

NOVELS

Death at the President's Lodging. London: Gollancz, 1936. U.S.: *Seven Suspects.* New York: Dodd, Mead, 1937; Dolphin/Doubleday, 1962.

Hamlet, Revenge! London: Gollancz, 1937; New York: Dodd, Mead, 1937; Crowell/Collier, 1962.

Lament for a Maker. London: Gollancz, 1938; New York: Dodd, Mead, 1938.

Stop Press: A Novel. London: Gollancz, 1939. U.S.: *The Spider Strikes: A Detective Story.* New York: Dodd, Mead, 1939.

The Secret Vanguard. London: Gollancz, 1940; New York: Dodd, Mead, 1941; Harper & Row/Perrenial, 1982.

There Came Both Mist and Snow. London: Gollancz, 1940. U.S.: *A Comedy of Terrors.* New York: Dodd, Mead, 1940.

Appleby on Ararat. London: Gollancz, 1941; New York: Dodd, Mead, 1941.

The Daffodil Affair. London: Gollancz, 1942; New York: Dodd, Mead, 1942.

The Weight of the Evidence New York: Dodd, Mead, 1943; London: Gollancz, 1944.

Appleby's End. New York: Dodd, Mead, 1945; London: Gollancz, 1946.

From "London" Far. London: Gollancz, 1946; Harmondsworth, England: Penguin, 1981. U.S.: *The Unsuspected Chasm.* New York: Dodd, Mead, 1946.

What Happened at Hazelwood. London: Gollancz, 1946. U.S.: *What Happened at Hazlewood?* New York: Dodd, Mead, 1946.

A Night of Errors. New York: Dodd, Mead, 1947; London: Gollancz, 1948.

The Journeying Boy. London: Gollancz, 1949; Harmondsworth, England: Penguin, 1964. U.S.: *The Case of the Journeying Boy.* New York: Dodd, Mead, 1949.

Operation Pax. London: Gollancz, 1951. U.S.: *The Paper Thunderbolt.* New York: Dodd, Mead, 1951.

A Private View. London: Gollancz, 1952. U.S.: *One-Man Show.* New York: Dodd, Mead, 1952; Ballantine, 1975. Also published as *Murder Is an Art.* New York: Avon, 1959.

Christmas at Candleshoe. London: Gollancz, 1953; New York: Dodd, Mead, 1953. U.S.: *Candleshoe.* Harmondsworth, England: Penguin, 1978.

The Man from the Sea. London: Gollancz, 1955; New York: Dodd, Mead, 1955. Also published as *Death by Moonlight.* New York: Avon, 1955.

Old Hall, New Hall. London: Gollancz, 1956. U.S.: *A Question of Queens.* New York: Dodd, Mead, 1956.

Appleby Plays Chicken. London: Gollancz, 1957. U.S.: *Death on a Quiet Day.* New York: Dodd, Mead, 1957.

The Long Farewell. London: Gollancz, 1958; New York: Dodd, Mead, 1958.

Hare Sitting Up. London: Gollancz, 1959; New York: Dodd, Mead, 1959.

The New Sonia Wayward. London: Gollancz, 1960. U.S.: *The Case of Sonia Wayward.* New York: Dodd, Mead, 1960. Also published as *The Last of Sonia Wayward.* New York: Crowell/Collier, 1962.

Silence Observed. London: Gollancz, 1961; New York: Dodd, Mead, 1961.

A Connoisseur's Case. London: Gollancz, 1962. U.S.: *The Crabtree Affair.* New York: Dodd, Mead, 1962.

Money from Holme. London: Gollancz, 1964; New York: Dodd, Mead, 1965.

The Bloody Wood. London: Gollancz, 1966; New York: Dodd, Mead, 1966.

A Change of Heir. London: Gollancz, 1966; New York: Dodd, Mead, 1966.

Appleby at Allington. London: Gollancz, 1968. U.S.: *Death by Water.* New York: Dodd, Mead, 1968.

A Family Affair. London: Gollancz, 1969. U.S.: *Picture of Guilt.* New York: Dodd, Mead, 1969.

Death at the Chase. London: Gollancz, 1970; New York: Dodd, Mead, 1970.

An Awkward Lie. London: Gollancz, 1971; New York: Dodd, Mead, 1971.

The Open House. London: Gollancz, 1972; New York: Dodd, Mead, 1972.

Appleby's Answer. London: Gollancz, 1973; New York: Dodd, Mead, 1973.

Appleby's Other Story. London: Gollancz, 1974; New York: Dodd, Mead, 1974.

The Mysterious Commission. London: Gollancz, 1974; New York: Dodd, Mead, 1975.

The "Gay Phoenix." London: Gollancz, 1976. U.S.: *The Gay Phoenix.* New York: Dodd, Mead, 1977.

Honeybath's Haven. London: Gollancz, 1977; New York: Dodd, Mead, 1978.

The Ampersand Papers. London: Gollancz, 1978; New York: Dodd, Mead, 1979.

Going It Alone. London: Gollancz, 1980; New York: Dodd, Mead, 1980.

Lord Mullion's Secret. London: Gollancz, 1981; New York: Dodd, Mead, 1981.

Sheiks and Adders. London: Gollancz, 1982; New York: Dodd, Mead, 1982.

Appleby and Honeybath. London: Gollancz, 1983; New York: Dodd, Mead, 1983.

Carson's Conspiracy. London: Gollancz, 1984; New York: Dodd, Mead, 1984.

Appleby and the Ospreys. London: Gollancz, 1986; New York: Dodd, Mead, 1986.

COLLECTED WORKS

Appleby Talking: Twenty-three Detective Stories. London: Gollancz, 1954. U.S.: *Dead Man's Shoes.* New York: Dodd, Mead, 1954.

Appleby Talks Again: Eighteen Detective Stories. London: Gollancz, 1956; New York: Dodd, Mead, 1957.

Appleby Intervenes: Three Tales from Scotland Yard. New York: Dodd, Mead, 1965. Contains *There Came Both Mist and Snow, The Secret Vanguard,* and *One-Man Show.*

The Appleby File: Detective Stories. London: Gollancz, 1975; New York: Dodd, Mead, 1976.

The Michael Innes Omnibus. Harmondsworth, Eng.: Penguin, 1983. Contains *Death at the President's Lodging, Hamlet, Revenge!,* and *The Daffodil Affair.*

The Second Michael Innes Omnibus. Harmondsworth, Eng.: Penguin, 1983. Contains *The Journeying Boy, Operation Pax,* and *The Man from the Sea.*

OTHER WRITINGS

Three Tales of Hamlet (with Rayner Heppenstall). London: Gollancz, 1950. Includes "The Hawk and the Handsaw" and "The Mysterious Affair at Elsinore."

"Death As a Game." *Esquire* 63: 55–56 (January 1965).

"John Appleby." In *The Great Detectives.* Edited by Otto Penzler. Boston: Little, Brown, 1978; Harmondsworth, Eng.: Penguin, 1979. Pp. 11–15.

WORKS OF J. I. M. STEWART

FICTION

Mark Lambert's Supper. London: Gollancz, 1954; New York: Norton, 1954.

The Man Who Wrote Detective Stories: And Other Stories. London: Gollancz, 1959; New York: Norton, 1959.

The Man Who Won the Pools. London: Gollancz, 1961; New York: Norton, 1961; Harmondsworth, Eng.: Penguin, 1963.

An Acre of Grass. London: Gollancz, 1965; New York: Norton, 1965.

The Gaudy. London: Gollancz, 1974; New York: Norton, 1975. Vol. 1 of *A Staircase in Surrey.*

Young Pattullo. London: Gollancz, 1975; New York: Norton, 1976. Vol. 2 of *A Staircase in Surrey.*

A Memorial Service. London: Gollancz, 1976; New York: Norton, 1976. Vol. 3 of *A Staircase in Surrey.*

The Madonna of Astrolabe. London: Gollancz, 1977; New York: Norton, 1977. Vol. 4 of *A Staircase in Surrey.*

Full Term. London: Gollancz, 1978; New York: Norton, 1979. Vol. 5 of *A Staircase in Surrey.*

The Bridge at Arta and Other Stories. London: Gollancz, 1981; New York: Norton, 1982.

Parlour 4 and Other Stories. London: Gollancz, 1986; New York: Norton, 1986.

NONFICTION

Montaigne's Essays: John Florio's Translation. Edited by J. I. M. Stewart. London: Longmans, Green, 1931.

Educating the Emotions. Adelaide: New Education Fellowship/South Australian Section, 1944

Character and Motive in Shakespeare: Some Recent Appraisals Examined. London and New York: Longmans, Green, 1949.

James Joyce. Writers and Their Work series, no. 91. London: Longmans, Green/for the British Council, 1957.

Thomas Love Peacock. Writers and Their Work series, no. 156. London: Longmans, Green/for the British Council, 1963.

Eight Modern Writers, vol. 12 of the *Oxford History of English Literature.* Oxford: Clarendon Press, 1963.

"An Edinburgh Boyhood." *Holiday* 38: 60–71, 101 (August 1965).

"Introduction" to *The Moonstone* by Wilkie Collins. Harmondsworth, Eng.: Penguin, 1966.

Rudyard Kipling. London: Gollancz, 1966, 1976; New York: Dodd, Mead, 1966.

Joseph Conrad. London: Longmans, 1968; New York: Dodd, Mead, 1968.

Thomas Hardy: A Critical Biography. London: Longmans, 1971; New York: Dodd, Mead, 1971.

Myself and Michael Innes: A Memoir. London: Gollancz, 1987.

BIOGRAPHICAL AND CRITICAL STUDIES

Auden, W. H. "The Guilty Vicarage." In *Detective Fiction: A Collection of Critical Essays.* Edited by Robin Winks. Englewood Cliffs, N.J.: Prentice-Hall, 1980. Rev. ed., Woodstock, Vt.: Countryman Press, 1988.

Barnes, Melvyn. *Best Detective Fiction: A Guide from Godwin to the Present.* London: Bingley, 1975; Hamden, Conn.: Linnet Books, 1975. Rev. ed. published as *Murder in Print: A Guide to Two Centuries of Crime Fiction.* London: Barn Owl Books, 1986.

Blake, Nicholas. "Dons and Beaks." Review of *Death at the President's Lodging* and others. *Spectator* 157: 770 (30 October 1936).

Champigny, Robert. *What Will Have Happened? A Philosophical and Technical Essay on Mystery Stories.* Bloomington: Indiana University Press, 1977.

Charney, Hanna. *The Detective Novel of Manners: Hedonism, Morality, and the Life of Reason.* Rutherford, N.J.: Fairleigh Dickinson University Press, 1981.

Cuppy, Will. "Mystery and Adventure," Review of *The Case of the Journeying Boy* and others. *New York Herald Tribune Weekly Book Review,* 17 April 1949: 12.

De Quincey, Thomas. "Murder Considered As One of the Fine Arts." In *Thomas De Quincey.* Edited by Bonamy Dobrée. New York: Schocken Books, 1965.

Filstrupp, Jane Merrill. "The Shattered Calm: Libraries in Detective Fiction." *Wilson Library Bulletin* 53: 320–327 (December 1978); 53: 392–396 (January 1979).

Gill, Richard. *Happy Rural Seat: The English Country House and the Literary Imagination.* New Haven: Yale University Press, 1972.

Günther, Vincent. "Spiegelungen Hamlets im Roman und im Drama: Goethe, Innes Brešan." In *Teilnahme und Spiegelung: Festschrift für Horst Rüdiger.* Edited by Bede Allemann and Erwin Koppen. Berlin and New York: Walter de Gruyter, 1975. Pp. 165–172.

Harper, Ralph. *The World of the Thriller.* Cleveland: Case Western Reserve University Press, 1969.

Haycraft, Howard. *Murder for Pleasure: The Life and Times of the Detective Story.* New York: Appleton, Century, 1941.

———, ed. *The Art of the Mystery Story: A Collection of Critical Essays.* New York: Simon & Schuster, 1946; Carroll & Graf, 1983.

Klein, H. M. "Stewart, J I M." In *Contemporary Novelists,* 3d ed. Edited by James Vinson. New York: St. Martin's Press, 1982. Pp. 610–611.

Krause, Agate Nesaule, and Margot Peters. "Murder in Academe." *Southwest Review* 62: 371–378 (autumn 1977).

Kunitz, Stanley, and Howard Haycraft, eds. *Twentieth Century Authors: A Biographical Dictionary of Modern Literature.* New York: Wilson, 1942. Pp. 1348–1349.

Mayne, Richard. Review of *An Acre of Grass,* by J. I. M. Stewart. *New Statesman,* 20 August 1965: 206.

Neuhaus, Volker. "Michael Innes. *From "London" far:* Spiel und Glasperlenspiel im Detektivroman." *Euphorion: Zeitschrift für Literaturgeschichte* 71: 195–206 (1977).

Neville, John D. "Michael Innes." *Clues* 5, no. 2: 119–130 (fall/winter 1984).

Nicolson, Marjorie. "The Professor and the Detective." In *The Art of the Mystery Story: A Collection of Critical Essays.* Edited by Howard Haycraft. New York: Simon & Schuster, 1946; Carroll & Graf, 1983.

Panek, LeRoy. "The Novels of Michael Innes." *Armchair Detective* 16, no. 2: 116–130 (spring 1983).

Partridge, Ralph. Review of *Hamlet, Revenge!* and others. *New Statesman,* 7 August 1937: 225.

———. Review of *The Secret Vanguard* and others. *New Statesman,* 19 October 1940: 392.

Priessnitz, Horst. "Shakespeare-Bearbeitungen als Shakespearekritik: Funkspiele um Hamlet von Rayner Heppenstall, 'Michael Innes,' Herbert Read und G. W. Stonier." In *Anglo-Amerikanische Shakespeare-Bearbeitungen des 20. Jahrhunderts.* Edited by Horst Priessnitz. *Ars Interpretandi,* Band 9. Darmstadt: Wissenschaftliche Buchgesellschaft, 1980. Pp. 203–218.

Rosenbaum, Jane. "Michael Innes." In *Critical Survey of Mystery and Detective Fiction,* vol. 3. Edited by Frank N. Magill. Pasadena: Salem Press, 1988. Pp. 922–927.

Routley, Erik. *The Puritan Pleasures of the Detective Story: A Personal Monograph.* London: Gollancz, 1972.

Scheper, George L. *Michael Innes.* New York: Ungar, 1985.

———. "Bodley Harm: Libraries in British Detective Fiction." *Popular Culture in Libraries* 2, no. 1: 1–20 (1994).

Slung, Michele. "Innes, Michael." In *Twentieth-Century Crime and Mystery Writers.* Edited by John Reilly. New York: St. Martin's Press, 1980. Pp. 844–848.

"States and Transitions." Review of *The Man Who Won the Pools,* by J. I. M. Stewart. *Times Literary Supplement,* 19 May 1961: 313.

Symons, Julian. *Bloody Murder. From the Detective Story to the Crime Novel: A History.* London: Faber, 1972; New York: Viking, 1985. Also published as *Mortal Consequences.* New York: Harper & Row, 1972.

Watson, Colin. *Snobbery with Violence: Crime Stories and Their Audience.* London: Eyre & Spottiswoode, 1971; rev. ed., 1979.

Wilson, A. N. "Gentle Malice." Review of *The Bridge at Arta,* by J. I. M. Stewart. *Spectator* 247: 22 (31 October 1981).

Winks, Robin, ed. *Detective Fiction: A Collection of Critical Essays.* Englewood Cliffs, N.J.: Prentice-Hall, 1980; rev. ed., Woodstock, Vt.: Countryman Press, 1988. Includes "The Guilty Vicarage" by W. H. Auden.

P. D. JAMES
(b. 1920)

DENNIS PORTER

P. D. JAMES is the consciously gender-neutral pen name of Phyllis Dorothy James White, who was born in Oxford, England, on 3 August 1920, into an English middle-class family. Her mother was Amelia Hone James; her father, Sidney James, was a middle-level civil servant in the British Inland Revenue Service. Phyllis James was the first-born of three children. In 1931 her family settled in the city of England's other great medieval university, Cambridge, where she attended the Cambridge Girls' High School until the age of sixteen. The background of her adolescent years is significant in that the city and university of Cambridge and, beyond them, the land- and seascapes of East Anglia as a whole furnish some of the most haunting locales of her detective novels. Ironically, since her father did not believe in higher education for girls and there was little in the way of scholarship money in 1930s Britain, James did not go on to university, like the great majority of middle-class and upper-middle-class girls of her generation. She was not to know from the inside the Cambridge colleges she so much admired from outside. Instead, she followed in her father's footsteps to the extent that she left school to work in a tax office. The few years she spent there were not apparently to her liking, and she eventually took a more stimulating job as an assistant stage manager at the Festival Theatre in Cambridge.

In 1941, at the age of twenty-one, James married a young medical student from Cambridge, Ernest Connor Bantry White. White served in the Royal Army Medical Corps during World War II, but when the war ended in 1945, he returned to England a broken man, suffering from the schizophrenia that made the practice of medicine virtually impossible throughout the rest of his life. (White died in 1964.) It seems more than likely that this personal experience of one of the most shattering forms of human psychopathology conditioned James's subsequent career choices as well as many of the locales and the chastened moral vision that one typically finds at the core of her fictional works.

The couple had two daughters in the early years of their marriage: Clare, who was born in 1942, and Jane, named after James's favorite author, Jane Austen, in 1944. Because she needed to earn a living, James took a job as a clerk in the National Health Service that had only recently been created by Clement Attlee's first postwar Labour Government. While raising her two daughters and working during the day, she also went to night school and earned diplomas in medical research and hospital administration. She went on to work as an administrative assistant in the field of mental health at a regional hospital board in London, and later as a fellow of the Institute of Hospital Administration. In 1968 she had the distinction of being appointed to the Home Office, where she worked as a principal in the police department, and then in the criminal department, becoming a specialist in the field of juvenile delinquency.

The professional administrator's inside knowledge of the policies and workings of these government departments subsequently played a crucial role in the representation of the institutions and procedures of criminal investigation that lend such an air of authenticity to her novels. It is hard to find a predecessor writing in the genre of detective fiction, in fact, who can be said to have had better preparation for a career as a crime writer, certainly no one among Golden Age British women writers of detective fiction from the 1920s through the 1940s with whom she is frequently compared. In the life and works of P. D. James one finds no sign of that cult of the inspired amateur which was, at least into the early 1960s, an important aspect of British class society, in general (from its civil service to its cricket and tennis), and of mainstream British detective fiction since Arthur Conan Doyle, in particular. In all aspects of her life and work, James projects the image of the well-informed and disciplined, yet compassionate, professional—an image that suggests the extent to which her favorite fictional detective, Adam Dalgliesh of the London Metropolitan Police, is in many respects an alter ego.

According to her own testimony, from childhood on James had the ambition to be a writer, an ambition that was reinforced by the English novelists whom she came to know and admire as she was growing up, especially Jane Austen. But the circumstances of her early womanhood, of full-time work, marriage to a mentally ill husband, and motherhood, did not afford her that indispensable minimum of freedom necessary for creative work. It was not until she was thirty-nine, in fact, that she came to the realization that if she was ever to be a writer she could wait no longer, and she began to write. From the beginning of her new career, there was apparently no hesitation about the kind of novel she wanted to write. Thus, setting aside the two hours before breakfast between 6 A.M. and 8 A.M., she started work on what was to become her first novel, *Cover Her Face* (1962), a work that broadly respects the familiar conventions of the classic British tradition with which she was thoroughly familiar.

Completed in 1960, *Cover Her Face* was brought out two years later by the first publisher to whom she submitted the manuscript, Faber and Faber. The publication of that work launched a remarkable career spanning four decades at a rhythm of approximately three to four novels per decade. Although her earliest work was an accomplished exercise in the manner of the classic British mystery story, there is no doubt that there was substantial growth in the richness, complexity, and moral seriousness of her subsequent novels. By the late 1990s, James was celebrated, along with Ruth Rendell, as the most accomplished and popular contemporary British practitioner of the genre, and was routinely hailed by reviewers as "the Queen of Crime."

The Early Novels of P. D. James

One of the most distinctive characteristics of James's body of work is that she remains true throughout to the conventions of the genre she inherited. Only one of her novels, the relatively late *Children of Men* (1992), belongs to an entirely different genre, that of the futuristic, dystopian novel associated with Aldous Huxley and George Orwell. Yet unlike *Brave New World* or *Nineteen Eighty-Four, The Children of Men* ends with an ambiguous promise of regeneration in the form of a miraculous birth that also has the character of a distinctly Christian second coming. (Only once, in *Innocent Blood* [1980], did she write a novel without a professional investigator at its center.) At the same time, the social world she represents has evolved significantly. The changes that have occurred in British society between the late 1950s, when James began to write, and the late 1990s, when her most recent work, *A Certain Justice* (1997), was published, are immense; part of the interest in reading James is to see the way she accommodates her writing—and particularly her depiction of human behavior, attitudes, and values—to these changes. For the most part the fit between form and material in her works is convincing, provided one accepts the conventions of the genre in the first place, but there are occasions when the artificiality of those conventions obtrudes on the complexity of the issues raised: the trained instincts of the professional genre writer undercut the high purposes of the chronicler of social life and the reflective moralist—in the French as well as the English sense of that word. Before exploring more fully the originality of James's contribution to the genre, it is helpful to take a quick look at the development of James's oeuvre over four decades.

As might be expected, although James's three earliest works, *Cover Her Face, A Mind to Murder* (1963), and *Unnatural Causes* (1967), have notable strengths, they show her still clearly in the process of discovering where her distinctive talents lie. Thus the first and third of these early works also possess concomitant weaknesses. *Cover Her Face* is the most conventional, harking back as it does to many of the techniques, devices, and social types, and even the prewar linguistic register, of the Golden Age works of her British predecessors. Nowhere, in fact, in her subsequent fictions will an opening sentence—"Exactly three months before the killing at Martingale Mrs. Maxie gave a dinner party"—and an opening chapter—an evocation of that upper-middle-class dinner party and its complement of family members, local dignitaries, and domestics—recall so obviously the already dated style and content of an Agatha Christie novel.

This first work takes up the traditional setting of the country house for its opening murder, along with the familiar device of the closed community and a limited cast of mainly upper-middle-class suspects, all of whom have a potential motive. There is a puzzle to be solved and a thoroughly professional detective who, in spite of a typical supply of distractions, false clues, and red herrings, is in the end more than up to the job of solving it. The novel is notable above all perhaps because it introduces James's poet-detective hero, Superintendent Adam Dalgliesh, fully formed at least in the broad outlines of his solitary life, career, and character, down to the way he practices his troubling profession and to his highly personal ethics. At this stage, however, the more interesting aspects of his worldview, which James develops from novel to novel, are only briefly outlined.

Unnatural Causes moves back and forth between a Suffolk village and London, but concentrates once again on a small community composed chiefly of literati and their friends, lovers, relatives, servants, and assistants. The most archly self-referential of James's works, the novel begins with the murder of a mystery-novel writer, and its characters include other novelists, a lady writer of romance, a drama critic, an editor and essayist, and even the poet Adam Dalgliesh in his off-duty mode. Probably the most notable episode in this exercise in satirical comedy of manners, however, is the description of a London organization called the Cadaver Club, whose all-male habitués are themselves writers of crime fiction as well as being criminal lawyers. The difficulty that is not satisfactorily resolved in this work is that of reconciling the tone and material. The novel reads, on the one hand, like lighthearted parody of the genre—including send-ups of the inbred community of writers, its pretensions, backbiting, envy, and narcissism. On the other hand, it offers frequently violent—indeed lurid—action sequences: along with a number of brutal murders, there is an ending that can only be described as overwrought, comprising a huge North Sea storm, coastal flooding, a violent encounter between three characters in a cottage, and the handicapped murderer flailing away with her crutches before she is swept out to sea. Nevertheless, *Unnatural Causes* does have an undeniably clever plot, in which a character's idea for a detective novel—an opening scene in which a handless corpse drifts ashore in a rowboat—is enacted in the real life of the fiction.

The most successful of these three early novels, however, is *A Mind to Murder*. Like the great majority of James's subsequent works, this novel has as its setting an institutional milieu—in this case, a London psychiatric clinic. The clinic, its office routines and professional practices, along with its cast of socially and psychologically differentiated characters, is rendered with great verisimilitude. James clearly makes good use of her inside knowledge of such institutions. In this her second novel many of the characteristics of her mature fiction are present. It is once again a case involving a closed community. The opening crime is arrestingly bizarre as well as violent—it involves a murder by means of a carved fetishistic object and a chisel. The puzzle is heightened along with the suspense, as in traditional locked-door mysteries, because the murderer cannot have left the premises and must be one of the staff. The character of Dalgliesh assumes center stage and is notably developed. At the same time the range of characters is enriched in terms of professional standing, social situation, age, sex, and psychic need; and for the first time questions of faith in a postreligious age are raised. Finally, all of the above are located in a work that is also a consciously realist novel of manners which sets out to represent the quality of the material and moral life of contemporary Britain. In short, in *A Mind to Murder* one can see how the violent crimes at issue are designed both to raise age-old questions about human nature and its propensity to evil, and to focus attention on the difficulty of living the good life, given the pressures and demands of the modern world.

Novels of the 1970s

During the 1970s James achieved her full maturity as a writer of thoughtfully crafted, carefully written, socially conscious detective fiction. The four novels of the decade—*Shroud for a Nightingale* (1971), *An Unsuitable Job for a Woman* (1972), *The Black Tower* (1975), and *Death of an Expert Witness* (1977)—demonstrate her tendency to vary between two polarities: that of realism and of the novel of manners, and that of the romantic gothic, whose origins go back to the late eighteenth century. In James's gothic settings one even finds echoes of the haunted residences, entrapment motifs, and lurid writing of America's most famous gothic writer and the inventor of short detective fiction, Edgar Allan Poe. Where *Shroud for a Nightingale* and *Death of an Expert Witness* are set in a suburban London hospital and in a forensic laboratory in semirural Essex, respectively, the action of *The Black Tower* is located in a nursing home for the incurably ill on the Dorset coast.

An Unsuitable Job for a Woman, which opens in London and moves to Cambridgeshire, marks an interesting departure to the extent that, strictly speaking, it fits into neither of the above categories. The novel introduces a British private detective who is professionally inexperienced but independent-minded and resourceful—a young woman named Cordelia Gray. Relatively short for James by this stage in her career, it is perhaps her wittiest and most focused detective novel of manners, using its central character and an apparent suicide, redolent of kinky sex gone wrong, in order to explore the increasingly fashionable topic of gender relations in modern Britain and the rapidly evolving morals of British society, in general (including those of its younger generations, in particular). Most remarkable is that in setting out to draw a moral which demonstrates the inaccuracy of her ironic title, James chooses to create a character who in her independence of spirit, innocence, and capacity to learn is a modern version of one of her favorite author's favorite characters, namely, Jane Austen's Emma.

This work followed what remains in many ways one of James's densest and most accomplished works, *Shroud for a Nightingale*. Most impressive here is the way in which

James manages to contain a complex, richly textured novel of sustained moral and social commentary within the frame of a detective-story plot that has its own suggestive resonance. The work opens with a spectacular murder before an audience of student nurses and their supervisors—a student nurse dies a horrible death by poison in the course of a demonstration of intragastric feeding. There are two further murders and, it turns out, two murderers. Notable features of this novel are, first, the way in which the psychological and historical past comes fatally to invade an apparently orderly present, and second, the fact that the three murders are motivated not by hate, jealousy, or greed, but by love and loyalty or pity—the third is essentially a mercy killing. Further, the denouement of this work is characteristic of the way in which James comes increasingly to incorporate moral ambiguities and troubling ironies into her best fictions: Dalgliesh knows but is unable to prove who committed this final murder, yet its sympathetic perpetrator ends up committing suicide in a manner that gives new meaning to the term "rough justice."

The least satisfying of James's novels of the 1970s is *The Black Tower,* a work that manages to plunge a convalescing, self-doubting Adam Dalgliesh into the unbalanced gothic world of a gloom-ridden nursing home for the incurably sick of all ages. With its cast of physically disabled and psychically wounded patients and staff, its unfrocked physician and his alcoholic wife, its guilty nurse, ex-convict help, and spiritually fraudulent warden, James reaches an outer limit in the representation of human misery and venality. This unsavory tale of multiple murders is an attempt to fuse the history of a late Georgian great house and its folly (the black tower of the title haunted by its legend of death by incarceration), set in a bleak locale on windswept Dorset cliffs, with a modern story of international drug dealing centered on the ironically improbable city of Lourdes. Thus does the modern world profane one of its notoriously dubious sacred sites. Given what precedes, it is no surprise, therefore, if the work tends to unravel by the time it reaches a climactic, overwrought action sequence in which a physically debilitated Dalgliesh fights the villain to the death at the edge of a cliff.

Novels of the 1980s

Innocent Blood (1980) marks another notable departure in the range of James's work. This is one of her most ambitious and probing studies of character and contemporary values, of human vulnerability, capacity for violence, and the search for meaning. The novel is located, in a way that was by now becoming typical, in various realistically rendered social milieus of modern Britain, milieus that are for the most part remote from the country-house settings of her predecessors in the genre. Abandoning for the first and only time the formal structure of a novel of detection, *Innocent Blood* nevertheless involves an investigation and its complement of violent crime. The difference in this case is that the initiating "crime" is the giving up of a child for adoption; and the search for the perpetrators of that act, that is, the biological parents, is undertaken by an eighteen-year-old woman whose deeper goal is a search for an identity of which she feels herself wrongfully robbed. However, like a modern Oedipus, James's heroine uncovers a paternity and a maternity that are both uniquely shattering: her father was a convicted child rapist and her mother a child murderer. Finally, if this baggage were not potent enough for what can only be described as a realist crime thriller, James adds to it the figure of the stalking father of the murdered child, intent on exacting his own bloody revenge on the murderer once she is released from prison.

James's other works of the 1980s, *The Skull Beneath the Skin* (1982), *A Taste for Death* (1986), and *Devices and Desires* (1989), represent a return to the formula and techniques of the detective novel, a genre on which she had previously put her own highly individual stamp. But it is a sign of her evolving practice that her later works are, on the whole, substantially longer and even more complex and multilayered. In the nature of the puzzle it poses, in its setting in a great house on an island off the coast of Dorset, in its closed community of sophisticated, upper-middle-class characters who have in common a professional relationship to theater, *The Skull Beneath the Skin* comes as close as any detective novel James has written since her very first to the locales and milieus of Agatha Christie, if not to that author's more limited social and moral horizons. In spite of the fact that James chooses again as her investigator the very modern, young private eye, Cordelia Gray, of *An Unsuitable Job for a Woman*, there is a substantial dose of romantic gothic. This is to be found both in the overall setting and in the macabre artifacts collected there, as well as in the Poe-like chamber of horror at sea level in the depths of the house. Crimes from the past, including the recent past of World War II, are reenacted there in the present, in the form of an incarceration and a death by drowning with the rising tide. Veering between gothic overstatement, on the one hand, and parody and satirical comedy of manners, on the other, *The Skull Beneath the Skin* largely eschews the verisimilitude that characterizes James's best work.

A Taste for Death brings back Adam Dalgliesh and locates the brutal double murder with which it opens in a high Victorian, romanesque church in the Paddington, Notting Hill, Holland Park area of London. The two victims, a tramp and a member of the nobility, embody the wide social range of characters evoked here along with the very different material worlds they inhabit—from an elegant Sir John Soane house in Holland Park to the British equivalent of a run-down urban project not too far away. The murder mystery turns, as frequently in James, on the working out in the present of tormented familial relations from the past.

A Taste for Death is an example of James's realism of contemporary manners at its best: its descriptions of very different London neighborhoods are done with a convincing precision; the author reveals once again her genuine feel for the fears and turmoil in which some of the most vulnerable members of contemporary society are forced to live; she proves a knowledgeable guide to the attitudes and ideologies of the rising generation, including its young political radicals; and above all her sympathetic vignettes of a number of her characters give the work a moral density that is exceptional in the genre. This is nowhere truer than in the thoughtful portrait of her young woman detective inspector, Kate Miskin, who displaces Dalgliesh in some of the most interesting sections of the novel. A highly competent young professional, she is another of James's orphaned heroines, who has come up the hard way and is forced, in a manner that is both unique and familiar, to balance a demanding career with care for the aging grandmother who raised her. Moreover, this novel concludes with one of the most convincing and emotionally complex action sequences James has written: it includes the unbalanced murderer with gun in hand; Kate Miskin, trying to cook spaghetti Bolognese; and her terrified, bound granny, who at one point finds herself on the toilet seat with her knickers around her ankles.

With *Devices and Desires* James returns to what over the years has proved to be her favorite English region, East Anglia—in this case Norfolk. But in this novel the archaic, elemental seascapes of that area, which constitute an important part of the threatening physical and moral ambience of earlier novels set in the same location, are less significant than the monumental silhouette of a late-twentieth-century image of potential horror—that is, a nuclear power station. In another layered, complex novel James creates a cast of more socially heterogeneous, contemporary British social and psychic types, whose function is to contribute their troubled past and complicated web of relationships to the disturbing intrigue. The device of a (relatively) closed community is retained, composed this time of those who work at the power plant and a cross section of local types and outsiders, who bring distinctly modern attitudes and ideologies to the ancient coast, including a faith in science and technology, an oppositional environmentalism, international terrorism, and the new taste for gourmet cooking that is sweeping contemporary Britain. Once again James fashions a plot of multiple murders, although this time there are two very different murderers, who are motivated by drives that seem to be in conscious contrast. The result in any case is that James introduces new and unexpected themes into her work.

If anyone needed reminding of how far James has come from the squeamishness of Golden Age writing, the macabre serial murders with which the novel begins are proof enough: dressed as a woman, the so-called Whistler strangles his female victims, carves an L into their foreheads, and stuffs their pubic hair into their mouths. Yet the serial murders of the first half of the novel are at least motivated on the familiarly old-fashioned grounds of sexual pathology. In the second half the narrative shifts to other murders and other murderers, including politically motivated murder. The implication seems to be that the old and familiar forms of evil that have always existed in the world are now being updated by means of other, distinctly contemporary forms, including modern terrorism. Moreover, in this story as in a number of previous ones, James chooses to place Dalgliesh at the site purely by accident and have a local, less worldly detective inspector conduct the investigation. It is, however, of symbolic significance that Dalgliesh is staying in the converted and nonfunctional windmill inherited from a beloved aunt—at the site, that is, of a much older, more environmentally friendly form of power than nuclear power.

Novels of the 1990s

In *Original Sin* (1994), James does for the world of publishing—its chief-executive officers, directors, authors, editors, accountants, secretaries, temps, packers, and cleaning ladies—what she had done for psychiatric clinics, nursing homes, teaching hospitals, and forensic laboratories in earlier works. The main difference is that here she pulls out all the stops in imagining and re-creating an eighteenth-century Venetian palace transposed to the south bank of the river Thames. This folly is on the grandest and most elaborately decorative of scales; and the "original sin" that made it possible—the murder of a wife in order to inherit her fortune and complete the structure—overlaps through a series of murders in the present with a very twentieth-century "original sin" associated with the Holocaust and with a form of *raison d'état*. In this case, Commander Dalgliesh is the lead investigator, aided once again by Kate Miskin as well as by Detective Inspector Daniel Aaron, whose Jewish blood understandably causes him in the end to seriously compromise his professional conduct. He fails to arrest an assassin who was motivated in his acts of revenge by the death of his Jewish wife and their two children in Nazi death camps during the German occupation of France.

A Certain Justice possesses that combination of qualities discussed above that are the hallmark of James's mature fiction. Like *Original Sin*, it has a London setting (apart from a brief excursion into Suffolk at its denouement). It also has a typically strong opening, in which the forthcoming murder of the novel's dominant character and first victim, the brilliant criminal lawyer Venetia Aldridge, is announced, even as she is in the process of conducting the successful defense, in Court Number One of the Old Bailey, of her young and disturbing client, Garry Ashe, who has himself been charged with the brutal murder of his sluttish aunt. *A Certain Justice* is thoughtfully plotted in a way that disturbs and surprises down to the end. It evokes with typical skill the intersecting lives of a broad cast of more or less complex characters of both sexes and of different classes, professions, and generations, and it situates them in different London neighborhoods in a city that is represented as endlessly destroying and re-creating itself even as certain fundamental traditions and monuments survive. Commander Dalgliesh and Detective Inspector Kate Miskin return once again to conduct an investigation that begins with the lurid murder scene in Venetia's office at her law chambers, and by the end they unravel the tangled network of human relations that motivate this original crime and give rise to two further murders by a different hand.

The work starts out, conventionally enough, like any other closed community mystery story. The locked outer door to the chambers points to an insider as the murderer in a milieu composed of lawyers, their secretarial staff, and their cleaners. From the beginning, however, the gruesome murder that is the subject of the trial with which the novel opens establishes a link between the apparently privileged, upper-middle-class world of the barristers' chambers and the wider and much more turbulent world outside. It is this link that the novel goes on to explore on a number of levels. The central theme is that of the moral ambiguities associated with the function of a criminal defense lawyer. Her task, as Venetia herself points out, is not to establish the truth of what happened but to challenge the prosecution's presentation of the evidence in a way that casts sufficient doubt for her client to be acquitted. This circumstance comes back to haunt her in the form of a distraught grandmother who returns like a Greek fury to exact revenge in a form that ironically fits the perceived crime. Janet Carpenter's granddaughter was murdered by a pedophile client of Venetia's who, thanks to her remarkable legal skills, had previously been acquitted of a similar offense. In obtaining Garry Ashe's acquittal, Venetia unknowingly supplies the instrument Janet Carpenter will use to punish her through her own daughter. The full ironic significance of the ambivalent title is only revealed at the end. The presumption of innocence and the adversarial system that are at the heart of British criminal law do not guarantee that the author of a criminal act will be found guilty, even if he is brought to trial. The consequences of these safeguards may be grave indeed. Even the best of human justice has its troubling limits.

The Originality of P. D. James

The late-middle-aged murderer of *Original Sin* and the motivation of his crime are reminders that James belongs to a generation that came to maturity in the late 1930s, a generation for which World War II was the determinative historical experience. Growing up at a time when the British Empire was still a dominant force in world politics, James was witness to the decline of British global power, to the frequently wrenching economic and social changes that accompanied that decline, and to renewal at home, from the postwar years of austerity through the emergence of an increasingly prosperous Britain in the 1990s. Although such socioeconomic matters are reflected only obliquely in her novels, James has developed over the decades into a social novelist of manners in the most profound meaning of that term: her stories of crime and detection consciously set out to represent the changing face of British society insofar as it is manifested in the material life, behavior, attitudes, beliefs, values, and speech of her characters.

James started out working in the tradition of British Golden Age detective fiction that was exemplified at its best in the works of Agatha Christie, Dorothy L. Sayers, Margery Allingham, and Ngaio Marsh; and many of the principal features of that tradition persist down into the works of her maturity—the initiating crime as puzzle to be solved, the carefully wrought plot, the (over)explicit denouements, the closed community of suspects, the great house as the site of murder, a village community as background, the sophisticated detective, the cultivated narrator, the literary references and quotations. Nevertheless, James has also contributed in a number of important ways to updating the genre and, without diminishing its power as literate entertainment, to turning it into a medium for probing commentary on human behavior in the contemporary world.

Without belonging, strictly speaking, to the police procedural, in the interest of realism most of her works employ many of the elements of that subgenre. James implicitly recognized, therefore, the need to avoid boring the reader with the painstaking and time-consuming processes associated with the actual work of the police. The problem is posed in a comment made by the narrator in *A Mind to Murder:* "Most police work consists of the boring, repetitive and meticulous checking of detail. Most murders are sordid little crimes bred out of ignorance and despair" (p. 90).[1] It is the paradoxical task of James's novels both to confirm the truth of this, for reasons of verisimilitude, and at the same time to refute it by the power of her art, for reasons of pleasure and interest. That she does so consistently and successfully and in a variety of ways is a tribute to her remarkable skills as a novelist.

To begin with, her novels are usually cleverly plotted in a manner that stimulates the reader's interest, produces sustained suspense relative to the source of the violence and the outcome of the investigation, and gives rise to denouements that are often unexpected or disturbing and, for the most part, satisfyingly plausible. The plots themselves are complex in ways that open up issues of significant contemporary interest but that have nevertheless developed into a recognizable formula: an initial vicious murder that is inherently mysterious is followed sooner or later by one or more enigmatic murders as the circle tightens and the unidentified criminal grows increasingly desperate to cover his or her tracks. There is in the end plenty of guilt to be shared, and it often turns out that one crime or one criminal uncovers another. Employing many of the techniques and routines of the police procedural, James presents objectively detailed descriptions of the spectacle of the victims' bodies along with an evocation of the scene of crime. Then comes the arrival of the investigating officers and the activities of the scene-of-crime–investigation team, who go on to record information and sift through clues, including the clues associated with the work of the pathologist and, later, of the forensic scientists. There follow equally detailed evocations of the voyeuristic task of hunting through the victims' living spaces and personal belongings. Interviews with witnesses and potential suspects typically involve swift socially and psychologically grounded vignettes of the characters concerned and, frequently, visits to their homes or places of work.

Subsequently, one encounters the familiar process of sorting through the clues, eliminating suspects, and following up on visits, along with sudden revelations, fresh acts of violence and fresh victims, and the progressive narrowing of the focus of the investigation; the investigator's discovery of the truth is usually withheld until the end in the interest of suspense. Some time before the denouement there is frequently a dramatic climax that involves Adam Dalgliesh, Cordelia Gray, or Kate Miskin in a life-and-death struggle with the criminal or the criminal's surrogate (*Unnatural Causes, An Unsuitable Job for a Woman, The Black Tower, Shroud for a Nightingale,* and *Devices and Desires,* and in a different mode, *Innocent Blood*). These scenes reveal James's talent for a kind of action writing traditionally associated with the hard-boiled genre, although they occasionally tilt into the melodramatic (*Unnatural Causes, The Black Tower*).

Further, throughout her works James consistently adopts the technique of the omniscient narrator. This enables her to shift the point of view at will, and often with telling effect, from that of one or more of the investigating officers to that of a suspect or casual witness, or, relatively rare in the genre, to that of panicked victim at the point of death, or even that of a murderer stalking his victim (a technique used most successfully in *Innocent Blood*). The novel that at first sight seems to constitute an exception to the formula, *Innocent Blood*, in fact, substitutes for a profes-

1. All page numbers refer to the Penguin editions listed in the bibliography.

sional investigator a young woman in search of her biological parents; and it turns out that in her behavior, highly contemporary attitudes, and investigative techniques, Phillipa Palfrey is not that different from the apprentice private detective of *An Unsuitable Job for a Woman*, Cordelia Gray.

James's overall mastery of the conventions and techniques of the genre is nowhere more apparent than in her strong openings, in which she renders with convincing and suggestive realist detail the sudden shift out of circumstances of ordinariness and order (*A Mind to Murder, Shroud for a Nightingale, Devices and Desires*) into the shock of violent crime. *A Taste for Death*, for example, opens with a description of the seediness of a marginal, racially mixed London neighborhood with its run-down, sixties apartment blocks, its garish ethnic restaurants, and the dilapidated Victorian church with its shrunken congregation that is the site of the double murder. It is not just the site of crime, however, that is rendered with suggestive precision but also the sympathetic and socially marginal odd couple who first come upon the crime scene—a lonely, sixty-five-year-old cleaning lady and the ten-year-old truant boy she has befriended—and, after them, the figure of the weak and unkempt Anglican vicar, who might have come out of a novel by Graham Greene. Further, the shocking mystery that immediately engages the attention is that of two men with their throats slashed: joined in the final equality of death, as they would never have been in life, are a homeless tramp and a recently resigned government minister and baronet.

Golden Age novels of detection frequently combine the ethos of a comedy of manners with their focus on crime and detection; although it is a combination one finds intermittently in parts of James's works, it is not maintained consistently or for long. James seems to take crime and the world, not to speak of her writer's task, too seriously for that. Nevertheless, the two novels in which Cordelia Gray appears begin with a series of witty, satirical scenes that more than confirm James's comic talent, as does the pathetically hilarious ballroom dancing scene in *Shroud for a Nightingale*. This dimension of her writing appears more fully developed, however, in those works where she combines a sly evocation of writers and writing with her tale of crime, that is, for example, in *Unnatural Causes* and *The Skull Beneath the Skin*. What modern critical theory has come to call intertextuality—a more or less explicit reference within one literary text to another—is used by James for satirical and occasionally parodistic ends there.

Unnatural Causes is intended as a tour de force that, in effect, has it both ways. It works on three levels. First, it satirizes the work and the inbred milieu of the covey of writers of novels, mystery stories, and romance novels, as well as critics and editors, that share the same Suffolk village. Second, it draws attention to its own status as fiction by cleverly opening with a scene of crime that was originally suggested by one of the characters for a work of fiction. Third, it attempts to set itself apart from what it satirizes by obliging the reader to take it seriously after all through the power of its art. Moreover, something similar could be said about *The Skull Beneath the Skin*, which does for the world of theater what *Unnatural Causes* does for writers of fiction.

Nevertheless, such teasing intertextual references, which only enhance the sense of the artfulness of the detective-novel genre, are far from the norm in James's best works. Indeed, it has grown increasingly apparent over the years that the tradition on which James draws in her writing is not simply that of British mystery fiction but also that of the British novel in general. More self-consciously than her acknowledged predecessors in the genre of the detective novel, James displays many of the strengths that characterize the British novel since Jane Austen, but that were given a new orientation and a new social thickness of texture in the mystery novels of Charles Dickens and Wilkie Collins. Those strengths include a curiosity in representing contemporary manners in realist settings, in the appearance of a thickened material world, in class difference within a broad social context, in character both as social type and as the expression of powerful individuality, in the extraordinary and disturbing variety of human behavior, and in moral conduct. To some extent, the frequent references to canonical English poets, dramatists, and novelists throughout her novels—and the resonant literary quotations from John Bunyan, Shakespeare, and John Webster to John Donne and A. E. Housman—are a sign of her ambition. They raise the ante by implying a standard by which her own work might be measured. Thus, if James provides something more than what is usually meant by "a good read," it is because her narratives stimulate and go on to satisfy an informed reader's curiosity about the who, what, when, how, and where of things.

Local Knowledge

From *A Mind to Murder* on, the pleasures and discriminations to be found in James's best works begin with what anthropologists call "local knowledge." She is herself "an expert witness" in at least two important senses. In the most obvious sense, she has a professional's inside knowledge of the workings of government agencies and institutions concerned with the practice of justice and criminal law in Britain, including its criminal investigation departments, its forensic science laboratories, and its law courts. She is also an acute observer and chronicler of contemporary British manners and mores, especially of its lower-middle to upper-middle classes. One can learn a lot about "middle England" from James's astute commentary on the material circumstances, tastes and values, prejudices, anxieties, fears, hopes and ambitions, generational conflicts, and personal relations evoked in her fictions.

Nothing characterizes a detective novel by P. D. James more obviously than a sense of place. Her crimes of violence are invariably located in a carefully evoked site that includes typically a more or less grand historical building, that may or may not have fallen on hard times, and a circumambient landscape that is both singular and steeped in disturbing associations. All of James's novels are set in England as opposed to Britain. Aside from London, which is the home base of Superintendent (and later, Commander) Dalgliesh of New Scotland Yard, the geographical region that figures most prominently in her works is East Anglia, including the flat fen country of Cambridgeshire (*Death of an Expert Witness*) and the two counties that thrust out into the forbidding seascape of the North Sea, Suffolk (*Unnatural Causes*) and Norfolk (*Devices and Desires*). On other occasions, she has ventured into the very different landscapes of southwest England, namely, into the county of Dorset (*The Black Tower* and *The Skull Beneath the Skin*), whose cliffs rise up dramatically above the Channel coast. What all these sites have in common is that they are represented as emotionally charged or burdened by history in a variety of ways. Thus, if James shows a special fondness for her northern seascapes, it is because of the way in which the fierceness and immensity of the nature they suggest dominate the lives of the human societies that live precariously on their edge—particularly where the sea has taken its toll in human lives and continues to encroach on the land or where storms batter human habitations.

At least as important for James as her natural landscapes and their weather are the links they have to English history, especially through the towns, villages, great houses, and country churches located in them. Nothing associates James's work more directly with the tradition of Golden Age British detective fiction, in fact, than her propensity to set her narratives of violent crime in great houses. Sometimes the house's original grandeur has managed to survive into a contemporary Britain more or less in its original form (the Elizabethan manor house of *Cover Her Face;* the monumental, late Victorian, island-fortress residence of *The Skull Beneath the Skin;* the Sir John Soane town house in *A Taste for*

Death); sometimes it has been transformed by modern bureaucrats (usually unsympathetically and tastelessly) into offices for institutions or agencies (the Georgian town house that houses the psychiatric clinic in *A Mind to Murder*; the surburban London mansion that is a nurses' residence in *Shroud for a Nightingale*; the forensic laboratory housed in a Palladian-style mansion in *Death of an Expert Witness*; the nursing home located in an ugly late-Georgian residence with its attendant tower in *The Black Tower*; and, most memorable of all, the publishing house in the extravagant, eighteenth-century Venetian folly in *Original Sin*).

Yet the significance of such buildings in James's works is, for the most part, different from what it is in the works of her predecessors. Representative of different ages of grand domestic architecture in Britain, the point for James of such buildings is that they are typically monuments to ostentatious wealth, ambition, and folly as much as to enlightened patronage and to taste. Thus, although they do sometimes point by contrast to a beauty and a grandeur gone from the modern world, in their origins they also frequently recall the continuity over generations of the human propensity for violence. Nowhere is this more apparent than in the incongruous Venetian palazzo James sites on the south bank of the Thames in *Original Sin*. The novel's title, in fact, refers among other things to the fact that the murders which take place there in the historical present are reenactments in a different guise of the violence which made the palace possible in the first place—the blood stain on its marble floor that, legend has it, can never be cleaned away is that of the original owner's wife, murdered by her husband so that construction could be completed.

The fact that James seems to be preoccupied with great houses from the English past does not mean that she is turning her back on the modern world. On the contrary, what interests her above all is the contrast, and the way in which the past invades the present. It is also important to note that the vast building that dominates the landscape in *Devices and Desires*, a nuclear power station, embodies a threat that is peculiarly modern—although in the end most of the brutal murders committed in its shadow are motivated by old-fashioned drives.

Far more of modern Britain is represented in James's fictions than the lives lived in its grand houses. James also extends her realist studies of manners into the mundane domestic interiors that include familiar urban terrace houses, suburban villas, village semidetached homes, country cottages, and even the caravan homes of the least affluent Britons. *A Mind to Murder, An Unsuitable Job for a Woman, Shroud for a Nightingale, Death of an Expert Witness, Innocent Blood*, and *A Taste for Death* open doors into the modest lives, both strange and humdrum, contented sometimes but more often than not unhappy, lonely, desperate, and driven, that are lived there. James seems to have a special interest, in fact, for failed and failing marriages, the tortuousness of relationships between the sexes in the modern world, the anxieties of childhood and adolescence, and varieties of domestic turmoil, in general. That is why she frequently ventures into the blighted areas of inner-city London and into apartment buildings that are malodorous as well as insalubrious.

In order to represent the remarkable changes in British mores over the past quarter century or so, James also goes out of her way to update the language spoken by her characters, if not always that of her narrator. As an observer of the social scene in her time, she could hardly have avoided noting the extent to which British speech has grown coarser in recent decades, both in everyday exchanges between ordinary people, particularly young people, and in the media. And something of the increasingly casual recourse to common scatological expressions once taboo in more or less polite society emerges in the works of her maturity. In this respect, the gap between her earliest novel—which is redolent of the polite discourse associated with the Golden

Age tradition—and her novels in the 1980s and 1990s is especially marked. Thus it comes as no surprise, in a scene that combines farce and a grim pathos, to hear the manner in which the very middle-class Philippa Palfrey of *Innocent Blood* denounces her adoptive father when she comes upon him in flagrante delicto with one of his students: "I would have thought you'd have more pride than to bring her here, to fuck her on your own bed" (p. 266).

In her fondness for the portrayal of character, a notable feature of her work, James draws once again on one of the strengths of the British tradition of the novel as a whole. Almost from the beginning her fiction is peopled by a relatively wide range of human and contemporary social types who are at once recognizable and suggestively idiosyncratic. This is true of many of her major characters, especially the principal suspects. It is also true of a great many of the secondary characters, vignettes of whose lives are sketched with insight and understanding, and who, it often turns out, are irrelevant to the crimes on which the plot turns.

Noticeable in this respect, too, are the alternating attitudes of compassion and distaste that her narrator expresses for her large cast of characters—from cleaning ladies, secretaries, temps, porters, single mothers on welfare, and out-of-work artists and actors or political radicals, to former school teachers, psychiatrists, surgeons, obstetricians, a variety of scientists, social scientists, literary editors, high-powered executives, and even a government minister. The compassion typically is reserved for struggling, ordinary people (including on occasion the perpetrators of crime), whose courage and folk wisdom often seem to have a special appeal to James; the distaste, on the other hand, focuses most obviously on the ambitious, the arrogant, and the driven, especially successful professional men, society women, and a new breed of worldly and successful women, all of whom are indifferent to others' needs.

Adam Dalgliesh and Cordelia Gray

The most developed of all her character studies is that of her detective, Adam Dalgliesh, who has appeared in each of her novels except *Innocent Blood* and *The Skull Beneath the Skin*, even if occasionally he only has a minor role or ostensibly plays second fiddle to a local detective. The man who comes increasingly to be described in professional superlatives such as "New Scotland Yard's most respected investigator" is crucial to an understanding of the highly individual moral ethos that James is at pains to project in her work, a moral ethos that is at the heart of her original contribution to the genre in the late twentieth century.

From the earliest novels, we learn that Dalgliesh is a loner, a widower who lost both his beloved wife and child as the result of a difficult birth. However, the mark that distinguishes him most obviously and immediately from all other fictional detectives is the fact that he is a poet. A "poet-detective" might seem an oxymoron, representing two ways of living in the world that are hard to reconcile. This sense that Dalgliesh is a living contradiction is reinforced by the fact that his favorite hobby is visiting English country churches. The figure James projects is that of a man who can be trusted with the awesome power that is vested in a senior police detective because he is sufficiently introspective to be aware of the temptations of power and the sinfulness of arrogance. There is, in fact, no doubt that from his author's point of view Dalgliesh is an ideal human type for the role he is called upon to play in the modern world. He is, on the one hand, the detached yet passionate observer of life, with a heightened sensibility and an intense relationship to language, who works in isolation at his difficult craft. On the other hand, he is the trained, seasoned professional, a member of a hierarchical institution not noted for its sensitivity who nonetheless acts professionally and with the requisite compassion in dealing, on a daily basis, with human life at its crudest and most brutal. Dalgliesh has the poise to confront humanity in all its forms and at a variety of social levels, and he has mastered his own passions in applying the techniques and technology of criminal investigation in a disciplined way. In the imbalance between his personal and his public life, he is also a clearly recognizable modern type. Whereas his professional life is a great success—he is after all Commander Dalgliesh—his private life, if not a failure, remains dissatisfying, open-ended, unresolved.

The risk for the novelist in such a figure is that he may appear too austere, patriarchal, and aloof for the taste of modern readers—Dalgliesh tends to have a distant and occasionally downright hostile relationship with most of his peers and subordinates, and expresses little fondness for children. James overcomes the problem at least in part by humanizing him in various ways—not only by focusing on the pain of his early loss, which makes him distrust life, but also through evocations of his self-doubt or of his filial relationship with an aging aunt, and above all by representing, however sketchily, his relations with women, including Deborah Riscoe, whom he thinks of marrying.

In fact, along with his obvious intelligence, it is his loneliness and his physical, emotional, and spiritual need—an apparent agnostic unhappy with his choice—that explain in large part his appeal as a character. He is designed to have the mysterious aura of the inconsolable bachelor for whom the writing of poetry is both an honorable craft and a consolation, a way of coming to terms with the suffering and evil he encounters in the world—although to judge from the single example of his poetry quoted in *Unnatural Causes,* Dalgliesh as poet is far from being a modernist. It is, finally, convenient for the author if Dalgliesh remains unattached: first, because he is free to set out unencumbered on a fresh investigative adventure with each new novel; and, second, because it gives her the opportunity to add an element of erotic suspense to the suspense of the mystery novel by promising, and then deferring, the possibility of real or potential relationships with different female characters.

Nevertheless, Dalgliesh seems above all intended to embody a duality expressive of the moral ethos characteristic of James's fictional universe. He is in a sense a convenient alter ego for his author because he is in this world—indeed, frequently in this world at its cruelest and ugliest—but he is not always of it. Dalgliesh is the most explicit embodiment of James's worldview, the figure who enables her to bring most directly a critical and moral dimension to her chronicles of modern life.

Among the other detectives who play significant roles in James's fictions, the most important is Cordelia Gray, since she is the central reflector and principal investigator in two novels, *An Unsuitable Job for a Woman* and *The Skull Beneath the Skin.* James gives her character special prominence in the earlier novel, a work that starts out with all the vivacity and satirical humor of a comedy of manners and manages to marry the style of Jane Austen to the sordid world of Raymond Chandler—until the colors darken rapidly once the murder investigation begins.

The apprentice Cordelia on her first case alone is one of James's most sustained sympathetic portraits in all her fiction. From the point of view of character, it is obviously significant that she shares a name with the youngest and only honest and loving one of King Lear's three daughters—something that is signaled in the novel by a mocking comment on "her sisters." The combined circumstances of a mother lost at birth and a foolish, irresponsible father confirm the allusion. Cordelia is nevertheless represented as a very modern young woman. A childhood that involves virtual orphanhood and a succession of foster homes requires her to make her own way in the world. If she succeeds in becoming a heroic type for the times, therefore, it is because she is intelligent, independent, resourceful, sexually experienced, not easily intimidated, physically strong, ethical, and above all, like Dalgliesh, compassionate.

Further, like many of James's more sympathetic characters, including Dalgliesh (his father was a country parson), she has an association with traditional religious life. Having received a convent education by accident, Cordelia retains an enduring respect for the nuns who raised her and for their school as an oasis of order and beauty. Also, like her author, Cordelia is obliged to forgo higher education in spite of her obvious ability because of demands made upon her by an egotistical and eccentric father. In *The Skull Beneath the Skin,* following in the footsteps of her folksy mentor, Bernie Pryde, whose untimely suicide opens the work, she does in the end get her man in the person of a prominent, but cruelly arrogant, scientific entrepreneur. If there is a feminist perspective in the works of James, it manifests itself here in the way in which the lonely, young, female outsider unmasks the sinister machinations of a male establishment figure at the height of his power. Thus does she demonstrate her suitability for her chosen profession.

Other, more or less conventional detective inspectors, along with pathologists and various kinds of forensic scientists, appear in almost all the novels. Their role is to play foil to Dalgliesh, to relay him at various junctures for reasons of verisimilitude or to give variety. They range from the traditionally manly, reliable, and stolid (Martin and Reckless), to the intelligent but overly ambitious son of a lord (Massingham), to the local Suffolk officer yearning for his absent wife (Rickards), to James's determined, independent, and thoroughly professional young women (as with Kate Miskin, who has risen from life in a London tenement and is not ready to make a permanent commitment in her own personal life).

Moral Vision

James intentionally creates in Dalgliesh a character who embodies a fundamental pessimism about life in the world, in general, and about humanity, in particular. The recurring spectacle of violent crime and its murdered victims leaves him a chastened observer of the human scene in his time; in this he is at one with James's omniscient narrator. The point to note is that although from the beginning James has worked almost exclusively in the popular genre of the detective novel, in the broad sense of that term, she has consistently invested it with a seriousness of moral purpose that is rare. The representation of murder in her hands sooner or later becomes a pretext to reflect on the motivation and larger meaning of that act; it typically leads her to explore what is widely considered a very unscientific and even an anachronistic idea, namely, the presence of evil in the modern world. The word itself is invoked at intervals in many of her novels with the result that, behind the psychological and sociological dimensions of crime associated with the realist strain in detective fiction of which she is herself a practitioner, there invariably resonates the notion of more disturbing, atavistic forces at work. On one level, motivation for murder is explained in a popular formula repeated in slightly different versions, which is expressed by an old detective sergeant in *A Taste for Death:* "Love, Lust, Loathing, Lucre, the four L's of murder, laddie" (p. 129). On another level, for James the formula signifies the sad fact of the fixity of the human animal over the millennia.

The overall impression her works leave in any case is that of human beings as creatures who are frequently desperate, driven, lonely, arrogant, deeply egotistical, or some combination of these qualities, who are capable of rising above themselves through love and compassion but who, under extreme conditions, are also potentially capable of destroying their kind out of rage or frustration, a desire for revenge, or the ruthless commitment to a cause or idea. James, then, is a student of human behavior—in it she sees reminders of the theological categories of good and evil. Original sin is not just the title of one of her most disturbing works, it is a pervading possibility. The only solution to original sin, she occasionally suggests, is a form of grace. The tormented stories told in *Innocent Blood* and *A Taste for Death* both end with a silent prayer—in the shadow of King's College Chapel, Cambridge, and in a Victorian London church, respectively—and the last word of the former is, in fact, "grace."

Similarly, the title of *Devices and Desires* is from archaic church English and refers to the deviousness of the desires of the flesh. Early in the novel, a quotation from Ecclesiastes offers a religious perspective on a modern world that includes nuclear power plants: "That which hath been is now; and that which is to be hath already been; and God requireth that which is past" (p. 22). The theological attitude expressed here explains in part why one frequently encounters in James's works evocations of the celebrants—priests, vicars, and nuns—and institutions of the religous life—churches, chapels, and convents. At the same time a great many of her most memorable characters give expression to what can only be called a nostalgia for faith. They are typically like Cordelia Gray, who is diagnosed as "incurably agnostic but prone to unpredictable lapses into faith" (*An Unsuitable Job for a Woman,* p. 177). Such characters are sensitive to the moving power of spiritual values, to the ideas of order, harmony, beauty, and a life of service, but they rarely encounter them in the largely desacralized world in which they live.

Finally, if there is one recurring motif to be found throughout James's novels, it is that of an irreparable, familial loss. Many of her principal characters, including three of her leading detectives, have experienced the death either of one or more parents early in life or of a spouse or child: in Dalgliesh's case, of course, the loss of a wife and a child in childbirth; in Cordelia Gray's, that of a mother when she herself was born and a feckless father in early womanhood; in Kate Miskin's, that of a mother in infancy and a father she never knew. Gabriel Dauntsey in *Original Sin* has lost both his wife and two children to the forces of the Holocaust. Probably most common, however, is the motif of orphanhood along with the sense of abandonment associated with it. *Innocent Blood* knowingly combines two themes of familial loss, in the apparently deliberate giving up of a child through adoption and—perhaps the cruelest loss of all—the death of a child who was first raped by a man and then murdered by his wife. After so much anguish, it is remarkable that the same novel concludes with a wish in the form of a prayer. The last words James chooses for this difficult novel show her main character reaching out for love and forgiveness: "And perhaps to be able to wish him well with all that she could recognise of her unpractised heart, to say a short, untutored prayer for him and his Violet, was in itself a small accession of grace" (p. 313). P. D. James knows humanity still needs all the help it can get.

In sum, the ethical code at the heart of her moral vision is a form of Saint Paul's *caritas:* that is, what in the King James version of the bible in English was translated as "charity" and what is now rendered as "love" in the sense of a selfless love for others. Part of the meaning James attaches to the concept is effectively summed up in a flash of memory Dalgliesh has in the denouement of *A Taste for Death.* At the small wake organized by Kate Miskin for her murdered granny, he is moved to recall an insight he first experienced as an adolescent on a similar occasion: "he had felt for the first time an adult and almost overwhelming sense of the sadness at the heart of life and had marveled at the grace with which the poor and the humble could meet it" (p. 507).

Selected Bibliography

WORKS OF P. D. JAMES

NOVELS

Cover Her Face. London: Faber, 1962; New York: Scribners, 1966. Harmondsworth, Eng.: Penguin, 1989.

A Mind to Murder. London: Faber, 1963; New York: Scribners, 1967.

Unnatural Causes. London: Faber, 1967; New York: Scribners, 1967.

The Maul and the Pear Tree: The Ratcliffe Highway Murders, 1811 (with T. A. Critchley). London: Constable, 1971.

Shroud for a Nightingale. London: Faber, 1971; New York: Scribners, 1971.

An Unsuitable Job for a Woman. London: Faber, 1972; New York: Scribners, 1973. Harmondsworth, Eng.: Penguin, 1989.

The Black Tower. London: Faber, 1975; New York: Scribners, 1975.

Death of an Expert Witness. London: Faber, 1977; New York: Scribners, 1977.

Innocent Blood. London: Faber, 1980; New York: Scribners, 1980. Harmondsworth, Eng.: Penguin, 1989.

The Skull Beneath the Skin. London: Faber, 1982; New York: Scribners, 1982.

A Taste for Death. London: Faber, 1986; New York: Scribners, 1986. Harmondsworth, Eng.: Penguin, 1989.

Devices and Desires. London: Faber, 1989; New York: Scribners, 1989. Harmondsworth, Eng.: Penguin, 1990.

The Children of Men. London: Faber, 1992; New York: Knopf, 1993.

Original Sin. London: Faber, 1994; New York: Scribners, 1994.

A Certain Justice. London: Faber, 1997; New York: Knopf, 1997.

STORIES

"Moment of Power." In *Ellery Queen's Murder Menu*. Edited by Ellery Queen. New York: World, 1969. Pp. 167–184.

"Murder, 1986." In *Ellery Queen's Masters of Mystery*. Edited by Ellery Queen. New York: Dial Press, 1975. Pp. 191–210.

"A Very Desirable Residence." In *Winter's Crimes 8*. Edited by Hilary Watson. New York: St. Martin's Press, 1977. Pp. 154–167.

"Great-Aunt Allie's Flypapers." In *Verdict of Thirteen*. Edited by Julian Symons. New York: Harper, 1978. Pp. 1–24.

"The Victim." In *John Creasey's Crime Collection 1982*. Edited by Herbert Harris. New York: St. Martin's Press, 1982. Pp. 71–84.

"The Girl Who Loved Graveyards." In *Winter's Crimes 15*. Edited by George Harding. New York: St. Martin's Press, 1984. Pp. 51–65.

"The Murder of Santa Claus." In *Great Detectives*. Edited by David Willis McCullough. New York: Pantheon, 1984. Pp. 534–553.

ARTICLES

"A Fictional Prognosis." In *Murder Ink*. Edited by Dilys Winn. New York: Workman, 1977. Pp. 339–342.

"Ought Adam to Marry Cordelia?" In *Murder Ink*. Edited by Dilys Winn. New York: Workman, 1977. Pp. 68–69.

"Dorothy L. Sayers: From Puzzle to Novel." In *Crime Writers: Reflections on Crime Fiction*. Edited by H. R. F. Keating. London: BBC Publications, 1978. Pp. 67–75.

"The Heart-Pounding Pleasure of Whodunits." *Family Weekly*, 22 August 1982: 6–8.

"A Series of Scenes." In *Whodunit*. Edited by H. R. F. Keating. New York: Van Nostrand Reinhold, 1982. Pp. 85–86.

BIOGRAPHICAL AND CRITICAL STUDIES

Bakerman, Jane S. Interview with P. D. James. *Armchair Detective* 10: 55–57 (January 1977).

Benstock, Bernard. "The Clinical World of P. D. James." In *Twentieth-Century Women Novelists*. Edited by Thomas F. Staley. Totowa, N.J.: Barnes and Noble, 1982. Pp. 104–129.

Cooper-Clark, Diana. *Designs of Darkness: Interviews with Detective Novelists*. Bowling Green, Ohio: Bowling Green State University Popular Press, 1983. Pp. 15–32.

Craig, Patricia. Interview with P. D. James. *Times Literary Supplement*, 5 June 1981: 642–643.

Gidez, Richard B. *P. D. James*. Boston: Twayne, 1986.

Harkness, Bruce. "P. D. James." In *Essays on Detective Fiction*. Edited by Bernard Benstock. London: Macmillan, 1983. Pp. 119–141.

Heilbrun, Carolyn G. "P. D. James." In *Twentieth-Century Crime and Mystery Writers*. Edited by John M. Reilly. New York: St. Martin's, 1980. Pp. 855–857.

Herbert, Rosemary. "P. D. James." In *The Fatal Art of Entertainment: Interviews with Mystery Writers*. New York: Hall, 1994. Pp. 55–83.

Hubly, Erlene. "Adam Dalgliesh: Byronic Hero." *Clues* 3: 40–46 (fall/winter 1982).

———. "The Formula Challenged: The Novels of P. D. James." *Modern Fiction Studies* 29: 511–521 (autumn 1983).

Joyner, Nancy Carol. "P. D. James." In *Ten Women of Mystery*. Edited by Earl F. Bargainner. Bowling Green, Ohio: Bowling Green State University Popular Press, 1981. Pp. 107–123.

Porter, Dennis. "Detection and Ethics: The Case of P. D. James." In *The Sleuth and the Scholar*. Edited by Barbara A. Rader and Howard G. Zettler. New York: Greenwood Press, 1988. Pp. 11–18.

Siebenheller, Norma. *P. D. James*. New York: Ungar, 1981.

Smyer, Richard I. "P. D. James: Crime and the Human Condition." *Clues* 3: 49–61 (spring/summer 1982).

Torre de la, Lillian. "Cordelia Gray: The Thinking Man's Heroine." In *Murderess Ink*. Edited by Dilys Winn. New York: Workman, 1979. Pp. 111–113.

Winks, Robin W. "Murder and Dying." *New Republic*, 31 July 1976: 31–32.

Wyndham, Francis. "The Civilized Art of Murder." *Times Literary Supplement*, 13 December 1974: 1419.

Ronald A. Knox

(1888–1957)

SUSAN OLEKSIW

RONALD ARBUTHNOTT KNOX was born on 17 February 1888 in Leicestershire to a family of long religious service in Protestant denominations. His parents, Ellen Penelope French and the Reverend Edmund Arbuthnott Knox, later bishop of Manchester, produced six children, of which Ronald was the youngest. When his mother died in the summer of 1892, Ronald and his brother Wilfred went to live with an uncle for four years. In 1895 Edmund Knox married Ethel Newton, daughter of a vicar and twenty years the bishop's junior. In 1896 Ronald went to Summer Fields School, near Oxford, where he made several strong friendships, excelled in academics, and developed his skills in oratory, for which he would become well known. He went on to Eton in 1900, a school he loved above all others; this affection prompted him later to translate a manuscript, published in 1923, on the miracles of Henry VI, the school's founder. In 1906, while still at Eton, Knox published his first book, a collection of poetry written in English, Latin, and Greek titled *Signa Severa.* In the same year he founded a journal, *The Outsider,* whose satirical bent was to become a standard feature of his later secular writing. Ronald entered Balliol College, Oxford, in 1906, where his intellectual abilities and knack for abiding friendship flourished. After a short trip on the Continent following graduation in 1910, he accepted a fellowship and chaplaincy at Trinity College, Oxford. He was ordained deacon in the Anglican Church in 1911 and priest in 1912. Around this time he began to publish his sermons and religious essays as well as short pieces on more popular topics.

World War I was a period of deep religious questioning for Knox; he resolved his doubts by converting to Roman Catholicism on 22 September 1917. He explained this passage in his religious life in *A Spiritual Aeneid* (1918). Despite his fervent prayers for peace and the death of many friends, Knox worked in the War Office until the end of 1918. He was ordained a Roman Catholic priest in 1919. Because the Church had not paid for his religious education, he was free to choose the path of his service, providing the responsible bishop approved; an inheritance from his mother and his own earning capacity as a writer also gave him financial flexibility. In 1926 he became Roman Catholic chaplain at Oxford, where he remained until 1939.

From 1919 to 1926 Knox taught at St. Edmund's College in Hertfordshire, where he wrote his first mystery novel, *The Viaduct Murder* (1925), three noncrime novels, and numerous essays. Between 1927 and 1934, he published five other mystery novels, as well as essays and sermons. His most important contribution to the study of crime fiction came in an introduction to a short-story collection published in 1929, in which Knox listed ten rules of detective fiction, which he called the Decalogue. He became a popular critic of contemporary life through his essays and sermons. In *Caliban in Grub Street* (1930) Knox turned his satirical eye on the religious views expressed during a symposium attended by, among others, Arnold Bennett, Sir Hugh Walpole, Sir Arthur Conan Doyle, E. Phillips Oppenheim, and Israel Zangwill. Symposia at which established, usually popular writers of the time discussed theological and other various topics of interest to the general public were popular during the 1920s, and newspapers published the results in book form. *Caliban* was Knox's commentary on this particular symposium, written by invitation of Frank Sheed, of the publishing house Sheed & Ward. His last secular work, *Let Dons Delight* (1939), is a witty review of 350 years of history from the perspective of an Oxford common room.

In 1939 Knox retired from Oxford in order to translate the New Testament into English and to serve at Aldenham as private chaplain to Lord John and Lady Daphne Acton, who had become Knox's close friends when he agreed to instruct Lady Daphne, a Protestant, in her husband's faith in 1937. Knox's plans for a quiet scholarly life were disrupted, however, by World War II and the installation at the Aldenham estate of a Roman Catholic convent school. He actively participated in the students' religious life and did his best to help maintain Aldenham in the face of chronic labor shortages. For the most part the 1940s and 1950s were difficult years for Knox as a writer. The *Manual of Prayers,* which he had been asked to revise in 1937, was repudiated by his superiors in 1942–1943. Only after careful scrutiny, minute criticism, and a three-year delay was the New Testament published in 1945; the Old Testament appeared in 1948–1949. The complete text of the Bible, incorporating hundreds of revisions suggested by the overseeing committee, was published in 1955. *God and the Atom* (1945), which Knox wrote in response to the attack on Hiroshima, was coldly received by the public. In 1947 Lord Acton decided to move his family to Southern Rhodesia, leaving Knox to find another home at the age of sixty. His predicament was resolved by an invitation to take up the chaplaincy at an old friend's estate in Mells; he moved there in 1947 and continued his work as a translator.

If praise for his work was rare, honors were abundant. In 1941 he received an honorary fellowship at Trinity College, Oxford, which greatly pleased him. In 1949 he was elected to the Old Brotherhood of the English Secular Clergy, a society founded in 1623. In 1951 he was appointed prothonotary apostolic *ad instar,* which was more title than anything else; in 1954 he received an honorary doctorate of letters from the National University of Ireland in Dublin. Knox's health began to decline in 1956; he underwent surgery early in the following year but managed to give the Romanes Lecture at Oxford in June 1957. He died on 24 August 1957 at Mells.

Sherlock Holmes Studies

In 1911, as a newly appointed Oxford don, Knox lectured in subjects that had long been dear to his heart—logic and the Greek and Roman epic poets Homer and Virgil. A traditionalist who believed in the historical personage of Homer, Knox deplored the trend among British and German scholars to apply to the study of the Greek epics the techniques of a form of criticism developed to identify the sources, authorship, time of composition, and the like of the books of the Bible; he especially disliked the extreme conclusions its practitioners sometimes reached. Named the higher criticism by W. R. Smith in *The Old Testament in the Jewish Church* (1881), this methodology led to the then-surprising conclusion that neither Homeric epic was the work of a single hand. Knox set out to ridicule the methodology of higher criticism by applying it to a body of popular literature whose origins and composition were not in question. The result was the satirical essay "Studies in the Literature of Sherlock Holmes," which he read as a paper in 1911 to the Gryphon Club,

Trinity, and published the following year in the *Blue Book 1912.* In this thirty-page essay Knox mimics the techniques, arguments, and style of the higher criticism in order to reach outrageously absurd conclusions on the composition and authorship of the stories about Sherlock Holmes.

Knox announces his intent in the opening paragraph: "It is the method by which we treat as significant what the author did not mean to be significant." This method can be relied upon to glean "economic evidence from Aristophanes . . . [who] knew nothing of economics" and "cryptograms from Shakespeare" (p. 145). Knox is especially intrigued with the idea of applying this technique to Sherlock Holmes because it is, after all, "Holmes's own method" and because "anything is worthy of study, if that study be thorough and systematic" (p. 146). All this, delivered in Knox's jaunty style, sounds reasonable enough, but it is, nevertheless, based on an absurd premise that Knox slips past the reader—that the literary character Sherlock Holmes is a real person.

At every point Knox makes what seems at first a reasonable statement and then underlines its absurdities. He cites the conclusions of other scholars, examining their evidence and arguments against or in support of one another. Knox painstakingly goes over various inconsistencies found in the Holmes stories, which include such momentous matters as Holmes's change in manners and what he regards as inaccurate details, such as the statement that Holmes attended college for only two years in "The Gloria Scott" (pp. 148–149). Knox presents his own theory—that Dr. Watson, after faithfully recording a number of stories for his friend Holmes up to the time of the fatal events at Reichenbach Falls, himself falls on hard times and "is forced to earn a livelihood by patching together clumsy travesties of the wonderful incidents of which he was once the faithful recorder" (p. 154).

Knox continues with an exploration of literary points, discussing a theory on the construction of the stories that identifies eleven parts in the ideal story, each with a Greek title. He caps this with a search for literary affinities for Watson's style, dismissing such well-known authors of mystery and detective fiction as Edgar Allan Poe, Emile Gaboriau, and Wilkie Collins in favor of Plato's *Dialogues* and Greek drama. The association is developed through an analogy linking Socrates and Holmes, the Greek chorus and Watson, and the Sophists and Inspector Lestrade. Knox reinforces his comparison between Watson and the Greek chorus with what he suggests are parallel passages from Doyle's "The Speckled Band" and Aeschylus' *Agamemnon.* He concludes this part of the essay with a flourish about the significance of Watson's bowler, raising it to the level of icon.

As Knox points out according to the methodology of higher criticism, the criminals "are only secondary figures" (p. 165). But they must be the best sort of criminals in order to interest, challenge, and, in fact, be caught by the best detective. Knox then segues into a brief biography of Sherlock Holmes, marshaling the data to determine his background, education, and general knowledge. Knox had an especial dislike of careless thinkers, and he subjects Holmes's method to sharp analysis, drawing a precise distinction between observation and inference and, later, between observation and deduction.

Knox ends his essay with a topic that softened the satirical point, the epigram that is unique to Sherlock Holmes, which Knox named the "Sherlockismus." This is the dialogue in which Holmes startles his interlocutor with an observation or riposte only Holmes could make. The best-known example is taken from "Silver Blaze" (1894). Holmes is investigating the disappearance of a favorite racehorse and the murder of its trainer. The local inspector questions Holmes:

> "Is there any point to which you would wish to draw my attention?"
>
> "To the curious incident of the dog in the night-time."
>
> "The dog did nothing in the night-time."

"That was the curious incident," remarked Sherlock Holmes.

In his study of the stories of Sherlock Holmes, Knox highlights all the practices he detested in contemporary criticism: major conclusions based on minor points; absurd generalizations based on a distortion of simple facts; a metaphorical comment by one scholar taken literally by another and then refuted rigorously; teasing out meaning from the nuances and subtleties of the English language and then exhibiting a woodenness and insensitivity to its finer features in one's own writing; and a tone of righteous indignation and self-importance informing the simplest statements. The roster of invented critics' names—the great Sauwosch, Backnecke, M. Piff-Pouff, Bilgemann, Prof. J. A. Smith, Blunt, Ratzegger, Professor Sabaglione, M. Papier Maché, M. Binsk—indicates Knox's opinion of contemporary scholars.

Knox considered higher criticism a waste of time and an insult to both the creators and readers of literature; he found in this work nothing that addressed literature as literature, nothing to expand the taste and knowledge of the reader and deepen his or her sense of the human condition. Instead of saying so directly, however, he used lighthearted, gentle satire and instigated an entirely new field of writing—the study of the literature of Sherlock Holmes.

The Decalogue

In 1929 Knox edited a volume of detective stories with an introduction containing his ten commandments of crime fiction. This part of the essay, known as the Decalogue, articulated the contract established between writer and reader at the beginning of a tale.

Knox was not the first reader to catalog features of this genre, but he was the first to identify the core of this fiction as a contest that depended on fair play between reader and writer; in addition, he mocked the more obvious weaknesses of the form. Knox's list is not, therefore, to be taken literally, but it is to be taken seriously as a guide to writing the detective story.

The ten rules fall roughly into two groups. Rules one, two, six, seven, and eight establish the principles of fair play to be adhered to by the writer. The remaining refer to specific failings of writers and therefore serve as examples of devices or shortcuts to be avoided. In rule one Knox states: "The criminal must be someone mentioned in the early part of the story, but must not be anyone whose thoughts the reader has been allowed to follow" (p. 12). He was concerned here with two principles. First, that the writer who failed to work out the details of the crime and its solution did not get himself out of his dilemma by making up a character at the last minute and introducing him or her late in the story. The reader must have the same opportunity as the detective to observe the behavior of all suspects; he or she cannot guess who the murderer is if this person is not introduced until the end of the book. Second, this rule ensures that the story will follow what Knox considered the correct form—the presentation of a crime, including all relevant players, early in the novel. The detective story, in Knox's view, is about unraveling a crime, not about building up to the commission of one.

Knox clarified the second part of the rule in order to acknowledge Agatha Christie's tour de force in *The Murder of Roger Ackroyd* (1926) by saying that "the author must not imply an attitude of mystification in the character who turns out to be the criminal" (p. 13). Following the thoughts of a murderer is allowable as long as the writer is scrupulously honest with what is observed and recorded. Knox in effect applauded Christie's trick.

In rule two Knox excludes recourse to supernatural or divine agencies to extricate the writer from her difficulties of finding a solution to the crime. This should be obvious, but Knox found the introduction of the divine in the Father Brown stories by G. K. Chesterton an unsettling element transforming them into something other than detective stories.

Despite efforts by many writers, this rule seems impossible to break satisfactorily.

In rule six Knox forbids happy "accidents" and "intuition." Early mystery writers had trouble developing the skill of detection, which meant that in order to bring about resolution the murderer had to confess. In Knox's view only the detective can solve the crime and must do so by relying solely on his or her wits. The detective may find things others cannot, but he does so by using his imagination, reason, and logic, not by luck. If during a search of the suspect's home the detective locates, in her files, an envelope with incriminating telephone numbers on it, it is because he knows the woman he is investigating is both careless (she uses old envelopes for notes) and logical (she files everything alphabetically). He succeeds in his investigation by using his imagination to think like the suspect, so that whatever he finds seems reasonable to the reader.

In rule seven Knox states that the "detective must not himself commit the crime" (p. 15). Here Knox is referring to instances in which the author clearly establishes that the character introduced as the detective is legitimate and not someone in disguise. Writers are especially fond of playing with this rule. Although some readers cry foul, these stories are fair, by Knox's reckoning, as long as the writer presents clues to the false detective's true identity, throughout the story.

In rule eight Knox insists that the detective reveal all clues he or she discovers. This is perhaps the sine qua non of detective fiction as distinguished from thrillers or other subtypes of the genre. Characterized as a game between reader and writer, detective fiction is specifically an intellectual entertainment. If each and every clue is not available to the reader, the game is flawed, and the reader is cheated of a fair chance to hit on the solution and thus enjoy a significant pleasure.

These five commandments establish the rules of the game and guarantee that the question posed in the beginning—who murdered X?—can be answered just as readily by an astute reader as by a great detective. Once the writer engages the reader's curiosity by presenting a murder, he must stick to his side of the bargain.

The second set of five commandments highlights the kind of absurdities and infelicities that writers should avoid. In rule three Knox forbids more than one secret room or passage; and even that one is forbidden unless the writer can establish that it is a reasonable device for the setting. Knox used a secret passage in his first novel, *The Viaduct Murder,* after giving the reader what he considered ample warning by relating the history of the old dower house. In rule four Knox forbids hitherto unknown poisons; no reader can guess how a person was murdered, and therefore who might have done the deed, if the means itself is not common knowledge. This rule also bars complicated scientific inventions that require long explanations at the end of the story. Many readers found tedious the detective novels of R. Austin Freeman, which he infused with his scientific expertise, but since then writers have combed the world of science for intriguing methods of murder and modes of investigation. Rule five contains the well-known stricture against a Chinaman. Fiction has always been fertile ground for stereotypes, and Knox rightly complains against characters whose cliché-bound descriptions inevitably cripple a story. Knox invoked the most egregious example of stereotyping of the period to make his point, but mystery writers of all periods have given rein to various forms of racism, including anti-Semitism. All forms violate the rule of reason and fair-mindedness essential to the detective story, and were especially offensive to Knox.

In rule ten Knox forbids twins and other kinds of doubles, unless the reader is fully prepared for them. In a version of the introduction published posthumously as "Detective Stories" (1958) Knox omits rule ten and hints he would substitute for it a ban on romance, for "this intrusion of life's backstairs introduces an element of unfair mystification" (pp. 197–198).

Rule nine concerns the character now called the Watson in honor of the chronicler in the Sherlock Holmes stories. The Watson is not necessary but is introduced as "a sparring partner" for the reader. According to Knox, the writer must not conceal any of the Watson's thoughts, and he must make the Watson less intelligent than the average reader. This is a practical detail that, if not followed, can wreak havoc. If the Watson is too smart, the reader will be denied the pleasure of figuring out the plot and instead will feel baffled and put off. The "stupid friend of the detective," as Knox characterizes him, is just slow enough to make the reader feel intelligent and in league with the Great Detective. We are fond of Watson, but we prefer to think we are like Holmes.

Even though every one of his rules has been broken many times over—all of them by Agatha Christie alone—no other critic grasped as well as Knox did the essential points of the detective story during its Golden Age. Knox identifies the features that distinguish the detective story from other kinds of fiction—the cerebral pleasure of exploring a question in a rational way through materials supplied by the writer—and in doing so articulates the fundamental agreement between reader and writer that writers ignore at their peril. The detective story should be fair and well written—signs of respect for the reader.

There is a note of parody in Knox's Decalogue, an element of fun that was not lost on his colleagues in The Detection Club, a society of mystery writers founded in 1928 by Anthony Berkeley whose early members included Chesterton, Dorothy L. Sayers, and Christie. With a deep bow to Knox's rules against intuition, acts of God, and the like, The Detection Club wittily adapted his prescriptions to their membership oath. One line of the oath reads: "Do you promise to observe a seemly moderation in the use of Gangs, Conspiracies, Death-Rays, Ghosts, Hypnotism, Trap-Doors, Chinamen, Super-Criminals and Lunatics; and utterly and for ever to forswear mysterious Poisons unknown to Science?" It is difficult to imagine any group of equally successful writers inventing anything quite as playful today—a sign perhaps of how much the field of writing in this genre has changed—but Knox perfectly captured the attitude of Golden Age writers, who devoted their considerable intelligence and long hours to careful plotting rather than to character studies. Although stories conforming to the Decalogue seem dated now, the standards of fair play and good writing still command respect.

Essays on Detective Fiction

Although Knox is known primarily as the author of the Decalogue, he wrote three other essays on detective fiction whose overall sensibleness, intelligence, and perceptiveness have been overshadowed by his satirical writings on the genre. Since he regularly published his essays only after having delivered them several times as talks, modifying and developing them as appropriate, his ideas received greater circulation than his limited record in this area of publishing would suggest.

In an essay entitled "Mystery Stories," contributed to the 1929 edition of the *Encyclopaedia Britannica,* Knox declares that the detective story deserved "to be classed as a separate branch of fiction from the very nature of its construction." He defines the formula of the genre as "an initial *fait accompli,* the unravelling of which is the principal interest of the book."

In "Detective Stories" Knox argues that detective fiction is "a highly specialized art-form, and deserves, as such, its own literature" (p. 181). He again develops the argument that detective fiction works backward, from a crime committed in the early chapters to the original impetus driving the criminal. In a well-constructed mystery there is no need for romance or the suspense of the thriller, for "the story derives its romantic excitement only from the danger of the criminal getting off scot free, or some innocent person being condemned in his place" (p. 184).

In seeking to identify the literary antecedents of detective fiction, Knox rejects the stories of the Jewish Apocrypha of the Book of Daniel, which Dorothy L. Sayers accepts in her introduction to *The Omnibus of Crime* (1928). Knox concedes that Daniel demonstrates the art of detection in the story of Susanna, for example, but he points out that there is no effort to conceal the truth of events and withhold the solution until the end (pp. 185–186). Knox turns instead to Sophocles' *Oedipus Tyrannus,* which is "constructed as a detective story; the truth about the past gradually coming out, and revealing itself to the actors in the drama one by one according to their various grades of intelligence" (p. 187). In his comparison, Creon is the Watson, Oedipus is the Scotland Yard detective (as well as the murderer), and Teiresias is the private detective. Knox's choice of a literary precedent illustrates several of his own rules, particularly the subtleties of rule seven; Oedipus promises to uncover the truth and punish the king's murderer, but the astute viewer will weigh every clue given by the Oracle and others before placing his faith in Oedipus' or anyone else's innocence. Sophocles does not mislead: he challenges us to question everyone to listen without bias, and to learn the truth gradually, as Oedipus does.

Like many other writers, Knox feared that the detective story had been overdone, that the game was "getting played out" and becoming a literature of stereotypes. The problem was that the writer is forever looking for ways to trick the reader, and the reader is becoming increasingly alert to these tricks. Knox feared that writers would resort to the qualities of the ordinary novel, drawing on romance and psychology instead of clever plotting. He did not care for contemporary fiction and did not see how the detective story could survive. In this he was not alone, but he was wrong.

In "Father Brown" (in *Literary Distractions,* 1958) Knox analyzed G. K. Chesterton's Father Brown stories, focusing on the character of the detective. Knox argues that it is the personality of the detective that counts; moreover, "he must appeal to us through weakness" (p. 171). When we meet Father Brown, we do not expect this unassuming man to be able to solve a crime, but in his gentle way this priest of the confessional exposes the mealinesses of the human heart that lead to crime. Concerned with the great moral and ethical questions of his time, Chesterton refused to be satisfied with delivering a clever plot; he instead used the plot to explore larger themes. The Father Brown stories slip into the reader's thought issues and ideas that detective fiction is supposed to help us escape, a weakness in Knox's view. He concludes that these stories are not always good mysteries, but they are very good Chesterton.

Fiction

Knox published six mystery novels and three short stories between 1925 and 1937 and contributed to three novels written jointly by members of The Detection Club. His fiction has been neglected since his death, dismissed as puzzle stories with little depth. There is some truth to this assessment, for Knox wrote precisely the kind of tale that fit his definition of the detective story as a game between reader and writer in which all clues were fairly presented and psychological and romantic themes did not figure.

Knox admitted, in *Literary Distractions,* that he wrote his first mystery novel, *The Viaduct Murder,* as "a satire on detective stories," but "the public insisted on taking it as a bad detective story" (p. 196). Nevertheless, this novel contains all the features he considered essential to good detective fiction: an abundance of physical clues, including ciphers, timetables and train or car journeys, footprints or fingerprints, maps, and cryptic notes, and long passages during which the detective and his companions reason their way through what they surmise to be the suspect's bluffs and double bluffs, giving Knox ample opportunity to lecture on the differences between observation, inference, deduction, and outrageous conclusions. As a writer, Knox is strong on setting the scene but almost completely ignores "stage business"—the reader never knows which character is sitting where and doing what while another talks. He had no interest in character development, but as a priest he could not resist opportunities to discuss moral issues; he has no sympathy for the murderer, much for the victim usually, and no sense of self-righteous vengeance, yet his endings are often sophisticated in their moral complexity.

In *The Viaduct Murder* two friends and golfing companions come upon the body of a man beneath a viaduct; with two other friends, including an Anglican priest, they decide to investigate the death, producing implausible theories to account for the clues found on and around the corpse. The murderer turns out to be the most obvious suspect, and all the efforts of the amateur detectives are shown to be the unfounded speculations of overheated imaginations. The characters are entertaining, and their dialogue is witty and vivid.

In *The Three Taps: A Detective Story Without a Moral* (1927) a millionaire decides to test the ethics of a Roman Catholic bishop but by accident asphyxiates himself, and what was supposed to be a subterfuge leads to a murder investigation. In this novel Knox introduces his series characters. Miles Bredon is an investigator for the Indescribable Insurance Company, which insures anyone against almost anything. He engages in charming banter with his wife, Angela, his boss, Sholto, and his colleague in Scotland Yard, Inspector Leyland. With the assistance of this crew, Bredon catches criminals with his cerebral methods, which include letting his unconscious do the heavy work while he loses himself in a game of patience. Except for his repartee with Angela, Miles is not deeply imagined and none of the characters changes or grows from novel to novel. Knox preferred to focus his attention on varying the crime and its outcome.

In *The Footsteps at the Lock* (1928) Derek and Nigel, two young cousins who do not get along, are persuaded to take a boat trip together down the Thames. Dissolute and sickly, Derek is due to inherit a substantial sum in a few days, on his twenty-fifth birthday; if his health fails before that date, Nigel will inherit. Derek disappears, and Nigel is suspected of his murder. Derek ultimately turns up in Europe, where he is killing himself with drugs and waiting to hear Nigel has been hanged for murder before returning to claim his inheritance.

In *The Body in the Silo* (1933) Mr. and Mrs. Halliford host a houseparty that includes a late-night car race, dubbed the elopement game, in which two guests slip away and race for the Welsh border before the remaining guests notice they are gone and set out to catch them. The following morning, an influential political figure is found dead in a silo. Miles Bredon's investigations reveal that the wrong man was murdered and his body removed to the silo; a second attempt is made, during which the murderer again bungles the mechanical aspects of the crime and ends up dead. Critics have called this Knox's best mystery; he keeps the focus on the crime at all times, and the characters have distinct personalities. Beginning with *The Body in the Silo,* Knox gives page numbers in footnotes to every clue that Bredon or any other character refers to during the explication of the crime; the reader is thus able to verify Knox's explanation.

For all of Knox's dislike of modern values, Bredon acts very much like a modern man when he finds himself faced with a situation that he dislikes and can alter. In *Still Dead* (1934) Colin Reiver is sent on a cruise after killing a young boy in a car accident. Almost a month later, on a Monday morning, a laborer discovers Colin's body, but when he returns with help, the body is gone. Two days later the body is discovered again, in the same place and same posture. The question of when Colin died is important, for his life was insured and the premium did not reach the insurance-company offices until early Monday morning. Bredon decides in the end to tell the truth to the company but to prevent any publicity; the murderer is left to deal with his guilt in his own way.

Critics consider *Double Cross Purposes* (1937) Knox's least successful effort. Bredon is sent to the Scottish Highlands to keep an eye on two men, Vernon Lethaby and Digger Henderson, who are searching for Prince Charlie's treasure; the company has insured one of the men against the loss of the treasure once it is found. Various maneuvers by Lethaby and Henderson lead to a fire in which a body is found burned beyond recognition. In the end there is no murder, only the exhumation of a corpse from a nearby cemetery to stand in for Henderson and enable him, presumably dead, to continue his work in secret.

Although Knox is severely criticized for poor character development, he can surprise the reader with his insight into the minds of those who have lost their moral bearings. Some recover themselves, others do not. In *Footsteps at the Lock,* Nigel is surprised to discover in himself doubt about how to treat the cousin who tried to incriminate him for murder and feels his way to a moral and charitable conclusion. In *Double Cross Purposes* Knox creates in Lethaby one of the most unsavory character types of the times—the man whose morals are only an extension of his opportunism. Amoral, arrogant, shallow, Lethaby is bold and shameless as he describes what he has done, and, as Knox makes clear, there is not much anyone can do about someone like that.

Legacy

As a young man, Knox excelled in the traditional education that calls for a quick mind, ready wit, and sense of fun, and he took these qualities with him into adulthood. He disliked the trends of the modern world toward undisciplined thought and unmoored lives, but instead of challenging the modern way directly, he turned to satire. This was his best medium, allowing him to exhibit his boyish charm and incisive humor as well as his kindly spirit. His essay on Sherlock Holmes, meant to chide modern literary critics, shines with affection for Sir Arthur Conan Doyle and his creation and led to an entirely new field of scholarship, the study of the chronicles by Dr. Watson. Knox was appalled at the results, but his work and its imitators continue to delight fans of Sherlock Holmes.

Knox's insistence that detective fiction deserved to be recognized as a distinct literature was more modern than he realized, and he made a valuable contribution to that literature in his essays. His Decalogue set forth standards that both writers and readers could point to and underscored the finer qualities of the genre. Though not an original or brilliant novelist or thinker, Knox brought intelligence and warmth to the study of the genre and demonstrated its best qualities—fun and fair play—in his own fiction.

Selected Bibliography

WORKS OF RONALD A. KNOX

ESSAYS

"Studies in the Literature of Sherlock Holmes." *Blue Book 1912.* Repr. of *The Blue Book: The Undergraduate Review.* London: Crosby, Lockwood & Son. One vol., 6 issues, May 1912–June 1913. Repr. in his *Essays in Satire.* London: Sheed & Ward, 1928. Pp. 145–175.

"Decalogue." Introduction to *The Best English Detective Stories: First Series.* Edited by Father Ronald Knox and H. Harrington. New York: Horace Liveright, 1929. Pp. 9–23. Repr. as "A Detective Story Decalogue" in *The Art of the Mystery Story: A Collection of Critical Essays.* Edited by Howard Haycraft. New York: Simon & Schuster, 1946. New York: Carroll & Graf, 1983. Pp. 194–196.

"Mystery Stories." In *Encyclopaedia Britannica,* 14th ed. London: Encyclopaedia Britannica, 1929.

"Detective Stories." In his *Literary Distractions.* New York: Sheed & Ward, 1958. Pp. 180–198.

"Father Brown." In his *Literary Distractions.* New York: Sheed & Ward, 1958. Pp. 170–179.

FICTION

The Viaduct Murder. London: Methuen, 1925.

The Three Taps: A Detective Story Without a Moral. London: Methuen, 1927.

The Footsteps at the Lock. London: Methuen, 1928.

The Scoop (with other members of The Detection Club). Serialized in *The Listener* (1930).

Behind the Screen (with other members of The Detection Club). Serialized in *The Listener* (1931).

"Solved by Inspection." In *My Best Detective Story: An Anthology of Stories Chosen by Their Own Authors.* London: Faber, 1931. Pp. 171–182.

The Floating Admiral (with other members of The Detection Club). London: Hodder and Stoughton, 1931; Garden City, N.Y.: Doubleday, 1932.

The Body in the Silo. London: Hodder and Stoughton, 1933. U.S.: *Settled out of Court.* New York: Dutton, 1934.

Still Dead. London: Hodder and Stoughton, 1934.

"The Fallen Idol." In *Six Against the Yard, in which Margery Allingham, Anthony Berkeley, Freeman Wills Crofts, Father Ronald Knox, Dorothy L. Sayers, Russell Thorndike Commit the Crime of Murder Which ex-Superintendent Cornish, C.I.D., Is Called Upon to Solve.* London: Selwyn & Blount, 1935.

Double Cross Purposes. London: Hodder and Stoughton, 1937.

"The Motive." In *The Second Century of Detective Stories.* Edited by E. C. Bentley. London: Hutchinson, 1938. Pp. 349–363.

BIOGRAPHICAL AND CRITICAL STUDIES

Corbishley, Thomas. *Ronald Knox, the Priest.* London: Sheed & Ward, 1964.

Donaldson, Norman. "Ronald Arbuthnott Knox." *The Armchair Detective* 7: 235–246 (August 1974).

Fitzgerald, Penelope. *The Knox Brothers.* London: Macmillan, 1977; New York: Coward, McCann, and Geoghegan, 1977.

Kingman, James. "In Defense of Ronald Knox." *The Armchair Detective* 11: 299 (July 1978).

Reynolds, William. "The Detective Novels of Ronald Knox: Toward a Reassessment." *The Armchair Detective* 14: 275–283 (summer 1981).

Speaight, Robert. *Ronald Knox, the Writer.* London: Sheed & Ward, 1966.

Waugh, Evelyn. *Ronald Knox: A Biography.* London: Chapman and Hall, 1959. Repr., London: Cassell, 1988.

JOHN LE CARRÉ
(b. 1931)

LYNNDIANNE BEENE

Like most artists, I'm an irreconcilable mixture of different people. If you have a talent and you know you have, you look after it, like a baby. So I do see David Cornwell as the guy who looks after John le Carré.

(David Cornwell, *Los Angeles Times,* 31 May 1989)

IN INTERVIEWS, NONFICTION, and best-seller after best-seller, David John Moore Cornwell, better known to his avid readers by the pseudonym John le Carré, adopts various personae. As a worried man, he discusses the many ways power degrades the precarious balance between governments and their citizens; for example, officials who circulate disinformation or shade the truth to benefit one group over another irreversibly sever the bond they have with their constituents. As a teacher, le Carré lectures readers on the moral obligations individuals have to one another. Betraying a friend to gain acceptance by a group degrades an individual's ethics irreparably in his work. As a novelist, le Carré explores sexual and emotional relationships among men and women. He makes his characters try on masks in the hope that they and, vicariously, his readers, will understand what it is to value another human being above oneself. Individuals who never move beyond a self-oriented love never complete their identities. But those who recognize that the love of another human being requires surrendering self, and often professional obligations, take on a new persona, one that is vulnerable but secured by commitment.

To produce characters representative of his various personae, le Carré fills his writing with barbed descriptions of venal politicians, agents, and bureaucrats who concoct international intrigues and feel satisfaction when their schemes end by destroying the moral and spiritual fiber of individuals. Ever the cleric and commentator, Cornwell religiously points out these dangers lest we, our loved ones, or our leaders forget. Unlike other espionage writers' timeworn plots and characters, technological wizardry, derring-do, and hackneyed themes, le Carré's fiction engages the mind and soul. His backdrops are the romanticism and individualism common to the work of Joseph Conrad and Graham Greene, and his settings are frequently drawn from real-world events, such as wars in the Middle East, superpower breakups, and national takeovers of internationally sensitive locations. Yet his focus stays on the deeper psychological facets that are pivotal in all human relationships. Directing his creative energies this way has not only led le Carré to reshape the public expectations and literary reputation of the spy fiction genre, it has also given him a means through which he can confront the duplicities of life, his own and others'.

Life

Bookish, courteous, and gentle spoken, David John Moore Cornwell exudes a distinctively patrician manner. He seems the product of a proper, aristocratic rearing because he has the educated deportment characteristic of the alumni of the most snobbish British schools. Cornwell, however, learned the ways of the gentry rather than came to them by birth. In fact, his upbringing is closer to that of one of his discredited characters than to an aristocrat's. His childhood experiences, and the ways he has reinterpreted them as an adult, shape his views of deception, betrayal, and the redemptive power of guileless love that buttress all his writing.

The observant watcher, natural spy, and future best-selling author was born in the genteel costal town of Poole, Dorset, England, on 19 October 1931. He learned to respect virtuous behavior and loyalty from his maternal grandfather, a nonconformist lay preacher. But his parents undercut these lessons. His mother, Olive (Glassy) Cornwell, was an emotionally distant caretaker, and his father, Ronald "Ronnie" Thomas Archibald Cornwell, was a flamboyant con man. His mother deserted her sons, Tony and David, early in their lives and left them feeling a need for love and approval but without a parental role model for such experiences. Cornwell, as an adult, publicly reconciled with his mother before her death, but he never forgot this childhood deprivation. He did not, however, reconcile with his unscrupulous father during his father's lifetime.

Undoubtedly the most important family influence on le Carré's fiction was his father, a Micawber-like character who was in and out of prison and whose schemes turned his children's early lives into survival by dissembling. Ronnie desperately wanted his children elevated to the respectability that he could not achieve, so he sent his sons and daughter, Charlotte, to schools he could not afford. His aspirations forced young David to change his voice, pretend to have a normal home life, and wonder, as he once told interviewer Tim Sullivan, "who his father's mistress-of-the-moment would be once the chauffeur drove them home." He also recalls times when Ronnie betrayed him. In one instance, during what was supposed to be a vacation, he and Tony sweated in a cellar in Aberdeen, squeezing figs and prunes into a mush that Ronnie rolled in glucose and sold as laxative pills. Another time Ronnie sent him to retrieve his luggage in Switzerland, where Cornwell was met by an irate hotel manager demanding immediate settlement of his father's unpaid bills. Several times later in life le Carré had to explain himself to women he had never met because his father had romanced them using the name le Carré. While many of these betrayals, taken individually, have a comic side, taken together they drove a wedge between father and son that was repaired only after Ronnie's death. These essential lessons about subterfuge, complicated schemes and operations, betrayal, and the elusiveness of unselfish love filled young Cornwell's imagination.

Moreover, Cornwell's formal education reinforced his father's amoral teachings. As a child, he attended St. Andrew's Preparatory and Sherborne School, the scene of James Hilton's *Goodbye, Mr. Chips,* where he endured the finest of British public school bigotry and repression. He rebelled from this hypocritical rigidity and fled to Switzerland, where he attended the University of Bern in 1948–1949 but left without a formal degree. He returned to England and joined the Army Intelligence Corps as part of his National Service before continuing his education. His language facility and firsthand knowledge of Europe ensured him such a posting. This child of a broken home now helped debrief defectors and interview Soviet-bloc refugees who had never had homes. The irony of the experience left a lasting impression on him. Throughout his fiction, refugees long for a safe house, a home, but seldom find one. Cornwell sought such a safe house in Lincoln College, Oxford University, where he studied linguistics, modern literature, and philosophy—particularly German aesthetics. He took a B.A. (honors) in modern languages and literature in 1956 and began working as a full-time teacher and part-time illustrator.

While at Lincoln, Cornwell met and married Alison Ann Veronica Sharp, the daughter of a much decorated Royal Air Force air marshal. Helped by an insider, Cornwell took teaching positions first at Millfield Junior School in Glastonbury, Somerset, then at prestigious Eton, institutions he excoriates in his fiction. Teaching, however, was never one of Cornwell's enthusiasms, in part because he chafed under the repression typical of long-standing bureaucracies and in part because of his own cynicism about the elitism such education abets. The harder he tried to conform to Eton's uncompromising dictates, the more the irony of becoming a member of the British gentry that he censured made him restless. Underpaid and unhappy, Cornwell fell back on his National Service contacts to secure an appointment with the Foreign Service as a low-level diplomat and occasional agent, a post he held from 1959 to 1964. Espionage, even of a rudimentary sort, suited him. He could stay emotionally aloof from institutions and their moral and ethical transgressions while still making himself into a plastic Everyman capable of straddling various social, political, and ethnic groups.

Shortly after entering the service, Cornwell returned to his passion, writing, because, as a new MI-6 recruit, he needed to earn more money to support Ann and their three sons, Simon, Stephen, and Timothy. Once again his past experience aided him; his stint teaching had taught him the principles of storytelling, and his work composing reports in the service disciplined his writing. He filled notebooks with story ideas and characters as he traveled by bus into London for work; for all his writing, he mined his own experiences as a rough template for his brand of genre fiction. But he shunned escapism and adventure in favor of didacticism. Every day his job with a secret service that was frequently ruthless in its dealings with friend and foe collided with his idealistic belief that, even in enemy territory, people who favor individuality and altruistic love are more ethical than any agency can be. With this bias guiding him, Cornwell wrote *Call for the Dead*, a novel that both heeds and violates the genre's criteria. *Call for the Dead* moves away from detective fiction as escapist literature by introducing psychological complexity, particularly in the main character and his search for identities. It seems that Cornwell turned to detective fiction early on as a way to escape truths about himself but could not, even in his first novel, avoid painful self-examination.

When London publisher Victor Gollancz accepted *Call for the Dead* for publication, Cornwell faced another problem: how to reconcile the low profile required of a secret-service agent and the high visibility common to authors of popular fiction. His official duties with the British secret service and, even more importantly, the strictures of the Official Secrets Act forced him to seek a pseudonym. Thus, a curious mixture of an alienated childhood, a chameleon nature, driving personal ambition, and professional restrictions allowed David Cornwell to reinvent himself as John le Carré and begin his long, productive writing career. Out of touch and in need of love, John le Carré created personae of all sorts to face the truths about David Cornwell.

Remaking a Genre

In his first three novels—*Call for the Dead* (1961), *A Murder of Quality* (1962), and his genre-breaking blockbuster *The Spy Who Came in from the Cold* (1963)—le Carré sets out themes that recur in all of his work. Basic to his novels are the issues of human values conflicting with pragmatic actions, the moral ambivalence and duplicity of intelligence services, the transforming, ennobling power that love can have, and a suspicion of debased language. Human values struggle to transcend big events and causes, such as the Israeli-Palestinian quagmire, in a world of disinformation and spy versus spy. Intelligence services thrive on duplicity that inevitably leads spies to self-destruction and a dehumanizing imbalance between feelings and reason. Feeling unselfish love for another is the only way for individuals to redeem themselves and achieve unity. But such affection cannot compete with the allure and false sense of control that undercover work proffers. Honorable actions cannot overtake empty language. Rather, close interrogations, wordplay, equivocation, and double entendre rule. Even in the best of circumstances, individuals find themselves manipulating language in heartless, deceiving ways, limiting their understanding, creating their own legends, or, worst of all, deceiving themselves. Le Carré's most rounded character, the diffident knight George Smiley, who appears in nine of his novels, manages to wield language in all these ways.

Given his interest in these larger issues, it is easy to see how le Carré is no mere writer of thrillers like Robert Ludlum, reporter like Frederick Forsyth, technology expert like Tom Clancy, or wham-bam-thank-you-ma'am escapist like Ian Fleming. He uses the scaffolding of espionage fiction to produce a tension common to mainstream literature. In his novels, a spy's inherent dilemma—that one must suspend one's convictions in order to champion their tenets—is common to many people. Hence, he makes the spy an archetype for the modern hero and shuns cardboard figures such as Robert Ludlum's Jason Bourne, Frederick Forsyth's the Jackal, Tom Clancy's Jack Ryan, and Ian Fleming's James Bond. Le Carré's characters repeat that "In the beginning was the deed" and will argue that one cannot believe in an ideology without taking action for an institution. But in taking action, characters discover that uncertainty rules. The motivation for le Carré's few admirable characters is redemptive love. It is the one worthwhile value left to modern individuals, who have been stripped of tradition, family, honor, and an understanding of virtue, and it condemns those who lose or reject it.

In other words, when le Carré's characters decide they must take action, they are given no quarter. Whether a novice but ambitious field agent, a seasoned professional, a child, or an individual trying to act responsibly, characters are bedeviled by ambitious spymasters, international political ideologies, drug cartels and money laundering, the deaths of innocent bystanders, the dehumanizing effects of institutions and the people who find their identities through those institutions. Heroes and lesser figures struggle with loyalty, betrayal, true friendship, honor, and love. Le Carré makes his readers think about these issues even though they may dip into his fiction for the escapism customarily promised by the spy genre.

Early Novels

Le Carré has said that telling a story of a cat sitting on a mat does not create a viable narrative. However, telling of a cat sitting on a dog's mat produces a story of tension, danger, and interest. It shapes out of a seemingly monotonous and everyday event a tale with a beginning, middle, and end that, while imaginary rather than factual, becomes so credible that it teaches its readers moral lessons while engaging them in a fictional world. In order to spin a yarn complex enough to keep readers interested in learning his characters' painful lessons, le Carré hit on a formula that places opposing characters in a house of distorted mirrors and forces them to confront their own misgivings. *Call for the Dead, A Murder of Quality,* and *The Spy Who Came in from the Cold* set this pattern and ended the traditional subjects and themes of espionage fiction.

Call for the Dead introduces readers to George Smiley, the most interesting recurring character in le Carré's oeuvre. A short, fat, toadish scholar of German poetry and philosophy turned professional spy, Smiley has virtually no parents or background to define him; thus, whenever he wishes, he can build a totally fictitious but nonetheless credible legend for himself. Over the course of eight novels, Smiley marries unwisely, leaves his Oxford teaching position during World War II to join other amateurs in intelligence, establishes himself as a professional agent and spymaster, divorces his unfaithful wife, sacrifices his psyche to best his totalitarian counterpart, Karla, and, finally, reclaims the limelight as the grand master of spying by lecturing new recruits. Pride, the need to belong, and a fascination with vicarious adventure draw Smiley to espionage. But the spiritual collapse inherent to his profession damns him. His errant spouse, Lady Ann Sercomb, sleeps with strangers and Smiley's colleagues because he enshrines rather than loves her. Much the same is true of his relation to his service, the Cambridge Circus. He can see but will not accept the inhumanity and consequences of the job. Rightly, Circus officials replace St. George, as Smiley is humorously called behind his back, when his attempts to maintain its honor become inconvenient to its political liaisons. Even Smiley's academic career turns sour when his students repudiate his ideals by burning their books. Personally and professionally ostracized, Smiley lets the contest between morality and ignominious habit destroy him. He betrays his own principles when he condones Liz Gold's murder in *The Spy Who Came in from the Cold,* orders Westerby's assassination in *The Honourable Schoolboy,* uses Karla's schizophrenic daughter, Tatania, to blackmail his adversary into defecting in *Smiley's People,* and glosses over espionage's questionable ethics in *The Secret Pilgrim.* But, because he is both spymaster and moralist, Smiley never has a choice.

Like the protagonists in all of le Carré's novels, Smiley best defines himself when he faces doppelgängers. In *Call for the Dead,* for example, Smiley mirrors the loyalty of his colleague Samuel Fennan and the dedication to service of his former, prize student Dieter Frey. In this way, Smiley sees himself as Fennan's advocate when the Circus investigates Fennan's activities much as Fennan sees himself as the protector of his wife, Elsa, against those who would harm her. Yet Fennan knows that Elsa, left only with pain from Holocaust experiences, has betrayed him by passing British secrets to her controller, Frey. To shield his beloved wife from the Circus, he unwittingly becomes her and Smiley's victim. When Smiley investigates Fennan to clear up Circus suspicions, his inquiries alert Frey, who murders Fennan and, later, Elsa. Frey acts nobly for his cause, making his murders of the disheartened couple operationally justified. But when he confronts Smiley, Frey's affection for his mentor demands that he step back and allow the older man to best him in hand-to-hand combat. Frey sacrifices himself for his former teacher and dies Smiley's moral superior, leaving Smiley to anguish over which man is the more ethical.

In *A Murder of Quality,* Smiley, the outsider, faces not a person but a complex social and educational milieu. The town and school of Carne symbolize the same sort of closed society as the Circus. Steeped in British public school snobbery, Carne justifies bigotry by passing it off as aberrant behavior. The school, in particular, protects individuals who pervert the town's disreputable past into its present grandeur. The mystery's victim, Stella Rode, a malevolent hypocrite and extortionist, is perfectly at home in this community; her murderer, the untenured and untenurable Terence Fielding, is an oppressed victim of his debased sexuality, Stella's blackmail schemes, and Carne's vicious imprudence. To Smiley's dismay, Fielding typifies Carne's decaying social structure. Rather than being satisfied with unraveling this mystery, Smiley labors to remain an outsider. He comes into the case as a favor to Circus head Control's former secretary Alisia "Brim" Brimley and believes he can remain aloof from the personalities he investigates. However, Smiley is always the worried humanist. He finds he cannot avoid becoming involved with Carne's denizens. He empathizes with Stanley Rode, the victim's enervated husband; with "Crazy" Jane, the town eccentric; with Tim Perkins, the young blackmailer; and even with the murderer. Smiley cringes from Carne's morally dubious protector, Felix D'Arcy, and the town's "faded Valkyrie" Shane Hecht, particularly when she reminds him that Carne is Lady Ann's ancestral home. Fighting to keep his emotional balance, Smiley reads into

Carne his own conflicting sense of isolation and futile hope for salvation. Carne is Smiley stripped of human awareness, and he knows it. He solves the case but, in restoring Carne's status quo, reinstates its hypocrisy.

The Spy Who Came in from the Cold broke both publishing records and the mystery genre's mold. It masterfully reinterprets events from *Call for the Dead* and applies the moral ambivalence associated with the doppleganger. Smiley, though in the background, mirrors Control and the naive dogsbody Alec Leamas. They, in turn, are distorted reflections of each other. Bureaucrats and sentimentalists, Smiley and Control nurture their agents, question and play on their sense of professionalism, and use subtlety and ironic symbols when interrogating. Prophetically, both embody the standards of their communities, albeit from seemingly opposite viewpoints. Smiley and Leamas are multilingual, European educated, World War II amateur recruits who have left the Circus only to return. But where Smiley is sagacious and angst ridden, Leamas is brutish and predisposed to accept illusion for truth. For Smiley thought paralyzes action, but for Leamas action deadens thought.

The more germane contrast, however, is between Control and Leamas. Both posture as honorable patriot-warriors, but Control more easily equivocates. Both seek revenge on Dieter Frey's spymaster Hans Mundt, and both prefer artifice to substance, serving the system to fighting for their humanity. Leamas, however, survives only when his unselfish love for Liz Gold forces him to question his complicity with the system. He eventually chooses honor through suicide rather than sustain his profession's rampant amorality. To succeed as a member of this society, Leamas must abdicate his humanity because the price of remaining an individual is high.

The Spy Who Came in from the Cold set a high standard against which le Carré's subsequent novels, as well as the cartoonish antics of traditional spy fiction (à la James Bond), are judged. Although in his later novels le Carré achieved a higher degree of sophistication and narrative complexity, in *The Spy Who Came in from the Cold* he began using metaphors, particularly in dialogue, that prevent characters from ever voicing their real meaning. The narrative moves with a slow, deliberate pace that reflects the nature of spying. Nonetheless, all the themes, images, structural patterns, and ambiguities of his later novels are present. After *The Spy Who Came in from the Cold,* other mystery and mainstream writers have been measured against the ways le Carré complicates confrontations and dilemmas, moves between international intrigue and interpersonal relationships, and preaches to readers the values of individuality, scrutiny, and unselfish empathy.

Financially secure as a result of the enormous sales of *The Spy Who Came in from the Cold,* Cornwell began writing full-time; yet his next three novels failed to approach the critical acclaim or financial success of *The Spy Who Came in from the Cold.* In the successor to this novel, *The Looking-glass War* (1965), le Carré cynically reprises a Peter Pan theme. Burned-out professionals, headed by a soon-to-retire Le Clerc, resist facing adult responsibilities by trying to return to their World War II operational glory. Joined by novice agent John Avery, they convince an aging Polish émigré, Fred Leiser, to undertake a dangerous mission without adequate background, training, or supplies. Both Avery and Leiser are outsiders desperately seeking acceptance. Avery dreams of being one of the Circus' elect; Leiser, like Leamas, upholds an ideal of honor that he thinks he can make compatible with Le Clerc's duplicitous world. Neither man understands the nuances of language that "espiocrats" such as Le Clerc use to manipulate others and then excuse their treacherous actions. As a result, the payoffs are all too obvious. Leiser is killed by a stunned enemy sentry, and Avery destroys his family and his spirit. To justify his actions, Le Clerc argues to Smiley and Control that history, not individuals, controls events and that wartime winners have no right to deny financially strapped or moribund agencies their return to glory. Le Carré paints a now familiar landscape in which a world that forgets individuals and the history they create, that uses people and their pasts for private, institutional ends, ensures that no absolutes are possible other than deceit and betrayal.

The ability to manipulate language plays a major role in le Carré's fifth novel, *A Small Town in Germany* (1968). Written agreements (both public and confidential), placards, files, summaries, and slogans plastered to walls feed the paranoia and inhumanity found in the British diplomatic corps. Leo Harting, a refugee like Fred Leiser, has disappeared from his "temporary" job of twenty years at the British embassy in Bonn. With him have gone several confidential files that Chancery head Rawley Bradfield cannot afford to have made public. Intelligence agent and outsider Alan Turner is sent to find Harting, recover the files without questioning what is in them, and keep up the Chancery's facade of stability and control. Bradfield, Turner's detestable counterpart, clearly and meticulously articulates the results of Britain's failed empire. To impress on the coarse, working-class Turner how Harting's disappearance handicaps Britain's negotiating position, Bradfield carefully selects the metaphor of a poker game played by ill-matched conspirators. The British are gambling, he says, but without credit or resources: "That smile is all we have. . . . Our situation is as delicate as that; and as mysterious. And as critical" (p. 58). Turner searches for truth, but Bradfield obscures salient facts to steer him toward expedient political realities. While Turner's idealism is ethically preferable, Bradfield's fascism supports his country's mission. A failed empire needs a disguise, and Bradfield's facility with words successfully obfuscates diplomatic reality.

An able detective, Turner uncovers Bradfield's misguided effort to ingratiate the British with Bonn's chief of police and German government spy, Ludwig Siebkron, and with a political faction of radical young Germans. Bradfield hopes that by secretly dealing with these immoral politicos he can obtain greater influence and a better economic future for Britain. But Turner's real search is for a black-and-white truth that will replace his lost family, love, and status. He sees himself as "a cynic in search of God" (p. 259), but he is little more than a patsy. He is wedded to his own version of class bigotry and morality. Initially, for instance, he does not question the embassy's condemnation of Harting as a traitor. Doggedly he pursues Harting only to discover that, because they share an unfounded idealism and unrewarded patriotism, he and his quarry are imperfect mirror images. Turner fails to save Harting's honor and life. Bradfield fails to silence the anti-British movement or East German conspirator Dr. Klaus Karfeld's protests against British entry into the European Economic Community.

Based on the success of *The Spy Who Came in from the Cold,* le Carré had money, prestige, and an open contract with British and American publishers. Nonetheless, *The Looking-glass War* and *A Small Town in Germany* were critical washouts. Readers complained that the novels depended too heavily on convoluted action, insider minutiae, and confusing interrelationships of morality, justice, and love. Unlike *The Spy Who Came in from the Cold,* these were long and sometimes taxing books. The public adulation and the suspicion among critics that he might be a one-novel writer confounded le Carré and further wore on his secretive nature. He became wary, more secretive, and, it might be argued, more determined to be taken as a literary novelist. He told Arthur Cooper in a *Saturday Review* interview that he would not "plod like an old athlete around the same track just because it makes money" (8 January 1972). Artistic discord, as well as marital friction, intensified when he published his one nongenre novel, *The Naive and Sentimental Lover* (1971). It was met with critical disdain and labeled maudlin and overwritten. Even worse, le Carré exposed a scandalous love triangle he previously had sought to keep private. *The Naive and Sentimental Lover* draws its themes from his espionage fiction, its metaphors from the aesthetic theories of German playwright and philosopher Friedrich von

Schiller, and its romance from Cornwell's private life.

Le Carré's one venture into the literary mainstream exemplifies his artistic strengths as much as his weaknesses. He can juggle narrative techniques, confuse and blend chronological sequences, balance betrayal and perversity against the possibility of familial and sexual love, but, without the trappings of political intrigue, he cannot sustain a convincing story. In many ways he needs the conventions of mystery fiction in order to subvert its limitations and successfully give voice to his mainstream themes. *The Naive and Sentimental Lover* loosely retells Cornwell's turbulent love affair with Susan, the long-suffering wife of Scottish novelist James Kennaway. Cornwell, a respected writer and family man, saw Kennaway as a romantic antihero trapped by his own violent love, speech, actions, and thoughts. Kennaway saw Cornwell as an intelligent, deliberate artist, strongly advocating individualism and romanticism. Susan fell in between James and David as Kennaway's verbally abused spouse who found solace but not peace as Cornwell's secret love.

In *The Naive and Sentimental Lover,* husband and wife Shamus and Helen freeload on an all-too-willing Aldo Cassidy. Shamus breaks into houses, takes up residence, and justifies his actions because he is a one-novel sensation. Helen delicately serves Shamus' ego and physical needs. She finds comfort in Aldo's studied facade, even though she knows it hides shallowness, emotional displacement, and fear of aging. Aldo has a belittling wife and spoiled child but no idea how to care for a family because his parents taught him nothing. His mother, Ella, abandoned him, and his swindler father, Hugo, prospers from his short-lived romantic liaisons and considerable ability to exaggerate.

The novel culminates much as the Kennaway-Cornwell affair did—in a bizarre confrontation at a Swiss skiing lodge. No institutions are skewered, no moral ambivalence lies exposed. Shamus and Helen disappear, and Aldo retreats to another facade, the life of a displaced country squire controlled by a family that needs a meal ticket. Le Carré turned his attachment to the Kennaways into a tome on the destructive potential inherent when shallow characters betray themselves and their infatuations. Le Carré resolved his artistic angst with *The Naive and Sentimental Lover,* but he lost his wife to divorce. He then returned, with greater success, to the mystery genre he had redefined.

The Question of Karla and Smiley

Markus Wolf, deputy minister of the East German State Security Ministry from 1953 to 1986, was more commonly known both within and outside the German Democratic Republic as the Stasi. In it, he headed the foreign-espionage branch, roughly equivalent in function to the U.S. Central Intelligence Agency (CIA) and in fact called the Central Intelligence Administration. He was also, according to speculation, the real-life model for le Carré's fictional Karla. But le Carré has discredited this story, claiming instead that Wolf is only one of many espionage figures fictionalized in his work.

Certainly the most fruitful source for spy-fiction writers has been Harold Adrian Russell "Kim" Philby (1912–1988). Born in India and educated at Cambridge, Philby was already a Soviet double agent when the British Secret Intelligence Service (SIS) recruited him to head anti-Communist counterespionage in 1944. He rose quickly through the old boy–Oxbridge network of the service, eventually becoming the first secretary of the British embassy in Washington, D.C., and working in close liaison with the CIA (1949–1951). Philby gave British and U.S. secrets to the Soviets for ideological, not monetary, gains. The betrayal made the Americans furious with the British, driving a wedge between their cooperative relations that continues to this day. Philby's actions stung Britons even more deeply because, in his duplicity, he partially blamed his homeland for his renounced loyalties. Britain trained Philby and others of his economic and political class to rule an empire that, by the time Philby came of age, no longer existed. This decline left such young men, as they saw it, without a means to remedy social and international ills. As college students, they were attracted to a Marxist political philosophy that promised solutions. Moreover, they secretly allied themselves with a struggling Soviet Union that seemed determined to put this philosophy into practice. To accomplish these goals, Philby and his ilk (Guy Burgess, Donald D. Maclean, Sir Anthony Blunt, John Carincross) undercut the values of their native country and class. Philby, the most destructive and unrepentant of the traitors, thereby made himself the prototype for betrayal, one that has been grist for the mill of fiction writers such as Alan Bennett, Len Deighton, Reginald Hill, Joseph Hone, Alan Williams, Graham Greene, and John le Carré.

For some, such as Greene in *The Human Factor* (1978), Philby's treason was horrific but explicable. Le Carré, however, could not countenance this argument. While he intellectualizes the circumstances that led to Philby's decision (in the introduction to *The Philby Conspiracy,* by Bruce Page, David Leitch, and Phillip Knightley), le Carré cannot tolerate Philby's faithlessness. Philby betrayed at the deepest human level, and no rationale or ideology can absolve his behavior. After the anticlimactic sequels to *The Spy Who Came in from the Cold,* marriage to Hodder and Stoughton editor Valerie Jane Eustace in 1972, and the birth of his fourth child, Nicholas, le Carré turned his attention to this ultimate example of betrayal. He wrote a trilogy that tracks the cancerous results of a Philby-like betrayal on George Smiley, his wife and associates, and his beloved Circus.

Tinker, Tailor, Soldier, Spy (1974), *The Honourable Schoolboy* (1977), and *Smiley's People* (1980), collectively known as the Quest for Karla, put Smiley center stage as he seeks out the double agent (the mole Bill Haydon) handpicked by his Moscow Centre counterpart (code name "Karla"), runs down Karla's Asian network, and, finally, forces Karla to defect. Le Carré not only won a prestigious literary award for *The Honourable Schoolboy,* he also enjoyed the most productive phase of his professional career. But he still faced his own deepest betrayal when, as he was writing the Quest for Karla trilogy in 1975, his father died. It would be more than a decade before le Carré could purge himself of his ghosts by fictionalizing his childhood memories and his ambivalent relationship with his father, Ronnie Cornwell.

The shifting world of betrayal, the value of knowing one's ancestry, the skill required to get information through subtle interrogation of hostile adversaries, the necessity of working outside to cauterize wounds inside, and the emotional and spiritual degradation that corrupts the lives of children and true believers all intertwine to make *Tinker, Tailor, Soldier, Spy* one of the most complex anatomies of betrayal ever written. *Tinker, Tailor, Soldier, Spy* opens with Smiley again the outsider. Although his work on the Leamas-Mundt operation was a success beyond his service's expectations, Smiley and others lose their positions with the Circus. Among the dismissed are loyal field agent Jim Prideaux ("the Circus' Number One Leper") and Connie Sachs ("Mother Russia"), Circus historian. In effect Karla, through his mole, manipulates British politics and its espionage wing to sever the main stem of loyalty from the Circus, leaving only lower-level agents, such as perpetual yeoman Peter Guillam, ineffectual operative Toby Esterhase, and occasional agent Jerry Westerby. Tipped off by obscure sources, Cabinet Minister Oliver Lacon unofficially brings Smiley back to unearth the double agent. Lacon ruefully attributes the Circus' problem to Smiley's Oxbridge generation. Who better then than Smiley, "out of date, but loyal to his own time," to "spy on the spies" (p. 25)? Painstakingly studying documents purloined by Guillam, interrogating dismissed Circus associates, and matching dates with suppressed initiatives and operations, Smiley discovers the mole he already knew, his social equal and Ann's lover, Bill Haydon. Smiley tries to intellectualize Haydon's betrayal by listening to his coldly egotistical rationalizations but cannot interpret his motivation. Smiley has to accept that no one can ever know the inner heart of another. Foreshadowing imagery dominates Smiley's interrogation of the traitor as "the unyielding face of Karla replaced Bill Haydon's crooked death mask" (p. 354), and Smiley, stunned by Karla's first assault, retreats into remorseful evaluation of his allegiances. Before the Circus can barter Haydon for its own British agents, Prideaux snaps his neck, exacting a revenge their contemporaries cannot.

In the trilogy's longest novel, *The Honourable Schoolboy,* Smiley moves into Control's job and tracks, travelogue style, Karla's lucrative networks across Southeast Asia. In this novel, le Carré complicates a relatively straightforward counterespionage operation by including emotional betrayals of lovers, colleagues, and family. Increasingly obsessed with the chase and his doppelgänger, Smiley traps Karla's Chinese mole, Nelson Ko, and thereby damages Karla's standing in Moscow Centre. Pivotal to his success is Jerry Westerby, another patriotic drudge, who betrays Smiley's orders to save the woman he loves, the ironically named Lizzie Worthington. Westerby is a womanizing journalist, failed novelist, good-hearted eccentric, zealous part-time field operative, and the child of a salacious con artist. Like Smiley, he abandoned his family (Tuscan mistress and beloved daughter, Catherine) for the Circus. But, like Leamas, Westerby is ultimately betrayed by his service. More damningly, Smiley pays for his operational success with his spirit, as he did when he killed his former student Dieter Frey in *Call for the Dead.* Smiley, in frustration, "orders" Westerby's assassination. Struggling with the human consequences of his betrayal, Smiley removes himself from the Circus once again.

Smiley's quest for Karla ends much as it began, with Smiley unofficially called back to the Circus to clean up a Moscow hit and to metaphorically gather together his people. *Smiley's People* leads St. George to Maria Andreyevna Ostrakova, a Russian emigré living in Paris and one of le Carré's most convincingly drawn female characters. Ostrakova's desperate search for her daughter, Alexandra, had prompted Karla to order her assassination, and through Smiley's discoveries about that sacrificed daughter he brings Karla down. But to succeed, Smiley threatens to expose that Karla has secreted his own schizophrenic daughter, Tatania. In other words, by betraying Karla's cherished family, Smiley assassinates Karla's spirit as surely as he kills his own. Watching Karla defect, Smiley imagines himself and Karla as a union of Joseph Conrad's idealist turned monster (Mr. Kurtz) and T. S. Eliot's paralyzed hollow men. The betrayal he has fought against defeats the humanity he has striven to save, and the realization overwhelms him. He has destroyed Karla "with the weapons I abhorred, and they are his" (p. 370). Smiley is left to ponder, once again, who is the better man.

A doubling imagery designed to suggest potential betrayal permeates *Smiley's People,* in which Smiley exists in a dual world of private citizen and agent at risk. When not brooding "half awake," "half aware," and with "half a network" over Karla's motives and his schizophrenic daughter Tatiana/Alexandra, Smiley agonizes over Ann's recent "half breed" lover as he pursues the twin proofs (the duplicated clues resolving the mystery) of the murdered former agent, Vladimir, and his murderer, Karla. Splitting wholes into halves confuses the chronology of the narrative, and Smiley's mission blurs. In Connie Sachs's view, Smiley and Karla are "half-angels fighting half-devils. No one knows where the lines are" (p. 202).

The trilogy's notions of honor and love for country and family reveal themselves as empty platitudes akin to Philby's hollow justifications. The events of the Quest for Karla unite Smiley's halves and, ironically, obliterate him. Through seven novels, and, later, in his eighth and final appearance, Smiley has professed enduring beliefs in the power of individualism, in the morality of means over questionable ends, and in the redemptive qualities of selfless love. Yet he ends as vacant as Aldo Cassidy, fully aware that these decencies are illusions. Nowhere in the trilogy does le Carré seriously evaluate political or emotional issues, yet, in the end, he has Smiley accept that the naive spirit must balance the sentimental man, that ideals become quickly tarnished, that democratic action will be compromised as surely as ends will sully means, and that love reclaims humanity only in defeat.

The Cold War To the New World

After the incredible success of the Quest for Karla trilogy, le Carré turned his uneasy eyes to the Israeli-Palestinian conflict in *The Little Drummer Girl* (1983), to the fragmenting of the superpowers in *The Russia House* (1989), to redefining espionage and its bureaucracies in *The Secret Pilgrim* (1991), to the rise of global "espiocrats" in *The Night Manager* (1993), to the paranoia of a life without safe houses in *Our Game* (1995), and to redressing human pain in the midst of international diplomacy in *The Tailor of Panama* (1996). While exploring these wider vistas, however, le Carré faced his own demons in the autobiographical *A Perfect Spy* (1986).

In *A Perfect Spy* le Carré coils a search for double agent Magnus Pym by British, Czechoslovakian, and American secret services into and around Pym's autobiographical suicide letter to his son, Tom, and, secondarily, to his wife, Mary, and his rival controllers. Pym feels free to write about a life that has never been his own by the unexpected death of his father, Richard "Rick" Pym. The chronologically shifting narrative moves deftly from ironically humorous memories of Rick's con games to the secret services' search, and back to Pym's bitter denunciations of his profession and his substitute fathers, Jack Brotherhood and Herr Axel. Magnus dissembles the grounds for his treason. Nowhere in the recounting of his youth, recruitment, or lifetime of multiple public and personal treasons does he face his true demon, his own intellectual and spiritual abyss.

If Magnus is his father's more aware half, Jack Brotherhood, a senior officer in the brotherhood of the Firm (SIS), mirrors Herr Axel, Magnus' Czech spymaster and friend. As a single image, Brotherhood and Axel connote the ideological poles dividing the world communities. With his indomitable, class-confident outlook, Brotherhood projects the image of an upper-class father. Axel allegorically stands for a larger, less patrician world outside the decayed English system. They struggle within and between themselves, fully knowing how their battle desecrates friends and foes alike. Behind their spirited attacks on snobbery, lineage, class systems, and unwarranted privileges lies the debased reasoning of Philby and Haydon. As le Carré constantly affirms, betrayal strips one of humanity, individuality, and salvation. Again this lesson carries deadly consequences. Before his "tidy" suicide, Magnus comes as close as he can to defining himself honestly. Addressing his vision of his father, Magnus sees how Rick's "mantle had passed to me, leaving you [his father] a naked little man, and myself the biggest con I knew" (p. 465).

When Ronnie Cornwell died in 1975, his son paid for the funeral but could not settle his emotional obligations to his father until writing *A Perfect Spy* in 1986. Le Carré had seen his father as making a home for him in a clandestine kingdom; his surrogate parents, the British educational system and the intelligence community, made him an aristocrat within that kingdom. He extricated himself from this nightmare of public, professional, and family demands by accepting, without strings, himself and his humorously unconventional father. Closing his narrative brings Pym full circle as surely as writing *A Perfect Spy* healed David Cornwell's wounds. Pym destroys out of love, not hate. So, in his own way, did Ronnie Cornwell. Once exposed, Pym dies without a clear national or individual identity but with the knowledge that his greatest treacheries, those he commits against his service but for his loved ones, make him a good man. That freedom brought joy. Le Carré told Stephen Schiff he "cried and cried when it [*A Perfect Spy*] was over" and believed that "writing *A Perfect Spy* is probably what a very wise shrink would have advised" (*Vanity Fair*, p. 89).

Le Carré ventures out of British espionage and into the Israeli-Palestinian conflict in one of his most artistically challenging and variously received novels, *The Little Drummer Girl*. From the novel's carefully worded preface to its nearly hopeful conclusion, le Carré does all he can to hide his sympathies with the Palestinians and to put a human face on the seemingly endless conflict. His goal here, as in all his novels, is to explicate why, in no uncertain terms, neither the Israeli nor the Palestinian professional combatants warrant pity. His success came, not too curiously, in the form of political denunciation. Although *The Little Drummer Girl* was a critical blockbuster, it was also the target of intense condemnation by both Jews and Palestinians.

The protagonist, Charlie, is masterfully portrayed as a complex, confused, immature, and slightly neurotic actor whose personal challenges—lack of a real family, isolation, romantic difficulties—are set against the backdrop of two morally ambiguous sides of violence and deception. Success comes in her convincing a Palestinian guerrilla unit that her allegiance is with its people's struggle for autonomy (a cause she truly supports) while infiltrating their hierarchy and setting up their leader, the terrorist-bomber Khalil, for Israeli agents to assassinate. She accepts the role as a double agent because the part requires her greatest acting skills. The offer, quite simply, is the greatest role she as an actor could play. Yet, like Smiley and countless other compromising and compromised characters, she excels in the part only by bankrupting her integrity and spirit. For this "theatre of the real" (p. 106), Charlie serves not herself but two implacable totalitarians: her Israeli controllers, surrogate father-figure Kurtz and her "demon lover" Joseph/Gadi Becker; and her Palestinian family, Khalil, his loving sister Fatmeh, and a host of abused Palestinian innocents. Placing herself between these forces, Charlie has as much chance at survival as do children caught in a terrorist bombing or as does a mature Lady Ann pleading with Smiley for understanding.

The advice "if it ain't broke, don't fix it" certainly fits le Carré's writing. The demise of the Cold War and the relative calm of hot wars such as the Israeli-Palestinian conflict may have frustrated other espionage novelists, but le Carré's formula and the inexhaustible sources for personal betrayal kept him writing. He told a *New York Times* interviewer in 1991 he was "heartily sick" of the cold war and delighted with the challenge of dissecting other varieties of intelligence organizations and their motivations, chronicling the ambiguity of human relationships, pursuing the sense of humor he mined in *A Perfect Spy*, and lamenting individuals' spiritual decline. All that changed for him was the venue. Now relationships take place in the uncertain age of perestroika and glasnost, when insane alliances are made between publicly righteous, multinational spokespersons and international thugs. The entrepreneurial Circus seems bumbling and Edwardian compared to the businesslike professionalism of the contemporary Firm. Ambivalent but ultimately loyal, spies are now fully manipulative bureaucrats or scared, witless espiocrats.

The combinations, however, are not always delightful. The ambiguities of the cold war made writing complex psychological studies easier for le Carré because it gave him ready mirror images. In the confused and confusing post-cold-war era, le Carré, more confident in his own identity and place in literature, is inclined more to sarcastic critiques than to close psychological examinations of characters in search of themselves. He excoriates the Circus' successor, the Firm, while indulging in a more traditional spy novel in *The Russia House*. Horatio Benedict "Harry" dePalfrey, the Firm's shyster, epitomizes the new order's compromised professionals. Distantly reminiscent of Joseph Conrad's unreliable narrator Marlow in *Heart of Darkness* (1902), Harry obediently provides equivocal answers to his

Russia House colleagues' banal questions and happily takes on the role of secret sharer to protagonist Bartholomew "Barley" Scott Blair and his alter ego, Ned, the Firm's top linguist-interrogator. Despicable himself, Harry makes them all look good. The novel's plot is ripe with double twists, but, unlike the Quest for Karla trilogy, *The Russia House* has a relatively clean, tightly crafted quest structure. Failing book publisher qua reluctant spy Barley Blair, one of le Carré's rare moral winners, takes possession of a bizarre manuscript that details plans, empty missile silos, official meetings, mathematical formulas, and strange references. He remembers, after some prodding, that he promised its author, the Russian dissident physicist Yakov (code name "Goethe"), he would publish it. The problem is Barley was very drunk when he made the promise, a condition Harry finds comforting. Hearing of the manuscript, spymaster Ned and his British and CIA colleagues try to recruit the rather cynical, independent Blair to contact Goethe and confirm that the Soviet behemoth is an empty threat. The fragmenting Soviet Union has bankrupted itself trying to build weapons of mass destruction. For years its government has faked new systems and armaments to keep the Western allies on alert. If Goethe is correct, then governments across the world have wasted their citizens' money on a useless arms race.

Barley Blair is the only one Goethe trusts, so he must be the contact. Barley enters the operation flippantly but becomes seriously involved when he falls in love with Yekaterina "Katya" Borisovna, as ill matched a lover for Barley as Lady Ann is for Smiley, Helen for Cassidy, Lizzie for Westerby, or Liz for Leamas. Katya, "the strong, the virtuous, the brave, the beautiful" (p. 47), has been Goethe's lover; hence, she becomes his courier, despite the considerable danger to herself, her son, and her aging uncle. Goethe expresses the novel's theme succinctly when, drunk with Barley, he notes that "today, one must think like a hero to behave like a merely decent human being" (p. 104). And that is what Barley must do. He betrays Ned and the operation to the Russians in the hope that they will release Katya and her family to join him in Lisbon. It is a deal made with a devil he does not know, but he bargains that he is better off with the devil he does not know than the one he does.

Barley finds a way for love to lead to redemption while Ned ends by embracing dePalfrey's cynicism. Barley betrays Ned without any assurance that Goethe, his Soviet source, is sane; that the silent KGB will honor the bargain; that the Firm will not subsequently assassinate him; or that he will not become as disillusioned as Harry or Ned. Where dePalfrey, Ned, and other professionals bury love in their infinite capacity for distrust, Barley acts from love and walks away a qualified winner.

Ned, loyal foot solider in the Firm's mostly illusory battles for international prestige, finds himself demoted to wet nurse for newly matriculated recruits in *The Secret Pilgrim*. Here, he arranges a standard graduation service for the new agents with a noteworthy but unexpected speaker, retired senior agent George Smiley. Smiley tries to guide the new spies toward a study of the past so they will be better equipped to face an uncertain, post-cold-war future. Inspired by Smiley's insights, Ned recounts to himself forty years of cold-war espionage and the roles he took on in life. He finds himself shifting back and forth in time, recalling and contrasting ambiguous triumphs and humorous mishaps with often brutal, decidedly worldly compromises.

Smiley sits counterpoised before Ned, clearly understanding the spiritual price he has paid for a lifetime of facades. Smiley quietly warns the recruits that, "by being all things to all spies, one does rather run the risk of becoming nothing to oneself." His scars will never heal, so he can, from experience, sadly advise them not to "ever imagine you'll be unscathed by the methods you use. The end may justify the means—if it wasn't supposed to, I dare say you wouldn't be here. But there's a price to pay, and the price does tend to be oneself. Easy to sell one's soul at your age. Harder later" (p. 10). Yet Ned cannot disavow his betrayals, cannot readily give up the professional mask he has worn for so long, cannot move beyond his own cynicism. Hence, he cannot bring himself to warn the Firm's new agents of the human price they will pay. An aging spy, Ned is called back for a last official act: he confronts Sir Anthony Joyston Bradshaw, a particularly unsavory representative of the British aristocracy. Bradshaw has brokered numerous shady deals for his own financial benefit, oblivious to the consequences of these transactions for others. During his interrogation of Bradshaw, Ned realizes that this elitist will be the service's new adversary, but resigns himself to the fact that others will have to take on the Bradshaws of the world. "In the face of an absolute," Ned is mute. A full member of the establishment, Ned has "battled against an institutionalized evil" all his life: "It had had a name, and most often a country as well. . . . But the evil that stood before me now was a wrecking infant in our own midst, and I became an infant in return, disarmed, speechless, and betrayed" (p. 334).

A mark of his style, le Carré picks up a character's story and weaves it into a subsequent novel, this time *The Night Manager.* One of Bradshaw's infamies involves English financial wizard Sir Richard Onslow Roper, "the world's worst man" and hotel night manager Jonathan Pine's alter ego. At the CIA's connivance, it seems, Roper trades arms, acquired from Bradshaw's sources, for cocaine. He then sells the drugs so he, his toadies, and his mistress, Jed, can lounge around in luxury hotels in Zurich and Cairo, on the yacht *Iron Pasha,* and on a private island in the Caribbean. Pine is charged with keeping Roper's entourage content during its stay at Zurich's Hotel Meister Palace. The first few chapters of *The Night Manager* set Pine up as a superhuman flunky who becomes mesmerized by Roper's high style and Jed's numbing beauty. But this is the face Pine shows to a suspicious world, and it masks his soul. He knows Roper from an earlier tragedy in which he failed to protect an Arab courtesan from Roper's violence. He now sells himself to a bigger British agency devoted to "pure intelligence" to avenge himself on Roper. He enters the operation with the same determination that lures Leamas in *The Spy Who Came in from the Cold* back into the game. And, like Leamas, Pine willingly lives various personae to ingratiate himself with Roper's inner circle. But he is an open psychological wound masquerading as James Bond. Repeatedly, Pine is described as needing to complete himself, to find that other half that will heal him. Once a Roper insider, he falls deeply in love with Jed and takes on the unselfish identity that will save them both. This affair reanimates Pine; it causes him to sacrifice his vengeful goals for Jed's happiness. Pine and Jed win their lives, perhaps the clearest instance in le Carré's fiction of the redemptive power of love.

Of all le Carré's novels, *The Night Manager* comes closest to fulfilling his requirements for existential love. It also most obviously follows the typical criteria of the genre. Eric Ambler's generation of interwar radicals in search of arms, chronicled in the two-novel series *The Light of Day* (1962) and *Dirty Story* (1967), are Roper and Bradshaw retailored. The intricate discussions of arms, while less technical, are nonetheless very similar to Tom Clancy's. Jed echoes Fleming's more flamboyant heroines, such as Pussy Galore. And Roper flies planes, drinks expensive wines, and easily manipulates any type of firearm much as James Bond does. One can only wonder whether Pine serves Roper his martinis shaken or stirred!

An impossible love triangle and metaphors of abandonment replay with little variation in le Carré's next novel, *Our Game,* turning the tale from a history lesson into a morality play. At the heart of the complex narrative is a variation on a classic le Carré question: What happens to individuals, relationships, and nations when everything that can be betrayed has been? After betraying its people for generations, the former Soviet Union has disintegrated. Nationalistic fervor, born of age-old ethnic conflicts, feeds the bloody separatist war in the former Soviet Muslim province of

Chechnya. From all sides, former espionage professionals feel betrayed by their services for pensioning them off and leaving them emotionally bankrupt shells. One superhero and former double agent for the British and Russians, Lawrence "Larry" Pettifer, has taken a teaching position at Bath University that, compared to his late profession, leaves him bored and restless. Artless and frequently gauche, Pettifer sees himself as a latter-day Lord Byron dying for Greece. At least, as he hints to his longtime friend and past British handler Timothy "Timbo" D'Abell Cranmer, he feels a Byronic passion for smaller, suffering nations such as Chechnya. The novel opens in this irresolute atmosphere with Pettifer, more than thirty-seven million pounds from the Russian government, and Cranmer's childlike mistress, Emma Manzini, gone.

The plot, however, plays only a minor key against the complex psychological interactions of the three main characters, Cranmer, Pettifer, and Emma. Cranmer knows that "if you encourage a man to dissemble and steal hearts, you have only yourself to thank when he turns around and robs you of your secrets and whatever else you've got" (p. 29). He taught Pettifer to be "a directionless English middle-class revolutionary, a permanent dissident, a dabbler, a dreamer, a habitual rejecter; a ruthless, shiftless, philandering, wasted semicreative failure, too clever not to demolish an argument, too mulish to settle for a flawed one" (p. 24). Yet Pettifer stole Emma, and Cranmer continually asks himself what he has done to make Pettifer betray him. Hauled back from forced retirement to account for Pettifer, Cranmer finds himself physically, emotionally, politically, and morally immobilized. He is not, nor will he ever be, admirable and, when he is moved to act, probably warrants responsibility for betraying Pettifer and Emma to their pursuers if they are caught. Hedonistic, elitist, and blind to his own bigotry, Cranmer may even have been Pettifer's partner in crime or may have killed Pettifer in a jealous fury; certainly he has driven Emma into the arms of the much younger, more charismatic missing agent. Cranmer, at the end of his quest for Pettifer and Emma, finds himself trapped in the Caucasus no longer sure of whether his friend and lover are alive or dead and still asking why.

Much as he has done with characters throughout his fiction, le Carré creates Harry Pendel, the protagonist of *The Tailor of Panama,* from whole cloth. Pendel cuts and shapes himself to fit those around him. He believes, as tailor-spy, he is "your ideal cutter . . . your born . . . impersonator. His job is to place himself in the clothes of whomever he is cutting for, and become that person until the rightful owner returns" (p. 15). The people he fits become "understandable members of his internal universe" (p. 52), ripe for his—and his creator's—manipulation. In his sixteenth novel, le Carré hits upon a character ideally suited to his shifting persona. Pendel, proprietor of Pendel & Braithwaite Co., Limitada, claims to be a transplanted Savile Row craftsman with serendipitous access to Panama's highest government officials and leading dissidents and, importantly, their secrets. But it is all "fluence," the quality of "running ahead of events and waiting for them to catch up. It was making people bigger or smaller according to whether they enhanced or threatened his existence. . . . Its purpose was to provide a hostile world with whatever made it feel at ease with itself. To make it tolerable. To befriend it. To draw its string" (p. 53). Harry flees Britain just three days after his release from prison for committing arson. Pendel & Braithwaite is "a load o' bollocks," and Arthur Braithwaite, "one of the great characters o' fiction" (p. 41). He failed to absorb some of his swindler uncle Benny; as a result, he is deeply in debt having been conned into a shady real estate venture.

The answer to his financial prayers walks into his shop in the person of a new recruit, Andrew "Andy" Osnard, who offers to be the answer to Pendel's prayers. Osnard, in his late twenties and cynical and seductive, is a spy for "Merrie England" intent on moving rapidly up the corporate ranks by mining Pendel's fertile imagination. Osnard has little to lose and much to gain, he believes, by identifying himself intimately with his service. He is pure superficiality, semiliterate, "unfettered by principle," with "no craft or qualifications, no proven skills outside the golf course and the bedroom." He is perfect for the British espionage community because "what he understood best was English rot, and what he needed was a decaying English institution that would restore to him what other decaying institutions had taken away" (p. 164).

Pendel, barely "restraining his eternal impulse to be of service" (p. 44), willingly obliges with conspiracies that are equal to le Carré's model, Graham Greene's vacuum-cleaner salesman Wormold in *Our Man in Havana* (1958), or to any imaginative thread John Buchan could weave. Were Pendel an individual untainted by his inconsistent past or willing to accept the consequences of his attachments, Osnard could never corrupt him. But Pendel lives to mime other lives. He savors his fantasies about Panamanian corruptions and near revolutionary coups d'état and goes to great lengths to edit and touch them up. The looking-glass world that Pendel creates and Osnard and his London superiors relish becomes a reality from which Pendel cannot escape. Even with broad, farcical humor, le Carré warns against the dehumanization that comes from wearing false masks. Continuing to favor ceremony over individuality, group conformity over personal allegiance, and "fluence" over reflection courts humanitarian disaster.

Recognizing Personae

A master of metaphor and language and an architect of the tortured soul for nearly forty years, le Carré has written about people straining under ideological conflicts, about betrayal in all its forms, and about irreconcilable problems that dispirited individuals confront trying to maintain their humanity in impossible situations. His talent has rewarded him with public accolades. *Call for the Dead* was a finalist in the prestigious British Crime Writers Association awards. *The Spy Who Came in from the Cold* earned him an international reputation as well as, in 1964, the British Crime Writers Association Golden Dagger, the Somerset Maugham Award, and the Edgar Allan Poe Award from the Mystery Writers of America. He won another Golden Dagger for *The Honourable Schoolboy* in 1977 and the Crime Writers Association Diamond Award for his outstanding contributions to genre fiction in 1988. And, as these last novels confirm, le Carré's landscapes may have changed, but the enriched themes, innovative narrative approaches, incisive metaphors, objects of satire, and virtuosity with language that he used to invigorate the genre have not. When faceless Soviet agents disappear, they are replaced by nationless, faceless alliances of cartel bosses. The protagonists may no longer be compromised British agents, but they are as unprepared for the human degradation guilt brings as any trained professionals. Each of his novels refines and advances a fiction unique to John le Carré. Unlike the good guys–bad guys simplicity and stereotypes of popular entertainments, his books depend for their intrigue on political, social, and cultural criticism and on the personal effects of betrayal and love. As reviewer Roy Neel commented, le Carré "entertains with the language, not the Luger."

Freed from the contorted motives for betrayal found in his cold-war fiction, le Carré sees his 1990s fiction as the beginning of an exciting artistic rejuvenation in which his element, his genre, "is no longer at the center of our concerns." And while some critics do not fully share this optimism, longtime le Carré readers do. Readers value his most convincing novels in which love and individuality—not spy fiction's superficial patriotism, nor adventure fiction's surreptitious excitement, nor mainstream literature's manifest self-awareness—determine a protagonist's fate. They relish le Carré's ability to create atmosphere or lay out labyrinthine plots. They know that espionage fiction has given him a ready form and that his experimentations with themes, characters, and structures elevate his work above the genre's often slapdash formulas. No matter what the critics argue, readers tolerate those occasional times when the novelist's worrisome nature spills over into his fiction. His best work is more than a vehicle for his public commentaries and satiric darts because it rivals the psychological and moral complexities of much contemporary mainstream fiction. The enduring novels attest to le Carré's unswerving confidence in the redemptive power of love after the experience of perfidy. Moreover, given his background and literary penchants, le Carré seems destined to continue to probe contemporary events through the timeless theme of love. Finally, in le Carré's personae, readers come to recognize the author himself.

Selected Bibliography

WORKS OF JOHN LE CARRÉ

NOVELS

Call for the Dead. London: Victor Gollancz, 1961.

A Murder of Quality. London: Victor Gollancz, 1962.

The Spy Who Came in from the Cold. London: Victor Gollancz, 1963.

The Looking-glass War. New York: Coward-McCann, 1965.

A Small Town in Germany. London: Heinemann, 1968; New York: Coward-McCann, 1968.

The Naive and Sentimental Lover. London: Hodder and Stoughton, 1971.

Tinker, Tailor, Soldier, Spy. London: Hodder and Stoughton, 1974; New York: Knopf, 1974.

The Honourable Schoolboy. London: Hodder and Stoughton, 1977; New York: Knopf, 1977.

Smiley's People. London: Hodder and Stoughton, 1980; New York: Knopf, 1980.

The Little Drummer Girl. London: Hodder and Stoughton, 1983; New York: Knopf, 1983.

A Perfect Spy. New York: Knopf, 1986.

The Russia House. London: Hodder and Stoughton, 1989; New York: Knopf, 1989.

The Secret Pilgrim. London: Hodder and Stoughton, 1991; New York: Knopf, 1991.

The Night Manager. London: Hodder and Stoughton, 1993.

Our Game. London: Hodder and Stoughton, 1995.

The Tailor of Panama. London: Hodder and Stoughton, 1996; New York: Knopf, 1996.

SHORT STORIES

"You Can't Sack a College Boy." *Spectator,* 27 November 1964: 699–700.

"Wrong Man on Crete." *Holiday,* December 1965: 74–75.

"Dare I Weep, Dare I Mourn?" *Saturday Evening Post,* 28 January 1967: 54, 56, 60.

"What Ritual Is Being Observed Tonight?" *Saturday Evening Post,* November 1968: 60–62, 64–65.

"Pym Takes Cover." *New York Times Magazine,* 15 March 1986: 42.

"Personal for Mr. Bartholomew Scott Blair, Urgent." *New York Times Book Review,* 23 April 1989: 1, 25–27.

"Smiley's Gift." *Esquire,* December 1990: 129–136.

NONFICTION

"The Writer and the Spy." *Daily Telegraph,* 29 March 1964: 18.

"What Every Writer Wants to Know." *Harper's,* November 1965: 142–145.

"To Russia, with Greetings: An Open Letter to the Moscow *Literary Gazette.*" *Encounter,* May 1966: 3–6.

"The Spy to End Spies: On Richard Sorge." *Encounter,* November 1966: 88–89.

"Wardrobe of Disguises: *The Man from Moscow* and *Shadow of a Spy.*" *The Sunday Times,* 10 September 1967: 31.

"A Writer and a Gentleman." *Saturday Review,* 30 November 1968: 4, 6.

"Vocation in a World of Pain." *Sunday Times,* 25 October 1970: 25.

"Well Played, Wodehouse." *Sunday Times,* 10 October 1971: 35.

"In a Small Place in Cornwall." *Sunday Telegraph Magazine,* 6 September 1974: 39, 40, 45, 46.

"In England Now." *New York Times Magazine,* 23 October 1977: 34–35, 86–87.

"England Made Me." *Observer,* 13 November 1977: 25.

"An American Spy Story." Review of *The Man Who Kept the Secrets: Richard Helms and the CIA,* by Thomas Powers. *New York Times Book Review,* 14 October 1979: 1, 46–48.

"At Last, It's Smiley." *Sunday Telegraph Magazine,* 21 October 1979: 105, 106, 111, 112.

"Tinker, Tailor, and the Mole that Never Was." *The Guardian,* (Manchester), 7 November 1979: 14.

"Siege." *Observer,* 1 June 1980: 25.

"McCullin's World." *Sunday Times Magazine,* 26 October 1980: 50, 51, 53, 55, 57, 58, 61. Repr. as introduction to *Hearts of Darkness,* by Don McCullin. New York: Knopf, 1981.

Introduction to *The Philby Conspiracy,* by Bruce Page, David Leitch, and Phillip Knightley. New York: Ballantine, 1981.

"Unlicensed to Quote." *Times* (London), 17 March 1981: 13.

"World Service." *Times* (London), 1 July 1981: 15.
"Optical Illusion." *Times* (London), 22 March 1982: 11.
"Memories of a Vanished Land." *Observer,* 13 June 1982: 9–10.
"Exiles in the White House." *Observer,* 26 June 1983: 25–26.
"Betrayal." *Observer,* 3 July 1983: 23–24.
"Spying on My Father." *Sunday Times* (London), 16 March 1986: 33–35.
"Don't Be Beastly to Your Secret Service." *Sunday Times* (London), 23 March 1986: 41–42.
"The Clandestine Muse." *Johns Hopkins Magazine* 38 (August 1986): 11–16. Repr. as "Readings: Le Carré: The Dishonorable Spy." *Harper's,* December 1986: 17–19.
"Inside Books: John le Carré on Perfect Spies and Other Characters." *Writer's Digest,* February 1987: 20–21.
Vanishing England (with Gareth W. Davies). New York: Salem House, 1987.
"Rushdie in Hiding" (with John Cunningham). *World Press Review,* March 1990: 74–75.
"The Secret Pilgrim." *Monologues from Contemporary Literature,* vol. 1. Edited by Eric Kraus. Newbury, Vt.: Smith and Kraus, 1992.
"Tinpots, Saviors, Lawyers, Spies." *New York Times,* 4 May 1993: A19, A25.
"The Shame of the West." *New York Times,* 14 December 1994: A19, A23.
"My New Friends in the New Russia: In Search of a Few Good Crooks, Cops, and Former Agents." *New York Times Book Review,* 19 February 1995: 3.
"Quel Panama!" *New York Times Magazine,* 13 October 1996: 52.

BIOGRAPHICAL AND CRITICAL STUDIES

BOOKS

Barley, Tony. *Taking Sides: The Fiction of John le Carré.* Philadelphia, Pa.: Open University, 1986.
Beene, LynnDianne. *John le Carré.* Boston: Twayne, 1992.
Bloom, Harold, ed. *John le Carré: Modern Critical Views.* New York: Chelsea House, 1987.
Bold, Alan, ed. *The Quest for le Carré.* New York: St. Martin's Press, 1988.
Campbell, Anthony. "Dialectical Discourses: A Study of John le Carré." M.A. thesis, University of Alberta, 1991.
Cobbs, John L. *Understanding John le Carré.* Columbia: University of South Carolina Press, 1997.
Dobler, George David. "The Novels of John le Carré: Children, Women, Religion." Ph.D. diss., University of Iowa, 1989.
Homberger, Eric. *John le Carré.* New York: Methuen, 1986.
Lewis, Peter. *John le Carré.* New York: Ungar, 1985.
Monaghan, David. *The Novels of John le Carré: The Art of Survival.* New York: Basil Blackwell, 1985.
———. *Smiley's Circus: A Guide to the Secret World of John le Carré.* New York: St. Martin's Press, 1986.
Powell, Cheryl C. "Redemption for the Protagonist in Three Novels by John le Carré." Ph.D. diss., Florida State University, 1991.
Sauerberg, Lars Ole. *Secret Agents in Fiction: Ian Fleming, John le Carré, and Len Deighton.* London: Macmillan, 1984.
Wolfe, Peter. *Corridors of Deceit: The World of John le Carré.* Bowling Green, Ohio: Bowling Green State University Popular Press, 1987.

SECTIONS OF BOOKS

Adams, Michael. "John le Carré/David John Moore Cornwell." In *Critical Survey of Mystery and Detective Fiction Authors,* 4 vols. Edited by Frank N. Magill. Englewood Cliffs, N.J.: Salem Press, 1988.
Bradbury, Richard. "Reading John le Carré." In *Spy Thrillers: From Buchan to Le Carré.* Edited by Clive Bloom. New York: St. Martin's Press, 1990.
Cawelti, John G., and Bruce A. Rosenberg. "The Complex Vision of John le Carré." In their *The Spy Story.* Chicago, Ill.: University of Chicago Press, 1987.
East, Andy. "Le Carré, John." In his *The Cold War File.* Metuchen, N.J.: Scarecrow, 1983.
Hayes, Michael J. "Are You Telling Me Lies David?: The Work of John le Carré." In *Spy Thrillers: From Buchan to le Carré.* Edited by Clive Bloom. London: Macmillan, 1990; New York: St. Martin's Press, 1990.
Jeffares, A. Norman. "John le Carré." In *Contemporary Novelists,* 21st ed. Edited by James Vinson. New York: St. Martin's Press, 1976.
Masters, Anthony. "John le Carré: The Natural Spy." In his *Literary Agents: The Novelist as Spy.* New York: Basil Blackwell, 1987.
Most, Glenn W. "The Hippocratic Smile: John le Carré and the Traditions of the Detective Novel." In *The Poetics of Murder: Detective Fiction and Literary Theory.* Edited by Glenn W. Most and William W. Stowe. San Diego: Harcourt Brace Jovanovich, 1983.
Panek, LeRoy L. "John le Carré." In his *The Special Branch: The British Spy Novel, 1890–1980.* Bowling Green, Ohio: Bowling Green University Popular Press, 1981.
Rao, K. Bhaskara. "John le Carré." In *Critical Survey of Long Fiction: English Language Series.* Edited by Frank N. Magill. Englewood Cliffs, N.J.: Salem Press, 1984.
Rutherford, Andrew. "The Spy as Hero: Le Carré and the Cold War." In his *The Literature of War: Five Studies in Heroic Virtue.* New York: Barnes and Noble, 1978.
Seed, David. "The Well-Wrought Structures of John le Carré's Early Fiction." In *Spy Thrillers: From Buchan to le Carré.* Edited by Clive Bloom. New York: St. Martin's Press, 1990.

JOHN LE CARRÉ

ESSAYS

Banks, R. Jeff, and Harry D. Dawson. "Le Carré's Spy Novels." *Mystery Fancier* 2: 22–25 (September–October 1978).

Beard, David. "Verdana." *Sun-Sentinel* (South Florida), 16 February 1997.

Becker, Jens P. "John le Carré's Smiley-Saga: 'Nostalgia for a Lost Paradise.' " *Anglistik & Englischunterricht* 37: 99–111 (1989).

Brady, Charles, A. "John le Carré's Smiley Saga." *Thought* 60: 275–296 (September 1985).

Buzard, James Michael. "Faces, Photos, Mirrors: Image and Ideology in the Novels of John le Carré." *Works and Days* 7, no. 1: 53–75 (spring 1989). Repr. in *Image and Ideology in Modern/Postmodern Discourse*. Edited by David B. Downing and Susan Bazargan. Albany: State University of New York Press, 1991.

Calendrillo, Linda T. "Role Playing and 'Atmosphere' in Four Modern British Spy Novels." *Clues* 3, no. 1: 111–119 (1982).

Cohn, Jack R. "The Watch on John le Carré." *Studies in the Novel* 20: 323–337 (fall 1988).

Cooper, Arthur. "Review of 'the Naive and Sentimental Lover.' " *Saturday Review* (8 January 1972).

Dawson, Harry D. "The Fathers and Sons of John le Carré." *Mystery Fancier* 5: 15–17 (May–June 1981).

Diamond, Julie. "Spies in the Promised Land." *Race & Class* 25: 35–40 (1984).

Dobel, J. Patrick. "The Honorable Spymaster: John le Carré and the Character of Espionage." *Administration and Society* 15: 191–215 (August 1988).

Garson, Helen S. "Enter George Smiley: Le Carré's *Call for the Dead*." *Clues* 3: 93–99 (fall–winter 1982).

Halperin, John. "Between Two Worlds: The Novels of John le Carré." *South Atlantic Quarterly* 79: 17–37 (spring 1980).

Hughes, Celia. "Serious Reflection on Light Reading: The World of John le Carré." *Theology* 84: 274–279 (July 1981).

Kemp, Percy. "Les Nouveaux Traitres de John Le Carré." *Esprit* 157: 95–99 (December 1989).

King, Holly Beth. "Child's Play in John le Carré's *Tinker, Tailor, Soldier, Spy*." *Clues* 3: 87–92 (fall–winter 1982).

———. "George Smiley: The Reluctant Hero." *Clues* 2: 70–76 (spring–summer 1981).

Knight, Stephen. "Re-Formations of the Thriller: Raymond Chandler and John le Carré." *Sydney Studies in English* 12: 78–91 (1986–1987).

Lasseter, Victor. "John le Carré's Spy Jargon: An Introduction and Lexicon." *Verbatim* 8: 1–2 (spring 1982).

Maddox, Tom. "Spy Stories: The Life and Fiction of John le Carré." *Western Quarterly* 158–170 (fall 1986).

Mathews, Tom. "In from the Cold." *Newsweek*, 5 June 1989: 52–57.

Monaghan, David. "John le Carré and England: A Spy's-Eye View." *Modern Fiction Studies* 29: 569–582. (fall 1983).

Neuse, Steven M. "Bureaucratic Malaise in the Modern Spy Novel: Deighton, Greene, and LeCarré." *Public Administration* 60: 293–306 (fall 1982).

Noland, Jack Edmund. "LeCarré, Deighton, Hall, and the Screen's Tired Spies." *Mystery Reader's Newsletter* 4: 23–28 (1970).

Noland, Richard W. "The Spy Fiction of John le Carré." *Clues* 1, no. 2: 54–70 (1980).

Rothbert, Abraham. "The Decline and Fall of George Smiley: John le Carré and English Decency." *Southwest Review* 66: 377–393 (fall 1981).

Schiff, Stephen. "The Secret Life of John le Carré." *Vanity Fair*, June 1989: 189.

Silver, Brenda R. "Woman as Agent: The Case of le Carré's *Little Drummer Girl*." *Contemporary Literature* 28, no. 1: 14–40 (1987).

Vogt, Jochen. "Halb-Engel gegen Halb-Teufel: Der endlose Schattenkrieg des John le Carré." *Die Horen* 34, no. 2: 49–59 (1989).

Wallace, Douglas. "John le Carré: The Dark Side of Organizations." *Harvard Business Review* 63: 6, 7, 10, 12, 14 (January–February 1985).

Walling, William. "John le Carré: The Doubleness of Class." *Columbia Library Columns* 37: 23–32 (February 1988).

MISCELLANEOUS

Cryer, Dan. "Le Carré Lightens Up on Spying." (21 October 1996): http://www.newsday.com.

Gray, Paul. "A Man, a Plan, a Canal: John le Carré Weaves a Terrific Tale About a British Spy in Pursuit of a Conspiracy That Doesn't Exist." *Time* (28 October 1996): http://www.pathfinder.com/@@ea@VCQF9GAAAQM6Q / time / magazine / domestic / 1996 / 961028/bks.spy.html.

Rohter, Larry. "In Land of the Big Ditch, le Carré's in Hot Water." *New York Times News Service* (1996): http://www.latinolink.com/art/1119acar.html.

Ross, Andrew, interviewer. "The Salon Interview: John le Carré." (27 August 1996): http://www.salon1996.com/weekly/lecarre961021.html#lecarrel.

Sullivan, Tim, interviewer. "John le Carré, Still Holding Back Some Secrets." Associated Press Interview (22 November 1996): http://canoe2.canoe.ca/JamBooksFeatures/lecarre john.html.

Walton, David. "A Tip of the Panama Hat to John le Carré's latest." *Detroit News Home Page* (4 November 1996): http://detnews.com/1996/menu/stories/72812.html.

Elmore Leonard

(b. 1925)

EDWARD GORMAN
ROBERT SKINNER
ROBERT GLEASON

ALTHOUGH HIS RELATIONSHIP with Hollywood has often been characterized as combative, Elmore Leonard's career as a writer actually began at the age of eleven in the darkness of a movie theater as he watched Gary Cooper play the role of Wild Bill Hickok in *The Plainsman* (1936). Cooper's portrayal of a violent, reckless man who was yet gentle and possessed a streak of goodness had a profound impact on the impressionable youngster. In later years the thin line that separated heroism from villainy would become a hallmark of his novels and screenplays.

Leonard was born in New Orleans on 11 October 1925. In 1934 his family moved to Detroit, where he remained for the rest of his formative years. From published accounts, it would appear that his boyhood was unremarkable in many respects. His main passion, aside from movies, was baseball. He was nicknamed "Dutch" by his pals, after a player on the Washington Senators that he admired.

In 1943 he entered the U.S. Navy and served in the Pacific with the Seabees until 1946. Following his discharge, he returned to Detroit, attended the University of Detroit, and graduated with majors in English and philosophy.

His first marriage was to Beverly Cline in 1949. The couple had five children and ten grandchildren, but were divorced in 1977. He remarried in 1979, to Joan Shepard, whom he later credited for helping him create strong, realistic women characters.

Leonard joined the Campbell-Ewald Advertising Agency in 1950 and made his living as an advertising copywriter until 1963. Between 1961 and 1963 he supplemented his income as a scriptwriter for educational films. In 1963 he left Campbell-Ewald and briefly ran his own advertising firm before sales to publishers and movie producers enabled him to become a full-time writer.

As he began his life as an advertising man, he also laid the foundation for his career as a writer of adventure stories. Probably because of the lingering impact of watching Gary Cooper in the middle 1930s, Leonard began getting up early every morning to write western short stories. He made his first sale, "Trail of the Apache," to *Argosy,* a top-rated men's adventure magazine, in 1951.

From the beginning, Leonard was well regarded. Even though he was years away from developing his own true voice, his earliest work shows an awareness of style and form rarely seen in western pulps. It also shows that Leonard was already as interested in techniques of suspense as he was in the techniques of the traditional western. Before many years had passed, he would begin to sell the movie rights to his stories "3:10 to Yuma" and "The Tall T," and his award-winning novel *Hombre.*

Themes

Elmore Leonard, like many authors, was influenced by a wide variety of books and writers, but his early interest in Ernest Hemingway's *For Whom the Bell Tolls* (1940) is telling and provides us with a prism through which we can view Leonard's development. Throughout his long career, beginning with his story "3:10 to Yuma," Leonard's protagonists have shared certain characteristics with Hemingway's Robert Jordan. Jordan is not a professional soldier, but rather a teacher who has been caught up in a war. Leonard likewise chooses his protagonists from unlikely places. Ironworkers, automotive engineers, bail bondsmen, process servers, farmers, and honorable thieves make up his universe. Like Jordan, they are not knights-errant. There is no grail, and little hope that good will triumph. Victories, to the extent there are victories, are relative to the universe in which they occur. They are qualified victories, at best.

Like Jordan, Leonard's characters are vulnerable. They are sometimes anxious, unsure, even frightened. Often they get hurt, and sometimes they die, just as Jordan did. Their women share their anxieties and sometimes, like Jordan's lover, Maria, they suffer torture and humiliation, and even die, as they are swept up in the violence swirling around them. Leonard is unusual for the ease with which he kills his protagonists, or, if they are criminal antiheroes, sends them to prison.

Another trademark Leonard shares with Hemingway is that while his protagonists are not intrinsically wicked, they are often forced to contend with an evil world. He continually asks how people with a code of honor can prevail over those who have none. To paraphrase Raymond Chandler, how can people who are not themselves mean walk down the world's meanest streets? Like Hemingway's protagonists, Leonard's heroes have been to the wars. They are proficient with weapons, but, more important, they are resourceful. All of Hemingway's heroes are quintessentially competent, and it is that competence and courage under fire that enables them to prevail over both enemies and fear, rather than any heroic transcendence or superior physical ability they may have.

Leonard's heroes are singularly gentle and mild-mannered, a quality that draws the women in his stories to them, but all know something about the business of killing. Passive town constable Bob Valdez (*Valdez Is Coming*) was a U. S. Cavalry scout in his early life. Automotive industrialist Harry Mitchell (*52 Pick-up*) was a fighter ace. Motel owner George Moran (*Cat Chaser*) was a soldier who served under fire in the Dominican Republic.

The cultural subtext of Leonard's protagonists is trickier, but again it reflects Hemingway's sense of the Lost Generation, people who, like Robert Jordan, live between two tribes, the decent and the indecent. But Leonard's heroes are a bit too knowing about the dark side of life and are too proficient at swimming with the sharks, perhaps because within the enemy they recognize something of themselves.

One often gets the sense from Leonard's characters that they have a dual nature, another person living inside them. Sometimes, as in the case of John Russell (*Hombre*), they recall past lives they've led, and use the remembered identity to deal with the new situation they're in. Others, like Vincent Majestyk (*Mr. Majestyk*), Joe LaBrava (*LaBrava*), George Moran (*Cat Chaser*) and Harry Mitchell (*52 Pick-up*), have engaged in occupations that taught them to kill, and they reach within themselves to find those violent qualities. There are times, too, when even villains will reach within for some latent part of themselves, as does the former movie star Jean Shaw (*LaBrava*) who takes on the qualities of the film noir bad girls she portrayed in her movies in her attempt to extort $600,000 from a wealthy Miamian, or Frank Braden's *segundo* (*Valdez Is Coming*), who finds more to admire in Bob Valdez than in Braden, who pays his salary.

Leonard makes this point rather strongly in *Split Images* from both the standpoint of hero and villain. The corrupt cop Walter Kouza thinks he likes killing until the psychopath Robbie Daniels crosses a line that Kouza didn't know was there. Gentle detective Bryan Hurd allows two rednecks in a restaurant to abuse and insult him until he gets his girlfriend, Angela, out of harm's way. Then Hurd savagely attacks the men, putting them in the hospital to make sure they'll stay away from her while he's out of town investigating his case.

In these examples, we see the protagonist summon forth a quasi-psychopath and find in this alter ego the necessary violence and cunning to extricate the innocent from harm's way, and vanquish the villain. The villain finds, unbidden, the good in himself, and either self-destructs from the weight of the realization, or puts his life on the line to help the hero. We immediately think of Shane in Jack Shaefer's classic western novel of the same name (1949), who recognizes his emotional connection to his farmer friend and at the same time his spiritual connection with the powerful rancher he must kill to save his friend's life and bring peace to the valley.

An archetypal example of a Leonard character lost between two cultures, two natures, is John Russell in *Hombre* (1961). Because the pattern can be found throughout Leonard's novels, it is worth examining. Russell is a white man who was raised by Apaches. He's seen the evil treatment of the Apaches by the white race. He has the strength and honor of the Apache, as well as their capacity for violence, from living among them, but he is also a white man collecting a lucrative inheritance from white society. He understands and forgives the brutality of the Apaches, just as Jordan forgives the brutal violence of the Spanish guerrillas with whom he is allied. Both lower castes are unlettered and disadvantaged, but Jordan and Russell believe the privileged castes whom they oppose should be enlightened enough to know better and lift those below them from their ignorance, rather than trying to exterminate them.

Russell rejects white society but benefits from his connection to it, and unlike his friends on the reservation, he can leave the Apache world whenever he chooses. He can never be completely white or Apache, and is forever lost between tribes. Perhaps it is this sense of displacement, of not belonging anywhere, that causes him to risk all he has for people to whom he has only a nebulous connection.

In the ultimate showdown, Russell must face the lone Mexican member of the white gang of desperadoes that are trying to kill Russell and his fellow stagecoach passengers. The Mexican gunman, ostensibly a villain, shares Russell's plight. He, too, is a man forced to live between two tribes. When he is mortally wounded in the gun battle with Russell, the Mexican expresses his kinship to Russell by asking, with his dying breath, to know the name of the man who bested him.

In *Valdez Is Coming* (1970), peace-loving town constable Bob Valdez petitions wealthy rancher Frank Braden for a pension to help the pregnant widow of a cowboy wrongly killed for a crime he didn't commit. Braden's contempt for Valdez escalates to hatred when Valdez refuses to be brushed off. Braden has his men, many of whom are, like Valdez, of Mexican descent, beat and torture Valdez and leave him for dead. As he recovers from his ordeal, Valdez recalls his past identity of cavalry scout and gunfighter, and dons the raiment and arms of that past identity.

Much of the rest of the story deals with Valdez's war against Braden, in which he stalks and kills Braden's men from ambush with his buffalo rifle. A tension-building chase culminates in Valdez's inevitable capture. By now, however, the Mexican contingent of Braden's force of men, with the unnamed *segundo*, or foreman, as their spokesperson, have seen something ennobling in Valdez's one-man fight for justice and recognize a long ignored resentment of their employer's racism. In the final scene, Braden is forced by his own men to stand alone against Valdez in a classic western face-off. His choice is to agree to Valdez's demand that he help the widow, or fight Valdez himself, without the help of his men. Although Leonard does not tell us directly what the decision will be, it is obvious that Braden will back down.

The pattern reappears in much of Leonard's subsequent work. The protagonist, often of Hispanic origin, struggles within a violent multicultural milieu. Frequently the cultures are multiracial, but that can be seen primarily as metaphor. Rudyard Kipling said there is no color, creed, or geography when strong individuals with a code of honor meet face to face, though they may come from opposite ends of the earth. Ethically, Leonard makes no ethnic distinctions. Heroes and villains in his universe come from all races, creeds, and colors. Honor and resourcefulness are the only dividing lines.

Westerns and Early Suspense Novels

Leonard's earliest masterpiece is the short story "3:10 to Yuma," published in *Dime Western* in 1953. The plot revolves around a town marshal charged with getting a convicted outlaw aboard the train to the territorial prison. Standing in the way are seven of the outlaw's gang, who are intent on setting him free. At the narrative level, the story is swift, exciting, and believable; in characterization it is a knowing and fascinating study. As the two men wait they talk about their lives, and out of the conversation comes, if not precisely a friendship, perhaps a level of understanding, even a bit of admiration. After the crisis passes and they board the train, there is the suggestion that they will remember each other, that perhaps the admiration will endure beyond the brief time they shared. Leonard's mastery of character is matchless here. The slight shift in the roles of the two characters is subtle and moving, and the ending is a masterstroke of storytelling. It is unfortunate that the story has not been reprinted or collected in the years since its original appearance, because in it one can see the true beginnings of Leonard's signature style.

It was also during the early 1950s that he began making his first Hollywood connections. Both "3:10 to Yuma" and "The Tall T" were adapted into films—connections that would eventually open the way to full-time freelance writing.

Leonard built on his career as a pulp storyteller with a series of western novels that show a growing sensitivity to the complexities of character and an increasing facility with the varied idioms of American language. We see other Leonard preoccupations forming as well. In this later work, the hero often must endure a ritual humiliation at the hands of his enemies. A chase through wild and rugged territory is a device used to build tension in the story. Finally, we begin to note a duality of nature in the hero (and sometimes in a villain), the man he *is* as opposed to the man he *seems* to others.

In spite of his skill in this arena, Leonard's career was forced into a sharp detour when the market for print and celluloid westerns dried up in the early 1960s. Many reasons for this demise have been offered, but the simple truth may be that the sheer remoteness of modern America from the days of the frontier simply made it impossible for consumers to relate to it any longer. That Leonard recognized this and shifted his focus is a tribute to his savvy and to his survival skills. By this time he was plagued by alcoholism, and his marriage was failing, factors that would have ended the career of a lesser man, but which he somehow survived to prosper anew.

Leonard's first suspense effort was *The Big Bounce* (1969). It is reminiscent of Leonard's westerns in that the story is starkly told and devoid of humor. The plot is simplicity in itself: a tough, rootless drifter named Jack Ryan falls in with Nancy Hayes, a seductive, nihilistic con woman always in search of a bigger "bounce," or kick, partly to assuage her ennui and partly to fund her ambition to reach Hollywood and become a movie star.

Echoes of James M. Cain abound in this story: mutual lust leading to murder and theft, the criminals in the end turning on each other. But while in Cain's doxology life is terminally tragic, lust our fatal flaw, and people intrinsically dishonest, Leonard's leading characters cling to their frontier code. Actions have consequences, and no matter how straight the path, in Leonard's universe there are always fateful choices to be made. Later Leonard characters reflect Jack and Nancy's shared trail of violence and lust, but with far less of Cain's cynicism, and they find love. Barbara and Harry Mitchell in *52 Pick-up* (1974), his next urban thriller, are more illustrative of Leonard's later lovers, and they blaze a trail of violence and lust in league with honor and love that provides a baseline for later protagonists. Likewise, later villains follow the path of Leo, Alan, and Bobby (also of *52 Pick-up*), trading a path of darkly comedic wit and startling violence for subsequent psycho- and sociopaths to follow.

We notice a significant change in style as Leonard moves from frontier drama more deeply into the urban milieu. Aristotle wrote more than two thousand years ago that we cannot separate form from substance, and that is the case with Leonard. His style is inseparable from his concept of characterization. When writing traditional westerns with characters far less colorful than those in later novels, his prose was of a straightforward style, and the style served the characters.

It is worthwhile, too, to reflect here on the American interpretation of the word "frontier." The European definition was literally the border between two countries. In America, almost from the earliest time, frontier denoted the line where civilized territory ended and uncivilized savagery began. Leonard maintains the same sense of characterization and the same sense of setting. His characters continue to populate a frontier, albeit an urban one, in which violence is resolved personally and scores settled *mano a mano.* But in expanding his characterizations, he subsequently developed his style to reflect the changing face and "sound" of the American frontier.

Leonard's transition, however, was fraught with difficulty. In spite of his reputation in the marketplace, the initial reaction to his first crime novel was not positive. As he related in a brief essay in *Mysterious News,*

> The first time *The Big Bounce* was offered to publishers and film producers, in the fall of 1966, it was rejected 84 times within a period of three months. They said the writing was okay, the author showed promise, but none of the characters was worth caring about and the ending was a downer. The unanimous negative reaction of 84 professionals would suggest that I hide the manuscript away, maybe even *throw* it away, and move on to something with a more commercial ring to it, at least more easily recognizable good guys and bad guys. (p. 3)

On the advice of his agent, the legendary H. N. Swanson, Leonard produced a revision that was accepted into Fawcett's Gold Medal series and then adapted into a cinematic vehicle of the same title for actor Ryan O'Neal the next year. It was a movie that no one seemed to like, but it netted Leonard $50,000 and was the first real break of his career.

Leonard's next novel, *The Moonshine War* (1969), is such a departure from *The Big Bounce* that the two books might have been written by different authors. Set in Prohibition-era Kentucky, the story depicts the three-sided war that moonshiner Son Martin wages against a gang of Louisville gangsters, a former friend turned treasury agent, and the whiskey-hungry denizens of his hometown, all of whom want his hidden stash of the home brew. A much larger and more complex novel than *The Big Bounce, The Moonshine War* is Leonard's first real attempt to project comedy through the dialogue and antics of low-level criminals, and he succeeds admirably.

We begin to see, too, an early conscious attempt to use female characters as something more than love or sex objects. Son's lover and the gang's moll are both complex women who go their own roads, no matter what the men are doing. Leonard does not write vividly about the sexual behavior of his characters, and he is not particularly adept at the intimate conversation of men and women, but he does show the curious attraction that grows between Son and the moll that culminates in a love scene in the woods. He describes it sparely, but convincingly conveys the woman's change of allegiance as Son's lovemaking transports her to a new place, an almost girlish awakening to the mysteries of sex.

Urban Thrillers

Leonard did not produce another crime novel for five years, thanks to Hollywood's new interest in him. In 1970 he wrote the film adaptation of *The Moonshine War,* and in 1973 he produced original screenplays for the Clint Eastwood western *Joe Kidd* and Charles Bronson's feature *Mr. Majestyk.*

In 1974 Leonard returned to crime writing with the publication of *52 Pick-up.* In many respects, this is the first crime novel to bear the now recognizable Leonard stamp. Again, the plot is a simple one. Self-made millionaire Harry Mitchell has a midlife fling with a younger woman. Unknown to him, the girl is working with a trio of criminals: a business school grad, a fat and alcoholic pornographer, and a drug addicted thief, who film Mitchell's trysts with the girl in order to blackmail him. They show the films to Mitchell, kill the girl with Mitchell's gun, which they have previously stolen, and demand $105,000 from him. To their surprise, Mitchell goes on the offensive and begins to identify and close in on them.

When Mitchell begins to fight back, the blackmailers up the ante by kidnapping his wife, Barbara. Barbara is an early incarnation of what we might think of as "the Leonard woman." While not skilled in or capable of any physical derring-do, she is strong-willed. She keeps her wits about her, even when she is drugged, and does everything she can to hinder her captors.

Mitchell's unrelenting pressure on the gang causes it to rupture. The addict shoots the pornographer and then the business school graduate shoots the addict. Mitchell blows the remaining gang member up in a truck in which he expected to pick up the $52,000 Mitchell earlier promised to pay him.

Published the same year as *52 Pick-up* is the novelization of the film *Mr. Majestyk. Mr. Majestyk* (1974) is a far less complex story than its predecessor. It bears more resemblance to Leonard's westerns than to his crime fiction. The plotting is negligible. Vincent Majestyk, a former Special Forces man, now runs a commercial farm in Texas, and uses migrant farm help to run his operation. A gangster enters the picture, his intent being to cut himself a slice of the local agricultural buck. Majestyk calls up his long-dormant fighting skills and goes on the offensive, which culminates in a violent confrontation in the woods, where he is more at home than the men he vanquishes. Along for the ride comes a feisty farm union organizer, although the sexual chemistry is a little thin. A paperback original, *Mr. Majestyk* is a quick and briefly satisfying read, offering the bare bones of Leonard's evolving style.

Leonard's next novel, *Swag* (1976), is something of a comedy of errors in that it concerns the one-hundred-day spree of a couple of hapless stickup men, Ernest Stickley, Jr., and Frank Ryan. This novel and a sequel, *Stick* (1983), are Leonard's darkest, except perhaps for *Hombre* and *Valdez Is Coming.* In this particular book, there is a melancholy, even a wistfulness, in some of the scenes that you find nowhere else in Leonard. Maybe it's because the characters seem smarter than other of his protagonists, and because they pay a price for their intelligence. You wouldn't call Stick or Ryan sensitive, but they seem capable of sustaining an emotional hurt, and they hurt badly. Listen to Ryan, for example:

> "The myth of the pussy," Frank said again, solemnly. "It seems like a simple, harmless

> little thing, doesn't it? Something every broad in the world has. But you know what? They sit back on their little myth and watch guys break up homes over it, go in debt, mess up their lives. . . . Girls say, You're bigger and stronger than we are, buddy, but we got something you want, so watch it."

This is beyond doubt a quirky and strangely powerful novel.

The Hunted (1977) shows Leonard's frontier ethic still firmly in place in his only story to take place entirely in another country. Al Rosen, an American businessman hiding out in Israel from American gangsters against whom he testified to the Feds, happens to be photographed in the aftermath of a Jerusalem hotel fire, and the published photo comes to the attention of his enemies in America.

In his efforts to escape death, he falls in with David Davis, a Marine stationed at the U.S. Embassy in Jerusalem. Davis is in a state of emotional disarray because all he knows is fighting and he lives in a world with no war for him to fight. He faces an uncertain future until Rosen explains his plight. Rosen offers Davis the opportunity to use his infantry skills, and although he is initially suspicious, the fighting man inside Davis can't resist the challenge.

The bad guys, led by Kamal Rashad, one of Leonard's earliest jive-talking black killers, chase Davis and Rosen across the desert, where an epic battle ensues at a deserted house. The battle ends as one might expect, with the starkest kind of irony overlaying the triumph at arms.

Unknown Man No. 89 (1977) features, once again, Jack Ryan, the protagonist of *The Big Bounce.* This Ryan is a cleaned-up version of his earlier self, now working as a process server in a Detroit suburb, and we almost don't recognize him here. During the story, Ryan himself recalls that a friend of his once said, "Yeah, but at least you don't take any shit from anybody." Ryan replies, "I don't know, the way things are going, maybe it's about time I started taking some." He wouldn't be an Elmore Leonard protagonist if he didn't have such self-doubts, and in this novel the self-doubts run deeper than ever. Indeed, a fair number of reviewers called this Leonard's most deeply felt novel. The love story is not as ironic and cynical as usual, nor is Jack Ryan quite the scoundrel he was in *The Big Bounce.* The plot develops into a western-style shoot-out at the end (one that is brilliantly paced and choreographed), but the heart of the story is the relationship between the alcoholic woman, Lee, and the alcoholic man, Jack Ryan. There is no melodrama here. Leonard plays against it, understating everything, and makes their relationship all the more powerful for its quiet authenticity. There are many who feel that this is Leonard's masterpiece.

The Switch (1978) won Leonard an Edgar nomination for best paperback original. It was well deserved. It anticipates, in its broad-stroke plot and broadly drawn characters, the kind of black comedy he later refined in *Get Shorty* (1990) and *Maximum Bob* (1991). In this story, an unhappy Detroit housewife is kidnapped by two tough guys hired by her husband. Through them she learns that her sneaky husband not only has a million dollars stashed away but a mistress, too. The housewife wins the affection of one of the kidnappers and then uses him to pay her husband back for his duplicity in a smooth, swift comic adventure.

Here we see that in addition to being a great storyteller and fine crafter of dialogue, Leonard also excels at the comedy of manners, a kind of Henry James of the more luckless segments of the underworld.

City Primeval: High Noon in Detroit (1980) is a wry tip of the hat to Leonard's western beginnings, and perhaps a conscious attempt to draw a parallel between the lawless frontier of the nineteenth century and the urban landscape that gives nightmares to the shivering middle class who are forced to live in it. The hero, soft-spoken police detective Raymond Cruz, recalls Bob Valdez, the Hispanic hero of *Valdez Is Coming,* and provides a clue to the direction this story will take. This truly is a Detroit western, a colorful folk dance of action and reaction, that builds inevitably to a bloody conclusion. This novel is most notable for the way Leonard demonstrates his skills with pure narrative. The action scenes are perfectly paced and completely compelling. The book is nicely balanced between the characters' sardonic attitude (by this time Leonard had completely developed his own style, and his characters were his distinctive trademark) and the headlong action of the plot.

Gold Coast (1980), Leonard's last original publication in paperback, is one of his most tightly plotted and features a particularly hardheaded female protagonist. Beautiful Karen Dicilia was married to a Mafia boss. When he died, he left instructions with his chief lieutenant that she was to remain chaste and unmarried in order for her to keep control of his estate. Karen had no illusions about the life she was buying into, but she's young, her desires are still intact, and she has no intention of remaining celibate for the rest of her life. But there's a problem—her late husband's right-hand man makes it clear that he plans to follow his boss's instructions to the letter, and enforce her celibate lifestyle.

She enlists the aid of Calvin Maguire, a prototypical Leonard drifter/ex-con who has been making his living at a local aqua-park where killer whales and dolphins put on shows and the teen-aged showgirls don't offer much resistance to his romantic assaults. Karen is a classy woman—far beyond what he is used to, and he is more than ready to give her his all. Karen skillfully uses Maguire to defeat her late husband's enforcer, then rids herself of Maguire, freeing herself once and for all from any unwanted male domination. Once again, we see Leonard in a mood more comic than dramatic, though his comments on the caste system have real bite.

Split Images (1981) shows Leonard firming up his control of his characters, and writing some of the best dialogue of his career. The story opens as a burglar is caught in the home of millionaire Robbie Daniels, who needlessly and wantonly executes him. The police are called to the scene, and Daniels makes the acquaintance of Walter Kouza, a veteran police detective. In the aftermath of an open-and-shut investigation, the novice killer, Daniels, asks Kouza if he's ever shot anyone. Kouza replies:

> "As a matter of fact I have," Walter said . . . "I shot nine, I killed nine." Walter let himself grin when he saw [Daniels] begin to smile, eating it up. "They were all DOA except this one guy, a jig, hung on for 367 days, if you can believe it. So technically his death wasn't scored a hit. I mean he didn't die of a gunshot, he died of like kidney failure or some fucking thing. But it was a nine-millimeter hollow-nose, couple of them, put him in the hospital so . . . you be the judge." (p. 202)

Walter Kouza is the earliest of Leonard's star monologists, and through Kouza the reader begins to realize that Leonard doesn't simply put a personality down on paper who talks in slang—he feels an empathy for the characters he creates. Kouza is a lousy excuse for a human being, but inside him is an aging athlete living in his past victories in order to blot out his sense of failure and defeat. Readers grin along with Kouza because he reminds them of the high school star tackle who ended up jerking gasoline at the corner station.

Like many working-class people, Kouza admires Daniels for his money and the freedom it gives him. When he is finally made privy to Daniels' dream of killing for sport, he allows himself to be swept up in it and eventually becomes Daniels' retainer—someone to drive him around and videotape his killings. In the beginning, Kouza enjoys it because the people Daniels murders are lowlifes, but then Daniels kills an investigative reporter during a rampage.

Kouza's emotional deterioration from that moment is one of the dramatic high points of this story, and it is here that Leonard evokes true sympathy for this man who thought himself a hardened killer until he discovered limits he didn't even know he had.

Cat Chaser (1982) is the first of Leonard's novels to make use of political turmoil as a backdrop to the action. The hero, George Moran, was a soldier who saw active service in the Dominican Republic and now lives a quiet life running a small motel in Miami. He has a chance meeting with Mary de Boya, a woman he had a serious crush on years before, and they embark on an affair.

The fly in the ointment is that Mary is the wife of Andres de Boya, a former head of the Dominican secret police, known for sewing his victims' eyelids to their brows and then shining a bright light into their eyes until they tell him what he wants to know.

De Boya has escaped to the United States with a large sum of money, following the assassination of real-life Dominican dictator Rafael Leonidas Trujillo Molina. Other people want the money—among them a Dominican pimp, a corrupt ex-cop, and a former actor, and they work, seemingly together, to steal it.

De Boya discovers his wife's infidelity and brutally rapes and beats her for it. But he finds in Mary a worthy antagonist. With her spunk still in place, she steals the money and takes it to Moran, who reaches within himself for the courage to stand between Mary and the final reckoning.

Moran is not one of Leonard's most intelligent heroes. He seems to have little ambition and is content to run his small beachfront motel, until he meets Mary again. His love for her is so all-encompassing (if a bit banal) that he puts himself in harm's way for her, risking the possibility of a manslaughter charge so that he can make clear to the villain that a guy can't just lie down when a goon tries to take something away from him.

Leonard was near the peak of his powers with the ironic masterpiece *LaBrava* (1983). The hero of the story, Joe LaBrava, is a former Secret Service agent turned freelance photographer who works the boardwalk of Miami Beach. By chance he meets Jean Shaw, a fifty-year-old former movie star, famed in her day for playing the beautiful bad girl in noir crime films. Joe, who has been in love with her since the age of twelve, fulfills a romantic fantasy by taking up with her.

Not without fantasies of her own, Jean has plans to steal $600,000. She enlists the aid of sociopath Cundo Rey (one of Leonard's best villains), who entered Florida during the infamous "Marielto boat lift" from Cuba during the 1970s, and the redneck rent-a-cop Richard Nobles to help her carry out the plot.

What makes this particular book so memorable is the blurring of reality and fantasy within the minds of the characters. Street-smart ex-cop Joe LaBrava is so mesmerized by the object of his adolescent crush that it takes him some time to realize who the true villain is, even when she gives him the clues. In one scene, as he regrets the fact that she never once got to go off into the sunset with one of her male costars, Jean comments, "You can't have it both ways. I played Woman as Destroyer, and that gave me the lines. And I'd rather have the lines any day than end up with the star." Later, as she cold-bloodedly murders Richard Nobles, her memory flashes to a scene from one of her movies in which she shoots the actor Henry Silva and recalls that he fell with the same shocked expression as Richard Nobles does.

Leonard's most appealing woman also appears in this story. Frannie Kaufmann, an earthy New York Jewish girl who falls in with LaBrava, proves to be a capable associate and later delivers the most delightful and memorable pillow talk in Leonard's entire oeuvre. One almost wishes that Frannie would make a return appearance, because no previous or subsequent Leonard woman has had her appeal or her linguistic bite.

Stick, the sequel to *Swag,* never quite got its due. While critics seemed charmed by its protagonist, the indomitable ex-convict Ernest Stickley, many of them could not quite appreciate the charm (and complexity) of the plot, in which Stick sticks it to some very slick people who see him as not much more than human vermin. The director Billy Wilder once said that a good movie is one that has two or three great scenes that you keep with you long after leaving the theater. By that measure, *Stick* is one of Leonard's better novels. Stick's psychological problems are not only wry but sad, too.

Dark Comedy and Later Writings

Glitz (1985) was the book that finally put Leonard on the map, garnering him the most lavish praise of his career and prompting the publication of two hardcover collections of his earlier paperback work.

Although there are critics who feel that Leonard did nothing new in this particular book, it represents perhaps the ultimate refinement of his middle period. Vincent Mora, the hero, has his violent moments, but he utters in a single sentence what may be the best articulation of the Leonardian philosophy. Early in the book, recovering from a gunshot wound received in a battle in which he was the winner, Mora agonizes over the killing, telling a friend that he "didn't scare the guy enough." The act of violence, even though it was precipitated by a life-threatening situation, is an instance of failure in Mora's life, because his wits, his nerve, his sheer authority as a policeman weren't enough to prevent the shooting. It is an ominous chord, since a particularly murderous antagonist, the psycho necrophiliac Teddy Magyk, is on the way.

Teddy Magyk is, far and away, the ultimate Leonard villain. He is a sadistic lunatic who believes himself to be a cool stud. In one scene, he entices an old woman beneath the boardwalk at Atlantic City, kills her with a beer bottle, and rapes her, while making jokes to himself about the texture of her pubic hair. It is the darkest kind of humor, the type to provoke nervous laughter and utter revulsion at the same time. And yet even with Teddy, Leonard provides a point of reference to an ordinary person: he has an irascible mother who drives him to distraction.

Bandits (1987), which is the first and only book to take place in Leonard's hometown of New Orleans, is slickly done but lacks the vitality of *Glitz* and the menace of *52 Pick-up* or *LaBrava*. Ex-con and mortuary worker Jack Delaney goes to the Public Health leprosarium at Carville, Louisiana, to pick up what he thinks is a dead body. What he finds instead is a pretty young Nicaraguan girl on the run from a murderous lover and a stylish and tough young woman he learns is a former Catholic nun named Lucy Nichols.

Soon Jack realizes that the lover who wants to kill the young woman is Colonel Dagoberto Godoy, a corrupt Contra officer who is ostensibly in the country to collect money for his government's fight against the Sandinistas, but who, in reality, plans to take the money, donated by wealthy Americans (among them Lucy's father), and run off with it.

After seeing to the safety of the Nicaraguan girl and weathering the company of her right-wing millionaire father, Lucy decides that she will steal Godoy's ill-gotten gains and take the money back to Central America and put it to good use. Jack, by now half in love with Lucy, signs on to help and brings with him an ex-con and ex-cop, Roy Hicks.

Floating around the edges of the story is Franklin De Dios, a Moskito Indian who works for Godoy largely as an assassin. He and Delaney have several encounters, during which Delaney plants a seed in Franklin's mind that causes him to have one of those interior dialogues for which Leonard is famous, an epiphany that stands the story on its head.

The similarity of *Bandits* to *Cat Chaser* is so strong that it almost seems a reprise. Like the earlier book, the story has all the right elements, but in many ways it fails to satisfy. The confrontations between good and bad lack the menacing resonance of other books, and the hero seems more pallid and less physically capable than other Leonard protagonists. Lucy seems, if anything, a bit too enigmatic and really comes to life only when she realizes that one can't successfully fight evil with words and prayers alone, that sometimes it takes a loaded .38 and the will to use it.

Franklin De Dios literally steals the show. His simplicity and innocence, his lethal profession notwithstanding, are appealing and funny, and his realization of his true place in the universe is perhaps the most dramatic event in the story.

In 1987, with the success of *LaBrava, Glitz,* and *Bandits* having made his name a household word, Leonard finally saw the release of a book he had written and sold several years before. *Touch* (1987) is a novel that defies easy classification, even though it contains most of Leonard's recognizable hallmarks. The story concerns a former Franciscan lay brother who calls himself Juvenal. Juvenal once worked in South America and spent four years in the seminary before leaving the church. For reasons no one can understand, Juvenal included, he is occasionally beset by stigmata, at which times he is capable of performing healing miracles.

Juvenal is caught between Bill Hill, a con artist and revival minister who wants to exploit his abilities, and August Murray, the leader of an ultraconservative Catholic group, who sees Juvenal as a threat to his plan to return the Church to traditional values.

More a satire on American mores and the two extremes of modern religious conviction, *Touch* is an experiment that few readers or critics understood, although it is a highly original concept and remains unique in Leonard's oeuvre.

Freaky Deaky (1988), named for a 1960s dance, is another of Leonard's books that makes use of political turmoil. Skip Gibbs and Robin Abbott are a pair of ex-cons and former student radicals who served time for blowing up government buildings. They hatch a plot to extort money from the Ricks brothers, a couple of wealthy wastrels, one of whom turned Skip and Robin in to the Feds. Robin manipulates both brothers with sex, intending to kill them when she gets their money. She manages to kill Mark Ricks, which brings detective Chris Mankowski, a former bomb squad member, into the case.

The rest of the story is a comedy of errors that includes Greta Wyatt, an inept actress who claims to have been raped by Woody Ricks, and Donnell Lewis, a big, capable black man who happens to work for Woody, keeping him placated with drugs and booze while running his house. The climax comes as Robin, trying to eliminate everyone in order to make off with the money, falls into a clever trap set by Mankowski.

Although this story lacks much in the way of tension or a genuine sense of menace, it is one of Leonard's more comical efforts, with Donnell Lewis, another of Leonard's wonderfully drawn black antiheroes, garnering most of the best lines and laughs.

Leonard returned to his true form in *Killshot* (1989), the story of ironworker Wayne Colson and his realtor wife, Carmen, who are mistakenly attacked by Armand Degas, a mob hit man, and his psychopathic partner, Richie Nix. The story is something of a throwback to Leonard's western days, in that the Colsons run from their pursuers, with the help of the Federal Witness Protection Program. That proves equally as dangerous, when Carmen finds herself sexually harassed by the U.S. Marshal assigned to protect them. Inevitably, the feisty Carmen is pushed into a corner where she alone must stand and deliver.

The story benefits from the presence of Degas, one of the most humorless and brooding villains Leonard has ever created, and the self-sufficient Carmen, who proves more than a match for her male antagonists. The ineptitude and vicious behavior of both local and federal police show Leonard at his most cynical and most humorless. Throughout the story, it is plain that the Colsons are in as much danger from their so-called protectors as they are from the actual killers, which brings their frontier resourcefulness to the surface.

The best work of Leonard's later career has to be *Get Shorty,* a novel that works on several levels and is perhaps best appreciated by those who know of Leonard's disdain for the Hollywood mentality. The novel chronicles the adventures of Chili Palmer, a loan shark, who goes to Hollywood to collect a gambling debt from Harry Zimm, a director of schlock horror movies. Along the way, Chili becomes seduced by the image of moviemaking, and he comes up with the idea for a movie about a heroic loan shark, strangely similar to himself. In the course of pitching his idea, Chili becomes Harry Zimm's unofficial partner and falls in love with Karen Flores, once a horror movie "scream queen," who knows more about the business than Harry. Meanwhile he out-schemes Ray Barboni, an old antagonist from Miami, and dodges Bo Catlett, a drug dealer with his own dreams of becoming a movie producer.

Throughout *Get Shorty,* the most striking characteristic is that nearly everybody must cope with the two identities inside them. Most often the real self becomes lost or overwhelmed by the glamorized self. Bo Catlett's glamorized self finally gets him killed, while Chili's writer-producer self ends up subsuming his identity as loan shark and changing his life.

Maximum Bob is both redneck comedy and romantic tragedy. Most of the action revolves around Judge Bob Isom Gibbs, famed for his harsh sentences, politically incorrect attitudes, and womanizing. As the story opens, he is scheming to rid himself of his wife, Leanne, formerly a water-park performer and now deeply involved in mysticism and out-of-body experiences, something that embarrasses Gibbs.

Dr. Tommy Vasco, a physician confined by Gibbs to long-term house arrest after being convicted of drug dealing, wants Gibbs dead, and hires Elvin Crowe, Jr., a convicted murderer, to kill him.

Crowe's probation officer, Kathy Baker, and a police detective, Gary Hammond, who meet at Gibbs's house after Elvin's first attempt on his life, are both drawn into the case as they fall in love with each other. Elvin recognizes the threat from them and sets in motion the events that ultimately lead to a unique and unexpected climax.

Leonard, who had previously shown an interest in mysticism, has a lot of fun with Leanne, allowing her spirit guide, Wanda Grace, to appear several times. On each occasion the spirit of the black slave girl sends a chill into the story line with a prediction that eventually comes true.

Gary Hammond's cold-blooded murder by Elvin Crowe is a jarring note in a story with more than its share of slapstick overtones. It is not the first time a Leonard protagonist dies, but it injects an unpleasant note of reality into the often unreal proceedings. Kathy Baker, who shows her mettle more than once by rejecting Judge Gibbs's clumsy sexual overtures, proves to be the strongest character of all and the true hero of the story.

Rum Punch (1992) has a large cast of characters and at the heart of it a middle-aged love fantasy. Jackie Burke, a pretty, but mildly dishonest flight attendant who has been transporting money for a black arms dealer named Ordell Robbie, is caught entering the country with $50,000 of Ordell's undeclared money and a small stash of cocaine. Her arrest brings her into contact with Max Cherry, an ex-cop turned bail bondsman. Max, although he is still married, has been separated from an uncaring wife for some time and quickly falls under Jackie's spell.

The federal agent and the Florida state cop who arrested Jackie don't want her as badly as they want Ordell; she finds herself in a squeeze between the cops and Ordell and decides to play both sides against each other. She tells the cops that she'll help them if they let her continue to fly and then warns Ordell about what the police suspect. She agrees to bring all of Ordell's money to him, but she will hand it off to a second party to confuse the police. Later she tells Max that she's agreed to help the police but doesn't tell him about the bait and switch.

Succeeding chapters chronicle a complex series of meetings in Macy's department store in which money is shifted from one character to another. The upshot is that Jackie manages to separate half a million dollars out before passing it to one of Ordell's women. The hand of James M. Cain is particularly evident here, as lust and money drive the villains to turn on one another in a violent feeding frenzy.

Jackie Burke is perhaps Leonard's best heroine to date, tough without appearing masculine and quietly competent in a way that puts most of the men in the cast to shame.

Rum Punch is one of Leonard's more complex plot lines, but he handles it well, gradually building and holding the tension until the climax.

In *Pronto* (1993) and its sequel, *Riding the Rap* (1995), Leonard gives us a hero who truly evokes Leonard's boyhood image of Gary Cooper in U.S. Marshal Raylan Givens. Tall and lanky, with a slow drawl and a fast gun, Givens takes us back to Leonard's early career and reminds us once again of Leonard's mastery of the western and of the obvious parallels to be drawn between his work in both genres. It is interesting, too, that Leonard has very deliberately written two very similar adventures around him, both of which include hard-luck bookmaker Harry Arno and his on-again off-again girlfriend, Joyce. In each story, Harry finds himself in jeopardy, and Raylan comes to his rescue. Both plots feature standup confrontations between the stalwart marshal and the bad guys, and *Pronto* even has a climax in which Raylan gives a gangster twenty-four hours to leave town before beating him to the draw.

Both stories involve a lot of chasing around, including a round-trip from America to Italy in *Pronto,* and rather complex plotting with a number of oddball secondary characters. Leonard is at his most wacky in *Riding the Rap,* giving us one of his best characterizations in Dawn Navarro, a glamorous psychic who ends up stealing Raylan's heart in spite of her involvement with Harry Arno's kidnappers. These two stories are among Leonard's most heavily plot-driven and the least concerned with character. Raylan, Harry, and Joyce do not provide much in the way of surprises for us, and it is left to the secondary characters to keep the reader on his toes.

Out of Sight (1996) features the most minimal of Leonard's plots but is the most affecting love story he has ever written. Jack Foley, one of the most successful bank robbers in American history, breaks out of a Florida prison and runs into the beautiful U.S. Marshal Karen Sisco, who is there to serve a complaint on the prison administration. She is taken hostage by Jack and his friend, Buddy Bragg, and forced to endure a ride in the trunk of a car with Jack until they get out of sight of the prison.

The interlude, which is chiefly a discussion about movies, is sufficient for Jack to fall in love with Karen and for her to become intrigued by him. After she escapes, she finds that she cannot forget him. She continues to search for him, ostensibly to put him back in prison, but when they finally meet again in Detroit, they spend the night together and find a deep, if momentary, romantic fulfillment. But romance seldom conquers all in Leonard's universe. As Jack and Karen revert to their true natures, a violent climax makes any but the toughest kind of love impossible.

In *Cuba Libre* (1998), Leonard proved that he was still full of surprises. Set at the time of the Spanish-American War, the story follows the adventures of an American gunrunner and a beautiful Cuban revolutionary. In the late 1990s it stood as Leonard's only historical novel, owing more to his earlier career as a western novelist than to his more recent work in modern urban crime.

Conclusion

Leonard's influence on other writers is not properly appreciated. While others, most notably Raymond Chandler, employed wit and irony in dialogue and description, Leonard was the first to use these gifts to systematically create colorful female protagonists and comical psychopaths. Leonard's villains have become his trademark and have multiplied like lemmings in contemporary books and films. It is worthy of note that the highly praised noir filmmaker Quentin Tarantino has publicly anointed himself Leonard's cinematic heir. Tarantino and Leonard collaborated in 1997, bringing *Rum Punch* to the screen as *Jackie Brown.*

Above and beyond writers such as Tom Kakonis and Carl Hiassen, even critically acclaimed artists seem to take their cues from Leonard. In Robert Stone's National Book

Award-winning novel *Dog Soldiers* (1974), we find the spoor of Leonard's *Hombre.* Like John Russell, Stone's Ray Hicks lives between the brown and the white races. He plies the seas, lost between two tribes, and is not eager to return to white America. A debt of honor, also consisting of ill-gained lucre, brings him back. Like John Russell, he is pursued by outlaws and lawmen gone bad, and ends up at the top of a hill. The spouse of a thief is down below, and he can buy her freedom, but only with a bag of contraband, plundered from the brown people he loves. Like Hemingway before him, who sent Robert Jordan down from a mountain to blow a bridge, redeem a ravaged girl, and by extension save a ravaged world, Leonard's hero will not let us down. Nor will Stone's. Hicks and Russell, outmanned and outgunned, fill their sacks with a worthless substitute, forsaking their mountains and facing the wrath of violent men. Mortally wounded, they slay the slayers, redeem the troubled girls, and by extension, save us all, a weak, ungrateful breed, disdainful of their code and unworthy of their love.

Leonard has been called a genius and the natural heir to the Chandler-Hammett-MacDonald crown by both book and film critics, a group more often given to type than true artistic analysis. He is so much his own writer, however, that it seems not only unnecessary, but also unhelpful to compare him to any predecessors. For one thing, Leonard isn't a mystery writer. He more closely resembles Charles Dickens or Victor Hugo (both of whom were looked upon as "genre" writers in their day) than Chandler and Hammett. For another, by focusing on the dialogue and development of his characters, rather than putting all of his efforts into devising an elaborate mystery for them to solve, Leonard has given us a remarkably consistent body of character studies, which he has set against the vivid backdrop of a darkly forbidding urban landscape.

In the late 1990s Leonard was undeniably one of the most visible and popular writers on the American stage, and his name had become practically a household word, if not for his books then for the highly successful movies that had been adapted from them. Leonard has been part showman, and the successful showman knows his audience and plays to it. Leonard has been a past master at this, but his popularity should not draw attention away from his artistic skill. He is a more consistent and prolific writer than Chandler, and although he maintains a certain rigidity in his plotting, his dialogue and characterizations give his work a freshness that the critically acclaimed Ross Macdonald and such younger writers as Robert B. Parker and Sue Grafton have rarely achieved.

Selected Bibliography

WORKS OF ELMORE LEONARD

NOVELS

The Bounty Hunters. Boston: Houghton Mifflin, 1954.
The Law at Randado. Boston: Houghton Mifflin, 1955.
Escape from Five Shadows. Boston: Houghton Mifflin, 1956.
Last Stand at Saber River. New York: Dell, 1959.
Hombre. New York: Ballantine, 1961.
The Big Bounce. Greenwich, Conn.: Fawcett, 1969.
The Moonshine War. Garden City, N.Y.: Doubleday, 1969.
Valdez Is Coming. Greenwich, Conn.: Fawcett, 1970.
Forty Lashes Less One. New York: Bantam, 1972.
Mr. Majestyk. New York: Dell, 1974.
52 Pick-up. New York: Delacorte, 1974.
Swag. New York: Delacorte, 1976.
Unknown Man No. 89. New York: Delacorte, 1977.
The Hunted. New York: Dell, 1977.
The Switch. New York: Bantam, 1978.
Gunsights. New York: Bantam, 1979.
Gold Coast. New York: Bantam, 1980.
City Primeval: High Noon in Detroit. New York: Arbor House, 1980.
Split Images. New York: Arbor House, 1981.
Cat Chaser. New York: Arbor House, 1982.
Stick. New York: Arbor House, 1983.
LaBrava. New York: Arbor House, 1983.
Glitz. New York: Arbor House, 1985.
Bandits. New York: Arbor House, 1987.
Touch. New York: Arbor House, 1987.
Freaky Deaky. New York: Arbor House, 1988.
Killshot. New York: Arbor House, 1989.
Get Shorty. New York: Delacorte, 1990.

Maximum Bob. New York: Delacorte, 1991.
Rum Punch. New York: Delacorte, 1992.
Pronto. New York: Delacorte, 1993.
Riding the Rap. New York: Delacorte, 1995.
Out of Sight. New York: Delacorte, 1996.
Cuba Libre. New York: Delacorte, 1998.

COLLECTED WORKS

Dutch Treat. New York: Arbor House, 1985. Intro. by George F. Will. Includes *The Hunted, Swag,* and *Mr. Majestyk.*
Double Dutch Treat. New York: Arbor House, 1986. Intro. by Bob Green. Includes *The Moonshine War, Gold Coast,* and *City Primeval.*

COLLECTED SHORT FICTION

"Hard Way." In *Branded West.* Edited by Don Ward. New York: Houghton Mifflin, 1956.
"Rancher's Lady." In *Wild Streets.* Edited by Don Ward. New York: Doubleday, 1958.
"Only Good Ones." In *Western Roundup.* Edited by Nelson Nye. New York: Macmillan, 1961.
"The Boy Who Smiled." In *The Arbor House Treasury of Great Western Stories.* Edited by Bill Pronzini and Martin Harry Greenberg. New York: Arbor House, 1982.
"The Tonto Woman." In *Roundup.* Edited by Steven Overholster. New York: Doubleday, 1982.

BIOGRAPHICAL AND CRITICAL STUDIES

Geherin, David. *Elmore Leonard.* New York: Continuum, 1989.
Leonard, Elmore. "Elmore Leonard on *The Big Bounce.*" *Mysterious News,* September 1986: 1, 3.
Lupica, Mike. "St. Elmore's Fire." *Esquire,* April 1987.
Prescott, Peter S. "Making a Killing." *Newsweek,* 22 April 1985.
Skinner, Robert E. "Collecting Elmore Leonard." *Firsts: The Book Collector's Magazine,* February 1996: 32–42.

Robert Ludlum

(b. 1927)

ROY S. GOODMAN

The details of Robert Ludlum's life are well-known, well-documented, and rather monotonously lacking in setbacks and suspense. Most would-be writers and performers dream of the time when they can quit their day jobs; Ludlum has barely had a day job to quit. He was married to actress Mary Ryducha for forty-six years until she died in late 1996. He has since gone on to remarry.

Born in New York City on 25 May 1927 to George Hartford Ludlum and Margaret Wadsworth Ludlum, Robert Ludlum became interested in drama as a boy, and at age fourteen he appeared in his first professional production. During World War II, Ludlum traveled to Toronto and attempted to join the Royal Canadian Air Force. Presumably, he felt it would be easier to falsify his name and age in a foreign country. This attempt failed; Ludlum did not enter military service until 1944, too late to see combat. He went from the Marines to Wesleyan University and from Wesleyan to a career as an actor, appearing on and off Broadway and on television. Looking for more control in his life, he then became a producer and was quite successful both artistically and financially, but in the late 1960s he became more interested in writing. Finally he sat down to write *The Scarlatti Inheritance* (1971), and after ten rejections the book became the first in a long string of highly successful novels.

Staples of the Thriller

Robert Ludlum does not view himself as a mystery writer, although his tales always involve mysterious goings-on and his characters must get to the bottom of puzzling circumstances. Working in the genre of suspense, Ludlum has created nearly two dozen thrillers. Although his books often deal with fairly conventional subjects, they are far from conventional in their tone and themes. To see just how different Ludlum's writing is, we can examine the way he handles the staples of the thriller: heroes and villains, science and technology, sex and violence.

In most thrillers, the hero is a full-time secret agent or at least a military or government professional. The amateur hero, the ordinary man or woman sucked into a vortex of international intrigue, is hardly unique to Ludlum—Helen MacInnes had created many amateur heroes and heroines before *The Scarlatti Inheritance* appeared—but few if any authors have used the device as often. The hero of Ludlum's debut novel is accountant Matthew Canfield. He has had some on-the-job training in derring-do before the main plot opens, but he is still an amateur. In *The Osterman Weekend* (1972), John Tanner must outwit the intelligence professionals to save himself and his family. James Matlock (*The Matlock Paper,* 1973) is a college professor; Alex McAuliff

(*The Cry of the Halidon,* 1974) is a surveyor; Vittorio Fontini-Cristi (*The Gemini Contenders,* 1976) is apparently a full-time rake and wastrel; and his son Adrian Fontine is a lawyer. Andrew Trevayne (*Trevayne,* 1973) is an industrialist; Noel Holcroft (*The Holcroft Covenant,* 1978) is an architect; and Joel Converse (*The Aquitaine Progression,* 1984) is an attorney.

Although Ludlum's amateur heroes lack formal training in cloak-and-dagger technique, many of them have special skills that come in handy. Like the hero of James Grady's *Six Days of the Condor* (1974), who knows undercover techniques because he is a thriller reader, Peter Chancellor (*The Chancellor Manuscript,* 1977) knows undercover techniques because he is a thriller writer. His vicarious knowledge is so helpful that at one point "the amateur [is] leading the professional." Evan Kendrick in *The Icarus Agenda* (1988) once ran a construction company in the Middle East and still has special knowledge and connections that prove invaluable. Jean-Pierre Villiers (*The Apocalypse Watch,* 1995) uses his skills as an actor to go undercover.

Joel Converse retains his reflexes and training from his days in Vietnam. In *The Aquitaine Progression* he overcomes at least four armed men whose combat training is up-to-date, and he is able to pilot a plane when called upon to do so. Joel is joined by his ex-wife Valerie, who becomes an amateur heroine herself. Her parents happen to have been in the Resistance during World War II, and she is able to enlist the support of a group of aging Resistance veterans. The men and women of the Resistance, who also appear in *The Apocalypse Watch,* are perhaps the ultimate amateur heroes. They were civilians until they were swept up in the tides of war, and they were happy to return to civilian life—but nothing in their lives was ever as exciting as clandestine warfare, and they jump at the chance to return to it.

While many of Ludlum's amateur heroes have the skills to function like professionals, his professional heroes would usually prefer to be amateurs. Jason Bourne is Ludlum's perennial secret agent. When we first meet him in *The Bourne Identity* (1980), he has lost his memory and he reenters the world of intrigue because it finds him, not because he finds it. Given the choice, he comes in from the cold; as *The Bourne Supremacy* (1986) opens, he is married and teaching Oriental studies at a small New England university. Michael Havelock (*The Parsifal Mosaic,* 1982) would also prefer to leave behind his career as a secret agent, and Tyrell Hawthorne (*The Scorpio Illusion,* 1993) has dropped out of intelligence work because his wife was killed in its dirty games. This seems like a normal reaction, but the typical secret agent of thriller fiction is not an ordinary person and does not react like one. James Bond's new bride is gunned down while he watches (Ian Fleming, *On Her Majesty's Secret Service* [1963]), and his reaction is to strap on his Walther PPK and set out for revenge. One Ludlum intelligence professional, Laurence Fassett of *The Osterman Weekend,* is also motivated by revenge, and remains in the game after his wife is killed by Soviet agents.

When Ludlum does cast a professional as the protagonist, he includes amateurs as well. Jason Bourne has a supporting cast of resourceful amateur assistants, including his wife Marie, his psychiatrist Mo Panov, and a gin-soaked former lawyer named Brendan Prefontaine; David Spaulding (*The Rhinemann Exchange,* 1974), Brandon Scofield (*The Matarese Circle,* 1979), and Drew Latham (*The Apocalypse Watch*) find paramours and amateur assistants in (respectively) Jean Cameron, Antonia Gravet, and Karen De Vries. (The last is not strictly an amateur, but then Drew Latham seems a remarkably unprofessional professional.)

Ludlum's professional heroes usually take up their adventures reluctantly, and once on the case they behave far differently from the usual secret agent. The average undercover operative has healthy instincts for self-preservation, but he knows he is in a dangerous profession and he views his own death as a reasonable occupational hazard. Ludlum's characters take danger personally; Drew Latham challenges the would-be Fourth Reich and then complains about attempts on his life.

Ludlum's novels mention sangfroid, but his characters rarely exhibit it. Most are nervous at best and at tight moments become panicky and often hysterical. When Peter Chancellor is trapped inside a burning house with armed fanatics outside, an FBI agent advises him: "They want us to panic; they're counting on it." "Why shouldn't we panic?" Chancellor replies. It's a great line and it emphasizes Chancellor's amateur status, but it's a bad idea.

Why shouldn't they panic? For the same reason that Dale Brown's and Tom Clancy's characters maintain a ritualized flat affect in the direst situations: it keeps them and those around them thinking straight. A U.S. Marine says as much to Drew Latham when Latham asks how he can remain "polite" in a tight spot. Unfortunately neither the character nor the author takes this lesson to heart. A Ludlum character would never say, "Houston, we have a problem." Instead he might become, as the head of an intelligence agency does at a critical moment in *The Apocalypse Watch,* "barely audible with fear." Ludlum's lavish use of italics contributes to an air of desperate and counterproductive alarm.

The conventional thriller villain schemes, spies, sabotages, and murders for power or money, or because he is a loyal agent of the Third Reich or the USSR. Ludlum created his share of conventional villains. The major villains of *The Icarus Agenda, The Rhinemann Exchange, The Matarese Circle,* and *The Bourne Ultimatum* (1990) are all motivated strictly by profit. The assassination ring in *The Bourne Identity* is an apolitical business venture, and in *The Scorpio Illusion* we likewise see terrorism for hire. The false Bourne of *The Bourne Supremacy* knows he's a sadist and works as an assassin for kicks. And the Brotherhood of the Watch (*The Apocalypse Watch*) may try to couch their ambitions in noble-sounding terms, but they are neo-Nazis and clearly racists.

What distinguishes Ludlum's villains is that many of them have well-meaning or even legitimately honorable intentions. Some are obviously misguided—Eye Corps (*The Gemini Contenders*) wants to blackmail the Pentagon into reforms that it feels are needed; Parsifal (*The Parsifal Mosaic*) hopes to build a better world after blowing up the present one; Aquitaine (*The Aquitaine Progression*) expects that chaos will lead to military rule, which can then be replaced by benevolent despotism—but they are genuinely convinced that they are doing right. Others really are doing right. The Halidon (*The Cry of the Halidon*) wants to create a free Jamaica, even if it must resort to violent means. The vice ring in *The Matlock Paper* is the ultimate university fund-raiser. Genessee Industries (*Trevayne*) uses its ill-gotten resources to benefit society. And Inver Brass (*The Chancellor Manuscript, The Icarus Agenda*), Ludlum's "benevolent society of misfits," has a long history of behind-the-scenes manipulation with noble goals if not always noble methods. Of course, their efforts to end the Great Depression just happened to create the Third Reich, but social engineering is never an exact science and that was an unforeseen side effect.

Villains with noble motives are characteristic of the blurring of good and evil in Ludlum's work. As *The Scorpio Illusion* opens, Arab terrorists are paddling ashore for a raid near Tel Aviv. They are surprised by Israeli troops who slaughter them in a burst of excessive violence, *but* then we learn that many of the Israelis have lost family members to terrorism, *but* the Israelis realize they have done wrong and institute a cover-up, and much later we learn that powerful, shadowy forces intended the raid to fail bloodily so that its leader would be seen as a martyr. We learn in lurid detail how the horrific events of Amaya Bajaratt's violent childhood have shaped her into a conscienceless killer, but Ludlum makes it clear that while her background explains her behavior, it does not excuse it. Peter Chancellor has a character in his manuscript say "You're no better than he [J. Edgar Hoover, who was presumably using his files for blackmail purposes] is" but later he learns more about Inver Brass and must concede "You're better than he was." In *The Icarus Agenda,* Inver Brass hopes to fast-forward Evan Kendrick's career and put him in the White House. The reader is all for it because the protagonist Kendrick has laudable ideals—but is it worth tampering with the political process and killing the president? It is no wonder that Ludlum gave one character the code name "Ambiguity."

Characters in the average thriller use gadgets freely; often the hero is trying to steal technology or prevent the villains from doing so. Aircraft and watercraft, computers and phone scramblers appear in Ludlum's books, but the details are severely limited compared to the usual thriller. This may be because of Ludlum's virtual technophobia—he writes his first drafts with a number-two pencil, and a secretary transcribes his sheets of yellow paper onto a word processor for later editing. *The Apocalypse Watch* is perhaps the most high-tech of his works, with a subplot involving brain control through computerized implants, but even here Ludlum avoids detailed technical description. We do not even see the make-up "technology" or acting technique used by Jean-Pierre Villiers in his undercover role. Assassins inexplicably smuggle an ice pick past metal detectors (another author would give them a purpose-built nonmetallic weapon), and Drew Latham, an intelligence professional, is amazed (and shaken, typical panic-prone Ludlum hero that he is) to learn that there are bullets that can penetrate bulletproof cars. "There's another world out there, and you haven't got a clue about it," the hero of *The Scorpio Illusion* angrily explains to a computer and communications genius, "It's called the human quotient." Ludlum clearly feels that the human quotient is more important than technology, and accordingly he focuses on people rather than aircraft and submarines.

Firearms are a staple of thriller fiction, but Ludlum remains for the most part resolutely ignorant. He occasionally read up on terminology because he felt obligated but then promptly forgot it. When he does bother to specify, he does so to good effect: his Gestapo raiding party (*The Gemini Contenders*) is characterized by its Schmeissers as much as by its wardrobe of black leather overcoats; Herr Oberst (*The Holcroft Covenant*) is marked misleadingly as a bad guy by his Luger; tradition-minded Sicilians carry "lupo," sawed-off shotguns (*The Matarese Circle, The Scorpio Illusion*). Yet Ludlum can just as easily refer to the grip of a pistol as the handle, or to the same gun alternately as a revolver and an automatic.

Sex figures prominently in most thrillers, and in Ludlum's as well. Joel Converse (*The Aquitaine Progression*) is enthusiastic about his own private sex life, but he finds the public displays of sexuality in Amsterdam inappropriate and embarrassing. Robert Ludlum apparently feels the same way. He has referred to the movie version of *The Osterman Weekend* as "adult pornography," yet the trysts on the screen are all marital sex. John Hurt's bony buttocks are hardly the stuff of fantasy, his on-screen wife is built like an ordinary woman but thinner, and their one love scene is brief and hardly graphic. Ludlum's characters often tumble into bed as readily as the randiest secret agent, but shortly thereafter the protagonists become very commitment minded and generally go on to marry. Only two sympathetic characters are swingers—Janet Scarlett (*The Scarlatti Inheritance*) and Vittorio Fontini-Cristi (*The Gemini Contenders*)—and both settle down quickly.

Sex in Ludlum's books is not the conventional earthshaking variety. Peter Chancellor (*The Chancellor Manuscript*) has strange, unsatisfactory sex with a terrified reporter. When he lands on the couch with his eventual true love, "the comfort [is] splendid." In *The Apocalypse Watch,* Ludlum emphasizes the "comfortable afterglow" of sex and the "comfort" of a trysting place.

Characters having sex outside of a committed relationship often fare as badly as the horny teenagers in a slasher movie. Johann von Tiebolt (*The Holcroft Covenant*) has been having an unsavory incestuous affair with his sister and kills her to tie up a few loose ends. Carlos' cousin and incestuous lover (*The Bourne Identity*) is killed by the husband she has betrayed. The stoned couple who invite James Matlock (*The Matlock Paper*) to join them in an awkward ménage à trois survive the book, but they certainly make fools of themselves. Amaya Bajaratt (*The Scorpio Illusion*) orders the murder of the young stud who has been her lover. Furthermore, in *The Scorpio Illusion,* Ludlum blurs the distinction between the two varieties of sex; Dominique Montaigne, whose love "nurtured [Tyrell Hawthorne] back to sanity" after his wife was killed, is really the villainous sexual predator Amaya Bajaratt in disguise. She has murder in her heart but apparently some genuine feelings for her paramour, and the result is confusion and an overwhelming sense of betrayal for both characters.

Thriller readers can easily become jaded with fictitious sex and inured to fictitious violence. In J. C. Pollock's *Crossfire* (1985), a surprisingly intelligent thriller despite the triteness of the title and the picture of a Green Beret on the Dell paperback cover, the hero efficiently dispatches two Czech policemen to avoid compromising his mission, and American special forces troops blow away a few dozen border guards to rescue one of their fellows—and readers find this typical and acceptable, although the victims are working stiffs with no evil intentions. Ludlum claims to abhor violence, and his protagonists kill only when absolutely necessary, but his books are laced with violence. In fact, few authors achieve comparable body counts without resorting to mass destruction such as shooting down airliners or nuking the Super Bowl. The corpses that litter Ludlum's literary landscape are not all evildoers getting their just deserts; many are innocent bystanders, good guys, or anybody whose continued existence is at all inconvenient to the villains. The violence is rarely clean, satisfying retribution; it is messy, personal, and scary. Ludlum's heroes react to violence with appropriate disgust, the way the average reader would; this is the one advantage of their lack of sangfroid.

Manipulation, Power, Betrayal

Ludlum handles some elements of the thriller in relatively conventional ways, but his writing remains distinctive. All thriller authors exaggerate, but Ludlum exaggerates more. His fanatics are more fanatical, his conspiracies more conspiratorial, his powerful organizations more powerful.

Blackmail is a frequent element in thrillers; in Ludlum's world it is a way of life. A character in *The Scorpio Illusion* explains the standard tactics: "extortion, blackmail, and guaranteed destruction if the candidates don't comply; guaranteed compensation if they do." "Is [the president] blackmailable?" a character asks in *The Apocalypse Watch.* "Everybody is, especially presidents," comes the reply. *The Chancellor Manuscript* is all about blackmail; J. Edgar Hoover created extensive dossiers with which to blackmail public figures, and now two shadowy groups want the files so that they can do the same for their own purposes. In the back-story of an intelligence master, we learn that the Pentagon routinely creates suspicious-looking gaps in the service records of promising young officers so that they can be blackmailed and controlled later. In *The Scarlatti Inheritance,* the matriarch Elizabeth Scarlatti forces her own daughter-in-law to cooperate with a mission of amateur heroics and a powerful cabal to drop its nefarious plans, both through blackmail. In *The Osterman Weekend,* agents of Omega will blackmail key executives; in *The Matlock Paper,* coeds are blackmailed into becoming hookers. In *Trevayne,* shadowy forces go to great lengths to set up the title character for blackmail; someone plants a quarter million dollars' worth of heroin at a party where Trevayne's daughter is busted, then kills a hapless motorist to make it look like his son caused the accident while driving drunk. In *The Road to Gandolfo* (1975), Sam Devereaux joins MacKenzie Hawkins' team only because he is blackmailed, and later he will blackmail four shady characters into donating ten million dollars each as operating funds. This book is a comedy, but the themes are pure Ludlum.

Most thriller writers create powerful organizations to provide antagonists for their protagonists; Ludlum creates his because he is genuinely concerned about the abuse of power. Shadowy organizations are present in often confusing profusion. In *The Aquitaine Progression,* an international consortium of influence traders wars with the mysterious anti-Aquitaine organization. In *The Holcroft Covenant,* the Odessa wants to establish the Fourth Reich, and the Rache will kill to prevent this—there is another group using both, as well as a second covert anti-Nazi group. In *The Apocalypse Watch,* there are likewise the Brotherhood and its enemies the Antinayous. "Our vehicles constantly roam the city," proclaims a member of the latter. *The Scorpio Illusion* is rich in secret organizations. The Baaka Valley is home base to an international syndicate of terrorism for hire that has "resources beyond any previous estimates." Then we have the Scorpios, who have infiltrated the highest levels of American politics, and for whom "if a day passed without realizing at least a million dollars, it was a day wasted." The Scorpios are controlled by the mysterious Providers—we learn the identity of this group about four hundred pages into the book—and another mysterious group is also pulling subtle, hidden strings.

Ludlum is especially concerned about government abuse of power. *Trevayne* was written specifically in response to Watergate; when Ludlum wrote the introduction to the 1989 edition, he was clearly still angry. So while most thriller heroes are working for benevolent governments and benevolent agencies, Ludlum's secretary of state in *The Scorpio Illusion* confesses, "We're a government of opportunists or benign reformers, of inconsequential minds, too often predators who have no right to govern." A few thrillers depict governments that deal shabbily with their agents; in Ludlum's work it is routine for the government and its agencies to abuse the protagonist. As one complains (in *The Scorpio Illusion*), "I've got a long litany of Washington double-crosses." The plot of *The Matlock Paper* centers around a government anti-drug investigation that may cost James Matlock his life. Ralph Loring, an agent of the Justice Department, Narcotics Bureau, speaks out against the cynical strategy presented at a government planning session, but he is soundly outvoted. At the end of *The Gemini Contenders,* the outraged Adrian Fontine wants to expose the evils of Eye Corps; the government vetoes this plan because it would damage the military. Adrian is forced to cooperate when the inspector general's office threatens to release material that would wreck his career (more blackmail, typical of the machinations in Ludlum). *The Chancellor Manuscript* includes a background story in which a genocidal massacre is arranged just to avoid exposing an intelligence operation.

In all thrillers, including Ludlum's, villains routinely terminate employees who become even minor liabilities (when his subordinates fail in their jobs, Carlos in *The Bourne Identity* delivers performance evaluations with a bullet in the throat). In Ludlum's world, benevolent governments sometimes do the same. In *The Matarese Circle,* Consular Operations decides on permanent retirement for a difficult agent. In *The Bourne Identity,* a covert agency called Treadstone Seventy-One Corporation declares Bourne "beyond salvage." In *The Parsifal Mosaic,* the president finally learns that Michael Havelock is on the side of right—but orders him killed anyway to conceal the government's knowledge of Parsifal.

Another of Ludlum's concerns is fanaticism, and he frequently illustrates the dangers of fanatical behavior. In *The Matarese Circle,* three assassins kill themselves rather than be captured, and Guillaume de Matarese has his staff and himself killed for security reasons. The Blitzkriegers of *The Apocalypse Watch* are moderate by comparison: they are happy to kill themselves over their own mistakes, but not over the mistakes of others. Not only the villains are fanatical. In *The Gemini Contenders,* a priest kills his brother and then himself to protect the location of hidden documents. In *The Icarus Agenda,* Israel's Masada Brigade is sent to rescue hostages at the U.S. embassy in Oman. One of the hostages is a leader of Mossad (Israeli intelligence), and if he cannot be rescued the commandos will kill him to protect his secrets—even though their leader is his son.

Thriller characters routinely lie to each other and manipulate each other, but nowhere is this more pronounced than in Ludlum's work. The basic plot of *The Osterman Weekend* is a CIA scheme to make four suburban couples profoundly paranoid about one another. In *The Holcroft Covenant,* Noel Holcroft's father manipulates him from beyond the grave. His legacy is intended not to atone for the Third Reich, but to establish the Fourth. In *The Scarlatti Inheritance,* Matthew Canfield is sent off on a potentially doomed mission by his cynical superiors. "There was no question about it. The fastest way to solve the mystery behind the Scarlattis was for Matthew Canfield to become a pawn. A pawn who trapped himself." Ludlum expresses his opinion of this treatment through the major villain of *The Scorpio Illusion;* in a rare moment of compassion she reflects, "it was a chess game invented in hell, the kings and pawns irrevocably at odds, unable to eliminate one another without a breakthrough that could destroy them both."

Ludlum's work offers the usual thriller contrivance in which a loyal CIA agent finds himself working with a loyal KGB agent: in *The Osterman Weekend,* Soviet moderates tip off the CIA to the hard-liners' drastic Omega plot; in *The Matarese Circle,* mortal enemies Brandon Scofield and Vasili Taleniekov are forced to work together; in *The Bourne Ultimatum,* both the KGB and the CIA are after Carlos, and KGB veteran Dimitri "Kruppie" Krupkin is a charming boulevardier who is happy to work with the West. But more unusual alliances occur as well, and the Mafia figures prominently in many of them. There is a Mafia industrial complex that influences U.S. government policy in *Trevayne.* In *The Bourne Ultimatum,* the Mafia, the Medusa (a group of financial pirates), and the Soviets all work together when it suits them. Later the Mafia tips off Carlos for its own purposes. In *The Scorpio Illusion,* the peripheral backstory of a minor character finds the Mafia organizing matters in Buenos Aires, "working with the generals, of course." In *The Apocalypse Watch,* the villains tap the expertise of the Mafia and find themselves with an unwanted partner. In *The Road to Omaha* (1992), the head of the CIA is a mafioso (again a Ludlum theme and typical Ludlum paranoia surface even in a comedy).

The Aquitaine council of *The Aquitaine Progression* is another collection of odd bedfellows: influence brokers from Germany, South Africa, France, Israel, and Britain. In *The Icarus Agenda,* Evan Kendrick assembles a commando force of Omani Royal Guards, Palestinians, and Israelis, plus himself, his glamorous paramour, and the young Sultan of Masqat.

The plot of *The Rhinemann Exchange* is the ultimate in Ludlum's unlikely, unsavory alliances. The Third Reich is short of industrial diamonds required to build V-2 rockets; the United States needs better gyroscopes to make a new bombsight work properly. Dishonest industrialists from the two sides work out a diamonds-for-designs deal as though they were general managers trading a hard-throwing left-hander for a shortstop and a player to be named later. "We've got a common enemy," one of the schemers announces, "and it isn't each other."

A Complicated World

Robert Ludlum's gift for inventing intricate stories is so active that there is often more than enough plot to fill his lengthy novels. The Omega plan of *The Osterman Weekend* is a brilliant scheme and would make a fascinating novel in its own right, yet Ludlum never unleashes it. Soviet deep-cover agents are a thriller staple; Ludlum's version is perhaps the best thought out, especially when it comes to keeping sleeper agents motivated and loyal while they are living as Westerners. His training facility at Novgorod is perhaps the most comprehensive and best conceived in thriller fiction. You could write an entire novel about it (Nelson De Mille did—it is called *The Charm School*), but Ludlum burns it to the ground (*The Bourne Ultimatum*).

At times Ludlum's fertile imagination gets away from him. In *The Gemini Contenders*, Vittorio Fontini-Cristi has the ingenious idea of training "accountants from hell" and sending his undercover inefficiency experts to wreck the Third Reich's bookkeeping. It could be the basis of a wildly unconventional thriller, but Ludlum simply mentions it and goes on. The first one-third of *The Icarus Agenda* has enough plot for an entire thriller, including a full-fledged resolution—and it is just the introduction. In *The Cry of the Halidon* we are intrigued by the mysterious Colonel of the Maroon, but he is apparently forgotten and we never meet him. And in *The Apocalypse Watch*, Jean-Pierre Villiers has the makings of a classic Ludlum amateur hero, but after a few promising adventures he virtually disappears.

As he has mentioned in several interviews, Robert Ludlum is meticulously careful to avoid having his own work influenced by others, even unintentionally. Accordingly he reads next to no fiction; his own reading is confined mainly to history and politics, whence he derives his concepts of nefarious machinations and his often bleak view of human nature.

Despite Ludlum's enormous commercial success, by the late 1990s few if any authors had intentionally or unintentionally tried to emulate him. Graham Masterton's *Ikon* (1983) is reminiscent of Ludlum's work in the sheer scope of its sprawling conspiracy. *By Order of the President* (1986), by Michael Kilian, is very much in the Ludlum mold, with a lone amateur pitted against powerful conspirators. The movies *F/X* and *Total Recall* emphasize manipulation of the hero. Perhaps the most Ludlum-like work of fiction in present memory is *Extreme Measures*, more so in the movie than in Michael Palmer's original novel. The villains have seemingly unlimited resources and genuinely noble motives. The hero is an amateur to intrigue, helped by other amateurs but manipulated and betrayed.

What kind of world does Robert Ludlum create for his characters and his audience? It is a question his characters repeatedly ask each other, and their answers summarize much about his philosophies. In a few of his books, the world of intrigue and treachery is the ordinary workaday world that we take for granted, and the secret war rages beneath a thin veneer of civilization. "What kind of world do you people live in?" asks John Tanner in *The Osterman Weekend*. "The same one you do," a cynical CIA agent replies. In *The Parsifal Mosaic*, Michael Havelock gives almost the same reply to the same question: "The same one you do, only we've been in it a little longer, a little deeper." *The Matlock Paper* provides a perfect illustration of the overlap between the "normal" world and the world of shadows; scratch the surface of the placid, prosperous country club facade, and you will find a hotbed of vice.

In most of Ludlum's books, the secret world is different from "real life." In *The Bourne Ultimatum*, Bourne's brother-in-law asks, "What kind of world do you live in?" Bourne replies, "One that I'm sorry you ever became a part of." David Spaulding (*The Rhinemann Exchange*) is asked the same question by his paramour and replies, "One that you'll help me leave." The sympathetic Munro St. Clair entreats Peter Chancellor (*The Chancellor Manuscript*), "Go back to that world [of fiction]; leave this one to others." Karin de Vries has a similar plea for Drew Latham (*Apocalypse Watch*): leave the undercover work "to those who *have* been in that world." And Tyrell Hawthorne (*The Scorpio Illusion*) views the world of intrigue and treachery as different and separate from "the good world."

"What kind of world do you live in?" Another answer in *The Rhinemann Exchange* sums up one of the qualities that have endeared Robert Ludlum's novels to millions of readers: "It's complicated."

Bibliography

NOVELS BY ROBERT LUDLUM

The Scarlatti Inheritance. Cleveland, Ohio: World, 1971.
The Osterman Weekend. Cleveland, Ohio: World, 1972.
The Matlock Paper. New York: Dial Press, 1973.
Trevayne. By "Jonathan Ryder." New York: Delacorte, 1973.
The Cry of the Halidon. By "Jonathan Ryder." New York: Delacorte, 1974.
The Rhinemann Exchange. New York: Dial Press, 1974.
The Road to Gandolfo. By *"Michael Shepherd."* New York: Dial Press, 1975.
The Gemini Contenders. New York: Dial Press, 1976.
The Chancellor Manuscript. New York: Dial Press, 1977.
The Holcroft Covenant. New York: Richard Marek, 1978.
The Matarese Circle. New York: Richard Marek, 1979.
The Bourne Identity. New York: Richard Marek, 1980.
The Parsifal Mosaic. New York: Random House, 1982.
The Aquitaine Progression. New York: Random House, 1984.
The Bourne Supremacy. New York: Random House, 1986.
The Icarus Agenda. New York: Random House, 1988.
The Bourne Ultimatum. New York: Random House, 1990.
The Road to Omaha. New York: Random House, 1992.
The Scorpio Illusion. New York: Bantam, 1993.
The Apocalypse Watch. New York: Bantam, 1995.

BIOGRAPHICAL AND CRITICAL STUDIES

Baxter, Susan and Mark Nichols. "Robert Ludlum and the Realm of Evil." *Maclean's,* 9 April 1984: 50–52.
Greenberg, Martin H., ed. *The Robert Ludlum Companion.* New York: Bantam, 1993.
Moritz, Charles, ed. *1982 Current Biography.* New York: H. W. Wilson Company, 1982. Pp. 247–250.
Skarda, Patricia L. "Robert Ludlum." *Dictionary of Literary Biography Yearbook.* Edited by Richard Ziegfield. Detroit: Gale, 1983.

JOHN D. MACDONALD
(1916–1986)

LEWIS D. MOORE

IT IS SOMEWHAT surprising that John D. MacDonald became a professional writer—moving from short stories to science fiction to mystery, detective, and suspense fiction to traditional novels of manners and morals—since he was nearly thirty before he apparently gave any serious thought to a writing career. Nothing in his background, however, militated against such a move. Born on 24 July 1916 in Sharon, Pennsylvania, to Eugene Andrew and Marguerite Dunn MacDonald, John MacDonald contracted scarlet fever when he was ten years old and spent a year in bed reading. This might have been the earliest influence on his choice to become a writer. His family moved to Utica, New York, when he was twelve, where, in 1932, he graduated from the Utica Free Academy. His father worked for the Savage Arms Company and provided the family with a comfortable lifestyle. MacDonald attended the Wharton School of Finance at the University of Pennsylvania for two years before transferring to Syracuse University, from which he graduated with a bachelor of science in business administration in 1938. He received a master's in business administration from the Harvard Business School in 1939 and first worked for Guardian Life Insurance Company in Syracuse.

Not particularly successful in business, MacDonald responded to an invitation to join the army in 1940, accepting a commission as a first lieutenant. MacDonald married Dorothy Mary Prentiss in 1937, and their one son, Maynard, was born in 1939. During the war, MacDonald served in New York State and then in the China-Burma-India theater, where he joined the Office of Strategic Services, the predecessor of the Central Intelligence Agency. The sale of "Interlude in India," a story he sent in a letter to his wife during the war, to *Story* for twenty-five dollars encouraged him to attempt a writing career after his release from the army in the fall of 1945. By the end of 1946 he had earned six thousand dollars through his writing.

From 1946 to 1949 MacDonald and his wife successively lived in Ingram in the Texas hills country north of San Antonio; Clinton, New York, to be near the academic environment of Hamilton College; and Cuernavaca, Mexico. Subsequently, he and Dorothy lived in Clearwater Beach, Florida, from 1949 until 1951 and then in the Sarasota area from the winter of 1951 until MacDonald's and his wife's deaths in 1986 and 1989, respectively. In the summers, and when they were not on one of their worldwide cruises or visiting their son and his family in Christchurch, New Zealand, MacDonald and Dorothy lived at Piseco Lake, New York. Florida, especially, became an important element in MacDonald's fiction as his interest in the environment grew. The Travis

McGee series and novels contemporaneous with it reflect his concern for man's careless and purposeful despoliation of the natural world. MacDonald not only included this theme in his fiction but also wrote essays on the subject and served on environmental committees in Sarasota. Both his fictional and personal actions in this cause have increased the awareness among other writers, especially in Florida, to environmental dangers.

From MacDonald's beginning as a writer for the pulps, he decided to write what he wanted and not tailor his work to a particular magazine. MacDonald admired a wide range of authors, among them, Joseph Conrad, Raymond Chandler, Dashiell Hammett, Ernest Hemingway, Charles Dickens, Leo Tolstoy, Fyodor Dostoyevsky, and Jack London. They helped shape his style and outlook, as did his own experiences and talent, but initially the constrictions of the magazine format affected what he could do. When he turned to the novel in 1950, he showed his greater abilities as a writer and began to influence others as well.

Contemporary Florida authors such as Paul Levine, James W. Hall, and Randy Wayne White acknowledge their debt to MacDonald. Upon his death from heart disease on 28 December 1986, Ross Thomas and Elmore Leonard published tributes to his accomplishments. Novelists George Garrett, Charles Willeford, and Kurt Vonnegut are effusive in praising MacDonald, and he remains a popular writer today, testified to by Fawcett's reissue of the Travis McGee series with new covers and a brief introduction, printed in each, by the mystery writer Carl Hiaasen. Critical attention to MacDonald has grown since the early 1970s. The first John D. MacDonald conference was held in 1978 at the University of South Florida in Tampa with MacDonald in attendance, and subsequent ones were convened in 1988, 1990, 1992, 1994, and 1996 at various Florida venues under the directorship of Dr. Edgar W. Hirshberg. Numerous essays in scholarly publications and papers at scholarly conferences testify to the continued critical interest in MacDonald. In addition, three critical books have appeared on his life and/or work.

Short Stories

MacDonald published five collections of short stories, and another (*Two,* 1983) was issued without his consent. He stated in an author's foreword to *More Good Old Stuff* (1984) that these were the last ones he would republish. The six collections represent sixty-five stories written over a period of twenty-five years. Given MacDonald's other literary output, this is a respectable showing and especially helpful in understanding the genesis of later characters in his novels and in revealing his thematic range.

End of the Tiger and Other Stories (1966) is an impressive collection. Among the fifteen stories, "The Big Blue" and "The Trap of Solid Gold" demonstrate MacDonald's strongest narrative abilities. In "The Big Blue," Jimmy Gerran, a young American traveling in Mexico, achieves a measure of maturity and independence through his actions in rejecting Lew Wolta's attempts to bully him and in landing by his own efforts a blue marlin off the coast of Mexico. For all that, Gerran receives praise from those who helped him land the giant marlin and poses triumphantly with them and the fish, but he is still alone, not part of any long-standing community except of those who have faced life and learned one of its many harsh lessons. "Trap of Solid Gold" is one of MacDonald's middle-class narratives, with a business background that risks falling into stereotype but superbly avoids it. Ben and Ginny Weldon have a comfortable lifestyle but live above their means. In the conflict between family and work, Ben chooses the former while recognizing that he no longer will have a chance to move to the top rung of management.

Selected stories from four of the other five collections are important for their thematic content and connection to character types in MacDonald's novels. "The Willow Pool"

(*S*E*V*E*N,* 1971) is a story of sexual abuse and madness. "The Annex," from the same collection, focuses on illness and death and includes science fantasy elements that led to its later inclusion in MacDonald's book of science fiction stories, *Other Times, Other Worlds* (1978). "Ring Around the Redhead" (*Other Times, Other Worlds*); "Murder for Money," "Murder in Mind," and "She Cannot Die" (*The Good Old Stuff,* 1982); and "Deadly Damsel," "Death for Sale," "A Corpse in His Dreams," and "Unmarried Widow" (*More Good Old Stuff*) are examples of MacDonald's very frequent mingling of romance, adventure, and suspense. Among his early works, adventure-suspense novels make up the largest proportion, and he liberally incorporates these themes in the Travis McGee series.

MacDonald also demonstrates an interest in the relationship between reason and emotion in such stories as "A Child Is Crying," "But Not to Dream," and "The Miniature," all from *Other Times, Other Worlds.* "They Let Me Live" (*The Good Old Stuff*) is a post–World War II story set in Ceylon (now Sri Lanka), where MacDonald served during the war. Finally, three stories introduce early versions of Travis McGee. In the series, a desire for independence, a degree of emotional isolation, and the selective use of violence become defining elements of McGee's personality. Park Falkner in "Breathe No More" and "From Some Hidden Grave" and Shay Pritchard in "A Trap for the Careless" (*The Good Old Stuff*) reveal MacDonald's efforts to clarify the kind of character that he later produces in McGee.

Early Novels

MacDonald's biography is truly a life in story. As evidenced by his numerous short stories, the forty-two novels he wrote from 1950 to 1963, and the four books he wrote from 1967 to 1986 while working on the Travis McGee series, MacDonald saw the world through narrative. If MacDonald has a permanent place in American fiction, the time and effort he gave to learning his craft is partly responsible. His early novels reflect a sense of plot, character, pace, and theme that only his long apprenticeship as a short-story writer could have provided. They also reveal an experimentation with novel types that lasted throughout his career, continuing through the last four non–Travis McGee novels.

The list of his first ten novels contains works of mystery-detection, adventure-suspense, science fiction, and manners and morals. *The Brass Cupcake* (1950) is an example of the first type; *Murder for the Bride* (1951), *Judge Me Not* (1951), *Weep for Me* (1951), *The Damned* (1952), *Dead Low Tide* (1953), and *The Neon Jungle* (1953) represent the second; *Wine of the Dreamers* (1951) and *Ballroom of the Skies* (1952) exemplify the third; and *Cancel All Our Vows* (1953) illustrates the fourth type. While MacDonald wrote only one more science fiction novel, *The Girl, the Gold Watch, and Everything,* (1962), he produced several more novels of manners and morals, mystery-detection, and adventure-suspense.

Every fictional genre in which MacDonald wrote brings to light the thematic depth of his early novels, but his mystery-detective and adventure-suspense fiction embody it best. These two categories are where MacDonald best explores the themes of violence, deception and betrayal, romantic love, sexual passion and desire, and the environment, which he returns to again and again, reexamining and rethinking them in different dramatic settings. *The Brass Cupcake* is a work of mature fiction, and in it MacDonald explores the violence and political corruption in a small Florida resort town through his protagonist Cliff Bartells. *Judge Me Not* contains the recognizable MacDonald mixture of sexual tension and desire, corruption both personal and social, striking violence, and a romantic interest between the protagonists Teed Morrow and Barbara Heddon that leads to partial recovery of emotional health.

MacDonald's pre–Travis McGee novels consist of seven mystery-detective works, twenty adventure-suspense, three works of science fiction, twelve novels of morals and manners, and one novelization of a movie, *I Could Go on Singing* (1963). Of the seven mystery-detective novels, four have a protagonist with an investigative background. Besides *The Brass Cupcake,* these works include *Deadly Welcome* (1959), *Where Is Janice Gantry?* (1961), and *The Drowner* (1963). Paul Stanial, in the last novel, is the only protagonist who is a licensed private detective. Each novel in this first category also has strong elements of adventure-suspense, and there are, moreover, protagonists caught up in the action of these novels who function like detectives.

MacDonald's many adventure-suspense novels represent an impressive variety of characters and plot structures. The novels appeared between 1950 and 1963, and for all their variety, MacDonald's consistently employed themes, listed earlier, make known his main preoccupations. These themes intertwine, organizing and developing the action while leaving room for other ideas to operate. Violence and deception and betrayal feature prominently in *Weep for Me,* with the added themes of passion and desire. Kyle Cameron becomes a thief and a murderer because of his obsession with the enigmatic Emily Rudolph. As if to balance the morbid atmosphere of *Weep for Me, The Damned* and *Dead Low Tide* mix violence and romantic love. Bill Danton and Linda Gerrold in *The Damned* find love in the artificial situation created by an inoperative ferry on the Rio Conchos in Mexico. In *Dead Low Tide,* Andrew McClintock's boss, John Long, is murdered, and he must find out who did it and then protect Christy Hallowell, the woman he loves, from Roy Kenney, the killer. As another example of the adventure-suspense drama, *April Evil* (1956), employing violence and betrayal centered on the family, introduces in Ronald Crown one of MacDonald's earliest examples of the amoral predator, a character type that he uses effectively in the Travis McGee series.

A few novels in this category especially emphasize suspense as a narrative device. Employing the themes of violence, deception, and betrayal, *Linda,* published with *Border Town Girl* (1956), and *The Executioners* (1958) illustrate MacDonald at the height of his abilities in this area. He uses two very different plotlines to achieve the suspense. *Linda* presents a husband falsely accused of murdering a friend's wife; *The Executioners* develops in Max Cady one of MacDonald's most striking sociopaths, a man who threatens Sam Bowden's family with seeming impunity. The two films based on the latter work, both entitled *Cape Fear,* visually demonstrate the riveting suspense generated by the novel. In *The Empty Trap* (1957), MacDonald uses suspense at a less intense, but still constant level. When Lloyd Westcott and Sylvia Danton run away from Harry Danton, Sylvia's husband, to Mexico, Danton sends three men to find and kill them. They kill Sylvia and beat Lloyd before putting him and the dead Sylvia into his Pontiac and pushing them off a mountain road. Lloyd survives and returns to Oasis Springs in Nevada to avenge Sylvia's murder. He later returns to Isabella, the Mexican-Indian woman who saved his life after he went over the cliff.

Of MacDonald's remaining adventure-suspense novels, romantic love and violence figure prominently in *The Beach Girls* (1959) and *The Only Girl in the Game* (1960). Leo Harrison in *The Beach Girls* and Hugh Darren in *The Only Girl in the Game* play romantic roles that lead to different results. Harrison comes to Elihu Beach, Florida, to investigate the circumstances of his wife's death. In the process, he falls in love with the wholesome Christy Yale, a character reminiscent of Christy Hallowell in *Dead Low Tide* in her bouncy energy and basically good character. Through her influence, he refrains from killing Rex Rigsby, a modern Lovelace, the notorious seducer in Samuel Richardson's *Clarissa,* and thus does not waste his life on him.

The Only Girl in the Game's Homer Gallowell foreshadows Sam Kimber in *The Drowner* and Jass Yeoman in *A Purple Place for Dying* (1964) as the wealthy, experienced older man who has a profound impact on the novel's direction. Here Gallowell aids the two lovers, Hugh Darren and Betty Dawson. After Dawson's death, Gallowell helps Darren manipulate the Las Vegas crime figures responsible for it into killing one another. Finally, *The End of the Night* (1960), mixing the themes of weakness and violence, features four people on a murder spree. Nicknamed the Wolf Pack, they proceed cross-country from the southwest to the northeast, killing those who have the misfortune to become involved with them. The four, Kirby Stassen, Sander Golden, Nanette Koslov, and Robert Hernandez, are all disaffected failures, each coming to their present actions for different reasons but dying in the electric chair one after the other.

MacDonald published three science fiction novels, *Wine of the Dreamers, Ballroom of the Skies,* and *The Girl, the Gold Watch, and Everything,* and the collection of science fiction stories *Other Times, Other Worlds.* The first and third of these novels are the most interesting in that they show a greater depth of ideas and intensity of action than appear in the second work. *Wine of the Dreamers* presents parallel worlds and characters, with the earth as a place of longing for the dreamers Raul and Leesa Kinson, who, at first indifferently, interfere with the lives of those whom they contact in the other world. When the focus of their dreams becomes the two earth protagonists, Dr. Bard Lane and Dr. Sharan Inly, they join them. Leesa falls in love with Bard and Raul with Sharan. Their escape from their dying planet symbolizes a hope for life.

The Girl, the Gold Watch, and Everything employs the device of a talisman. When the gold watch of the title is set properly, time slows for everyone but the watch's possessor. Omar Krepps leaves it to his nephew, Kirby Winter, as an enigmatic gift. Krepps did not tell Winter about the watch's powers before his death, but apparently believed that if Winter were worthy of his uncle's legacy he would discover its properties and know how to regulate its use wisely. Krepps' trust, after many twists, some humorous, proves well founded.

MacDonald employed four to five major themes in his novels of manners and morals. Family and marriage are especially crucial ideas in these works. The cultural emphasis on family in the 1950s possibly accounts for their inclusion, but MacDonald frequently set these ideas in a quagmire of deception and betrayal. Passion and desire lead characters to destabilize their lives. But even more important, MacDonald works his moral concerns into the stories. As Edgar Hirshberg remarks, "The primary characteristic of his fiction . . . is its reliance on moralistic themes" (p. 110).

In *Cancel All Our Vows* and *The Deceivers* (1958), MacDonald starkly poses uncontrolled desire as a threat to married life. Two families unravel when Fletcher Wyant and Laura Corban in the former novel and Carl Garrett and Cindy Cable in the latter begin affairs that increasingly disrupt their and their spouses' lives. In *Clemmie* (1958), Craig Fitz, roiled in a conflict of lust and regret, pursues the young, rich, and irresponsible Clemmie Bennet while his wife and children are out of town. In other novels, MacDonald adds a strong business focus to his thematic mix. In *A Man of Affairs* (1957) and *Slam the Big Door* (1960), the central protagonists, Sam Glidden and Mike Rodenska, respectively, are strong, practical men who control their desires and offer others help, however unsuccessfully. MacDonald limits any sense of infallibility when Rodenska accepts information from Purdy Elmarr, another wise old man like Homer Gallowell in *The Only Girl in the Game* and Judge Rufus Wellington in *Pale Gray for Guilt* (1968).

Two of MacDonald's most impressive novels of manners and morals, *A Key to the Suite* (1962) and *A Flash of Green* (1962), rival *One More Sunday* (1984), discussed below, in their depth of characterization and thematic complexity. In both works, the protagonists are accused of betrayal, but MacDonald includes an element of ethical ambiguity in each work, especially in the case of Jimmy Wing in *A Flash of Green.* In *A Key to the Suite,* Floyd Hubbard betrays his wife with Corinna Barlund at a business convention. Business and marriage, both losers in this case, merge once again in MacDonald's fiction to create dramatic tension. Wing, a reporter in *A Flash of Green,* is a different character altogether. Believing in no one, not even himself, he betrays both sides in a wetlands dispute. MacDonald's opposition of corrupt and greedy developers against those who wish to protect the environment, a combination he made dramatic use of again fifteen years later in *Condominium* (1977), emphasizes his strong moral interests.

Travis McGee

MacDonald's Travis McGee series helped lead the rejuvenation of the hard-boiled detective novel in the 1960s. Although neither licensed nor calling himself a private detective, McGee possesses most attributes of that literary type and functions squarely in the tradition. Except for the occasional guest, McGee lives alone on the *Busted Flush* at Slip F-18, Bahia Mar, Fort Lauderdale, Florida. He won the boat in a poker game, using the cunning and deception for which he is known. These attributes and his physical abilities enable him to thrive as a salvage consultant. In this capacity he attempts to retrieve whatever someone has lost for 50 percent of its value. MacDonald develops the image of McGee as a knight-errant but, ironically, more as a Don Quixote type, fighting against seemingly hopeless odds, than as a shining hero of medieval legend. Meyer, McGee's economist friend who lives on the nearby *John Maynard Keynes* and later the *Thorstein Veblen,* brings his formidable intelligence to their friendship and ultimately to McGee's salvage activities. In their leisure time they play chess, and their intense games become symbolic of their personalities and friendship.

Each novel in the series has a color in the title. MacDonald states that he chose that device in order to make them easier for readers to identify. He connects the colors in the titles to the actions and themes in various ways. Sometimes a color refers to an aspect of a character or an event related to a character. For example, McGee wraps the dead Maureen Pike in *The Girl in the Plain Brown Wrapper* (1968) in brown paper. The eye referred to in *One Fearful Yellow Eye* (1966) belongs to the murdered Saul Gorba. *Cinnamon Skin* (1982) describes Barbara Castillo's skin tone. MacDonald also elicits moods with colors, for example, in *The Deep Blue Good-by* (1964) and *The Lonely Silver Rain* (1985). The allusion to Raymond Chandler's *The Long Goodbye* (1953) is clear in the former title.

One of the principal conventions of the hard-boiled detective is that he acts alone. Carroll John Daly's Race Williams, Dashiell Hammett's Continental Op and Sam Spade, Chandler's Philip Marlowe, and Ross Macdonald's Lew Archer establish this image from the beginning of the genre. At the start of *The Deep Blue Good-by,* McGee contemplates moving the *Busted Flush* from Bahia Mar. Chookie McCall, however, urges him to stay and help her fellow dancer Cathy Kerr, for which McGee will charge his 50 percent fee. Kerr wishes McGee to recover whatever (it turns out to be gems) Junior Allen, her former lover, has stolen from her. Sergeant Dave Berry, Kerr's father, smuggled the gems into the United States after World War II and hid them on his Candle Key, Florida, property. McGee only gets a few of them, sells them in New York, and gives most of the money to Kerr, thus going against his own 50 percent terms. Since McGee lives on his boat, MacDonald shifts the image of the detective's locus of work from the seedy office with its grim furnishings to the intimacy of a home, a comfortable space that radiates a sense of self-sufficiency more than despair and loneliness exuded by the home and office of Chandler's Marlowe:

> Home is where the privacy is. Draw all the opaque curtains, button the hatches, and with the whispering drone of the air conditioning masking all the sounds of the outside world, you are no longer cheek to jowl with the random activities aboard the neighbor craft. You could be in a rocket beyond Venus, or under the icecap. (*Blue,* 1964, p. 5)

McGee is also part of a community. In *The Green Ripper* (1979), McGee reflects, at the funeral of his lover Gretel Howard, that those present are "my village and my people" (p. 37). The presence of characters from earlier novels underscores this idea of a web of relationships. Whether from the influence of the hard-boiled detective tradition or from his development of McGee as a character, MacDonald portrays him as experiencing both joy and despair. This blend of real-life experience and literary convention gives the series one of its main strengths.

Emphasizing McGee's occasional sense of personal and social isolation, MacDonald employs the first-person point of view in the series. This narrative device offers the self in all its immediacy. Every thought carries the narrator's special tone and imbues events and other people with his unique perspective. One hears his voice, indicating present and past worries as well as future possibilities overladen with the burden of personality. Although some have wondered if McGee represents MacDonald's thinking, Raymond D. Fowler writes of an experiment he conducted with MacDonald. The author took the Minnesota Multiphasic Personality Inventory as McGee, as himself, and as Meyer. MacDonald's results corresponded closely to Meyer's and much less so to McGee's.

In the course of the twenty-one novels, McGee's retrogressive moves are some of the most impressive in terms of character development. These negative emotional swings usually occur in moments of crisis. Cathy Kerr, McGee's client in *The Deep Blue Good-by,* nurses him back to health in that novel and in *The Scarlet Ruse* (1973). In *The Deep Blue Good-by,* Junior Allen's murder of Lois Atkinson devastates McGee because of their deepening personal involvement. Searching for Allen earlier, McGee finds Lois, a victim of Allen's sexual depredations and general physical abuse, and nurses her back to health, literally saving her life according to Dr. Ramirez whom McGee calls in after discovering Lois. But when he asks Cathy to come to the *Busted Flush* to receive her share of what he recovered from Allen, McGee can barely function. Paradoxically, Cathy offers herself to him in an almost motherly fashion, and eventually he goes back with her to her home on Candle Key, south of Miami, where she mends him as much as he can be mended. McGee's relationships with Lois and Cathy are the first two instances of sex as therapy in the series, with McGee in the roles of both healer and healed. In *The Scarlet Ruse,* McGee's recovery is more physical than emotional.

In a darker vein, MacDonald develops a side of McGee in which alienation, a feeling of separateness, arises from the act of living. MacDonald said in *Clues,* in a reply to the papers given at the first John D. MacDonald conference, that he tries to write his suspense fiction as close as possible to the "novels of manners and morals" ("Introduction and Comment," p. 73). In a flashback in *The Scarlet Ruse,* McGee describes his feelings of despair to Meyer, who responds with apparently genuine surprise by asking if McGee is unaware that this is what all people experience: "'But we are *all* like that!' he said. 'That's the way it *is.* For everyone in the world. Didn't you know?'" (1973, p. 265). While both McGee and Meyer have their dark moments, Meyer's become more philosophical as the series progresses and McGee's more personal.

As the series starts, McGee's dissatisfactions are largely social. His complaints cover a general tawdriness in American society (*The Deep Blue Good-by*), New York City (*Nightmare in Pink,* 1964), education (*A Purple Place for Dying* and *A Deadly Shade of Gold,* 1965), San Francisco (*The Quick Red Fox,* 1964), the Everglades (*Bright Orange for the Shroud,* 1965), race (*Darker than Amber,* 1966, and *The Girl in the Plain Brown Wrapper*), and condominiums (*A Tan and Sandy Silence,* 1971). From this last novel onward, McGee frequently loses a sense of himself and feels a separation from others. Meyer, however, states his unhappiness with American society in near cataclysmic terms in *The Dreadful Lemon Sky* (1975) and especially in *The Green Ripper.* MacDonald said that when he put the color black in a title he would kill off his hero, but he left no such novel. McGee is, on the whole, little preoccupied with death, but he is conscious of a loss of vitality and the richness of life in the later novels.

Coupled with McGee's loss of vitality is the passage of time and its effects on his life. MacDonald addresses this early in McGee's portrait when he says of Nina Gibson in *Nightmare in Pink,* the second novel in the series, that she is his "very last bitter-sweet girl" (p. 57). MacDonald ages McGee, as he states in the article in *Clues,* one year for every three years in real time. This aging produces cycles of loss and recovery of spirit, with each return of vigor less than the last. Measured against this, McGee's gaining a daughter in *The Lonely Silver Rain* (his child with Puss Killian, his lover and helper from *Pale Gray for Guilt*), and his transferring most of his money to a trust fund for her have an almost wistful note. His subsequent statement that he needs to find another salvage does not ring with the same desire for the hunt as in previous novels. The entrance of Jean Killian, however, a daughter and thus a real family, provides an escape from the feelings of isolation and gloom and helps revive his friendship with Meyer as well. During the course of the novel, they become irritable with one another, but McGee admits at the very end that the problem lay within himself. Another example of the effects of time on his life occurs when Anne Renzetti breaks up with McGee in *Free Fall in Crimson* (1981) because she feels he is never really present in the relationship. Through McGee's relationship with Gretel Howard in *The Empty Copper Sea* (1978), MacDonald seems to make McGee emotionally whole, but her death in *The Green Ripper* throws him back into a state of emptiness and despair. Her loss marks him, creates too many echoes that make his affair with Anne less certain of fulfillment.

Violence is a defining element in the Travis McGee series. McGee deals with dangerous people who prey on others and who have little sense of the physical or emotional pain suffered by their victims. He spaces these amoral predators evenly throughout the series, and nearly every novel adds another striking example of human brutality. Howie Brindle, in *The Turquoise Lament* (1973), is arguably the most extreme figure in his willingness to kill with little or no emotional involvement in the act. As McGee, who has assumed the name Tom McGraw, lies in the bunk with Stella, a member of a Church of the Apocrypha terrorist group, in *The Green Ripper* and as she describes mass killings and her training to destroy society's infrastructure of bridges, tunnels, pipelines, and so on, one understands the profound difference between the emotional states of aggressor and victim. In this instance, MacDonald has chosen as a spokesperson for violence a seemingly innocuous young woman almost totally robbed of identity by the Church of the Apocrypha. There is a sense of a physical displacement as she speaks her paradoxical words of human slaughter. One expects the representation of a monster for such monstrous statements, and yet Stella is the opposite. How she would react to the actual killings is unknown, but some of MacDonald's predators have little sense of the humanity of their victims.

In *A Tan and Sandy Silence,* Paul Dissat, one of the most violent of McGee's killers, appears to see those whom he tortures and kills as arrangements of flesh, bone, and sensations, the last linked to his own emotional state. Dissat lovingly describes a future course of human destruction, one that becomes a necessity once he learns the joys of his new avocation first practiced on Mary Broll. McGee cuts short Dissat's activities by burying him under the hot asphalt that had been destined to cover Meyer and himself as it previously served to kill Harry Broll, Mary's husband.

Cody T. W. Pittler in *Cinnamon Skin* differs strikingly from Dissat in that he reveals no awareness of his pleasure in killing, though he is one of MacDonald's most forbidding serial murderers. Except when provoked by McGee's list of his murders not only to admit to them but to add ones not uncovered by McGee and Meyer's search of his past,

Pittler makes no statement about the chilling details or the horror felt by his victims. Pittler blows up the boat carrying Norma Greene Lawrence—his own wife and Meyer's niece—and MacDonald implies a similar suddenness in the other women's deaths. Desensitized, Pittler apparently has no fear for his own safety.

As an animal might have physical responses to certain conditions but not, especially in the case of predators, what humans call fear, so Pittler, Junior Allen in *The Deep Blue Good-by,* Boone Waxwell in *Bright Orange for the Shroud,* and Howie Brindle in *The Turquoise Lament* appear at times as natural forces in human form. Just as McGee throws an anchor at Allen near the end of *The Deep Blue Good-by* and he still seems unstoppable and as Waxwell appears reborn from the Florida swamps at the end of *Bright Orange for the Shroud* to shock McGee and his companions, so McGee's glimpse of the sheer animality of the real Brindle startles him and reminds him of a look given by a bear whom he surprised one morning with her cubs. Allen, Waxwell, and Brindle do not feel more for their victims than does Dissat, but they employ violence differently. Dissat experiences the pleasure of inflicting harm, while Allen, Waxwell, and Brindle use it as a tool to gain their ends. Brindle, especially, seems to be indifferent to using violence. It is quick and ends problems, but he has no stated need to kill. Rather, he slaughters as ferociously as a wild animal and with as little apparent effect on himself.

MacDonald states that some people are naturally evil, not made evil by a genetic imbalance or family dysfunction. Placing evil in a moral context does not account for them. Although their actions devastate people's lives, one cannot include them in a moral universe in which the will to do something matters. Amoral characters live outside the boundaries within which one makes moral decisions. Big, physically healthy Mary Alice McDermitt in *The Scarlet Ruse* seems impervious to the effects of killing her coworker Jane Lawson, the mother of two daughters. McGee puzzles and irritates her by discussing it as if it changes anything in their relationship. After he finds out about Jane's murder from Meyer, McGee becomes temporarily impotent as he and Mary Alice begin to make love, and he later attributes it to an unconscious awareness of what she did and of what she is.

One of MacDonald's subtleties in character development is that neither Junior Allen nor Cody Pittler fits the image of natural evil. MacDonald suggests that prison has affected Allen, and it turns out that Pittler may have killed his stepmother and his father during a struggle after he surprised them making love. Dissat (and to a lesser extent Waxwell in his swamp habitat), on the other hand, does fit this model as he discovers in himself, with no explanation as to its source, the evil he wishes to practice. It is buried deeply and comes out fully when he is an adult. Desmin Grizzel, in *Free Fall in Crimson,* is willing to murder, but his violence is always connected to personal gain. Ruffino Marino, in *The Lonely Silver Rain,* is a somewhat anomalous figure with regard to natural evil. He kills three young people when a drug deal goes bad, and he corrupts Angie Casak, Irina Casak's eleven-year-old daughter, as he hides in their home. Moral weakness, with no restraint, seems to dominate his actions, rather than a settled propensity to commit evil deeds.

MacDonald not only depicts violence committed by unfeeling killers or those with a natural dose of evil but also shows that McGee is capable of intentionally inflicting harm either to save someone's life or gain information. The latter situation occurs in *The Deep Blue Good-by* as McGee tries to find out what Junior Allen stole from Cathy Kerr. He nearly scalds George Brell in that novel and threatens to kill Carl Abelle in *The Quick Red Fox.* McGee subsequently recoils from his behavior in both novels. Almah Hichin, in *A Deadly Shade of Gold,* has information McGee needs regarding Sam Taggart and certain gold statues owned by Carlos Menterez and stolen by Taggart. Luring Almah into the jungle near the village of Puerto Altamura,

Mexico, where Sam worked as a boat captain, McGee ties her up and seems to be ready to kill her before Almah gives him the information he wants. He considers and accepts the idea that he has broken her spirit and that she will be prey to any who encounter her in the future. Her murder by Miguel Alconedo shortly after McGee's actions against her curtails that bleak prospect.

Regardless of McGee's regret at what he has done to a fellow human, his application of violent means to achieve what he feels is a justified end occurs again in *The Turquoise Lament.* McGee's search for an explanation of Howie Brindle's nature and actions leads him to Pidge Brindle's banker, Lawton Hisp, and finally to her lawyer, Tom Collier. Both men conspired to defraud Pidge's estate, and Collier employed Brindle to marry and then get rid of her. McGee does not easily get the information he needs from Collier and, after abducting him from a party at his Florida ranch, threatens to bury him alive. McGee forces him to dig a grave in an isolated part of the ranch and, when Collier will not talk, matter-of-factly binds and gags him and throws him into the hole. He promptly starts filling the grave, and the shattered Collier signals his desire to speak. His volubility is in direct proportion to the fear created in him by both McGee's actions and his manner while performing them.

MacDonald's female characters play a major role in the series. Every novel places a woman in a position from which she controls or affects the action. They usually relate directly to McGee, though MacDonald uses the device of flashback to include women from his past who are no longer living, such as Helena Pearson in *The Girl in the Plain Brown Wrapper.* McGee helped her husband, Mick Pearson, some years before, and now, knowing she is dying, Helena writes and asks McGee to help her daughter Maureen. Sometimes MacDonald uses two female characters as counterpoints to each other. In *The Quick Red Fox,* Dana Holtzer works for the movie star Lysa Dean. Through an intermediary, Dean learns that McGee does favors for friends, and she employs him to protect her from a blackmail scheme. Dean sends Holtzer to McGee to make the necessary arrangements and help him recover a set of photos secretly taken during her participation in an orgy in California. Holtzer stands in sharp moral contrast to Dean. She lacks her employer's dangerous self-indulgence as well as her reliance on her looks and sexual allure. In addition, Holtzer's husband lies in a coma, and her child is severely retarded. She supports her family with her highly efficient administrative skills.

In *Bright Orange for the Shroud,* Chookie McCall's wholesome sexuality is in marked contrast to Wilma Ferner's corrupt use of her physical attractiveness. Arthur Wilkinson successively marries Ferner and McCall and is happy with the second wife. While Lysa Dean in *The Quick Red Fox* is by no means as morally obtuse as Wilma Ferner, her extreme focus on self excludes others and the possibility of any real closeness. Of Dean, Holtzer, McCall, and Ferner, McGee has an affair only with Holtzer and seems committed to a permanent relationship. Attempting to escape near the end of the novel, the murderer hits Holtzer beside the head and puts her in a coma. Holtzer and McGee were having an affair, but once she recovers consciousness, she decides to return to her very ill husband and child. In approximately half of the novels, MacDonald employs these oppositional female figures, most often with a clear moral divide between them.

Women as McGee's lovers, whether the relationships succeed or fail, are a principal focus in the series. Some of the most perceptive criticism on MacDonald also comes from female scholars writing on McGee's numerous romantic involvements. The very large number of lovers might give one pause in determining whether McGee is capable of seeing them as individuals or responds solely on a physical level. The critics Peggy Moran and Carol Cleveland, while acknowledging the latter aspect of McGee's character, decide on the whole that he is not a user of women. Most male critics come to the same conclusion, looking beyond ideology to the novels' contexts.

One factor is that some series characters need freedom of movement, notably hard-boiled private detectives like McGee, and a permanent love relationship might inhibit the formula's operation in this regard. Consequently, McGee at times wants a long-term relationship, but events intervene. *The Deep Blue Good-by* especially illustrates this problem. The death of Lois Atkinson, McGee's first lover in the series, functions as a real and permanent alteration of his life. His acknowledgment at the end of the novel that some losses cannot be completely healed supports this conclusion. Gretel Howard's death in *The Green Ripper* is McGee's last and probably most profound loss in the series. MacDonald spaces these deeply meaningful love affairs in the series, thus not stretching the reader's credulity as to what is emotionally possible.

In addition to Lois Atkinson in *The Deep Blue Good-by* and Dana Holtzer in *The Quick Red Fox,* McGee has at least four other relationships that seem headed for some kind of permanence. The next occurs in *Pale Gray for Guilt,* the ninth novel in the series. Puss Killian is the epitome of the good-time girl. She never seems to take anything seriously, and it is only when McGee becomes obviously desirous of a committed relationship that she leaves. Not long afterward, he receives a lengthy letter explaining her flight. She writes that she has returned to her husband and is dying of a brain tumor. McGee had been unaware of either her husband or her illness. He also does not know where she has gone. McGee attempts to dismiss her from his mind but cannot. In the series' last novel, *The Lonely Silver Rain,* Jean Killian confronts McGee about his rejection of her and her mother, and McGee takes her to his safety deposit box at a local bank to show her Puss's letter. It is unlikely that MacDonald knew he would use this letter twelve novels later or give McGee a daughter, but this subplot works well to impart meaning to both their lives, a fitting novelistic theme for both MacDonald's announced intentions for the series and the novel.

Six novels after *Pale Gray for Guilt,* McGee falls in love in *The Turquoise Lament* with Pidge Brindle, the daughter of his dead friend, Ted Lewellen. This is likely McGee's most improbable affair, since he had known Pidge as a love-struck teenager who once stowed away on his boat. More important, McGee meets Gretel Howard, mentioned earlier, in *The Empty Copper Sea.* Divorced and living with her brother, John Tuckerman, in Flamingo, a west coast Florida town, Gretel becomes the complete woman for McGee. Since the disappearance (and presumed death) of Tuckerman's friend Hubbard Lawless, Tuckerman, his personal assistant, has seemed disoriented, and Gretel acts somewhat as a caretaker. They live in a cabin on the beach south of Flamingo, and when McGee and Meyer go there to talk to Tuckerman about Lawless's whereabouts, McGee sees Gretel and knows immediately that she will be someone special in his life. He responds to other women in the series, but to no woman does he orient himself so quickly and so thoroughly.

McGee eventually tells Gretel that they must be together permanently, even if she refuses to stay with him on the *Busted Flush.* She does accept the idea that they are a couple. Their developing affair in *The Empty Copper Sea* so dominates the novel that it partially moves it out of the category of a hard-boiled detective work and possibly accounts for the difficulty in successfully filming it. A made-for-television movie, *Travis McGee: The Empty Copper Sea,* appeared in 1983 and starred Sam Elliot as Travis, Gene Evans as Meyer, and Katharine Ross as Gretel. Gretel's illness in *The Green Ripper* provokes McGee into identifying himself at the hospital as her common-law husband, something he never did with any other woman and never does again. Gretel's death leads McGee on a hunt for those responsible and for the members of the terrorist cell of the Church of the Apocrypha. His recovery from the deep depression he experiences near the end of the novel occurs after he senses that his past exists across a wide chasm: "There was a black, deep, dreadful ravine separating me from all my previous days" (p. 219). Even as he begins to enjoy life and plans a cruise with Lady Vivian Stanley-Tucker, the reader realizes that MacDonald has shifted McGee back into an earlier mode of relating to women, more superficial and controlled.

McGee's relationship with Anne Renzetti in *Free Fall in Crimson,* the nineteenth novel in the series, reveals MacDonald's psychological acuity in developing McGee's personality. McGee agrees to look into the year-old death of Ellis Esterland, Ron Esterland's father. Renzetti, Esterland's former secretary and lover, manages a hotel in Naples, on the west coast of Florida. McGee and Renzetti sleep together the first night they meet. This disturbs her and sets the tone for their affair: "I don't know what the hell I was thinking of" (p. 47). In *Cinnamon Skin,* Anne claims that their affair seems too easy for him. Initially, he reminds her that their relationship is mutual and that she has also made choices and finds pleasure in it. While she agrees with his statements, something more than being thought too easy lies below her occasional irritations. Finally, she confesses that she believes he never fully engages with her, that he always withholds part of himself. McGee protests, however hollowly, that this is not so, but the events with Gretel in *The Empty Copper Sea* and *The Green Ripper* loom too large.

Whether he is too wary ever to be fully committed to a woman again after losing Gretel or whether he has temporarily used up his emotional stock, McGee does not confront his feelings. MacDonald indirectly reveals the possibilities for them through Anne Renzetti's reactions. She is whole and ready for a committed love relationship but knows that he is not. Their geographical separation parallels their gradual emotional estrangement until MacDonald magnifies it when Renzetti takes a new job in Hawaii. McGee has the chance to relocate with her (after all he can perform his salvage operations from anywhere), but this never becomes a serious option, and in *Cinnamon Skin,* a few phone calls are a coda to the affair. His loss of Gretel remains paramount in his emotional life.

No analysis of the Travis McGee series would be complete without a discussion of the relationship between McGee and Meyer. Fidelity and trust best exemplify this friendship. From the brief introduction of Meyer in *A Purple Place for Dying* to *The Lonely Silver Rain* and the posthumously published *Reading for Survival* (1987), their developing bond gives a special flavor to the series. Meyer deepens McGee's character in ways that McGee could not achieve himself. An economist with an international reputation, Meyer has a full place in the larger world-that MacDonald wonderfully underplays. He knows many things that McGee does not know, and he can live both within himself and with others.

McGee says that Meyer's knowledge of the world is available to him as if it were sorted into many places, a description recalling Sir Philip Sidney's method of aiding one's memory, described in *A Defence of Poetry* (1595), by arranging items in a room. Meyer can lean back, shut his eyes, and wander from place to place, from music to literature to history. Meyer not only knows things, however, he thinks about them, with no pretension, and adds to McGee's understanding of the world. When he is gloomy, and this is rarely so, Meyer's fears for the future direction of humanity, as Joseph Marotta observes, verge on nihilism. His view of looming social and moral corruption in *The Green Ripper* has a sense of irreversible decline that can lead only to despair. He later reminds McGee of this prediction, made earlier in the novel, after McGee has killed the Church of the Apocrypha terrorists in Ukiah, California. McGee recovers his spirits despite the death of his lover Gretel Howard and the killings and, possibly, because Meyer has shared his own sense of hopelessness.

Meyer first extensively participates in one of McGee's cases in *Darker than Amber* and more fully in *Dress Her in Indigo* (1969). McGee trusts Meyer completely and often consults with him about his salvage work because Meyer can act as a sounding board and clarify elements for McGee. McGee is careful not to endanger Meyer, but in *Dress Her in Indigo,* Wally McLeen, looking for his missing daughter Minda, seriously injures him. Of course, McGee no more sees the harmless-looking McLeen as threatening than does Meyer and barely escapes injury himself as McLeen wields his ancient-style Indian weapon. Meyer is also hurt in *The Long Lavender Look* (1970) and endangered in *A Tan and Sandy Silence* and *The Scarlet Ruse.* Once fully engaging him in the series, MacDonald shifts Meyer from his place as sedentary academic to the role of sharing in McGee's adventures. In *The Long Lavender Look,* the police hold McGee and Meyer on suspicion of murdering Frank Baither. While they are in jail, Deputy Lew Arnstead severely beats Meyer. The events leading up to this incident happen so quickly that McGee cannot protect his friend, and once he is released, Meyer must be taken to Fort Lauderdale for medical care.

The danger to Meyer from the killer Paul Dissat in *A Tan and Sandy Silence* arises as a result of his friendship with McGee. Knowing that McGee's way of life puts him at risk of danger, Meyer shows no desire to retreat from the friendship. When McGee asks him to be part of the plan in *The Scarlet Ruse* to lure Frank Sprenger to his death, Meyer agrees. Sprenger injures McGee so badly that Meyer, hurt himself, must rescue his friend and clean up the mess resulting from the violent confrontation. Meyer aids McGee in *The Dreadful Lemon Sky* and *The Empty Copper Sea,* escaping serious injury in the former novel when someone plants a bomb on the *Busted Flush. Free Fall in Crimson* clarifies the division between McGee the hard-boiled detective and Meyer the academic. Desmin Grizzel surprises Meyer on his boat and forces Meyer to get him aboard the *Busted Flush,* where Grizzel plans to kill both men. McGee understands that Meyer, by his failure to protect either of them from Grizzel, has also failed to live up to some image of himself, that he is not a man of action and adventure like McGee. However, his recovery of a sense of self-esteem in *Cinnamon Skin* and his recognition that he is an "academic" and not "some sort of squatty superman" (p. 13) lead, paradoxically, to his being primarily responsible for Pittler's death. Once Meyer accepts who he is and what he is capable of doing in *Cinnamon Skin,* he can end Pittler's life with a sense of fulfillment; justice has been served. *Darker than Amber, Pale Gray for Guilt,* and *The Lonely Silver Rain* also reveal the value to McGee of Meyer's presence and reasoning abilities. In addition to being McGee's friend and supporter, Meyer provides McGee with solutions to various problems, for example, Vangie Bellemer's past, Tush Bannon's financial problems, and Billy Ingraham's stolen boat, respectively.

Later Novels

From 1967 to 1986 MacDonald wrote four works of fiction in addition to the Travis McGee novels. Two of these, *The Last One Left* (1967) and *Condominium,* are adventure-suspense novels, and two are novels of manners and morals, *One More Sunday* and *Barrier Island* (1986). Garry Staniker and Cristen Harkinson attempt in *The Last One Left* to steal eight hundred thousand dollars from Bixby Kayd. But to do so, they must kill everyone on Kayd's boat, *Muneca.* The adventure-suspense elements of the plot lie in the murders; the sinking of Kayd's boat; Leila Boylston's survival and rescue by the strange Sargeant Corpo, a World War II veteran; and Cristen Harkinson's follow-up murders. Parallel and essential to these violent actions, MacDonald tells the story of Sam and Lydia Boylston's marital difficulties; his love for his sister, Leila; and the way in which Sam and Lydia resolve their problems.

Against the background of man's damage to the environment, MacDonald constructs in *Condominium* a novel of corruption and greed, heroism and struggle worked out in the face of a devastating hurricane and high tide.

Revisiting the scene of natural catastrophe from *Murder in the Wind* (1956), MacDonald broadens it with the political corruption and cheap construction practices, against which certain characters, namely, Gus Garver, Sam Harrison, and LeGrande Messenger, struggle with mixed results. Nature's power, however, brings out a basic decency of mutual aid that demonstrates MacDonald's theme of mankind's struggle to cope.

One More Sunday and *Barrier Island,* MacDonald's last novel, tell different stories but use his familiar themes of human weakness and courage. *Barrier Island* dramatizes a scheme to defraud the federal government through buying barrier islands off the coast of Mississippi and creating false developmental plans to support a claim for compensation. MacDonald's focus on environmental preservation underlies the novel's action. *One More Sunday* deals with the more problematic idea of loss of faith and hope. John Tinker Meadows, the novel's protagonist, is basically an empty shell who goes through the motions of running the Eternal Church of the Believer with his sister, Mary Margaret Meadows. He creates unease among his associates who help run the church and its many ancillary activities. Written before the unraveling of several fundamentalist churches in the past decade, the book examines the effects of size on a church's mission and the possibility that growth will outweigh any salvational purpose. The irony of a charismatic preacher leading his television-driven church, but without any religious purpose of his own, becomes especially apparent when the backwoods preacher, the Reverend Tom Daniel Birdy, refuses to join John and Mary Margaret. *One More Sunday* equals MacDonald's best Travis McGee novels in its sure sense of its novelistic aims and its success in carrying them to fruition.

Nonfiction

MacDonald is not primarily known as a nonfiction writer, yet he published four books and a monograph as well as numerous essays on writing and the environment, among other topics. During the 1960s he wrote *The House Guests* (1965) and *No Deadly Drug* (1968). *Nothing Can Go Wrong* appeared in 1981, coauthored by Captain John H. Kilpack. In 1986 he published *A Friendship: The Letters of Dan Rowan and John D. MacDonald, 1967–1974,* and in 1987 *Reading for Survival* came out. *The House Guests* narrates the story of the animals, principally cats, that he and Dorothy owned or with whom they cohabited for nearly thirty years. It also provides the only sustained view of his life, at least to 1965. *No Deadly Drug* presents MacDonald as an objective reporter who obviously found the hearing and trials of Dr. Carl Coppolino, a doctor accused of killing his wife and a neighbor, fascinating, especially because he was represented by the young and now famous attorney F. Lee Bailey. *Nothing Can Go Wrong* narrates the mishaps experienced on the SS *Mariposa* by the MacDonalds on one of their cruises. Captain Kilpack's struggles with the problems of running and repairing the ship and MacDonald's observations on the passengers combine in a sometimes humorous book.

MacDonald's last two nonfiction works are revealing in different ways. *A Friendship* discloses his personality, especially as manifested through private relationships. One admires that MacDonald reprinted the letters, seemingly with all of his and the comedian Dan Rowan's virtues and flaws intact. This openness reflects the basic emotional and intellectual honesty that he appears to strive for in his fiction. In addition, these letters contain much important information about his writing. *Reading for Survival,* a dialogue between McGee and Meyer about the value of the written word, combines both MacDonald's fictional and real voices in a convincing manner to achieve his didactic purpose. The strongest sense one gains from this monograph is that MacDonald takes a stand. He admits no ambiguity about reading's value for the human race. To live or die is the clear choice, and reading is the path to life. Fittingly, Meyer speaks almost exclusively throughout the work, supporting Raymond Fowler's claim that Meyer represents MacDonald. It would be difficult to imagine a more proper end to his writing life than this passionate argument for the written word in a narrative dialogue.

Selected Bibliography

WORKS OF JOHN D. MACDONALD

TRAVIS MCGEE NOVELS

The Deep Blue Good-by. Greenwich, Conn.: Fawcett, 1964; Philadelphia: Lippincott, 1975.

Nightmare in Pink. Greenwich, Conn.: Fawcett, 1964; Philadelphia: Lippincott, 1976.

A Purple Place for Dying. Greenwich, Conn.: Fawcett, 1964; Philadelphia: Lippincott, 1976.

The Quick Red Fox. Greenwich, Conn.: Fawcett, 1964; Philadelphia: Lippincott, 1974.

A Deadly Shade of Gold. Greenwich, Conn.: Fawcett, 1965; Philadelphia: Lippincott, 1974.

Bright Orange for the Shroud. Greenwich, Conn.: Fawcett, 1965; Philadelphia: Lippincott, 1972.

Darker than Amber. Greenwich, Conn.: Fawcett, 1966; New York: Philadelphia, 1970.

One Fearful Yellow Eye. Greenwich, Conn.: Fawcett, 1966; Philadelphia: Lippincott, 1977.

Pale Gray for Guilt. Greenwich, Conn.: Fawcett, 1968; Philadelphia: Lippincott, 1971.

The Girl in the Plain Brown Wrapper. Greenwich, Conn.: Fawcett, 1968; Philadelphia: Lippincott, 1973.

Dress Her in Indigo. Greenwich, Conn.: Fawcett, 1969; Philadelphia: Lippincott, 1971.

The Long Lavender Look. Greenwich, Conn.: Fawcett, 1970; Philadelphia: Lippincott, 1972.

A Tan and Sandy Silence. Greenwich, Conn.: Fawcett, 1971; Philadelphia: Lippincott, 1979.

The Scarlet Ruse. Greenwich, Conn.: Fawcett, 1973; New York: Lippincott & Crowell, 1980.

The Turquoise Lament. Philadelphia: Lippincott, 1973.

The Dreadful Lemon Sky. Philadelphia: Lippincott, 1975.

The Empty Copper Sea. Philadelphia: Lippincott, 1978.

The Green Ripper. Philadelphia: Lippincott, 1979.

Free Fall in Crimson. New York: Harper & Row, 1981.

Cinnamon Skin: The Twentieth Adventure of Travis McGee. New York: Harper & Row, 1982.

The Lonely Silver Rain. New York: Knopf, 1985.

MYSTERY-DETECTIVE NOVELS

The Brass Cupcake. Greenwich, Conn.: Fawcett, 1950.

A Bullet for Cinderella. New York: Dell, 1955.

You Live Once. New York: Popular Library, 1956.

Deadly Welcome. New York: Dell, 1959.

Where Is Janice Gantry? Greenwich, Conn.: Fawcett, 1961.

The Drowner. Greenwich, Conn.: Fawcett, 1963.

On the Run. Greenwich, Conn.: Fawcett, 1963.

NOVELS OF MANNERS AND MORALS

Cancel All Our Vows. New York: Appleton-Century-Crofts, 1953.

Contrary Pleasure. New York: Appleton-Century-Crofts, 1954.

Cry Hard, Cry Fast. New York: Popular Library, 1955.

Murder in the Wind. New York: Dell, 1956.

A Man of Affairs. New York: Dell, 1957.

The Deceivers. New York: Dell, 1958.

Clemmie. Greenwich, Conn.: Fawcett, 1958.

The Crossroads. New York: Simon & Schuster, 1959.

Please Write for Details. New York: Simon & Schuster, 1959.

Slam the Big Door. Greenwich, Conn.: Fawcett, 1960; New York: Mysterious Press, 1987.

A Key to the Suite. Greenwich, Conn.: Fawcett, 1962; New York: Mysterious Press, 1989.

A Flash of Green. New York: Simon & Schuster, 1962.

I Could Go On Singing. Greenwich, Conn.: Fawcett, 1963.

One More Sunday. New York: Knopf, 1984.

Barrier Island. New York: Knopf, 1986.

ADVENTURE-SUSPENSE NOVELS

Murder for the Bride. Greenwich, Conn.: Fawcett, 1951.

Judge Me Not. Greenwich, Conn.: Fawcett, 1951.

Weep for Me. Greenwich, Conn.: Fawcett, 1951.

The Damned. Greenwich, Conn.: Fawcett, 1952.

Dead Low Tide. Greenwich, Conn.: Fawcett, 1953.

The Neon Jungle. Greenwich, Conn.: Fawcett, 1953.

Area of Suspicion. New York: Dell, 1954.

All These Condemned. Greenwich, Conn.: Fawcett, 1954.

April Evil. New York: Dell, 1956.

Border Town Girl. New York: Popular Library, 1956. Includes *Linda.*

Death Trap. New York: Dell, 1957.

The Empty Trap. New York: Popular Library, 1957.

The Price of Murder. New York: Dell, 1957.

Soft Touch. New York: Dell, 1958.

The Executioners. New York: Simon & Schuster, 1958.

The Beach Girls. Greenwich, Conn.: Fawcett, 1959.

The Only Girl in the Game. Greenwich, Conn.: Fawcett, 1960.

The End of the Night. New York: Simon & Schuster, 1960.

One Monday We Killed Them All. Greenwich, Conn.: Fawcett, 1961.

The Last One Left. Garden City, N.Y.: Doubleday, 1967.

Condominium. Philadelphia: Lippincott, 1977.

SCIENCE FICTION

Wine of the Dreamers. New York: Greenberg, 1951.
Ballroom of the Skies. New York: Greenberg, 1952.
The Girl, the Gold Watch, and Everything. Greenwich, Conn.: Fawcett, 1962.

SHORT STORY COLLECTIONS

End of the Tiger and Other Stories. Greenwich, Conn.: Fawcett, 1966.
*S*E*V*E*N.* Greenwich, Conn.: Fawcett, 1971.
Other Times, Other Worlds. Edited by Martin Greenberg. New York: Fawcett, 1978.
The Good Old Stuff: Thirteen Early Stories. Edited by Martin H. Greenberg, Francis M. Nevins, Jr., and Walter and Jean Shine. New York: Harper & Row, 1982.
Two. New York: Carroll & Graf, 1983.
More Good Old Stuff. New York: Knopf, 1984.

NONFICTION

"How to Live with a Hero." *Writer,* September 1964: 14–16.
The House Guests. Garden City, N.Y.: Doubleday, 1965.
No Deadly Drug. Garden City, N.Y.: Doubleday, 1968.
"How a Character Becomes Believable." In *Mystery Writer's Handbook,* rev. ed. Edited by Herbert Brean. Cincinnati: Writer's Digest, 1976. Pp. 113–122.
"Introduction and Comment." *Clues* 1, no. 1: 63–74 (1980).
Nothing Can Go Wrong (with John H. Kilpack). New York: Harper & Row, 1981.
Reading for Survival. Washington, D.C.: Library of Congress, 1987.

LETTERS

A Friendship: The Letters of Dan Rowan and John D. MacDonald, 1967–1974. New York: Knopf, 1986.

BIBLIOGRAPHIES AND ARCHIVE

MacDonald's papers are deposited in the Special Collections Division, University Libraries, University of Florida at Gainesville.

Shine, Walter, and Jean Shine, eds. *A Bibliography of the Published Works of John D. MacDonald,* Gainesville, Fla.: Patrons of the Library of the University of Florida, 1980. With selected biographical materials and critical essays.
———. *Rave or Rage: The Critics and John D. MacDonald.* Gainesville, Fla.: University of Florida, George A. Smathers Libraries, 1993.
Shine, Walter, et al., comps. *A MacDonald Potpourri—Being a Miscellany of Post-perusal Pleasure of the John D. MacDonald Books for Bibliophiles, Bibliographers, and Bibliomaniacs.* Gainesville, Fla.: University of Florida Libraries, 1988.

BIOGRAPHICAL AND CRITICAL STUDIES

Abrahams, Etta C. "Travis McGee: The Thinking Man's Robin Hood." In *New Dimensions in Popular Culture.* Edited by Russel B. Nye. Bowling Green, Ohio: Bowling Green State University Popular Press, 1972. Pp. 236–246.
———. "Cops and Detectives." *Clues* 1, no. 1: 96–98 (1980).
Alderman, Taylor. "Hedonist, Therapist, Lover: The Sexual Roles of Travis McGee." *JDM Bibliophile* 46: 17–21 (December 1990).
Benjamin, David A. "Key Witness: J. D. MacDonald." *New Republic,* 26 July 1975: 28–31.
Black, David. "The Moralism of John D. MacDonald." *Boston Phoenix,* 3 August 1982: 1, 12.
Brittin, Norman A. "The Joys and Troubles of Children and Adolescents in the Work of John D. MacDonald." *JDM Bibliophile* 36: 19–25 (July 1985).
Cleveland, Carol. "Travis McGee: The Feminists' Friend." *Armchair Detective* 16: 407–413 (winter 1983).
Cook, Wister. "John D. MacDonald: A Little Ecology Goes a Long Way." *Clues* 1, no. 1: 57–61 (1980).
Doulis, Thomas. "John D. MacDonald: The Liabilities of Professionalism." *Journal of Popular Culture* 10: 38–53 (summer 1976).
Ecenbarger, William. "Violence on Violet Nights." *Inquirer: Philadelphia Inquirer Magazine,* 17 March 1985: 20–25.
Feetenby, John. "Pigments of the Imagination." *Million: The Magazine About Popular Culture* 14: 4–8 (March/June 1993).
Fowler, Raymond D. "The Case of the Multicolored Personality." *Psychology Today,* November 1986: 38–40, 42, 46–47, 49.
Geherin, David. *John D. MacDonald.* New York: Ungar, 1982.
Green, Martin Burgess. "Our Detective Heroes." In his *Transatlantic Patterns: Cultural Comparisons of England with America.* New York: Basic Books, 1977. Pp. 101–130.
Grimes, Larry E. "The Reluctant Hero: Reflections on Vocation and Heroism in the Travis McGee Novels of John D. MacDonald." *Clues* 1, no. 1: 103–108 (1980).
Hirshberg, Edgar W. *John D. MacDonald.* Boston: Twayne, 1985.
Holtsmark, Erling B. "Travis McGee as Traditional Hero." *Clues* 1, no. 1: 99–102. (1980).
Hoyt, Charles Alva. "*The Damned:* Good Intentions: The Tough Guy as Hero and Villain." In *Tough Guy Writers of the Thirties.* Edited by David Madden. Carbondale: Southern Illinois University Press, 1968. Pp. 224–230.
Jackman, Mary K. "A Question of Survival: Feminine Narratives in John D. MacDonald's *The Deep Blue*

Good-by." JDM Bibliophile 50: 41–48 (December 1992).

Jackson, S. H. "The Enlightened but Earthbound Detective Hero in Novels by Ross MacDonald and John D. MacDonald." *JDM Bibliophile* 46: 6–10 (December 1990).

Jeffrey, David K. "The Mythology of Crime and Violence." *Clues* 1, no. 1: 75–81 (1980).

Kaler, Anne K. "Cats, Colors, and Calendars: The Mythic Basis of the Love Story of Travis McGee." *Clues* 7, no. 2: 147–157 (1986).

Keefer, T. Frederick. "Albert Camus' American Disciple: John D. MacDonald's Existentialist Hero, Travis D. McGee." *Journal of Popular Culture* 19, no. 2: 33–48 (1985).

Kelly, R. Gordon. "The Precarious World of John D. MacDonald." In *Dimensions of Detective Fiction.* Edited by Larry N. Landrum, Pat Browne, and Ray B. Browne. Bowling Green, Ohio: Bowling Green State University Popular Press, 1976. Pp. 149–161.

Lane, Thomas D. "MacDonald's Villians: Assumptions on Their Origin and Selection." *Clues* 11, no. 1: 21–29 (1990).

———. "Criticizing the Critics: A Reader's Response to Commentary on John D. MacDonald." *JDM Bibliophile* 46: 42–48 (December 1990).

Lott, Rock. "Signs and Portents: John D. MacDonald's Apocalyptic Vision." *JDM Bibliophile* 44: 8–15 (December 1989). Repr. *University of Mississippi Studies in English,* New Series 10:181–190 (1992).

Marotta, Joseph. "The Disorderly World of John D. MacDonald; or, Travis McGee Meets Thomas Pynchon." *Clues* 3, no. 1: 105–110 (1982).

Meyer, Sam. "Color and Cogency in Titles of John D. MacDonald's Travis McGee Series." *Rhetoric Society Quarterly* 18: 259–260 (summer–fall 1988).

Moore, Lewis D. *Meditations on America: John D. MacDonald's Travis McGee Series and Other Fiction.* Bowling Green, Ohio: Bowling Green State University Popular Press, 1994.

———. "The Natural World and Human Desire in John D. MacDonald's Fiction." *JDM Bibliophile* 54: 11–20 (December 1994).

———. "John D. MacDonald's Fiction and the Idea of Identity." *JDM Bibliophile* 58: 38–46 (December 1996).

Moran, Peggy. "McGee's Girls." *Clues* 1, no. 1: 82–88 (1980).

Nelson, John Wiley. "Travis McGee, Tarnished Knight in Modern Armor." In his *Your God Is Alive and Well and Appearing in Popular Culture.* Philadelphia: Westminster Press, 1976. Pp. 170–192.

Nevins, Francis M., Jr. "The Making of a Tale-Spinner: John D. MacDonald's Early Pulp Mystery Stories." *Clues* 1, no. 1: 89–95 (1980).

Peek, George S. "Conquering the Stereotypes: On Reading the Novels of John D. MacDonald." *Armchair Detective* 13: 90–93 (spring 1980).

———. "Beast Imagery and Stereotypes in the Novels of John D. MacDonald." *Clues* 2, no. 1: 91–97 (1981).

Phillips, Robert K. "Travis McGee—Androgynous Existentialist." *JDM Bibliophile* 46: 29–33 (1990).

Sanders, Joe. "Science Fiction and Detective Fiction: The Case of John D. MacDonald." *Science-Fiction Studies* 7, no. 2: 157–165 (1980).

Smead, James D. "The Landscape of Modernity: Rationality and the Detective." In *Digging into Popular Culture: Theories and Methodologies in Archeology, Anthropology, and Other Fields.* Edited by Ray B. Browne and Pat Browne. Bowling Green, Ohio: Bowling Green State University Popular Press, 1991. Pp. 165–171.

Tolley, Michael J. "Color Him Quixote: McDonald's Strategy in the Early McGee Novels." *Armchair Detective* 10: 6–13 (January 1977).

Vander Van, Karen. "Psychological Genesis of the Prototype Hero in Mystery/Detective Fiction as Embodied by Travis McGee: A Retrospective Analysis of His Development as a Child and Youth." *Clues* 11, no. 1: 31–56 (1990).

Vatai, Frank L. "John D. MacDonald and Calvinism: Some Key Themes." *Clues* 11, no. 1: 9–19 (1990).

Note: The *JDM Bibliophile* is published out of the Department of English, University of South Florida in Tampa. It specializes in the work of John D. MacDonald and his contemporaries.

823.087
MYS
Mystery and suspense writers

Date Due

FRANKLIN REGIONAL
SENIOR HIGH
LIBRARY